PAN BOOKS E

Cassell's Spanish - English English - Spanish Dictionary

This dictionary aims to provide a modern reference book for most general purposes.

The emphasis is on words used in normal contemporary speech and writing, as well as the technical vocabulary that is more and more widely used in the twentieth century.

It also bears in mind the current variations in Spanish America, literary and poetical terms for students of classical literature, and idiomatic and slang expressions.

It is ideal for the student of Spanish from the very beginning to college-level studies, and also for the businessman, traveller and tourist.

PAN BOOKS EDITION OF

Pequeño Diccionario Cassell Español - Inglés

Inglés - Español

Redactado por

Brian Dutton

MA, PhD, Professor of Spanish,
University of Georgia

L. P. Harvey

MA, DPhil, Professor of Spanish,
Queen Mary College, University of London

Roger M. Walker

BA, Lecturer in Spanish
Birkbeck College, University of London

Pan Books Ltd : Londres

Advice to the User

Arrangement of Entries

Entries are given in strict alphabetical order, in both English and Spanish. The sequence of definitions is based on frequency. Similar meanings are separated by a comma, distinct meanings by a semicolon. Idiomatic phrases are entered after the definitions of the individual word. Usually idioms occur under the first noun, verb, adjective or adverb which is present in the idiom.

Words that are spelt alike but semantically quite distinct are given separate numbered entries.

Grammar

Parts of speech are indicated by abbreviations in italics (*a.*, *v.t.* etc.), all of which are included in the List of Abbreviations.

Genders are indicated in both halves of the dictionary by *m.* or *f.* following the word. In the English-Spanish half, a group of two or more nouns followed by one of these two letters will be nouns of the same gender, although no genders have been indicated for masculine words in **–o** or feminine words in **–a.**

Verbs. Irregular verbs in both Spanish and English have been listed in tables. In the Spanish-English section verbs having orthographic changes are indicated with a letter that refers to the explanatory table. A verb indicated by a number is irregular in form as well as spelling and will be listed in the corresponding table. Where a verb has both a spelling and a form difference, such as **rogar** (**ruego, rogué**) it will bear both a letter and a number.

The suffix **-se** has been omitted from Spanish reflexive verbs when they occur as keywords.

Variants

Usually variant forms are listed as separate entries with a reference in small capitals to the commonest form.

Accents

The latest rulings of the Real Academia de la Lengua have been observed.

Phonetics

The symbols of the International Phonetic Association have been used as far as possible, with some slight simplifications. Phonetic transcriptions are given only for English words, given the ease with which Spanish pronunciation can be determined by the spelling. A key to the I.P.A. symbols and to Spanish pronunciation is given. In the phonetic transcriptions, the mark ′ precedes the stressed syllable.

Preface

This Compact Dictionary aims to provide the user with a modern reference book that will serve for most general purposes. The listings have been carefully selected with regard to both frequency and importance in normal speech and writing, as well as technical vocabulary that is more and more frequent in the twentieth century.

The base-language is the Spanish of Spain, though we have given close attention to the current variations in Spanish America. The definitions have been selected on the basis of similarity of register, e.g. **barriga** is defined *belly*, not *stomach*, since *belly*/**barriga** have a very similar tone and level.

The dictionary also bears in mind school and college users who read classical literature, and so lists literary and poetical items with appropriate equivalents. On the other hand, racy expressions common in normal day-to-day speech are also listed abundantly, sometimes uniquely.

In order to contain so much in a compact dictionary, certain word-groups of the type **geólogo, geología, geológico; biólogo, biología, biológico** are often represented only by the **-ía** form. Similarly, adverbs in **-mente** have been omitted where they simply correspond to the adjective + *ly* in English.

The listing of irregularities in verbs has been carried out in a very clear tabular form, with references in the text of the dictionary.

In general, this dictionary should be sufficient for the student of Spanish from the very beginning to college-level studies, and also for the traveller and tourist.

B.D.

PAN BOOKS EDITION OF

Cassell's Compact Spanish - English English - Spanish Dictionary

Compiled by

Brian Dutton

MA, PhD, Professor of Spanish
University of Georgia

. P. Harvey

A, DPhil, Professor of Spanish,
Queen Mary College, University of London

oger M. Walker

, Lecturer in Spanish,
kbeck College, University of London

n Books Ltd : London

Also available in this series

Cassell's Compact German-English English-German Dictionary

Cassell's Compact French-English English-French Dictionary

The large Cassell Dictionaries are available only in hardbound editions and include:
Cassell's English
Cassell's French-English, English-French
Cassell's German-English, English-German
Cassell's Spanish-English, English-Spanish
Cassell's Italian-English, English-Italian
Cassell's Dutch-English, English-Dutch
Cassell's Latin-English, English-Latin

Cassell's Compact Spanish-English English-Spanish Dictionary first published 1969 by Cassell & Co Ltd
This edition published 1973 by Pan Books Ltd, Cavaye Place, London SW10 9PG

2nd printing 1975

ISBN 0 330 23559 1

Printed in Great Britain by
Cox & Wyman Ltd, London, Reading and Fakenham

Contents

Variantes regionales
Dentro de los límites de un diccionario de este tamaño, hemos intentado dar variantes americanas tanto del inglés como del español. Las palabras que son exclusivamente británicas o españolas peninsulares han sido indicadas a veces como tales.

Registro
Cuando una palabra en un idioma se usa solamente en un nivel específico (poético, literario, familiar, vulgar etc.) hemos seleccionado el equivalente en el otro idioma para coincidir lo más posible con el tono del original.

Ortografía
Se han adoptado las normas ortográficas usuales de la Real Academia Española. Se han indicado en los artículos los cambios ortográficos de sustantivos y adjetivos, a excepción de la simple adición de **-s** para formar el plural.

Key to Pronunciation

PHONETIC SYMBOLS; ENGLISH TRANSCRIPTIONS

Phonetic symbol	English example		Rough Spanish equivalent
VOWELS			
i:	[si:t]	seat	como la *i* de fin
i	[fiʃ]	fish	*i* muy corta
e	[nek]	neck	*e* de perro
æ	[mæn]	man	*a* muy corta, casi *e* corta
ɑ:	[pɑ:t]	part	*a* muy larga
ɔ	[blɔk]	block	*o* muy corta
ɔ:	[ʃɔ:l]	shawl	*o* de torre
u	[gud]	good	*u* muy corta
u:	[mu:n]	moon	*u* de luna
ʌ	[kʌt]	cut	*u* muy corta, casi *a*
ə:	[sə:tʃ]	search	vocal larga relajada
ə	['nevə]	never	vocal corta relajada
DIPHTHONGS			
ei	[reit]	rate	*ey* de l*ey*
ou	[stou]	stow	*ou* portuguesa
ai	[hai]	high	h*ay*
au	[kraud]	crowd	*au* de c*au*to
ɔi	[bɔi]	boy	*oy* de v*oy*
iə	[stiə]	steer	*ía* de p*ía*, pero con un *a* muy relajada
ɛə	[hɛə]	hair	*e* de sierra más *a* muy relajada
uə	[muə]	moor	*u* de l*u*na más *a* muy relajada
CONSONANTS			
p	[peil]	pail	*p* de *p*aso
b	[beil]	bail	*b* de *b*ajo
t	[teil]	tail	*t* de al*t*o
d	[deil]	dale	*d* de bal*de*
k	[keil]	kale	*k* de *k*ilo
g	[geil]	gale	*g* de *g*anas
m	[meil]	male	*m* de *m*ás
n	[neil]	nail	*n* de *n*o
ŋ	[siŋ]	sing	*n* de ta*n*go
f	[feil]	fail	*f* de *f*ino
v	[veil]	veil	*v* valenciana, *f* sonora
θ	[θin]	thin	*c* de *c*inco
ð	[ðain]	thine	*d* de na*d*a
s	[seil]	sail	*s* de e*s*to
z	[leiz]	laze	*s* de de*s*de
ʃ	[ʃeil]	shale	*s* portuguesa, *sch*
ʒ	['viʒən]	vision	*ll* argentina de ca*ll*e
r	[reil]	rail	*r* de pasa*r*
h	[heil]	hail	*j* suave andaluza
x	[lɔx]	loch (Scots)	*j* castellana
SEMI-CONSONANTS			
j	[jeil]	Yale	*y* de va*y*a
w	[weil]	wail	*hu* de *hu*evo

Key to Pronunciation

PHONETIC VALUES OF SPANISH (CASTILIAN)

	Phonetic symbol	Spanish example		Rough English equivalent
VOWELS				
i	i	fin	[fin]	*ee* in seen
e	e	leche	['letʃe]	*a* in late
a	a	saca	['saka]	*a* in past (Northern English)
o	o	solo	['solo]	*o* in soldier
u	u	luna	['luna]	*oo* in boot
DIPHTHONGS				
ie	je	tiene	['tjene]	*ya* in *Ya*le
ei	ej	peine	['pejne]	*ay* in p*ay*ing
eu	ɛu	deuda	['dɛuða]	ɛ as *ai* in *ai*r; ***ai-oo* run together**
ai, ay	aj	baile	['bajle]	*y* in sk*y*
au	aw	cauto	['kawto]	*ow* in c*ow*
oi, oy	oj	doy	[doj]	*oy* in b*oy*
ue	we	bueno	['bweno]	*way*
CONSONANTS				
b, v (initial)	b	beso	['beso]	*b* in *b*est
		vaso	['baso]	
b, v (intervocalic)	β	cabo, cavo	['kaβo]	like *b* without lips touching
ca, co, cu	k	coca	['koka]	*k* in *k*ind
		cuna	['kuna]	
que, qui, k	k	que	[ke]	
		quiso	['kiso]	
		kilo	['kilo]	
ce, ci	θ	cero	['θero]	*th* in *th*ink
		cinco	['θiŋko]	
z	θ	caza	['kaθa]	
		zona	['θona]	
d (initial)	d	dice	['diθe]	*d* in *d*ear
d (intervocalic)	ð	nada	['naða]	*th* in *th*ere
f	f	fino	['fino]	*f* in *f*ind
g	g	gana	['gana]	*g* in *g*ain
h	zero	hace	['aθe]	*h* in *h*onour
ch	tʃ	chico	['tʃiko]	*ch* in *ch*oose, ri*ch*
j, ge, gi	x	gigante	[xi'gante]	*ch* in lo*ch* (Scots)
		caja	['kaxa]	
l	l	bala	['bala]	*l* in *l*ong
ll	λ	calla	['caλa]	*lli* in mil*li*on
m	m	mozo	['moθo]	*m* in *m*ice
n	n	gana	['gana]	*n* in ba*n*ner
ñ	ɲ	caña	['kaɲa]	*ni* in o*ni*on
p	p	capa	['kapa]	*p* in co*pp*er
r	r	caro	['karo]	*r* in Scots la*r*ge
rr	r̄	carro	['kar̄o]	*r* in Scots *r*ound
s	s	casa	['kasa]	*s* in goo*s*e
t	t	tanto	['tanto]	*t* in *t*ank
w	treated like *v*, *b*, occurs only in foreign words			
x	gz	examen	[eg'zamen]	*gs* in e*gg*s
	s	extremo	[es'tremo]	*s* in be*s*t
y	j	vaya	['baja]	*y* in la*y*er

Key to Pronunciation

American Spanish

The following are the major features which distinguish the pronunciation of American from that of Castilian Spanish; they also occur in Southern Spain:

ci, *ce* and *z* are all pronounced as *s*.

Castilian		*American*
casa	['kasa]	['kasa]
caza	['kaθa]	['kasa]
has	[as]	[as]
haz	[aθ]	[as]
ase	['ase]	['ase]
hace	['aθe]	['ase]

ll is pronounced in many regions as y [j], both in Spain and Spanish America. It is also pronounced [ʒ] (=the *s* in plea*s*ure) in Argentina and Uruguay.

Castilian		*Regional pronunciations*	
haya	['aja]	['aʒa]	
halla	['aʎa]	['aja, 'aʒa]	
cayó	[ka'jo]	[ka'ʒo]	
calló	[ka'ʎo]	[ka'jo]	[ka'ʒo]

s at the end of a word or before a consonant is pronounced as a weak *h* in parts of Southern Spain and America:

Castilian		*Regional*
esto	['esto]	['ehto]
los mismos	[los 'mizmos]	[loh 'mihmoh]

List of Abbreviations

a.	adjective
abbrev.	abbreviation
adv.	adverb
aer.	aeronautics
agr.	agriculture
anat.	anatomy
arch.	architecture
art.	arts
astr.	astronomy
aut.	automobiles
aux.	auxiliary
Bibl.	Biblical
biol.	biology
bot.	botany
Brit.	British
C.A.	Central America
carp.	carpentry
chem.	chemistry
cin.	cinema
com.	commerce
compar.	comparative
cond.	conditional
conj.	conjunction
cul.	culinary
dial.	dialect
dem.	demonstrative
eccl.	ecclesiastical
educ.	education
elec.	electricity
eng.	engineering
ent.	entomology
esp.	especially
f.	feminine
fam.	familiar
fig.	figurative
fut.	future
gem.	precious stones
geog.	geography
geol.	geology
gram.	grammar
her.	heraldry
hist.	history
hunt.	hunting
i.	intransitive
ichth.	ichthyology
impers.	impersonal
indef.	indefinite
inf.	infinitive
interj.	interjection
interrog.	interrogative
inv.	invariable
iron.	ironic
irr.	irregular
joc.	jocular
jur.	jurisprudence
Lat.	Latin
lit.	literary
m.	masculine
math.	mathematics
mech.	mechanics
med.	medicine
metal.	metallurgy
mil.	military
min.	mining
mus.	music
myth.	mythology
n.	noun
naut.	nautical
nav.	naval
neg.	negative
neol.	neologism
obs.	obsolete
orn.	ornithology
p.p.	past participle
paint.	painting
pej.	pejorative
pers.	personal
phot.	photography
phr.	phrase
phys.	physics
pl.	plural
poet.	poetic
pol.	politics
poss.	possessive
prep.	preposition
pret.	preterite
print.	printing
pron.	pronoun
prov.	provincial
r.	reflexive
rad.	radio
rail.	railways
rel.	relative
S.A.	South America
s.o.	someone
s.th.	something
sg.	singular
Sp.	Spain
sup.	superlative
t.	transitive
T.V.	television
taur.	bullfighting
tech.	technical
tel.	telephone
theat.	theatre
theol.	theology
U.S.	United States
v.	verb
var.	variant
vet.	veterinary
vulg.	vulgar; popular
zool.	zoology

A, a, *n.f.* first letter of the Spanish alphabet.
a, *prep.* to; on; by; at.
abad, *n.m.* abbot.
abadesa, *n.f.* abbess.
abadía, *n.f.* abbey; dignity of abbot.
abajo, *adv.* under(neath), below.—*interj.* **¡abajo . . .!** down with . . .!
abalanzar [C], *v.t.* balance; throw.—*v.r.* rush.
abalorio, *n.m.* glass bead.
abanderado, *n.m.* colour-sergeant.
abanderamiento, *n.m.* (*naut.*) registration.
abandonado, -da, *a.* forsaken; forlorn; profligate.
abandonar, *v.t.* forsake; leave; give up.—*v.r.* give oneself up.
abandono, *n.m.* forlornness; slovenliness; debauchery.
abanicar, *v.t.* fan.
abanico, *n.m.* fan.
abano, *n.m.* hanging-fan, punkah.
abarca, *n.f.* rawhide *or* rubber sandal.
abarcar [A], *v.t.* clasp; cover, take up; include.
abarloar, *v.t.* (*naut.*) dock, bring alongside.
abarquillar, *v.t., v.r.* curl up, warp.
abarrancadero, *n.m.* precipice; steep slope.
abarrancar [A], *v.t.* erode.—*v.i.* (*naut.*) run aground.—*v.r.* fall into a hole.
abarrote, *n.m.* (*naut.*) packing; stop-gap.—*pl.* (*S.A.*) groceries.
abastar, *v.t.* supply, provision.
abastecedor, -ra, *a.* providing.—*n.m.f.* victualler, caterer.
abastecer [9], *v.t.* supply, provision.—*v.r.* obtain supplies; provision oneself (***de,*** with).
abastecimiento, abasto, *n.m.* provisioning; provision(s), supplies.
abatimiento, *n.m.* depression; (*naut.*) leeway; (*aer.*) drift.
abatir, *v.t.* throw down; demolish.—*v.r.* be downcast; (*naut.*) have leeway.
abdicación, *n.f.* abdication.
abdicar [A], *v.t.* abdicate; renounce.
abdomen, *n.m.* abdomen.
abdominal, *a.* abdominal.
abecé, *n.m.* A.B.C., alphabet.
abedul, *n.m.* (*bot.*) birch.
abeja, *n.f.* (*ent.*) bee.
abejarrón, *n.m.* (*ent.*) bumble-bee, humble-bee.
abejón, *n.m.* (*ent.*) hornet.
aberración, *n.f.* aberration; deviation.
abertura, *n.f.* opening; gap.
abierto, -ta, *a.* open; frank, sincere.—*p.p.* [ABRIR].
abigarrado, -da, *a.* motley, particoloured; variegated.
Abisinia, *n.f.* Abyssinia.
abisinio, -nia, *a., n.m.f.* Abyssinian.
abismal, *a.* abysmal.
abismo, *n.m.* abyss, depths.
abjurar, *v.t.* abjure, forswear.
ablandador de agua, *n.m.* water-softener.
ablandante, *a.* soothing, mollifying.
ablandar, ablandecer [9], *v.t.* soften, mollify, assuage.—*v.i.* soften, mellow.
ablativo, -va, *a., n.m.* (*gram.*) ablative.
ablución, *n.f.* ablution, washing.
abnegación, *n.f.* self-denial, abnegation.
abnegar [1B], *v.t.* renounce.—*v.r.* deny oneself.
abobar, *v.t.* stupefy.—*v.r.* grow stupid.
abocar [A], *v.t.* decant; bring near.—*v.r.* meet by agreement.
abocardar, *v.t.* (*eng.*) ream; countersink.
abocetar, *v.t.* (*art.*) sketch roughly.
abochornar, *v.t., v.r.* wilt, shrivel (*plants*); (*fig.*) (make) blush.
abofetear, *v.t.* slap.
abogacía, *n.f.* advocacy, pleading; Bar, profession of barrister.
abogado, *n.m.* barrister, lawyer, advocate.
abogar [B], *v.i.* plead; — ***por,*** advocate.
abolengo, *n.m.* ancestry; (*jur.*) inheritance.
abolición, *n.f.* abolition.
abolicionista, *a., n.m.f.* abolitionist.
abolir [Q], *v.t.* revoke, abolish.
abollar, *v.t.* dent; bruise; emboss.
abombar, *v.t.* make bulge; (*fam.*) stun.
abominable, *a.* abominable.
abominación, *n.f.* abomination.
abominar, *v.t.* abominate, detest.
abonado, -da, *a., n.m.f.* subscriber (*to magazine*); season-ticket holder (*person*).
abonar, *v.t.* certify, vouch for; fertilize, manure.—*v.r.* take out a subscription.
abonaré, *n.m.* (*com.*) (promissory) note; debenture.
abono, *n.m.* guarantee; subscription; (*com.*) credit entry; fertilizer, manure.
abordaje, *n.m.* (*naut.*) collision.
abordar, *v.t.* (*naut.*) run foul of; board; approach.
aborigen, *a.* (*pl.* **aborígenes**) aboriginal.—*n.m.* aborigine.
aborrascar [A], *v.r.* get stormy.
aborrecer [9], *v.t.* hate, detest.
aborrecible, *a.* abhorrent, detestable.
aborrecimiento, *n.m.* abhorrence, hate.
abortar, *v.t.* make abortive.—*v.i.* miscarry; have a miscarriage; abort.
abortivo, -va, *a.* abortive.
aborto, *n.m.* abortion; miscarriage; aborted fœtus.
abotonar, *v.t.* button.—*v.i.* bud; crack in boiling (*egg*).
abovedar, *v.t.* arch, vault, groin.
abozalar, *v.t.* muzzle.
abra, *n.f.* bay, cove; (*S.A.*) clearing; crack.
abrasar, *v.t.* set fire to; nip (*frost*).—*v.i.* burn.
abrasión, *n.f.* abrasion.
abrasivo, -va, *a.* abrasive, abradent.
abrazadera, *n.f.* clamp, clasp; (*print.*) bracket.
abrazar [C], *v.t.* embrace; (*fig.*) accept.—*v.r.* embrace.

abrazo, *n.m.* embrace.
ábrego, *n.m.* south-west wind.
abrelatas, *n.m. inv.* tin-opener, (*esp. U.S.*) can-opener.
abrevadero, *n.m.* water-hole; trough.
abrevar, *v.t.* water.
abreviación, *n.f.* abbreviation; abridgement.
abreviar, *v.t.* shorten; abridge.
abrigar [B], *v.t.* shelter, protect; (*fig.*) cherish.—*v.r.* take shelter; wrap up warmly.
abrigo, *n.m.* shelter; overcoat; (*naut.*) haven; ***al — de,*** under protection of.
abril, *n.m.* April.
abrillantar, *v.t.* polish; cut (*diamonds*).
abrir [*p.p.* **abierto**], *v.t., v.i.* open.—*v.r.* open; unbosom oneself; gape.
abrochar, *v.t.* button; buckle.
abrogación, *n.f.* abrogation, repeal.
abrogar [B], *v.t.* abrogate, annul.
abrojo, *n.m.* (*bot.*) thistle; (*fig. esp. pl.*) difficulty.
abrumar, *v.t.* crush, overwhelm; weary.—*v.r.* become foggy; worry.
abrupto, -ta, *a.* abrupt; craggy, rugged.
abrutado, -da, *a.* brutish, bestial.
absceso, *n.m.* (*med.*) abscess.
absentismo, *n.m.* absenteeism.
ábside, *n.m.f.* (*arch.*) apse.
absintio, *n.m.* wormwood, absinthe.
absolución, *n.f.* absolution.
absoluta, *n.f.* dogma, dictum; (*mil.*) discharge *or* exemption.
absolutismo, *n.m.* despotism, autocracy.
absolutista, *a., n.m.f.* absolutist.
absoluto, -ta, *a.* absolute; despotic; ***en —,*** absolutely (*negative*).
absolvente, *a.* absolving.
absolver [5, *p.p.* **absuelto**], *v.t.* absolve; acquit.
absorbencia, *n.f.* absorbence, absorption.
absorbente, *a.* absorbent; (*fig.*) engrossing.
absorber, *v.t.* absorb; (*fig.*) engross.
absorción, *n.f.* absorption.
absorto, -ta, *a.* absorbed, wrapped in thought.
abstemio, -mia, *a.* abstemious.
abstención, *n.f.* abstention.
abstener [33], *v.r.* abstain, forbear (**de,** from).
abstinencia, *n.f.* abstinence, self-denial, fasting.
abstinente, *a.* abstemious.
abstracto, -ta, *a., n.m.* abstract.
abstraer [34], *v.t.* abstract.
abstruso, -sa, *a.* abstruse, difficult.
absuelto, -ta, *p.p.* [ABSOLVER].
absurdidad, *n.f.* absurdity.
absurdo, -da, *a.* absurd, nonsensical.—*n.m.* absurdity.
abubilla, *n.f.* (*orn.*) hoopoe.
abuela, *n.f.* grandmother; ***tía —,*** great-aunt.
abuelo, *n.m.* grandfather; ***tío —,*** great-uncle.—*n.m.pl.* grandparents; forefathers.
abundamiento, *n.m.* abundance; ***a mayor —,*** furthermore.
abundancia, *n.f.* abundance; fertility.
abundar, *v.i.* abound.
abundoso, -sa, *a.* abundant.
aburilar, *v.t.* engrave.
aburrar, *v.r.* become brutish.
aburrido, -da, *a.* bored; boring.
aburrimiento, *n.m.* boredom, tedium.
aburrir, *v.t.* annoy, vex, bore, weary.—*v.r.* be bored.
abusar, *v.t.* abuse, misuse; profit unduly from; impose upon.
abusivo, -va, *a.* abusive.
abuso, *n.m.* abuse, misuse.
abyección, *n.f.* abjectness.
abyecto, -ta, *a.* abject; servile.
acá, *adv.* here; this way; ***desde entonces —,*** from that time on.
acabado, -da, *a.* perfect, consummate; (*fam.*) shabby.—*n.m.* (*tech.*) finish.
acabamiento, *n.m.* end, completion; (*fig.*) death.
acabar, *v.t., v.i.* finish, end, conclude; ***— de*** (+ *inf.*), have just (*done something*); ***— con,*** put an end to, finish off.—*v.r.* end; run out.
acacia, *n.f.* (*bot.*) acacia.
academia, *n.f.* academy.
académico, -ca, *a.* academic.—*n.m.f.* academician.
acaecer [9], *v.i.* happen.
acaecimiento, *n.m.* event, incident.
acalenturar, *v.r.* become feverish.
acalorar, *v.t.* warm; urge on, encourage.—*v.r.* (*fig.*) grow excited.
acallar, *v.t.* quiet, hush.
acampamento, *n.m.* (*mil.*) encampment camp.
acampar, *v.t., v.i., v.r.* encamp, camp.
acanalar, *v.t.* make a channel in; (*arch.*) flute; (*carp.*) groove.
acantilado, -da, *a.* steep, sheer.—*n.m.* cliff.
acanto, *n.m.* (*bot., arch.*) acanthus.
acantonar, *v.t.* (*mil.*) quarter (*troops*).
acaparar, *v.t.* monopolize.
acápite, *n.m.* (*S.A.*) paragraph.
acar(e)ar, *v.t.* confront.
acariciar, *v.t.* caress; fondle; cherish.
acarrear, *v.t.* carry, transport; cause.
acarreo, *n.m.* carrying, freight.—*pl.* supplies.
acaso (1), *n.m.* chance.
acaso (2), *adv.* perhaps, maybe; ***por si —,*** just in case.
acatamiento, *n.m.* esteem; view.
acatar, *v.t.* respect, esteem.
acatarrar, *v.r.* catch cold.
acaudalado, -da, *a.* wealthy, opulent.
acaudalar, *v.t.* hoard.
acaudillar, *v.t.* lead, command.
acceder, *v.i.* accede, agree, consent.
accesibilidad, *n.f.* accessibility.
accesible, *a.* accessible.
accesión, *n.f.* accession; (*med.*) access.
acceso, *n.m.* access; (*jur.*) accession (*to property*); (*med.*) attack.
accesorio, -ria, *a. n.m.* accessory.—*n.f.* outbuilding.
accidentado, -da, *a.* broken (*ground*); eventful.
accidental, *a.* accidental, fortuitous.
accidente, *n.m.* accident, chance.
acción, *n.f.* action; (*com.*) share.
accionar, *v.t.* (*mech.*) operate.—*v.i.* gesticulate.
accionista, *n.m.f.* (*com.*) shareholder.
acebo, *n.m.* (*bot.*) holly.
acebuche, *n.m.* (*bot.*) wild olive-tree.
acecinar, *v.t.* salt and smoke *or* dry (*meat*).
acechanza, *n.f.* [ACECHO].
acechar, *v.t.* waylay, lie in ambush for; (*fig.*) watch closely for.

acecho, *n.m.* waylaying, ambush.
acedar, *v.t., v.r.* sour.
acedera, *n.f.* (*bot.*) sorrel.
acedía, *n.f.* acidity; heartburn.
acedo, -da, *a.* acid, sour; (*fig.*) harsh, cutting.
acéfalo, -la, *a.* acephalous, headless.
aceitar, *v.t.* oil, lubricate.
aceite, *n.m.* oil.
aceitero, -ra, *a.* relative to oil.—*n.f.* **oil-cruet**; oil-can.
aceitoso, -sa, *a.* oily, greasy.
aceituna, *n.f.* olive.
aceituno, *n.m.* (*bot.*) olive-tree.
aceleración, *n.f.* acceleration.
acelerador, *n.m.* accelerator.
acelerar, *v.t.* accelerate, hasten, expedite.
acelga, *n.f.* (*bot.*) salt-wort; (*cul.*) spinach-beet.
acémila, *n.f.* mule.
acendrar, *v.t.* refine; (*fig.*) purify.
acento, *n.m.* accent, stress.
acentuación, *n.f.* accentuation.
acentuar, *v.t.* accentuate, stress.
aceña, *n.f.* water-mill (*for corn*).
acepción, *n.f.* acceptation; (*gram.*) acceptation, sense, meaning; — ***de personas,*** favouritism.
acepillar, *v.t.* (*carp.*) plane; brush (*clothes*).
aceptable, *a.* acceptable.
aceptación, *n.f.* acceptance; approbation.
aceptar, *v.t.* accept.
acequia, *n.f.* channel (*for irrigation*).
acera, *n.f.* pavement, (*U.S.*) sidewalk.
acerbo, -ba, *a.* tart; (*fig.*) cruel, severe.
acerca de, *prep.* about, concerning.
acercar [A], *v.t.* bring near, draw up.—*v.r.* approach (***a***).
acero, *n.m.* steel.
acerolo, *n.m.* (*bot.*) hawthorn, may.
acérrimo, -ma, *sup. a.* very harsh; very strong (*taste, smell*); (*fig.*) very staunch.
acertar [1], *v.t.* hit the mark; hit by chance; guess correctly.—*v.i.* succeed.
acertijo, *n.m.* riddle.
acetato, *n.m.* acetate.
acetileno, *n.m.* acetylene.
acetona, *n.f.* acetone.
aciago, -ga, *a.* unfortunate, sad.
acíbar, *n.m.* aloe(s).
acicalar, *v.t.* burnish.
acicate, *n.m.* long spur; (*fig.*) spur.
acidez, *n.f.* acidity.
acidificar, *v.t.* acidify.
ácido, -da, *a.* acid, sour.—*n.m.* acid.
acierto, *n.m.* good shot; dexterity; success; right answer.
aclamación, *n.f.* acclamation.
aclamar, *v.t.* acclaim.
aclarar, *v.t.* make clear, clarify; explain; rinse.—*v.i., v.r.* clear up (*weather*).
aclaratorio, -ria, *a.* explanatory.
aclimatación, *n.f.* acclimatization; absorption (*of immigrants*).
aclimatar, *v.t.* acclimatize.
acne, *n.m.* (*med.*) acne.
acobardar, *v.t.* intimidate.—*v.r.* become daunted.
acoger [E], *v.t.* receive; welcome, shelter.—*v.r.* take shelter; (*fig.*) resort to (*a pretext*).
acogida, *n.f.* reception; place of meeting; ***dar — a una letra,*** (*com.*) honour a draft; ***buena —,*** welcome.
acólito, *n.m.* acolyte.
acometedor, -ra, *a.* aggressive.—*n.m.f.* aggressor.
acometer, *v.t.* attack; undertake; overcome, overtake.
acometida, *n.f.* attack; fit of illness.
acomodación, *n.f.* accommodation; integration, absorption (*of immigrants*).
acomodado, -ada, *a.* well-to-do; fond of comfort; convenient; reasonable.
acomodador, -ra, *a.* conciliating.—*n.m.* (*theat.*) usher.—*n.f.* usherette.
acomodar, *v.t.* accommodate, put up; compromise.—*v.i.* suit.—*v.r.* comply; put up (***a***, with).
acompañamiento, *n.m.* retinue; (*mus.*) accompaniment.
acompañar, *v.t.* accompany; (*com.*) enclose.
acompasado, -da, *a.* measured, rhythmic; (*fam.*) slow, monotonous.
acompasar, *v.t.* measure with dividers; (*mus.*) divide into bars (*score*).
acondicionar, *v.t.* prepare, arrange; condition.—*v.r.* qualify (*for a position*).
aconsejable, *a.* advisable.
aconsejar, *v.t.* advise, counsel.—*v.r.* consult (***con***, with).
aconsonantar, *v.t., v.i.* rhyme.
acontecedero, -ra, *a.* possible, eventual.
acontecer [9] (*used only in inf. and 3rd person*) *v.i.* happen.
acontecimiento, *n.m.* event, occurrence.
acopiar, *v.t.* collect, garner; corner (*goods*).
acopio, *n.m.* gathering; cornering.
acoplar, *v.t.* couple.—*v.t., v.r.* (*zool.*) mate.
acoquinar, *v.t.* (*fam.*) scare.
acorazado, *n.m.* battleship.
acorazar [C], *v.t.* armour-plate.
acorchar, *v.r.* shrivel; (*fig.*) go to sleep (*limbs*).
acordada, *n.f.* (*jur.*) order, decision.
acordar [4], *v.t.* remind; tune; make flush *or* level.—*v.i.* agree.—*v.r.* remember (***de***).
acorde, *a.* in tune; in accord.—*n.m.* (*mus.*) chord; harmony.
acordeón, *n.m.* (*mus.*) accordion.
acorralar, *v.t.* (*agr.*) round up, pen, (*U.S.*) corral; intimidate.
acorrer, *v.t.* avail.
acortar, *v.t.* shorten, lessen; obstruct.—*v.r.* shrivel; shrink; be bashful; (*mil.*) fall back.
acosar, *v.t.* harass.
acostar [4], *v.t.* lay down; put to bed.—*v.i.* (*naut.*) tilt.—*v.r.* lie down; go to bed.
acostumbrado, -da, *a.* usual, customary.
acostumbrar, *v.t.* accustom.—*v.i.* be accustomed to, be used to.—*v.r.* become accustomed (***a***, to).
acotación, *n.f.* bounds, limit; annotation; (*theat.*) directions.
acotar, *v.t.* limit; banish; annotate; accept for a certain price; vouch for.
acotillo, *n.m.* sledge-hammer.
acre, *a.* acrid.
acrecentar [1], **acrecer** [9], *v.t., v.r.* increase; advance.
acreditar, *v.t.* assure; verify; (*com.*) guarantee; authorize; prove.—*v.r.* gain a reputation (***de***, as).
acribar, *v.t.* sift; (*fig.*) riddle.

acriminar, *v.t.* accuse.
acrimonia, *n.f.* acrimony.
acrisolar, *v.t.* (*metal.*) refine; (*fig.*) purify; (*fig.*) clear up.
acróbata, *n.m.f.* acrobat.
acrobático, -ca, *a.* acrobatic.
acta, *n.f.* record of proceedings, minutes; certificate.
actitud, *n.f.* attitude.
activar, *v.t.* make active, activate; expedite.
actividad, *n.f.* activity; nimbleness.
activo, -va, *a.* active; quick.—*n.m.* (*com.*) assets.
acto, *n.m.* act; event; public function; (*theat.*) act.
actor, *n.m.* actor; (*jur.*) plaintiff.
actriz, *n.f.* actress.
actuación, *n.f.* actuation, action; performance; (*jur.*) proceedings.
actual, *a.* present, current.
actualidad, *n.f.* present time.—*pl.* current events.
actualmente, *adv.* at present.
actuar [M], *v.t.* actuate, set in action.—*v.i.* act (*de,* as); perform; perform judicial acts.
actuario, *n.m.* clerk of the court; actuary.
acuarela, *n.f.* (*art.*) water-colour.
Acuario, *n.m.* (*astr.*) Aquarius; **acuario,** *n.m.* aquarium.
acuartelar, *v.t.* (*mil., her.*) quarter.
acuático, -ca, *a.* aquatic.
acuatizar [C], *v.i.* (*aer.*) alight on the water.
acucia, *n.f.* zeal, diligence; longing.
acuciar, *v.t.* stimulate, hasten; covet.
acuclillar, *v.r.* crouch, squat.
acuchillado, -da, *a.* (*fig.*) toughened by experience.
acuchillar, *v.t.* stab, cut, slash.
acudir, *v.i.* resort; assist; attend.
acueducto, *n.m.* aqueduct.
acuerdo, *n.m.* resolution; remembrance; agreement, pact; harmony; ***de* —,** in agreement; agreed.
acuitar, *v.t.* afflict.
acullá, *adv.* yonder.
acumulación, *n.f.* accumulation.
acumular, *v.t.* accumulate, hoard; impute to.
acumulativo, -va, *a.* joint; cumulative.
acuñar (1), *v.t.* mint, coin.
acuñar (2), *v.t.* wedge.
acuoso, -sa, *a.* watery, aqueous.
acurrucar [A], *v.r.* huddle.
acusación, *n.f.* accusation.
acusado, -da, *a., n.m.f.* accused; marked.
acusar, *v.t.* accuse; prosecute; show; (*com.*) acknowledge (*receipt*).
acusativo, -va, *a., n.m.* (*gram.*) accusative.
acuse, *n.m.* (*com.*) acknowledgement.
acusón, -sona, *a., n.m.f.* tell-tale.
acústico, -ca, *a.* acoustic.—*n.f.* acoustics.
achacar [A], *v.t.* impute, blame.
achacoso, -sa, *a.* ailing.
achaparrado, -da, *a.* thick-set; stunted.
achaque, *n.m.* ailment; failing; excuse.
achicar [A], *v.t.* reduce, diminish.
achicoria, *n.f.* (*bot.*) chicory.
achochar, *v.r.* (*fam.*) become senile.
adagio (1), *n.m.* adage.
adagio (2), *n.m.* (*mus.*) adagio.
adalid, *n.m.* (*obs.*) chief, champion.
adaptable, *a.* adaptable.
adaptación, *n.f.* adaptation.
adaptar, *v.t.* adapt, fit.
adarga, *n.f.* (oval) shield.
adarme, *n.m.* small amount.
adecuado, -da, *a.* adequate.
adecuar, *v.t.* fit, accommodate.
adefesio, *n.m.* (*fam.*) extravagance, folly; ridiculous person.
adelantado, -da, *a.* advanced; forward; fast (*clock*); early (*fruit*); ***por* —,** in advance.—*n.m.* governor of a province.
adelantamiento, *n.m.* progress; betterment; anticipation.
adelantar, *v.t.* advance; promote; pay in advance.—*v.i.* be fast, gain (*clock*).—*v.r.* take the lead; overtake (***a***).
adelante, *adv.* ahead; forward.—*interj.* come in!
adelanto, *n.m.* advance; (*com.*) advance payment.
adelfa, *n.f.* (*bot.*) oleander.
adelgazar [C], *v.t.* make thin; taper; attenuate.—*v.i., v.r.* slim; taper off.
ademán, *n.m.* gesture; manner; ***en* — *de,*** about to, prepared to.—*pl.* manners.
además, *adv.* moreover; besides.—*prep.* **— *de,*** besides.
adentro, *adv.* within, inside; ***mar* —,** out to sea.—*n.m.pl.* innermost thoughts; ***para sus adentros,*** to oneself.
adepto, -ta, *a.* adept, initiated.
aderezar [C], *v.t.* adorn; (*cul.*) cook; (*cul.*) dress (*salad*).
aderezo, *n.m.* dressing; finery.
adestrar [1], *v.t.* lead; train.—*v.r.* practise.
adeudar [P], *v.t.* owe; (*com.*) debit.—*v.r.* run into debt.
adeudo, *n.m.* indebtedness; (*com.*) debit.
adherencia, *n.f.* adhesion, adherence; bond.
adherente, *a.* adhesive.—*n.m.* adherent, follower; accessory, equipment.
adherir [6], *v.t., v.r.* adhere, stick.
adhesión, *n.f.* adhesion, adherence.
adhesivo, -va, *a.* adhesive.—*n.m.* adhesive, glue.
adición, *n.f.* addition.
adicional, *a.* additional.
adicto, -ta, *a.* addicted; attached.
adiestramiento, *n.m.* training.
adiestrar, *v.t., v.r.* practise.
adinerado, -da, *a.* well-to-do, wealthy.
¡adiós! *interj.* good-bye! good day!
adiposo, -sa, *a.* adipose, fat.
aditamento, *n.m.* addition; attachment.
aditivo, -va, *a., n.m.* additive.
adivinaja, *n.f.* conundrum.
adivinar, *v.t.* foretell; guess right.
adivino, -va, *n.m.f.* soothsayer, fortune-teller; guesser.
adjetival, *a.* adjectival.
adjetivo, -va, *a., n.m.* adjective.
adjudicar [A], *v.t.* adjudge, adjudicate; sell (*at auction*).—*v.r.* appropriate.
adjunta, *n.f.* (*com*). enclosure (*in letter*).
adjunto, -ta, *a.* enclosed; associate.
administración, *n.f.* administration; (*com. etc.*) management.
administrador, *n.m.* administrator; manager; (*com.*) director; trustee.
administrar, *v.t.* administer; govern.
administrativo, -va, *a.* administrative; managerial.
admirable, *a.* admirable; marvellous.

admiración, *n.f.* admiration; wonder; (*gram.*) exclamation mark.
admirar, *v.t.* admire; marvel at; cause to wonder.—*v.r.* wonder, be astonished (***de,*** at).
admisible, *a.* admissible.
admisión, *n.f.* admission, acceptance; input.
admitir, *v.t.* receive, admit; permit.
adobar, *v.t.* prepare (*food*); pickle (*meat*); tan (*hide*).
adobe, *n.m.* mud brick, adobe.
adobo, *n.m.* repairing; pickle sauce; dressing.
adolecente, *a.* suffering.
adolecer [9], *v.i.* suffer (***de,*** from).—*v.r.* condole.
adolescencia, *n.f.* adolescence.
adolescente, *a.*, *n.m.f.* adolescent.
adonde, *adv.* where, whither. (*As interrog.* **¿adónde?**).
adopción, *n.f.* adoption.
adoptar, *v.t.* adopt.
adoptivo, -va, *a.* adoptive; foster.
adoquier, adoquiera, *adv.* anywhere.
adoquín, *n.m.* paving-stone; (*fig.*) rogue.
adorable, *a.* adorable.
adoración, *n.f.* adoration.
adorar, *v.t.* adore, worship.
adormecer [9], *v.t.* lull.—*v.r.* fall asleep.
adormilar, adormitar, *v.r.* doze, drowse.
adornamiento, *n.m.* adornment.
adornar, *v.t.* adorn, embellish, ornament.
adorno, *n.m.* ornament; accomplishment; furniture.
adquirir [6], *v.t.* acquire, obtain.
adquisición, *n.f.* acquisition.
adrede, *adv.* on purpose, deliberately.
adriático, -ca, *a.* Adriatic.
aduana, *n.f.* customs.
aduanero, -ra, *a.* customs.—*n.m.* customs officer.
aducir [15], *v.t.* adduce.
adueñar, *v.r.* take possession.
adulación, *n.f.* adulation, flattery.
adular, *v.t.* adulate, flatter.
adulteración, *n.f.* adulteration.
adulterar, *v.t.* adulterate.—*v.i.* commit adultery.
adulterino, -na, *a.* adulterine.
adulterio, *n.m.* adultery.
adúltero, -ra, *a.* adulterous.—*n.m.* adulterer. —*n.f.* adulteress.
adulto, -ta, *a.*, *n.m.f.* adult, grown-up.
adusto, -ta, *a.* parched; austere; sullen, dour.
advenidizo, -za, *a.*, *n.m.f.* immigrant; outsider, newcomer; parvenu, upstart.
advenimiento, *n.m.* arrival; accession (*of ruler*).
adventicio, -cia, *a.* adventitious.
adverbial, *a.* adverbial.
adverbio, *n.m.* adverb.
adversario, -ria, *n.m.f.* opponent, foe, adversary.
adversidad, *n.f.* adversity, misfortune.
adverso, -sa, *a.* adverse, calamitous, unfavourable.
advertencia, *n.f.* admonition; remark; foreword.
advertido, -da, *a.* intelligent; sagacious.
advertir [6], *v.t.* observe; give warning of; advise (*person*).
Adviento, *n.m.* (*eccl.*) Advent.
adyacente, *a.* adjacent.
aeración, *n.f.* aeration.
aéreo, -rea, *a.* aerial, by air; (*fig.*) airy.
aerodeslizador, *n.m.* hovercraft.
aerodinámica, *n.f.* aerodynamics.
aerodinámico, -ca, *a.* aerodynamic.
aeródromo, *n.m.* aerodrome, airfield, airport.
aerógrama, *n.m.* air letter.
aerolito, *n.m.* aerolite, meteorite.
aeronáutico, -ca, *a.* aeronautical.—*n.f.* aeronautics.
aeronave, *n.f.* (*aer.*) aircraft, air liner; airship.
aeroplano, *n.m.* (*aer.*) aeroplane, airplane, aircraft.
aeropuerto, *n.m.* airport.
aerosol, *n.m.* aerosol.
aerostato, *n.m.* aerostat.
afabilidad, *n.f.* affability, approachableness.
afable, *a.* affable, approachable.
afamar, *v.t.* make famous.
afán, *n.m.* anxiety; eagerness; toil.
afanadamente, *adv.* laboriously; anxiously.
afanar, *v.t.* press, urge.—*v.i.*, *v.r.* toil.
afanoso, -sa, *a.* anxious; painstaking.
afear, *v.t.* deform; (*fig.*) decry.
afección, *n.f.* affection, fondness; (*med.*) affection.
afectación, *n.f.* affectation; (*com.*) earmarking (*funds*).
afectado, -da, *a.* affected, foppish.
afectar, *v.t.* affect; (*mil.*) attach.—*v.r.* be moved.
afecto, -ta, *a.* affectionate; fond (***a,*** of).—*n.m.* affection; (*med.*) affect.
afectuoso, -sa, *a.* affectionate.
afeitar, *v.t.*, *v.r.* make up; shave; ***máquina de* —,** (electric) shaver; ***maquinilla de* —,** safety razor.
afeite, *n.m.* cosmetic, make-up; shave.
afeminar, *v.t.* make effeminate.
aferrado, -da, *a.* headstrong, obstinate.
aferrar, *v.t.* grasp.—*v.r.* (*fig.*) persist obstinately (***a,*** in).
el Afganistán, *n.m.* Afghanistan.
afgano, -na, *a.*,*n.m.f.* Afghan.
afianzar [C], *v.t.* guarantee, go bail for; prop.
afición, *n.f.* affection (***a,*** for); enthusiasm.
aficionado, -da, *a.* fond (***a,*** of).—*n.m.* amateur; (*fam.*) fan.
aficionar, *v.t.* give a liking (***a,*** for).—*v.r.* take a fancy (***a,*** to).
afilar, *v.t.* sharpen; taper.
afiliar, *v.t.* adopt; affiliate.
afilón, *n.m.* whetstone; smoothing steel.
afín, *a.* contiguous, close by.—*n.m.f.* relation by affinity; (*fam.*) in-law.
afinación, *n.f.* (*mus.*, *T.V.*) tuning; (*metal.*) refining.
afinar, *v.t.* complete; (*mus.*, *T.V.*) tune; (*metal.*) refine.
afincar [A], *v.i.*, *v.r.* acquire real estate.
afinidad, *n.f.* relationship.
afirmar, *v.t.* make fast; affirm.
afirmativo, -va, *a.* affirmative.
aflicción, *n.f.* affliction.
aflictivo, -va, *a.* distressing; ***pena aflictiva,*** corporal punishment.
afligir [E], *v.t.* afflict.—*v.r.* grieve.
aflojar, *v.t.* loosen, slacken.—*v.i.*, *v.r.* grow weak; slack.
aflorar, *v.t.* sift (*flour*).

afluencia, *n.f.* abundance; general rush; fluency.
afluente, *a.* abundant; affluent.—*n.m.* (*geog.*) tributary.
afluir [O], *v.i.* congregate; flow (into).
aflujo, *n.m.* inrush; (*med.*) afflux.
afondar, *v.t.*, *v.i.*, *v.r.* sink.
aforar, *v.t.* gauge, appraise.
aforismo, *n.m.* aphorism, maxim.
aforro, *n.m.* lining.
afortunado, -da, *a.* fortunate, lucky.
afrancesar, *v.t.* gallicise, frenchify.
afrenta, *n.f.* insult, affront.
africano, -na, *a.*, *n.m.f.* African.
afrodisíaco, -ca, *a.* aphrodisiac.
afrontar, *v.t.* confront.—*v.i.* face.
afuera, *adv.* outside.—*n.f.pl.* outskirts; surrounding country.
agachadiza, *n.f.* (*orn.*) snipe.
agachar, *v.t.* bow down.—*v.r.* crouch.
agalla, *n.f.* oak-apple.
agalludo, -da, *a.* (*S.A.*) stingy; (*S.A.*) foxy.
agareno, -na, *a.* Mohammedan; Arab.
agarrado, -da, *a.* tight-fisted.
agarrar, *v.t.* grasp, seize.—*v.r.* hold on (***de***, to).
agarre, *n.m.* grip, gripping.
agarrotar, *v.t.* garrotte; compress (*bales*).
agasajar, *v.t.* receive kindly, fête; fondle.
agasajo, *n.m.* friendly treatment; reception, party; kindness; gift.
ágata, *n.f.* (*gem.*) agate.
agencia, *n.f.* agency, bureau.
agenda, *n.f.* note-book; diary.
agente, *n.m.* agent.
agigantado, -da, *a.* gigantic.
ágil, *a.* agile, nimble.
agilidad, *n.f.* agility.
agitación, *n.f.* agitation; stirring; (*naut.*) choppiness.
agitador, -ra, *n.m.f.* agitator.
agitar, *v.t.* agitate; stir.
aglomeración, *n.f.* agglomeration.
aglomerado, *n.m.* briquette.
aglomerar, *v.t.* agglomerate.
aglutinación, *n.f.* agglutination.
aglutinante, *n.m.* cement.
aglutinar, *v.t.* agglutinate.
agnóstico, -ca, *a.*, *n.m.f.* agnostic.
agobiar, *v.t.* bow down; (*fig.*) oppress, overwhelm.
agolpar, *v.t.* pile up.—*v.r.* crowd.
agonía, *n.f.* agony; pangs of death.
agonioso, -sa, *a.* importunate, persistent.
agonizante, *a.* dying.—*n.m.f.* person on the point of death.
agonizar [C], *v.i.* be dying.
agorar [10], *v.t.* divine, foretell.
agostar, *v.t.* parch; consume.
agosto, *n.m.* August; harvest; ***hacer su —***, get rich quick(ly), make hay while the sun shines.
agotado, -da, *a.* out of print.
agotar, *v.t.* exhaust; use up.—*v.r.* go out of print; become exhausted.
agraciar, *v.t.* embellish; favour.
agradable, *a.* agreeable, pleasant.
agradar, *v.i.* please.
agradecer [9], *v.t.* thank for; be grateful for.
agradecido, -da, *a.* grateful.
agradecimiento, *n.m.* gratitude.
agrado, *n.m.* agreeableness; pleasure; gratitude; liking.
agramilar, *v.t.* point (*brickwork*).
agrandamiento, *n.m.* enlargement; aggrandisement.
agrario, -ria, *a.* agrarian.
agravación, *n.f.* aggravation.
agravar, *v.t.* exaggerate; oppress.—*v.r.* become grave.
agraviador, -ra, *n.m.f.* injurer; offender.
agraviante, *a.* wronging; aggravating.
agraviar, *v.t.* wrong, harm.—*v.r.* take offence.
agravio, *n.m.* offence; harm; grievance.
agravioso, -sa, *a.* offensive; injurious.
agraz, *n.m.* (*pl.* **-aces**) unripe grape; (*fam.*, *fig.*) displeasure; ***en —***, unripe, premature.
agredir, *v.t.* attack, assault.
agregado, *n.m.* aggregate; attaché.
agregar, *v.t.* aggregate; add.
agresión, *n.f.* aggression.
agresividad, *n.f.* aggressiveness.
agresivo, -va, *a.* aggressive.
agresor, -ra, *n.m.f.* aggressor.
agreste, *a.* rustic; wild (*plant*); (*fam.*) uncouth.
agriar [L *or regular*], *v.t.* make sour.
agrícola, *a.* agricultural.
agricultor, *n.m.* farmer, agriculturist.
agricultura, *n.f.* agriculture.
agridulce, *a.* bitter-sweet.
agrietar, *v.t.*, *v.r.* crack, split.
agrimensor, *n.m.* land-surveyor.
agrio, -ria, *a.* sour, sharp; (*bot.*) citrous.
agro, -ra, *a.* [AGRIO].—*n.m.* citron.
agronomía, *n.f.* agronomy, agriculture.
agrónomo, -ma, *n.m.f.* agronomist, agricultural expert.
agrupar, *v.t.* group.—*v.r.* cluster.
agua, *n.f.* water; ***aguas mayores***, excrement; ***aguas menores***, urine.
aguacate, *n.m.* avocado pear.
aguacero, *n.m.* downpour.
aguaducho, *n.m.* refreshment stall.
aguafiestas, *n.m.f.* (*fam.*) kill-joy, wet blanket.
aguafuerte, *n.f.* etching.
aguaje, *n.m.* tidal wave; sea current; wake.
aguamanil, *n.m.* water-jug; washstand.
aguamarina, *n.f.* aquamarine.
aguamiel, *n.f.* honey and water; mead.
aguanieve, *n.f.* sleet.
aguantar, *v.t.* suffer, endure; put up with.—*v.r.* forbear.
aguar [H], *v.t.* dilute with water, water; (*fig.*) mar.
aguardar, *v.t.* wait for, await.—*v.i.* wait.
aguardiente, *n.m.* spirits; brandy.
aguarrás, *n.m.* turpentine.
aguaturma, *n.f.* (*bot.*) Jerusalem artichoke.
agudeza, *n.f.* sharpness; acuteness; wit.
agudo, -da, *a.* sharp; acute; clever; (*mus.*) high-pitched.
agüero, *n.m.* augury.
aguijada, *n.f.* spur, goad.
aguijar, *v.t.* spur, goad.—*v.i.* hasten.
aguijón, *n.m.* sting; spur, goad.
águila, *n.f.* eagle.
aguileño, -ña, *a.* aquiline.—*n.f.* (*bot.*) columbine.
aguilón, *n.m.* boom (*of crane*).
aguilucho, *n.m.* eaglet.
aguinaldo, *n.m.* New Year's present; Christmas box.

aguja, *n.f.* needle; (*rail.*) point; hand (*of watch*); (*arch.*) spire.
agujazo, *n.m.* prick.
agujerear, *v.t.* pierce, prick.
agujero, *n.m.* hole.
agujeta, *n.f.* lace (*for shoes etc.*).—*pl.* pins-and-needles, cramp.
agujón, *n.m.* hatpin.
¡agur! *interj.* (*fam.*) good-bye!
agusanar, *v.r.* become worm-eaten.
Agustín, *n.m.* Augustine.
agustiniano, -na, agustino, -na, *a., n.m.f.* (*eccl.*) Augustinian, (*obs.*) Austin.
aguzanieves, *n.m. inv.* (*orn.*) wagtail.
aguzar [C], *v.t.* sharpen, whet.
ahechar, *v.t.* winnow.
ahí, *adv.* there; yonder; ***por* —,** that way; somewhere over there.
ahijada, *n.f.* god-daughter.
ahijado, *n.m.* god-son.
ahilar, *v.r.* become faint; turn sour.
ahilo, *n.m.* faintness.
ahinco, *n.m.* earnestness; ardour.
ahitar, *v.t., v.r.* surfeit, gorge.
ahito, -ta, *a.* satiated, gorged; bored.—*n.m.* surfeit; indigestion.
ahogadizo, -za, *a.* heavier than water, sinkable.
ahogador, *n.m.* hangman.
ahogamiento, *n.m.* drowning; suffocation.
ahogar [B], *v.t., v.r.* stifle; choke; drown.
ahogo, *n.m.* anguish; suffocation; penury.
ahondar, *v.t.* go deep into.—*v.i.* go deep; investigate.
ahonde, *n.m.* excavation, sinking.
ahora, *adv.* now; ***de — en adelante,*** from now on, henceforward.
ahorcar [A], *v.t.* hang.
ahorita, *adv.* (*fam.*) right away.
ahormar, *v.t.* fit, shape.
ahorrado, -da, *a.* unencumbered, exempt.
ahorramiento, *n.m.* saving.
ahorrar, *v.t.* save; spare.
ahorrativo, -va, *a.* thrifty; sparing.
ahorro, *n.m.* economy.—*pl.* savings; ***caja de ahorros,*** savings-bank.
ahuecar [A], *v.t.* excavate; hollow.—*v.r.* become hollow; put on airs.
ahumado, -da, *a.* smoky; smoked, smoke-cured.—*n.m.* smoking, curing.
ahumar, *v.t.* smoke; fumigate.—*v.i.* smoke, emit smoke.—*v.r.* get smoky.
ahusar, *v.t.* taper.
ahuyentar, *v.t.* frighten away; put to flight. —*v.r.* flee.
airado, -da, *a.* angry, wrathful.
airar [P], *v.t.* anger, irritate.—*v.r.* grow angry.
aire, *n.m.* air; (*mus.*) air; choke (*in cars*); ***al — libre,*** in the open air; ***hacer* —,** be windy.
airear, *v.t.* ventilate.—*v.r.* take the air.
airoso, -sa, *a.* airy, windy; graceful; successful.
aislamiento, *n.m.* isolation; (*phys.*) insulation.
aislar [P], *v.t.* isolate; (*phys.*) insulate.
¡ajá! *interj.* aha!
ajado, -da (1), *a.* garlicky.—*n.f.* garlic sauce.
ajado, -da (2), *a.* withered.
ajar, *v.t.* spoil, mar; tarnish.
ajedrecista, *n.m.f.* chess-player.
ajedrez, *n.m.* chess.
ajenjo, *n.m.* (*bot.*) wormwood; absinthe; (*fig.*) bitterness.
ajeno, -na, *a.* belonging to another; foreign; strange.
ajetreo, *n.m.* fatigue; agitation.
ají, *n.m.* (*bot.*) chili, capsicum.
ajimez, *n.m.* arched (Moorish) window divided by a central pillar.
ajo, *n.m.* garlic; (*fam.*) oath.
ajobo, *n.m.* burden.
ajuar, *n.m.* trousseau; household furniture.
ajustador, *n.m.* brassière.
ajustar, *v.t.* adjust; regulate; make (*an agreement*); reconcile; settle (*accounts*).
ajuste, *n.m.* adjustment; settlement; coupling.
ajusticiar, *v.t.* execute, put to death.
al [A EL].
ala, *n.f.* wing; brim (*hat*).
Alá, *n.m.* Allah.
alabanza, *n.f.* praise.
alabar, *v.t.* praise, extol.—*v.r.* boast; show oneself pleased (***de,*** at).
alabarda, *n.f.* halberd.
alabardero, *n.m.* halberdier; (*theat.*) member of the claque.
álabe, *n.m.* blade, vane (*of turbine*).
alabear, *v.t., v.r.* warp.
alacena, *n.f.* cupboard; closet; (*naut.*) locker.
Alacrán, *n.m.* (*astr.*) Scorpio; **alacrán,** *n.m.* scorpion.
alacridad, *n.f.* alacrity.
alambicar [A], *v.t.* distil; refine excessively (*style*).
alambique, *n.m.* still.
alambrada, *n.f.* barbed-wire entanglement.
alambrado, *n.m.* wiring.
alambrar, *v.t.* wire; fasten with wire.
alambre, *n.m.* wire; ***— de púas*** or ***espinas,*** barbed-wire.
alambrera, *n.f.* wire netting; wire cover (*for food etc.*).
alameda, *n.f.* poplar grove; public avenue.
álamo, *n.m.* poplar; ***— temblón,*** aspen.
alano, *n.m.* mastiff.
alar, *n.m.* overhanging roof.
alarbe, *a., n.m. f.* (*obs.*) Arab; Arabian.
alarde, *n.m.* parade, (*mil.*) review; ostentation.
alardear, *v.i.* boast, brag.
alargar [B], *v.t.* lengthen, extend; hand out; increase; protract.—*v.r.* become longer; move off.
alarido, *n.m.* outcry; scream.
alarma, *n.f.* alarm.
alarmante, *a.* alarming.
alavés, -vesa, *a., n.m.f.* rel. to Alava.
alazán, -zana, *a.* sorrel-coloured.
alaba, *n.f.* dawn; (*eccl.*) alb.
albacea, *n.m.* executor.—*n.f.* executrix.
albada, *n.f.* aubade, dawn song.
albahaca, *n.f.* (*bot.*) sweet-basil.
albalá, *n.m.f.* (*obs.*) royal letters patent.
albanega, *n.f.* hair net.
albanés, -nesa, *a., n.m.f.* Albanian.
albañal, *n.m.* sewer.
albañil, *n.m.* mason; bricklayer.
albañilería, *n.f.* masonry.
albarán, *n.m.* 'to let' sign.
albarda, *n.f.* packsaddle.
albardilla, *n.f.* small packsaddle; (*cul.*) batter; coping-stone.
albaricoque, *n.m.* apricot.
albaricoquero, *n.m.* apricot-tree.

albatros, *n.m. inv.* (*orn.*) albatros.
albayalde, *n.m.* white lead.
albear, *v.i.* glow white.
albedrío, *n.m.* free-will.
albéitar, *n.m.* horse-doctor.
alberca, *n.f.* pond; tank; vat.
albérchigo, *n.m.*, **albérchiga,** *n.f.* peach-apricot.
albergar [B], *v.t.*, *v.i.*, *v.r.* lodge, shelter.
albergue, *n.m.* lodging, shelter, hostel; den.
alberguería, *n.f.* inn; poorhouse.
albino, -na, *a.* albino.
albo, -ba, *a.* (*poet.*) white.
albogue, *n.m.* pastoral flute.
albollón, *n.m.* sewer; drain.
albóndiga, *n.f.* rissole; meat-dumpling.
albor, *n.m.* dawn; whiteness; (*fig.*) beginning.
alborada, *n.f.* dawn; dawn serenade.
albornoz, *n.m.* burnoose; dressing-gown.
alborotado, -da, *a.* turbulent, restive.
alborotar, *v.t.* disturb, excite.—*v.i.*, *v.r.* get excited; riot.
alboroto, *n.m.* disturbance; riot, outcry.
alborozar [C], *v.t.* exhilarate.
alborozo, *n.m.* merriment, gaiety.
albricias, *n.f.pl.* reward for bringing good news; expression of joy.
álbum, *n.m.* album.
albúmina, *n.f.* (*chem.*) albumin.
albuminoso, -sa, *a.* albuminous.
albura, *n.f.* whiteness; white of egg.
alca, *n.f.* (*orn.*) razorbill.
alcabala, *n.f.* excise.
alcachofa, *n.f.* (*bot.*) artichoke.
alcahueta, *n.f.* bawd, procuress.
alcahuete, *n.m.* pimp, procurer.
alcahuetear, *v.t.*, *v.i.* pander, procure (*women*).
alcaide, *n.m.* (*obs.*) governor, warden.
alcalde, *n.m.* mayor; justice of the peace.
alcaldía, *n.f.* office of ALCALDE.
álcali, *n.m.* (*chem.*) alkali.
alcalino, -na, *a.* (*chem.*) alkaline.
alcalizar [C], *v.t.* (*chem.*) alkalize.
alcaloide, *n.m.* alkaloid.
alcance, *n.m.* reach, scope, range; (*print.*) stop-press; (*com.*) deficit.
alcancía, *n.f.* money-box, (child's) piggy-bank.
alcanfor, *n.m.* camphor.
alcantarilla, *n.f.* culvert; sewer.
alcanzado, -da, *a.* necessitous; indebted.
alcanzar [C], *v.t.* follow; catch up with; overtake; get to; reach.
alcaparra, *n.f.*, **alcaparro,** *n.m.* (*bot.*) caper-bush; caper.
alcaraván, *n.m.* (*orn.*) stone-curlew.
alcaravea, *n.f.* (*bot.*) caraway seed.
alcatraz (1), *n.m.* (*orn.*) pelican, gannet.
alcatraz (2), *n.m.* (*bot.*) arum.
alcazaba, *n.f.* (*mil.*) keep, donjon.
alcázar, *n.m.* castle, fortress; (*naut.*) quarter-deck.
alce (1), *n.m.* moose, elk.
alce (2), *n.m.* cut (*at cards*); (*print.*) gathering.
alcista, *n.m.* (*com.*) bull (*Stock Exchange*).
alcoba, *n.f.* bedroom; alcove.
alcohol, *n.m.* alcohol; kohl, eye-shadow.
alcohólico, -ca, *a.* alcoholic.
alcor, *n.m.* hill.
alcornoque, *n.m.* cork-tree.
alcorza, *n.f.* (*cul.*) icing.
alcotana, *n.f.* pickaxe.
alcuña, alcurnia, *n.f.* ancestry, lineage.
alcuza, *n.f.* oil-bottle; oilcan.
alcuzcuz, *n.m.* (*cul.*) couscous.
aldaba, *n.f.* door-knocker; (*eng.*) iron flap.
aldabonazo, *n.m.* knock on the door.
aldea, *n.f.* village, hamlet.
aldeano, -na, rel. to a village; rustic.—*n.m.f.* villager; peasant.
aleación, *n.f.* (*metal.*) alloy; alloying.
alear (1), *v.t.* alloy.
alear (2), *v.i.* flutter.
aledaño, -ña, *a.* bordering.—*n.m.* boundary, border.
alegación, *n.f.* allegation; argument.
alegar [B], *v.t.* allege, affirm; quote.
alegato, *n.m.* (*jur.*) allegation, summing-up.
alegoría, *n.f.* allegory.
alegórico, -ca, *a.* allegorical.
alegorizar [C], *v.t.* allegorize.
alegrar, *v.t.* gladden; enliven.—*v.r.* be glad, rejoice (*de*, at).
alegre, *a.* merry, gay; funny; tipsy.
alegría, *n.f.* mirth; joy; pleasure.
alegro, *n.m.* (*mus.*) allegro.
Alejandría, *n.f.* Alexandria.
alejandrino, -na, *a.*, *n.m.* alexandrine.
Alejandro, *n.m.* Alexander.
alejar, *v.t.* remove to a distance; separate.—*v.r.* recede.
aleluya, *n.f.* hallelujah, alleluia; joy; doggerel.
alemán, -mana, *a.*, *n.m.f.* German.
Alemania, *n.f.* Germany.
alentador, -ra, *a.* encouraging, cheering.
alentar [1], *v.t.* inspire; encourage.—*v.i.* breathe.
alerce, *n.m.* (*bot.*) larch.
alero, *n.m.* eaves, gable-end.
alerón, *n.m.* (*aer.*) aileron.
alerta, *n.m.* (*mil.*) alert.—*interj.* watch out!
alertar, *v.t.* put on guard.—*v.r.* be on one's guard.
alerto, -ta, *a.* alert, vigilant.
aleta, *n.f.* (*ichth.*) fin; (*Brit.*) mudguard; (*U.S.*) fender; (*aer.*) flap, fin.
aletear, *v.i.* flutter, flap.
aleve, *a.* perfidious.
alevosía, *n.f.* perfidy.
alevoso, -sa, *a.* perfidious.
alfabético, -ca, *a.* alphabetical.
alfabeto, *n.m.* alphabet.
alfalfa, *n.f.* alfalfa, lucerne.
alfanje, *n.m.* scimitar; cutlass.
alfaquí, *n.m.* fakir.
alfarería, *n.f.* pottery, earthenware.
alfarero, -ra, *n.m.f.* potter.
alféizar, *n.m.* (*arch.*) embrasure.
alfeñicado, -da, *a.* weakly; finicky.
alfeñique, *n.m.* sugar paste; (*fam.*) delicate person.
alférez, *n.m.* (*mil.*) ensign; second lieutenant.
alfil, *n.m.* bishop (*chess*).
alfiler, *n.m.* pin; brooch.—*pl.* pin-money.
alfolí, *n.m.* granary; salt warehouse.
alfombra, *n.f.* carpet; rug, mat.
alfonsí, *a.* Alfonsine.
alforja, *n.f.* saddle-bag; pannier.
alforza, *n.f.* plait; tuck.
alga, *n.f.* (*bot.*) alga, seaweed.
algalia, *n.f.* civet (*perfume*).—*n.m.* civet-cat.
algara, *n.f.* raiding party.
algarabía, *n.f.* Arabic; jargon; clamour.

algarroba, *n.f.* carob-bean.
álgebra, *n.f.* algebra.
algebraico, -ca, *a.* algebraic.
algo, *pron.* something.—*adv.* somewhat, rather.
algodón, *n.m.* cotton; — ***hidrófilo,*** cotton wool; — ***pólvora,*** gun cotton.
algodonoso, -sa, *a.* cottony; insipid (*of fruit*).
alguacil, *n.m.* constable.
alguien, *pron.* somebody.
algún, *a. m. contracted form of* ALGUNO *before n.m.sg.*
alguno, -na, *a.* some, any; — ***que otro,*** a few. —*pron.* somebody, someone.
alhaja, *n.f.* jewel; highly prized thing; showy furniture.
al(h)elí, *n.m.* (*bot.*) wallflower; stock.
alheña, *n.f.* (*bot.*) privet; henna (*dye*); (*agr.*) rust.
alhóndiga, *n.f.* public granary.
alhucema, *n.f.* lavender.
aliado, -da, *a.* allied.—*n.m.f.* ally.
alianza, *n.f.* alliance, league; wedding-ring; (*Bibl.*) covenant.
aliar [L], *v.r.* form an alliance.
alias, *adv.* (*Lat.*) alias.—*n.m.* alias.
alicaído, -da, *a.* with drooping wings; (*fig.*) discouraged.
alicantino, -na, *a., n.m.f.* (one) from Alicante.
alicates, *n.m.pl.* pliers, pincers, nippers.
aliciente, *n.m.* attraction, inducement.
alienable, *a.* alienable.
alienación, *n.f.* (*med., jur.*) alienation.
alienar, *v.t.* alienate.
aliento, *n.m.* breath; inspiration; bravery.
aligerar, *v.t.* lighten; ease.
alijar, *v.t.* (*naut.*) lighten (*cargo*); gin (*cotton*); smuggle; (*carp.*) sandpaper.
alijo, *n.m.* (*naut.*) lightening (*cargo*); ginning (*cotton*); smuggling.
alimaña, *n.f.* (*pej.*) animal.
alimentación, *n.f.* nutrition; feeding.
alimentar, *v.t.* feed; nourish.
alimenticio, -cia, *a.* nutritious.
alimento, *n.m.* food, nutriment.—*pl.* (*jur.*) alimony.
alineación, *n.f.* alignment.
aliñar, *v.t.* adorn; (*cul.*) dress.
aliño, *n.m.* ornament; preparation.
alisadura, *n.f.* smoothing; planing.—*pl.* shavings.
alisios, *n.m.pl.* trade winds.
aliso, *n.m.* (*bot.*) alder; — ***blanco,*** (*bot.*) birch.
alistar, *v.t., v.r.* enlist, enrol; get ready.
aliteración, *n.f.* alliteration.
aliviar, *v.t.* lighten, relieve.
alivio, *n.m.* relief; comfort.
aljama, *n.f.* mosque; synagogue; assembly (*of Moors* or *Jews*).
aljamía, *n.f.* Moorish name for Spanish; Spanish written with Arabic characters.
aljibe, *n.m.* cistern; well.
aljófar, *n.m.* asymmetrical pearl; (*poet.*) dewdrop.
alma (1), *n.f.* soul, spirit.
alma (2), *n.f.* (*arch.*) scaffold pole.
almacén, *n.m.* warehouse, store, shop; naval arsenal.
almádena, *n.f.* sledge-hammer.
almadía, *n.f.* raft.
almadreña, *n.f.* clog.
almagra, *n.f.,* **almagre,** *n.m.* red ochre.
almanaque, *n.m.* almanac.
almeja (1), *n.f.* (*zool.*) cockle; clam.
almeja (2), *n.f.* grab (*cranes*).
almendra, *n.f.* almond.
almendrado, *n.m.* macaroon.
almendrilla, *n.f.* gravel; nuts (*coal*); file.
almendro, *n.m.* almond-tree.
almiar, *n.m.* haystack.
almíbar, *n.m.* syrup.
almibarar, *v.t.* (*cul.*) preserve in syrup *or* sugar; (*fig.*) conciliate.
almidón, *n.m.* starch.
almidonar, *v.t.* starch.
alminar, *n.m.* minaret.
almirantazgo, *n.m.* admiralty.
almirante, *n.m.* admiral.
almirez, *n.m.* (*pl.* **-eces**) mortar.
almizcle, *n.m.* (*bot.*) musk.
almocafre, *n.m.* (*agr.*) dibble; hoe.
almofrej, almofrez (*S.A.*), *n.m.* (*pl.* **-eces**) bedding roll.
almohada, *n.f.* pillow; cushion.
almohadilla, *n.f.* cushion; pad.
almojarife, *n.m.* king's tax-gatherer.
almoneda, *n.f.* auction.
almorzar [4C], *v.i.* lunch; breakfast.
almud, *n.m.* a dry measure; half an acre.
almuédano, *n.m.* muezzin.
almuerzo, *n.m.* lunch, luncheon; breakfast.
alnada, *n.f.* step-daughter.
alnado, *n.m.* step-son.
alocución, *n.f.* allocution, address.
áloe, *n.m.* aloes.
aloja, *n.f.* mead.
alojamiento, *n.m.* lodging.
alojar, *v.t., v.i.* lodge; (*mil.*) (be) billet(ed).
alondra, *n.f.* (*orn.*) lark.
alongar [4B], *v.t.* enlarge; extend; separate.
alotropia, *n.f.* (*chem.*) allotropy.
alpaca, *n.f.* (*zool., textile*) alpaca.
alpargata, *n.f.* rope-soled sandal.
alpinismo, *n.m.* mountaineering.
alquería, *n.f.* (isolated) farmhouse.
alquilar, *v.t.* let, hire, rent.
alquiler, *n.m.* wages; fee; hire, rent.
alquilona, *n.f.* charwoman.
alquimia, *n.f.* alchemy.
alquitrán, *n.m.* tar, pitch.
alquitranado, *n.m.* tarpaulin.
alrededor, *adv.* around.—*prep.* around about (*de*).—*n.m.pl.* outskirts, environs.
altanería, *n.f.* haughtiness.
altanero, -ra, *a.* haughty, insolent; proud.
altar, *n.m.* altar.
altavoz, *n.m.* (*rad.*) loudspeaker.
alteración, *n.f.* alteration; change; taint.
alterar, *v.t.* alter, change (*for the worse*); debase; weather.
altercación, *n.f.* altercation, wrangle.
alternación, *n.f.* alternation.
alternadamente, *adv.* alternately.
alternar, *v.t.* alternate.—*v.i.* alternate; have friendly relations with, (*fam.*) hob-nob with.
alternativa, *n.f.* alternative, turn; (*taur.*) ceremony of becoming a matador.
alternativamente, *adv.* alternatively.
alternativo, -va, alterno, -na, *a.* alternate, by turns; (*elec.*) alternating.
Alteza, *n.f.* Highness (*title*); **alteza,** *n.f.* height.

altibajo(s), *n.m.(pl.)* ups and downs.
altímetro, *n.m.* (*aer.*) altimeter.
altisonante, *a.* high-sounding, grandiloquent, (*fam.*) high-falutin.
altitud, *n.f.* altitude; height.
altivez, *n.f.* haughtiness, pride.
altivo, -va, *a.* haughty.
alto (1) **-ta,** *a.* high, lofty, tall; (*mus.*) alto; — ***horno,*** blast furnace; ***dar de alta,*** pronounce fit; ***en voz alta,*** out loud, in a loud voice.
¡alto! (2), *interj.* halt!
altramuz, *n.f.* (*bot.*) lupin.
altura, *n.f.* height; altitude; (*naut.*) latitude; ***estar a la — de,*** be equal to, be up to.
alubia, *n.f.* bean.
alucinación, *n.f.,* **alucinamiento,** *n.m.* hallucination; spell.
alucinar, *v.t.* hallucinate; delude; fascinate.
alucón, *n.m.* tawny owl.
alud, *n.m.* avalanche.
aludir, *v.i.* allude, refer.
alumbrado, -da, *a.* (*fam.*) tipsy; enlightened. —*n.m.* lighting.
alumbramiento, *n.m.* illumination; childbirth.
alumbrar, *v.t.* illuminate, light.
alumbre, *n.m.* alum.
alumino, *n.m.* (*Brit.*) aluminium, (*U.S.*) aluminum.
alumno, -na, *n.m.f.* foster-child; pupil; student.
alusión, *n.f.* allusion.
aluvión, *n.m.* (*geol.*) alluvium.
alveolar, *a.* alveolar.
alza, *n.f.* (*com.*) rise (*in price*); (*mil.*) sight (*guns*).
alzado, *n.m.* fraudulent bankrupt; (*arch.*) elevation.
alzamiento, *n.m.* raising; raising a bid; rising, insurrection.
alzaprima, *n.f.* crowbar, lever; (*mech.*) fulcrum.
alzar [C], *v.t.* raise; cut (*cards*); (*naut.*) heave. —*v.r.* rise (*in revolt*); rise; (*com.*) embezzle.
allá, *adv.* there, in that place; ***por* —,** thereabouts.
allanar, *v.t.* level, flatten.—*v.r.* acquiesce (***a,*** in).
allegar [B], *v.t.* reap; collect; procure.—*v.r.* approach.
allende, *adv.* on the far side.
allí, *adv.* there, in that place.
ama, *n.f.* mistress of the house; owner; ***— de llaves,*** housekeeper; ***— de cría,*** wet-nurse.
amabilidad, *n.f.* amiability; kindness.
amable, *a.* amiable; kind.
amado, -da, *a.* beloved.—*n.m.f.* beloved, sweetheart.
amador, *n.m.* lover.
amaestrado, -da, *a.* experienced; schooled.
amaestrar, *v.t.* instruct, teach.
amagar [B], *v.t.* threaten; show signs of; feign. —*v.i.* threaten; be impending.
amago, *n.m.* threatening; hint; empty promise.
amainar, *v.t.* relax.—*v.i.* subside; lessen.
amalgama, *n.f.* (*metal.*) amalgam.
amalgamar, *v.t.* amalgamate.
amamantar, *v.t.* suckle.
amancebamiento, *n.m.* concubinage.
amancebar, *v.r.* live in concubinage.
amancillar, *v.t.* stain, pollute.
amanecer [9], *v.i.* dawn; be (at a place) at dawn.—*n.m.* dawn.
amanerar, *v.r.* become affected.
amansar, *v.t.* tame, domesticate, break in (*horses*).
amante, *a.* loving.—*n.m.f.* lover; sweetheart.
amanuense, *n.m.f.* amanuensis, clerk.
amañar, *v.t.* do cleverly, doctor (*accounts etc.*).—*v.r.* be handy.
amapola, *n.f.* poppy.
amar, *v.t.* love.
amargar [B], *v.t.* make bitter; embitter.—*v.i.* be bitter.
amargo, -ga, *a.* bitter.
amargón, *n.m.* (*bot.*) dandelion.
amargor, *n.m.,* **amargura,** *n.f.* bitterness.
amaricado, -da, *a.* (*fam., pej.*) effeminate, sissy.
amarillez, *n.f.* yellowness.
amarillo, -lla, *a.* yellow.—*n.m.* jaundice.
amarra, *n.f.* (*naut.*) cable, hawser.
amarre, *n.m.* (*naut.*) mooring, tying-up.
amartelar, *v.t.* court; love devotedly.—*v.r.* fall in love.
amartillar, *v.t.* hammer.
amasadera, *n.f.* kneading-trough.
amasadora, *n.f.* mixer (*dough etc.*).
amasar, *v.t.* knead, mould; (*med.*) massage.
amasijo, *n.m.* dough; kneading; mortar.
amatista, *n.f.* (*gem.*) amethyst.
amayorazgar [B], *v.t.* (*jur.*) entail.
amazona, *n.f.* riding habit; horsewoman; (*myth.*) Amazon.
Amazonas, *n.m.sg.* Amazon (*river*).
amazónico, -ca, *a.* Amazonian.
ambages, *n.m.pl.* circumlocutions.
ámbar, *n.m.* amber.
ambición, *n.f.* ambition.
ambicionar, *v.t.* aspire to.
ambicioso, -sa, *a.* ambitious; covetous.
ambidextro, -tra, *a.* ambidextrous.
ambiente, *n.m.* environment; atmosphere.
ambigüedad, *n.f.* ambiguity.
ambiguo, -gua, *a.* ambiguous, doubtful.
ámbito, *n.m.* circuit; compass; scope.
ambos, -bas, *a., pron. pl.* both.
ambulancia, *n.f.* ambulance.
ambulante, *a.* ambulant; ***vendedor* —,** pedlar, itinerant salesman.
ameba [AMIBA].
amedrantar, *v.t.* frighten.
amén, *n.m.* amen.—*prep.* beside, in addition to (***de***).
amenaza, *n.f.* threat.
amenazante, *a.* menacing.
amenazar [C], *v.t.* threaten, menace (***con,*** with, to).
amenidad, *n.f.* amenity; urbanity.
ameno, -na, *a.* pleasant; elegant; urbane.
americana, *n.f.* jacket.
americanismo, *n.m.* (*gram.*) Americanism.
americano, -na, *a., n.m.f.* American (*esp. applied to S.A.*).
amerindio, -dia, *a., n.m.f.* Amerindian.
ametrallador, *n.m.* machine gunner.
ametralladora, *n.f.* machine-gun.
ametrallar, *v.t.* machine-gun, strafe.
amiba, *n.f.* amoeba.
amiga (1), *n.f.* friend; mistress, concubine.
amiga (2), *n.f.* (*prov., obs.*) dame-school.
amigablemente, *adv.* amicably.
amígdalas, *n.f.pl.* (*med.*) tonsils.

amigdalitis, *n.f.* (*med.*) tonsillitis.
amigo, *n.m.* friend; lover.
amistad, *n.f.* friendship; concubinage.
amistoso, -sa, *a.* friendly, amicable.
amistar, *v.t.* bring together.—*v.r.* make friends.
amnesia, *n.f.* (*med.*) amnesia.
amnistía, *n.f.* amnesty.
amnistiar [L], *v.t.* amnesty.
amo, *n.m.* master; employer; (*fam.*) boss.
amodorrar, *v.r.* drowse.
amodorrido, -da, *a.* drowsy.
amojamado, -da, *a.* dried-up.
amoladora, *n.f.* (*eng.*) grinder, grinding machine.
amolar [4], *v.t.* whet, grind; (*fam*). bore.
amoldar, *v.t.* mould; adjust.—*v.r.* adapt oneself.
amonestación, *n.f.* advice; warning.—*pl.* banns.
amonestar, *v.t.* advise, counsel.
amoníaco, *n.m.* (*chem.*) ammonia.
amontillado, *n.m.* variety of pale dry sherry, amontillado.
amontonar, *v.t.* heap; pile; accumulate.—*v.r.* (*fam.*) fly into a rage; (*fam.*) live in sin.
amor, *n.m.* love.
amoral, *a.* amoral.
amordazar [C], *v.t.* gag, muzzle.
amorfo, -fa, *a.* amorphous.
amorío, *n.m.* love-affair, amour.
amoroso, -sa, *a.* amorous; loving.
amortajar, *v.t.* shroud.
amortiguar [H], *v.t.* deaden; absorb; temper.
amortizable, *a.* (*com.*) redeemable.
amortizar [C], *v.t.* amortize, write off.
amotinar, *v.t.* incite to rebellion.—*v.r.* rebel.
amparar, *v.t.* shelter; protect; support.—*v.r.* claim protection; seek shelter.
amparo, *n.m.* protection; aid.
amperaje, *n.m.* (*elec.*) amperage.
amperio, *n.m.* (*elec.*) ampere.
ampliación, *n.f.* extension; (*phot. etc.*) enlargement.
ampliar [L], *v.t.* amplify, enlarge.
amplificación, *n.f.* enlargement.
amplificador, -ra, *a.* enlarging, amplifying.—*n.m.* (*photo., rad.*) amplifier.
amplio, -lia, *a.* ample; large, roomy.
amplitud, *n.f.* extent; largeness; (*phys. etc.*) amplitude.
ampolla, *n.f.* blister; bulb (*lamp*); bubble.
amputación, *n.f.* amputation.
amueblar, *v.t.* furnish.
amurallar, *v.t.* wall up; surround with walls.
anacoreta, *n.m.* (*eccl.*) anchorite, hermit.
anacronismo, *n.m.* anachronism.
anadón, *n.m.* duckling.
anagrama, *n.m.* anagram.
anal, *a.* anal.
anales, *n.m.pl.* annals.
analfabetismo, *n.m.* illiteracy.
analfabeto, -ta, *a.* illiterate.
análisis, *n.m. inv.* or *f. inv.* analysis.
analizar [C], *v.t.* analyse.
analogia, *n.f.* analogy.
analógico, -ca, *a.* analogical.
análogo, -ga, *a.* analogous.
ananás, *n.f.* (*bot.*) pineapple.
anaquel, *n.m.* shelf.
anarquía, *n.f.* anarchy.
anárquico, -ca, *a.* anarchic(al).
anarquismo, *n.m.* anarchism.
anatema, *n.m.* or *f.* anathema.
anatematizar [C], *v.t.* anathematize, excommunicate.
anatomía, *n.f.* (*med.*) anatomy; dissection.
anatómico, -ca, *a.* anatomical.—*n.m.f.* anatomist.
anca, *n.f.* croup; haunch.
anciano, -na, *n.m.f.* elderly person, elder.
ancla, *n.f.* anchor.
ancladero, *n.m.* anchorage.
anclar, *v.i.* cast anchor, anchor.
ancón, *n.m.* small cove, inlet.
áncora, *n.f.* anchor.
ancho, -cha, *a.* broad, wide, large.—*n.m.* width, breadth; (*rail.*) gauge; ***a sus anchas,*** at one's ease.
anchoa, *n.f.* anchovy.
andada, *n.f.* track, trail; ***volver a las andadas,*** backslide.
andaluz,-za, *a., n.m.f.* (*pl.* **-uces, -uzas**) Andalusian.
andaluzada, *n.f.* (*fam.*) long yarn, tall story.
andamiaje, *n.m.* scaffolding.
andamio, *n.m.* scaffold, platform.
andante, *a.* walking; errant (*knight*).—*n.m.* (*mus.*) andante.
andanza, *n.f.* occurrence.
andar [11], *v.i.* go, come; walk; ***¡anda!*** come on! gracious!
andariego, -ga, *a.* restless, roving.
andarrío, *n.m.* (*orn.*) wagtail.
andas, *n.f.pl.* litter.
andén, *n.m.* (*rail*). platform, footpath.
andino, -na, *a.* Andean.
andrajo, *n.m.* rag.
andrajoso, -sa, *a.* ragged.
andurriales, *n.m.pl.* by-roads.
anea, *n.f.* (*bot.*) rush; basket-work.
anécdota, *n.f.* anecdote.
anecdótico, -ca, *a.* anecdotal.
anegable, *a.* submersible; floodable.
anegar [B], *v.t.* inundate; submerge; drown.—*v.r.* become flooded *or* submerged *or* soaked.
anejo, -ja, *a.* annexed, joined.—*n.m.* annexe.
aneldo, *n.m.* (*bot.*) common dill.
anemia, *n.f.* (*med.*) anaemia.
anémona, anémone, *n.f.* (*bot.*) anemone.
anestesiar, *v.t.* anaesthetize.
anexo-xa, *a.* [ANEJO].
anfibio, -bia, *a.* amphibious.
anfiteatro, *n.m.* amphitheatre; lecture-theatre.
angarillón, *n.m.* large basket.
ángel, *n.m.* angel; ***tener —,*** have a way with one.
angélica, *n.f.* (*bot., med.*) angelica.
angina, *n.f.* (*med.*) angina.—*pl.* sore throat.
anglicano, -na, *a., n.m.f.* Anglican.
anglicismo, *n.m.* (*gram.*) Anglicism.
anglo, -gla, *a.* Anglian,—*n.m.f.* Angle.
angloamericano, -na, *a.* Anglo-American.
anglófilo, -la, *a., n.m.f.* Anglophile.
anglófobo, -ba, *a., n.m.f.* Anglophobe.
anglomanía, *n.f.* Anglomania.
anglosajón, -jona, *a., n.m.f.* Anglo-Saxon; British and American.
angosto, -ta, *a.* narrow; insufficient.
angostura, *n.f.* narrowness; narrows.
anguila, *n.f.* (*ichth.*) eel.

angular, *a.* angular; ***piedra* —,** cornerstone.
ángulo, *n.m.* angle, corner.
angustia, *n.f.* anguish, affliction.
angustiar, *v.t.* anguish, afflict.
anhelar, *v.t.* long for, covet.—*v.i.* fight for breath.
anhelo, *n.m.* anxiousness; vehement desire.
anheloso, -sa, *a.* breathless; anxious (***de***, to, for).
anidar, *v.i.* nest.
anilina, *n.f.* (*chem.*) aniline.
anillo, *n.m.* ring; (*pol.*) ***de* —,** honorary.
ánima, *n.f.* soul; (*mil.*) bore.
animación, *n.f.* animation, bustle, liveliness.
animado, -da, *a.* lively.
animadversión, *n.f.* animadversion, remark.
animal, *a.*, *n.m.* animal, brute.
animar, *v.t.* animate; enliven; inspire, encourage.—*v.r.* cheer up; grow energetic; take courage.
ánimo, *n.m.* soul, spirit; valour, bravery.—*interj.* come on!
animosidad, *n.f.* valour; animosity.
animoso, -sa, *a.* bold.
aniquilación, *n.f.* annihilation.
aniquilar, *v.t.* annihilate.
anís, *n.m.* (*bot.*) anise; aniseed; anisette.
anisar, *v.t.* flavour with aniseed.
anisete, *n.m.* anisette.
aniversario, -ria, *a.*, *n.m.* anniverary.
ano, *n.m.* (*med.*) anus.
anoche, *adv.* last night.
anochecer [9], *v.i.* grow dark; be (at a place) at nightfall.—*v.r.* grow dark.—*n.m.* dark, dusk.
anochecida, *n.f.* nightfall.
anodino, -na, *a.* (*med.*) anodyne; (*fig.*) inoffensive.
ánodo, *n.m.* (*phys.*) anode.
anónimo, -ma, *a.* anonymous.—*n.m.* anonymity.
anormal, *a.* abnormal.
anormalidad, *n.f.* abnormality.
anotación, *n.f.* annotation, note.
anotar, *v.t.* annotate.
ánsar, *n.m.* goose; **— *macho*,** gander.
ansarino, -na, *a.* goose.—*n.m.* gosling.
ansarón, *n.m.* big goose.
ansia, *n.f.* anxiety; anguish; longing.
ansiar, *v.t.* desire, hanker for *or* after.
ansioso, -sa, *a.* anxious; eager.
anta (1), *n.f.* (*zool.*) elk.
anta (2), *n.f.* obelisk; pillar.
antagonismo, *n.m.* antagonism.
antaño, *adv.* yesteryear.
antártico, -ca, *a.* Antarctic.
ante (1), *prep.* before; in the presence of; **— *todo*,** above all.
ante (2), *n.m.* (*zool.*) elk; doeskin; suede; buff (*colour*).
anteanoche, *adv.* the night before last.
anteayer, *adv.* the day before yesterday.
antebrazo, *n.m.* fore-arm.
antecámara, *n.f.* antechamber, lobby.
antecedencia, *n.f.* antecedence; lineage.
antecesor, -ra, *a.* antecedent.—*n.m.f.* predecessor.—*n.m.pl.* ancestors.
antedicho, -cha, *a.* aforesaid.
con antelación, de antemano, *adv. phr.* beforehand.
antena, *n.f.* (*rad.*) aerial; (*ent.*) antenna; (*naut.*) lateen yard.
antenatal, *a.* pre-natal, ante-natal.
anteojera, *n.f.* spectacle-case.—*pl.* blinkers eyeflaps.
anteojo, *n.m.* telescope; (*obs.*) spy-glass.—*pl.* spectacles; ***anteojos de camino***, goggles.
antepasado, -da, *a.* passed, elapsed.—*n.m.pl.* ancestors, forebears.
anteponer [25], *v.t.* prefer; place before.—*v.r.* push oneself forward.
antepuesto, -ta, *a.* preferred.—*p.p.* [ANTEPONER].
anterior, *a.* anterior, former, previous.
anterioridad, *n.f.* priority; precedence; ***con* —,** previously.
antes, *adv.* before(hand); first; rather; ***cuanto* —,** as quickly as possible.—*prep.* before (***de***).—*conj.* before. (***que, de que***).
antesala, *n.f.* anteroom, antechamber.
anticiclón, *n.m.* anticyclone.
anticipación, *n.f.* anticipation; foretaste; ***con* —,** in advance.
anticipado, -da, *a.* in advance.
anticipar, *v.t.* anticipate; forestall; advance.
anticipo, *n.m.* anticipation; advance, advance payment *or* loan.
anticombustible, *a.* non-inflammable.
anticoncepcionismo, *n.m.* contraception.
anticoncepcionista, *a.* contraceptive.
anticongelante, *n.m.* anti-freeze.
anticuado, -da, *a.* antiquated.
anticuario, -ria, *a.*, *n.m.f.* antiquarian.
antídoto, *n.m.* antidote.
antiestético, -ca, *a.* unaesthetic.
antifaz, *n.m.* mask.
antífona, *n.f.* antiphon.
antigualla, *n.f.* monument of antiquity; antique; out-of-date custom *or* object.
antiguamente, *adv.* in ancient times; formerly.
antigüedad, *n.f.* antiquity; seniority.
antiguo, -gua, *a.* antique, old, ancient; former.—*n.m.* veteran, senior.
antihigiénico, -ca, *a.* unhygienic.
antílope, *n.m.* (*zool.*) antelope.
antillano, -na, *a.*, *n.m.f.* West Indian.
Antillas, *n.f.pl.* West Indies, Antilles.
antiministerial, *a.* opposition.—*n.m.* member of the opposition.
antioxidante, *a.* rust-preventive.
antipara, *n.f.* screen.
antipartícula, *n.f.* (*phys.*) antiparticle.
antipatía, *n.f.* antipathy; dislike.
antipático, -ca, *a.* disagreeable, unpleasant.
antípoda, *a.* antipodal.—*n.f.pl.* Antipodes.
antiquísimo, -ma, *sup. a.* very ancient; (*fam.*) out of the Ark.
antirrino, *n.m.* (*bot.*) antirrhinum.
antisemita, *a.* anti-Semitic.—*n.m.f.* anti-Semite.
antiséptico, -ca, *a.*, *n.m.* (*med.*) antiseptic.
antítesis, *n.f.* antithesis.
antitético, -ca, *a.* antithetic(al).
antitoxina, *n.f.* (*med.*) antitoxin.
antojadizo, -za, *a.* capricious, whimsical; fickle.
antojar, *v.r.* long for, fancy; surmise.
antojo, *n.m.* whim, caprice; longing; surmise.
antología, *n.f.* anthology.
antonomasia, *n.f.* antonomasia; **... *por* —** the outstanding example of . . .
antorcha, *n.f.* torch, cresset.

antracita, *n.f.* (*min.*) anthracite.
ántrax, *n.m.* (*med.*) anthrax.
antro, *n.m.* (*poet.*) cavern, grotto; (*fam.*) night-club.
antropófago, -ga, *a.*, *n.m.f.* cannibal.
antropoide, *a.* anthropoid.
antropología, *n.f.* anthropology.
antuvión, *n.m.* (*fam.*) sudden attack; ***de* —,** unexpectedly.
anual, *a.* annual, yearly.
anualidad, *n.f.* annuity; annual instalment.
anuario, *n.m.* year-book; directory.
anublar, *v.t.* cloud, overcast.—*v.r.* become cloudy.
anublo, *n.m.* mildew.
anudar, *v.t.* knot; unite.—*v.r.* become knotted.
anular (1), *v.t.* annul, make void, rescind.—*v.r.* (*math.*) vanish.
anular (2), *a.* annular, ring-shaped; ***dedo* —,** ring-finger.
Anunciación, *n.f.* (*eccl.*) Annunciation; **anunciación,** *n.f.* announcement.
anunciar, *v.t.* announce; notify; advertise.
anuncio, *n.m.* announcement; prediction; advertisement.
anzuelo, *n.m.* fish-hook; (*fig.*) allurement; fritters.
añadidura, *n.f.*, **añadimiento,** *n.m.* addition; increase.
añadir, *v.t.* add; increase.
añafea, *n.f.* ***papel de* —,** brown paper.
añafil, *n.m.* Moorish trumpet.
añagaza, *n.f.* lure, decoy.
añejo, -ja, *a.* old; mature (*wine etc.*); stale (*news*).
añicos, *n.m.pl.* smithereens.
añil, *n.m.* indigo.
año, *n.m.* year.
añoranza, *n.f.* homesickness, nostalgia.
añorar, *v.t.*, *v.i.* long (for); regret.
aojar, *v.t.* bewitch, cast the evil eye upon.
aojo, *n.m.* fascination; evil eye.
aovado, -da, *a.* egg-shaped.
aovillar, *v.t.* wind (*into balls*).—*v.r.* roll oneself into a ball; shrink.
apabilar, *v.t.* trim (*wick*).—*v.r.* lose courage.
apacentar [1], *v.t.* graze (*cattle*); feed on.
apacible, *a.* peaceable; placid.
apaciguar [H], *v.t.* pacify.—*v.r.* calm down.
apadrinar, *v.t.* act as godfather to; act as second to; patronize.
apagadizo, -za, *a.* which burns badly.
apagado, -da, *a.* dull (*colour*); submissive; humble.
apagafuegos, *n.m. inv.* fire-extinguisher.
apagaincendios, *n.m. inv.* fire-engine; fire-extinguisher.
apagar [B], *v.t.* extinguish; put out; soften (*colours*); quench (*thirst*).
apalear, *v.t.* drub, beat.
apanalado, -da, *a.* honey-combed.
apantanar, *v.t.* flood.
apañado, -da, *a.* skilful; (*fam.*) suitable.
apañador, -ra, *a.* pilfering.—*n.m.f.* pilferer.
apañar, *v.t.* seize; pilfer; dress; fit close.—*v.r.* be skilful; manage, contrive.
apaño, *n.m.* seizing; knack; patch.
aparador, *n.m.* sideboard, dresser; workshop; display window.
aparato, *n.m.* apparatus; device, appliance; pomp; system; party machine.
aparatoso, -sa, *a.* showy, pompous.
aparcamiento, *n.m.* parking (*cars*); car-park.
aparcar [A], *v.t.* park (*car*).
aparcero, *n.m.* (*agr.*) partner; share-cropper.
aparear, *v.t.* match, mate, couple.
aparecer [9], *v.i.*, *v.r.* appear, turn up.
aparecido, *n.m.* ghost.
aparejador, *n.m.* master-builder; general foreman; (*aer.*) rigger.
aparejar, *v.t.* prepare, get ready; saddle.
aparejo, *n.m.* preparation; harness, gear; tackle.—*pl.* tools.
aparente, *a.* apparent; manifest.
aparición, *n.f.* apparition; coming into sight.
apariencia, *n.f.* appearance, aspect; likeness; probability.
apartadero, *n.m.* (*rail.*) siding, (*U.S.*) side-track; lay-by.
apartadizo, -za, *a.* unsociable.—*n.m.f.* recluse.—*n.m.* small (partitioned) room.
apartado, -da, *a.* remote; separate.—*n.m.* separate room; Post Office box; (*taur.*) shutting up bulls before a fight.
apartamiento, *n.m.* separation; apartment, flat; (*com.*) waiver.
apartar, *v.t.* separate; (*rail.*) shunt; sort.—*v.r.* withdraw; retire.
aparte, *n.m.* paragraph; section; (*theat.*) aside; ***punto y* —,** new paragraph.—*adv.* aside; apart.
apasionar, *v.t.* impassion; afflict.—*v.r.* become passionately fond (***de, por***, of).
apatía, *n.f.* apathy.
apátrida, *a.*, *n.m.f.* stateless (person).
apeadero, *n.m.* horseblock; (*rail.*) halt; pied-à-terre.
apeador, *n.m.* land-surveyor.
apear, *v.t.* set down; survey; hobble.—*v.r.* alight, dismount.
apedrear, *v.t.* stone, lapidate.—*v.i.* hail.—*v.r.* be injured by hail.
apegar [B], *v.r.* become attached (***a***, to).
apego, *n.m.* attachment.
apelación, *n.f.* (*jur.*) appeal.
apelado, -da, *n.m.f.* (*jur.*) successful appellant.
apelante, *n.m.f.* (*jur.*) appellant.
apelar, *v.i.* (*jur.*) appeal; have recourse (***a***, to).
apelmazar [C], *v.t.* compress, make hard and lumpy.
apelotonar, *v.t.* wind into a ball.
apellidar, *v.t.* name; call by name.
apellido, *n.m.* surname, family name.
apenar, *v.t.* cause pain.—*v.r.* grieve.
apenas, *adv.* hardly, scarcely.
apéndice, *n.m.* appendix.
apendicitis, *n.f.* appendicitis.
apercibimiento, *n.m.* foresight; preparation; advice; (*jur.*) summons.
apercibir, *v.t.* provide; get ready; warn; (*jur.*) summon.
aperitivo, -va, *a.* aperitive, appetizing.—*n.m.* cocktail snack, canapé.
apero, *n.m.* tool(s), equipment; sheep-fold.
apertura, *n.f.* (solemn) opening.
apesadumbrar, *v.t.* sadden.—*v.r.* grieve.
apesgar [B], *v.t.* overburden.—*v.r.* become aggrieved.
apestar, *v.t.* infect with the plague; (*fig.*) pester.—*v.i.* stink.
apetecer [9], *v.t.* long for, crave.—*v.i.* appeal to.

apetecible, *a.* desirable.
apetencia, *n.f.* appetite; hunger; desire.
apetito, *n.m.* appetite.
apiadar, *v.t.* inspire pity.—*v.r.* take pity (***de,*** on).
apicarar, *v.r.* become roguish.
ápice, *n.m.* apex; iota.
apicultor, -ra, *n.m.f.* apiarist, bee-keeper.
apilar, *v.t., v.r.* pile up.
apimpollar, *v.r.* sprout.
apiñadura, *n.f.,* **apiñamiento,** *n.m.* crowding, congestion.
apiñar, *v.t., v.r.* crowd.
apisonadora, *n.f.* (steam-)roller, road-roller.
aplacar [A], *v.t.* appease; calm.
aplacible, *a.* pleasant.
aplanar, *v.t.* level.
aplastar, *v.t.* flatten; crush.—*v.r.* collapse.
aplaudir, *v.t.* applaud.
aplauso, *n.m.* applause; praise.
aplazar [C], *v.t.* convene; postpone.
aplazo, *n.m.* postponement.
aplicación, *n.f.* application; assiduity; appliqué-work.
aplicado, -da, *a.* industrious.
aplicar [A], *v.t.* apply; destine.—*v.r.* apply oneself.
aplomo, *n.m.* tact, prudence; aplomb; (*tech.*) plumb.
apocamiento, *n.m.* bashfulness, diffidence.
apocar [A], *v.t.* lessen.—*v.r.* belittle oneself.
apócope, *n.f.* (*gram.*) apocope; apocopation.
apócrifo, -fa, *a.* apocryphal.—*n.m.pl.* (*Bib.*) Apocrypha.
apodar, *v.t.* give nick-names to; ridicule.
apoderar, *v.t.* empower.—*v.r.* take possession (***de,*** of).
apodo, *n.m.* nick-name.
apogeo, *n.m.* apogee; peak.
apolilladura, *n.f.* moth-hole.
apolillar, *v.t.* (*of moths*) eat holes in.—*v.r.* become moth-eaten.
apologia, *n.f.* apologia, defence.
apólogo, *n.m.* apologue, fable.
apoltronar, *v.r.* grow lazy *or* cowardly.
apoplejía, *n.f.* apoplexy.
aporrar, *v.i.* (*fam.*) stand tongue-tied.—*v.r.* (*fam.*) become importunate.
aporrear, *v.t.* beat, cudgel.—*v.r.* cudgel one's brains, study hard.
aportación, *n.f.* contribution.
aportar, *v.t.* bring, contribute.—*v.i.* (*naut.*) make port.
aposentar, *v.t., v.r.* lodge.
aposento, *n.m.* room; inn.
apostar [4], *v.t.* bet, wager; post (*troops*); ***apostarlas*** or ***apostárselas a*** or ***con alguien,*** compete with s.o.—*v.i.* contend.
apostasía, *n.f.* apostasy.
apóstata, *n.m.f.* apostate.
apostema, *n.f.* (*med.*) abscess.
apostilla, *n.f.* marginal note, gloss.
apóstol, *n.m.* apostle.
apostolado, *n.m.* apostleship, apostolate; the twelve apostles.
apostrofar, *v.t.* apostrophize.
apóstrofe, *n.f.* (*rhetoric*) apostrophe.
apóstrofo, *n.m.* (*gram.*) apostrophe.
apostura, *n.f.* gentleness, pleasant disposition.
apoteosis, *n.f.* apotheosis.
apoyabrazo, *n.m.* arm-rest.
apoyadero, *n.m.* prop, support.
apoyar, *v.t.* rest, lean (***en,*** on); support; bear out.—*v.i.* rest.—*v.r.* depend (***en,*** upon), rely (***en,*** upon); lean (***en,*** on, against).
apoyo, *n.m.* prop, support; help; backing.
apreciable, *a.* valuable; respectable; ***Apreciable Señor,*** Dear Sir (*showing respect*).
apreciación, *n.f.* valuation.
apreciar, *v.t.* estimate; esteem, appreciate.
apreciativo, -va, *a.* appreciative.
aprecio, *n.m.* valuation; appreciation.
apremiante, *a.* urgent, pressing.
apremiar, *v.t.* press, urge; oblige.
apremio, *n.m.* constraint.
aprender, *v.t.* learn.
aprendiz, -za, *n.m.f.* apprentice, trainee.
aprendizaje, *n.m.* apprenticeship.
aprensivo, -va, *a.* apprehensive.
apresador, *n.m.* (*naut.*) privateer.
apresar, *v.t.* seize, capture; take captive.
aprestar, *v.t.* prepare.
apresurar, *v.t.* hasten.—*v.r.* make haste.
apretador, *n.m.* tightener; waistcoat; hairnet.
apretar [1], *v.t.* tighten; compress; clench; squeeze.—*v.i.* pinch (*of shoes*); begin (***a,*** to).
apretón, *n.m.* pressure; squeeze; handshake.
apretura, *n.f.* confined space; (*fig.*) straits.
aprieto, *n.m.* crowd; stringency; danger; (*fam.*) tight spot.
aprisa, *adv.* swiftly.
aprisco, *n.m.* sheep-fold.
aprisionar, *v.t.* imprison.
aprobable, *a.* approvable.
aprobar [4], *v.t.* approve; pass (*an examinee*).—*v.i.* pass.
apropiar, *v.t.* give possession of; adapt, fit.—*v.r.* appropriate, take possession of.
apropincuar, *v.r.* (*joc.*) approach.
aprovechable, *a.* available; useful, utilizable.
aprovechar, *v.t.* make good use of.—*v.i.* be useful *or* profitable; make progress; ***que (le) aproveche,*** I hope you enjoy your meal.—*v.r.* avail oneself (***de,*** of).
aprovisionar, *v.t.* victual, supply.
aproximar, *v.t.* approximate; move near.—*v.r.* move near (***a,*** to).
aptitud, *n.f.* aptitude, ability.
apto, -ta, *a.* fit, apt.
apuesta, *n.f.* bet, wager.
apuesto, -ta, *a.* elegant; spruce, well-dressed.
apuntación, *n.f.* note; (*mus.*) notation.
apuntador, *n.m.* (*theat.*) prompter; (*mil.*) gun layer.
apuntalar, *v.t.* prop, shore up.
apuntar, *v.t.* point at; note; stitch; (*theat.*) prompt.—*v.i.* begin to appear.—*v.r.* begin to go sour.
apunte, *n.m.* note; (*theat.*) promptbook.
apuñalar, *v.t.* stab.
apuñear, apuñetear, *v.t.* punch.
apuradamente, *adv.* (*fam.*) in the nick of time, exactly; precisely.
apurado, -da, *a.* destitute, hard-up; dangerous.
apurar, *v.t.* purify; verify; finish; annoy.—*v.r.* worry; (*S.A.*) hasten; strive (***por hacer,*** to do).
apuro, *n.m.* want, need; sorrow; (*S.A.*) urgency; (*fam.*) difficult situation, tight spot.

aquel, aquella, *dem. a.* (*pl.* **aquellos, aquellas**) that.—*pl.* those.
aquél, aquélla, *dem. pron.* (*pl.* **aquéllos, aquéllas**) that one; the former.—*pl.* those. —*n.m.* (*fam.*) appeal, it.
aquelarre, *n.m.* witches' Sabbath.
aquello, *dem. pron. neuter.* that, that thing *or* matter.
aquende, *adv.* (*obs., lit.*) on this side.
aquerenciar, *v.r.* become fond (*de*, of).
aquí, *adv.* here; hither.
aquilatar, *v.t.* assay; (*fig.*) weigh the merits of.
aquilea, *m.f.* (*bot.*) arrow.
Aquiles, *n.m.* (*myth.*) Achilles.
aquilón, *n.m.* (*poet.*) north wind.
Aquisgrán, *n.m.* Aachen, Aix-la-Chapelle.
aquistar, *v.t.* acquire.
ara, *n.f.* altar.
árabe, *a.* Arabic.—*n.m.f.* Arab.—*n.m.* Arabic.
arabesco, -ca, *a.* (*art.*) arabesque; [ÁRABE].—*n.m.* (*art.*) arabesque.
la Arabia Saudita, *n.f.* Saudi Arabia.
arábigo, -ga, *a.* Arabic; Arabian.—*n.m.* Arabic.
arabio, -bia, *a.* [ÁRABE]; Arabian.
arabismo, *n.m.* Arabism.
arabizar [C], *v.t.* Arabize.—*v.i., v.r.* go Arab.
arable, *a.* (*agr.*) arable.
arada, *n.f.* (*agr.*) ploughed land; ploughing.
arado, *n.m.* (*agr.*) plough; ploughshare.
aragonés, -nesa, *a.* Aragonese.
arambel, *n.m.* tatter.
aramio, *n.m.* fallow.
arancel, *n.m.* tariff, rate (*customs etc.*).
arándano, *n.m.* (*bot.*) cranberry; (*S.A.*) bilberry, whortleberry.
arandela, *n.f.* (*mech.*) washer, ring; candlestick.
araña, *n.f.* (*zool.*) spider; (*bot.*) love-in-a-mist; chandelier; (*fam.*) thrifty person; whore.
arañada, *n.f.* scratch.
arañar, *v.t.* scratch; score; scrape.
arañazo, *n.m.* scratch.
arar, *v.t.* plough.
araucano, -na, *a., n.m.f.* Araucanian.
arbitrador, -ra, *a.* arbitrating.—*n.m.* arbitrator, umpire, referee.—*n.f.* arbitress.
arbitrar, *v.t.* arbitrate; referee, umpire (*sports*).—*v.r.* manage well.
arbitrariedad, *n.f.* arbitrariness.
arbitrario, -ria, *a.* arbitrary; (*jur.*) arbitral.
arbitrio, *n.m.* free will; arbitration; arbitrariness; ways, means.—*pl.* excise taxes.
arbitrista, *n.m.f.* schemer.
árbitro, -tra, *a.* autonomous.—*n.m.f.* referee, umpire; arbiter.—*n.f.* arbitress.
árbol, *n.m.* tree; (*mech.*) shaft, spindle; (*naut.*) mast.
arbolado, -da, *a.* wooded.—*n.m.* woodland.
arboladura, *n.f.* (*naut.*) masts and spars.
arbolar, *v.t.* hoist.
arboleda, *n.f.* grove.
arbollón, *n.m.* outlet; gutter.
arbusto, *n.m.* shrub.
arca, *n.f.* chest, coffer; safe; reservoir; — ***de Noé***, Noah's ark; (*fam.*) treasure-house.
arcabuz, *n.m.* (*pl.* **-uces**) arquebus.
arcada, *n.f.* retch; (*arch.*) arcade.
arcaduz, *n.m.* (*pl.* **-uces**) conduit; pipe.
arcaico, -ca, *a.* archaic.
arcaismo, *n.m.* archaism.
arcángel, *n.m.* archangel.
arce, *n.m.* (*bot.*) maple.
arcediano, *n.m.* (*eccl.*) archdeacon.
arcilla, *n.f.* clay.
arcipreste, *n.m.* (*eccl.*) archpriest.
arco, *n.m.* bow; (*math., elec.*) arc; (*arch.*) arch; — ***iris***, rainbow.
arcón, *n.m.* bin, large chest, linen-chest.
archidiácono, *n.m.* (*eccl.*) archdeacon.
archiduque, *n.m.* archduke.
archimillonario, -ria, *a., n.m.f.* multi-millionaire.
archipiélago, *n.m.* (*geog.*) archipelago.
archivar, *v.t.* deposit in an archive; (*com. etc.*) file.
archivo, *n.m.* archive, archives; file, filing cabinet; (*S.A.*) office.
arder, *v.t., v.i.* burn.
ardid, *n.m.* stratagem, ruse, trick.
ardido, -da, *a.* bold, brave.
ardiente, *a.* burning, fervent; ardent, passionate; (*poet.*) glowing red.
ardilla, *n.f.* (*zool.*) squirrel.
ardite, *n.m.* farthing.
ardor, *n.m.* ardour; vehemence; intrepidity.
arduo, -dua, *a.* arduous, hard.
área, *n.f.* area; are (*unit of measure*).
arena, *n.f.* sand; arena; (*med.*) gravel.
arenal, *n.m.* sandy ground; quicksand; sand-pit.
arengar, *v.t.* harangue.
arenisca, *n.f.* (*min.*) sandstone.
arenque, *n.m.* (*ichth.*) herring.
arete, *n.m.* ear-ring.
argamasa, *n.m.* mortar, cement.
argamasar, *v.t.* cement; plaster.—*v.i.* mix cement *or* mortar.
árgana, *n.f.*, **árgano,** *n.m.* (*industry*) crane; pannier.
argayo, *n.m.* landslide.
Argel, *n.m.* Algiers.
Argelia, *n.f.* Algeria.
argelino, -na, *a., n.m.f.* Algerian.
argentar, *v.t.* plate; (*fig.*) silver.
la Argentina, *n.f.* Argentina, the Argentine.
argentino (1), **-na,** *a.* silvery.
argentino (2), **-na,** *a. n.m.f.* Argentine, Argentinian.
argolla, *n.f.* large ring, staple.
argucia, *n.f.* subtlety, sophistry.
argüir [I], *v.t.* imply.—*v.i.* argue.
argumentación, *n.f.* argumentation.
argumento, *n.m.* argument; plot (*of a story*).
aria, *n.f.* (*mus.*) aria; tune.
aridez, *n.f.* aridity, drought.
árido, -da, *a.* arid, barren.—*n.m.pl.* dry goods.
ariete, *n.m.* battering-ram; (*tech.*) ram.
ario, -ria, *a., n.m.f.* Aryan.
arisco, -ca, *a.* churlish; surly; dour.
arista, *n.f.* (*arch.*) arris; edge.
aristocracia, *n.f.* aristocracy.
aristócrata, *n.m.f.* aristocrat.
aristocrático, -ca, *a.* aristocratic.
Aristóteles, *n.m.* Aristotle.
aristotélico, -ca, *a., n.m.f.* Aristotelian.
aritmético, -ca, *a.* arithmetical.—*n.m.f.* arithmetician.—*n.f.* arithmetic.
arlequín, *n.m.* harlequin; Neapolitan ice-cream.

arma, *n.f.* arm, weapon; — ***blanca,*** sword etc., cold steel; — ***de fuego,*** firearm.
armada, *n.f.* (*naut.*) fleet, navy, Armada.
armadía, *n.f.* raft.
armadijo, *n.m.* trap, snare.
armadura, *n.f.* armour; (*elec.*) armature; (*arch.*) framework.
armamento, *n.m.* armament; (*naut.*) fitting-out.
armar, *v.t.* arm; assemble; equip, fit out; reinforce (*concrete*); load (*weapon*); (*fam.*) cause, stir up; ***armarla,*** start a row.—*v.r.* arm; arm oneself (**de,** with).
armario, *n.m.* closet; wardrobe; cupboard.
armazón, *n.f.* framework.
armiño, *n.m.* (*zool., her.*) ermine.
armisticio, *n.m.* armistice.
armonía, *n.f.* harmony.
armónico, -ca, *a.* harmonious; harmonic.—*n.m.* harmonic.—*n.f.* harmonica.
armonio, *n.m.* (*mus.*) harmonium.
armonioso, -sa, *a.* harmonious.
arnés, *n.m.* harness; armour.
aro, *n.m.* hoop; rim; staple; — ***de émbolo,*** piston ring.
aroma, *n.m.* aroma, perfume.
aromático, -ca, *a.* aromatic.
arpa, *n.f.* (*mus.*) harp.
arpar, *v.t.* rend, claw.
arpista, *n.m.f.* (*mus.*) harpist.
arpón, *n.m.* harpoon.
arpon(e)ar, *v.t.* harpoon.
arquear, *v.t.* arch; (*naut.*) gauge.—*v.i.* retch.
arqueo, *n.m.* arching; (*naut.*) tonnage; (*com.*) audit.
arquelogía, *n.f.* archeology.
arqueólogo, -ga, *n.m.f.* archeologist.
arquero, *n.m.* treasurer; archer.
arquetipo, *n.m.* archetype.
arquiepiscopal, *a.* archiepiscopal.
arquitecto, *n.m.* architect.
arquitectónico, -ca, *a.* architectural, archi-tectonic.
arquitectura, *n.f.* architecture.
arrabal, *n.m.* suburb, quarter.
arrabalero, -ra, *a.* suburban; ill-bred.
arraigado, -da, *a.* rooted, secure; inveterate.
arraigar [B], *v.i., v.r.* take root.
arrancar [A], *v.t.* root up; extirpate; pull out.—*v.i.* start off; originate (**de,** in).
arranque, *n.m.* extirpation; sudden impulse; starting-up; starter.
arras, *n.f.pl.* deposit; pledge; dowry.
arrasar, *v.t.* raze; smooth; fill to the brim.—*v.i., v.r.* clear up.
arrastrar, *v.t.* drag (along); drag down.—*v.r.* creep, crawl; follow (*suit at cards*).
arrastre, *n.m.* dragging, haulage, towage (*taur.*) towing out the dead bull.
arrayán, *n.m.* (*bot.*) myrtle.
¡arre! *interj.* gee up!
arrear, *v.t.* drive, urge on (*mules etc.*).
arrebatadamente, *adv.* headlong; recklessly.
arrebatado, -da, *a.* sudden; violent; im-petuous.
arrebatar, *v.t.* carry off (**a,** from); captivate.—*v.r.* get carried away; (*cul.*) get burnt.
arrebato, *n.m.* surprise; sudden attack; paroxysm; rapture.
arrebol, *n.m.* red glow (*in the sky*); rosiness (*of cheeks*); rouge.
arrebolar, *v.t.* redden; rouge.—*v.r.* redden.
arrebujar, *v.t.* jumble together; huddle.—*v.r.* cover oneself up well.
arreciar, *v.i., v.r.* grow stronger *or* more severe.
arrecife, *n.m.* (*naut.*) reef.
arrecir [Q], *v.r.* become numb.
arrechucho, *n.m.* (*fam.*) fit, impulse; (*fam.*) slight indisposition.
arredrar, *v.t.* drive back; frighten.—*v.r.* draw back; be frightened.
arregazar [C], *v.t.* tuck up.
arreglar, *v.t.* adjust, regulate; settle; arrange; repair.—*v.r.* get ready; come to terms (**con,** with); ***arreglárselas,*** to manage as best one can.
arreglo, *n.m.* adjustment; arrangement; agreement; ***con* — *a,*** in accordance with.
arrejaco, arrejaque, *n.m.* (*orn.*) swift; (*S.A.*) blackmartin.
arremangar [B], *v.r.* roll *or* tuck up one's sleeves.
arremeter, *v.t., v.i.* attack.
arrendajo, *n.m.* (*orn.*) jay; (*S.A., U.S.*) mocking-bird.
arrendar [1], *v.t.* rent, lease; tie (*a horse*); mimic.
arrendatario, -ria, *n.m.f.* lessee, leaseholder, renter.
arreo, *n.m.* dress; ornament.—*pl.* harness, trappings.
arrepentimiento, *n.m.* repentance.
arrepentir [6], *v.r.* repent, be sorry (**de,** for).
arrequives, *n.m.pl.* finery; attendant cir-cumstances.
arrestado, -da, *a.* bold, audacious.
arrestar, *v.t.* arrest; stop.
arresto, *n.m.* detention, arrest, imprisonment.
arria, *n.f.* drove (*of beasts*).
arriano, -na, *a., n.m.f.* (*eccl.*) Arian.
arriar [L], *v.t.* flood; (*naut.*) dip, strike; (*naut.*) slacken.
arriata, *n.f.,* **arriate,** *n.m.* (herbaceous) border.
arriaz, *n.m.* (*pl.* **-aces**) quillion, hilt.
arriba, *adv.* above, over, overhead; upstairs; (*naut.*) aloft; ***¡ — el rey!*** long live the King!
arribaje, *n.m.* (*naut.*) arrival.
arribar, *v.i.* arrive; (*naut.*) put in; (*fam.*) make a come-back.
arriero, *n.m.* muleteer.
arriesgado, -da, *a.* dangerous; daring.
arriesgar [B], *v.t.* risk; jeopardize.—*v.r.* run a risk; ***arriesgarse a hacer,*** risk doing; ***arriesgarse en hacer,*** venture on doing.
arrimar, *v.t.* bring close; (*naut.*) stow.—*v.r.* lean (**a,** against); depend (**a,** upon).
arrinconamiento, *n.m.* seclusion.
arroba, *n.f.* arroba (*Spanish measure of weight 25 lb. approx.*).
arrobamiento, *n.m.* ecstasy, rapture.
arrobar, *v.t.* charm, transport.—*v.r.* be enraptured.
arrodillar, *v.t.* make (*s.o.*) kneel.—*v.i., v.r.* kneel (down).
arrogancia, *n.f.* arrogance, haughtiness.
arrogante, *a.* haughty; arrogant.
arrogar [B], *v.t.* adopt.—*v.r.* arrogate (*to oneself*).
arrojallamas, *n.m. inv.* (*mil.*) flame-thrower.
arrojar, *v.t.* fling; dash; shed; (*fam.*) vomit.

arrojo, *n.m.* boldness.
arrollamiento, *n.m.* (*elec.*) winding.
arrollar, *v.t.* roll (up); wind, coil; rout.
arrope, *n.m.* grape syrup, boiled must.
arrostrar, *v.t.*, *v.i.* face.—*v.r.* fight face to face; ***arrostrarse con,*** to defy.
arroyo, *n.m.* stream, brook.
arroyuelo, *n.m.* rill, rivulet.
arroz, *n.m.* rice.
arruga, *n.f.* wrinkle, pucker, crease.
arrugar [B], *v.t.* wrinkle; corrugate.
arruinar, *v.t.* ruin; demolish; destroy.—*v.r.* fall into ruin; go bankrupt.
arrullar, *v.t.* lull.—*v.i.* coo; bill and coo.
arrullo, *n.m.* cooing; lullaby.
arrumbar, *v.t.* cast aside; (*naut.*) take bearings.—*v.i.* steer a course.—*v.r.* take bearings; get seasick.
arrurruz, *n.m.*(*cul.*) arrowroot.
arsenal, *n.m.* arsenal; dockyard.
arsénico, *n.m.* arsenic.
arte, *n.f.* or *m.* art; cunning; tackle.
artefacto, *n.m.* device, appliance; artefact.
artejo, *n.m.* knuckle.
arteria, *n.f.* (*med.*) artery; (*rail.*) trunk line; (*elec.*) feeder.
artería, *n.f.* artifice; cunning.
artero, -ra, *a.* cunning, artful.
artesa, *n.f.* trough, kneading trough.
artesanía, *n.f.* crafstmanship; artisan class.
artesano, *n.m.* artisan, craftsman.
artesiano, -na, *a.* artesian.
artesonado, -da, *a.* panelled.—*n.m.* panelled roof.
ártico, -ca, *a.* arctic.
articular, *v.t.* articulate.
artículo, *n.m.* article; joint, articulation; (*gram.*) article.
artífice, *n.m.f.* artificer; craftsman.
artificial, *a.* artificial; ***fuegos artificiales,*** fireworks.
artificiero, *n.m.* (*mil.*) artificer; fireworks manufacturer.
artificio, *n.m.* artifice, craft; device, contrivance.
artificioso, -sa, *a.* ingenious; crafty, artful.
artilugio, *n.m.* (*pej.*) contraption.
artillería, *n.f.* artillery.
artillero, *n.m.* gunner, artilleryman.
artimaña, *n.f.* trap, trick.
artimón, *n.m.* (*naut.*) mizzen.
artista, *n.m.f.* artist.
artístico, -ca, *a.* artistic.
artritis, *n.f.* (*med.*) arthritis.
Arturo, (*obs.* **Artús**), *n.m.* Arthur.
arveja, *n.f.* (*bot.*) vetch; tare; (*bot.*) carob; (*S.A.*) green pea.
arzobispado, *n.m.* (*eccl.*) archbishopric.
arzobispal, *a.* archiepiscopal.
arzobispo, *n.m.* archbishop.
arzón, *n.m.* saddle-tree.
as, *n.m.* ace (*also fig.*).
asa, *n.f.* handle.
asado, *n.m.* roast; — ***de vaca,*** roast beef.
asador, *n.m.* (*cul.*) spit.
asadura, *n.f.* offal, entrails.
asalariado, -da, *a.*, *n.m.f.* wage-earner, employee.
asaltar, *v.t.* assault.
asalto, *n.m.* assault; (*sport*) round.
asamblea, *n.f.* assembly.
asar, *v.t.* roast.
asaz, *adv.* (*poet.*, *obs.*, *joc.*) enough.
asbesto, *n.m.* asbestos.
ascalonia, *n.f.* (*bot.*) shallot.
ascendencia, *n.f.* lineage, ancestry.
ascendente, *a.* ascendent.
ascender [2], *v.t.* promote.—*v.i.* ascend, climb; (*com.*) amount (***a,*** to).
ascendiente, *a.* ascendent.—*n.m.f.* ancestor, forebear.—*n.m.* ascendency.
Ascensión, *n.f.* Ascension.
ascenso, *n.m.* ascent; rise, (*U.S.*) raise; promotion.
ascensor, *n.m.* lift, (*U.S.*) elevator; hoist.
asceta, *n.m.f.* ascetic.
asceticismo, *n.m.* asceticism.
asco, *n.m.* disgust; disgusting thing; (*fam.*) ***dar*** —, make sick.
ascua, *n.f.* ember; ***en ascuas,*** agitated.
asechamiento, *n.m.*, **asechanza,** *n.f.* snare, waylaying.
asechar, *v.t.* waylay, ambush.
asediador, -ra, *a.* besieging.—*n.m.f.* besieger.
asediar, *v.t.* besiege; blockade; (*fig.*) importune.
asedio, *n.m.* siege.
aseguración, *n.f.* insurance (*policy*).
asegurar, *v.t.* make safe; assure; insure.
asemejar, *v.t.* compare.—*v.i.*, *v.r.* be like (***a***).
a asentadillas, *adv. phr.* sidesaddle.
asentamiento, *n.m.* establishment; settlement; judgement.
asentar [1], *v.t.* seat; establish; hone, sharpen; (*jur.*) award; tamp down.—*v.i.* be becoming.—*v.r.* sit down; settle down.
asentimiento, *n.m.* assent.
asentir [6], *v.i.* assent.
aseo, *n.m.* cleanliness; tidiness; toilet; ***cuarto de*** —, bathroom, cloakroom.
asepsia, *n.f.* (*med.*) asepsis.
asequible, *a.* obtainable, accessible.
aserrador, -ra, *a.* saw, sawing.—*n.m.* sawyer.—*n.f.* circular saw.
aserradura, *n.f.* saw-cut.
aserrar [1], *v.t.* saw.
aserruchar, *v.t.* saw (*by hand*).
asesinar, *v.t.* assassinate, murder.
asesinato, *n.m.* assassination, murder.
asesino, -na, *a.* murderous.—*n.m.* murderer, assassin.—*n.f.* murderess.
asestar, *v.t.* aim; shoot; deal (*a blow*).
aseverar, *v.t.* assert.
asfaltar, *v.t.* asphalt.
asfalto, *n.m.* asphalt.
asfixia, *n.f.* asphyxia, asphyxiation.
asfixiante, *a.* asphyxiating.
asfixiar, *v.t.* asphyxiate.
asfódelo, *n.m.* (*bot.*) asphodel.
así, *adv.* thus, so; — ***como,*** — ***que,*** as soon as.
asiático, -ca, *a.*, *n.m.f.* Asiatic.
asidero, *n.m.* handle, grip.
asiduidad, *n.f.* assiduity.
asiduo, -dua, *a.* assiduous; persistent.
asiento, *n.m.* seat; bottom; sediment; wisdom: agreement.
asignación, *n.f.* assignation; salary.
asignar, *v.t.* assign.
asignatura, *n.f.* course, subject (*at school etc.*).
asilar, *v.t.* shelter; put in an asylum.
asilo, *n.m.* asylum; home (*for poor etc.*); refuge.
asimétrico, -ca, *a.* asymmetrical.

asimilación, *n.f.* assimilation.
asimilar, *v.t., v.i., v.r.* assimilate.
asimismo, *adv.* likewise.
asir [12], *v.t.* grasp, seize.—*v.i.* take root.—*v.r.* take hold (**de,** of); grapple (**con,** with).
asistencia, *n.f.* attendance; assistance; social service.
asistenta, *n.f.* charwoman, daily help.
asistente, *a.* assisting.—*n.m.f.* attendant; assistant; (*mil.*) orderly.
asistir, *v.t.* attend; assist, help.—*v.i.* be present; follow suit.
asma, *n.f.* (*med.*) asthma.
asmático, -ca, *a., n.m.f.* asthmatic.
asna, *n.f.* she-ass.—*pl.* (*carp.*) rafters.
asno, *n.m.* ass, donkey.
asociación, *n.f.* association.
asociado, -da, *a.* associate, associated.—*n.m.f.* associate, partner.
asociar, *v.t.* associate.—*v.r.* associate; become a partner.
asolar (1), *v.t.* parch.—*v.r.* become parched.
asolar (2) [4], *v.t.* destroy, raze.
asolear, *v.r.* get sunburnt; bask.
asomar, *v.t.* show, stick out (*the head etc.*).—*v.i.* appear, come into view.—*v.r.* appear, lean out (*of a window etc.*).
asombrar, *v.t.* shade; darken (*colours*); frighten; astonish.—*v.r.* be frightened; be amazed.
asombro, *n.m.* fear; astonishment.
asombroso, -sa, *a.* amazing.
asomo, *n.m.* appearance; indication.
asonancia, *n.f.* (*lit.*) assonance.
asonante, *a.* assonant.
asosegar [1B], *v.t.* calm.—*v.i., v.r.* calm down.
aspa, *n.f.* cross; sail of a windmill.
aspar, *v.t.* reel; crucify.—*v.r.* take great pains.
aspaviento, *n.m.* fuss, excitement.
aspecto, *n.m.* aspect.
aspereza, *n.f.* roughness; bitterness; coarseness; ruggedness (*of ground*); asperity.
áspero, -ra, *a.* rough; harsh; sour; rugged, craggy.
aspérrimo, -ma, *a. sup. of* ÁSPERO.
áspid, áspide, *n.m.* (*zool.*) asp.
aspidistra, *n.f.* (*bot.*) aspidistra.
aspillera, *n.f.* (*mil.*) embrasure, loophole.
aspiración, *n.f.* aspiration; inhalation; suction.
aspirador, -ra, *a.* relative to suction.—*n.m.* or *f.* vacuum cleaner.
aspirante, *a.* aspiring; aspirating.—*n.m.f.* applicant, candidate; (*mil.*) cadet.
aspirar, *v.t.* suck in; inhale; aspirate.—*v.i.* aspire.
aspirina, *n.f.* (*med.*) aspirin.
asquerosidad, *n.f.* loathsomeness.
asqueroso, -sa, *a.* loathsome, disgusting; squeamish.
asta, *n.f.* shaft; spear; mast; flagpole; handle; horn (*of an animal*).
astado, -da, *a.* horned.—*n.m.* (*taur.*) bull.
asterisco, *n.m.* asterisk.
asteroide, *a., n.m.* asteroid.
astil, *n.m.* handle (*of an axe*); shaft (*of an arrow*); beam (*of a balance*).
astilla, *n.f.* splinter.
astillero, *n.m.* shipyard; rack for spears.
astringente, *a., n.m.* astringent.
astro, *n.m.* (*poet.*) star; heavenly body luminary.
astrolabio, *n.m.* (*astr.*) astrolabe.
astrología, *n.f.* astrology.
astrólogo, *n.m.* astrologer.
astronauta, *n.m.* astronaut.
astronomía, *n.f.* astronomy.
astronómico, -ca, *a.* astronomic(al).
astrónomo, *n.m.* astronomer.
astroso, -sa, *a.* unfortunate; contemptible.
astucia, *n.f.* cunning; astuteness.
astur, -ra, asturiano, -na, *a., n.m.f.* Asturian.
asturión, *n.m.* (*ichth.*) sturgeon; pony.
astuto, -ta, *a.* astute; cunning.
asueto, *n.m.* (*esp. educ.*) short holiday; half holiday.
asumir, *v.t.* assume.
asunción, *n.f.* assumption.
asunto, *n.m.* subject, matter; business, affair.
asustar, *v.t.* scare, frighten.—*v.r.* to be frightened (**de, con,** at).
atabal, *n.m.* kettledrum.
atacante, *a.* attacking.—*n.m.f.* attacker.
atacar [A], *v.t.* attack; pack, ram (down); fit.
atado, -da, *a.* timid; irresolute; hammered.—*n.m.* bundle.
atadura, *n.f.* tying, fastening, bond.
ataguía, *n.f.* coffer-dam.
atajar, *v.t.* cut short; partition; interrupt.—*v.i.* take a short cut.—*v.r.* be abashed.
atajo, *n.m.* short cut; cross cut.
atalaya, *n.f.* watch-tower, gazebo.—*n.m.* guard.
atanor, *n.m.* pipe.
atañer [K], *v.t.* concern.
ataque, *n.m.* attack.
atar, *v.t.* tie, fasten.
ataracea, *n.f.* (*carp.*) marquetry.
atarantar, *v.t.* stun.
atarazana, *n.f.* arsenal; (*slang*) fence.
atardecer, *n.m.* late afternoon, evening.
atarear, *v.t.* allot a task to.—*v.r.* toil; ***atarearse a hacer,*** be busy doing.
atarjea, *n.f.* culvert; drainpipe; sewer.
atascadero, *n.m.* mudhole, bog; obstruction.
atascar [A], *v.t.* clog.—*v.r.* clog; get bogged down; stuff oneself; jam.
atasco, *n.m.* clogging; jamming; — ***de circulación,*** traffic jam.
ataúd, *n.m.* coffin.
ataviar [L], *v.t.* adorn.
atavío, *n.m.* dress, adornment.
ateísmo, *n.m.* atheism.
atención, *n.f.* attention.—*interj.* watch out!
atender [2], *v.t.* attend to.—*v.i.* pay attention.
atener [33], *v.r.* abide (**a,** by); depend.
atentadamente, *adv.* illegally; cautiously.
atentado, -da, *a.* prudent, cautious.—*n.m.* transgression, offence.
atentar, *v.t.* attempt to commit (*a crime*).—*v.i.* attempt a crime.
atento, -ta, *a.* attentive, kind; polite.—*n.f.* (*com.*) favour (*i.e. letter*).
atenuación, *n.f.* attenuation; extenuation.
atenuar [M], *v.t.* attenuate; extenuate.
ateo, atea, *a., n.m.f.* atheist.
aterecer [9], **aterir** [Q], *v.r.* become numb (*with cold*).
aterrador, -ra, *a.* dreadful, terrifying.
aterrajar, *v.t.* (*tech.*) thread, tap.
aterraje, *n.m.* (*aer.*) landing.
aterrar (1), *v.t.* terrify.

aterrar (2) [1], *v.t.* demolish; earth up.—*v.i.* (*aer.*) land.—*v.r.* (*naut.*) stand inshore.
aterrizaje, *n.m.* (*aer.*) landing.
aterrizar [C], *v.i.* (*aer.*) land.
aterrorizar [C], *v.t.* terrorize.
atesar [1], [ATIESAR].
atesorar, *v.t.* treasure up; hoard up.
atestación, *n.f.* attestation, deposition.
atestadura, *n.f.*, **atestamiento,** *n.m.* cramming, stuffing.
atestar (1), *v.t.* (*jur.*) attest.
atestar (2) [1], *v.t.* cram, stuff, fill.
atestiguación, *n.f.*, **atestiguamiento,** *n.m.* attestation, deposition.
atestiguar [H], *v.t.* testify, depose.—*v.i.* attest (to).
atiborrar, *v.t.* stuff.
at(i)esar, *v.t.* stiffen.
atildado, -da, *a.* neat, stylish.
atildar, *v.t.* put a tilde over; adorn; find fault with.
atinado, -da, *a.* keen; pertinent.
atinar, *v.t.* come upon, find.—*v.i.* guess (right).
atisbar, *v.t.* spy on, watch.
atisbo, *n.m.* prying; slight likeness.
atizador, -ra, *a.* stirring; inciting.—*n.m.* poker.
atizar [C], *v.t.* stir; rouse.
Atlante, *n.m.* (*myth.*) Atlas.
atlántico, -ca, *a.*, *n.m.* Atlantic.
atlas, *n.m. inv.* atlas.
atleta, *n.m.f.* athlete.
atlético, -ca, *a.* athletic.
atletismo, *n.m.* athletics.
atmósfera, *n.f.* atmosphere.
atmosférico, -ca, *a.* atmospheric.
atocha, *n.f.* esparto.
atolón, *n.m.* (*geog.*) atoll.
atolondrado, -da, *a.* scatterbrained.
atolondrar, *v.t.* amaze; bewilder.
atollar, *v.i.*, *v.r.* get stuck in the mud.
atómico, -ca, *a.* atomic.
atomizar [C], *v.t.* atomize.
átomo, *n.m.* atom.
atónito, -ta, *a.* astonished; aghast.
átono, -na, *a.* atonic, unstressed.
atontar, *v.t.* stun; bewilder.
atormentar, *v.t.* torment.
atosigar [B], *v.t.* poison; harass.—*v.r.* be hurried.
atóxico, -ca, *a.* non-poisonous.
atrabancar [A], *v.t.* hurry through (*work*).
atracar [A], *v.t.* (*naut.*) bring alongside; hold-up, assault.—*v.i.* (*naut.*) come alongside; (*S.A.*) quarrel.
atracción, *n.f.* attraction.
atraco, *n.m.* hold-up, attack.
atractivo, -va, *a.* attractive.—*n.m.* attractiveness, attraction.
atraer [34], *v.t.* attract.
atrafagar [B], *v.i.* toil.
atrampar, *v.r.* be trapped, get stuck, get blocked.
atramuz, *n.m.* (*pl.* **-uces**) (*bot.*) lupin.
atrancar [A], *v.t.* obstruct.—*v.i.* take large strides.
atranco, atranque, *n.m.* difficulty.
atrapar, *v.t.* (*fam.*) catch.
atrás, *adv.* back(ward)(s); behind; previously.
atrasado, -da, *a.* backward; slow (*clock*); late; in arrears.
atrasar, *v.t.* slow; put back (*clock*); leave behind; delay; postdate.—*v.i.* go slow; be late; fall behind.
atraso, *n.m.* delay; lateness; backwardness.
atravesar [1], *v.t.* put *or* lay across; cross; go through.—*v.r.* get in the way (**en,** of); have an encounter *or* a fight with.
atreguar [H], *v.t.* grant a truce *or* an extension to.
atrever, *v.r.* dare; ***atreverse a,*** venture to.
atrevido, -da, *a.* bold; impudent.
atrevimiento, *n.m.* boldness; effrontery.
atribuir [O], *v.t.* attribute.
atril, *n.m.* lectern.
atrincherar, *v.t.* entrench.
atrocidad, *n.f.* atrocity; (*fam.*) enormous amount.
atronar [4], *v.t.* deafen; stun.
atropellado, -da, *a.* hasty; violent; tumultuous.
atropellar, *v.t.* trample down; run over; violate.
atropello, *n.m.* trampling; running over; outrage.
atroz, *a.* (*pl.* **-oces**) atrocious; (*fam.*) enormous.
atuendo, *n.m.* pomp; dress, adornment.
atún, *n.m.* (*ichth.*) tuna, tunny.
aturdido, -da, *a.* reckless; scatter-brained.
aturdimiento, *n.m.* amazement; stunning.
aturdir, *v.t.* stun; amaze.
audacia, *n.f.* audacity.
audaz, *a.* (*pl.* **-aces**) audacious.
audición, *n.f.* audition, hearing.
audiencia, *n.f.* audience, hearing; (*jur.*) superior court.
audífono, *n.m.* audiphone, hearing aid.
auditivo, -va, *a.* auditory.—*n.m.* (*tel.*) earpiece.
auditor, *n.m.* (*jur.*) judge; (*com.*) auditor.
auditorio, *n.m.* (*theat. etc.*) audience; auditorium.
auge, *n.m.* (*astr.*) apogee; boom, vogue.
augurio, *n.m.* augury.
augusto, -ta, *a.* august.
aula, *n.f.* (lecture) hall; (*poet.*) palace.
aulaga, *n.f.* (*bot.*) furze, gorse.
aullar [P], *v.i.* howl.
aullido, *n.m.* howl.
aumentar, *v.t.*, *v.i.*, *v.r.* augment, increase.
aumento, *n.m.* increase; augmentation.
aun, *adv.* still, even.
aún, *adv.* still, yet.
aunque, *conj.* although, even though.
¡aúpa! *interj.* up! — ***de*** —, (*fam.*) swanky.
aupar [P], *v.t.* (*fam.*) give a hoist up, hitch up.
aura, *n.f.* gentle breeze; acclamation.
áureo, -rea, *a.* aureate, golden.
aureola, *n.f.* aureole; halo.
auricular, *a.* auricular; ***dedo* —,** little finger. —*n.m.* (*tel.*) receiver.
ausencia, *n.f.* absence.
ausentar, *v.t.* send away.—*v.r.* absent oneself.
ausente, *a.* absent.
ausentismo, *n.m.* absenteeism.
auspicio, *n.m.* auspice (*usually pl.*).
austeridad, *n.f.* austerity.
austero, -ra, *a.* austere.
Australia, *n.f.* Australia.
australiano, -na, *a.*, *n.m.f.* Australian.
Austria, *n.f.* Austria.

austríaco, -ca, *a., n.m.f.* Austrian.
austro, *n.m.* south wind.
autarcía, autarquía, *n.f.* (*pol.*) autarchy, (*U.S.*) autarky; home-rule.
auténtico, -ca, *a.* authentic, genuine, real.—*n.f.* certificate.
auto (1), *n.m.* (*jur.*) decree; writ; (*theat.*) auto.—*pl.* proceedings.
auto (2), *n.f.* (*fam.*) [AUTOMÓVIL].
autobiografía, *n.f.* autobiography.
autobote, *n.m.* power boat.
autobús, *n.m.* omnibus, bus.
autocar, *n.m.* motor coach, (*U.S.*) interurban bus.
autocracia, *n.f.* (*pol.*) autocracy.
autocrático, -ca, *a.* autocratic.
autocrítica, *n.f.* self-criticism.
autóctono, -na, *a.* autochthonous, native.
autodeterminación, *n.f.* (*pol.*) self-determination.
autodidacto, -ta, *a.* self-taught, self-educated.
autodirigido, -da, *a.* homing (*missile*).
autógrafo, -fa, *a., n.m.* autograph.
automacia, *n.f.* automation.
autómata, *n.m.* automaton.
automaticidad, *n.f.* automatic nature; automation.
automático, -ca, *a.* automatic.
automotor, -ra, *a.* self-propelled.—*n.m.* rail-car.
automóvil, *a.* self-propelled.—*n.m.* (motor) car, (*U.S.*) automobile.
automovilista, *a.* rel. to motoring.—*n.m.f.* driver, motorist.
autonomía, *n.f.* (*pol.*) autonomy, home rule; (*aer.*) operational range.
autónomo, -ma, *a.* autonomous.
autopista, *n.f.* motorway, (*U.S.*) turnpike.
autopropulsado, -da, *a.* self-propelled.
autopsia, *n.f.* autopsy.
autor, -ra, *n.m.f.* author; (*obs. theat.*) manager.
autoridad, *n.f.* authority.
autorizar [C], *v.t.* authorize (*a*, to).
autorretrato, *n.m.* (*art.*) self-portrait.
auxiliante, *a.* helping.
auxiliar (1), *a.* auxiliary.—*n.m.* (*educ.*) assistant.
auxiliar (2) [L *or regular*], *v.t.* help; attend (*dying person*).
auxilio, *n.m.* help; relief; — ***social,*** social service.
avalar, *v.t.* (*com.*) stand security for.
avaluar [M], *v.t.* estimate.
avance, *n.m.* advance; (*tech.*) feed.
avanzar [C], *v.t.* advance.—*v.i.* (*com.*) have a credit balance.
avaricia, *n.f.* avarice.
avaricioso, -sa, *a.* avaricious.
avariento, -ta, avaro, -ra, *a.* avaricious.—*n.m.f.* miser.
avasallar, *v.t.* subject, enslave.
ave, *n.f.* bird; — ***de rapiña,*** bird of prey.
avecindar, *v.t.* domicile.—*v.r.* set up residence.
avefría, *n.f.* (*orn.*) lapwing.
avellana, *n.f.* hazel-nut, filbert, cob.
avellano, *n.m.* hazel (*bush*).
avena, *n.f.* oats; ***harina de —,*** oatmeal.
avenencia, *n.f.* bargain; agreement.
avenida, *n.f.* avenue; flood, inflow.
avenir [36], *v.t.* reconcile.—*v.r.* agree (*a*, to); ***avenirse con,*** get along with.
aventajado, -da, *a.* superior, outstanding.
aventajar, *v.t.* advance, raise, give an advantage to, prefer.—*v.r.* excel.
aventar [1], *v.t.* fan; winnow.—*v.r.* swell up; (*fam.*) run away.
aventura, *n.f.* adventure; risk.
aventurado, -da, *a.* venturesome; hazardous.
aventurar, *v.t.* adventure, hazard.
aventurero, -ra, *a.* adventurous.—*n.m.* adventurer.—*n.f.* adventuress.
avergonzar [10C], *v.t.* shame.—*v.r.* be ashamed (*de*, to).
avería (1), *n.f.* breakdown, failure, defect; (*naut.*) average.
avería (2), *n.f.* aviary.
averiar [L], *v.t.* damage.—*v.r.* break down.
averiguable, *a.* ascertainable.
averiguación, *n.f.* ascertainment; investigation.
averiguar [H], *v.t.* ascertain, verify.
aversión, *n.f.* aversion.
avestruz, *n.m.* (*pl.* **-uces**) (*orn.*) ostrich.
avetoro, *n.m.* (*orn.*) bittern.
avezar [C], *v.t.* accustom.—*v.r.* become accustomed (*a*, to).
aviación, *n.f.* aviation; (*mil.*) air force.
aviador, -ra, *a.* rel. to flying; equipping.—*n.m.f.* aviator.
aviar [L], *v.t., v.r.* get ready, prepare.
avidez, *n.f.* eagerness, avidity; covetousness.
ávido, -da, *a.* eager, anxious (*de*, for); covetous (*de*, of).
avieso, -sa, *a.* distorted; perverse.
avilés, -lesa, *a.* rel. to Avila.—*n.m.f.* inhabitant of Avila.
avinagrar, *v.t.* make sour.
avío, *n.m.* preparation; money advanced.—*pl.* equipment.
avión, *n.m.* (*aer.*) aeroplane, airplane; (*orn.*) martin.
avisado, -da, *a.* prudent, wise; ***mal —,*** rash.
avisador, -ra, *a.* warning.—*n.m.f.* informer; adviser.—*n.m.* electric bell; alarm.
avisar, *v.t.* advise; inform; warn.
aviso, *n.m.* advice; notice; warning.
avispa, *n.f.* (*ent.*) wasp.
avispero, *n.m.* wasps' nest; (*fam.*) mess.
avispón, *n.m.* (*ent.*) hornet.
avistar, *v.t.* descry.—*v.r.* have a meeting (***con,*** with).
avivar, *v.t.* revive; enliven.
avutarda, *n.f.* (*orn.*) bustard; (*S.A.*) wild turkey.
axioma, *n.m.* axiom.
axiomático, -ca, *a.* axiomatic.
¡ay! *interj.* oh! ouch! alas! ***¡— de mí!*** woe is me!
aya, *n.f.* governess, nurse.
ayer, *adv.* yesterday.
ayo, *n.m.* tutor.
ayuda, *n.f.* aid, help.—*n.m.* page, aide.
ayudanta, *n.f.* female assistant; relief teacher; maid.
ayudante, *n.m.* assistant; (*mil.*) aide-de-camp; adjutant.
ayudar, *v.t.* help, aid, assist.
ayunar, *v.i.* fast.
ayuno, -na, *a.* fasting.—*n.m.* fast; fasting; ***en ayunas,*** on an empty stomach.

ayuntamiento, *n.m.* town council, municipal government.
azabache, *n.m.* (*min.*) jet.
azada, *n.f.* hoe; spade.
azadón, *n.m.* hoe; — ***de peto,*** pick-axe.
azafata, *n.f.* (*aer.*) air hostess; (*obs.*) lady of the wardrobe.
azafate, *n.m.* tray.
azafrán, *n.m.* (*bot.*) saffron.
azafranar, *v.t.* flavour *or* colour with saffron.
azahar, *n.m.* orange blossom.
azar, *n.m.* chance; fate; hazard; ***al* —,** at random.
azaroso, -sa, *a.* hazardous.
ázimo, -ma, *a.* azymous, unleavened.
azimut, *n.m.* (*pl.* **-s**) (*astr.*) azimuth.
azogar [B], *v.t.* coat with quicksilver, silver.—*v.r.* have mercurialism; (*fam.*) shake.
azogue, *n.m.* quicksilver, mercury.
azor, *n.m.* (*orn.*) goshawk.
azorar, *v.t.* abash; excite.
azotaina, *n.f.* (*fam.*) spanking.
azotar, *v.t.* whip, lash.
azote, *n.m.* whip, lash; (*fig.*) scourge.
azotea, *n.f.* flat roof, terrace.
azteca, *a., n.m.f.* Aztec.
azúcar, *n.m.* sugar.
azucarar, *v.t.* sugar; ice.
azucarero, -ra, *a.* rel. to sugar *or* the sugar industry.—*n.m.* sugar producer *or* dealer; sugar-bowl.
azucena, *n.f.* (*bot.*) Madonna lily.
azud, *n.m.,* **azuda,** *n.f.* weir; water wheel.
azuela, *n.f.* adze.
azufre, *n.m.* (*chem.*) sulphur, (*U.S.*) sulfur; brimstone.
azul, *a., n.m.* blue; — ***celeste,*** sky-blue; — ***marino,*** navy-blue.
azulado, -da, *a.* blue, bluish.
azulejo, *n.m.* glazed (coloured) tile; (*orn.*) bee-eater.
azumbre, *n.m.* azumbre (*a liquid measure, about 4 pints*).
azuzar [C], *v.t.* set on (*a dog*); (*fig.*) incite.

B

B, b, *n.f.* second letter of the Spanish alphabet.
baba, *n.f.* slobber; slime.
babador, *n.m.* bib.
babear, *v.i.* slobber, drool.
Babel, *n.m.* or *f.* Babel; (*fig.*) babel.
babero, -ra, *n.m.f.* bib.
Babia, *n.f.* area of León; ***estar en* —,** be in the clouds, be absent-minded.
babieca, *a., n.m.f.* (*fam.*) fool.
babilónico, -ca, *a.* Babylonian; (*fig.*) sumptuous.
babilonio, -nia, *a., n.m.f.* Babylonian.
bable, *n.m.* Asturian dialect.
babor, *n.m.* (*naut.*) port (*side*).
babosa, *n.f.* (*zool.*) slug.
babosear, *v.t.* drool over; (*C.A.*) hoodwink.
baboso, -sa, *a.* slobbery; callow.—*n.m.* (*S.A.*) fool; (*C.A.*) rotter.
babucha, *n.f.* Moorish slipper.
babuíno, *n.m.* baboon.
baca, *n.f.* top (*of vehicle*).
bacalada, *n.f.* cured cod.
bacalao, *n.m.* cod; dried salt cod.
bacanal, *a.* bacchanal.—*n.f.* orgy.
bacante, *n.f.* bacchante; (*fig.*) drunken hussy.
bacía, *n.f.* basin; shaving dish.
bacilo, *n.m.* bacillus.
bacín, *n.m.* urinal; poor box; wastrel.
Baco, *n.m.* Bacchus.
bacteria, *n.f.* microbe, bacterium.
bactericida, *a.* bactericidal.—*n.m.* bactericide.
bacteriología, *n.f.* bacteriology.
bacteriológico, -ca, *a.* bacteriological.
báculo, *n.m.* staff; crook; crozier; (*fig.*) aid, comfort.
bache, *n.m.* pothole, rut; air-pocket.
bachiller, -ra, *n.m.f.* bachelor (*degree*); (*fam.*) wiseacre.
bachillerato, *n.m.* baccalaureate, bachelor's degree; school-leaving examination.
badajo, *n.m.* bell-clapper; chatterbox.
badana, *n.f.* sheep leather; (*fam.*) hide, skin.
badea, *n.f.* tasteless melon; (*fam.*) dimwit; (*fam.*) bauble, nothing.
badén, *n.f.* ford; open drain.
badulaque, *n.m.* (*fam.*) nincompoop; (*S.A.*) scoundrel.
bagaje, *n.m.* (*mil.*) baggage; baggage mule.
bagatela, *n.f.* trifle, bagatelle.
bagre, *a.* (*S.A.*) showy, vulgar; loose, immoral.—*n.m.* catfish.
bahía, *n.f.* bay, bight.
bahorrina, *n.f.* bilge; (*fam.*) riff-raff.
bailable, *n.m.* (*fam.*) dance-tune.
bailadero, *n.m.* dance hall.
bailador, -ra, *a.* dancing.—*n.m.f.* dancer.
bailar, *v.t., v.i.* dance.
bailarín, -rina, *a.* dancing.—*n.m.f.* dancer.—*n.f.* ballerina.
baile, *n.m.* dance, dancing; dance, ball.
bailotear, *v.i.* dance badly, jig about.
baja, *n.f.* fall (*in price*); (*mil.*) casualty, loss; (*fig.*) withdrawal, resignation; ***dar* —, *ir en* —,** lose value, wane; ***estar de* —,** be on the decline.
bajada, *n.f.* descent; way down; drop.
bajamar, *n.f.* low tide.
bajar, *v.t.* lower; bring *or* take down.—*v.i.* descend, go *or* come down; alight, get off; drop.—*v.r.* dismount; stoop.
bajel, *n.m.* vessel, ship.
bajeza, *n.f.* lowness, meanness; lowliness.
bajío, *n.m.* (*naut.*) sandbank, shallow; (*S.A.*) lowland, plain.
bajista, *n.m.* (*com.*) bear (*in shares*).
bajo, -ja, *a.* low, lower; short; base, vulgar; ground (*floor*).—*n.m.* (*naut.*) shallow, shoal; (*mus.*) bass.—*adv.* below, down; in a low voice.—*prep.* under(neath).
bajón (1), *n.m.* decline, drop; relapse.
bajón (2), *n.m.* bassoon.
bajorelieve, *n.m.* bas-relief.
bajura, *n.f.* lowness; shortness; lowlands.
bala, *n.f.* bullet, shell; bale.
balada, *n.f.* ballad; ballade.
baladí, *a.* (*pl.* **-íes**) paltry, worthless.
baladrar, *v.i.* screech, whoop.
baladrón, -ona, *a.* boastful.—*n.m.f.* braggart.

balance, *n.m.* swaying, vacillation; (*com.*) balance sheet.
balancear, *v.t.* balance.—*v.i.*, *v.r.* rock, swing; waver; sway.
balancín, *n.m.* balance beam; balancing pole; see-saw; (*mech.*) crank.
balanza, *n.f.* scales, balance; judgement.
balar, *v.i.* bleat.
balaustrada, *n.f.* balustrade.
balaustre, *n.m.* baluster, banister.
balazo, *n.m.* shot; bullet wound.
balbucear, *v.i.* stammer, stutter; mumble.
balbucencia, *n.f.*, **balbuceo,** *n.m.* stammer, stutter, mumbling.
balbucir [Q] [BALBUCEAR].
Balcanes, *n.m.pl.* the Balkans.
balcánico, -ca, *a.* Balkan.
balcón, *n.m.* balcony.
baldaquín, baldaquino, *n.m.* canopy, baldaquin.
baldar, *v.t.* cripple, maim; trump.
balde (1), *n.m.* baling bucket.
balde (2), *adv.* ***de* —,** gratis, free; ***en* —,** in vain; ***estar de* —,** stand idle.
baldío, -día, *a.* idle (*land*); useless, pointless.
baldón, *n.m.* insult.
baldonar, *v.t.* affront, insult.
baldosa, *n.f.* floor tile; (*S.A.*) gravestone.
balear (1), *a.* Balearic.—*n.m.f.* native of the Balearic Islands.
balear (2), *v.t.* (*S.A.*) shoot at, shoot.
Baleares, *n.f.pl.* Balearic Islands.
baleárico, -ca, *a.* Balearic.
balido, *n.m.* bleat.
balístico, -ca, *a.* ballistic.—*n.f.* ballistics.
baliza, *n.f.* buoy.
balneario, -ria, *a.* rel. to a spa.—*n.m.* spa, hydro, watering-place.
balompié, *n.m.* football (*game*).
balón, *n.m.* (foot)ball; balloon; bale.
baloncesto, *n.m.* basketball.
balonvolea, *n.m.* volley-ball.
balotaje, *n.m.* balloting.
balotar, *v.i.* ballot.
balsa, *n.f.* pond, pool; raft; (*bot.*) balsa.
balsámico, -ca, *a.* balsamic, soothing.
bálsamo, *n.m.* balsam, balm.
báltico, -ca, *a.* Baltic.
baluarte, *n.m.* bulwark, rampart.
balumba, *n.f.* bulk, mass; (*S.A.*) uproar.
ballena, *n.f.* whale; whalebone.
ballenero, -ra, *a.* whaling.—*n.m.* whaler.
ballesta, *n.f.* cross-bow; bird snare; (*mech.*) vehicle spring.
ballestero, *n.m.* cross-bowman.
ballet, *n.m.* (*pl.* **-s**) ballet.
bambalina, *n.f.* (*theat.*) fly drop, back-cloth.
bambolear, *v.t.*, *v.i.* swing, sway, totter.
bamboleo, *n.m.* swaying, swinging, wobbling, tottering.
bambú, *n.m.* (*pl.* **-úes**) bamboo.
banana, *n.f.* banana tree; (*S.A.*) banana.
banano, *n.m.* banana tree.
banasta, *n.f.* large basket.
banasto, *n.m.* large round basket; (*low*) jug, jail.
banca, *n.f.* bench, form; market stall; (*com.*) banking.
bancal, *n.m.* vegetable plot.
bancario, -ria, *a.* banking.
bancarrota, *n.f.* bankruptcy; ***hacer* —,** go bankrupt.
bance, *n.m.* rail, bar.
banco, *n.m.* bank; bench; shoal; sandbank; ***— de hielo,*** iceberg.
banda, *n.f.* sash; band, gang; riverbank; (*mus.*) military band; (*naut.*) gunwale.
bandada, *n.f.* covey, flock; ***a bandadas,*** (*fam.*) in droves.
bandeado, -da, *a.* striped.
bandeja, *n.f.* tray; (*S.A.*) serving dish.
bandera, *n.f.* flag, banner.
banderilla, *n.f.* (*taur.*) barbed decorated dart.
banderillero, *n.m.* (*taur.*) bullfighter who inserts the banderillas.
banderín, *n.m.* small flag; pennant; military colours; leading soldier; recruiting office.
bandidaje, banditismo, *n.m.* banditry.
bandido, *n.m.* bandit, outlaw; (*fam.*) crook, twister.
bando, *n.m.* edict; faction, band; shoal.
bandolera, *n.f.* bandolier; gangsters' moll.
bandolerismo, *n.m.* banditry, brigandage.
bandolero, *n.m.* bandit, brigand.
bandolín, *n.m.* (*mus.*) mandolin.
bandolina, *n.f.* hair-grease; (*S.A.*) mandolin.
bandurria, *n.f.* (*mus.*) bandore.
banquero, *n.m.* banker.
banqueta, *n.f.* foot-stool; (*C.A.*) pavement, (*U.S.*) sidewalk.
banquete, *n.m.* banquet; small stool.
banquillo, *n.m.* (*jur.*) dock; small bench.
banzo, *n.m.* jamb.
bañado, *n.m.* chamber-pot; (*S.A.*) floodlands.
bañador, -ra, *n.m.f.* bather.—*n.m.* swimsuit.
bañar, *v.t.* bath; bathe; drench.—*v.r.* have a bath; bathe; (*C.A.*) do well (*in business*).
bañera, *n.f.* bath, bath-tub.
baño, *n.m.* bath; bathe; spa; Turkish prison.
baque, *n.m.* thud, bump.
baquelita, *n.m.* bakelite.
baqueta, *n.f.* (*mil.*) ramrod; horse-switch; drumstick; ***carrera de baquetas,*** running the gauntlet.
baquía, *n.f.* familiarity with tracks *etc.* of a region; (*S.A.*) dexterity, skill.
baquiano, -na, *a.* skilled, experienced.—*n.m.* scout, path-finder, guide.
báquico, -ca, *a.* Bacchic; bacchanal.
bar, *n.m.* bar, café.
barahunda, *n.f.* hurly-burly, din, rumpus.
baraja, *n.f.* pack (*of cards*); row, quarrel.
barajar, *v.t.* shuffle; (*S.A.*) understand.—*v.i.* squabble.—*v.r.* get mixed up.
baranda, *n.f.* railing, edge.
barandilla, *n.f.* railing, guard-rail.
barata, *n.f.* barter; cheapness; ***a la* —,** confusedly.
baratear, *v.t.* cheapen, sell under value.
baratija, *n.f.* knick-knack, trinket.
baratillo, *n.m.* second-hand shop; bargain counter.
barato, -ta, *a.* cheap.—*n.m.* bargain sale.—*adv.* cheap, cheaply; ***de* —,** gratis, interest free; ***echar*** or ***meter a* —,** heckle; ***dar de* —,** grant, admit.
báratro, *n.m.* (*poet.*) hell.
baratura, *n.f.* cheapness.
baraúnda [BARAHUNDA].
baraustar [P], *v.t.* aim; ward off.
barba, *n.f.* beard; chin; burr, frayed edge; ***hacer la* —,** shave; annoy; cajole.
barbacoa, barbacúa, *n.f.* (*S.A.*) barbecue; various lattice structures.

la Barbada, *n.f.* Barbados.
barbaridad, *n.f.* barbarism, barbarity; rashness, rudeness; (*fam.*) vast amount; **¡que —!** what a nerve! how shocking!
barbarie, *n.f.* barbarism, cruelty, savagery.
barbarismo, *n.m.* barbarism.
barbarizar [C], *v.t.* barbarize.—*v.i.* say outrageous things.
bárbaro, -ra, *a.* barbaric, barbarous; (*fam.*) terrific, fantastic.—*n.m.f.* barbarian.
barbear, *v.t.* reach with the chin; (*S.A.*) shave; (*S.A.*) flatter; **— con,** be as high as.
barbecho, *n.m.* fallow, fallow land.
barbería, *n.f.* barber's shop.
barbero, *n.m.* barber; (*S.A.*) flatterer.
barbiblanco, -ca, *a.* white-bearded.
barbilampiño, -ña, *a.* smooth-faced, beardless.
barbilla, *n.f.* tip of the chin; barbel.
barbiponiente, *a.* beginning to grow a beard. —*n.m.f.* beginner, novice.
barbiturato, *n.m.* barbiturate.
barbo, *n.m.* (*ichth.*) barbel.
barbón, *n.m.* bearded man; billy goat; (*fam.*) old fuddy duddy.
barbot(e)ar, *v.t.*, *v.i.* mumble.
barbudo, -da, *a.* heavy-bearded.
barbulla, *n.f.* (*fam.*) hullabaloo.
barbullar, *v.i.* gabble, jabber.
barca, *n.f.* rowing boat.
barcaza, *n.f.* (*naut.*) lighter.
barcelonés, -nesa, *a.* rel. to Barcelona.—*n.m.f.* person from Barcelona.
barco, *n.m.* boat, ship.
barda, *n.f.* horse armour; wall-thatch; (*naut.*) low dark cloud.
bardaguera, *n.f.* osier.
bardo, *n.m.* bard.
bario, *n.m.* barium.
barítono, *n.m.* baritone.
barjuleta, *n.f.* knapsack, tool-bag.
barloar, *v.t.* (*naut.*) bring alongside.
barloventear, *v.i.* (*naut.*) ply windward; (*fig.*) rove about.
barlovento, *n.m.* windward.
barman, *n.m.* barman.
barniz, *n.m.* varnish; pottery glaze; (*fig.*) smattering.
barnizar [C], *v.t.* varnish; glaze.
barómetro, *n.m.* barometer.
barón, *n.m.* baron.
baronesa, *n.f.* baroness.
baronía, *n.f.* barony, baronage.
barquero, *n.m.* boatman.
barquía, *n.f.* rowing boat.
barquilla, *n.f.* (*cul.*) cake mould; airship car; balloon basket; (*naut.*) log.
barquillo, *n.m.* tiny boat; ice-cream cornet; wafer biscuit.
barra, *n.f.* bar, rod; ingot; (*mech.*) lever; (*naut.*) sand-bar; (*law, mus.*) bar; ***— de labios,*** lipstick.
barraca, *n.f.* rustic cottage; (*S.A.*) storage shed.
barranca, *n.f.*, **barranco,** *n.m.* gully, ravine; great difficulty, snag.
barrar, *v.t.* bar; mire.
barreda, *n.f.* barrier, fence.
barredero, -ra, *a.* sweeping; (*fig.*) sweeping all before.
barrena, *n.f.* drill-bit; (*aer.*) spin; ***— de mano,*** (*carp.*) gimlet.
barrenar, *v.t.* drill, bore; scuttle; break (*the law*).
barrendero, *n.m.* sweeper.
barreno, *n.m.* large bit, auger; drilled hole; (*S.A.*) mania, whim.
barreño, *n.m.* earthenware bowl.
barrer, *v.t.* sweep (away); brush against.
barrera, *n.f.* barrier; barricade; front seats in bullring; clay-pit; crockery cupboard; ***— del sonido,*** sound barrier.
barrero, *n.m.* potter; clay-pit; (*S.A.*) saltpetre marsh.
barriada, *n.f.* quarter, ward, precinct.
barrial, *n.m.* (*S.A.*) quagmire.
barrica, *n.f.* medium barrel.
barricada, *n.f.* barricade.
barriga, *n.f.* (*fam.*) belly; (*fig.*) bulge.
barril, *n.m.* cask, barrel; water jug.
barrio, *n.m.* quarter, district, suburb.
barrisco, *only in* ***a —,*** *adv. phr.* pell-mell, indiscriminately.
barrizal, *n.m.* quagmire.
barro, *n.m.* mud, clay; earthenware; red pimple; (*S.A.*) unintended *or* thoughtless harm; ***— cocido,*** terra cotta.
barroco, -ca, *a.*, *n.m.* baroque.
barroquismo, *n.m.* baroque style; extravagance, bad taste.
barroso, -sa, *a.* muddy; pimply.
barruntar, *v.t.* foresee, conjecture.
barrunte, *n.m.* presentiment; indication.
barrunto, *n.m.* guess, conjecture, presentiment.
bartola, *n.f. only in* ***a la —,*** *adv.phr.* (*fam.*) in a lazy old way.
bártulos, *n.m.pl.* gear, paraphernalia, belongings.
baruca, *n.f.* (*fam.*) wangle, trick; (*fam.*) snag.
barullero, -ra, *a.* clumsy, bungling.—*n.m.f.* bungler; rowdy.
barullo, *n.m.* (*fam.*) rumpus; mess.
barullón, -llona [BARULLERO].
basa, *n.f.* (*arch.*) base, pedestal.
basalto, *n.m.* (*geol.*) basalt.
basar, *v.t.* base (***en,*** on).
basca, *n.f.* queasiness; (*fam.*) tantrum.
bascoso, -sa, *a.* queasy; (*S.A.*) foul.
báscula, *n.f.* platform scale.
base, *n.f.* base, basis; (*mil.*) base; ***a — de,*** on the basis of, with, using.
básico, -ca, *a.* basic.
basílica, *n.f.* basilica.
basilisco, *n.m.* basilisk; (*fig.*) furious person.
basquear, *v.i.* feel queasy.
basquiña, *n.f.* overskirt, basquine.
bastante, *a.* enough, sufficient.—*adv.* enough; rather, fairly.
bastar, *v.i.* be enough, suffice.—*v.r.* be self-sufficient.
bastardilla, letra bastardilla, *n.f.* italics.
bastardo, -da, *a.* illegitimate, bastard; degenerate; spurious, mongrel.
bastedad, basteza, *n.f.* coarseness, roughness.
bastidor, *n.m.* frame; (*mech.*) chassis; (*art.*) easel; (*theat.*) flat; ***entre bastidores,*** behind the scenes, off stage.
bastilla, *n.f.* hem.
bastimento, *n.m.* provisions, victuals; (*obs.*) ship.
bastión, *n.m.* bastion.
basto, -ta, *a.* coarse, crude, rough.—*n.m.* club (*in cards*).

bastón, *n.m.* cane, walking stick; (*mil*). baton.
bastonada, *n.f.*, **bastonazo,** *n.m.* blow with stick, bastinado.
bastonera, *n.f.* umbrella-stand.
basura, *n.f.* rubbish, refuse, trash; manure, ordure.
basurero, *n.m.* dustman, (*U.S.*) trash collector; rubbish dump.
bata, *n.f.* dressing gown; smock; (*S.A.*) bat.
batacazo, *n.m.* thud, bump; (*fam.*) let-down, failure.
batalla, *n.f.* battle; fight; joust.
batallar, *v.i.* battle, fight; waver, struggle with oneself.
batallón, -llona, *a.* moot, debatable; causing discord.—*n.m.* battalion.
batán, *n.m.* fulling mill; (*S.A.*) flourmill.
batata, *n.f.* sweet potato, yam; (*S.A.*) jitters, fear.
batayola, *n.f.* (*naut.*) rail.
bate, *n.m.* (*S.A.*) baseball bat.
batea, *n.f.* wooden tray, wooden vessel; flat-bottomed boat; (*rail.*) flat wagon.
batería, *n.f.* (*mil., elec.*) battery; drums, drummer; (*S.A.*) nuisance; (*theat.*) footlights.
batido, -da, *a.* shot (*silk, etc.*); well-beaten (*road*).—*n.m.* batter; milk-shake.
batidor, *n.m.* (*mil.*) scout, outrider; (*cul.*) whisk; (*hunt.*) beater; comb.
batiente, *n.m.* door-jamb; piano damper.
batihoja, *n.m.* gold-beater; sheet-metal worker.
batín, *n.m.* smoking jacket.
batintín, *n.m.* gong.
batir, *v.t.* beat; clap; overcome, ruin; strike (*coins*); patrol.—*v.r.* fight.
bato, *n.m.* ninny.
batueco, -ca, *a.* simple, yokelish; addled.
baturro, -rra, *a.* yokelish, simple.—*n.m.f.* Aragonese peasant; ninny.
batuta, *n.f.* (*mus.*) baton; ***llevar la —***, (*fam.*) be in charge.
baúl, *n.m.* trunk, chest; (*fam*). belly.
bauprés, *n.m.* (*naut.*) bowsprit.
bausán, *n.m.* (*mil.*) strawman, dummy; (*fam.*) fool, dummy.
bautismal, *a.* baptismal.
bautismo, *n.m.* baptism.
bautista, *n.m.* baptizer; baptist.
bautizar [C], *v.t.* baptize, christen; (*fam.*) dilute (*wine*).
bautizo, *n.m.* christening.
bávaro, -ra, *a., n.m.f.* Bavarian.
Baviera, *n.f.* Bavaria.
baya (1), *n.f.* berry.
bayeta, *n.f.* baize; floor-cloth.
bayo, -ya (2) *a., n.m.f.* bay (*horse*).
bayoneta, *n.f.* bayonet.
baza (1), *n.f.* trick (*cards*); ***hacer —***, prosper; ***meter —***, (*fam.*) stick an oar in.
bazar, *n.m.* bazaar; department store.
bazo, -za (2), *a.* yellow-brown.—*n.m.* spleen.
bazofia, *n.f.* pig-swill; garbage.
bazucar [A], **bazuquear,** *v.t.* shake (*liquid in container*); meddle with, tamper with.
be (1), *n.m.* bleat.
be (2), *n.f.* name of letter B; ***— por —***, in detail.
beatería, *n.f.* bigotry.
beatificar [A], *v.t.* beatify.
beatitud, *n.f.* beatitude.
beato, -ta, *a.* blessed; happy; devout; bigoted.—*n.m.f.* bigot; prude.
beatón, -tona, *a.* bigoted, sanctimonious.—*n.m.f.* prude; bigot.
bebé, *n.m.* baby; doll.
bebedero, -ra, *a.* drinking, drinkable.—*n.m.* watertrough; spout.
bebedizo, -za, *a.* drinkable.—*n.m.* potion, philtre; poison.
beber, *n.m.* drink.—*v.t.* drink; absorb.—*v.i.* drink, tipple.—*v.r.* drink, swallow.
bebida, *n.f.* drink, beverage.
bebido, -da, *a.* drunk, tipsy, merry.
bebistrajo, *n.m.* (*fam.*) rot-gut, nasty drink.
beca, *n.f.* scholarship, studentship; academic sash.
becario, -ria, *n.m.* scholarship holder.
becerrada, *n.f.* yearling bullfight.
becerro, *n.m.* yearling calf; calfskin; cartulary.
becuadro, *n.m.* (*mus.*) natural sign.
bedel, *n.m.* university porter.
beduino, -na, *a., n.m.f.* Bedouin.
befa, *n.f.* taunt.
befar, *v.t.* jeer at.
befo, -fa, *a.* blubber-lipped; knock-kneed.—*n.m.* blubber lip.
behetría, *n.f.* (*hist.*) free city; (*fam.*) pandemonium.
bejín, *n.m.* (*bot.*) puff-ball; (*fam.*) touchy person.
bejuco, *n.m.* rattan, liana.
beldad, *n.f.* beauty.
beldar [1], *v.t.* winnow (*with a fork*).
Belén, *n.m.* Bethlehem; **belén,** *n.m.* crib; (*fam.*) bedlam; (*fam.*) risky business.
beleño, *n.m.* (*bot.*) henbane; poison.
belfo, -fa, *a.* blubber-lipped.—*n.m.* lip (*of animal*).
belga, *a., n.m.f.* Belgian.
Bélgica, *n.f.* Belgium.
bélgico, -ca, *a.* Belgian.
bélico, -ca, *a.* warlike; rel. to war.
belicoso, -sa, *a.* bellicose, aggressive.
beligerante, *a., n.m.* belligerent.
belitre, *a.* (*fam.*) mean, vile.—*n.m.* wretch, cur.
bellaco, -ca, *a.* knavish, villainous, cunning.—*n.m.f.* scoundrel.
belladona, *n.f.* belladonna.
bellaquería, *n.f.* villainy, roguery.
belleza, *n.f.* beauty.
bello, -lla, *a.* beautiful, fine; ***el — sexo,*** the fair sex; ***bellas artes,*** fine arts.
bellota, *n.f.* acorn; (*fam.*) Adam's apple.
bembo, -ba, *a.* (*S.A.*) thick-lipped, Negroid.
bemol, *a., n.m.* (*mus.*) flat.
bencina, *n.f.* benzine.
bendecir [17, *but p.p.* **bendecido,** *rarely* **bendito**; *fut.* **bendeciré,** *cond.* **bendeciría**], *v.t.* bless.
bendición, *n.f.* blessing.
bendito, -ta, *a.* blessed, happy; (*fam.*) confounded; (*fam.*) simple, silly.—*n.m.* simpleton.
benedictino, -na, *a., n.m.f.* Benedictine.
beneficencia, *n.f.* charity, welfare.
beneficentísimo, -ma, *sup. of* BENÉFICO.
beneficiación, *n.f.* benefit; cultivation, tilling; (*min.*) exploitation; (*industry*) processing; (*com.*) concession, discount.
beneficiar, *v.t.* benefit; cultivate, till; exploit (*mines*); process (*raw materials*); (*com.*)

allow a discount to; (*S.A.*) slaughter (*stock*). —*v.r.* avail oneself (***de,*** of); (*S.A.*) kill, account for.
beneficiario, -ria, *n.m.f.* beneficiary.
beneficio, *n.m.* benefaction; benefit; benefice; (*theat., sport*) benefit; (*agr.*) cultivation; (*min.*) yield; (*com.*) profit; (*S.A.*) slaughtering; (*S.A.*) processing plant; (*S.A.*) fertilizer.
beneficioso, -sa, *a.* profitable, advantageous.
benéfico, -ca, *a.* beneficent, charitable; beneficial.
la Benemérita, *n.f.* (*Sp.*) Civil Guard.
benemérito, -ta, *a., n.m.f.* worthy; — ***de la patria,*** national hero.
beneplácito, *n.m.* approval, consent.
benevolencia, *n.f.* benevolence.
benévolo, *a.* benevolent [*sup.* **benevolentísimo, -ma**].
benignidad, *n.f.* kindness.
benigno, -na, *a.* benignant, kind; mild.
Benito, *n.m.* Benedict; **benito, -ta,** *n.m.f.* Benedictine.
beodez, *n.f.* drunkenness.
beodo, -da, *a.* drunk.—*n.m.f.* drunkard.
berberecho, *n.m.* (*zool.*) cockle.
Berbería, *n.f.* Barbary.
berberisco, -ca, *a.* Berber.
berbiquí, *n.m.* (*carp.*) brace and bit.
bereber, *a., n.m.f.* Berber.
berenjena, *n.f.* eggplant, aubergine.
berenjenal, *n.m.* eggplant plot; (*fig.*) predicament.
bergante, *n.m.* scoundrel.
bergantín, *n.m.* (*naut.*) brig; (*S.A.*) black-eye.
berilo, *n.m.* (*gem.*) beryl.
berlina, *n.f.* berlin; ***en —,*** in the cart, in a silly position.
berlinés, -nesa, *a., n.m.f.* Berliner.
bermejear, *v.i.* look *or* become bright red.
bermejo, -ja, *a.* vermilion.
bermellón, *n.m.* vermilion.
Bermudas, *n.f.pl.* Bermuda.
bernadina, *n.f.* tall story, cock-and-bull story.
berrear, *v.i.* low, bellow.
berrenchín, *n.m.* (*fam.*) tantrum; bad breath.
berrido, *n.m.* lowing, bellow.
berrín, *n.m.* (*fam.*) touchy person *or* child.
berrinche, *n.m.* (*fam.*) tantrum, rage; (*S.A.*) squabble.
berro, *n.m.* watercress.
berza, *n.f.* cabbage.
besana, *n.f.* furrow; arable land.
besar, *v.t.* kiss; (*fam.*) brush against.—*v.r.* (*fam.*) collide; — ***la mano*** or ***los pies a,*** pay one's respects to.
beso, *n.m.* kiss; (*fam.*) bump.
bestia, *n.f.* beast.—*n.m.f.* brute, boor, lout.
bestiaje, *n.m.* beasts of burden.
bestial, *a.* bestial, beastly; (*fam.*) terrific.
bestialidad, *n.f.* beastliness.
besucar [A], *v.t., v.i.* kiss and cuddle.
besucón, -cona, *a., n.m.f.* (person) much given to kissing.—*n.m.* (*fam.*) big kiss.
besugo, *n.m.* sea-bream.
besuquear [BESUCAR].
besuqueo, *n.m.* kissing, billing and cooing.
betarraba (*S.A.*), **betarraga** (*Sp.*), *n.f.* beetroot.
bético, -ca, *a.* Andalusian.
betún, *n.m.* bitumen; shoe polish; pitch; asphalt.
bezo, *n.m.* thick lip.
biberón, *n.m.* baby's feeding bottle.
Biblia, *n.f.* Bible.
bíblico, -ca, *a.* biblical.
bibliófilo, *n.m.* bibliophile.
bibliografía, *n.f.* bibliography.
bibliógrafo, *n.m.* bibliographer.
biblioteca, *n.f.* library; large bookcase.
bibliotecario, -ria, *n.m.f.* librarian.
bicarbonato, *n.m.* bicarbonate (*esp. of soda*).
bicentenario, -ria, *a., n.m.* bicentenary.
bíceps, *n.m.* biceps.
bicerra, *n.f.* wild goat.
bicicleta, *n.f.* bicycle.
bicoca, *n.f.* (*fam.*) trifle, small thing.
bicolor, *a.* bicoloured.
bicornio, *n.m.* two-pointed hat.
bicha, *n.f.* (*dial.*) snake; (*obs.*) caryatid.
bichar, *v.t.* spy on.—*v.i.* pry.
bichero, *n.m.* boathook.
bicho, *n.m.* bug; (*fam.*) anything living; ***mal —,*** (*fam.*) ugly customer; savage bull; (*S.A.*) spite.
bidé, *n.m.* bidet.
biela, *n.f.* (*mech.*) connecting rod.
bielda, *n.f.,* **bieldo, bielgo,** *n.m.* winnowing fork.
bien, *n.m.* good, welfare.—*pl.* property, goods. —*adv.* well; properly; very; really; — ***a —,*** willingly; — ***que,*** although; ***en — de,*** for the good of; ***hombre de —,*** honest man; ***no —,*** as soon as; ***o —,*** or else, otherwise; ***¡qué — !*** splendid! ***si —,*** although.
bienal, *a.* biennial.
bienandante, *a.* prosperous, happy.
bienandanza, *n.f.* prosperity, success.
bienaventurado, -da, *a.* blissful, blessed.
bienaventuranza, *n.f.* bliss.—*pl.* (*eccl.*) Beatitudes.
bienestar, *n.m.* well-being.
bienhechor, -ra, *a.* charitable, kind.—*n.m.* benefactor.—*n.f.* benefactress.
bienhechuría, *n.f.* (*S.A.*) improvements (*to property*).
bienintencionado, -da, *a.* well-meaning.
bienllegada, *n.f.* welcome.
bienmandado, -da, *a.* compliant, obedient.
bienoliente, *a.* fragrant.
bienquerencia, *n.f.* goodwill, affection.
bienquerer [26], *v.t.* be fond of, be well disposed towards.—*n.m.* goodwill, affection.
bienquisto, -ta, *a.* well-loved; widely esteemed.
bienvenido, -da, *a., n.f.* welcome; ***dar la bienvenida a,*** welcome.
bife, *n.m.* (*S.A.*) beefsteak; (*S.A., fam.*) biff.
bifocal, *a.* bifocal.
biftec, *n.m.* beefsteak.
bifurcación, *n.f.* bifurcation; (*rail.*) branch; fork (*in road*).
bigamia, *n.f.* bigamy; (*jur.*) second marriage.
bígamo, -ma, *a.* bigamous.—*n.m.f.* bigamist; remarried person.
bigardía, *n.f.* hoodwinking; lechery.
bigardo, -da, *a.* wanton.
bigornia, *n.f.* anvil.
bigote, *n.m.* moustache; (*print.*) ornate dash.—*pl.* moustache.
bigotudo, -da, *a.* moustachioed.

bilbaino, -na, *a., n.m.f.* (*person*) native of Bilbao.
bilingüe, *a.* bilingual.
bilioso, -sa, *a.* (*med.*) bilious; (*fig.*) tetchy.
bilis, *n.f.* bile; ***descarger la* —,** vent one's spleen.
billar, *n.m.* billiards; billiard-table; billiard-room.
billete, *n.m.* ticket; note; banknote; **— *de ida y vuelta,*** return ticket; **— *de abonado,*** season ticket; **— *kilométrico,*** mileage ticket.
billón, *n.m.* (*Brit.*) billion, (*U.S.*) trillion (10^{12}).
billonario, -ria, *a., n.m.f.* billionaire.
bimba, *n.f.* (*fam.*) top hat.
bimembre, *a.* two-part.
bimensual, *a.* twice-monthly.
bimestre, bimestral, *a.* bi-monthly.—*n.m.* two months.
bimotor, -ra, *a., n.m.f.* twin-engine(d).
binóculo, *n.m.* binoculars; lorgnette.
biografía, *n.f.* biography.
biógrafo, -fa, *n.m.f.* biographer.
biología, *n.f.* biology.
biológico, -ca, *a.* biological.
biólogo, *n.m.* biologist.
biombo, *n.m.* folding screen.
bioquímica, *n.f.* biochemistry.
bióxido, *n.m.* dioxide.
bípede, bípedo, -da, *a., n.m.f.* biped.
biplano, *n.m.* (*aer.*) biplane.
birlar, *v.t.* (*fam.*) bring down with one blow *or* shot; (*fam.*) pinch, filch.
birlocha, *n.f.* kite (*toy*).
a la birlonga, *adv. phr.* (*fam.*) sloppily.
Birmania, *n.f.* Burma.
birmano, -na, *a., n.m.f.* Burmese.
birreta, *n.f.* cardinal's hat.
birrete, *n.m.* academic *or* judge's cap.
bis, *interj.* (*theat., mus.*) encore! (*mus.*) bis.
bisabuelo, -la, *n.m.f.* great-grandfather, great-grandmother.
bisagra, *n.f.* door-hinge.
bisar, *v.t.* (*mus.*) repeat.—*v.i.* give an encore.
bisbisar, *v.t.* (*fam.*) mutter.
bisbita, *n.f.* (*orn.*) pipit.
bisecar [A], *v.t.* bisect.
bisector, -triz, *a.* bisecting.—*n.f.* bisector.
bisel, *n.m.* bevel.
bisemanal, *a.* twice-weekly.
bisiesto, *a.* ***año* —,** leap year.
bismuto, *n.m.* bismuth.
bisnieto,-ta, *n.m.f.* great-grandson, great-granddaughter.
bisojo, -ja, *a.* squinting, cross-eyed.
bisonte, *n.m.* bison.
bisoño, -ña, *a.* (*mil.*) raw.—*n.m.f.* novice, greenhorn; raw recruit.
bistec, *n.m.* beefsteak.
bisturí, *n.m.* (*pl.* **-íes**) scalpel.
bisulfato, *n.m.* bisulphate.
bisulfuro, *n.m.* bisulphide.
bisunto, -ta, *a.* greasy, dirty.
bisutería, *n.f.* imitation jewellery, paste.
bituminoso, -sa, *a.* bituminous.
bizantino, -na, *a., n.m.f.* Byzantine.
bizarría, *n.f.* valour; magnanimity; splendour.
bizarro, -rra, *a.* valiant; magnanimous; splendid.
bizcar [A], *v.t.* wink (*one's eye*).—*v.i.* squint.
bizco, -ca, *a.* cross-eyed, squinting; (*fam.*) dumbfounded.
bizcocho, *n.m.* cake (*esp. sponge-cake*); biscuit.
bizma, *n.f.* poultice.
blanco, -ca, *a.* white; blank; (*fam.*) yellow, cowardly. ***quedarse en* —,** not understand. —*n.m.* white; blank; target; (*fam.*) coward; ***dar en el* —,** hit the mark. —*n.f.* ***estar sin blanca,*** be penniless.
blancor, *n.m.*, **blancura,** *n.f.* whiteness.
blandear, *v.t.* mollify, persuade; brandish.—*v.i., v.r.* soften, give in.
blandir [Q], *v.t.* brandish.—*v.i., v.r.* wave about, shake.
blando, -da, *a.* soft; smooth; mild; weak; timid; (*mus.*) flat.—*adv.* gently, softly.
blandura, *n.f.* softness, gentleness; flattery, blandishment; flabbiness; weakness.
blanquear, *v.t.* whiten, bleach; whitewash; blanch; (*S.A.*) hit *or* kill with the first shot. —*v.i., v.r.* turn white, blanch.
blanquecino, -na, *a.* whitish.
blanqueo, *n.m.* whitening, bleaching; white-washing; blanching.
blasfemar, *v.i.* blaspheme.
blasfemia, *n.f.* blasphemy.
blasfemo, -ma, *a.* blasphemous.—*n.m.f.* blasphemer.
blasón, *n.m.* heraldry; coat of arms; (*fig.*) glory.
blasonar, *v.t.* emblazon.—*v.i.* boast (**de,** of being).
blasonería, *n.f.* bragging.
bledo, *n.m.* (*bot.*) goosefoot; (*fam.*) tinker's cuss.
blenda, *n.f.* (*geol.*) blende.
blindaje, *n.m.* armour plating.
blindar, *v.t.* (*mil.*) armour-plate.
blofear, *v.t.* (*S.A.*) bluff.
blondo, -da, *a.* flaxen, blond; (*S.A.*) curly.
bloque, *n.m.* block; note-pad; lot; (*S.A.*) block (of houses).
bloquear, *v.t.* blockade; brake; (*com.*) block, freeze.
bloqueo, *n.m.* blockade.
blusa, *n.f.* blouse; smock.
boa, *n.f.* boa constrictor.
boato, *n.m.* pomp.
bobada, *n.f.* stupidity.
bobalicón, -cona, *a., n.m.f.* fool.
bobear, *v.i.* act the fool; dawdle.
bobería, *n.f.* stupidity; trifle, trinket, knick-knack.
bobina, *n.f.* bobbin; (*elec.*) coil.
bobo, -ba, *a.* stupid, daft; ***estar* — *con,*** be mad on.—*n.m.f.* simpleton, dolt; clown.
boca, *n.f.* mouth; (*fig.*) flavour; ***a pedir de* —,** to one's heart's desire; ***se me viene a la* —,** it tastes horrid to me.
bocacalle, *n.f.* end of a street.
bocadillo, *n.m.* roll, sandwich; morsel; snack.
bocado, *n.m.* mouthful, morsel; bit, bridle.
bocallave, *n.f.* keyhole.
bocamanga, *n.f.* cuff.
bocanada, *n.f.* mouthful; puff; rush; gust; (*fam.*) boast.
bocel, *n.m.* (*arch.*) moulding; (*carp.*) moulding plane.
bocera, *n.f.* smear (*on lips*).
boceto, *n.m.* sketch, outline.
bocina, *n.f.* trumpet, horn; car horn, hooter; (*S.A.*) blowgun.
bocio, *n.m.* goitre.
bock, *n.m.* (*pl.* **-cks**) small beer glass.

bocudo, -da, *a.* big-mouthed.
bocha, *n.f.* bowl (*ball*).
bochar, *v.t.* hit the jack (*in bowls*); (*S.A.*) snub; fail (*an examinee*).
boche, *n.m.* marble hole; Boche; (*S.A.*) squabble, row; ***dar — a,*** (*S.A.*) snub.
bochinche, *n.m.* din, uproar, to-do; (*S.A.*) pub.
bochinchero, -ra, *a.* rowdy, trouble-making. —*n.m.f.* rowdy, hooligan.
bochorno, *n.m.* sultry weather; flush, embarrassment.
bochornoso, -sa, *a.* sultry, sweltering; embarrassing.
boda(s), *n.f. pl.* wedding; (*fig.*) feast; bear-garden; ***bodas de plata,*** silver wedding *or* jubilee.
bodega, *n.f.* wine vault, wine cellar; pantry; (*naut.*) hold; (*S.A.*) grocer's shop.
bodegón, *n.m.* cheap restaurant, inn; (*art.*) still life.
bodeguero, -ra, *n.m.f.* wine dealer; (*S.A.*) grocer.
bodigo, *n.m.* votive bread.
bodijo, *n.m.* (*fam.*) ill-matched couple; quiet wedding.
bodoque, *n.m.* (*fam.*) dimwit; (*C.A.*) botched job.
bodrio, *n.m.* hodge-podge; bad meal; pig pudding.
bofe, *n.m.*, **bofena,** *n.f.* light, animal lung.
bofetada, *n.f.* slap.
bofetón, *n.m.* hard slap.
boga, *n.f.* vogue; rowing; kind of fish.
bogar [B], *v.i.* row, sail.
bogavante, *n.m.* leading oarsman; lobster.
bogotano, -na, *a., n.m.f.* Bogotan.
bohemiano, -na, *a., n.m.f.* (*geog.*) Bohemian.
bohemio, -mia, *a., n.m.f.* Bohemian; bohemian.
boicotear, *v.t.* boycott.
boicoteo, *n.m.* boycott.
boina, *n.f.* beret.
boj, *n.m.* (*bot.*) box.
bojiganga, *n.f.* strolling players; weird dress; sham.
bol, *n.m.* punch-bowl; net; red earth.
bola, *n.f.* ball; shoe-polish; (*cards*) abundance; (*fam.*) swindle, lie; (*C.A.*) shindig; ***hacer bolas,*** play truant.
bolada, *n.f.* ball-throw; (*S.A.*) cinch, bargain.
bolchevique, *a., n.m.f.* Bolshevik.
bolcheviquista, bolchevista, *n.m.f.* Bolshevist.
bolear, *v.t.* (*fam.*) chuck, throw.—*v.i.* play (*a game for fun only*); (*fam.*) fib.—*v.r.* (*S.A.*) stumble.
bolero, -ra, *a.* (*fam.*) lying.—*n.m.f.* truant; fibber.
boleta, *n.f.* ticket, pass; (*mil.*) billet; warrant; (*S.A.*) certificate; voting slip.
boleto, *n.m.* (*bot.*) boletus; (*S.A.*) ticket, form.
bolichada, *n.f.* (*fam.*) windfall.
boliche, *n.m.* bowl, jack; (*S.A.*) cheap shop *or* bar; dragnet.
bólido, *n.m.* shooting-star; hot-rod (*car*).
bolígrafo, *n.m.* ball-point pen.
bolina, *n.f.* (*naut.*) bowline; flogging; (*fam.*) shindy.
boliviano, -na, *a., n.m.f.* Bolivian.
bolo, *n.m.* skittle, ninepin; ignoramus; company of strolling players.
bolsa, *n.f.* purse, pouch, bag; stock exchange; (*S.A.*) pocket; sack; ***— de trabajo,*** labour exchange.
bolsillo, *n.m.* pocket.
bolsista, *n.m.* stock-broker; (*S.A.*) pick-pocket.
bolso, *n.m.* bag; handbag.
bolsón, *n.m.* large bag; (*S.A.*) satchel, brief-case.
bollo, *n.m.* bun; bump, dent; row, shindy.
bollón, *n.m.* stud (*nail*).
bomba, *n.f.* bomb; pump; fire-engine; (*S.A.*) fire-cracker; (*S.A.*) lie; rumour; (*C.A.*) drunkenness; ***— atómica,*** atom bomb; ***— de hidrógeno,*** hydrogen bomb.
bombar, *v.t.* pump.
bombardear, *v.t.* bomb, bombard.
bombardeo, *n.m.* bombing, bombardment.
bombardero, *n.m.* bomber.
bombástico, -ca, *a.* bombastic.
bombazo, *n.m.* bomb explosion *or* hit.
bombear, *v.t.* bomb; make bulge; (*S.A.*) spy out.
bombilla, *n.f.* (*elec.*) bulb; (*naut.*) lantern.
bombillo, *n.m.* hand-pump; (*S.A., elec.*) bulb.
bombita, *n.f.* firework; (*S.A.*) shame.
bombo, -ba, *a.* (*fam.*) flabbergasted.—*n.m.* big bass drum; fulsome praise, ballyhoo; (*naut.*) sea-barge.
bombón, *n.m.* sweet, candy.
Bona, *n.f.* Bonn.
bonachón, -chona, *a.* good-natured, credulous.
bonaerense, *a., n.m.f.* rel. to, *or* native of, Buenos Aires.
bonanza, *n.f.* (*naut.*) fair weather; (*fig.*) prosperity, bonanza.
bonazo, -za, *a.* (*fam.*) good-natured.
bondad, *n.f.* goodness, kindness; ***tener la — de,*** be kind enough to.
bondadoso, -sa, *a.* kind, good-natured.
bonete, *n.m.* bonnet, hat; academic cap; ***a tente —,*** (*fam.*) all agog; ***gran —,*** (*fam.*) big-wig.
boniato, *n.m.* sweet potato.
bonico, -ca, *a.* pretty; cute.
bonísimo, -ma, *sup. of* BUENO.
bonítalo, *n.m.* (*ichth.*) bonito.
bonito, -ta, *a.* pretty, nice; (*fig.*) crafty.—*n.m.* (*ichth.*) bonito.
bono, *n.m.* voucher; bond.
boqueada, *n.f.* last gasp, dying breath.
boquear, *v.t.* utter.—*v.i.* breathe one's last; (*fam.*) tail off.
boquerón, *n.m.* anchovy; large opening.
boquiabierto, -ta, *a.* open-mouthed, gaping.
boquilla, *n.f.* mouthpiece; cigarette holder; lamp burner; opening; cigarette tip.
boquimuelle, *a.* (*fam.*) easily imposed on.
boquirroto, -ta, *a.* (*fam.*) wordy.—*n.m.f.* chatterbox.
boquiverde, *a.* (*fam.*) smutty.—*n.m.f.* dirt-peddler.
bórax, *n.m.* borax.
borbollar, borbollear, *v.i.* bubble.
borbollón, *n.m.* bubble, bubbling.
Borbón, *n.m.* Bourbon.
borbotar, *v.i.* bubble.
borbotón, *n.m.* bubble.
borceguí, *n.m.* laced boot.
bordado, *n.m.* embroidery.

bordar, *v.t.* embroider.
borde, *n.m.* edge, side, fringe; bastard.
bordear, *v.t.* skirt.—*v.i.* be *or* go along the edge; (*naut.*) sail windward.
bordillo, *n.m.* kerb.
bordo, *n.m.* (*naut.*) board; ***a* —,** on board; ***al* —,** alongside; ***de alto* —,** large (*vessel*); (*fam.*) high-ranking.
bordón, *n.m.* pilgrim's staff; refrain, burden.
bordonear, *v.i.* rove, roam; (*S.A.*) buzz.
Borgoña, *n.f.* Burgundy; **borgoña,** *n.m.* burgundy.
borgoñés, -ñesa, borgoñón, -ñona, *a., n.m.f.* Burgundian.
borinqueño, -ña, *a., n.m.f.* Puerto Rican.
borla, *n.f.* tassel; powder puff, (*fig.*) doctorate.
borne, *n.m.* (*elec.*) terminal.
bornear, *v.t.* twist, warp; set; size up.—*v.i.* (*naut.*) lie at anchor.—*v.r.* warp.
borní, *n.m.* (*orn.*) lanner; harrier.
boro, *n.m.* boron.
borra, *n.f.* young ewe; flock, raw wool; fluff; borax.
borrachera, borrachería, borrachez, *n.f.* drunkenness; carousal; folly.
borracho, -cha, *a.* drunk; violet coloured.—*n.m.f.* drunkard.
borrador, *n.m.* rough draft; note book; (*S.A.*) eraser.
borradura, *n.f.* erasure.
borraj, *n.m.* borax.
borrajear, *v.t.* doodle, scribble.
borrajo, *n.m.* embers.
borrar, *v.t.* erase; efface; blot, smear.
borrasca, *n.f.* tempest, storm; (*fam.*) spree.
borrascoso, -sa, *a.* stormy.
borrego, -ga, *n.m.f.* young sheep; (*fam.*) nitwit.—*n.m.pl.* fleecy clouds.
borrico, -ca, *n.m.f.* ass, donkey.—*n.m.* (*carp.*) trestle.
borricón, borricote, *n.m.* plodder, drudge.
borrón, *n.m.* blot; draft.
borronear, *v.i.* doodle.
borroso, -sa, *a.* blurred; fluffy.
boscaje, *n.m.* grove, coppice.
boscoso, -sa, *a.* (*S.A.*) well-wooded.
bosque, *n.m.* wood, woods.
bosquejar, *v.t.* sketch, outline.
bosquejo, *n.m.* sketch.
bosquete, *n.m.* spinney, coppice.
bostezar [C], *v.i.* yawn.
bostezo, *n.m.* yawn.
bota (1), *n.f.* boot.
bota (2), *n.f.* leather wine bottle; butt (*measure*).
botadura, *n.f.* launching.
botamen, *n.m.* phials and jars; (*naut.*) water store.
botana, *n.f.* bung, plug; patch, scar; (*S.A.*) [TAPA].
botánico, -ca, *a.* botanical.—*n.m.f.* botanist.—*n.f.* botany.
botar, *v.t.* hurl, throw away; launch; (*S.A.*) squander, get rid of.—*v.i.* bounce; buck.
botarate, *n.m.* (*fam.*) blusterer, show-off. (*S.A.*) spendthrift.
bote, *n.m.* thrust, bounce, bucking; tin; pot; rowing boat; (*fam.*) clink, jail; ***de* — *en* —,** (*fam.*) packed tight; ***en el* —,** (*fam.*) in the bag.
botella *n.f.* bottle.
botero, *n.m.* maker *or* repairer of BOTAS (2); boatman.
botica, *n.f.* chemist's shop; (*fam.*) shop.
boticario, *n.m.* apothecary.
botija, *n.f.* earthen water-jug.
botijo, *n.m.* unglazed BOTIJA; (*fam.*) Tubby (*person*).
botillo, *n.m.* wineskin.
botín, *n.m.* booty; gaiter, spat; (*S.A.*) sock.
botina, *n.f.* boot.
botiquín, *n.m.* first aid box, medicine chest; (*S.A.*) wine shop.
boto, -ta, *a.* blunt, dull.
botón, *n.m.* button; knob; bud; (*S.A., fam.*) cop, policeman; **— *de oro*,** buttercup.
botonero, *n.m.* buttonmaker; (*elec.*) control buttons.
botones, *n.m. inv. pl.* pageboy, (*U.S.*) bellhop.
bóveda, *n.f.* vault; crypt, cavern.
bovino, -na, *a.* bovine.
boxear, *v.t.* box.
boxeo, *n.m.* boxing.
boya, *n.f.* buoy.
boyada, *n.f.* drove of oxen.
boyante, *a.* buoyant; lucky, successful.
boyar, *v.i.* float.
boyera, boyeriza, *n.f.* ox-stall.
boyerizo, boyero, *n.m.* ox-drover.
boyuno, -na, *a.* bovine.
bozal, *a.* pure-blooded (*Negro*); callow, green; stupid; wild; (*S.A.*) speaking broken Spanish.—*n.m.* muzzle.
bozo, *n.m.* down on face; headstall.
braceaje, *n.m.* coining; furnace tapping; brewing; (*naut.*) fathoming.
bracear, *v.t.* tap (*furnace*); brew; fathom, sound.—*v.i.* swing the arms; wrestle.
braceo, *n.m.* arm swing; crawl (*swimming*).
bracero, -ra, *a.* manual, thrown.—*n.m.* escort; day labourer; brewer; ***de* —** or ***de bracete*,** arm in arm.
braga, *n.f.* hoisting rope; baby's napkin.—*pl.* knickers, panties.
bragazas, *n.m. inv.* (*fam.*) hen-pecked husband; weak-willed man.
bragueta, *n.f.* fly (*of trousers*).
bramar, *v.i.* roar, bellow, howl.
bramido, *n.m.* bellow, howl, roar.
bramón, -mona, *n.m.f.* (*fam.*) squealer, stool-pigeon.
brasa, *n.f.* live coal.
brasero, *n.m.* brazier; place for burning heretics.
Brasil, *n.m.* Brazil.
brasileño, -ña, *a., n.m.f.* Brazilian.
bravata, *n.f.* bravado; ***echar bravatas*,** talk big, make boastful threats.
bravear, *v.i.* boast, bully.
braveza, *n.f.* ferocity; courage; fury.
bravío, -vía, *a.* wild.—*n.m.* fierceness.
bravo, -va, *a.* manful, brave; wild; (*fam.*) bullying; (*fam.*) cussed; (*fam.*) classy pricey; ***fiesta brava*,** bull-fighting.—*n.m. interj.* bravo!
bravucón, -cona, *a.* swaggering, bragging.—*n.m.f.* braggart.
bravura, *n.f.* fierceness; courage; bravado.
braza, *n.f.* (*naut.*) fathom; breaststroke.
brazada, *n.f.* armstroke; armful; stroke (*swimming*).
brazado, *n.m.* armful.

brazal, *n.m.* armband; branch channel; headrail.
brazalete, *n.m.* bracelet.
brazo, *n.m.* arm; foreleg; ***a — partido,*** hand to hand (*fighting*); ***de —,*** (*S.A.*) arm in arm. —*pl.* hands, workers; sponsors, backers.
brea, *n.f.* pitch, tar; resin.
brebaje, *n.m.* nasty potion; (*naut.*) grog.
brécol(es), *n.m.* (*pl.*) broccoli.
brecha, *n.f.* breach; impact, impression.
brega, *n.f.* struggle, fight; trick.
bregar [B], *v.t.* knead.—*v.i.* toil; struggle.
breña, *n.f.* rough scrubland.
breñoso, -sa, *a.* rough (*ground*); craggy, rocky.
Bretaña, *n.f.* Brittany; ***(la) Gran —,*** Great Britain; **bretaña,** *n.f.* (*bot.*) hyacinth.
brete, *n.m.* fetter; (*fig.*) tight spot.
bretón, -tona, *a., n.m.f.* Breton.
bretones, *n.m.pl.* sprouts, kale.
breva, *n.f.* cinch, bargain; early fig; flat cigar.
breve, *a.* short, brief; ***en —,*** shortly; in short. —*n.m.* papal brief.—*n.f.* (*mus.*) breve.
brevedad, *n.f.* brevity.
brevete, *n.m.* memorandum.
breviario, *n.m.* breviary; short treatise.
brezal, *n.m.* heath, moor.
brezo, *n.m.* (*bot.*) heather, heath.
bribón, -bona, *n.m.f.* scoundrel, loafer.
bribonería, *n.f.* roguery.
brida, *n.f.* bridle; (*fig.*) curb.
brigada, *n.f.* brigade.—*n.m.* sergeant major.
Briján, *n.m.* ***saber más que —,*** (*idiom*) know what's what, be as wise as an owl.
brillante, *a.* brilliant, shining; outstanding; gaudy.—*n.m.* brilliant, diamond.
brillantez, *n.f.* brilliance, splendour.
brillantina, *n.f.* hair grease; metal polish.
brillar, *v.i.* shine, beam.
brillo, *n.m.* shine, splendour, brilliance.
brincar [A], *v.t.* bounce; (*fam.*) skip, pass over.—*v.i.* skip, gambol; (*fam.*) be touchy.
brinco, *n.m.* leap, bound, hop.
brindar, *v.t.* offer.—*v.i.* drink the health (***a,*** of).—*v.r.* offer to.
brindis, *n.m. inv.* toast; offer, invitation.
brinquillo, brinquiño, *n.m.* trinket; sweetmeat; ***hecho un brinquiño,*** (*fam.*) all dolled up.
brinza, *n.f.* (*bot.*) sprig, blade.
brío, *n.m.* mettle, vigour, spirit.
brioso, -sa, *a.* mettlesome, spirited, lively.
briqueta, *n.f.* briquette.
brisa, *n.f.* breeze.
británico, -ca, *a.* British.
britano, -na, *a.* British.—*n.m.f.* Briton.
briza, *n.f.* haze.
brizna, *n.f.* chip, splinter; string, filament; blade.
briznoso, -sa, *a.* splintery; stringy.
brizo, *n.m.* cradle.
broa (1), *n.f.* biscuit.
broa (2), *n.f.* (*naut.*) creek.
broca, *n.f.* shuttle bobbin; drill bit; nail.
brocal, *n.m.* edge, rim, mouth; scabbard.
brocino, *n.m.* lump, bump.
bróculi, *n.m.* broccoli.
brocha, *n.f.* brush; ***de — gorda,*** (*fam.*) slapdash.
brochada, *n.f.* brush stroke.
broche, *n.m.* clasp; brooch; (*S.A.*) paperclip.
brocheta, *n.f.* skewer.
broma, *n.f.* joke, fun; (*zool.*) woodworm; (*S.A.*) disappointment; ***de —,*** in fun; ***dar — a,*** tease; ***en —,*** jokingly.
bromato, *n.m.* bromate.
bromear, *v.i., v.r.* joke; have a good time.
bromista, *n.m.f.* joker, practical joker, merry person.
bromo, *n.m.* bromine.
bromuro, *n.m.* bromide.
bronca, *n.f.* (*fam.*) row, quarrel; ***soltar una — a,*** rant and rave at.
bronce, *n.m.* bronze, brass.
broncear, *v.t., v.r.* bronze; sun-tan.
bronco, -ca, *a.* rough, harsh; abrupt, crusty; brittle.
bronquedad, *n.f.* roughness; gruffness; brittleness.
bronquial, *a.* bronchial.
bronquitis, *n.f.* bronchitis.
brontosauro, *n.m.* brontosaurus.
broquel, *n.m.* (*poet.*) shield, buckler.
broquelillo, *n.m.* ear-ring.
broqueta, *n.f.* skewer.
brota, *n.f.* shoot, bud.
brotadura, *n.f.* budding, sprouting; (*med.*) rash.
brotar, *v.t.* sprout, send out.—*v.i.* sprout, bud; break out (*in a rash*).
brote, *n.m.* shoot, sprout; (*med.*) rash.
broza, *n.f.* brushwood; garden rubbish; printer's brush.
bruces, de, *adv. phr.* face down.
bruja, *n.f.* witch; (*fam.*) old hag; (*orn.*) barn owl; (*S.A.*) spook.—*a. inv.* (*S.A.*) broke, penniless.
Brujas, *n.f.* Bruges.
brujería, *n.f.* witchcraft.
brujir [GRUJIR].
brujo, -ja, *a.* magic—*n.m.* sorcerer, wizard.
brújula, *n.f.* compass, magnetic needle; gunsight; peephole; ***perder la —,*** lose the knack.
brujulear, *v.t.* scrutinise, examine; (*fam.*) suspect; (*S.A.*) plot; (*S.A.*) have a spree.
brulote, *n.m.* fireship; (*S.A.*) swear word.
bruma, *n.f.* mist, fog.
brumazón, *n.m.* thick fog.
brumoso, -sa, *a.* foggy, misty.
bruno, -na, *a.* dark brown.
bruñido, *n.m.*, **bruñidura,** *n.f.*, **bruñimiento,** *n.m.* burnishing, polishing.
bruñir [K], *v.t.* burnish.
brusco, -ca, *a.* gruff, abrupt, brusque.
bruselas, *n.f.pl.* tweezers.
Bruselas, *n.f.* Brussels.
brusquedad, *n.f.* abruptness, brusqueness.
brutal, *a.* brutal; sudden; (*fam.*) stunning, terrific.—*n.m.* brute.
brutalidad, *n.f.* brutality; (*fam.*) terrific amount.
brutalizar [C], *v.t.* brutalize.
brutesco, -ca, *a.* grotesque.
bruteza, *n.f.* brutishness; roughness.
bruto, -ta, *a.* brutish; crude, rough.—*n.m.* brute, beast.
bruza, *n.f.* brush, bristle brush.
bu, *n.m.* (*fam.*) bogeyman.
búa, buba, *n.f.* (*med.*) pustule; (*med.*) bubo.
bubón, *n.m.* tumour.
bubónico, -ca, *a.* bubonic.
bucanero, *n.m.* buccaneer.

bucear, *v.i.* dive; (*fig.*) delve (***en,*** into).
bucle, *n.m.* curl, ringlet, loop.
buco, *n.m.* gap, opening; (*zool.*) buck; (*S.A.*) yarn.
bucólico, -ca, *a.* bucolic.—*n.m.* pastoral poet.—*n.f.* pastoral poetry; (*fam.*) grub, food.
buchada, *n.f.* (*fam.*) mouthful.
buche, *n.m.* craw, crop (*of birds*); belly; ***sacar el — a uno,*** (*fam.*) make s.o. spill the beans.
buchón, -ona, *a.* (*fam.*) baggy, bulging.—*n.f.* pouter pigeon.
budín, *n.m.* (*S.A.*) pudding.
budismo, *n.m.* Buddhism.
budista, *a., n.m.f.* Buddhist.
buen, *a.m. contracted form of* BUENO *before n.m.sg.*
buenamente, *adv.* willingly; easily.
buenaventura, *n.f.* good luck, good fortune.
buenazo, -za, [BONAZO].
bueno, -na, *a.* good; kind; fit; ***de buenas a primeras,*** suddenly; ***estar de buenas,*** be in a good mood.
buenparecer, *n.m.* good appearance; good opinion.
buey, *n.m.* ox, bullock; ***a paso de —,*** at a snail's pace.
¡buf! *interj.* ugh!
bufa, *n.f.* jest.
búfalo, *n.m.* buffalo.
bufanda, *n.f.* scarf.
bufar, *v.i.* snort, puff.
bufete, *n.m.* desk; lawyer's office; (*S.A.*) buffet, snack.
bufido, *n.m.* snort.
bufo, -fa, *a.* farcical.—*n.m.* buffoon, clown.
bufonada, *n.f.* buffoonery.
bugle, *n.m.* bugle.
buharda, *n.f.* garret; dormer window.
buhardilla, *n.f.* [BUHARDA]; (*S.A.*) skylight.
buharro, *n.m.* (*orn.*) eagle-owl.
buhedera, *n.f.* loophole.
buho, *n.m.* eagle-owl; tawny owl; (*fam.*) miser, misery; (*fam.*) squealer.
buhón, buhonero, *n.m.* pedlar.
buhonería, *n.f.* peddling.
buitre, *n.m.* vulture.
buitrero, -ra, *a.* vulturine.
buje, *n.m.* axle-box.
bujería, *n.f.* bauble, trinket.
bujeta, *n.f.* box made of boxwood.
bujía, *n.f.* candle; sparking plug.
bula, *n.f.* (*eccl.*) bull.
bulbo, *n.m.* (*bot., med.*) bulb.
bulboso, -sa, *a.* bulbous.
bulevar, *n.m.* boulevard.
búlgaro, -ra, *a., n.m.f.* Bulgarian.
bulto, *n.m.* bulk, mass; bundle; (*S.A.*) brief-case; ***a —,*** broadly, by and large; ***de —,*** evident; (*S.A.*) important.
bulla, *n.f.* din, uproar.
bullanga, *n.f.* tumult, riot.
bullanguero, -ra, *a.* riotous.—*n.m.f.* rioter.
bullarengue, *n.m.* (*fam.*) bustle (*of dress*); (*S.A.*) dud, anything false.
bullicio, *n.m.* bustle, noise, excitement.
bullicioso, -sa, *a.* restless, noisy, turbulent.
bullir [J], *v.t.* move, stir.—*v.i.* boil; teem, swarm; bustle; budge.—*v.r.* budge, stir.
bullón, *n.m.* ornamental stud; boiling dye.
buñuelo, *n.m.* bun, doughnut; (*fam.*) botched job.
buque, *n.m.* ship, vessel; hull; ***— cisterna,*** tanker; ***— de desembarco,*** landing craft; ***— de guerra,*** warship; ***— lanzaminas,*** minelayer; ***— mercante,*** merchant ship.
buqué, *n.m.* wine bouquet.
burato, *n.m.* crêpe; transparent veil.
burbuja, *n.f.* bubble.
burbujear, *v.i.* bubble, burble.
burbujeo, *n.m.* bubbling.
burdel, *n.m.* brothel.
Burdeos, *n.f.* Bordeaux.
burdeos, *n.m. inv.* claret.
burdo, -da, *a.* coarse, common.
bureta, *n.f.* burette.
burgalés, -lesa, *a., n.m.f.* rel. to, *or* native of, Burgos.
burgo, *n.m.* (*obs.*) township, borough.
burgomaestre, *n.m.* burgomaster.
burgués, -guesa, *a., n.m.f.* bourgeois.—*n.m.f.* burgess.
burguesía, *n.f.* bourgeoisie, middle class.
buriel, *a.* dark red.—*n.m.* coarse woollen cloth.
buril, *n.m.* burin, engraver; dentist's probe.
burilar, *v.t.* engrave.
burjaca, *n.f.* beggar's pouch.
burla, *n.f.* mocking; joke, jest; trick, hoax; gibe; ***— burlando,*** gently, on the quiet; ***de burlas,*** jokingly.
burlador, -ra, *a.* joking, mocking.—*n.m.f.* wag, practical joker.—*n.m.* seducer.
burlar, *v.t.* gibe at; hoax; outwit; evade (*the law*).—*v.r.* make fun (***de,*** of).
burlería, *n.f.* drollery; hoaxing; yarn.
burlesco, -ca, *a.* (*fam.*) funny, comic, ludicrous.
burlón, -lona, *a.* mocking, joking.—*n.m.f.* banterer.
buró, *n.m.* bureau.
burocracia, *n.f.* bureaucracy.
burócrata, *n.m.f.* bureaucrat.
burocrático, -ca, *a.* bureaucratic.
burra, *n.f.* she-ass; drudge (*woman*).
burro, -rra, *a.* stupid.—*n.m.f.* donkey, ass; sawing horse; windlass; (*S.A.*) stepladder.
bursátil, *a.* rel. to stock exchange *or* to shares.
busca, *n.f.* search; pursuit.—*pl.* (*S.A. coll.*) perks.
buscada, *n.f.* search.
buscapié, *n.m.* hint, clue.
buscapiés, *n.m. inv.* jumping jack, firework.
buscapleitos, *n.m. inv.* (*S.A.*) shyster, trouble-maker; touting lawyer.
buscar [A], *v.t.* look for, seek; (*fam.*) pinch, filch; ***se la busca,*** (*fam.*) he's asking for it!
buscavidas, *n.m.f. inv.* busybody, snooper.
buscón, -cona, *a.* seeking.—*n.m.f.* cheat, petty pilferer.
busilis, *n.m.* (*fam.*) trouble, tricky problem; (*fam.*) cash.
búsqueda, *n.f.* search.
busto, *n.m.* bust.
butaca, *n.f.* easy chair; (*theat.*) stalls seat.
butano, *n.m.* butane.
buzo, *n.m.* diver.
buzón, *n.m.* pillar box, post box; conduit; lid; sluice.

C

C, c, *n.f.* third letter of the Spanish alphabet.
ca, *conj.* (*obs.*) for, since.—*interj.* no! never!
cabal, *a.* exact; complete; ***no estar en sus cabales,*** not to be in one's right mind.—*adv.* exactly.—*interj.* right! fine!
cábala, *n.f.* cabal; intrigue; superstition.
cabalgada, *n.f.* cavalry sortie.
cabalgadura, *n.f.* mount; beast of burden.
cabalgar [B], *v.i.* ride (***en, sobre,*** on).
cabalgata, *n.f.* cavalcade.
cabalista, *n.m.f.* cabalist; intriguer.
caballar, *a.* equine.
caballerear, *v.i.* simulate gentility.
caballeresco, -ca, *a.* courteous; gentlemanly; chivalric.
caballería, *n.f.* (*mil.*) cavalry; chivalry; mount.
caballeriza, *n.f.* stable.
caballerizo, *n.m.* groom.
caballero, *n.m.* gentleman; knight; horseman; ***— de industria,*** sharper, confidence man; ***armar a uno —,*** knight.
caballerosidad, *n.f.* gentlemanliness, chivalry.
caballeroso, -sa, *a.* gentlemanly, chivalrous.
caballete, *n.m.* ridge (*roof, furrow*); bridge (*nose*); trestle; easel; torture horse.
caballista, *n.m.* horseman, horse-breaker.—*n.f.* horsewoman.
caballito, *n.m.* small horse; hobbyhorse; ***— del diablo,*** dragonfly; ***— de mar,*** sea horse.
caballo, *n.m.* horse; knight (*chess*); (*S.A.*) blockhead; ***— de vapor*** or ***de fuerza,*** horsepower; ***a mata —,*** full tilt; ***— blanco,*** sponsor, backer.
caballuno, -na, *a.* horselike; equine.
cabaña, *n.f.* hut; herd; track.
cabaret, *n.m.* cabaret, night-club.
cabecear, *v.t.* head; thicken (*letters*).—*v.i.* shake one's head; nod (*in sleep*); lurch; (*naut.*) pitch.
cabeceo, *n.m.* shake, nod; lurch; (*naut.*) pitching.
cabecera, *n.f.* head (*bed, table etc.*); regional capital; headline; bolster; ***— de puente,*** (*mil.*) bridge-head.
cabecilla, *n.m.* ringleader.
cabellera, *n.f.* locks, hair.
cabello, *n.m.* hair; ***traerlo por los cabellos,*** drag it in, mention it somehow.
cabelludo, -da, *a.* hairy.
caber [13], *v.i.* fit, have room; befall; ***no cabe duda,*** there's no room for doubt; ***no cabe en sí,*** he is beside himself; ***no cabe más,*** that's the end; ***todo cabe,*** everything goes.
cabestrante, *n.m.* capstan.
cabestrillo, *n.m.* sling (*for arm*); small halter.
cabestro, *n.m.* halter; lead ox.
cabeza, *n.f.* head; chief; top; ***dar de —,*** (*fam.*) come a cropper; ***irse de la —,*** (*fam.*) go off one's head.
cabezada, *n.f.* butt; nod.
cabezalero, *n.m.* executor.
cabezo, *n.m.* hillock; reef, rock.
cabezón, -zona, *a.* large-headed; (*fam.*) stubborn.
cabezota, *a.* stubborn.—*n.m.f.* mulish person.
cabezudo, -da, *a.* large-headed; (*fam.*) stubborn.—*n.m.* man wearing huge mask (*in festive processions*).
cabida, *n.f.* space, room; ***tener gran — con,*** (*fam.*) have great influence with.
cabildear, *v.i.* lobby.
cabildero, *n.m.* lobbyist.
cabildo, *n.m.* (*eccl.*) chapter; council.
cabina, *n.f.* (*aer.*) cabin; telephone kiosk.
cabizbajo, -ja, *a.* crestfallen.
cable, *n.m.* cable; lifeline.
cablegrafiar [L], *v.t., v.i.* cable.
cablegrama, *n.m.* cable, cablegram.
cabo, *n.m.* end, tip; (*geog.*) cape; handle; (*naut.*) rope; foreman; (*mil.*) corporal; ***al fin y al —,*** after all; ***dar — a,*** complete; ***llevar a —,*** carry out.—*pl.* odds and ends; ***atar cabos,*** (*fam.*) put two and two together.
cabra, *n.f.* goat; loaded dice; (*med.*) leg blister.
cabrahigo, *n.m.* wild fig.
cabrero, -ra, *n.m.f.* goatherd, goatherdess.
cabrestante, *n.m.* capstan.
cabria, *n.f.* three-legged hoist.
cabrilla, *n.f.* (*carp.*) sawing horse; (*med.*) leg blister; whitecap (*wave*).
cabrio, *n.m.* (*carp.*) roof spar, beam, joist.
cabrío, -ría, *a.* rel. to goats.—*n.m.* herd of goats.
cabriola, *n.f.* gambol, somersault, caper.
cabriolar, *v.i.* gambol, caper.
cabrito, *n.m.* kid (*goat*).
cabrón, *n.m.* male goat. [*Avoid: use* **macho cabrío** *instead*].
cabruno, -na, *a.* rel. to goats.
cacahuete, *n.m.* peanut, groundnut.
cacao, *n.m.* cacao; (*S.A.*) chocolate.
cacaraña, *n.f.* pock, pit.
cacarear, *v.t.* (*fam.*) crow about.—*v.i.* cackle, crow.
cacareo, *n.m.* crowing, cackling; (*fam.*) bragging.
cacatúa, *n.f.* cockatoo.
cacería, *n.f.* hunt; hunting party; game caught, bag.
cacerola, *n.f.* (*cul.*) pot, casserole.
cacique, *n.m.* Indian chief; (*fam.*) bossy fellow; (*fam.*) string-puller; (U.S.) political boss.
caciquismo, *n.m.* (*fam.*) string-pulling; (*U.S.*) bossism.
cacofonía, *n.f.* cacophony.
cacto, *n.m.* cactus.
cacumen, *n.m.* (*fam.*) nous, acumen.
cachano, *n.m.* (*fam.*) Old Nick; ***llamar a —,*** (*fam.*) waste one's breath.
cachar, *v.t.* shatter; harrow; (*S.A.*) mock; cheat; (*S.A.*) catch (*Anglicism: all meanings*).
cacharro, *n.m.* crock, pot; crockery; (*fam.*) bone-shaker, rickety machine; (*C.A.*) (*coll.*) jug, jail.
cachaza, *n.f.* (*fam.*) slowness, phlegm.
cachazudo, -da, *a.* (*fam.*) slow, phlegmatic.—*n.m.f.* slowcoach, sluggard.
cachear, *v.t.* frisk (*a suspect*).
cachete, *n.m.* (*taur.*) dagger; slap (*on face*); cheek.
cachetina, *n.f.* (*fam.*) scuffle, brawl.
cachicán, *n.m.* overseer; (*fam.*) sharper.
cachidiablo, *n.m.* hobgoblin; (*fam.*) imp, rogue.

cachifollar, *v.t.* (*fam.*) snub; cheat.
cachillada, *n.f.* litter (*of young*).
cachimba, *n.f.* pipe (*smoking*).
cachiporra, *n.f.* club, cudgel.
cachivache, *n.m.* (*fam.*) thingummy, contraption; (*fam.*) wretch, fool; (*fam.*) pot, pan, *etc.*
cacho, -cha, *a.* bent.—*n.m.* bit; slice; (*ichth.*) chub; (*S.A.*) (*zool.*) horn; (*S.A.*) yarn, fib.
cachón, *n.m.* (*naut.*) breaker.
cachondeo, *n.m.* (*low*) larking, messing about.
cachorro, -rra, *n.m.f.* puppy; cub.
cachucha, *n.f.* small boat; cap; Andalusian dance.
cachupín, -pina, *n.m.f.* (*C.A. pej.*) Spanish settler.
cada, *a. inv.* each, every; — ***cual,*** each one, one and all; — ***quisque,*** (*fam.*) every man jack.
cadalso, *n.m.* scaffold; platform.
cadáver, *n.m.* corpse.
cadavérico, -ca, *a.* cadaverous.
cadena, *n.f.* chain; chain gang; — ***perpetua,*** life imprisonment.
cadencia, *n.f.* cadence; (*mus.*) cadenza.
cadencioso, -sa, *a.* rhythmical, cadenced.
cadente, *a.* moribund; rhythmic.
cadera, *n.f.* hip.
cadetada, *n.f.* prank.
cadete, *n.m.* cadet.
caducar [A], *v.i.* expire, lapse; dodder; wear out.
caducidad, *n.f.* expiry, caducity; decrepitude.
caduco, -ca, *a.* expired; decrepit.
caduquez, *n.f.* dotage; decrepitude.
caedizo,-za, *a.* ready to fall.—*n.m.* (*S.A.*) lean-to.
caer [14], *v.i.* fall, drop; decline; suit, fit; lie, be located; — ***del burro,*** see one's mistake; — ***en la cuenta,*** see the point; ***¡ya caigo!*** I get it! Oh, I see!—*v.r.* fall down; lie.
café, *n.m.* coffee; café; — ***solo,*** black coffee; — ***con leche,*** white coffee.
cafeína, *n.f.* caffeine.
cafetero, -ra, *a.* coffee.—*n.m.f.* coffee worker. —*n.f.* coffee pot.
cafeto, *n.m.* coffee bush.
cáfila, *n.f.* (*fam.*) bunch, troop.
cafre, *a., n.m.f.* Kaffir; (*fig.*) savage.
cagafierro, *n.m.* slag.
cagalaolla, *n.m.* (*fam.*) clown.
cagatintas, *n.m. inv.* (*fam., pej.*) pen-pusher.
caída, *n.f.* fall; collapse; flop; setting (*of sun*).
caído, -da, *a.* fallen; drooping; dejected.—*n.m.pl.* the fallen; income due; (*min.*) rubble. [CAER].
caigo [CAER].
caimán, *n.m.* alligator; (*fam.*) shark, crook.
caimiento, *n.m.* fall; droop; dejection.
Caín, *n.m.* (*Bib.*) Cain; ***pasar las de*** —, go through hell.
el Cairo, *n.m.* Cairo.
caja, *n.f.* box, chest; cash-desk, cashier's office; casing; drum; body (*of vehicle*); well (*stairs, lift*); fund; (*carp.*) mortise; — ***de ahorros,*** savings bank; — ***fuerte,*** safe; — ***de registro,*** manhole; — ***registradora,*** till, cash register; ***despedir con cajas destempladas,*** send packing.
cajero, -ra, *n.m.f.* cashier.
cajetilla, *n.f.* packet; matchbox.
cajista, *n.m.* (*print.*) compositor.
cajón, *n.m.* case, crate; drawer; stall, stand; caisson; (*C.A.*) shop; (*S.A.*) gorge; — ***de sastre,*** muddle; ***de*** —, two-a-penny.
cajonería, *n.f.* chest of drawers.
cal, *n.f.* lime; ***de — y canto,*** (*fam.*) hefty.
cala, *n.f.* inlet; (*min.*) test boring; (*naut.*) hold; probe.
calabacear, *v.t.* (*fam.*) plough (*examinee*); (*fam.*) give the brush off to.
calabaza, *n.f.* pumpkin; marrow.—*n.m.f.* (*fam.*) bonehead; ***dar calabazas a,*** give the brush off to; ***salir*** —, (*fam.*) be a wash-out.
calabobos, *n.m.sg.* (*fam.*) drizzle.
calabozo, *n.m.* dungeon, cell.
calabrote, *n.m.* hawser.
calada, *n.f.* soaking; plunge, swoop.
calado, *n.m.* fretwork; drawn thread work; stencil; depth; (*naut.*) draught.
calafate, *n.m.* shipwright; caulker.
calafatear, *v.t.* caulk; point (*walls*); plug up.
calamar, *n.m.* (*zool.*) squid.
calambre, *n.m.* (*med.*) cramp.
calamidad, *n.f.* calamity.
calamita, *n.f.* loadstone; magnetic needle.
calamitoso, -sa, *a.* calamitous.
cálamo, *n.m.* reed; (*poet.*) pen, flute.
calamoco, *n.m.* icicle.
calandrajo, *n.m.* tatter; (*fam.*) scruff.
calandria, *n.f.* (*orn.*) calandria lark; calender (*press*); treadmill.—*n.m.f.* malingerer, lead-swinger.
calaña, *n.f.* pattern; calibre, character.
calar (1), *a.* limy.—*n.m.* limestone quarry.—*v.t.* lime.
calar (2), *v.t.* pierce, penetrate; soak; do CALADO work; test-bore; fix (*bayonet*); lower (*nets etc.*); (*naut.*) draw; (*fam.*) size up (*someone*); (*fam.*) see through (*someone*); (*fam.*) pick (*pockets*); (*S.A.*) stare at.—*v.r.* get soaked *or* drenched; squeeze in; swoop down; (*fam.*) stick on (*hat etc.*).
calavera, *n.f.* skull.—*n.m.* rake (*person*).
calaverada, *n.f.* escapade, tomfoolery.
calcañar, calcaño, *n.m.* heel.
calcar [A], *v.t.* trace, copy; model (***en, on***); trample on.
calce, *n.m.* iron tip, edge *or* rim.
calceta, *n.f.* hose, stocking; knitting.
calcetero, -ra, *n.m.f.* hosier.
calcetín, *n.m.* sock (*men's*).
calcio, *n.m.* calcium.
calco, *n.m.* tracing, copy.
calcografía, *n.f.* calchography, engraving.
calcomanía, *n.f.* transfer (*picture*).
calcular, *v.t.* calculate.
calculista, *a.* scheming; (*S.A.*) prudent.—*n.m.f.* schemer.
cálculo, *n.m.* calculation; calculus; gallstone.
calda, *n.f.* heating; (*fig.*) encouragement.
caldear, *v.t.* heat; weld.—*v.r.* get hot.
caldeo, *n.m.* heating; welding.
caldera, *n.f.* cauldron, pot; (*S.A.*) kettle; tea- *or* coffee-pot; (*eng.*) boiler.
calderero, *n.m.* boilermaker; tinker.
caldereta, *n.f.* cooking pot; stew.
calderilla, *n.f.* small change, coppers.
caldero, *n.m.* large cauldron.
calderoniano, -na, *a.* Calderonian.
caldillo, *n.m.* gravy.

caldo, *n.m.* broth; stock; salad dressing.
caldoso, -sa, *a.* thin, brothy.
cale, *n.m.* (*fam.*) tap, flip.
calefacción, *n.f.* heating; — ***central,*** central heating.
calendario, *n.m.* calendar.
calentador, -ra, *a.* heating, warming.—*n.m.* heater.
calentar [I], *v.t.* heat, warm; urge on; (*fam.*) thrash, beat.—*v.r.* get warm; (*fig.*) get heated; ***calentarse los sesos*** or ***la cabeza,*** rack one's brains.
calentura, *n.f.* fever.
calenturiento, -ta, *a.* feverish.
calera, *n.f.* limestone quarry; lime kiln.
caleta, *n.f.* small cove; (*S.A.*) dockers' union; (*S.A.*) minor port.
caletre, *n.m.* (*fam.*) nous, acumen.
calibrador, *n.m.* callipers.
calibrar, *v.t.* calibrate, gauge.
calibre, *n.m.* calibre; gauge.
calicanto, *n.m.* roughcast.
calicata, *n.f.* (*min.*) prospecting.
calicó, *n.m.* (*pl.* **-cós**) calico.
caliche, *n.m.* flake (*of plaster etc.*).
calidad, *n.f.* quality, worth; condition; capacity; ***en — de,*** in the capacity of.
cálido, -da, *a.* warm.
calidoscopio, *n.m.* kaleidoscope.
caliente, *a.* warm, hot; (*fig.*) heated.
califa, *n.m.* caliph.
califato, *n.m.* caliphate.
calificación, *n.f.* assessment; mark (*in exam.*); qualification.
calificado, -da, *a.* qualified; competent; sound; important.
calificar [A], *v.t.* assess; justify; qualify; describe; ennoble.
calificativo, -va, *a.* qualifying.
calígine, *n.f.* (*poet.*) murk; (*fam.*) sultry weather.
caligrafía, *n.f.* calligraphy.
calígrafo, *n.m.* calligrapher.
calina, *n.f.* light mist.
cáliz, *n.m.* chalice; calyx.
calizo, -za, *a.* limy.—*n.f.* chalk.
calmante, *a.* calming.—*n.m.* sedative.
calmar, *v.t.* calm.—*v.i.* calm down, abate.
calmo, -ma, *a.* treeless; calm.—*n.f.* calm; lull; ***calma chicha,*** dead calm.
calmoso, -sa, *a.* calm; (*fam.*) slow.
caló, *n.m.* Spanish gipsy dialect.
calofriar [L], *v.r.* shiver.
calofrío, *n.m.* shiver, chill.
calor, *n.m.* heat, warmth; ***hace —,*** it is hot (*weather*); ***tengo —,*** I am hot.
caloría, *n.f.* calorie.
calorífero, -ra, *a.* giving heat.—*n.m.* heater.
calorífico, -ca, *a.* calorific.
calorífugo, -ga, *a.* heat insulating; fire-proof.
caloroso, -sa, *a.* hot, warm.
calumnia, *n.f.* slander, calumny.
calumniar, *v.t.* slander, calumniate.
calumnioso, -sa, *a.* slanderous, calumnious.
caluroso, -sa, *a.* hot, warm; heated.
calvario, *n.m.* Calvary; (*fam.*) Baldy; (*fam.*) troubles.
calvatrueno, *n.m.* bald head.
calvero, *n.m.* clearing (*in woods*).
calvicie, *n.f.* baldness.
calvinismo, *n.m.* Calvinism.
calvinista, *a., n.m.f.* Calvinist.
Calvino, *n.m.* Calvin.
calvo, -va, *a.* bald; barren; threadbare.—*n.f.* bald spot; clearing.
calza, *n.f.* hose.—*pl.* tights.
calzado, -da, *a.* shod.—*n.m.* footwear.—*n.f.* causeway; Roman road.
calzador, *n.m.* shoehorn.
calzar [C], *v.t.* wear (*shoes*); put on (*shoes*); wedge; fit.—*v.r.* put on (*shoes etc.*); (*fig.*) make one's fortune.
calzo, *n.m.* (*mech.*) wedge, chock; shoe.
calzón, *n.m.*, **calzones,** *n.m.pl.* breeches.
calzonarias, *n.f.pl.* (*S.A.*) braces, (*U.S.*) suspenders.
calzonazos, *n.m. inv.* weak-willed husband *or* man.
calzoncillos, *n.m.pl.* underpants.
callada, *n.f.* silence; lull; ***de —*** or ***a las calladas,*** stealthily, on the quiet.
callado, -da, *a.* silent; secret; vague.
callandico, callandito, *adv.* stealthily, on the quiet.
callar, *v.t.* silence; keep quiet; not mention.—*v.i., v.r.* be silent; become silent.
calle, *n.f.* street; (*fam.*) let-out (*of predicament*); ***— mayor,*** main street; ***hacer —*** or ***abrir —,*** clear the way.
calleja, *n.f.* narrow street; (*fam.*) bolt-hole, way out.
callejear, *v.i.* loiter about.
callejeo, *n.m.* loitering, loafing.
callejero, -ra, *a.* of the street, low.—*n.m.f.* gadabout, loiterer.
callejón, *n.m.* alley; ***— sin salida,*** blind alley.
callejuela, *n.f.* alley, side-street; (*fam.*) way-out, dodge.
callicida, *n.m.* corn-remover.
callo, *n.m.* corn, callosity.—*pl.* cooked tripe.
calloso, -sa, *a.* calloused, horny.
cama, *n.f.* bed; bedding; ***caer en (la) —,*** fall ill; ***guardar (la) —,*** be ill in bed.
camada, *n.f.* litter, brood; layer.
camafeo, *n.m.* cameo.
camaleón, *n.m.* chameleon.
camándula, *n.f.* rosary; (*fam.*) trickery.
camandulero, -ra, *a.* (*fam.*) slippery, sly.—*n.m.f.* (*fam.*) sly one, slippery customer.
cámara, *n.f.* chamber, hall; (*aer.*) cockpit; (*jur.*) camera; berth; ***— de aire,*** inner tube; ***— de comercio,*** chamber of commerce.
camarada, *n.m.f.* comrade, friend.
camaradería, *n.f.* comradeship.
camaranchón, *n.m.* attic.
camarera, *n.f.* waitress; chamber maid; lady-in-waiting.
camarero, *n.m.* waiter; steward; valet.
camarilla, *n.f.* pressure group, clique.
camarín, *n.m.* small room; niche; (*theat.*) dressing room.
camarlengo, *n.m.* chamberlain.
cámaro, camarón, *n.m.* shrimp.
camarote, *n.m.* (*naut.*) cabin.
camasquince, *n.m. inv.* (*fam.*) Nosey Parker.
camastro, *n.m.* bunk, rickety bed.
camastrón, -rona, *n.m.f.* (*fam.*) twister, double-dealer.
cambalachear, *v.t.* (*fam.*) swap, swop.
cámbaro, *n.m.* crayfish.
cambiadiscos, *n.m. inv.* record-changer.
cambial, *a.* (*com.*) rel. to exchange.
cambiamiento, *n.m.* change, alteration.

cambiante, *a.* changing.—*n.m.f.* money-changer.
cambiar, *v.t.* change; exchange (***por,*** for); convert (***en,*** into).—*v.i.* alter, change.—*v.r.* change, be changed; — ***de propósito,*** change plans.
cambio, *n.m.* change; exchange; (*com.*) share quotation; exchange rate; (*rail.*) points; (*mech.*) — ***de marchas,*** gear change; ***en* —,** on the other hand; ***libre* —,** free trade.
cambista, *n.m.* money-changer; banker.
Camboya, *n.f.* Cambodia.
camboyano, -na, *a., n.m.f.* Cambodian.
camelar, *v.t.* (*fam.*) flirt with; seduce.
camelia, *n.f.* camelia.
camelo, *n.m.* (*fam.*) flirtation; (*fam.*) letdown.
camello, *n.m.* camel.
Camerón, *n.m.* Cameroons.
camilla, *n.f.* stretcher; couch.
camillero, *n.m.* stretcher-bearer.
caminante, *a.* walking.—*n.m.f.* walker, traveller.
caminar, *v.t., v.i.* travel, walk.
caminata, *n.f.* (*fam.*) stroll, trip.
caminero, -ra, *a.* rel. to roads.
camino, *n.m.* road; ***a medio* —,** half-way; ***en* —,** on the way.
camión, *n.m.* lorry, (*U.S.*) truck; (*S.A.*) bus.
camioneta, *n.f.* van, small lorry.
camisa, *n.f.* shirt; chemise; (*bot.*) skin; lining; mantle; — ***de fuerza,*** strait jacket.
camisería, *n.f.* draper's.
camiseta, *n.f.* vest, (*U.S.*) undershirt.
camisola, *n.f.* blouse, shirt (*ruffled*).
camisón, *n.m.* nightdress.
camomila, *n.f.* camomile.
camorra, *n.f.* (*fam.*) row, quarrel.
campal, *a.* pitched (*battle*).
campamento, *n.m.* camp, encampment.
campana, *n.f.* bell.
campanada, *n.f.* stroke of bell; (*fig.*) scandal.
campanario, *n.m.* belfry, steeple.
campanear, *v.t., v.i.* peal, chime.
campaneo, *n.m.* peal, pealing.
campanilla, *n.f.* hand bell; door-bell; bubble; tassel.
campanillear, *v.i.* tinkle, ring.
campante, *a.* outstanding; (*fam.*) glad, self-satisfied.
campanudo, -da, *a.* bell-shaped; (*fam.*) high-flown.
campaña, *n.f.* open countryside; campaign; (*naut.*) cruise.
campar, *v.i.* stand out; (*mil.*) camp; — ***por su respeto,*** act independently.
campeador, *n.m.* valiant warrior (*said of* **El Cid**).
campear, *v.t.* (*S.A.*) survey, look for.—*v.i.* campaign; graze.
campechanía, campechanería, *n.f.* (*fam.*) heartiness.
campechano, -na, *a.* (*fam.*) hearty, lively.
campeón, *n.m.* champion.
campeonato, *n.m.* championship.
campesino, -na, *a.* rural, rustic.—*n.m.f.* peasant.
campestre, *a.* rural.
campiña, *n.f.* farmlands.
campo, *n.m.* country, countryside; field; background; ***a* — *traviesa*** or ***travieso,*** across country; ***dar* — *a,*** give free range to.
camposanto, *n.m.* cemetery, grave-yard.
camueso, -sa, *n.m.* pippin tree.—*n.f.* pippin apple.
camuflaje, *n.m.* camouflage.
camuflar, *v.t.* camouflage.
can, *n.m.* dog, hound; Khan.
cana, *n.f.* grey hair; ***echar una* — *al aire,*** have a good time; ***peinar canas,*** be getting on (*old*).
Canadá, *n.m.* Canada.
canadiense, *a., n.m.f.* Canadian.
canal, *n.m.* canal; channel.—*n.f.* gutter; trough; conduit, pipe; carcass; ***el Canal de la Mancha,*** the English Channel.
canalización, *n.f.* canalization; conduits, piping; (*elec.*) wiring.
canalizar [C], *v.t.* channel, canalize.
canalón, *n.m.* water spout.
canalla, *n.f.* rabble, canaille.—*n.m.* (*fig.*) swine, rotter.
canallada, *n.f.* filthy trick.
canallesco, -ca, *a.* low, swinish.
canape, *n.m.* sofa, settee.
Canarias, *n.f.* Canaries, Canary Islands.
canariense, *a., n.m.f.* Canarian.
canario, -ria, *a., n.m.f.* Canarian; canary (*bird*).
canasta, *n.f.* large basket; canasta; layette; bottom drawer.
canastillo, -lla, *n.m.f.* small basket, wicker tray.
canasto, canastro, *n.m.* tall round basket.
cancamurria, *n.f.* (*fam.*) the blues.
cancamusa, *n.f.* (*fam.*) stunt, trick.
cancán, *n.m.* cancan.
cáncano, *n.m.* (*fam.*) louse, bug.
cancel, *n.m.* porch; (*C.A.*) screen.
cancela, *n.f.* lattice gate.
cancelación, canceladura, *n.f.* cancellation.
cancelar, *v.t.* cancel.
cancelario, *n.m.* chancellor.
Cáncer, *n.m.* (*astr.*) Cancer; **cáncer,** *n.m.* cancer.
cancerar, *v.t.* canker.—*v.r.* become cancerous.
canceroso, -sa, *a.* cancerous.
cancilla, *n.f.* half-door.
canciller, *n.m.* chancellor.
cancilleresco, -ca, *a.* rel. to chancellery.
cancillería, *n.f.* chancellery; Foreign Ministry.
canción, *n.f.* song; (*lit.*) canzone.
cancionero, *n.m.* song-book.
cancionista, *n.m.f.* song-writer; singer.
cancro, *n.m.* canker.
cancha, *n.f.* arena; (*S.A.*) open space.
cancho, *n.m.* boulder.
candado, *n.m.* padlock.
cande, *a.* candied.
candela, *n.f.* candle; (*fam.*) light.
candelabro, *n.m.* candelabra.
Candelaria, *n.f.* Candlemas.
candelero, *n.m.* candlestick; (*fig.*) high office.
candelilla, *n.f.* small candle; (*med.*) catheter; (*S.A.*) glow-worm, firefly, weevil.
candelizo, *n.m.* icicle.
candencia, *n.f.* white heat.
candente, *a.* white hot; ***cuestión* —,** burning question.
candi, *a.* candied; ***azúcar* —,** sugar candy.
candidato, -ta, *n.m.f.* applicant; candidate.
candidatura, *n.f.* candidature.

candidez, *n.f.* whiteness; candour; naïveté.
cándido, -da, *a.* candid, naïve; white.
candil, *n.m.* oil lamp.
candileja, *n.f.* tiny lamp.—*pl.* (*theat.*) footlights.
candor, *n.m.* candour; whiteness.
candoroso, -sa, *a.* frank, sincere.
canelo, -la, *a.* cinnamon coloured.—*n.f.* cinnamon; (*fam.*) peach, fine thing.
canelón, *n.m.* spout; icicle; piping (*sewing*).
canevá, *n.m.* canvas.
cangrejo, *n.m.* crab; crayfish.
canguro, *n.m.* kangaroo.
caníbal, *a., n.m.f.* cannibal.
canibalino, -na, *a.* cannibalistic.
canibalismo, *n.m.* cannibalism.
canica, *n.f.* marble (*toy*).
canicie, *n.f.* whiteness (*of hair*).
canícula, *n.f.* (*astr.*) dog star; dog days.
canijo, -ja, *a.* ailing, infirm.—*n.m.f.* weakling, invalid.
canilla, *n.f.* arm *or* shin bone; tap, cock; bobbin.
canino, -na, *a.* canine.
canje, *n.m.* exchange.
canjear, *v.t.* exchange.
cano, -na, *a.* grey, hoary.
canoa, *n.f.* canoe.
canon, *n.m.* (*pl.* **cánones**) (*eccl.*) canon precept.—*pl.* canon law.
canónico, -ca, *a.* canonical.
canónigo, *n.m.* (*eccl.*) canon (*person*).
canonizar [C], *v.t.* (*eccl.*) canonize.
canonjía, *n.f.* canonry; (*fam.*) soft job.
canoro, -ra, *a.* melodious.
canoso, -sa, *a.* grey- *or* white-haired.
cansado, -da, *a.* tired, weary; wearisome.
cansancio, *n.m.* tiredness, weariness.
cansar, *v.t.* tire, weary.—*v.r.* get tired.
cansera, *n.f.* (*fam.*) wearisome pest.
cantábrico, -ca, *a.* Cantabrian.
cantada, *n.f.* (*mus.*) cantata; (*C.A.*) folk song.
cantal, *n.m.* stone block; stony ground.
cantaleta, *n.f.* tin-pan serenade, mockery.
cantante, *a.* singing.—*n.m.f.* professional singer.
cantar, *n.m.* song; singing.—*v.t., v.i.* sing; (*fam.*) split, squeal.
cantarín, *a.* singing.—*n.m.f.* singer.
cántaro, *n.m.* pitcher; ***llover a cántaros,*** rain cats and dogs.
cantata, *n.f.* (*mus.*) cantata.
cantatriz, *n.f.* (*pl.* **-ices**) singer.
cante, *n.m.* singing; **— *hondo,* — *flamenco,*** Andalusian styles of singing.
cantera, *n.f.* quarry; (*fig.*) gift, talent.
cantero, *n.m.* stonemason.
cántico, *n.m.* canticle; song.
cantidad, *n.f.* quantity.
cantiga, *n.f.* lay, song.
cantilena, *n.f.* song, ballad; ***la misma* —,** (*fam.*) the same old song.
cantillo, *n.m.* pebble; corner.
cantimplora, *n.f.* water bottle, canteen.
cantina, *n.f.* canteen, buffet; wine cellar.
cantizal, *n.m.* stony ground.
canto (1), *n.m.* song; canto; singing.
canto (2), *n.m.* edge, corner; stone; pebble.
cantonada, *n.f.* corner; ***dar* — *a,*** (*fam.*) shake off, dodge.
cantonear, *v.i.* lounge on street corners.
cantonera, *n.f.* corner piece *or* guard.
cantor, -ra, *a.* sweet-singing.—*n.m.* songster, choirmaster; bard.—*n.f.* songstress.
Cantórbery, *n.m.* Canterbury.
cantoso, -sa, *a.* rocky, stony.
cantueso, *n.m.* lavender.
canturrear, canturriar, *v.i.* (*fam.*) hum, sing.
canturreo, *n.m.,* **canturria,** *n.f.* humming, singing.
caña, *n.f.* cane; reed, stalk; pipe, tube; beer glass; **— *del timón,*** helm.
cañada, *n.f.* track; dale.
cañamazo, *n.m.* canvas, hempcloth.
cañamo, *n.m.* hemp.
cañavera, *n.f.* reed-grass.
cañería, *n.f.* pipe(s); **— *maestra,*** main.
cañero, *n.m.* pipe-maker; plumber.
cañizal, *n.m.* reed bed.
caño, *n.m.* pipe; (*naut.*) channel.
cañón, *n.m.* gun-barrel; cannon; shaft; quill; gorge, canyon.
cañonazo, *n.m.* artillery shot; (*fam.*) big surprise.
cañonería, *n.f.* cannon, artillery.
caoba, *n.f.* mahogany.
caolín, *n.m.* kaolin.
caos, *n.m. sg.* chaos.
caótico, -ca, *a.* chaotic.
capa, *n.f.* cloak, coat; layer; ***de* — *caída,*** in a bad way, in decline.
capacidad, *n.f.* capacity.
capacitar, *v.t.* enable; empower.
capacho, *n.m.* tool basket.
capar, *v.t.* geld.
caparazón, *n.m.* caparison; shell; chicken frame.
capataz, *n.m.* foreman.
capaz, *a.* (*pl.* **-aces**) capable; capacious; holding.
capcioso, -sa, *a.* captious.
capear, *v.t.* (*taur.*) wave the cape at; (*fam.*) fool.
capellán, *n.m.* chaplain, priest.
Caperucita Roja, *n.f.* Red Riding Hood.
caperuza, *n.f.* hood.
capilla, *n.f.* chapel; **— *ardiente,*** funeral chapel; ***en* (*la*) —,** (*fam.*) on tenterhooks.
capillo, *n.m.* baby's hood; toe-cap.
capirote, *n.m.* conical hood; hood, (*U.S.*) top (*of car*); fillip.
capital, *a.* capital, main; basic, important.—*n.m.* capital (*money*).—*n.f.* capital (*city*).
capitalismo, *n.m.* capitalism.
capitalista, *a., n.m.f.* capitalist.
capitalizar [C], *v.t.* capitalize.
capitán, *n.m.* (*mil.*) captain; (*aer.*) squadron leader; **— *de corbeta,*** (*naut.*) lieutenant-commander; **— *de fragata,*** (*naut.*) commander; **— *de navío,*** (*naut.*) captain.
capitana, *n.f.* (*naut.*) flagship; (*fam.*) captain's wife.
capitanear, *v.t.* lead, captain.
capitanía, *n.f.* captaincy.
capitel, *n.m.* (*arch.*) capital.
Capitolio, *n.m.* Capitol.
capitulación, *n.f.* capitulation.—*pl.* marriage contract.
capitular, *a.* capitular.—*v.t.* accuse; settle.—*v.i.* capitulate.
capítulo, *n.m.* chapter.
capón, *n.m.* capon; rap; faggot.
caporal, *n.m.* overseer.

capotaje, *n.m.* overturning.
capotar, *v.i.* overturn.
capote, *n.m.* cloak; greatcoat; cover.
capotear, *v.t.* dodge; wave (*cloak*); (*theat.*) cut.
Capricornio, *n.m.* Capricorn.
capricho, *n.m.* caprice, whim.
caprichoso, -sa, *a.* whimsical, capricious.
caprino, -na, *a.* caprine, goatish.
cápsula, *n.f.* capsule.
captación, *n.f.* attraction; catchment; (*rad.*) tuning.
captar, *v.t.* catch; attract, win over; (*rad.*) tune in to.—*v.r.* win, attract.
captura, *n.f.* capture.
capturar, *v.t.* capture.
capucha, *n.f.* cowl; circumflex (^).
capuchino, *n.m.* (*eccl.*, *zool.*) capuchin.
capucho, *n.m.* hood; cowl.
capullo, *n.m.* bud, bloom; cocoon.
caqui, *a.*, *n.m.* khaki.
cara, *n.f.* face; — ***de hereje,*** (*fam.*) ugly mug; — ***de pascua,*** cheerful face; — ***y cruz,*** heads and tails.
carabela, *n.f.* caravel.
carabina, *n.f.* carbine; (*joc.*) chaperon.
carabinero, *n.m.* customs guard.
caracol, *n.m.* snail; curl; spiral.
carácter, *n.m.* (*pl.* **caracteres**) character; nature.
característico, -ca, *a.*, *n.f.* characteristic.
caracterizar [C], *v.t.* characterize.
carado, -da, *a.* faced.
¡caramba! *interj.* dear me! well, well!
carámbano, *n.m.* icicle.
carambola, *n.f.* cannon (*billiards*); (*fam.*) ruse.
caramelo, *n.m.* caramel.
caramillo, *n.m.* thin flute; jumble; false rumour.
carantamaula, *n.f.* (*fam.*) ugly mug.
carantoña, *n.f.* (*fam.*) ugly mug; (*fam.*) dolled-up old hag.—*pl.* wheedling.
carapacho, *n.m.* shell, carapace.
carátula, *n.f.* mask; (*fig.*) the boards, theatre.
caravana, *n.f.* caravan.
caray, *n.m.* tortoise.—*interj.* gosh!
carbohidrato, *n.m.* carbohydrate.
carbólico, -ca, *a.* carbolic.
carbón, *n.m.* charcoal; coal.
carbonato, *n.m.* carbonate.
carbonera, *n.f.* charcoal kiln; coal shed.
carbonero, -ra, *a.* rel. to coal.—*n.m.* coalman; (*orn.*) great *or* coal tit.
carbónico, -ca, *a.* carbonic.
carbonilla, *n.f.* coal dust; coking, carbonizing (*car*).
carbonizar [C], *v.t.*, *v.r.* carbonize, char.
carbono, *n.m.* (*chem.*) carbon.
carborundo, *n.m.* carborundum.
carbunclo, *n.m.* carbuncle.
carburador, *n.m.* carburettor.
carburo, *n.m.* carbide.
carcaj, *n.m.* quiver, holder.
carcajada, *n.f.* guffaw.
carcamán, *n.m.* (*naut.*) old tub.
cárcava, *n.f.* gully, ditch; grave.
cárcel, *n.f.* prison; clamp.
carcelario, -ria, *a.* rel. to prison.
carcelería, *n.f.* imprisonment.
carcelero, *n.m.* jailer.
carcoma, *n.f.* woodworm; (*fig.*) gnawing worry.
carcomer, *v.t.* gnaw away.—*v.r.* become worm-eaten.
cardenal, *n.m.* cardinal; bruise.
cardenillo, *n.m.* verdigris.
cárdeno, -na, *a.* violet, rich purple.
cardíaco, -ca, *a.* cardiac.
cardinal, *a.* cardinal.
cardiografía, *n.f.* cardiography.
cardo, *n.m.* thistle.
carear, *v.t.* bring face to face.—*v.r.* face (**con,** up to).
carecer [9], *v.i.* lack (***de***), be lacking (***de,*** in).
carencia, *n.f.* need; shortage.
carente, *a.* lacking (***de,*** in), devoid (***de,*** of).
careo, *n.m.* confronting.
carestía, shortage, scarcity; rising prices.
careta, *n.f.* mask.
carey, *n.m.* turtle.
carga, *n.f.* load; charge.
cargadero, *n.m.* loading bay.
cargamento, *n.m.* load, cargo.
cargante, *a.* (*fam.*) crushing, boring.
cargar [B], *v.t.* load, overload; charge; (*fam.*) bore.—*v.r.* (*fam.*) put paid (***de,*** to).
cargazón, *n.f.* cargo; heaviness (*health, weather*).
cargo, *n.m.* load; charge; office, duty; ***hacerse — de,*** undertake (to).
cargoso, -sa, *a.* onerous, bothersome.
cari, *n.m.* (*cul.*) curry.
cariacontecido, -da, *a.* woebegone.
el Caribe, *n.m.* the Caribbean.
caribe, *a.*, *n.m.* Carib; (*fig.*) savage.
caricatura, *n.f.* caricature, cartoon.
caricia, *n.f.* caress.
caridad, *n.f.* charity.
caridoliente, *a.* glum.
carilucio, -cia, *a.* shiny-faced.
carillón, *n.m.* carillon, chime.
carinegro, -gra, *a.* swarthy.
cariño, *n.m.* love, affection; darling.
cariñoso, -sa, *a.* loving, affectionate.
caritativo, -va, *a.* charitable.
cariz, *n.m.* aspect, look.
carlinga, *n.f.* (*aer.*) cockpit; saloon.
carlismo, *n.m.* Carlism.
carlista, *a.*, *n.m.f.* Carlist.
Carlomagno, *n.m.* Charlemagne.
Carlos, *n.m.* Charles.
carmelita, *a.*, *n.m.f.* Carmelite.
Carmen, *n.f.* Carmen; Carmelite Order; **carmen,** *n.m.* song, poem, carmen; villa.
carmesí, *a.*, *n.m.* (*pl.* **-íes**) crimson.
carmín, *n.m.* carmine, cochineal; wild rose; lip-stick.
carnadura, *n.f.* (*low*) beefiness, muscularity.
carnal, *a.* carnal; related by blood.—*n.m.* non-Lenten period.
carnaval, *n.m.* carnival; ***martes de Carnaval,*** Shrove Tuesday.
carnavalesco, -ca, *a.* rel. to carnival.
carne, *n.f.* flesh, meat; ***echar carnes,*** to put on weight; — ***de gallina,*** goose pimples; ***ser uña y —,*** be very intimate.
carnestolendas, *n.f.pl.* Shrovetide.
carnet, *n.m.* identity card; licence; note book.
carnicería, *n.f.* butcher's shop; butchery.
carnicero, -ra, *a.* carnivorous.—*n.m.* butcher.
carniseco, -ca, *a.* lean, scraggy.

carnívoro, -ra, *a.* carnivorous.—*n.m.* carnivore.
carnoso, -sa, *a.* fleshy, meaty.
caro, -ra, *a.* dear.—*adv.* dear, dearly.
carolingio, -gia, *a.* Carolingian.
Carón, Caronte, *n.m.* Charon.
carpa, *n.f.* (*ichth.*) carp; (*S.A.*) tent.
carpeta, *n.f.* folder, portfolio.
carpetazo, *n.m.* ***dar — a,*** shelve, file away.
carpintería, *n.f.* carpentry, joinery; carpenter's shop.
carpintero, *n.m.* carpenter, joiner; (*orn.*) woodpecker.
carpir, *v.t.* (*S.A.*) weed.
carraca, *n.f.* (*naut.*) carrack, old tub; rattle.
carrada, *n.f.* cartload.
carrasca, *n.f.* holm oak.
carraspear, *v.i.* croak, be hoarse.
carraspeño, -ña, *a.* gruff, hoarse.
carrera, *n.f.* race, course; career; row, line; way; girder, beam; ladder (*in stocking*); — ***armamentista,*** arms race.
carrerista, *n.m.f.* punter, race-goer; racer.
carrero, *n.m.* carter.
carreta, *n.f.* ox-cart.
carrete, *n.m.* bobbin; fishing reel; (*elec.*) coil; (*phot.*) spool.
carretear, *v.t.* haul, cart; (*aer.*) (also *v.i.*) taxi.
carretera, *n.f.* road, highway.
carretero, *n.m.* carter, cartwright.
carretilla, *n.f.* truck, wheelbarrow; ***saber de* —,** know parrot-fashion.
carretón, *n.m.* pushcart; — ***de remolque,*** trailer.
carril, *n.m.* rail; lane; rut.
carrilera, *n.f.* rut.
carrizo, *n.m.* reed-grass.
el Carro, *n.m.* (*astr.*) the Plough.
carro, *n.m.* cart; (*mech.*) carriage; truck; (*S.A.*) car.
carrocería, *n.f.* body shop; body-work.
carrocero, *n.m.* coachbuilder.
carroña, *n.f.* carrion.
carroñ(os)o, -ñ(os)a, *a.* rotten, putrid.
carroza, *n.f.* coach, carriage.
carruaje, *n.m.* vehicle.
carruco, *n.m.* primitive cart.
carrucha, *n.f.* pulley.
carta, *n.f.* letter; card; chart; charter; ***a — cabal,*** thoroughly, completely; — ***blanca,*** carte blanche.
cartaginense, cartaginés, -nesa, *a.* Carthaginian.
Cartago, *n.f.* Carthage.
cartapacio, *n.m.* writing-case; dossier; notebook; satchel.
cartear, *v.r.* correspond (with), write letters to (***con***).
cartel, *n.m.* poster, placard; cartel.
cartelera, *n.f.* bill-board.
carteo, *n.m.* correspondence.
cárter, *n.m.* (*mech.*) casing, case.
cartera, *n.f.* wallet; brief-case; (*pol.*) portfolio.
carterista, *n.m.* pickpocket.
cartero, *n.m.* postman.
cartesiano, -na, *n.m.f.* Cartesian.
cartílago, *n.m.* cartilage, gristle.
cartilla, *n.f.* note; primer (*book*); dossier.
cartografía, *n.f.* cartography, map-making.
cartón, *n.m.* cardboard; carton; cartoon; papier-mâché.
cartoné, *n.m.* boards (*bookbinding*).
cartucho, *n.m.* cartridge; paper cornet.
Cartuja, *n.f.* Carthusian order.
cartujo, -ja, *a., n.m.f.* Carthusian.
cartulario, *n.m.* cartulary.
cartulina, *n.f.* fine cardboard.
carura, *n.f.* (*S.A.*) [CARESTIA].
casa, *n.f.* house; home; — ***de correos,*** post office; ***a* —,** home (*to one's home*); ***en* —,** at home; ***poner* —,** set up house.
casaca, *n.f.* great coat.
casación, *n.f.* cassation.
casadero, -ra, *a.* marriageable.
casal, *n.m.* country house; (*S.A.*) couple, pair.
casalicio, *n.m.* dwelling, house.
casamentero, -ra, *a.* match-making.—*n.m.f.* match-maker.
casamiento, *n.m.* wedding, marriage.
casar (1), *n.m.* hamlet.
casar (2), *v.t.* marry, marry off; (*jur.*) annul.—*v.i.* marry; to match (***con***).—*v.r.* ***casarse con,*** marry, get married to.
casarón, *n.m.* big rambling house.
casatienda, *n.f.* dwelling shop.
casca, *n.f.* grape-skin; tanning bark.
cascabel, *n.m.* tinkle bell.
cascabelear, *v.t.* (*fam.*) bamboozle.—*v.i.* (*fam.*) be feather-brained; (*S.A.*) tinkle, jingle.
cascabelero, -ra, *a.* (*fam.*) feather-brained. —*n.m.f.* (*fam.*) feather-brain.—*n.m.* baby's rattle.
cascada, *n.f.* cascade.
cascajo, *n.m.* gravel; nuts; (*fam.*) junk, old wreck.
cascanueces, *n.m. inv.* nut-crackers.
cascar [A], *v.t.* split, crack; (*fam.*) bust.—*v.i.* chatter.—*v.r.* break (*voice*); (*fam.*) fail (*health*).
cáscara, *n.f.* shell, rind, bark; cascara.
cascarón, *n.m.* eggshell.
cascarria, *n.f.* mud-splash.
casco, *n.m.* helmet; skull; potsherd; (*naut.*) hull, hulk; — ***urbano,*** built-up area.—*pl.* (*fam.*) brains, head.
cascote, *n.m.* rubble, debris.
casería, *n.f.* manor, farm; (*S.A.*) clientele.
caserío, *n.m.* hamlet.
casero, -ra, *a.* home-made, homely.—*n.m.f.* tenant; caretaker.—*n.m.* landlord.—*n.f.* landlady.
caserón, *n.m.* big rambling house.
caseta, *n.f.* bathing hut.
casi, *adv.* almost, nearly.
casilla, *n.f.* hut, kiosk; pigeon-hole; square (*chess*).
casillero, *n.m.* pigeon holes.
casino, *n.m.* club, casino.
caso, *n.m.* event; (*jur., med., gram.*) case; matter; ***al* —,** to the point; ***hacer — de,*** take notice of.
casorio, *n.m.* (*fam.*) hasty marriage.
caspa, *n.f.* scurf, dandruff.
¡cáspita! *interj.* by Jove!
casquete, *n.m.* helmet; skull-cap.
casquijo, *n.m.* gravel.
casquillo, *n.m.*, ferrule, tip.
casquivano, -na, *a.* feather-brained.
casta, *n.f.* caste, lineage.
castañeta, *n.f.* snap, click; castanet.
castañetazo, *n.m.* click, snap, crack.
castañetear, *v.t.* snap (*fingers*).—*v.i.* play castanets; chatter (*teeth*); crack (*joints*).

castaño, -ña, *a.* chestnut.—*n.m.* chestnut tree; — ***de Indias,*** horse chestnut.—*n.f.* chestnut; bun (*of hair*).
castañuela, *n.f.* castanet.
castellanismo, *n.m.* Castilianism.
castellanizar [C], *v.t.* Castilianize, Hispanicize.
castellano, -na, *a.*, *n.m.f.* Castilian; (*S.A.*) Spanish.
casticidad, *n.m.* purity, correctness.
casticismo, *n.m.* purism.
castidad, *n.f.* chastity.
castigar [B], *v.t.* punish.
castigo, *n.m.* punishment.
Castilla, *n.f.* Castile; — ***la Nueva*** (***la Vieja***), New (Old) Castile.
castillejo, *n.m.* scaffolding.
castillo, *n.m.* castle.
castizo, -za, *a.* pure (*language, blood*).
casto, -ta, *a.* chaste.
castor, *n.m.* beaver.
castrar, *v.t.* castrate; prune.
castrense, *a.* military, army.
casual, *a.* accidental, casual; (*gram.*) rel. to case.
casualidad, *n.f.* accident, chance.
casuca, casucha, *n.f.* shanty, slum house.
casuista, *a.*, *n.m.f.* casuist.
casuístico, -ca, *a.* casuistic(al).—*n.f.* casuistry.
casulla, *n.f.* chasuble.
cata, *n.f.* taste, sample; sampling.
catacaldos, *n.m.f. inv.* (*fam.*) rolling stone; meddler.
cataclismo, *n.m.* cataclysm.
catacumba, *n.f.* catacomb.
catadura, *n.f.* sampling; (*obs.*) mien.
catafalco, *n.m.* catafalque.
catalán, -lana, *a.*, *n.m.f.* Catalan, Catalonian.
catalanismo, *n.m.* Catalanism; Catalan nationalism.
catalanista, *n.m.f.* Catalan nationalist; Catalan scholar.
catalejo, *n.m.* spying glass.
Catalina, *n.f.* Catherine.
catálisis, *n.f.* catalysis.
catalizador, *n.m.* catalyst.
catalogación, *n.f.* cataloguing.
catalogar [B], *v.t.* catalogue.
catálogo, *n.m.* catalogue.
Cataluña, *n.f.* Catalonia.
catamarán, *n.m.* catamaran.
cataplasma, *n.f.* poultice.
¡cataplum! *interj.* bump!
catapulta, *n.f.* catapult.
catar, *v.t.* taste, sample; (*obs.*) look at.
catarata, *n.f.* cataract.
catarro, *n.m.* heavy cold; catarrh.
catarroso, -sa, *a.* prone to catarrh.
catarsis, *n.f.* catharsis.
catástrofe, *n.f.* catastrophe.
catastrófico, -ca, *a.* catastrophic.
catavinos, *n.m. inv.* wine-taster; (*fam.*) pub-crawler.
catear, *v.t.* seek; sample; (*S.A.*) search.
catecismo, *n.m.* catechism.
catecúmeno, -na, *a.*, *n.m.f.* catechumen.
cátedra, *n.f.* cathedra, chair, professorship.
catedral, *n.f.* cathedral.
catedrático, -ca, *n.m.f.* professor.
categoría, *n.f.* category.
categórico, -ca, *a.* categorical.
catequesis, *n.f.*, **catequismo,** *n.m.* religious instruction.
catequista, *n.m.f.* catechist.
catequizar [C], *v.t.* catechize.
caterva, *n.f.* throng, mob.
cateto, -ta, *n.m.f.* (*pej.*) bumpkin.
catilinaria, *n.f.* violent diatribe.
cátodo, *n.m.* cathode.
catolicidad, *n.f.* catholicity; Catholicity.
catolicismo, *n.m.* Catholicism.
católico, -ca, *a.*, *n.m.f.* catholic; Catholic; (*fam.*) ***no estar muy*** **—,** to be off colour.
Catón, *n.m.* Cato; **catón,** *n.m.* reading primer.
catorce, *a.*, *n.m.* fourteen.
catorceno, -na, *a.* fourteenth.
catre, *n.m.* cot; — ***de tijera,*** camp bed.
caucásico, -ca, *a.* Caucasian.
Cáucaso, *n.m.* Caucasus.
cauce, *n.m.* river bed; ditch; course.
caución, *n.f.* caution; pledge.
caucionar, *v.t.* caution; guard against.
cauchal, *n.m.* rubber plantation.
cauchero, -ra, *a.* rubber.—*n.m.f.* rubber worker.
caucho, *n.m.* rubber; — ***esponjoso,*** sponge rubber.
caudal, *a.* large.—*n.m.* wealth; volume (*of water*).
caudaloso, -sa, *a.* of heavy flow (*rivers*).
caudatorio, *n.m.* bishop's attendant; (*fam.*) yes-man.
caudillaje, *n.m.* leadership; (*S.A.*) political bossism.
caudillo, *n.m.* leader; (*S.A.*) political boss.
causa, *n.f.* cause; lawsuit; ***a* — *de,*** on account of.
causal, *a.* causal.
causalidad, *n.f.* causality.
causante, *a.* causing; (*fam.*) responsible.—*n.m.f.* litigant.
causar, *v.t.* cause; (*jur.*) sue.
causativo, -va, *a.* causative.
causticidad, *n.f.* causticness.
cáustico, -ca, *a.* caustic.
cautela, *n.f.* caution, heed; artfulness.
cautelar, *v.t.*, *v.r.* guard (***de,*** against).
cauteloso, -sa, *a.* wary; cunning.
cauterizar [C], *v.t.* cauterize.
cautivar, *v.t.* capture; captivate.
cautiverio, *n.m.*, **cautividad,** *n.f.* captivity.
cautivo, -va, *a.*, *n.m.f.* captive.
cauto, -ta, *a.* cautious.
cavadura, *n.f.* digging.
cavar, *v.t.* dig.
cavazón, *n.f.* digging.
caverna, *n.f.* cavern.
cavernícola, *n.m.f.* cave-dweller.
cavernoso, -sa, *a.* cavernous.
cavial, caviar, *n.m.* caviare.
cavidad, *n.f.* cavity.
cavilación, *n.f.* cavilling.
cavilar, *v.t.* cavil at.
caviloso, -sa, *a.* captious, cavilling.
cayada, *n.f.*, **cayado,** *n.m.* shepherd's crook; crozier.
Cayena, *n.f.* Cayenne.
cayente, *a.* falling.
caza, *n.f.* hunt, chase; game, quarry; ***a* — *de,*** hunting for; — ***de grillos,*** wild-goose chase; — ***mayor,*** big game.—*n.m.* (*aer.*) fighter.

cazabe, *n.m.* cassava.
cazabombadero, *n.m.* (*aer.*) fighter-bomber.
cazador, -ra, *a.* hunting.—*n.m.* hunter; (*mil.*) chasseur; — ***furtivo,*** poacher.—*n.f.* huntress.
cazar [C], *v.t.* hunt, chase; (*fam.*) catch, take in; (*fam.*) wangle.
cazatorpedero, *n.m.* (*naut.*) destroyer.
cazcalear, *v.i.* (*fam.*) bumble about.
cazcorvo, -va, *a.* bowlegged.
cazo, *n.m.* ladle; saucepan.
cazolero, *a.m.* old-womanish.—*n.m.* fuss-pot, "old woman".
cazoleta, *n.f.* pipe-bowl; sword guard; pan.
cazuela, *n.f.* casserole, pan, dish; (*theat.*) upper gallery, (*obs.*) women's gallery.
cazumbre, *n.m.* oakum.
cazurro, -rra, *a.* (*obs.*) vulgar; (*fam.*) grumpy.—*n.m.* (*obs.*) low minstrel.
ce, *n.f.* name of letter C; — ***por be,*** in detail. —*interj.* hey!
cebada, *n.f.* barley.
cebadura, *n.f.* fattening; priming.
cebar, *v.t.* fatten (*cattle etc.*); stoke; bait; prime; start (*a motor*); nourish (*passions*).—*v.i.* bite (*nail, screw*).—*v.r.* rage (*disease*); ***cebarse en,*** gloat over; devote oneself to.
cebellina, *n.f.* sable (fur).
cebo, *n.m.* animal feed; bait; priming.
cebolla, *n.f.* onion; bulb; nozzle.
cebón, -bona, *a.* fattened.—*n.m.* fattened animal.
cebra, *n.f.* zebra.
cebrado, -da, *a.* zebra-striped.
ceca, *only in* ***de — en Meca,*** *adv. phr.* hither and thither.
cecear, *v.i.* lisp; pronounce *s* as *z* [θ] in Spanish.
ceceo, *n.m.* lisp, lisping.
ceceoso, -sa, *a.* lisping.
cecial, *n.m.* dried fish.
cecina, *n.f.* dried meat.
cecografía, *n.f.* braille.
ceda (1), *n.f.* bristle.
ceda (2), *n.f.* name of letter Z.
cedazo, *n.m.* riddle, sieve.
ceder, *v.t.* give up, cede.—*v.i.* yield, give in.
cedilla, *n.f.* cedilla.
cedro, *n.m.* cedar.
cédula, *n.f.* slip, form; charter; patent.
céfiro, *n.m.* zephyr.
cegajoso, -sa, *a.* bleary, watery (*eyes*).
cegar [1B], *v.t.* blind; block up.—*v.i.* go blind.
cegarra, *a. inv.,* **cegato, -ta,** *a.* (*fam.*) short-sighted.
ceguedad, ceguera, *n.f.* blindness.
Ceilán, *n.m.* Ceylon.
ceilanés, -nesa, *a., n.m.f.* Ceylonese.
ceja, *n.f.* eyebrow; brow.
cejar, *v.i.* back; slacken off.
cejijunto, -ta, *a.* (*fam.*) heavy browed, scowling.
cejo, *n.m.* morning mist; esparto cord.
cejudo, -da, *a.* bushy-browed.
celada, *n.f.* ambush, trap; (*obs.*) helmet.
celaje, *n.m.* scattered cloud; skylight; foretaste.
celar, *v.t.* show zeal in; keep an eye on; hide; engrave.—*v.i.* watch (***sobre, por,*** over).
celda, *n.f.* cell.
celebérrimo, -ma, *a. sup.* very celebrated.
celebración, *n.f.* celebration.
celebrante, *a.* celebrating.—*n.m.f.* celebrator. —*n.m.* celebrant.
celebrar, *v.t.* celebrate; be glad about, hold (*meetings etc.*).—*v.i.* be glad to.—*v.r.* take place.
célebre, *a.* celebrated; (*fam.*) cute.
celebridad, *n.f.* celebrity; celebration.
celemín, *n.m.* Spanish dry measure (= 1 *gallon approx.*).
celeridad, *n.f.* celerity.
celeste, *a.* celestial (*rel. to sky*); sky blue. —*n.m.* sky blue.
celestial, *a.* heavenly, celestial; (*fam.*) silly.
celestina, *n.f.* bawd, procuress.
celibato, *n.m.* celibacy; (*fam.*) bachelor.
célibe, *a., n.m.f.* celibate.
celidonia, *n.f.* celandine.
celo, *n.m.* zeal; rut, heat; ***en —,*** on heat.—*pl.* jealousy; ***dar celos a,*** make jealous; ***tener celos,*** be jealous.
celofán, -fana, celófana, *n.m.* or *f.* cellophane.
celosía, *n.f.* lattice (*over window*), grill, grating.
celoso, -sa, *a.* jealous; zealous; (*S.A.*) tricky, unsafe.
celsitud, *n.f.* grandeur; highness.
celta, *a., n.m.* Celtic.—*n.m.f.* Celt.
celtibérico, -ca, celtíbero, -ra, *a., n.m.f.* Celtiberian.
céltico, -ca, *a.* Celtic.
célula, *n.f.* (*biol., elec., pol.*) cell.
celular, *a.* cellular.
celuloide, *n.f.* celluloid.
celulosa, *n.f.* cellulose.
cementar, *v.t.* cement (*metals*); precipitate.
cementerio, *n.m.* cemetery.
cemento, cimento, *n.m.* cement; — ***armado,*** reinforced concrete.
cena, *n.f.* supper.
cenaoscuras, *n.m.f. inv.* (*fam.*) recluse; skinflint.
cenáculo, *n.m.* cenacle; Cenacle.
cenacho, *n.m.* carrier basket.
cenador, -ra, *n.m.f.* diner.—*n.m.* summer-house, arbour.
cenagal, *n.m.* quagmire.
cenagoso, -sa, *a.* marshy, muddy.
cenar, *v.t.* eat for supper.—*v.i.* have supper.
cenceño, -ña, *a.* thin, lean; unleavened.
cencerrear, *v.i.* clatter, clang.
cencerro, *n.m.* cow-bell.
cendal, *n.m.* gauze, tulle.
cendolilla, *n.f.* flighty girl.
cendra, cendrada, *n.f.* cupel paste.
cenicero, *n.m.* ash-tray, ash-box.
ceniciento, -ta, *a.* ashen, ashy; ***la Cenicienta,*** Cinderella.
cenit, *n.m.* zenith.
ceniza, *n.f.* ash, ashes.
cenizo, -za, *a.* ashy, ashen.—*n.m.f.* (*fam.*) wet-blanket, Jonah, jinx.
cenobio, *n.m.* monastery, cenoby.
cenobita, *n.m.f.* cenobite.
cenotafio, *n.m.* cenotaph.
censar, *v.t.* (*S.A.*) take a census of.
censo (1), *n.m.* census.
censo (2), *n.m.* tax; lien, mortgage; (*fam.*) burden, drain.
censor, *n.m.* censor, proctor; accountant.
censura, *n.f.* censure; censorship; auditing.
censurar, *v.t.* censure; censor.

censurista, *a.* censorious.—*n.m.f.* fault-finder.
centauro, *n.m.* centaur.
centavo, -va, *a.* hundredth.—*n.m.* hundredth; cent.
centella, *n.f.* lightning flash; (*fig.*) spark.
centellar, centellear, *v.i.* flash, sparkle.
centelleo, *n.m.* flash, sparkle.
centena, *n.f.* a hundred (*approx.*).
centenada, *n.f.*, **centenar,** *n.m.* about a hundred.
centenario, -ria, *a.* age-old, centenarian, centenary.—*n.m.f.* centenarian.—*n.m.* centenary.
centeno, *n.m.* rye.
centesimal, *a.* centesimal.
centésimo, -ma, *a.* hundredth.—*n.m.* cent.
centígrado, *n.m.* centigrade.
centilitro, *n.m.* centilitre.
centímetro, *n.m.* centimetre.
céntimo, -ma, *a.* hundredth.—*n.m.* cent.
centinela, *n.f.* sentinel, guard, sentry.
centípedo, *n.m.* centipede.
centiplicado, -da, *a.* hundredfold.
centón, *n.m.* patchwork quilt; cento.
central, *a.* central.—*n.f.* head office; power station; (*tel.*) exchange.
centralismo, *n.m.* centralism.
centralista, *a.*, *n.m.f.* centralist.
centralizar [C], *v.t.*, *v.r.* centralize.
centrar, *v.t.* centre; square up.
céntrico, -ca, *a.* central.
centrífugo, -ga, *a.* centrifugal.—*n.f.* centrifuge.
centrípeto, -ta, *a.* centripetal.
centro, *n.m.* centre; aim, object.
Centro América, *n.f.* Central America.
centroamericano, -na, *a.*, *n.m.f.* Central American.
centroeuropeo, -pea, *a.*, *n.m.f.* Central European.
centuplicar [A], *v.t.* centuple, centuplicate.
centuria, *n.f.* century.
centurión, *n.m.* centurion.
cénzalo, *n.m.* mosquito.
ceñido, -da, *a.* thrifty; close-fitting.
ceñidor, *n.m.* belt, girdle, sash.
ceñidura, *n.f.* girding; limiting.
ceñir [8K], *v.t.* gird, girdle; encircle; limit, shorten.—*v.r.* tighten one's belt; ***ceñirse a,*** limit oneself to.
ceño, *n.m.* frown; hoop, band.
ceñoso, -sa, ceñudo, -da, *a.* frowning, stern.
cepa, *n.f.* stump, bole, stock.
cepillar, *v.t.* brush; (*carp.*) plane.
cepillo, *n.m.* brush; (*carp.*) smoothing plane.
cepo, *n.m.* bough; stump; trap; pillory; poor-box.
cera, *n.f.* wax; wax polish.
cerámico, -ca, *a.* ceramic.—*n.f.* ceramics.
cerbatana, *n.f.* peashooter; blowgun; ear trumpet.
cerca (1), *n.f.* fence, wall; — ***viva,*** hedge.
cerca (2), *adv.* near, nearby; almost, about.—*prep.* near (***de***), close (***de,*** to); nearly (***de***); ***de*** —, near, at close range.
cercado, *n.m.* enclosure; fence.
cercanía, *n.f.* nearness.—*pl.* outskirts.
cercano, -na, *a.* nearby, adjoining.
cercar [A], *v.t.* fence in, enclose; surround, besiege.
a cercén, *adv. phr.* completely, to the root.
cercenar, *v.t.* clip, trim, curtail.
cerciorar, *v.t.* inform, assure.—*v.r.* find out, assure oneself (***de,*** about), ascertain (***de***).
cerco, *n.m.* siege; ring, rim; frame; circle; (*S.A.*) fence.
cerda, *n.f.* bristle; sow; snare.
Cerdeña, *n.f.* Sardinia.
cerdo, *n.m.* hog, pig, boar; — ***marino,*** porpoise.
cerdoso, -sa, *a.* bristly.
cereal, *a.*, *n.m.* cereal.
cerebración, *n.f.* cerebration.
cerebral, *a.* cerebral.
cerebro, *n.m.* brain.
ceremonia, *n.f.* ceremony.
ceremonial, *a.*, *n.m.* ceremonial.
ceremoniático, -ca, *a.* extremely formal.
ceremoniero, -ra, ((*fam.*) **ceremonioso, -sa**) ceremonious, formal.
céreo, -rea, *a.* waxen.
cerero, *n.m.* wax dealer; chandler.
cerevisina, *n.f.* brewer's yeast.
cereza, *n.f.* cherry.
cerezal, *n.m.* cherry orchard.
cerezo, *n.m.* cherry-tree.
cerilla, *n.f.* match; earwax; taper.
cerillo, *n.m.* taper; (*C.A.*) match.
cerner [2], *v.t.* sift; scan.—*v.i.* bud; drizzle.—*v.r.* hover; waddle.
cernícalo, *n.m.* (*orn.*) kestrel; (*fam.*) lout.
cernidillo, *n.m.* drizzle; waddle.
cernir [3], *v.t.* sift.
cero, *n.m.* zero.
ceroso, -sa, *a.* waxy.
cerote, *n.m.* cobbler's wax; (*fam.*) funk.
cerquillo, *n.m.* tonsure, hair ring.
cerquita, *adv.* quite near.
cerradero, -ra, *a.* locking.—*n.m.* lock, bolt; purse string.
cerrado, -da, *a.* close; overcast; heavy (*accent*).
cerradura, *n.f.* lock; closing.
cerraja, *n.f.* lock; thistle.
cerrajero, *n.m.* locksmith.
cerrajón, *n.m.* steep hill, cliff.
cerramiento, *n.m.* closing; enclosure; partition.
cerrar [1], *v.t.* shut; close, lock.—*v.r.* close.
cerrazón, *n.f.* darkness, overcast sky.
cerrejón, *n.m.* hillock.
cerrero, -ra, cerril, *a.* wild; brusque.
cerro, *n.m.* hill; backbone; ***en*** —, bareback; ***por los cerros de Úbeda,*** up hill and down dale.
cerrojillo, *n.m.* (*orn.*) coaltit.
cerrojo, *n.m.* bolt, latch.
certamen, *n.m.* contest.
certero, -ra, *a.* accurate.
certeza, certidumbre, *n.f.* certainty.
certificado, *n.m.* certificate; registered letter.
certificar [A], *v.t.* register (*mail*); certify.
certitud, *n.f.* certainty.
cerúleo, -lea, *a.* cerulean.
cerval, *a.* deerlike, rel. to deer.
cervantino, -na, *a.* Cervantine.
cervantista, *n.m.f.* Cervantist.
cervato, *n.m.* fawn.
cervecería, *n.f.* brewery; beer house.
cervecero, -ra, *a.* brewing.—*n.m.f.* brewer.
cerveza, *n.f.* beer; — ***negra,*** stout.
cerviz, *n.f.* (*pl.* **-ices**) neck, nape.
cesación, *n.f.*, **cesamiento,** *n.m.* cessation.

cesante, *a.* forced to retire on half pay.—*n.m.f.* civil servant so retired.
cesantía, *n.f.* condition of a CESANTE.
César, *n.m.* Caesar.
cesar, *v.i.* cease, stop; **— *de*,** stop (+*gerund*).
cesáreo, -rea, *a.* Caesarean; caesarean.
cese, *n.m.* dismissal.
cesionario, -ria, *n.m.f.* assignee.
césped, *n.m.* turf, lawn.
cesta, *n.f.* basket.
cestería, *n.f.* basketry.
cesto, *n.m.* large basket; cestus.
cesura, *n.f.* caesura.
cetina, *n.f.* whale oil.
cetrería, *n.f.* falconry.
cetrino, -na, *a.* citrine, lemon; gloomy.
cetro, *n.m.* sceptre; roost.
ceutí, *a.* (*pl.* **-íes**) rel. to Ceuta.—*n.m.f.* native of Ceuta.
cianhídrico, -ca, *a.* hydrocyanic.
cianotipo, *n.m.* blueprint, cyanotype.
cianuro, *n.m.* cyanide.
ciática, *n.f.* sciatica.
cicatero, -ra, *a.* niggardly.—*n.m.f.* skinflint.
cicatriz, *n.f.* scar.
cicatrizar [C], *v.r.* heal (*of wound*).
cícero, *n.m.* pica type.
Cicerón, *n.m.* Cicero.
cicerone, *n.m.* cicerone.
ciceroniano, -na, *a.* Ciceronian.
cíclico, -ca, *a.* cyclic(al).
ciclismo, *n.m.* cycling; cycle racing.
ciclista, *n.m.f.* cyclist.
ciclo, *n.m.* cycle (*not bicycle*).
ciclón, *n.m.* cyclone.
Cíclope, *n.m.* Cyclops.
ciclostil(o), *n.m.* cyclostyle, mimeograph.
cicuta, *n.f.* hemlock.
cidra, *n.f.* citrus, citron.
cidrada, *n.f.* candied peel.
cidro, *n.m.* citrus *or* citron tree.
ciego, -ga, *a.* blind; blocked.—*n.m.* blindman.—*n.f.* blind woman; ***a ciegas*,** blindly.
cielo, *n.m.* sky; heaven, Paradise; roof, canopy; ***a — raso*,** in the open air.
ciempiés, *n.m. inv.* centipede; (*fam.*) (written) drivel.
cien, *a.* a hundred.—*n.m.* (*fam.*) a hundred, [CIENTO].
ciénaga, *n.f.* bog, quagmire.
ciencia, *n.f.* science, learning.
cieno, *n.m.* mud, silt.
científico, -ca, *a.* scientific.—*n.m.f.* scientist.
ciento, *a., n.m.* a hundred, one hundred; ***por* —,** per cent. [*As a. before nouns* CIEN].
cierne, *n.m.* blooming, burgeoning.
cierre, *n.m.* closure; lock, latch; **— *metálico*,** metal roller-blind; **— *cremallera*** or ***relámpago*,** zip, zipper.
cierto, -ta, *a.* certain, sure; right; a certain; ***por* —,** certainly.
ciervo, -va, *n.m.f.* deer.—*n.m.* stag.—*n.f.* hind, doe.
cierzo, *n.m.* north wind.
cifra, *n.f.* number; code, cypher; monogram.
cifrar, *v.t.* code, cypher; summarize; **— *la esperanza en*,** put one's hopes in.
cigala, *n.f.* crayfish, squilla.
cigarra, *n.f.* (*ent.*) cicada.
cigarrero, -ra, *n.m.f.* cigar maker *or* seller.—*n.f.* cigar box.
cigarrillo, *n.m.* cigarette.
cigarro, *n.m.* cigar, cigarette; **— *puro*,** cigar.
cigoñal, *n.m.* crankshaft; winch.
cigüeña, *n.f.* (*orn.*) stork; (*mech.*) winch.
cilicio, *n.m.* hairshirt, sackcloth.
cilindrada, *n.f.* cylinder capacity.
ciliandrar, *v.t.* roll.
cilíndrico, -ca, *a.* cylindrical.
cilindro, *n.m.* cylinder; roller.
cillero, *n.m.* store; tithe man.
cima, *n.f.* summit, top; ***dar — a*,** round off.
cimarrón, -rrona, *a.* (*S.A.*) wild; fugitive, gone wild.
címbalo, *n.m.* cymbal.
cimborio, cimborrio, *n.m.* (*arch.*) dome.
cimbr(e)ar, *v.t., v.r.* sway; bend.
cimbreño, -ña, *a.* supple, willowy.
cimentación, *n.f.* foundation.
cimentar, *v.t.* lay the foundation for.
cimento [CEMENTO].
cimera, *n.f.* plume, crest.
cimero, -ra, *a.* uppermost, crowning.
cimiento, *n.m.* foundation, groundwork.
cimitarra, *n.f.* scimitar.
cinabrio, *n.m.* cinnabar.
cinc, *n.m.* zinc.
cincel, *n.m.* graver, chisel.
cincelar, *v.t.* chisel, carve, engrave.
cinco, *a., n.m.* five.
cincuenta, *a., n.m.* fifty.
cincuentavo, -va, *a.* fiftieth.
cincuentenario, -ria, *a., n.m.* semicentenary.
cincuentena, *n.f.* fifty (*approx.*).
cincuentón, -tona, *a., n.m.f.* (*fam.*) fifty-year-old.
cincha, *n.f.* girth, cinch.
cinchar, *v.t.* cinch, band, hoop.
cincho, *n.m.* girdle, sash; girth; hoop.
cine, *n.m.* cinema; **— *hablado*,** talkie; **— *mudo*,** silent film.
cineasta, *n.m.f.* film producer; film actor *or* actress.
cinedrama, *n.m.* film drama, photoplay.
cinemático, -ca, *a.* kinematic.
cinematografía, *n.f.* cinematography.
cinematografiar [L], *v.t.* film.
cinematográfico, -ca, *a.* cinematographic.
cinematógrafo, *n.m.* cinematograph; filming; cinema.
cinéreo, -rea, *a.* ash-grey, cinerous.
cinético, -ca, *a.* kinetic.—*n.f.* kinetics.
cíngaro, -ra, *a., n.m.f.* zingaro, gipsy.
cinglar (1), *v.t.* forge (*iron*).
cinglar (2), *v.t., v.i.* scull (*boat*).
cíngulo, *n.m.* cingulum.
cínico, -ca, *a.* cynical; (*fig.*) brazen, immoral.—*n.m.f.* cynic, Cynic.
cinismo, *n.m.* cynicism, Cynicism; (*fig.*) brazen immorality.
cinta, *n.f.* ribbon, tape; strip; film; kerb.
cintarazo, *n.m.* blow with flat of sword.
cintero, -ra, *n.m.f.* ribbon seller.—*n.m.* belt, sash; rope.
cintillo, *n.m.* hat-band.
cinto, *n.m.* girdle, belt.
cintra, *n.f.* (*arch.*) curvature, arching.
cintura, *n.f.* waist; girdle.
cinturón, *n.m.* belt.
ciño, etc. [CEÑIR].
ciprés, *n.m.* cypress.
ciprino, -na, ciprio, -ria, *a., n.m.f.* Cypriot.
circo, *n.m.* circus, amphitheatre; coomb.
circuir [O], *v.t.* encircle.

circuito, *n.m.* circuit; ***corto* —,** (*elec.*) short circuit.
circulación, *n.f.* circulation; traffic.
circular, *a.*, *n.f.* circular.—*v.t.*, *v.i.* circulate, circularize.
circularidad, *n.f.* circularity.
circulatorio, -ria, *a.* circulatory.
círculo, *n.m.* circle; club; — ***polar ártico,*** Arctic Circle.
circuncidar, *v.t.* circumcise.
circuncisión, *n.f.* circumcision.
circundar, *v.t.* surround.
circunferencia, *n.f.* circumference.
circunflejo, -ja, *a.*, *n.m.* circumflex.
circunlocución, *n.f.*, **circunloquio,** *n.m.* circumlocution.
circunnavegar [B], *v.t.* circumnavigate.
circunscribir, *v.t.* (*p.p.* **circunscrito**) circumscribe.
circunscripción, *n.f.* circumscription; territorial division.
circunspección, *n.f.* circumspection.
circunspecto, -ta, *a.* circumspect.
circunstancia, *n.f.* circumstance.
circunstanciado, -da, *a.* detailed.
circunstancial, *a.* circumstantial.
circunstante, *a.* surrounding; present.—*n.m.f.* onlooker, bystander.
circunvalar, *v.t.* circumvallate, surround.
circunvención, *n.f.* circumvention.
circunvenir [36], *v.t.* circumvent.
circunvolar [4], *v.t.* fly round.
circunvolución, *n.f.* circumvolution.
cirigallo, -lla, *n.m.f.* layabout, gadabout.
cirio, *n.m.* (*eccl.*) large candle.
cirolero, *n.m.* plum-tree.
ciruela, *n.f.* plum; — ***pasa,*** prune.
ciruelo, *n.m.* plum-tree; (*fam.*) numskull.
cirugía, *n.f.* surgery.
cirujano, *n.m.* surgeon.
cisco, *n.m.* slack, fine charcoal; (*fam.*) row, din; ***meter* —,** stir up trouble.
ciscón, *n.m.* cinders.
cisión, *n.f.* incision, cut.
cisma, *n.f.* schism.
cismático, -ca, *a.*, *n.m.f.* schismatic.
cisne, *n.m.* swan.
Cister, *n.m.* Cistercian Order.
cisterciense, *a.*, *n.m.f.* Cistercian.
cisterna, *n.f.* tank, cistern.
cisura, *n.f.* fissure; incision.
cita, *n.f.* appointment, date; quotation.
citación, *n.f.* summons; quotation.
citano, -na, *n.m.f.* (*fam.*) so-and-so.
citar, *v.t.* make an appointment with; quote, cite; summon; (*taur.*) provoke.
cítara, *n.f.* zither; cithern.
cítrico, -ca, *a.* citric.
citrón, *n.m.* lemon.
ciudad, *n.f.* city.
ciudadanía, *n.f.* citizenship.
ciudadano, -na, *a.* civic; town-bred.—*n.m.f.* citizen; townsman, townswoman.
ciudadela, *n.f.* citadel.
civeta, *n.f.* civet.
cívico, -ca, *a.* civic.—*n.m.* (*fam.*) copper, policeman.
civil, *a.* civil; civilian.—*n.m.f.* civilian; policeman.
civilidad, *n.f.* civility.
civilización, *n.f.* civilization.
civilizar [C], *v.t.* civilize.
civismo, *n.m.* civicism; patriotism.
cizaña, *n.f.* darnel, tare; (*fig.*) discord.
cinzañero, -ra, *n.m.f.* (*fam.*) troublemaker.
clamor, *n.m.* clamour, outcry; knell.
clamoreada, *n.f.* outcry; shrieking.
clamorear, *v.t.* clamour for.—*v.i.* toll; clamour (***por***, for).
clandestino, -na, *a.* clandestine.
clangor, *n.m.* (*poet.*) blare, clarion.
claque, *n.m.* claque.
claraboya, *n.f.* skylight.
clarear, *v.t.* brighten; dawn.—*v.r.* be transparent.
clarecer [9], *v.i.* dawn.
clareo, *n.m.* clearing (*in woods*).
clarete, *n.m.* claret.
clareza (*lit.*), **claridad,** *n.f.* clarity, clearness; brightness; daylight.—*pl.* plain truths.
clarificación, *n.f.* clarification.
clarificar [A], *v.t.* clarify; brighten.
clarín, *n.m.* clarion; trumpeter.
clarinada, *n.f.* clarion call; (*fam.*) uncalled-for remark.
clarinero, *n.m.* bugler.
clarinete, *n.m.* clarinet.
clarioncillo, *n.m.* crayon.
clarividencia, *n.f.* clairvoyance; perspicacity.
clarividente, *a.* clairvoyant; perspicacious.
claro, -ra, *a.* clear, bright; light; obvious; famous.—*n.m.* blank, gap; clearing; skylight.—*n.f.* egg white; thin patch; break, bright patch.—*adv.* clearly.—*interj.* of course! naturally! ***poner en* —,** make clear; ***a las claras,*** clearly.
claror, *n.m.* brightness, splendour, light.
claroscuro, *n.m.* (*art.*) chiaroscuro.
clarucho, -cha, *a.* (*fam.*) watery thin.
clase, *n.f.* class.
clasicismo, *n.m.* classicism.
clasicista, *n.m.f.* classicist.
clásico, -ca, *a.* classic(al).—*n.m.* classic; classicist.
clasificador, -ra, *a.* classifying.—*n.m.* filing cabinet.
clasificar [A], *v.t.* classify.—*v.r.* qualify.
claudicación, *n.f.* limping; bungling.
claudicar [A], *v.i.* limp; bungle.
claustral, *a.* cloistral.
claustro, *n.m.* cloister; university council.
claustrofobia, *n.f.* claustrophobia.
cláusula, *n.f.* clause.
clausura, *n.f.* cloistered life; close, closure.
clausurar, *v.t.* adjourn; close.
clavado, -da, *a.* studded; sharp, punctual; stopped (*watch*); (*fam.*) to the life.
clavar, *v.t.* nail; drive in (*nail, dagger etc.*); fix; (*fam.*) cheat.
clavazón, *n.f.* nails.
clave, *n.f.* key (*to code*); (*mus.*) clef.—*n.m.* harpsichord.
clavel, *n.m.* carnation, pink.
clavellina, *n.f.* (*bot.*) pink.
clavero (1), **-ra,** *n.m.f.* keeper of the keys.
clavero (2), *n.m.* clove tree.
claveta, *n.f.* peg.
clavete, *n.m.* tack; plectrum.
clavicordio, *n.m.* clavichord.
clavícula, *n.f.* clavicle, collar-bone.
clavija, *n.f.* peg; (*elec.*) plug.

clavijero, *n.m.* coat rack; peg-box; (*tel.*) switch board.
clavo, *n.m.* nail; (*cul.*) clove; (*fig.*) pain, anguish; (*med.*) corn; ***dar en el —,*** hit the nail on the head.
clemencia, *n.f.* clemency.
clemente, *a.* clement.
cleptomanía, *n.f.* kleptomania.
cleptómano, -na, *a., n.m.f.* kleptomaniac.
clerecía, *n.f.* clergy.
clerical, *a.* clerical.—*n.m.* clericalist.
clericalismo, *n.m.* clericalism.
clericato, *n.m.,* **clericatura,** *n.f.* clergy, priesthood.
clerigalla, *n.f.* (*pej.*) priests, dog-collar men.
clérigo, *n.m.* clergyman, cleric.
clerigón, *n.m.* acolyte, server.
clero, *n.m.* clergy.
clerofobia, *n.f.* hatred of priests.
clerófobo, -ba, *a.* priest-hating.—*n.m.f.* priest-hater.
cliché, *n.m.* cliché.
cliente, *n.m.f.* client, customer.
clientela, *n.f.* clientele; customers, custom; patronage.
clima, *n.m.* climate, (*poet.*) clime.
climactérico, -ca, *a.* climacteric.
climático, -ca, *a.* climatic.
clínico, -ca, *a.* clinical.—*n.m.f.* clinical doctor.—*n.f.* clinic; clinical medicine.
clíper, *n.m.* (*naut., aer.*) clipper.
clisar, *v.t.* stereotype.
clisé, *n.m.* (*phot., print.*) plate; stencil.
cloaca, *n.f.* sewer.
clocar [4A], **cloquear,** *v.i.* cluck.
clorhídrico, -ca, *a.* hydrochloric.
cloro, *n.m.* chlorine.
clorofila, *n.f.* chlorophyll.
cloroformizar [C], *v.t.* chloroform.
cloroformo, *n.m.* chloroform.
cloruro, *n.m.* chloride.
club, *n.m.* (*pl.* **-bs** *or* **-bes**) club.
clubista, *n.m.f.* club member.
clueco, -ca, *a.* broody.—*n.f.* broody hen.
cluniacense, *a., n.m.* Cluniac.
coacción, *n.f.* coercion.
coaccionar, *v.t.* force, compel.
coactivo, -va, *a.* coercive.
coagulación, *n.f.* coagulation.
coagular, *v.t., v.r.* coagulate.
coalición, *n.f.* coalition.
coartada, *n.f.* alibi.
coartar, *v.t.* limit, restrict.
coautor, -ra, *n.m.f.* co-author, fellow author.
coba, *n.f.* (*fam.*) leg-pull; cajolery, wheedling.
cobalto, *n.m.* cobalt.
cobarde, *a.* cowardly.—*n.m.f.* coward.
cobardía, *n.f.* cowardice.
cobayo, -ya, *n.m.f.* guinea-pig.
cobertera, *n.f.* pot cover; bawd.
cobertizo, *n.m.* lean-to; cover.
cobertor, *n.m.* coverlet.
cobertura, *n.f.* covering, cover; knighting.
cobija, *n.f.* cover.—*pl.* bedclothes.
cobijar, *v.t.* cover, shelter; lodge.
cobijo, *n.m.* shelter, cover.
cobista, *n.m.f.* (*fam.*) cajoler, smooth-tongued character.
cobra, *n.f.* (*hunt.*) retrieving; (*zool.*) cobra.
cobrable, cobrandero, -ra, *a.* collectable, recoverable.
cobrador, *n.m.* bus conductor; collector; retriever.
cobranza, *n.f.* recovery, retrieving; cashing.
cobrar, *v.t.* recover, collect; cash; acquire; (*hunt.*) retrieve.—*v.r.* recover (**de,** from).
cobre, *n.m.* copper.—*pl.* (*mus.*) brass.
cobreño, -ña, *a.* made of copper.
cobrizo, -za, *a.* coppery.
cobro, *n.m.* collection, cashing; ***en —,*** in a safe place.
coca, *n.f.* (*bot.*) coca; berry; rap; (*fam.*) head.
cocaína, *n.f.* cocaine.
cocción, *n.f.* baking, cooking.
cocear, *v.i.* kick; jib, balk.
cocer [5D], *v.t.* cook, bake, boil; seethe.—*v.r.* suffer agonies.
coces [COZ].
cocido, *n.m.* Spanish stew with chick peas.—*p.p.* [COCER].
cociente, *n.m.* quotient.
cocimiento, *n.m.* cooking, baking; decoction.
cocina, *n.f.* kitchen; cuisine, cookery.
cocinar, *v.t.* cook; (*fam.*) meddle.
cocinero, -ra, *n.m.f.* cook.
cocinilla, *n.f.* kitchenette; camping stove.
coco, *n.m.* coconut; coconut palm; coccus; (*fam.*) bogeyman; ***hacer cocos,*** (*fam.*) pull faces; make eyes.
cocodrilo, *n.m.* crocodile.
cocoliche, *n.m.* (*S.A.*) broken Spanish.
cócora, *a.* pestering, pesky.—*n.m.f.* pest, bore.
cocotero, *n.m.* coconut palm.
coctel, *n.m.* cocktail.
coctelera, *n.f.* cocktail shaker.
cochambre, *n.m.* (*fam.*) greasy filth.
coche, *n.m.* coach; car; bus; ***en el — de San Francisco,*** on Shanks's pony.
coche-cama, *n.m.* (*pl.* **coches-cama**) (*rail.*) sleeper, wagon-lit.
cochera, *n.f.* coach-house, garage.
cochero, *n.m.* coachman.
cochinilla, *n.f.* cochineal, cochineal beetle; woodlouse.
cochinillo, *n.m.* sucking-pig; piglet.
cochino, -na, *a.* piggish.—*n.m.f.* pig.—*n.m.* hog.—*n.f.* sow.
cochite-hervite, *adv.* helter skelter; slap-dash.
cochitril [CUCHITRIL].
cochura, *n.f.* baking; dough.
codal, *a.* rel. to elbow, cubital.—*n.m.* strut, brace.
codazo, *n.m.* nudge, poke.
codear, *v.i.* elbow; (*S.A.*) cadge; ***codearse con,*** hob-nob with.
codera, *n.f.* elbow-patch.
códice, *n.m.* codex, manuscript.
codicia, *n.f.* greed, lust.
codiciar, *v.t., v.i.* covet.
codicilo, *n.m.* codicil.
codicioso, -sa, *a.* covetous; (*fam.*) hard-working.
codificar [A], *v.t.* codify.
código, *n.m.* (*jur.*) statute book; code.
codo, *n.m.* elbow, cubit; ***por los codos,*** (*fam.*) nineteen to the dozen.
codoñate, *n.m.* quince fondant.
codorniz, *n.f.* (*pl.* **-ices**) (*orn.*) quail.
coeducación, *n.f.* co-education.
coeducacional, *a.* co-educational.
coeficiente, *a., n.m.* coefficient.

coercer [D], *v.t.* coerce.
coerción, *n.f.* coercion.
coetáneo, -nea, *a.* contemporary.
coevo, -va, *a.* coeval.
coexistencia, *n.f.* coexistence.
coexistente, *a.* coexistent.
coexistir, *v.i.* coexist.
cofia, *n.f.* coif.
cofrade, *n.m.f.* fellow member; member of COFRADÍA.
cofradía, *n.f.* confraternity, guild.
cofre, *n.m.* coffer, chest; — ***fuerte,*** safe.
cofto, -ta, *a.* Coptic.—*n.m.f.* Copt.
cogedero, -ra, *a.* ready for picking.—*n.m.* handle.
cogedor, -ra, *n m.f.* picker, gatherer.—*n.m.* shovel; rubbish box.
cogedura, *n.f.* picking, gathering.
coger [E], *v.t.* seize; catch; gather; pick up; hold; cover; (*taur.*) toss.—*v.i.* be situated; (*fam.*) fit. [*This word NEVER used in Argentina*].
cogida, *n.f.* gathering; catch; (*taur.*) toss.
cognado, -da, *a., n.m.f.* cognate.
cognición, *n.f.* cognition.
cogollo, *n.m.* (*bot.*) heart; shoot; tree-top; (*fig.*) pick, best.
cogolludo, -da, *a.* (*fam.*) terrific, great, fine.
cogorza, *n.f.* ***coger una —,*** (*fam.*) get tipsy.
cogotazo, *n.m.* rabbit punch, blow on nape.
cogote, *n.m.* nape, back of neck.
cogotudo, -da, *a.* thick-necked; (*fam.*) stiff-necked, proud.
cogujada, *n.f.* (*orn.*) crested lark.
cogulla, *n.f.* cowl.
cohabitar, *v.i.* cohabit.
cohechar, *v.t.* bribe; plough.
cohecho, *n.m.* bribe.
coherencia, *n.f.* coherence.
coherente, *a.* coherent.
cohesión, *n.f.* cohesion.
cohete, *n.m.* rocket; jet, rocket motor.
cohetería, *n.f.* rocketry.
cohibir, *v.t.* inhibit.
cohombrillo, *n.m.* gherkin.
cohombro, *n.m.* cucumber.
cohonestar, *v.t.* gloss over.
cohorte, *n.m.* cohort.
coincidencia, *n.f.* coinciding; coincidence.
coincidir, *v.i.* coincide; concur.
coipo, coipú, *n.m.* (*zool.*) coypu, nutria.
cojear, *v.i.* limp, wobble; (*fam.*) slip up.
cojera, *n.f.* limp.
cojijo, *n.m.* (*ent.*) insect, (*fam.*) creepy-crawly; moan, grouse.
cojijoso, -sa, *a.* peevish, grumpy.
cojín, *n.m.* cushion.
cojinete, *n.m.* pad; (*mech.*) bearing.
cojo, -ja, *a.* lame, limping; crippled; wobbly, shaky.—*n.m.f.* cripple, lame person.
cok, [COQUE].
col, *n.f.* cabbage.
cola, *n.f.* tail; train (*of dress*); queue; glue; ***hacer (la) —,*** queue up, (*U.S.*) make a line.
colaboración, *n.f.* collaboration.
colaborador, -ra, *a.* collaborating.—*n.m.f.* collaborator.
colaborar, *v.i.* collaborate.
colación, *n.f.* collation; conferment; glebe; ***sacar a —,*** (*fam.*) bring up, mention.
colada, *n.f.* soaking; lye; wash(ing); track; ravine.
coladizo, -za, *a.* runny.
colador, *n.m.* colander; strainer.
coladura, *n.f.* straining; (*fam.*) slip-up.
colanilla, *n.f.* small bolt, catch.
colapso, *n.m.* collapse; — ***nervioso,*** nervous breakdown.
colar [4], *v.t.* strain; boil (*clothes*); pour; bore.—*v.i.* squeeze through; ooze, leak; (*fam.*) booze.—*v.r.* seep; slip in; — ***a fondo,*** (*naut.*) sink; ***eso no cuela,*** (*fam.*) that's impossible.
colateral, *a., n.m.f.* co-lateral.
colcrén, *n.m.* cold cream.
colcha, *n.f.* quilt, bedspread.
colchón, *n.m.* mattress.
colear, *v.t.* throw (*cattle*).—*v.i.* wag one's tail; (*fam.*) remain unsettled.
colección, *n.f.* collection.
coleccionar, *v.t.* collect (*as hobby*).
coleccionista, *n.m.f.* collector.
colecta, *n.f.* (*eccl.*) collect.
colectividad, *n.f.* collectivity; community.
colectivismo, *n.m.* collectivism.
colectivización, *n.f.* collectivization.
colectivizar [C], *v.t.* collectivize.
colectivo, -va, *a.* collective.—*n.m.* (*S.A.*) bus.
colector, *n.m.* collector, gatherer; drain; (*elec.*) commutator.
colega, *n.m.f.* colleague.
colegiata, *n.f.* collegiate church.
colegio, *n.m.* college; high school.
colegir [8E], *v.t.* gather, infer.
cólera, *n.f.* bile, wrath.—*n.m.* cholera.
colérico, -ca, *a., n.m.f.* choleric, angry, wrathful; choleraic.
coleta, *n.f.* (*taur.*) bullfighter's pigtail; queue; postscript.
coletillo, *n.m.* waistcoat.
coleto, *n.m.* doublet; (*fam.*) oneself.
colgadero, *n.m.* hanger.
colgadizo, -za, *a.* hanging.—*n.m.* lean-to.
colgado, -da, *a.* drooping; unsettled; thwarted.
colgadura, *n.f.* drapery, hangings.
colgajo, *n.m.* tatter.
colgante, *a.* hanging; ***puente —,*** suspension bridge.
colgar [4B], *v.t.* hang; drape; fail (*an examinee*).—*v.i.* hang, dangle.
colibrí, *n.m.* (*pl.* **-íes**) humming bird.
cólico, -ca, *a., n.m.* colic.
coliflor, *n.f.* cauliflower.
coligación, *n.f.* union, alliance.
coligado, -da, *n.m.f.* ally.
coligar [B], *v.r.* join forces.
colijo [COLEGIR].
colilla, *n.f.* end, butt (*cigar etc.*).
colina, *n.f.* hill.
colindante, *a.* adjacent.
coliseo, *n.m.* coliseum.
colisión, *n.f.* collision.
colmar, *v.t.* fill to the brim; fulfil; overwhelm (***de,*** with).
colmena, *n.f.* beehive.
colmillo, *n.m.* canine tooth, eye-tooth; tusk; fang.
colmilludo, -da, *a.* tusked, fanged; (*fam.*) canny.
colmo, -ma, *a.* full to the brim.—*n.m.* height, peak; overflowing; (*fam.*) the last straw.
colocación, *n.f.* collocation; job.
colocar [A], *v.t.* place; locate.

colofón, *n.m.* colophon.
colombiano, -na, *a., n.m.f.* Colombian.
colombino, -na, *a.* rel. to Columbus, Columbine.
Colón, *n.m.* Columbus; **colón,** *n.m.* (*anat., gram.*) colon.
colonato, *n.m.* colonization.
Colonia, *n.f.* Cologne; **colonia,** *n.f.* colony; eau-de-Cologne.
colonial, *a.* colonial.—*n.m.pl.* imported foods.
colonización, *n.f.* colonization.
colonizar [C], *v.t.* colonize.
colono, -na, *n.m.f.* settler; colonial; tenant farmer.
coloquio, *n.m.* colloquy, talk.
color, *n.m.* colour; ***de* —,** coloured; ***so* — *de,*** on pretext of.
coloración, *n.f.* coloration.
colorado, -da, *a.* red; coloured; blue (*joke*); specious.
colorante, *a., n.m.* colouring.
colorar, *v.t.* colour.
colorativo, -va, *a.* colouring.
colorear, *v.t.* colour; palliate.—*v.i.* turn red, ripen.
colorete, *n.m.* rouge.
colorido, -da, *a.* colourful.—*n.m.* colouring.
colorín, *n.m.* bright colour; (*orn.*) goldfinch.
colorir [Q], [COLOREAR].
colorista, *n.m.f.* colourist.
colosal, *a.* colossal.
coloso, *n.m.* colossus.
coludir, *v.i., v.r.* act in collusion.
columbino, -na, *a.* columbine, dovelike.
columbrar, *v.t.* discern, glimpse.
columbrete, *n.m.* reef, islet.
columna, *n.f.* column.
columnata, *n.f.* colonnade.
columpiar, *v.t., v.r.* swing, rock.
columpio, *n.m.* swing.
colusión, *n.f.* collusion.
colusorio, -ria, *a.* collusive.
collado, *n.m.* hill; mountain pass.
collar, *n.m.* necklace; collar (*for dogs, slaves etc.*).
collazo, *n.m.* farmhand; (*obs.*) serf.
coma, *n.f.* (*gram.*) comma.—*n.m.* (*med.*) coma.
comadre, *n.f.* midwife; grandmother; (*fam.*) gossip; (*fam.*) woman friend.
comadrear, *v.i.* (*fam.*) gossip, chin-wag.
comadreja, *n.f.* weasel.
comadrero, -ra, *a.* (*fam.*) gossipy.—*n.m.f.* gossip.
comadrona, *n.f.* midwife.
comandancia, *n.f.* (*mil.*) high command.
comandante, *n.m.* (*mil.*) commander, commandant, major; (*aer.*) wing commander.
comandar, *v.t.* (*mil.*) command.
comandita, *n.f.* sleeping partnership.
comanditar, *v.t.* invest (*in a business*).
comando, *n.m.* (*mil.*) commando; command, control.
comarca, *n.f.* region, district.
comarcal, *a.* regional, local.
comarcano, -na, *a.* neighbouring, bordering.
comarcar [A], *v.i.* border.
comatoso, -sa, *a.* comatose.
comba (1), *n.f.* bend, curve, camber.
comba (2), *n.f.* skipping; skipping-rope; ***saltar a la* —,** skip.
combadura, *n.f.* bend, camber; sag.
combar, *v.t.* bend, warp.—*v.r.* sag, bulge, bend.
combate, *n.m.* fight, combat; ***fuera de* —,** out of action, hors de combat.
combatiente, *a., n.m.* combatant.
combatir, *v.t.* fight, combat; harass.—*v.i., v.r.* struggle, fight.
combatividad, *n.f.* combativeness; fighting spirit.
combinación, *n.f.* combination; (*rail.*) connexion.
combinar, *v.t.* combine; work out.
combo, -ba, *a.* bulging, bent, warped.
combustible, *a.* combustible.—*n.m.* fuel.
combustión, *n.f.* combustion.
comedero, -ra, *a.* eatable.—*n.m.* manger.
comedia, *n.f.* play, drama; comedy; (*fig.*) shamming.
comediante, -ta, *n.m.* actor.—*n.f.* actress; (*fig.*) hypocrite.
comediar, *v.t.* halve.
comedido, -da, *a.* courteous, moderate.
comedimiento, *n.m.* politeness, moderation.
comedio, *n.m.* middle; interval.
comedir [8], *v.r.* be polite *or* moderate.
comedor, -ra, *a.* eating much.—*n.m.* dining room.
comején, *n.m.* termite; fretter moth.
comendador, *n.m.* commander (*of an Order*).
comensal, *n.m.f.* retainer; fellow diner.
comentador, -ra, *n.m.f.* commentator.
comentar, *v.t.* comment (on).—*v.i.* (*fam.*) natter.
comentario, *n.m.* commentary; comment.
comentarista, *n.m.* commentator.
comento, *n.m.* comment; falsehood.
comenzar [1C], *v.t., v.i.* begin, commence (***a,*** to, ***por,*** by).
comer, *n.m.* food; eating.—*v.t.* eat, eat away. —*v.i.* eat; have lunch; itch.
comerciable, *a.* marketable; sociable.
comercial, *a.* commercial.
comercialización, *n.f.* commercialization.
comercializar [C], *v.t.* commercialize.
comerciante, *a.* trading.—*n.m.f.* trader, merchant.
comerciar, *v.t.* trade, deal (**con,** with).
comercio, *n.m.* commerce, business; intercourse.
comestible, *a.* edible.—*n.m.pl.* food.
cometa, *n.m.* comet.—*n.f.* kite (*toy*).
cometer, *v.t.* commit; assign.
cometido, *n.m.* assignment, commitment.
comezón, *n.f.* itch.
comicidad, *n.f.* comicality.
cómico, -ca, *a.* comic, comical; dramatic.—*n.m.* actor; comedian.—*n.f.* actress; comedienne.
comida, *n.f.* lunch; meal; food.
comidilla, *n.f.* (*fam.*) right thing, "cup of tea"; (*fam.*) hobby; (*fam.*) gossip, talk, scandal.
comienzo, *n.m.* beginning; ***dar* —,** begin.
comilón, -lona, *a.* (*fam.*) guzzling.—*n.m.f.* (*fam.*) guzzler, big eater.—*n.f.* spread, big meal.
comillas, *n.f.pl.* quotation marks.
cominero, *n.m.* "old woman", fuss-pot.
comino, *n.m.* (*bot.*) cumin.
comiquear, *v.i.* put on amateur plays.
comisar, *v.t.* impound.
comisaría, *n.f.* police station.

comisariato, *n.m.* commissariat.
comisario, *n.m.* commissioner, commissar.
comisión, *n.f.* committee; commission.
comisionista, *n.m.f.* commission agent.
comiso, *n.m.* seizure, impounding.
comisquear, *v.t.* nibble.
comistrajo, *n.m.* rotten meal, hodge-podge.
comité, *n.m.* committee.
comitente, *n.m.f.* client, constituent.
comitiva, *n.f.* retinue, party.
como, *adv.* like, as; how; about; as if.—*conj.* as; when; how; so that; if; ***así* —,** as soon as; just as; **— *que*,** seeing that; **— *quien dice*,** so to speak.
cómo, *adv. interrog.* how ? what ?—*interj.* how! what! **¿— *no*?** why not ? for sure, yes.
comóda, *n.f.* commode.
comodidad, *n.f.* comfort, ease, convenience.
comodín, *n.m.* joker (*in cards*); gadget; alibi, excuse.
comodista, *a.* selfish, comfort-loving.—*n.m.f.* self-seeker, comfort-lover.
cómodo, -da, *a.* convenient; comfortable.
comodón, -dona, *a.* comfort-loving.
comodoro, *n.m.* commodore.
compacidad, *n.f.* compressibility, compactness.
compactar, *v.t.* make compact.
compacto, -ta, *a.* compact.
compadecer [9], *v.t.* pity, feel sorry for.—*v.r.* concur, tally; sympathize (***de***, with).
compadraje, *n.m.* clique, ring.
compadrar, *v.i.* become a godfather; become friends.
compadre, *n.m.* godfather; (*fam.*) mate, chum; (*S.A.*) swanker.
compadrear, *v.i.* (*fam.*) be matey.
compaginación, *n.f.* pagination; arranging.
compaginar, *v.t.* arrange; page.—*v.r.* fit. agree.
compañerismo, *n.m.* companionship; comradeship.
compañero, -ra, *n.m.f.* companion, fellow, friend, comrade.
compañía, *n.f.* company.
comparable, *a.* comparable.
comparación, *n.f.* comparison.
comparar, *v.t.* compare.
comparativo, -va, *a., n.m.* comparative.
comparecer [9], *v.i.* (*jur.*) appear.
comparsa, *n.f.* (*theat.*) extras.—*n.m.f.* extra.
compartimiento, *n.m.* division, compartment.
compartir, *v.t.* share, divide.
compás, *n.m.* compass; compasses; (*mus.*) time, beat; (*mus.*) bar.
compasado, -da, *a.* moderate, measured.
compasar, *v.t.* cut to size, adapt.
compasión, *n.f.* compassion.
compasivo, -va, *a.* compassionate.
compatibilidad, *n.f.* compatibility.
compatible, *a.* compatible.
compatriota, *n.m.f.* compatriot, fellow countryman *or* -woman.
compeler, *v.t.* compel.
compendiar, *v.t.* summarize.
compendio, *n.m.* summary, compendium.
compendioso, -sa, *a.* compendious.
compenetrar, *v.r.* interpenetrate; ***compenetrarse de***, absorb, immerse oneself in; ***compenetrarse con***, understand.
compensación, *n.f.* compensation.
compensar, *v.t.* compensate (for).
competencia, *n.f.* competence; competition.
competente, *a.* competent, adequate.
competer, *v.i.* appertain, concern.
competición, *n.f.* competition.
competidor, -ra, *a.* competing.—*n.m.f.* competitor.
competir [8], *v.i.* compete.
compilación, *n.f.* compilation.
compilar, *v.t.* compile.
compinche, *n.m.f.* (*fam.*) crony.
complacencia, *n.f.* pleasure, satisfaction.
complacer [23], *v.t.* please; humour.—*v.r.* be pleased (***de, con, en***, with).
complaciente, *a.* complaisant, pleasing.
complejidad, *n.f.* complexity.
complejo, -ja, *a., n.m.* complex.
complementar, *v.t.* complete, complement.
complementario, -ria, *a.* complementary.
complemento, *n.m.* complement; completion.
completar, *v.t.* complete.
completo, -ta, *a.* complete; full (*vehicle*).—*n.f.pl.* (*eccl.*) compline.
complexidad, *n.f.* complexity.
complexión, *n.f.* (*med.*) constitution.
complexo [COMPLEJO].
complicación, *n.f.* complication.
complicar [A], *v.t.* complicate.
cómplice, *n.m.f.* accomplice, accessory.
complicidad, *n.f.* complicity.
complot, *n.m.* plot.
complutense, *a.* rel. to Alcalá.
componedor, -ra, *n.m.f.* compositor; composer, arbitrator.
componenda, *n.f.* compromise, settlement.
componente, *a., n.m.* (*mech. n.f.*) component.
componer [25], *v.t.* compose, arrange; mend, trim; reconcile.—*v.r.* come to terms; be composed (***de***, of).
comportamiento, *n.m.* conduct, behaviour.
comportar, *v.t.* bear; (*S.A.*) entail.—*v.r.* behave.
comporte, *n.m.* bearing, behaviour.
composición, *n.f.* composition; settlement.
compositor, -ra, *n.m.f.* (*mus.*) composer.
compostelano, -na, *a., n.m.f.* Compostelan (*rel. to Santiago de Compostela*).
compostura, *n.f.* structure; settlement; composure; repair.
compota, *n.f.* stewed fruit.
compra, *n.f.* shopping, purchase; ***ir de compras***, go shopping.
comprar, *v.t.* buy, purchase.—*v.i.* shop.
compraventa, *n.f.* transaction; second-hand business.
comprender, *v.t.* understand; comprise.
comprensible, *a.* understandable.
comprensión, *n.f.* understanding; comprehension.
comprensivo, -va, *a.* comprehensive; understanding.
compresa, *n.f.* compress; sanitary towel.
compresible, *a.* compressible.
compresión, *n.f.* compression.
compresor, -ra, *a.* compressing.—*n.m.* (*med.*) *n.f.* (*mech.*) compressor.
comprimido, *n.m.* tablet.—*p.p.* [COMPRIMIR].
comprimir, *v.t.* compress, condense; repress.
comprobación, *n.f.* proof, verification.
comprobante, *a.* proving.—*n.m.* proof; voucher.
comprobar [4], *v.t.* prove, verify, check.

comprometer, *v.t.* oblige; compromise.—*v.r.* undertake (***a***, to).
comprometido, -da, *a.* embarrassing.
comprometimiento, *n.m.* compromise; predicament.
compromisario, -ria, *n.m.f.* arbitrator.
compromiso, *n.m.* compromise; commitment; embarrassment, compromising situation.
compuerta, *n.f.* sluice gate, lock gate; half door.
compuesto, -ta, *a.* compound, composed, composite—*p.p.* [COMPONER].—*n.m.* compound.
compulsa, *n.f.* collation; authenticated copy.
compulsación, *n.f.* collation.
compulsar, *v.t.* collate, check.
compulsión, *n.f.* compulsion.
compulsivo, -va, *a.* compulsive; compulsory.
compunción, *n.f.* compunction.
compungir [E], *v.t.* move to remorse.—*v.r.* feel remorse.
compuse [COMPONER].
computación, *n.f.* computation.
computador, *n.m.* (*S.A.*), **computadora,** *n.f.* (*Sp.*) computer.
computar, *v.t.* compute.
cómputo, *n.m.* computation, calculation.
comulgante, *n.m.f.* (*eccl.*) communicant.
comulgar [A], *v.t.* (*eccl.*) administer communion to.—*v.i.* communicate, receive communion; — ***con,*** (*fig.*) agree with.
comulgatorio, *n.m.* communion rail.
común, *a.* common.—*n.m.* commonalty; the common run; lavatory, toilet; ***por lo —,*** commonly, generally.
comuna, *n.f.* commune; (*S.A.*) township.
comunal, *a.* common; communal.—*n.m.* the common people.
comunero, -ra, *a.* popular.—*n.m.* joint owner; (*hist.*) commoner.
comunicable, *a.* communicable.
comunicación, *n.f.* communication.
comunicado, *n.m.* communiqué.
comunicante, *a.*, *n.m.f.* communicant.
comunicar [A], *v.t.* communicate.
comunicativo, -va, *a.* communicative.
comunidad, *n.f.* community; ***Comunidad Británica de Naciones,*** British Commonwealth.
comunión, *n.f.* communion.
comunismo, *n.m.* Communism.
comunista, *a.*, *n.m.f.* Communist.
comunizante, *n.m.f.* fellow-traveller, Communist sympathizer.
comunizar [C], *v.t.* communize.—*v.r.* turn Communist.
con, *prep.* with; in spite of; by; — ***que,*** so that; — ***tal que,*** provided that; — ***todo,*** nevertheless.
conato, *n.m.* endeavour; attempt.
concadenación, concatenación, *n.f.* concatenation.
concadenar, concatenar, *v.t.* concatenate.
cóncavo, -va, *a.* concave.—*n.m.f.* concavity.
concebible, *a.* conceivable.
concebir [8], *v.t.* conceive.
conceder, *v.t.* concede, grant.
concejal, *n.m.* alderman, councillor.
concejo, *n.m.* council.
concentración, *n.f.* concentration.
concentrado, -da, *a.* (*fig.*) retiring.—*n.m.* concentrate.
concentrar, *v.t.* concentrate.—*v.r.* concentrate (***en,*** on); be centred (***en,*** on, around).
concéntrico, -ca, *a.* concentric.
concepción, *n.f.* conception.
conceptismo, *n.m.* conceptism.
conceptista, *a.*, *n.m.f.* conceptist.
conceptivo, -va, *a.* conceptive.
concepto, *n.m.* concept, opinion; conceit, witticism.
conceptual, *a.* conceptual.
conceptuar [M], *v.t.* deem.
conceptuoso, -sa, *a.* epigrammatic, witty, conceited (*style*).
concerniente, *a.* concerning.
concernir [3Q], *v.t.* concern, apply to.
concertar [1], *v.t.* arrange, harmonise, mend.—*v.i.* agree.—*v.r.* come to terms.
concertina, *n.f.* concertina.
concertista, *n.m.f.* concert performer.
concesible, *a.* allowable.
concesión, *n.f.* concession.
conciencia, *n.f.* conscience; consciousness.
concienzudo, -da, *a.* conscientious.
concierto, *n.m.* agreement, harmony; (*mus.*) concert; concerto.
conciliación, *n.f.* conciliation.
conciliar, *a.* rel. to council.—*n.m.* councillor.—*v.t.* conciliate; gain.—*v.r.* win, earn (*esteem etc.*)
conciliatorio, -ria, *a.* conciliatory.
concilio, *n.m.* council; council decrees.
concisión, *n.f.* concision.
conciso, -sa, *a.* concise.
concitar, *v.t.* incite.
conciudadano, -na, *a.* fellow-citizen.
cónclave, conclave, *n.m.* conclave.
concluir [O], *v.t.* conclude; convince.—*v.i., v.r.* conclude, end.
conclusión, *n.f.* conclusion.
conclusivo, -va, *a.* concluding.
concluso, -sa, *a.* concluded.
concluyente, *a.* conclusive.
concomer, *v.r.* fidget; shrug; be impatient.
concomitante, *a.* concomitant.
concordancia, *n.f.* concordance, concord.
concordante, *a.* concordant.
concordar [4], *v.t.* harmonize.—*v.i.* agree (***con,*** with).
concordato, *n.m.* concordat.
concorde, *a.* agreeing, in agreement.
concordia, *n.f.* concord.
concretar, *v.t.* limit; make concrete *or* definite, substantiate.—*v.r.* confine oneself (***a***, to).
concreto, -ta, *a.* concrete; definite.—*n.m.* concrete; concretion.
concubina, *n.f.* concubine.
por concuerda, *adv. phr.* accurately (*copied*).
conculcar [A], *v.t.* trample on, violate.
concupiscencia, *n.f.* concupiscence.
concupiscente, *a.* concupiscent.
concurrencia, *n.f.* concurrence; gathering, assembly; competition.
concurrente, *a.* concurrent; competing.—*n.m.f.* competitor.
concurrido, -da, *a.* crowded, much frequented.
concurrir, *v.i.* concur; assemble; compete.
concurso, *n.m.* concourse; contest; show, exhibition.

concusión, *n.f.* concussion; extortion.
concusionario, -ria, *n.m.f.* extortioner.
concha, *n.f.* shell, conch, shellfish; (*theat.*) prompter's box.
conchabanza, *n.f.* comfort; (*fam.*) conniving.
conchabar, *v.t.* blend, join; (*S.A.*) employ, obtain a job.—*v.r.* (*fam.*) connive.
conchabo, *n.m.* (*S.A.*) employment (*esp. as servant*).
conchudo, -da, *a.* crustacean, shell-covered; (*fam.*) crafty, sly.
condado, *n.m.* county; earldom.
conde, *n.m.* count, earl; (*dial.*) foreman.
condecoración, *n.f.* decoration, honour.
condecorar, *v.t.* decorate, honour.
condena, *n.f.* (*jur.*) conviction, sentence.
condenacíon, *n.f.* condemnation; damnation.
condenado, -da, *a.* condemned, damned.—*n.m.f.* condemned prisoner; (*fam.*) blighter.
condenar, *v.t.* condemn, damn.
condensación, *n.f.* condensation.
condensador, -ra, *a.* condensing.—*n.m.* (*elec.*) condenser.
condensar, *v.t.*, *v.r.* condense.
condesa, *n.f.* countess.
condescendencia, *n.f.* condescendence, condescension.
condescender [2], *v.i.* acquiesce (*a*, to, in).
condescendiente, *a.* acquiescent.
condestable, *n.m.* constable.
condición, *n.f.* condition; ***a* — (*de*) *que*,** on condition that.
condicional, *a.* conditional.
condicionar, *v.t.* condition, adjust.—*v.i.* agree.
condigno, -na, *a.* appropriate (***de***, to).
condimentar, *v.t.* season, condiment.
condimento, *n.m.* seasoning, condiment.
condiscípulo, -la, *n.m.f.* fellow-student.
condolencia, *n.f.* condolence.
condoler [5], *v.r.* condole, sympathize (***de***, with).
condominio, *n.m.* condominium.
condonar, *v.t.* condone, pardon.
cóndor, *n.m.* condor.
conducción, *n.f.* conduction; driving; transport; piping.
conducir [15], *v.t.* guide, lead, conduct; drive; convey.—*v.r.* behave, conduct oneself.
conducta, *n.f.* conduct; guidance, management; conveyance.
conductividad, *n.f.* conductivity.
conductivo, -va, *a.* conductive.
conducto, *n.m.* conduit, duct; agency.
conductor, -ra, *a.* leading, guiding, conducting.—*n.m.f.* conductor, leader, guide; driver; (*S.A.*) bus conductor.
conectar, *v.t.* connect.
conectivo, -va, *a.* connective.
conejero, -ra, *a.* rabbit-hunting.—*n.f.* rabbit-warren *or* hutch; (*fam.*), dive, den.
conejillo de Indias, *n.m.* guinea-pig.
conejo, *n.m.* rabbit.
conejuno, -na, *a.* rel. to rabbits.—*n.f.* coney fur.
conexión, *n.f.* connexion.
conexionar, *v.t.* connect.
conexo, -xa, *a.* connected.
confabulación, *n.f.* confabulation.
confabular, *v.i.*, *v.r.* confabulate.

confección, *n.f.* ready-made suit; making concoction.
confederación, *n.f.* confederation, confederacy.
confederado, -da, *a.*, *n.m.f.* confederate.
confederar, *v.t.*, *v.r.* confederate.
conferencia, *n.f.* lecture; conference; (*t*... trunk call.
conferenciante, *n.m.f.* lecturer.
conferenciar, *v.i.* confer, discuss.
conferir [6], *v.t.* confer, bestow, discuss.
confesado, -da, *n.m.f.* penitent.
confesante, *n.m.f.* penitent, one who confesses (*guilt etc.*).
confesar [1], *v.t.*, *v.r.* confess.
confesión, *n.f.* confession.
confesor, *n.m.* confessor (*priest, believer*).
confeti, *n.m.* confetti.
confiable, *a.* reliable.
confiado, -da, *a.* trusting, confident.
confianza, *n.f.* confidence; informality; ***de* —**, reliable; intimate.
confianzudo, -da, *a.* (*fam.*) forward, t... informal.
confiar [L], *v.t.*, *v.i.* trust, confide (***en, de***, in).—*v.r.* rely (***en, de***, on).
confidencia, *n.f.* confidence, secret.
confidencial, *a.* confidential.
confidente, *a.* faithful; reliable.—*n.m.f.* confidant(e), informer.
configuración, *n.f.* configuration.
configurar, *v.t.* shape, form.
confín, *a.* bordering.—*n.m.* border, confine.
confinar, *v.t.* confine.—*v.i.* border (***con***, on).
confinidad, *n.f.* proximity.
confirmación, *n.f.* confirmation.
confirmador, -ra, confirmante, *a.* confirming, confirmatory.—*n.m.f.* confirmant, confirmer.
confirmar, *v.t.* confirm.
confiscación, *n.f.* confiscation.
confiscar [A], *v.t.* confiscate.
confitar, *v.t.* preserve, candy.
confite, *n.m.* preserve, toffee, candy.
confitería, *n.f.* confectionery.
confitura, *n.f.* jam, preserve.
conflagración, *n.f.* conflagration.
conflagrar, *v.t.* set ablaze.
conflicto, *n.m.* conflict, struggle, fight; anguish.
confluencia, *n.f.* confluence.
confluente, *a.* confluent.—*n.m.* confluence.
confluir [O], *v.i.* flow together, meet.
conformación, *n.f.* conformation.
conformar, *v.t.* comfort; invigorate.
conforme, *a.* agreeable, agreeing; fitting.—*adv.* accordingly.—*conj.* as, just as, according to what.
conformidad, *n.f.* conformity, agreement.
conformista, *a.*, *n.m.f.* conformist.
confort, *n.m.* comfort, ease.
confortable, *a.* comforting, comfortable.
confortación, *n.f.*, **confortamiento,** *n.m.* comfort; encouragement.
confortante, *a.* comforting; invigorating.—*n.m.* tonic; mitten.
confortar, *v.t.* comfort; invigorate.
confraternar, confraternizar [C], *v.i.* fraternize.
confrontación, *n.f.* comparison, checking; confrontation.

onfrontar, *v.t.* confront, compare.—*v.i.*, *v.r.* border (on); agree (*con*, with).
onfucio, *n.m.* Confucius.
nfundir, *v.t.* confuse, confound; mix (up). —*v.r.* get confused, make a mistake.
fusión, *n.f.* confusion.
fuso, -sa, *a.* confused.
futación, *n.f.* confutation.
futar, *v.t.* confute.
gelación, *n.f.* freezing, congealing.
gelante, *a.* freezing.
gelar, *v.t.*, *v.r.* freeze, congeal.
génere, *a.* congeneric.
genial, *a.* congenial.
geniar, *v.i.* be congenial; get on well *on*, with).
génito, -ta, *a.* congenital.
gerie, *n.f.* mass, congeries.
gestión, *n.f.* congestion.
gestionar, *v.t.* congest.
glomeración, *n.f.* conglomeration.
glomerar, *v.t.*, *v.r.* conglomerate.
ngo, *n.m.* the Congo.
igo, -ga, *a.*, *n.m.f.* Congolese.—*n.f.* conga.
goja, *n.f.* anguish, grief.
gojoso, -sa, *a.* grievous, anguished.
ngoleño, -ña, congolés, -lesa, *a.*, *n.m.f.* Congolese.
ngraciamiento, *n.m.* ingratiation.
ngraciar, *v.t.* win over, ingratiate.
ngratulación, *n.f.* congratulation.
ngratular, *v.t.* congratulate (*de*, *por*, on). —*v.r.* rejoice (*de*, at).
ongratulatorio, -ria, *a.* congratulatory.
ongregación, *n.f.* congregation.
congregar [B], *v.t.*, *v.r.* congregate.
congresal, *n.m.* (*S.A.*) [CONGRESISTA].
congresional, *a.* congressional.
congresista, *n.m.f.* member of a congress.
congreso, *n.m.* congress.
congrio, *n.m.* conger eel; (*fam.*) mutt, fool.
congruencia, *n.f.* congruence, congruity.
congruente, *a.* congruent.
congruo, -rua, *a.* congruous.
cónico, -ca, *a.* conical, conic.
conífero, -ra, *a.* coniferous.—*n.f.* conifer.
conjetura, *n.f.* conjecture.
conjectural, *a.* conjectural.
conjecturar, *v.t.* conjecture, surmise.
conjugación, *n.f.* conjugation.
conjugar [B], *v.t.* conjugate.
conjunción, *n.f.* conjunction.
conjunctivo, -va, *a.* conjunctive.
conjunto, -ta, *a.* conjunct, allied.—*n.m.* entirety, whole; *en —*, as a whole.
conjura, conjuración, *n.f.* conspiracy.
conjurado, -da, *n.m.f.* conspirator.
conjurar, *v.t.* entreat, conjure; exorcize.—*v.i.* *v.r.* conspire.
conjuro, *n.m.* conjuration, entreaty.
conllevar, *v.t.* share (*burden*); bear with, suffer.
conmemoración, *n.f.* commemoration.
conmemorar, *v.t.* commemorate.
conmemorativo, -va, *a.* commemorative.
conmensurable, *a.* commensurable, commensurate.
conmigo, *adv.* with me.
conminar, *v.t.* threaten.
conmiseración, *n.f.* commiseration.
conmisto, -ta, *a.* mingled, (*obs.*) commixed.
conmoción, *n.f.* commotion.
conmovedor, -ra, *a.* moving, touching.
conmover [5], *v.t.* move, touch.—*v.r.* be moved.
conmutable, *a.* commutable.
conmutación, *n.f.* commutation.
conmutar, *v.t.* commute.
conmutatriz, *n.f.* (*elec.*) converter (*of A.C. or D.C.*).
connaturalizar [C], *v.r.* become acclimatized.
connivencia, *n.f.* connivance.
connivente, *a.* conniving.
connotación, *n.f.* connotation.
connotar, *v.t.* connote.
cono, *n.m.* cone.
conocedor, -ra, *a.* knowledgeable, well-informed, expert.—*n.m.f.* connoisseur, expert.
conocencia, *n.f.* (*jur.*) statement, confession.
conocer [9], *v.t.* know, be acquainted with; get to know; (*jur.*) try (*a case*).—*v.i.* know (*en*, *de*, about).
conocible, *a.* knowable.
conocido, -da, *a.* familiar; well-known.—*n.m.f.* acquaintance.
conocimiento, *n.m.* knowledge; consciousness; (*com.*) bill of lading; acquaintance; (*jur.*) substantiation.
conque, *conj.*, *adv.* so that, so then, then.—*n.m.* (*fam.*) terms, condition; (*S.A.*) wherewithal.
conquista, *n.f.* conquest.
conquistador, *n.m.* conqueror; conquistador; (*fam.*) lady-killer.
conquistar, *v.t.* conquer; capture; win over gain.
consabido, -da, *a.* aforesaid; well-known.
consagración, *n.f.* consecration.
consagrar, *v.t.* consecrate, dedicate.
consanguíneo, -nea, *a.* consanguineous.
consciente, *a.* conscious, aware; conscientious.
conscripción, *n.f.* conscription, (*U.S.*) draft.
conscripto, *n.m.* conscript, (*U.S.*) draftee.
consecución, *n.f.* acquisition.
consecuencia, *n.f.* consequence.
consecuente, *a.* consequent, coherent.
consecutivo, -va, *a.* consecutive.
conseguir [8G], *v.t.* obtain, attain; bring about.—*v.i.* manage, succeed.
conseja, *n.f.* yarn, tale.
consejero, -ra, *a.* advisory.—*n.m.f.* counsellor; councillor.
consejo, *n.m.* advice, counsel; council, board; *— de guerra*, court martial.
consenso, *n.m.* assent; consensus.
consentido, -da, *a.* spoiled (*child*); complaisant (*husband*); (*S.A.*) haughty.
consentimiento, *n.m.* consent.
consentir [6], *v.t.* permit, allow; pamper.—*v.i.* consent (*en*, to); believe.—*v.r.* come apart; (*S.A.*) be haughty.
conserje, *n.m.* concierge.
conserjería, *n.f.* porter's desk *or* room *or* position.
conserva (1), *n.f.* preserves; jam; pickles; ***conservas alimenticias***, tinned food.
conserva (2), *n.f.* (*naut.*) convoy.
conservación, *n.f.* maintenance; preservation, conservation.
conservador, -ra, *a.* preservative; (*pol.*) conservative.—*n.m.f.* conservative, (*pol.*) Conservative.—*n.m.* curator.
conservaduría, *n.f.* curatorship.

conservar, *v.t.* conserve, preserve, keep, save. —*v.r.* look after oneself; keep, last well.
conservatismo, *n.m.* conservatism.
conservatorio, -ria, *a., n.m.* conservatory.
conservería, *n.f.* canning, preserving; canning factory.
considerable, *a.* considerable.
consideración, *n.f.* consideration; importance; regard.
considerado, -da, *a.* considerate; considered; esteemed.
considerar, *v.t.* consider.
consigna, *n.f.* (*mil.*) order, charge; (*rail.*) left-luggage office.
consignación, *n.f.* consignment; apportionment.
consignar, *v.t.* consign; apportion; state; deliver.
consignatorio, -ria, *n.m.f.* (*com.*) consignee.
consigo, *adv.* with him, her, it, them; with you; with himself, herself *etc.*
consiguiente, *a.* consequent, consequential; ***por* —,** consequently.
consistencia, *n.f.* consistency.
consistente, *a.* consistent; consisting (***en,*** of, in).
consistir, *v.i.* consist (***en,*** of, in).
consistorio, *n.m.* consistory, council.
consola, *n.f.* console.
consolación, *n.f.* consolation.
consolador, -ra, *a.* consoling.—*n.m.f.* consoler.
consolar [4], *v.t.* console, comfort.
consolidación, *n.f.* consolidation.
consolidados, *n.m.pl.* consols.
consolidar, *v.t., v.r.* consolidate.
consonancia, *n.f.* consonance, rhyme; harmony.
consonantado, -da, *a.* rhymed.
consonante, *a.* consonant; rhyming.—*n.m.* rhyme word.—*n.f.* consonant.
consonántico, -ca, *a.* consonantal.
consonar [4], *v.t.* rhyme; harmonize.
consorcio, *n.m.* consortium.
consorte, *n.m.f.* consort; partner; accomplice.
conspicuo, -cua, *a.* outstanding; conspicuous.
conspiración, *n.f.* conspiracy.
conspirado, *n.m.*, **conspirador, -ra,** *n.m.f.* conspirator.
conspirar, *v.i.* conspire.
constancia, *n.f.* constancy; proof, evidence.
constante, *a., n.f.* (*math.*) constant.
constar, *v.i.* be clear, certain, right; **— *de*** consist of.
constatación, *n.f.* proof, proving.
constatar, *v.t.* prove, establish.
constelación, *n.f.* constellation; climate.
constelar, *v.t.* spangle.
consternación, *n.f.* consternation.
consternar, *v.t.* distress, dismay.
constipado, *n.m.* head cold.
constipar, *v.r.* catch cold; ***estar constipado,*** have a cold.
constitución, *n.f.* constitution.
constitucional, *a.* constitutional.
constituir [O], *v.t.* constitute, establish; force into (***en***).—*v.r.* set oneself up, be established (***en, por,*** as).
constituyente, *a., n.m.* (*pol. etc.*) constituent.
constreñimiento, *n.m.* constraint; (*med.*) constipation.
constreñir [8K], *v.t.* constrain; (*med.*) constipate.
constricción, *n.f.* constriction.
construcción, *n.f.* construction, structure.
constructivo, -va, *a.* constructive.
constructor, -ra, *a.* constructing.—*n.m.* constructor; builder.
construir [O], *v.t.* construct.
consuelo, *n.m.* consolation, comfort; ***sin* —** to excess, inconsolably.
consueta, *n.m.* (*theat.*) prompter.
cónsul, *n.m.* consul.
consulado, *n.m.* consulate; consulship.
consular, *a.* consular.
consulta, consultación, *n.f.* consultation.
consultar, *v.t.* consult; discuss; advise.
consultivo, -va, *a.* consultative.
consultor, -ra, *a.* consulting.—*n.m.f.* consultant.
consultorio, *n.m.* advice bureau; clinic.
consumación, *n.f.* consummation.
consumar, *v.t.* consummate.
consumición, *n.f.* consumption; drink, food.
consumir, *v.t.* consume; take communion; (*fam.*) vex, wear down.—*v.r.* pine, waste away; be consumed.
consumo, *n.m.* consumption; consumers.—*pl.* octroi, excise.
consunción, *n.f.* (*med. etc.*) consumption.
de consuno, *adv. phr.* jointly, in accord.
consuntivo, -va, *a.* consumptive.
contabilidad, *n.f.* accountancy, book-keeping.
contabilista, *n.m.* accountant.
contable, *n.m.f.* book-keeper.
contacto, *n.m.* contact.
contadero, -ra, *a.* countable, to be counted. —*n.m.* turnstile.
contado, -da, *a.* scarce, infrequent; (*obs.*) famous; ***al* —,** for cash; ***por de* —,** of course.
contador, *n.m.* counter, meter; auditor; till; **— *de Geiger,*** Geiger counter.
contaduría, *n.f.* accountancy; accountant's office; (*theat.*) box office; treasury.
contagiar, *v.t.* infect.—*v.r.* become infected (***de,*** with).
contagio, *n.m.* contagion.
contagioso, -sa, *a.* contagious.
contaminación, *n.f.* contamination.
contaminar, *v.t.* contaminate; infringe; corrupt.
contante, *a.* ready (*cash*); (*fam.*) ***dinero* — *y sonante,*** ready cash.
contar [4], *v.t.* count; tell, narrate; debit; consider; **— *con,*** count on, rely on.
contemplación, *n.f.* contemplation.
contemplar, *v.t.* contemplate; be lenient towards.
contemplativo, -va, *a.* contemplative; condescending.
contemporáneo, -nea, *a., n.m.f.* contemporary.
contención, *n.f.* contention, strife.
contencioso, -sa, *a.* contentious.
contender [2], *v.i.* contend.
contendiente, *n.m.* contender.
contener [33], *v.t.* contain.
contenido, -da, *a.* restrained.—*n.m.* contents.
contenta, *n.f.* gift, treat; (*com.*) endorsement.
contentadizo, -za, *a.* easy to please; ***mal* —,** hard to please.
contentamiento, *n.m.* contentment.

contentar, *v.t.* content, please.—*v.r.* be content (***de, con,*** with).
contento, -ta, *a.* glad, content.—*n.m.* contentment.
contera, *n.f.* metal tip; refrain; bell; (*fam.*) the end.
conterráneo, -nea, *a., n.m.f.* person *or* thing from the same country *or* region.
contestable, *a.* answerable.
contestación, *n.f.* answer, reply; dispute.
contestar, *v.t.* answer; confirm.—*v.i.* reply (***a,*** to); agree.
contexto, *n.m.* context; interweaving.
contienda, *n.f.* dispute, fight.
contigo, *adv.* with you, with thee.
contiguo, -gua, *a.* contiguous.
continental, *a., n.m.f.* continental.
continente, *a.* continent.—*n.m.* container; continent; countenance.
contingencia, *n.f.* contingency.
contingente, *a.* contingent.—*n.m.* contingent; quota; contingency.
contingible, *a.* possible.
continuación, *n.f.* continuation; ***a —,*** below, as follows.
continuadamente, *adv.* continuously; continually.
continuar [M], *v.t.* continue.—*v.i., v.r.* be adjacent (***con,*** to); ***continuará,*** to be continued.
continuidad, *n.f.* continuity.
continuo, -nua, *a.* continual; continuous; perservering; ***de —,*** continuously.
contómetro, *n.m.* comptometer.
contonear, *v.r.* strut, swagger, waddle.
contoneo, *n.m.* strut, swagger, waddle.
contorcer [5D], *v.r.* writhe.
contorción, *n.f.* writhing, contortion.
contorno, *n.m.* outline; contour; ***en —,*** round about.—*pl.* environs.
contorsión, *n.f.* contortion.
contorsionista, *n.m.f.* contortionist.
contra, *n.m.* contra, con.—*n.f.* (*fam.*) bother, pest; (*S.A.*) antidote; ***llevar la — a,*** (*fam.*) go against.—*prep.* against; facing.—*prefix.* counter-, contra-.
contraalmirante, *n.m.* rear-admiral.
contraatacar [A], *v.t., v.i.* counter-attack.
contraataque, *n.m.* counter-attack.
contrabajo, *n.m.* (*mus.*) double bass.
contrabalancear, *v.t.* counterbalance.
contrabalanza, *n.f.* counterbalance, counterpoise.
contrabandear, *v.i.* smuggle.
contrabandista, *n.m.f.* smuggler.
contrabando, *n.m.* contraband; smuggling.
contrabarrera, *n.f.* (*taur.*) second row seats.
contracción, *n.f.* contraction.
contracifra, *n.f.* cypher-key.
contráctil, *a.* contractile.
contracto, -ta, *a.* contracted.
contractual, *a.* contractual.
contradecir [17], *v.t.* contradict.
contradicción, *n.f.* contradiction.
contradictorio, -ria, *a.* contradictory.
contradicho [CONTRADECIR].
contraer [34], *v.t.* contract; condense.—*v.r.* contract.
contraespionaje, *n.m.* counterespionage.
contrafigura, *n.f.* counterpart.
contrafuerte, *n.m.* girth strap; stiffener; buttress.
contrahacedor, -ra, *a.* counterfeiting.—*n.m.f.* counterfeiter; imitator.
contrahacer [20], *v.t.* counterfeit; imitate; feign.
contrahaz, *n.f.* (*pl.* **-aces**) reverse side.
contrahecho [CONTRAHACER].
contrahechura, *n.f.* counterfeit, forgery.
a contrahilo, *adv. phr.* on the cross, against the grain.
contraigo [CONTRAER].
contralto, *n.m.f.* contralto.
contraluz, *n.f.* view (*facing the light*); ***a —,*** against the light.
contramaestre, *n.m.* overseer; (*naut.*) petty officer, bosun.
contramandar, *v.t.* countermand.
a contramano, *adv. phr.* in the wrong direction.
contramarcha, *n.f.* countermarch; reverse.
contramarchar, *v.i.* countermarch; reverse.
contranatural, *a.* unnatural, against nature.
a contrapelo, *adv. phr.* against the (*lie of the*) hair; (*fig.*) against the grain.
contrapesar, *v.t.* counterbalance.
contrapeso, *n.m.* counterbalance; ***puente de —,*** cantilever bridge.
contraponer [25], *v.t.* compare; oppose.
contraposición, *n.f.* contraposition, contrast.
contraproducente, *a.* self-defeating.
contrapuerta, *n.f.* screen door, storm door.
contrapuesto [CONTRAPONER].
contrapunto, *n.m.* counterpoint; sarcasm.
contrapuse [CONTRAPONER].
contrariar [L], *v.t.* oppose, run counter to; disappoint, annoy.
contrariedad, *n.f.* obstacle; contrariness; opposition.
contrario, -ria, *a.* contrary, opposite.—*n.m.f.* opponent, adversary.—*n.m.* impediment; contradiction; ***al —*** or ***por (el) —,*** on the contrary; ***llevar la contraria a,*** (*fam.*) go against, oppose.
Contrarreforma, *n.f.* (*hist.*) Counter-Reformation.
contrarrestar, *v.t.* counteract, resist.
contrarrevolución, *n.f.* counterrevolution.
contrasentido, *n.m.* misinterpretation; contradiction.
contraseña, *n.f.* countersign; counterfoil; ticket.
contrastar, *v.t.* resist; assay.—*v.i.* resist; contrast.
contraste, *n.m.* contrast; resistance; assay, assaying; hall-mark.
contrata, *n.f.* contract.
contratante, *a.* contracting.—*n.m.f.* contractor.
contratar, *v.t.* engage, hire; trade.
contratiempo, *n.m.* contretemps.
contratista, *n.m.* contractor.
contrato, *n.m.* contract.
contravención, *n.f.* contravention.
contraveneno, *n.m.* antidote.
contravenir [36], *v.i.* contravene, violate (***a***).
contraventana, *n.f.* shutter.
contraventor, -ra, *a.* contravening.—*n.m.f.* contravener.
contravine [CONTRAVENIR].
contrayente, *a., n.m.f.* contracting party.
contrecho, -cha, *a.* crippled.
contribución, *n.f.* contribution; tax.
contribuir [O], *v.t., v.i.* contribute.

contributivo, -va, *a.* contributive; tax, rel. to taxes.
contribuyente, *n.m.f.* contributor; taxpayer.
contrición, *n.f.* contrition.
contrincante, *n.m.* rival, competitor.
contristar, *v.t.* sadden.
contrito, -ta, *a.* contrite.
control, *n.m.* control; inspection, supervision.
controlar, *v.t.* control; supervise, inspect.
controversia, *n.f.* controversy.
controvertir [6], *v.t.* controvert, call in question.
contumacia, *n.f.* contumacy; (*jur.*) contempt.
contumaz, *a.* (*pl.* **-aces**) contumacious; (*med.*) disease-carrying; (*jur.*) guilty of contempt.
contumelia, *n.f.* contumely.
contundente, *a.* bruising, blunt; forceful.
contundir, *v.t.* bruise, contuse.
conturbación, *n.f.* anxiety, perturbation.
conturbar, *v.t.* perturb, disquiet.
contusión, *n.f.* contusion.
contuso, -sa, *a.* contused, bruised.
contuve [CONTENER].
convalecencia, *n.f.* convalescence.
convalecer [9], *v.i.* convalesce, recover.
convaleciente, *a.*, *n.m.f.* convalescent.
convalidar, *v.t.* ratify, confirm.
convección, *n.f.* convection.
convecino, -na, *a.* neighbouring.—*n.m.f.* next-door neighbour.
convencer [D], *v.t.* convince.
convención, *n.f.* convention.
convencional, *a.* conventional.
conveniencia, *n.f.* conformity; settlement; suitability; convenience, advantage.—*pl.* wealth; proprieties, social conventions.
convenienciero, -ra, *a.* self-centred, selfish.
conveniente, *a.* appropriate; convenient, advantageous.
convenio, *n.m.* pact; settlement.
convenir [36], *v.i.* be appropriate; suit, be advantageous *or* important; agree (*en*, to).—*v.r.* come to an agreement; ***conviene a saber***, that is to say, namely.
conventillo, *n.m.* (*S.A.*) tenement house.
convento, *n.m.* convent; monastery.
convergencia, *n.f.* convergence; concurrence.
convergente, *a.* convergent.
converger, convergir [E], *v.i.* converge; concur.
conversable, *a.* sociable.
conversación, *n.f.* conversation.
conversador, -ra, *a.* conversing.—*n.m.f.* conversationalist.
conversar, *v.i.* converse; (*mil.*) wheel about.
conversión, *n.f.* conversion.
converso, -sa, *a.* converted.—*n.m.f.* convert; lay brother.
convertibilidad, *n.f.* convertibility.
convertible, *a.* convertible.
convertir [6], *v.t.* convert.—*v.r.* be converted; turn, change.
convexidad, *n.f.* convexity.
convexo, -xa, *a.* convex.
convicción, *n.f.* conviction.
convicto, -ta, *a.* convicted.—*n.m.f.* convict.
convidado, -da, *n.m.f.* guest.
convidar, *v.t.* invite; treat.—*v.r.* offer one's services.
convincente, *a.* convincing.
convine [CONVENIR].
convite, *n.m.* invitation; treat; banquet.
convivencia, *n.f.* coexistence; life together.
convivir, *v.i.* coexist, live together.
convocación, *n.f.* convocation.
convocar [A], *v.t.* convoke.
convocatorio, -ria, *a.* convoking, summoning.—*n.f.* summons, call.
convolución, *n.f.* convolution.
convoy, *n.m.* convoy; cruet set; (*fam.*) retinue; (*S.A.*) train.
convoyar, *v.t.* convoy.
convulsión, *n.f.* convulsion.
convulsionar, *v.t.* convulse.
convulsivo, -va, *a.* convulsive.
convulso, -sa, *a.* convulsed.
conyugal, *a.* conjugal.
cónyuge, *n.m.f.* spouse.
coñac, *n.m.* cognac, brandy.
cooperación, *n.f.* co-operation.
cooperar, *v.i.* co-operate.
cooperativo, -va, *a.*, *n.f.* co-operative.
coordinación, *n.f.* co-ordination.
coordinar, *v.t.* co-ordinate.
copa, *n.f.* wine- *or* spirit-glass, goblet; tree-top; crown (*of hat*); (*sport, fig.*) cup.
copar, *v.t.* take by surprise; (*fam.*) sweep (*election*).
coparticipación, *n.f.* copartnership.
copartícipe, *n.m.f.* copartner.
copero, *n.m.* cup-bearer; cocktail cabinet.
copeta, *n.f.* small wine glass.
copete, *n.m.* forelock; tuft; crest; top; (*fig.*) haughtiness; ***de alto* —**, high-ranking, aristocratic.
copetudo, -da, *a.* crested, tufted; (*fig.*) snobbish, haughty.
copia (1), *n.f.* plenty, abundance.
copia (2), *n.f.* copy.
copiante, *n.m.f.* copier, copyist.
copiar, *v.t.* copy.
copioso, -sa, *a.* copious.
copista, *n.m.f.* copyist.
copla, *n.f.* couplet; stanza; popular song; ***coplas de ciego***, doggerel.
coplero, -ra, coplista, *n.m.f.* ballad-monger; poetaster.
copo, *n.m.* skein; (snow)flake.
coposo, -sa, *a.* bushy; woolly.
copra, *n.f.* copra.
cóptico, -ca, *a.* Coptic.
copto, -ta, *a.* Coptic.—*n.m.f.* Copt.
cópula, *n.f.* copula.
copulativo, -va, *a.*, *n.f.* copulative.
coque, *n.m.* coke.
coqueluche, *n.f.* whooping cough.
coquera, *n.f.* cavity; coke-scuttle.
coqueta, *a.* coquettish.—*n.f.* coquette, flirt; dressing-table.
coquetear, *v.i.* flirt, be coquettish.
coquetería, *n.f.* flirtation; flirtatiousness; coquetry; affectation; (*S.A.*) good taste.
coquetismo, *n.m.* coquetry.
coquetón, -tona, *a.* coquettish.—*n.m.* lady-killer.
coquito, *n.m.* amusing grimace.
coraje, *n.m.* anger; mettle.
corajina, *n.f.* (*fam.*) tantrum, outburst.
corajudo, -da, *a.* (*fam.*) bad-tempered.
coral (1), *a.* choral.—*n.m.* chorale.
coral (2), *n.m.* coral.—*pl.* coral beads.
Corán, *n.m.* Koran.

coránico, -ca, *a.* Koranic.
coraza, *n.f.* cuirass; armour.
corazón, *n.m.* heart; core; (*fig.*) courage; ***de* —,** sincerely; ***hacer de tripas* —,** find courage in fear.
corazonada, *n.f.* impulse; hunch; (*fam.*) guts.
corbata, *n.f.* tie, cravat.
corbatín, *n.m.* bow-tie.
corbeta, *n.f.* (*naut.*) corvette; ***capitán de* —,** lieutenant commander.
Córcega, *n.f.* Corsica.
corcel, *n.m.* charger, steed.
corcova, *n.m.* hump, hunch.
corcovado, -da, *a.* hunch-backed.—*n.m.f.* hunchback.
corcovar, *v.t.* bend.
corcovear, *v.i.* buck; (*S.A.*) grumble; (*C.A.*) be afraid.
corcovo, *n.m.* buck, bucking; (*fam.*) crookedness.
corcusir, *v.t.* (*fam.*) mend roughly.
corcha, *n.f.* raw cork.
corcheta, *n.f.* eye (*of fastening*).
corchete, *n.m.* hook (*of fastening*); fastener; square bracket [ ]; (*obs.*) constable.
corcho, *n.m.* cork; cork, stopper.
corchoso, -sa, *a.* corky.
cordaje, *n.m.* strings (*of guitar*); (*naut.*) rigging.
cordal, *n.m.* (*mus.*) string-bar; wisdom tooth.
cordel, *n.m.* cord; ***a* —,** in a straight line.
cordelazo, *n.m.* lash *or* blow with rope.
cordelería, *n.f.* cordmaking, cordage; (*naut.*) rigging.
cordería, *n.f.* cordage.
corderino, -na, *a.* rel. to lambs.—*n.f.* lambskin.
cordero, -ra, *n.m.f.* lamb.
cordial, *a.*, *n.m.* cordial.
cordialidad, *n.f.* cordiality.
cordillera, *n.f.* chain *or* range of mountains.
cordita, *n.f.* cordite.
Córdoba, *n.f.* Cordova.
cordobán, *n.m.* cordovan (*leather*).
cordobés, -besa, *a.*, *n.m.f.* Cordovan.
cordón, *n.m.* cord; cordon; strand; lace.—*pl.* aiguillettes.
cordoncillo, *n.m.* braid; milled edge.
cordura, *n.f.* wisdom, good sense.
Corea, *n.f.* Korea.
coreano, -na, *a.*, *n.m.f.* Korean.
corear, *v.t.*, *v.i.* chorus; choir.
coreografía, *n.f.* choreography.
coreógrafo, *n.m.* choreographer.
corezuelo, *n.m.* piglet; crackling.
Corinto, *n.f.* Corinth; ***pasa de* —,** currant.
corista, *n.m.f.* chorister.—*n.f.* (*theat.*) chorus girl.
corladura, *n.f.* gold varnish.
corma, *n.f.* wooden stocks; (*fig.*) hindrance.
cormorán, *n.m.* (*orn.*) cormorant.
cornada, *n.f.* horn thrust *or* wound.
cornadura, cornamenta, *n.f.* horns, antlers.
cornamusa, *n.f.* bagpipes; brass horn.
córnea, *n.f.* cornea.
corneal, *a.* corneal.
cornear, *v.t.* butt, gore.
corneja, *n.f.* crow; scops owl.
córneo, -nea, *a.* horny.
córner, *n.m.* corner (*in football*).
corneta, *n.f.* (*mus.*) cornet; bugle; pennant.—*n.m.* bugler.
cornetilla, *n.f.* hot pepper.
cornezuelo, *n.m.* (*bot.*) ergot.
córnico, -ca, *a.* Cornish.
cornisa, *n.f.* cornice.
corno, *n.m.* dogwood; (*mus.*) horn.
Cornualles, *n.m.* Cornwall.
cornucopia, *n.f.* cornucopia.
cornudo, -da, *a.* horned.—*a.m.*, *n.m.* cuckold.
cornúpeta, cornupeto, *a.m.* butting.—*n.m.* (*fam.*) bull.
coro (1), *n.m.* choir; chorus; ***hacer* — *a*,** echo, second; ***a coros*,** alternately.
coro (2), ***de* —,** by heart.
corolario, *n.m.* corollary.
corona, *n.f.* crown; tonsure; corona; wreath; coronet; ***ceñir(se) la* —,** come to the throne.
coronación, *n.f.* coronation; crowning.
coronamiento, *n.m.* completion, termination.
coronar, *v.t.* crown; cap; complete.
coronel, *n.m.* colonel; (*aer.*) group captain.
coronela, *n.f.* colonel's wife.
coronilla, *n.f.* crown (*of the head*); ***estar hasta la* — (*de*),** (*fam.*) be fed up (with).
corotos, *n.m.pl.* (*S.A.*) gear, tackle.
coroza, *n.f.* conical cap (*for criminals*); peasant cap.
corpa(n)chón, *n.m.* (*fam.*) big carcass; fowl's carcass.
corpazo, *n.m.* (*fam.*) big body.
corpecico, corpiño, *n.m.* small body; bodice.
corporación, *n.f.* corporation.
corporal, *a.* corporal, bodily.
corporativo, -va, *a.* corporat(iv)e.
corpóreo, -ea, *a.* corporeal.
corpulencia, *n.f.* corpulence.
corpulento, -ta, *a.* corpulent.
Corpus, *n.m.* Corpus Christi.
corpúsculo, *n.m.* corpuscle; particle.
corral, *n.m.* yard, farm yard; (*obs.*) open-air theatre; corral; ***hacer corrales*,** (*fam.*) play truant.
correa, *n.f.* belt, strap; leatheriness; ***besar la* —,** eat humble pie; ***tiene mucha* —,** (*fam.*) he can take it! **— *de seguridad*,** safety belt.
correcalles, *n.m. inv.* idler, loafer.
corrección, *n.f.* correction; correctness.
correccional, *a.* correctional.—*n.m.* reformatory.
correctivo, -va, *a.*, *n.m.* corrective.
correcto, -ta, *a.* correct.
corrector, -ra, *a.* correcting.—*n.m.f.* corrector; proof-reader.
corredera (1), *n.f.* track, rail; runner; slide valve; (*naut.*) log line; (*S.A.*) rapids; ***de* —,** sliding (*door etc.*).
corredera (2), *n.f.* (*ent.*) cockroach.
corredizo, -za, *a.* running (*knot*), sliding.
corredor, -ra, *a.* running.—*n.m.f.* runner.—*n.m.* corridor; gallery; (*com.*) broker; (*mil. obs.*) scout.
corredura, *n.f.* overflow.
corregidor, -ra, *a.* correcting.—*n.m.* (*obs.*) corregidor, Spanish magistrate.
corregir [8E], *v.t.* correct.
correlación, *n.f.* correlation.
correlacionar, *v.t.* correlate.
correlativo, -va, *a.*, *n.m.* correlative.
correntío, -tía, *a.* runny, running; (*fig.*) easy going.

correo, *n.m.* post, mail; post office; mail train; courier; — ***aéreo,*** airmail; ***echar al —,*** post.
correón, *n.m.* large strap.
correoso, -sa, *a.* leathery.
correr, *v.t.* run; travel over; chase; overrun; slide, draw; shame, confuse; (*taur.*) fight; auction; (*fam.*) pinch, steal.—*v.i.* run; flow; pass; be current; be valid; ***correrla,*** (*fam.*) spend a night on the town; ***a todo —,*** at full speed; ***que corre,*** current.—*v.r.* run, drip; (*fam.*) overstep the mark; (*fam.*) become embarrassed; slide, slip; turn.
correría, *n.f.* incursion; excursion.
correspondencia, *n.f.* correspondence; harmony; connexion; intercourse.
corresponder, *v.i.* correspond; communicate; — ***a,*** return, reciprocate; concern, be the duty of.
correspondiente, *a.* corresponding.—*n.m.f.* correspondent.
corresponsal, *n.m.f.* (*press, com.*) correspondent.
corretear, *v.t.* (*S.A.*) chase, pester.—*v.i.* (*fam.*) gad about, race around.
correve(i)dile, *n.m.f.* (*fam.*) gossip, tell-tale.
corrido, -da, *a.* surplus; cursive; fluent; experienced; continuous; (*fam.*) flummoxed.—*n.m.* lean-to; ***de —,*** fluently, without pause.—*n.f.* bullfight; run, race; (*S.A.*) binge; ***de corrida,*** without pausing.
corriente, *a.* running, flowing; current; ordinary, common; normal.—*n.m.* current month; ***al — de,*** posted on, up to date with. —*n.f.* current; stream; draught.—*interj.* fine! all right!
corrillo, *n.m.* clique, coterie.
corrimiento, *n.m.* running; flow; abashment; landslide.
corrincho, *n.m.* bunch of no-goods, riff-raff.
corro, *n.m.* group, circle; ring, space.
corroboración, *n.f.* corroboration.
corroborar, *v.t.* corroborate; fortify.
corroborativo, -va, *a.* corroborative.
corroer [29], *v.t.* corrode, eat away.
corromper, *v.t.* corrupt; rot; (*fam.*) bother.
corrosión, *n.f.* corrosion.
corrosivo, -va, *a., n.m.* corrosive.
corrugación, *n.f.* contraction; corrugation.
corrumpente, *a.* corrupting; (*fam.*) bothersome.
corrupción, *n.f.* corruption; rotting.
corruptela, *n.f.* corruption; abuse.
corruptible, *a.* corruptible.
corrusco, *n.m.* (*fam.*) chunk of bread, crust.
corsario, -ria, *a.* (*naut.*) privateering.—*n.m.* privateer, pirate.
corsé, *n.m.* corset.
corsear, *v.i.* (*naut.*) privateer.
corso, -sa, *a., n.m.f.* Corsican.—*n.m.* privateering; (*S.A.*) promenade.
corta, *n.f.* felling, cutting.
cortacorriente, *n.m.* (*elec.*) switch.
cortada, *n.f.* (*S.A.*) cut; haircut.
cortado, -da, *a.* proportioned; jerky (*style*); with a little milk (*coffee*); (*S.A.*) broke, hard up.—*n.m.* caper, leap; small glass.
cortador, -ra, *a.* cutting.—*n.m.* cutter (*person*); butcher.—*n.f.* cutter; slicer; mower.
cortadura, *n.f.* cutting; cut, gash.—*pl.* trimmings, cuttings.
cortafuego, *n.m.* fire barrier.
cortalápices, *n.m. inv.* pencil-sharpener.
cortante, *a.* cutting, sharp.—*n.m.* butcher's knife.
cortapicos, *n.m. inv.* (*ent.*) earwig; — ***y callares,*** (*fam.*) less lip! (*to children*).
cortaplumas, *n.m. inv.* penknife.
cortar, *v.t.* cut; cut off, out, down, up; (*elec.*) switch off; — ***de vestir,*** (*fam.*) backbite.—*v.r.* become speechless; chap; curdle.
cortavidrios, *n.m. inv.* glass cutter.
cortaviento, *n.m.* windshield.
la Corte, *n.f.* Madrid.—*pl.* Spanish Parliament.
corte (1), *n.m.* cut; cutting; cutting edge; (*elec.*) break; ***darse —,*** (*S.A.*) put on airs.
corte (2), *n.f.* court, royal household; (*S.A.*) law court; ***hacer la — a,*** pay court to, court.
cortedad, *n.f.* shortness; scantiness; timidity.
cortejar, *v.t.* court; escort.
cortejo, *n.m.* courtship; entourage; cortège; (*fam.*) beau, lover.
cortero, *n.m.* (*S.A.*) day labourer.
cortés, *a.* courteous, polite.
cortesanía, *n.f.* courtliness; flattery.
cortesano, -na, *a.* courtly.—*n.m.* courtier.—*n.f.* courtesan.
cortesía, *n.f.* courtesy; bow, curtsy.
corteza, *n.f.* bark; peel, rind; crust; coarseness; (*orn.*) sand grouse.
cortezudo, -da, *a.* barky, crusty; boorish, coarse.
cortical, *a.* cortical.
cortijo, *n.m.* farm, farmhouse.
cortil, *n.m.* farmyard.
cortina, *n.f.* curtain; screen; ***correr la —,*** open *or* close the curtain.
cortinaje, *n.m.* curtaining.
cortinilla, *n.f.* window netting; curtain.
cortisona, *n.f.*, **cortisono,** *n.m.* cortisone.
corto, -ta, *a.* short; scanty; weak; shy; wanting; — ***de oído,*** hard of hearing; — ***de vista,*** short-sighted; ***corta edad,*** early childhood.
cortocircuito, *n.m.* (*elec.*) short circuit.
la Coruña, *n.f.* Corunna
coruñes, -sa, *a.* rel. to Corunna.—*n.m.f.* native of Corunna.
coruscar [A], *v.i.* (*poet.*) glow, shine.
corvadura, *n.f.* curvature, bend.
corvejón, *n.m.* hock; spur (*of cock*).
córvidos, *n.m.pl.* (*orn.*) Corvidae.
corvino, -na, *a.* corvine, raven-like.
corvo, -va, *a.* curved, arched.—*n.m.* hook.
corzo, -za, *n m f.* roe-deer, fallow-deer.
cosa, *n.f.* thing; ***a — hecha,*** as good as done; ***como si tal —,*** (*fam.*) as if nothing had happened; — ***de,*** a matter of, about; — ***que,*** (*S.A.*) so that, in order that.
cosaco, -ca, *a., n.m.f.* Cossack.
coscarse, *v.r.* (*fam.*) shrug.
coscoja, *n.f.* kermes oak.
coscojita, *n.f.* hop-scotch.
coscón, -cona, *a.* (*fam.*) crafty, sly.
coscorrón, *n.m.* bump (*on the head*), bruise.
cosecante, *n.f.* (*math.*) cosecant.
cosecha, *n.f.* harvest, crop; ***de su —,*** (*fam.*) out of his own head.
cosechar, *v.t.* harvest, reap.
cosechero, -ra, *n.m.f.* harvester.
coseno, *n.m.* (*math.*) cosine.
coser, *v.t.* sew; join closely.

cosicosa, *n.f.* riddle, puzzle.
cosido, *n.m.* sewing.
cosmético, -ca, *a., n.m.* cosmetic.
cósmico, -ca, *a.* cosmic.
cosmopolita, *a., n.m.f.* cosmopolitan.
cosmos, *n.m. sg.* cosmos.
coso (1), *n.m.* bullring.
coso (2), *n.m.* wood-worm.
cosquillas, *n.f.pl.* ticklishness; (*fig.*) touchiness; (*fig., fam.*) weak spot; ***tener* —,** be ticklish; ***tener malas* —,** be touchy.
cosquillear, *v.t.* tickle.
cosquilleo, *n.m.* tickling.
cosquilloso, -sa, *a.* ticklish; touchy.
costa (1), *n.f.* cost.
costa (2), *n.f.* coast; ***Costa de Marfil,*** Ivory Coast.
costado, *n.m.* side; (*mil.*) flank.
costal, *n.m.* sack.
costanero, -ra, *a.* coastal; sloping.—*n.f.* slope; rafter.
costanilla, *n.f.* narrow steep street.
costar [4], *v.t.* cost.
costarricense, costarriqueño, -ña, *a., n.m.f.* Costa Rican.
coste, *n.m.* cost, price.
costear, *v.t.* pay the cost of; (*naut.*) coast.
costeño, -ña, *a.* coastal.
costero, -ra, *a.* coastal.—*n.m.* side.—*n.f.* side; slope; coast; fishing season.
costilla, *n.f.* rib; (*fam.*) better half, wife.—*pl.* back, shoulders.
costilludo, -da, *a.* (*fam.*) well-built (*person*).
costo, *n.m.* cost; ***el* — *de la vida,*** the cost of living.
costoso, -sa, *a.* costly.
costra, *n.f.* scab; crust.
costroso, -sa, *a.* crusty; scaled; scabby.
costumbre, *n.f.* custom; habit; ***de* —,** usual; usually; ***tener la* — *de,*** be in the habit of.
costumbrista, *a., n.m.f.* (*lit.*) author who chronicles the customs of his period.
costura, *n.f.* seam; sewing.
costurera, *n.f.* seamstress, dressmaker.
costurón, *n.m.* (*pej.*) thick seam; (*fig.*) heavy scar.
cota, *n.f.* coat (*of mail etc.*); quota; elevation (*in maps*).
cotangente, *n.f.* (*math.*) cotangent.
cotarrera, *n.f.* (*fam.*) chin-wagger; (*pej.*) slut.
cotarro, *n.m.* side of a ravine; doss-house.
cotejar, *v.t.* compare.
cotejo, *n.m.* comparison; comparing.
cotidiano, -na, *a.* daily, everyday.
cotillo, *n.m.* hammer-head *or* -face.
cotillón, *n.m.* cotillion.
cotización, *n.f.* quotation (*of price*); quota.
cotizar [C], *v.t.* quote (*a price*); impose, collect *or* pay dues.—*v.r.* be esteemed *or* valued.
coto (1), *n.m.* estate, preserve; boundary stone; ***poner* — *a,*** put a stop to.
coto (2), *n.m.* (*ichth.*) chub.
coto (3), *n.m.* (*S.A.*) goitre.
cotón, *n.m.* printed cotton; (*S.A.*) smock.
cotonada, *n.f.* printed cotton.
cotorra, *n.f.* (*orn.*) parakeet; magpie; (*fam.*) gossiper, chatterer.
cotorrear, *v.i.* chatter, gossip.
cotufa, *n.f.* Jerusalem artichoke; titbit; (*S.A.*) pop-corn.
coturna, *n.m.* buskin.
covacha, *n.f.* small cave; (*S.A.*) box-room; (*C.A.*) shanty.
covachuelista, *n.m.* (*fam.*) civil servant.
coy, *n.m.* (*naut.*) hammock.
coyote, *n.m.* coyote, prairie wolf.
coyunda, *n.f.* yoking strap; (*fam.*) marriage; (*fig.*) bondage.
coyuntura, *n.f.* joint; juncture.
coz, *n.f.* (*pl.* **coces**) kick; recoil; return blow, (*fam.*) churlishness.
crac, *n.m.* crash, failure.
crampón, *n.m.* crampon.
cran, *n.m.* (*print.*) nick.
cráneo, *n.m.* cranium, skull.
crápula, *n.f.* dissipation.
crapuloso, -sa, *a.* crapulous, dissolute.
crascitar, *v.i.* caw.
crasitud, *n.f.* fatness; (*fam.*) stupidity.
craso, -sa, *a.* thick, greasy; crass, gross.
cráter, *n.m.* crater.
creación, *n.f.* creation.
creador, -ra, *a.* creating, creative.—*n.m.f.* creator.
crear, *v.t.* create.
creativo, -va, *a.* creative.
crecer [9], *v.i.* grow, increase; swell.—*v.r.* acquire more authority.
creces, *n.f.pl.* increase; extra; ***con* —,** abundantly, with interest.
crecida, *n.f.* swelling (*of rivers*).
crecido, -da, *a.* large, big; swollen.
creciente, *a.* growing; crescent.—*n.m.* crescent.—*n.f.* flood-tide; crescent moon.
crecimiento, *n.m.* growth; increase.
credencial, *a., n.f.* credential.
credibilidad, *n.f.* credibility.
crediticio, -cia, *a.* rel. to credit.
crédito, *n.m.* credit.
credo, *n.m.* creed, credo; (*fam.*) trice, moment; ***con el* — *en la boca,*** with his heart in his mouth.
credulidad, *n.f.* credulity.
crédulo, -la, *a.* credulous.
creedero, -ra, *a.* credible, believable.
creedor, -ra, *a.* credulous.
creencia, *n.f.* credence, credit; belief; creed.
creer [N], *v.t.* believe, think; — ***en,*** to believe in; ***¡ya lo creo!*** of course!—*v.r.* believe oneself to be.
creíble, *a.* believable, credible.
creído, -da, *a.* (*S.A.*) credulous; vain.
crema (1), *n.f.* cream.
crema (2), *n.f.* diaeresis (¨).
cremación, *n.f.* cremation.
cremallera, *n.f.* (*mech.*) rack, toothed bar; zip.
crematorio, -ria, *a.* crematory.—*n.m.* crematorium.
crémor tártaro, *n.m.* cream of tartar.
crencha, *n.f.* parting (*in hair*).
creosota, *n.f.* creosote.
crep, crepé, *n.m.* crêpe.
crepitación, *n.f.* crepitation, crackling.
crepitar, *v.i.* crepitate, crackle.
crepuscular, crepusculino, -na, *a.* crepuscular, twilight.
crepúsculo, *n.m.* twilight, crepuscule.
cresa, *n.f.* larva, maggot.
Creso, *n.m.* Croesus; **creso,** *n.m.* wealthy man.
crespo, -pa, *a.* curly; crispy; (*fig.*) angry; (*fig.*) over-elegant.

crespón, *n.m.* crêpe; crape.
cresta, *n.f.* crest.
crestado, -da, *a.* crested.
crestomatía, *n.f.* chrestomathy.
crestón, *n.m.* large crest; (*min.*) outcrop.
crestudo, -da, *a.* large-crested; (*fam.*) haughty.
Creta, *n.f.* Crete; **creta,** *n.f.* chalk.
cretáceo, -cea, *a.* cretaceous.
cretense, *a., n.m.f.* Cretan.
cretino, -na, *a.* cretinous.—*n.m.f.* cretin.
cretona, *n.f.* cretonne.
creyente, *a.* believing.—*n.m.f.* believer.
cría, *n.f.* brood; breeding; (*S.A.*) stock, lineage.
criadero, -ra, *a.* prolific.—*n.m.* nursery; hatchery; (*min.*) seam.
criado, -da, *a.* bred.—*n.m.f.* servant.—*n.f.* maid, servant.
criador, -ra, *a.* fruitful; raising.—*n.m.f.* creator; raiser.—*n.m.* God, the Creator.—*n.f.* wet-nurse.
crianza, *n.f.* rearing; nursing; breeding, manners.
criar [L], *v.t.* rear, bring up; nurse; grow, raise; create.
criatura, *n.f.* creature; baby, child.
criba, *n.f.* riddle, screen.
cribar, *v.t.* sieve, screen.
cribo, *n.m.* sieve, riddle.
cric, *n.m.* jack, lifting jack.
crimen, *n.m.* crime.
criminal, *a.* criminal.
criminalidad, *n.f.* criminality.
criminalista, *n.m.* criminologist; criminal lawyer.
criminar, *v.t.* incriminate; censure.
criminología, *n.f.* criminology.
criminoso, -sa, *a., n.m.f.* criminal, delinquent.
crin, *n.f.* mane; horse-hair.
crinolina, *n.f.* crinoline.
crío, *n.m.* (*fam.*) nipper, child; young (*of animals etc.*).
criollo, -lla, *a., n.m.f.* Creole; (*S.A.*) American-born.
cripta, *n.f.* crypt.
criptografía, *n.f.* cryptography.
crisálida, *n.f.* chrysalis, pupa.
crisantema, -mo, *n.f.* or *m.* chrysanthemum.
crisis, *n.f. inv.* crisis; judgement; — ***de la vivienda,*** housing shortage; — ***nerviosa,*** nervous breakdown.
crisma, *n.m.* or *f.* (*eccl.*) chrism; (*fam.*) noddle, head.
crisol, *n.m.* crucible.
crispar, *v.t.* convulse.—*v.r.* twitch.
cristal, *n.m.* crystal; glass; pane; mirror; — ***hilado,*** glass wool.
cristalino, -na, *a.* crystalline.
cristalización, *n.f.* crystallization.
cristalizar [C], *v.t., v.r.* crystallize.
cristalografía, *n.f.* crystallography.
cristalógrafo, -fa, *n.m.f.* crystallographer.
cristianar, *v.t.* (*fam.*) christen.
cristiandad, *n.f.* Christendom.
cristianismo, *n.m.* Christianity; (*fam.*) christening.
cristianizar [C], *v.t.* christianize.
cristiano, -na, *a., n.m.f.* Christian.—*n.m.* soul, person; (*fam.*) the Spanish language; ***vino*** **—,** (*joc.*) watered-down wine.
Cristo, *n.m.* Christ; crucifix.
Cristóbal, *n.m.* Christopher.
cristus, *n.m.* Christ-cross (*beginner's primer*); (*fig.*) the rudiments.
criterio, *n.m.* criterion; judgement.
criticar [A], *v.t.* criticize.
criticismo, *n.m.* (*philos.*) Criticism.
crítico, -ca, *a.* critical.—*n.m.f.* critic; (*fam.*) pedant.—*n.f.* criticism; critique.
criticón, -cona, *a.* fault-finding.—*n.m.f.* (*fam.*) fault-finder.
critiquizar [C], *v.t.* (*fam.*) be over-critical.
croar, *v.i.* croak (*frogs*).
croco, *n.m.* crocus.
croché, *n.m.* crochet.
cromar, *v.t.* chrome, chromium-plate.
cromático, -ca, *a.* chromatic.—*n.f.* chromatics.
cromo, *n.m.* chromium, chrome; chromolithograph.
cromosoma, *n.m.* chromosome.
crónica, *n.f.* chronicle; news, report.
cronicidad, *n.f.* chronic nature *or* condition.
crónico, -ca, *a.* chronic.
cronicón, *n.m.* short chronicle.
cronista, *n.m.f.* chronicler; reporter, (*U.S.*) newsman.
cronístico, -ca, *a.* rel. to chronicles, news.
cronología, *n.f.* chronology.
cronológico, -ca, *a.* chronological.
cronometraje, *n.m.* (*sport*) timing.
cronometrar, *v.t.* (*sport*) time.
cronómetro, *n.m.* chronometer.
croqueta, *n.f.* croquette.
croquis, *n.m. inv.* sketch.
crótalo, *n.m.* rattle-snake; castanet.
cruce, *n.m.* crossing, cross; intersection, crossroads.
crucero, *n.m.* crossing; cruise; cross-beam; (*naut.*) cruiser.
cruceta, *n.f.* cross-piece; cross-tree.
crucial, *a.* crucial.
crucificar [A], *v.t.* crucify.
crucifijo, *n.m.* crucifix.
crucifixión, *n.f.* crucifixion.
cruciforme, *a.* cruciform.
crucigrama, *n.m.* crossword puzzle.
crudelísimo, -ma, *a. sup.* most *or* very cruel.
crudeza, *n.f.* rawness; crudity; hardness; harshness.
crudo, -da, *a.* raw; hard; harsh; crude; boastful.
cruel, *a.* cruel.
crueldad, *n.f.* cruelty.
cruento, -ta, *a.* bloody.
crujidero, -ra, *a.* creaking; rustling; crackling.
crujido, *n.m.* creak; rustle; clatter; crackle.
crujir, *v.i.* creak; rustle; clatter; crackle.
crúor, *n.m.* (*poet.*) blood; (*med.*) cruor.
crup, *n.m.* (*med.*) croup.
crustáceo, -cea, *a.* crustaceous.—*n.m.* crustacean.
cruz, *n.f.* (*pl.* **cruces**) cross; tails (*of coin*); plus sign; (*vet.*) withers; ***¡— y raya!*** (*fam.*) enough! no more of that!
cruzado, -da, *a.* crossed; cross (*bred*).—*n.m.* crusader.—*n.f.* crusade; intersection.
cruzamiento, *n.m.* crossing.
cruzar [C], *v.t.* cross; decorate, honour.—*v.i.* cruise.—*v.r.* cross paths; cross.

cu, *n.f.* name of letter Q.
cuaderno, *n.m.* exercise book; (*print.*) gathering.
cuadra, *n.f.* stable; large room; ward, dormitory; rump, croup; (*S.A.*) block (*of houses*).
cuadradillo, *n.m.* square rule; sugar cube.
cuadrado, -da, *a.* square; complete.—*n.m.* square; ruler.
cuadragenario, -ria, *a.*, *n.m.f.* quadragenarian.
cuadragésimo, -ma, *a.* fortieth.—*n.f.* (*eccl.*) Lent; Quadragesima.
cuadral, *n.m.* truss, angle-brace.
cuadrángulo, -la, *a.* quadrangular.—*n.m.* quadrangle.
cuadrante, *n.m.* fourth; face (*of watch*); quadrant; angle-brace; — ***solar,*** sun dial.
cuadrar, *v.t.* square; suit perfectly.—*v.i.* fit; suit, please.—*v.r.* square one's shoulders; (*fam.*) become solemn; (*C.A.*) strike it rich.
cuadricular, *a.* checkered, ruled in squares.—*v.t.* graticulate.
cuadrienio, *n.m.* quadrennium.
cuadrilátero, -ra, *a.*, *n.m.* quadrilateral.
cuadrilongo, -ga, *a.*, *n.m.* oblong.
cuadrilla, *n.f.* gang, team, crew; quadrille.
cuadrillero, *n.m.* gang leader, squad leader.
cuadripartido, -da, *a.* quadripartite.
cuadrivio, *n.m.* crossroads; quadrivium.
cuadro, *n.m.* square; picture, painting; frame; cadre; panel; (*theat.*) scene; ***en —,*** square; (*fam.*) on one's uppers; ***a cuadros,*** squared.
cuadrúpedo, -da, *a.*, *n.m.* quadruped.
cuajado, -da, *a.* (*fam.*) flabbergasted.—*n.m.* mincemeat.—*n.f.* curds.
cuajaleche, *n.m.* (*bot.*) cheese rennet.
cuajar, *v.t.* curdle; coagulate; cake; set, thicken; over-decorate.—*v.i.* turn out well; (*C.A.*) natter.—*v.r.* curdle, go sour; set, go thick; sleep well; (*fam.*) get crowded (***de,*** with).
cuajarón, *n.m.* clot.
cuákero, -ra [CUÁQUERO].
cual, *rel. a.*, *rel. pron.* (*pl.* **cuales**) which; who, whom; as, such as; — . . . ***tal,*** like . . . like, just as . . . so; ***por lo —,*** for which reason. (*As interrog.* **cuál, cuáles.**)
cualesquier(a) [CUALQUIER(A)].
cualidad, *n.f.* characteristic, quality.
cualitativo, -va, *a.* qualitative.
cualquier, *indef. a.*, *contracted form of* CUALQUIERA *used before noun or other a.*
cualquier(a), *indef. a.* (*pl.* **cualesquier(a)**) any, some or other.—*rel. a.* whichever.—*indef. pron.* anyone.—*rel. pron.* whoever, whichever.—*n.m.* (*fam.*) a nobody.
cuan, *adv.* (*contracted form of* CUANTO *used before a. or other adv.*).
cuán, *adv. interrog.*, *interj.* how, how much.
cuando, *adv.*, *conj.* when; although; ***de — en —,*** from time to time; — ***más*** (***menos***), at most (least); — ***quiera,*** whenever.—*prep.* (*fam.*) at the time of, during. (*As interrog.* **cuándo**).
cuantía, *n.f.* amount, quantity; importance, rank.
cuantiar [L], *v.t.* appraise.
cuantioso, -sa, *a.* substantial, large.
cuantitativo, -va, *a.* quantitative.
cuanto (1), **-ta,** *a.*, *rel. pron.*, *adv.* as much as, as many as, whatever; as soon as; whilst; all that; — ***antes,*** as soon as possible; — ***más . . . tanto más,*** the more . . . the more; ***en —,*** as soon as; ***en — a,*** as regards, as for; ***por —,*** inasmuch as; ***cuantos,*** all those who, all those that.
cuanto (2), *n.m.* (*pl.* **cuanta**) (*phys.*) quantum.
cuánto, -ta, *interrog.*, *adv.*, *pron.* how much? how many? how long?—*interj.* how much! how many! how long!
cuáquero, -ra, *a.*, *n.m.f.* Quaker.
cuarenta, *a.*, *n.m.* forty.
cuarentavo, -va, *a.* fortieth.
cuarentena, *n.f.* two score; quarantine; forty days *or* nights *or* years.
cuarentón, -tona, *a.*, *n.m.f.* forty-year-old.
cuaresma, *n.f.* Lent.
cuaresmal, *a.* Lenten.
cuartago, *n.m.* pony.
cuartana, *n.f.* quartan fever.
cuartazos, *n.m.* (*fam.*, *pej.*) fatty.
cuartear, *v.t.* quarter; zig-zag along; (*C.A.*) whip.—*v.i.* dodge.—*v.r.* crack; dodge.
cuartel, *n.m.* barracks; quarter, section; quarter, mercy; — ***general,*** (*mil.*) headquarters.—*pl.* quarters.
cuartelada, *n.f.* (*S.A.* **cuartelazo,** *n.m.*) military revolt.
cuartelero, -ra, *a.* rel. to barracks *or* camp.—*n.m.* (*mil.*) camp policeman.
cuarterón, -rona, *a.*, *n.m.f.* quadroon.—*n.m.* quarter; door panel; postern.
cuarteta, *n.f.* quatrain.
cuartete, cuarteto, *n.m.* quartet(te); quatrain.
cuartilla, *n.f.* quart; quarto; sheet (*paper*).
cuartillo, *n.m.* quart; pint; (*obs.*) groat.
cuarto, -ta, *a.*, *n.m.* fourth.—*n.m.* quarter; room; quarto; (*fam.*) bean, penny; ***de tres al —,*** (*fam.*) ten a penny.—*n.f.* quarter; palm-span; (*C.A.*) whip.
cuartucho, *n.m.* hovel.
cuarzo, *n.m.* quartz.
cuasi, *adv.* quasi.
cuatrero, *n.m.* rustler, horse *or* cattle thief.
cuatrillizo, -za, *n.m.f.* quadruplet.
cuatrillón, *n.m.* quadrillion.
cuatrimestre, *a.* four-monthly.—*n.m.* four months.
cuatrinca, *n.f.* foursome.
cuatro, *a.*, *n.m.* four.
cuatrocientos, -tas, *a.*, *n.m.* four hundred.
Cuba, *n.f.* Cuba; **cuba,** *n.f.* barrel, cask, vat.
cubano, -na, *a.*, *n.m.f.* Cuban.
cubeta, *n.f.* keg; pail; cup; dish.
cubicar [A], *v.t.* calculate the volume of; cube.
cúbico, -ca, *a.* cubic.
cubículo, *n.m.* cubicle.
cubierta, *n.f.* cover; covering; envelope; car bonnet, (*U.S.*) hood; dust jacket (*of book*); (*naut.*) deck; casing.
cubierto, -ta, *a.* covered.—*p.p.* [CUBRIR].—*n.m.* cover, shelter; table service, place at table; fixed-price meal; ***a —,*** under cover.
cubil, *n.m.* lair, den; river bed.
cubillo, -lla, *n.m.f.* Spanish fly.—*n.m.* earthenware jug (*for cooling water*).
cubismo, *n.m.* Cubism.
cubista, *a.*, *n.m.f.* Cubist.
cubo, *n.m.* bucket, pail; cube; hub; socket; (*mech.*) drum.
cubrecadena, *n.m.* or *f.* chain-cover (*of bicycle*).

cubrecama, *n.m.* bedspread.
cubrefuego, *n.m.* curfew.
cubretetera, *n.f.* tea cosy.
cubrir [*p.p.* **cubierto**], *v.t.* cover, cover over *or* up.
cucamonas, *n.f.pl.* (*fam.*) sweet nothings, wheedling.
cucaña, *n.f.* greasy pole; (*fam.*) walk-over, cinch.
cucar, *v.t.* wink; (*fam.*) tease.
cucaracha, *n.f.* cockroach; cochineal beetle.
cucarda, *n.f.* cockade.
cuclillas, *adv.* ***en* —,** squatting; ***ponerse en* —,** squat, crouch.
cuclillo, *n.m.* (*orn.*) cuckoo; (*fam.*) cuckold.
cuco, -ca, *a.* sly; spruce, smart.—*n.m.* cuckoo.—*n.m.f.* caterpillar; (*fam.*) gambler.
cucú, *n.m.* (*pl.* **-úes**) cuckoo (*call*).
cuculla, *n.f.* cowl.
cucurucho, *n.m.* paper cone.
cuchara, *n.f.* spoon; ladle, scoop; (*S.A.*) trowel; ***media* —,** (*fam.*) wet hen, ungifted person; ***meter su* —,** (*fam.*) stick one's oar in.
cucharada, *n.f.* spoonful, ladleful.
cucharear, *v.t.* spoon out, ladle out.
cucharilla, cucharita, *n.f.* teaspoon.
cucharón, *n.m.* tablespoon; ladle; (*fam.*) the pickings.
cuchichear, *v.i.* whisper.
cuchicheo, *n.m.* whisperings.
cuchichero, -ra, *n.m.f.* whisperer.
cuchilla, *n.f.* blade; carver, cleaver; (*S.A.*) penknife.
cuchillada, *n.f.* cut, gash, slash.—*pl.* fight, squabble.
cuchillo, *n.m.* knife; (*carp.*) upright; ***pasar a* —,** put to the sword.
cuchitril, *n.m.* cubby-hole; hovel.
cuchuchear, *v.i.* whisper; (*fam.*) gossip.
cuchufleta, *n.f.* (*fam.*) joke, fun.
cuelga, *n.f.* bunch; (*fam.*) birthday present.
cuello, *n.m.* neck; collar; ***levantar el* —,** get on one's feet again.
cuenca, *n.f.* river basin; wooden bowl; eye socket.
cuenco, *n.m.* earthenware bowl; cavity.
cuenta, *n.f.* count, calculation; account; bill; bead; ***a* (*buena*) —,** on account; ***caer en la* —,** (*fam.*) see the point, get it; ***dar* — *de*,** account, for; (*coll.*) use up, finish off; ***darse* — *de*,** realize; ***de* —,** of some account; ***por la* —,** apparently; ***tener en* —,** take into account; **— *corriente*,** current account; ***cuentas galanas*,** (*fam.*) day-dreams, castles in Spain; ***en resumidas cuentas*,** in short; ***a fin de cuentas*,** when all's said and done.
cuentacorrentista, *n.m.f.* person having current account.
cuentagotas, *n.m. inv.* dropper, drop-bottle.
cuentakilómetros, *n.m. inv.* milometer.
cuentero, -ra, *a.* (*fam.*) fibbing.—*n.m.f.* fibber, gossip.
cuentista, *n.m.f.* story writer *or* teller; (*fam.*) fibber.
cuento, *n.m.* story, tale; yarn; count; (*obs.*) million; prop; (*fam.*) trouble; ***a* —,** opportune(ly); ***sin* —,** countless.
cuerda, *n.f.* string, rope, cord; watch spring; fishing line; ***dar* — *a*,** wind up (*watch*); give free rein to; ***bajo* —,** underhandedly.
cuerdo, -da, *a.* wise, sensible.
cuerna, *n.f.* horn; antler.
cuerno, *n.m.* horn; (*ent.*) antenna.
cuero, *n.m.* leather; hide; wineskin; (*S.A.*) whip; ***en cueros* (*vivos*),** stark naked.
cuerpo, *n.m.* body; substance; corpus; (*mil.*) corps; **— *a* —,** hand to hand; ***hurtar el* — *a*,** dodge, avoid.
cuervo, *n.m.* raven; **— *marino*,** cormorant.
cuesta (1), *n.f.* hill, slope; **— *abajo*,** downhill; **— *arriba*,** uphill; ***a cuestas*,** on one's shoulders *or* back.
cuesta (2), **cuestación,** *n.f.* charity appeal.
cuestión, *n.f.* question, matter, affair.
cuestionable, *a.* questionable.
cuestionar, *v.t.* call in question, dispute.
cuestionario, *n.m.* questionnaire.
cuesto, *n.m.* hill.
cuestuario, -ria, cuestuoso, -sa, *a.* lucrative.
cueto, *n.m.* crag; fortified crag.
cueva, *n.f.* cave; cellar.
cuévano, *n.m.* grape basket.
cuico, -ca, *a.* (*S.A.*) half-breed.—*n.m.f.* (*S.A., pej.*) foreigner; (*S.A.*) Indian.
cuidado, *n.m.* care; heed; caution; worry; ***tener* —,** be careful (***con*,** with, of).—*interj.* look out! be careful!
cuidadoso, -sa, *a.* careful; concerned.
cuidar, *v.t.* care for, mind, take care of.—*v.i.* take care (***de*,** of).—*v.r.* be careful (***de*,** of, to); look after oneself.
cuido, *n.m.* care.
cuita, *n.f.* woe, travail; (*C.A.*) dung.
culantro, *n.m.* coriander.
culata, *n.f.* buttock; butt (*of gun*); cylinder head.
culatada, *n.f.*, **culatazo,** *n.m.* recoil; butt-blow.
culebra, *n.f.* snake; (*fam.*) rowdy disturbance; (*fam.*) lark, trick.
culebrazo, *n.m.* lark, trick.
culebrear, *v.i.* wriggle (along).
culebreo, *n.m.* wriggling.
culebrino, -na, *a.* snaky.
culera (1), *n.f.* seat-patch (*in trousers*).
culero (1), **-ra** (2), *a.* lazy.
culero (2), *n.m.* nappy, (*U.S.*) diaper.
culí, *n.m.* (*pl.* **-íes**) coolie.
culinario, -ria, *a.* culinary.
culminación, *n.f.* culmination.
culminante, *a.* predominating, supreme.
culminar, *v.t.* culminate.
culo, *n.m.* (*low*) rump, bottom; **— *de vaso*,** cheap jewel.
culpa, *n.f.* blame, fault, guilt; ***tener la* — (*de*),** be to blame (for).
culpabilidad, *n.f.* culpability.
culpable, culpado, -da, *a.* guilty.—*n.m.f.* culprit.
culpar, *v.t.* blame; accuse (***de*,** of).—*v.r.* take the blame (***de*,** for).
cultedad, *n.f.* fustian; (*joc.*) culture vulture.
culteranismo, *n.m.* (*lit.*) Spanish euphuism.
culterano, -na, *a.* euphuistic; fustian.—*n.m.* euphuist.
cultismo, *n.m.* euphuism; learned word.
cultivación, *n.f.* cultivation.
cultivador, -ra, *a.* cultivating.—*n.m.f.* farmer, cultivator.
cultivar, *v.t.* cultivate.
cultivo, *n.m.* cultivation.

culto, -ta, *a.* cultured; learned.—*n.m.* worship; cult.
cultor, -ra, *a.* worshipping; cultivating.—*n.m.f.* worshipper; cultivator.
cultura, *n.f.* culture.
cultural, *a.* cultural.
culturar, *v.t.* cultivate.
cumbre, *n.f.* summit; (*fig.*) pinnacle.
cumbrera, *n.f.* ridge coping; lintel; (*S.A.*) summit.
cumpa, *n.m.* (*S.A., low*) mate, pal.
cúmplase, *n.m.* official confirmation.
cumpleaños, *n.m. inv.* birthday.
cumplidero, -ra, *a.* be completed; expiring; requisite, necessary.
cumplido, -da, *a.* full, complete; polite correct.—*n.m.* compliment, courtesy.
cumplimentar, *v.t.* compliment, congratulate; fulfil (*an order*).
cumplimiento, *n.m.* compliment; fulfilment; formality.
cumplir, *v.t.* fulfil; reach (*an age*).—*v.i.* expire; fall due; — ***con,*** fulfil (*duty etc.*); behave correctly towards; ***cumple a Pedro hacerlo,*** it behoves Peter to do it.—*v.r.* be fulfilled, come true.
cumquibus, *n.m.* (*fam.*) wherewithal, cash.
cúmulo, *n.m.* heap, pile; cumulus.
cuna, *n.f.* cradle; orphans' home; (*fig.*) family.
cundir, *v.i.* spread; swell; multiply.
cunero, -ra, *n.m.f.* foundling; (*pol.*) outside candidate, carpet-bagger.
cuneta, *n.f.* ditch.
cuña, *n.f.* wedge; cobblestone; (*S.A.*) bigwig.
cuñada, *n.f.* sister-in-law.
cuñado, *n.m.* brother-in-law.
cuñete, *n.m.* keg.
cuño, *n.m.* coin die; (*fig.*) stamp, mark.
cuodlibeto, *n.m.* quodlibet; witticism.
cuota, *n.f.* quota; dues.
cuotidiano, -na, *a.* daily, quotidian.
cupe, *etc.* [CABER].
cupé, *n.m.* coupé.
Cupido, *n.m.* Cupid; **cupido,** *n.m.* gallant, lover; cupid.
cupo, *n.m.* quota, share.—*v.* [CABER].
cupón, *n.m.* coupon; ***cupón-respuesta,*** reply coupon.
cúprico, -ca, *a.* cupric.
cuproso, -sa, *a.* cuprous.
cúpula, *n.f.* cupola, dome; (*bot.*) cupule; (*naut.*) turret.
cuquería, *n.f.* slyness.
cura, *n.m.* parish priest; ***este —,*** (*fam.*) yours truly.—*n.f.* cure, curing; — ***de almas,*** care of souls.
curaca, *n.m.* (*S.A.*) Indian chief.
curación, *n.f.* healing, treatment.
curador, -ra, *n.m.f.* guardian; curator; curer.
curandero, -ra, *n.m.f.* quack, medicaster; witch-doctor.
curar, *v.t.* cure, heal; dry.—*v.i.* recover; pay attention; — ***de,*** recover from; look after *or* to.—*v.r.* heal up; recover; take a cure; (*S.A.*) get drunk; ***curarse de,*** recover from.
curare, *n.m.* curare.
curatela, *n.f.* (*jur.*) guardianship.
curativo, -va, *a., n.f.* curative.
curato, *n.m.* curacy; parish.
curazao, *n.m.* curaçao.
cúrcuma, *n.f.* curcumin, turmeric.
curdo, -da, *a.* Kurdish.—*n.m.f.* Kurd; ***coger una curda,*** (*fam.*) get canned, drunk.
cureña, *n.f.* gun carriage.
curia, *n.f.* curia.
curial, *a.* curial.—*n.m.* (*jur.*) clerk.
curialesco, -ca, *a.* (*pej.*) legalistic.
curiosear, *v.i.* (*fam.*) pry, snoop.
curiosidad, *n.f.* curiosity; curio; care.
curioso, -sa, *a.* curious; diligent; tidy.—*n.m.f.* busy-body, snooper; (*S.A.*) quack doctor.
Curro, *n.m.* (*fam.*) form of Francisco; **curro, -rra,** *a.* (*fam.*) flashy, loud.
curruca, *n.f.* (*orn.*) warbler; whitethroat.
currutaco, -ca, *a.* dandyish, fashion-conscious.—*n.m.* dandy, (*U.S.*) dude.
cursado, -da, *a.* versed, skilled.
cursante, *a.* attending, studying.—*n.m.f.* pupil, student.
cursar, *v.t.* frequent; study; expedite.
cursería [CURSILERÍA].
cursi, *a.* (*pl.* **-sis** *or* (*low*) **cúrsiles**) (*fam.*) flashy, shoddy, vulgar.
cursilería, *n.f.* flashiness, vulgarity.
cursillista, *n.f.* student on short course.
cursillo, *n.m.* short course.
cursivo, -va, *a.* cursive.
curso, *n.m.* course; academic year; — ***legal,*** legal tender.
curtido, *n.m.* tanning.—*pl.* leather.
curtidor, *n.m.* tanner.
curtiente, *a.* tanning.—*n.m.* tanning material.
curtimiento, *n.m.* tanning.
curtir, *v.t.* tan; sunburn; inure, season.
curuca, curuja, *n.f.* barn owl.
curva, *n.f.* curve, bend.
curvado, -da, *a.* curved.
curvatura, *n.f.* curvature.
curvilíneo, -nea, *a.* curvilinear.
curvo, -va, *a.* curved.
cusir, *v.t.* (*fam.*) sew badly.
cúspide, *n.f.* apex; cusp; vertex.
custodia, *n.f.* custody; guard; (*eccl.*) monstrance.
custodiar, *v.t.* guard, take care of.
custodio, *n.m.* custodian, guard.
cúter, *n.m.* (*naut.*) cutter.
cutí, *n.m.* (*pl.* **-íes**) ticking.
cutícula, *n.f.* cuticle.
cutio, *n.m.* labour.
cutir, *v.t.* knock, hit.
cutis, *n.m. inv.* skin; complexion.
cutre, *a.* miserly.—*n.m.f.* skinflint.
cuy, *n.m.* (*S.A.*) guinea-pig.
cuyo, -ya, *rel. a.* whose (*obs. as interrog.*).—*n.m.* (*fam.*) beau, lover.
¡cuz! *interj.* here! (*to dog*).
czar [ZAR].

Ch

Ch, ch, *n.f.* fourth letter of the Spanish alphabet.
cha, *n.m.* (*S.A.*) tea.

chabacanada, chabacanería, *n.f.* vulgarity, grossness.
chabacano, -na, *a.* vulgar, gross, crude.
chacal, *n.m.* jackal.
chacolotear, *v.i.* clatter (*hooves*).
chacota, *n.f.* noisy mirth.
chacra, *n.f.* (*S.A.*) farm, plantation.
chacha, *n.f.* (*fam.*) lass; (*fam.*) nurse.
cháchara, *n.f.* (*fam.*) blather, chatter.
chacho, *n.m.* (*fam.*) lad.
chafaldita, *n.f.* (*fam.*) little joke.
chafallar, *v.t.* (*fam.*) patch up, botch.
chafallo, *n.m.* (*fam.*) botched repair.
chafallón, -llona, *a.* (*fam.*) botching.—*n.m.f.* botcher.
chafandín, *n.m.* (*fam.*) vain clot, fool.
chafarrinada, *n.f.* blotch, daub.
chafarrinar, *v.t.* blotch, stain.
chaflán, *n.m.* chamfer, bevel.
chagrín, *n.m.* shagreen.
chah, *n.m.* shah.
chal, *n.m.* shawl.
chalado, -da, *a.* (*fam.*) daft, silly, infatuated.
chalán, -lana, *a.* horse-dealing.—*n.m.f.* horse-dealer.
chalana, *n.f.* lighter, flatboat.
chalar, *v.t.* (*fam.*) drive daft *or* crazy.—*v.r.* be gone, be daft (***por***, on).
chaleco, *n.m.* waistcoat.
chalet, *n.m.* chalet.
chalina, *n.f.* neckerchief.
chalote, *n.m.* (*bot.*) shallot.
chalupa, *n.f.* sailing boat; lifeboat.
chamar, *v.t.* (*fam.*) barter, swap.
chámara, chamarasca, *n.f.* brushwood.
chamarillero, -ra, *n.m.f.* scrap dealer.
chamarra, *n.f.* sheepskin jacket.
chamba, *n.f.* (*fam.*) fluke.
chambelán, *n.m.* chamberlain.
chambergo, -ga, *a.* Schomberg.—*n.m.* slouch hat.
chambón, -bona, *a.* (*fam.*) clumsy.—*n.m.f.* blunderer.
chamiza, *n.f.* thatching reed; twigs.
chamizo, *n.m.* half-burnt tree *or* log; cottage; hovel.
chamorrar, *v.t.* (*fam.*) crop (*hair*).
Champaña, *n.f.* Champagne; **champán, champaña,** *n.m.* champagne.
champiñón, *n.m.* mushroom.
champú, *n.m.* (*pl.* **-úes**) shampoo.
champurrar, *v.t.* (*fam.*) mix (*drinks*).
chamuscar [A], *v.t.* singe, scorch.
chamusco, *n.m.* singe, scorch.
chamusquina, *n.f.* singe; (*fam.*) row, squabble; ***oler a* —,** (*fam.*) be fishy.
chanada, *n.f.* (*fam.*) swindle.
chancear, *v.i.*, *v.r.* joke.
chancero, -ra, *a.* joking, merry.
chanciller, *n.m.* chancellor.
chancillería, *n.f.* chancery.
chancla, *n.f.* old shoe; slipper.
chanclo, *n.m.* clog; pattern; galosh.
chancho, -cha, *a.* (*S.A.*) filthy.—*n.m.f.* (*S.A.*) pig.
chanchullo, *n.m.* (*fam.*) twist, sharp practice.
chanfaina, *n.f.* offal stew.
chanflón, -lona, *a.* misshapen.
changüí, *n.m.* (*pl.* **-íes**) (*fam.*) trick, hoax.
chantaje, *n.m.* blackmail.
chantajista, *n.m.f.* blackmailer.
chantre, *n.m.* precentor.
chanza, *n.f.* joke, fun.
chanzoneta, *n.f.* chansonnette; (*fam.*) lark, joke.
chapa, *n.f.* metal plate, sheet; veneer; (*fam.*) nous, sense.—*pl.* tossing coins; (*fam.*) blush, redness.
chapado, -da, *a.* plated; veneered; ***— a la antigua***, olde-worlde, old-fashioned.
chapalear, *v.i.* lap, splash; patter.
chapaleteo, *n.m.* splashing, lapping; patter.
chapapote, *n.m.* asphalt.
chapar [CHAPEAR].
chaparra, *n.f.* brush oak; scrub.
chaparrada, *n.f.* shower, downpour.
chaparro, *n.m.* oak scrub.
chaparrón, *n.m.* heavy shower.
chapear, *v.t.* plate; veneer; (*C.A.*) weed.—*v.i.* clatter.
chapería, *n.f.* metal-plating.
chapetón, -tona, *a.* (*S.A.*) new, green (*immigrant*); novice.
chapitel, *n.m.* (*arch.*) spire, pinnacle; capital.
chapón, *n.m.* blot.
chapotear, *v.t.* sponge; damp.—*v.i.* splash.
chapucear, *v.t.* bungle, botch; dabble in.
chapucería, *n.f.* botching; botched job; fib, lie.
chapucero, -ra, *a.* botchy.—*n.m.f.* dabbler; bungler; fibber.
chapurrar, *v.t.* jabber, (*fam.*) murder (*a language*); mix (*drinks*).
chapurrear, *v.t.*, *v.i.* jabber.
chapuz, *n.m.* botching; ducking (*in water*); (*naut.*) spar.
chapuza, *n.f.* botched job.
chapuzar, *v.t.* duck (*in water*).
chapuzón, *n.m.* ducking.
chaqué, *n.m.* morning-coat.
chaqueta, *n.f.* jacket.
chaquira, *n.f.* (*S.A.*) bead.
charabán, *n.m.* charabanc.
charada, *n.f.* charade.
charanga, *n.f.* (*mus.*) brass band.
charanguero, -ra, *a.* [CHAPUCERO].
charca, *n.f.* pool.
charco, *n.m.* puddle; (*fam.*) pond, sea.
charla, *n.f.* (*fam.*) chat; (*orn.*) missel thrush.
charlar, *v.i.* chatter; chat.
charlatán, -tana, *a.* prattling.—*n.m.f.* prattler; charlatan.
charlatanería, *n.f.* quackery; prattle.
charnela, *n.f.* hinge; (*mech.*) knuckle.
charol, *n.m.* varnish; patent leather.
charpa, *n.f.* gun-belt; arm-sling.
charqui, *n.m.* (*S.A.*) dried meat.
charrada, *n.f.* peasant dance; loutishness; over-ornamentation.
charrán, *n.m.* scoundrel.
charrasca, *n.f.* (*joc.*) sword; throat-cutter.
charrería, *n.f.* over-ornamentation.
charretera, *n.f.* (*mil.*) epaulet.
charro, -rra, *a.* churlish; (*fam.*) tawdry.—*n.m.f.* Salamantine peasant.
charrúa, *n.f.* (*naut.*) tug.
chascar, *v.t.* click (*tongue*); crush up.—*v.i.* [CHASQUEAR].
chascarrillo, *n.m.* (*fam.*) spicy yarn.
chasco, -ca, *a.* (*S.A.*) curly, thick (*hair*).—*n.m.* disappointment; joke.
chasis, *n.m. inv.* chassis; (*phot.*) plate-frame.
chasponazo, *n.m.* bullet mark.

chasquear, *v.t.* crack (*a whip*); disappoint.—*v.i.* crack.—*v.r.* be disappointed.
chasquido, *n.m.* snap, crack.
chatarra, *n.f.* scrap iron.
chato, -ta, *a.* flat, snub-nosed.—*n.m.* (*fam.*) wine-glass; glass of wine.
chatre, *a.* (*S.A.*) dolled-up.
chauvinismo, *n.m.* chauvinism, jingoism.
chaval, -la, *n.m.* (*fam.*) laddie, lad.—*n.f.* lass, lassie.
chaveta, *n.f.* (*mech.*) cotter pin.
che (1), *n.f.* name of letter CH.
¡che! (2), *interj.* (*dial., S.A.*) oy! hey!
checa (1), *n.f.* police terrorist group, cheka.
checo -ca (2), *n.m.f.* Czech.
checoslovaco, -ca, *a., n.m.f.* Czechoslovak.
Checoslovaquia, *n.f.* Czechoslovakia.
chelín, *n.m.* shilling.
cheque, *n.m.* cheque, (*U.S.*) check.
chica, *n.f.* girl.
chicarrón, -rrona, *a.* (*fam.*) forward, overgrown (*child*).
chicle, *n.m.* chicle; chewing gum.
chico, -ca, *a.* small.—*n.m.* boy; youth.—*n.f.* girl.—*n.m.f.* child.
chicolear, *v.i.* (*fam.*) pay compliments.—*v.r.* (*S.A.*) have a good time.
chicoría, *n.f.* chicory.
chicote, -ta, *n.m.f.* (*fam.*) strapping youth.—*n.m.* cigar; cigar butt; (*S.A.*) lash.
chicha, *n.f.* (*fam.*) meat; (*S.A.*) chicha (*drink*).
chícharo, *n.m.* (*bot.*) pea.
chicharra, *n.f.* (*ent.*) cicada.
chicharrón, *n.m.* crackling; burnt food.
chichear, *v.t., v.i.* hiss.
chichisbeo, *n.m.* passionate wooing; cicisbeo.
chichón, *n.m.* lump, bruise.
chifla, *n.f.* whistle; hiss.
chiflado, -da, *a.* (*fam.*) daft.—*n.m.f.* (*fam.*) crank, nut-case.
chifladura, *n.f.* (*fam.*) barminess; silly whim.
chiflar, *v.t.* whistle at; hiss, boo.—*v.r.* (*fam.*) be crazy (*por,* about).
chiflato, chiflete, chiflido, chiflo, *n.m.* whistle.
Chile, *n.m.* Chile; **chile,** *n.m.* chili.
chileno, -na, chileño, -ña, *a., n.m.f.* Chilean.
chiltipiquín, *n.m.* chili.
chillar, *v.i.* scream, shriek, squeal; sizzle.
chillido, *n.m.* shriek, screech, scream.
chillón, -ona, *a.* (*fam.*) shrieking; shrill; loud (*colour*).—*n.m.f.* (*S.A.*) squealer, informer.
chimenea, *n.f.* chimney; fire-place; (*naut.*) funnel; (*min.*) shaft.
chimpancé, *n.m.* chimpanzee.
China, *n.f.* China; **china,** *n.f.* pebble; [CHINO], china.
chinchar, *v.t.* (*fam.*) pester, bother.—*v.r.* get fed up.
chinche, *n.m.* or *f.* bug; drawing-pin, (*U.S.*) thumbtack; (*fam.*) pest.
chincheta, *n.f.* drawing-pin, (*U.S.*) thumbtack.
chinchilla, *n.f.* (*zool.*) chinchilla.
chinchín, *n.m.* street-music; (*fam.*) ballyhoo.
chinchoso, -sa, *a.* (*fam.*) bothersome.
chinela, *n.f.* slipper.
chinesco, -ca, *a.* Chinese.
chino, -na, *a., n.m.f.* Chinese; (*S.A.*) half-breed; (*S.A.*) love, dearie (*mode of address*).
de chipé(n), *a. phr.* (*fam.*) first-rate.
Chipre, *n.f.* Cyprus.
chipriota, chipriote, *a., n.m.f.* Cypriot.
chiquillada, *n.f.* child's prank.
chiquillo, -lla, *n.m.f.* *diminutive of* CHICO.
chiquirritico, -ca; -tillo, -lla; -tín, -tina; chiquitín, -tina, *a.* (*fam.*) tiny, weeny; very young.
chiribitil, *n.m.* attic, cubby-hole.
chirimbolo, *n.m.* (*fam.*) gadget, utensil.
chirimía, *n.f.* (*mus.*) flagoelet.
chirimoya, *n.f.* (*bot.*) custard apple.
chiripa, *n.f.* fluke.
chirivía, *n.f.* parsnip.
chirlar, *v.i.* (*fam.*) yell, gabble.
chirle, *a.* (*fam.*) flat, tasteless.—*n.m.* dung.
chirlo, *n.m.* slash, scar (*on face*).
chirlomirlo, *n.m.* morsel; (*orn.*) blackbird.
chirriadero, -ra, chirriante, *a.* squeaking, shrieking.
chirriar, *v.i.* squeak, shriek; chirp; caterwaul; sizzle.
chirrido, *n.m.* shriek, squeak, creak; sizzling.
chirumen, *n.m.* (*fam.*) gumption.
¡chis! *interj.* sh! hush! ***¡ chis chis !*** hey!
chiscón, *n.m.* hovel.
chisgarabís, *n.m.* (*fam.*) Nosey Parker.
chisguete, *n.m.* (*fam.*) swig, drink.
chisme, *n.m.* titbit of gossip; (*fam.*) thingummy.
chismear, *v.i.* tale-tattle, gossip.
chismería, *n.f.* tale-tattling, gossip.
chismero, -ra, *a.* gossiping.—*n.m.f.* gossip.
chismorrear, *v.i.* (*fam.*) [CHISMEAR].
chismoso, -sa, *a.* gossipy.—*n.m.f.* gossip, tattler.
chispa, *n.f.* spark, (*fam.*) live wire; flash (*of lightning*); drop (*of liquid*); drunkenness; ***echar chispas,*** be furious.
chispazo, *n.m.* spark; sparking; tale, gossip.
chispeante, *a.* sparkling.
chispear, *v.i.* sparkle; spark; drizzle.
chispero, *n.m.* blacksmith; (*fam.*) spiv, sharper.
chispo, -pa, *a.* (*fam.*) tipsy.—*n.m.* (*fam.*) swig, drink.
chispoleto, -ta, *a.* lively.
chisporrotear, *v.i.* (*fam.*) throw sparks.
chisposo, -sa, *a.* sparking.
chistar, *v.i.* say a word; ***sin — (ni mistar),*** (*fam.*) without saying a word.
chiste, *n.m.* joke, witticism.
chistera, *n.f.* fish basket; cesta; top-hat.
chistoso, -sa, *a.* witty.—*n.m.f.* wit (*person*).
chita, *n.f.* anklebone; quoit; ***a la — callando,*** (*fam.*) as quiet as a mouse.
¡chitón! *interj.* sh! hush!
chivato, *n.m.* kid, young goat; (*fam.*) cant, tell-tale.
chivo, -va, *n.m.f.* goat.—*n.m.* billy-goat.
chocante, *a.* surprising, shocking; (*S.A.*) pesky.
chocar, *v.t.* shock, shake; (*low*) [GUSTAR].—*v.i.* collide; clash.
chocarrero, -ra, *a.* coarse, ribald.
choclo, *n.m.* clog; (*S.A.*) maize, cob.
chocolate, *n.m.* chocolate.
chocha, *n.f.* (*orn.*) woodcock.
chochear, *v.i.* dodder, dote.
chochera, chochez, *n.f.* dotage, doting.
chochita, *n.f.*, **chochín,** *n.m.* (*orn.*) wren.
chocho, -cha, *a.* doddering; doting.
chofe [BOFE].

chófer, chofer, *n.m.* (*pl.* **chóferes, choferes, chofers**) driver; chauffeur.
cholo, -la, *a., n.m.f.* (*S.A.*) Indian; mestizo.—*n.f.* [CHOLLA].
cholla, *n.f.* (*fam.*) noddle, head; nous.
chopo, *n.m.* black poplar; (*fam.*) gun.
choque, *n.m.* shock; collision, impact; clash.
choricero, -ra, *n.m.f.* CHORIZO maker *or* seller; (*fam.*) [EXTREMEÑO].
chorizo, *n.m.* smoked seasoned pork sausage.
chorlito, *n.m.* plover; stone-curlew; (*fam.*) ***cabeza de* —,** ninny, bird-brain.
chorrear, *v.i.* gush, spurt; drip,
chorrera, *n.f.* spout; gulley; rapids; water stains.
chorrillo, *n.m.* (*fam.*) stream (*of money etc.*); ***irse por el* —,** follow the herd.
chorro, *n.m.* jet; flow; ***propulsión a* —,** jet propulsion; ***a chorros,*** in large amounts.
chotacabras, *n.m.* (*orn.*) nightjar.
choto, -ta, *n.m.f.* kid, sucking kid.
chova, *n.f.* (*orn.*) chough; rook.
choz, *n.f.* novelty, surprise; ***hacer* — *a,*** surprise.
choza, *n.f.* hut, cabin.
chubasco, *n.m.* rain storm, downpour; squall.
chucruta, *n.f.* sauerkraut.
chuchear, *v.i.* whisper.
chuchería (1), *n.f.* tit-bit; trinket.
chuchería (2), *n.f.* snaring.
chucho, -cha, *n.m.f.* (*fam.*) dog.—*interj.* down! away! (*to dogs*).—*n.f.* spree; laziness.
chueca, *n.f.* hockey; (*fam.*) lark, joke.
chufa, *n.f.* (*bot.*) chufa; scoffing, mockery.
chufar, *v.t., v.i., v.r.* scoff (*at*).
chufleta [CUCHUFLETA].
chulada, *n.f.* vulgarity; (*fam.*) carefree wit.
chulería, *n.f.* (*fam.*) sparkle, wit, flashiness; bunch of CHULOS.
chuleta, *n.f.* chop, cutlet; (*carp.*) chip; (*educ. fam.*) crib.
chulo, -la, *a.* snappy, flashy; vulgar.—*n.m.* or *f.* flashy type from Madrid slums. —*n.m.* bullfighter's assistant.
chumacera, *n.f.* rowlock; (*mech.*) journal bearing.
chumbera, *n.f.* (*bot.*) prickly-pear cactus.
chumbo, higo chumbo, *n.m.* prickly-pear.
chunga, *n.f.* larking, joking; ***de* —,** in a merry mood.
chupada, *n.f.* suck, sucking.
chupado, -da, *a.* (*fam.*) scrawny.
chupador, *n.m.* teething ring, dummy, (*U.S.*) pacifier.
chupar, *v.t.* suck; sip; (*S.A.*) smoke *or* tipple. —*v.r.* waste away; ***chuparse los dedos,*** (*fig.*) smack one's lips.
chupatintas, *n.m.f. inv.* (*fam.*) pen-pusher.
chupete, *n.m.* baby's dummy, (*U.S.*) pacifier; ***de* —,** tasty.
chupetón, *n.m.* suck, sucking.
churra, *n.f.* (*orn.*) sand-grouse.
churrasco, *n.m.* (*S.A.*) barbecue, roast.
churre, *n.m.* (*fam.*) muck, dirt.
churrero, -ra, *n.m.f.* CHURRO maker *or* seller.
churrete, *n.m.* dirty mark (*on person*).
churriburri, *n.m.* (*fam.*) rotter.
churriento, -ta, *a.* filthy.
churrigueresco, -ca, *a.* (*arch.*) churrigueresque; tawdry, overdone.
churro, *n.m.* doughnut finger, Spanish sweetmeat.
churrullero, -ra, *a.* chattering.—*n.m.f.* chatterer.
churruscar [A], *v.t.* burn (*food*).
churrusco, *n.m.* burnt crust.
¡chus! *interj.* here! (*to dog*); ***sin decir* — *ni mus,*** without saying a word.
chusco, -ca, *a.* funny.
chusma, *n.f.* galley slaves; rabble.
chutar, *v.t., v.i.* shoot (*in football*).
chuzo, *n.m.* (*mil.*) pike; (*fam.*) boast; ***llover a chuzos,*** rain in buckets.
chuzón, -zona, *a.* sharp, waggish.

D

D, d, *n.f.* fifth letter of the Spanish alphabet.
dable, *a.* feasible.
dáctilo, *n.m.* dactyl.
dactilografía, *n.f.* typewriting.
dadaísmo, *n.m.* (*lit., art.*) Dadaism.
dádiva, *n.f.* gift, bounty.
dadivoso, -sa, *a.* bountiful.
dado (1), **-da,** *a., p.p.* given; **— *que,*** granted that; provided that.
dado (2), *n.m.* die; (*mech.*) block.—*pl.* dice.
dador, -ra, *a.* giving.—*n.m.f.* giver, donor; bearer; (*com.*) drawer.
daga, *n.f.* dagger.
daguerrotipo, *n.m.* daguerreotype.
dalia, *n.f.* (*bot.*) dahlia.
Dalila, Dálila, *n.f.* (*Bib.*) Delilah.
dálmata, *a., n.m.f.* Dalmatian (*also dog*).
dalmático, -ca, *a.* Dalmatian.—*n.f.* dalmatic.
dama, *n.f.* lady; dame; (*chess*) queen.—*pl.* draughts, (*U.S.*) checkers.
damajuana, *n.f.* demijohn.
damasceno, -na, *a., n.m.f.* Damascene.
Damasco, *n.m.* Damascus; **damasco,** *n.m.* damask; damson.
damasquina (1), *n.f.* French marigold.
damasquino, -na (2), *a.* damascene.
damería, *n.f.* prudery.
damisela, *n.f.* maiden.
damnación, *n.f.* damnation.
damnificar [A], *v.t.* hurt, damage.
dandismo, *n.m.* dandyism.
danés, -nesa, *a.* Danish.—*n.m.f.* Dane.—*n.m.* Danish.
dánico, -ca, *a.* Danish.
dantesco, -ca, *a.* Dantesque; (*fam.*) fantastic.
Danubio, *n.m.* Danube.
danza, *n.f.* dance; (*fam.*) merry dance; squabble.
danzante, *a.* dancing.—*n.m.f.* dancer.
danzar [C], *v.t., v.i.* dance; (*fam.*) butt in.
danzarín, -rina, *a.* dancing.—*n.m.f.* good dancer.
dañable, *a.* prejudicial.
dañado, -da, *a.* wicked; spoiled.—*n.m.f.* damned soul.
dañar, *v.t.* damage; harm, hurt.
dañino, -na, *a.* harmful, destructive.

daño, *n.m.* harm, hurt; damage; ***en — de,*** to the detriment of; ***hacer —,*** harm, hurt, damage.
dañoso, -sa, *a.* harmful.
dar [16], *v.t.* give, provide.—*v.i.* strike (*the hour*); fall; **— *a,*** give onto, overlook; **— *con,*** come across, bump into; **— *de sí,*** give, stretch; **— *en,*** hit, hit on, get; give onto; run *or* fall into; **— *por,*** consider to be; **— *sobre,*** give onto; **— *tras,*** chase, pursue.—*v.r.* yield; occur; ***darse contra,*** run into, come up against; ***dárselas de,*** put on a show of being; ***darse por,*** be thought to be; consider oneself to be.
dardo, *n.m.* dart; spear.
dares y tomares, *n.m.pl.* (*fam.*) give and take; (*fam.*) squabbles, rowing.
dársena, *n.f.* dock, harbour.
darviniano, -na, *a.* Darwinian.
darvinismo, *n.m.* Darwinism.
data, *n.f.* date; (*com.*) item.
datar *v.t.*, *v.i.* date.
dátil, *n.m.* (*bot.*) date.
datilera, *n.f.* date palm.
dativo, -va, *a.*, *n.m.* (*gram.*) dative.
dato, *n.m.* fact, datum.
de (1), *n.f.* name of letter D.
de (2), *prep.* of; from; by; with; **— *ser así,*** if it should be so.
dé [DAR].
dea, *n.f.* (*poet.*) goddess.
deán, *n.m.* (*eccl.*) dean.
debajo, *adv.* underneath, below.—*prep.* underneath, below (***de***).
debate, *n.m.* debate; struggle.
debatir, *v.t.* debate; fight.—*v.r.* struggle.
debe, *n.m.* (*com.*) debit.
debelación, *n.f.* conquest.
debelar, *v.t.* conquer.
deber, *n.m.* duty; debt; homework.—*v.t.* owe; must; should; ***debe haber venido,*** he should have come; ***debe de haber venido,*** he must have come.
debido, -da, *a.* due, proper, fit.
débil, *a.* weak.
debilidad, *n.f.* weakness.
debilitación, *n.f.* debilitation.
debilitar, *v.t.* debilitate.—*v.r.* grow weak.
debitar, *v.t.* (*com.*) debit.
débito, *n.m.* debit; duty.
debut, *n.m.* début.
debutante, *n.m.* débutant.—*n.f.* débutante.
debutar, *v.i.* make a début.
década, *n.f.* decade.
decadencia, *n.f.* decadence.
decadente, *a.* decadent.
decadentismo, *n.m.* (*lit.*) decadence.
decaer [14], *v.i.* decline, fade, decay.
decagramo, *n.m.* decagramme.
decaimiento, *n.m.* decline, decay.
decalitro, *n.m.* decalitre.
decálogo, *n.m.* decalogue.
decalvar, *v.t.* crop, shave (*convicts*).
decámetro, *n.m.* decametre.
decampar, *v.i.* decamp.
decano, *n.m.* (*educ.*) dean; doyen.
decantar, *v.t.* decant; exaggerate.
decapitación, *n.f.* decapitation.
decapitar, *v.t.* decapitate.
decárea, *n.f.* decare (1000 *sq. metres*).
decasílabo, -ba, *a.* decasyllabic.—*n.m.* decasyllable.
decena, *n.f.* ten.
decenal, *a.* decennial.
decencia, *n.f.* decency, decorum.
decenio, *n.m.*, decade.
decentar [1], *v.t.* start on; begin to lose (*health etc.*).
decente, *a.* decent, proper; reasonable.
decepción, *n.f.* disappointment; deception.
decepcionar, *v.t.* disappoint.
decibel, decibelio, decíbelo, *n.m.* (*phys.*) decibel.
decible, *a.* utterable.
decidero, -ra, *a.* mentionable.
decidir, *v.t.* decide; persuade (***a,*** to).—*v.r.* decide (***a,*** to, ***por,*** on).
decidor, -ra, *a.* witty, fluent.—*n.m.f.* witty talker.
deciduo, -dua, *a.* deciduous.
décima, *n.f.* tenth; Spanish verse metre.
decimación, *n.f.* decimation.
decimal, *a.*, *n.m.* decimal.
decímetro, *n.m.* decimetre.
décimo, -ma, *a.* tenth.—*n.m.* tenth; tenth of lottery ticket.
décimoctavo, -va, *a.*, *n.f.* eighteenth.
décimocuarto, -ta, *a.*, *n.f.* fourteenth.
décimonono, -na, décimonoveno, -na, *a. n.m.* nineteenth.
décimoquinto, -ta, *a.*, *n.f.* fifteenth.
décimoséptimo, -ma, *a.*, *n.f.* seventeenth.
décimosexto, -ta, *a.*, *n.f.* sixteenth.
décimotercero, -ra, décimotercio, -cia, *a.*, *n.f.* thirteenth.
decir, *n.m.* saying; gossip.—[17], *v.t.* say; tell; call; fit, suit; ***como quien dice,*** so to speak; ***como quien no dice nada,*** now this is important; **— *entre*** or ***para sí,*** say to oneself; **— *por* —,** say for saying's sake; **— *que sí,*** say yes; ***¡diga!*** hello! (*on telephone*); ***es* —,** that is to say; ***mejor dicho*** or ***por mejor* —,** rather; ***querer* —,** mean; **se dice,** people say, it is said.
decisión, *n.f.* decision.
decisivo, -va, *a.* decisive.
declamación, *n.f.* declamation.
declamar, *v.t.*, *v.i.* declaim.
declaración, *n.f.* declaration; statement.
declarar, *v.t.* state, declare; explain. —*v.i.* testify.—*v.r.* arise, break out.
declinable, *a.* declinable.
declinación, *n.f.* declination; (*gram*). declension.
declinar, *v.t.* decline.
declive, *n.m.* slope; decline.
declividad, *n.f.*, **declivio,** *n.m.* slope, declivity.
decoloración, *n.f.* decoloration.
decoración, *n.f.* decoration; decorating.—*pl.* (*theat.*) scenery.
decorado, *n.m.* decoration; (*theat.*) decor.
decorador, -ra, *n.m.f.* decorator.
decorar, *v.t.* decorate; (*obs.*) memorize.
decorativo, -va, *a.* decorative.
decoro, *n.m.* decorum; respect.
decoroso, -sa, *a.* decorous.
decrecer [9], *v.i.* decrease.
decreciente, *a.* decreasing, diminishing.
decrecimiento, *n.m.* decrease.
decrepitar, *v.i.* crackle.
decrépito, -ta, *a.* decrepit.
decrepitud, *n.f.* decrepitude.
decretal, *a.*, *n.f.* decretal.

decretar, *v.t.* decree.
decreto, *n.m.* decree.
dechado, *n.m.* model, example; pattern; sampler.
dedada, *n.f.* drop, touch.
dedal, *n.m.* thimble; finger-stall.
dedalera, *n.f.* (*bot.*) foxglove.
dedicación, *n.f.* dedication.
dedicante, *a.* dedicating.—*n.m.f.* dedicator.
dedicar [A], *v.t.* dedicate, devote.—*v.r.* devote oneself; be dedicated *or* devoted (***a,*** to).
dedicatorio, -ria, *a.* dedicatory.—*n.f.* dedication (*in book etc.*).
dedil, *n.m.* finger-stall.
dedillo, *n.m.* little finger; ***al* —,** perfectly.
dedo, *n.m.* finger; toe; ***a dos dedos de,*** within an ace of.
deducción, *n.f.* deduction.
deducir [15], *v.t.* deduce (***de, por,*** from); deduct.
deductivo, -va, *a.* deductive.
defección, *n.f.* defection.
defeccionar, *v.i.* desert.
defectible, *a.* faulty, unsure.
defecto, *n.m.* defect, failing; lack.
defectuoso, -sa, *a.* faulty, defective.
defendedero, -ra, *a.* defensible.
defendedor, -ra, *a.* defending.—*n.m.f.* defender.
defender [2], *v.t.* defend; hinder; (*obs.*) forbid.
defendible, *a.* defendable; defensible.
defensa, *n.f.* defence.—*n.m.* (*sport*) back, defence.
defensión, *n.f.* protection, defence, safeguard.
defensivo, -va, *a.* defensive.—*n.m.* defence, safeguard; ***a la defensiva,*** on the defensive.
defensor, -ra, *n.m.f.* defender; (*jur.*) counsel for the defence.
deferencia, *n.f.* deference.
deferente, *a.* deferential.
deficiencia, *n.f.* deficiency, defect.
deficiente, *a.* deficient, defective.
déficit, *n.m.* *inv.* deficit.
definible, *a.* definable.
definición, *n.f.* definition.
definido, -da, *a.* definite; defined.
definir, *v.t.* define.
definitivo, -va, *a.* definitive; ***en definitiva,*** definitely.
deflector, *n.m.* deflector.
deflexión, *n.f.* deflection.
deformación, *n.f.* deformation; (*rad.*) distortion.
deformar, *v.t.* deform, distort.
deforme, *a.* deformed.
deformidad, *n.f.* deformity.
defraudación, *n.f.* defrauding, fraud; usurping.
defraudar, *v.t.* defraud; disappoint.
defuera, *adv.* outside.
defunción, *n.f.* demise, decease.
degeneración, *n.f.* degeneration, degeneracy.
degenerado, -da, *a.*, *n.m.f.* degenerate.
degenerar, *v.i.* degenerate.
degollación, *n.f.* beheading.
degolladura, *n.f.* throat-cutting; décolletage.
degollar [10], *v.t.* cut the throat of; cut low (*clothes*); ruin, spoil, murder; (*fam.*) bore to tears.
degollina, *n.f.* (*fam.*) slaughter.
degradación, *n.f.* degradation.
degradante, *a.* degrading.
degradar, *v.t.* degrade; demote.
degüello, *n.m.* throat-cutting.
degustación, *n.f.* tasting, sampling.
degustar, *v.t.* taste, sample.
dehesa, *n.f.* pasture, meadow.
deicida, *a.* deicidal.—*n.m.f.* deicide (*person*).
deicidio, *n.m.* deicide (*act*).
deidad, *n.f.* deity.
deificación, *n.f.* deification.
deificar [A], *v.t.* deify.
deísmo, *n.m.* deism.
deísta, *a.* deistic.—*n.m.f.* deist.
dejación, *n.f.* relinquishment.
dejadez, *n.f.* laziness, slovenliness; low spirits.
dejado, -da, *a.* negligent, slovenly; dejected; ***— de la mano de Dios,*** Godforsaken.
dejamiento, *n.m.* relinquishment; slovenliness; dejection.
dejar, *v.t.* leave; let, allow; produce; lend; ***— caer,*** drop. *v.i.* cease, stop; ***— de,*** leave off, give up; ***no — de,*** not fail to.—*v.r.* be slipshod; allow oneself.
deje, dejillo, *n.m.* regional accent, lilt; after-taste.
dejo, *n.m.* relinquishment; end; regional accent; after-taste; carelessness; drop (*in voice*).
del [DE EL].
delación, *n.f.* denunciation, betrayal, informing.
delantal, *n.m.* apron, pinafore.
delante, *adv.* before, in front, ahead.—*prep.* in front (***de,*** of).
delantero, -ra, *a.* forward, foremost, front. —*n.m.* (*sport*) forward; postillion.—*n.f.* front front row; lead, advantage.
delatar, *v.t.* denounce, inform on, betray.
delator, -ra, *a.* denouncing, betraying.—*n.m.f.* accuser, informer.
deleble, *a.* erasable.
delectación, *n.f.* delectation.
delegación, *n.f.* delegation.
delegado, -da, *n.m.f.* delegate; (*com.*) agent.
delegar [B], *v.t.* delegate.
deleitar, *v.t.* delight.—*v.r.* delight, take delight (***en,*** in).
deleite, *n.m.* delight.
deleitoso, -sa, *a.* delightful.
deletéreo, -rea, *a.* deleterious; poisonous (*gas*).
deletrear, *v.t.* spell; decipher.
deletreo, *n.m.* spelling.
deleznable, *a.* slippery; crumbly; perishable.
délfico, -ca, *a.* Delphic.
delfín, *n.m.* dolphin; Dauphin.
Delfos, *n.f.* Delphi.
delgadez, *n.f.* slenderness; lightness; sharpness.
delgado, -da, *a.* thin, slender; sharp, fine.
delgaducho, -cha, *a.* lanky, spindly.
deliberación, *n.f.* deliberation.
deliberar, *v.t.*, *v.i.* deliberate, decide.
deliberativo, -va, *a.* deliberative.
delicadez, *n.f.* delicateness, weakness; touchiness.
delicadeza, *n.f.* delicacy; ingenuity; scrupulosity; good manners.
delicado, -da, *a.* delicate; sharp, clever; touchy; chary.
delicia, *n.f.* delight.

delicioso, -sa, *a.* delicious, delightful.

delictivo, -va, delictuoso, -sa, *a.* criminal.

delimitar, *v.t.* delimit.

delincuencia, *n.f.* delinquency.

delincuente, *a., n.m.f.* delinquent.

delineante, *n.m.* designer, draughtsman.

delinear, *v.t.* delineate.

delinquimiento, *n.m.* transgression.

delinquir [F], *v.i.* transgress, be delinquent.

deliquio, *n.m.* swoon.

delirante, *a.* delirous, raving.

delirar, *v.i.* be delirious, rave.

delirio, *n.m.* delirium; raving, nonsense.

delito, *n.m.* crime.

delta, *n.f.* delta.

deludir, *v.t.* delude.

delusivo, -va, delusorio, -ria, *a.* delusive, delusory.

demacrar, *v.t.* emaciate.—*v.r.* waste away.

demagogia, *n.f.* demagogy.

demagógico, -ca, *a.* demagogic.

demagogo, -ga, *a.* demagogic.—*n.m.f.* demagogue.

demanda, *n.f.* demand; claim; request; ***en — de,*** in search of; ***tener —,*** be in demand.

demandante, *n.m.f.* (*jur.*) plaintiff.

demandar, *v.t.* demand, request, desire; (*jur.*) sue.

demarcación, *n.f.* demarcation.

demarcar [A], *v.t.* demarcate.

demás, *a.* rest of the; (***los — días, las — personas***).—*pron.* the rest (***lo —, las*** or ***los —***); ***estar —,*** be in the way, be useless; ***por —,*** in vain; excessively; ***por lo —,*** as for the rest, furthermore.

demasía, *n.f.* excess, surplus; audacity; outrage.

demasiadamente, *adv.* too much, too.

demasiado, -da, *a., pron.* too much, too many.—*adv.* too, too much.

demasiar, *v.r.* (*fam.*) overdo it, go too far.

demediar, *v.t.* halve; reach the middle of.—*v.i.* be cut in half.

demencia, *n.f.* dementia, madness.

dementar, *v.t.* drive mad.

demente, *a.* demented.—*n.m.* madman.—*n.m.f.* lunatic.

demérito, *n.m.* demerit.

demisión, *n.f.* submission, humility.

democracia, *n.f.* democracy.

demócrata, *a.* democratic.—*n.m.f.* democrat.

democrático, -ca, *a.* democratic.

democratizar [C], *v.t., v.r.* democratize.

demografía, *n.f.* demography.

demoler [5], *v.t.* demolish.

demolición, *n.f.* demolition.

demonche, *n.m.* (*fam.*) devil.

demoníaco, -ca, *a., n.m.f.* demoniac.

demonio, *n.m.* demon, devil.

demonismo, *n.m.* demonism

demontre, *n.m.* (*fam.*) devil.—*interj.* the deuce!

demora, *n.f.* delay; (*naut.*) bearing.

demorar, *v.t., v.i.* delay; halt; (*naut.*) bear.

Demóstenes, *n.m.* Demosthenes.

demostrable, *a.* demonstrable.

demostración, *n.f.* demonstration.

demostrar [4], *v.t.* demonstrate; show clearly.

demostrativo, -va, *a., n.m.* (*gram.*) demonstrative.

demótico, -ca, *a.* demotic.

demudar, *v.t.* alter, change; disguise.—*v.r.* change, alter.

denario, *a.* denary.—*n.m.* denarius.

dende, *adv.* (*dial., obs.*) thence.

denegación, *n.f.* denial, refusal.

denegar [1B], *v.t.* deny, refuse.

denegrecer [9], *v.t.* blacken, darken.

denegrido, -da, *a.* blackened.

dengoso, -sa, *a.* fussy, (*fam.*) finicky.

dengue, *n.m.* affectedness, fastidiousness; long cape; (*med.*) dengue.

denigración, *n.f.* denigration.

denigrante, *a.* denigrating.

denigrar, *v.t.* denigrate, defame.

denodado, -da, *a.* bold, daring.

denominación, *n.f.* denomination.

denominador, -ra, *a.* denominating.—*n.m.* (*math*) denominator.

denominar, *v.t.* denominate.

denostar [4], *v.t.* revile.

denotar, *v.t.* denote.

densidad, *n.f.* density; obscurity.

densificar [A], *v.t.* densify.

denso, -sa, *a.* dense; obscure; crowded.

dentado, -da, *a.* toothed, dentate; perforated. —*n.m.* perforation (*on stamps*).

dentadura, *n.f.* denture.

dental, *a., n.f.* dental.

dentar [1], *v.t.* tooth; perforate (*stamps*).—*v.i.* teethe; ***sin —,*** imperforate (*stamps*).

dentellada, *n.f.* bite; gnashing; tooth-mark.

dentellado, -da, *a.* denticulated, serrated.

dentellar, *v.i.* gnash the teeth; chatter (*teeth*).

dentellear, *v.t.* nibble.

dentera, *n.f.* tingle (*sensation in teeth as reaction to certain tastes, sounds etc.*); eagerness; envy; ***dar — a,*** set (*s.o.'s*) teeth on edge; whet the appetite of.

dentezuelo, *n.m.* small tooth.

dentición, *n.f.* dentition.

dentífrico, -ca, *a.* for the teeth.—*n.m.* dentifrice, tooth-paste.

dentista, *n.m.f.* dentist.

dentistería, *n.f.* dentistry.

dentro, *adv.* inside, within.—*prep.* inside (*space*) (*de*); within (*time*) (*de*).

denudar, *v.t.* lay bare, denude.—*v.r.* be stripped bare.

denuedo, *n.m.* daring.

denuesto, *n.m.* affront, abuse.

denuncia, *n.f.* announcement, proclamation; denunciation.

denunciación, *n.f.* denunciation.

denunciar, *v.t.* denounce; proclaim; foretell.

deparar, *v.t.* provide; present.

departamental, *a.* departmental.

departamento, *n.m.* department; compartment; (*S.A.*) flat.

depauperar, *v.t.* impoverish; debilitate.

dependencia, *n.f.* dependence; dependency; agency; branch; employees.

depender, *v.i.* depend (**de,** on).

dependienta, *n.f.* shop assistant (*female*).

dependiente, *a.* dependant.—*n.m.f.* dependent; shop-assistant; employee, clerk.

deplorable, *a.* deplorable.

deplorar, *v.t.* deplore.

deponente, *a., n.m.f.* (*gram., jur.*) deponent.

deponer [25], *v.t.* depose; put aside; take down; testify, affirm.

deportación, *n.f.* deportation.

deportar, *v.t.* deport.

deporte, *n.m.* sport.
deportismo, *n.m.* sport, sports.
deportista, *n.m.* sportsman.—*n.f.* sportswoman.
deportivo, -va, *a.* sporting, rel. to sport.
deposición, *n.f.* deposition.
depositar, *v.t.* deposit.—*v.r.* settle (*as sediment*).
depósito, *n.m.* depot; deposit; reserve; tank, reservoir.
depravación, *n.f.* depravity.
depravar, *v.t.* deprave.
deprecar [A], *v.t.* entreat.
depreciación, *n.f.* depreciation.
depreciar, *v.t.*, *v.i.* depreciate.
depredación, *n.f.* depredation.
depredar, *v.t.* depredate; pillage.
depresión, *n.f.* depression, drop, dip.
depresivo, -va, *a.* depressive.
deprimente, *a.* depressing, depressive.
deprimir, *v.t.* depress; dent; lower.
depuesto, *p.p.* [DEPONER].
depurar, *v.t.* purify, cleanse, refine.
depuse [DEPONER].
derecha, *n.f.* right (*side, political*).
derechera, *n.f.* straight road.
derechista, *a.* (*pol.*) rightwing.—*n.m.f.* right-winger.
derecho, -cha, *a.* right-hand, right-handed; upright; straight.—*n.m.* law (*as subject*); right; ***no hay* —,** nobody has the right to do *or* say that.—*pl.* dues, taxes.—*n.f.* right side; right wing.—*adv.* rightly; directly.
deriva, *n.f.* drift; ***a la* —,** adrift.
derivación, *n.f.* derivation; diverting; (*elec.*) shunt.
derivado, -da, *a.*, *n.m.* derivative.—*n.m.* by-product.
derivar, *v.t.* derive; divert; (*elec.*) shunt.—*v.i.*, *v.r.* derive (***de***, from); drift.
derivativo, -va, *a.*, *n.m.* derivative.
dermatitis, *n.f.* dermatitis.
derogación, *n.f.* repeal, annulment; deterioration.
derogar [B], *v.t.* abolish, destroy; reform.
derramadero, *n.m.* dump; overspill.
derramamiento, *n.m.* spilling, shedding, over-flow; scattering; waste.
derramar, *v.t.* pour; spread; spill, shed; waste.—*v.r.* spread; overflow.
derrame, *n.m.* [DERRAMAMIENTO]; chamfer, bevel; (*med.*) discharge.
derredor, *n.m.* circumference; ***al*** or ***en* —,** round, round about; ***al* — *de*,** around.
derrelicto, *n.m.* (*naut.*) wreck; jetsam.
derrelinquir [F], *v.t.* abandon, forsake.
derrengar [1B, *modern* B], *v.t.* maim, break the back of; twist.
derretido, -da, *a.* (*fam.*) love-lorn.—*n.m.* concrete.
derretimiento, *n.m.* melting, thaw; (*fam.*) crush, passion.
derretir [8], *v.t.* melt, thaw; squander; (*fam.*) change (*money*).—*v.r.* melt, thaw; (*fam.*) fall in love easily; (*fam.*) be like a cat on hot bricks.
derribar, *v.t.* demolish; knock down; overthrow.—*v.r.* tumble down; collapse.
derribo, *n.m.* demolition; overthrow.—*pl.* debris.
derrocadero, *n.m.* precipice.
derrocar [4A, *modern* A], *v.t.* fling *or* throw down; knock down, destroy; oust.
derrochar, *v.t.* squander.
derroche, *n.m.* waste, squandering.
derrota, *n.f.* rout, defeat; route; (*naut.*) course.
derrotar, *v.t.* rout; wear down; squander; ruin.—*v.r.* (*naut.*) stray off course.
derrotero, *n.m.* (*naut.*) course.
derrotismo, *n.m.* defeatism.
derrotista, *a.*, *n.m.f.* defeatist.
derruir [O], *v.t.* ruin, destroy.
derrumbamiento, *n.m.* plunge, fall; collapse; landslide.
derrumbar, *v.t.* fling down, throw flat.—*v.r.* fall flat; collapse, cave in.
derrumbe, *n.m.* precipice; landslide.
derviche, *n.m.* dervish.
desabarrancar [A], *v.t.* pull out, extricate.
desabollar, *v.t.* planish, flatten.
desabor, *n.m.* tastelessness.
desaborido, -da, *a.* tasteless, insipid; flimsy; (*fam.*) boring, dull.
desabotonar, *v.t.* unbutton.—*v.i.* bloom.
desabrido, -da, *a.* tasteless; gruff, harsh; bleak.
desabrigar [B], *v.t.* expose, uncover; bare.
desabrigo, *n.m.* nakedness; exposure.
desabrimiento, *n.m.* insipidity; severity; glumness.
desabrochar, *v.t.* unbutton, unfasten; reveal.
desacalorar, *v.r.* cool off.
desacatar, *v.t.* behave disrespectfully towards.
desacato, *n.m.* disrespect.
desacertar [1], *v.i.* be in error, err.
desacierto, *n.m.* error, blunder.
desacomodar, *v.t.* inconvenience; dismiss.—*v.r.* lose one's job.
desacomodo, *n.m.* dismissal.
desaconsejar, *v.t.* dissuade.
desacoplar, *v.t.* uncouple.
desacordar, *v.t.* ill-tune.—*v.r.* be out of tune; forget.
desacorde, *a.* out of tune; discordant.
desacostumbrado, -da, *a.* unusual, unaccustomed.
desacostumbrar, *v.t.* break (*s.o.*) of a habit.—*v.r.* lose the habit (***de***, of).
desacreditar, *v.t.* discredit.
desacuerdo, *n.m.* disagreement; forgetting.
desafección, *n.f.* dislike.
desafecto, -ta, *a.* disaffected, opposed.—*n.m.* ill-will.
desafiador, -ra, *a.* challenging, defiant.—*n.m.f.* challenger; duellist.
desafiar [L], *v.t.* challenge; defy; rival.
desafición, *n.f.* dislike.
desaficionar, *v.t.* stop the desire to.—*v.r.* lose one's liking (***de***, for).
desafilar, *v.t.* blunt, dull.
desafinar, *v.i.*, *v.r.* get out of tune; (*fam.*) speak indiscreetly.
desafío, *n.m.* challenge; rivalry.
desaforado, -da, *a.* disorderly, lawless; uncalled-for.
desaforar [4], *v.t.* encroach on the rights of.—*v.r.* overstep the mark.
desafortunado, -da, *a.* unfortunate.
desafuero, *n.m.* excess, outrage; encroachment.
desagradable, *a.* unpleasant.

desagradar, *v.t.* displease.
desagradecer [9], *v.t.* be ungrateful for.
desagradecido, -da, *a.* ungrateful.
desagradecimiento, *n.m.* ingratitude.
desagrado, *n.m.* displeasure.
desagraviar, *v.t.* make amends to.
desagravio, *n.m.* amends.
desagregar [B], *v.t., v.r.* disintegrate.
desaguar [H], *v.t.* drain; squander.
desagüe, *n.m.* drainage; outlet.
desahogado, -da, *a.* brazen; roomy; comfortable; carefree; easy.
desahogar [B], *v.t.* ease, relieve; give vent to. —*v.r.* recover, take it easy; get free of one's difficulties; open one's heart (***de,*** about).
desahogo, *n.m.* easement, comfort; relief; vent, free rein; unburdening.
desahuciar, *v.t.* drive to despair; despair of; evict.—*v.r.* despair.
desahucio, *n.m.* eviction.
desairado, -da, *a.* graceless; thwarted.
desairar, *v.t.* slight, snub.
desaire, *n.m.* lack of charm; slight.
desajuste, *n.m.* fault, break-down; disagreement.
desalado, -da, *a.* hasty, eager.
desalar (1), *v.t.* remove the salt from.
desalar (2), *v.t.* clip the wings of.—*v.r.* rush; yearn (***por,*** for).
dasalentar [1], *v.t.* make breathless; discourage.—*v.r.* get out of breath; get discouraged.
desaliento, *n.m.* depression, discouragement.
desaliñar, *v.t.* rumple.
desaliño, *n.m.* slovenliness; neglect.
desalmado, -da, *a.* merciless, inhuman.
desalmar, *v.r.* crave (***por,*** for).
desalojar, *v.t.* dislodge; evict.—*v.i.* move away.
desalterar, *v.t.* allay, assuage.
desamar, *v.t.* dislike, detest; stop loving.
desamor, *n.m.* coldness; hatred; dislike.
desamortizar [C], *v.t.* disentail.
desamparar, *v.t.* desert; forsake, abandon.
desamparo, *n.m.* abandonment; helplessness.
desamueblado, -da, *a.* unfurnished.
desandar [11], *v.t.* retrace (***lo andado,*** one's steps).
desangrar, *v.t., v.i.* bleed heavily.
desanimación, *n.f.* down-heartedness.
desanimar, *v.t.* deject, dishearten.
desánimo, *n.m.* low spirits.
desanublar, *v.t.* clarify.—*v.r.* clear up (*weather*).
desanudar, *v.t.* untie; disentangle.
desapacible, *a.* disagreeable.
desaparecer [9], *v.t.* make disappear.—*v.i., v.r.* disappear.
desaparición, *n.f.* disappearance.
desaparroquiar, *v.t.* take customers away from.—*v.r.* lose trade.
desapasionado, -da, *a.* dispassionate.
desapego, *n.m.* indifference, coolness, dislike.
desaplacible, *a.* unpleasant.
desaplicación, *n.f.* idleness, laziness.
desaplicar [A], *v.t.* make idle.—*v.r.* be idle.
desapoderado, -da, *a.* impetuous, wild.
desapoderar, desaposesionar, *v.t.* dispossess.
desapreciar, *v.t.* underestimate.
desaprensar, *v.t.* take the shine off; free, ease.
desaprensivo, -va, *a.* unworried; unscrupulous.
desaprobación, *n.f.* disapproval.
desaprobar [4], *v.t.* disapprove of.
desapropiar, *v.t.* divest, deprive (***de,*** of).—*v.r.* surrender, give up (*property*).
desaprovechado, -da, *a.* unrewarding, unproductive.
desaprovechar, *v.t.* fail to make use of.
desarbolar, *v.t.* unmast; clear (*woodland*).
desarmar, *v.t.* disarm; dismantle.—*v.r.* disarm.
desarme, *n.m.* disarmament; dismantling.
desarraigar [B], *v.t.* root out; extirpate.
desarrapado, -da, *a.* ragged.
desarrebujar, *v.t.* disentangle, unravel.
desarreglar, *v.t.* disarrange, put out of order, derange.
desarreglo, *n.m.* disorder, confusion.
desarrimar, *v.t.* separate; dissuade.
desarrollar, *v.t., v.i., v.r.* develop, unfold, unroll.
desarrollo, *n.m.* development, unfolding.
desarrugar [B], *v.t., v.r.* smooth out.
desarticular, *v.t.* disarticulate, dislocate.
desaseo, *n.m.* slovenliness, untidiness.
desasir [12], *v.t.* let go, release.—*v.r.* let go of, give up (***de***).
desasociar, *v.t.* dissociate.
desasosegar [1B], *v.t.* disquiet.
desasosiego, *n.m.* uneasiness, anxiety.
desastrado, -da, *a.* unfortunate; ragged.
desastre, *n.m.* disaster; misfortune.
desastroso, -sa, *a.* wretched, unfortunate.
desatar, *v.t.* untie, undo.—*v.r.* run wild; break out.
desatascar [A], *v.t.* extricate.
desate, *n.m.* loosening, untying; looseness; lack of restraint.
desatención, *n.f.* disregard.
desatender [2], *v.t.* disregard.
desatento, -ta, *a.* inattentive, thoughtless.
desatiento, *n.m.* anxiety, worry.
desatinado, -da, *a.* unwise, extravagant, unruly.—*n.m.f.* madcap: blunderer.
desatinar, *v.t.* bewilder, derange.—*v.i.* act *or* speak wildly; reel.—*v.r.* get confused.
desatino, *n.m.* folly; bewilderment; tactlessness.
desaturdir, *v.t.* bring round, rouse.
desautorizar [C], *v.t.* deprive of authority; discredit.
desavahar, *v.t.* air, cool.—*v.r.* cheer up.
desavenencia, *n.f.* disagreement; misunderstanding.
desavenir [36], *v.t.* cause trouble with.—*v.r.* disagree, quarrel (***de, con,*** with).
desaventajado, -da, *a.* disadvantageous.
desaviar [L], *v.t.* mislead; ill-equip; deprive.
desavisado, -da, *a.* uninformed; ill-advised.
desayudar, *v.t.* hinder.
desayunar, *v.i.* have breakfast.—*v.r.* breakfast (***con,*** on); hear (***de,*** of) for the first time.
desayuno, *n.m.* breakfast.
desazón, *n.f.* tastelessness; displeasure, discomfort; poor heart, poverty (*of land*).
desazonado, -da, *a.* indisposed; peevish; poor (*land*).
desazonar, *v.t.* make tasteless; annoy embitter.
desbancar [A], *v.t.* oust.

desbandada, *n.f.* disbandment; ***a la* —,** helter-skelter.
desbandar, *v.r.* flee in disorder; desert.
desbarajustar, *v.t.* throw into confusion.
desbarajuste, *n.m.* disorder, confusion.
desbaratar, *v.t.* destroy; waste; ruin; (*mil.*) rout.—*v.i.*, *v.r.* be unreasonable.
desbarate, desbarato, *n.m.* ruin; waste; rout.
desbarbar, *v.t.* shave; trim.
desbarrar, *v.t.* unbar.—*v.i.* slip away; be foolish.
desbarretar, *v.t.* unbolt.
desbarro, *n.m.* slip, folly; quiet departure.
desbastar, *v.t.* rough-hew; waste; weaken; educate.
desbocado, -da, *a.* wide-mouthed; broken-edged; runaway; foul-mouthed.
desbocar [A], *v.t.* break the spout, mouth *or* edge of.—*v.i.* run into, meet (*rivers, streets*).—*v.r.* run wild, break loose; swear, curse; become licentious.
desbordamiento, *n.m.* overflowing.
desbordar, *v.i.*, *v.r.* overflow; lose self-control.
desborde, *n.m.* overflowing; inundation.
desbragado, -da, *a.* (*fam.*) scruffy, ragged.
desbravar, *v.t.* break in, tame.—*v.i.*, *v.r.* get tame, calm down.
desbravecer [9], *v.i.*, *v.r.* [DESBRAVAR].
desbrazar [C], *v.r.* wave one's arms violently.
desbridar, *v.t.* unbridle.
desbrujar, *v.t.* wear away.
desbuchar, *v.t.* disgorge (*of birds*); reveal (*secrets*).
descabal, *a.* imperfect.
descabalgar [B], *v.t.*, *v.i.* dismount.
descabellado, -da, *a.* wild, rash; dishevelled.
descabellar, *v.t.* dishevel, rumple; (*taur.*) kill the bull by piercing the nape of his neck.
descabezado, -da, *a.* rash, headstrong.
descabezamiento, *n.m.* beheading; quandary.
descabezar [C], *v.t.* behead; lop off; (*fam.*) break the back of (*a task*); **— *un sueño*,** take a nap.—*v.r.* rack one's brains.
descabullir [J], *v.r.* sneak away.
descaecer [9], *v.t.* languish.
descalabrar, *v.t.* brain; harm, ruin.—*v.r.* hurt one's head.
descalabro, *n.m.* misfortune, damage, loss.
descalificar [A], *v.t.* disqualify.
descalzado, -da, *a.* bare-foot, bare-footed.
descalzar [C], *v.t.* take one's shoes off; undermine.
descalzo, -za, *a.* bare-foot, unshod; (*eccl.*) discalced.
descambiar, *v.t.* exchange again (*esp. goods bought in error*).
descaminar, *v.t.* mislead.—*v.r.* go astray; run off the road.
descamino, *n.m.* leading *or* going astray.
descamisado, -da, *a.* ragged, shirtless.—*n.m.f.* ragamuffin, wretch.
descampado, -da, *a.* open (*terrain*).
descansadero, *n.m.* resting place.
descansado, -da, *a.* rested; unworried, tranquil.
descansar, *v.t.* rest; help out.—*v.i.* rest; stop work; lean.
descanso, *n.m.* rest, peace, quiet; interval, break; support; relief, aid; stair-landing.
descantillar, *v.t.* pare.
descapotable, *a.*, *n.m.* convertible (*car*).
descarado, -da, *a.* brazen, shameless.
descarar, *v.r.* be shameless *or* impudent; have the nerve (***a***, to).
descarburar, *v.t.* decarbonize.
descarga, *n.f.* unloading; discharge; discount; customs clearance.
descargadero, *n.m.* unloading bay; wharf.
descargar [B], *v.t.* unload; discharge; clear; strike (*a blow*).—*v.i.* discharge, open, burst, empty.—*v.r.* get rid (***de***, of); free oneself of.
descargo, *n.m.* unloading; exoneration; discharge.
descargue, *n.m.* unloading.
descariño, *n.m.* lovelessness, indifference, coolness.
descarnado, -da, *a.* thin, lean; (*fig.*) bald, plain.—*n.f.* death.
descarnar, *v.t.* remove the flesh from; wear down.—*v.r.* lose weight.
descaro, *n.m.* effrontery, sauciness.
descarriar, *v.t.* [DESCAMINAR].—*v.r.* get separated (***de***, from); go wrong.
descarrilamiento, *n.m.* derailment.
descarrilar, *v.t.* derail.—*v.i.*, *v.r.* be derailed.
descarrío, *n.m.* erring; ruin.
descartar, *v.t.* discard, reject.—*v.r.* shirk (***de***).
descarte, *n.m.* rejection; shirking.
descasar, *v.t.* annul the marriage of; disturb the good order of.—*v.r.* have one's marriage annulled; be deranged.
descascar [A], *v.t.* shell, peel.—*v.r.* shatter; blabber.
descastar, *v.t.* exterminate (*pests*).—*v.r.* lose one's natural affections.
descatolizar [C], *v.t.* cause to lapse.—*v.r.* lapse (*said of Catholics*).
descendencia, *n.f.* descent, descendants.
descendente, *a.* descending.
descender [2], *v.t.* descend; lower; bring down; take down.—*v.i.* descend; go *or* come down; descend, derive (***de***, from); stoop (***a***, to).
descendiente, *n.m.f.* descendant.
descensión, *n.f.* descent, descending.
descenso, *n.m.* descent; drop, decline.
descentralizar [C], *v.t.* decentralize.
desceñir [8K], *v.t.* ungird.
descercar [A], *v.t.* tear down the fences of; break the siege of.
descerebrar, *v.t.* brain.
descerrajado, -da, *a.* (*fig.*) corrupt, evil.
descerrajar, *v.t.* break the lock of; (*fig.*) fire (*shots*).
descifrar, *v.t.* make out, decipher.
descivilizar [C], *v.t.* barbarize, decivilize.
desclasificar [A], *v.t.* disqualify.
descocado, -da, *a.* (*fam.*) cheeky, saucy.
descocer [5D], *v.t.* digest.
descoco, *n.m.* (*fam.*) cheek, nerve.
descolar, *v.t.* dock; (*S.A.*) snub; dismiss (*employees*).
descolgar [4B], *v.t.* unhang.—*v.r.* fall down, drop; (*fam.*) blurt (***con***, out).
descolocado, -da, *a.* misplaced, out of place.
descoloramiento, *n.m.* discoloration.
descolorar, *v.t.* discolour.
descolorido, -da, *a.* discoloured.
descolorimiento, *n.m.* discoloration.
descolorir [DESCOLORAR].
descollar [4], *v.t.* stand out.

descomedido, -da, *a.* excessive; impolite.
descomedimiento, *n.m.* disrespect.
descomedir [8], *v.r.* be rude.
descomodidad, *n.f.* discomfort.
descompás, *n.m.* excess.
descompasado, -da, *a.* immoderate.
descomponer [25], *v.t.* upset; decompose; alienate.—*v.r.* decompose; change for the worse; alter (*of the face*); fall out (**con,** with).
descomposición, *n.f.* decomposition; disorder, confusion; disagreement; discomposure.
descompostura, *n.f.* decomposition; disorder; brazenness.
descompresión, *n.f.* decompression.
descompuesto, -ta, *a.* impudent; exasperated; out of order.—*p.p.* [DESCOMPONER].
descomulgado, -da, *a.* wicked, evil.
descomulgar [B], *v.t.* excommunicate.
descomunal, *a.* huge; extraordinary.
desconceptuar [M], *v.t.* discredit.
desconcertar [1], *v.t.* disconcert, baffle, disturb; dislocate.—*v.r.* get upset; be reckless.
desconcierto, *n.m.* disorder; imprudence; mismanagement; disagreement; dismay.
desconectar, *v.t.* disconnect.
desconexión, *n.f.* disconnexion.
desconfiado, -da, *a.* distrustful.
desconfianza, *n.f.* distrust.
desconfiar [L], *v.i.* distrust (*de*).
desconforme, *a.* disagreeing; unlike.
desconformidad, *n.f.* disagreement; disparity; discord.
descongelar, *v.t., v.i., v.r.* melt, defrost.
descongestionar, *v.t.* clear.
desconocer [9], *v.t.* not know (*about*); ignore, snub; disown.—*v.r.* be unrecognizable.
desconocido, -da, *a.* unknown; strange; ungrateful.—*n.m.f.* stranger.
desconocimiento, *n.m.* disregard; ingratitude; ignorance.
desconsiderado, -da, *a.* inconsiderate; ill-considered.
desconsolar [4], *v.t., v.i.* grieve.
desconsuelo, *n.m.* distress, grief.
descontagiar, *v.t.* disinfect.
descontaminación, *n.f.* decontamination.
descontaminar, *v.t.* decontaminate.
descontar [4], *v.t.* discount; take for granted.
descontentadizo, -za, *a.* hard to please.
descontentamiento, *n.m.* discontentment; disagreement.
descontentar, *v.t.* displease, dissatisfy.
descontento, -ta, *a.* discontent(ed), displeased.—*n.m.* discontent.
descontinuar [M], *v.t.* discontinue.
descontinuo, -nua, *a.* discontinuous.
desconvenible, *a.* unsuitable, incompatible.
desconveniencia, *n.f.* inconvenience; discord.
desconveniente, *a.* inconvenient; discordant.
desconvenir [36], *v.i., v.r.* disagree; match badly.
descorazonar, *v.t.* dishearten.
descorchar, *v.r.* uncork.
descorrer, *v.t.* draw back.—*v.i.* flow.
descortés, *a.* discourteous.
descortesía, *n.f.* discourtesy.
descortezar [C], *v.t.* strip; (*fam.*) polish (*manners*).
descoser, *v.t.* rip, unstitch.—*v.r.* prattle; come unstitched.
descosido, -da, *a.* indiscreet; disjointed; unstitched.—*n.m.f.* (*fam.*) rip, tear-away (*wild person*).—*n.m.* rip.
descote [ESCOTE].
descoyuntar, *v.t.* disjoint; (*fig.*) vex.
descrédito, *n.m.* discredit.
descreer [N], *v.t.* disbelieve; deny due credit to.
descreído, -da, *a.* unbelieving.—*n.m.f.* unbeliever.
describir [*p.p.* **descrito**], *v.t.* describe.
descripción, *n.f.* description.
descriptible, *a.* describable.
descriptor, -ra, *a.* descriptive.—*n.m.f.* describer.
descrito, *p.p.* [DESCRIBIR].
descuajar, *v.t.* dissolve; uproot; dispirit.
descuartizar [C], *v.t.* quarter; carve up.
descubierta, *n.f.* reconnaissance, scanning.
descubierto, -ta, *a.* manifest; bare-headed, unveiled; exposed.—*p.p.* [DESCUBRIR].—*n.m.* exposition of the Eucharist; discovery; ***al* —,** openly; ***en* —,** (*com.*) overdrawn.
descubridor, -ra, *a.* discovering.—*n.m.f.* discoverer; (*mil.*) scout.
descubrimiento, *n.m.* discovery.
descubrir [*p.p.* **descubierto**] *v.t.* discover; disclose; uncover; (*mil.*) reconnoitre.—*v.r.* take off one's hat.
descuello, *n.m.* excellence, prominence; great stature.
descuento, *n.m.* discount; deduction.
descuidado, -da, *a.* careless.
descuidar, *v.t.* neglect, overlook; distract.—*v.i., v.r.* be careless; not worry (*de*, about).
descuido, *n.m.* carelessness; neglect, omission.
desde, *prep.* from (*place*); since (*time*); — ***entonces,*** ever since; — ***luego,*** at once; admittedly; of course.
desdecir [17], *v.i.* degenerate; be unworthy (*de*, of).—*v.r.* gainsay, retract (*de*).
desdén, *n.m.* disdain, contempt.
desdentado, -da, *a.* toothless.
desdeñable, *a.* despicable.
desdeñar, *v.t.* disdain, scorn.—*v.r.* be disdainful; loathe; not deign (*de*, to).
desdeñoso, -sa, *a.* disdainful, scornful.
desdibujar, *v.r.* become blurred.
desdicha, *n.f.* misfortune, misery.
desdichado, -da, *a.* unfortunate, wretched.
desdoblar, *v.t., v.r.* unfold, spread out.
desdorar, *v.t.* take the gilt off; tarnish, sully.
deseable, *a.* desirable.
desear, *v.t.* want, desire, wish.
desecar [A], *v.t., v.r.* desiccate.
desechar, *v.t.* reject; expel; underrate; turn (*keys*).
desecho, *n.m.* residue; debris; rejection; (*S.A.*) short-cut.
desedificar [A], *v.t.* set a bad example for.
desembalar, *v.t.* unpack.
desembarazado, -da, *a.* open, easy, free.
desembarazar [C], *v.t.* free, disencumber.—*v.r.* get free; be cleared.
desembarazo, *n.m.* ease, freedom.
desembarcadero, *n.m.* quay, pier.
desembarcar [A], *v.t., v.i., v.r.* disembark.
desembarco, *n.m.* disembarkation.
desembargar [B], *v.t.* free, disembargo.

desembarque, *n.m.* unloading; disembarkation.
desembarrar, *v.t.* clean of mud.
desembocadero, desemboque, *n.m.*, **desembocadura,** *n.f.* estuary; outlet.
desembocar [A], *v.i.* flow (**en,** into); end at, lead into (**en**).
desembolsar, *v.t.* disburse.
desembolso, *n.m.* outlay, expenditure.
desemborrachar, *v.t., v.r.* sober up.
desemboque, [DESEMBOCADERO].
desembragar [B], *v.t.* (*mech.*) disengage, declutch.
desembrollar, *v.t.* unravel.
desemejante, *a.* different (**de,** from).
desemejanza, *n.f.* dissimilarity, difference.
desemejar, *v.t.* disfigure.—*v.i.* differ.
desempacho, *n.m.* ease, forwardness.
desempatar, *v.t.* decide, replay.
desempate, *n.m.* deciding game, vote *etc.* after a tie; replay, decider.
desempeñar, *v.t.* carry out; play (*a part*); redeem; free.
desempeño, *n.m.* fulfilment, discharge; redemption.
desempleo, *n.m.* unemployment.
desempolvar, *v.t.* dust; (*fig.*) brush up.
desenamorar, *v.t.* disenchant.
desencadenamiento, *n.m.* unchaining; outbreak.
desencadenar, *v.t.* unchain, unleash.—*v.r.* break loose *or* out.
desencajar, *v.t.* disjoint.—*v.r.* look distorted.
desencajonar, *v.t.* unpack; (*taur.*) release bulls from their travelling boxes.
desencallar, *v.t.* refloat.
desencantar, *v.t.* disenchant, disillusion.
desencanto, *n.m.* disillusionment; disenchantment.
desencapotar, *v.r.* take one's cloak off; clear up (*sky*); calm down (*person*).
desencoger [E], *v.t.* unfold.—*v.r.* grow bold.
desencogimiento, *n.m.* ease, assuredness.
desencolerizar [C], *v.t., v.r.* calm down.
desenconar, *v.t.* calm. allay.—*v.r.* calm down, soften.
desencono, *n.m.* calming, allaying.
desenchufar, *v.t.* unplug.
desendiosar, *v.t.* humble, bring down to earth.
desenfadado, -da, *a.* free and easy, carefree; roomy.
desenfadar, *v.t.* appease; cheer.—*v.r.* calm down, cheer up.
desenfado, *n.m.* ease, calm.
desenfrenado, -da, *a.* unbridled, wanton.
desenfrenar, *v.t.* unbridle.—*v.r.* lose all restraint.
desenfreno, *n.m.* wantonness, unruliness.
desenganchar, *v.t.* unhook, undo.
desengañar, *v.t.* disabuse; disillusion.—*v.r.* get disillusioned.
desengaño, *n.m.* disillusion; disappointment; bitter truth.
desengranar, *v.t.* put out of gear.
desenjaezar [C], *v.t.* unharness.
desenjaular, *v.t.* uncage, let out.
desenlace, *n.m.* outcome, dénouement.
desenlazar [C], *v.t.* untie; unravel.—*v.r.* unfold (*story, plot etc.*).
desenlodar, *v.t.* remove the mud from.
desenmarañar, *v.t.* disentangle.
desenmascaradamente, *adv.* bare-facedly.
desenmascarar, *v.t.* unmask.
desenojar, *v.t.* calm the anger of.—*v.r.* calm down.
desenojo, *n.m.* appeasement; composure.
desenredar, *v.t.* disentangle, sort out.—*v.r.* extricate oneself.
desenredo, *n.m.* disentanglement; dénouement.
desenrollar, *v.t.* unroll, unfurl, unwind.
desenroscar [A], *v.t.* unscrew.
desensillar, *v.t.* unsaddle.
desentender, *v.r.* take no part (**de,** in).
desentendido, -ida, *a.* unmindful, feigning ignorance.
desenterramiento, *n.m.* disinterment; unearthing.
desenterrar [I], *v.t.* unearth; disinter exhume; dig up.
desentonar, *v.t.* humble.—*v.i.* be out of tune.—*v.r.* overstep the mark.
desentono, *n.m.* false note; disrespect.
desentrañar, *v.t.* disembowel; figure out.—*v.r.* bleed oneself white.
desenvainar, *v.t.* unsheathe, draw.
desenvoltura, *n.f.* free-and-easy ways; wantonness.
desenvolver [5, *p.p.* **desenvuelto**], *v.t.* unfold, unroll; develop; unravel.—*v.r.* develop, evolve; extricate oneself; be too forward.
desenvolvimiento, *n.m.* unfolding; development; sorting out.
desenvuelto, -ta, *a.* wanton, impudent; free-and-easy.
deseo, *n.m.* desire, wish.
deseoso, -sa, *a.* desirous; eager.
desequilibrar, *v.t.* unbalance.
deserción, *n.f.* desertion.
desertar, *v.t.* desert; (*jur.*) forfeit.—*v.i.* desert (**de, a,** from, to).
desertor, *n.m.* deserter.
deservicio, *n.m.* disservice.
deservir [8], *v.t.* do (a) disservice to.
desesperación, *n.f.* despair, desperation.
desesperado, -da, *a.* desperate; hopeless.
desesperante, *a.* despairing; exasperating.
desesperanza, *n.f.* hopelessness.
desesperanzar [C], *v.t.* deprive of hope.—*v.r.* lose hope.
desesperar, *v.t.* drive to despair.—*v.i., v.r.* despair.
desespero, *n.m.* [DESESPERACIÓN].
desestima, desestimación, *n.f.* lack of esteem, low regard.
desfachatado, -da, *a.* (*fam.*) brazen, hard-faced.
desfachatez, *n.f.* (*fam.*) cheek, impudence.
desfalcar [A], *v.t.* lop off; embezzle.
desfalco, *n.m.* lopping off; embezzlement.
desfallecer [9], *v.t., v.i.* weaken.
desfalleciente, *a.* languishing.
desfallecimiento, *n.m.* weakening; languor; fainting.
desfavorable, *a.* unfavourable.
desfavorecer [9], *v.t.* disfavour; despise; injure.
desfiguración, *n.f.* disfigurement; distortion.
desfigurar, *v.t.* disfigure; disguise; cloud; distort.
desfiladero, *n.m.* pass, defile.
desfilar, *v.i.* defile, march past, parade.

desfile, *n.m.* parade, march-past.
desflorar, *v.t.* deflower; skim over.
desflorecer [9], *v.i.*, *v.r.* wither, fade.
desflorecimiento, *n.m.* withering, fading.
desfogar [B], *v.t.* give vent to; slake.—*v.i.* break (*storm clouds*).—*v.r.* vent one's anger.
desfrenar, *v.i.* take off the brakes; [DESENFRENAR].
desgaire, *n.m.* slovenliness; scorn.
desgajar, *v.t.* tear off, break off.—*v.r.* come off, break off; pour with rain.
desgalgadero, *n.m.* cliff, precipice.
desgana, *n.f.* lack of appetite *or* interest; ***a* —,** unwillingly.
desganar, *v.t.* take away interest *or* appetite. —*v.r.* lose one's appetite *or* interest.
desgañitar, *v.r.* (*fam.*) yell and bawl.
desgarbado, -da, *a.* graceless, uncouth.
desgargantar, *v.r.* (*fam.*) shout oneself blue in the face.
desgaritar, *v.i.* go astray.—*v.r.* lose one's way; give up a job.
desgarrado, -da, *a.* tattered, torn; shameless.
desgarrar, *v.t.* tear; ruin.—*v.r.* retire.
desgarro, *n.m.* tear, tatter; effrontery; boasting; outburst.
desgarrón, *n.m.* tear, rent; shred, tatter.
desgastar, *v.t.*, *v.r.* wear away.
desgaste, *n.m.* wear; attrition.
desgaznatar, *v.r.* (*fam.*) yell and scream.
desgobernado, -da, *a.* uncontrollable.
desgobernar [1], *v.t.* misgovern; dislocate.
desgobierno, *n.m.* misgovernment; mismanagement; dislocation.
desgonzar [C], **desgoznar,** *v.t.* unhinge.
desgracia, *n.f.* misfortune; disfavour; gracelessness; ***por* —,** unfortunately.
desgraciado, -da, *a.* unfortunate, luckless; graceless; unpleasant; wretched.
desgraciar, *v.t.* displease; spoil.—*v.r.* decline; quarrel; fail.
desgranar, *v.t.* thresh, shell, husk, pick.—*v.r.* drop off.
desgravar, *v.t.* lower the tax on.
desgreñar, *v.t.* dishevel.
deshabitado, -da, *a.* uninhabited.
deshabitar, *v.t.* abandon, leave (*a dwelling*).
deshabituar, *v.t.* break of a habit.—*v.r.* become unaccustomed.
deshacer [20], *v.t.* undo; take apart; use up; spoil; right (*wrongs*).—*v.r.* fall to pieces; melt; get rid (***de,*** of); strive (***por,*** to).
deshambrido, -da, *a.* starving.
desharrapado, -da, *a.* ragged.
deshecha, *n.f.* feint, evasion; farewell.
deshechizo, *n.m.* breaking of a spell; disappointment.
deshecho, -cha, *a.* hard, violent; ruined.—*p.p.* [DESHACER].
deshelar [1], *v.t.* thaw; de-ice.
desherbar [1], *v.t.* weed.
desheredado, -da, *a.* disinherited; underprivileged.
desheredar, *v.t.* disinherit.—*v.r.* betray one's heritage.
deshidratar, *v.t.* dehydrate.
deshielo, *n.m.* thaw; defrosting.
deshierba, *n.f.* weeding.
deshilachar, *v.r.* fray.
deshilado, -da, *a.* in single file; ***a la deshilada,*** single file; secretly.
deshilar, *v.t.* draw (*threads*).
deshilvanado, -da, *a.* disjointed.
deshipotecar [A], *v.t.* end the mortgage on.
deshojar, *v.t.* strip of leaves; tear the pages from.—*v.r.* lose its leaves; fall to bits (*book*).
deshollinador, *n.m.* chimney-sweep.
deshollinar, *v.t.* sweep (*chimneys*); (*fam.*) eye all over.
deshonestidad, *n.f.* indecency.
deshonesto, -ta, *a.* indecent, immodest.
deshonor, *n.m.* dishonour.
deshonorar, *v.t.* dishonour.
deshonra, *n.f.* dishonour, disgrace.
deshonrar, *v.t.* dishonour; defame.
deshonroso, -sa, *a.* dishonourable.
deshora, *n.f.* inopportune moment; ***a* —,** inopportunely.
desiderátum, *n.m.* (*pl.* **-rata**) desideratum.
desidioso, -sa, *a.* indolent.
desierto, -ta, *a.* deserted.—*n.m.* desert.
designación, *n.f.* designation.
designar, *v.t.* designate; design.
designio, *n.m.* purpose, design.
desigual, *a.* unequal; unlike; uneven; difficult.
desigualar, *v.t.* make unequal.—*v.r.* excel.
desigualdad, *n.f.* unevenness; inequality.
desilusión, *n.f.* disillusionment.
desilusionar, *v.t.* disillusion.—*v.r.* be disillusioned.
desimanar, *v.t.* demagnetize.
desimpresionar, *v.t.* undeceive.
desinencia, *n.f.* (*gram.*) ending, inflexion.
desinfección, *n.f.* disinfection.
desinfectante, *a.*, *n.m.* disinfectant.
desinfectar, desinficionar, *v.t.* disinfect.
desinflamar, *v.t.* reduce the inflammation in.
desintegración, *n.f.* disintegration.
desintegrar, *v.t.*, *v.r.* disintegrate.
desinterés, *n.m.* disinterest.
desinteresado, -da, *a.* disinterested, impartial.
desistir, *v.i.* desist (***de,*** from); (*jur.*) waive a right.
desjarretar, *v.t.* hamstring.
desjuiciado, -da, *a.* senseless, brainless.
desjuntar, *v.t.*, *v.r.* sever.
deslabonar, *v.t.* unlink; break up.
deslavado, -da, *a.* barefaced.
desleal, *a.* disloyal.
deslealtad, *n.f.* disloyalty.
deslenguado, -da, *a.* foul-mouthed.
deslenguar, *v.t.* cut the tongue out of.—*v.r.* (*fam.*) blab.
desliar [L], *v.t.* untie; unroll; unravel.
desligar [B], *v.t.* untie; unravel; exempt.
deslindador, *n.m.* surveyor.
deslindamiento, *n.m.* demarcation.
deslindar, *v.t.* mark the boundaries of; (*fig.*) define.
desliz, *n.m.* (*pl.* **-ices**) slip (*also fig.*).
deslizadizo, -za, *a.* slippery.
deslizamiento, *n.m.* slip, slide.
deslizar [C], *v.t.* (make) slide; let slip.—*v.i.* slip, slide.—*v.r.* slip, slide, glide; slip out; get away.
deslucido, -da, *a.* dull, uninteresting.
deslucir [9], *v.t.* dull, tarnish.
deslumbramiento, *n.m.* glare; bafflement.
deslumbrante, *a.* dazzling; bewildering.
deslumbrar, *v.t.* dazzle; baffle.
deslustrar, *v.t.* tarnish; frost (*glass*).
deslustre, *n.m.* tarnish, dullness; discredit.

deslustroso, -sa, *a.* unbecoming, ugly.
desmadejar, *v.t.* enervate.
desmadrado, -da, *a.* motherless, abandoned.
desmagnetizar [C], *v.t.* demagnetize.
desmán, *n.m.* mishap; excess, misbehaviour.
desmanchar, *v.t.* (*S.A.*) clean (*clothes*).
desmandado, -ada, *a.* lawless, out of hand.
desmandar, *v.t.* countermand, revoke.—*v.r.* be unruly.
desmantelamiento, *n.m.* dismantling; dilapidation.
desmantelar, *v.t.* dismantle; dilapidate; (*naut.*) demast.—*v.r.* fall into disrepair.
desmaña, *n.f.* clumsiness.
desmañado, -da, *a.* clumsy, fumbling, awkward.
desmayado, -da, *a.* languid; dull (*colour*).
desmayar, *v.t., v.i.* dismay.—*v.r.* faint.
desmayo, *n.m.* swoon; dismay; faltering.
desmazalado, -da, *a.* dispirited, dejected.
desmedido, -da, *a.* excessive.
desmedir [8], *v.r.* forget oneself.
desmedrar, *v.t.* impair.—*v.r.* deteriorate.
desmedro, *n.m.* detriment, decay.
desmejorar, *v.t.* spoil, make worse.—*v.i., v.r.* get worse; fade.
desmelenar, *v.t.* dishevel.
desmembración, *n.f.* dismembering.
desmembrar, *v.t.* dismember.—*v.r.* break up.
desmemoriado, -da, *a.* forgetful.
desmemoriar, *v.r.* lose one's memory.
desmenguar [H], *v.t.* diminish.
desmentida, *n.f.* denial, giving the lie.
desmentir [6], *v.t.* give the lie to, belie; hide.
desmenuzar [C], *v.t.* crumble; scrutinize.—*v.r.* crumble.
desmerecer [9], *v.t.* be unworthy of.—*v.i.* lose worth; look bad in comparison.
desmerecimiento, *n.m.* unworthiness.
desmesura, *n.f.* immoderation.
desmesurado, -da, *a.* immoderate; uncouth.
desmesurar, *v.t.* discompose, disorder.—*v.r.* be insolent.
desmigajar, desmigar [B], *v.t., v.r.* crumble.
desmilitarización, *n.f.* demilitarization.
desmilitarizar [C], *v.t.* demilitarize.
desmirriado, -da, *a.* (*fam.*) low, off-colour.
desmochar, *v.t.* poll(ard); dehorn; abridge.
desmonetizar [C], *v.t.* demonetize.
desmontable, *a.* detachable; collapsible.
desmontadura, *n.f.,* **desmontaje,** *n.m.* dismantling.
desmontar, *v.t.* dismantle; clear of trees; level off (*ground*); uncock; unhorse.—*v.i., v.r.* dismount.
desmonte, *n.m.* felling; levelling; (*S.A.*) mine rubble.
desmoralización, *n.f.* demoralization.
desmoralizar [C], *v.t.* demoralize.—*v.r.* become demoralized.
desmoronamiento, *n.m.* crumbling, decay.
desmoronar, *v.t.* wear away.—*v.r.* crumble.
desmovilización, *n.f.* demobilization.
desmovilizar [C], *v.t.* demobilize.
desnacionalizar [C], *v.t.* denationalize.
desnatar, *v.t.* skim (*milk*).
desnaturalizar [C], *v.t.* denaturalize; pervert.—*v.r.* become unnatural; lose citizenship.
desnivel, *n.m.* unevenness; drop.
desnivelar, *v.t.* make uneven.
desnucar [A], *v.t.* break the neck off.—*v.r.* break one's neck.
desnudar, *v.t.* undress; strip; reveal.—*v.r.* undress; get rid (*de*, of); shed (*de*).
desnudez, *n.f.* nakedness.
desnudo, -da, *a.* naked, bare, nude; (*fam.*) broke, penniless.
desnutrición, *n.f.* malnutrition.
desnutrido, -da, *a.* undernourished.
desobedecer [9], *v.t.* disobey.
desobediencia, *n.f.* disobedience.
desobediente, *a.* disobedient.
desobligar [B], *v.t.* release from an obligation; disoblige, alienate.
desocupación, *n.f.* leisure; unemployment.
desocupado, -da, *a.* vacant, free; unemployed.—*n.m.f.* unemployed person.
desocupar, *v.t.* empty, vacate.—*v.r.* be doing nothing.
desodorante, *a., n.m.* deodorant.
desoír [22], *v.t.* ignore, not heed.
desolación, *n.f.* desolation.
desolar [4], *v.t.* desolate, lay waste.
desollado, -da, *a.* (*fam.*) brazen, cheeky.
desolladura, *n.f.* flaying, fleecing; graze, hurt.
desollar [4], *v.t.* skin, flay; (*fam.*) fleece; condemn.
desorbitado, -da, *a.* (*S.A.*) wild-eyed.
desorden, *n.m.* disorder.
desordenado, -da, *a.* unruly, disorderly.
desordenar, *v.t.* disorder.—*v.r.* get out of order.
desorganizar [C], *v.t.* disorganize.
desorientar, *v.t.* confuse.—*v.r.* lose one's bearings, get lost.
desovillar, *v.t.* unravel, disentangle.
despabilado, -da, *a.* wide-awake, smart.
despabilar, *v.t.* snuff (*candles*); (*fam.*) eat up; kill off; fritter away; liven up.—*v.r.* wake up; (*S.A.*) go away.
despacio, *adv.* slowly; gently.—*interj.* steady!—*n.m.* (*S.A.*) delay.
despacioso, -sa, *a.* slow, sluggish.
despacito, *adv.* (*fam.*) very slowly.
despachaderas, *n.f.pl.* (*fam.*) wit, resourcefulness.
despachante, *n.m.* (*S.A.*) shop assistant.
despachar, *v.t.* dispatch; attend to; send, ship; sell.—*v.i., v.r.* hurry; get things settled; give birth.
despacho, *n.m.* dispatch; office, study; shop; sending, shipping; message.
despachurrar, *v.t.* (*fam.*) squash, mangle.
despampanante, *a.* (*fam.*) shaking, stunning.
despampanar, *v.t.* prune (*vines*); (*fam.*) shake, dumbfound.—*v.i.* (*fam.*) tell all.—*v.r.* (*fam.*) come a cropper.
desparejo, -ja, *a.* uneven; unsteady.
desparpajar, *v.t.* tear to bits; (*S.A.*) spill.—*v.i.* (*fam.*) gabble.
desparpajo, *n.m.* (*fam.*) cheek, nerve; (*C.A.*) chaos.
desparramado, -da, *a.* wide, open.
desparramamiento, *n.m.* scattering, spilling; prodigality.
desparramar, *v.t.* scatter; spill; squander.—*v.r.* scatter; be spilled; revel, carouse.
despartir, *v.t.* separate, part.
despear, *v.t.* damage the feet of.—*v.r.* get sore feet.

despectivo, -va, *a.* pejorative, disparaging.
despechar, *v.t.* spite, enrage.—*v.r.* fret; give up hope.
despecho, *n.m.* spite; despair; ***a — de,*** despite.
despedazar [C], *v.t., v.r.* break into pieces.
despedida, *n.f.* farewell, parting; dismissal.
despedimiento, *n.m.* parting, farewell.
despedir [8], *v.t.* hurl; give off; dismiss; see off.—*v.r.* take one's leave (***de,*** of).
despegado, -da, *a.* (*fam.*) gruff, surly.
despegar [B], *v.t.* unstick, open, detach.—*v.i.* (*aer.*) take off.—*v.r.* come loose; become distant.
despego, *n.m.* coldness; surliness.
despegue, *n.m.* (*aer.*) take-off.
despeinar, *v.t.* ruffle, muss, let down (*hair*).
despejado, -da, *a.* cloudless; bright, smart.
despejar, *v.t.* clear, clear up.—*v.r.* be bright; clear up (*weather*); get better.
despejo, *n.m.* clearing; ability; brightness.
despeluzar [C], *v.t.* ruffle the hair of; make the hair stand on end.
despeluznante, *a.* hair-raising.
despeluznar [DESPELUZAR].
despellejar, *v.t.* skin, flay; (*fam.*) back-bite.
despenar, *v.t.* console; (*fam.*) kill.
despensa, *n.f.* pantry, larder; provisions.
despensero, -ra, *n.m.f.* steward, storekeeper.
despeñadamente, *adv.* rashly.
despeñadero, -ra, *a.* steep.—*n.m.* precipice, cliff; danger.
despeñadizo, -za, *a.* steep, precipitous.
despeñar, *v.t.* throw over a cliff.—*v.r.* fall from rocks; plunge.
despeño, *n.m.* throwing *or* falling from a cliff; failure, ruin, fall.
despepitar, *v.t.* remove seed.—*v.r.* scream with fury; yearn (***por,*** for).
desperdiciar, *v.t.* waste; lose, miss.
desperdicio, *n.m.* waste.—*pl.* waste, **by-**products.
desperdigar [B], *v.t.* scatter.
desperezar [C], *v.r.* stretch (*limbs on waking etc.*).
desperfecto, *n.m.* flaw, blemish.
despernar [1], *v.t.* injure the legs of.
despertador, *n.m.*, **despertadora,** *n.f.* alarm-clock; (*fig.*) warning.
despertamiento, *n.m.* awakening.
despertar [1], *v.t.* wake, rouse.—*v.r.* wake up, awake, stir.
despiadado, -da, *a.* merciless.
despicar [A], *v.t.* satisfy, make amends.—*v.r.* have one's honour satisfied.
despichar, *v.t.* dry out.—*v.i.* (*low*) snuff it (*die*).
despierto, -ta, *a.* awake.
despilfarrado, -da, *a.* ragged; wasteful.—*n.m.f.* squanderer.
despilfarrar, *v.t.* squander, waste.—*v.r.* (*fam.*) blue it in (*money*).
despilfarro, *n.m.* squandering, waste; shabbiness.
despintar, *v.t.* strip the paint off; spoil.—*v.r.* fade, wash off.
despique, *n.m.* requital, satisfaction.
despistar, *v.t.* throw off the scent.—*v.r.* lose the track; get muddled.
despiste, *n.m.* losing the way; putting off the scent; muddle, mistake; lack of care.
despizcar [A], *v.t.* crush, grind up.
desplacer, *n.m.* displeasure.—*v.t.* [23] displease.
desplantar, *v.t.* dig up; throw out of the vertical.—*v.r.* lose the upright position.
desplante, *n.m.* bad posture; (*S.A.*) impudence.
desplazar [C], *v.t.* displace; supplant.—*v.r.* move.
desplegar [1B], *v.t.* unfold, unroll; display; deploy.—*v.r.* unfold; deploy.
despliegue, *n.m.* unfolding; display; deployment.
desplomar, *v.t.* put out of plumb.—*v.r.* move out of plumb; collapse; faint; fall; (*aer.*) pancake.
desplome, *n.m.* collapse; fall; downfall.
desplomo, *n.m.* leaning, tilting.
desplumar, *v.t.* pluck; (*fam.*) fleece.—*v.r.* moult.
despoblación, *n.f.* depopulation.
despoblado, *n.m.* deserted place, wilds.
despoblar [4], *v.t.* depopulate; lay waste.—*v.r.* become depopulated.
despojar, *v.t.* plunder, despoil, divest.—*v.r.* undress; divest oneself (***de,*** of).
despolvar, *v.t.* dust; (*S.A.*) sprinkle.
despopularizar [C], *v.t.* make unpopular.
desportillar, *v.t.* chip, nick.
desposado, -da, *a.* handcuffed.—*a., n.m.f.* newly-wed.
desposar, *v.t.* betroth, marry.—*v.r.* get engaged *or* married.
desposeer [N], *v.t.* dispossess.
desposorios, *n.m.pl.* betrothal; **nuptials.**
déspota, *n.m.* despot.
despótico, -ca, *a.* despotic.
despotismo, *n.m.* despotism.
despotizar [C], *v.t.* (*S.A.*) tyrannize.
despotricar [A], *v.i., v.r.* (*fam.*) rant, rave.
despreciable, *a.* contemptible.
despreciar, *v.t.* despise; slight; reject.—*v.r.* not deign (***de,*** to).
desprecio, *n.m.* contempt, scorn; slight.
desprender, *v.t.* unfasten, separate; emit.—*v.r.* come loose; be clear (***de,*** from); give up (***de***).
desprendido, -da, *a.* unselfish.
desprendimiento, *n.m.* coming loose; release; generosity; landslide.
despreocupación, *n.f.* freedom from bias; unconcernedness.
despreocupado, -da, *a.* unconcerned; unconventional.
despreocupar, *v.r.* forget one's cares.
desprestigiar, *v.t.* bring into disrepute.—*v.r.* lose one's good standing.
desprestigio, *n.m.* loss of standing; unpopularity.
desprevención, *n.f.* unpreparedness.
desprevenido, -da, *a.* unprepared; unawares.
desproporción, *n.f.* disproportion.
desproporcionado, -da, *a.* disproportionate.
despropositado, -da, *a.* absurd, nonsensical.
despropósito, *n.m.* absurdity, nonsense.
desprovisto, -ta, *a.* deprived of, lacking entirely in (***de***).
después, *adv.* after, later, next.—*prep.* after (***de***).—*conj.* after (***de que*** or ***de***).
despuntar, *v.t.* take the edge *or* point off; nibble.—*v.i.* start sprouting; dawn; stand out.
despunte, *n.m.* blunting.

desquiciar, *v.t.* unhinge; upset; (*fam.*) spoil things for.—*v.r.* come unhinged; collapse.
desquijarar, *v.t.* break the jaw of.—*v.r.* roar (*de risa,* with laughter).
desquilatar, *v.t.* alloy (*gold*); devaluate.
desquitar, *v.t.* recoup; avenge.—*v.r.* recoup; get even (*con,* with).
desquite, *n.m.* recouping, recovery; retaliation, getting even.
desrazonable, *a.* unreasonable.
desreputación, *n.f.* bad name, disrepute.
destacado, -da, *a.* outstanding.
destacamento, *n.m.* (*mil.*) detachment.
destacar [A], *v.t.* highlight; (*mil.*) detail.—*v.r.* stand out, excel.
destajar, *v.t.* let out (*work*) on piece-rate; cut (*cards*).
destajo, *n.m.* job, piece-work; *a —,* on piece-rate, by the job; eagerly.
destapar, *v.t.* uncover; uncork.
destaponar, *v.t.* uncork, open.
destartalado, -da, *a.* shabby, jumbled, ill-furnished.
destejer, *v.t.* unweave, ravel.
destellar, *v.i.* flash, beam, sparkle.
destello, *n.m.* flash.
destemplanza, *n.f.* lack of moderation *or* regularity.
destemplar, *v.t.* put out of tune; disconcert. —*v.r.* become irregular; be indisposed; act immoderately.
destemple, *n.m.* dissonance; lack of moderation; indisposition.
desteñir [8K], *v.t., v.r.* fade.
desternillar, *v.r.* split one's sides.
desterrar [1], *v.t.* exile, banish.
a destiempo, *adv. phr.* inopportunely.
destierro, *n.m.* exile, banishment; wilds.
destilación, *n.f.* distillation, distilling.
destilar, *v.t.* distil; filter.—*v.r.* drip, ooze.
destilería, *n.f.* distillery.
destinación, *n.f.* destination, assignment.
destinar, *v.t.* destine (*a,* to, *para,* for); assign.
destinatario, -ria, *n.m.f.* addressee.
destino, *n.m.* destiny; destination; employment; *con — a,* bound for.
destitución, *n.f.* destitution; dismissal.
destituir [O], *v.t.* deprive; dismiss.
destorcer [5D], *v.t., v.r.* untwist.
destornillado, -da, *a.* reckless, crazy.
destornillador, *n.m.* screwdriver.
destornillar, *v.t.* unscrew.—*v.r.* (*fig.*) be rash.
destral, *n.m.* hatchet.
destrejar, *v.i.* act with dexterity.
destreza, *n.f.* skill, dexterity.
destripar, *v.t.* disembowel; smash; (*fam.*) spoil, ruin.
destripaterrones, *n.m. inv.* (*fam.*) clodhopper.
destrísimo, -ma, *a.* most skilful.
destrizar [C], *v.t.* tear to shreds.—*v.r.* be furious.
destronamiento, *n.m.* dethronement.
destronar, *v.t.* dethrone.
destrozar [C], *v.t.* destroy, shatter, smash; squander.
destrozo, *n.m.* havoc, ruin, destruction.
destrucción, *n.f.* destruction.
destructivo, -va, *a.* destructive.
destructor, -ra, *a.* destroying.—*n.m.* (*mil.*) destroyer.
destruir [O], *v.t.* destroy.
desudar, *v.t.* wipe the sweat off.
desuello, *n.m.* skinning; brazenness; (*fam.*) daylight robbery (*exorbitant price*).
desuetud, *n.f.* desuetude.
desunión, *n.f.* disunion.
desunir, *v.t., v.r.* disunite.
desusado, -da, *a.* obsolete, out of use.
desusar, *v.t.* disuse.—*v.r.* become disused.
desuso, *n.m.* disuse.
desvaído, -da, *a.* spindly; dull (*colour*).
desvalido, -da, *a.* destitute, helpless.
desvalijar, *v.t.* steal (*from baggage*); plunder, rob.
desvalimiento, *n.m.* helplessness.
desvalorar, *v.t.* devalue.
desvalorización, *n.f.* devaluation.
desvalorizar [C], *v.t.* devaluate.
desván, *n.m.* loft, attic.
desvanecer [9], *v.t.* make vanish; dissipate. —*v.r.* disappear, vanish; swoon.
desvanecido, -da, *a.* faint; haughty.
desvanecimiento, *n.m.* disappearance; vanity; faintness, swoon.
desvariado, -da, *a.* nonsensical; luxuriant.
desvariar [L], *v.i.* rave, be delirious.
desvarío, *n.m.* delirium, raving; extravagance, whim.
desvelado, -da, *a.* watchful, wakeful; worried.
desvelar, *v.t.* keep awake; unveil.—*v.r.* stay awake, not sleep; be very worried (*por,* about).
desvelo, *n.m.* wakefulness; sleeplessness; worry.
desvencijado, -da, *a.* rickety.
desvencijar, *v.t.* pull to bits, loosen.—*v.r.* come loose, come to bits.
desvendar, *v.t.* unbandage.
desventaja, *n.f.* disadvantage.
desventajoso, -sa, *a.* disadvantageous.
desventura, *n.f.* misfortune.
desventurado, -da, *a.* unfortunate; mean, miserable; faint-hearted.
desvergonzado, -da, *a.* shameless.
desvergonzar [4C], *v.r.* be shameless, be insolent (*con,* to).
desvergüenza, *n.f.* shamelessness.
desvestir [8], *v.t., v.r.* undress.
desviación, *n.f.* deflection.
desviado, -da, *a.* devious; astray.
desviar [L], *v.t.* divert, deflect, avert; dissuade.—*v.r.* deviate, wander, swerve.
desvío, *n.m.* deviation, diversion, deflection; dislike; detour; (*rail.*) siding.
desvirtuar [M], *v.t.* detract from, spoil.
desvivir, *v.r.* be eager (*por,* to, for).
desvolver [5, *p.p.* **desvuelto**], *v.t.* change the shape of; till (*the soil*); unscrew.
detallar, *v.t.* detail; retail.
detalle (1), *n.m.* detail; (*fam.*) sign of good manners.
detalle (2), *n.m.* (*S.A.*) retail.
detallista (1), *n.m.f.* retailer.
detallista (2), *n.m.f.* person fond of detail.
detective, *n.m.* detective.
detector, *n.m.* (*rad.*) detector.
detención, *n.f.* detention; delay; meticulousness; arrest.

detener [33], *v.t.* detain, delay, check, arrest, retain.—*v.r.* stop; linger, pause.
detenido, -da, *a.* sparing; lengthy; careful; hesitant.
detenimiento, *n.m.* [DETENCIÓN].
detergente, *a.*, *n.m.* detergent.
deteriorar, *v.t.*, *v.r.* deteriorate.
deterioro, *n.m.* deterioration; damage, wear.
determinable, *a.* determinable.
determinación, *n.f.* determination.
determinado, -da, *a.* determined; determinate; (*gram.*) definite.
determinante, *a.*, *n.m.* determinant.
determinar, *v.t.* determine; induce; specify. —*v.r.* decide, determine (***a***, to).
determinismo, *n.m.* determinism.
detestación, *n.f.* detestation; cursing.
detestar, *v.t.* curse; detest.—*v.i.* detest (***de***).
detonación, *n.f.* detonation.
detonador, *n.m.* detonator.
detonante, *a.* detonating.
detonar, *v.i.* detonate.
detorsión, *n.f.* (*med.*) sprain.
detracción, *n.f.* detraction.
detractar, *v.t.* detract, defame.
detractor, -ra, *a.* detracting.—*n.m.f.* detractor.
detraer [34], *v.t.* detract; libel.
detrás, *adv.* behind.—*prep.* behind (***de***).
detrimento, *n.m.* detriment, harm, damage.
detrito, *n.m.* detritus; debris.
deuda, *n.f.* debt; fault.
deudo, -da, *n.m.f.* relative, kinsman *or* kinswoman.—*n.m.* kinship.
deudor, -ra, *n.m.f.* debtor.
Deuteronomio, *n.m.* (*Bib.*) Deuteronomy.
devanar, *v.t.* wind, spool.—*v.r.* (*S.A.*) writhe; ***devanarse los sesos,*** cudgel one's brains.
devanear, *v.i.* rave; fritter time away.
devaneo, *n.m.* frenzy, raving; time-wasting; flirting.
devastación, *n.f.* devastation.
devastar, *v.t.* devastate.
devengar [B], *v.t.* earn, receive.
devenir [36], *v.i.* happen; (*phil.*) become.
devoción, *n.f.* devotion.
devocionario, *n.m.* prayer-book.
devolución, *n.f.* return, restitution.
devolver [5, *p.p.* **devuelto**], *v.t.* return, give back, pay back; (*fam.*) vomit.—*v.r.* (*S.A.*) come back.
devorante, *a.* devouring.
devorar, *v.t.* devour.
devotería, *n.f.* bigotry; sanctimoniousness.
devoto, -ta, *a.* devout; devoted.—*n.m.f.* devotee.
devuelto, *n.m.* (*fam.*) vomiting.—*p.p.* [DEVOLVER].
día, *n.m.* day; daylight; ***al —,*** per day; up to date; ***buenos días,*** good morning; ***dar los días a,*** wish many happy returns to; ***de —,*** in the daytime; ***del —,*** in fashion; today's; ***— de guardar*** or ***de precepto,*** holiday; ***— de Reyes,*** Epiphany; ***— onomástico,*** saint's day; ***— útil*** or ***laborable,*** working day; ***el — menos pensado,*** (*fam.*) ***al menor —,*** when you least expect it; ***en el — de hoy,*** these days; ***en pleno —,*** in broad daylight; ***en su —,*** in due course, at the proper time; ***entrado en días,*** advanced in years; ***vivir al —,*** live for the day *or* moment, live from day to day.
diabetes, *n.f.* (*med.*) diabetes.
diabético, -ca, *a.*, *n.m.f.* diabetic.
diablesa, *n.f.* (*fam.*) she-devil.
diablillo, *n.m.* imp; (*fam.*) schemer.
diablo, *n.m.* devil.
diablura, *n.f.* devilment, devilry; escapade, naughtiness.
diabólico, -ca, *a.* diabolical, devilish.
diácono, *n.m.* deacon.
diadema, *n.f.* diadem, tiara.
diado, -da, *a.* appointed (*day*).
diáfano, -na, *a.* diaphanous.
diafragma, *n.m.* diaphragm.
diagnosis, *n.f. inv.* diagnosis.
diagnosticar [A], *v.t.* diagnose.
diagnóstico, -ca, *a.*, *n.m.* diagnostic.—*n.m.* diagnosis.
diagonal, *a.*, *n.f.* diagonal.
diagrama, *n.m.* diagram.
dialectal, *a.* dialectal.
dialéctico, -ca, *a.* dialectic.—*n.f.* dialectics.
dialecto, *n.m.* dialect.
dialogar [B], *v.i.* maintain a dialogue.
diálogo, *n.m.* dialogue.
diamantado, -da, *a.* diamond-like.
diamante, *n.m.* diamond.
diamantino, -na, *a.* rel. to diamonds; (*poet.*) adamantine.
diamantista, *n.m.* diamond cutter *or* merchant.
diametral, *a.* diametrical.
diámetro, *n.m.* diameter.
diana, *n.f.* (*mil.*) reveille.
dianche, diantre, *n.m.* (*fam.*) the devil.—*interj.* the deuce!
diapasón, *n.m.* (*mus.*) diapason; tuning fork; pitch-pipe.
diapositiva, *n.f.* (*phot.*) diapositive; slide.
diario, -ria, *a.* daily.—*n.m.* daily (*paper*); diary; daily allowance; day book; ***a —,*** every day.
diarismo, *n.m.* (*S.A.*) journalism.
diarista, *n.m.f.* diarist; (*S.A.*) journalist.
diarrea, *n.f.* (*med.*) diarrhoea.
Diáspora, *n.f.* (*Bib.*) Diaspora.
diatriba, *n.f.* diatribe.
dibujante, *n.f.* drawer, illustrator.—*n.m.* draughtsman.
dibujar, *v.t.* draw, sketch; depict; outline.—*v.r.* take shape, appear.
dibujo, *n.m.* drawing.
dicaz, *a.* (*pl.* **-aces**) sarcastic.
dicción, *n.f.* diction; word.
diccionario, *n.m.* dictionary.
diccionarista, *n.m.f.* lexicographer.
diciembre, *n.m.* December.
diciente, *a.* saying.
dicotomía, *n.f.* dichotomy.
dictado, *n.m.* dictation; title, honour.—*pl.* dictates.
dictador, *n.m.* dictator.
dictadura, *n.f.* dictatorship.
dictáfono, *n.m.* dictaphone.
dictamen, *n.m.* opinion, dictum.
dictaminar, *v.i.* pass judgement, express an opinion.
dictar, *v.t.* dictate; suggest; (*S.A.*) give (*lectures*).
dictatorial, dictatorio, -ria, *a.* dictatorial.

dicterio, *n.m.* taunt.
dicha, *n.f.* happiness, luck.
dicharachero, -ra, *a.* (*fam.*) foul-mouthed.
dicharacho, *n.m.* (*fam.*) smuttiness, obscenity.
dicho, -cha, *a.* said.—*p.p.* [DECIR].—*n.m.* saying; promise; witticism; (*fam.*) insult; — ***y hecho,*** no sooner said than done.
dichoso, -sa, *a.* happy, lucky; (*fam. iron.*) blessed.
didáctico, -ca, *a.* didactic(al).
diecinueve, *a.*, *n.m.* nineteen.
dieciochesco, -ca, *a.* eighteenth-century.
dieciocho, *a.*, *n.m.* eighteen.
dieciséis, *a.*, *n.m.* sixteen.
diecisiete, *a.*, *n.m.* seventeen.
Diego, *n.m.* James.
diente, *n.m.* tooth; fang; tusk; cog; ***a regaña dientes,*** grudgingly; — ***de león,*** (*bot.*) dandelion; ***dar — con —,*** (*fam.*) chatter (*of teeth*); ***estar a —,*** (*fam.*) be famished.
diéresis, *n.f.* diaeresis.
diesel, *n.m.* diesel engine.
diestro, -tra, *a.* skilful, expert, dexterous; shrewd; propitious; right; (*her.*) dexter.—*n.m.* bullfighter; master fencer.
dieta, *n.f.* diet; ***a —,*** on a diet.—*pl.* daily fee.
dietar, *v.t.*, *v.r.* diet.
dietario, *n.m.* day book.
dietético, -ca, *a.* dietary, dietetic.—*n.f.* dietetics.
diez, *a.*, *n.m.* ten.
diezmal, *a.* decimal.
diezmar, *v.t.* decimate; tithe.
diezmo, *n.m.* tithe.
difamación, *n.f.* defamation.
difamar, *v.t.* defame.
difamatorio, -ria, *a.* defamatory.
diferencia, *n.f.* difference; (*obs.*) delay; ***a — de,*** unlike.
diferenciación, *n.f.* differentiation.
diferencial, *a.*, *n.f.* (*math.*, *mech.*) differential.
diferenciar, *v.t.* differentiate.—*v.i.*, *v.r.* differ.
diferente, *a.* different.
diferir [6], *v.t.* defer.—*v.i.*, *v.r.* differ.
difícil, *a.* difficult, hard (***de,*** to).
difícilmente, *adv.* with difficulty.
dificultad, *n.f.* difficulty.
dificultar, *v.t.* make difficult, impede; consider difficult.—*v.i.* raise objections.—*v.r.* get difficult.
dificultoso, -sa, *a.* difficult, troublesome.
difidencia, *n.f.* distrust.
difidente, *a.* distrustful.
difracción, *n.f.* diffraction.
difractar, *v.t.* diffract.
difteria, *n.f.* (*med.*) diphtheria.
difundido, -da, *a.* widespread, widely known.
difundir, *v.t.* spread, broadcast.
difunto, -ta, *a.*, *n.m.f.* deceased; ***día de los Difuntos,*** All Souls' Day.
difusión, *n.f.* diffusion; spreading; broadcasting.
difusivo, -sa, *a.* diffusive.
difuso, -sa, *a.* diffuse.
digerir [6], *v.t.* digest; bear, suffer.
digestión, *n.f.* digestion.
digestivo, -va, *a.*, *n.m.* digestive.
digesto, *n.m.* (*jur.*) digest.
digital, *a.* digital.—*n.f.* (*bot.*) digitalis.
dígito, *n.m.* digit.
dignar, *v.r.* deign to.
dignatario, *n.m.* dignitary.
dignidad, *n.f.* dignity.
dignificar [A], *v.t.* dignify; honour.
digno, -na, *a.* worthy (***de,*** of); fitting.
digo [DECIR].
digresión, *n.f.* digression.
digresivo, -va, *a.* digressive.
dije, *n.m.* amulet; (*fam.*) a gem (*good person*); (*fam.*) toff (*smart person*).—*pl.* bragging [DECIR].
dilación, *n.f.* delay.
dilapidación, *n.f.* dilapidation; wasting.
dilapidar, *v.t.* dilapidate; squander.
dilatación, *n.f.* dilation; prolixity; serenity (*in grief*).
dilatado, -da, *a.* vast; prolix; dilated.
dilatar, *v.t.* dilate; defer; spread.—*v.r.* dilate, expand; be prolix; be deferred.
dilecto, -ta, *a.* beloved, loved.
dilema, *n.m.* dilemma.
diletante, *a.*, *n.m.f.* dilettante.
diletantismo, *n.m.* dilettantism.
diligencia, *n.f.* diligence; stage-coach; speed; errand.
diligenciar, *v.t.* expedite.
diligente, *a.* diligent; prompt.
dilucidar, *v.t.* elucidate.
dilución, *n.f.* dilution.
diluir [O], *v.t.* dilute.
diluviar, *v.i.* pour with rain.
diluvio, *n.m.* deluge; (*Bib.*) the Flood.
dimanar, *v.i.* spring, arise (***de,*** from).
dimensión, *n.f.* dimension.
dimensional, *a.* dimensional.
dimes, *n.m. pl.* ***andar en — y diretes,*** (*fam.*) squabble, bicker (***con,*** with).
diminución, *n.f.* diminution.
diminuir [O], *v.t.*, *v.i.*, *v.r.* diminish.
diminutivo, -va, *a.* diminutive.
diminuto, -ta, *a.* diminutive; imperfect.
dimisión, *n.f.* resignation.
dimisionario, -ria, dimitente, *a.* resigning.—*n.m.f.* person resigning.
dimitir, *v.t.* resign from, renounce.—*v.i.* resign.
Dinamarca, *n.f.* Denmark.
dinamarqués, -quesa [DANÉS].
dinámico, -ca, *a.* dynamic.—*n.f.* dynamics.
dinamita, *n.f.* dynamite.
dinamitar, *v.t.* dynamite.
dinamitero, -ra, *a.* rel. to dynamite.—*n.m.f.* dynamiter.
dínamo, *n.m.* dynamo.
dinastía, *n.f.* dynasty.
dinerada, *n.f.*, **dineral,** *n.m.* large sum of money, (*fam.*) fortune.
dinero, *n.m.* money; currency.
dineroso, -sa, *a.* moneyed.
dingo, *n.m.* (*zool.*) dingo.
dinosaurio, *n.m.* dinosaur.
dintel, *n.m.* (*arch.*) lintel.
diocesano, -na, *a.* diocesan.
diócesi(s), *n.f.* (*pl.* **-sis**) diocese.
Dionisio, *n.m.* Dionysius; Denis.
Dios, *n.m.* God; ***a la buena de —,*** (*fam.*) goodnaturedly, without malice; ***¡ por — !*** for goodness' sake! ***¡ válgame — !*** bless me! ***¡ vaya con — !*** God speed!; be off! ***¡ vive — !*** by heaven! **dios,** *n.m.* god.
diosa, *n.f.* goddess.
diploma, *n.m.* diploma; document.

diplomacia, *n.f.* diplomacy.
diplomado, -da, *a., n.m.f.* graduate.
diplomático, -ca, *a.* diplomatic.—*n.m.f.* diplomat.—*n.f.* diplomatics; diplomacy.
dipsomanía, *n.f.* dipsomania.
dipsomaníaco, -ca, dipsómano, -na, *a., n.m.f.* dipsomaniac.
diptongar [B], *v.t., v.r.* diphthongize.
diptongo, *n.m.* diphthong.
diputación, *n.f.* deputation; (*hist.*) ruling council when the Cortes were not in session.
diputado, -da, *n.m.f.* deputy; member (*of Parliament*).
diputar, *v.t.* depute; deputize.
dique, *n.m.* dyke, dam; dry dock; (*fig.*) check.
diré [DECIR].
dirección, *n.f.* direction; management; steering; trend; address; — ***única,*** one-way (*streets etc.*).
direccional, *a.* directional.
directo, -ta, *a.* direct; clear; straight.
director, -ra, *a.* directing, guiding.—*n.m.f.* director; manager; principal; editor (*of paper*); (*mus.*) conductor.
directorado, *n.m.* directorship.
directorio, -ria, *a.* directory; directorial.—*n.m.* directory; directorship; board of directors; directive.
directriz, *n.f.* (*pl.* **-ices**) directive.
dirigente, *n.m.f.* head, director, manager; ruler, minister.
dirigible, *a., n.m.* dirigible.
dirigir [E], *v.t.* direct, manage; conduct; address; steer.—*v.r.* address (***a***); apply (***a,*** to).
dirimir, *v.t.* annul; pour; settle.
discante, *n.m.* descant; treble.
discerniente, *a.* discerning.
discernimiento, *n.m.* discernment.
discernir [3], *v.t.* discern; (*jur.*) entrust.
disciplina, *n.f.* discipline; education; lash.
disciplinar, *v.t.* discipline; educate; whip.
disciplinario, -ria, *a.* disciplinary.
disciplinazo, *n.m.* lash.
discípulo, -la, *n.m.f.* disciple; pupil, student.
disco, *n.m.* gramophone record; disc, disk, discus; (*rail.*) signal; tap washer; (*tel.*) dial.
díscolo, -la, *a.* unruly, wayward.
disconforme, *a.* disagreeing.
disconformidad, *n.f.* non-, in- *or* disconformity; disagreement.
discontinuar [M], *v.t.* discontinue.
discordante, *a.* discordant.
discordar [4], *v.i.* disagree, be out of tune (***de,*** with).
discorde, *a.* discordant, dissonant.
discordia, *n.f.* discord.
discoteca, *n.f.* record cabinet.
discreción, *n.f.* discretion; prudence; wit.
discrecional, *a.* discretional, optional.
discrepancia, *n.f.* discrepancy; disagreement.
discrepante, *a.* discrepant; disagreeing.
discrepar, *v.i.* disagree, differ.
discretear, *v.i.* attempt cleverness.
discreto, -ta, *a.* discreet, prudent; witty; discrete.
discrimen, *n.m.* risk; difference.
discriminación, *n.f.* discrimination.
discriminante, *a.* discriminating.
discriminar, *v.t., v.i.* discriminate, differentiate.
disculpa, *n.f.* apology; excuse.
disculpable, *a.* excusable.
disculpar, *v.t.* excuse, pardon.—*v.r.* apologize (***con,*** to, ***de,*** for).
discurrir, *v.t.* contrive; conjecture.—*v.i.* roam; flow; reason; discourse.
discursear, *v.i.* (*fam.*) speechify.
discursivo, -va, *a.* reflective.
discurso, *n.m.* speech; passage (*of time*).
discusión, *n.f.* discussion.
discutible, *a.* arguable.
discutir, *v.t.* discuss; argue about.—*v.i.* argue (***sobre,*** about).
disecación, *n.f.* dissection.
disecar [A], *v.t.* dissect; stuff.
disección, *n.f.* dissection; taxidermy.
disector, *n.m.* dissector.
diseminación, *n.f.* dissemination.
diseminar, *v.t.* disseminate.—*v.r.* spread.
disensión, *n.f.* dissension.
disenso, *n.m.* dissent.
disentería, *n.f.* (*med.*) dysentery.
disentimiento, *n.m.* dissension.
disentir [6], *v.i.* dissent.
diseñar, *v.t.* design, draw.
diseño, *n.m.* design, sketch.
disertación, *n.f.* dissertation.
disertar, *v.i.* discourse.
disfavor, *n.m.* disfavour.
disforme, *a.* deformed; monstrous, ugly.
disfraz, *n.m.* (*pl.* **-aces**) disguise.
disfrazar [C], *v.t.* disguise.
disfrutar, *v.t.* enjoy; have at one's disposal.—*v.i.* take pleasure (***con,*** in); — ***de,*** enjoy, have the benefit of.
disfrute, *n.m.* use, enjoyment, benefit.
disgregar [B], *v.t., v.r.* disintegrate.
disgustado, -da, *a.* annoyed; insipid.
disgustar, *v.t.* displease.—*v.r.* be displeased (***con, de,*** with, about).
disgusto, *n.m.* displeasure, annoyance; worry, sorrow; squabble; ***a* —,** against one's will.
disgustoso, -sa, *a.* unpleasant.
disidencia, *n.f.* dissidence.
disidente, *a.* dissident.—*n.m.f.* dissenter.
disidir, *v.i.* dissent.
disímil, *a.* dissimilar.
disimilación, *n.f.* dissimilation.
disimilitud, *n.f.* dissimilarity.
disimulación, *n.f.* dissembling.
disimulado, -da, *a.* underhand; reserved.
disimular, *v.t.* hide, pretend not to have *or* to be, dissemble; forgive.
disimulo, *n.m.* dissembling; toleration.
disipación, *n.f.* dissipation.
disipar, *v.t.* dissipate.—*v.r.* be dissipated, vanish.
dislate, *n.m.* nonsense, absurdity.
dislocación, dislocadura, *n.f.* dislocation.
dislocar [A], *v.t., v.r.* dislocate.
disminución, *n.f.* diminution.
disminuir [O], *v.t., v.i., v.r.* diminish, decrease.
disociar, *v.t., v.r.* dissociate.
disoluble, *a.* dissoluble.
disolución, *n.f.* dissolution; disoluteness.
disoluto, -ta, *a.* dissolute.—*n.m.f.* debauchee.
disolver [5, *p.p.* **disuelto**], *v.t., v.r.* dissolve.
disonancia, *n.f.* dissonance.
disonante, *a., n.m.* dissonant.
disonar [4], *v.i.* be dissonant; grate, jar.
dísono, -na, *a.* dissonant.

dispar, *a.* unlike, unmatched, disparate.
disparadero, disparador, *n.m.* trigger; catch.
disparar, *v.t.* shoot, fire; hurl.—*v.i.* talk rubbish.—*v.r.* dash off; go off (*gun*); bolt.
disparatado, -da, *a.* absurd, foolish.
disparatar, *v.i.* talk rubbish; blunder.
disparate, *n.m.* piece of foolery, blunder; (*fam.*) scandal, outrage.
disparidad, *n.f.* disparity.
disparo, *n.m.* shot, discharge; nonsense.
dispendio, *n.m.* waste, squandering.
dispensa, dispensación, *n.f.* dispensation.
dispensar, *v.t.* dispense; excuse, pardon (***de***, for).—*v.i.* dispense (***con***, with).
dispensario, *n.m.* dispensary.
dispersar, *v.t.*, *v.r.* disperse.
dispersión, *n.f.* dispersal, dispersion.
disperso, -sa, *a.* scattered, dispersed; worried.
displicencia, *n.f.* lukewarmness; discouragement.
displiciente, *a.* disagreeable; peevish.
disponer [25], *v.t.* arrange; direct.—*v.i.* dispose, make use, have the use (***de***, of).—*v.r.* get ready, prepare (***a***, ***para***, to).
disponibilidad, *n.f.* availability.
disponible, *a.* available.
disposición, *n.f.* disposition; arrangement; inclination; lay-out; disposal.
dispositivo, *n.m.* device.
dispuesto, -ta, *a.* disposed; ready, willing; sprightly.—*p.p.* [DISPONER].
disputa, *n.f.* dispute.
disputable, *a.* disputable.
disputar, *v.t.* dispute; fight for.—*v.i.* argue, fight (***de***, ***por***, ***sobre***, over, about).
disquisición, *n.f.* disquisition.
distancia, *n.f.* distance.
distanciar, *v.t.* outdistance; place apart.
distante, *a.* distant.
distar, *v.i.* be distant, be far.
distender [2], *v.t.*, *v.r.* distend.
distensión, *n.f.* distension.
distinción, *n.f.* distinction.
distinguible, *a.* distinguishable.
distinguir [G], *v.t.* distinguish.
distintivo, -va, *a.* distinctive.—*n.m.* mark, badge, insignia.
distinto, -ta, *a.* different; distinct.—*pl.* various.
distorsión, *n.f.* distortion.
distracción, *n.f.* distraction; amusement; embezzlement.
distraer [34], *v.t.* distract, divert; seduce; misappropriate; amuse.
distraído, -da, *a.* absent-minded; dissolute; (*S.A.*) slovenly.
distribución, *n.f.* distribution; supply system; (*mech.*) gear system.
distribuidor, -ra, *a.* distributing.—*n.m.f.* distributor.
distribuir [O], *v.t.* distribute.
distributivo, -va, *a.* distributive.
distrito, *n.m.* district.
disturbar, *v.t.* disturb.
disturbio, *n.m.* disturbance.
disuadir, *v.t.* dissuade (***de***, from).
disuasión, *n.f.* dissuasion.
disuasivo, -va, *a.* dissuasive.
disuelto, *p.p.* [DISOLVER].
disyuntivo, -va, *a.* disjunctive.—*n.f.* dilemma.
dita, *n.f.* surety, bond; (*S.A.*) debt; credit.
diva, *n.f.* (*poet.*) goddess; (*mus.*) diva.
divagación, *n.f.* wandering, divagation.
divagar [B], *v.i.* ramble, digress.
diván, *n.m.* divan.
divergencia, *n.f.* divergence.
divergente, *a.* divergent.
divergir [E], *v.i.* diverge.
diversidad, *n.f.* diversity, variety.
diversificación, *n.f.* diversification.
diversificar [A], *v.t.*, *v.r.* diversify.
diversión, *n.f.* diversion; amusement.
diverso, -sa, *a.* diverse, different.—*pl.* several.
divertido, -da, *a.* funny; (*S.A.*) merry.
divertimiento, *n.m.* amusement; distraction.
divertir [6], *v.t.* amuse, divert.—*v.r.* have fun, enjoy oneself (***en***, by).
dividendo, *n.m.* dividend.
dividir, *v.t.*, *v.r.* divide.
divieso, *n.m.* (*med.*) boil.
divinidad, *n.f.* divinity; adored person.
divino, -na, *a.* divine; ***a lo* —**, rewritten to convey religious concepts.
divisa, *n.f.* emblem, device; foreign currency; (*taur.*) breeder's colours.
divisar, *v.t.* espy, perceive.
divisible, *a.* divisible.
división, *n.f.* division.
divisor, -ra, *a.* dividing.—*n.m.f.* divider.—*n.m.* (*math.*, *rad.*) divisor.
divisorio, -ria, *a.* dividing.—*n.f.* dividing-line; (*geol.*) divide.
divo, -va, *a.* (*poet.*) godlike.—*n.m.* (*poet.*) god; (*mus.*) opera singer. [DIVA].
divorciar, *v.t.* divorce, end the marriage of.—*v.r.* get a divorce, divorce (***de***).
divorcio, *n.m.* divorce.
divulgación, *n.f.* divulging.
divulgar [B], *v.t.* divulge, reveal, spread.
do (1), *adv.* (*obs.*, *poet.*) [DONDE].
do (2), *n.m.* (*mus.*) (key of) C; **— *de pecho*,** top C (*also fig.*).
dobladillo, *n.m.* hem.
doblado, -da, *a.* stocky; uneven; deceitful.
dobladura, *n.f.* fold, crease.
doblamiento, *n.m.* folding, doubling.
doblar, *v.t.* fold, crease; turn (*a corner*); dissuade; dub (*films*); double.—*v.i.* double; toll; turn.—*v.r.* fold, bend; stoop; yield.
doble, *a.* double; thickset; deceitful.—*n.m.* double, twice the amount; double, stand-in; fold; toll(ing); deceitfulness.—*adv.* doubly; ***al* —**, doubly; double.
doblegable, *a.* easily folded, pliant.
doblegar [B], *v.t.* fold, bend; dissuade; overcome; brandish.—*v.r.* yield; fold.
doblete, *a.* medium.—*n.m.* imitation gem; doublet.
doblez, *n.f.* crease, fold, pleat; turn-up.—*n.m.* or *f.* duplicity.
doblón, *n.m.* doubloon.
doce, *a.*, *n.m.* twelve.
docena, *n.f.* dozen.
docente, *a.* teaching.
dócil, *a.* docile; ductile.
docto, -ta, *a.* learned.—*n.m.f.* scholar.
doctor, -ra, *n.m.f.* doctor.—*n.f.* (*fam.*) doctor's wife; (*fam.*) blue-stocking.
doctorado, *n.m.* doctorate.
doctoral, *a.* doctoral.

doctorar, *v.t.* award a doctorate to.—*v.r.* obtain one's doctorate (***por*** (***la Universidad de***), at).
doctrina, *n.f.* doctrine.
doctrinal, *a.*, *n.m.* doctrinal.
doctrinar, *v.t.* indoctrinate, instruct.
doctrinario, -ria, *a.* doctrinaire.
doctrino, *n.m.* charity child; (*fig.*) timid person.
documentación, *n.f.* documentation; documents.
documental, *a.*, *n.m.* documentary.
documentar, *v.t.* document.
documento, *n.m.* document.
dogal, *n.m.* halter; noose.
dogma, *n.m.* dogma.
dogmático, -ca, *a.* dogmatic.
dogmatismo, *n.m.* dogmatism.
dogmatizar [C], *v.t.*, *v.i.* dogmatize; teach heresies.
dogo, -ga, *n.m.f.* bulldog.
dolamas, *n.f.pl.*, **dolames,** *n.m.pl.* (*vet.*) defects; (*S.A.*) ailment.
dolar [4], *v.t.* hew.
dólar, *n.m.* dollar.
dolencia, *n.f.* ailment, complaint.
doler [5], *v.t.* hurt, pain; distress.—*v.i.* ache. —*v.r.* complain (***de,*** about); feel sorry (***de,*** for).
doliente, *a.* ailing; sorrowing.—*n.m.f.* patient, sick person; mourner.
dolo, *n.m.* guile.
dolor, *n.m.* pain; sorrow, grief; repentance.
dolorido, -da, *a.* painful; heart-broken.
doloroso, -sa, *a.* painful; dolorous.—*n.f.* Mater Dolorosa.
doloso, -sa, *a.* deceitful.
doma, *n.f.* breaking, taming.
domador, -ra, *a.* taming.—*n.m.* horse-breaker.
domar, *v.t.* tame, break in (*horses*); master.
domeñar, *v.t.* tame; master.
domesticación, *n.f.* domestication.
domesticidad, *n.f.* domesticity.
doméstico, -ca, *a.*, *n.m.f.* domestic.
domestiquez, *n.f.* tameness.
domiciliar, *v.t.* domicile.—*v.r.* settle.
domicilio, *n.m.* dwelling; home address.
dominación, *n.f.* domination, dominance.
dominante, *a.* dominant; domineering, overbearing.
dominar, *v.t.* dominate; know completely *or* perfectly; domineer.—*v.r.* control oneself.
domingo, *n.m.* Sunday.
dominguero, -ra, *a.* (*fam.*) Sunday.
dominical, *a.* rel. to the Sabbath; feudal; ***la oración —,*** the Lord's Prayer.
dominicano, -na, *a.*, *n.m.f.* (*eccl.*, *geog.*) Dominican.
dominio, *n.m.* dominion (*jur.*) ownership; domain; knowledge (*of a subject*).
dominó, *n.m.* (*pl.* **-ós**) domino; dominoes.
dómino, *n.m.* dominoes.
Don, *n.m.* Don, Sir; **don,** *n.m.* gift; talent.
donación, *n.f.* donation.
donador, -ra, *n.m.f.* donor.
donaire, *n.m.* elegant clever wit; graceful witticism.
donairoso, -sa, *a.* witty, clever; graceful.
donante, *n.m.f.* donor.
donar, *v.t.* donate, give.
donativo, *n.m.* gift, donation.
doncel, *n.m.* knight's page; virgin.
doncella, *n.f.* maiden, virgin.
doncellez, *n.f.* maidenhood, virginity.
doncellueca, *n.f.* (*fam.*) old maid, spinster.
donde, *conj.* where; wherever; in which.—*prep.* (*S.A.*) at *or* to the home, office, shop *etc.* of (*like Fr.* chez); ***por —,*** through which, whereby; ***— no,*** otherwise.
¿dónde? *interrogative adv.* where?
dondequiera, *adv.* anywhere.
dondiego, *n.m.* dandy; (*bot.*) morning glory.
donjuanesco, -ca, *a.* like Don Juan.
donoso, -sa, *a.* witty, graceful.
donostiarra, *a.*, *n.m.f.* rel. to *or* native of San Sebastian.
donosura, *n.f.* wittiness; elegance.
Doña, *n.f.* Miss, Mrs., Madam (*title used before Christian name of ladies*).
doñear, *v.t.* woo.—*v.i.* (*fam.*) womanize.
doquier(a), *adv.* wherever.
dorado, -da, *a.* golden, gilt.—*n.m.* gilding, gilt; (*ichth.*) dorado.
dorar, *v.t.* gild; (*fig.*) sugar-coat; (*cul.*) brown.
dórico, -ca, *a.* Doric.
dormida, *n.f.* sleeping; night's sleep; lair, den; (*S.A.*) bedroom; night's lodgings.
dormidero, -ra, *a.* soporific.—*n.f.* (*bot.*) opium poppy.—*pl.* sleepiness.
dormido, -da, *a.* asleep; sleepy.
dormilón, -lona, *a.* (*fam.*) sleepy.—*n.m.f.* (*fam.*) sleepyhead; pyjama-case.—*n.f.* ear-ring (*for small child*).
dormir [7], *v.t.* sleep; sleep off; (*S.A.*) deceive.—*v.i.* sleep.—*v.r.* go to sleep, fall asleep.
dormitar, *v.i.* snooze, doze.
dormitorio, *n.m.* bedroom; dormitory.
Dorotea, *n.f.* Dorothy.
dorsal, *a.* dorsal.
dorso, *n.m.* back, dorsum.
dos, *a.*, *n.m.* two; ***en un — por tres,*** (*fam.*) in a flash.
doscientos, -tas, *a.*, *n.m.* two hundred.
dosel, *n.m.* canopy.
dosificación, *n.f.* dosage, dosing.
dosificar [A], *v.t.* dose; measure out.
dosis, *n.f. inv.* dose.
dotación, *n.f.* endowment; dowry; (*naut.*, *aer.*) complement, crew; equipment.
dotar, *v.t.* give a dowry to; endow; equip; man; staff.
dote, *n.m.* or *f.* dowry.—*n.f.* gift, talent.
doy [DAR].
dozavado, -da, *a.* twelve-sided.
dozavo, -va, *a.*, *n.m.* twelfth; ***en —,*** 12°.
dracma, *n.f.* drachma; dram, drachm.
draga, *n.f.* dredging; (*naut.*) dredger.
dragaminas, *n.m. inv.* (*naut.*) mine-sweeper.
dragar [B], *v.t.* dredge.
dragomán, *n.m.* dragoman.
dragón, *n.m.* dragon; (*mil.*) dragoon.
dragona, *n.f.* (*mil.*) shoulder tassel; (*C.A.*) cape.
dragoncillo, *n.m.* (*bot.*) tarragon.
dragonear, *v.i.* (*S.A.*) boast (***de,*** *of being*); flirt.
drama, *n.m.* drama.
dramático, -ca, *a.* dramatic; theatrical.—*n.m.f.* dramatist; actor.—*n.f.* drama, the dramatic art.
dramatismo, *n.m.* dramatic quality, drama.
dramatización, *n.f.* dramatization.

dramatizar [C], *v.t.* dramatize.
dramaturgo, *n.m.* dramatist.
drástico, -ca, *a.* drastic.
dren, *n.m.* drain.
drenaje, *n.m.* draining.
drenar, *v.t.* drain.
dril, *n.m.* drill (*cloth*).
driza, *n.f.* (*naut.*) halyard.
droga, *n.f.* drug; swindle; pest; (*S.A.*) bad debt; (*fam.*) white elephant (*useless object*).
drogmán, *n.m.* dragoman.
droguería, *n.f.* pharmacy.
droguero, -ra, *n.m.f.* druggist, pharmacist; (*S.A.*) bad debtor; cheat.
droguista, *n.m.f.* cheat; (*S.A.*) druggist.
dromedario, *n.m.* dromedary.
druida, *n.m.* druid.
dual, *n.m.* dual.
dualidad, *n.f.* duality.
dualismo, *n.m.* dualism.
dualista, *a.* dualistic.—*n.m.f.* dualist.
dubitación, *n.f.* dubitation, doubt.
dubitativo, -va, *a.* dubitative.
ducado, *n.m.* duchy, dukedom; ducat.
ducal, *a.* ducal.
dúctil, *a.* ductile.
ductivo, -va, *a.* conducive.
ducha, *n.f.* shower-bath; douche, shower.
duchar, *v.t.* douche; give a shower to.—*v.r.* take a shower.
duda, *n.f.* doubt.
dudable, *a.* doubtful.
dudar, *v.t., v.i.* doubt; — ***en,*** hesitate to.
dudoso, -sa, *a.* doubtful, dubious.
duelista, *n.m.* duellist.
duelo (1), *n.m.* duel.
duelo (2), *n.m.* sorrow, grief; bereavement. —*pl.* travails.
duende, *n.m.* elf, goblin; spirit.
duendo, -da, *a.* tame, domestic.
dueño, -ña, *n.m.f.* owner.—*n.m.* landlord; master; — ***de sí mismo,*** self-controlled; ***ser — de,*** be quite at liberty to.—*n.f.* landlady; mistress; matron; duenna, chaperone.
duermevela, *n.f.* (*fam.*) doze, snooze.
dulce, *a.* sweet; mild; soft; fresh (*water*).—*n.m.* sweet, toffee; — ***de membrillo,*** quince jelly.
dulcería, *n.f.* sweet-shop.
dulcero, -ra, *a.* (*fam.*) sweet-toothed.—*n.m.f.* confectioner.
dulcificar [C], *v.t.* sweeten; dulcify.
dulcinea, *n.f.* (*fam.*) lady-love; (*fig.*) dream.
dulzaino, -na, *a.* (*fam.*) over-sweet, sickly.—*n.f.* (*mus.*) flageolet; (*fam.*) sweet sticky mess.
dulz(arr)ón, -ona, *a.* (*fam.*) too sweet, sickly.
dulzor, *n.m.* sweetness; pleasantness.
dulzura, *n.f.* sweetness, mildness.
duna, *n.f.* dune.
Dunquerque, *n.m.* Dunkirk.
dúo, *n.m.* (*mus.*) duet.
duodecimal, *a.* duodecimal.
duodécimo, -ma, *a.* twelfth.
duplicación, *n.f.* duplication.
duplicado, *n.m.* duplicate; ***por —,*** in duplicate.
duplicar [A], *v.t.* duplicate; (*jur.*) reply to.
dúplice, *a.* double.
duplicidad, *n.f.* duplicity.
duplo, -la, *a., n.m.* double.
duque, *n.m.* duke.
duquesa, *n.f.* duchess.
dura (*fam.*), **durabilidad,** *n.f.* durability.
durable, *a.* durable.
duración, *n.f.* duration; durability.
duradero, -ra, *a.* durable, lasting.
durante, *prep.* during.
durar, *v.i.* last; last well, wear well.
durazno, *n.m.* peach.
dureza, *n.f.* hardness.
durmiente, *a.* sleeping.—*n.m.f.* sleeper.—*n.m.* cross-beam, tie; (*S.A., rail.*) sleeper.
duro, -ra, *a.* hard; tough; rough; cruel; harsh.—*n.m.* duro, five pesetas.—*adv.* hard.

E

E, e, *n.f.* sixth letter of the Spanish alphabet.
e, *conj.* and (*used instead of* y *before* i *or* hi, *but not before* hie *or at the beginning of a sentence*).
¡ea! *interj.* hey!
ebanista, *n.m.* cabinet-maker.
ébano, *n.m.* ebony.
ebriedad, *n.f.* drunkenness.
ebrio, -ria, *a., n.m.f.* drunk.
ebrioso, -sa, *a.* drunken.
ebulición, ebullición, *n.f.* ebullition, boiling.
ebúrneo, -nea, *a.* ivory.
eclecticismo, *n.m.* electicism.
ecléctico, -ca, *a.* eclectic.
eclesiástico, -ca, *a.* ecclesiastical.—*n.m.* ecclesiastic.
eclipsar, *v.t.* eclipse.—*v.r.* be eclipsed.
eclipse, *n.m.* eclipse.
eclíptico, -ca, *a., n.f.* ecliptic.
eco, *n.m.* echo.
ecología, *n.f.* ecology.
ecómetro, *n.m.* echo-meter.
economato, *n.m.* co-operative store.
economía, *n.f.* economy; frugality.—*pl.* savings.
económico, -ca, *a.* economic; economical, thrifty.
economista, *n.m.f.* economist.
economizar [C], *v.t., v.i.* economize.
ecónomo, *n.m.* trustee.
ecuación, *n.f.* equation.
Ecuador, *n.m.* Ecuador; **ecuador,** *n.m.* equator.
ecuánime, *a.* calm, equanimous.
ecuanimidad, *n.f.* equanimity; impartiality.
ecuatorial, *a.* equatorial.
ecuatoriano, -na, *a., n.m.f.* Ecuadorian.
ecuestre, *a.* equestrian.
ecuménico, -ca, *a.* ecumenical.
eczema, *n.m.* (*med.*) eczema.
echadizo, -za, *a.* waste; foundling; spying.—*n.m.f.* foundling; spy.
echado, -da, *a.* lying down; (*S.A.*) lazy.

echar, *v.t.* throw, fling; dismiss; pour; emit; turn (*a key*); put on (*a play*); begin to grow (*shoots etc.*); cut (*teeth*); deal (*cards*); cast (*a glance*); shed (*blood*); post, mail (*letters*); ***echarla de,*** (*fam.*) claim to be; — ***a perder,*** spoil; — ***por,*** turn towards; — ***a pique,*** sink; ***echarse a hacer,*** begin to do; ***echarse sobre,*** rush upon.
echazón, *n.m.* (*naut.*) jettison.
edad, *n.f.* age; epoch; — ***media,*** Middle Ages.
edecán, *n.m.* (*mil.*) aide-de-camp.
edición, *n.f.* edition; impression; publication.
edicto, *n.m.* edict.
edificación, *n.f.* construction; edification.
edificante, *a.* edifying.
edificar [A], *v.t.* construct; edify.
edificio, *n.m.* building; edifice.
Edimburgo, *n.m.* Edinburgh.
Edipo, *n.m.* (*myth.*) Oedipus.
editar, *v.t.* publish, edit (*a text*).
editor, -ra, *a.* publishing.—*n.m.f.* publisher.
editorial, *a.* publishing; editorial.—*n.m.* editorial (*article*).—*n.f.* publishing house.
editorialista, *n.m.f.* (*S.A.*) leader-writer.
edredón, *n.m.* eiderdown.
educable, *a.* educable, teachable.
educación, *n.f.* education; good manners, politeness.
educador, -ra, *a.* educating.—*n.m.f.* education(al)ist.
educando, -da, *n.m.f.* student (*in a college*).
educar [A], *v.t.* educate, train; bring up.
educativo, -va, *a.* educational.
educir [15], *v.t.* educe, bring out.
efe, *n.f.* name of letter F.
efectivamente, *adv.* effectively; really; actually; quite so.
efectivo, -va, *a.* real, actual; effective, effectual; permanent (*employment*).—*n.m.* cash.—*pl.* (*mil.*) effectives, troops.
efecto, *n.m.* effect; end; impression; ***en —,*** in effect; indeed.—*pl.* effects, assets; ***efectos de consumo,*** consumer goods.
efectuar [M], *v.t.* effect, carry out.
efeméride, *n.f.* anniversary.—*pl.* diary.
efervescencia, *n.f.* effervescence.
eficacia, *n.f.* efficacy, effectiveness.
eficaz, *a.* (*pl.* **-aces**) effective, effectual.
eficiencia, *n.f.* efficiency.
eficiente, *a.* efficient.
efigie, *n.f.* effigy.
efímero, -ra, *a.* ephemeral.—*n.f.* may-fly.
eflorescencia, *n.f.* (*chem., bot.*) efflorescence; (*med.*) eruption.
efluente, *a., n.m.* effluent.
efluvio, *n.m.* effluvium, emanation.
efusión, *n.f.* effusion; — ***de sangre,*** bloodshed.
efusivo, -va, *a.* effusive.
egida, égida, *n.f.* aegis.
egipcio, -cia, *a., n.m.f.* Egyptian.
egiptología, *n.f.* Egyptology.
égloga, *n.f.* eclogue.
egoísmo, *n.m.* selfishness, egoism.
egoísta, *a.* selfish, egoistic(al).—*n.m.f.* egoist.
egotismo, *n.m.* egotism.
egotista, *a.* egotistic(al), self-centred.
egregio, -gia, *a.* distinguished, eminent.
egresar, *v.t.* (*S.A.*) withdraw (*money*).—*v.i.* (*S.A.*) leave; (*S.A.*) graduate.
egreso, *n.m.* debit; expense; (*S.A.*) graduation; (*S.A.*) departure.
¡eh! *interj.* ah! here!
eje, *n.m.* axle; spindle; axis.
ejecución, *n.f.* execution; implementation.
ejecutante, *a.* executing.—*n.m.f.* performer.
ejecutar, *v.t.* execute; implement.
ejecutivo, -va, *a.* executive; insistent.
ejecutor, -ra, *a.* executive.—*n.m.f.* executive; executor, executrix.
ejecutoria, *n.f.* title of nobility.
ejecutoriar, *v.t.* confirm (*a judicial sentence*).
ejecutorio, -ria, *a.* (*jur.*) executory.
ejemplar, *a.* exemplary.—*n.m.* copy (*of a book*), sample, model; example.
ejemplaridad, *n.f.* exemplary nature.
ejemplificar [A], *v.t.* exemplify.
ejemplo, *n.m.* example, instance.
ejercer [D], *v.t.* practise, exercise.
ejercicio, *n.m.* exercise; drill; exertion; fiscal year.
ejercitar, *v.t.* exercise (*a profession etc.*); train.
ejército, *n.m.* army; — ***del aire,*** air force.
ejido, *n.m.* common land.
el, *definite article, m.* (*pl.* **los**) the.
él, *pers. pron. m.* (*pl.* **ellos**) he; him; it.—*pl.* they; them.
elaboración, *n.f.* elaboration; processing, manufacture.
elaborar, *v.t.* elaborate; process, manufacture.
elación, *n.f.* haughtiness; magnanimity; pomposity.
elasticidad, *n.f.* elasticity.
elástico, -ca, *a.* elastic.—*n.m.* elastic.—*n.f.* undervest.—*n.f.pl.* (*S.A.*) braces, (*U.S.*) suspenders.
ele, *n.f.* name of letter L.
elección, *n.f.* election; choice.
electivo, -va, *a.* elective.
electo, -ta, *a.* chosen, elect.
elector, -ra, *a.* electing.—*n.m.f.* elector.
electorado, *n.m.* electorate.
electoral, *a.* electoral.
electricidad, *n.f.* electricity.
electricista, *n.m.* electrician.
eléctrico, -ca, *a.* electric(al).
electrificación, *n.f.* electrification.
electrificar [A], *v.t.* electrify.
electrizar [C], *v.t.* electrify.—*v.r.* become charged with electricity.
electro, *n.m.* amber; electrum.
electrocución, *n.f.* electrocution.
electrocutar, *v.t.* electrocute.
electrodeposición, *n.f.* electric plating.
electrodo, eléctrodo, *n.m.* electrode.
electroimán, *n.m.* electromagnet.
electrólisis, *n.f.* electrolysis.
electrolizar [C], *v.t.* electrolyze.
electromotora, *n.f.* electric motor.
electrón, *n.m.* electron.
electrónico, -ca, *a.* electronic.—*n.f.* electronics.
electrotecnia, *n.f.* electrical engineering.
electrotipia, *n.f.* (*print.*) electrotyping.
electuario, *n.m.* electuary.
elefante, -ta, *n.m.f.* elephant.
elefantino, -na, *a.* elephantine.
elegancia, *n.f.* elegance.
elegante, *a.* elegant, stylish.
elegía, *n.f.* elegy.

elegíaco, -ca, *a.* elegiac.
elegibilidad, *n.f.* eligibility.
eligible, *a.* eligible.
elegir [8E], *v.t.* elect; select.
elemental, *a.* elementary; elemental, fundamental.
elemento, *n.m.* element; member; (*elec.*) cell.
elenco, *n.m.* index, list; selection.
elevación, *n.f.* elevation.
elevador, *n.m.* hoist; lift, (*U.S.*) elevator.
elevar, *v.t.* elevate.—*v.r.* rise, ascend.
Elías, *n.m.* (*Bib.*) Elijah, Elias.
elidir, *v.t.* (*gram.*) elide.
eliminación, *n.f.* elimination.
eliminador, -ra, *a.* eliminating.—*n.m.f.* eliminator.—*n.m.* (*rad., T.V.*) suppressor.
eliminar, *v.t.* eliminate.
elipse, *n.f.* ellipse.
elipsis, *n.f. inv.* (*gram.*) ellipsis.
elíptico, -ca, *a.* elliptic(al).
Elíseo (1), *n.m.* Elisha.
Elíseo (2), *n.m.* (*myth.*) Elysium.
elíseo, -sea, elisio, -sia, *a.* Elysian.
elisión, *n.f.* elision.
elíxir, elixir, *n.m.* elixir.
elocución, *n.f.* elocution.
elocuencia, *n.f.* eloquence.
elocuente, *a.* eloquent.
elogiar, *v.t.* praise, eulogize.
elogio, *n.m.* eulogy, praise.
elogioso, -sa, *a.* eulogistic.
elucidar, *v.t.* elucidate.
eludible, *a.* avoidable.
eludir, *v.t.* elude, avoid.
ella, *pers. pron. f.* (*pl.* **ellas**) she; her; it.—*pl.* they; them.
elle, *n.f.* name of letter LL.
ello, *pers. pron. neuter,* it.
ellos, ellas, *pers. pron. pl.* they; them.
emanación, *n.f.* emanation.
emanar, *v.i.* emanate, proceed from.
emancipación, *n.f.* emancipation.
emancipar, *v.t.* emancipate.
emascular, *v.t.* emasculate.
embadurnar, *v.t.* daub, smear, coat.
embajada, *n.f.* embassy.
embajador, *n.m.* ambassador.
embajadora, *n.f.* ambassadress; ambassador's wife.
embajatorio, -ria, *a.* ambassadorial.
embalador, -ra, *n.m.f.* packer.
embalaje, embalamiento, *n.m.* packing; package; rush, hurry.
embalar, *v.t.* pack, bale.—*v.r.* rush.
embaldosado, *n.m.* tile paving.
embalsadero, *n.m.* swamp.
embalsamar, *v.t.* embalm.
embalsar, *v.t.* dam; put on a raft.
embalse, *n.m.* dam; damming.
embarazada, *a.f.* pregnant.—*n.f.* pregnant woman.
embarazadamente, *adv.* with difficulty.
embarazar [C], *v.t.* hinder; make pregnant. —*v.r.* be obstructed; become pregnant.
embarazo, *n.m.* embarrassment, obstacle; pregnancy.
embarazoso, -sa, *a.* embarrassing; complicated.
embarcación, *n.f.* vessel, ship; embarcation; **— *de alijo*,** lighter.
embarcadero, *n.m.* pier; loading dock.
embarcar [A], *v.t.* embark.
embarco, *n.m.* embarcation.
embargar [B], *v.t.* embargo; impede; stupefy.
embargo, *n.m.* embargo; (*jur.*) seizure; ***sin* —,** however, nevertheless.
embarque, *n.m.* shipment, embarcation (*of goods*).
embarrar, *v.t.* splash with mud; smear.
embarullar, *v.t.* (*fam.*) muddle.
embastecer [9], *v.i.* get fat *or* flabby.—*v.r.* become coarse.
embate, *n.m.* sudden attack; dashing (*of the waves*).
embaucar [A], *v.t.* deceive, trick.
embeber, *v.t.* absorb, soak up; shrink (*of cloth*); soak.—*v.i.* shrink, contract.—*v.r.* be enchanted; become well versed (**de,** in).
embeleco, *n.m.* fraud, imposture.
embelesar, *v.t.* charm, enrapture.
embeleso, *n.m.* entrancement; fascination.
embellecer [9], *v.t.* embellish.
emberrenchinar, emberrinchinar, *v.r.* (*fam.*) fly into a rage.
embestida, *n.f.* attack, assault.
embestir [8], *v.t.* assail, attack; charge.
embetunar, *v.t.* cover with pitch.
emblanquecer [9], *v.t.* bleach; whiten.—*v.r.* turn white.
emblema, *n.m.* emblem.
emblemático, -ca, *a.* emblematic.
embobar, *v.t.* fascinate; amuse.—*v.r.* stand gaping.
embobecer [9], *v.t.* make foolish.
embocadero, *n.m.* outlet, mouth.
embocadura, *n.f.* nozzle; mouthpiece; outlet, mouth; taste (*of wine*); (*arch.*) proscenium arch; tip (*of a cigarette*).
embocar [A], *v.t.* put into the mouth; put through a narrow passage.
embolada, *n.f.* stroke (*of a piston*).
embolia, *n.f.* (*med.*) embolism, blood-clot.
embolismo, *n.m.* intercalation (*in the calendar*).
émbolo, *n.m.* piston; (*med.*) blood-clot.
embolsar, *v.t.* pocket.
embolso, *n.m.* pocketing.
emboquillar, *v.t.* tip (*cigarettes*).
emborrachar, *v.t.* intoxicate.—*v.r.* get drunk.
emborrar, *v.t.* pad.
emborrascar [A], *v.t.* provoke.—*v.r.* become stormy; fail (*of a business, a mine*).
emborronar, *v.t.* cover with blots; scribble.
emboscada, *n.f.* ambush.
emboscar [A], *v.t.* ambush.—*v.r.* lie in ambush; go deep into the woods.
embotar, *v.t.* blunt; dull.
embotellamiento, *n.m.* bottling; traffic-jam.
embotellar, *v.t.* bottle.
embotijar, *v.t.* put into jars.—*v.r.* be in a rage.
embovedar, *v.t.* arch, vault.
embozalar, *v.t.* muzzle.
embozar [C], *v.t.* muffle; disguise.
embozo, *n.m.* muffler; turn-over of a sheet; ***sin* —,** frankly.
embragar [B], *v.t.* throw in the clutch, couple.
embrague, *n.m.* clutch; engaging the clutch.
embrazadura, *n.f.* clasp.
embrazar [C], *v.t.* clasp; buckle.—*v.i.* engage (*of gears*).

embriagar [B], *v.t.* intoxicate.
embriaguez, *n.f.* intoxication; rapture.
embrión, *n.m.* embryo.
embrionario, -ria, *a.* embryonic.
embroca, embrocación, *n.f.* embrocation.
embrocar [A], *v.t.* place upside down; tack (*soles*); (*taur.*) toss between the horns.
embrollar, *v.t.* embroil.
embrollo, *n.m.* imbroglio.
embromar, *v.t.* tease; cheat.
embrujar, *v.t.* bewitch.
embrutecer [9], *v.t.* brutalize.
embuchado, *n.m.* sort of sausage.
embuchar, *v.t.* stuff; cram down (*food*).
embudo, *n.m.* funnel; trick.
embullo, *n.m.* (*C.A.*) excitement.
embuste, *n.m.* trick, fraud.
embustero, -ra, *a.* lying, deceitful.—*n.m.f.* cheat, fraud.
embutido, *n.m.* sausage; marquetry.
embutir, *v.t.* stuff; inlay; set flush.
eme, *n.f.* name of letter M.
emergencia, *n.f.* emergence; emergency.
emergente, *a.* emergent.
emerger [E], *v.i.* emerge.
emético, -ca, *a.* emetic.
emigración, *n.f.* emigration.
emigrado, -da, *n.m.f.* emigrant, émigré.
emigrar, *v.i.* emigrate.
emigratorio, -ria, *a.* rel. to emigration.
eminencia, *n.f.* eminence.
emisario, -ria, *n.m.f.* emissary.
emisión, *n.f.* emission; issue (*of money*); (*rad.*) broadcast, programme; (*phys.*) radiation.
emisor, -ra, *a.* emitting.—*n.m.* (*rad.*) transmitter.—*n.f.* (*rad.*) station.
emitir, *v.t.* emit; (*rad.*) broadcast; issue.
emoción, *n.f.* emotion.
emocional, *a.* emotional.
emocionante, *a.* touching; stirring, exciting.
emocionar, *v.t.* touch; stir.—*v.r.* be moved *or* stirred; get excited.
emoliente, *a.*, *n.m.* emollient.
emolumento, *n.m.* emolument.
emotivo, -va, *a.* emotive.
empacar [A], *v.t.* pack, bale; (*S.A.*) anger.—*v.r.* get angry.
empachar, *v.t.* hinder; surfeit.—*v.r.* feel ashamed *or* bashful.
empacho, *n.m.* bashfulness; obstacle; surfeit.
empachoso, -sa, *a.* shameful; embarrassing.
empadronamiento, *n.m.* census.
empadronar, *v.t.*, *v.r.* register.
empalagar [B], *v.t.* surfeit; weary.
empalago, empalagamiento, *n.m.* surfeit.
empalagoso, -sa, *a.* cloying, sickening.
empalar, *v.t.* impale.
empaliada, *n.f.* bunting.
empalizada, *n.f.* pallisade, stockade.
empalizar [C], *v.t.* fence in, stockade.
empalmadura, *n.f.* [EMPALME].
empalmar, *v.t.* join, connect.—*v.i.* connect.
empalme, *n.m.* joint; splice; (*rail.*) connexion; (*rail.*) junction.
empanado, -da, *a.* windowless.—*n.f.* pasty, pie; fraud.
empantanar, *v.t.* flood, swamp.
empañadura, *n.f.* swaddling clothes.
empañar, *v.t.* swaddle; blur; tarnish.
empapar, *v.t.*, *v.r.* soak.
empapelado, *n.m.* wall-paper; paper-hanging; paper-lining.
empapelador, -ra, *n.m.f.* paper-hanger.
empaque, *n.m.* packing; appearance; stiffness; (*S.A.*) brazenness.
empaquetar, *v.t.* pack; stuff.
emparedado, *n.m.* sandwich.
emparedar, *v.t.* wall in; immure.
emparejar, *v.t.* pair; match; level off.—*v.i.* be even (**con,** with).
emparentar [1], *v.i.* become related (*by marriage*).
emparrado, *n.m.* bower.
empastar, *v.t.* cover *or* fill with paste; fill (*a tooth*).
empaste, *n.m.* filling (*of a tooth*).
empastelar, *v.t.* botch; compromise.
empatar, *v.t.*, *v.i.*, *v.r.* tie, draw (*in sport etc.*).
empate, *n.m.* draw, tie; hindrance.
empavesar, *v.t.* bedeck with flags, (*naut.*) dress.
empecinado, -da, *a.* (*S.A.*) stubborn.
empedernir [Q], *v.t.* harden.—*v.r.* get hard, harden.
empedrado, -da, *a.* flecked, dappled.—*n.m.* stone pavement.
empedrar [1], *v.t.* pave; bespatter.
empega, *n.f.* pitch, tar.
empegado, *n.m.* tarpaulin.
empegar [B], *v.r.* coat *or* mark with pitch.
empeine, *n.m.* groin; instep.
empelotar, *v.r.* (*fam.*) get tangled up; (*C.A.*) strip.
empellón, *n.m.* push, shove.
empenta, *n.f.* prop, stay.
empeñado, -da, *a.* persistent; heated (*argument*).
empeñar, *v.t.* pawn; pledge.—*v.r.* persist (**en,** in).
empeño, *n.m.* pledge; persistence, perseverance.
empeoramiento, *n.m.* deterioration.
empeorar, *v.t.* make worse.—*v.r.* get worse.
emperador, *n.m.* emperor.
emperatriz, *n.f.* (*pl.* **-ices**) empress.
emperezar [C], *v.t.* make lazy.—*v.r.* be *or* become lazy.
empero, *conj.* (*obs.*) however, yet.
empezar [1C], *v.t.*, *v.i.* begin (***a,*** to, ***por,*** by).
empicotar, *v.t.* pillory.
empilar, *v.t.* pile up.
empinado, -da, *a.* high; steep; conceited.
empinar, *v.t.* raise; — ***el codo,*** (*fam.*) drink heavily.
empíreo, -rea, *a.*, *n.m.* empyrean.
empírico, -ca, *a.* empirical.
empirismo, *n.m.* empiricism.
empizarrar, *v.t.* slate.
emplastadura, *n.f.*, **emplastamiento,** *n.m.* plastering.
emplastar, *v.t.* plaster; smear; (*fam.*) obstruct.
emplastecer [9], *v.t.* stop (*cracks before painting*).
emplasto, *n.m.* plaster, poultice; tyre patch.
emplazar [C], *v.t.* summon; site, locate.
empleado, -da, *n.m.f.* employee; clerk.
emplear, *v.t.* employ.—*v.r.* be employed; (*fam.*) ***le esté bien empleado,*** it serves him right.
empleo, *n.m.* employment, occupation, job; public office.

emplomar, *v.t.* lead; seal with lead.
emplumar, *v.t.* put feathers *or* plumes on; tar and feather; ***emplumarlas,*** (*S.A. fam.*) beat it.
emplumecer [9], *v.i.* fledge.
empobrecer [9], *v.t.* impoverish.
empodrecer [9], *v.i.*, *v.r.* rot.
empolvar, *v.t.* cover with dust.
empollador, *n.m.* incubator.
empolladura, *n.f.* (*fam.*) swotting, grinding (*for examinations*).
empollar, *v.t.* hatch, brood; (*fam.*) swot.
empollón, -llona, *n.m.f.* (*pej.*) swot, (*U.S.*) grind.
emponzoñar, *v.t.* poison.
emporio, *n.m.* emporium.
empotrar, *v.t.* (*arch.*) embed, fix in a wall, build-in.
emprender, *v.t.* undertake.
empreñar, *v.t.* impregnate.
empresa, *n.f.* enterprise, undertaking; design; firm.
empresario, -ria, *n.m.f.* contractor; impresario.
empréstito, *n.m.* loan.
emprimar, *v.t.* prime (*with paint*); (*fam.*) hoodwink.
empujadora, *n.f.* bulldozer.
empujar, *v.t.* push.
empuje, *n.m.* push; (*phys.*) thrust; energy.
empujón, *n.m.* push, shove.
empulgueras, *n.f.pl.* thumbscrews.
empuñadura, *n.f.* hilt; beginning of a story.
empuñar, *v.t.* clutch, grasp.
emulación, *n.f.* emulation.
emular, *v.t.* emulate.
emulsión, *n.f.* emulsion.
en, *prep.* in; at; on; for.
enagua, *n.f.* (*esp. pl.*) underskirt(s), petticoat.
enajenación, *n.f.*, **enajenamiento,** *n.m.* alienation; distraction; madness; rapture.
enajenar, *v.t.* alienate, transfer; enrapture.
enamoradizo, -za, *a.* susceptible (*to passion*).
enamorado, -da, *a.* in love.—*n.m.f.* lover, sweetheart.
enamorar, *v.t.* enamour; make love to.—*v.r.* fall in love (***de,*** with).
enano, -na, *a.*, *n.m.f.* dwarf.
enarbolar, *v.t.* hoist (*flags etc.*).
enardecer [9], *v.t.* inflame.—*v.r.* be inflamed.
encabalgamiento, *n.m.* gun-carriage; (*poet.*) enjambement.
encabezamiento, *n.m.* census; headline, title, heading.
encabezar [C], *v.t.* draw up (*a list*); put a heading to; fortify (*wine*); be at the head (of).
encadenar, *v.t.* chain; enchain; brace.
encajar, *v.t.* insert, fit; tell (*a story etc.*) inopportunely.
encaje, *n.m.* insertion; recess; lace.
encajonar, *v.t.* box, crate.—*v.r.* become narrow (*of a river*).
encalar, *v.t.* whitewash; (*agr.*) lime.
encalmado, -da, *a.* (*naut.*) becalmed; (*com.*) quiet (*market*).
encallar, *v.i.* run aground.
encallecer [9], *v.i.* get corns *or* calluses.
encaminadura, *n.f.*, **encaminamiento,** *n.m.* directing, forwarding.
encaminar, *v.t.* direct, put on the right track; forward.—*v.r.* set out, be on the way (***a,*** to).
encanalar, encanalizar [C], *v.t.* channel.
encanallar, *v.t.* corrupt.—*v.r.* become corrupt *or* depraved.
encanecer [9], *v.i.* turn grey.
encantado, -da, *a.* delighted, enchanted; absent-minded.
encantador, -ra, *a.* enchanting.—*n.m.* charmer, enchanter.—*n.f.* enchantress.
encantamiento, *n.m.* enchantment.
encantar, *v.t.* bewitch; charm, delight.
encante, *n.m.* auction.
encanto, *n.m.* charm.
encañada, *n.f.* gorge.
encañado, *n.m.* conduit.
encapotar, *v.t.* cloud; veil.—*v.r.* get cloudy; (*fig.*) glower.
encaprichar, *v.r.* persist in one's fancy.
encaramar, *v.t.* raise; extol.—*v.r.* get on top.
encarar, *v.t.* face; aim.—*v.r.* face, confront (***con***).
encarcelar, *v.t.* imprison; (*carp.*) clamp.
encarecer [9], *v.t.* raise the price of; extol; recommend.
encarecimiento, *n.m.* overrating; enhancement; augmentation; ***con —,*** earnestly.
encargado, -da, *n.m.f.* person in charge; manager; ***— de negocios,*** chargé d'affaires.
encargar [B], *v.t.* entrust; urge, warn; order (*goods*); request.—*v.r.* take charge (***de,*** of).
encargo, *n.m.* charge; assignment; (*com.*) order.
encariñar, *v.t.* inspire affection.—*v.r.* become fond (***de,*** of).
encarnación, *n.f.* incarnation.
encarnadino, -na, *a.* incarnadine, reddish-pink.
encarnado, -da, *a.* incarnate; flesh-coloured.
encarnar, *v.t.* incarnate.—*v.i.* become incarnate.
encarnecer [9], *v.i.* grow fat.
encarnizado, -da, *a.* bloody; fierce.
encarnizar [C], *v.t.* flesh (*a hound*); infuriate.—*v.r.* be infuriated.
encaro, *n.m.* stare; aim.
encartar, *v.t.* outlaw; enrol; lead (*at cards*).—*v.r.* be unable to discard (*at cards*).
encartonar, *v.t.* cover *or* protect with card-board; bind (*books*).
encasar, *v.t.* set (*bones*).
encasillar, *v.t.* pigeonhole, classify.
encasquetar, *v.t.* clap on (*a hat*); put (*an idea*) in someone's mind.—*v.r.* clap on (*one's hat*); get (*an idea*) fixed in one's mind.
encastillado, -da, *a.* castellated; proud.
encastillador, *n.m.* scaffolder.
encastillar, *v.t.* fortify; scaffold.—*v.r.* withdraw; be stubborn.
encastrar, *v.t.* engage (*gears*).
encauchar, *v.t.* coat with rubber.
encáustico, -ca, *a.* encaustic.
encauzamiento, *n.m.* channelling.
encauzar [C], *v.t.* channel; guide.
encebollado, *n.m.* stewed steak and onions.
encenagar [B], *v.r.* get into the mire, wallow.
encendedor, -ra, *a.* lightning.—*n.m.* lighter, igniter.
encender [2], *v.t.* light, kindle; (*fig.*) inflame.—*v.r.* catch fire.
encendido, -da, *a.* inflamed, flushed.—*n.m.* (*auto.*) ignition.
encendimiento, *n.m.* lighting; incandescence; ardour.

encepar, *v.t.* put in the stocks; stock.—*v.i.*, *v.r.* take root.
encerado, -da, *a.* waxy; hard-boiled (*eggs*).—*n.m.* oilcloth; tarpaulin; blackboard; waxing (*furniture etc.*).
encerar, *v.t.* wax.
encerradura, *n.f.*, **encerramiento,** *n.m.* locking up; imprisonment.
encerrar [1], *v.t.* shut in, lock up; contain, include.
encerrona, *n.f.* (*fam.*) voluntary confinement; trap.
encía, *n.f.* (*anat.*) gum.
enciclopedia, *n.f.* encylopedia.
enciclopédico, -ca, *a.* encyclopedic.
encierro, *n.m.* locking up; enclosure; (*taur.*) driving bulls into the pen (*before the fight*); retreat.
encima, *adv.* above, over; besides.—*prep.* on, upon, above (**de**).
encina, *n.f.* (*bot.*) holm oak, ilex.
encinal, encinar, *n.m.* wood *or* grove of holm oaks.
encinta, *a.f.* pregnant.
encintado, *n.m.* kerb, (*U.S.*) curb.
encintar, *v.t.* beribbon; kerb.
enclaustrar, *v.t.* cloister; hide.
enclavar, *v.t.* nail; pierce.
enclave, *n.m.* (*geog.*) enclave.
enclavijar, *v.t.* peg (together), dowel.
enclenque, *a.* weak, sickly, puny.
enclítico, -ca, *a.* (*gram.*) enclitic.
enclocar [4A], *v.i.*, *v.r.* go broody, brood.
encobar, *v.i.*, *v.r.* brood.
encofrar, *v.t.* (*min.*) timber; (*arch.*) shutter (*concrete*).
encoger [E], *v.t.* shrink; intimidate.—*v.i.* shrink.—*v.r.* shrink; cringe; be bashful.
encogimiento, *n.m.* shrinking; timidity; crouching.
encojar, *v.t.* cripple.—*v.r.* go lame; (*fam.*) malinger.
encolar, *v.t.* glue, size; clarify (*wine*).
encolerizar [C], *v.t.* anger.—*v.r.* become angry.
encomendar [1], *v.t.* entrust; give an ENCOMIENDA.—*v.i.* hold an ENCOMIENDA.—*v.r.* commend oneself; send one's compliments.
encomiador, -ra, *a.* eulogistic, panegyric.—*n.m.f.* panegyrist.
encomiar, *v.t.* eulogize.
encomienda, *n.f.* (*hist.*) encomienda, grant of crown land; commandership (*in a military order*); badge of a knight commander; charge, commission; commendation; (*S.A.*) parcel-post; ***en* —,** (*eccl.*) in commendam.
encomio, *n.m.* eulogy.
enconamiento, *n.m.* (*med.*) inflammation; (*fig.*) rancour.
enconar, *v.t.* irritate, inflame.—*v.r.* be irritated; fester.
encono, *n.m.* rancour; sore spot.
enconoso, -sa, *a.* sore; malevolent.
encontradizo, -za, *a.* likely to be met with.
encontrado, -da, *a.* opposite; opposing; at odds (**con,** with).
encontrar [4], *v.t.* meet, encounter.—*v.r.* be situated; ***encontrarse con,*** meet; run across.
encontrón, *n.m.* collision.
encopetar, *v.t.* arrange (*the hair*) high.—*v.r.* become conceited.
encorar [4], *v.t.* cover with leather.—*v.i.*, *v.r.* heal over, grow new skin.
encorchetar, *v.t.* fasten with hooks and eyes; sew hooks and eyes on.
encordelar, encordonar, *v.t.* tie (*with string*).
encoriación, *n.f.* healing (*of a wound*).
encornadura, *n.f.* (*esp. taur.*) horns, shape of the horns.
encornudar, *v.t.* cuckold.—*v.i.* grow horns.
encorrear, *v.t.* strap.
encorvada, *n.f.* bending; ***hacer la* —,** (*fam.*) malinger.
encorvar, *v.t.* bend.—*v.r.* stoop; be biased.
encostrar, *v.t.* encrust, crust.
encovar [4], *v.t.* put in the cellar.
encrasar, *v.t.* thicken; (*agr.*) fertilize.
encrespador, *n.m.* curling-tongs.
encrespamiento, *n.m.* curling; roughness (*of the sea*).
encrespar, *v.t.* curl; ruffle (*feathers etc.*).—*v.r.* curl; become rough (*of waves etc.*); get angry.
encrucijada, *n.f.* crossroads, (*U.S.*) intersection; ambush.
encuadernación, *n.f.* (book-)binding.
encuadernar, *v.t.* bind (*books*); ***sin* —,** unbound.
encuadrar, *v.t.* frame; insert.
encuadre, *n.m.* film version (*of a book etc.*).
encubierto, -ta, *p.p.* [ENCUBRIR].—*n.f.* fraud.
encubridor, -ra, *n.m.f.* concealer; (*jur.*) accessory.
encubrir [*p.p.* **encubierto**], *v.t.* hide.
encuentro, *n.m.* meeting, encounter.
encuesta, *n.f.* enquiry; poll.
encumbrar, *v.t.* raise.—*v.r.* rise; be proud.
encurtir, *v.t.* pickle.
enchapado, *n.m.* veneer; plywood; overlay cladding.
enchapar, *v.t.* veneer; overlay, clad.
encharcada, *n.f.* puddle.
encharcar [A], *v.t.* turn into a puddle.—*v.r.* be inundated; stagnate.
enchufar, *v.t.* connect (*two pipes etc.*); (*elec.*) plug in; ***estar bien enchufado,*** be able to pull strings.
enchufe, *n.m.* socket, coupling; (*elec.*) plug; contact; (*fam.*) contact; (*fam.*) fat job.
por ende, *adv. phr.* (*obs.*) therefore.
endeble, *a.* feeble.
endeblez, *n.f.* feebleness.
endecágono, *n.m.* hendecagon.
endecasílabo, -ba, *a.* hendecasyllabic.—*n.m.* hendecasyllable.
endecha, *n.f.* dirge.
endechadera, *n.f.* hired mourner.
endechar, *v.t.* bewail.—*v.r.* grieve.
endémico, -ca, *a.* endemic.
endentar [1], *v.t.*, *v.r.* mesh, engage (*gears*).
endentecer [9], *v.i.* teethe.
enderezadamente, *adv.* rightly, honestly.
enderezar [C], *v.t.* straighten; regulate; direct.—*v.i.* go straight.—*v.r.* straighten up.
endeudar, *v.r.* run into debt.
endiablar, *v.t.* corrupt.
endibia, *n.f.* (*bot.*) endive; chicory.
endilgar [B], *v.t.* (*fam.*) direct; (*fam.*) help; (*fam.*) spring (*a surprise*) on.
endomingar, *v.r.* put on one's Sunday best.
endorsar, endosar, *v.t.* (*com.*) endorse.

endosante, *n.m.f.* (*com.*) endorser.
endosatorio, -ria, *n.m.f.* (*com.*) endorsee.
endriago, *n.m.* dragon, fabulous monster.
endrino, -na, *a.* sloe-coloured.—*n.m.* (*bot.*) sloe (*tree*).—*n.f.* sloe (*fruit*).
endulzar [C] *v.t.* sweeten.
endurador, -ra, *a.* parsimonious.—*n.m.f.* miser.
endurancia, *n.f.* (*sport*) endurance.
endurar, *v.t.* harden; endure.
endurecer [9], *v.t.* harden.
ene, *n.f.* name of letter N.
enea, *n.f.* (*bot.*) rush.
eneágono, *n.m.* nonagon.
eneasílabo, -ba, *a.* of nine syllables.—*n.m.* nine-syllable line.
enebro, *n.m.* (*bot.*) juniper.
eneldo, *n.m.* (*bot.*) common dill.
enemigo, -ga, *a.* hostile, enemy.—*n.m.f.* enemy.
enemistad, *n.f.* enmity.
enemistar, *v.t.* make an enemy of.—*v.r.* become enemies; become an enemy (**con,** of).
energía, *n.f.* energy.
enérgico, -ca, *a.* energetic.
enero, *n.m.* January.
enervación, *n.f.* enervation.
enervar, *v.t.* enervate.—*v.r.* become enervated *or* effeminate.
enésimo, -ma, *a.* (*math.*) nth.
enfadar, *v.t.* offend.—*v.r.* become annoyed.
enfado, *n.m.* anger; trouble.
enfadoso, -sa, *a.* bothersome.
enfangar [B]. *v.t.* soil with mud.—*v.r.* sink in the mud.
enfardelador, -ra, *n.m.f.* packer.—*n.f.* baler, baling press.
enfardelar, *v.t.* bale.
énfasis, *n.m.* or *f. inv.* emphasis
enfático, -ca, *a.* emphatic.
enfermar, *v.t.* make sick.—*v.i.* fall ill (**de,** with).
enfermedad, *n.f.* sickness, illness, disease.
enfermería, *n.f.* infirmary; sanatorium; (*naut., mil.*) sick bay.
enfermero, -ra, *n.m.f.* nurse.
enfermizo, -za, *a.* sickly.
enfermo, -ma, *a.* sick, ill.—*n.m.f.* patient.
enfeudar, *v.t.* (*jur.*) enfeoff.
enfilar, *v.t.* line up; (*mil.*) enfilade; string (*beads*).
enflaquecer [9], *v.t.* make thin.—*v.i.* get thin; lose heart.—*v.r.* get thin.
enfocar [A], *v.t.* focus; (*fig.*) visualise (*from a certain viewpoint*).
enfoque, *n.m.* focus, focusing; (*fig.*) viewpoint, approach.
enfoscar [A], *v.t.* fill in (*with mortar*).—*v.r.* become grumpy.
enfrascar [A], *v.t.* bottle.—*v.r.* become involved.
enfrenar, *v.t.* bridle, check, curb.
enfrentar, *v.t.* confront.—*v.r.* meet face to face; stand up (**con,** to).
enfrente, *adv.* opposite.—*prep.* opposite (**de**); against (**de**).
enfriar [L], *v.t.* refrigerate, cool, chill.
enfurecer [9], *v.t.* infuriate.—*v.r.* rage.
engalanar, *v.t.* deck, adorn.
enganchar, *v.t.* hook; couple, connect; (*fam.*) inveigle (*esp. into the army*).—*v.r.* (*fam.*) enlist (*in the army etc.*).
enganche, *n.m.* hooking; coupling; (*fam.*) enlistment.
engañadizo, -za, *a.* easily deceived.
engañador, -ra, *a.* deceptive.—*n.m.f.* cheat.
engañapastores, *n.m. inv.* (*orn.*) nightjar.
engañar, *v.t.* mislead, deceive.—*v.r.* make a mistake.
engaño, *n.m.* fraud, deceit.
engañoso, -sa, *a.* deceitful, fraudulent.
engarce, *n.m.* mounting; (*gem*) setting; linking.
engarzar [C], *v.t.* link; set (*gems*).
engastar, *v.t.* set (*gems*).
engaste, *n.m.* setting (*of gems*).
engatusar, *v.t.* (*fam.*) inveigle.
engendrar, *v.t.* engender, beget.
engendro, *n.m.* foetus; misbegotten creature.
englobar, *v.t.* enclose, lump together.
engolosinar, *v.t.* allure.—*v.r.* take a liking (**con,** to).
engordar, *v.t.* fatten.
engorroso, -sa, *a.* troublesome.
engoznar, *v.t.* put hinges on, hang (*a door*).
engranaje, *n.m.* (*tech.*) gearing.
engranar, *v.t., v.i.* gear, mesh.
engrandecer [9], *v.t.* enlarge, magnify.—*v.i.* grow big(ger).
engrandecimiento, *n.m.* enlargement, amplification.
engrasar, *v.t.* lubricate, grease.
engrase, *n.m.* lubrication; fouling (*sparking plugs*).
engreimiento, *n.m.* vanity.
engreír [28], *v.t.* make vain.—*v.r.* become vain.
engrosar [4], *v.t.* broaden; enlarge.—*v.i.* get fat.—*v.r.* broaden; become enlarged.
engrudar, *v.t.* paste, glue.
engrudo, *n.m.* paste, glue.
engruesar, *v.i.* get fat.
enguirnaldar, *v.t.* garland, bedeck.
engullir [J], *v.t.* gulp down, swallow.
enhebrar, *v.t.* string, thread (*a needle*).
enherbolar, *v.t.* poison (*with herbs*).
enhestar [1], *v.t.* erect; hoist.—*v.r.* stand upright; tower.
enhiesto, -ta, *a.* erect, upright.
enhilar, *v.t.* thread.
enhorabuena, *adv.* well and good, all right.—*n.f.* congratulations.
enhoramala, *adv.* unluckily, in an evil hour.
enigma, *n.m.* puzzle.
enigmático, -ca, *a.* enigmatic(al).
enjabonar, *v.t.* soap; (*fam.*) soft-soap; (*fam.*) give a good dressing down (to).
enjaezar [C], *v.t.* harness, adorn.
enjaguar [H], [ENJUAGAR].
enjalbegado, *n.m.* whitewashing.
enjalbegar [B], *v.t.* whitewash.
enjalma, *n.f.* light packsaddle.
enjambrar, *v.t.* empty (*a hive*).—*v.i.* swarm.
enjambre, *n.m.* swarm.
enjarciar, *v.t.* rig (*a ship*).
enjebe, *n.m.* alum; lye.
enjergar [B], *v.t.* (*fam.*) start up (*a business etc.*).
enjertación, *n.f.* grafting.
enjertar, *v.t.* engraft.
enjerto, *n.m.* graft, grafted plant.
enjoyar, *v.t.* bejewel.

enjuagadientes, *n.m. inv.* mouthwash.
enjuagar [B], *v.t.* rinse.
enjuagatorio, *n.m.* rinsing; finger-bowl.
enjuague, *n.m.* rinsing; finger-bowl; plot, scheme.
enjugador, *n.m.* drier; clothes-horse; squeegee.
enjugar [B], *v.t.* dry.
enjuiciar, *v.t.* (*jur.*) sue, indict; (*jur.*) sentence.
enjundia, *n.f.* kidney-fat; grease; (*fig.*) force, substance.
enjundioso, -sa, *a.* fatty; substantial.
enjunque, *n.m.* (*naut.*) heavy ballast, kentledge.
enjuto, -ta, *a.* lean; dried.—*n.m.pl.* tinder, brushwood; salty tit-bits.
enlabiar, *v.t.* wheedle; bamboozle.
enlace, *n.m.* connexion; link; (*chem.*) linkage; (*rail.*) connexion; marriage.
enladrillado, *n.m.* brick pavement; brickwork.
enladrillar, *v.t.* brick; pave with bricks *or* red tiles.
enlatar, *v.t.* tin, (*esp. U.S.*) can; (*S.A.*) roof with tin.
enlazar [C], *v.t.* tie; link; lasso; (*rail.*) connect.—*v.r.* be joined (*in wedlock*).
enlistonar, *v.t.* lath.
enlodar, *v.t.* soil with mud, bemire.
enloquecer [9], *v.t.* madden, drive to distraction.—*v.i.* go mad.
enlosar, *v.t.* pave with flagstones.
enlucir [10], *v.t.* plaster; polish (*metal*).
enlutar, *v.t.* put into mourning.—*v.r.* wear mourning.
enmaderar, *v.t.* board, plank.
enmagrecer [9], *v.t.* make thin.—*v.i., v.r.* grow thin.
enmarañamiento, *n.m.* entanglement.
enmarañar, *v.t.* entangle.
enmascarar, *v.t.* mask.—*v.r.* masquerade.
enmasillar, *v.t.* putty.
enmendación, *n.f.* emendation.
enmendar [1], *v.t.* correct; amend.
enmienda, *n.f.* correction, amendment; amends.
enmohecer [9], *v.t.* mildew, mould (*U.S.* mold), rust.—*v.r.* go mouldy, rust.
enmudecer [9], *v.t.* hush.—*v.i.* fall silent.
ennegrecer [9], *v.t.* blacken; denigrate.—*v.r.* turn *or* be black.
ennoblecer [9], *v.t.* ennoble.—*v.r.* become ennobled.
ennoblecimiento, *n.m.* ennoblement.
enodio, *n.m.* fawn.
enojar, *v.t.* anger; offend; annoy.—*v.r.* be angry; be offended.
enojo, *n.m.* anger, passion; annoyance.
enojoso, -sa, *a.* annoying; troublesome.
enorgullecer [9], *v.r.* make proud.—*v.r.* be proud (***de,*** of); pride oneself (***de,*** on).
enorme, *a.* enormous; huge.
enormidad, *n.f.* enormity.
enquiciar, *v.t.* put on hinges, hang (*a door*).
enquillotrar, *v.t.* (*fam.*) fall in love.
enrabiar, *v.t.* enrage.—*v.i.* have rabies.—*v.r.* become enraged.
enraizar [C & P], *v.i.* take root.
enredadera, *n.f.* (*bot.*) bindweed, climbing plant.
enredar, *v.t.* entangle; ensnare.—*v.i.* romp.—*v.r.* become entangled.
enredo, *n.m.* tangle; mischief; intricacy; plot (*of a play etc.*).
enredoso, -sa, *a.* intricate.
enrejado, *n.m.* trellis, lattice; ***— de alambre,*** wire netting.
enrejar, *v.t.* surround with a trellis *or* a grating.
enriar [L], *v.t.* ret.
enrielar, *v.t.* cast into ingots; (*S.A.*) lay rails on (*a road*); (*S.A. fig.*) put on the right track.
Enrique, *n.m.* Henry.
enriquecer [9], *v.t.* enrich.
enriscado, -da, *a.* craggy, mountainous.
enriscar [A], *v.t.* raise.—*v.r.* take refuge in the rocks.
enristrar, *v.t.* couch (*the lance*); string (*onions*); straighten out (*a difficulty*).
enrocar [A], *v.t., v.i.* castle (*in chess*).
enrojar, enrojecer [9], *v.t., v.r.* redden; flush.
enrollar, *v.t.* roll, wind.
enromar, *v.t.* blunt.
enronquecer [9], *v.t.* make hoarse.—*v.r.* become hoarse.
enroque, *n.m.* castling (*in chess*).
enroscar [A], *v.t.* twist.—*v.r.* curl, coil.
enrubiar, *v.t.* bleach (*the hair*).
enrubio, *n.m.* bleaching, dyeing blond; blond dye.
ensaimada, *n.f.* kind of bun.
ensalada, *n.f.* salad; hodge-podge.
ensaladera, *n.f.* salad-bowl.
ensalmador, -ra, *n.m.f.* bone-setter; quack.
ensalmar, *v.t.* set (*bones*).
ensalmista, *n.m.f.* quack, charlatan.
ensalmo, *n.m.* spell, charm.
ensalzar [C], *v.t.* extol.—*v.r.* boast.
ensamblador, *n.m.* (*carp.*) joiner.
ensambladura, *n.f.*, **ensamble,** *n.m.* joinery; joint.
ensamblar, *v.t.* join; assemble; (*carp.*) joint.
ensanchador, -ra, *a.* expanding, stretching.—*n.m.* stretcher, expander.
ensanchar, *v.t.* widen; stretch; let out (*clothes*).—*v.r.* widen; be high and mighty.
ensanche, *n.m.* widening; extension.
ensandecer [9], *v.i.* grow crazy *or* stupid.
ensangrentar [1], *v.t.* stain with blood.—*v.r.* cover oneself with gore; (*fig.*) have murderous thoughts (***con uno,*** about s.o.).
ensañamiento, *n.m.* cruelty; (*jur.*) aggravating circumstance.
ensañar, *v.t.* irritate; enrage.—*v.r.* be ruthless.
ensartar, *v.t.* string (*beads*); thread (*a needle*).
ensayador, -ra, *n.m.f.* assayer; rehearser.
ensayista, *n.m.f.* essayist.
ensayo, *n.m.* trial; assay; essay; rehearsal; (*com.*) sample.
ensebar, *v.t.* grease, tallow.
ensenada, *n.f.* inlet, cove.
enseña, *n.f.* ensign, standard.
enseñable, *a.* teachable.
enseñamiento, *n.m.*, **enseñanza,** *n.f.* teaching, education.
enseñar, *v.t.* teach, instruct; point out, show the way.—*v.r.* school oneself; become inured.

enseñorear, *v.t.* domineer.—*v.r.* take possession (*de,* of).
enseres, *n.m.pl.* chattels, implements; fixtures.
ensilar, *v.t.* (*agr.*) put into a silo, ensile.
ensillar, *v.t.* saddle.
ensimismar, *v.r.* become absent-minded *or* lost in thought.
ensoberbecer [9], *v.t.* make proud.—*v.r.* become proud.
ensombrecer [9], *v.t.* darken.
ensordecer [9], *v.t.* deafen.—*v.i.* grow deaf; become silent.
ensordecimiento, *n.m.* deafness.
ensortijar, *v.t.* curl, form ringlets in.
ensuciar, *v.t.* pollute, defile, soil.
ensueño, *n.m.* illusion, daydream, dream.
entablación, *n.f.* (*carp.*) flooring; boarding.
entabladura, *n.f.* flooring; boarding.
entablamento, *n.m.* (*arch.*) entablature.
entablar, *v.t.* floor; board; start, initiate.
entable, *n.m.* position (*of chessmen*); (*S.A.*) circumstances.
entalegar [B], *v.t.* bag; hoard.
entallador, *n.m.* engraver; carver.
entalladura, *n.f.*, **entallamiento,** *n.m.* carving; engraving; slot.
entallar, *v.t.* carve; engrave; slot.
entapizar [C], *v.t.* drape, hang with tapestry; upholster.
entarimar, *v.t.* floor; put a parquet *or* inlaid floor on.
ente, *n.m.* being; entity; (*fam.*) queer fish.
entena, *n.f.* (*naut.*) lateen yard.
entenado, -da, *n.m.f.* stepchild.
entendedor, -ra, *n.m.f.* understander, one who understands.
entender [2], *v.t.*, *v.i.* understand, comprehend; — ***de,*** be familiar with; be experienced as; — ***en,*** be in charge of.—*v.r.* be meant; ***entenderse con,*** get along with.
entendidamente, *adv.* knowingly.
entendido, -da, *a.* expert, trained; prudent; ***darse por —,*** take a hint.
entendimiento, *n.m.* understanding.
enterar, *v.t.* acquaint, inform.
entereza, *n.f.* integrity; entirety; — ***virginal,*** virginity.
entérico, -ca, *a.* enteric.
enterizo, -za, *a.* in one piece.
enternecer [9], *v.t.* soften, move.—*v.r.* be moved (*to pity etc.*).
enternecimiento, *n.m.* pity, compassion.
entero, -ra, *a.* entire, whole; honest; (*math.*) integral, whole; strong (*cloth*).—*n.m.* (*math.*) integer.
enterrador, *n.m.* grave-digger.
enterramiento, *n.m.* burial, interment.
enterrar [1], *v.t.* inter, bury.
entesar [1], *v.t.* stretch, make taut.
entibar, *v.t.* prop (*esp. min.*).—*v.i.* rest, lean.
entibiar, *v.t.* make lukewarm, moderate.—*v.r.* cool off.
entibo, *n.m.* (*min.*) pit-prop; foundation.
entidad, *n.f.* entity.
entierro, *n.m.* burial, interment.
entoldar, *v.t.* cover with an awning; adorn with hangings.
entomología, *n.f.* entomology.
entonación, *n.f.* intonation, intoning; blowing the bellows.
entonar, *v.t.* intone; sing (*something*) in tune; harmonize; blow (*an organ*) with bellows.—*v.r.* sing in tune; assume grand airs.
entonces, *adv.* then; ***en aquel —,*** at that time.
entono, *n.m.* intonation; arrogance.
entontecer [9], *v.t.* make foolish.—*v.i.*, *v.r.* grow foolish.
entontecimiento, *n.m.* foolishness.
entorchado, *n.m.* gold braid; (*fig.*) promotion.
entornado, -da, *a.* ajar, half-closed.
entornillar, *v.t.* thread (*a screw*); screw (up).
entorpecer [9], *v.t.* benumb; obstruct; clog (*machines*).—*v.r.* stick, jam.
entortar [4], *v.t.* bend.
entosigar [B], *v.t.* poison.
entrado, -da, *a.* — ***en años,*** advanced in years.—*n.f.* entrance; admission; admission ticket; (*cul.*) entrée; (*min.*) shift; (*com.*) entry.
entrambos, -bas, *a.*, *pron.* (*obs.*) both.
entrante, *a.* entering, incoming; ***el mes —,*** (*com.*) prox.—*n.m.f.* entrant.
entraña, *n.f.* entrail, bowel; (*fig.*) heart, affection.
entrañable, *a.* intimate; deep (*affection*).
entrañar, *v.t.* contain; bury deep.
entrar, *v.t.* bring *or* show in; invade.—*v.i.* enter (***en***); begin (***a,*** to).
entre, *prep.* between; among; — ***mí,*** to myself, myself; — ***tanto,*** meanwhile.
entreabierto, -ta, *a.* ajar, half-open.
entreabrir [*p.p.* **entreabierto**], *v.t.* half open.
entreacto, *n.m.* (*theat.*) interval, intermission; entr'acte.
entrecano, -na, *a.* greying (*hair*).
entrecejo, *n.m.* space between the eyebrows; frown.
entrecoger [E], *v.t.* catch; compel (*by arguments*).
entrecoro, *n.m.* (*arch.*) chancel.
entrecortado, -da, *a.* intermittent, faltering.
entrecruzar [C], *v.t.*, *v.r.* interweave.
entrecuesto, *n.m.* (*cul.*) loin, sirloin; backbone.
entrechoque, *n.m.* collision.
entredicho, *n.m.* prohibition, interdict.
entrega, *n.f.* delivery; batch, instalment, issue.
entregar [B], *v.t.* deliver; surrender, hand over.—*v.r.* surrender; take charge (***de,*** of).
entrelazar [C], *v.t.* interweave, interlace.
entrelucir [10], *v.i.* show through.
entremedias, *adv.* in the meantime; half-way.
entremés, *n.m.* (*cul.*) hors d'oeuvre; (*theat.*) interlude.
entremeter, *v.t.* insert.—*v.r.* meddle; butt in.
entremetido, -da, *a.* meddlesome, officious.
entremezclar, *v.t.*, *v.r.* intermingle.
entrenamiento, *n.m.* (*sport*) training.
entrenar, *v.t.*, *v.r.* (*sport*) train.
entrepaño, *n.m.* (*arch.*) bay; panel.
entreparecer [9], *v.r.* show through.
entrepierna, *n.f.* (*esp. pl.*) crotch, fork.
entreponer [25], *v.t.* interpose.
entresacar [A], *v.t.* select; thin out (*plants*).
entresuelo, *n.m.* mezzanine, entresol.
entretalla, entretalladura, *n.f.* bas-relief.
entretallar, *v.t.* carve in bas-relief.—*v.r.* fit together.
entretanto, *adv.* meanwhile.
entretejer, *v.t.* interweave.

entretela, *n.f.* interlining.—*pl.* (*fam., fig.*) heart.
entretención, *n.f.* (*S.A.*) amusement, pastime.
entretenedor, -ra, *a.* entertaining.—*n.m.f.* entertainer.
entretener [33], *v.t.* entertain, amuse; delay; (*neol.*) maintain.—*v.r.* amuse oneself.
entretenido, -da, *a.* entertaining.
entretenimiento, *n.m.* entertainment; delay; (*neol.*) maintenance.
entretiempo, *n.m.* spring *or* autumn.
entrever [37], *v.t.* glimpse; guess.
entreverado, -da, *a.* streaky (*bacon etc.*).
entreverar, *v.t.* mingle.
entrevista, *n.f.* interview, meeting.
entrevistar, *v.r.* have a meeting *or* an interview.
entripado, -da, *a.* intestinal; not gutted (*dead animal*).—*n.m.* veiled anger *or* displeasure.
entristecer [9], *v.t.* sadden.—*v.r.* grieve.
entronar, *v.t.* enthrone.
entroncar [A], *v.i., v.r.* be descended from the same stock, be related (**con,** to); (*C.A. rail.*) connect.
entronizar [C], *v.t.* enthrone, exalt.
entuerto, *n.m.* injustice, wrong.
entumecer [9], *v.t.* benumb.—*v.r.* become numb, (*fam.*) go to sleep; surge.
entupir, *v.t.* compress; block.
enturbiar, *v.t.* stir up, muddy; obscure.
entusiasmar, *v.t.* enrapture.—*v.r.* be enthusiastic.
entusiasmo, *n.m.* enthusiasm.
entusiasta, *a.* enthusiastic.—*n.m.f.* enthusiast.
entusiástico, -ca, *a.* enthusiastic.
enumeración, *n.f.* enumeration.
enumerar, *v.t.* enumerate.
enunciar, *v.t.* enunciate.
envainar, *v.t.* sheathe.
envalentonar, *v.t.* embolden.—*v.r.* pluck up courage; brag.
envarar, *v.t.* benumb.
envasador, -ra, *n.m.f.* filler; packer.—*n.m.* funnel.
envasar, *v.t.* pack; bottle.—*v.i.* (*fam.*) booze.
envase, *n.m.* packing; bottling, canning; bottle, jar, can.
envejecer [9], *v.t.* age.—*v.i.* age, grow old.
envenenar, *v.t.* poison, envenom.
enverdecer [9], *v.i., v.r.* turn green.
envergadura, *n.f.* span (*of wings etc.*), spread, compass; (*fig.*) scope, importance.
envergue, *n.m.* sail-rope, rope-band.
envero, *n.m.* golden red, ripeness.
envés, *n.m.* wrong side, back; ***al* —,** inside out.
envestidura, *n.f.* investiture.
enviada, *n.f.* consignment.
enviado, *n.m.* envoy.
enviar [L], *v.t.* send, remit.
enviciar, *v.t.* corrupt, vitiate.—*v.r.* become addicted (**con,** to).
envidador, -ra, *n.m.f.* bidder (*at cards*).
envidar, *v.t.* bid against.
envidia, *n.f.* envy; desire.
envidiable, *a.* enviable.
envidiar, *v.t.* envy; covet.
envidioso, -sa, *a.* envious.
envilecer [9], *v.t.* degrade; vilify.
envío, *n.m.* shipment, consignment; remittance.
envite, *n.m.* stake (*at cards*); invitation; push; ***al primer* —,** at once.
envoltorio, *n.m.* bundle; knot (*in cloth*).
envoltura, *n.f.* wrapping.—*n.f.pl.* swaddling clothes.
envolver [5, *p.p.* **envuelto**], *v.t.* wrap; wind; swaddle; (*mil.*) surround.—*v.r.* become involved.
envuelto, -ta, *p.p.* [ENVOLVER].
enyesado, *n.m.,* **enyesadura,** *n.f.* plasterwork.
enyesar, *v.t.* plaster.
enyugar [B], *v.t.* yoke.
enzainar, *v.r.* look askance; (*fam.*) become crooked.
enzima, *n.f.* (*chem.*) enzyme.
enzímico, -ca, *a.* (*chem.*) enzymatic.
eñe, *n.f.* name of letter Ñ.
eón, *n.m.* aeon.
epactilla, *n.f.* liturgical calendar.
epéntesis, *n.f. inv.* epenthesis.
eperlano, *n.m.* (*ichth.*) smelt.
épico, -ca, *a.* epic.—*n.f.* epic poetry.
epicúreo, -rea, *a.* epicurean.
epidemia, *n.f.* epidemic.
epidemial, epidémico, -ca, *a.* epidemic.
epidermis, *n.f. inv.* epidermis.
Epifanía, *n.f.* Epiphany.
epiglotis, *n.f. inv.* epiglottis.
epígrafe, *n.m.* inscription; epigraph.
epigrafía, *n.f.* epigraphy.
epigrama, *n.m.* or *f.* epigram.
epigramático, -ca, *a.* epigrammatic.
epilepsia, *n.f.* (*med.*) epilepsy.
epiléptico, -ca, *a., n.m.f.* epileptic.
epílogo, *n.m.* epilogue.
episcopado, *n.m.* bishopric; episcopacy.
episcopal, *a.* episcopal.
episodio, *n.m.* episode; digression; subplot.
epístola, *n.f.* epistle.
epistolar, *a.* epistolary.
epitafio, *n.m.* epitaph.
epíteto, *n.m.* (*gram.*) epithet.
epitomar, *v.t.* epitomize.
época, *n.f.* epoch, era, age.
epónimo, -ma, *a.* eponymous.
epopeya, *n.f.* epic poem.
epsomita, *n.f.* Epsom salts.
equidad, *n.f.* equity.
equidistante, *a.* equidistant.
equilibrar, *v.t., v.r.* balance; counterbalance.
equilibrio, *n.m.* equilibrium; balance.
equilibrista, *n.m.f.* rope-dancer, tight-rope-walker.
equinoccial, *a.* equinoctial.
equinoccio, *n.m.* equinox.
equipaje, *n.m.* luggage; (*naut.*) crew; (*mil.*) baggage-train.
equipar, *v.t.* equip, fit out.
equiparable, *a.* comparable.
equiparar, *v.t.* compare.
equipo, *n.m.* fitting out, equipment; (*sport*) team.
equis, *n.f.* name of letter X.
equitación, *n.f.* equitation.
equitativo, -va, *a.* equitable, fair.
equivalencia, *n.f.* equivalence; compensation.
equivalente, *a.* equivalent, tantamount; compensatory.

equivaler [35], *v.i.* be of equal value; be equivalent.
equivocación, *n.f.* blunder, misconception, mistake.
equivocar [A], *v.t.* mistake.—*v.r.* be mistaken; make a mistake.
equívoco, -ca, *a.* equivocal, ambiguous.—*n.m.* equivocation; pun; mistake.
era (1), *n.f.* era, age, epoch.
era (2), *n.f.* threshing-floor.
era (3), [SER].
erario, *n.m.* exchequer, public treasury.
ere, *n.f.* name of letter R.
erección, *n.f.* erection; elevation; establishment.
erector, -ra, *a.* erecting.—*n.m.f.* erector, founder.
eres [SER].
ergio, *n.m.* (*phys.*) erg.
ergotizar [C], *v.i.* argue, split hairs.
erguir [8 *or* 3, *in which case initial* i *is changed to* y: *yergo etc.*], *v.t.* erect, raise up.
erial, *a.* unploughed, barren.—*n.m.* waste land.
erica, *n.f.* (*bot.*) heath, heather.
erigir [E], *v.t.* erect, build; set up.
erío, ería, *a.* unploughed, barren.
erizar [C], *v.t.* set on end.—*v.r.* bristle, stand on end.
erizo, *n.m.* (*zool.*) hedgehog; prickly husk; (*ichth.*) sea-urchin.
ermita, *n.f.* hermitage.
ermitaño, -ña, *n.m.f.* hermit.—*n.m.* hermit-crab.
erosión, *n.f.* erosion.
erótico, -ca, *a.* erotic.
erotismo, *n.m.* eroticism.
errabundo, -da, *a.* wandering, errant.
e(r)radicación, *n.f.* eradication.
e(r)radicar [A], *v.t.* eradicate.
erraj, *n.m.* fuel made from olive stones.
errante, *a.* errant, wandering, itinerant.
errar [1; *initial* i *is changed to* y: *yerro etc.*], *v.t.* miss.—*v.i.*, *v.r.* wander; be mistaken, err; sin.
errata, *n.f.* erratum; ***fe de erratas,*** (*print.*) errata.
errático, -ca, *a.* erratic, vagabond.
erre, *n.f.* name of letter RR.
erróneo, -nea, *a.* erroneous, mistaken.
error, *n.m.* error, mistake.
eructar, *v.i.* belch.
eructo, *n.m.* eructation, belch(ing).
erudición, *n.f.* erudition, scholarship.
erudito, -ta, *a.* erudite, learned, scholarly.
erumpir, *v.i.* erupt (*of a volcano*).
erupción, *n.f.* eruption.
ervilla [ARVEJA].
es [SER].
esbeltez, esbelteza, *n.f.* slenderness, litheness; gracefulness.
esbelto, -ta, *a.* slender, svelte; graceful.
esbirro, *n.m.* bailiff; hired thug.
esbozar [C], *v.t.* sketch.
esbozo, *n.m.* sketch.
escabechar, *v.t.* pickle, souse; (*fam.*, *pej.*) paint (*the face*), dye (*the hair*); plough, (*U.S.*) flunk (*an examination*).
escabeche, *n.m.* pickle.
escabel, *n.m.* stool; (*fig.*) stepping-stone.
escabioso, -sa, *a.* scabious, mangy.—*n.f.* (*bot.*) scabious.
escabro, *n.m.* sheep-scab.
escabrosidad, *n.f.* scabrousness.
escabroso, -sa, *a.* scabrous; harsh, rough.
escabullir [J], *v.r.* escape, slip off.
escafandra, *n.f.*, **escafandro,** *n.m.* diving suit; — ***spacial,*** space suit.
escala, *n.f.* ladder, step-ladder; (*math.*, *mus.*) scale; (*naut.*) port of call.
escalada, *n.f.* climbing, escalade.
escalador, -ra, *a.* burglarious.—*n.m.f.* housebreaker, cat burglar.
escalafón, *n.m.* register, graded list of established staff.
escalamera, *n.f.* rowlock.
escalamiento, *n.m.* scaling; burglary.
escalar, *v.t.* climb, scale; burgle.
Escalda, *n.m.* (*geog.*) Scheldt.
escaldar, *v.t.* scald; make red-hot.
escalera, *n.f.* stairs, staircase, stairway; ladder; — ***de caracol,*** spiral staircase; — ***doble,*** pair of steps, step-ladder; — ***extensible,*** extension ladder; — ***mecánica,*** moving staircase, escalator.
escalfar, *v.t.* (*cul.*) poach (*eggs*).
escalmo, *n.m.* rowlock.
escalofrío, *n.m.* shiver; shudder.
escalón, *n.m.* step, stair; rung; grade; (*mil.*) échelon; (*rad.*) stage.
escaloña, *n.f.* (*bot.*) shallot.
escalpelo, *n.m.* scalpel.
escama, *n.f.* (*ichth.*) scale; (*fig.*) grudge.
escamar, *v.t.* scale (*fish*): (*fam.*) arouse the suspicions of.
escamocho, *n.m.* left-overs, dregs.
escamondar, *v.t.* prune.
escamoso, -sa, *a.* scaly, squamous.
escamotear, *v.t.* palm away, whisk away; (*fam.*) swipe, pinch.
escamoteo, *n.m.* sleight of hand; (*fam.*) swiping.
escampada, *n.f.* clear spell, bright interval (*weather*).
escampar, *v.t.* clear out (*a place*).—*v.i.* clear up (*of the weather*), stop raining.
escampo, *n.m.* clearing out (*a place*); clearing up (*of the weather*).
escanciar, *v.t.* pour out (*wine*).
escandalizar [C], *v.t.* scandalize.—*v.r.* be scandalized; be angered.
escándalo, *n.m.* scandal; commotion.
escandaloso, -sa, *a.* scandalous; turbulent.
Escandinavia, *n.f.* Scandinavia.
escandinavo, -va, *a.*, *n.m.f.* Scandinavian.
escandio, *n.m.* (*chem.*) scandium.
escandir, *v.t.* scan (*verse*).
escansión, *n.f.* scansion.
escaño, *n.m.* settle, bench; (*S.A.*) park bench.
escañuelo, *n.m.* foot-stool.
escapada, *n.f.* escape; ***en una —,*** at full speed.
escapar, *v.t.* free, deliver; drive hard (*a horse*).—*v.i.* escape.—*v.r.* escape; run away (***a,*** from); ***se me escapó el tren,*** I just missed the train.
escaparate, *n.m.* show cabinet, window display, shop window.
escapatoria, *n.f.* escape; (*fig.*) subterfuge.
escape, *n.m.* flight, escape; escapement (*of a watch*); exhaust; ***a —,*** on the run.
escapulario, *n.m.* scapulary.
escaque, *n.m.* square (*of a chessboard*).
escaqueado, -da, *a.* chequered.

scarabajo, *n.m.* (*ent.*) black-beetle; (*fig. esp. pl.*) scrawl.
scaramujo, *n.m.* (*bot.*) dog-rose.
scaramuza, *n.f.* skirmish.
scaramuzar [C], *v.i.* skirmish.
scarbar, *v.t.* scrape, scratch; poke (*the fire*).
scarbo, *n.m.* scraping, scratching.
scarcha, *n.f.* hoar frost, rime.
scarchar, *v.t.* ice (*cakes*).—*v.i.* freeze.
scardador, -ra, *a.* weeding.—*n.m.f.* weeder.—*n.m.* hoe.
scardar, escardillar, *v.t.* weed.
scarlata, *n.f.* scarlet; scarlet cloth.
scarlatina, *n.f.* scarlet fever.
scarmentar, *v.t.* inflict an exemplary punishment on.—*v.i.* take warning.
scarmiento, *n.m.* warning; chastisement.
scarnecer [9], *v.t.* mock at, ridicule.
scarnio, *n.m.* jeer; ridicule.
scarola, *n.f.* (*bot.*) endive.
scarpa, *n.f.* bluff, slope; (*esp. mil.*) escarpment, scarp.
scarpia, *n.f.* tenterhook.
scarpín, *n.m.* dancing pump (*shoe*).
scasear, *v.t.* give sparingly; spare.—*v.i.* be scarce; grow less.
scasez, *n.f.* scarcity; meanness; lack.
scaso, -sa, *a.* scarce, scanty; little; lacking in.
scatimar, *v.t.* curtail; scrimp.
scatimoso, -sa, *a.* malicious, cunning.
scatología (1), *n.f.* eschatology.
scatología (2), *n.f.* scatology.
scayola, *n.f.* plaster (*of Paris*).
scayolar, *v.t.* put in plaster.
scena, *n.f.* stage; scene.
scenario, *n.m.* stage; (*cine.*) scenario.
scénico, -ca, *a.* scenic, rel. to the stage *or* stage effects.
scenografía, *n.f.* (*theat.*) stage-setting, set designing.
scepticismo, *n.m.* scepticism.
scéptico, -ca, *a.*, *n.m.f.* sceptic.
scila, *n.f.* (*myth.*) Scylla; **escila,** *n.f.* (*bot.*) squill.
scinca, *n.f.* (*zool.*) skink.
scisión, *n.f.* division.
scita, *a.*, *n.m.f.* Scythian.
sclarecer [9], *v.t.* illuminate; elucidate; enlighten.—*v.i.* dawn.
sclavitud, *n.f.* slavery, servitude.
sclavizar [C], *v.t.* enslave.
sclavo, -va, *a.* enslaved.—*n.m.f.* slave.
sclavón, -vona [ESLAVO].
clusa, *n.f.* sluice.
coba, *n.f.* broom; (*bot.*) broom.
cobajo, *n.m.* old broom; stalk of a bunch of grapes.
cobar, *v.t.* sweep.
cobilla, *n.f.* brush.
cocer [5D], *v.t.* irritate.—*v.i.* smart.
cocés, -cesa, *a.* Scottish, Scots.—*n.m.f.* Scot.
scocia, *n.f.* Scotland.
cofina, *n.f.* rasp.
coger [E], *v.t.* select, choose.
colar, *a.* scholastic.—*n.m.* school-boy, scholar.
colástico, -ca, *a.* scholastic.—*n.m.* (*hist.*) schoolman.
scolio, *n.m.* gloss.
scolopendra, *n.f.* (*zool.*) centipede.

escolta, *n.f.* (*mil.*) escort.
escollera, *n.f.* breakwater.
escollo, *n.m.* reef; (*fig.*) difficulty.
escombro (1), *n.m.* rubbish; debris.
escombro (2), *n.m.* (*ichth.*) mackerel.
esconder, *v.t.* hide; disguise.
a escondidas, *adv. phr.* on the sly.
escondite, *n.m.* hiding-place.
escopeta, *n.f.* shotgun.
escopetero, *n.m.* musketeer.
escoplo, *n.m.* (*carp.*) chisel.
escorbuto, *n.m.* (*med.*) scurvy.
escorchar, *v.t.* flay (*hides*).
escoria, *n.f.* slag, dross.
escorial, *n.m.* slag-heap.
Escorpión, *n.m.* (*astr.*) Scorpio; **escorpión,** *n.m.* (*zool.*) scorpion.
escorzar [C], *v.t.* (*art.*) foreshorten.
escorzón, *n.m.* (*zool.*) toad.
escotado, *n.m.*, **escotadura,** *n.f.* low neck (*in dress*).
escotar, *v.t.* cut to fit; cut low at the neck.—*v.i.* club together, go Dutch.
escote, *n.m.* low neck (*in dress*), décolleté.
escotilla, *n.f.* hatch.
escotillón, *n.m.* hatchway; (*theat.*) trapdoor.
escozor, *n.m.* smarting; affliction.
escribanía, *n.f.* court clerkship; escritoire.
escribano, *n.m.* court clerk; notary; (*naut.*) purser.
escribir [*p.p.* **escrito**], *v.t.*, *v.i.* write; ***— a máquina,*** type; ***máquina de —,*** typewriter.—*v.r.* enroll.
escrito, -ta, *p.p.* [ESCRIBIR].—*n.m.* writing; document; (*jur.*) writ.
escritor, -ra, *n.m.f.* writer, author.
escritorio, *n.m.* desk; study, office.
escritura, *n.f.* handwriting, writing; scripture; deed.
escrófula, *n.f.* (*med.*) scrofula, king's evil.
escroto, *n.m.* scrotum.
escrúpulo, *n.m.* scruple; scruple (20 *grains*).
escrupulosidad, *n.f.* scrupulosity, scrupulousness.
escrupuloso, -sa, *a.* scrupulous.
escrutación, *n.f.* scrutiny.
escrutar, *v.t.* scrutinize; invigilate; count votes.
escrutinio, *n.m.* scrutiny; counting of votes.
escuadra, *n.f.* set-square; angle-iron; squad; (*naut.*) squadron.
escuadrilla, *n.f.* (*aer.*) squadron.
escuadro, *n.m.* (*ichth.*) skate.
escuadrón, *n.m.* (*mil.*) squadron (*of cavalry*); swarm.
escualidez, *n.f.* squalor.
escuálido, -da, *a.* squalid; weak.
escualo, *n.m.* (*ichth.*) spotted dogfish.
escuchar, *v.t.* listen to; heed.
escudero, *n.m.* page, squire, shield-bearer, esquire.
escudilla, *n.f.* bowl.
escudo, *n.m.* shield, escutcheon.
escudriñar, *v.t.* scrutinize, pry into.
escuela, *n.f.* school.
escuerzo, *n.m.* (*zool.*) toad.
escueto, -ta, *a.* disengaged; plain, unadorned.
esculpir, *v.t.* sculpt, carve.
escultor, -ra, *n.m.f.* sculptor, sculptress.
escultura, *n.f.* sculture.
escultural, *a.* sculptural.
escupidura, *n.f.* spittle.

escupir, *v.t., v.i.* spit.
escurreplatos, *n.m. inv.* plate-rack.
escurridizo, -za, *a.* slippery.
escurridor, *n.m.* colander; plate-rack.
escurriduras, escurrimbres, *n.f.pl.* rinsings, dregs.
escurrir, *v.t.* drain; wring out.—*v.i.* drip, trickle, ooze; slip out.
esdrújulo, -la, *a.* proparoxytonic, proparoxytonal.—*n.m.* proparoxyton.
ese (1), *n.f.* name of letter S.
ese (2), **esa,** *a., dem. m.f.* (*pl.* **esos, esas**) that.—*pl.* those.
ése, ésa, *pron. dem. m.f.* (*pl.* **ésos, ésas**) that, that one.—*pl.* those, those ones.
esencia, *n.f.* essence.
esencial, *a.* essential.
esfera, *n.f.* sphere; dial (*of a clock*).
esferal, esférico, -ca, *a.* spherical, globular.
esfinge, *n.f.* sphinx.
esforzado, -da, *a.* valiant; vigorous, enterprising.
esforzar [4C], *v.t.* strengthen; encourage.—*v.r.* exert oneself.
esfuerzo, *n.m.* effort; vigour.
esfumar, *v.t.* blur, (*art.*) stump; (*art.*) tone down, soften.
esgrima, *n.f.* (*sport*) fencing.
esgrimidor, -ra, *n.m.f.* fencer.
esgrimir, *v.t.* wield; brandish.—*v.i.* fence.
esguince, *n.m.* dodge, twist; sprain.
eslabón, *n.m.* link; steel (*for striking fire or for sharpening*).
eslavo, -va, *a., n.m.f.* Slav.
eslovaco, -ca, *a., n.m.f.* Slovak.
esloveno, -na, *a., n.m.f.* Slovene.
esmaltar, *v.t.* enamel; (*fig.*) adorn.
esmalte, *n.m.* enamel, enamelling; **— *de uñas*,** nail-polish.
esmerado, -da, *a.* painstaking; highly finished.
esmeralda, *n.f.* (*gem*) emerald.
esmerar, *v.t.* polish.—*v.r.* take great pains; do one's best.
esmeril, *n.m.* emery.
esmero, *n.m.* careful attention; correctness.
eso, *pron. dem. neuter* (*pl.* **esos**) that; **— *es*,** that's it; ***a — de las cinco*,** at about five o'clock.—*pl.* those, those ones.
esotérico, -ca, *a.* esoteric.
espabilar, *v.t.* to snuff (*a candle*).—*v.r.* (*fam.*) look lively.
espaciar, *v.t.* space.—*v.r.* expatiate; relax; walk to and fro.
espacio, *n.m.* space; period, interval; delay.
espaciosidad, *n.f.* spaciousness.
espacioso, -sa, *a.* spacious.
espada, *n.f.* sword; spade (*at cards*); (*ichth.*) swordfish.—*n.m.* (*taur.*) bullfighter.
espadachín, *n.m.* swordsman; bully.
espadaña, *n.f.* (*bot.*) bulrush, reed-mace; belfry.
espadilla, *n.f.* scull; jury rudder; ace of spades; hair bodkin; (*bot.*) gladiolus.
espadín, *n.m.* rapier.
espadón, *n.m.* broadsword; (*mil. fam.*) brass hat.
espadrapo [ESPARADRAPO].
espalda, *n.f.* back; shoulder; ***de espaldas*,** with the back turned (***a*,** towards).
espaldar (1), *n.m.* back (*of a seat etc.*).
espaldar (2), *n.m.* (*bot.*) espalier.
espaldera, *n.f.* (*bot.*) espalier.
espaldilla, *n.f.* shoulder-blade.
espaldudo, -da, *a.* broad-shouldered.
espantable, *a.* frightful.
espantadizo, -za, *a.* shy, easily frightened.
espantajo, *n.m.* scarecrow.
espantar, *v.t.* scare, frighten; drive away.—*v.r.* be surprised *or* astonished.
espanto, *n.m.* fright; threat; (*S.A.*) ghost.
espantoso, -sa, *a.* frightful, dreadful; wonderful.
España, *n.f.* Spain.
español, -la, *a.* Spanish.—*n.m.f.* Spaniard.—*n.m.* Spanish (*language*).
esparadrapo, *n.m.* plaster, sticking-plaster.
esparaván, *n.m.* (*vet.*) spavin; (*orn.*) sparrow-hawk.
esparcimiento, *n.m.* scattering; amusement, recreation.
esparcir [D], *v.t.* scatter.—*v.r.* amuse oneself.
espárrago, *n.m.* (*bot.*) asparagus.
espartano, -na, *a.* Spartan.
esparto, *n.m.* (*bot.*) esparto-grass.
espasmo, *n.m.* spasm.
espasmódico, -ca, *a.* spasmodic.
espato, *n.m.* (*min.*) spar.
espátula, *n.f.* spatula, putty knife; (*orn.*) spoonbill.
espaviento, *n.m.* consternation, fuss.
espavorido, -da, *a.* terrified.
especia, *n.f.* spice.
especial, *a.* special, especial.
especialidad, *n.f.* speciality, (*U.S.*) specialty
especialista, *a., n.m.f.* specialist.
especialización, *n.f.* specialization.
especializar [C], *v.t., v.i., v.r.* specialize.
especiar, *v.t.* spice.
especie, *n.f.* kind, sort; matter, affair; (*zool. etc.*) species; ***en* —,** in kind.
especiería, *n.f.* spice store.
especificación, *n.f.* specification.
especificar [A], *v.t.* specify.
especificativo, -va, *a.* specificatory; (*gram.*) restrictive.
específico, -ca, *a.* specific.—*n.m.* paten[t] medicine.
espécimen, *n.m.* (*pl.* **especímenes**) specimen
especiosidad, *n.f.* beauty; speciosity.
especioso, -sa, *a.* beautiful; specious.
espectacular, *a.* spectacular.
espectáculo, *n.m.* spectacle, show.
espectador, -ra, *a.* observing.—*n.m.f.* spectator, onlooker.
espectro, *n.m.* spectre, phantom; spectrum
especulación, *n.f.* speculation, contemplation; (*com.*) speculation.
especulador, -ra, *a.* speculating.—*n.m.* speculator.
especular, *v.t.* inspect; speculate on.—*v.* speculate (*esp. com.*).
especulativo, -va, *a.* speculative.
espejeo, espejismo, *n.m.* mirage.
espejo, *n.m.* mirror, looking-glass.
espelunca, *n.f.* cavern.
espeluznante, *a.* hair-raising.
espeluznar, *v.t.* set the hair of (*s.o.*) on en[d], ruffle (*U.S.* muss) the hair of (*s.o.*).
espera, *n.f.* expectation; waiting; (*mu[s.]*) pause, rest.
esperanza, *n.f.* hope; expectancy.
esperar, *v.t.* expect; hope.—*v.r.* stay, wai[t]
esperezar, *v.r.* stretch (*one's arms and legs*)
esperma, *n.f.* sperm.

espermático, -ca, *a.* spermatic, seminal.
esperpento, *n.m.* (*fam.*) absurdity; absurd person; fright.
espesar, *v.t.* thicken, inspissate; coagulate.
espeso, -sa, *a.* thick, dense; bulky, heavy; slovenly.
espesor, *n.m.* thickness, gauge (*of plates etc.*); density.
espesura, *n.f.* density, closeness; thicket; slovenliness.
espetar, *v.t.* skewer.
espetera, *n.f.* dresser, kitchen-rack.
espetón, *n.m.* spit; poker.
espía, *n.m.f.* spy.
espiar [L], *v.t.* spy on.—*v.i.* spy.
espicanardi, *n.f.*, **espicanardo,** *n.m.* (*bot.*) spikenard.
espichar, *v.t.* prick.—*v.i.* (*fam.*) peg out, die.
espiche, *n.m.* spigot.
espiga, *n.f.* spike; ear (*of grain*); (*carp.*) tenon; shank; fuse (*of a bomb*); (*naut.*) masthead.
espigar [B], *v.t.* glean; tenon, pin.—*v.i.* form ears.—*v.r.* grow tall.
espigón, *n.m.* sting (*of a bee*); point; breakwater.
espín, *n.m.* ***puerco* —,** porcupine.
espina, *n.f.* thorn; spine; fishbone splinter; (*fig.*) doubt, uncertainty; ***— de pescado,*** herringbone (*cloth*).
espinaca, *n.f.* (*bot.*) spinach.
espinal, *a.* spinal.
espinazo, *n.m.* backbone.
espinel, *n.m.* trawl.
espinera, *n.f.* (*bot.*) hawthorn.
espingarda, *n.f.* long Moorish musket; (*obs.*) sort of cannon.
espinilla, *n.f.* shin-bone; blackhead.
espino, *n.m.* (*bot.*) hawthorn.
espinoso, -sa, *a.* thorny; bony (*fish*).—*n.m.* (*ichth.*) stickleback.
espiocha, *n.f.* pickaxe.
espión, *n.m.* spy.
espionaje, *n.m.* espionage, spying.
espira, *n.f.* coil, turn.
espiral, *a.* spiral.—*n.m.* hairspring.—*n.f.* (*geom.*) spiral.
espirar, *v.t.*, *v.i.* breathe, exhale.
espiritar, *v.t.* possess with the devil; agitate. —*v.r.* get agitated.
espiritismo, *n.m.* spiritualism, spiritism.
espiritoso, -sa, *a.* spirited; spirituous.
espíritu, *n.m.* spirit; (*gram.*) breathing; ***— de cuerpo,*** esprit de corps; ***Espíritu Santo,*** Holy Spirit, Holy Ghost.
espiritual, *a.* spiritual.—*n.f.* spiritual (*song*).
espiritualidad, *n.f.* spirituality.
espiritualismo, *n.m.* spirituality.
espirituoso, -sa [ESPIRITOSO].
espiroqueta, *n.f.* (*med.*) spirochete.
espita, *n.f.* cock, tap, spigot.
espitar, *v.t.* tap (*a barrel*).
esplendidez, *n.f.* splendour, magnificence.
espléndido, -da, *a.* splendid, magnificent; resplendent.
esplendor, *n.m.* splendour.
esplendoroso, -sa, *a.* resplendent; magnificent.
esplenético, -ca, esplénico, -ca, *a.* splenetic.
espliego, *n.m.* (*bot.*) lavender.
espolada, *n.f.* spurring, prick with the spur.
espolear, *v.t.* spur; (*fig.*) spur on.
espoleta, *n.f.* fuse (*of a bomb*); wishbone.
espolón, *n.m.* spur (*of a cock*); (*geog.*) spur; (*naut.*) beak, ram; mole, jetty; (*arch.*) buttress; (*mil.*) trail spade (*of a gun*); chilblain.
espondaico, -ca, *a.* (*poet.*) spondaic.
espondeo, *n.m.* (*poet.*) spondee.
esponja, *n.f.* sponge; (*fig.*) sponger.
esponjar, *v.t.* sponge, soak.—*v.r.* become puffed up (*with conceit*); glow with health.
esponjosidad, *n.f.* sponginess.
esponjoso, -sa, *a.* spongy.
esponsales, *n.m.pl.* betrothal, engagement.
espontanear, *v.r.* own up, come forward.
espontaneidad, *n.f.* spontaneity, spontaneousness.
espontáneo, -nea, *a.* spontaneous.—*n.m.* spectator who jumps into the bull-ring.
espora, *n.f.* (*bot. etc.*) spore.
esporádico, -ca, *a.* sporadic.
esportilla, *n.f.* small basket.
esportillero, *n.m.* errand boy, carrier.
esportillo, *n.m.* basket, frail.
esposo, -sa, *n.m.f.* spouse.—*n.m.* husband.—*n.f.* wife.—*n.f.pl.* handcuffs.
espuela, *n.f.* spur.
espuerta, *n.f.* basket (*esp. as used by labourers*); ***a espuertas,*** in abundance.
espulgar [B], *v.t.* delouse; clean of fleas.
espuma, *n.f.* foam; spume; scum; ***goma —*** or ***de caucho,*** foam rubber.
espumajoso, -sa, *a.* frothy, foamy.
espumante, *a.* frothy, foaming; sparkling (*wine*).
espumar, *v.t.* scum, skim.—*v.i.* froth.
espumosidad, *n.f.* frothiness; foaminess.
espurio, -ria, *a.* spurious; illegitimate.
esputo, *n.m.* sputum, spittle.
esquela, *n.f.* note; announcement.
esquelético, -ca, *a.* skeletal, very thin.
esqueleto, *n.m.* skeleton; (*C.A.*) (application *etc.*) form.
esquema, *n.m.* scheme; schema.
esquemático, -ca, *a.* schematic.
esquematismo, *n.m.* schematism.
esquena, *n.f.* spine.
esquí, *n.m.* ski.
esquiar [L], *v.i.* ski.
esquiciar, *v.t.* sketch.
esquicio, *n.m.* sketch.
esquife, *n.m.* skiff, small boat.
esquila, *n.f.* small bell; prawn; water-spider; (*bot.*) squill.
esquilar, *v.t.* shear; (*fig.*) fleece.
esquilmar, *v.t.* harvest; impoverish.
esquilón, *n.m.* small bell.
esquimal, *a.*, *n.m.f.* Eskimo.
esquina, *n.f.* corner.
esquinco, *n.m.* (*zool.*) skink.
esquirla, *n.f.* splinter (*of bone, glass etc.*).
esquirol, *n.f.* strike-breaker, blackleg.
esquisto, *n.m.* (*geol.*) schist.
esquivar, *v.t.* avoid, elude.—*v.r.* withdraw.
esquivez, *n.f.* coyness; disdain; scorn.
esquivo, -va, *a.* shy; elusive; reserved.
estabilidad, *n.f.* stability; constancy.
estabilizar [C], *v.t.* stabilize.
estable, *a.* stable, permanent.
establecer [9], *v.t.* establish, found; decree.—*v.r.* settle (*in a place*).
establecimiento, *n.m.* establishment, settlement; store; institution; decree.
establo, *n.m.* stable.

estaca, *n.f.* picket, stake; cudgel.
estacada, *n.f.* stockade, palisade.
estacar [A], *v.t.* stake; enclose.
estación, *n.f.* condition, situation; season; (*rail.*) station.
estacional, *a.* seasonal.
estacionar, *v.r.* remain stationary; (*auto.*) park.
estacionario, -ria, *a.* stationary, fixed.
estadio, *n.m.* stadium.
estadista, *n.m.f.* statesman; statistician.
estadístico, -ca, *a.* statistical.
estado, *n.m.* state; condition; estate (*of the realm*); — ***mayor,*** (*mil.*) staff; ***Estados Unidos,*** United States.
estafa, *n.f.* swindle, trick.
estafador, -ra, *n.m.f.* swindler.
estafar, *v.t.* swindle.
estafeta, *n.f.* courier.
estafilococo, *n.m.* (*med.*) staphylococcus.
estalactita, *n.f.* (*geol.*) stalactite.
estalagmita, *n.f.* (*geol.*) stalagmite.
estallar, *v.i.* explode; (*fig.*) break out.
estallido, *n.m.* crack, report.
estambre, *n.m.* yarn, worsted; (*bot.*) stamen.
estameña, *n.f.* serge.
estampa, *n.f.* print; engraving; printing press.
estampar, *v.t.* print, imprint; impress, stamp.
estampida, *n.f.* (*S.A.*) stampede.
estampido, *n.m.* crack, report; crash.
estampilla, *n.f.* small print; (*S.A.*) postage-stamp.
estancar [A], *v.t.* staunch; check; (*com.*) monopolize; embargo.—*v.r.* be stagnant.
estancia, *n.f.* stay, sojourn; dwelling; living-room; (*poet.*) stanza; (*S.A.*) farm, estate.
estanciero, *n.m.* owner of an estate; farm-overseer.
estanco, -ca, *a.* watertight; seaworthy.—*n.m.* monopoly; shop for monopoly goods (*esp. tobacco and postage-stamps*); repository.
estandar(d), *n.m.* (*neol.*) standard.
estandar(d)izar, *v.t.* standardize.
estandarte, *n.m.* standard, banner.
estanque, *n.m.* pond; reservoir.
estanquero, -ra, *n.m.f.* retailer of monopoly goods, esp. tobacco; keeper of reservoirs.
estante, *a.* being; permanent.—*n.m.* shelf.
estantería, *n.f.* shelving; bookcase.
estantigua, *n.f.* procession of phantoms and hobgoblins; (*fam.*) fright, scarecrow.
estañar, *v.t.* tin; solder.
estaño, *n.m.* tin.
estar [18], *v.i.* be (*temporarily, or in a state or condition*); ***estamos a lunes,*** it is Monday; — ***con,*** have (*a disease*); — ***de viaje,*** be on a journey; — ***de (capitán),*** be acting as (captain); ***estoy en lo que Vd. me dice,*** I follow what you are telling me; — ***para,*** be about to; ***estoy por romperle la cabeza,*** I have a good mind to break his head; ***está por hacer,*** it remains to be done; — ***sobre un negocio,*** conduct a business well.—*v.r.* stay, remain.
estático, -ca, *a.* static.—*n.f.* statics.
estatua, *n.f.* statue.
estatuario, -ria, *a.* statuary.—*n.m.* sculptor.
estatuir [O], *v.t.* ordain, establish.
este (1), *n.m.* east.
este (2), **esta,** *a. dem.* (*pl.* **estos, estas**) this; latter.—*pl.* these.
éste, ésta, *pron. dem.* (*pl.* **éstos, éstas**) this; the latter.—*pl.* these.
estela, *n.f.* (*naut.*) wake; (*aer.*) trail.
estelar, *a.* stellar, sidereal.
estenografía, *n.f.* stenography, shorthand.
estenográfico, -ca, *a.* shorthand.
estenógrafo, -fa, *n.m.f.* stenographer, shorthand-writer.
estepa (1), *n.f.* (*bot.*) rock-rose.
estepa (2), *n.f.* (*geog.*) steppe.
estera, *n.f.* mat, matting.
estercolar, *n.m.* manure heap, dunghill.—*v.t.* [4] dung, manure.
estereotipar, *v.t.* stereotype (*also fig.*).
estereotipia, *n.f.* stereotype.
estéril, *a.* sterile; fruitless.
esterilidad, *n.f.* sterility.
esterilizador, -ra, *a.* sterilizing.—*n.m.* sterilizer (*apparatus*).
esterilizar, *v.t.* sterilize.
esterilla, *n.f.* small mat; hopsack (*textile weave*); (*S.A.*) canvas.
esterlina, *n.f.* sterling.
esternón, *n.m.* (*anat.*) sternum, breastbone.
estero, *n.m.* matting; tidal marsh; (*S.A.*) swamp: (*S.A.*) stream.
estertor, *n.m.* noisy breathing; death rattle.
esteta, *n.m.f.* aesthete.
estético, -ca, *a.* aesthetic.—*n.f.* aesthetics.
esteva, *n.f.* plough-handle.
estiaje, *n.m.* low-water mark.
estibador, *n.m.* stevedore, docker, (*U.S.*) longshoreman.
estibar, *v.t.* pack, (*naut.*) stow.
estibio, *n.m.* (*chem.*) stibium.
estiércol, *n.m.* dung, manure.
estigio, -gia, estigioso, -sa, *a.* Stygian.
estigma, *n.m.* stigma.
estigmatismo, *n.m.* (*med.*) stigmatism.
estigmatizar [C], *v.t.* stigmatize.
estilete, *n.m.* stiletto; style, stylus (*of recording instrument*); (*med.*) stylet.
estilista, *n.m.f.* (*lit.*) stylist.
estilístico, -ca, *a.* (*lit.*) stylistic.—*n.f.* stylistics.
estilización, *n.f.* stylization.
estilo, *n.m.* style; stylus; ***por el*** —, of that kind.
estilográfico, -ca, *a.* stylographic.—*n.f.* fountain pen.
estima, *n.f.* esteem.
estimable, *a.* estimable, worthy.
estimación, *n.f.* estimation; esteem.
estimar, *v.t.* esteem, respect; judge; (*fam.*) be fond of.
estimulación, *n.f.* stimulation.
estimulante, *a.* stimulating.—*n.m.* stimulant.
estimular, *v.t.* stimulate; irritate; goad.
estímulo, *n.m.* stimulus, sting.
estío, *n.m.* summer.
estipendio, *n.m.* stipend, salary.
estipulación, *n.f.* stipulation.
estipular, *v.t.* stipulate.
estirable, *a.* stretchable.
estirar, *v.t.* draw, stretch; — ***la pata,*** (*fam.*) die.—*v.r.* stretch; put on airs.
estirón, *n.m.* stretch; strong pull.
estirpe, *n.f.* stock, race.
estival, estivo, -va, *a.* summer.
esto, *pron. dem. neuter* this.
estocada, *n.f.* thrust, stab.
Estocolmo, *n.m.* Stockholm.

estofa, *n.f.* (*rare*) quilted material; (*fig.*) stuff, quality.
estofado, *n.m.* meat stew.
estofar, *v.t.* quilt; stew.
estoicismo, *n.m.* Stoicism.
estoico, -ca, *a.* stoic(al).—*n.m.f.* stoic.
estomagar [B], *v.t.* upset (*the stomach*); pall; (*fam.*) annoy.
estómago, *n.m.* stomach.
estonio, -nia, *a., n.m.f.* Estonian.
estopa, *n.f.* tow, oakum.
estopilla, *n.f.* fine flax; cambric.
estoque, *n.m.* rapier; (*bot.*) gladiolus.
estorbar, *v.t.* hinder, impede, hamper.
estorbo, *n.m.* impediment, hindrance.
estorboso, -sa, *a.* hindering, in the way.
estornino, *n.m.* (*orn.*) starling.
estornudar, *v.i.* sneeze.
estornudo, *n.m.* sneeze.
estrabismo, *n.m.* (*med.*) strabismus, squint.
estrada, *n.f.* causeway; highway.
estrado, *n.m.* dais; drawing-room; lecturing platform.—*pl.* court of justice.
estrafalario, -ria, *a.* (*fam.*) slovenly; (*fam.*) outlandish.
estragamiento, *n.m.* corruption.
estragar [B], *v.t.* corrupt, deprave, spoil.
estrago, *n.m.* damage, havoc, devastation; depravity.
estragón, *n.m.* (*bot.*) tarragon.
estrambote, *n.m.* (*poet.*) burden (*of a song*).
estrambótico, -ca, *a.* (*fam.*) odd, freakish.
estrangulación, *n.f.* strangulation; choke (*in machinery*).
estrangulador, *n.m.* throttle, choke (*in machinery*).
estrangular, *v.t.* throttle, strangle, choke.
estraperlista, *a.* rel. to the black market.—*n.m.f.* black marketeer.
estraperlo, *n.m.* black market.
estratagema, *n.f.* stratagem.
estrategia, *n.f.* strategy.
estratégico, -ca, *a.* strategic(al).
estratificar [A], *v.t., v.r.* stratify.
estrato, *n.m.* layer, stratum.
estratosfera, *n.f.* stratosphere.
estraza, *n.f.* rag.
estrechar, *v.t.* tighten; constrict; narrow; press; — ***la mano,*** shake hands (***a,*** with).—*v.r.* become narrow; reduce expenses; come closer together.
estrechez, *n.f.* narrowness; tightness; penury.
estrecho, -cha, *a.* narrow; tight; intimate; stingy.—*n.m.* (*geog.*) strait; (*fig.*) danger, predicament.
estrechón, *n.m.* (*fam.*) handshake.
estrechura, *n.f.* narrowness; closeness, familiarity; predicament; penury.
estregadera, *n.f.* scrubbing brush.
estregar [1B], *v.t.* scrub, scour; rub.
estrella, *n.f.* star; ***estrellas y listas,*** Stars and Stripes.
estrelladera, *n.f.* (*cul.*) slice, turnover (*implement*).
estrellar, *v.t.* (*fam.*) break; (*cul.*) scramble (*eggs*); crash.—*v.r.* crash (**contra,** into).
estrellón, *n.m.* large star; (*S.A.*) collision.
estremecer [9], *v.t.* shake.—*v.r.* shake, shiver.
estremecimiento, *n.m.* shaking, shivering.
estrena, *n.f.* gift (*of appreciation*); (*obs.*) first use.
estrenar, *v.t.* use *or* wear *or* stage (*etc.*) for the first time.—*v.r.* make one's début, appear (*etc.*) for the first time.
estreno, *n.m.* beginning; début; first performance.
estrenuo, -nua, *a.* strenuous.
estreñimiento, *n.m.* constipation.
estreñir [8K], *v.t.* bind, tighten; constipate.—*v.r.* be constipated.
estrépito, *n.m.* noise, racket; fuss.
estrepitoso, -sa, *a.* noisy; notorious.
estriadura, *n.f.* fluting; striation.
estriar [L], *v.t.* flute; striate.
estribar, *v.i.* rest (***en,*** on).
estribillo, *n.m.* (*poet.*) burden, refrain.
estribo, *n.m.* stirrup; (*geog.*) spur.
estribor, *n.m.* (*naut.*) starboard.
estricto, -ta, *a.* strict.
estridente, *a.* strident.
estridor, *n.m.* stridence, loud noise.
estrige, *n.f.* (*orn.*) barn owl.
estro (1), *n.m.* (*poet.*) inspiration.
estro (2), *n.m.* (*ent.*) botfly.
estrofa, *n.f.* strophe.
estrófico, -ca, *a.* strophic.
estroncio, *n.m.* (*chem.*) strontium.
estropajo, *n.m.* (*bot.*) loofah; dishcloth, dishmop.
estropear, *v.t.* abuse; spoil; cripple.—*v.r.* spoil; fail.
estropeo, *n.m.* mistreatment; damage.
estructura, *n.f.* structure.
estruendo, *n.m.* clamour; turmoil, uproar.
estrujar, *v.t.* squeeze, press, crush.
estuario, *n.m.* estuary.
estuco, *n.m.* stucco.
estuche, *n.m.* case, box, casket.
estudiante, *n.m.f.* student.
estudiantina, *n.f.* group of students; students' band.
estudiar, *v.t., v.i.* study.
estudio, *n.m.* study; studio.
estudioso, -sa, *a.* studious.
estufa, *n.f.* stove; hothouse; sweating room.
estufador, *n.m.* stew-pan.
estufilla, *n.f.* foot-warmer.
estulto, -ta, *a.* silly.
estupefaciente, *a., n.m.* narcotic.
estupefacto, -ta, *a.* dumbfounded; petrified.
estupendo, -da, *a.* stupendous, wonderful; (*fam.*) marvellous.
estupidez, *n.f.* stupidity.
estúpido, -da, *a.* stupid.
estupor, *n.m.* stupor.
estuprar, *v.t.* rape, violate.
estupro, *n.m.* rape.
esturión, *n.m.* (*ichth.*) sturgeon.
estuve, estuvo, *etc. preterite of* ESTAR.
etapa, *n.f.* stage (*of a journey; rad.*).
etcétera, et cetera.—*n.f.* (*print.*) ampersand.
éter, *n.m.* (*chem.*) ether.
etéreo, -ea, *a.* ethereal.
eternal, *a.* eternal.
eternidad, *n.f.* eternity.
eternizar [C], *v.t.* make eternal.—*v.r.* go on for ever.
eterno, -na, *a.* eternal.
ético, -ca (1), *a.* ethical, moral.
ético, -ca (2), *a.* (*med.*) consumptive.
etilo, *n.m.* ethyl.
etimología, *n.f.* etymology.
etimológico, -ca, *a.* etymological.

etíope, etiopio, -pia, *a., n.m.f.* Ethiopian.
Etiopía, *n.f.* Ethiopia.
etiqueta, *n.f.* etiquette; label, price-tag; *de* —, formal.
étnico, -ca, *a.* ethnic.
etnografía, *n.f.* ethnography.
etnología, *n.f.* ethnology.
eucalipto, *n.m.* (*bot.*) eucalyptus.
eucaristía, *n.f.* (*eccl.*) eucharist, communion.
euclidiano, -na, *a.* Euclidean.
eufemismo, *n.m.* euphemism.
eufonía, *n.f.* euphony.
eufónico, -ca, *a.* euphonic, euphonious.
euforia, *n.f.* euphoria, sense of well-being.
eunuco, *n.m.* eunuch.
eupéptico, -ca, *a.* eupeptic, digestive.
eurasiano, -na, *a., n.m.f.* Eurasian.
euro, *n.m.* (*poet.*) east wind.
Europa, *n.f.* (*geog., myth.*) Europe.
europeizar [C], *v.t.* Europeanize.
europeo, -pea, *a., n.m.f.* European.
europio, *n.m.* (*chem.*) europium.
éuscaro, -ra, eusquero, -ra, *a., n.m.f.* Basque.—*n.m.* Basque (*language*).
eutanasia, *n.f.* euthanasia.
evacuación, *n.f.* evacuation.
evacuar, *v.t., v.i.* evacuate.
evacuatorio, -ria, *a.* evacuant.—*n.m.* pubiic convenience.
evadir, *v.t.* avoid, evade.—*v.r.* flee, escape.
evaluación, *n.f.* evaluation.
evaluar [M], *v.t.* evaluate.
evanescente, *a.* evanescent.
evangélico, -ca, *a.* evangelic; evangelical.
Evangelio, *n.m.* Gospel; (*fam.*) gospel truth.
evangelista, *n.m.* evangelist; gospeller.
evangelizar [C], *v.t., v.i.* evangelize.
evaporable, *a.* evaporable.
evaporación, *n.f.* evaporation.
evaporar, *v.t., v.r.* evaporate.
evaporizar [C], *v.t.* vaporize.
evasión, *n.f.* evasion; escape.
evasivo, -va, *a.* evasive, elusive.
evento, *n.m.* contingency, chance event; ***a todo*** —, (prepared *etc.*) for any eventuality.
eventual, *a.* eventual, fortuitous.
eventualidad, *n.f.* eventuality.
evicción, *n.f.* (*jur.*) eviction, dispossession.
evidencia, *n.f.* evidence.
evidenciar, *v.t.* make evident.—*v.r.* be evident.
evidente, *a.* evident.
evitable, *a.* avoidable.
evitar, *v.t.* avoid, shun.
evocación, *n.f.* evocation.
evocar [A], *v.t.* evoke.
evolución, *n.f.* evolution; change (*in ideas*).
evolucionar, *v.i.* evolve; (*mil.*) manoeuvre.
evolucionismo, *n.m.* evolutionism, Darwinism.
evolutivo, -va, *a.* evolutionary.
ex, *prefix.* ex-; — ***mujer***, ex-wife.
ex abrupto, *n.m.* outburst; sudden violent remark.
exacerbar, *v.t.* exacerbate.—*v.r.* become exacerbated.
exactitud, *n.f.* exactitude.
exacto, -ta, *a.* exact, accurate; punctual.
exageración, *n.f.* exaggeration.
exagerar, *v.t.* exaggerate.
exaltación, *n.f.* exaltation.
exaltado, -da, *a.* hot-headed; ultra-radical; extremist.
exaltar, *v.t.* exalt.—*v.r.* become excited.
examen, *n.m.* examination.
examinador, -ra, *a.* examining.—*n.m.f.* examiner.
examinando, -da, *n.m.f.* examinee.
examinar, *v.t.* examine, inspect.—*v.t.* take an examination (***de***, in).
exangüe, *a.* bloodless; anaemic.
exánime, *a.* lifeless; fainting.
exasperación, *n.f.* exasperation.
exasperar, *v.t.* exasperate.
excarcelar, *v.t.* release (*from prison*).
excavación, *n.f.* excavation.
excavador, -ra, *a.* excavating.—*n.m.f.* excavator.—*n.f.* steam shovel.
excavar, *v.t.* excavate.
excedente, *a.* excess; redundant.—*n.m.* excess.
exceder, *v.t., v.i.* exceed.—*v.r.* go too far; ***excederse a sí mismo,*** outdo oneself.
Excelencia, *n.m.f.* Excellency (*title*); **excelencia,** *n.f.* excellence; ***por*** **—,** par excellence.
excelsitud, *n.f.* sublimity.
el Excelso, *n.m.* the Most High; **excelso, -sa,** *a.* lofty, sublime.
excentricidad, *n.f.* eccentricity.
excéntrico, -ca, *a.* eccentric.
excepción, *n.f.* exception; ***a* — *de*,** except, with the exception of.
excepcional, *a.* exceptional.
excepto, *prep.* except(ing), but.
exceptuar [M], *v.t.* except; exempt.
excesivo, -va, *a.* excessive, immoderate.
exceso, *n.m.* excess; — ***de peso,*** excess weight.
excitable, *a.* excitable.
excitación, *n.f.* excitation, excitement.
excitante, *a.* exciting.
excitar, *v.t.* excite.
exclamación, *n.f.* exclamation.
exclamar, *v.i.* exclaim.
exclamativo, -va, exclamatorio, -ria, *a.* exclamatory.
exclaustrar, *v.t.* secularize (*a monk*).
excluir [O], *v.t.* exclude.
exclusión, *n.f.* exclusion; ***con* — *de*,** with the exclusion of, excluding.
exclusive, *adv.* exclusively.
exclusivo, -va, *a.* exclusive.—*n.f.* refusal; exclusive rights.
excomulgar [B], *v.t.* excommunicate; (*fam.*) send to Coventry.
excomunión, *n.f.* excommunication.
excoriar, *v.t.* excoriate.—*v.r.* skin.
excrecencia, *n.f.* excrescence.
excremental, *a.* excremental.
excrementar, *v.i.* move the bowels.
excrementicio, -cia, *a.* excremental.
excremento, *n.m.* excrement.
excretar, *v.t., v.i.* excrete.
exculpación, *n.f.* exculpation.
exculpar, *v.t.* exculpate.
excursión, *n.f.* excursion, trip.
excursionista, *a.* rel. to an excursion.—*n.m.f.* excursionist, tripper.
excusa, *n.f.* excuse.
excusable, *a.* excusable, pardonable.
excusadamente, *adv.* unnecessarily.
excusado, -da, *a.* exempt; unnecessary reserved, private.—*n.m.* lavatory.

excusar, *v.t.* excuse; avoid; hinder; exempt; ***excusas venir,*** you do not have to come.—*v.r.* make one's apologies; decline (***de hacer,*** to do).
execrable, *a.* execrable.
execración, *n.f.* execration.
exención, *n.f.* exemption.
exencionar, *v.t.* exempt.
exentar, *v.t.* exempt.
exento, -ta, *a.* exempt.
exequible, *a.* attainable, feasible.
exhalación, *n.f.* exhalation; shooting star; fume; ***como una* —,** (*fam.*) like a shot.
exhalar, *v.t.* exhale, emit (*vapours*).—*v.r.* exhale; breathe hard.
exhaustivo, -va, *a.* exhaustive.
exhausto, -ta, *a.* exhausted.
exheredar, *v.t.* disinherit.
exhibición, *n.f.* exhibition.
exhibir, *v.t.* exhibit.
exhilarante, *a.* exhilarating; laughing (*gas*).
exhortar, *v.t.* exhort.
exhumar, *v.t.* exhume.
exigencia, *n.f.* exigency.
exigente, *a.* exacting, demanding, exigent.
exigible, exigidero, -ra, *a.* exigible.
exigir [E], *v.t.* exact, demand.
exiguo, -gua, *a.* exiguous.
exil(i)ar, *v.t.* exile.
exilio, *n.m.* exile.
eximio, -mia, *a.* select, choice.
eximir, *v.t.* exempt.
existencia, *n.f.* existence.—*pl.* stock(s).
existencial, *a.* existential.
existencialista, *a.*, *n.m.f.* existentialist.
existente, *a.* existent; extant; (*com.*) to hand.
existir, *v.i.* exist.
éxito, *n.m.* outcome, result; success.
éxodo, *n.m.* exodus.
exogamia, *n.f.* exogamy.
exonerar, *v.t.* exonerate, acquit.—*v.r.* relieve nature.
exorbitante, *a.* exorbitant.
exorcismo, *n.m.* exorcism.
exorcizar [C], *v.t.* exorcize.
exordio, *n.m.* exordium.
exornar, *v.t.* adorn.
exoticidad, *n.f.* exoticism.
exótico, -ca, *a.* exotic; foreign-grown (*timber etc.*).
exotismo, *n.m.* exoticism.
expansible, *a.* expansible, dilatable.
expansión, *n.f.* expansion; expansiveness; recreation.
expansivo, -va, *a.* expansive.
expatriado, -da, *a.* expatriate.—*n.m.f.* expatriate; displaced person.
expatriar, *v.t.* expatriate.—*v.r.* go *or* settle abroad.
expectación, *n.f.* expectation, expectance.
expectante, *a.* expectant.
expectativa, *n.f.* expectation.
expectorar, *v.t.* expectorate.
expedición, *n.f.* expedition; shipment, despatch.
expedicionario, -ria, *a.* expeditionary.
expedidor, -ra, *a.* (*com.*) forwarding, shipping.—*n.m.f.* (*com.*) shipper, merchant.
expediente, *n.m.* expedient; (*jur.*) proceedings, dossier; motive.
expedir [8], *v.t.* send, ship, remit; expedite.
expeditivo, -va, expedito, -ta, *a.* expeditious.
expeler, *v.t.* expel.
expendedor, -ra, *a.* spending.—*n.m.f.* dealer, agent; utterer (*of coins*).
expendeduría, *n.f.* retail shop (*for monopoly goods*).
expender, *v.t.* spend, expend; sell (*retail*); (*jur.*) pass (*counterfeit coins*).
expendio, *n.m.* expense; (*S.A.*) retail store; (*S.A.*) retailing.
expensas, *n.f.pl.* expenses.
experiencia, *n.f.* experience; experiment.
experimentado, -da, *a.* experienced, expert.
experimentar, *v.t.* experience; test; undergo.—*v.i.* experiment.
experimento, *n.m.* experiment, test.
experto, -ta, *a.*, *n.m.f.* expert.
expiable, *a.* expiable.
expiar, *v.t.* expiate.
expiración, *n.f.* expiration.
expirante, *a.* expiring.
expirar, *v.i.* expire.
explanada, *n.f.* esplanade.
explanar, *v.t.* level; explain.
explayar, *v.t.* extend.—*v.r.* dwell upon a subject; unbosom oneself.
expletivo, -va, *a.* expletive.
explicable, *a.* explainable, explicable.
explicación, *n.f.* explanation.
explicar [A], *v.t.* explain.—*v.r.* give an explanation; understand.
explicativo, -va, *a.* explanatory.
explícito, -ta, *a.* explicit.
exploración, *n.f.* exploration.
explorador, -ra, *a.* exploring; scouting.—*n.m.f.* explorer; boy-scout; (*mil.*) scout.—*n.m.* (*T.V.*) scanner.
explorar, *v.t.* explore; investigate; (*mil.*) scout; (*T.V.*) scan.
exploratorio, -ria, *a.* exploratory.
explosión, *n.f.* explosion, burst.
explosivo, -va, *a.* explosive.
explotable, *a.* exploitable.
explotación, *n.f.* exploitation; (*min.*) working; operation.
explotar, *v.t.* exploit; operate (*an airline etc.*); (*neol.*) explode (*also v.i.*).
exponente, *a.* exponent.—*n.m.f.* exponent; (*com.*) exhibitor.
exponer [25], *v.t.* expose; expound; disclose; exhibit.—*v.r.* run a risk.
exportación, *n.f.* export, exportation.
exportador, -ra, *a.* exporting.—*n.m.f.* exporter.
exportar, *v.t.* export.
exposición, *n.f.* display, exhibition; (*phot.*) exposure; explanation; (*eccl.*) Benediction.
expositivo, -va, *a.* explanatory.
expósito, -ta, *a.*, *n.m.f.* foundling.
expositor, -ra, *a.* explaining; exhibiting.—*n.m.f.* expounder; exhibitor.
expresado, -da, *a.* aforesaid.
expresar, *v.t.* express; utter.
expresión, *n.f.* expression; gift; pressing out.
expresivo, -va, *a.* expressive.
expreso, -sa, *a.* expressed; express.—*adv.* on purpose.—*n.m.* express train.
exprimidera, *n.f.* squeezer.
exprimir, *v.t.* squeeze (out).
expropiación, *n.f.* expropriation.
expropiar, *v.t.* expropriate.

expuesto, -ta, *a.* exposed; liable, in danger.—*p.p.* [EXPONER].
expugnar, *v.t.* (*mil.*) take by storm.
expulsar, *v.t.* eject, drive out.
expulsión, *n.f.* expulsion.
expulso, -sa, *a.* expelled; ejected, outcast.
expurgar [B], *v.t.* expurgate.
exquisito, -ta, *a.* exquisite.
extasiar [L], *v.r.* be delighted; go into ecstasies.
éxtasis, *n.f. inv.* ecstasy.
extático, -ca, *a.* ecstatic.
extemporaneamente, *adv.* untimely; extempore.
extemporáneo, -nea, *a.* ill-timed.
extender [2], *v.t., v.r.* extend, stretch; widen.
extensión, *n.f.* extension; stretch.
extensivo, -va, *a.* extensive.
extenso, -sa, *a.* extensive; extended; ***por* —,** in full.
extenuar [M], *v.t.* attenuate, diminish.—*v.r.* languish.
exterior, *a.* exterior; external; foreign; overlooking the street (*room*).—*n.m.* exterior, outside; abroad.
exteriorizar [C], *v.t.* make manifest.—*v.r.* unbosom oneself.
exterminar, *v.t.* exterminate.
exterminio, *n.m.* extermination.
externado, *n.m.* day-school.
externo, -na, *a.* external; outward; exterior.—*n.m.f.* day-pupil.
extinción, *n.f.* extinction.
extinguible, *a.* extinguishable.
extinguir [G], *v.t.* extinguish, quench; extirpate.
extinto, -ta, *a.* extinguished; extinct; (*S.A.*) deceased.
extintor, *n.m.* fire-extinguisher.
extirpación, *n.f.* extirpation.
extirpar, *v.t.* extirpate.
extorsión, *n.f.* extortion.
extra, *prefix.* extra-; **— *de*,** in addition to.—*n.m.f.* (*theat.*) extra.—*n.m.* tip.
extracción, *n.f.* extraction.
extracto, *n.m.* extract; abstract; summary.
extradición, *n.f.* extradition.
extraer [34], *v.t.* extract.
extranjero, -ra, *a.* foreign.—*n.m.f.* foreigner.—*n.m.* ***en*** or ***a* —,** abroad.
extrañamiento, *n.m.* alienation; deportation.
extrañar, *v.t.* alienate; expatriate; find strange; be surprised at.—*v.i.* be strange.—*v.r.* be surprised; wonder; refuse.
extrañez, extrañeza, *n.f.* strangeness.
extraño, -ña, *a.* strange; foreign; extraneous.—*n.m.f.* stranger; foreigner.
extraordinario, -ria, *a.* extraordinary, out of the ordinary; extra; ***horas extraordinarias*,** overtime.
extrarradio, *n.m.* outskirts.
extravangancia, *n.f.* extravagance; oddness.
extravagante, *a.* extravagant; eccentric.
extraviar [L], *v.t.* mislead; misplace; embezzle.—*v.r.* go astray; err.
extravío, *n.m.* deviation, aberration.
extremado, -da, *a.* extreme, consummate.
extremeño, -ña, *a.* (*geog.*) rel. to Extremadura.
extremidad, *n.f.* extremity.
extremista, *a., n.m.f.* extremist.
extremo, -ma, *a.* extreme, last.—*n.m.* extreme.
exuberancia, *n.f.* exuberance.
exudar, *v.t., v.i.* exude.
exultación, *n.f.* exultation.
exvoto, *n.m.* (*relig.*) votive offering.
eyacular, *v.t.* (*med.*) ejaculate.
eyección, *n.f.* ejection.
eyector, *n.m.* ejector (*of a gun*).
Ezequías, *n.m.* (*Bib.*) Hezekiah.
Ezequial, *n.m.* (*Bib.*) Ezekiel.

F

F, f, *n.f.* seventh letter of the Spanish alphabet.
fa, *n.m.* (*mus.*) (key of) F.
fabada, *n.f.* pork and beans.
fábrica, *n.f.* factory, mill; building, structure, (*esp. eccl.*) fabric.
fabricación, *n.f.* manufacture.
fabricante, *a.* manufacturing.—*n.m.f.* manufacturer.
fabricar [A], *v.t.* manufacture, make; devise.
fábula, *n.f.* fable.
fabuloso, -sa, *a.* fabulous.
faca, *n.f.* sheath-knife.
facción, *n.f.* faction; (*esp. pl.*) feature (*face*); (*mil.*) duty.
faccioso, -sa, *a.* factious.—*n.m.f.* agitator.
faceta, *n.f.* facet.
facial, *a.* facial; ***valor* —,** face value.
facies, *n.f.* (*med.*) facies, appearance.
fácil, *a.* easy; facile; compliant; probable.
facilidad, *n.f.* facility, ease.
facilitar, *v.t.* facilitate; provide.
facineroso, -sa, *a.* villainous.—*n.m.f.* rascal; criminal.
facistol, *n.m.* lectern.
facsímil, facsímile, *n.m.* facsimile.
factible, *a.* feasible.
facticio, -cia, *a.* factitious.
factor, *n.m.* factor; freight agent; victualler.
factoría, *n.f.* factory, trading post; factorage.
factura, *n.f.* execution, workmanship; invoice, bill.
facturar, *v.t.* invoice; (*rail.*) register, (*U.S.*) check.
facultad, *n.f.* faculty; permission, licence.
facultar, *v.t.* authorize, empower.
facultativo, -va, *a.* optional, facultative.—*n.m.* physician; surgeon.
facundia, *n.f.* eloquence.
facundo, -da, *a.* eloquent; loquacious.
facha, *n.f.* (*fam.*) face, appearance.
fachada, *n.f.* façade; frontispiece (*of a book*).
fachado, -da, *a.* ***bien*** (or ***mal***) **—,** good- (*or* unpleasant-) looking.
fada, *n.f.* fairy; witch; (sort of) apple.
faena, *n.f.* task, chore, job; (*mil.*) fatigue; each part of a bull-fight.
faenero, *n.m.* (*S.A.*) farm labourer.
fagocita, *n.m.* (*med.*) phagocyte.
fagot, *n.m.* (*mus.*) bassoon; bassoonist.
fagotista, *n.m.f.* (*mus.*) bassoonist.

faisán, *n.m.* pheasant.
faja, *n.f.* sash, girdle, belt, cummerbund; wrapper (*book*); zone; (*rad.*) channel; (*aer.*) strip; (*aer.*) apron (*airport*); (*arch.*) fascia; swaddling clothes.
fajar, *v.t.* swaddle, swathe; girdle; (*S.A.*) thrash; — ***con***, (*S.A.*) set upon.
fajardo, *n.m.* (*cul.*) meat pie; vol-au-vent.
fajina, *n.f.* faggot; (*mil.*) lights out, retreat; (*agr.*) shock, stook.
fajo, *n.m.* bundle, sheaf.
falacia, *n.f.* fraud, deceit.
Falange, *n.f.* (*pol.*) Falange; **falange**, *n.f.* phalanx.
falangero, *n.m.* (*zool.*) phalanger.
falangia, *n.f.*, **falangio**, *n.m.* (*zool.*) daddy-long-legs.
falangista, *a.*, *n.m.f.* (*pol.*) Falangist.
falaz, *a.* (*pl.* **-aces**) deceitful; treacherous.
falca, *n.f.* weatherboard; (*naut.*) gunwale.
falce, *n.f.* sickle.
falda, *n.f.* skirt; lower slope (*of a hill*); loin (*of meat*); (*esp. pl.*, *fam.*) women.
faldero, -ra, *a.* rel. to the lap; ***perro*** —, lap-dog.
faldeta, *n.f.* small skirt; (*theat.*) drop-curtain.
faldillas, *n.f.pl.* skirts; coat-tails.
faldistorio, *n.m.* (*eccl.*) faldstool.
faldón, *n.m.* coat-tail; shirt-tail; flap; hip (*roof*).
faldriquera, *n.f.* pocket.
falencia, *n.f.* fallacy; mistake; (*S.A.*) bankruptcy.
falible, *a.* fallible.
fálico, -ca, *a.* phallic.
falo, *n.m.* phallus.
de falondres, *adv.phr.* (*naut.*, *S.A.*) suddenly, briskly.
falsario, -ria, *a.* falsifying.—*n.m.f.* forger.
falsear, *v.t.* falsify, forge, counterfeit; pierce. —*v.i.* sag; be out of tune (*string*).
falsedad, *n.f.* falsehood; deceit; perfidy.
falseo, *n.m.* bevelling.
falsete, *n.m.* spigot, (*U.S.*) tap; small door; falsetto.
falsificación, *n.f.* falsification.
falsificar [A], *v.t.* falsify; forge, counterfeit.
falso, -sa, *a.* untrue; false; sham, mock.—*n.m.* facing (*clothes*).—*n.f.* (*mus.*) dissonance.
falta, *n.f.* lack; want; fault; flaw; (*med.*) missed period; ***a — de***, for want of; ***hacer*** —, be necessary; ***me hacían*** —, I needed them, I missed them; — ***de pago***, non-payment; ***sin*** —, without fail.
faltante, *a.* wanting, missing.
faltar, *v.t.* offend.—*v.i.* be wanting; be missing *or* deficient; lack; fall short; — ***a su palabra***, be untrue to one's word; ***¡ no faltaba más !*** but of course!
falto, -ta, *a.* wanting, lacking; mean; short (*weight*).
faltoso, -sa, *a.* (*fam.*) non compos mentis.
faltriquera, *n.f.* pocket; pouch.
falúa, *n.f.* (*naut.*) gig, tender.
falucho, *n.m.* (*naut.*) felucca, lateen-rigged vessel.
falla, *n.f.* (*S.A.*) defect, fault; (*geol.*) fault, break; (*dial.*) float.
fallar, *v.t.* trump, ruff (*at cards*).—*v.i.* fail, be deficient; break, give way.
falleba, *n.f.* latch, bolt, fastener.
fallecer [9], *v.i.* die, pass away; expire.
fallecimiento, *n.m.* decease.
fallido, -da, *a.* frustrated; bankrupt.
fallo, -lla, *a.* (*S.A.*) simple, silly; (*cards*) — ***a***, lacking in; ***estoy — a bastos***, I have no clubs.—*n.m.* judgement, decision.
fama, *n.f.* fame; reputation; rumour.
famélico, -ca, *a.* hungry, ravenous.
familia, *n.f.* family; household.
familiar, *a.* domestic; familiar.—*n.m.* household servant; familiar spirit; (*eccl.*) familiar.
familiaridad, *n.f.* familiarity.
familiarizar [C], *v.t.* familiarize; popularize. —*v.r.* accustom oneself (***con***, to).
famoso, -sa, *a.* celebrated; famous; notorious.
fámulo, -la, *n.m.f.* (*fam.*) servant.
fanal, *n.m.* lighthouse.
fanático, -ca, *a.* fanatic.
fanatismo, *n.m.* fanaticism.
fandango, *n.m.* fandango; disorder.
fanega, *n.f.* a grain measure (*c.* 1.5 *bushels*); a surface measure (*c.* 1.5 *acres*).
fanfarria, *n.f.* (*fam.*) arrogance, swagger.
fanfarrón, -rrona, *a.* swaggering, boasting; bullying.
fanfarronear, *v.i.* bluster.
fangal, fangar, *n.m.* swamp, bog.
fango, *n.m.* mud; ooze; sludge.
fangoso, -sa, *a.* muddy.
fantasear, *v.t.* dream of.—*v.i.* daydream.
fantasía, *n.f.* imagination; fancy; fantasy, caprice; (*mus.*) fantasia; ***de*** —, fancy.
fantasma, *n.m.* phantom; apparition, ghost.
fantasmagoría, *n.f.* phantasmagoria.
fantasmagórico, -ca, *a.* phantasmagoric.
fantástico, -ca, *a.* imaginary; fantastic; conceited.
fantoche, *n.m.* puppet; (*fam.*) nincompoop.
farad, faradio, *n.m.* (*elec.*) farad.
farallón, *n.m.* headland, cliff; outcrop.
faramalla, *n.f.* (*fam.*) cajoling; claptrap.
farándula, *n.f.* (*obs.*) strolling troupe; (*S.A.*) bunch, crowd; din.
faraón, *n.m.* pharaoh; faro (*cards*).
faraute, *n.m.* herald, messenger; prologue (*actor*).
fardel, *n.m.* bag, bundle.
fardela, *n.f.* (*orn.*) shearwater.
fardo, *n.m.* bale, bundle.
fárfara, *n.m.* (*bot.*) coltsfoot; membrane (*of an egg*); ***en*** —, immature, (*fam.*) half-baked.
farfolla, *n.f.* husk (*maize*); (*fam.*) sham, fake.
farfullar, *v.t.* gabble; stumble through (*a lesson*).
fargallón, -llona, *a.* (*fam.*) slapdash.—*n.m.f.* botcher; bungler.
farináceo, -cea, *a.* farinaceous.
fariseo, *n.m.* Pharisee.
farmacéutico, -ca, *a.* pharmaceutical.—*n.m.f.* pharmacist, dispensing chemist.—*n.f.* pharmaceutics.
farmacia, *n.f.* pharmacy, (*Brit.*) chemist's shop, (*U.S.*) drugstore.
farmacología, *n.f.* pharmacology.
farmacológico, -ca, *a.* pharmacological.
farmacólogo, -ga, *n.m.f.* pharmacologist.
farmacopea, *n.f.* pharmacopoeia.
faro, *n.m.* lighthouse; (*auto.*) headlight; beacon.
farol, *n.m.* lantern; street lamp; (*fam.*) conceited fellow.
farola, *n.f.* large street lamp; beacon.

farra, *n.f.* (*ichth.*) sea trout; (*S.A.*) spree.
fárrago, *n.m.* farrago; hodgepodge.
farro, *n.m.* peeled barley; spelt wheat.
farsa, *n.f.* farce.
farsante, *a.*, *n.m.f.* humbug.
fascículo, *n.m.* fascicle *or* fascicule.
fascinación, *n.f.* fascination, bewitchment.
fascinador, *a.* fascinating.—*n.m.f.* charmer.
fascinante, *a.* fascinating.
fascinar, *v.t.* fascinate, bewitch; allure.
fascismo, *n.m.* fascism.
fascista, *a.*, *n.m.f.* fascist.
fase, *n.f.* phase, stage.
fásol, *n.m.* (*esp. pl.*) French bean; string bean.
fastidiar, *v.t.* sicken; annoy; disappoint.
fastidio, *n.m.* squeamishness; loathing; boredom; fatigue.
fastidioso, -sa, *a.* sickening; annoying; boring; vexed.
fastigio, *n.m.* pinnacle.
fasto, -ta, *a.* auspicious (*event*).—*n.m.* pomp, pageantry.—*pl.* annals.
fastoso, -sa, *a.* pompous, ostentatious.
fatal, *a.* fatal; mortal, deadly; (*fam.*) inevitable.
fatalidad, *n.f.* destiny; ill-fortune; necessity.
fatalismo, *n.m.* fatalism.
fatídico, -ca, *a.* fatidic; fateful.
fatiga, *n.f.* weariness; fatigue; stress.
fatigante, fatigador, -ra, *a.* [FATIGOSO].
fatigar [B], *v.t.* tire; annoy; strain.—*v.r.* get tired.
fatigoso, -sa, *a.* troublesome; wearisome, tiring; tedious.
fatuidad, *n.f.* fatuity; stupidity.
fatuo, -tua, *a.* fatuous; conceited; ***fuego* —,** will-o'-the-wisp.
fauno, *n.m.* faun.
fausto, -ta, *a.* fortunate; prosperous.—*n.m.* splendour; pomp.
faustoso, -sa, *a.* pompous, luxurious.
fautor, -ra, *n.m.f.* abettor, one who countenances.
favor, *n.m.* favour; ***por* —,** please.
favorable, *a.* favourable.
favorecer [9], *v.t.* favour.—*v.r.* avail oneself (***de***, of).
favorito, -ta, *a.*, *n.m.f.* favourite.
fayanca, *n.f.* unsteady posture; ***de* —,** carelessly.
faz, *n.m.* (*pl.* **faces**) face; (*fig.*) **— *a* —,** face to face.
fe, *n.f.* faith; religion; certificate; testimony; ***dar* — *de*,** attest to; **— *de erratas*,** errata slip.
fealdad, *n.f.* ugliness; turpitude.
feble, *a.* feeble, weak; light-weight (*coin*).—*n.m.* foible.
Febo, *n.m.* (*myth.*) Phoebus.
febrero, *n.m.* February.
febril, *a.* febrile.
fécal, *a.* faecal.
fécula, *n.f.* starch.
feculento, -ta, *a.* feculent; starchy.
fecundante, *a.* fertilizing, fecundating.
fecundar, *v.t.* fertilize, fecundate.
fecundidad, *n.f.* fecundity, fruitfulness.
fecundo, -da, *a.* fecund.
fecha, *n.f.* date, time.
fechador, *n.m.* (*S.A.*) cancelling stamp.
fechar, *v.t.* date (*a letter*).
fechoría, *n.f.* misdeed.
federación, *n.f.* federation.
federal, *a.* federal.
federalismo, *n.m.* federalism.
federar, *v.t.* federate.
Federico, *n.m.* Frederick.
fehaciente, *a.* (*jur.*) authentic.
feldespato, *n.m.* (*min.*) feldspar.
felicidad, *n.f.* felicity.
felicitación, *n.f.* congratulation, felicitation.
felicitar, *v.t.* congratulate, felicitate.
félido, -da, *a.* feline.—*n.m.* (*zool.*) felid.
feligrés, -gresa, *n.m.f.* parishioner.
feligresía, *n.f.* parish.
felino, -na, *a.*, *n.m.* feline, (*zool.*) felid.
Felipe, *n.m.* Philip.
feliz, *a.* (*pl.* **-ices**) happy; lucky.
felón, -lona, *a.* treacherous; felonious, criminal.
felonía, *n.f.* treachery.
felpa, *n.f.* plush; (*fam.*) good dressing-down.
felpado, -da, *a.* plushy, velvety.
felpilla, *n.f.* chenille.
felposo, -sa, *a.* plushy, velvety; downy.—*n.m.* mat.
felpudo, *n.m.* mat.
femenil, *a.* feminine, womanish.
femenino, -na, *a.* feminine; (*bot.*) female.
feminidad, *n.f.* feminity.
feminismo, *n.m.* feminism.
fenda, *n.f.* crack, split.
fenecer [9], *v.t.* finish, terminate.—*v.i.* end, die.
fenecimiento, *n.m.* end, termination; death.
fenicio, -cia, *a.*, *n.m.f.* Phoenician.
fénico, -ca, *a.* carbolic.
fénix, *n.m.* (*myth.*) phoenix.
fenol, *n.m.* phenol, carbolic acid.
fenomenal, *a.* phenomenal.
fenómeno, *n.m.* phenomenon.
feo, fea, *a.* ugly; alarming.
feraz, *a.* (*pl.* **-aces**) fertile.
féretro, *n.m.* bier.
feria, *n.f.* fair, market; weekday; holiday; (*S.A.*) tip.
feriado, -da, *a.* ***día* —,** holiday.
feriar, *v.t.* buy; sell.—*v.i.* take a holiday.
ferino, -na, *a.* wild; savage; ***tos ferina*,** whooping cough.
fermentable, *a.* fermentable.
fermentación, *n.f.* fermentation.
fermentar, *v.t.*, *v.i.* ferment.
fermento, *n.m.* ferment, leaven.
Fernando, *n.m.* Ferdinand.
ferocidad, *n.f.* ferocity.
feroz, *a.* (*pl.* **-oces**) ferocious, savage.
ferrar [1], *v.t.* cover with iron.
ferrato, *n.m.* (*chem.*) ferrate.
férreo, -rrea, *a.* iron, ferreous; ***vía férrea*,** railway.
ferrería, *n.f.* ironworks, foundry.
ferrete, *n.m.* sulphate of copper; iron punch.
ferretería, *n.f.* ironmongery, hardware store.
férrico, -ca, *a.* ferric.
ferrocarril, *n.m.* railway, (*U.S.*) railroad.
ferrocarrilero, -ra, *a.*, *n.m.f.* (*S.A.*) railway employee.
ferroconcreto, ferrohormigón, *n.m.* ferroconcrete.
ferroso, -sa, *a.* ferrous.
ferrovía, *n.f.* railway, (*U.S.*) railroad.
ferrovial, *a.* rel. to the railway.

ferroviario, -ria, *a.* rel. to the railway.—*n.m.f.* railway employee.
ferruginoso, -sa, *a.* ferruginous, iron.
fértil, *a.* fertile.
fertilidad, *n.f.* fertility.
fertilización, *n.f.* fertilization.
fertilizante, *a.* fertilizing.—*n.m.* fertilizer (*manure*).
fertilizar [C], *v.t.* fertilize.
férula, *n.f.* ferule, cane; (*fig.*) yoke; (*med.*) splint.
férvido, -da, *a.* fervid.
ferviente, *a.* fervent.
fervor, *n.m.* fervour.
fervoroso, -sa, *a.* fervent.
festejar, *v.t.* fête, entertain; court; (*S.A.*) thrash.
festejo, *n.m.* feast, entertainment; courtship.
festín, *n.m.* banquet.
festival, *n.m.* festival.
festividad, *n.f.* festivity; witticism.
festivo, -va, *a.* gay; festive; witty; ***día —,*** holiday.
fetal, *a.* foetal.
fetiche, *n.m.* fetish.
fetichismo, *n.m.* fetishism.
fetidez, *n.f.* fetidity; stink.
fétido, -da, *a.* fetid, stinking.
feto, *n.m.* foetus.
feudal, *a.* feudal.
feudalidad, *n.f.*, **feudalismo,** *n.m.* feudalism.
feudo, *n.m.* fief; feudal due.
fiable, *a.* trustworthy.
fiado, -da, *a.* trusting; ***al —,*** on credit; ***en —,*** on bail.
fiador, -ra, *n.m.f.* bondsman, guarantor, bail, surety.—*n.m.* pawl; trigger; safety-catch; tumbler (*of lock*).
fiambre, *a.* served cold (*of food*).—*n.m.* cold meat; cold lunch; (*fig.*) stale joke, chestnut.
fiambrera, *n.f.* lunch basket; dinner pail, snap tin.
fianza, *n.f.* guarantee, surety.
fiar [L], *v.t.* guarantee, go surety for; entrust; sell on trust.—*v.r.* trust (***a, de,*** in).
fiasco, *n.m.* fiasco.
fibra, *n.f.* fibre; grain (*of wood*); (*fig.*) vigour.
fibravidrio, *n.m.* fibreglass.
fibroideo, -dea, *a.* fibroid.
fibroso, -sa, *a.* fibrous.
ficción, *n.f.* fiction.
ficcionario, -ria, *a.* fictional.
fice, *n.m.* (*ichth.*) whiting; hake.
ficticio, -cia, *a.* fictitious.
ficha, *n.f.* counter, chip; index-card; (*police*) dossier; ***— perforada,*** punched card.
fichador, -ra, *a.* filing.—*n.m.f.* filing clerk.
fichar, *v.t.* file (*cards, papers etc.*); play (*a piece at dominoes*); (*fam.*) black-list.
fichero, *n.m.* filing cabinet; file.
fidedigno, -na, *a.* reliable, trustworthy.
fideicomisario, *n.m.* trustee; fideicommissary.
fidelidad, *n.f.* fidelity; punctiliousness.
fidelísimo, -ma, *a. sup. of* FIEL.
fideos, *n.m.pl.* vermicelli.
fiduciario, -ria, *a.* fiduciary.
fiebre, *n.f.* fever.
fiel, *a.* faithful, honest; punctilious.—*n.m.* inspector of weights and measures; pointer (*of scales*).
fieltro, *n.m.* felt.
fiereza, *n.f.* ferocity, cruelty; ugliness.
fiero, -ra, *a.* fierce; terrible; cruel; ugly; proud, haughty; wild.—*n.m.pl.* beasts.—*n.f.* wild animal; (*taur.*) bull.
fiesta, *n.f.* feast, holy day; holiday; festivity; ***— brava,*** bullfighting.
figura, *n.f.* figure; countenance; face-card; (*theat.*) character.
figuración, *n.f.* figuration; (*theat.*) extras; (*S.A.*) rôle in society.
figuranta, *n.f.* figurante, ballet-dancer.
figurante, *n.m.* figurant, ballet-dancer.
figurar, *v.t.* figure; depict; feign.—*v.i.* figure, participate.—*v.r.* imagine.
figurativo, -va, *a.* figurative.
figurilla, figurita, *n.f.* figurine; (*fam.*) runt.
figurín, *n.m.* dummy, lay figure; (*fig.*) dandy.
figurón, *n.m.* (*fam.*) pretentious nobody; (*naut.*) ***— de proa,*** figurehead.
fijación, *n.f.* fixation; fastening.
fijador, -ra, *a.* fixing.—*n.m.f.* fixer.—*n.m.* (*phot.*) fixing solution; ***— de pelo,*** hair cream.
fijar, *v.t.* fix, fasten; glue; settle, establish; (*phot.*) fix.—*v.r.* settle; ***fijarse en,*** notice; look closely at.
fijeza, *n.f.* firmness; fixity.
fijo, -ja, *a.* fixed, permanent; firm; secure; ***de —,*** (*S.A.*) ***a la fija,*** surely; without doubt.
fila, *n.f.* row, file, rank; ***en filas,*** (*mil.*) on active service.
filamento, *n.m.* filament.
filantropía, *n.f.* philanthropy.
filantrópico, -ca, *a.* philanthropic(al).
filatelia, *n.f.* philately.
filatura, *n.f.* spinning; spinning-mill.
filete, *n.m.* fillet (*of meat*); welt; thread (*of a screw*).
filfa, *n.f.* (*fam.*) fib, fake, hoax.
filiación, *n.f.* filiation; relationship.
filial, *a.* filial.—*n.f.* (*com.*) affiliate, subsidiary.
filibustero, *n.m.* freebooter.
filigrana, *n.f.* filigree; watermark.
las Filipinas, *n.f.pl.* the Philippines.
filipino, -na, *a.* Filipino *or* Philippine.—*n.m.f.* Filipino.
filisteo, -tea, *a.*, *n.m.f.* Philistine.
film, *n.m.* (*cine.*) film.
filmar, *v.t.* (*cine.*) film.
filo, *n.m.* edge, cutting edge; dividing-line; arris; ***dar — a,*** sharpen; ***por —,*** exactly.
filología, *n.f.* philology.
filológico, -ca, *a.* philological.
filón, *n.m.* (*min.*) vein; lode; (*fig.*) gold mine.
filoseda, *n.f.* silk and wool *or* cotton.
filosofal, *a.* ***piedra —,*** philosopher's stone.
filosofar, *v.i.* philosophize.
filosofía, *n.f.* philosophy.
filosófico, -ca, *a.* philosophic(al).
filtración, *n.f.* filtration.
filtrador, *n.m.* filter.
filtrar, *v.t.* filter.—*v.i.*, *v.r.* filter through, seep through.
filtro, *n.m.* filter; philtre.
filván, *n.m.* wire-edge (*on a tool*).
fimo, *n.m.* dung.
fin, *n.m.* or *f.* end, conclusion.—*n.m.* end, object, purpose; ***al —,*** at last; ***en —, por —,*** finally; ***a fines de,*** towards the end of; ***un sin — de,*** an infinity of.
finado, -da, *a.* dead, deceased, late.

final, *a.* final.—*n.m.* end, conclusion.
finalidad, *n.f.* end, purpose.
finalizar [C], *v.t., v.i.* conclude.
finamiento, *n.m.* decease.
financiero, -ra, *a.* financial.—*n.m.f.* financier.
finar, *v.i.* die.—*v.r.* long for, (*fam.*) be dying for.
finca, *n.f.* property, (real) estate; farm.
fincar [A], *v.i.* buy real estate.—*v.r.* (*esp. S.A.*) reside.
finés, -nesa, *a.* Finnish.—*n.m.f.* Finn.—*n.m.* Finnish (*language*).
fineza, *n.f.* fineness; favour.
fingir [E], *v.t., v.i.* feign, pretend.—*v.r.* pretend to be.
finiquito, *n.m.* (*com.*) final settlement.
finito, -ta, *a.* finite.
finlandés, -desa, *a.* Finnish.—*n.m.f.* Finn.—*n.m.* Finnish (*language*).
Finlandia, *n.f.* Finland.
fino, -na, *a.* fine; sheer; courteous, refined, polite; cunning, shrewd.
finura, *n.f.* fineness; courtesy.
firma, *n.f.* signature; (*com.*) firm.
firmamento, *n.m.* firmament.
firmante, *a., n.m.f.* signatory.
firmar, *v.t., v.i.* sign.
firme, *a.* firm, steady; ***de* —,** steadily, constantly; ***¡ firmes !*** (*mil.*) attention!
firmeza, *n.f.* firmness; resolution.
fiscal, *a.* fiscal.—*n.m.* attorney-general; district attorney.
fiscalizar [C], *v.t.* prosecute; criticize; pry into; inspect; (*rad.*) monitor.
fisco, *n.m.* exchequer, treasury.
fisga, *n.f.* harpoon; banter, chaff.
fisgar [B], *v.t.* harpoon; pry into.—*v.i.* pry; mock.—*v.r.* mock.
fisgón, -na, *n.m.f.* jester, joker; nosey-parker.
físico, -ca, *a.* physical.—*n.m.f.* physicist.—*n.m.* physique; (*obs.*) physician.—*n.f.* physics.
físil, *a.* fissile.
fisiología, *n.f.* physiology.
fisiológico, -ca, *a.* physiological.
fisión, *n.f.* (*phys.*) fission.
fisionomía, *n.f.* physiognomy.
fisioterapia, *n.f.* physiotherapy.
fisonomía, *n.f.* physiognomy.
fistol, *n.m.* crafty person; (*S.A.*) scarf pin.
fístula, *n.f.* (*med.*) fistula; (*mus.*) reed; conduit.
fisura, *n.f.* fissure.
fláccido, -da, *a.* flaccid, soft, lax.
flaco, -ca, *a.* weak; frail; lank, lean.—*n.m.* foible.
flacura, *n.f.* thinness; weakness.
flagelante, *a., n.m.f.* flagellant.
flagelar, *v.t.* flagellate, scourge, flay.
flagelo, *n.m.* whip, scourge.
flagrancia, *n.f.* flagrancy; ardour.
flagrante, *a.* (*poet.*) ardent; rampant; ***en* —,** in the act, red-handed.
flagrar, *v.i.* (*poet.*) blaze.
flamante, *a.* bright; brand-new; spick and span.
flamear, *v.i.* flame; (*naut., aer.*) flutter.
flamenco, -ca, *a.* Flemish; buxom; Andalusian gypsy, flamenco.—*n.m.f.* Fleming.—*n.m.* Flemish (*language*); (*orn.*) flamingo.
flamenquilla, *n.f.* (*bot.*) marigold.
flameo, *n.m.* (*aer.*) flutter.
flámula, *n.f.* streamer.

flan, *n.m.* (*cul.*) crème caramel; custard.
flanco, *n.m.* flank, face; side wall (*of tyre*).
Flandes, *n.m.* (*geog.*) Flanders.
flanquear, *v.t.* flank.
flanqueo, *n.m.* flanking, out-flanking.
flaquear, *v.i.* weaken, flag.
flaqueza, *n.f.* weakness; faintness.
flato, *n.m.* flatus, wind; (*S.A.*) gloominess.
flatulencia, *n.f.* flatulence, wind.
flatulento, -ta, *a.* flatulent.
flauta, *n.f.* (*mus.*) flute.
flautín, *n.m.* (*mus.*) piccolo.
flautista, *n.m.f.* flautist, flute-player.
fleco, *n.m.* fringe.
flecha, *n.f.* arrow.
flechador, *n.m.* archer.
flechar, *v.t.* draw (*the bow*); wound (*with an arrow*); (*fam.*) infatuate.
flechazo, *n.m.* shot with an arrow; love at first sight.
fleje, *n.m.* hoop; strip steel.
flema, *n.f.* phlegm; low wines (*alcohol*).
flemático, -ca, *a.* phlegmatic.
flequillo, *n.m.* fringe (*of hair*).
Flesinga, *n.f.* (*geog.*) Flushing.
fletador, *n.m.* (*naut., aer.*) charterer.
fletamento, *n.m.* chartering; charter party.
fletante, *n.m.* ship-owner.
fletar, *v.t.* (*naut., aer.*) charter; load; (*S.A.*) hire (*animal*).—*v.r.* (*S.A.*) vamoose.
flete, *n.m.* (*naut.*) cargo; (*naut.*) freightage; (*S.A.*) freight; (*S.A.*) horse.
flexibilidad, *n.f.* flexibility.
flexible, *a.* flexible, soft.—*n.m.* (*elec.*) cord, flex.
flexión, *n.f.* flexion; inflexion.
flexional, *a.* flexional; inflexional.
flirtear, *v.i.* flirt.
flojear, *v.i.* slacken.
flojedad, *n.f.* looseness, slackness, laxity.
flojel, *n.m.* nap (*of cloth*); down; ***pato del* —,** (*orn.*) eider.
flojo, -ja, *a.* loose, slack, sagging.
flor, *n.f.* flower; (*fig.*) compliment; ***— de harina,*** fine flour; ***a — de,*** flush with, along the surface of; ***dar en la* —,** get the knack.
floral, *a.* floral.
florar, *v.i.* flower, bloom.
florear, *v.t.* adorn with flowers; bolt (*flour*).—*v.i.* flourish a sword; pay compliments.
florecer [9], *v.i.* flower, bloom; flourish.—*v.r.* go mouldy.
floreciente, *a.* flourishing; blooming.
Florencia, *n.f.* (*geog.*) Florence.
florentino, -na, *a., n.m.f.* Florentine.
floreo, *n.m.* flourish (*in fencing* or *music*); idle talk.
florero, -ra, *a.* flattering; jesting.—*n.m.f.* flatterer; jester; florist.—*n.m.* flowerpot.
floresta, *n.f.* forest, grove; rural pleasance; anthology.
florete, *a.* (*com.*) top-grade.—*n.m.* foil (*in fencing*).
floretear, *v.t.* decorate with flowers.—*v.i.* fence.
Florida, *n.f.* Florida.
florido, -da, *a.* flowery, full of flowers; florid; choice; ***pascua florida,*** Easter.
floridano, -na, *a. n.m.f.* Floridan *or* Floridian.
florilegio, *n.m.* anthology.

florista, *n.m.f.* florist; maker of artificial flowers.
flota, *n.f.* fleet (*ships, cars etc.*).
flotable, *a.* floatable.
flotación, *n.f.* flotation.
flotante, *a.* floating; flowing (*beard*).
flotar, *v.i.* float.
flote, *n.m.* floating; ***a* —,** afloat.
flotilla, *n.f.* flotilla.
flox, *n.m.* (*bot.*) phlox.
fluctuación, *n.f.* fluctuation.
fluctante, *a.* fluctuating.
fluctuar [M], *v.i.* fluctuate.
fluencia, *n.f.* flowing; creep (*metals*).
fluidez, *n.f.* fluidity; fluency (*of style*).
flúido, -da, *a.* fluid; fluent (*language*).—*n.m.* fluid; **— *eléctrico,*** electric current.
fluir [O], *v.i.* flow.
flujo, *n.m.* flow; discharge; flux; rising tide.
flúor, *n.m.* (*chem.*) fluorine.
fluorescente, *a.* fluorescent.
fluorhídrico, -ca, *a.* (*chem.*) hydrofluoric.
fluórico, -ca, *a.* fluoric.
fluorina, fluorita, *n.f.* (*chem.*) fluor spar, fluorite.
fluorización, *n.f.* fluoridation.
fluoruro, *n.m.* (*chem.*) fluoride.
fluvial, *a.* fluvial.
flux, *n.m.* flush (*at cards*); ***hacer* —,** (*fam.*) go bust.
fluxión, *n.f.* fluxion; catarrh, cold in the head.
foca, *n.f.* (*zool.*) seal.
focal, *a.* focal.
foco, *n.m.* focus; centre; core; (*theat.*) spot(light); (*S.A.*) electric light.
focha, *n.f.* (*orn.*) coot.
fofo, -fa, *a.* spongy, soft.—*n.m.* bulk (*papers*).
fogata, *n.f.* blaze; bonfire; fougasse.
fogón, *n.m.* hearth; (cooking) stove; galley; flash-hole.
fogosidad, *n.f.* vehemence; dash, spirit.
fogoso, -sa, *a.* ardent; impetuous.
foja, *n.f.* (*obs., jur.*) leaf, sheet.
foliación, *n.f.* foliation; (*geol.*) rock cleavage.
folio, *n.m.* folio, leaf; ***al primer* —,** straight off; ***de a* —,** (*fam.*) enormous.
folklórico, -ca, *a.* rel. to folklore.
folla, *n.f.* medley, hodge-podge.
follada, *n.f.* (*cul.*) puff-pastry patty.
follaje, *n.m.* foliage; (*fig.*) fustian.
follar (1), *v.t.* foliate, shape like a leaf.
follar (2) [4], *v.t.* blow (*bellows*).
folletín, *n.m.* feuilleton; serial, story.
folletinesco, -ca, *a.* rel. to serial stories; cheap.
folleto, *n.m.* pamphlet, tract, brochure.
follón, -llona, *a.* lazy, indolent; cowardly; laggard.—*n.m.* knave, good-for-nothing.
fomentación, *n.f.* (*med.*) fomentation.
fomentar, *v.t.* foment; promote; encourage, foster.
fomento, *n.m.* development; encouragement; (*med.*) fomentation.
fon, *n.m.* (*phys.*) phone.
fonda, *n.f.* inn; restaurant.
fondillos, *n.m.pl.* seat (*of trousers*).
fondista, *n.m.* innkeeper.
fondo, *n.m.* bottom; back; background; (*fig.*) fund, reserve; ***a* —,** thoroughly; ***artículo de* —,** leading article.—*pl.* funds.
fondón, -dona, *a.* flabby, old.
fonema, *n.m.* phoneme.
fonémico, -ca, *a.* phonemic.—*n.f.* phonemics.
fonético, -ca, *a.* phonetic.—*n.f.* phonetics.
fonetista, *n.m.f.* phonetician.
fonógrafo, *n.m.* gramophone, (*U.S. coll.*) phonograph.
fonología, *n.f.* phonology.
fontanal, fontanar, *n.m.* spring.
fontanería, *n.f.* plumbing; pipelaying; water-supply system.
fontanero, *n.m.* plumber; pipelayer.
foquito, *n.m.* (*S.A.*) flashlight bulb.
forajido, -da, *a., n.m.f.* outlaw.
foral, *a.* (*jur.*) statutory.
forastero, -ra, *a.* outside, strange.—*n.m.f.* outsider, stranger.
forcej(e)ar, *v.i.* struggle.
forcej(e)o, *n.m.* struggling; contention.
forcejudo, -da, *a.* robust, (*U.S. coll.*) husky.
forense, *a.* forensic.
forero, -ra, *a.* statutory.—*n.m.f.* leaseholder.
forestal, *a.* rel. to a forest.
forja, *n.f.* forge, foundry.
forjar, *v.t.* forge (*metal*); forge, falsify.
forma, *n.f.* form; way; format; ***de* — *que,*** so that.
formación, *n.f.* formation; training.
formal, *a.* formal; serious; proper, reliable, definite.
formalidad, *n.f.* formality; seriousness; reliability.
formalismo, *n.m.* formalism; red-tape.
formalizar [C], *v.t.* formalize; formulate.—*v.r.* grow serious; take offence.
formar, *v.t.* form; educate.
formativo, -va, *a.* formative.
formidable, *a.* formidable.
formón, *n.m.* (*carp.*) chisel.
fórmula, *n.f.* formula.
formulación, *n.f.* formulation.
formular, *v.t.* formulate.
fornicación, *n.f.* fornication.
fornicar [A], *v.i.* fornicate.
fornido, -da, *a.* robust, (*U.S. coll.*) husky.
foro, *n.m.* (*hist.*) forum; (*jur.*) bar; rear (*of stage*).
forraje, *n.m.* fodder, forage.
forrajear, *v.t., v.i.* forage.
forrar, *v.t.* line (*clothes*); cover (*books*).
forro, *n.m.* lining; (*naut.*) planking.
fortalecer [9], *v.t.* strengthen; fortify.
fortalecimiento, *n.m.* fortification; tonic.
fortaleza, *n.f.* fortitude, courage; fortress.
fortificación, *n.f.* fortification.
fortificante, *a.* fortifying.
fortificar [A], *v.t.* fortify; corroborate.
fortuito, -ta, *a.* fortuitous.
fortuna, *n.f.* fortune, chance; tempest; ***por* —,** luckily.
forúnculo, *n.m.* (*med.*) boil.
forzado, -da, *a.* forced.—*n.m.* convict, galley-slave.
forzador, *n.m.* ravisher.
forzal, *n.m.* back (*of a comb*).
forzar [4C], *v.t.* force; constrain.
forzoso, -sa, *a.* unavoidable, obligatory; strong.
forzudo, -da, *a.* robust, (*U.S. coll.*) husky.
fosa, *n.f.* grave; pit; **— *séptica,*** septic tank.
fosca, *n.f.* haze.
fosco, -ca, *a.* sullen, dour.
fosfático, -ca, *a.* (*chem.*) phosphatic.
fosfato, *n.m.* (*chem.*) phosphate.

fosforecer [9], *v.i.* phosphoresce.
fosforero, -ra, *n.m.f.* match-seller.—*n.f.* matchbox.
fosforescencia, *n.f.* phosphorescence.
fosforescente, *a.* phosphorescent.
fosfórico, -ca, *a.* (*chem.*) phosphoric.
fósforo, *n.m.* (*chem.*) phosphorus; match; (*poet.*) morning star.
fosforoso, -sa, *a.* phosphorous.
fosfuro, *n.m.* (*chem.*) phosphide.
fósil, *a.* fossile.—*n.m.* fossil (*also fig.*).
fosilización, *n.f.* fossilization.
fosilizar [C], *v.r.* become fossilized.
foso, *n.m.* pit, hole; moat.
fotingo, *n.m.* (*S.A. coll.*) jalopy.
fotocelda, fotocélula, *n.f.* photocell.
fotograbado, *n.m.* photogravure.
fotografía, *n.f.* photography; photograph.
fotografiar [L], *v.t., v.i.* photograph.
fotográfico, -ca, *a.* photographic.
fotógrafo, -fa, *n.m.f.* photographer.
fototipia, *n.f.* phototypy.
foz [HOZ].
frac, *n.m.* swallow-tailed coat, tails.
fracasar, *v.i.* fail.
fracaso, *n.m.* failure, collapse.
fracción, *n.f.* fraction.
fraccionar, *v.t.* divide into fractions, break up; crack (*oil*).
fraccionario, -ria, *a.* fractional.
fractura, *n.f.* fracture.
fracturar, *v.i., v.r.* fracture.
fragancia, *n.f.* fragrance.
fragante, *a.* fragrant; ***en* —,** [EN FLAGRANTE].
fragata, *n.f.* (*naut.*) frigate; ***capitán de* —,** commander.
frágil, *a.* fragile, frail; weak (*morally*); (*S.A.*) needy.
fragilidad, *n.f.* fragility; moral lapse.
fragmentación, *n.f.* fragmentation.
fragmentar, *v.t.* fragment.
fragmentario, -ria, *a.* fragmentary.
fragmento, *n.m.* fragment.
fragor, *n.m.* din, uproar.
fragosidad, *n.f.* roughness (*of terrain*).
fragoso, -sa, *a.* rough (*terrain*); noisy.
fragua, *n.f.* forge, smithy; (*fig.*) hotbed.
fraguar [H], *v.t.* forge (*iron, lies, plots*).—*v.i.* set (*concrete*).
fraile, *n.m.* friar; — ***rezador,*** (*ent.*) praying mantis.
frailecillo, *n.m.* (*orn.*) lapwing; puffin.
frailengo, -ga, fraileño, -ña, frailuno, -na, *a.* monkish, friar-like.
frambesia, *n.f.* (*med.*) yaws.
frambuesa, *n.f.* raspberry (*fruit*).
frambueso, *n.m.* raspberry(-cane).
francachela, *n.f.* (*fam.*) feast, spread.
francés, -cesa, *a.* French.—*n.m.* Frenchman; French (*language*).—*n.f.* Frenchwoman; ***irse a la francesa,*** take French leave.
Francia, *n.f.* France.
franciscano, -na, *a., n.m.f.* Franciscan.
francmasón, *n.m.* Freemason, mason.
francmasonería, *n.f.* Freemasonry.
franco, -ca, *a.* frank; liberal; free; Frankish; — ***a bordo,*** free on board; — ***de porte,*** postpaid; ***puerto* —,** free port.—*n.m.f.* Frank.—*n.m.* franc.
francoalemán, -mana, *a.* Franco-German.
francobordo, *n.m.* (*naut.*) freeboard.
franchote, -ta, franchute, -ta, *n.m.f.* (*pej.*) Frenchy, Froggy.
franela, *n.f.* flannel (*also fig.*).
frangible, *a.* brittle.
franja, *n.f.* fringe, strip.
franquear, *v.t.* exempt; enfranchise; manumit; frank (*a letter*).—*v.r.* yield; unbosom oneself.
franqueo, *n.m.* manumission; postage.
franqueza, *n.f.* liberty; sincerity.
franquicia, *n.f.* franchise; exemption, privilege.
franquista, *a., n.m.f.* rel. to supporters of Gen. Franco.
frasco, *n.m.* flask.
frase, *n.f.* phrase; sentence; epigram.
fraternal, *a.* fraternal.
fraternidad, *n.f.* fraternity.
fraternizar [C], *v.i.* fraternize.
fraterno, -na, *a.* fraternal.—*n.f.* reprimand.
fratría, *n.f.* phratry, siblings.
fratricida, *a.* fratricidal.—*n.m.f.* fratricide (*person*).
fratricidio, *n.m.* fratricide (*crime*).
fraude, *n.m.* fraud.
fraudulento, -ta, *a.* fraudulent.
fray, *n.m.* Brother (*title used in certain orders*), Fra.
frazada, *n.f.* blanket.
frecuencia, *n.f.* frequency.
frecuentación, *n.f.* frequentation.
frecuentar, *v.t.* frequent, haunt; repeat.
frecuente, *a.* frequent.
fregadero, *n.m.* sink.
fregador, -ra, *n.m.f.* dish-washer.—*n.m.* dish-cloth, dish-mop.
fregadura, *n.f.,* **fregamiento,** *n.m.* dish-washing, (*Brit.*) washing-up.
fregar [1B], *v.t.* rub; scrub; mop, scour; (*Brit.*) wash up, (*U.S.*) wash (*the dishes*); (*S.A.*) annoy.
fregona, *n.f.* kitchen-maid.
freidura, *n.f.* frying.
freile, *n.m.* knight *or* priest of a military order.
freír [28, *p.p.* **frito**], *v.t.* fry.
fréjol [FRIJOL].
frenar, *v.t.* brake, check; lock (*nuts*).
frenero, *n.m.* bridle-maker; (*rail.*) brakeman.
frenesí, *n.m.* (*pl.* **-íes**) frenzy, madness.
frenético, -ca, *a.* mad, frantic.
freno, *n.m.* bit; bridle; brake; restraint.
frenología, *n.f.* phrenology.
frental, *a.* frontal, rel. to the forehead.
frente, *n.f.* forehead, brow; countenance.—*n.m.* or *f.* front, fore part; obverse.—*n.m.* (*mil., pol.*) front.—*prep.* — ***a,*** opposite; vis-à-vis; ***en* — *de,*** opposite.—*adv.* ***a* —,** straight ahead; ***al* —,** (*com.*) carried forward; ***del* —,** (*com.*) brought forward; ***de* —,** forward, abreast.
fresa, *n.f.* strawberry; milling tool, cutter.
fresadora, *n.f.* milling machine, miller.
fresal, *n.m.* strawberry bed.
fresar, *v.t.* mill.
frescachón, -chona, *a.* bouncing, buxom.
frescal, *a.* slightly salted.
fresco, -ca, *a.* fresh, cool; recent; (*fam.*) fresh, cheeky; fresh (*breeze*); ruddy; ***quedarse tan* —,** not turn a hair.—*n.m.* fresh air; (*S.A.*) cool drink; (*art.*) fresco.—*n.f.* fresh air, cool.

frescor, *n.m.* freshness; (*art.*) flesh tint.
frescura, *n.f.* coolness; cheek, insolence.
fresneda, *n.f.* ash-grove.
fresno, *n.m.* ash-tree.
fresquera, *n.f.* ice-box, meat-safe.
frey, *n.m.* Brother (*title used in certain military orders*).
frez, *n.f.* dung.
freza, *n.f.* dung; spawning season; spawn.
frezar [C], *v.i.* dung; spawn; root (*of pigs*).
friabilidad, *n.f.* friability, brittleness.
friable, *a.* friable; brittle.
frialdad, *n.f.* coldness; frigidity.
fricasé, *n.m.* (*cul.*) fricassee.
fricción, *n.f.* friction; embrocation.
friega, *n.f.* rubbing, massage; (*S.A.*) drubbing, (*S.A.*) nuisance.
friera, *n.f.* chilblain.
frigidez, *n.f.* frigidity, coldness.
frigorífico, -ca, *a.* refrigerating.—*n.m.* refrigerator; cold-store; (*S.A.*) meat-packing plant.
fríjol, frijol, *n.m.* kidney-bean; ***frijol de media luna,*** butter-bean, (*U.S.*) Lima bean.
frijolar, *n.m.* bean-patch.
frío, fría, *a.* cold; ***hacer* —,** be cold (*weather*); ***tener* —,** be cold (*person*); ***tomar* —,** catch cold.—*n.m.* cold(ness).
friolento, -ta, *a.* chilly.
friolera, *n.f.* trifle, bauble.
frisa, *n.f.* frieze; gasket.
frisar, *v.t.* frieze, frizz (*cloth*); (*naut.*) pack.—*v.i.* resemble; **— *con,*** border on, approach.
frisón, -sona, *a., n.m.f.* Friesian.
frito, -ta, *p.p.* [FREIR].—*n.m.* fry.
frivolidad, *n.f.* frivolity.
frívolo, -la, *a.* frivolous.
frondosidad, *n.f.* foliage, luxuriant growth.
frondoso, -sa, *a.* leafy.
frontal, *a.* frontal, rel. to the forehead.—*n.m.* frontal.
frontera, *n.f.* frontier, border, boundary; frontage.
frontero, -ra, *a.* opposite.
frontispicio, *n.m.* frontispiece.
frontón, *n.m.* (*arch.*) pediment; front wall (*in pelota*); (fives-)court (*for pelota*).
frotador, -ra, *a.* rubbing.—*n.m.* (*elec.*) shoe, brush.
frotante, *a.* rubbing.
frotar, *v.t.* rub.
fructificar [A], *v.i.* bear fruit.
fructuoso, -sa, *a.* fruitful, profitable.
fruente, *a.* enjoying.
frugal, *a.* frugal.
frugalidad, *n.f.* frugality.
frugívoro, -ra, *a.* frugivorous, fruit-eating.
fruición, *n.f.* fruition; enjoyment.
fruir [O], *v.i.* be gratified, enjoy oneself.
frunce, *n.m.* gather, shirr (*sewing*).
fruncir [D], *v.t.* pucker; shirr (*sewing*).—*v.r.* affect modesty.
fruslería, *n.f.* bauble.
fruslero, -ra, *a.* trifling, futile.—*n.f.* bauble.
frustración, *n.f.* frustration.
frustrar, *v.t.* frustrate, disappoint, baulk.—*v.r.* miscarry, fall through.
fruta, *n.f.* fruit (*esp. as food*); result; **— *de sartén,*** pancake.
frutal, *a.* fruit (*tree*).—*n.m.* fruit-tree.
frutería, *n.f.* fruit-shop, fruiterers.
frutero, -ra, *a.* rel. to fruit.—*n.m.f.* fruiterer.—*n.m.* fruit dish.
fruto, *n.m.* fruit (*as containing seed*); (*esp. fig.*) fruit(s), result; ***dar* —,** yield fruit; ***sin* —,** fruitlessly.
¡fu! *interj.* fie! faugh! phooey!
fucilar, *v.i.* flash.
fucilazo, *n.m.* (heat-)lightning.
fucsia, *n.f.* (*bot.*) fuchsia.
fue [SER *&* IR].
fuego, *n.m.* fire; light (*for a cigarette etc.*); hearth; (*mil.*) fire; ***fuegos artificiales,*** fireworks.
fuelle, *n.m.* bellows; blower.
fuente, *n.f.* fountain, spring; source; font; platter, dish; **— *de gasolina,*** petrol pump.
fuer, *adv.* ***a* — *de,*** in the manner of.
fuera, *adv.* without, outside; **— *de,*** out of besides; **— *de sí,*** beside oneself; ***estar* —,** not be at home.
fuero, *n.m.* law, statute; privilege, charter; **— *interior* or *interno,*** conscience.
fuerte, *a.* strong; heavy-weight; hard.—*adv.* hard; loud; heavily.—*n.m.* fort.
fuerza, *n.f.* strength; power; (*phys.*) force.—*n.f.pl.* forces, troops.
fuete, *n.m.* (*S.A.*) whip.
fuga, *n.f.* escape, leak; flight; ardour; (*mus.*) fugue.
fugar [B], *v.r.* flee, run away.
fugaz, *a.* (*pl.* **-aces**) fleeting, fugitive, brief.
fugitivo, -va, *a.* fugitive, brief.
fuina, *n.f.* (*zool.*) marten.
fulano, -na, *n.m.f.* such a one, so-and-so; **—, *zutano y mengano,*** Tom, Dick and Harry.
fulcro, *n.m.* fulcrum.
fulgente, *a.* refulgent.
fulgor, *n.m.* resplendence.
fulgurante, *a.* resplendent.
fulgurar, *v.i.* flash.
fuliginoso, -sa, *a.* fuliginous, obscure.
fulminante, *a.* fulminating.—*n.m.* percussion cap.
fulminar, *v.t., v.i.* fulminate.
fullero, -ra, *a.* cheating.—*n.m.f.* cheat, crook.
fumable, *a.* smokable.
fumadero, *n.m.* smoking-room.
fumador, -ra, *n.m.f.* smoker.
fumante, *a.* smoking; fuming.
fumar, *v.t., v.i.* smoke.—*v.r.* waste; ***fumarse la clase,*** to play truant.
fumigar [B], *v.t.* fumigate.
fumigatorio, -ria, *a.* fumigatory.
fumista, *n.m.* stove maker; stove repairer.
funambulesco, -ca, *a.* funambulatory; extravagant.
funámbulo, -la, *n.m.f.* tight-rope walker.
función, *n.f.* function.
funcional, *a.* functional.
funcionar, *v.i.* work, function; be in working order.
funcionario, -ria, *n.m.f.* functionary, civil servant.
funda, *n.f.* case; sheath; cover; holdall; **— *de almohada,*** pillow-slip.
fundación, *n.f.* foundation.
fundadamente, *adv.* with good reason.
fundador, -ra, *a.* founding.—*n.m.f.* founder.
fundamental, *a.* fundamental.
fundamentar, *v.t.* found; lay the basis for.

fundamento, *n.m.* foundation; grounds; trustworthiness; weft, woof.
fundar, *v.t.* found, base.
fundente, *a.* fusing, melting.—*n.m.* (*chem.*) flux, fluxing agent.
fundería, *n.f.* foundry.
fundible, *a.* fusible.
fundición, *n.f.* fusion; fuse, blow-out; melting; (*print.*) fount.
fundillo, *n.m.* (*S.A.*) behind.—*pl.* seat (*of trousers*).
fundir, *v.t.* fuse; smelt; cast; merge.—*v.r.* melt; fuse; merge.
fundo, *n.m.* rural property.
fúnebre, *a.* funereal; funeral.
funeral, *a.* funereal; funeral.—*n.m. esp. pl.* funeral.
funerario, -ria, *a.* funeral, funerary.—*n.m.* undertaker, (*U.S.*) mortician.—*n.f.* undertaking establishment.
funesto, -ta, *a.* fatal, ill-fated; doleful.
fungir [E], *v.i.* (*S.A.*) function, be employed.
fungoso, -sa, *a.* fungous.
funicular, *a.*, *n.m.* funicular.
furgón, *n.m.* van.
furgoneta, *n.f.* light truck, delivery truck *or* van.
furia, *n.f.* fury; rage.
furibundo, -da, *a.* furious.
furioso, -sa, *a.* furious, infuriated.
furor, *n.m.* fury; rage.
furriel, furrier, *n.m.* quartermaster.
furtivo, -va, *a.* furtive.
furúnculo, *n.m.* (*med.*) boil.
fusa, *n.f.* (*mus.*) demi-semiquaver.
fusco, -ca, *a.* brown, dark.
fuselaje, *n.m.* (*aer.*) fuselage.
fusibilidad, *n.f.* fusibility.
fusible, *a.* fusible.—*n.m.* fuse.
fusil, *n.m.* rifle, gun.
fusilar, *v.t.* shoot, kill by shooting.
fusión, *n.f.* fusion, melting; — ***de empresas,*** (*com.*) merger.
fusta (1), *n.f.* brushwood.
fusta (2), *n.f.* (*naut.*) small lateen-rigged vessel.
fustán, *n.m.* fustian.
fuste, *n.m.* wood; shaft; shank; substance, importance.
fustigar [B], *v.t.* lash; censure severely.
fútbol, *n.m.* football.
futbolista, *n.m.* footballer.
futesa, *n.f.* trifle.
fútil, *a.* futile; worthless.
futilidad, *n.f.* futility.
futre, *n.m.* (*S.A.*) fop, (*U.S.*) dude.
futuro, -ra, *a.* future, forthcoming.—*n.m.f.* (*fam.*) fiancé(e).—*n.m.* (*gram.*) future; future.

G

G, g, *n.f.* eighth letter of the Spanish alphabet.
gabacho, -cha, *a.*, *n.m.f.* (*fam. pej.*) Froggie, Frenchie.
gabán, *n.m.* overcoat.
gabardina, *n.f.* gabardine; raincoat.
gabarra, *n.f.* lighter, barge.
gabarro, *n.m.* flaw; error; bother.
gabela, *n.f.* tax, duty.
gabinete, *n.m.* study; cabinet; boudoir; lavatory.
gacel, -la, *n.m.f.* (*zool.*) gazelle.
gaceta, *n.f.* gazette; (*S.A.*) newspaper.
gacetero, *n.m.* gazetteer; newspaper vendor.
gacetilla, *n.f.* gossip column.
gacetillero, *n.m.* gossip writer.
gacha, *n.f.* mush.—*pl.* pap, sops.
gacho, -cha, *a.* drooping; ***a gachas,*** (*fam.*) on all fours.
gachón, -chona, *a.* (*fam.*) nice, sweet.
gachumbo, *n.m.* (*S.A.*) gourd, pot.
gachupín, -pina, *n.m.f.* (*C.A. pej.*) Spanish settler.
gaditano, -na, *a.*, *n.m.f.* rel. to *or* native of Cadiz.
gafa, *n.f.* hook.—*pl.* glasses, spectacles.
gafar, *v.t.* hook, claw.
gafe, *n.m.* (*fam.*) jinx, Jonah.
gafete, *n.m.* hook and eye.
gafo, -fa, *a.* claw-handed, leprous.—*n.m.* (*fam.*) jinx.
gago, -ga, *a.* (*S.A.*, *dial.*) stammering.
gaita, *n.f.* bagpipe; (*fam.*) neck; (*fam.*) bother.
gaje, *n.m.* wage; ***gajes del oficio,*** (*joc.*) snags that go with the job, occupational hazards.
gajo, *n.m.* broken branch; cluster; pip; quarter (*of lemon etc.*); prong; spur; foothills.
gala, *n.f.* gala, elegance, finery; ***de —,*** in full dress; ***hacer — de,*** show off, glory in.—*pl.* regalia; talents; delights.
galafate, *n.m.* sneak-thief.
galaico, -ca, *a.* Galician.
galán, *a.* [GALANO].—*n.m.* gallant, beau; (*theat.*) male lead.
galano, -na, *a.* smart, spruce, elegant.
galante, *a.* elegant, courtly; attentive to women; coquettish.
galantear, *v.t.* woo, flirt with.
galanteo, *n.m.* wooing, flirting.
galantería, *n.f.* courtesy, elegance; gallantry; generosity.
galanura, *n.f.* finery, elegance; charm.
galápago, *n.m.* tortoise, turtle; ingot; (*fam.*) sharper.
galardón, *n.m.* reward, guerdon.
galaxia, *n.f.* (*astr.*) Galaxy, Milky Way.
galbana, *n.f.* (*fam.*) idleness, laziness.
galbanoso, -sa, *a.* (*fam.*) shiftless, idle.
galeón, *n.m.* (*naut.*) galleon.
galeote, *n.m.* galley slave; (*obs.*) convict.
galera, *n.f.* (*naut.*, *print.*) galley; large cart; hospital ward; women's prison; (*carp.*) jack plane.—*pl.* galleys (*as penal sentence*).
galería, *n.f.* gallery.
galerín, *n.m.* (*print.*) galley.
Gales, *n.f.* ***el país de —,*** Wales.
galés, -lesa, *a.*, *n.m.* Welsh.—*n.m.f.* Welshman, Welshwoman.
galfarro, *n.m.* loafer.
galgo, -ga, *n.m.f.* greyhound.
Galia, *n.f.* Gaul.
gálibo, *n.m.* template.
galicano, -na, *a.* (*eccl.*) Gallican.
Galicia, *n.f.* Galicia.
galicismo, *n.m.* Gallicism.

galicista, *a.* gallicizing.—*n.m.f.* gallicizer.
galimatías, *n.m.* rigmarole, gibberish.
galiparla, *n.f.* Frenchified Spanish.
galo, -la, *a.* Gallic.—*n.m.f.* Gaul.
galocha, *n.f.* wooden shoe.
galófobo, -ba, *a., n.m.f.* Gallophobe.
galomanía, *n.f.* Gallomania.
galón, *n.m.* galloon, braid; gallon.
galonear, *v.t.* braid.
galopada, *n.f.* gallop, galloping.
galopar, *v.i.* gallop.
galope, *n.m.* gallop.
galopear, *v.i.* gallop.
galopillo, *n.m.* scullion.
galopo, *n.m.* rogue.
galvanismo, *n.m.* galvanism.
galvanizar [C], *v.t.* galvanize.
gallardear, *v.i., v.r.* be elegant, gallant.
gallardete, *n.m.* pennant, riband.
gallardía, *n.f.* elegance, nobility, gallantry.
gallardo, -da, *a.* elegant, gallant, brave; strong.
gallego, -ga, *a., n.m.f.* Galician; (*S.A.*) Spaniard.
gallera, *n.f.* cockpit.
galleta, *n.f.* biscuit; anthracite; (*fam.*) slap.
gallina, *n.f.* hen.—*n.m.f.* (*fam.*) coward, chicken.
gallinazo, -za, *n.m.f.* (*S.A.*) buzzard.—*n.f.* hen dung.
gallinero, -ra, *n.m.f.* chicken merchant.—*n.m.* hencoop; (*theat.*) gods, gallery; bedlam.
gallipuente, *n.m.* foot-bridge.
gallito, *n.m.* beau, coxcomb.
gallo, *n.m.* cock; false note; (*fam.*) boss; (*fam.*) cockiness; — ***en la garganta,*** frog in the throat.
gallofero, -ra, gallofo, -fa, *a.* begging, scrounging.—*n.m.f.* beggar, scrounger.
gallón, *n.m.* clod, sod.
gama, *n.f.* gamut; [GAMO].
gamba, *n.f.* shrimp, prawn.
gamberrismo, *n.m.* hooliganism.
gamberro, -rra, *a., n.m.f.* rowdy, hooligan.
gambeta, *n.f.* prance, caper.
gambito, *n.m.* gambit.
gamo, -ma, *n.m.f.* (*zool.*) fallow-deer.
gamuza, *n.f.* chamois.
gana, *n.f.* desire; ***de buena —,*** willingly; ***de mala —,*** unwillingly; ***me da la — de,*** I feel like (*doing etc.*); ***tener ganas de,*** feel like, have a mind to.
ganadería, *n.f.* ranch; ranching; livestock.
ganadero, -ra, *a.* ranching, rel. to cattle breeding.—*n.m.f.* stock breeder, cattle raiser.
ganado, *n.m.* cattle; livestock; (*fam.*) swarm, mob; — ***caballar,*** horses; — ***lanar,*** sheep; — ***mayor,*** cattle, horses, mules; — ***menor,*** sheep, goats, pigs.
ganador, -ra, *a.* earning.—*n.m.f.* winner; earner.
ganancia, *n.f.* profit, gain.
ganancioso, -sa, *a.* profitable; gaining.
ganapán, *n.m.* odd-job man; lout.
ganar, *v.t.* win, gain; earn; beat, defeat; reach.—*v.i.* win, gain.—*v.r.* earn; win over; (*S.A.*) run off.
ganchillo, *n.m.* crocheting hook; crochet.
gancho, *n.m.* hook; (*fam.*) sponger.
ganchoso, -sa, ganchudo, -da, *a.* hooked.
gándara, *n.f.* wasteland.
gandaya, *n.f.* loafing, scrounging.
gandul, -la, *a.* (*fam.*) bone-idle.—*n.m.f.* idler.
gandulear, *v.i.* laze, loaf.
gandulería, *n.f.* (*fam.*) idleness, laziness.
ganga, *n.f.* (*orn.*) sand grouse; (*fig.*) bargain.
gangoso, -sa, *a.* snuffling, with a cold in the nose.
gangrena, *n.f.* gangrene.
gángster, *n.m.* gangster.
gangsterismo, *n.m.* gangsterism.
ganguear, *v.i.* snuffle.
ganguero, -ra, ganguista, *n.m.f.* self-seeker; bargain-hunter; (*fam.*) lucky blighter.
ganoso, -sa, *a.* desirous.
gansarón, *n.m.* gander.
ganso, -sa, *n.m.f.* ninny, bumpkin.—*n.m.* (*orn.*) goose, gander.
Gante, *n.f.* Ghent.
ganzúa, *n.f.* lock-picker; (*fig.*) wheedler.
gañán, *n.m.* farm labourer.
gañido, *n.m.* yelp, yell, howl.
gañir, *v.i.* yelp, howl; croak.
gañón, gañote, *n.m.* (*fam.*) gizzard, throat.
garabatear, *v.t.* scribble.—*v.i.* hook; mess about.
garabato, *n.m.* hook; pothook, scrawl.
garabatoso, -sa, *a.* scribbly; attractive.
garabito, *n.m.* market stall.
garage, garaje, *n.m.* garage.
garambaina, *n.f.* ugly trinket.—*pl.* (*fam.*) simpering; (*fam.*) scrawl.
garante, *n.m.* guarantor.
garantía, *n.f.* guarantee.
garantir [Q], **garantizar** [C], *v.t.* guarantee.
garañón, *n.m.* stud donkey; (*S.A.*) stallion.
garapiña, *n.f.* (*cul.*) icing; braid.
garapiñar, *v.t.* ice, sugar-coat.
garatusa, *n.f.* (*fam.*) wheedling.
garbanzo, *n.m.* chick-pea.
garbear, *v.i.* put on airs.
garbillo, *n.m.* sieve.
garbo, *n.m.* jauntiness, elegance; nobility.
garboso, -sa, *a.* jaunty, elegant.
garbullo, *n.m.* rumpus, ructions.
garceta, *n.f.* egret.
garduño, -ña, *n.m.f.* sneak-thief.—*n.f.* (*zool.*) marten.
garfa, *n.f.* claw.
garfio, *n.m.* gaff, hook; climbing iron.
gargajear, *v.i.* clear one's throat.
gargajeo, *n.m.* clearing of one's throat, spitting.
gargajo, *n.m.* phlegm.
garganta, *n.f.* throat, neck; gorge.
gargantear, *v.i.* warble.
gárgara, *n.f.* gargle, gargling.
gargarismo, *n.m.* gargle (*liquid*).
gargarizar [C], *v.i.* gargle.
garita, *n.f.* box, cabin.
garlocha, *n.f.* goad.
garra, *n.f.* claw, talon; (*fig.*) clutch.
garrafa, *n.f.* carafe.
garrafiñar, *v.t.* (*fam.*) grab, snatch.
garramar, *v.t.* (*fam.*) pinch, steal.
garrapata, *n.f.* (*zool.*) tick.
garrapatear, *v.i.* scribble.
garrapato, *n.m.* pothook, scrawl.
garrido, -da, *a.* comely.
garrocha, *n.f.* goad; vaulting pole.
garrón, *n.m.* talon, spur.

garrote, *n.m.* cudgel; garrotte; (*C.A.*) brake.
garrotero, *n.m.* (*S.A.*) thug; (*C.A.*) brakeman.
garrotillo, *n.m.* (*med.*) croup.
garrucha, *n.f.* pulley.
gárrulo, -la, *a.* garrulous.
garulla, *n.f.* (single) grape; (*fam.*) bunch, mob.
garza, *n.f.* (*orn.*) heron; crane.
garzo, -za, *a.* blue.
garzón, *n.m.* lad, stripling.
garzota, *n.f.* (*orn.*) night heron; plume.
gas, *n.m.* gas; — ***de guerra*** or ***tóxico,*** poison gas; — (*ex*)***hilarante,*** laughing gas.
gasa, *n.f.* muslin; mourning crêpe.
gascón, -cona, *a., n.m.f.* Gascon.
gasconada, *n.f.* gasconade, bravado.
gaseoso, -sa, *a.* gaseous.—*n.f.* mineral water, (*fam.*) pop.
gasificar [A], *v.t.* gasify.
gasista, *n.m.* gas fitter.
gasolina, *n.f.* petrol; (*U.S.*) gasoline, gas.
gasómetro, *n.m.* gasometer.
gastado, -da, *a.* spent, worn-out.
gastamiento, *n.m.* consumption, wear.
gastar, *v.t.* spend; use up; waste; use very often; play (*jokes*); wear out.
gasto, *n.m.* outlay, expense; wear, use; waste.
gastoso, -sa, *a.* costly; wasteful.
gástrico, -ca, *a.* gastric.
gastronomía, *n.f.* gastronomy.
gastronómico, -ca, *a.* gastronomic.
gastrónomo, -ma, *n.m.f.* gastronome, gourmet.
gata, *n.f.* she-cat; (*fam.*) Madrid woman; ***a gatas,*** on all fours.
gatallón, *n.m.* (*fam.*) cheat, rogue.
gatatumba, *n.f.* (*fam.*) pretence, shamming, show.
gatear, *v.t.* (*fam.*) scratch; (*fam.*) pinch, steal.—*v.i.* clamber; crawl; (*S.A.*) philander.
gatería, *n.f.* bunch of cats; (*fam.*) gang; (*fam.*) guile.
gatillo, *n.m.* trigger, hammer (*of gun*).
gato, *n.m.* cat, tom-cat; money-bag; (*mech.*) jack; clamp; (*fam.*) pickpocket; (*fam.*) Madrid man; hook; — ***encerrado,*** fly in the ointment; ***vender — por liebre,*** (*fam.*) pull a fast one.
gatuno, -na, *a.* catlike.
gauchesco, -ca, *a.* Gaucho.
gaucho, -cha, *a., n.m.f.* Gaucho; (*fig.*) rustic.
gaveta, *n.f.* drawer (*in desk*); till.
gavia, *n.f.* ditch; (*orn.*) gull; padded cell; (*naut.*) top-sail.
gavieta, *n.f.* (*naut.*) crow's nest.
gavilán, *n.m.* (*orn.*) sparrow-hawk; hair-stroke (*in penmanship*); quillon (*of sword*); metal tip.
gavilla, *n.f.* sheaf; (*fam.*) gang.
gaviota, *n.f.* (*orn.*) sea-gull.
gavota, *n.f.* gavotte.
gaya, *n.f.* stripe; magpie.
gayo, -ya, *a.* merry, gay; ***gaya ciencia,*** poesy.—*n.m.* jay.
gayola, *n.f.* cage; (*fam.*) clink; vineyard watch-tower.
gazapa, *n.f.* (*fam.*) fib, lie.
gazapatón, *n.m.* (*fam.*) howler, bloomer.
gazapina, *n.f.* gang; brawl.
gazapo, *n.m.* young rabbit; (*fam.*) twister; (*fam.*) howler.
gazmoñero, -ra, gazmoño, -ña, *a.* prudish, priggish.
gaznápiro, *n.m.* boob, churl.
gaznate, *n.m.* gullet; fritter.
gazpacho, *n.m.* gazpacho, cold soup.
gazuza, *n.f.* (*fam.*) hunger.
ge, *n.f.* name of letter G.
gea, *n.f.* mineral geography.
géiser, *n.m.* geyser.
gelatina, *n.f.* gelatine.
gélido, -da, *a.* (*poet.*) gelid, frigid.
gema, *n.f.* gem; (*bot.*) bud.
gemelo, -la, *a., n.m.f.* twin.—*n.m.pl.* pair of theatre glasses *or* cuff links; (*astr.*) Gemini.
gemido, *n.m.* groan, moan.
Geminis, *n.m.* (*astr.*) Gemini.
gemir [8], *v.i.* groan; whine; roar.
gen, *n.m.* gene.
genealogía, *n.f.* genealogy.
genealógico, -ca, *a.* genealogical.
genealogista, *n.m.f.* genealogist.
generación, *n.f.* generation.
generador, -ra, *a.* generating.—*n.m.* generator.
general, *a., n.m.* general; (*aer.*) air marshal; — ***de brigada,*** brigadier.
generala, *n.f.* general's wife; call to arms.
generalidad, *n.f.* generality; Catalonian Parliament.
generalísimo, *n.m.* generalissimo.
generalización, *n.f.* generalization.
generalizar [C], *v.t.* generalize.—*v.r.* become general.
generar, *v.t.* generate.
genérico, -ca, *a.* generic; common (*noun*).
género, *n.m.* kind, type; genus, class; genre; gender; — ***humano,*** human race, mankind. —*pl.* goods, wares.
generosidad, *n.f.* generosity; nobility.
generoso, -sa, *a.* generous; noble; brave; superb.
Génesis, *n.m.* (*Bib.*) Genesis; **génesis,** *n.f.* genesis.
genet(ic)ista, *n.m.f.* geneticist.
genético, -ca, *a.* genetic.—*n.f.* genetics.
genetista, *n.m.f.* geneticist.
geniado, *a.* ***bien* —,** good-tempered; ***mal* —,** bad-tempered.
genial, *a.* brilliant, of genius; temperamental; pleasant.
genialidad, *n.f.* natural disposition; genius.
genio, *n.m.* temperament, disposition; character, spirit; genius; genie, jinn; ***mal* —,** bad temper.
genital, *a.* genital.
genitivo, -va, *a., n.m.* (*gram.*) genitive.
genocidio, *n.m.* genocide.
Génova, *n.f.* Genoa.
genovés, -vesa, *a., n.m.f.* Genoese.
gente, *n.f.* people; troops; nation; (*fam.*) family; (*S.A.*) a somebody; — ***de bien,*** decent people; — ***principal,*** gentry.
gentecilla, *n.f.* the rabble.
gentil, *a.* genteel; Gentile.—*n.m.f.* Gentile.
gentileza, *n.f.* gentility, elegance; courtesy.
gentilhombre, *n.m.* gentleman; good man.
gentilicio, -cia, *a.* national, family.
gentílico, -ca, *a.* heathen.
gentilidad, *n.f.,* **gentilismo,** *n.m.* heathendom.

gentío, *n.m.* throng, crowd.
gentualla, gentuza, *n.f.* rabble, mob.
genuflexión, *n.f.* genuflexion.
genuino, -na, *a.* genuine.
geofísica, *n.f.* geophysics.
geografía, *n.f.* geography.
geográfico, -ca, *a.* geographic(al).
geógrafo, *n.m.* geographer.
geología, *n.f.* geology.
geológico, -ca, *a.* geological.
geólogo, *n.m.* geologist.
geometría, *n.f.* geometry.
geométrico, -ca, *a.* geometric(al).
geopolítico, -ca, *a.* geopolitical.—*n.f.* geopolitics.
geórgica, *n.f.* georgic.
geranio, *n.m.* (*bot.*) geranium.
gerencia, *n.f.* management.
gerente, *n.m.* manager; director.
gerifalte, *n.m.* (*orn.*) gerfalcon.
germanesco, -ca, *a.* rel. to underworld slang.
germanía, *n.f.* underworld slang; criminals' fraternity.
germánico, -ca, *a.* Germanic.
germano, -na, *a.* Germanic, Teutonic.—
—*n.m.f.* German, Teuton; (*obs.*) member of thieves' fraternity.
germen, *n.m.* germ.
germicida, *a.* germicidal.—*n.m.* germicide.
germinación, *n.f.* germination.
germinar, *v.i.* germinate.
gerundio, *n.m.* (*gram.*) gerund; (*fam.*) windbag.
gerundivo, *n.m.* (*gram.*) gerundive.
gesta, *n.f.* (*obs.*) gest; feat.
gestación, *n.f.* gestation.
gestear, *v.i.* pull faces.
gesticulación, *n.f.* facial expression; gesture.
gesticular, *v.i.* make faces; gesture.
gestión, *n.f.* management; measure, action, step.
gestionar, *v.t.* negotiate; take steps to obtain.
gesto, *n.m.* facial expression; gesture; (*fig.*) mood.
gestor, *n.m.* agent, manager.
Getsemaní, *n.m.* (*Bib.*) Gethsemane.
giba, *n.f.* hump; (*fam.*) bugbear.
gibón, *n.m.* (*zool.*) gibbon.
giboso, -sa, *a.* humped, gibbous.
Gibraltar, *n.m.* Gibraltar.
gibraltareño, -ña, *a., n.m.f.* Gibraltarian.
giga, *n.f.* (*mus.*) jig [JIGA].
giganta, *n.f.* giantess.
gigante, *a., n.m.* giant.
gigantesco, -ca, *a.* gigantic.
gigantez, *n.f.* gigantic size.
gigantón, -tona, *n.m.f.* giant figure in festival processions.
gigote, *n.m.* potted meat.
Gil, *n.m.* Giles.
gilí, *a.* (*pl.* **-íes**) (*fam.*) daft.
gimnasia, *n.f.* gymnastics.
gimnasio, *n.f.* gymnasium.
gimnasta, *n.m.f.* gymnast.
gimnástico, -ca, *a.* gymnastic.—*n.f.* gymnastics.
gimotear, *v.i.* (*fam.*) whimper, whine.
Ginebra, *n.f.* Geneva.
ginebra (1), *n.f.* gin.
ginebra (2), *n.f.* bedlam.
ginecología, *n.f.* gynaecology.
ginecólogo, *n.m.* gynaecologist.
gira, *n.f.* outing, trip [JIRA].
giralda, *n.f.* weathervane.
girante, *a.* rotating.
girar, *v.t.* (*com.*) draw.—*v.i.* revolve, turn.
girasol, *n.m.* sunflower.
giratorio, -ria, *a.* revolving.—*n.f.* revolving stand.
giro, *n.m.* turn, rotation; trend; turn of phrase; bragging; money order; gash.
girocompás, *n.m.* gyrocompass.
giroscopio, giróscopo, *n.m.* gyroscope.
gitanear, *v.i.* live like a gipsy; fawn.
gitanería, *n.f.* gipsies; fawning.
gitanesco, -ca, *a.* gipsy, romany.
gitanismo, *n.m.* gipsyism, gipsy lore.
gitano, -na, *a.* gipsy; artful; flattering.—*n.m.f.* gipsy.
glacial, *a.* glacial; icy.
glaciar, *n.m.* glacier.
glaciario, -ria, *a.* glacial.
gladiador, *n.m.* gladiator.
glándula, *n.f.* gland.
glandular, *a.* glandular.
glauco, -ca, *a.* glaucous.
gleba, *n.f.* plough-land.
glera, *n.f.* sandy place.
glicerina, *n.f.* glycerine.
global, *a.* total; global.
globo, *n.m.* globe; balloon; ***en* —,** in general; in bulk.
globoso, -sa, *a.* globose, spherical.
globular, *a.* globular.
glóbulo, *n.m.* globule; (*anat.*) corpuscle.
gloglò [GLUGLÚ].
gloria, *n.f.* glory.—*n.m.* (*eccl.*) Gloria; (*theat.*) curtain call; ***oler*** or ***saber a* —,** smell *or* taste heavenly; ***en sus glorias,*** in one's glory.
gloriar [L], *v.r.* glory (***de, en,*** in).
glorieta, *n.f.* summer-house; roundabout, square.
glorificación, *n.f.* glorification.
glorificar [C], *v.t.* glorify.—*v.r.* win glory.
la Gloriosa, *n.f.* Our Lady.
glorioso, -sa, *a.* glorious; vainglorious.
glosa, *n.f.* gloss.
glosar, *v.t.* gloss.
glosario, *n.m.* glossary.
glosopeda, *n.f.* (*vet.*) foot-and-mouth disease.
glotis, *n.f. inv.* (*anat.*) glottis.
glotón, -tona, *a.* gluttonous.—*n.m.f.* glutton.
glotonear, *v.i.* gormandise.
glotonería, *n.f.* gluttony.
glucosa, *n.f.* glucose.
gluglú, *n.m.* glug, gurgle; turkey's gobble.
gluglutear, *v.i.* gobble (*of turkeys*).
glutinoso, -sa, *a.* glutinous.
gnomo, *n.m.* gnome.
gnóstico, -ca, *a., n.m.f.* gnostic.
gobelino, *n.m.* goblin.
gobernable, *a.* governable, controllable.
gobernación, *n.f.* home affairs; ***Ministerio de la Gobernación,*** Home Office.
gobernador, -ra, *a.* governing.—*n.m.* governor.—*n.f.* governor's wife.
gobernalle, *n.m.* helm, rudder.
gobernante, *a.* ruling.—*n.m.f.* ruler.
gobernar [1], *v.t.* govern; steer; control.
gobernoso, -sa, *a.* (*fam.*) orderly.
gobiernista, *a.* (*S.A.*) governmental.

gobierno, *n.m.* government; control; steering; guidance; — ***doméstico,*** housekeeping.
goce, *n.m.* pleasure, enjoyment.
gocho, -cha, *n.m.f.* (*fam.*) pig, porker.
godesco, -ca, *a.* cheery, merry.
godo, -da, *a.* Gothic.—*n.m.f.* Goth; blue-blooded person; (*S.A., pej.*) Spaniard.
gofo, -fa, *a.* crude, boorish.
gol, *n.m.* (*sport*) goal.
gola, *n.f.* gullet; (*mil.*) gorget.
goleta, *n.f.* schooner.
golfín, *n.m.* dolphin.
golfista, *n.m.f.* golfer.
golfo, -fa, *n.m.f.* street urchin.—*n.m.* gulf, bay; main, open sea; mass; mess.
Gólgota, *n.f.* Golgotha.
Goliat, *n.m.* Goliath.
golilla, *n.f.* ruff, gorget; (*S.A.*) tie.
golondrina, *n.f.* (*orn.*) swallow.
golondrino, *n.m.* (*mil.*) deserter.
golondro, *n.m.* (*fam.*) desire, whim.
golosina, *n.f.* tit-bit; eagerness.
goloso, -sa, *a.* greedy; sweet-toothed.—*n.m.f.* gourmand.
golpazo, *n.m.* thump.
golpe, *n.m.* blow, knock; shock, clash; mass, abundance; surprise; wittiness; ***dar* —,** be a hit; ***de* —,** suddenly; — ***de estado,*** coup d'état; — ***de gracia,*** coup de grâce; — ***de mano,*** surprise attack; — ***de teatro,*** dramatic turn of events; — ***de vista*** or ***de ojo,*** glance, look.
golpear, *v.t.* beat, knock, bump.
golpeo, *n.m.* beating, knocking, bumping.
golpetear, *v.t.* hammer, pound.
gollería, *n.f.* morsel; (*fam.*) pernicketiness.
golletazo, *n.m.* breaking (*of bottle-neck*); abrupt finishing; (*taur.*) thrust through bull's lungs.
gollete, *n.m.* neck.
goma, *n.f.* rubber, gum; (rubber) eraser; rubber band; tyre; (*S.A.*) hangover; — ***de mascar,*** chewing gum; — ***espumosa,*** foam rubber.
gomoso, -sa, *a.* gummy; rubbery.—*n.m.* fop, coxcomb.
gonce [GOZNE].
góndola, *n.f.* gondola.
gondolero, *n.m.* gondolier.
gongo, *n.m.* gong.
gongorino, -na, *a., n.m.f.* Gongorist.
gongorismo, *n.m.* Gongorism (*Spanish euphuism*).
gordiano, -na, *a.* Gordian.
gordi(n)flón, -lona, *a.* (*fam.*) tubby, pudgy.
gordo, -da, *a.* fat, plump; greasy; large, big; thick, coarse; ***se armó la gorda,*** (*fam.*) there was hell to pay.—*n.m.* fat; first prize in lottery.
gordura, *n.f.* fatness; fat.
Gorgona, *n.f.* (*myth.*) Gorgon.
gorgorito, *n.m.* (*fam.*) trill.
gorgorotada, *n.f.* gulp.
gorgotear, *v.i.* gurgle.
gorgoteo, *n.m.* gurgle.
gorguera, *n.f.* ruff; gorget.
gorila, *n.m.* (*zool.*) gorilla.
gorja, *n.f.* throat; ***estar de* —,** (*fam.*) be full of fun.
gorjear, *v.i.* warble.—*v.r.* gurgle.
gorjeo, *n.m.* warbling; gurgle.
gorra (1), *n.f.* cap.
gorra (2), *n.f.* sponging; ***de* —,** on the sponge; ***colarse de* —,** (*fam.*) gate-crash.
gorrero, -ra, *n.m.f.* cap-maker; (*fam.*) sponger.
gorrino, -na, *n.m.f.* piglet; (*fam.*) pig.
gorrión, *n.m.* sparrow.
gorrionera, *n.f.* den of thieves.
gorrista, *a.* sponging.—*n.m.f.* sponger.
gorro, *n.m.* cap; bonnet.
gorrón (1), **-rrona,** *a.* sponging.—*n.m.f.* sponger.
gorrón (2), *n.m.* pebble; (*mech.*) pivot.
gorronear, *v.i.* sponge.
gorullo, *n.m.* ball, lump.
gota, *n.f.* drop; (*med.*) gout.
gotear, *v.i.* drip; splatter.
goteo, *n.m.* dripping.
gotera, *n.f.* dripping; leak.
gótica, *n.f.* (*print.*) gothic type.
gótico, -ca, *a.* Gothic; noble.
gotoso, -sa, *a.* gouty.—*n.m.f.* gout sufferer.
gozar [C], *v.t.* enjoy, possess.—*v.i.* enjoy, rejoice (***de,*** in).—*v.r.* enjoy oneself; delight (***en,*** in).
gozne, *n.m.* hinge.
gozo, *n.m.* joy, glee; mirth.
gozoso, -sa, *a.* joyful, merry.
gozque(jo), *n.m.* small dog.
grabado, *n.m.* engraving; print.
grabar, *v.t.* engrave; record (*sounds*).—*v.r.* be fixed *or* engraved (*on one's memory*).
gracejar, *v.i.* be a charmer.
gracejo, *n.m.* wit, charm; (*C.A.*) clowner.
gracia, *n.f.* grace; piece of wit; funniness; ***de* —,** gratis; ***en* — *a,*** because of; ***hacer* —,** amuse, be funny; ***hacer* — *de,*** let (*s.o.*) off; ***pedir una* —,** ask a favour; ***tener* —,** be funny, amusing.—*pl.* thanks, thank-you.
grácil, *a.* gracile, slender.
gracioso, -sa, *a.* graceful, gracious; funny, witty; gratuitous.—*n.m.* (*theat.*) comic, comic rôle.
grada, *n.f.* grandstand; step; tier; (*naut.*) slipway, (*agr.*) harrow.—*pl.* steps.
gradación, *n.f.* gradation; (*gram.*) comparison.
gradería, *n.f.* stand, row of seats; steps.
gradiente, *n.m.* (*math.*) gradient; (*S.A.*) slope, gradient.
gradilla, *n.f.* step-ladder.
grado, *n.m.* step, tread (*of stair*); grade; degree; (*mil.*) rank; ***de*** (***buen***) **—,** gladly, willingly; ***en alto* —,** to a high degree.
graduación, *n.f.* graduation; grading; rank.
graduado, -da, *a., n.m.f.* graduate.
gradual, *a.* gradual.
graduar [M], *v.t.* graduate; evaluate, grade; (*mil.*) confer the rank (***de,*** of) on.—*v.r.* graduate (***de,*** as).
grafía, *n.f.* graphy, graph.
gráfico, -ca, *a.* graphic(al); rel. to printing.—*n.m.* diagram.—*n.f.* graph.
grafito, *n.m.* graphite; graffito.
gragea, *n.f.* tiny sweet.
grajo, -ja, *n.m.f.* (*orn.*) rook; jackdaw; chough.
gramática, *n.f.* grammar; — ***parda,*** (*fam.*) slyness, cunning.
gramatical, *a.* grammatical.
gramático, -ca, *a.* grammatical.—*n.m.f.* grammarian.
gramo, *n.m.* gramme.

gramófono, *n.m.* gramophone.
gramola, *n.f.* record-player and cabinet.
gran, *a. contracted form of* GRANDE, *before sg. nouns.*
grana (1), *n.f.* running to seed.
grana (2), *n.f.* kermes; red cloth.
granada, *n.f.* pomegranate; grenade, shell.
granadero, *n.m.* grenadier.
granadino, -na, *a., n.m.f.* rel. to *or* native of Granada.
granado (1), **-da,** *a.* notable; expert; seedy; large.
granado (2), *n.m.* pomegranate-tree.
granalla, *n.f.* filings, granules.
granar, *v.t.* coarse-grind.—*v.i.* run to seed, fruit.
grande, *a.* big, large; great; ***en* —,** largely. [GRAN].—*n.m.* grandee.
grandeza, *n.f.* greatness; size; grandeur.
grandilocuente, grandílocuo, -cua, *a.* grandiloquent.
grandillón, -llona, *a.* (*fam.*) over-big.
grandiosidad, *n.f.* grandeur.
grandioso, -sa, *a.* grandiose.
grandor, *n.m.* size.
granear, *v.t.* sow; stipple.
granero, -ra, *a.* rel. to grain.—*n.m.f.* grain-merchant.—*n.m.* granary.
granillo, *n.m.* fine corn; profit.
granilloso, -sa, *a.* granular.
granito, *n.m.* granite.
granizada, *n.f.* hail-storm; (*S.A.*) iced drink.
granizar [C], *v.t., v.i.* hail.
granizo, *n.m.* hail.
granja, *n.f.* dairy farm; dairy grange.
granjear, *v.t.* win, earn.—*v.r.* win over, gain.
granjeo, *n.m.* winning; gain.
granjería, *n.f.* gain; husbandry.
granjero, -ra, *n.m.f.* farmer.
grano, *n.m.* grain; berry, bean, grape; pimple; ***ir al* —,** get to the point.—*pl.* corn, grain.
granuja, *n.f.* (single) grape; pip.—*n.m.* rogue.
granular, *a.* granular.—*v.t.* granulate.
gránulo, *n.m.* granule.
granza, *n.f.* (*bot.*) madder.—*pl.* chaff; dross.
grao, *n.m.* shore; beach-port.
grapa, *n.f.* clamp; staple.
grasa, *n.f.* fat, grease.—*pl.* slag.
graseza, *n.f.* fattiness.
grasiento, -ta, *a.* greasy.
graso, -sa, *a.* fatty.—*n.m.* fattiness.
grata (1), *n.f.* favour, esteemed (*letter*).
grata (2), *n.f.* wire brush.
gratificación, *n.f.* gratification; reward.
gratificar [A], *v.t.* gratify; reward, tip.
al gratín, *a., adv. phr.* (*cul.*) au gratin.
gratitud, *n.f.* gratitude.
grato, -ta, *a.* pleasing; gratuitous; (*S.A.*) grateful.
gratulación, *n.f.* felicitation.
gratular, *v.t.* congratulate.—*v.r.* rejoice.
grava, *n.f.* gravel.
gravamen, *n.m.* obligation; load, burden.
gravar, *v.t.* burden.
grave, *a.* heavy; grave; serious (*illness*); difficult.
gravedad, *n.f.* gravity.
gravedoso, -sa, *a.* pompous, ponderous.
gravidez, *n.f.* pregnancy.
grávido, -da, *a.* gravid; pregnant.
gravitación, *n.f.* gravitation.
gravitacional, *a.* gravitational.
gravitar, *v.i.* gravitate; rest; be a burden (***sobre,*** to).
gravoso, -sa, *a.* onerous.
graznar, *v.i.* caw, croak.
graznido, *n.m.* caw, croak.
Grecia, *n.f.* Greece.
greco, -ca, *a., n.m.f.* Greek.
grecolatino, -na, *a.* Graeco-Latin.
grecorromano, -na, *a.* Graeco-Roman.
greda, *n.f.* marl, fuller's earth.
gregario, -ria, *a.* gregarious; slavish.
Gregorio, *n.m.* Gregory.
greguería, *n.f.* din, hubbub.
gregüescos, *n.m.pl.* 17th century breeches.
gremial, *a.* rel. to union *or* guild.—*n.m.* guildsman, trade-unionist.
gremio, *n.m.* guild, trade union; lap.
greña, *n.f.* mop, shock, tangled hair; ***andar a la* —,** (*fam.*) squabble, fight.
gresca, *n.f.* uproar; wrangle.
grey, *n.f.* flock; herd; nation.
Grial, *n.m.* Grail.
griego, -ga, *a., n.m.f.* Greek.
grieta, *n.f.* crack, split.
grietar, *v.t.* crack, split.
grietoso, -sa, *a.* cracked, crannied.
grifo, -fa, *a.* curly.—*n.m.* tap, (*U.S.*) faucet; (*myth.*) griffin.
grifón, *n.m.* spigot, faucet.
grilla, *n.f.* (*rad.*) grid; (*fam.*) fib.
grillete, *n.m.* shackle, fetter.
grillo (1), *n.m.* (*ent.*) cricket.
grillo (2), *n.m. usually pl.* fetters, irons; drag, impediment; ***andar a grillos,*** (*fam.*) fritter time away.
grima, *n.f.* horror; ***dar* — *a,*** irritate.
gringo, -ga, *a., n.m.f.* (*pej.*) Gringo (*Anglo-Saxon*).
gripe, *n.f.* influenza.
gris, *a.* grey.—*n.m.* cold weather; grey.
grisáceo, -cea, *a.* greyish.
grisú, *n.m.* (*min.*) fire-damp.
grita, *n.f.* shouting.
gritar, *v.i.* shout; scream; cry out.
gritería, *n.f.*, **griterío,** *n.m.* outcry, clamouring, shouting.
grito, *n.m.* shout, cry; scream; ***poner el* — *en el cielo,*** (*fam.*) raise the roof (***contra,*** against).
groenlandés, -desa, *a., n.m.f.* Greenlander.
Groenlandia, *n.f.* Greenland.
grosella, *n.f.* currant.
grosería, *n.f.* coarseness; stupidity.
grosero, -ra, *a.* coarse; vulgar; stupid.
grosísimo, -ma, *a. sup. of* GRUESO.
grosor, *n.m.* thickness, bulk.
grosura, *n.f.* fat, suet; meat diet; offal.
grúa, *n.f.* crane, derrick, hoist.
grueso, -sa, *a.* thick, bulky, massive; coarse, rough; dense; (*fig.*) stupid.—*n.m.* bulk; size, thickness.—*n.f.* gross (144).
grulla, *n.f.* (*orn.*) crane.
grumo, *n.m.* clot; lump.
gruñente, *a.* grunting.
gruñido, *n.m.* grunt; growl.
gruñir [K], *v.i.* grunt; growl; creak.
gruñón, -ñona, *a.* (*fam.*) grumpy.
grupa, *n.f.* croup, rump.
grupera, *n.f.* crupper; pillion.
grupo, *n.m.* group; (*mech.*) unit.
gruta, *n.f.* grotto, cave.

guaca, *n.f.* (*S.A.*) Indian tomb; (*fig.*) hidden treasure; nest-egg.
guachapear, *v.t.* kick, splash (*water with feet*); (*fam.*) botch.—*v.i.* rattle.
guácharo, -ra, *a.* ailing, sickly.
guachinango, -ga, *a.* (*C.A.*) crafty, cunning. —*n.m.f.* (*C.A. pej.*) Mex, Mexican.
guacho, -cha, *a.* orphaned.—*n.m.* chick.
guadamací *or* **-cil, guadamecí** *or* **-cil,** *n.m.* embossed leather.
guadaña, *n.f.* scythe.
guadañar, *v.t.* mow, scythe.
guagua, *n.f.* trifle; (*S.A.*) kid, baby; (*dial., C.A.*) bus.
guaita, *n.f.* night-guard.
guajiro, -ra, *a.* (*Cuba*) rustic.—*n.m.f.* white Cuban peasant.
gualdo, -da, *a.* weld, yellow.
gualdrapa, *n.f.* trappings; (*fam.*) tatter.
guano, *n.m.* guano.
guantada, *n.f.*, **guantazo,** *n.m.* slap *or* blow with glove.
guante, *n.m.* glove.
guantelete, *n.m.* gauntlet.
guapear, *v.i.* (*fam.*) show off.
guapeza, *n.f.* (*fam.*) good looks; (*fam.*) daring; (*fam.*) showing-off.
guapo, -pa, *a.* (*fam.*) good-looking; showy.—*n.m.* bully; (*fam.*) girl-chaser; (*fam.*) chum (*in vocative*).
guapura, *n.f.* (*fam.*) good looks.
guarapo, *n.m.* sugar-cane juice.
guarda, *n.m.f.* guard, keeper.—*n.m.* guard, ranger, officer.—*n.f.* guard, keeping; fly-leaf.
guardabarreras, *n.m.* (*rail.*) gate-keeper.
guardabarros, *n.m. inv.* mudguard, (*U.S.*) fender.
guardabosque, *n.m.* gamekeeper.
guardabrisa, *n.f.* windscreen, (*U.S.*) windshield.
guardacadena, *n.m.* or *f.* chain-guard.
guardacostas, *n.m. inv.* coast-guard cutter.—*pl.* coast-guard service.
guardafrenos, *n.m. inv.* (*rail.*) brakeman.
guardainfante, *n.m.* farthingale.
guardalado, *n.m.* rails, railing.
guardalmacén, *n.m.f.* store-keeper.
guardalodos, *n.m. inv.* (*S.A.*) mudguard.
guardamano, *n.m.* hand-guard of sword.
guardamarina, *n.m.* (*naut.*) midshipman.
guardameta, *n.m.* (*sport*) goalkeeper.
guardapuerta, *n.f.* storm-door.
guardar, *v.t.* guard; keep; look after; observe, obey; save.—*v.r.* be on one's guard; guard (***de***, against); look out (***de***, for).
guardarropa, *n.f.* wardrobe; cloakroom.—*n.m.f.* costumier.
guardarropía, *n.f.* (*theat.*) wardrobe, props.; ***de —***, make-believe, sham.
guardasilla, *n.f.* chair-rail.
guardavía, *n.m.* (*rail.*) linesman.
guardería, *n.f.* guard; day-nursery.
guardia, *n.m.* policeman, guard.—*n.f.* guard, watch; protection; duty; ***de —***, on guard; on duty; — ***civil***, *m.* country policeman; *f.* country police; — ***de corps***, bodyguard (*m. person*; *f. team*).
guardián, -diana, *n.m.f.* guardian.
guardilla, *n.f.* attic; end-guard.
guardoso, -sa, *a.* careful; mean, stingy.
guarecer [9], *v.t.* shelter.—*v.r.* take refuge *or* shelter.
guarida, *n.f.* den, lair; shelter.
guarín, *n.m.* piglet.
guarismo, *n.m.* cypher, number.
guarnecer [9], *v.t.* garnish; edge; provide; plaster; equip; garrison, man.
guarnición, *n.f.* trimmings, edging; setting; sword-guard; garrison; harness; (*mech.*) lining, bush; (*cul.*) garnish.—*pl.* fixtures, fittings.
guarnicionar, *v.t.* garrison.
guarro, -rra, *n.m.f.* pig.
¡guarte! *interj.* look out!
guasa, *n.f.* (*fam.*) dullness; (*fam.*) joking.
guaso, -sa, *a.* (*S.A.*) churlish.—*n.m.f.* peasant.
guasón, -sona, *a.* (*fam.*) churlish; (*fam.*) waggish.—*n.m.f.* (*fam.*) lout; (*fam.*) wag.
guatemalteco, -ca, *a.*, *n.m.f.* Guatemalan.
¡guau! *n.m.*, *interj.* bow-wow!
¡guay! *interj.* (*poet.*) alack!
guaya, *n.f.* lament, plaint.
guayaba, *n.f.* guava; (*S.A.*, *fam.*) fib, yarn.
Guayana, *n.f.* Guyana.
guayanés, -nesa, *a.*, *n.m.f.* Guyanese.
gubernamental, *a.* governmental; pro-government.
gubernativo, -va, *a.* governmental.
gubia, *n.f.* (*carp.*) gouge.
guedeja, *n.f.* mane (*of lion*); long hair.
güero, -ra, *a.* (*C.A.*) blond(e).—*n.m.f.* (*C.A., fam.*) dear.
guerra, *n.f.* war, warfare; ***dar —***, (*fam.*) be a nuisance; — ***fría***, cold war; ***Guerra Mundial***, World War; — ***relámpago***, blitzkrieg.
guerrear, *v.i.* war, fight.
guerrero, -ra, *a.* warlike, warring, war.—*n.m.f.* fighter, warrior, soldier.
guerrilla, *n.f.* guerrilla band *or* warfare.
guerrillero, *n.m.* guerrilla.
guía, *n.m.f.* guide; leader.—*n.f.* guide, guidance; marker, post; (*rail.*) timetable; handle-bars; — ***sonora***, (*cine.*) sound-track; — ***telefónica***, telephone directory.
guiar [L], *v.t.* lead; drive, pilot, steer.—*v.r.* be guided (***de***, ***por***, by).
guija, *n.f.* pebble.—*pl.* (*fam.*) go, energy.
guijarro, *n.m.* cobble, large pebble.
guijo, *n.m.* gravel; (*mech.*) gudgeon.
Guillermo, *n.m.* William.
guillotina, *n.f.* guillotine; ***de —***, sash (*window*).
guillotinar, *v.t.* guillotine.
guinchar, *v.t.* goad, prick.
güinche, *n.m.* (*S.A.*) winch.
guincho, *n.m.* goad, pricker.
guinda, *n.f.* mazard, sour cherry.
guindal, *n.m.*, **guindaleza,** *n.f.* (*naut.*) hawser.
guindar, *v.t.* hoist; (*fam.*) snap up.
guindilla, *n.f.* small sour cherry; pepper (*fruit*).—*n.m.* (*fam.*) copper (*policeman*).
guindo, *n.m.* sour-cherry-tree.
guindola, *n.f.* bosun's chair; lifebuoy.
Guinea, *n.f.* Guinea.
guineo, -ea, *a.*, *n.m.f.* Guinean.—*n.f.* guinea (*coin*).
guiñada, *n.f.* wink; (*naut.*) lurch.
guiñapo, *n.m.* tatter; ragamuffin.
guiñar, *v.t.* wink.—*v.i.* wink; (*naut.*) lurch.
guiño, *n.m.* wink; grimace.

guión, *n.m.* guide; hyphen, dash; outline, notes; script; scenario.
guionista, *n.m.f.* scriptwriter; (*cine.*) scenarist; dubber.
guirlache, *n.m.* almond brittle.
guirnalda, *n.f.* garland.
guisa, *n.f.* way, wise; ***a — de,*** as, in the manner of.
guisado, *n.m.* stew.
guisante, *n.m.* pea.
guisar, *v.t.* cook; stew; arrange.
guiso, *n.m.* dish, stew; seasoning.
guita, *n.f.* twine; (*fam.*) cash.
guitarra, *n.f.* guitar.
guitarrear, *v.i.* strum a guitar.
guitarreo, *n.m.* strumming (*of guitar*).
guitarrista, *n.m.f.* guitarist.
guitarro, *n.m.* small four-stringed guitar.
guitarrón, *n.m.* big guitar; (*fam.*) sly boots.
guitón, -tona, *n.m.f.* tramp, vagrant; (*fam.*) scamp.
guizque, *n.m.* boat-hook.
gula, *n.f.* gluttony.
guloso, -sa, *a.* gluttonous.
gulusmear, *v.i.* hang around the food.
gullería [GOLLERÍA].
gurdo, -da, *a.* silly.
guripa, *n.m.* (*low*) soldier; scoundrel.
gurriato, *n.m.* young sparrow.
gurrufero, *n.m.* broken-down old horse.
gurrumino, -na, *a.* weak, wretched; (*S.A.*) cowardly.—*n.m.* (*fam.*) doting *or* henpecked husband.—*n.f.* luxuriousness.—*n.m.f.* (*C.A.*) kid, child.
gurullo, *n.m.* lump; knot.
gusanear, *v.i.* teem.
gusanera, *n.f.* worm heap; (*fam.*) mania.
gusanillo, *n.m.* small grub *or* worm; silk twist; threaded tip.
gusano, *n.m.* grub, worm, maggot.
gustación, *n.f.* tasting, taste.
gustadura, *n.f.* tasting, sampling.
gustar, *v.t.* please; taste, try.—*v.i.* be nice; please; — ***de,*** like, enjoy; ***me gusta leer,*** I like to read, ***me gusta el pan,*** I like bread; ***como Vd. gusta,*** as you please, as you will.
gustatorio, -ria, *a.* gustatory.
gustazo, *n.m.* delight; malignant delight.
gustillo, *n.m.* trace, slight taste.
gusto, *n.m.* pleasure; whim; taste, flavour; ***a —,*** at will; ***con mucho —,*** only too happy, delighted; ***dar —,*** be very pleasant, please; ***estar a —,*** be happy, be in one's element; ***tomar — a,*** take a liking to.
gustoso, -sa, *a.* glad, delighted; tasty; pleasant.
gutapercha, *n.f.* gutta-percha.
gutural, *a., n.f.* guttural.

H

H, h, *n.f.* ninth letter of the Spanish alphabet.
ha [HABER].
haba, *n.f.* bean; broad bean.
habado, -da, *a.* dappled.
la Habana, *n.f.* (*geog.*) Havana.
habanero, -ra, *a.* rel. to Havana.—*n.f.* habanera (*dance*).
habano, -na, *a.* from Havana (*tobacco*).—*n.m.* Havana cigar.
haber (1) [19], *v.t.* (*obs.*) have.—*v.i.* (*impersonal: pres.* **hay**) there to be; ***tres años ha,*** three years ago.—*v.r.* ***habérselas con,*** have it out with; deal with.—*auxiliary v.* have; — ***que hacer,*** be necessary to do; — ***de***: ***he de salir temprano,*** I am to leave early; ***he de escribir,*** I have to write, I must write.
haber (2), *n.m.* (*com.*) credit (*side*); income; (*esp. pl.*) property, wealth.
habichuela, *n.f.* kidney bean; ***habichuelas verdes,*** French beans.
hábil, *a.* skilful, able; (*jur.*) fit, qualified; ***día —,*** working day.
habilidad, *n.f.* ability; skill; cunning.
habilitación, *n.f.* qualification; (*naut.*) fitting out.
habilitar, *v.t.* entitle, qualify; finance; equip, fit out.
habitable, *a.* habitable, inhabitable.
habitación, *n.f.* dwelling; room; habitat.
habitar, *v.t.* inhabit.
hábito, *n.m.* dress, habit; habit, custom.
habituación, *n.f.* habituation.
habitual, *a.* habitual; usual.
habituar [M], *v.t.* accustom, habituate.
habitud, *n.f.* habit, custom; connexion.
habla, *n.f.* speech; language, dialect; ***al —,*** (*tel.*) speaking.
hablador, -ra, *a.* talkative.—*n.m.f.* gossip.
habladuría, *n.f.* idle talk; gossip.
hablante, *a.* speaking.—*n.m.f.* speaker.
hablar, *v.t., v.i.* speak; talk.
hablilla, *n.f.* rumour; gossip.
hacanea, *n.f.* nag.
hacedero, -ra, *a.* feasible.
Hacedor, *n.m.* Maker.
hacedor, *n.m.* (farm-)manager.
hacendado, -da, *a.* landed, property-owning.—*n.m.f.* property-owner; (*S.A.*) rancher.
hacendar [1], *v.t.* transfer (*property*).—*v.r.* buy property.
hacendero, -ra, *a.* industrious; sedulous.—*n.f.* public work.
hacendista, *n.m.* economist.
hacendoso, -sa, *a.* diligent.
hacer [20], *v.t.* make; do; act; believe (s.o. to be): ***yo hacía a Juan en París,*** I thought John was in Paris.—*v.r.* become; ***hacerse a,*** become accustomed to; ***hace,*** ago: ***hace un año,*** a year ago; ***desde hace,*** for: ***está aquí desde hace un mes,*** he has been here (for) a month; ***hacer hacer,*** have done; — ***de,*** act as.
hacia, *prep.* toward(s); about; — ***adelante,*** forward(s).
hacienda, *n.f.* landed property; farm, ranch; (*S.A.*) livestock; (*pol.*) Treasury.—*pl.* chores.
hacina, *n.f.* stack; pile.
hacinamiento, *n.m.* accumulation.
hacinar, *v.t.* stack; pile.
hacha (1), *n.f.* axe.
hacha (2), *n.f.* torch.
hache, *n.f.* aitch, name of letter H.
hach(e)ar, *v.t.* hew.

hachero, *n.m.* woodcutter; (*mil.*) sapper, pioneer.
hacheta, *n.f.* small axe; small torch.
hachich, *n.m.* hashish.
hacho, *n.m.* firebrand, torch; beacon (*hill*).
hada, *n.f.* fairy.
hadar, *v.t.* foretell; fate.
hado, *n.m.* fate.
hagiografía, *n.f.* hagiography.
hagiógrafo, *n.m.* hagiographer.
hago [HACER].
Haití, *n.m.* Haiti.
haitiano, -na, *a.* Haitian.
¡hala! *interj.* get up! gee up!
halagador, -ra, *a.* flattering.
halagar [B], *v.t.* flatter; cajole; fondle.
halago, *n.m.* (*esp. pl.*) flattery; cajolery; caress.
halagüeño, -ña, *a.* attractive; flattering.
halar, *v.t.* (*naut.*) haul.—*v.i.* (*naut.*) pull ahead.
halcón, *n.m.* falcon.
halconear, *v.i.* (*fam.*) be brazen.
halconero, *n.m.* falconer.
halda, *n.f.* skirt; burlap (*for packing*).
haldudo, -da, *a.* full-skirted.
haleche, *n.m.* (*ichth.*) anchovy.
hálito, *n.m.* breath; (*poet.*) breeze.
halo, *n.m.* halo.
hallar, *v.t.* find.—*v.r.* find oneself; be (situated).
hallazgo, *n.m.* finding, discovery; reward for discovery.
hamaca, *n.f.* hammock; deck-chair.
hámago, *n.m.* beebread; nausea.
hambre, *n.f.* hunger; famine.
hambrear, *v.t.*, *v.i.* starve.
hambriento, -ta, *a.* hungry (**de,** for).
hamo, *n.m.* fish-hook.
hampa, *n.f.* low-life, underworld.
hampesco, -ca, *a.* villainous.
hampón, *n.m.* bully, lout.
hangar, *n.m.* (*aer.*) hangar.
haragán, -gana, *a.* idle, loafing.—*n.m.f.* idler, loafer.
haraganear, *v.i.* idle, loaf.
harapiento, -ta, haraposo, -sa, *a.* ragged.
harapo, *n.m.* tatter, rag.
harén, *n.m.* harem.
harija, *n.f.* mill-dust, flour-dust.
harina, *n.f.* flour; ***ser — de otro costal,*** be quite a different kettle of fish.
harinero, -ra, rel. to flour.—*n.m.* flour-dealer.
harinoso, -sa, *a.* mealy; farinaceous.
harmonía [ARMONÍA].
harnero, *n.m.* sieve, riddle.
harón, -rona, *a.* lazy.—*n.m.* loafer.
harpa, *n.f.* harp.
harpía, *n.f.* harpy.
harpillera, *n.f.* burlap, sack-cloth.
hartar, *v.t.* sate; stuff.—*v.i.* be satiated.—*v.r.* be satiated; be bored, fed up (**de,** with).
hartazgo, *n.m.* fill, glut, (*fam.*) bellyful.
harto, -ta, *a.* full, satiated; fed up (**de,** with). —*adv.* sufficiently; exceedingly.
hartura, *n.f.* satiety; abundance.
hasta, *adv.* even.—*prep.* until, as far as, (*U.S.*) through; ***— luego*** or ***la vista,*** good-bye, until we meet again.
hastial, *n.m.* (*arch.*) gable-end; yokel.
hastiar [L], *v.t.* surfeit; cloy; disgust.
hastío, *n.m.* disgust, nausea; surfeit; boredom.
hastioso, -sa, *a.* sickening, disgusting; boring.
hataca, *n.f.* large wooden spoon; rolling-pin.
hatear, *v.t.* (*fam.*) pack up.—*v.i.* pack one's equipment.
hatería, *n.f.* equipment; provision for several days.
hato, *n.m.* herd, flock; (shepherds') lodge *or* hut, bothie; outfit, clothes; gang.
haxix [HACHICH].
hay, *v. impers.* there is *or* are [HABER (1)].
La Haya, *n.f.* The Hague.
haya (1), *n.f.* (*bot.*) beech.
haya (2), [HABER (1)].
hayaca, *n.f.* (*S.A.*) mince-pie.
hayal, hayedo, *n.m.* beech grove.
hayo, *n.m.* (*S.A. bot.*) coca.
hayuco, *n.m.* beech mast.
haz (1), *n.m.* (*pl.* **haces**) bundle, sheaf; beam; jet (*cathode ray*).
haz (2), *n.m.* (*pl.* **haces**) troops drawn up in array; (*mil.*) file.
haz (3), *n.f.* (*pl.* **haces**) (*esp. fig.*) face; surface; upper side (*leaf*).
haz (4), [HACER].
haza, *n.f.* field (*arable*).
hazaña, *n.f.* exploit, deed.
hazañería, *n.f.* fuss, dismay.
hazañero, -ra, *a.* easily dismayed *or* fussed.
hazañoso, -sa, *a.* heroic, valiant.
hazmerreír, *n.m.* laughing-stock.
he (1), *adv.* here is *or* are; ***heme aquí,*** here I am.
he (2), [HABER (1)].
hebdómada, *n.f.* period of seven days *or* years.
hebdomadario, -ria, *a.* hebdomadal, hebdomadary, weekly.
hebilla, *n.f.* buckle, clasp.
hebra, *n.f.* fibre; thread; grain (*of wood*).
hebraico, -ca, *a.* Hebrew, Hebraic.
hebraizar [C & P], *v.i.* Hebraize; Judaize.
hebreo, -rea, *a.* Hebrew.—*n.m.f.* Hebrew.—*n.m.* Hebrew (*language*); (*pej.*) usurer.
Hébridas, *n.f.pl.* Hebrides.
hebroso, -sa, *a.* stringy, fibrous.
hectárea, *n.f.* hectare.
héctico, -ca, *a.* (*med.*) consumptive.
hectiquez, *n.f.* (*med.*) consumption, phthisis.
hectolitro, *n.m.* hectolitre.
hectómetro, *n.m.* hectometre.
hechicería, *n.f.* sorcery, witchcraft; glamour.
hechicero, -ra, *a.* enchanting; charming.—*n.m.* wizard.—*n.f.* witch.
hechizar [C], *v.t.* bewitch, enchant.
hechizo, -za, *a.* artificial; fake; detachable; (*S.A.*) home-produced.—*n.m.* spell; magic; glamour.
hecho, -cha, *p.p.* [HACER].—*a.* accustomed; perfect; ready-made.—*n.m.* act; event; fact; ***de —,*** in fact, (*jur.*) de facto.
hechura, *n.f.* making; workmanship; creature; shape; (*S.A.*) treat.
hedentina, *n.f.* stink.
heder [2], *v.t.* annoy.—*v.i.* stink.
hediondez, *n.f.* stink.
hediondo, -da, *a.* stinking, fetid; lewd.—*n.m.* (*bot.*) wild Syrian rue; (*zool.*) skunk.
hedonismo, *n.m.* hedonism.
hedor, *n.m.* stink.
hegemonía, *n.f.* hegemony.
hégira, *n.f.* Hegira.

heladería, *n.f.* (*esp. S.A.*) ice-cream parlour.
helado, -da, *a.* frozen; frost-bitten; chilly.—*n.m.* ice-cream.—*n.f.* frost.
helar [1], *v.t.* freeze; discourage.—*v.i.* freeze.—*v.r.* freeze; be frost-bitten.
helecho, *n.m.* (*bot.*) fern.
helénico, -ca, *a.* Hellenic.
helenismo, *n.m.* Hellenism.
helenístico, -ca, *a.* Hellenistic.
heleno, -na, *a.* Hellenic.—*n.m.f.* Hellene.
helero, *n.m.* snow-cap; glacier.
helgado, -da, *a.* jag-toothed.
helgadura, *n.f.* gap (*in the teeth*).
hélice, *n.f.* heliz, spiral; screw, propeller.
hélico, -ca, *a.* helical.
helicoide, *n.m.* helicoid.
helicóptero, *n.m.* (*aer.*) helicopter.
helio, *n.m.* helium.
heliotropio *or better* **heliotropo,** *n.m.* (*bot., min.*) heliotrope.
helvecio, -cia, *a., n.m.f.* Helvetian.
helvético, -ca, *a.* Helvetic.—*n.m.f.* Helvetian.
hematíe, *n.m.* (*med.*) red (blood) cell.
hembra, *n.f.* female (*of animals and plants*); (*low*) woman; eye (*of a hook*); female part (*of plug etc.*), socket; gudgeon.
hembrilla, *n.f.* small socket *or* staple.
hemeroteca, *n.f.* newspaper library.
hemiciclo, *n.m.* semicircle.
hemisferio, *n.m.* hemisphere.
hemistiquio, *n.m.* hemistich.
hemofilia, *n.f.* (*med.*) hemophilia.
hemoglobina, *n.f.* (*med.*) hemoglobin.
hemorragia, *n.f.* hemorrhage.
hemorroida, hemorroide, *n.f.* (*esp. pl.*) (*med.*) hemorrhoids.
henal, *n.m.* hayloft.
henar, *n.m.* hayfield.
henchimiento, *n.m.* filling-up; abundance; repletion.
henchir [8], *v.t.* fill; stuff.
hendedura, *n.f.* crack, fissure.
hender [2], *v.t.* split, cleave, crack.
hendible, *a.* cleavable.
hendidura, *n.f.* crack, fissure.
henil, *n.m.* hayloft.
heno, *n.m.* hay.
heñir [8K], *v.t.* knead.
heptagonal, *a.* heptagonal.
heptágono, -na, *a.* heptagonal.—*n.m.* heptagon.
heptámetro, *n.m.* heptameter.
heptasílabo, -ba, *a.* heptasyllabic.—*n.m.* heptasyllable.
heráldico, -ca, *a.* heraldic.—*n.f.* heraldry.
heraldo, *n.m.* herald, king-at-arms.
herbáceo, -cea, *a.* herbaceous.
herbaje, *n.m.* pasture, herbage.
herbaj(e)ar, *v.t., v.i.* graze.
herbario, -ria, *a.* herbal.—*n.m.* herbarium; herbalist.
herbero, *n.m.* oesophagus (*of a ruminant*).
herbicida, *a., n.m.* herbicide, weed-killer.
herbívoro, -ra, *a.* herbivorous.
herbolario, *n.m.* herbalist; (*fam.*) scatter-brain.
herborizar [C], *v.i.* herbalize.
herboso, -sa, *a.* grassy.
herciano, -na, *a.* (*phys.*) Hertzian.
hercúleo, -lea, *a.* Herculean.
heredable, *a.* inheritable, hereditable.
heredamiento, *n.m.* inheritance; landed estate, hereditament.
heredar, *v.t.* inherit; institute as heir.
heredero, -ra, *a.* inheritable; inheriting.—*n.m.* heir, inheritor; — ***presunto,*** heir presumptive.—*n.f.* heiress, inheritor.
hereditario, -ria, *a.* hereditary.
hereje, *n.m.f.* heretic.
herejía, *n.f.* heresy.
herén, *n.m.* vetch.
herencia, *n.f.* inheritance; heritage.
herético, -ca, *a.* heretical.
herido, -da, *a.* wounded; hurt.—*n.m.f.* injured *or* wounded person, casualty.—*n.f.* wound.
herir [6], *v.t.* hurt, injure; wound; strike; pluck (*an instrument*); touch, offend.
hermana, *n.f.* sister [HERMANO].
hermanar, *v.t.* match; join; harmonize.—*v.r.* match; love one another as brothers.
hermanastra, *n.f.* step-sister.
hermanastro, *n.m.* step-brother.
hermanazgo, *n.m.* brotherhood.
hermandad, *n.f.* brotherhood; fraternity; conformity.
hermanear, *v.t.* call brother; treat as a brother.
hermano, -na, *a.* sister (*language*); matched (*objects*).—*n.m.* brother; mate, companion; — ***carnal,*** full brother; — ***de leche,*** foster brother; ***medio*** —, half-brother; — ***político,*** brother-in-law; ***hermanos siameses,*** Siamese twins.
hermético, -ca, *a.* hermetic; air-tight; (*fig.*) impenetrable.
hermosear, *v.t.* beautify.
hermoso, -sa, *a.* beautiful, handsome, comely.
hermosura, *n.f.* beauty, handsomeness; belle.
hernioso, -sa, *a.* herniated, suffering from hernia.
héroe, *n.m.* hero.
heroico, -ca, *a.* heroic(al).
heroína, *n.f.* heroine.
heroismo, *n.m.* heroism.
herrada, *n.f.* wooden pail.
herradero, *n.m.* place *or* season for branding cattle.
herrador, *n.m.* smith.
herradura, *n.f.* horse-shoe.
herraj [ERRAJ].
herramental, *n.m.* tool-box; tool-bag.
herramienta, *n.f.* tool, implement; set of tools; (*fam.*) horns; (*fam.*) teeth.
herrar [1], *v.t.* shoe (*horses*); brand (*cattle*); hoop, bind with iron.
herrén, *n.m.* mixed fodder.
herrería, *n.f.* smithy.
herrerico, herrerillo, *n.m.* (*orn.*) blue tit; great tit; marsh tit.
herrero, *n.m.* smith, blacksmith; — ***de obra,*** structural steelworker, scaffolder.
herreruelo, *n.m.* (*orn.*) coal tit.
herrete, *n.m.* ferrule, metal tip.
herrín, *n.m.* rust (*iron*).
herrón, *n.m.* quoit; washer.
herrumbre, *n.f.* rust (*iron*).
herrumbroso, -sa, *a.* rusty.
herventar, *v.t.* boil.
hervidor, *n.m.* boiler (*domestic*), kettle.
hervir [6], *v.i.* boil; seethe.

hervor, *n.m.* boiling; vigour; — ***de la sangre,*** rash.
hervoroso, -sa, *a.* ardent, impetuous.
hesitación, *n.f.* (*rare*) hesitation.
heteróclito, -ta, *a.* (*gram.*) heteroclite.
heterodoxia, *n.f.* heterodoxy.
heterodoxo, -xa, *a.* heterodox.
heterogeneidad, *n.f.* heterogeneity.
heterogéneo, -nea, *a.* heterogeneous.
hético, -ca [HÉCTICO].
hetiquez [HECTIQUEZ].
hexagona, *a.* hexagonal.
hexágono, -na, *a.* hexagonal.—*n.m.* hexagon.
hexámetro, *n.m.* hexameter.
hez, *n.f.* (*pl.* **heces**) sediment; dregs; scum, dross; (*fig.*) dregs, scum.—*pl.* excrement.
hiato, *n.m.* hiatus; gap.
hibernar, *v.i.* hibernate.
hibernés, -esa, hibernio, -nia, *a.* Hibernian.
híbrido, -da, *a.* hybrid.
hice [HACER].
hidalgo, -ga, *a.* noble.—*n.m.f.* noble.—*n.m.* nobleman.—*n.f.* noblewoman.
hidalguez, hidalguía, *n.f.* nobility.
hidrato, *n.m.* (*chem.*) hydrate.
hidráulico, -ca, *a.* hydraulic(al).—*n.f.* hydraulics.
hidroavión, *n.m.* seaplane; flying-boat.
hidrocarburo, *n.m.* (*chem.*) hydrocarbon.
hidrodeslizador, *n.m.* hydroplane.
hidroeléctrico, -ca, *a.* hydro-electric.
hidrófilo, -la, *a.* (*chem.*) hydrophilic; absorbent (*cotton*).
hidrófugo, -ga, hidrofugante, *a.* water-repellent.
hidrógeno, *n.m.* hydrogen.
hidrógrafo, *n.m.* hydrographer.
hidromel, hidromiel, *n.m.* hydromel, mead.
hidropesía, *n.f.* (*med.*) dropsy.
hidrópico, -ca, *a.* hydropic, dropsical.
hidroplano, *n.m.* hydroplane; seaplane, flying-boat.
hidrosulfuro, *n.m.* (*chem.*) hydrosulphide.
hidrotecnia, *n.f.* hydraulic engineering.
hidruro, *n.m.* (*chem.*) hydride.
hiedra, *n.f.* (*bot.*) ivy.
hiel, *n.f.* gall, bile; bitterness.
hielo, *n.m.* ice; frost; cold; ***punto de —,*** freezing-point.
hiemal, *a.* hibernal, winter.
hiena, *n.f.* hyena.
hienda, *n.f.* dung.
hierba, *n.f.* grass; herb; ***mala —,*** weed. —*pl.* pasture; herbal poison; herb soup.
hierbabuena, *n.f.* (*bot.*) mint.
hierro, *n.m.* iron; brand; weapon; — ***albo,*** white-hot iron; — ***colado,*** cast iron; — ***de fragua,*** wrought iron; — ***a Vizcaya,*** coals to Newcastle.—*pl.* irons (*shackles*).
higa, *n.f.* amulet; mockery.
hígado, *n.m.* liver.—*pl.* (*fam.*) guts; ***malos hígados,*** ill-will.
higiene, *n.f.* hygiene; sanitation.
higiénico, -ca, *a.* hygienic(al); ***papel —,*** lavatory paper.
higo, *n.m.* fig; (*vet.*) thrush; (*fig.*) rap, fig; — ***chumbo,*** prickly pear.
higuera, *n.f.* (*bot.*) fig-tree; — ***chumba,*** prickly pear; — ***del diablo*** or ***infernal,*** castor-oil plant.
hija, *n.f.* daughter [HIJO].
hijastro, -tra, *n.m.f.* stepchild.—*n.m.* stepson. —*n.f.* stepdaughter.
hijo, -ja, *n.m.f.* child; young (*of animals*); issue, product.—*n.m.* son; — ***político,*** son-in-law.—*n.f.* daughter.
hijodalgo, *n.m.* [HIDALGO].
hijuela, *n.f.* little daughter; gore, gusset; branch drain *or* path *etc.*
hijuelo, *n.m.* little son; (*bot.*) sucker.
hila, *n.f.* row, line; spinning.—*pl.* (*med.*) lint; (*S.A.*) cotton waste.
hilacha, *n.f.,* **hilacho,** *n.m.* loose thread; fraying; (*S.A.*) tatter, rag.
hilado, *n.m.* spinning; thread.
hilandería, *n.f.* spinning-mill.
hilandero, -ra, *n.m.f.* spinner.—*n.m.* spinning mill.
hilar, *v.t., v.i.* spin.
hilarante, *a.* mirthful; laughing (*gas*).
hilaridad, *n.f.* hilarity.
hilatura, *n.f.* spinning.
hilaza, *n.f.* yarn; uneven thread.
hilera, *n.f.* row, line.
hilo, *n.m.* thread; linen; yarn; edge (*of a blade*); filament; wire; — ***de perlas,*** string of pearls; ***a —,*** successively; ***al —,*** with the thread.
hilván, *n.m.* tacking (*in sewing*); (*S.A.*) hem; ***de —,*** rapidly.
hilvanar, *v.t.* tack (*in sewing*); (*fig.*) throw together in a hurry; (*S.A.*) hem.
La Himalaya, *n.f.* the Himalayas.
himalayo, -ya, *a.* Himalayan.
himnario, *n.m.* hymnal.
himno, *n.m.* hymn; — ***nacional,*** national anthem.
himnología, *n.f.* hymnology.
hin, *n.m.* neigh.
hincadura, *n.f.* driving; thrusting.
hincapié, *n.m.* ***hacer — en algo,*** insist on s.th.
hincar [A], *v.t.* fix, drive in (*a nail etc.*); — (***la rodilla***), bend (*the knee*).—*v.r.* kneel (down).
hincón, *n.m.* hitching- *or* mooring-post.
hincha, *n.f.* (*fam.*) grudge.—*n.m.* (*fam.*) fan, supporter.
hinchar, *v.t.* inflate, swell.—*v.r.* swell (up); become puffed up.
hinchazón, *n.m.* swelling; vanity.
hindú, -dúa, *a., n.m.f.* (*pl.* **-úes, -úas**) Hindu; Indian.
hiniesta, *n.f.* (*bot.*) broom.
hinojo (1), *n.m.* (*bot.*) fennel; — ***marino,*** samphire.
hinojo (2), *n.m.* (*obs.*) knee; ***de hinojos,*** on one's knees.
hipar, *v.i.* hiccup; pant (*of dogs*); whine; (*fig.*) — ***por,*** long for.
hipérbola, *n.f.* (*geom.*) hyperbola.
hipérbole, *n.f.* (*lit.*) hyperbole.
hiperbólico, -ca, *a.* (*geom., lit.*) hyperbolical.
hipercrítico, -ca, *a.* hypercritical.—*n.m.f.* severe critic.—*n.f.* severe criticism.
hipertensión, *n.f.* (*med.*) hypertension; high blood-pressure.
hípico, -ca, *a.* equine.—*n.f.* show-jumping; horse-racing.
hipido, *n.m.* whining.
hipismo, *n.m.* horse-training; equestrianism.
hipnosis, *n.f. inv.* hypnosis.

hipnótico, -ca, *a., n.m.f.* hypnotic.—*n.m.* hypnotic (*drug*).
hipnotismo, *n.m.* hypnotism.
hypnotizar [C], *v.t.* hypnotize.
hipo, *n.m.* hiccup; longing; grudge.
hipocampo, *n.m.* sea-horse.
hipocondría, *n.f.* hypochondria.
hipocondriaco, hipocondríaco, hipocóndrico, -ca, *a., n.m.f.* hypochondriac.
hipocrás, *n.m.* hippocras, grog.
hipocrático, -ca, *a.* Hippocratic.
hipocresía, *n.f.* hypocrisy.
hipócrita, *a.* hypocritical.—*n.m.f.* hypocrite.
hipodérmico, -ca, *a.* hypodermic.
hipódromo, *n.m.* hippodrome.
hipopótamo, *n.m.* hippopotamus.
hiposo, -sa, *a.* having hiccups.
hipoteca, *n.f.* mortgage.
hipotecable, *a.* mortgageable.
hipotecar [A], *v.t.* mortgage, hypothecate.
hipotensión, *n.f.* (*med.*) low blood-pressure.
hipotenusa, *n.f.* hypotenuse.
hipótesis, *n.f. inv.* hypothesis.
hipotético, -ca, *a.* hypothetical.
hiriente, *a.* stinging, cutting, hurting.
hirma, *n.f.* selvedge.
hirsuto, -ta, *a.* hirsute; (*fig.*) gruff.
hirviente, *a.* boiling.
hisca, *n.f.* bird-lime.
hisop(e)ar, *v.t.* (*eccl.*) asperse.
hisopillo, *n.m.* small aspergill; mouth-swab; (*bot.*) winter-savory.
hisopo, *n.m.* (*bot.*) hyssop; (*eccl.*) hyssop, aspergill.
hispalense, *a.* rel. to Seville.
hispánico, -ca, *a.* Hispanic.
hispanidad, *n.f.* Spanish character *or* spirit; Spanish-speaking community.
hispanismo, *n.m.* Hispanicism, Spanish idiom *or* turn of phrase; Spanish studies.
hispanista, *n.m.f.* Hispanist, Spanish scholar.
hispanizar [C], *v.t.* Hispanicize.
hispano, -na, *a.* Spanish, Hispanic.—*n.m.f.* Spaniard, man *or* woman of Spanish stock.
Hispanoamérica, *n.f.* Spanish America, Latin America.
hispanoamericano, -na, *a.* Spanish American, Latin American.
hispanohablante, *a.* Spanish-speaking.—*n.m.f.* speaker of Spanish.
histérico, -ca, *a.* hysterical.
histerismo, *n.m.* hysteria.
histología, *n.f.* histology.
historia, *n.f.* history; tale, story; — ***natural,*** natural history; ***de*** —, infamous, notorious.
historiador, -ra, *n.m.f,* historian.
historial, *a.* historical.—*n.m.* record sheet.
historiar, *v.t.* relate (*history, story*); (*art.*) depict, illustrate.
histórico, -ca, *a.* historic(al).
historieta, *n.f.* anecdote.
hita, *n.f.* brad, panel-pin, nail.
hito, -ta, *a.* (*obs.*) adjoining (*house, street*).—*n.m.* landmark; milestone; target; ***dar en el*** —, hit the nail on the head.
hitón, *n.m.* large headless cut nail.
hocico, *n.m.* snout; ***poner*** —, pout.
hocicón, -cona, hocicudo, -da, *a.* big-snouted.
hocino, *n.m.* sickle, bill-hook; gorge.
hogaño, *adv.* (*obs.*) this year.
hogar, *n.m.* hearth, fire-place; fire-chamber, furnace; home; hostel.
hogaza, *n.f.* large loaf.
hoguera, *n.f.* bonfire.
hoja, *n.f.* leaf (*of plant, book, door*); — ***de ruta,*** waybill.
hojalata, *n.f.* tin, tin-plate.
hojaldre, *n.m.* or *f.* puff-pastry.
hojear, *v.t.* leaf through, skim through.—*v.t.* flutter (*of leaves*).
hojuela, *n.f.* small leaf; pancake; foil.
¡hola! *interj.* hello!
Holanda, *n.f.* Holland; **holanda,** *n.f.* cambric, (*U.S.*) chambray.
holandés, -desa, *a.* Dutch.—*n.m.* Dutchman; Dutch (*language*).—*n.f.* Dutchwoman.
holgadomente, *adv.* amply; easily.
holganza, *n.f.* ease; leisure; enjoyment.
holgar [4B], *v.i.* rest; be idle; be unnecessary; be too loose; be glad (***con,*** at).—*v.r.* be idle; amuse oneself.
holgazán, -zana, *a.* idle, indolent.—*n.m.f.* idler, loafer.
holgazanear, *v.i.* idle; loiter.
holgorio, *n.m.* mirth; spree.
holgura, *n.f.* mirth; spree; ease; looseness, (*mech.*) play.
holocausto, *n.m.* holocaust; burnt-offering.
hológrafo, -fa, *a.* holograph.
hollar [4], *v.t.* trample, tread upon.
hollejo, *n.m.* skin, peel, husk.
hollín, *n.m.* soot, smut.
holliniento, -ta, *a.* sooty, fuliginous.
hombracho, *n.m.* well-built man.
hombradía, *n.f.* manliness.
hombre, *n.m.* man; mankind; (*low*) husband; ombre (*cards*); — ***de estado,*** statesman.
hombrear, *v.i.* shoulder, vie (***con,*** with).—*v.r.* vie (***con,*** with).
hombrecillo, *n.m.* little man; (*bot.*) hop.
hombrera, *n.f.* epaulette; shoulder-strap.
hombría, *n.f.* manliness.
hombrillo, *n.m.* yoke (*of a shirt*).
hombro, *n.m.* shoulder.
hombruno, -na, *a.* mannish (*of a woman*).
homenaje, *n.m.* homage.
Homero, *n.m.* Homer.
homicida, *a.* homicidal, murderous.—*n.m.* murderer.—*n.f.* murderess.
homicidio, *n.m.* murder, homicide, manslaughter.
homilía, *n.f.* homily.
homogeneidad, *n.f.* homogeneity.
homogen(e)izar [C], *v.t.* homogenize; normalize (*steel*).
homogéneo, -nea, *a.* homogeneous.
homologar [B], *v.t.* validate (*a record*).
homólogo, -ga, *a.* homologous.
homonimia, *n.f.* homonymy.
homónimo, -ma, *a.* homonymous.—*n.m.f.* namesake.—*n.m.* homonym.
honda, *n.f.* sling.
hondo, -da, *a.* deep; low.—*n.m.* depth; bottom.
hondón, *n.m.* bottom (*of cup*); eye (*of needle*); dell; hole.
hondonada, *n.f.* dell, ravine.
hondura, *n.f.* depth; profundity.
Honduras, *n.f.pl.* (*geog.*) Honduras.
hondureño, -ña, *a., n.m.f.* Honduran.
honestidad, *n.f.* modesty; decency; honourableness.

honesto, -ta, *a.* decent, chaste; honourable.
hongo, *n.m.* mushroom, fungus; bowler hat.
honor, *n.m.* honour; reputation.
honorable, *a.* honourable.
honorario, -ria, *a.* honorary.—*n.m.* honorarium.
honorífico, -ca, *a.* honorific, honourable.
honra, *n.f.* honour; reputation.—*pl.* obsequies.
honradez, *n.f.* integrity.
honrado, -da, *a.* honest, honourable, upright.
honrar, *v.t.* honour.—*v.r.* deem it an honour (***de,*** to).
honrilla, *n.f.* keen sense of honour.
honroso, -sa, *a.* honourable (*action*).
hopo, *n.m.* bushy tail, brush.
hora, *n.f.* hour; time; — ***de cenar,*** supper time; ***a la —,*** on time; ***¿qué — es?*** what is the time? ***horas extraordinarias,*** overtime.
Horacio, *n.m.* Horace.
horadar, *v.t.* perforate, bore.
horario, -ria, *a.* hour.—*n.m.* hour-hand; time-table.
horca, *n.f.* gallows, gibbet; pitch-fork.
a horcajadas, a horcajadillas, *adv.phr.* astride.
horchata, *n.f.* horchata, orgeat.
horda, *n.f.* horde.
hordiate, *n.m.* pearl barley.
horizontal, *a.* horizontal.
horizonte, *n.m.* horizon.
horma, *n.f.* mould, last.
hormiga, *n.f.* ant.
hormigón, *n.m.* concrete; — ***armado,*** reinforced concrete.
hormigonera, *n.f.* concrete mixer.
hormiguear, *v.i.* itch; swarm (*as with ants*).
hormigueo, *n.m.* crawling sensation; itch.
hormiguero, *n.m.* ant-hill.
hormiguillo, *n.m.* (*vet.*) founders; human chain.
hormón, *n.m.* hormone.
hormonal, *a.* hormone.
hornero, -ra, *n.m.f.* baker.
hornillo, *n.m.* stove (*for cooking*).
horno, *n.m.* oven, kiln, furnace; ***alto —,*** blast furnace.
horóscopo, *n.m.* horoscope.
horquilla, *n.f.* fork; fork-socket; (*mil.*) bracket (*in gunnery*); (*naut.*) rowlock.
horrendo, -da, *a.* horrible, awful.
hórreo, *n.m.* granary.
horrible, *a.* horrible.
horridez, *n.f.* dreadfulness.
hórrido, -da, horrífico, -ca, *a.* horrible, horrific.
horripilante, *a.* horrifying.
horro, -rra, *a.* free; freed; barren.
horror, *n.m.* horror.
horrorizar [C], *v.t.* horrify.
horroroso, -sa, *a.* horrible.
hortaliza, *n.f.* (*fresh*) vegetable, garden produce.
hortelano, -na, *a.* rel. to gardens.—*n.m.f.* gardener.
hortensia, *n.f.* (*bot.*) hydrangea.
hortícola, *a.* horticultural.
horticultura, *n.f.* gardening, horticulture.
hosco, -ca, *a.* swarthy; sullen, dour.
hospedaje, *n.m.* lodging.
hospedar, *v.t.* lodge, give lodging, put up.—*v.i., v.r.* lodge, stop at.
hospedería, *n.f.* hostelry, hostel, guest-house.
hospicio, *n.m.* hospice; asylum.
hospital, *n.m.* hospital, infirmary.
hospitalario, -ria, *a.* hospitable.—*n.m.* (*hist.*) Hospitaller.
hospitalidad, *n.f.* hospitality.
hostal, *n.m.* hostelry.
hostia, *n.f.* (*eccl.*) host, wafer.
hostigar [B], *v.t.* lash; chastise; censure severely; trouble.
hostigo, *n.m.* lash.
hostil, *a.* hostile.
hostilidad, *n.f.* hostility.
hostilizar [C], *v.t.* harass, raid.
hotel, *n.m.* hotel; mansion; — ***de ventas,*** auction rooms.
hotelero, -ra, *a.* rel. to hotels.—*n.m.* hotelier hotel-keeper.
hoy, *adv.* today; — ***día*** or — ***en día,*** nowadays; — ***por la tarde,*** this evening.
hoya, *n.f.* hole, pit; grave.
hoyo, *n.m.* hole, pit; grave.
hoyoso, -sa, *a.* pitted.
hoyuelo, *n.m.* dimple.
hoz, *n.f.* sickle, bill-hook; ravine.
hozar [C], *v.t.* root (*as pigs*).
hua- *see also* [GUA-].
huacal, *n.m.* crate.
hucha, *n.f.* large chest; money-box, (*child's*) piggy-bank.
hueco, -ca, *a.* hollow.—*n.m.* hollow; gap.
huelga, *n.f.* rest; strike (*in industry*).
huelgo, *n.m.* breath (*mech.*) clearance, slack.
huelguista, *n.m.f.* striker.
huella, *n.f.* footprint; trace.
huello, *n.m.* trodden path; treading.
huérfano, -na, *a., n.m.f.* orphan.
huero, -ra, *a.* addled; empty, vain; (*C.A.*) blond(e) [GÜERO].
huerta, *n.f.* stretch of irrigable land; market-gardening region.
huerto, *n.m.* orchard; fruit and vegetable garden.
huesa, *n.f.* grave.
hueso, *n.m.* bone; stone, core.
huesoso, -sa, *a.* bony, osseous.
huésped, -da, *n.m.f.* guest; host; innkeeper.
hueste, *n.f.* host, army.
huesudo, -da, *a.* bony.
hueva, *n.f.* spawn, roe.
huevera, *n.f.* egg-woman; ovary (*of fowls*); egg-cup.
huevo, *n.m.* egg.
huida, *n.f.* flight; escape.
huidizo, -za, *a.* fugitive, fleeting.
huir, *v.i., v.r.* flee.
hule, *n.m.* oil-cloth, American cloth; (*S.A.*) rubber.
hulla, *n.f.* (pit-)coal.
hullero, -ra, *a.* rel. to coal.—*n.m.* colliery.
humanidad, *n.f.* humanity.—*pl.* humanities.
humanismo, *n.m.* humanism.
humanista, *n.m.* humanist.
humanitario, -ria, *a.* humanitarian.
humano, -na, *a.* human; humane.—*n.m.* human being.
humarada, humareda, *n.f.* cloud of smoke.
humeante, *a.* smoking, fuming.
humear, *v.i.* smoke, emit smoke.
humedad, *n.f.* humidity.

humedecer [9], *v.t.* moisten.
húmedo, *a.* humid; wet, damp.
húmero, *n.m.* (*anat.*) humerus, funny-bone.
humildad, *n.f.* humility, modesty, lowliness.
humilde, *a.* humble; modest.
humillación, *n.f.* humiliation.
humillante, *a.* humiliating.
humillar, *v.t.* humiliate, humble.—*v.r.* humble oneself.
humo, *n.m.* smoke; fume.
humor, *n.m.* humour; disposition; (*med.*) humour; ***buen* —,** good nature; ***mal* —,** ill-temper.
humorismo, *n.m.* (*med.*) theory of the humours; humourous style.
humorístico, -ca, *a.* comic, humorous.
hundible, *a.* sinkable.
hundimiento, *n.m.* subsidence; sinking; downfall.
hundir, *v.t.* sink; immerse; pull down; ruin. —*v.r.* sink; collapse.
húngaro, -ra, *a., n.m.f.* Hungarian.
Hungría, *n.f.* Hungary.
huno, -na, *a.* Hunnish.
hupe, *n.f.* touchwood, tinder.
huracán, *n.m.* hurricane.
huraño, -ña, *a.* shy, wild.
hurgar [B], *v.t.* poke (*fire*); stir up.
hurgón, *n.m.* poker; ash rake.
hurón, -rona, *a.* shy; intractable.—*n.m.f.* ferret.
¡hurra! *interj.* hurrah!
a hurtadillas, *adv. phr.* stealthily.
hurtar, *v.t.* steal.—*v.r.* steal off.
hurto, *n.m.* theft, robbery.
husma, *n.f.* (*fam.*) snooping.
husmear, *v.t.* scent, get wind of; (*fam*) pry. —*v.i.* smell high.
husmo, *n.m.* high smell; ***andarse al* —,** be on the scent.
huso, *n.m.* spindle; bobbin; gore (*of parachute*).
huta, *n.f.* hut; (*huntsman's*) hide.
hutía, *n.f.* (*zool.*) hutia, Cuban rat.
¡huy! *interj.* expressing surprise, grief *or* pain.

I

I, i, *n.f.* tenth letter of the Spanish alphabet.
iba [IR].
ibérico, -ca, iberio, -ria, *a.* Iberian.
ibero, -ra, *a., n.m.f.* Iberian.
iberoamericano, -na, *a., n.m.f.* Ibero-American.
íbice, *n.m.* ibex.
ibicenco, -ca, *a., n.m.f.* rel. to *or* native of Ibiza, Iviza.
ibis, *n.f.* ibis.
Ibiza, *n.f.* Ibiza, Iviza.
icón, *n.m.* icon.
iconoclasia, *n.f.,* **iconoclasmo,** *n.m.* iconoclasm.
iconoclasta, *a.* iconoclastic.—*n.m.f.* iconoclast.
ictericia, *n.f.* (*med.*) jaundice.
ictiología, *n.f.* ichthyology.
ida, *n.f.* going, departure; impetuosity; trail; sally; ***de* — *y vuelta,*** return (*ticket*); ***idas y venidas,*** comings and goings.
idea, *n.f.* idea.
ideal, *a., n.m.* ideal.
idealismo, *n.m.* idealism.
idealista, *a.* idealist(ic).—*n.m.f.* idealist.
idealización, *n.f.* idealization.
idealizar [C], *v.t.* idealize.
idear, *v.t.* plan, contrive.
ideario, *n.m.* ideology, idearium.
ideático, -ca, *a.* (*S.A.*) whimsical.
idéntico, -ca, *a.* identical.
identidad, *n.f.* identity; identicalness.
identificable, *a.* identifiable.
identificación, *n.f.* identification.
identificar [A], *v.t.* identify.
ideograma, *n.m.* ideogram.
ideología, *n.f.* ideology.
ideológico, -ca, *a.* ideological.
ideólogo, *n.m.* ideologist.
idílico, -ca, *a.* idyllic.
idilio, *n.m.* idyll.
idioma, *n.m.* language; parlance, jargon, idiom.
idiomático, -ca, *a.* idiomatic.
idiosincrasia, *n.f.* idiosyncrasy.
idiosincrático, -ca, *a.* idiosyncratic.
idiota, *a., n.m.f.* idiot.
idiotez, *n.f.* idiocy.
idiótico, -ca, *a.* idiotic.
idiotismo, *n.m.* idiom; crass ignorance.
ido, -da, *a.* (*fam.*) gone, daft; tipsy, drunk.—*p.p.* [IR].
idólatra, *a.* idolatrous.—*n.m.* idolater, idolizer.—*n.f.* idolatress, idolizer.
idolatrar, *v.t.* idolize; idolatrize.
idolatría, *n.f.* idolatry; idolization.
ídolo, *n.m.* idol.
idóneo, -nea, *a.* suitable, proper.
idus, *n.m.pl.* ides.
iglesia, *n.f.* church.
iglú, *n.m.* (*pl.* **-úes**) igloo.
Ignacio, *n.m.* Ignatius.
ignaro, -ra, *a.* ignorant.
ignición, *n.f.* ignition.
ignícola, *n.m.f.* fire-worshipper.
ignifugar [B], *v.t.* flame-proof (*cloth etc.*).
ignoble, *a.* ignoble.
ignominia, *n.f.* ignominy.
ignominioso, -sa, *a.* ignominious.
ignorancia, *n.f.* ignorance; unawareness.
ignorante, *a.* ignorant; unaware.—*n.m.f.* ignoramus.
ignorar, *v.t.* not know.
ignoto, -ta, *a.* unknown.
igual, *a.* equal; level, even; consistent; same, alike.—*adv.* the same, similarly; ***al* — *que,*** just as, like; ***en* — *de,*** in lieu of; ***por* —,** equally; ***me es* —,** it's all the same to me; ***sin* —,** matchless, unequalled.
iguala, *n.f.* equalization; agreement; stipend.
igualación, *n.f.* equalization; levelling; matching; agreement.
igualar, *v.t.* equalize; level off; match, pair; equate; settle, adjust, iron out.—*v.i., v.r.* be equal.
igualdad, *n.f.* equality; levelness; sameness; evenness.
igualitario, -ria, *a., n.m.f.* egalitarian.
igualmente, *adv.* likewise; (*fam.*) the same to you.

iguana, *n.f.* iguana.
ijada, *n.f.* flank; loin; stitch, pain in side; (*fig.*) weak spot.
ijadear, *v.i.* pant.
ijar, *n.m.* flank, loin.
ilegal, *a.* illegal, unlawful.
ilegalidad, *n.f.* illegality.
ilegibilidad, *n.f.* illegibility.
ilegible, *a.* illegible.
ilegitimidad, *n.f.* illegitimacy.
ilegítimo, -ma, *a.* illegitimate.
ileso, -sa, *a.* unharmed.
Ilíada, *n.f.* Iliad.
ilícito, -ta, *a.* illicit.
ilimitado, -da, *a.* unlimited, limitless.
ilógico, -ca, *a.* illogical.
iludir, *v.t.* mislead, delude.
iluminación, *n.f.* illumination; enlightenment.
iluminado, -da, *a.* illuminated; enlightened. —*n.m.pl.* illuminati.
iluminar, *v.t.* illuminate; enlighten.
ilusión, *n.f.* illusion.
ilusionar, *v.t.* fascinate, give illusions to.—*v.r.* have illusions.
ilusionista, *n.m.f.* illusionist.
ilusivo, -va, *a.* illusive.
iluso, -sa, *a.* deluded; visionary.
ilusorio, -ria, *a.* illusory.
ilustración, *n.f.* illustration; learning, enlightenment; ennobling.
ilustrado, -da, *a.* illustrated; learned; enlightened.
ilustrar, *v.t.* illustrate; ennoble; inspire; educate.
ilustrativo, -va, *a.* illustrative.
ilustre, *a.* illustrious.
imagen, *n.f.* (*pl.* **imágenes**) image.
imaginable, *a.* imaginable.
imaginación, *n.f.* imagination.
imaginar, *v.t.*, *v.i.*, *v.r.* imagine.
imaginario, -ria, *a.* imaginary.—*n.f.* (*mil.*) reserves.
imaginería, *n.f.* imagery; statuary.
imán, *n.m.* magnet, lodestone; magnetism; (*relig.*) imam.
iman(t)ación, *n.f.* magnetizing.
iman(t)ar, *v.t.* magnetize.
imbécil, *a.*, *n.m.f.* imbecile.
imbecilidad, *n.f.* imbecility.
imberbe, *a.* beardless; raw, green.
imborrable, *a.* ineradicable, indelible.
imbuir [O], *v.t.* imbue (***de, en,*** with).
imitación, *n.f.* imitation.
imitador, -ra, *a.* imitative.—*n.m.f.* imitator.
imitar, *v.t.* imitate.
impaciencia, *n.f.* impatience.
impacientar, *v.t.* make impatient.—*v.r.* get impatient.
impaciente, *a.* impatient.
impacto, *n.m.* impact.
impago, -ga, *a.* (*S.A.*) unpaid.
impalpabilidad, *n.f.* impalpability.
impalpable, *a.* impalpable.
impar, *a.* odd, uneven.—*n.m.* odd number.
imparcial, *a.* impartial, disinterested.
imparcialidad, *n.f.* impartiality.
imparidad, *n.f.* oddness, imparity.
impartir, *v.t.* impart.
impasible, *a.* impassive.
impavidez, *n.f.* intrepidity.
impávido, -da, *a.* dauntless, intrepid.
impecable, *a.* impeccable.
impedido, -da, *a.* disabled.
impedimenta, *n.f.* impedimenta.
impedimento, *n.m.* impediment.
impedir [8], *v.t.* prevent, impede.
impeler, *v.t.* propel, impel.
impenetrabilidad, *n.f.* impenetrability.
impenetrable, *a.* impenetrable.
impenitente, *a.* impenitent.
impensado, -da, *a.* unforeseen.
imperar, *v.i.* rule, hold sway.
imperativo, -va, *a.*, *n.m.* imperative.
imperceptible, *a.* imperceptible.
imperdible, *n.m.* safety-pin.
imperdonable, *a.* unpardonable.
imperecedero, -ra, *a.* imperishable.
imperfecto, -ta, *a.*, *n.m.* imperfect.
imperforable, *a.* imperforable; puncture-proof.
imperial, *a.* imperial.—*n.f.* top-deck.
imperialismo, *n.m.* imperialism.
imperialista, *a.*, *n.m.f.* imperialist.
impericia, *n.f.* inexpertness, lack of skill.
imperio, *n.m.* empire; dominion, sway.
imperioso, -sa, *a.* imperious.
imperito, -ta, *a.* inexpert.
impermanente, *a.* impermanent.
impermeabilizar [C], *v.t.* waterproof.
impermeable, *a.* impermeable; waterproof. —*n.m.* raincoat.
impersonal, *a.* impersonal.
impersonalidad, *n.f.* impersonality.
impertérrito, -ta, *a.* dauntless.
impertinencia, *n.f.* impertinence.
impertinente, *a.* impertinent.—*n.m.pl.* lorgnettes.
imperturbabilidad, *n.f.* imperturbability.
imperturbable, *a.* imperturbable.
impetrar, *v.t.* entreat; get by entreaty.
ímpetu, *n.m.* impetus; impetuousness.
impetuosidad, *n.f.* impetuosity.
impetuoso, -sa, *a.* impetuous.
impiedad, *n.f.* impiety; pitilessness.
impío, -pía, *a.* impious, godless; cruel.
implacabilidad, *n.f.* implacability.
implacable, *a.* implacable.
implantar, *v.t.* implant, introduce.
implicación, *n.f.* contradiction; implication.
implicar [A], *v.t.* imply; implicate.—*v.i.* oppose, contradict.
implícito, -ta, *a.* implicit.
implorar, *v.t.* implore.
impolítico, -ca, *a.* impolitic; impolite.—*n.f.* discourtesy.
imponderable, *a.*, *n.m.* imponderable.
imponente, *a.* imposing, impressive.
imponer [25], *v.t.* impose; invest; acquaint (***en,*** with), instruct (***en,*** in); impute falsely. —*v.i.* command respect, be imposing.—*v.r.* dominate; acquaint oneself (***de,*** with); ***se impone,*** it becomes essential (to).
impopular, *a.* unpopular.
importación, *n.f.* importing, imports.
importador, -ra, *a.* importing.—*n.m.f.* importer.
importancia, *n.f.* importance; concern.
importante, *a.* important; considerable.
importar, *v.t.* amount to, be worth; imply; concern; (*com.*) import.—*v.i.* matter, be important.
importe, *n.m.* amount; value.
importunación, *n.f.* importuning.

importunar, *v.t.* importune, pester.
importunidad, *n.f.* importunity.
importuno, -na, *a.* importunate; inopportune.
imposibilidad, *n.f.* impossibility.
imposibilitar, *v.t.* render unable; make impossible; disable.—*v.r.* become unable; be disabled; become impossible.
imposible, *a.* impossible.
imposición, *n.f.* imposition.
impostor, -ra, *a.* cheating.—*n.m.f.* impostor.
impostura, *n.f.* imposture; false accusation.
impotencia, *n.f.* impotence.
impotente, *a.* impotent.
impracticable, *a.* impracticable; impassable.
impráctico, -ca, *a.* impractical.
imprecación, *n.f.* imprecation.
imprecar [A], *v.t.* imprecate, curse.
impreciso, -sa, *a.* imprecise, indefinite.
impregnación, *n.f.* impregnation.
impregnar, *v.t.* impregnate, saturate.
impremeditado, -da, *a.* unpremeditated.
imprenta, *n.f.* printing; press; printed matter; impress(ion).
imprescindible, *a.* indispensable.
impresión, *n.f.* printing; impression; stamp; (*phot.*) print; — ***digital,*** finger print.
impresionable, *a.* impressionable.
impresionante, *a.* impressing, impressive.
impresionar, *v.t.* impress; (*phot.*) expose.
impresionismo, *n.m.* Impressionism.
impresionista, *a., n.m.f.* Impressionist.
impreso, -sa, *a.* printed.—*n.m.* printed book. —*pl.* printed matter.
impresor, -ra, *n.m.f.* printer.
imprevisible, *a.* unforseeable.
imprevisión, *n.f.* improvidence.
imprevisto, -ta, *a.* unforeseen.
imprimir, *v.t.* print; impress; stamp.
improbabilidad, *n.f.* improbability.
improbable, *a.* improbable.
improbar, *v.t.* disapprove, censure.
ímprobo, -ba, *a.* dishonest; laborious.
improcedente, *a.* unlawful; inappropriate.
impronta, *n.f.* stamp, mark.
impronunciable, *a.* unpronounceable.
improperio, *n.m.* insult, affront.
impropiedad, *n.f.* impropriety.
improprio, *a.* improper (***a, de, en, para,*** to); alien.
impróvido, -da, *a.* improvident.
improvisación, *n.f.* improvisation; impromptu; unmerited success.
improvisar, *v.t., v.i.* improvise.
improviso, -sa, improvisto, -ta, *a.* unforeseen, unexpected; ***al*** or ***de*** —, or ***a la improvista,*** unexpectedly.
imprudente, *a.* imprudent.
impudencia, *n.f.* shamelessness, impudence.
impudente, *a.* shameless, impudent.
impúdico, -ca, *a.* immodest, shameless.
impuesto, *a.* imposed; informed (***de,*** about). —*n.m.* tax, duty.—*p.p.* [IMPONER].
impugnar, *v.t.* contest, impugn.
impulsar, *v.t.* impel; (*mech.*) drive.
impulsión, *n.f.* impulsion; impulse.
impulsivo, -va, *a.* impulsive.
impulso, *n.m.* impulse; impulsion.
impulsor, -ra, *a.* impelling; (*mech.*) driving.
impune, *a.* unpunished.
impunidad, *n.f.* impunity.
impureza, impuridad, *n.f.* impurity.
impuro, -ra, *a.* impure.
impuse, -so [IMPONER].
imputación, *n.f.* imputation.
imputar, *v.t.* impute; (*com.*) credit on account.
inabordable, *a.* unapproachable.
inacabable, *a.* interminable, endless.
inaccessibilidad, *n.f.* inaccessibility.
inaccessible, *a.* inaccessible.
inacción, *n.f.* inaction.
inaceptable, *a.* unacceptable.
inactividad, *n.f.* inactivity.
inactivo, -va, *a.* inactive.
inadecuado, -da, *a.* inadequate.
inadmisible, *a.* inadmissible.
inadvertencia, *n.f.* inadvertency; oversight.
inadvertido, -da, *a.* unnoticed; inadvertent.
inagotable, *a.* inexhaustible.
inaguantable, *a.* intolerable.
inajenable, *a.* inalienable.
inalterable, *a.* unalterable.
inalterado, -da, *a.* unchanged.
inane, *a.* inane.
inanidad, *n.f.* inanity.
inanimado, -da, *a.* inanimate.
inapagable, *a.* inextinguishable.
inapelable, *a.* without appeal; unavoidable.
inapetencia, *n.f.* lack of appetite.
inaplicable, *a.* inapplicable.
inaplicación, *n.f.* indolence, inapplication.
inaplicado, -da, *a.* indolent, careless.
inapreciable, *a.* inappreciable; inestimable.
inapto, -ta, *a.* inapt.
inarticulado, -da, *a.* inarticulate.
inasequible, *a.* unattainable, inaccessible.
inatención, *n.f.* inattention.
inatento, -ta, *a.* inattentive.
inaudible, *a.* inaudible.
inauguración, *n.f.* inauguration; opening, opening ceremony.
inaugural, *a.* inaugural.
inaugurar, *v.t.* inaugurate.
inaveriguable, *a.* unverifiable.
inca, *n.m.f.* Inca.
incaico, -ca, *a.* Inca.
incalculable, *a.* incalculable.
incalificable, *a.* unspeakable.
incambiable, *a.* unchangeable.
incandescencia, *n.f.* incandescence.
incandescente, *a.* incandescent.
incansable, *a.* tireless.
incapacidad, *n.f.* incapacity; incapability.
incapacitar, *v.t.* incapacitate; make impossible; declare incapable.
incapaz, *a.* (*pl.* **-aces**) incapable; incompetent.
incásico, -ca [INCAICO].
incautar, *v.r.* (*jur.*) seize, attach.
incauto, -ta, *a.* incautious, unwary.
incendiar, *v.t.* set fire to.—*v.r.* catch fire.
incendiario, -ria, *a., n.m.f.* incendiary.
incendio, *n.m.* fire, blaze.
incensar [I], *v.t.* incense, cense.
incensario, *n.m.* censer.
incentivo, -va, *a., n.m.* incentive.
incertidumbre, incertitud, *n.f.* uncertainty.
incesable, incesante, *a.* incessant, ceaseless.
incesto, *n.m.* incest.
incestuoso, -sa, *a.* incestuous.
incidencia, *n.f.* incidence; incident.
incidental, *a.* incidental.
incidente, *a., n.m.* incident.

incidir, *v.t.* (*med.*) make an incision.—*v.i.* fall (***en,*** into).
incienso, *n.m.* incense.
incierto, -ta, *a.* uncertain; untrue.
incineración, *n.f.* incineration, cremation.
incinerar, *v.t.* incinerate, cremate.
incipiente, *a.* incipient.
incircunciso, -sa, *a.* uncircumcised.
incisión, *n.f.* incision.
incisivo, -va, *a.* incisive.
incitación, *n.f.* inciting, incitement.
incitante, *a.* inciting; tempting.
incitar, *v.t.* incite (***a,*** to).
incivil, *a.* uncivil, incivil.
incivilidad, *n.f.* incivility.
incivilizado, -da, *a.* uncivilized.
inclasificable, *a.* unclassifiable.
inclemencia, *n.f.* inclemency; ***a la —,*** exposed to the elements.
inclemente, *a.* inclement.
inclinación, *n.f.* inclination; bow; gradient.
inclinar, *v.t.* incline.—*v.i.*, *v.r.* incline, be inclined; bow.
ínclito, -ta, *a.* renowned, illustrious.
incluir [O], *v.t.* include; enclose.
inclusión, *n.f.* inclusion; acquaintanceship.
inclusive, *a.* inclusively.
inclusivo, -va, *a.* inclusive.
incluso, -sa, *a.* enclosed.—*adv.* even; included, besides.
incoativo, -va, *a.* inchoative.
incógnito, -ta, *a.* unknown, incognito; ***de —,*** incognito.—*n.m.* incognito.—*n.f.* (*math.*) unknown quantity.
incoherencia, *n.f.* incoherence.
incoherente, *a.* incoherent.
íncola, *n.m.f.* inhabitant.
incoloro, -ra, *a.* colourless.
incólume, *a.* safe, unharmed.
incombustible, *a.* incombustible.
incomible, *a.* uneatable.
incomodar, *v.t.* inconvenience.—*v.r.* get angry.
incomodidad, *n.f.* inconvenience; uncomfortableness; vexation.
incómodo, -da, *a.* uncomfortable; inconvenient; cumbersome.—*n.m.* discomfort; inconvenience.
incomparable, *a.* incomparable.
incomparado, -da, *a.* matchless.
incompasivo, -va, *a.* pitiless.
incompatibilidad, *n.f.* incompatibility.
incompatible, *a.* incompatible.
incompetencia, *n.f.* incompetence, (*jur.*) incompetency.
incompetente, *a.* incompetent.
incompleto, -ta, *a.* incomplete.
incomprensible, *a.* incomprehensible.
incomprensión, *n.f.* lack of understanding.
incomunicable, *a.* untransferable.
incomunicación, *n.f.* solitary confinement, isolation.
incomunicado, -da, *a.* incommunicado.
inconcebible, *a.* inconceivable.
inconciliable, *a.* irreconcilable.
inconcluso, -sa, *a.* unfinished; inconclusive.
inconcuso, -sa, *a.* unquestionable.
incondicional, *a.* unconditional.
inconexión, *n.f.* incoherence; lack of connexion.
inconexo, -xa, *a.* unconnected, incoherent.
inconfundible, *a.* unmistakable.
incongruencia, *n.f.* incongruence, incongruity.
incongruente, *a.* incongruent.
incongruidad, *n.f.* incongruity.
incongruo, -rua, *a.* incongruous.
inconmensurable, *a.* incommensurable; immense.
inconmovible, *a.* unmovable, unyielding.
inconocible, *a.* unknowable.
inconquistable, *a.* impregnable; incorruptible.
inconsciencia, *n.f.* unconsciousness; unawareness.
inconsciente, *a.* unconscious; unknowing, unaware.
inconsecuencia, *n.f.* inconsequence.
inconsecuente, *a.* inconsequent; inconsistent.
inconsideración, *n.f.* inconsideration.
inconsiderado, -da, *a.* inconsiderate; unconsidered.
inconsiguiente, *a.* inconsistent.
inconsistencia, *n.f.* inconsistency.
inconsistente, *a.* inconsistent.
inconstancia, *n.f.* inconstancy.
inconstante, *a.* inconstant.
inconstitucional, *a.* unconstitutional.
incontable, *a.* uncountable, countless.
incontaminado, -da, *a.* uncontaminated.
incontestable, *a.* unquestionable, indisputable.
incontestado, -da, *a.* undisputed.
incontinencia, *n.f.* incontinence.
incontinente, *a.* incontinent.—*adv.* (*also* **incontinenti**) at once.
incontrastable, *a.* irresistible; unquestionable; unshakable.
incontrovertible, *a.* incontrovertible.
inconvenible, *a.* inconvenient; uncompromising.
inconveniencia, *n.f.* inconvenience; unfitness; impropriety; unlikeliness.
inconveniente, *a.* inconvenient; impolite; unsuitable.—*n.m.* objection, difficulty.
incorporación, *n.f.* incorporation.
incorporar, *v.t.* incorporate; embody.—*v.r.* sit up.
incorpóreo, -rea, *a.* incorporal.
incorrecto, -ta, *a.* incorrect.
incorregible, *a.* incorrigible.
incorruptible, *a.* incorruptible.
incorrupto, -ta, *a.* incorrupt, uncorrupted.
increado, -da, *a.* uncreated.
incredibilidad, *n.f.* incredibility.
incredulidad, *n.f.* incredulousness.
incrédulo, -la, *a.* incredulous.—*n.m.f.* unbeliever.
increíble, *a.* incredible, unbelievable.
incrementar, *v.t.* increase.
incremento, *n.m.* increment.
increpar, *v.t.* chide, rebuke.
incriminación, *n.f.* incrimination.
incriminar, *v.t.* incriminate.
incrustación, *n.f.* incrustation.
incrustar, *v.t.* encrust.
incubación, *n.f.* incubation, hatching.
incubar, *v.t.* incubate, hatch.
íncubo, *n.m.* incubus.
inculcar [A], *v.t.* inculcate.—*v.r.* be stubborn
inculpable, *a.* blameless.
inculpar, *v.t.* accuse, inculpate.
inculto, -ta, *a.* uncultured, uncivilized uncultivated.

incultura, *n.f.* lack of culture.
incumbencia, *n.f.* incumbency, concern.
incumbente, *a.* incumbent.
incumbir, *v.i.* be incumbent (***a,*** on).
incumplido, -da, *a.* unfulfilled.
incunable, *n.m.* incunabulum.
incurable, *a., n.m.f.* incurable.
incurrir, *v.i.* lapse; incur, become liable (***en,*** to).
incursión, *n.f.* incursion, inroad.
indagación, *n.f.* investigation.
indagar [B], *v.t.* investigate.
indebido, -da, *a.* undue; improper; uncalled-for.
indecencia, *n.f.* indecency.
indecente, *a.* indecent.
indecible, *a.* unspeakable.
indecisión, *n.f.* indecision.
indeciso, -sa, *a.* indecisive, undecided; vague.
indecoroso, -sa, *a.* indecorous.
indefectible, *a.* unfailing, indefectible.
indefendible, indefensable, indefensible, *a.* indefensible.
indefenso, -sa, *a.* defenceless.
indefinible, *a.* undefinable.
indefinido, -da, *a.* indefinite; undefined.
indeleble, *a.* indelible.
indelicadeza, *n.f.* indelicacy.
indelicado, -da, *a.* indelicate.
indemnidad, *n.f.* indemnity.
indemnizar [C], *v.t.* indemnify.
independencia, *n.f.* independence.
independiente, *a.* independent (***de,*** of).
indescifrable, *a.* undecipherable.
indescriptible, *a.* indescribable.
indeseable, *a., n.m.f.* undesirable.
indestructible, *a.* indestructible.
indeterminable, *a.* indeterminable.
indeterminación, *n.f.* indetermination.
indeterminado, -da, *a.* indeterminate.
la India, *n.f.* India.
indiano, -na, *a., n.m.f.* Indian (*West, East*). —*n.m.* nabob, emigrant who returns rich from the Americas.
Indias, *n.f.pl.* the Indies (*esp. West Indies*).
indicación, *n.f.* indication.
indicador, -ra, *a.* indicating.—*n.m.f.* indicator.
indicar [A], *v.t.* indicate.
indicativo, -va, *a., n.m.* indicative.
índice, *n.m.* index; index finger.
indicio, *n.m.* sign, mark, token; ***indicios vehementes,*** (*jur.*) circumstantial evidence.
índico, -ca, *a.* (East) Indian.
indiferencia, *n.f.* indifference.
indiferente, *a.* indifferent; immaterial.
indígena, *a., n.m.f.* native.
indigencia, *n.f.* indigence.
indigente, *a.* indigent.
indigestión, *n.f.* indigestion.
indigesto, -ta, *a.* indigestible; undigested.
indignación, *n.f.* indignation.
indignar, *v.t.* anger.—*v.r.* become indignant.
indignidad, *n.f.* indignity; unworthiness.
indigno, -na, *a.* unworthy.
índigo, *n.m.* indigo.
indio (1), **-dia,** *a., n.m.f.* Indian.
indio (2), *a.* blue.
indirecto, -ta, *a.* indirect.—*n.f.* innuendo hint.
indisciplina, *n.f.* indiscipline.
indisciplinado, -da, *a.* undisciplined.
indiscreción, *n.f.* indiscretion.
indiscreto, -ta, *a.* indiscreet.
indisculpable, *a.* inexcusable.
indiscutible, *a.* unquestionable, undeniable.
indisoluble, *a.* indissoluble.
indispensable, *a.* unpardonable; indispensable.
indisponer [25], *v.t.* indispose; prejudice.—*v.r.* become indisposed; quarrel; be cross.
indisposición, *n.f.* disinclination; indisposition.
indispuesto, -ta, *a.* indisposed; at variance. —*p.p.* [INDISPONER].
indisputable, *a.* indisputable.
indistinguible, *a.* indistinguishable.
indistinto, -ta, *a.* indistinct; joint (*account*).
individual, *a.* individual.
individualidad, *n.f.* individuality.
individualismo, *n.m.* individualism.
individualista, *a., n.m.f.* individualist.
individualizar [C], *v.t.* individualize.
individuo, -dua, *a.* individual.—*n.m.f.* member, fellow; individual; (*fam.*) character; self.
indivisible, *a.* indivisible.
indiviso, -sa, *a.* undivided.
indo, -da, *a., n.m.f.* Hindu.
indócil, *a.* indocile, unteachable.
indocto, -ta, *a.* unlearned.
la Indochina, *n.f.* Indo-China.
indochino, -na, *a., n.m.f.* Indo-Chinese.
indoeuropeo, -pea, *a., n.m.f.* Indo-European.
indogermánico, -ca, *a., n.m.* Indo-Germanic.
índole, *n.f.* disposition, temper; class, kind.
indolencia, *n.f.* indolence.
indolente, *a.* indolent.
indoloro, -ra, *a.* painless.
indómito, -ta, *a.* indomitable; unruly.
la Indonesia, *n.f.* Indonesia.
indonésico, -ca, indonesio, -sia, *a., n.m.f.* Indonesian.
inducción, *n.f.* inducing; induction.
inducido, *n.m.* (*elec.*) armature.
inducir [15], *v.t.* induce; lead (***en,*** into).
inductivo, -va, *a.* inductive.
indudable, *a.* indubitable, undoubted.
indulgencia, *n.f.* indulgence.
indulgente, *a.* indulgent.
indultar, *v.t.* pardon.
indulto, *n.m.* (*jur.*) pardon.
indumentario, -ria, *a.* rel. to clothing.—*n.f.* attire, garb.
indumento, *n.m.* attire, apparel.
industria, *n.f.* industry; industriousness; profession; ***de —,*** on purpose.
industrial, *a.* industrial.—*n.m.* industrialist.
industrialismo, *n.m.* industrialism.
industrializar [C], *v.t.* industrialize.
industriar, *v.r.* find a way, manage.
industrioso, -sa, *a.* industrious.
induzco [INDUCIR].
inédito, -ta, *a.* unpublished.
inefable, *a.* ineffable.
ineficacia, *n.f.* inefficacy.
ineficaz, *a.* ineffectual.
ineficiencia, *n.f.* inefficiency.
ineficiente, *a.* inefficient.
inelegante, *a.* inelegant.
ineluctable, *a.* inevitable.
ineludible, *a.* unavoidable.

inepcia, ineptitud, *n.f.* ineptitude, inaptitude.
inepto, -ta, *a.* inept, inapt.
inequívico, -ca, *a.* unequivocal.
inercia, *n.f.* inertia.
inerme, *a.* unarmed.
inerrable, *a.* unerring.
inerte, *a.* inert.
inescrutable, *a.* inscrutable.
inesperado, -da, *a.* unexpected.
inestable, *a.* unstable.
inestimable, *a.* inestimable.
inevitable, *a.* inevitable.
inexactitud, *n.f.* inexactitude.
inexacto, -ta, *a.* inexact; incorrect.
inexcusable, *a.* inexcusable.
inexistente, *a.* non-existent.
inexorable, *a.* inexorable.
inexperiencia, *n.f.* inexperience.
inexperto, -ta, *a.* inexpert; inexperienced.
inexplicable, *a.* inexplicable.
inexplorado, -da, *a.* unexplored.
inexpresivo, -va, *a.* inexpressive.
inexpugnable, *a.* impregnable.
inextinguible, *a.* inextinguishable.
inextricable, *a.* inextricable.
infalibilidad, *n.f.* infallibility.
infalible, *a.* infallible.
infamación, *n.f.* defamation.
infamador, -ra, *a.* defamatory.—*n.m.f.* defamer, slanderer.
infamar, *v.t.* defame, slander.
infame, *a.* infamous; sordid.—*n.m.f.* infamous wretch.
infamia, *n.f.* infamy.
infancia, *n.f.* infancy; infants.
infanta, *n.f.* infanta (*Spanish king's daughter*).
infante, *n.f.* infante (*Spanish king's son*); infantryman.
infantería, *n.f.* infantry.
infanticida, *a.* infanticidal.—*n.m.f.* infanticide (*person*).
infanticidio, *n.m.* infanticide (*crime*).
infantil, *a.* infantile; children's; childish.
infatigable, *a.* indefatigable, tireless.
infatuación, *n.f.* infatuation; vanity.
infatuar, *v.t.* make vain.—*v.r.* become vain.
infausto, -ta, *a.* luckless, unfortunate.
infección, *n.f.* infection.
infeccioso, -sa, *a.* infectious.
infectar, *v.t.* infect.
infecto, -ta, *a.* infected; foul.
infecundidad, *n.f.* infertility.
infecundo, -da, *a.* infertile.
infelicidad, *n.f.* unhappiness.
infeliz, *a.* (*pl.* **-ices**) unhappy.—*n.m.f.* (*fam.*) poor devil.
inferencia, *n.f.* inference.
inferior, *a.* inferior; lower (***a***, than).—*n.m.f.* inferior.
inferioridad, *n.f.* inferiority.
inferir [6], *v.t.* infer; inflict; entail.—*v.r.* follow, be deduced.
infernal, *a.* infernal.
infernar [I], *v.t.* (*fam.*) upset.
infestación, *n.f.* infestation.
infestar, *v.t.* infest.
inficionar, *v.t.* infect.
infidelidad, *n.f.* infidelity; infidels.
infidente, *a.* disloyal, faithless.
infiel, *a.* unfaithful; disloyal.—*a.*, *n.m.f.* infidel.
infiernillo, *n.m.* chafing dish; stove.
infierno, *n.m.* hell.
infiltración, *n.f.* infiltration.
infiltrar, *v.t.*, *v.r.* infiltrate.
ínfimo, -ma, *a.* lowest, worst.
infinidad, *n.f.* infinity.
infinitesimal, *a.* infinitesimal.
infinitivo, -va, *a.*, *n.m.* infinitive.
infinito, -ta, *a.*, *n.m.* infinite.—*adv.* immensely.
infinitud, *n.f.* infinitude.
inflación, *n.f.* inflation; vanity.
inflacionismo, *n.m.* inflationism.
inflacionista, *a.* inflationary, inflationist. —*n.m.f.* inflationist.
inflador, *n.m.* pump (*for tyres, balls etc.*).
inflamable, *a.* inflammable.
inflamación, *n.f.* inflammation; ardour.
inflamar, *v.t.* inflame; set on fire.—*v.r.* become inflamed; catch fire.
inflamatorio, -ria, *a.* inflammatory.
inflar, *v.t.* blow up, inflate.
inflexible, *a.* inflexible.
inflexión, *n.f.* bending; inflexion.
inflexionar, *v.t.* inflect.
infligir [E], *v.t.* inflict (***a***, on).
influencia, *n.f.* influence.
influenciar, *v.t.* influence.
influir [O], *v.i.* have (an) influence (***en, sobre***, on, over).
influjo, *n.m.* influence; (*naut.*) rising tide.
influyente, *a.* influential.
infolio, *n.m.* folio volume.
información, *n.f.* information; inquiry; report; (*jur.*) brief.
informal, *a.* irregular, unreliable, improper; informal.
informalidad, *n.f.* breach of etiquette; informality.
informante, *a.* informing.—*n.m.f.* informer, informant.
informar, *v.t.* inform, apprise; shape.—*v.r.* find out (***de***, about).
informativo, -va, *a.* informative.
informe, *a.* shapeless, formless; misshapen.—*n.m.* report; piece of information.—*pl.* information.
infortunado, -da, *a.* unfortunate, ill-starred.
infortunio, *n.m.* misfortune.
infracción, *n.f.* infringement, breach.
infractor, -ra, *n.m.f.* violator, transgressor.
infrangible, *a.* unbreakable.
infranqueable, *a.* impassable.
infrarrojo, -ja, *a.* infra-red.
infrascri(p)to, -ta, *a.*, *n.m.f.* undersigned, undermentioned.
infrecuente, *a.* infrequent.
infringir [E], *v.t.* infringe.
infructuoso, -sa, *a.* fruitless, unfruitful.
infundado, -da, *a.* unfounded.
infundio, *n.m.* (*fam.*) rumour, fib.
infundir, *v.t.* infuse, imbue.
infusión, *n.f.* infusion.
ingeniar, *v.t.* contrive, think up.—*v.r.* manage (***a, para***, to).
ingeniería, *n.f.* engineering.
ingeniero, *n.m.* engineer.
ingenio, *n.m.* mind, intelligence, wit; talent, skill; engine.
ingenioso, -sa, *a.* talented, ingenious.
ingénito, -ta, *a.* innate; unbegotten.
ingente, *a.* huge, immense.

ingenuidad, *n.f.* ingeniousness.
ingenuo, -ua, *a.* ingenuous, naïve; open, frank.
ingerir [6], *v.t.* consume, swallow. [INJERIR].
Inglaterra, *n.f.* England.
ingle, *n.f.* groin.
inglés, -lesa, *a., n.m.* English.—*n.m.* Englishman.—*n.f.* Englishwoman.—*n.m.f.* (*iron.*) creditor.
inglesismo, *n.m.* Anglicism.
ingratitud, *n.f.* ingratitude.
ingrato, -ta, *a.* ungrateful; thankless; unpleasant; fruitless.
ingravidez, *n.f.* weightlessness (*of spacemen*).
ingrávido, -da, *a.* weightless (*spaceman*).
ingrediente, *n.m.* ingredient.
ingresar, *v.t.* deposit; put in.—*v.i.* enter (***en***); accrue.—*v.r.* (*C.A.*) enlist.
ingreso, *n.m.* entrance, entry.—*pl.* receipts, income.
íngrimo, -ma, *a.* (*S.A.*) all alone.
inhábil, *a.* incompetent, incapable.
inhabilidad, *n.f.* inability, incompetency.
inhabilitar, *v.t.* incapacitate; disqualify.
inhabitable, *a.* uninhabitable.
inhabitado, -da, *a.* uninhabited.
inhalar, *v.t.* inhale.
inherente, *a.* inherent.
inhibición, *n.f.* inhibition.
inhibir, *v.t.* inhibit; (*jur.*) stay.—*v.r.* keep out (***de***, of).
inhospitalario, -ria, *a.* inhospitable.
inhumanidad, *n.f.* inhumanity.
inhumano, -na, *a.* inhuman.
inhumar, *v.t.* inter, inhume.
iniciación, *n.f.* initiation.
inicial, *a., n.f.* initial.
iniciar, *v.t.* initiate.
iniciativa, *n.f.* initiative.
inicuo, -cua, *a.* iniquitous; unjust.
inimaginable, *a.* unimaginable.
inimitable, *a.* inimitable.
ininteligente, *a.* unintelligent.
ininteligible, *a.* unintelligible.
iniquidad, *n.f.* iniquity; injustice.
injerir [6], *v.t.* (*agr.*) graft; insert.
injerta, *n.f.* blood orange.
injertar, *v.t.* (*agr., med.*) graft.
injerto, *n.m.* (*agr., med.*) graft.
injuria, *n.f.* offence, insult, wrong, harm.
injuriar, *v.t.* offend, wrong, insult.
injurioso, -sa, *a.* offensive, insulting, harmful.
injusticia, *n.f.* injustice.
injustificable, *a.* unjustifiable.
injustificado, -da, *a.* unjustified.
injusto, -ta, *a.* unjust.
la Inmaculada, *n.f.* Our Lady.
inmaculado, -da, *a.* immaculate, pure.
inmanejable, *a.* unmanageable.
inmanente, *a.* immanent.
inmarcesible, inmarchitable, *a.* unfading; imperishable.
inmaterial, *a.* immaterial.
inmaturo, -ra, *a.* immature.
inmediaciones, *n.f.pl.* environs, neighbourhood.
inmediato, -ta, *a.* immediate; close, next (***a***, to).—*n.f.pl.* crux; sore point.
inmejorable, *a.* unbeatable, peerless.
inmemorial, *a.* immemorial.
inmensidad, *n.f.* immensity.
inmenso, -sa, *a.* immense.
inmensurable, *a.* immeasurable.
inmerecido, -da, *a.* undeserved.
inmergir [E], *v.t.* immerse.—*v.r.* be immersed.
inmersión, *n.f.* immersion.
inmigración, *n.f.* immigration.
inmigrado, -da, inmigrante, *a., n.m.f.* immigrant.
inmigrar, *v.i.* immigrate.
inminencia, *n.f.* imminence.
inminente, *a.* imminent.
inmoble, *a.* immovable; firm.
inmoderación, *n.f.* immoderation.
inmoderado, -da, *a.* immoderate.
inmodestia, *n.f.* immodesty, indecency.
inmodesto, -ta, *a.* immodest, indecent.
inmolación, *n.f.* immolation.
inmolar, *v.t.* immolate, sacrifice.
inmoral, *a.* immoral.
inmoralidad, *n.f.* immorality.
inmortal, *a.* immortal.
inmortalidad, *n.f.* immorality.
inmortalizar [C], *v.t.* immortalize.
inmotivado, -da, *a.* motiveless, unfounded.
inmovible, *a.* immovable.
inmóvil, *a.* motionless; unshaken.
inmovilidad, *a.* immobility.
inmovilizar [C], *v.t.* immobilize.
inmundicia, *n.f.* filth; lewdness.
inmundo, -da, *a.* filthy; lewd.
inmune, *a.* immune (***contra***, to); exempt.
inmunidad, *n.f.* immunity.
inmunización, *n.f.* immunization.
inmunizar [C], *v.t.* immunize.
inmutable, *a.* immutable.
inmutar, *v.t., v.r.* change, alter.
innato, -ta, *a.* innate, inborn.
innatural, *a.* unnatural.
innavegable, *a.* unnavigable.
innecesario, -ria, *a.* unnecessary.
innegable, *a.* undeniable.
innoble, *a.* ignoble.
innocuo, -cua, *a.* innocuous.
innovación, *n.f.* innovation.
innovar, *v.t.* innovate.
innumerable, *a.* innumerable.
innúmero, -ra, *a.* numberless, countless.
inobediente, *a.* disobedient.
inobservado, -da, *a.* unobserved.
inocencia, *n.f.* innocence.
inocentada, *n.f.* (*fam.*) bloomer; stunt.
inocente, *a., n.m.f.* innocent; (*fam.*) gullible (*person*); ***día de los inocentes,*** All Fools' Day (*in Spain*, 28 *December*).
inoculación, *n.f.* inoculation.
inocular, *v.t.* inoculate; (*fig.*) pervert.
inocuo [INNOCUO].
inodoro, -ra, *a.* odourless.—*n.m.* deodorant.
inofensivo, -va, *a.* inoffensive.
inolvidable, *a.* unforgettable.
inoperable, *a.* (*med.*) inoperable.
inopia, *n.f.* penury.
inopinado, -da, *a.* unexpected.
inoportunidad, *n.f.* inopportuneness.
inoportuno, -na, *a.* inopportune, untimely.
inorgánico, -ca, *a.* inorganic.
inoxidable, *a.* inoxidizable, stainless (*steel etc.*).
inquietador, -ra, inquietante, *a.* disquieting, disturbing.
inquietar, *v.t.* disquiet, disturb, worry.—*v.r.* worry (***con, de, por***, about).

inquieto, -ta, *a.* worried, uneasy, anxious; restless.
inquietud, *n.f.* worry, anxiety; restlessness.
inquilinato, *n.m.* tenancy; rent; rates.
inquilino, -na, *n.m.f.* tenant.
inquina, *n.f.* dislike.
inquirir [3, *as if* **inquerir**], *v.t.* enquire into, investigate.
inquisición, *n.f.* inquisition.
inquisidor, *n.m.* inquisitor.
inquisitivo, -va, inquisitorio, -ria, *a.* investigatory.
inquisitorial, *a.* inquisitorial.
insaciable, *a.* insatiable, greedy.
insalubre, *a.* unhealthy, insalubrious.
insania, insanidad, *n.f.* insanity.
insano, -na, *a.* unhealthy; insane, mad.
insatisfecho, -cha, *a.* unsatisfied.
inscribir [*p.p.* **inscrito**], *v.t.* inscribe; enrol. —*v.r.* enrol, register.
inscripción, *n.f.* inscription; enrolment.
insecticida, *n.m.* insecticide.
insectívoro, -ra, *a.* insectivorous.—*n.m.* insectivore.
insecto, *n.m.* insect.
inseguridad, *n.f.* insecurity; uncertainty.
inseguro, -ra, *a.* insecure; unsafe; uncertain.
inseminación, *n.f.* insemination.
inseminar, *v.t.* inseminate.
insensatez, *n.f.* senselessness, folly.
insensato, -ta, *a.* senseless, insensate.
insensibilidad, *n.f.* insensibility; insensitivity.
insensibilizar [C], *v.t.* make insensible.
insensible, *a.* insensible; insensitive, unfeeling.
inseparable, *a.* inseparable.
inserción, *n.f.* insertion.
insertar, *v.t.* insert.
inserto, -ta, *a.* inserted.
inservible, *a.* useless, unserviceable.
insidioso, -sa, *a.* insidious.
insigne, *a.* celebrated, renowned, noted.
insignia, *n.f.* badge; banner, standard; medal; pennant.—*pl.* insignia.
insignificancia, *n.f.* insignificance.
insignificante, *a.* insignificant.
insincero, -ra, *a.* insincere.
insinuación, *n.f.* insinuation.
insinuar [M], *v.t.* insinuate, hint.—*v.r.* slip in, work one's way in (***en***).
insipidez, *n.f.* insipidity.
insípido, -da, *a.* insipid.
insipiente, *a.* unwise; ignorant.
insistencia, *n.f.* insistence.
insistente, *a.* insistent.
insistir, *v.i.* insist (***en, sobre,*** on).
insociable, insocial, *a.* unsociable.
insolación, *n.f.* insolation; (*med.*) sun-stroke.
insolar, *v.t.* insolate; expose to the sun.—*v.r.* get sun-stroke.
insolencia, *n.f.* insolence.
insolente, *a.* insolent.
insólito, -ta, *a.* unwonted, unaccustomed.
insolubilidad, *n.f.* insolubility.
insoluble, *a.* insoluble.
insolvencia, *n.f.* insolvency.
insolvente, *a.* insolvent.
insomne, *a.* sleepless, insomnious.
insomnio, *n.m.* insomnia, sleeplessness.
insoportable, *a.* intolerable.
insospechado, -da, *a.* unsuspected.
insostenible, *a.* indefensible.
inspección, *n.f.* inspection; control; inspectorate.
inspeccionar, *v.t.* inspect.
inspector, -ra, *a.* inspecting.—*n.m.f.* inspector.
inspiración, *n.f.* inspiration; inhalation.
inspirar, *v.t.* inspire; inhale.—*v.r.* be inspired (***en,*** by).
instalación, *n.f.* installation.—*pl.* plant, works, machinery, fittings.
instalar, *v.t.* install.
instancia, *n.f.* instance, entreaty; petition; ***de primera —,*** (*jur.*) of first instance; in the first place, originally.
instantáneo, -nea, *a.* instantaneous.—*n.f.* (*phot.*) snap, snapshot.
instante, *n.m.* instant, moment; ***al —,*** at once, this very minute.
instantemente, *adv.* insistently; instantly.
instar, *v.t.* urge, press (***a,*** to).—*v.i.* be urgent.
instaurar, *v.t.* restore; establish; install.
instigación, *n.f.* instigation.
instigador, -ra, *a.* instigating.—*n.m.f.* instigator.
instigar [B], *v.t.* instigate.
instilar, *v.t.* instil.
instintivo, -va, *a.* instinctive.
instinto, *n.m.* instinct.
institución, *n.f.* institution.
instituir [O], *v.t.* institute, found.
instituto, *n.m.* institute; high *or* grammar school; rule, constitution.
institutor, -ra, *a.* instituting, founding.—*n.m.f.* founder, institutor; grammar-school teacher.
institutriz, *n.f.* (*pl.* **-ices**) governess; teacher.
instrucción, *n.f.* instruction; education.
instructivo, -va, *a.* instructive.
instructor, -ra, *a.* instructing.—*n.m.* instructor.—*n.f.* instructress.
instruído, -da, *a.* educated.
instruir [O], *v.t.* instruct.
instrumentación, *n.f.* instrumentation.
instrumental, *a.* instrumental.—*n.m.* instruments.
instrumentista, *n.m.f.* instrumentalist; instrument-maker.
instrumento, *n.m.* instrument.
insubordinación, *n.f.* insubordination.
insubordinado, -da, *a.* insubordinate.
insubordinar, *v.r.* rebel.
insuficiencia, *n.f.* insufficiency.
insuficiente, *a.* insufficient.
insufrible, *a.* insufferable.
insular, *a.* insular.—*n.m.f.* islander.
insulina, *n.f.* (*med.*) insulin.
insulso, -sa, *a.* tasteless, insipid, dreary.
insultante, *a.* insulting.
insultar, *v.t.* insult.
insulto, *n.m.* insult; swoon.
insumergible, *a.* unsinkable.
insumiso, *a.* rebellious, unsubmissive.
insuperable, *a.* insuperable.
insurgente, *a., n.m.f.* insurgent.
insurrección, *n.f.* insurrection.
insurreccionar, *v.t.* incite to rebel.—*v.r.* rise in rebellion.
insurrecto, -ta, *a., n.m.f.* rebel.
intacto, -ta, *a.* intact.
intachable, *a.* irreproachable.
intangible, *a.* intangible.

integración, *n.f.* integration.
integral, *a.* integral.
integrante, *a.* component; integrant.
integrar, *v.t.* integrate; make up; reimburse.
integridad, *n.f.* integrity; maidenhead; whole.
íntegro, -ra, *a.* whole, integral; upright, honest.
intelectivo, -va, *a.* intellective.—*n.f.* understanding.
intelecto, *n.m.* intellect.
intelectual, *a., n.m.f.* intellectual.
inteligencia, *n.f.* intelligence.
inteligente, *a.* intelligent.
inteligible, *a.* intelligible.
intemperancia, *n.f.* intemperance.
intemperante, *a.* intemperate.
intemperie, *n.f.* rough weather, inclemency.
intempestivo, -va, *a.* untimely.
intención, *n.f.* intention; nasty temper (*in animals*); ***con*** or ***de*** —, deliberately, knowingly.
intencionado, -da, *a.* ***bien*** or ***mal*** —, well- *or* ill-intentioned.
intencional, *a.* intentional; inner, volitional.
intendencia, *n.f.* administration; intendancy.
intendente, *n.m.* intendant, manager, commander.
intensar, *v.t.* intensify.
intensidad, *n.f.* intensity.
intensificar [A], *v.t.* intensify.
intensivo, -va, *a.* intensive.
intenso, -sa, *a.* intense.
intentar, *v.t.* try out; attempt, try.
intento, *n.m.* purpose, intent; ***de*** —, on purpose.
intentona, *n.f.* (*pej.*) rash plan *or* attempt.
interacción, *n.f.* interaction.
intercalar, *v.t.* intersperse, intercalate.
intercambiar, *v.t.* interchange; exchange.
intercambio, *n.m.* interchange; exchange.
interceder, *v.i.* intercede.
interceptación, *n.f.* interception.
interceptar, *v.t.* intercept.
interceptor, *n.m.* (*aero.*) fighter.
intercesión, *n.f.* intercession.
intercomunicación, *n.f.* intercommunication.
intercontinental, *a.* intercontinental.
interdecir [17], *v.t.* interdict.
interdependencia, *n.f.* interdependence.
interdicción, *n.f.* interdiction.
interdicto, *n.m.* interdict.
interés, *n.m.* interest; ***intereses creados,*** vested interests.
interesado, -da, *a.* interested; self-interested.
interesante, *a.* interesting.
interesar, *v.t.* interest; affect.—*v.r.* be interested (***en, por,*** in).
interferencia, *n.f.* interference.
interfoliar, *v.t.* interleave.
ínterin, *n.m.* interim, meantime.—*adv.* meanwhile.—*conj.* (*fam.*) until, till; while.
interino, -na, *a.* interim, temporary.
interior, *a., n.m.* interior.
interioridad, *n.f.* inside, interior.—*pl.* family secrets.
interiormente, *adv.* inwardly.
interjección, *n.f.* interjection.
interlinear, *v.t.* interline.
interlocutor, -ra, *n.m.f.* interlocutor; (*rad.*) interviewer.
intérlope, *a.* (*com., pol.*) interloping.
interludio, *n.m.* interlude.
intermediar, *v.i.* intermediate; stand between.
intermediario, -ria, *a., n.m.f.* intermediary.
intermedio, -dia, *a.* intermediate; intervening.—*n.m.* interlude, intermission.
interminable, *a.* interminable.
intermisión, *n.f.* intermission.
intermitente, *a.* intermittent.
internacional, *a.* international.
internacionalismo, *n.m.* internationalism.
internacionalizar [C], *v.t.* internationalize.
internar, *v.t.* intern; send inland.—*v.i., v.r.* move inland; penetrate (***en,*** into).
interno, -na, *a.* internal, inward, inner.—*n.m.f.* (*educ.*) boarder.
interpaginar, *v.t.* interpage.
interpelar, *v.t.* appeal to; demand an explanation of; (*jur.*) summon.
interpenetración, *n.f.* interpenetration.
interplanetario, -ria, *a.* interplanetary.
interpolación, *n.f.* interpolation.
interpolar, *v.t.* interpolate.
interponer [25], *v.t.* interpose.—*v.r.* intervene.
interpretación, *n.f.* interpretation.
interpretar, *v.t.* interpret.
interpretativo, -va, *a.* interpretative.
intérprete, *n.m.f.* interpreter.
interpuesto, *p.p.* [INTERPONER].
interracial, *a.* interracial.
interregno, *n.m.* interregnum.
interrogación, *n.f.* interrogation, questioning.
interrogante, *a.* interrogating.—*n.m.f.* interrogator.—*n.m.* question-mark.
interrogar [B], *v.t.* interrogate, question.
interrogativo, -va, *a., n.m.* interrogative.
interrumpir, *v.t.* interrupt; break, switch off.
interrupción, *n.f.* interruption.
interruptor, -ra, *a.* interrupting.—*n.m.f.* interrupter.—*n.m.* (*elec.*) switch.
intersección, *n.f.* intersection.
intersticio, *n.m.* interstice; interval.
intervalo, *n.m.* interval.
intervención, *n.f.* intervention; inspection; control; (*med.*) operation; auditing.
intervenir [36], *v.t.* audit; supervise; (*med.*) operate; tap (*telephones*).—*v.i.* intervene; occur.
interventor, *n.m.* comptroller, superintendent; auditor.
intervievar, interviewar, *v.t.* [ENTREVISTAR].
interview, interviú, *n.m.* [ENTREVISTA].
intestado, -da, *a.* intestate.
intestinal, *a.* intestinal.
intestino, -na, *a.* inner, interior.—*n.m.* intestine.
intimación, *n.f.* intimation, announcement.
intimar, *v.t.* intimate, indicate.—*v.i., v.r.* become close friends.
intimidación, *n.f.* intimidation.
intimidad, *n.f.* intimacy.
intimidar, *v.t.* intimidate.
íntimo, -ma, *a.* intimate.
intitular, *v.t.* entitle, give a title to.
intocable, *a., n.m.f.* untouchable.
intolerable, *a.* intolerable.
intolerancia, *n.f.* intolerance.
intolerante, *a.* intolerant.
intonso, -sa, *a.* ignorant; uncut.

intoxicación, *n.f.* (*med.*) poisoning.
intoxicar [A], *v.t.* (*med.*) poison.
intraducible, *a.* untranslatable.
intranquilizar [C], *v.t.* disquiet, worry.—*v.r.* worry.
intranquilo, -la, *a.* uneasy, worried.
intransigencia, *n.f.* intransigence.
intransigente, *a.* intransigent.
intransitable, *a.* impassable.
intransitivo, -va, *a.*, *n.m.* intransitive.
intratable, *a.* unsociable, intractable.
intrepidez, *n.f.* intrepidity.
intrépido, -da, *a.* intrepid.
intricado, -da, *a.* intricate.
intriga, *n.f.* intrigue.
intrigante, *a.* intriguing.—*n.m.f.* intriguer.
intrigar [B], *v.t.*, *v.i.* intrigue.
intrincado, -da, *a.* intricate.
intrincar [A], *v.t.* entangle, complicate.
intríngulis, *n.m. inv.* (*fam.*) hidden motive; puzzle.
intrínseco, -ca, *a.* intrinsic(al).
introducción, *n.f.* introduction.
introducir [15], *v.t.* introduce.—*v.r.* get (***en,*** into); intervene, interfere.
introductivo, -va, *a.* introductive.
introductor, -ra, *a.* introductory.—*n.m.f.* introducer.
introito, *n.m.* (*eccl.*) introit; prologue.
introspectivo, -va, *a.* introspective.
intrusión, *n.f.* intrusion; quackery.
intruso, -sa, *a.* intruding, intrusive.—*n.m.f.* intruder; quack.
intuición, *n.f.* intuition.
intuir [O], *v.t.* intuit.
intuitivo, -va, *a.* intuitive.
intuito, *n.m.* view, glance.
inundación, *n.f.* inundation, flood.
inundar, *v.t.* inundate, flood.
inurbano, -na, *a.* uncivil.
inútil, *a.* useless.
inutilidad, *n.f.* uselessness.
inutilizado, -da, *a.* unused, unutilized.
inutilizar [C], *v.t.* make useless.—*v.r.* become useless *or* disabled.
invadir, *v.t.* invade.
invalidar, *v.t.* invalidate.
invalidez, *n.f.* invalidity.
inválido, -da, *a.*, *n.m.f.* invalid.
invariable, *a.* invariable.
invasión, *n.f.* invasion.
invasor, -ra, *n.m.f.* invader.
invectiva, *n.f.* invective.
invencible, *a.* invincible.
invención, *n.f.* discovery; invention.
inventar, *v.t.* invent; create.
inventario, *n.m.* inventory.
inventiva, *n.f.* inventiveness.
inventivo, -va, *a.* inventive.
invento, *n.m.* invention.
inventor, -ra, *n.m.f.* inventor.
invernáculo, *n.m.* greenhouse.
invernal, *a.* hibernal.
invernar [1], *v.i.* winter.
invernizo, -za, *a.* wintry.
inverosímil, *a.* unlikely, improbable.
inverosimilitud, *n.f.* unlikelihood, improbability.
inversión, *n.f.* inversion; investment.
inverso, -sa, *a.* inverse, opposite.
invertebrado, -da, *a.*, *n.m.* invertebrate.
invertir [6], *v.t.* invert; invest.
investidura, *n.f.* investiture.
investigación, *n.f.* investigation.
investigador, -ra, *a.* investigating.—*n.m.f.* investigator.
investigar [B], *v.t.* investigate.
investir [8], *v.t.* vest, invest, install.
inveterado, -da, *a.* inveterate.
inveterar, *v.r.* get old; become chronic.
invicto, -ta, *a.* unconquered.
invidente, *a.* sightless.
invierno, *n.m.* winter.
inviolabilidad, *n.f.* inviolability.
inviolable, *a.* inviolable.
inviolado, -da, *a.* inviolate, unviolated.
invisible, *a.* invisible.
invitación, *n.f.* invitation.
invitado, -da, *n.m.f.* guest, invited person.
invitar, *v.t.* invite; treat (***a,*** to).
invocación, *n.f.* invocation.
invocar [A], *v.t.* invoke.
involucrar, *v.t.* jumble up with, tangle.
involuntario, -ria, *a.* involuntary.
invulnerabilidad, *n.f.* invulnerability.
invulnerable, *a.* invulnerable.
inyección, *n.f.* injection.
inyectar, *v.t.* inject.
inyector, *n.m.* injector.
iñiguista, *a.*, *n.m.f.* Jesuit.
ion, *n.m.* (*phys.*) ion.
iota, *n.f.* iota.
ir [21], *v.i.* go, walk, move; be getting on (***para,*** for); go in (***por,*** for); go for (***por***).—*v.r.* go away; pass away; slip; leak; wear out.
ira, *n.f.* wrath, ire.
iracundo, -da, *a.* wrathful.
Irak, *n.m.* Iraq.
Irán, *n.m.* Iran.
iranio, -nia, *a.*, *n.m.f.* Iranian, Persian.
iraqués, -quesa, *a.*, *n.m.f.* Iraqi.
irascible, *a.* irascible.
iridescencia, *n.f.* iridescence.
iridiscente, *a.* iridescent.
iris, *n.m.* (*bot.*) iris; rainbow; (*anat.*) iris.
irisado, -da, *a.* rainbow-hued.
Irlanda, *n.f.* Ireland; Eire; **irlanda,** fine linen *or* cotton.
irlandés, -desa, *a.* Irish.—*n.m.* Irishman; Irish (*language*).—*n.f.* Irishwoman.
ironía, *n.f.* irony.
irónico, -ca, *a.* ironic(al).
ironizar [C], *v.i.* be ironic.
irracional, *a.* irrational.
irradiación, *n.f.* (ir)radiation; (*rad.*) broadcast.
irradiar, *v.t.* (ir)radiate; (*rad.*) broadcast.
irrazonable, *a.* unreasonable.
irrealizable, *a.* impossible, unrealizable.
irrebatible, *a.* irrefutable.
irreconciliable, *a.* irreconcilable.
irredimible, *a.* irredeemable.
irreducible, *a.* irreducible; stubborn.
irreemplazable, *a.* irreplaceable.
irrefrenable, *a.* uncontrollable, unbridled.
irrefutable, *a.* irrefutable.
irregular, *a.* irregular.
irregularidad, *n.f.* irregularity.
irreligión, *n.f.* irreligion.
irreligioso, -sa, *a.* irreligious.
irremediable, *a.* irremediable.
irreparable, *a.* irreparable.
irreprochable, *a.* irreproachable.

irresistible, *a.* irresistible.
irresoluto, -ta, *a.* irresolute.
irresponsabilidad, *n.f.* irresponsibility.
irresponsable, *a.* irresponsible.
irresuelto, -ta, *a.* irresolute; unsolved.
irreverencia, *n.f.* irreverence.
irreverente, *a.* irreverent.
irrevocable, *a.* irrevocable.
irrigación, *n.f.* irrigation.
irrigar [B], *v.t.* (*agr.*, *med.*) irrigate.
irrisible, *a.* laughable, risible.
irrisión, *n.f.* derision.
irrisorio, -ria, *a.* ridiculous.
irritabilidad, *n.f.* irritability.
irritable, *a.* irritable.
irritación, *n.f.* irritation; (*jur.*) invalidation.
irritante, *a.*, *n.m.* irritant.
irritar, *v.t.* irritate; (*jur.*) invalidate.—*v.r.* get *or* become irritated.
irruir [O], *v.t.* invade, to assail.
irrumpir, *v.i.* irrupt, burst (***en,*** into); invade.
irrupción, *n.f.* invasion, irruption.
Isabel, *n.f.* Elizabeth, Isabel(la).
isabelino, -na, *a.*, *n.m.f.* Isabeline; Elizabethan.
Isaías, *n.m.* (*Bib.*) Isaiah.
Isidoro, *n.m.* Isidore.
isidro, -ra, *n.m.f.* bumpkin.
isla, *n.f.* island; block of houses; — ***de seguridad,*** traffic island.
Islam, *n.m.* Islam.
islámico, -ca, *a.* Islamic.
islandés, -desa, *a.* Icelandic.—*n.m.* Icelandic (*language*).—*n.m.f.* Icelander.
Islandia, *n.f.* Iceland.
islándico, -ca, *a.* Icelandic.
isleño, -ña, *a.* rel. to an island.—*n.m.f.* islander.
isleta, *n.f.* islet.
islote, *n.m.* barren islet.
isobara, *n.f.* isobar.
isomórfico, -ca, *a.* isomorphic.
isósceles, *a.* isosceles.
isoterma, *n.f.* isotherm.
isótopo, *n.m.* isotope.
Israel, *n.m.* Israel.
israelí, *a.*, *n.m.f.* (*pl.* **-íes**) Israeli.
israelita, *a.*, *n.m.f.* Israelite.
Istambul, *n.f.* Istanbul.
istmo, *n.m.* isthmus.
Italia, *n.f.* Italy.
italiano, -na, *a.*, *n.m.f.* Italian.
itálico, -ca, *a.*, *n.f.* italic.
ítem, *adv.* item.—*n.m.* section, paragraph.
iterar, *v.t.* iterate.
itinerario, -ria, *a.*, *n.m.* itinerary.
izar [C], *v.t.* (*naut.*) hoist, haul up.
izquierda, *n.f.* left, left-hand; (*pol.*) the Left.
izquierdear, *v.i.* go wrong; (*pol.*) be Leftish.
izquierdista, *a.*, *n.m.f.* (*pol.*) Leftist.
izquierdo, -da, *a.* left, left-hand; left-handed; crooked.

J

J, j, *n.f.* eleventh letter of the Spanish alphabet.
¡ja! *interj.* ha!
jabalí, *n.m.* wild boar.
jabalina (1), *n.f.* javelin.
jabalina (2), *n.f.* wild sow.
jabardo, *n.m.* small swarm.
jábega, *n.f.* drag-net; fishing smack.
jabón, *n.f.* soap; (*fam.*) flattery; telling-off.
jabonar, *v.t.* soap; (*fam.*) tell off.
jaboncillo, *n.m.* toilet soap, tablet of soap.
jabonera, *n.f.* soap-dish.
jabonete, -ta, *n.m.* or *f.* tablet of soap.
jabonoso, -sa, *a.* soapy.
jaca, *n.f.* cob, nag, pony; (*S.A.*) fighting cock.
jacal, *n.m.* (*zool.*) jackal; (*C.A.*) hovel.
jácara, *n.f.* gay ballad; serenaders; story; pest.
jacarear, *v.i.* sing gay ballads; (*fam.*) be annoying.
jacarero, -ra, *a.* serenading; (*fam.*) waggish. —*n.m.f.* serenader; (*fam.*) wag, wit.
jácaro, -ra, *a.* bragging, bullying.—*n.m.* bully.
jacinto, *n.m.* hyacinth.
jacobino, -na, *a.*, *n.m.f.* Jacobin.
jacobita, *n.m.f.* pilgrim to St. James of Compostela; Jacobite.
Jacobo, *n.m.* James, Jacob.
jactancia, *n.f.* boasting, bragging.
jactancioso, -sa, *a.* boastful.
jactar, *v.r.* boast, brag.
jaculatorio, -ria, *a.* ejaculatory.—*n.f.* ejaculatory *or* short sudden prayer.
jade, *n.m.* jade.
jadeante, *a.* panting, out of breath.
jadear, *v.i.* pant.
jaez, *n.m.* (*pl.* **jaeces**) harness, trappings; (*fig.*) kind, type.
jaguar, *n.m.* jaguar.
Jaime, *n.m.* James.
jalar, *v.t.* (*fam.*) tug; (*C.A.*) flirt with.—*v.r.* (*S.A.*) get tipsy.
jalbegue, *n.m.* whitewash; (*fam.*) make-up.
jalde, jaldo, -da, *a.* bright yellow.
jalea, *n.f.* jelly.
jalear, *v.t.* cheer on; flirt with.—*v.r.* dance the JALEO; have noisy fun.
jaleo, *n.m.* noisy fun; jaleo, Spanish dance.
jaletina, *n.f.* gelatine.
jalifa, *n.f.* caliph.
jalisco, -ca, *a.* (*C.A.*) tipsy.
jalma, *n.f.* packsaddle.
jalón, *n.m.* surveyor's pole; stage, point; (*S.A.*) tug; (*C.A.*) swig.
jalonar, *v.t.* mark, stake out.
Jamaica, *n.f.* Jamaica; **jamaica,** *n.m.* rum.
jamaicano, -na, *a.*, *n.m.f.* Jamaican.
jamar, *v.t.* (*low*) gorge, guzzle (*eat*).
jamás, *adv.* never; ***nunca* —,** never ever; ***por siempre* —,** for ever and ever.
jamba, *n.f.* jamb.
jamelgo, *n.m.* (*fam.*) skinny horse.
jamón, *n.m.* ham.
jándalo, -la, *a.*, *n.m.f.* (*fam.*) Andalusian.
jangada, *n.f.* (*fam.*) stupid trick; raft.
Jano, *n.m.* (*myth.*) Janus.
el Japón, *n.m.* Japan.
japonés, -nesa, *a.*, *n.m.f.* Japanese.
jaque, *n.m.* check (*in chess*); (*fam.*) bully; ***dar — a,*** check; ***estar muy* —,** (*fam.*) be full of beans; — ***mate,*** checkmate; ***¡— de aquí!*** get out of here!
jaquear, *v.t.* check (*in chess*); harass.—*v.i.* (*fam.*) bully.

jaqueca, *n.f.* migraine.
jaquel, *n.m.* (*her.*) square.
jaquetón, *n.m.* shark; (*fam.*) bully.
jarabe, *n.m.* syrup; — ***de pico,*** (*fam.*) flattery, hot air, lip service.
jarana, *n.f.* (*fam.*) spree, larking, merriment.
jarano, *n.m.* Mexican sombrero.
jarcia, *n.f.* rigging; tackle; (*fam.*) jumble.
jardín, *n.m.* garden, flower garden; — ***zoológico,*** zoological gardens; — ***de la infancia,*** kindergarten.
jardinería, *n.f.* gardening.
jardinero, -ra, *n.m.f.* gardener.
jardinista, *n.m.f.* gardening expert.
jaro, *n.m.* thicket; (*bot.*) (*also* **jarillo**) arum.
jarocho, -cha, *a.* bluff, blunt.—*n.m.* John Blunt.
jarope, *n.m.* syrup; potion.
jarra, *n.f.* jar, jug, pitcher; ***de*** or ***en jarras,*** arms akimbo.
jarrero, -ra, *n.m.f.* potter.
jarrete, *n.m.* hock, gambrel.
jarretera, *n.f.* garter.
jarro, *n.m.* pitcher, ewer.
jarrón, *n.m.* urn, vase.
jaspe, *n.m.* jasper.
jaspear, *v.t.* marble.
Jauja, *n.f.* Shangri-La, El Dorado (*place of abundant wealth*).
jaula, *n.f.* cage.
jauría, *n.f.* pack (*of dogs*).
jayán, -yana, *n.m.f.* big, strong person.
jazmín, *n.m.* (*bot.*) jasmine.
¡je! *interj.* [JI].
jefa, *n.f.* woman head; (*fam.*) woman boss.
jefatura, *n.f.* chieftainship; headship; headquarters.
jefe, *n.m.* chief, head; boss; (*mil.*) field officer; ***en*** —, in chief; — ***del estado,*** head of state.
Jehová, *n.m.* Jehovah.
jengibre, *n.m.* ginger.
jeque, *n.m.* sheik.
jerarquía, *n.f.* hierarchy; ***altas jerarquías,*** personalities, high-ranking officials.
jerárquico, -ca, *a.* hierarchical.
Jeremías, *n.m.* Jeremiah.
jerez, *n.m.* sherry.
jerga, *n.f.* serge, coarse cloth; jargon; straw bed.
jergal, *a.* rel. to jargon.
Jericó, *n.f.* Jericho.
jerife, *n.m.* shereef.
jerigonza, *n.f.* slang, jargon; gibberish.
jeringa, *n.f.* syringe; hypodermic; grease gun; (*fam.*) pest.
jeringar, *v.t.* syringe, inject; (*fam.*) pester.
jeringazo, *n.m.* shot, injection.
jeringuilla (1), *n.f.* hypodermic syringe.
jeringuilla (2), *n.f.* (*bot.*) syringa.
jeroglífico, -ca, *a., n.m.* hieroglyphic.—*n.m.* hieroglyph.
jerónimo, -ma, *a., n.m.f.* Hieronymite.—*n.m.* Jerome.
jerosolimitano, -na, *a., n.m.f.* rel. to *or* native of Jerusalem.
jersey, *n.m.* jersey.
Jerusalén, *n.m.* Jerusalem.
Jesucristo, *n.m.* Jesus Christ.
jesuíta, *a., n.m.f.* Jesuit.
jesuítico, -ca, *a.* Jesuitical.
jesuitismo, *n.m.* Jesuitism.
Jesús, *n.m.* Jesus; ***en un*** —, in a moment.—*interj.* heavens!
jeta, *n.f.* pig's snout; blubber lips; (*fam.*) mug, face.
¡ji, ji! *interj.* tee-hee!
jíbaro, -ra, *a., n.m.f.* peasant.
jibia, *n.f.* (*zool.*) cuttlefish, sepia.
jícara, *n.f.* chocolate-cup; (*S.A.*) gourd.
jicarazo, *n.m.* poisoning.
jifa, *n.f.* offal.
jifero, *n.m.* butcher, slaughterman.
jiga, *n.f.* jig, dance, [GIGA].
jilguero, *n.m.* (*orn.*) goldfinch.
jilí, jilando, jilaza, *a.* (*fam.*) daft [GILÍ].
jineta, *n.f.* mode of riding with bent legs and high stirrups; (*zool.*) genet; ***tener los cascos a la*** —, (*fam.*) be hare-brained.
jinete, *n.m.* horseman, rider; thoroughbred horse.
jinetear, *v.t.* (*S.A.*) break in (*horses*).—*v.i.* ride about, show one's horsemanship.—*v.r.* (*S.A.*) show off, parade oneself.
jinglar, *v.t.* sway, rock.
jingoísmo, *n.m.* jingoism.
jingoista, *a., n.m.f.* jingoist.
jira, *n.f.* strip, shred, tatter; picnic [GIRA].
jirafa, *n.f.* giraffe.
jirón, *n.m.* shred, tatter; pennant; piece.
¡jo! *interj.* whoa!
Joaquín, *n.m.* Joachim.
jocoserio, -ria, *a.* seriocomic.
jocosidad, *n.f.* jocosity, jocularity.
jocoso, -sa, *a.* jocular; jocose.
jocundo, -da, *a.* jocund.
jofaina, *n.f.* wash-stand; wash-basin.
jolgorio, *n.m.* merrymaking, jollification.
jolito, *n.m.* calm, leisure; ***en*** —, in suspense; disappointed.
jollín, *n.m.* (*fam.*) uproar; spree.
Jonás, *n.m.* Jonah.
Jordán, *n.m.* Jordan; (*fig.*) fountain of youth.
jordano, -na, *a., n.m.f.* Jordanian.
Jorge, *n.m.* George.
jornada, *n.f.* day's journey; day's work; journey; (*theat.*) act; lifetime; passing on; (*mil.*) expedition; occasion; ***a grandes*** or ***largas jornadas,*** by forced marches.
jornal, *n.m.* day's wage, wages; day's work; diary.
jornalero, *n.m.* day-labourer, labourer.
joroba, *n.m.* hump, hunched back; (*fam.*) pest.
jorobado, -da, *a.* hunchbacked.—*n.m.f.* hunchback.
jorobar, *v.t.* (*fam.*) pester, annoy.
José, *n.m.* Joseph.
Josué, *n.m.* Joshua.
jota, *n.f.* name of letter J; jota, Aragonese dance; iota, tittle.
joven, *a.* (*pl.* **jóvenes**) young.—*n.m.f.* youth, young man, woman; ***de*** —, as a young man *or* woman.
jovial, *a.* jovial.
jovialidad, *n.f.* joviality.
joya, *n.f.* jewel.
joyel, *n.m.* gem.
joyelero, *n.m.* jewel case.
joyería, *n.m.* jeweller's shop; jewel(le)ry.
joyero, -ra, *n.m.f.* jeweller.—*n.m.* jewel case.
Juan, *n.m.* John; ***Buen*** —, dupe, Billy Muggins; — ***Soldado,*** Tommy Atkins.

Juana, *n.f.* Jane, Joan, Jean; **— *de Arco,*** Joan of Arc.
juanete, *n.m.* prominent cheek-bone; bunion; (*naut.*) top-gallant.
jubilación, *n.f.* pension; retirement.
jubilado, -da, *a.* retired; (*educ.*) emeritus.
jubilar, *v.t.* retire, pension off; (*fam.*) chuck out.—*v.i.* celebrate; retire.—*v.r.* retire; celebrate, rejoice.
jubileo, *n.m.* jubilee; ***por* —,** once in a blue moon.
júbilo, *n.m.* jubilation.
jubiloso, -sa, *a.* jubilant.
jubón, *n.m.* doublet, jerkin.
Judá, *n.m.* Judah.
judaico, -ca, *a.* Judaic.
judaísmo, *n.m.* Judaism.
judaizar [PC], *v.i.* Judaize.
Judas, *n.m.* Judas; **— *Iscariote,*** Judas Iscariot; ***estar hecho un* —,** look like a rag-bag.
judeo-español, -la, *a., n.m.* Judaeo-Spanish.
judería, *n.f.* Jewry; ghetto.
judía (1), *n.f.* Jewess.
judía (2), *n.f.* bean; **— *blanca,*** haricot bean; **— *pinta,*** red kidney bean; **— *verde,*** kidney bean; French bean.
judicatura, *n.f.* judgeship; judicature.
judicial, *a.* judicial, rel. to judge.
judiciario, -ria, *a.* astrological.—*n.m.f.* astrologer.
judío, -día, *a.* Jewish.—*n.m.f.* Jew, Jewess.
Judit, *n.f.* Judith.
judo, *n.m.* judo.
juego, *n.m.* game; play, playing; gambling, gaming; set; suite; working, movement; ***hacer el* — *a,*** play into the hands of; ***hacer* — *con,*** match; **— *de ajedrez,*** chess set *or* game of chess; **— *de bolas,*** (*mech.*) ball bearing.
juerga, *n.f.* (*fam.*) spree, binge.
juerguista, *n.m.f.* (*fam.*) reveller.
jueves, *n.m.* Thursday; ***cosa del otro* —,** a thing seldom seen.
juez, *n.m.* (*pl.* **jueces**) judge; **— *de guardia,*** coroner; **— *de instrucción,*** magistrate; (*sport*) umpire, linesman, starter, *etc.*
jugada, *n.f.* play; stroke, move, throw; dirty trick.
jugador, -ra, *n.m.f.* player; gambler.
jugar [4B, *conjugated as if* **jogar**], *v.t.* play; stake, gamble; wield.—*v.i.* match; work, function.—*v.r.* gamble, risk; **— *a,*** play (*games*); **— *con,*** match; **— *en,*** have a hand in.
juglar, *n.m.* (*obs.*) minstrel.
jugo, *n.m.* juice; gravy; (*fig.*) substance.
jugoso, -sa, *a.* juicy, succulent.
juguete, *n.m.* toy, plaything; (*theat.*) skit.
juguetear, *v.i.* frolic, sport, dally.
juguetón, -tona, *a.* playful, frolicsome.
juicio, *n.m.* judgement; (*jur.*) trial; reason, sense; wisdom; astrological forecast, horoscope; **— *de Dios,*** trial by ordeal; **— *de divorcio,*** divorce decree.
juicioso, -sa, *a.* judicious, wise.
julepe, *n.m.* julep; (*fam.*) reprimand; (*S.A.*) fright; (*C.A.*) busy time.
Julio, *n.m.* Julius, Julian; **julio,** *n.m.* July.
¡jum! *interj.* hum!
jumento, -ta, *n.m.f.* donkey.
juncia, *n.f.* (*bot.*) sedge; ***vender* —,** brag.
junco, *n.m.* (*bot.*) rush; rattan cane; (*naut.*) junk.
jungla, *n.f.* jungle.
junio, *n.m.* June.
junípero, *n.m.* juniper.
Juno, *n.f.* (*myth.*) Juno.
junquera, *n.f.* (*bot.*) rush.
junquillo, *n.m.* (*bot.*) jonquil; rattan, reed; (*carp.*) beading.
junta, *n.f.* board, council; session; union; junction, joint; coupling; washer, gasket; **— *de comercio,*** board of trade; **— *de sanidad,*** board of health; **— *militar,*** military junta.
juntamente, *adv.* together.
juntar, *v.t.* join, connect, unite; gather together; leave ajar.—*v.r.* assemble, gather; unite.
junto, -ta, *a.* united, joined.—*pl.* together.—*adv.* together; jointly; near (***a,*** to); ***por* —,** all together, in bulk.
juntura, *n.f.* joint, seam; connexion.
Júpiter, *n.m.* Jupiter.
jura, *n.f.* oath, swearing.
jurado, *n.m.* jury; juror.
juramentar, *v.t.* swear in, put on oath.—*v.r.* take the oath, be sworn in.
juramento, *n.m.* oath; **— *de Hipócrates,*** Hippocratic oath.
jurar, *v.t., v.i.* swear.—*v.r.* swear, curse.
jurídico, -ca, *a.* juridical.
jurisconsulto, *n.m.* jurisconsult, jurist.
jurisdicción, *n.f.* jurisdiction.
jurisperito, *n.m.* legal expert.
jurisprudencia, *n.f.* jurisprudence.
jurista, *n.m.* jurist.
justa, *n.f.* joust, tournament.
justamente, *adv.* justly; exactly, precisely.
justar, *v.i.* joust, tilt.
justicia, *n.f.* justice; (*fam.*) execution, death sentence; ***de* —,** duly, deservedly.
justiciable, *a.* actionable.
justiciero, -ra, *a.* stern, rigorous.
justificable, *a.* justifiable.
justificación, *n.f.* justification.
justificar [A], *v.t.* justify.
justiprecio, *n.m.* just appraisal.
justo, -ta, *a.* just; exact; right, correct; fair; honest; tight, flush.—*adv.* tightly; duly, rightly.
juvenil, *a.* youthful, juvenile.
juventud, *n.f.* youth.
juzgado, *n.m.* tribunal, court.
juzgar [B], *v.t.* judge.—*v.i.* judge, pass judgement (***de,*** on); ***a* — *por,*** judging by, to judge by.

K

K, k, *n.f.* twelfth letter of the Spanish alphabet.
ka, *n.f.* name of the letter K.
keroseno, kerosene, kerosén, *n.m.* kerosene, paraffin.
kiliárea, *n.f.* kiliare.
kilo, *n.m.* kilo.

kilociclo, *n.m.* kilocycle.
kilométrico, -ca, *a.* kilometric.
kilómetro, *n.m.* kilometre.
kilovatio, *n.m.* kilowatt.
kiosko, *n.m.* kiosk [QUIOSCO].
Kremlín, *n.m.* Kremlin.
Kuwait, Estado del, *n.m.* Kuwait.

L

L, l, *n.f.* thirteenth letter of the Spanish alphabet.
la (1), *f. def. art.* the.—*f. accus. pron.* her; it; you.
la (2), *n.m.* (*mus.*) (key of) A.
laberinto, *n.m.* labyrinth, maze.
labia, *n.f.* (*fam.*) gift of the gab.
labial, *a., n.f.* labial.
labihendido, -da, *a.* hare-lipped.
labio, *n.m.* lip.
labor, *n.f.* work, labour; needle-work; farm work; ***campo de —,*** tilled field.
laborable, *a.* tillable; working (day).
laboral, *a.* rel. to labour, work.
laborante, *a.* working.—*n.m.* political pressure-man.
laborar, *v.t.* work, till.—*v.i.* intrigue.
laboratorio, *n.m.* laboratory.
laborear, *v.t.* work (*a mine*).
laborioso, -sa, *a.* industrious; laborious.
laborismo, *n.m.* Labour, socialism.
laborista, *a.* Labour.—*n.m.f.* Labour supporter.
labradero, -ra, labradío, -día, *a.* arable, tillable.
labrador, -ra, *a.* working, farming.—*n.m.f.* farmer, peasant.—*n.m.* ploughman.
labrantío, -tía, *a.* arable, tillable.
labranza, *n.f.* farming, tillage; farm-land; working.
labrar, *v.t.* work, fashion; plough, till; construct; bring about.—*v.i.* make a strong impression (***en,*** on).
labriego, -ga, *n.m.f.* peasant.
laca, *n.f.* lac; lacquer, japan.
lacayo, *n.m.* lackey.
laceración, *n.f.* laceration.
lacerar, *v.t.* lacerate; damage.
laceria, *n.f.* misery.
lacio, -cia, *a.* withered; languid.
lacónico, -ca, *a.* laconic.
laconismo, *n.m.* laconism.
lacra, *n.f.* mark left by illness; defect; (*S.A.*) wound, sore.
lacrar, *v.t.* strike down; harm.—*v.r.* be stricken.
lacre, *n.m.* sealing wax.
lacrimógeno, -na, *a.* tear-causing.—*n.m.* or *f.* tear-gas.
lacrimoso, -sa, *a.* lachrymose.
lactación, lactancia, *n.f.* lactation.
lactar, *v.t., v.i.* suckle.
lácteo, -tea, *a.* lacteous, milky.
lacticinio, *n.m.* milk food.
láctico, -ca, *a.* lactic.
ladear, *v.t., v.i., v.r.* tilt, turn, level.
ladeo, *n.m.* tilt, turn, leaning.
ladera, *n.f.* hillside.
ladino, -na, *a.* crafty, cunning; Romansch; Sephardic Spanish.—*n.m.f.* Ladin.
lado, *n.m.* side; place; ***de —,*** sideways; ***hacer —,*** make room; ***hacerse a un —,*** step aside.—*pl.* advisers; ***por todos lados,*** on all sides, everywhere.
ladrar, *v.t., v.i.* bark.
ladrido, *n.m.* bark.
ladrillar, *v.t.* brick.
ladrillo, *n.m.* brick; tile.
ladrón, -rona, *a.* thieving.—*n.m.f.* thief, robber.
ladronear, *v.i.* thieve.
ladronería, *n.f.* thievery; thieves.
lagar, *n.m.* wine-press, press.
lagartija, *n.f.* small lizard.
lagarto, *n.m.* lizard; (*fam.*) sly man.
lago, *n.m.* lake.
lágrima, *n.f.* tear; drop, drip.
lagrimar, *v.i.* weep.
lagrimoso, -sa, *a.* tearful; runny (*eyes*).
laguna, *n.f.* lagoon, pool; lacuna.
lagunoso, -sa, *a.* fenny, marshy.
laical, *a.* lay.
laicizar [C], *v.t.* laicize, secularize.
laico, -ca, *a.* lay.—*n.m.f.* lay person.
laja, *n.f.* slab.
lama, *n.f.* slime, mud; lamé.—*n.m.* lama.
lamasería, *n.f.* lamasery.
lambrija, *n.f.* worm.
lamedura, *n.f.* licking.
lamentable, *a.* lamentable.
lamentación, *n.f.* lamentation.
lamentar, *v.t., v.i., v.r.* lament, weep (***de, por,*** for).
lamento, *n.m.* lament.
lamentoso, -sa, *a.* lamentable; mournful.
lamer, *v.t.* lick; lap against.
lámina, *n.f.* plate; sheet, lamina.
laminar, *v.t.* laminate; roll (*metals*).
lamoso, -sa, *a.* slimy.
lámpara, *n.f.* lamp; light bulb; radio valve; grease spot.
lamparilla, *n.f.* small lamp; night-light.
lamparón, *n.m.* grease spot; (*med.*) king's evil, scrofula.
lampazo, *n.m.* (*bot.*) dock; (*naut.*) swab.
lampiño, -ña, *a.* beardless, hairless.
lamprea, *n.f.* lamprey.
lampreazo, *n.m.* lash, stroke.
lana, *n.f.* wool.
lanar, *a.* rel. to wool; wool-bearing.
lance, *n.m.* cast, throw; stroke, move; catch; chance; juncture; affair; quarrel; ***de —,*** bargain, second hand.
lancero, *n.m.* lancer.
lanceta, *n.f.* lancet.
lancha, *n.f.* slab; (*naut.*) long-boat; lighter.
landa, *n.f.* lande, moor, woodland.
landó, *n.m.* landau.
lanería, *n.f.* woolshop.—*pl.* woollen goods.
lanero, -ra, *a.* rel. to wool, woollen.—*n.m.* wool-store; (*orn.*) lanner.
langosta, *n.f.* (*ent.*) locust; (*zool.*) lobster; (*fam.*) scourge.
langostín, langostino, *n.m.* crayfish.
languidecer [9], *v.i.* languish.
languidez, *n.f.* languor.
lánguido, -da, *a.* languid, languishing, languorous.

lanilla, *n.f.* nap; flannel.
lanolina, *n.f.* lanolin.
lanoso, -sa, lanudo, -da, *a.* woolly, fleecy.
lanza, *n.f.* lance, spear; nozzle; coach pole.
lanzabombas, *n.m. inv.* (*mil.*) mortar; (*aer.*) bomb-doors.
lanzacohetes, *n.m. inv.* (*mil.*) rocket-launcher.
lanzada, *n.f.* lance thrust *or* wound.
lanzadera, *n.f.* shuttle.
lanzallamas, *n.m. inv.* (*mil.*) flame-thrower.
lanzamiento, *n.m.* throw; launching; leap; ***plataforma de —,*** launching pad (*rockets etc.*).
lanzaminas, *n.m. inv.* (*naut.*) mine-layer.
lanzar [C], *v.t.* hurl, throw; launch; throw out.—*v.r.* rush, dash; leap.
Lanzarote, *n.m.* Lancelot.
laocio, -cia, *a., n.m.f.* Laotian.
Laos, *n.m.* Laos.
lapicero, *n.m.* pencil-case; drawing pencil.
lápida, *n.f.* stone tablet.
lapidario, -ria, *a., n.m.* lapidary.
lapislázuli, *n.m.* lapis lazuli.
lápiz, *n.m.* (*pl.* **lápices**) graphite, black lead; pencil; ***— de labios,*** lipstick; ***— tinta,*** indelible pencil.
lapo, *n.m.* (*fam.*) slap; swig, drink.
lapón, -pona, *a., n.m.f.* Lapp.
Laponia, *n.f.* Lapland.
lapso, *n.m.* lapse.
laquear, *v.t.* lacquer.
lard(e)ar, *v.t.* (*cul.*) baste; grease.
lardero, *a.* applied to Thursday before Lent.
lardo, *n.m.* lard.
largar [B], *v.t.* release, loosen; unfurl; (*fam.*) let slip, say.—*v.r.* set sail; (*fam.*) clear off.
largo, -ga, *a.* long; generous; ready, prompt; abundant.—*n.m.* length; (*mus.*) largo.—*interj.* be off! get out! ***a la larga,*** in the long run; ***a lo — de,*** along, throughout; ***— de uñas,*** light-fingered; ***pasar de —,*** pass by; pass over.
largueza, *n.f.* length; generosity.
larguirucho, -cha, *a.* (*fam.*) lanky.
largura, *n.f.* length.
laringe, *n.f.* larynx.
larva, *n.f.* (*ent.*) larva.
las, *f.pl. def. art.* the.—*f.pl. accus. pron.* them; those.
lascivia, *n.f.* lasciviousness.
lascivo, -va, *a.* lascivious; sportive.
lasitud, *n.f.* lassitude.
laso, -sa, *a.* weary; lax; unspun.
lastar, *v.t.* pay *or* suffer for another.
lástima, *n.f.* pity; plaint; pitiful object; ***¡ qué — !*** what a pity!
lastimar, *v.t.* hurt, bruise; pity.—*v.r.* feel sorry (***de,*** for), pity; complain (***de,*** about).
lastimero, -ra, *a.* pitiful; harmful.
lastimoso, -sa, *a.* pitiful.
lastra, *n.f.* slab.
lastrar, *v.t.* ballast.
lastre, *n.m.* ballast.
lata, *n.f.* tin, can; tin-plate; lath; small dog; (*fam.*) bore, drag; ***dar la —,*** be a nuisance.
latente, *a.* latent.
lateral, *a.* lateral.
látex, *n.m.* latex.
latido, *n.m.* beat, throb; yap, yelp.
latiente, *a.* heating, throbbing.
latifundio, *n.m.* large rural estate.
latifundista, *n.m.f.* big land-owner.
latigazo, *n.m.* lash, crack.
látigo, *n.m.* whip, lash; cinch-strap; (*fam.*) thin person.
latín, *n.m.* Latin (*language*); (*fam.*) Latinism; ***saber (mucho) —,*** be canny.
latinajo, *n.m.* (*fam.*) dog Latin; (*fam.*) Latin phrase.
latinidad, *n.f.* Latinity.
latinismo, *n.m.* Latinism.
latinista, *n.m.f.* Latinist.
latinizar, *v.t., v.i.* Latinize.
latino, -na, *a., n.m.f.* Latin.
latinoamericano, -na, *a.* Latin-American.
latir, *v.i.* beat, throb; yap, yelp.
latitud, *n.f.* latitude.
latitudinal, *a.* latitudinal.
lato, -ta, *a.* broad; general.
latón, *n.f.* brass.
latoso, -sa, *a.* (*fam.*) pesky, boring.
latrocinio, *n.m.* thievery, theft.
latvio, -via, *a., n.m.f.* Latvian.
laúd, *n.m.* lute.
laudable, *a.* laudable.
laude, *n.f.* grave-stone.—*pl.* lauds.
laudo, *n.m.* (*jur.*) findings.
laureado, -da, *a., n.m.f.* laureate; prize-winner.
laurear, *v.t.* crown with laurel, honour; award a degree to.
laurel, *n.m.* laurel; laurels.
láureo, -rea, *a.* rel. to laurel.—*n.f.* laurel wreath.
lauréola, *n.f.* laurel crown; halo.
lauro, *n.m.* laurel; laurels.
lauto, -ta, *a.* sumptuous.
lava, *n.f.* lava.
lavable, *a.* washable.
lavabo, *n.m.* wash-basin; lavatory.
lavadedos, *n.m. inv.* finger-bowl.
lavadero, *n.m.* wash-house; washing place; laundry.
lavado, -da, *a.* (*fam.*) brazen.—*n.m.* washing, laundry; ***— a seco,*** dry cleaning.
lavador, -ra, *a.* washing.—*n.f.* washing machine.
lavajo, *n.m.* pool, pond; morass.
lavamanos, *n.m. inv.* wash-basin, wash-stand.
lavanco, *n.m.* wild duck.
lavanda, *n.f.* lavender.
lavandera, *n.f.* laundress, washerwoman; (*orn.*) wagtail.
lavandería, *n.f.* laundry.
lavandero, *n.m.* launderer, laundryman.
lavaplatos, *n.m.* or *f. inv.* dishwasher.
lavar, *v.t.* wash.—*v.r.* wash, have a wash.
lavativa, *n.f.* enema; (*fam.*) pest.
lavatorio, *n.m.* wash; lavatory; (*med.*) lotion; (*eccl.*) Maundy.
lavazas, *n.f.pl.* dirty suds.
laxación, *n.f.* laxation, easing.
laxamiento, *n.m.* laxation; laxity.
laxante, *a., n.m.* (*med.*) laxative.
laxar, *v.t., v.r.* slacken, loosen.
laxidad, laxitud, *n.f.* laxity, laxness.
laxo, -xa, *a.* lax, slack.
laya, *n.f.* spade; kind, ilk; (*fam.*) shame.
lazar [C], *v.t.* snare, lasso.
lazareto, *n.m.* lazaretto.
lazarillo, *n.m.* blind man's guide.
lazarino, -na, *a., n.m.f.* leper.

Lázaro, *n.m.* Lazarus; **lázaro,** *n.m.* ragged pauper; ***hecho un* —,** covered in sores.
lazaroso, -sa, *a.* leprous.
lazo, *n.m.* bow, knot; loop; bond; lasso; snare, trap; tie.
le, *dat. pers. pron.* to him, to her, to it, to you. [SE].—*accus.* him, you.
leal, *a.* loyal, faithful, trustworthy.
lealtad, *n.f.* loyalty, faithfulness.
lebrato, lebratón, *n.m.* leveret.
lebrel, -la, *n.m.f.* whippet.
lebrero, -ra, *a.* hare-hunting.
lebrillo, librillo, *n.m.* washing-up bowl.
lebroncillo, *n.m.* leveret.
lebruno, -na, *a.* hare-like, leporine.
lección, *n.f.* lesson; reading, interpretation.
leccionista, *n.m.f.* tutor, coach.
lectivo, -va, *a.* term-time, school (*day, year etc.*).
lector, -ra, *n.m.f.* reader; (*educ.*) native language teacher, lector.
lectura, *n.f.* reading; lecture; reading matter.
lechada, *n.f.* lime-water; paper-pulp.
lechar, *v.t.* (*S.A.*) milk; (*C.A.*) whitewash.
leche, *n.f.* milk.
lechecillas, *n.f.pl.* sweetbreads; offal.
lechería, *n.f.* dairy.
lechero, -ra, *a.* milky, milk.—*n.m.* milkman, dairyman.—*n.f.* milkmaid, dairymaid; milk jug *or* churn.
lechida, *n.f.* litter, brood.
lecho, *n.m.* bed.
lechón, -chona, *n.m.f.* piglet.
lechoso, -sa, *a.* milky.
lechuga, *n.f.* lettuce.
lechugada, *n.f.* (*fam.*) flop, wash-out.
lechuguilla, *n.f.* wild lettuce; ruff, frill.
lechuguino, -na, *a.* stylish, natty.—*n.m.f.* young flirt.
lechuza, *n.f.* barn owl.
lechuzo, -za, *a.* owlish.—*n.m.* bailiff, debt collector.
ledo, -da, *a.* (*poet.*) happy, joyful.
leer [N], *v.t.* read.
lega, *n.f.* lay sister.
legación, *n.f.* legation.
legado, *n.m.* legate; legacy.
legajo, *n.m.* file, bundle; dossier.
legal, *a.* legal; correct, dutiful.
legalidad, *n.f.* legality.
legalizar [C], *v.t.* legalize; authorize.
légamo, *n.m.* ooze, slime, silt.
legaña, *n.f.* bleariness.
legar, *v.t.* bequeath; send as legate.
legendario, -ria, *a.* legendary.
legibilidad, *n.f.* legibility.
legible, *a.* legible.
legión, *n.f.* legion.
legionario, -ria, *a., n.m.f.* legionary.
legislación, *n.f.* legislation.
legislador, -ra, *a.* legislating.—*n.m.f.* legislator.
legislar, *v.i.* legislate.
legislativo, -va, *a.* legislative.
legislatura, *n.f.* legislature.
legisperito, legista, *n.m.* legal expert.
legitimación, *n.f.* legitimation.
legitimar, *v.t.* legitimize.
legítimo, -ma, *a.* legitimate; fair; genuine.
lego, -ga, *a.* lay.—*n.m.* layman; lay brother.
legón, *n.m.* hoe.
legrar, *v.t.* scrape.
legua, *n.f.* league (*about* 3 *miles*).
leguleyo, *n.m.* pettifogger, petty lawyer.
legumbre, *n.f.* vegetable; legume.
leguminoso, -sa, *a.* leguminous.
leíble, *a.* readable.
leísta, *n.m.f.* person who uses **le** instead of **lo.**
lejanía, *n.f.* distance, remoteness.
lejano, -na, *a.* far-away, distant.
lejía, *n.f.* lye; (*fam.*) dressing-down.
lejísimo(s), *adv. sup. of* LEJOS.
lejito(s), *adv.* pretty far.
lejos, *adv.* far, distant; ***a lo* —,** in the distance.
lelo, -la, *a.* silly, stupid.—*n.m.f.* fool, dolt.
lema, *n.m.* motto; theme.
lemosín, -sina, *a.* Limousin, Languedocian. —*n.m.* Langue d'Oc.
lencería, *n.f.* linenry.
lendroso, -sa, *a.* full of nits, lousy.
lene, *a.* gentle, soft, mild.
lengua, *n.f.* tongue; language; ***mala* —,** gossip; ***hacerse lenguas de,*** (*fam.*) to rave about.
lenguado, *n.m.* (*ichth.*) sole.
lenguaje, *n.m.* language, manner of speaking.
lenguaraz, lenguaz, *a.* (*pl.* **-aces**) loose-tongued; garrulous; foul-mouthed.
lengüeta, *n.f.* needle, pointer; shoe-tongue; tongue; wedge; (*mus.*) reed.
lenidad, *n.f.* lenity, leniency.
lenificar [A], *v.t.* soothe, ease.
Lenín, *n.m.* Lenin.
Leningrado, *n.m.* Leningrad.
lenitivo, -va, *a.* lenitive.
lente, *n.m.* or *f.* lens; magnifying glass.—*pl.* glasses; ***lentes de contacto,*** contact lenses.
lenteja, *n.f.* lentil; pendulum weight; duck-weed.
lentejuela, *n.f.* sequin.
lentitud, *n.f.* slowness.
lento, -ta, *a.* slow.
leña, *n.f.* firewood; (*fam.*) hiding, beating.
leñador, *n.m.* woodman.
leñame, *n.m.* timber; fire-wood.
leñero, *n.m.* fire-wood dealer; wood-shed.
leño, *n.m.* wood, timber; log; (*poet.*) bark ship; (*fam.*) dunce.
leñoso, -sa, *a.* woody.
León, *n.m.* Leo; Leon; **león,** *n.m.* lion.
leona, *n.f.* lioness.
leonado, -da, *a.* tawny.
leonera, *n.f.* lion cage; lion's den; (*fam.*) dive, joint; (*fam.*) loft.
leonés, -nesa, *a., n.m.f.* Leonese.
leonino, -na, *a.* leonine.
leopardo, *n.m.* leopard.
lepra, *n.f.* leprosy.
leproso, -sa, *a.* leprous.—*n.m.f.* leper.
lerdo, -da, *a.* slow, heavy; coarse.
les, *pron. m., pl. dative,* to them, to you. [SE]. —*accus.* them, you.
lesión, *n.f.* lesion; harm.
lesionar, *v.t.* hurt, harm, injure.
lesivo, -va, *a.* injurious, harmful.
leso, -sa, *a.* hurt; perverted; ***lesa majestad,*** lese-majesty.
letal, *a.* lethal.
letanía, *n.f.* litany.
letárgico, -ca, *a.* lethargic.
letargo, *n.m.* lethargy.
Lete, *n.m.* (*myth.*) Lethe.
letificar [A], *v.t.* animate, cheer.

letón, -tona, *a.*, *n.m.* Lettish.—*n.m.f.* Lett, Latvian.
letra, *n.f.* letter, character; handwriting; type face; words (*of song*); letter, strict sense; ***a la* —,** to the letter; **— *de cambio,*** (*com.*) bill of exchange.—*pl.* letters, literature; ***bellas letras,*** belles lettres; ***primeras letras,*** (*educ.*) the three R's.
letrado, -da, *a.* lettered, learned.—*n.m.* lawyer; man of letters.
letrero, *n.m.* sign, poster, label.
letrina, *n.f.* latrine.
letrista, *n.f.* lyricist.
leucemia, *n.f.* leukæmia.
leudar, *v.t.* leaven.
leva, *n.f.* (*naut.*) weighing anchor; (*mil.*) levy; (*naut.*) swell; (*mech.*) tooth, cog.
levadura, *n.f.* leaven, yeast.
levantamiento, *n.m.* raising; rising, insurrection; sublimity; **— *del censo,*** census taking.
levantar, *v.t.* raise, lift; rouse, agitate; clear (*the table*); build; make (*survey*); levy.—*v.r.* get up, rise; stand up; rebel.
Levante, *n.m.* Levant; East coast of Spain; **levante,** *n.m.* East, Orient.
levantino, -na, *a.*, *n.m.f.* Levantine.
levantisco, -ca, *a.* turbulent, restless.
leve, *a.* light; slight.
levedad, *n.f.* lightness; levity.
Leví, *n.m.* Levi.
leviatán, *n.m.* Leviathan.
levita (1), *n.m.* Levite; deacon.
levita (2), *n.f.* frock-coat.
levitación, *n.f.* levitation.
Levítico, *n.m.* (*Bib.*) Leviticus; **levítico, -ca,** *a.* Levitical.
léxico, -ca, *a.* lexical.—*n.m.* lexicon.
lexicografía, *n.f.* lexicography.
lexicográfico, -ca, *a.* lexicographical.
lexicógrafo, -fa, *n.m.f.* lexicographer.
lexicología, *n.f.* lexicology.
lexicológico, -ca, *a.* lexicological.
lexicólogo, *n.m.* lexicologist.
lexicón, *n.m.* lexicon.
ley, *n.f.* law; norm, standard; loyalty; grade (*of metal*); ***a* — *de caballero,*** on the word of a gentleman; ***de buena* —,** genuine, sterling.
leyenda, *n.f.* legend.
lía, *n.f.* esparto rope.—*pl.* lees.
liar [L], *v.t.* bind; tie *or* wrap up; roll (*cigarettes*); (*fam.*) draw in, embroil.—*v.r.* come together; form a liaison; (*fam.*) get mixed up *or* involved (***a, en,*** in); ***liarlas,*** (*fam.*) escape; (*fam.*) snuff it (*die*).
liatón, *n.m.* esparto cord.
libación, *n.f.* libation.
libanés, -nesa, *a.*, *n.m.f.* Lebanese.
Líbano, *n.m.* (the) Lebanon.
libar, *v.t.* suck; taste.—*v.i.* perform a libation.
libelista, *n.m.f.* lampooner, libeller.
libelo, *n.m.* lampoon, libel; (*jur.*) petition.
libélula, *n.f.* dragonfly.
liberación, *n.f.* liberation; settlement, quittance.
liberador, -ra, *a.* liberating.—*n.m.f.* liberator.
liberal, *a.*, *n.m.f.* liberal.
liberalidad, *n.f.* liberality.
liberalismo, *n.m.* liberalism.
liberalizar [C], *v.t.* liberalize.
liberar, *v.t.* free, liberate.
liberiano, -na, *a.*, *n.m.f.* Liberian.
libérrimo, -ma, *a. sup. of* LIBRE.
libertad, *n.f.* liberty, freedom.
libertado, -da, *a.* bold, taking liberties.
libertador, -ra, *a.* liberating.—*n.m.f.* liberator, deliverer.
libertar, *v.t.* free, liberate (***de,*** from).
libertario, -ria, *a.*, *n.m.f.* anarchist.
liberticida, *a.* liberticidal.—*n.m.f.* destroyer of freedom.
libertinaje, *n.m.* libertinism.
libertino, -na, *a.*, *n.m.f.* libertine.
liberto, -ta, *n.m.f.* freed slave.
Libia, *n.f.* Libya.
libídine, *n.f.* libido; lewdness.
libidinoso, -sa, *a.* libidinous, lewd.
libio, -bia, *a.*, *n.m.f.* Libyan.
Libra, *n.f.* (*astr.*) Libra; **libra,** *n.f.* pound (*£*, *lb.*).
librado, -da, *a.* (*fam.*) done-for.—*n.m.f.* (*com.*) drawee.
librador, -ra, *n.m.f.* deliverer; (*com.*) drawer; scoop.
libramiento, *n.m.* delivery; warrant.
libranza, *n.f.* (*com.*) draft, bill of exchange.
librar, *v.t.* free, deliver (***de,*** from); exempt; expedite; pass (*sentence*); issue (*a decree*); give (*battle*); (*com.*) draw.—*v.i.* give birth; ***a bien*** or ***buen* —,** as well as could be expected; **— *bien,*** succeed; **— *mal,*** fail.—*v.r.* escape; get rid (***de,*** of); ***librarse de buena,*** (*fam.*) have a close shave.
libre, *a.* free; loose, immoral; rash, brash; unmarried; innocent.
librea, *n.f.* livery.
librecambio, *n.m.* free trade.
librepensador, -ra, *n.m.f.* free-thinker.
librería, *n.f.* book-shop; library; book-case.
libreril, *a.* rel. to books *or* booksellers.
librero, *n.m.* bookseller.
libresco, -ca, *a.* bookish.
libreta, *n.f.* note-book; cheque book; (*Madrid*) loaf.
libreto, *n.m.* libretto.
librillo, *n.m.* packet; booklet. [LEBRILLO].
libro, *n.m.* book; (*fig.*) impost.
licencia, *n.f.* licence; permission, permit; leave, furlough: licentiate, bachelor's degree.
licenciado, -da, *a.* licensed; on leave; free; pedantic.—*n.m.f.* (*educ.*) bachelor, licentiate; discharged soldier; lawyer.
licenciamiento, *n.m.* (*educ.*) graduation; (*mil.*) discharge.
licenciatura, *n.f.* (*educ.*) graduation; licentiate, Spanish bachelor's degree.
licencioso, -sa, *a.* licentious.
liceo, *n.m.* lycée, lyceum.
licitar, *v.t.* bid for; (*S.A.*) buy *or* sell by auction.
lícito, -ta, *a.* licit, lawful; just.
licor, *n.m.* liquor; liqueur.
licoroso, -sa, *a.* spirituous; rich, generous (*wine*).
licuefacer [20], *v.t.*, *v.r.* liquefy.
licuescente, *a.* liquescent.
lid, *n.f.* fight; dispute.
líder, *n.m.* leader.
lidia, *n.f.* fight, battle, contest; bull-fight.
lidiador, -ra, *a.* fighting.—*n.m.f.* fighter.—*n.m.* bull-fighter.

lidiar, *v.t.* fight (*bulls*).—*v.i.* fight, battle.
liebre, *n.f.* hare; coward.
liendre, *n.f.* nit, louse egg.
lienzo, *n.m.* linen; piece of linen; (*paint.*) canvas; (*arch.*) face, facing.
liga, *n.f.* league, union; garter; alloy; bird-lime; mistletoe; rubber band.
ligación, *n.f.* bond; binding; alloying.
ligada, *n.f.* lashing, binding.
ligado, *n.m.* (*print.*, *mus.*) ligature.
ligadura, *n.f.* ligature; lashing, binding.
ligamaza, *n.f.* bird-lime.
ligamento, *n.m.* ligament.
ligar [B], *v.t.* bind, tie, lash; join; alloy; bind, oblige, commit.—*v.r.* form an alliance; bind oneself (*a*, to).
ligazón, *n.f.* bond, union, connexion.
ligereza, *n.f.* lightness; swiftness; levity, fickleness.
ligero, -ra, *a.* light; swift; flippant; fickle; ***de* —,** without thinking; **— *de cascos*,** feather-brained.
ligur, ligurino, -na, *a.*, *n.m.f.* Ligurian.
ligustro, *n.m.* (*bot.*) privet.
lija, *n.f.* sand-paper; (*ichth.*) dog-fish.
lijar, *v.t.* sand-paper, sand.
lila, lilac (*pl.* **lilaques**), *n.f.* (*bot.*) lilac.
lilaila, *n.f.* (*fam.*) wiliness.
lilao, *n.m.* (*fam.*) swank, empty show.
liliputiense, *a.*, *n.m.f.* Lilliputian.
lima, *n.f.* file, rasp; polish.
limadura, *n.f.* filing.
limalla, *n.f.* filings.
limar, *v.t.* file; touch up, polish.
limatón, *n.m.* rasp, rough round file.
limaza, *n.f.* (*zool.*) slug.
limbo, *n.m.* (*eccl.*) limbo; edge; (*astr.*, *bot.*) limb.
limen, *n.m.* threshold.
limeño, -ña, *a.*, *n.m.f.* rel. to *or* native of Lima.
limero, *n.m.* sweet-lime tree.
limitación, *n.f.* limitation.
limitar, *v.t.* limit (***a***, to); bound; constrict, reduce.
límite, *n.m.* limit, confine.
limítrofe, *a.* bordering, limiting, conterminous.
limo, *n.m.* slime, mud; (*S.A.*) [LIMERO].
limón, *n.m.* lemon; lemon-tree; shaft, pole.
limonado, -da, *a.* lemon.—*n.f.* lemonade.
limonar, *n.m.* lemon grove.
limonero, *n.m.* lemon-tree; lemon-seller.
limosina, *n.f.* limousine.
limosna, *n.f.* alms.
limosnear, *v.i.* beg alms.
limosnero, -ra, *a.* charitable.—*n.m.* almoner. —*n.m.f.* (*S.A.*) beggar.
limoso, -sa, *a.* slimy, muddy.
limpia, *n.f.* cleaning.
limpiabotas, *n.m. inv.* boot-black.
limpiachimeneas, *n.m. inv.* chimney-sweep.
limpiadientes, *n.m. inv.* toothpick.
limpiadura, *n.f.* cleaning.
limpiaparabrisas, *n.m. inv.* windscreen-wiper.
limpiar, *v.t.* clean; (*fam.*) steal; clean out.
límpido, -da, *a.* (*poet.*) limpid.
limpieza, *n.f.* cleanness, cleanliness; cleaning; purity; neatness.
limpio, -pia, *a.* clean, cleanly; neat; pure; free, clear; fair; ***en* —,** clearly, neatly; net.
linaje, *n.m.* lineage; progeny; extraction; (*fig.*) class.
linajista, *n.m.f.* genealogist.
linajudo, -da, *a.* high-born.
linaza, *n.f.* linseed.
lince, *a.*, *n.m.* lynx.
lincear, *v.t.* (*fam.*) see through, spot.
linchamiento, *n.m.* lynching.
linchar, *v.t.* lynch.
lindante, *a.* adjoining, contiguous.
lindar, *v.i.* border (***con***, on).
lindazo, *n.m.* boundary.
linde, *n.m.* or *f.* boundary, limit.
lindero, -ra, *a.* bordering.—*n.m.f.* edge border.
lindeza, *n.f.* prettiness.
lindo, -da, *a.* pretty; fine; ***de lo* —,** wonderfully.—*n.m.* fop, (*fam.*) sissy.
línea, *n.f.* line.
lineal, *a.* linear, lineal.
linear, *v.t.* outline, sketch; demarcate.
linfa, *n.f.* lymph.
linfático, -ca, *a.* lymphatic.
lingote, *n.m.* ingot, pig.
lingual, *a.*, *n.f.* lingual.
linguete, *n.m.* ratchet.
lingüista, *n.m.f.* linguist.
lingüístico, -ca, *a.* linguistic.—*n.f.* linguistics.
linimento, *n.m.* liniment.
lino, *n.m.* linen; flax; (*poet.*) sail.
linóleo, *n.m.* linoleum.
linón, *n.m.* lawn (*cloth*).
linotipia, *n.f.* linotype.
lintel, *n.m.* lintel.
linterna, *n.f.* lantern; torch.
lío, *n.m.* bundle, parcel; (*fam.*) mess, muddle; liaison; ***armar un* —,** (*fam.*) make trouble.
Liorna, *n.f.* Leghorn; **liorna,** *n.f.* (*fam.*) uproar.
lioso, -sa, *a.* (*fam.*) troublesome; trouble-making.
liquen, *n.m.* lichen.
liquidación, *n.f.* liquidation; settlement.
liquidar, *v.t.* liquidate; liquefy; settle.
liquidez, *n.f.* liquidity.
líquido, -da, *a.*, *n.m.* liquid; (*com.*) net.
lira, *n.f.* lyre; lyrical poetry; inspiration of poet; a verse form.
lírico, -ca, *a.* lyric(al); (*S.A.*) utopian, day-dreaming.—*n.m.f.* lyrical poet; (*S.A.*) utopian.—*n.f.* lyrical poetry.
lirio, *n.m.* (*bot.*) iris, flag; lily.
lirismo, *n.m.* lyricism.
lirón, *n.m.* dormouse; (*fam.*) sleepy-head.
lis, *n.m.* (*bot.*) iris; lily.
Lisboa, *n.f.* Lisbon.
lisbonense, lisbonés, -nesa, *a.*, *n.m.f.* rel. to *or* native of Lisbon.
lisiado, -da, *a.* crippled; wild, eager.—*n.m.f.* cripple.
lisiar, *v.t.* hurt, cripple.—*v.r.* become crippled.
liso, -sa, *a.* smooth; plain, simple; straightforward.
lisonja, *n.f.* flattery; (*her.*) lozenge.
lisonjear, *v.t.* flatter; delight.
lisonjero, -ra, *a.* flattering; pleasing.—*n.m.f.* flatterer.
lista, *n.f.* list; stripe; strip; muster, roll; **— *de correos*,** poste restante.
listar, *v.t.* list.
list(e)ado, -da, *a.* striped.

listeza, *n.f.* (*fam.*) alertness.
listo, -ta, *a.* ready; alert; prompt; clever.
listón, *n.m.* tape, ribbon; (*carp.*) lath.
lisura, *n.f.* smoothness; simplicity; sincerity; (*S.A.*) nerve, cheek.
litera, *n.f.* litter (*bed*); bunk, berth.
literal, *a.* literal.
literario, -ria, *a.* literary.
literato, -ta, *a.* lettered, literary, learned.—*n.m.f.* lettered *or* literary person.—*pl.* literati.
literatura, *n.f.* literature.
litigación, *n.f.* litigation.
litigante, *a.*, *n.m.f.* litigant.
litigar [B], *v.t.*, *v.i.* litigate.
litigio, *n.m.* lawsuit, litigation; dispute.
litografía, *n.f.* lithograph, lithography.
litografiar, *v.t.* lithograph.
litoral, *a.*, *n.m.f.* littoral, coast.
litro, *n.m.* litre.
Lituania, *n.f.* Lithuania.
lituano, -na, *a.*, *n.m.f.* Lithuanian.
liturgia, *n.f.* liturgy.
litúrgico, -ca, *a.* liturgical.
liviandad, *n.f.* lightness; frivolity; lewdness.
liviano, -na, *a.* light; frivolous; lewd.—*n.m.pl.* lungs, lights.
lividecer [9], *v.t.*, *v.r.* turn livid.
lividez, *n.f.* lividity, lividness.
lívido, -da, *a.* livid.
livor, *n.m.* livid colour; envy, malice.
liza, *n.f.* lists, tournament.
lo, *def. art. neuter*, the.—*accus. pron. m.* it, him; — ***bueno,*** what is good, the good thing; — ***rápido,*** the rapidness; how rapidly.
loa, *n.f.* praise; panegyric.
loable, *a.* praiseworthy.
loar, *v.t.* praise.
loba (1), *n.f.* she-wolf.
loba (2), *n.f.* cassock.
lobanillo, *n.m.* wen; gall.
lobato, lobezno, *n.m.* wolf cub.
lobo, *n.m.* wolf; lobe; ***coger un* —,** (*fam.*) get tight; ***desollar un* —,** (*fam.*) sleep it off; — ***marino,*** (*zool.*) seal; (*fam.*) sea-dog.
lóbrego, -ga, *a.* gloomy, murky.
lóbulo, *n.m.* lobule, lobe.
lobuno, -na, *a.* rel. to wolves, wolfish.
locación, *n.f.* (*jur.*) lease.
local, *a.* local.—*n.m.* premises.
localidad, *n.f.* locality; (*theat.*) seat, location.
localismo, *n.m.* localism.
localización, *n.f.* location; localization.
localizar [C], *v.t.* localize; locate.
locatario, -ria, *n.m.f.* tenant.
locería, *n.f.* china-shop; (*S.A.*) pottery.
loción, *n.f.* lotion; lavation.
loco, -ca, *a.* mad; (*fam.*) terrific, wonderful; wild, raging; enthusiastic (***por,*** about, ***de,*** with); ***estar* —,** be mad, angry *or* enthusiastic; ***ser un* —,** be insane; — ***de atar,*** — ***rematado***; raving mad; raving lunatic.—*n.m.f.* lunatic; ***la loca de la casa,*** the imagination.—*n.m.* madman.
locomoción, *n.f.* locomotion.
locomotivo, -va, *a.* locomotive.
locomotor, -ra (*f. also* **locomotriz,** *pl.* **-ices,** *as a.*), *a.* locomotive, locomotor.—*n.f.* (*rail.*) locomotive, engine.
locuacidad, *n.f.* loquacity.
locuaz, *a.* (*pl.* **-aces**) loquacious.
locución, *n.f.* expression; locution.
locuelo, -la, *a.* giddy, wild (*youth*).—*n.m.f.* madcap, giddy youth, giddy girl.—*n.f.* personal manner of speech.
locura, *n.f.* madness.
locutor, -ra, *n.m.f.* (*rad.*) announcer.
locutorio, *n.m.* telephone kiosk; locutory.
lodazal, lodazar, *n.m.* quagmire, muddy place.
lodo, *n.m.* mud.
lodoso, -sa, *a.* muddy.
logaritmo, *n.m.* logarithm.
logia, *n.f.* (Freemasons') lodge; loggia.
lógico, -ca, *a.* logical.—*n.m.f.* logician.—*n.f.* logic.
logístico, -ca, *a.* logistic(al).—*n.f.* logistics.
logrado, -da, *a.* successful.
lograr, *v.t.* gain, obtain; attain, produce; succeed, manage.—*v.i.* do well; manage (*to*), succeed (*in*).—*v.r.* be successful.
logrear, *v.i.* profiteer.
logrería, *n.f.* usury.
logrero, -ra, *a.* usurious, profiteering.—*n.m.f.* profiteer, usurer.
logro, *n.m.* gain, profit; attainment; usury, interest.
loísta, *a.*, *n.m.f.* said of those who use **lo** instead of **le**.
lombriz, *n.f.* (*pl.* **-ices**) worm, grub.
lomo, *n.m.* back; ridge.—*pl.* ribs.
lona, *n.f.* canvas, sailcloth.
londinense, *a.* London.—*n.m.f.* Londoner.
Londres, *n.m.* London.
longánimo, -ma, *a.* magnanimous.
longaniza, *n.f.* pork sausage.
longevidad, *n.f.* longevity.
longevo, -va, *a.* long-lived, longeval.
longitud, *n.f.* length; longitude.
longitudinal, *a.* longitudinal.
longuísimo, -ma, *a. sup. of* LUENGO.
lonja, *n.f.* slice, strip; slap, step; market, exchange; warehouse; portico; grocer's shop.
lonjista, *n.m.f.* grocer.
lontananza, *n.f.* (*art.*) background; distance.
loor, *n.m.* praise.
lopista, *a.* rel. to Lope de Vega.—*n.m.f.* Lope scholar.
loquear, *v.i.* rave, play the madman.
loquera, *n.f.* madhouse; (*S.A.*) madness.
loquesco, -ca, *a.* half-mad; (*fam.*) screamingly funny.
loranto, *n.m.* Eastern mistletoe.
lord, *n.m.* (*pl.* **lores**) lord, Lord.
Lorena, *n.f.* Lorraine.
Lorenzo, *n.m.* Laurence, Lawrence.
loriga, *n.f.* lorica, cuirass.
loro, -ra, *a.* dark brown.—*n.m.* parrot.
los, *def. article, m.pl.* the.—*pron. acc. pl.* them.—*demonstrative rel.* those.
losa, *n.f.* flagstone, slab.
losange, *n.m.* lozenge.
loseta, *n.f.* small flagstone; trap.
lote, *n.m.* lot, portion.
lotería, *n.f.* lottery.
loto, *n.m.* lotus.
loza, *n.f.* crockery.
lozanear, *v.i.*, *v.r.* be luxuriant; be lusty.
lozanía, *n.f.* luxuriance; elegance; lustiness; pride.
lozano, -na, *a.* luxuriant; lusty; haughty.
lubricación, *n.f.* lubrication.
lubricante, *a.*, *n.m.* lubricant.

lubricar [A], *v.t.* lubricate.
lúbrico, -ca, *a.* lubricious.
Lucano, *n.m.* Lucan.
Lucas, *n.m.* Luke.
lucero, *n.m.* Venus, morning star, evening star; bright star; small window; brilliance. —*pl.* (*poet.*) eyes.
Lucía, *n.f.* Lucy, Lucia.
lucidez, *n.f.* lucidity.
lúcido, -da, *a.* lucid.
lucido, -da, *a.* brilliant; gorgeous.
luciente, *a.* shining.
luciérnaga, *n.f.* (*ent.*) glow-worm.
lucífero, -ra, *a.* (*poet.*) shining, brilliant.
lucimiento, *n.m.* lustre, brilliance; success, applause.
lucio, -cia (1), *a.* bright, lucid.
lucio (2), *n.m.* (*ichth.*) pike.
lución, *n.m.* (*zool.*) slow worm.
lucir [9], *v.t.* illumine; display, sport; aid.—*v.i.* gleam, shine.—*v.r.* dress up; be brilliant (*fig.*).
lucrar, *v.t.* obtain.—*v.r.* make a profit.
lucrativo, -va, *a.* lucrative.
lucro, *n.m.* profit; lucre.
lucroso, -sa, *a.* profitable.
luctuoso, -sa, *a.* gloomy, mournful.
lucubración, *n.f.* lucubration.
lucubrar, *v.t., v.i.* lucubrate.
lucha, *n.f.* fight, struggle; strife; wrestling.
luchador, -ra, *n.m.f.* fighter; wrestler.
luchar, *v.i.* fight, struggle (***por,*** for); wrestle; contend.
ludibrio, *n.m.* mockery, derision.
luego, *adv.* presently, later; (*obs.*) immediately; then, next.—*conj.* then; so; ***desde —,*** naturally; at once; ***¡hasta —!*** cheerio! au revoir! — ***que,*** after, as soon as.
luengo, -ga, *a.* long.
lugar, *n.m.* place, site; room, space; village; chance, time, occasion; ***dar — a,*** give rise to; ***en — de,*** instead of; — ***común,*** commonplace; lavatory; ***no ha —,*** (*jur.*) petition not granted; ***tener —,*** take place; have time *or* the chance (***de,*** to).
lugarcillo, -rcito, -rejo, -rete, -rillo, *n.m.* hamlet.
lugareño, -ña, *a.* village.—*n.m.f.* villager.
lugarteniente, *n.m.* lieutenant, deputy.
lúgubre, *a.* lugubrious, dismal, gloomy.
Luis, *n.m.* Louis, Lewis; **luis,** *n.m.* louis (*coin*).
lujo, *n.m.* luxury; excess; ***de —,*** de luxe.
lujoso, -sa, *a.* luxurious.
lujuria, *n.f.* lechery, lust; excess.
lujuriante, *a.* luxuriant.
lujuriar, *v.i.* be lustful.
lujurioso, -sa, *a.* lustful, lecherous.—*n.m.f.* lecher.
Lulio, *n.m.* Lull.
lumbago, *n.m.* lumbago.
lumb(ra)rada, *n.f.* blaze, great fire.
lumbre, *n.f.* fire; light; brilliance; learning; ***dar — a,*** give a light to; — ***del agua,*** surface of the water.—*pl.* tinder-box.
lumbrera, *n.f.* light; air- *or* light-vent; shining light, high example.
luminar, *n.m.* luminary.
luminaria, *n.f.* (*eccl.*) altar light, monstrance lamp.—*pl.* illuminations, lights.
luminescencia, *n.f.* luminescence.
luminescente, *a.* luminescent.
luminosidad, *n.f.* luminosity light.
luminoso, -sa, *a.* luminous.
luna, *n.f.* moon; moonlight; mirror; (*fam.*) whim, mood; ***a la — de Valencia,*** left out in the cold; — ***de miel,*** honeymoon.
lunar, *a.* lunar.—*n.m.* mole; spot.
lunático, -ca, *a., n.m.f.* lunatic.
lunes, *n.m.* Monday.
luneta, *n.f.* eyeglass; (*theat.*) orchestra seat.
lunfardo, *n.m.* Argentine gangster; Argentine criminal slang.
lupa, *n.f.* magnifying glass.
lupino, -na, *a.* lupine.—*n.m.* lupin.
lúpulo, *n.m.* (*bot.*) hop, hops.
Lurdes, *n.f.* Lourdes.
lurio, -ria, *a.* (*C.A.*) love-crazed.
lusismo, lusitanismo, *n.m.* Lusitanism.
lusitano, -na, *a., n.m.f.* Lusitanian; Portuguese.
lustrar, *v.t.* polish; lustrate.—*v.i.* roam.
lustre, *n.m.* lustre, gloss, polish.
lustro, *n.m.* lustrum; chandelier.
lustroso, -sa, *a.* glossy, lustrous.
lúteo, -tea, *a.* luteous, miry; vile.
luterano, -na, *a., n.m.f.* Lutheran.
Lutero, *n.m.* Luther.
luto, *n.m.* mourning; bereavement; ***de —,*** in mourning.—*pl.* mourning clothes.
luz, *n.f.* (*pl.* **luces**) light; opening, window; ***dar a —,*** give birth to; publish; ***salir a —,*** come to light; appear (*book*).—*pl.* culture; ***a todas luces,*** anyway; everywhere; ***entre dos luces,*** at dusk *or* dawn.
luzco [LUCIR].

Ll

Ll, ll, fourteenth letter of the Spanish alphabet.
llaga, *n.f.* ulcer; wound.
llagar [B], *v.t.* wound, hurt.
llama (1), *n.f.* flame, blaze.
llama (2), *n.m.* or *f.* (*zool.*) llama.
llamada, *n.f.* call; ring, knock; signal, sign; peal.
llamado, *n.m.* call.
llamador, -ra, *n.m.f.* caller.—*n.m.* door-knocker; door-bell; messenger.
llamamiento, *n.m.* call; calling, vocation.
llamar, *v.t.* call; call upon, summon; name; attract.—*v.i.* knock, ring; have an appeal.—*v.r.* be named, be called.
llamarada, *n.f.* flare-up, flash; sudden blush.
llamativo, -va, *a.* flashy, showy.
llamear, *v.i.* flame, flash.
llanero, -ra, *n.m.f.* plain-dweller.
llaneza, *n.f.* simplicity, plainness.
llano, -na, *a.* level, smooth, plain, flat; homely, frank; simple, clear.—*n.m.* plain; stair-landing; ***de —*** or ***a la llana,*** simply, plainly.
llanta, *n.f.* (metal) tyre; wheel-rim.
llantén, *n.m.* (*bot.*) plantain.
llantera, *n.f.* (*fam.*) blubbering.
llanto, *n.m.* weeping.
llanura, *n.f.* levelness; plain.
llapa, *n.f.* (*S.A.*) extra bit, bonus.

llave, *n.f.* key; spanner, wrench; tap, faucet; (*elec.*) switch; — ***inglesa,*** monkey wrench.
llavero, -ra, *n.m.f.* turn-key.—*n.m.* key-ring.
llavín, *n.m.* latch key.
llegada, *n.f.* arrival.
llegar [B], *v.t.* move nearer.—*v.i.* arrive (***a,*** at), reach; amount (***a,*** to).—*v.r.* come *or* go nearer.
llena, *n.f.* overflow, flood.
llenar, *v.t.* fill; satisfy; cover; fulfil.—*v.r.* fill, get full; get covered (***de,*** with).
llenero, -ra, *a.* complete, entire.
lleno, -na, *a.* full.—*n.m.* fill, fullness, plenty; full moon; (*theat.*) full house; ***de*** —, entirely, fully.
llenura, *n.f.* fullness, plenty.
lleva, llevada, *n.f.* carrying.
llevadero, -ra, *a.* bearable.
llevar, *v.t.* carry, take; lead; carry off, take away; wear, have on; bear, suffer; run, manage.—*v.r.* carry off, take away; get on (***con,*** with); get carried away; ***lleva un año aquí,*** he has been here for a year; ***Paco me lleva dos años,*** Paco is two years older than I; ***nos llevan ocho horas,*** they are eight hours ahead of us.
llorar, *v.t.* weep, lament, mourn.—*v.i.* weep, cry; stream.
lloriquear, *v.i.* (*fam.*) whimper.
lloriqueo, *n.m.* (*fam.*) blubbering, whimpering.
lloro, *n.m.* weeping, mourning, crying.
llorón, -rona, *a.* weepy, tearful; weeping (*willow etc.*).—*n.m.f.* weeper, mourner.—*n.m.* plume.
lloroso, -sa, *a.* tearful; mournful.
llovedizo, -za, *a.* leaky; ***agua llovediza,*** rain-water.
llover [5], *v.t., v.i.* rain; ***como llovido,*** out of the blue; — ***sobre mojado,*** never to come alone (*said of misfortunes*); ***llueva o no,*** rain or shine; ***llueve,*** it is raining.—*v.r.* leak.
llovido, -da, *n.m.f.* stowaway.
llovizna, *n.f.* drizzle.
lloviznar, *v.i.* drizzle.
llueca, *a., n.f.* broody (*hen*).
lluvia, *n.f.* rain; rain-water; (*fig.*) abundance.
lluvioso, -sa, *a.* rainy, showery, wet.

M

M, m, *n.f.* fifteenth letter of the Spanish alphabet.
maca, *n.f.* blemish.
macabro, -ra, *a.* macabre
macadám, macadán, *n.m.* macadam.
macarrón, *n.m.* macaroon.—*pl.* macaroni.
macear, *v.t.* hammer.—*v.i.* (*fam.*) be a bore.
maceta, *n.f.* flower-pot; mallet; handle.
macfarlán, macferlán, *n.m.* rain-cape.
macicez, *n.f.* solidity.
macilento, -ta, *a.* lean, wan.
macillo, *n.m.* piano hammer.
macis, *n.f.* (*bot., cul.*) mace.
macizar [C], *v.t.* fill up *or* in.
macizo, -za, *a.* solid; massive.—*n.m.* massif; mass; bulk; flower-bed.
mácula, *n.f.* blemish; (*fam.*) trick; — ***solar,*** sun-spot.
machacar [A], *v.t.* crush, pound.—*v.i.* be persistent *or* a bore.
machado, *n.m.* hatchet.
a machamartillo, *adv. phr.* firmly, solidly.
machar, *v.t.* crush.
machete, *n.m.* machete, chopper.
machihembrar, *v.t.* (*carp.*) tongue and groove; mortise.
machina, *n.f.* derrick; pile-driver.
macho (1), *a. inv.* male; masculine; robust; stupid.—*n.m.* male; buttress; dolt; mule.
macho (2), *n.m.* sledge hammer; anvil.
machucar [A], *v.t.* batter, pound.
machucho, -cha, *a.* mature, wise; elderly.
machuno, -na, *a.* mannish; manly.
madamisela, *n.f.* (*pej.*) young lady.
madeja, *n.f.* hank, skein; — ***sin cuenda,*** wet blanket.
madera, *n.f.* wood, timber; (*fig.*) stuff, makings.—*n.m.* madeira (*wine*).
maderable, *a.* timber-yielding.
maderaje, maderamen, *n.m.* timber; wooden framework.
maderero, -ra, *a.* rel. to timber.—*n.m.* timber merchant.
madero, *n.m.* beam, log; dolt; (*poet.*) bark, ship.
madrastra, *n.f.* step-mother.
madre, *n.f.* mother; source, origin; river-bed; lees, mother; main channel; matrix; womb; main-beam; ***lengua*** —, mother tongue; — ***patria,*** mother country.
madreperla, *n.f.* pearl oyster; mother-of-pearl.
madreselva, *n.f.* honeysuckle.
madrigal, *n.m.* madrigal.
madriguera, *n.f.* warren; den.
madrileño, -ña, *a., n.m.f.* rel. to *or* native of Madrid.
madrina, *n.f.* godmother; protectress; — ***de boda,*** bridesmaid.
madroño, *n.m.* arbutus, strawberry-tree; fruit of same; tassel.
madrugada, *n.f.* the early hours, dawn.
madrugar [B], *v.i.* get up very early; (*fig.*) be well ahead.
madurar, *v.t., v.i., v.r.* ripen, mature, mellow.
madurez, *n.f.* ripeness; maturity.
maduro, -ra, *a.* ripe, mellow; mature.
maestra, *n.f.* mistress; schoolmistress; guide-line.
maestrazgo, *n.m.* (*hist.*) mastership of military order.
maestre, *n.m.* master of military order; (*naut.*) master.
maestrear, *v.t.* take charge of, direct.
maestría, *n.f.* mastery; mastership; stratagem.
maestro, -tra, *a.* master; main, major; trained; ***obra maestra,*** masterpiece.—*n.m.* master, schoolmaster; maestro.
magia, *n.f.* magic.
mágico, -ca, *a.* magic(al).—*n.m.f.* magician.—*n.f.* magic.
magín, *n.m.* (*fam.*) mind, imagination; gumption.

magisterial, *a.* rel. to teaching *or* schoolmasters.
magisterio, *n.m.* (school-)teaching; schoolteachers; teaching profession.
magistrado, *n.m.* magistrate.
magistral, *a.* masterly; magisterial.
magnanimidad, *n.f.* magnanimity.
magnánimo, -ma, *a.* magnanimous.
magnate, *n.m.* magnate.
magnesia, *n.f.* magnesia.
magnesio, *n.m.* magnesium; (*phot.*) flash.
magnético, -ca, *a.* magnetic.
magnetismo, *n.m.* magnetism.
magnetizar [C], *v.t.* magnetize.
magneto, *n.m.* or *f.* magneto.
magnetofónico, -ca, *a.* rel. to tape-recorder; ***cinta magnetofónica,*** recording tape.
magnetófono, magnetofón (*pl.* **-fones**), *n.m.* tape-recorder.
magnificar [A], *v.t.* magnify.
magníficat, *n.m.* Magnificat.
magnificencia, *n.f.* magnificence.
magnífico, -ca, *a.* magnificent; generous, liberal.
magnitud, *n.f.* magnitude.
magno, -na, *a.* Great; ***Alejandro Magno,*** Alexander the Great.
mago, -ga, *a.*, *n.m.f.* magian; ***los Reyes Magos,*** the Three Wise Men.—*n.m.* wizard.
magra, *n.f.* rasher, slice.
magro, -ra, *a.* thin, lean; scant.
maguer, *conj.* (*obs.*) albeit.
magullar, *v.t.* bruise.
Mahoma, *n.m.* Mohammed.
mahometano, -na, *a.*, *n.m.f.* Mohammedan.
mohametismo, *n.m.* Mohammedanism.
maído, *n.m.* mew, miaow.
maitines, *n.m.pl.* (*eccl.*) matins.
maíz, *n.m.* maize, Indian corn.
majada, *n.f.* sheepfold; dung; (*S.A.*) flock.
majadería, *n.f.* pest; silliness.
majadero, -ra, *a.* stupid, boring.—*n.m.f.* fool; bore.—*n.m.* pestle.
majadura, *n.f.* pounding.
majar, *v.t.* pound, crush; (*fam.*) pester.
majestad, *n.f.* majesty.
majestuoso, -sa, *a.* majestic.
majeza, *n.f.* (*fam.*) nattiness, bonniness.
majo, -ja, *a.* bonny, flashy, natty.—*n.m.* beau, young blood.—*n.f.* belle.
majuelo, *n.m.* (*bot.*) white hawthorn; young vine.
mal, *a. contracted form of* MALO, *before n.m.sg.*—*n.m.* evil; harm; wrong; damage; illness; fault; ***— de la tierra,*** homesickness; ***— de mar,*** seasickness; ***— de ojo,*** evil eye.—*adv.* badly, ill, wrongly; wickedly; hardly; ***de — en peor,*** from bad to worse; ***echar a —,*** despise; ***estar —,*** be ill; be on bad terms (***con,*** with); ***¡ — haya . . . !*** confound . . . ! ***— que bien,*** by hook or by crook.
malabarista, *n.m.f.* juggler.
Malaca, *n.f.* Malaya.
malacate, *n.m.* windlass, hoist.
malacostumbrado, -da, *a.* pampered; having bad habits.
malagueño, -ña, *a.*, *n.m.f.* rel. to *or* native of Malaga.
malamente, *adv.* badly; wrongly.
maladanza, *n.f.* misfortune, ill-chance.
malaria, *n.f.* malaria.
Malasia, *n.f.* Malaysia.
malasiano, -na, *a.*, *n.m.f.* Malaysian.
malaventura, *n.f.* misfortune.
malaventurado, -da, *a.* unfortunate, luckless.
Malaya, *n.f.* Malaya.
malayo, -ya, *a.*, *n.m.f.* Malayan, Malay.
malbaratar, *v.t.* cut the price of; squander.
malcasado, -da, *a.* ill-matched; unfaithful (*husband, wife*).
malcontento, -ta, *a.*, *n.m.f.* malcontent.
malcriar [L], *v.t.* spoil (*a child*).
maldad, *n.f.* evil, wickedness.
maldecir [17, *fut.* **maldeciré**; *p.p.* **maldito**], *v.t.* curse.—*v.i.* speak ill (***de,*** of).
maldiciente, *a.* cursing; slanderous.—*n.m.f.* slanderer.
maldición, *n.f.* malediction, curse.
maldito, -ta, *a.* cursed; wicked; (*fam.*) a single, any.
maleante, *a.*, *n.m.f.* miscreant.
malear, *v.t.* corrupt, spoil.
maledicencia, *n.f.* evil talk.
maleficiar, *v.t.* damage, harm; curse.
maleficio, *n.m.* harm; curse, evil spell.
maléfico, -ca, *a.* malicious, evil.
malestar, *n.m.* malaise; uneasiness.
maleta, *n.f.* suitcase.—*n.m.* (*fam.*) bungler.
maletín, *n.m.* satchel; attaché case.
malevolencia, *n.f.* malevolence.
malévolo, -la, *a.* malevolent.
maleza, *n.f.* weeds; scrub; (*S.A.*) pus.
malgastar, *v.t.* squander.
malhablado, -da, *a.* ill-spoken.
malhecho, -cha, *a.* malformed.—*n.m.* misdeed.
malhechor, -ra, *n.m.f.* malefactor.
malhumorado, -da, *a.* ill-humoured.
malicia, *n.f.* evil; malice; slyness.
maliciar, *v.t.* suspect maliciously.—*v.r.* go wrong, err.
malicioso, -sa, *a.* malicious; crafty, sly.
malignar, *v.t.* vitiate, deprave.—*v.r.* spoil; become depraved.
malignidad, *n.f.* malignance, malice.
maligno, -na, *a.* malignant, malign.
malintencionado, -da, *a.* intending evil.
malmandado, -da, *a.* disobedient, wayward.
malmaridada, *n.f.* faithless wife.
malmeter, *v.t.* estrange; waste.
malmirado, -da, *a.* disliked; indiscreet.
malo, -la, *a.* bad; ill; wicked; wrong.—*n.m.* wicked person; the Devil; ***por (las) malas o por (las) buenas,*** willy-nilly.
malogrado, -da, *a.* lamented, late, ill-fated.
malograr, *v.t.* miss, lose; spoil.—*v.r.* come amiss, fail; come to an untimely end.
malogro, *n.m.* failure; disappointment; untimely end.
maloliente, *a.* foul-smelling.
malparar, *v.t.* hurt, harm, ill-treat.
malparir, *v.i.* miscarry.
malparto, *n.m.* miscarriage.
malquerencia, *n.f.* ill-will, dislike.
malquerer [26], *v.t.* hate, dislike.
malquistar, *v.t.* estrange.
malquisto, -ta, *a.* unpopular, detested.
malsano, -na, *a.* unhealthy.
malsonante, *a.* offensive, sounding objectionable.
malsufrido, -da, *a.* impatient.
malta, *n.f.* malt; coffee substitute.

maltés, -tesa, *a., n.m.f.* Maltese.
maltratar, *v.t.* ill-treat, maltreat.
maltrato, *n.m.* maltreatment.
maltrecho, -cha, *a.* ill-treated, damaged, battered.
maltusiano, -na, *a.* Malthusian.
maluco, -ca, malucho, -cha, *a.* (*fam.*) sickly, poorly.
malva, *n.f.* (*bot.*) mallow; hollyhock; ***ser (como) una* —,** be kind and gentle.
malvado, -da, *a.* wicked.
malvasía, *n.f.* malmsey (*grape, wine*).
malvavisco, *n.m.* (*bot.*) marsh mallow.
malvender, *v.t.* sell at a loss.
malversación, *n.f.* embezzlement.
malversar, *v.t.* embezzle.
las Malvinas, *n.f.pl.* Falkland Islands.
malla, *n.f.* mesh; chain-mail.
mallete, *n.m.* mallet.
Mallorca, *n.f.* Majorca.
mallorquín, -quina, *a., n.m.f.* Majorcan.
mamá, *n.f.* (*pl.* **-áes**) (*fam.*) mummy.
mamar, *v.t.* suck (*mother's milk*); (*fam.*) gulp down; (*fam.*) wangle; (*fam.*) swallow, be fooled by.—*v.r.* (*low*) get sozzled; (*fam.*) wangle; ***mamarse el dedo,*** be fooled, be taken in.
mamarracho, *n.m.* (*fam.*) daub, mess; wretch.
mameluco, *n.m.* mameluke; (*fam.*) dolt.
mamífero, -ra, *a.* mammalian.—*n.m.* mammal.
mamola, *n.f.* chuck under the chin.
mamotreto, *n.m.* ledger; bundle of papers.
mampara, *n.f.* folding screen.
mamparo, *n.m.* (*naut.*) bulkhead.
mampostería, *n.f.* rubble-work.
mampuesto, *n.m.* rough stone; rubble; parapet; ***de* —,** spare, set aside.
mamut, *n.m.* (*pl.* **-ts**) (*zool.*) mammoth.
maná, *n.m.* manna.
manada, *n.f.* herd, drove, pack; handful.
manante, *a.* flowing.
manantial, *a.* flowing.—*n.m.* spring, source.
manantío, -tía, *a.* flowing.
manar, *v.t.* run with, pour forth.—*v.i.* pour, flow.
mancar [A], *v.t.* maim.
manceba, *n.f.* concubine.
mancebo, *n.m.* youth; bachelor; lad.
mancilla, *n.f.* stain, blot.
mancillar, *v.t.* blemish, stain.
manco, -ca, *a.* one-handed; one-armed; maimed.
de mancomún, *adv. phr.* by common consent, jointly.
mancomunar, *v.t.* pool, combine.
mancha, *n.f.* stain, blot; patch; **— *solar,*** sun-spot.
manchar, *v.t.* spot, strain.
manchego, -ga, *a., n.m.f.* rel. to *or* native of La Mancha.
mandadero, -ra, *n.m.f.* messenger.
mandado, *n.m.* order; errand.
mandamiento, *n.m.* (*Bib.*) commandment.
mandar, *v.t.* command; send; bequeath; **— *por,*** send for.—*v.r.* interconnect (***con,*** with); go (***por,*** through, up).
mandarín, *n.m.* mandarin.
mandarina, *n.f.* mandarin orange.
mandato, *n.m.* mandate; (*eccl.*) maundy.
mandíbula, *n.f.* mandible, jaw.
mandil, *n.m.* apron.
mando, *n.m.* command, authority; (*mech.*) control.
mandolina, *n.f.* mandolin.
mandria, *a. inv.* cowardly; worthless.
mandril, *n.m.* (*zool.*) mandrill; (*mech.*) chuck.
manducar [A], *v.t., v.i.* (*fam.*) eat, tuck in.
manear, *v.t.* hobble; wield.
manecilla, *n.f.* small hand; watch-hand; clasp; tendril.
manejar, *v.t.* manage; handle; (*S.A.*) drive (*cars*).
manejo, *n.m.* handling; management; stratagem.
manera, *n.f.* manner, way; kind, type; ***a* — *de,*** in the way of, like; ***de* — *que,*** so that; ***sobre* —,** exceedingly.
manezuela, *n.f.* small hand; handle.
manga, *n.f.* sleeve; hose, pipe; armed band; whirlwind; ***de* — *ancha,*** broad-minded.
manganeso, *n.m.* manganese.
mangle, *n.m.* (*bot.*) mangrove.
mango, *n.m.* handle; (*bot.*) mango (*fruit and tree*).
mangosta, *n.f.* (*zool.*) mongoose.
manguera, *n.f.* (*naut.*) hose; air-vent.
maní, *n.m.* (*pl.* **manises**) (*bot.*) pea-nut.
manía, *n.f.* mania.
maníaco, -ca [MANIÁTICO].
maniatar, *v.t.* tie the hands of.
maniático, -ca, *a., n.m.f.* maniac.
manicomio, *n.m.* lunatic asylum.
manicorto, -ta, *a.* stingy.
manicuro, -ra, *n.m.f.* manicurist.—*n.f.* manicure.
manido, -da, *a.* tattered; stale.—*n.f.* den, haunt.
manifacero, -ra, *a.* (*fam.*) meddlesome.
manifestación, *n.f.* manifestation; (*jur.*) writ of habeas corpus.
manifestar [I], *v.t.* show, reveal, manifest.
manifiesto, -ta, *a.* clear, obvious, manifest.—*n.m.* manifesto; (*com.*) manifest.
manija, *n.f.* handle, haft; clamp; shackles.
manilargo, -ga, *a.* long-handed; generous.
manilla, *n.f.* small hand; bracelet; manacle.
manillar, *n.m.* handle-bars.
maniobra, *n.f.* operation; (*mil., naut.*) manœuvre; (*rail.*) shunting.
maniobrar, *v.i.* perform; manœuvre; (*rail.*) shunt.
maniota, *n.f.* hobble; manacle.
manipulación, *n.f.* manipulation.
manipular, *v.t.* manipulate.
maniquí, *n.m.* (*pl.* **-íes**) manikin; (*fig.*) puppet.
manirroto, -ta, *a.* lavish, spendthrift.
manivela, *n.f.* (*mech.*) crank; lever.
manjar, *n.m.* morsel, dish.
mano, *n.f.* hand; forefoot, trotter; pestle; coat (*of paint*); elephant's trunk; reproof; ***a la* —,** to hand; ***a* —,** at *or* by hand; ***dar de manos,*** fall flat; ***echar* — *de,*** make use of; ***echar una* —,** lend a hand; **— *de gato,*** master touch; (*fam.*) face-paint;**— *de obra,*** labour; ***ser* —,** lead, be first (*in games*).—*pl.* labour, hands; ***entre manos,*** on hand; ***llegar a las manos,*** come to blows.
manojo, *n.m.* bunch.
Manolo, *n.m.* (*fam. form of*) MANUEL; **manolo, -la,** *n.m.f.* flashy young person of Madrid.
manopla, *n.f.* mitten.

manosear, *v.t.* paw, handle.
manotada, *n.f.*, **manotazo,** *n.m.* slap.
manotear, *v.t.* slap, cuff.—*v.i.* gesticulate.
manquear, *v.i.* feign a limp; be maimed.
manquedad, manquera, *n.f.* lack of hand *or* arm; defect.
a mansalva, *adv. phr.* without danger (***de,*** of, from).
mansedumbre, *n.f.* meekness, tameness.
mansión, *n.f.* sojourn; abode.
manso, -sa, *a.* gentle; tame.
manta, *n.f.* blanket; cloak.
mantear, *v.t.* toss in a blanket.
manteca, *n.f.* lard; butter.
mantecado, *n.m.* ice-cream; butter biscuit.
mantel, *n.m.* table-cloth; altar cloth.
mantelería, *n.f.* table-linen.
mantellina, *n.f.* mantilla.
mantenencia, *n.f.* maintenance.
mantener [33], *v.t.* maintain.—*v.r.* keep oneself; stay firm.
a manteniente, *adv.phr.* with might and main.
mantenimiento, *n.m.* maintenance, sustenance.
manteo, *n.m.* tossing in a blanket; mantle.
mantequera, *n.f.* butter-dish; churn; butter-girl.
mantequilla, *n.f.* butter.
mantilla, *n.f.* mantilla; horse-blanket.
manto, *n.m.* mantle, cloak.
mantón, *n.m.* shawl; stole.
mantuve [MANTENER].
manual, *a.* manual; handy.—*n.m.* manual.
manubrio, *n.m.* crank; handle.
Manuel, *n.m.* Emmanuel.
manufactura, *n.f.* manufacture; factory.
manufacturar, *v.t.* manufacture.
manufacturero, -ra, *a.* manufacturing.
manumitir, *v.t.* manumit.
manuscrito, -ta, *a.*, *n.m.* manuscript.
manutención, *n.f.* maintenance.
manzana, *n.f.* apple; block of houses; pommel.
manzanar, *n.m.* apple orchard.
manzanilla, *n.f.* camomile; manzanilla sherry; point of chin.
manzano, *n.m.* apple-tree.
maña, *n.f.* skill, knack; wile; trick; bad habit; ***darse* —,** manage (***para,*** to).
mañana, *n.f.* morning.—*n.m.* morrow.—*adv.* tomorrow.
mañear, *v.t.*, *v.i.* wangle.
mañero, -ra, *a.* cunning; easy.
maño, -ña, *a.*, *n.m.f.* (*fam.*) Aragonese.
mañoso, -sa, *a.* clever; cunning.
mapa, *n.m.* map.—*n.f.* (*fam.*) the tops, the cream.
mapamundi, *n.m.* map of the world.
maque, *n.m.* lacquer.
maqueta, *n.f.* (*arch.*) scale model.
maquivélico, -ca, *a.* Machiavellian.
maquiavelista, *a.*, *n.m.f.* Machiavellian.
Maquiavelo, *n.m.* Machiavelli.
maquillaje, *n.m.* make-up.
maquillar, *v.t.*, *v.r.* make up.
máquina, *n.f.* machine; engine; locomotive; contrivance; machination; vast structure; (*C.A.*) car; ***— de escribir,*** typewriter; ***escrito a —,*** typewritten.
maquinación, *n.f.* machination.
máquina-herramienta, *n.f.* machine-tool.
maquinal, *a.* mechanical.
maquinar, *v.t.* machinate.
maquinaria, *n.f.* machinery; mechanics.
maquinista, *n.m.f.* mechanic, machinist; engine-driver.
mar, *n.m.* or *f.* sea; (*fig.*) vast amount; ***alta —,*** the high seas; ***hacerse a la —,*** set sail; ***hablar de la —,*** (*fam.*) waffle; ***meterse — adentro,*** get into deep water; ***— alta,*** rough sea.
maraña, *n.f.* thicket; tangle; swindle; puzzle.
marañón, *n.m.* (*bot.*) cashew-tree *or* nut.
maravedí, *n.m.* (*pl.* **-ís, -íses** *or* **-íes**) marvedi, old small coin.
maravilla, *n.f.* wonder, marvel; surprise; (*bot.*) marigold; ***a —,*** wonderfully; ***por —,*** very seldom; ***a las mil maravillas,*** superbly.
maravillar, *v.t.* amaze, surprise.—*v.r.* marvel, be astonished (***con, de,*** at).
maravilloso, -sa, *a.* wonderful, marvellous; amazing.
marbete, *n.m.* label; edge.
marca, *n.f.* mark; brand; trade mark; (*sport*) record; measure; marker; march, frontier region; standard; size; ***de —,*** branded; outstanding.
marcar [A], *v.t.* mark; brand; embroider; (*tel.*) dial; designate; score; point out; show; (*naut.*) take bearings.
marcial, *a.* martial.
marcialidad, *n.f.* martialness.
marciano, -na, *a.*, *n.m.f.* Martian.
marco, *n.m.* frame; standard; mark (*coin*).
Marcos, *n.m.* (*Bib.*) Mark.
marcha, *n.f.* march; operation, action; speed; (*mech.*) gear; progress; ***en —,*** in motion, working.
marchar, *v.i.* march; run, function; progress. —*v.r.* go away.
marchitar, *v.t.*, *v.i.* wither, wilt.
marchitez, *n.f.* witheredness; languor.
marchito, -ta, *a.* wilted, withered; languid.
marea, *n.f.* tide; sea breeze; dew, drizzle.
marear, *v.t.* navigate; (*fam.*) pester.—*v.r.* get sea-sick *or* dizzy; suffer damage at sea; (*fam.*) get tiddly.
marejada, *n.f.* (*naut.*) swell; (*fig.*) commotion.
maremagno, mare mágnum, *n.m.* (*fam.*) mess, commotion; vast crowd.
mareo, *n.m.* nausea; sea- *or* travel-sickness; dizziness; (*fam.*) bother.
marfil, *n.m.* ivory.
margarina, *n.f.* margarine.
Margarita, *n.f.* Margaret; **margarita,** *n.f.* pearl; (*bot.*) common daisy.
margen, *n.m.* or *f.* (*pl.* **márgenes**) margin; occasion.
marginal, *a.* marginal.
marginar, *v.t.* annotate in the margin; margin.
María, *n.f.* Mary; **maría,** *n.f.* wax taper; ***al baño (de) —,*** (*cul.*) steamed.
mariano, -na, *a.* Marian.
marica, *n.f.* (*orn.*) magpie; cissy, pansy.
Maricastaña, *n.f.* ***en tiempo(s) de —,*** in days of yore.
maridaje, *n.m.* conjugal life; (*fig.*) union.
marido, *n.m.* husband.
mariguana, *n.f.* marijuana.
marimacho, *n.m.* (*fam.*) virago, mannish woman.
marimorena, *n.f.* (*fam.*) bust-up, fight.

marina, *n.f.* navy; sea-coast.
marinar, *v.t.* marinate, salt; man (*a ship*).
marinero, -ra, *a.* seaworthy; sea-going, seafaring.—*n.m.* mariner, sailor, seaman.
marinesco, -ca, *a.* nautical, sailorly.
marino, -na, *a.* marine, of the sea.—*n.m.* sailor, seaman.
marioneta, *n.f.* marionette.
mariposa, *n.f.* butterfly, moth; night-light; wing nut.
mariposear, *v.i.* flutter about, be fickle.
mariquita, *n.f.* (*fam.*) cissy; (*ent.*) ladybird.
marisabidilla, *n.f.* blue-stocking.
mariscal, *n.m.* marshal.
marisco, *n.m.* shell-fish.—*pl.* sea-food.
marisma, *n.f.* salt-marsh, fen.
marital, *a.* rel. to a husband; marital.
marítimo, -ma, *a.* maritime.
marjal, *n.m.* fen, boggy moor.
marjoleto, *n.m.* (*bot.*) hawthorn.
marmita, *n.f.* stew-pot.
marmitón, *n.m.* scullion.
mármol, *n.m.* marble.
marmóreo, -rea, *a.* rel. to *or* made of marble.
marmota, *n.f.* (*zool.*) marmot; (*fam.*) sleepy-head.
maroma, *n.f.* esparto rope; (*S.A.*) acrobatics.
marqués, *n.m.* marquis, marquess.
marquesa, *n.f.* marchioness.
marquesina, *n.f.* awning, marquee.
marquetería, *n.f.* marquetry.
marra (1), *n.f.* gap, lacuna.
marra (2), *n.f.* sledge-hammer.
marrajo, -ja, *a.* cunning, sly.—*n.m.* shark.
marrano, -na, *n.m.f.* pig.
marras, *adv.* ***de* —,** of yore.
marro, *n.m.* quoits; failure; swerve.
marrón, *a. inv.*, *n.m.* brown.
marroquí (*pl.* **-íes**), **marroquín, -quina, marrueco, -ca,** *a.*, *n.m.f.* Moroccan.
Marruecos, *n.m.* Morocco.
marrullería, *n.f.* cajolery.
marrullero, -ra, *a.* cajoling.—*n.m.f.* cajoler.
Marsella, *n.f.* Marseilles.
marsopa, *n.f.* (*zool.*) porpoise.
marsupial, *a.*, *n.m.* marsupial.
marta, *n.f.* (*zool.*) marten; — ***cebellina,*** sable.
martagón, -gona, *n.m.f.* (*fam.*) sly-boots.
Marte, *n.m.* (*myth.*, *astr.*) Mars.
martes, *n.m.* Tuesday.
martillar, *v.t.* hammer.
marillazo, *n.m.* hammer-blow.
martilleo, *n.m.* hammering.
martillo, *n.m.* hammer; (*fig.*) scourge; auction; ***a macha* —,** robustly, roughly.
Martín, *n.m.* Martin; ***le viene su San* —,** his time (*to pay etc.*) is coming; ***martín pescador,*** (*orn.*) kingfisher.
martinete, *n.m.* (*orn.*) night-heron; pile-driver; piano-hammer.
martingala, *n.f.* martingale.
martinico, *n.m.* (*fam.*) elf, ghost.
mártir, *n.m.* martyr.
martirio, *n.m.* martyrdom.
martirizar [C], *v.t.* martyr.
Maruja, *n.f.* (*fam. form of* MARÍA) Mary.
marullo, *n.m.* (*naut.*) swell.
marxismo, *n.m.* Marxism.
marxista, *a.*, *n.m.f.* Marxist.
marzo, *n.m.* March.
mas, *conj.* but.
más, *adv.* more, most; any more.—*n.m.* (*math.*) plus; more; ***a lo* —,** at most; ***a — de,*** besides; ***de* —,** in addition; in excess; — ***bien,*** rather; ***no . . .* —,** no longer; ***por — que,*** however much; ***sin — ni* —,** (*fam.*) with no more ado.
masa, *n.f.* dough; mass; mortar; disposition.
masacrar, *v.t.* (*S.A.*) massacre.
masada, *n.f.* farm-house.
masaje, *n.m.* massage.
masajista, *n.m.* masseur.—*n.f.* masseuse.
masar, *v.t.* knead; massage.
mascadura, *n.f.* chewing; fraying.
mascar [A], *v.t.* chew.—*v.r.* fray.
máscara, *n.f.* mask; masquerade.—*n.m.f.* masquerader.
mascarada, *n.f.* masked ball, masquerade.
mascarilla, *n.f.* small mask; death-mask.
mascarón, *n.m.* ugly person; gargoyle; (*naut.*) figurehead.
mascota, *n.f.* mascot.
masculinidad, *n.f.* masculinity.
masculino, -na, *a.* masculine.
mascullar, *v.t.* mutter.
masería, masía, *n.f.* farm-house.
masilla, *n.f.* putty.
masón(1), *n.m.* (free)mason.
masón (2), *n.m.* hen-mash.
masonería, *n.f.* freemasonry.
masónico, -ca, *a.* masonic.
mastelero, *n.m.* top-mast.
masticación, *n.f.* mastication.
masticar [A], *v.t.* masticate, chew.
mástil, *n.m.* mast; stem; upright; quill.
mastín, *n.m.* mastiff.
mastuerzo, *n.m.* (*bot.*) cress; (*fam.*) mutt, fool.
mata, *n.f.* bush; sprig; coppice; (*bot.*) mastic; tousled hair.
matacandelas, *n.m. inv.* candle-snuffer.
matachín, *n.m.* slaughterman; (*fam.*) bully.
matadero, *n.m.* slaughterhouse; drudgery.
matador, -ra, *a.* killing.—*n.m.* bullfighter; killer.
matafuego, *n.m.* fire extinguisher.
matalascallando, *n.m.f.* sly-boots, cunning person.
matamoros, *n.m. inv.* braggart; Moor-slayer.
matamoscas, *n.m. inv.* fly-swat; fly-paper.
matancero, *n.m.* (*S.A.*) slaughterman.
matanza, *n.f.* slaughter; massacre.
mataperros, *n.m. inv.* street-urchin.
matapolvo, *n.m.* drizzle.
matar, *v.t.* kill; put out; slake; gall; ***matarse por,*** be dying to *or* for.
matasanos, *n.m. inv.* (*fam.*) sawbones, medic.
matasellos, *n.m. inv.* postmark.
matasiete, *n.m.* bravo, bully.
mate, *a.* dull, matt.—*n.m.* (check)mate; (*bot.*, *cul.*) maté; — ***ahogado,*** stalemate; ***dar — (a),*** (check)mate.
matemática(s), *n.f.* (*pl.*) mathematics.
matemático, -ca, *a.* mathematical.—*n.m.* mathematician.
Mateo, *n.m.* Matthew.
materia, *n.f.* matter; material; subject-matter; (*med.*) pus; ***materias prim(er)as,*** raw materials.
material, *a.* material; physical; materialistic.—*n.m.* material; ingredient; (*print.*) copy.
materialidad, *n.f.* materiality; literalness.

materialismo, *n.m.* materialism.
materialista, *a.* materialistic.—*n.m.f.* materialist.
maternal, *a.* maternal, motherly.
maternidad, *n.f.* maternity, motherhood.
materno, -na, *a.* maternal, mother.
matinal, *a.* morning, matutinal.
matiné, *n.m.* matinée.
matiz, *n.m.* (*pl.* **-ices**) shade, hue, nuance.
matizar [C], *v.t.* shade, tint.
matón, *n.m.* (*fam.*) bully, braggart.
matorral, *n.m.* thicket, undergrowth.
matraca, *n.f.* wooden rattle; (*fam.*) banter.
matraquear, *v.i.* make a clatter; jeer.
matrero, -ra, *a.* cunning.—*n.m.* (*S.A.*) tramp, hobo.
matriarca, *n.f.* matriarch.
matriarcado, *n.m.* matriarchy.
matriarcal, *a.* matriarchal.
matricida, *n.m.f.* matricide (*person*).
matricidio, *n.m.* matricide (*act*).
matrícula, *n.f.* register; matriculation; registration; (*auto.*) registration-number.
matricular, *v.t.* register; enroll; matriculate.
matrimonesco, -ca (*fam.*); **matrimonial,** *a.* matrimonial.
matrimonio, *n.m.* matrimony, marriage; married couple; ***cama de —,*** double bed.
matritense [MADRILEÑO].
matriz, *n.f.* (*pl.* **-ices**) womb; matrix.
matrona, *n.f.* matron; midwife.
Matusalén, *n.m.* Methuselah.
matute, *n.m.* smuggling.
matutino, -na, matutinal, *a.* morning, matutinal.
maula, *n.f.* junk, rubbish; trickery.—*n.m.f.* (*fam.*) cheat, twister.
maulero, -ra, *n.m.f.* scrap dealer; twister.
maullar [P], *v.i.* miaow.
maullido, *n.m.* miaow.
Mauricio, *n.m.* Maurice, Morris.
mausoleo, *n.m.* mausoleum.
máxima, *n.f.* maxim.
máxime, *adv.* principally, especially.
máximo, -ma, *a.* very great, major, chief.—*n.m.* maximum.
maya, *a.*, *n.m.f.* Mayan.—*n.f.* daisy.
mayal, *n.m.* flail.
mayar, *v.i.* miaow.
mayestático, -ca, *a.* majestic, imperial.
mayo, *n.m.* May; maypole.
mayonesa, *n.f.* mayonnaise.
mayor, *a.* greater; larger; elder, older; greatest; largest; eldest, oldest; major, main; senior, adult.—*n.m.* major, chief, head; ***por —,*** wholesale.—*pl.* elders; ancestors.
mayoral, *n.m.* foreman, overseer; (*obs.*) coachman.
mayorazgo, *n.m.* primogeniture.
mayordomo, *n.m.* majordomo, steward.
mayoría, *n.f.* majority; superiority.
mayoridad, *n.f.* majority (*age*).
mayúscula, *a.f.*, *n.f.* capital (*letter*).
maza, *n.f.* mace, club; pestle; pile-driver.
mazapán, *n.m.* marzipan.
mazmorra, *n.f.* dungeon.
mazo, *n.m.* mallet; bunch; (*fig.*) botherer.
mazorca, *n.f.* ear, cob (*of maize*); spindle.
mazurca, *n.f.* (*mus.*) mazurka.
me, *personal pron.* me, to me.
meandro, *n.m.* meander.
mear, *v.t.*, *v.i.*, *v.r.* (*low*) urinate.
Meca, *n.f.* Mecca; [CECA].
mecánico, -ca, *a.* mechanical; (*fam.*) mean, low.—*n.m.* mechanic; driver.—*n.f.* mechanics; machinery; (*fam.*) chore; (*fam.*) mean ruse.
mecanismo, *n.m.* mechanism.
mecanización, *n.f.* mechanization.
mecanizar [C], *v.t.*, *v.r.* mechanize.
mecanografía, *n.f.* typewriting.
mecanografiar [L], *v.t.*, *v.i.* type.
mecanográfico, -ca, *a.* typewriting.
mecanógrafo, -fa, *n.m.f.* typist.
mecedor, *n.f.* rocking-chair.
Mecenas, *n.m.* Maecenas; **mecenas,** *n.m.* maecenas.
mecer [D], *v.t.* stir; rock.—*v.r.* swing; rock.
mecha, *n.f.* wick; fuse; lock of hair; tinder.
mechera, *n.f.* shoplifter.
mechero, *n.m.* burner; lighter.
medalla, *n.f.* medal, medallion.
medallón, *n.m.* medallion; locket.
media, *n.f.* stocking; (*S.A.*) sock; (*math.*) mean; ***a medias,*** half.
mediación, *n.f.* mediation.
mediado, -da, *a.* half-full; ***a mediados de mayo,*** about the middle of May.
mediador, -ra, *a.* mediating.—*n.m.f.* mediator.
medianero, -ra, *a.* dividing, intermediate.—*n.m.* mediator; next-door neighbour.
medianía, *n.f.* middle position, halfway; middlingness, mediocrity; (*fam.*) a nobody.
mediano, -na, *a.* middling; intermediate.
medianoche, *n.f.* midnight.
mediante, *prep.* by means of, through; ***Dios —,*** God willing.
mediar, *v.t.* half-fill.—*v.i.* be halfway; mediate; intervene; be in the middle; elapse; happen.
mediatizar [C], *v.t.* control, manipulate.
mediato, -ta, *a.* mediate.
medicación, *n.f.* medication.
medicamento, *n.m.* medicament.
medicina, *n.f.* medicine.
medicinal, *a.* medicinal.
medicinar, *v.t.* treat (*a patient*).
médico, -ca, *a.* medical.—*n.m.f.* doctor, physician.—*n.f.* woman doctor; doctor's wife.
medida, *n.f.* measure; moderation; ***a — de,*** according to; ***a — que,*** according as, as.
medieval, *a.* mediaeval.
medievo, *n.m.* Middle Ages.
medio, -dia, *a.* half; middle; average.—*n.m.* half; middle; centre; measure, step; means; medium.—*adv.* half; ***de por —,*** half; in between; ***en — de,*** in the midst of; ***estar de por —,*** mediate; ***quitar de en —,*** (*fam.*) get rid of.
mediocre, *a.* medium, mediocre.
mediocridad, *n.f.* mediocrity.
mediodía, *n.m.* noon, midday; south.
medioev- [MEDIEV-].
medir [8], *v.t.*, *v.i.* measure.—*v.r.* act with moderation.
meditabundo, -da, *a.* pensive.
meditación, *n.f.* meditation.
meditar, *v.t.*, *v.i.* meditate.
Mediterráneo, *n.m.*, **mediterráneo, -nea,** *a.* Mediterranean.

medrar, *v.i.* thrive, flourish.
medro, *n.m.* thriving.—*pl.* progress.
medroso, -sa, *a.* fearful, afraid.
médula, *n.f.* marrow, medulla, pith.
Mefistófeles, *n.m.* Mephistopheles.
mefistofélico, -ca, *a.* Mephistophelian.
megáfono, *n.m.* megaphone.
megalomanía, *n.f.* megalomania.
megalómano, -na, *a., n.m.f.* megalomaniac.
megatón, *n.m.* megaton.
mego (1), **-ga,** *a.* meek, gentle.
mego (2), *n.m.* (*obs.*) warlock.
mejicano, -na, *a., n.m.f.* Mexican.
Méjico, *n.m.* Mexico.—*n.f.* Mexico City.
mejilla, *n.f.* cheek.
mejillón, *n.m.* (*zool.*) mussel.
mejor, *a.* better; best.—*adv.* better; best; rather; ***a lo* —,** (*fam.*) perhaps, maybe; with any luck; **— *dicho*,** rather, better.
mejora, *n.f.* improvement; highest bid.
mejoramiento, *n.m.* amelioration.
mejorar, *v.t.* improve.—*v.i., v.r.* get better, improve.
mejoría, *n.f.* improvement, turn for the better.
melado, -da, *a.* honey-coloured.—*n.m.* honey cake.
melancolía, *n.f.* melancholy, melancholia.
melancólico, -ca, *a., n.m.f.* melancholic; melancholy.
melancolizar [C], *v.t.* make melancholy.—*v.r.* get melancholy.
melaza, *n.f.* molasses.
melena, *n.f.* forelock; long hair; mane (*of lion*).
melenudo, -da, *a.* hairy, with long hair.
melifluo, -lua, *a.* mellifluent, mellifluous.
melindre, *n.m.* (*cul.*) honey fritter, lady-finger.—*pl.* prudery, finickiness, fads.
melindrear, *v.i.* (*fam.*) be finicky.
melindrero, -ra, melindroso, -sa, *a.* finicky, faddy.
melocotón, *n.m.* peach.
melocotonero, *n.m.* peach-tree.
melodía, *n.f.* melody; melodiousness.
melodioso, -sa, *a.* melodious.
melodrama, *n.m.* melodrama.
melodramático, -ca, *a.* melodramatic.
melón, *n.m.* (*bot.*) melon (*plant, fruit*); nitwit, dolt; (*fam.*) pate, bald head.
meloso, -sa, *a.* honeyed, mellow.
mella, *n.f.* notch, gap; ***hacer* — *a*,** leave a mark on; ***hacer* — *en*,** harm, damage.
mellar, *v.t.* notch, groove; harm.
mellizo, -za, *a., n.m.f.* twin.
membrana, *n.f.* membrane; (*rad., tel.*) diaphragm.
membrete, *n.m.* memo, note; letter-head.
membrillo, *n.m.* (*bot.*) quince; ***carne*** or ***queso de* —,** quince jelly.
membrudo, -da, *a.* hefty, burly.
memo, -ma, *a.* simple.—*n.m.f.* simpleton.
memorable, memorando, -da, *a.* memorable.
memorándum, *n.m. inv.* memorandum; letter-head.
memoria, *n.f.* memory; memoir; ***de* —,** by heart; ***hacer* — *de*,** bring to mind.
memorial, *n.m.* petition; memorandum book; (*jur.*) brief.
menaje, *n.m.* furnishings; school equipment.
mención, *n.f.* mention.
mencionar, *v.t.* mention.
mendaz, *a.* (*pl.* **-aces**) mendacious.—*n.m.f.* liar.
mendicante, *a., n.m.f.* mendicant.
mendicidad, *n.f.* mendicancy.
mendigar [B], *v.t.* beg.
mendigo, -ga, *n.m.f.* beggar.
mendrugo, *n.m.* crust, scrap of bread.
menear, *v.t.* shake; wag; manage.—*v.r.* shake, wag, waggle; (*fam.*) get a move on; ***peor es meneallo*,** let sleeping dogs lie.
meneo, *n.m.* shaking, stirring, wagging; (*fam.*) thrashing.
menester, *n.m.* want, need, lack; job, métier; ***haber* —,** need; ***ser* —,** be necessary.
menesteroso, -sa, *a.* needy.—*n.m.f.* needy person.
menestra, *n.f.* vegetable stew; dried vegetable.
mengano, -na, *n.m.f.* (*fam.*) so-and-so, who's it (*after* FULANO).
mengua, *n.f.* decline; decrease; want; discredit.
menguado, -da, *a.* cowardly; silly; fatal.
menguante, *a.* declining, waning.—*n.f.* waning; ebb-tide; decline.
menguar, *v.t., v.i.* diminish, decrease; *v.i.* wane; fall.
menina, *n.f.* maid of honour.
menor, *a.* less, lesser; least; smaller; smallest; younger; youngest; minor.—*n.m.f.* minor; ***al por* —,** retail; ***por* —,** in detail; retail.
Menorca, *n.f.* Minorca.
menoría, *n.f.* minority (*age*).
menorquín, -quina, *a., n.m.f.* Minorcan.
menos, *adv.* less; least; rather not.—*prep.* less, minus, except, ***al* —,** or ***por lo* —,** at least; ***a* — *que*,** unless; ***de* —,** less; missing; ***echar* (*de*) —,** miss; ***no poder* — *de*,** not be able to help . . .; ***tener a*** or ***en* —,** think badly of; ***venir a* —,** decay, decline.
menoscabar, *v.t.* lessen; damage; discredit.
menoscabo, *n.m.* detriment; lessening.
menospreciar, *v.t.* underrate; despise.
menosprecio, *n.m.* underrating; scorn.
mensaje, *n.m.* message; errand.
mensajero, -ra, *a., n.m.f.* messenger.
menstruar [M], *v.i.* menstruate.
mensual, *a.* monthly.
mensualidad, *n.f.* monthly payment.
menta, *n.f.* (*bot.*) mint; peppermint.
mental, *a.* mental.
mentalidad, *n.f.* mentality.
mentar [1], *v.t.* mention, name.
mente, *n.f.* mind.
mentecato, -ta, *a.* foolish, silly.—*n.m.f.* fool.
mentido, -da, *a.* lying, false.
mentir [6], *v.t.* lie to, deceive.—*v.i.* lie; clash (*of colours*).
mentira, *n.f.* lie, falsehood; slip of the pen; ***parece* —,** it's unbelievable.
mentiroso, -sa, *a.* lying; deceitful; full of mistakes.—*n.m.f.* liar.
mentís, *n.m.* insult; lie; ***dar el* — *a*,** give the lie to.
mentol, *n.m.* menthol.
mentolado, -da, *a.* mentholated.
mentón, *n.m.* chin.
mentor, *n.m.* mentor.
menú, *n.m.* (*pl.* **-ús**) menu.
menudear, *v.t.* do frequently; detail; (*S.A.*) sell retail.—*v.i.* happen frequently; abound; go into detail.

menudencia, *n.f.* minuteness; trifle.—*pl.* offal.
menudeo, *n.m.* frequent repetition; great detail; retail.
menudillos, *n.m. pl.* giblets.
menudo, -da, *a.* tiny; worthless; common, vulgar; petty; (*fam.*) many a.—*adv.* ***a* —,** often; ***por* —,** in detail; at retail.—*n.m.pl.* small change; offal, giblets.
menuzo, *n.m.* fragment.
meñique, *a.* little (*finger*); (*fam.*) tiny.
meollo, *n.m.* (*anat.*) marrow; (*bot.*) pith; brains; gist.
mequetrefe, *n.m.* busybody.
merca, *n.f.* (*fam.*) buy.
mercader, -ra, *n.m.f.* merchant.
mercadería, *n.f.* merchandise.
mercado, *n.m.* market; — ***común,*** Common Market.
mercancía, *n.f.* trade; merchandise.—*pl.* goods, merchandise.
mercancías, *n.m. sg.* (*rail.*) goods train.
mercante, *a.* merchant (*navy*).—*n.m.f.* merchant.
mercantil, *a.* mercantile; mercenary.
mercantilismo, *n.m.* mercantilism; commercialization.
mercar [A], *v.t.* (*obs., dial.*) buy.
merced, *n.f.* favour, grace; mercy, pleasure; ***a merced(es),*** voluntarily, without stipend; ***vues(tr)a* —,** (*obs.*) sire, your honour; — ***a,*** thanks to.
mercedario, -ria, *a., n.m.f.* (*eccl.*) Mercedarian.
mercenario, -ria, *a., n.m.f.* mercenary; Mercedarian.
mercería, *n.f.* haberdashery; (*S.A.*) draper's.
mercurial, *a.* mercurial.
Mercurio, *n.m.* Mercury; **mercurio,** *n.m.* (*chem.*) mercury.
merecedor, -ra, *a.* deserving.
merecer [9], *v.t.* deserve, merit.—*v.i.* be worth. — ***la pena,*** be worthwhile.
merecido, *n.m.* deserts.
merecimiento, *n.m.* worth, value; merit.
merendar [1], *v.t.* have for afternoon tea.—*v.i.* have tea *or* a snack.
merendero, *n.m.* open-air snack shop *or* stall.
merengue, *n.m.* meringue.
meretriz, *n.f.* (*pl.* **-ices**) harlot.
meridiano, -na, *a.* meridian; clear, bright.—*n.m.* meridian.—*n.f.* midday nap; ***a la meridiana,*** at noon.
meridional, *a.* southern.—*n.m.f.* southerner.
merienda, *n.f.* afternoon tea, high tea; snack; ***juntar meriendas,*** (*fam.*) join forces.
merino, -na, *a., n.m.f.* merino (*sheep*).—*n.m.* (*hist.*) royal magistrate.
mérito, *n.m.* merit; worth; ***hacer* — *de,*** mention.
meritorio, -ria, *a.* meritorious.—*n.m.f.* volunteer; emeritus.
merluza, *n.f.* (*ichth.*) hake; ***coger una* —,** (*fam.*) get blotto, drunk.
merma, *n.f.* decrease, leakage, waste.
mermar, *v.t.* cut, decrease.—*v.i., v.r.* dwindle.
mermelada, *n.f.* marmalade; jam (*esp. apricot*).
mero (1), **-ra,** *a.* mere.
mero (2), *n.m.* (*ichth.*) Red Sea bass.
merodear, *v.i.* maraud.
merodeo, *n.m.* marauding.
mes, *n.m.* month; monthly pay.
mesa, *n.f.* table; counter; desk; facet; plateau.
mesar, *v.t.* pluck (*hair, beard*).
meseta, *n.f.* plateau, table-land, meseta.
mesiánico, -ca, *a.* Messianic.
Mesías, *n.m.* Messiah.
mesilla, *n.f.* small table; (*fam.*) dressing-down.
mesmerismo, *n.m.* mesmerism.
mesnada, *n.f.* retinue; band.
mesón, *n.m.* inn.
mesonero, -ra, *a.* rel. to inns.—*n.m.f.* innkeeper.
mesta, *n.f.* (*hist.*) stockmen's guild.
mestizo, -za, *a., n.m.f.* half-breed; mongrel; mestizo.
mesura, *n.f.* gravity, restraint, civility.
mesurado, -da, *a.* moderate; circumspect; grave; restrained.
mesurar, *v.t.* moderate.—*v.r.* act with restraint.
meta, *n.f.* goal.
metabolismo, *n.m.* metabolism.
metafísico, -ca, *a.* metaphysical.—*n.m.f.* metaphysician.—*n.f.* metaphysics.
metáfora, *n.f.* metaphor.
metafórico, -ca, *a.* metaphorical.
metal, *n.m.* metal; brass, bronze; mettle, quality.
metálico, -ca, *a.* metallic.—*n.m.* metalworker; hard cash.—*n.f.* metallurgy.
metalífero, -ra, *a.* metalliferous.
metalurgia, *n.f.* metallurgy.
metalúrgico, -ca, *a.* metallurgic(al).—*n.m.* metallurgist.
metamorfosi(s), *n.f.* (*pl.* **-fosis**) metamorphosis.
metano, *n.m.* methane.
metedor (1), **-ra,** *n.m.f.* smuggler.
metedor (2), *n.m.* napkin; (*U.S.*) diaper.
meteórico, -ca, *a.* meteoric.
meteorito, *n.m.* meteorite.
meteoro, metéoro, *n.m.* meteor, metereological phenomenon.
meteorología, *n.f.* meteorology.
meteorológico, -ca, *a.* meterological.
meteorologista, *n.m.f.* meteorologist.
meter, *v.t.* put; smuggle; cause; make (*noise etc.*); start (*rumours*).—*v.r.* project; butt in; get (*en*, into); meddle; ***meterse a,*** pass oneself off as; start to; ***meterse con,*** pick a quarrel with.
metesillas, *n.m. inv.* stage-hand.
meticuloso, -sa, *a.* timid, shy; meticulous.
metido, -da, *a.* rich, full, heavy; tight; involved; intimate.—*n.m.* punch, blow; (*sewing*) seam; napkin.
metilo, *n.m.* methyl.
metimiento, *n.m.* insertion; influence, sway.
metódico, -ca, *a.* methodic(al).
metodismo, *n.m.* Methodism.
metodista, *a., n.m.f.* Methodist.
método, *n.m.* method.
metomentodo, *n.m.f.* (*fam.*) Nosey Parker.
metonimia, *n.f.* metonymy.
metraje, *n.m.* length (*of cinema films*).
metralla, *n.f.* grape-shot; shrapnel.
métrico, -ca, *a.* metric(al).—*n.f.* prosody.
metro (1), *n.m.* metre.

metro (2), *n.m.* (*rail.*) Metro, (*U.S.*) subway, (*rail.*) Underground, (*coll.*) tube.
metrópoli, *n.f.* metropolis.
metropolitano, -na, *a.* metropolitan.—*n.m.* metropolitan; (*rail.*) Underground, (*U.S.*) subway.
México, *n.m.* (*S. & C.A.*) Mexico (*Sp.* MÉJICO).
mezcla, *n.f.* mixture.
mezclar, *v.t., v.r.* mix, blend, mingle; *v.r.* meddle.
mezcolanza, *n.f.* jumble, mix-up.
mezquindad, *n.f.* wretchedness; smallness.
mezquino, -na, *a.* poor; mean; tiny.
mezquita, *n.f.* mosque.
mi (1), *n.m.* (*mus.*) (key of) E.
mi (2), *a. poss.* my.
mí, *pron.* (*used after preps.*) me, myself.
miar [L], *v.t., v.i.* miaow.
miasma, *n.m.* miasma.
miau, *n.m.* miaow.
microanálisis, *n.m.* microanalysis.
microbio, *n.m.* microbe.
microcosmo, *n.m.* microcosm.
microfilm, *n.m.* microfilm.
micrófono, *n.m.* microphone.
microgramo, *n.m.* microgram.
micrómetro, *n.m.* micrometer.
microscópico, -ca, *a.* microscopic.
microscopio, *n.m.* microscope.
micho, -cha, *n.m.f.* puss, pussy.
miedo, *n.m.* fear; ***dar — a,*** frighten; ***tener —,*** be afraid (***de,*** of).
miedoso, -sa, *a.* (*fam.*) windy, scared, afraid.
miel, *n.f.* honey; molasses.
miembro, *n.m.* member; limb.
mientes, *n.f.pl.* (*obs.*) mind; ***caer en*** (***las***) ***—,*** come to mind; ***parar*** or ***poner — en,*** reflect on, consider.
mientras, *adv.* while.—*conj.* (*also* ***— que*** or ***— tanto***); while, whilst; whereas; ***— más ... más,*** the more . . . the more; ***— tanto,*** meanwhile.
miércoles, *n.m.* Wednesday; ***— corvillo*** or ***de ceniza,*** Ash Wednesday.
mierda, *n.f.* (*low*) dung; excrement.
mies, *n.f.* grain; harvest.
miga, *n.f.* crumb; (*fig.*) substance; bit, fragment; ***hacer buenas*** (***malas***) ***migas con,*** get on well (badly) with.
migaja, *n.f.* crumb, scrap, bit; smattering.
migar [B], *v.t.* crumble, crumb; add crumbs to.
migración, *n.f.* migration.
migraña, *n.f.* migraine, megrim.
migratorio, -ria, *a.* migratory.
Miguel, *n.m.* Michael.
mijo, *n.m.* millet; (*dial.*) maize, (*U.S.*) corn.
mil, *a., n.m.* a thousand; ***hasta las — y monas,*** (*fam.*) until the cows come home.
milagrero, -ra, *n.m.f.* miracle-monger, superstitious person.
milagro, *n.m.* miracle.
milagroso, -sa, *a.* miraculous.
milano (1), *n.m.* (*orn.*) kite.
milano (2), *n.m.* thistledown.
milenario, -ria, *a.* millennial.—*n.m.* millennium.
milenio, *n.m.* millennium.
milésimo, -ma, *a., n.m.* thousandth.
mili, *n.f.* (*fam.*) national service, conscription.
milicia, *n.f.* militia; soldiery; warfare.
miliciano, *n.m.* militiaman.
miligramo, *n.m.* milligram.
milímetro, *n.m.* millimetre.
militante, *a.* militant.
militar, *a.* military.—*n.m.* soldier, military man.—*v.i.* serve under arms; militate.
militarismo, *n.m.* militarism.
militarista, *a., n.m.f.* militarist.
militarizar [C], *v.t.* militarize.
milocha, *n.f.* kite (*toy*).
milor(d), *n.m.* milord; (*fam.*) lord.
milla, *n.f.* mile.
millar, *n.m.* thousand; ***a millares,*** in thousands.
millo, *n.m.* millet; (*S.A.*) maize, (*U.S.*) corn.
millón, *n.m.* million.
millonario, -ria, *a., n.m.f.* millionaire.
millonésimo, -ma, *a., n.m.* millionth.
mimar, *v.t.* fondle; pamper, spoil.
mimbre, *n.m.* or *f.* wicker, osier.
mimbrear, *v.i., v.r.* sway, bend.
mimbreño, -ña, *a.* willowy.
mimbrera, *n.f.,* **mimbrón,** *n.m.* (*bot.*) osier.
mimeografiar [L], *v.t.* mimeograph.
mímico, -ca, *a.* mimic; rel. to mimes.—*n.f.* mimicry; sign language.
mimo, *n.m.* mime; pampering; caress.
mimosa, *n.f.* (*bot.*) mimosa.
mimoso, -sa, *a.* pampered; finicky.
mina, *n.f.* (*min., mil.*) mine; ***volar la —,*** let the cat out of the bag.
minador, -ra, *a.* mining.—*n.m.* miner; minelayer.
minar, *v.t.* mine; undermine; strive for.
minarete, *n.m.* minaret.
mineraje, *n.m.* mining.
mineral, *a.* mineral.—*n.m.* mineral; ore; source.
minería, *n.f.* mining; miners.
minero, -ra, *a.* rel. to mines.—*n.m.* miner; (*fig.*) source, origin.
Minerva, *n.f.* Minerva; **minerva,** ***n.f. de su propia minerva,*** out of his own head.
miniar, *v.t.* illuminate, paint in miniature.
miniatura, *n.f.* miniature.
miniaturista, *n.m.* miniaturist.
mínimo, -ma, *a.* least; minimal; minimum; tiny.—*n.m.* minimum.
mínimum, *n.m.* minimum.
ministerial, *a.* ministerial.
ministerio, *n.m.* ministry.
ministrar, *v.t.* minister to; administer; supply.
ministro, *n.m.* minister; bailiff; ***— de la hacienda,*** Chancellor of the Exchequer; ***— sin cartera,*** minister without portfolio; ***primer —,*** prime minister.
mino, -na, *n.m.f.* pussy.
minorar, *v.t.* diminish.
minoría, *n.f.* minority.
minoridad, *n.f.* minority (*age*).
minoritario, -ria, *a.* rel. to a minority.
minucia, *n.f.* mite.—*pl.* minutiae.
minucioso, -sa, *a.* meticulous; detailed.
minué, minuete, *n.m.* minuet.
minúsculo, -la, *a.* tiny; small (*letter*).—*n.f.* small letter.
minuta, *n.f.* draft; list; memorandum; menu.
minutar, *v.t.* make a first draft of.
minutero, *n.m.* minute-hand (*of clock*).
minuto, -ta, *a., n.m.* minute.

miñoneta, *n.f.* (*bot.*) mignonette.
mío, mía, *a., pron. m.f.* mine; ***de* —,** of my own accord.
miope, *a.* myopic.—*n.m.f.* myope.
miopía, *n.f.* myopia, short-sightedness.
mira, *n.f.* sight (*of gun*); target; aim, object; ***a la* —,** on the look-out.
mirada, *n.f.* look, glance.
miradero, *n.m.* look-out; cynosure.
mirado, -da, *a.* circumspect, cautious; viewed.
mirador, -ra, *n.m.f.* spectator, looker-on.—*n.m.* balcony; watch-tower; bay window.
miramiento, *n.m.* look; care; regard.—*pl.* fussiness.
mirar, *v.t.* look at, watch; look to; **— *por,*** look after; **— *por encima,*** glance at. —*v.r.* take care; take an example (***en,*** from).
miríada, *n.f.* myriad.
mirilla, *n.f.* peep-hole.
miriñaque, *n.m.* bauble, trinket; crinoline.
mirlar, *v.r.* (*fam.*) put on airs.
mirlo, *n.m.* (*orn.*) blackbird; (*fam.*) airs, affectedness.
mirón, -rona, *a.* watching; nosy, prying.—*n.m.f.* onlooker; busybody.
mirra, *n.f.* myrrh.
mirto, *n.m.* (*bot.*) myrtle.
¡mis! *interj.* puss!
misa, *n.f.* (*eccl.*) Mass.
misacantano, *n.m.* (*eccl.*) priest, celebrant.
misal, *n.m.* missal.
misantrópico, -ca, *a.* misanthropic.
misántropo, *n.m.* misanthrope, misanthropist.
misar, *v.i.* (*fam.*) say *or* hear Mass.
misceláneo, -nea, *a.* miscellaneous.—*n.f.* miscellany.
miserable, *a.* wretched, miserable, niggardly. —*n.m.f.* wretch.
miserando, -da, *a.* pitiable.
miseria, *n.f.* misery, wretchedness, poverty; stinginess; (*fam.*) trifle, bit.
misericordia, *n.f.* compassion; mercy.
misericordioso, -sa, *a.* compassionate, merciful.
mísero, -ra, *a.* (*sup.* **misérrimo, -ma**) miserable.
misión, *n.m.* mission; sending.
misionar, *v.t.* to preach, to spread.
misionario, *n.m.* envoy; missionary.
misionero, *a., n.m.f.* (*eccl.*) missionary.
Misisipí, *n.m.* Mississippi.
misivo, -va, *a., n.f.* missive.
mismamente, *adv.* (*fam.*) exactly; likewise.
mismo, -ma, *a.* same; own; self.—*n.m.* same; self.—*adv.* right; ***aquí* —,** right here; ***así* —,** likewise; ***da lo* —,** it's all the same; ***lo* —,** the same, the same thing; ***por lo* —,** for that same reason; ***ella misma,*** herself, she herself.
misógino, *n.m.* misogynist.
mistar, *v.i.* to mumble.
misterio, *n.m.* mystery.
misterioso, -sa, *a.* mysterious.
misticismo, *n.m.* mysticism.
místico, -ca, *a.* mystic(al).—*n.m.f.* mystic.—*n.f.* mysticism.
mistificar [A], *v.t.* hoax, deceive; mystify.
mistura [MIXTURA].
Misurí, *n.m.* Missouri.

mitad, *n.f.* half; middle; ***cara* —,** (*fam.*) better half, wife.
mítico, -ca, *a.* mythical.
mitigación, *n.f.* mitigation.
mitigar [B], *v.t.* mitigate.
mitin, *n.m.* (*pl.* **mítines**) meeting.
mito, *n.m.* myth.
mitología, *n.f.* mythology.
mitológico, -ca, *a.* mythological.
mitón, *n.m.* mitten.
mitra, *n.f.* mitre.
mixtif- [MISTIF-].
mixto, -ta, *a.* mixed.—*n.m.* compound; match; explosive mixture.
mixtura, *n.f.* mixture.
mixturar, *v.t.* mix.
¡miz! *interj.* puss!
mnemónico, -ca, *a.* mnemonic.—*n.f.* mnemonics.
mobiliario, moblaje, *n.m.* furnishings.
moblar [4], *v.t.* furnish.
mocasín, *n.m.*, **mocasina,** *n.f.* mocassin.
mocear, *v.i.* be a wild youth.
mocedad, *n.f.* youth; wild oats; frolic.
mocetón, *n.m.* strapping youth.
mocetona, *n.f.* buxom lass.
moción, *n.f.* motion; leaning, bent.
moco, *n.m.* mucus; drippings; slag; ***a* — *de candil,*** by candlelight.—*pl.* (*fam.*) nose.
mocoso, -sa, *a.* snivelly; rude; cheeky; mean. —*n.m.f.* brat.
mochila, *n.f.* knapsack.
mocho, -cha, *a.* lopped, shorn.—*n.m.* butt-end.
mochuelo, *n.m.* (*orn.*) little owl; (*fam.*) the rough end.
moda, *n.f.* fashion; mode; ***a la* —** or ***de* —** in fashion.
modal, *a.* modal.—*n.m.pl.* manners.
modalidad, *n.f.* way, manner, modality.
modelar, *v.t.* model.—*v.r.* model oneself (***sobre,*** on).
modelo, *n.m.* model; pattern.—*n.m.f.* model, mannequin.
moderación, *n.f.* moderation.
moderado, -da, *a., n.m.f.* moderate.
moderador, -ra, *a.* moderating.—*n.m.f.* moderator.
moderantismo, *n.m.* moderation; (*pol.*) moderates.
moderar, *v.t.* moderate.
modernidad, *n.f.* modernity.
modernismo, *n.m.* modernism.
modernista, *a.* modernist(ic).—*n.m.f.* modernist.
modernización, *n.f.* modernization.
modernizar [C], *v.t.* modernize.
moderno, -na, *a., n.m.f.* modern.
modestia, *n.f.* decency, modesty.
modesto, -ta, *a.* decent, modest.
módico, -ca, *a.* moderate.
modificación, *n.f.* modification.
modificar [A], *v.t.* modify.
modismo, *n.m.* idiom.
modistilla, *n.f.* seamstress.
modisto, -ta, *n.m.f.* ladies' tailor.
modo, *n.m.* mode, manner, way; (*gram.*) mood; ***de* — *que,*** so that; ***sobre* —,** extremely; ***de todos modos,*** anyhow, anyway.

modorro, -rra, *a.* drowsy; stupid.—*n.f.* drowsiness.
modoso, -sa, *a.* well-behaved.
modulación, *n.f.* modulation.
modular, *v.t.* modulate.
mofa, *n.f.* mockery.
mofar, *v.i., v.r.* jeer (***de,*** at).
mogol, -la, *a., n.m.f.* Mongol.
Mogolia, *n.f.* Mongolia.
mogollón, *n.m.* intrusion.
mogote, *n.m.* hummock, knoll.
mohatra, *n.f.* fraudulent sale; swindle.
mohatrero, -ra, *n.m.f.* confidence-trickster.
mohiento, -ta, *a.* musty, mouldy.
mohín, *n.m.* grimace.
mohino, -na, *a.* gloomy; peevish.
moho, *n.m.* (*bot.*) moss; mould; rust.
mohoso, -sa, *a.* mossy; rusty; mouldy.
Moisés, *n.m.* Moses.
mojama, *n.f.* salted tunny.
mojar, *v.t.* wet, soak.—***v.r.*** get wet.
moje, *n.m.* gravy.
mojiganga, *n.f.* mummery; (*fam.*) hypocrisy.
mojigato, -ta, *a.* sanctimonious, prudish.—*n.m.f.* prude.
mojón, *n.m.* boundary stone; heap; milestone.
moldar, *v.t.* mould, shape.
molde, *n.m.* mould, matrix; form; good example; ***de* —,** just right.
moldear, *v.t.* cast, mould.
moldura, *n.f.* moulding, beading.
mole, *a.* soft.—*n.f.* mass, bulk.
molécula, *n.f.* molecule.
molecular, *a.* molecular.
moler [5], *v.t.* grind, mill; weary.
molestar, *v.t.* bother, disturb; annoy.—***v.r.*** be vexed; bother (***con,*** with).
molestia, *n.f.* bother; annoyance.
molesto, -ta, *a.* annoying; annoyed.
molicie, *n.f.* softness flabbiness.
molificar [A], *v.t.* soften, mollify.
molinero, -ra, *n.m.f.* miller.
molinete, *n.m.* small mill; air-vent; turnstile; windlass.
molinillo, *n.m.* hand-mill (*for coffee, pepper etc.*).
molino, *n.m.* mill; (*fig.*) power-house (*person*).
molusco, *n.m.* (*zool.*) mollusc.
mollear, *v.i.* give, be soft.
mollera, *n.f.* crown of head; (*fig.*) brains.
momentáneo, -nea, *a.* momentary.
momento, *n.m.* moment; momentum; importance; ***al* —,** at once; ***de* —,** suddenly.
momificar [A], *v.t., v.r.* mummify.
momio, -mia, *a.* meagre, lean.—*n.m.* (*fam.*) bargain, gift.—*n.f.* mummy.
momo, *n.m.* grimace, pulled face.
mona [MONO].
monacal, *a.* monastic, monkish.
monacato, *n.m.* monkhood, monasticism.
monada, *n.f.* wry face; fawning; (*fam.*) pet, dear, pretty thing.
monaguillo, *n.m.* altar-boy, acolyte.
monarca, *n.m.* monarch.
monarquía, *n.f.* monarchy.
monárquico, -ca, *a.* monarchic(al).
monarquismo, *n.m.* monarchism.
monarquista, *a., n.m.f.* monarchist.
monasterio, *n.m.* monastery.
monasticismo, *n.m.* monasticism.
monástico, -ca, *a.* monastic.
mondadientes, *n.m. inv.* tooth-pick.
mondadura, *n.f.* cleaning.—*pl.* trimmings.
mondar, *v.t.* clean; trim; peel; (*fam.*) fleece.
mondo, -da, *a.* clean, pure; ***— y lirondo,*** (*fam.*) pure; ***ser la monda,*** be ridiculously funny.
monear, *v.i.* act the goat.
moneda, *n.f.* coin; money; ***casa de la —,*** mint.
monedero, *n.m.* coiner, minter; money-bag, purse.
monería, *n.f.* wry face; charming antics; bauble.
monetario, -ria, *a.* monetary.
mongol- [MOGOL-].
monigote, *n.m.* lay brother; (*fam.*) booby.
monipodio, *n.m.* cabal, crooked plot.
monís, *n.m.* trinket.—*pl.* (*fam.*) cash.
monismo, *n.m.* monism.
monista, *a., n.m.f.* monist.
monitor, *n.m.* monitor.
monja, *n.f.* nun.
monje, *n.m.* monk.
monjil, *a.* monkish, nunnish.—***n.m.*** nun's habit.
mono, -na, *a.* pretty, nice, cute.—***n.m.*** monkey, ape; mimic, copycat; overalls; nitwit.—*n.f.* female monkey; Barbary ape; mimic; (*fam.*) ***coger una mona,*** get tipsy.
monocarril, *n.m.* monorail.
monocromo, -ma, *a., n.m.* monochrome.
monóculo, -la, *a.* monocular.—***n.m.*** monacle.
monogamía, *n.f.* monogamy.
monógamo, -ma, *a.* monogamous.—***n.m.f.*** monogamist.
monografía, *n.f.* monograph.
monograma, *n.m.* monogram.
monólogo, *n.m.* monologue.
monomanía, *n.f.* monomania.
monomaníaco, -ca, monómano, -na, *a. n.m.f.* monomaniac.
monoplano, *n.m.* (*aer.*) monoplane.
monopolio, *n.m.* monopoly.
monopolista, *n.m.f.* monopolist, monopolizer.
monopolizar [C], *v.t.* monopolize.
monorriel, *n.m.* monorail.
monosílabo, -ba, *a.* monosyllabic.—***n.m.*** monosyllable.
monoteísmo, *n.m.* monotheism.
monoteísta, *n.m.f.* monotheist.
monotonía, *n.f.* monotony.
monótono, -na, *a.* monotonous.
monseñor, *n.m.* monseigneur; monsignor.
monserga, *n.f.* (*fam.*) gibberish.
monstruo, *n.m.* monster; prodigy.
monstruoso, -sa, *a.* monstrous.
monta, *n.f.* sum; mounting; account, importance.
montadura, *n.f.* mounting; harness.
montaje, *n.m.* mounting; installing; setting; assembly.
montantada, *n.f.* boast; crowd.
montante, *n.m.* upright, post; amount.
montaña, *n.f.* mountain; (*S.A.*) woodland, forest.
montañ(er)ismo, *n.m.* mountaineering.
montañero, -ra, *n.m.f.* mountaineer.
montañés, -ñesa, *a.* highland, mountain.—*n.m.f.* highlander.
montañoso, -sa, *a.* mountainous.

montar, *v.t.* mount; ride; set up, install; amount to.—*v.i.* ride; matter.
montaraz, *a.* (*pl.* **-aces**) wild, untamed.—*n.m.* forester.
monte, *n.m.* hill, mountain; woodlands, woods; brush, scrub; (*fig.*) snag, obstacle; — ***de piedad,*** pawnshop; — ***pío,*** fund for widows *etc.*
montera, *n.f.* cap (*esp. bull-fighter's*).
montería, *n.f.* hunting, the chase.
montero, *n.m.* hunter, huntsman.
montés (*poet., f.* **-tesa**), **montesino, -na,** *a.* wild, feral.
montón, *n.m.* heap, pile; crowd, mass; (*fam.*) lots; ***del* —,** (*fam.*) ordinary; ***a montones,*** (*fam.*) by the hundred.
montura, *n.f.* mount; mounting.
monumental, *a.* monumental.
monumento, *n.m.* monument; (*eccl.*) altar of repose.
monzón, *n.m. or f.* monsoon.
moña, *n.f.* doll; hair ribbon.
moño, *n.m.* chignon, top-knot; tuft; airs and graces; whim.
moñudo, -da, *a.* crested, tufted.
moque(te)ar, *v.i.* snivel.
mora (1), *n.f.* delay.
mora (2), *n.f.* (*bot.*) blackberry; mulberry.
mora (3) [MORO].
morada, *n.f.* abode, dwelling; sojourn.
morado, -da, *a.* purple.
moral, *a.* moral.—*n.m.* (*bot.*) mulberry-tree. —*n.f.* morals; morale.
moraleja, *n.f.* moral (*of story*).
moralidad, *n.f.* morality; [MORALEJA].
moralista, *n.m.f.* moralist.
moralizar [C], *v.t., v.i.* moralize.
morar, *v.i.* dwell.
mórbido, -da, *a.* morbid; (*art.*) soft, gentle.
morbo, *n.m.* disease.
morboso, -sa, *a.* morbid, diseased.
morcilla, *n.f.* black sausage *or* pudding; (*fam.*) crack, gag; (*theat.*) actor's ad-libbing.
mordacidad, *n.f.* mordacity.
mordaz, *a.* (*pl.* **-aces**) mordant, mordacious.
mordaza, *n.f.* gag; grab, check.
mordedura, *n.f.* bite.
morder [5], *v.t.* bite; erode; backbite.
mordimiento, *n.m.* bite, biting.
mordiscar [A], *v.t.* nibble.
mordisco, *n.m.* nibble, bite.
moreno, -na, *a.* brown; dark-skinned; suntanned; (*S.A.*) mulatto.—*n.m.f.* dark-skinned person.—*n.f.* brunette.
morería, *n.f.* Moorish quarter; Moors.
Morfeo, *n.m.* (*myth.*) Morpheus.
morfina, *n.f.* morphine.
morfinómano, -na, *n.m.f.* drug addict.
morfología, *n.f.* morphology.
morfológico, -ca, *a.* morphological.
moribundo, -da, *a., n.m.f.* moribund.
morigerar, *v.t.* moderate.
morir [7, *p.p.* **muerto**], *v.t.* (*fam.*) kill.—*v.i.* die.—*v.r.* die; be dying.
morisco, -ca, *a.* Moorish.—*n.m.f.* Morisco; converted Moor.
morisma, *n.f.* Moordom, Mohammedanism.
morlaco, -ca, *a.* playing possum, feigning ignorance.—*n.m.* (*taur., fam.*) bull.
mormón, -mona, *n.m.f.* Mormon.
mormonismo, *n.m.* Mormonism.
moro, -ra (3), *a.* Moorish; Muslim; unwatered (*wine*).—*n.m.* Moor; Muslim; — ***de paz,*** peaceful person; ***moros en la costa,*** fly in the ointment, snag.—*n.f.* Mooress.
morón, *n.m.* mound.
morosidad, *n.f.* tardiness, slowness.
moroso, -sa, *a.* tardy, slow.
morral, *n.m.* nose-bag; kit-bag; game-bag.
morriña, *n.f.* (*vet.*) murrain; (*fam.*) blues, nostalgia.
morriñoso, -sa, *a.* rachitic; (*fam.*) blue, nostalgic.
morro, *n.m.* snout, thick lips; knob; knoll; pebble.
morrocotudo, -da, *a.* (*fam.*) thorny, tricky; whopping, massive.
morsa, *n.f.* (*zool.*) walrus.
mortadela, *n.f.* Bologna sausage.
mortaja, *n.f.* shroud; (*carp.*) mortise.
mortal, *a.* mortal; deadly; dying; certain; definite.—*n.m.f.* mortal.
mortalidad, *n.f.* mortality.
mortandad, *n.f.* mortality; massacre slaughter.
mortecino, -na, *a.* dead; dying; weak.
mortero, *n.m.* (*cul., mil., arch.*) mortar.
mortífero, -ra, *a.* lethal, deadly.
mortificación, *n.f.* mortification.
mortificar [A], *v.t.* mortify.
mortuorio, -ria, *a., n.m.* funeral.
moruno, -na, *a.* Moorish.
mosaico, -ca, *a.* Mosaic; mosaic.—*n.m.* mosaic.
mosca, *n.f.* fly; (*fam.*) pest, bother; (*fam.*) cash.—*pl.* sparks.
moscardón, *n.m.* horse-fly; hornet; bumblebee; (*fam.*) pesterer.
moscatel, *n.m.* muscatel; (*fam.*) bore.
mosco, *n.m.* mosquito.
moscón, *n.m.* big fly; (*fam.*) sly-boots; (*bot.*) maple.
moscovita, *a., n.m.f.* Muscovite.
Moscú, *n.f.* Moscow.
mosquear, *v.t.* swat (*flies*); retort; whip.—*v.r.* shake off impediments; take offence.
mosquero, *n.m.* fly-swatter; fly-paper.
mosquetazo, *n.m.* musket shot *or* wound.
mosquete, *n.m.* musket.
mosquetero, *n.m.* musketeer.
mosquitero, -ra, *n.m.* or *f.* mosquito-net.
mosquito, *n.m.* mosquito, gnat; (*fam.*) boozer.
mostacero, -ra, *n.m.f.* mustard-pot.
mostacho, *n.m.* moustache; (*fam.*) spot on one's face.
mostaza, *n.f.* mustard.
mósto, *n.m.* must, fresh juice.
mostrado, -da, *a.* accustomed.
mostrador, -ra, *a.* showing, pointing.—*n.m.* counter (*of shop*); clock-face.
mostrar [4], *v.t.* show.—*v.r.* show oneself; appear.
mostrenco, -ca, *a.* stray, homeless; (*fam.*) thick, stupid; (*fam.*) bulky, fat.—*n.m.f.* dolt; stray.
mota, *n.f.* speck, mote; knoll.
mote, *n.m.* nickname; riddle; motto, device.
motear, *v.t.* speckle.
motejar, *v.t.* call names, ridicule (***de,*** for, as).
motete, *n.m.* (*mus.*) motet, anthem.
motilar, *v.t.* crop (*hair*).
motín, *n.m.* mutiny, insurrection.
motivar, *v.t.* substantiate; motivate.

motivo, -va, *a., n.m.* motive; ***con — de,*** on the occasion of; because of; ***de su —,*** of his own accord.
moto, *n.f.* (*fam.*) motor-bike.
moto-, *prefix.* motor-.
motocicleta, *n.f.* motorcycle.
motociclista, *n.m.f.* motorcyclist.
motor, -ra (*f. also* **motriz**), *a.* motor, motive. —*n.m.* motor engine; mover, author; ***— a chorro,*** jet engine; ***— de combustión interna*** or ***de explosión,*** internal-combustion engine; ***— de reacción*** or ***— cohete,*** rocket motor; ***— diesel,*** Diesel motor.—*n.f.* motor boat.
motorismo, *n.m.* motoring; motor cycling.
motorista, *n.m.f.* motorist, driver.
motorización, *n.f.* motorization.
motorizar [C], *v.t.* motorize.
motril, *n.m.* errand-boy.
motriz [MOTOR].
movedizo, -za, *a.* movable, moving; shaky; fickle.
mover [5], *v.t.* move; wag, shake; stir up.—*v.r.* move.
movible, *a.* movable; fickle.
móvil, *a.* moving, mobile; fickle.—*n.m.* motive; moving body; revenue stamp.
movilidad, *n.f.* mobility.
movilización, *n.f.* mobilization.
movilizar [C], *v.t., v.i., v.r.* mobilize.
movimiento, *n.m.* movement; motion.
mozalbete, *n.m.* lad, stripling.
mozárabe, *a.* Mozarabic.—*n.m.f.* Mozarab.
mozo, -za, *a.* youthful; single.—*n.m.* lad; servant; porter; waiter; ***— de cordel*** or ***de cuerda*** or ***de requina,*** carrier, odd-jobber.—*n.f.* lass; servant, maid; wench.
mu, *n.m.* moo, bellow.—*n.f.* bye-byes, sleep (*infants' word*).
muchachada, muchachería, *n.f.* child's trick.
muchachez, *n.f.* childhood; childishness.
muchacho, -cha, *a.* (*fam.*) boyish, girlish.—*n.m.* boy.—*n.f.* girl; maid.
muchedumbre, *n.f.* crowd; mass.
mucho, -cha, *a.* much, a lot of.—*pl.* many.—*pron.* much.—*adv.* much, a lot, a great deal; hard; a long time; ***con —,*** by far; ***ni con —,*** not by a long shot; ***ni — menos,*** far from it; ***por — que,*** however much.
muda, *n.f.* change; moult; breaking of voice.
mudable, mudadizo, -za, *a.* changeable.
mudanza, *n.f.* change; house-moving; fickleness.
mudar, *v.t.* change; move (*house*).—*v.i.* change (*de*); moult.—*v.r.* change; (*fam.*) get changed (*change one's clothes*); move.
mudéjar, *a., n.m.f.* Mudejar.
mudez, *n.f.* dumbness; silence.
mudo, -da, *a.* dumb, mute, silent.—*n.m.f.* mute.
mueblaje, *n.m.* furnishings, furniture.
mueble, *a.* (*jur.*) movable.—*n.m.* piece of furniture.—*pl.* furniture.
mueca, *n.f.* pulled face, grimace; ***hacer muecas,*** pull faces.
muela, *n.f.* grindstone; hillock; (*anat.*) molar.
muelle, *a.* soft; luxurious, voluptuous.—*n.m.* (*mech.*) spring; (*naut.*) jetty, quay.
muérdago, *n.m.* mistletoe.
muerte, *n.f.* death; ***a —,*** to the death; ***de mala —,*** (*fam.*) lousy, worthless; ***de —,*** implacably; dangerously (*ill*); ***— chiquita,*** (*fam.*) nervous shiver.
muerto, -ta, *a.* dead; languid; lifeless; dull; slaked.—*n.m.* corpse; deceased.—*p.p.* MORIR.
muesca, *n.f.* mortise, socket.
muestra, *n.f.* sample; sign (*shop, inn etc.*); dial, face; indication, sign; ***pasar —,*** review; ***feria de muestras,*** trade fair.
muestro *etc.* [MOSTRAR].
muevo *etc.* [MOVER].
mugido, *n.m.* moo, bellow, lowing.
mugir [E], *v.i.* low; bellow; roar.
mugre, *n.f.* filth, grime, dirt.
mugriento, -ta, *a.* filthy, grimy.
mujer, *n.f.* woman; wife.
mujerero, -ra (*S.A.*), **mujeriego, -ga** (*Sp.*), *a.* womanly, womanish; womanizing.
mujeril, *a.* womanly; womanish.
mujerío, *n.m.* women; female population.
mujerona, *n.f.* matron, beefy woman.
mújol, *n.m.* (*ichth.*) mullet.
mula, *n.f.* mule; (*C.A.*) junk; ***en (la) — de San Francisco,*** on Shanks's pony; ***hacer la —,*** shirk.
muladar, *n.m.* dungheap; filth.
mular, *a.* rel. to mules.
mul(at)ero, *n.m.* muleteer.
mulato, -ta, *a., n.m.f.* mulatto.
muleta, *n.f.* crutch; (*fam.*) snack; (*taur.*) matador's red cape.
muletilla, *n.f.* (*taur.*) muleta; crutch; (*fam.*) theme-song, pet phrase.
mulo, *n.m.* mule.
multa, *n.f.* fine.
multar, *v.t.* fine.
multicolor, *a.* multicoloured.
multicopista, *n.m.* duplicating machine.
multiforme, *a.* multiform.
multilátero, -ra, *a.* multilateral.
multimillonario, -ria, *a. n.m.f.* multi-millionaire.
múltiple, *a.* multiple, manifold.—*n.m.* (*mech.*) manifold.
multiplicación, *n.f.* multiplication.
multiplicar [A], *v.t., v.r.* multiply.
multíplice, *a.* multiple.
multiplicidad, *n.f.* multiplicity.
múltiplo, -la, *a., n.m.* (*elec., math.*) multiple.
multitud, *n.f.* multitude.
mullido, -da, *a.* soft, fluffy.
mullir [J], *v.t.* fluff up; shake up (*beds*); soften; get ready.
mundanal, mundano, -na, *a.* wordly, mundane.
mundial, *a.* world-wide, international.
mundo, *n.m.* world; large trunk; (*fam.*) vast crowd; ***tener (mucho) —,*** be canny and experienced; ***todo el —,*** everybody.
munición, *n.f.* munition; supplies; charge (*of gun*); small shot.
municionar, *v.t.* (*mil.*) supply.
municipal, *a.* municipal.—*n.m.* policeman.
municipalizar [C], *v.t.* municipalize.
municipio, *n.m.* municipality; town council.
munificencia, *n.f.* magnificence.
munificente, munífico, -ca, *a.* (*sup.* **munificentísimo, -ma**) munificent.
muñeca, *n.f.* wrist; doll.
muñeco, *n.m.* doll; puppet; (*fam.*) cissy.
muñequera, *n.f.* wrist-watch strap.
muñidor, *n.m.* beadle; activist.

muñir [K], *v.t.* summon; (*fig.*) rig.
muñón, *n.m.* stump (*of amputated limb*); (*mech.*) swivel, gudgeon.
mural, *a.*, *n.m.* mural.
muralla, *n.f.* city wall, rampart.
murciano, -na, *a.*, *n.m.f.* Murcian.
murciégalo, murciélago, *n.m.* (*zool.*) bat.
murga, *n.f.* (*fam.*) street band; (*fam.*) pest.
murmullar, *v.i.* murmur.
murmullo, *n.m.* murmur; rustle; ripple.
murmuración, *n.f.* gossip, backbiting.
murmurar, *v.t.*, *v.i.* murmur; mutter (*de*, against, about).
muro, *n.m.* wall.
murria, *n.f.* melancholy; blues.
murrio, -rria, *a.* dejected, morose.
Musa, *n.f.* Muse.
musaraña, *n.f.* (*zool.*) shrew; spot (*speck in eye*).
muscular, *a.* muscular.
músculo, *n.m.* (*anat.*) muscle.
musculoso, -sa, *a.* muscular.
muselina, *n.f.* muslin.
museo, *n.m.* museum.
musgaño, *n.m.* (*zool.*) shrew.
musgo, *n.m.* (*bot.*) moss.
musgoso, -sa, *a.* mossy.
música, *n.f.* music; band; ***— celestial,*** (*fam.*) eyewash.
musical, *a.* musical.
músico, -ca, *a.* musical.—*n.m.f.* musician.
musitar, *v.i.* mumble, whisper.
muslime, *a.*, *n.m.f.* Muslim, Moslem.
muslo, *n.m.* thigh.
mustela, *n.f.* (*zool.*) weasel.
mustio, -tia, *a.* gloomy, sad; withered.
musulmán, -mana, *a.*, *n.m.f.* Mussulman, Moslem.
mutabilidad, *n.f.* mutability.
mutación, *n.f.* change; (*biol.*) mutation.
mutante, *n.m.* (*biol.*) mutant.
mutilación, *n.f.* mutilation.
mutilado, -da, *a.* crippled.—*n.m.f.* cripple.
mutilar, *v.t.* cripple; mutilate.
mútilo, -la, *a.* mutilated; defective.
mutis, *n.m.* (*theat.*) exit; ***hacer —,*** say nothing.
mutismo, *n.m.* mutism; silence.
mutual, *a.* mutual.
mutualidad, *n.f.* mutuality; cooperative.
mutuo, -tua, *a.* mutual.—*n.m.* (*jur.*) loan.
muy, *adv.* very; very much of a; ***— . . . para,*** too . . . to; ***— de noche,*** very late at night.

N

N, n, *n.f.* sixteenth letter of the Spanish alphabet.
nabo, *n.m.* (*bot.*) turnip.
nácar, *n.m.* mother-of-pearl.
nacencia, *n.f.* tumour, growth.
nacer [9], *v.i.* be born; rise.—*v.r.* sprout; split.
nacido, -da, *a.* inborn, innate; apt.—*n.m.* offspring; tumour.
naciente, *a.* recent; incipient; rising (*sun*).
nacimiento, *n.m.* birth; origin; spring; crib.
nación, *n.f.* nation.
nacional, *a.*, *n.m.f.* national.
nacionalidad, *n.f.* nationality.
nacionalismo, *n.m.* nationalism.
nacionalista, *a.*, *n.m.f.* nationalist.
nacionalización, *n.f.* nationalization.
nacionalizar [C], *v.t.* nationalize; naturalize.
nacista, *a.*, *n.m.f.* Nazi.
nada, *n.f.* nothingness, void.—*pron.* nothing.—*adv.* not very, not at all; ***de —,*** don't mention it.
nadar, *v.i.* swim; float.
nadería, *n.f.* trifle.
nadie, *n.m.*, *pron.* nobody, no one.
nadir, *n.m.* nadir.
a nado, *adv. phr.* swimming; floating.
nafta, *n.f.* naphtha.
naipe, *n.m.* playing card.
nalga, *n.f.* buttock.
nana, *n.f.* lullaby; (*fam.*) granny.
nao, *n.f.* (*poet.*) ship.
Napoleón, *n.m.* Napoleon.
napoleónico, -ca, *a.* Napoleonic.
Nápoles, *n.f.* Naples.
napolitano, -na, *a.*, *n.m.f.* Neopolitan.
naranja, *n.f.* orange; ***media —,*** (*fam.*) wife; bosom friend.
naranjado, -da, *a.* orange.—*n.f.* orangeade; (*fig.*) vulgarity.
naranjal, *n.m.* orange grove.
naranjo, *n.m.* orange-tree.
narciso, *n.m.* narcissus; fop.
narcótico, -ca, *a.*, *n.m.* narcotic.
narcotizar [C], *v.t.* drug.
narigón, -gona, *a.* big-nosed.—*n.m.* big nose.
narigudo, -da, *a.* [NARIGÓN].
nariz, *n.f.* (*pl.* **-ices**) nose; nostril.
narración, *n.f.* narration; telling.
narrar, *v.t.* narrate.
narrativo, -va, *a.*, *n.f.* narrative.
nasal, *a.*, *n.f.* nasal.
nasalizar [C], *v.t.* nasalize.
naso, *n.m.* (*fam.*) big nose.
nata, *n.f.* cream; ***(la) flor y (la) —,*** the cream, élite.
natación, *n.f.* swimming.
natal, *a.* native; natal.—*n.m.* birth; birthday.
natalicio, -cia, *a.* natal.—*n.m.* birthday.
natalidad, *n.f.* birth-rate.
natillas, *n.f.pl.* custard.
natío, -tía, *a.* native; ***de su —,*** naturally.
natividad, *n.f.* nativity.
nativo, -va, *a.* native.
nato, -ta, *a.* born.
natura, *n.f.* nature; genitalia.
natural, *a.* natural; native.—*n.m.f.* native.—*n.m.* disposition, nature.
naturaleza, *n.f.* nature; nationality.
naturalidad, *n.f.* naturalness; nationality.
naturalizar [C], *v.t.* naturalize.
naufragar [B], *v.i.* be (ship)wrecked; fail.
naufragio, *n.m.* shipwreck; failure.
náufrago, -ga, *a.* shipwrecked.—*n.m.f.* shipwrecked person.
náusea, *n.f.* nausea.
nauseabundo, -da, *a.* nauseating, loathsome.
nauseativo, -va, nauseoso, -sa, *a.* nauseating.
náutico, -ca, *a.* nautical.—*n.f.* nautics, navigation.

nava, *n.f.* plain between mountains.
navaja, *n.f.* razor; clasp-knife.
navajada, *n.f.,* **navajazo,** *n.m.* gash cut.
naval, *a.* naval.
Navarra, *n.f.* Navarre.
navarro, -rra, *a., n.m.f.* Navarrese.
nave, *n.f.* ship; (*arch.*) nave.
navegable, *a.* navigable (*water*).
navegación, *n.f.* navigation; voyage.
navegador, navegante, *n.m.* navigator.
navegar [B], *v.t.* sail, navigate.
Navidad, *n.f.* Christmas.
navi(da)deño, -ña, *a.* Christmas.
naviero, -ra, *a.* shipping.—*n.m.* ship-owner.
navío, *n.m.* ship, vessel.
nazareno, -na, *a., n.m.f.* Nazarene.
nazi, *a., n.m.f.* Nazi.
nazismo, *n.m.* Naz(i)ism.
neblina, *n.f.* mist, haze.
nebulosa, *n.f.* (*astr.*) nebula.
nebuloso, -sa, *a.* nebulous; cloudy; gloomy.
necedad, *n.f.* foolishness.
necesario, -ria, *a.* necessary.—*n.f.* lavatory.
neceser, *n.f.* sewing basket; toilet bag.
necesidad, *n.f.* necessity; need, want.
necesitado, -da, *a.* needy.
necesitar, *v.t.* need, require.—*v.i.* be in need (***de,*** of).
necio, -cia, *a.* foolish, stupid.—*n.m.f.* fool.
necrología, *n.f.* obituary.
necrópolis, *n.f. inv.* necropolis.
néctar, *n.m.* nectar.
nefando, -da, *a.* abominable.
nefario, -ria, *a.* nefarious.
nefasto, -ta, *a.* ominous, ill-omened.
negar [1B], *v.t.* deny; refuse; disown; hide.—*v.r.* pretend to be out; refuse (***a,*** to).
negativo, -va, *a., n.m.* negative.—*n.f.* refusal, denial; negative.
negligencia, *n.f.* negligence.
negligente, *a.* negligent.
negociable, *a.* negotiable.
negociación, *n.f.* negotiation.
negociador, -ra, *n.m.f.* negotiator.
negociante, *n.m.* dealer; business-man.
negociar, *v.t.* negotiate; arrange.—*v.i.* trade.
negocio, *n.m.* business; transaction.
negocioso, -sa, *a.* diligent, business-like.
negra, *n.f.* Negro woman *or* girl.
negrear, *v.i.* show black; be blackish.
negrecer [9], *v.i.* turn black(ish).
negrero, -ra, *a.* slaving, slave-driving.—*n.m.* slaver, slave-driver.
negrilla, negrita, *n.f.* (*print.*) bold-face.
negro, -ra, *a.* black; dismal; evil; Negro; (*fam.*) penniless.—*n.m.* Negro; ***pasar las negras,*** (*fam.*) have a bad time of it.
negroide, *a.* Negroid.
negror, *n.m.,* **negrura,** *n.f.* blackness.
negruzco, -ca, *a.* blackish.
nene, nena, *n.m.f.* (*fam.*) baby.
nenúfar, *n.m.* (*bot.*) water-lily.
neocelandés, -desa, *a.* New Zealand.—*n.m.f.* New Zealander.
neoclásico, -ca, *a.* neoclassic(al).—*n.m.f.* neoclassicist.
neolatino, -na, *a.* Neo-Latin; Romance.
neolítico, -ca, *a.* neolithic.
neologismo, *n.m.* neologism.
neón, *n.m.* (*chem.*) neon.
neoyorquino, -na, *a., n.m.f.* rel. to *or* native of New York.
Nepal, *n.m.* Nepal.
nepalés, -lesa, *a., n.m.f.* Nepalese.
nepotismo, *n.m.* nepotism.
Nerón, *n.m.* Nero.
nervio, *n.m.* nerve; mettle; ribbing.
nerviosidad, *n.f.,* **nerviosismo,** *n.m.* nervousness.
nervioso, -sa, nervoso, -sa, *a.* nervous; vigorous; sinewy.
nervudo, -da, *a.* sinewy; robust, vigorous.
neto, -ta, *a.* pure; (*com.*) net.
neumático, -ca, *a.* pneumatic.—*n.m.* tyre.
neumonía, *n.m.* pneumonia.
neuralgia, *n.f.* neuralgia.
neurólogo, *n.m.* neurologist.
neurosis, *n.f. inv.* neurosis.
neurótico, -ca, *a., n.m.f.* neurotic.
neutral, *a., n.m.f.* neutral.
neutralidad, *n.f.* neutrality.
neutralizar [C], *v.t.* neutralize.
neutro, -ra, *a.* neuter; (*chem., elec. etc.*) neutral.
nevada, *n.f.* snowfall.
nevado, -da, *a.* snow-covered; snowy.
nevar [1], *v.i.* snow.—*v.t.* whiten.
nevasca, *n.f.,* **nevazo,** *n.m.* snowstorm.
nevera, *n.f.* refrigerator, ice-box.
nevisca, *n.f.* fine snow.
neviscar [A], *v.i.* snow lightly.
nevoso, -sa, *a.* snowy.
nexo, *n.m.* nexus.
ni, *conj.* neither, not; ***ni . . . ni,*** neither . . . nor; — ***siquiera,*** not even.
nicaragüense, nicaragüeño, -ña, *a., n.m.f.* Nicaraguan.
Nicolás, *n.m.* Nicholas.
nicotina, *n.f.* nicotine.
nicho, *n.m.* niche.
nidada, *n.f.* brood.
nido, *n.m.* nest.
niebla, *n.f.* fog, mist.
nieto, -ta, *n.m.f.* grandchild.—*n.m.* grandson. —*n.f.* grand-daughter.
nieva *etc.* [NEVAR].
nieve, *n.f.* snow.
el Níger, *n.m.* the Niger.
nihilismo, *n.m.* nihilism.
nihilista, *a., n.m.f.* nihilist.
Nilo, *n.m.* Nile.
nilón, *n.m.* nylon.
nimbo, *n.m.* halo, nimbus.
nimiedad, *n.f.* prolixity; sparingness.
nimio, -mia, *a.* excessive; stingy.
ninfa, *n.f.* (*ent., myth.*) nymph.
ninfea, *n.f.* (*bot.*) water-lily.
ningún, *a.m. contracted form of* NINGUNO *before n.m. sg.*
ninguno, -na, *a.* no, not any.—*pron. m.f.* none; no one.
niña, *n.f.* girl, child; (*anat.*) pupil; — ***del ojo,*** apple of one's eye.
niñada, *n.f.* childishness.
niñera, *n.f.* nursemaid.
niñería, *n.f.* trifle; childishness.
niñez, *n.f.* childhood, infancy.
niño, -ña, *a.* young; child-like.—*n.m.f.* child. —*n.m.* boy; ***desde* —,** from childhood.—*n.f.* girl.
nipón, -pona, *a., n.m.f.* Japanese.
níquel, *n.m.* nickel.

niquelar, *v.t.* nickel-plate.
níspero, *n.m.* (*bot.*) medlar.
nitidez, *n.f.* clearness, sharpness.
nítido, -da, *a.* bright, clear, sharp.
nitrato, *n.m.* (*chem.*) nitrate.
nitro, *n.m.* nitre, salpetre.
nitrógeno, *n.m.* nitrogen.
nivel, *n.m.* level; — ***de vida,*** standard of living.
nivelar, *v.t.* level; survey.—*v.r.* come level.
Niza, *n.f.* Nice.
no, *adv.* no; not; ***¿ a que — ?*** (*fam.*) I bet it isn't! ***¿ cómo — ?*** why not? (*S.A.*) sure! — ***bien,*** no sooner.
nobilísimo, -ma, *a. sup. of* NOBLE.
noble, *a., n.m.f.* noble.—*n.m.* nobleman.
nobleza, *n.f.* nobility.
nocente, *a.* noxious; guilty.
noción, *n.f.* notion; rudiment.
nocivo, -va, *a.* harmful.
noctámbulo, -la, *a.* sleepwalking; night-wandering.—*n.m.f.* sleep-walker; night-bird.
nocturno, -na, *a.* nocturnal.—*n.m.* (*mus.*) nocturne.
noche, *n.f.* night; darkness; ***de —,*** at night; ***de la — a la mañana,*** all of a sudden; ***Noche buena,*** Christmas Eve;— ***toledana*** or ***en blanco,*** sleepless night; ***Noche vieja,*** New Year's Eve; ***buenas noches,*** good night!
nodriza, *n.f.* wet nurse; reserve tank (*in car*).
Noé, *n.m.* Noah.
nogal, *n.m.* walnut (*tree, wood*).
noguera, *n.f.* walnut-tree.
nómada, *a.* nomadic.—*n.m.f.* nomad.
nombradía, *n.f.* renown, fame.
nombrado, -da, *a.* renowned.
nombramiento, *n.m.* naming, appointment.
nombrar, *v.t.* name; appoint.
nombre, *n.m.* name; noun; password; ***no tener —,*** be unmentionable; — ***de pila,*** Christian name; — ***propio,*** proper noun; — ***de soltera,*** maiden name.
nomenclatura, *n.f.* nomenclature.
nomeolvides, *n.f.* (*bot.*) forget-me-not.
nómina, *n.f.* list, roll.
nominación, *n.f.* nomination.
nominal, *a.* nominal; substantival.
nominar, *v.t.* name; nominate.
nominativo, -va, *a., n.m.* nominative.
nominilla, *n.f.* voucher.
non, *a.* (*math.*) odd, uneven.—*n.m.* odd number; ***decir que nones,*** say no, refuse.
nona, *n.f.* (*eccl.*) nones.
nonada, *n.f.* trifle, nothing.
nonagenario, -ria, *a., n.m.f.* nonagenarian.
nonagésimo, -ma, *a., n.m.* ninetieth.
nono, -na, *a., n.m.* ninth.
nopal, *n.m.* (*bot.*) prickly pear.
norabuena, *n.f.* congratulation(s).—*adv.* fortunately.
noramala, nora tal, *adv.* [ENHORAMALA].
nordeste, *a., n.m.* north-east.
nórdico, -ca, *a., n.m.f.* Nordic. — *a., n.m.* Norse.
noria, *n.f.* draw-well; (*fam.*) chore.
norma, *n.f* standard, norm; (*carp.*) square.
normal, *a.* normal; perpendicular; ***según la —,*** at right angles.
normalidad, *n.f.* normality.
normalizar [C], *v.t.* normalize; standardize.
Normandía, *n.f.* Normandy.
normando, -da, normano, -na, *a., n.m.f.* Norman.
noroeste, *a.* north-western.—*n.m.* north-west.
norte, *n.m.* north; (*fig.*) pole-star.
Norteamérica, *n.f.* North America.
norteamericano, -na, *a., n.m.f.* North American, American.
norteño, -ña, *a.* northern.—*n.m.f.* northerner.
Noruega, *n.f.* Norway.
noruego, -ga, *a., n.m.f.* Norwegian.
nos, *pron.* us, to us; (to) ourselves; (*obs.*) we.
nosotros, -ras, *pron.* we; (*with prep.*) us.
nostalgia, *n.f.* nostalgia, homesickness.
nostálgico, -ca, *a.* nostalgic, homesick.
nota, *n.f.* note; (*educ.*) mark.
notabilidad, *n.f.* notability.
notable, *a., n.m.f.* notable.
notación, *n.f.* notation.
notar, *v.t.* note; notice; dictate.—*v.r.* be noticeable.
notario, *n.m.* notary.
noticia, *n.f.* piece of news; information; notion; knowledge.—*pl.* news.
noticiar, *v.t.* notify.
noticiario, -ria, *a., n.m.* news.
noticiero, *n.m.* news editor.
notición, *n.m.* (*fam.*) big news.
notificación, *n.f.* notification.
notificar [A], *v.t.* notify.
noto, -ta, *a.* noted; illegitimate.
notoriedad, *n.f.* fame.
notorio, -ria, *a.* widely known, well-known.
novador, -ra, *a.* innovating.
novato, -ta, *a.* new, green.—*n.m.f.* new-comer; novice; fresher.
novecientos, -tas, *a., n.m.pl.* nine hundred.
novedad, *n.f.* novelty; news; trouble; change; ***sin —,*** as usual; (*mil.*) all quiet.
novel, *a., n.m.* novice.
novela, *n.f.* novel.
novelar, *v.i.* romance; write novels.
novelero, -ra, *a.* fond of novel(tie)s; fickle: (*fam.*) gossiping.
novelesco, -ca, *a.* novelesque.
novelista, *n.m.f.* novelist.
noveno, -na, *a.* ninth.—*n.f.* (*eccl.*) novena.
noventa, *a., n.m.* ninety.
noventón, -tona, *n.m.f.* (*fam.*) nonagenarian.
novia, *n.f.* fiancée; bride.
noviazgo, *n.m.* betrothal, engagement.
novicio, -cia, *a., n.m.f.* novice; apprentice.
noviembre, *n.m.* November.
novilla, *n.f.* heifer.
novillada, *n.f.* bullfight (*of young bulls*).
novillero, *n.m.* (*taur.*) trainee bullfighter; (*fam.*) truant.
novillo, *n.m.* young bull; ***hacer novillos,*** (*fam.*) play truant.
novio, *n.m.* fiancé; bridegroom; suitor.—*pl* couple (*engaged* or *newly-wed*).
novísimo, -ma, *a. sup.* newest, latest.
nuba(rra)do, -da, *a.* cloudy.—*n.f.* shower.
nubarrón, *n.m.* dense, black cloud.
nube, *n.f.* cloud; ***andar por las nubes,*** cost a fortune; ***ponerle por las nubes*** or ***subirle a las nubes,*** praise him to the skies.
núbil, *a.* nubile.
nublado, -da, *a.* cloudy.—*n.m.* storm cloud gloom; mass.

nubloso, -sa, *a.* cloudy; gloomy.
nuca, *n.f.* (*anat.*) nape; scruff.
nuclear, *a.* nuclear.
núcleo, *n.m.* nucleus; kernel; (*elec.*) core.
nudillo, *n.m.* knuckle; nodule; knot.
nudismo, *n.m.* nudism.
nudista, *n.m.f.* nudist.
nudo, -da, *a.* naked, nude.—*n.m.* knot, bond; snag; node; crisis of drama; lump (*in throat*).
nudoso, -sa, *a.* knotty, knotted.
nuera, *n.f.* daughter-in-law.
nuestro, -ra, *a.* our.—*pron.* ours.
nueva, *n.f.* piece of news.
Nueva York, *n.f.* New York.
Nueva Zelandia, *n.f.* New Zealand.
nueve, *a., n.m.* nine.
nuevo, -va, *a.* new; ***de* —,** anew, again.
nuez, *n.f.* (*pl.* **nueces**) walnut; nut; kernel; Adam's apple.
nulidad, *n.f.* nullity; incompetence.
nulo, -la, *a.* null, void; useless.
numeración, *n.f.* numeration.
numeral, *a.* numeral.
numerar, *v.t.* number; calculate.
numerario, -ria, *a.* numerary.—*n.m.* coin, hard cash.
numérico, -ca, *a.* numerical.
número, *n.m.* number; ***sin* —,** countless; unnumbered.
numeroso, -sa, *a.* numerous.
numismático, -ca, *n.m.f.* numismatist.—*n.f.* numismatics.
nunca, *adv.* never; **— *jamás*,** never ever.
nuncio, *n.m.* nuncio; forerunner.
nupcial, *a.* nuptial.
nupcias, *n.f.* nuptials; ***casarse en segundas* —,** remarry.
nutr(i)a, *n.f.* (*zool.*) otter.
nutricio, -cia, *a.* nutritious.
nutrición, *n.f.* nutrition.
nutrido, -da, *a.* full (*of*), rich (*in*) (***de***).
nutrim(i)ento, *n.m.* nutriment, nourishment.
nutrir, *v.t.* nourish; enrich.
nutritivo, -va, *a.* nutritious.

Ñ

Ñ, ñ, *n.f.* seventeenth letter of the Spanish alphabet.
ñapa, *n.f.* (*S.A.*) extra, bonus.
ñaque, *n.m.* junk, rubbish.
ñeque, *n.m.* (*S.A.*) vim, pep, zest.
ñiqueñaque, *n.m.* (*fam.*) good-for-nothing; trash, bunk.
ñoñería, *n.f.* shyness; drivel.
ñoñez, *n.f.* sloppiness; timidity.
ñoño, -ña, *a.* (*fam.*) sloppy, feeble; (*S.A.*) doting.
ñu, *n.m.* (*zool.*) gnu.
ñubl- [NUBL-].
ñud- [NUD-].

O

O, o (1), *n.f.* eighteenth letter of the Spanish alphabet.
o (2), *conj.* or; **o . . . o . . .,** either . . . or . . .; ***o sea*,** that is to say.
¡o! (3), *interj.* oh!
oasis, *n.m.* oasis.
obcecación, *n.f.* obfuscation.
obedecer [9], *v.t., v.i.* obey; respond.
obediencia, *n.f.* obedience.
obediente, *a.* obedient.
obelisco, *n.m.* obelisk; (*print.*) dagger (†).
obertura, *n.f.* (*mus.*) overture.
obesidad, *n.f.* obesity.
obeso, -sa, *a.* obese.
óbice, *n.m.* obstacle, hindrance.
obispado, *n.m.* bishopric.
obispillo, *n.m.* boy bishop; rump (*of a fowl*), parson's nose; large black pudding.
obispo, *n.m.* bishop.
óbito, *n.m.* (*jur.*) demise.
obituario, *n.m.* obituary.
objetar, *v.t.* object.
objetividad, *n.f.* objectivity.
objetivo, -va, *a., n.m.* objective.
objeto, *n.m.* object; aim, end.
oblación, *n.f.* oblation.
oblato, -ta, *a., n.m.* oblate.
oblea, *n.f.* wafer.
oblicuángulo, -la, *a.* oblique-angled.
oblicuar, *v.t., v.i.* slant.
oblicuidad, *n.f.* obliquity.
oblicuo, -cua, *a.* oblique.
obligación, *n.f.* obligation; bond, debenture.
obligacionista, *n.m.f.* bond-holder.
obligado, -da, *a.* grateful.—*n.m.* (*mus.*) obbligato; public contractor.
obligar [B], *v.t.* oblige, force (**a,** to).—*v.r.* bind oneself (**a,** to).
obligatorio, -ria, *a.* obligatory.
obliteración, *n.f.* (*med.*) failing of memory; cancellation.
obliterar, *v.t.* obliterate.
oblongo, -ga, *a.* oblong.
oboe, *n.m.* oboe; oboist.
óbolo, *n.m.* (widow's) mite.
obra, *n.f.* work; **— *maestra*,** masterpiece; ***en obras*,** under repair *or* construction.
obrador, -ra, *a.* working.—*n.m.f.* worker.
obrar, *v.t.* work; act; construct; ***obra en mi poder*,** (*com.*) I have to hand.
obrerismo, *n.m.* Labour movement.
obrerista, *a.* rel. to Labour.—*n.m.f.* Labour supporter, (*U.S. pej.*) Laborite.
obrero, -ra, *a.* working; rel. to labour.—*n.m.f.* worker.
obscenidad, *n.f.* obscenity.
obsceno, -na, *a.* obscene.
obscurantismo, *n.m.* obscurantism.
obscuro, -ra [OSCURO].
obsecuente, *a.* submissive.
obsequiante, *a.* fawning, flattering.
obsequiar, *v.t.* pay attentions to; flatter, court.
obsequio, *n.m.* civility, attention; gift.
obsequioso, -sa, *a.* obliging; attentive.
observable, *a.* observable.
observación, *n.f.* observation.

observador, -ra, *a.* observant.—*n.m.f.* observer.
observancia, *n.f.* observance; regard, reverence.
observante, *a.* observant.
observar, *v.t.* observe.
observatorio, *n.m.* observatory.
obsesión, *n.f.* obsession.
obsesionante, *a.* haunting.
obsesionar, *v.t.* obsess.
obsesivo, -va, *a.* obsessive.
obstáculo, *n.m.* obstacle.
obstante, *a.* standing in the way; ***no* —,** notwithstanding; in spite of.
obstar, *v.i.* obstruct, stand in the way.
obstétricia, *n.f.* (*med.*) obstetrics.
obstétrico, -ca, *a.* obstetrical.—*n.m.* obstetrician.—*n.f.* obstetrics.
obstinación, *n.f.* obstinacy.
obstinado, -da, *a.* obstinate.
obstinar, *v.r.* be obstinate; persist.
obstrucción, *n.f.* obstruction.
obstructivo, -va, *a.* obstructive.
obstruir [O], *v.t.* obstruct.
obtener [33], *v.t.* obtain.
obtenible, *a.* obtainable.
obturador, -atriz, *a.* stopping, plugging.—*n.m.* plug, stopper; (*aut.*) choke; (*phot.*) shutter.
obturar, *v.t.* obturate, plug.
obtusángulo, -la, *a.* obtuse-angled.
obtuso, -sa, *a.* obtuse (*also fig.*).
obtuve, *etc.* [OBTENER].
obué, *n.m.* [OBOE].
obús, *n.m.* howitzer.
obvención, *n.f.* perquisite(s), (*fam.*) perks.
obviar, *v.t.* obviate.—*v.i.* hinder.
obvio, -via, *a.* obvious.
oca, *n.f.* goose.
ocasión, *n.f.* occasion, opportunity; ***de* —,** second-hand.
ocasional, *a.* chance, casual.
ocasionar, *v.t.* occasion.
ocaso, *n.m.* west, occident; setting (*of a star*); decline.
occidental, *a.* occidental, western.—*n.m.f.* Occidental, westerner.
occidentalización, *n.f.* westernization.
occidentalizar [C], *v.t.* westernize.
occidente, *n.m.* occident, west.
occipucio, *n.m.* (*anat.*) occiput.
occisión, *n.f.* violent death.
Oceanía, *n.f.* Oceania.
oceánico, -ca, *a.* oceanic.—*n.m.f.* South Sea Islander.
océano, *n.m.* ocean.
oceanógrafo, *n.m.* oceanographer.
ocelote, *n.m.* (*zool.*) ocelot.
ocio, *n.m.* idleness; leisure.
ociosidad, *n.f.* idleness.
ocioso, -sa, *a.* idle.
oclusión, *n.f.* occlusion.
oclusivo, -va, *a.*, *n.f.* occlusive.
ocre, *n.m.* ochre.
octagonal, *a.* octagonal.
octágono, -na, *a.* octagonal.—*n.m.* octagon.
octano, *n.m.* (*chem.*) octane.
octavín, *n.m.* (*mus.*) piccolo.
octavo, -va, *a.*, *n.m.* eighth.—*a.*, *n.f.* octave; ***en* —,** octavo.
octogenario, -ria, *a.*, *n.m.f.* octogenarian.
octogésimo, -ma, *a.*, *n.m.* eightieth.
octubre, *n.m.* October.
ocular, *a.* ocular.—*n.m.* eyepiece.
oculista, *n.m.f.* oculist.
ocultante, *a.* dense (*smoke*).
ocultar, *v.t.* hide, conceal (***a, de,*** from).
ocultismo, *n.m.* occultism.
oculto, -ta, *a.* hidden; occult; clandestine.
ocupación, *n.f.* occupation.
ocupado, -da, *a.* busy.
ocupador, -ra, *a.* occupying.—*n.m.f.* occupier.
ocupante, *a.* occupying.—*n.m.f.* occupant.
ocupar, *v.t.* occupy; keep busy.—*v.r.* be busy (***con, de, en,*** with).
ocurrencia, *n.f.* occurrence; witticism; bright idea.
ocurrente, *a.* witty.
ocurrir, *v.i.* occur; have recourse (***a,*** to).—*v.r.* come to mind.
ochavón, -vona, *n.m.f.* octoroon.
ochenta, *a.*, *n.m.* eighty.
ocho, *a.*, *n.m.* eight.
ochocientos, -tas, *a.*, *n.m.* eight hundred.
oda, *n.f.* ode.
odiar, *v.t.* hate.
odio, *n.m.* hatred, odium.
odioso, -sa, *a.* odious.
odontología, *n.f.* (*med.*) odontology.
odontólogo, -ga, *n.m.f.* odontologist, dentist.
odorante, *a.* fragrant.
odorífero, -ra, *a.* odoriferous.
odre, *n.m.* wine-skin.
odrina, *n.f.* wineskin made of cowhide.
oeste, *n.m.* west.
ofender, *v.t.*, *v.i.* offend.—*v.r.* take offence.
ofensa, *n.f.* offence.
ofensivo, -va, *a.* offensive.—*n.f.* offensive.
ofensor, -ra, *a.* offensive.—*n.m.f.* offender; attacker.
oferta, *n.f.* offer; ***— y demanda,*** supply and demand.
ofertorio, *n.m.* offertory.
oficial, *a.* official.—*n.m.* clerk; tradesman office-holder; (*mil.*) officer.
oficiala, *n.f.* workwoman, craftswoman.
oficialidad, *n.f.* official nature; body of officers.
oficiar, *v.t.* communicate officially.—*v.i.* officiate.
oficina, *n.f.* office; laboratory.
oficinista, *n.m.f.* office-worker.
oficio, *n.m.* occupation, work; (*eccl.*) office.
oficiosidad, *n.f.* officiousness.
oficioso, -sa, *a.* diligent; officious; unofficial; ***periódico* —,** government newspaper.
ofrecer [9], *v.t.*, *v.i.*, *v.r.* offer.
ofrecimiento, *n.m.* offer.
ofrenda, *n.f.* gift, offering, oblation.
oftálmico, -ca, *a.* ophthalmic.
oftalmología, *n.f.* ophthalmology.
ofuscar [A], *v.t.* obfuscate; confuse.
ogaño, *adv.*, (*obs.*) this year.
ogro, *n.m.* ogre.
¡oh! *interj.* oh!
ohmio, *n.m.* (*phys.*) ohm.
oíble, *a.* audible.
oída, *n.f.* hearing.
oído, *n.m.* (sense of) hearing; ear; inlet, ven
oidor, -ra, *n.m.f.* hearer.—*n.m.* judge.
oigo [OÍR].
oír [22], *v.t.* hear.
ojal, *n.m.* button-hole.

¡ojalá! *interj.* God grant!
ojeada, *n.f.* glance.
ojear, *v.t.* eye, stare at; beat (*game*).
ojén, *n.m.* anisette (*liqueur*).
ojera, *n.f.* eye-bath; rings under the eyes.
ojeriza, *n.f.* grudge.
ojeroso, -sa, ojerudo, -da, *a.* with rings under the eyes.
ojete, *n.m.* eyelet.
ojinegro, -ra, *a.* black-eyed.
ojituerto, -ta, *a.* cross-eyed.
ojiva, *n.f.* (*arch.*) ogive.
ojival, *a.* ogival.
ojizaino, -na, *a.* (*fam.*) squint-eyed.
ojo, *n.m.* eye; span (*of bridge*); ***hacer del* —,** wink; **— *con* . . .,** beware (of) . . . .
ola, *n.f.* wave.
¡olé! *interj.* bravo!
oleada, *n.f.* wave (*esp. fig.*).
oleaginoso, -sa, *a.* oleaginous, oily.
óleo, *n.m.* oil (*painting*); oil.
oleoducto, *n.m.* (oil) pipeline.
oleoso, -sa, *a.* oily, oleaginous.
oler [5: **huelo** *etc.*], *v.t.* smell.—*v.i.* smell (***a***, of).
olfatear, *v.t.* smell, scent.
olfato, *n.m.* (*sense of*) smell; flair.
olíbano, *n.m.* frankincense.
oligarca, *n.m.* oligarch.
oligárquico, -ca, *a.* oligarchic.
olimpiada, *n.f.* Olympiad; Olympic Games.
olímpico, -ca, *a.* Olympian; Olympic; haughty.
oliscar [A], *v.t.* smell (out).—*v.i.* smell (*high*).
oliva, *n.f.* olive (*fruit, colour*).
olivar, *a.* olive.—*n.m.* olive grove.
olivera, *n.f.* olive-tree.
olivo, *n.m.* olive-tree.
olmedo, *n.m.*, **olmeda,** *n.f.* elm-grove.
olmo, *n.m.* elm.
olor, *n.m.* odour; smell; stench; hope.
oloroso, -sa, *a.* fragrant; sweet (*sherry*).
olvidadizo, -za, *a.* forgetful.
olvidar, *v.t.* forget.
olvido, *n.m.* forgetfulness; oblivion.
olla, *n.f.* saucepan, stewpot, kettle; stew; whirlpool; **— *podrida,*** (sort of) Spanish stew; **— *exprés,* — *de*** or ***a presión,*** pressure cooker.
ollería, *n.f.* pottery.
ollero, -ra, *n.m.f.* potter; dealer in earthenware.
olluela, *n.f.* small pot.
ombligo, *n.m.* navel; umbilical cord; (*fig.*) centre.
ombría, *n.f.* shady place.
omega, *n.f.* omega.
ómicron, *n.f.* (*pl.* **omícrones**) omicron.
ominoso, -sa, *a.* ominous.
omisión, *n.f.* omission.
omiso, -sa, *a.* neglectful; remiss.
omitir, *v.t.* omit; overlook.
ómnibus, *n.m. inv.* (omni)bus; stopping train.
omnímodo, -da, *a.* all-embracing.
omnipotencia, *n.f.* omnipotence.
omnipotente, *a.* omnipotent.
omnisciencia, *n.f.* omniscience.
omniscio, -cia, *a.* omniscient.
omnívoro, -ra, *a.* omnivorous.
onagro, *n.m.* (*zool.*) onager, wild ass.
onanismo, *n.m.* onanism.
once, *a., n.m.* eleven.
onceno, -na, *a.* eleventh.
onda, *n.f.* wave.
ondatra, *n.m.* (*zool.*) musk-rat.
ondeante, *a.* undulating.
ondear, *v.t.* wave (*hair*).—*v.i.* wave, undulate.
ondoso, -sa, *a.* wavy.
ondulación, *n.f.* undulation; **— *permanente,*** permanent wave.
ondulado, -da, *a.* wavy; rolling (*country*).—*n.m.* wave (*in one's hair*).
ondulante, *a.* undulating.
ondular, *v.t.* wave (*hair*).—*v.i.* undulate.
ónice, ónique, ónix, *n.m.* onyx.
onomástico, -ca, *a.* onomastic.
onomatopeya, *n.f.* onomatopeia.
ontología, *n.f.* ontology.
onza (1), *n.f.* ounce; square (*of chocolate*).
onza (2), *n.f.* (*zool.*) snow-leopard, ounce.
opacidad, *n.f.* opacity.
opaco, -ca, *a.* opaque; gloomy, dark.
ópalo, *n.m.* (*min.*) opal.
ópera, *n.f.* opera.
operable, *a.* operable.
operación, *n.f.* operation (*also mil., med.*).
operacional, *a.* operational.
operador, -ra, *a.* operating.—*n.m.f.* operator.
operante, *a.* operating, active.
operar, *v.t.* (*med.*) operate (***a uno de algo,*** on s.o. for s.th.).—*v.i.* operate (*com., mil., med.*).
operario, -ria, *n.m.f.* operative.
operativo, -va, *a.* operative.
opereta, *n.f.* operetta.
operista, *n.m.f.* opera-singer.
operoso, -sa, *a.* hard-working; wearisome.
opiado, -da, opiato, -ta, *a., n.m.* opiate.
opinable, *a.* problematical.
opinar, *v.i.* opine.
opinión, *n.f.* opinion.
opio, *n.m.* opium.
oponer [25], *v.t.* oppose; set up against.—*v.r.* oppose; compete (***a***, for).
oporto, *n.m.* port (*wine*).
oportunidad, *n.f.* opportuneness; opportunity.
oportunismo, *n.m.* opportunism.
oportuno, -na, *a.* opportune.
oposición, *n.f.* opposition; competitive examination (*esp. pl.*).
opositor, -ra, *n.m.f.* competitor, candidate.
opresión, *n.f.* oppression.
opresor, -ra, *a.* oppressive.—*n.m.f.* oppressor.
oprimir, *v.t.* oppress.
oprobio, *n.m.* opprobrium.
optar, *v.t.* choose.—*v.i.* opt (***por***, to).
optativo, -va, *a., n.m.* optative.
óptico, -ca, *a.* optic.—*n.m.* optician.—*n.f.* optics.
optimismo, *n.m.* optimism.
optimista, *a.* optimistic.—*n.m.f.* optimist.
óptimo, -ma, *a.* optimum.
opuesto, -ta, *a.* opposite; contrary.—*p.p.* [OPONER].
opulencia, *n.f.* opulence.
opulento, -ta, *a.* opulent.
opúsculo, *n.m.* short work, opuscule.
de oque, *adv. phr.* (*fam.*) gratis.
oquedad, *n.f.* hollow; hollowness.
ora, *conj.* ***ora . . . ora . . .,*** now . . . then . . . .

oración, *n.f.* oration, speech; prayer; (*gram.*) clause.
oráculo, *n.m.* oracle.
orador, *n.m.* orator.
oral, *a.* oral, vocal.
orangután, *n.m.* orang-outang.
orar, *v.i.* pray; speak.
orate, *n.m.f.* lunatic.
oratorio, -ria, *a.* oratorical.—*n.m.* (*eccl.*) oratory; (*mus.*) oratorio.—*n.f.* oratory, eloquence.
orbe, *n.m.* orb, sphere.
órbita, *n.f.* orbit; eye-socket.
orbital, *a.* orbital.
las Órcadas, *n.f.pl.* Orkneys.
órdago, *n.m.* ***de* —,** (*fam.*) first class.
ordalías, *n.f.pl.* (*hist.*) (trial by) ordeal.
orden, *n.m.* (*pl.* **órdenes**) order (*sequence*); order (*peace*); order (*zool.*); **— *de batalla,*** battle array.—*n.f.* order (*command*); (*religious*) order.
ordenanza, *n.f.* method, order, ordinance.—*n.m.* (*mil.*) orderly.
ordenar, *v.t.* arrange; ordain.
ordeñador, -ra, *a., n.m.f.* milker.
ordeñar, *v.t.* milk.
ordinal, *a.* ordinal.
ordinariez, *n.f.* rude manners.
ordinario, -ria, *a.* ordinary; coarse.
orear, *v.t.* air.—*v.r.* become aired; take an airing.
orégano, *n.m.* (*bot.*) wild marjoram.
oreja, *n.f.* ear; tongue (*of a shoe*); (*eng.*) flange.
orejano, -na, *a.* unbranded.
orejera, *n.f.* earflap.
orejeta, *n.f.* lug.
orejón, *n.m.* dried peach; tug on the ear; dog-ear (*page*).
orfandad, *n.f.* orphanage; orphanhood.
orfebre, *n.m.* goldsmith, silversmith.
orfebrería, *n.f.* gold *or* silver work.
orgánico, -ca, *a.* organic.
organillo, *n.m.* barrel organ.
organismo, *n.m.* organism.
organista, *n.m.f.* organist.
organización, *n.f.* organization.
organizar [C], *v.t.* organize.
órgano, *n.m.* organ.
orgasmo, *n.m.* orgasm.
orgía, orgia, *n.f.* orgy.
orgullo, *n.m.* pride.
orgulloso, -sa, *a.* proud; haughty.
orientación, *n.f.* orientation.
oriental, *a.* oriental; eastern.—*n.m.f.* Oriental.
orientalista, *a., n.m.f.* Orientalist.
orientar, *v.t.* orientate, orient.—*v.r.* get one's bearings.
oriente, *n.m.* east; orient; origin.
orífice, *n.m.* goldsmith.
orificio, *n.m.* orifice.
origen, *n.m.* (*pl.* **orígenes**) origin; datum line *or* point.
original, *a.* original; odd.—*n.m.* original.
originalidad, *n.f.* originality.
originar, *v.t., v.r.* originate.
originario, -ria, *a.* original, primitive.
orilla, *n.f.* border, edge; selvedge; sidewalk; shoulder (*of road*); ***a orillas de,*** on the banks of.
orillar, *v.t.* border, trim; (*fig.*) settle, tie up.—*v.i., v.r.* skirt, come to the shore.
orillo, *n.m.* selvedge.
orín (1), *n.m.* rust.
orín (2), *n.m.* urine (*esp. pl.*).
orina, *n.f.* urine.
orinal, *n.m.* chamber pot.
orinar, *v.i.* urinate.
oriol, *n.m.* (*orn.*) oriole.
oriundez, *n.f.* origin.
oriundo, -da, *a.* originating (***de,*** from) native (***de,*** of).
orla, *n.f.* border; fringe; galosh.
orlar, *v.t.* border.
orlo, *n.m.* (*mus.*) Alpine horn.
ornamento, *n.m.* ornament.
ornato, *n.m.* adornment.
ornitología, *n.f.* ornithology.
oro, *n.m.* gold; suit of the Spanish card pack; — ***batido,*** gold-leaf; — ***de ley,*** hall-marked gold; — ***mate,*** matt gold.
orondo, -da, *a.* bulging; pompous.
oropel, *n.m.* tinsel (*also fig.*); imitation gold-leaf.
oropéndola, *n.f.* (*orn.*) golden oriole.
oroya, *n.f.* (*S.A.*) hanging basket for carrying people over a rope bridge.
orozuz, *n.m.* (*bot.*) liquorice plant.
orquesta, *n.f.* orchestra.
orquestación, *n.f.* orchestration.
orquestal, *a.* orchestral.
órquide, *n.m.* (*bot.*) orchis.
orquídea, *n.f.* (*bot.*) orchid.
en orre, *adv. phr.* in bulk.
ortega, *n.f.* sand grouse.
ortiga, *n.f.* nettle.
orto, *n.m.* rise (*of star*).
ortodoxia, *n.f.* orthodoxy.
ortodoxo, -xa, *a.* orthodox.
ortopédico, -ca, *a.* orthopaedic.
oruga, *n.f.* caterpillar; (caterpillar) track; (*bot.*) rocket.
orujo, *n.m.* oil greaves; marc.
orza, *n.f.* gallipot; preserve jar; (*naut.*) luff.
orzar, *v.i.* (*naut.*) luff.
orzuelo, *n.m.* (*med.*) sty; trap, snare.
os, *pron. pers. & r. pl.* (*obs. sg.*) you; yourselves.
osa, *n.f.* (*zool.*) she-bear.
osadía, *n.f.* boldness.
osado, -da, *a.* bold.
osambre, *n.m.,* **osamenta,** *n.f.* skeleton.
osar (1), *v.i.* dare.
osar (2), **osario,** *n.m.* ossuary; charnel house.
oscilación, *n.f.* oscillation.
oscilador, -ra, *a.* oscillating.—*n.m.* oscillator.
oscilante, *a.* oscillating.
oscilar, *v.i.* oscillate.
oscurantismo, *n.m.* obscurantism.
oscurecer [9], *v.t., v.i.* darken.
oscuridad, *n.f.* obscurity.
oscuro, -ra, *a.* dark; obscure.
óseo, -sea, *a.* osseous.
osera, *n.f.* bear's den.
osezno, *n.m.* bear cub.
osificación, *n.f.* ossification.
osificar, *v.r.* become ossified.
osmio, *n.m.* (*chem.*) osmium.
oso, *n.m.* bear; — ***blanco,*** polar bear; — ***marino,*** fur seal.
ososo, -sa, *a.* osseous.
ostensible, *a.* ostensible.

ostensivo, -va, *a.* ostensive, on show.
ostentación, *n.f.* ostentation.
ostentar, *v.t.* show, display.
ostento, *n.m.* spectacle; prodigy, portent.
ostentoso, -sa, *a.* ostentatious.
osteópata, *n.m.f.* osteopath.
ostra, *n.f.* oyster.
ostral, *n.m.* oyster bed.
ostro (1), *n.m.* south wind.
ostro (2), *n.m.* large oyster.
osudo, -da, *a.* bony.
osuno, -na, *a.* bearish.
otalgia, *n.f.* (*med.*) otalgia, earache.
otear, *v.t.* survey.
otero, *n.m.* hillock; knoll.
otomano, -na, *a., n.m.f.* Ottoman.—*n.f.* ottoman.
Otón, *n.m.* Otto.
otoñada, *n.f.* autumn season.
otoñal, *a.* autumn.
otoñar, *v.i.* spend the autumn.
otoño, *n.m.* autumn, (*U.S.*) fall.
otorgador, -ra, *a.* granting.—*n.m.f.* grantor.
otorgamiento, *n.m.* granting; approval; (*jur.*) execution (*of a document*).
otorgar [B], *v.t.* grant, consent; (*jur.*) execute (*a deed*).
otro, otra, *a.* other, another.—*pron.* other one, another one; ***al — día,*** on the next day; ***otra vez,*** again; another time.
otrosí, *adv.* (*obs., joc.*) furthermore.
ova, *n.f.* seawrack, seaweed.
ovación, *n.f.* ovation.
ovado, -da, oval, *a.* oval.
óvalo, *n.m.* oval.
ovar, *v.i.* lay eggs.
oveja, *n.f.* ewe, sheep.
overa, *n.f.* ovary (*of a bird*).
ovetense, *a.* rel. to Oviedo.—*n.m.f.* inhabitant of Oviedo.
Ovidio, *n.m.* Ovid.
óvido, -da, *a.* ovine.
ovil, *n.m.* sheep-cote.
ovillar, *v.t.* roll into balls.
ovillo, *n.m.* ball (*wool, yarn etc.*).
ovino, -na, *a., n.m.f.* ovine.
ovíparo, -ra, *a.* oviparous.
ovoso, -sa, *a.* full of roe.
ovulación, *n.f.* ovulation.
ovulo, *n.m.* (*med.*) ovum.
¡ox! *interj.* shoo!
oxálico, -ca, *a.* oxalic.
oxidable, *a.* oxidizable.
oxidación, *n.f.* oxidation.
oxidante, *a.* oxidizing.—*n.m.* oxidizer.
oxidar, *v.t., v.r.* oxidize; rust.
óxido, *n.m.* oxide; ***— de cinc,*** zinc oxide.
oxígeno, *n.m.* oxygen.
¡oxte! *interj.* keep off! shoo! ***sin decir — ni moxte,*** without a word; without so much as a by-your-leave.
oyente, *a.* hearing.—*n.m.f.* listener.
ozono, *n.m.,* **ozona,** *n.f.* ozone.

P

P, p, *n.f.* nineteenth letter of the Spanish alphabet.
pabellón, *n.m.* pavilion; flag.
pábilo, pabilo, *n.m.* wick.
pacer [9], *v.t., v.i.* graze.
paciencia, *n.f.* patience.
paciente, *a., n.m.f.* patient.
pacificar [A], *v.t.* pacify.—*v.r.* calm down.
pacífico, -ca, *a.* pacific, peaceful.—*n.m.* ***el Pacífico,*** the Pacific (Ocean).
Paco, *n.m.* (*fam. form of* FRANCISCO) Frank.
pacotilla, *n.f.* trash, gewgaws.
pactar, *v.t.* agree to.—*v.i.* come to an agreement.
pacto, *n.m.* pact, covenant.
pachorra, *n.f.* sluggishness.
padecer [9], *v.t.* suffer; endure.—*v.i.* suffer (***con, de,*** from).
padecimiento, *n.m.* suffering.
padrasto, *n.m.* stepfather; obstacle.
padre, *n.m.* father; stallion; (*eccl.*) father; ***— político,*** father-in-law.
padrenuestro, *n.m.* (*pl.* **padrenuestros**) Lord's Prayer.
padrino, *n.m.* godfather.—*pl.* godparents.
padrón, *n.m.* census; pattern, model.
paella, *n.f.* (*cul.*) rice with meat etc.
¡paf! *interj.* bang! wham!
paga, *n.f.* pay.
pagable, pagadero, -ra, *a.* payable.
pagam(i)ento, *n.m.* payment.
pagano, -na, *a.* pagan.
pagar [B], *v.t.* pay.
pagaré, *n.m.* (*com.*) I.O.U.
página, *n.f.* page.
pago, *a. inv.* (*fam.*) paid.—*n.m.* payment; district.
painel, *n.m.* panel.
país, *n.m.* country, land; landscape; ***País de Gales,*** Wales; ***Países Bajos,*** Low Countries, Netherlands.
paisaje, *n.m.* landscape.
paisano, -na, *a.* of the same country.—*n.m.f.* compatriot; ***de —,*** in civilian clothes.
paja, *n.f.* straw; (*fig.*) padding.
pajar, *n.m.* straw-rick; straw-loft.
pajarero, -ra, *a.* gaudy, gay.—*n.m.f.* bird dealer.—*n.f.* aviary.
pájaro, *n.m.* bird.
pajarota, *n.f.* canard; hoax.
paje, *n.m.* page (boy); cabin boy.
pajizo, -za, *a.* straw-coloured.
pakistano, -na, *a., n.m.f.* Pakistani.
pala, *n.f.* shovel; blade; racket.
palabra, *n.f.* word.
palabrería, *n.f.,* **palabrerío,** *n.m.* wordiness.
palabrero, -ra, *a.* wordy.
palabrota, *n.f.* coarse word *or* expression.
palaciego, -ga, *a.* palatial, palace.—*n.m.* courtier.
palacio, *n.m.* palace; mansion.
palacra, palacrana, *n.f.* (gold) nugget.
paladar, *n.m.* palate.
paladear, *v.t., v.r.* taste, relish.
paladeo, *n.m.* tasting, relishing.
paladino, -na, *a.* public.—*n.m.* paladin.
palafrén, *n.m.* palfrey.
palanca, *n.f.* lever, crowbar; ***— de mayúsculas,*** shift-key (*of typewriter*).
palancana, palangana, *n.f.* (wash-)basin.
palanqueta, *n.f.* small lever; dumb-bell.
palastro, *n.m.* sheet-iron.
palatal, *a., n.f.* palatal.
palco, *n.m.* (*theat.*) box.

palenque, *n.m.* palisade; enclosure.
palero, *n.m.* shoveller; (*mil.*) pioneer.
Palestina, *n.f.* Palestine.
palestino, -na, *a.* Palestinian.
paleta (1), *n.f.* fire shovel; paddle (*of a propeller etc.*); (*S.A.*) lollipop; **de —,** opportunely.
paleto, -ta (2), *n.m.f.* (*fam.*) bumpkin, yokel.
paliar, *v.t.* palliate.
paliativo, -va, *a.* palliative.
palidecer [9], *v.i.* turn pale.
palidez, *n.f.* pallor.
pálido, -da, *a.* pallid.
palillo, *n.m.* toothpick; drumstick; cocktail-stick; bobbin.—*pl.* chopsticks; castanets; trifles.
palinodia, *n.f.* recantation, palinode.
palio, *n.m.* (*eccl., hist.*) canopy; cloak.
palique, *n.m.* chit-chat.
paliza, *n.f.* beating, drubbing.
palizada, *n.f.* stockade.
palma, *n.f.* palm (*hand, tree*).—*pl.* clapping.
palmada, *n.f.* slap; clap.
palmario, -ria, *a.* obvious.
palmatoria, *n.f.* small candlestick.
palmeado, -da, *a.* web-footed.
palmera, *n.m.* palm-tree.
palmo, *n.m.* palm, span.
palo, *n.m.* stick; wood; hook (*of a letter*); (*naut.*) mast.—*pl.* beating, drubbing.
paloma, *n.f.* pigeon, dove.
palomar, *n.m.* dovecot.
palomilla, *n.f.* young pigeon; (*mech.*) journal bearing; wall bracket.
palomo, *n.m.* cock pigeon.
palor, *n.m.* pallor.
palpable, *a.* palpable.
palpar, *v.t.* feel.—*v.i.* grope.
párpebra, *n.f.* eyelid.
palpitación, *n.f.* palpitation.
palpitante, *a.* palpitating.
palpitar, *v.i.* throb, palpitate.
palúdico, -ca, *a.* marshy; malarial.
paludismo, *n.m.* (*med.*) malaria.
palurdo, *n.m.* rustic, boor.
palustre, *a.* marshy.—*n.m.* trowel.
pallete, *n.m.* (*naut.*) fender.
pampa, *n.f.* (*S.A.*) wide plain, pampas.
pampanilla, *n.f.* loin-cloth.
pámpano, *n.m.* vine-tendril.
pampeano, -na, *a.* (*S.A.*) rel. to the pampas.
pampero, -ra, *n.m.f.* (*S.A.*) dweller on the pampas.
pamplemusa, *n.f.* (*S.A.*) grapefruit (*tree, fruit*).
pamplina, *n.f.* chickweed.—*pl.* (*interj.*) nonsense! fiddlesticks!
pampringada, *n.f.* bread and dripping; (*fam.*) nonsense, frivolity.
pan, *n.m.* bread; loaf; cake (*of soap etc.*); piecrust.
pana, *n.f.* velveteen, corduroy; (*S.A.*) breakdown.
panadería, *n.f.* bakery; baker's shop.
panadero, -ra, *n.m.f.* baker.
panadizo, *n.m.* whitlow.
panado, -da, *a.* covered with bread-crumbs, pané.
panal, *n.m.* honeycomb.
Panamá, *n.m.* Panama.
panameño, -ña, *a.* Panamanian.
panamericano, -na, *a.* Pan-American.
panarra, *n.m.,* (*fam.*) blockhead.
pancada, *n.f.* bulk sale.
pancarta, *n.f.* (*S.A.*) placard.
Pancho, *n.m.* (*S.A.*) Frank; **pancho,** *n.m.* paunch.
panda, *n.f.,* (*zool.*) panda.
pandear, *v.i., v.r.* warp.
pandectas, *n.f.pl.* (*com.*) index-book.
pandeo, *n.m.* warping.
pandereta, *n.f.* tambourine.
pandero, *n.m.* tambourine; paper-kite.
pandilla, *n.f.* party, gang.
pando, -da, *a.* bulging; deliberate.
panecillo, *n.m.* roll.
panera, *n.f.* granary; bread-basket.
panfleto, *n.m.* (*S.A.*) pamphlet.
paniaguado, *n.m.* (*fam.*) protégé.
pánico, -ca, *a.* panicky.—*n.m.* panic.
panificación, *n.f.* bread-making.
panique, *n.m.* (*zool.*) flying-fox.
panizo, *n.m.* panic-grass; foxtail millet.
panocha, *n.f.* ear of corn.
pantalón, *n.m.* (*esp. pl.* **-lones**) trousers.
pantalla, *n.f.* screen (*film, T.V.*); lampshade.
pantano, *n.m.* marsh; reservoir; dam.
pantanoso, -sa, *a.* marshy.
panteísmo, *n.m.* pantheism.
pantera, *n.f.* (*zool.*) panther.
pantoque, *n.m.* (*naut.*) bilge.
pantorrilla, *n.f.* (*anat.*) calf.
pantuflo, -la, *n.m.f.* slipper.
panza, *n.f.* paunch.
panzudo, -da, *a.* paunchy.
pañal, *n.m.* napkin, (*U.S.*) diaper; shirt-tail.
pañería, *n.f.* draper's shop, (*U.S.*) dry-goods store.
pañero, *n.m.* draper, (*U.S.*) clothier.
paño, *n.m.* cloth; **al —,** (*theat.*) off-stage.
pañoso, -sa, *a.* ragged.
pañuelo, *n.m.* handkerchief; headscarf.
papa (1), *n.m.* pope.
papa (2), *n.f.* (*esp. S.A.*) potato; (*fam.*) food; fib.—*pl.* gruel, baby-food.
papá, *n.m.* papa, daddy.
papada, *n.f.* double chin, dewlap.
papado, *n.m.* papacy.
papafigo, *n.m.* (*orn.*) ortolan.
papagayo, *n.m.* parrot.
papal, *a.* papal.—*n.m.* (*S.A.*) potato patch.
papamoscas, *n.m. inv.* (*orn.*) fly-catcher; ninny.
papar, *v.t.* gulp down; gape.
páparo, *n.m.* gawk, churl.
paparrucha, *n.f.,* (*fam.*) hoax.
papaya, *n.f.* papaw (*fruit*).
papayo, *n.m.* papaw (*tree*).
papel (1), *n.m.* paper; piece of paper.
papel (2), *n.m.* rôle, character.
papelería, *n.f.* stationery; stationer's shop.
papelero, -ra, *a.* boastful; rel. to paper.—*n.m.* stationer.
papeleta, *n.f.* slip (*of paper*), file card.
papelón, -lona, *a.* (*fam.*) bluffing.
papera, *n.f.* mumps.
papilla, *n.f.* pap; guile.
papillote, *n.m.* curl-paper.
papiro, *n.m.* papyrus.
papo, *n.m.* dewlap.
paquebote, *n.m.* packet (*boat*).
paquete, *n.m.* parcel, packet; (*S.A.*) dandy.
paquetería, *n.f.* retail trade.
el Paquistán, *n.m.* Pakistan.

par, *a.* equal; even.—*n.m.* pair, couple; peer; even number; ***al* —,** jointly; ***de* — *en* —,** wide open; ***sin* —,** peerless; ***pares o nones,*** odds or evens.—*n.f.* par; ***a la* —,** jointly; at par.
para, *prep.* to, for; towards; by (*a time*); in order to; — ***con,*** towards; — ***que,*** in order that; ***¿* — *qué?*** for what reason?
parabién, *n.m.* congratulations.
parábola, *n.f.* parable; parabola.
parabrisas, *n.m. inv.* windscreen, (*U.S.*) windshield.
paracaídas, *n.m. inv.* parachute.
paracaidista, *n.m.f.* parachutist.
paracleto, paráclito, *n.m.* Paraclete.
parachoques, *n.m. inv.* bumper.
parada, *n.f.* halt, stop; (*mil.*) parade; (*mus.*) pause.
paradero, *n.m.* whereabouts.
paradigma, *n.m.* paradigm.
parado, -da, *a.* stopped; idle; listless.
paradoja, *n.f.* paradox.
paradójico, -ca, paradojo, -ja, *a.* paradoxical.
parador, *n.m.* inn, hostelry.
parafina, *n.f.* paraffin (*wax*).
parafrasear, *v.t.* paraphrase.
paráfrasis, *n.f.* paraphrase.
paraguas, *n.m. inv.* umbrella.
paraguayano, -na, paraguayo, -ya, *a. n.m.f.* Paraguayan.
paraíso, *n.m.* paradise.
paraje, *n.m.* place; condition.
paralelismo, *n.m.* parallelism.
paralelo, -la, *a., n.m.* parallel.
parálisis, *n.f. inv.* paralysis.
paralítico, -ca, *a.* paralytic.
paralizar [C], *v.t.* paralyze.
paramento, *n.m.* embellishment.
páramo, *n.m.* bleak wilderness.
parangón, *n.m.* paragon; comparison.
parangonar, *v.t.* compare.
paraninfo (1), *n.m.* assembly hall.
paraninfo (2), *n.m.* best man, groomsman.
parapeto, *n.m.* parapet.
parar, *v.t.* stop; stake; prepare; parry.—*v.i.* stop; put up (***en,*** at).—*v.r.* stop.
pararrayo, *n.m.,* **pararrayos,** *n.m. inv.* lightning conductor.
parasitario, -ria, *a.* parasitic.
parásito, -ta, *a.* parasitic.—*n.m.* parasite; (*rad. esp. pl.*) atmospherics.
parasol, *n.m.* sunshade, parasol.
paraviento, *n.m.* shield, screen.
parcamente, *adv.* parsimoniously.
parcela, *n.f.* plot (*of land*); particle.
parcelar, *v.t.* parcel out.
parcial, *a.* partial; partisan.
parco, -ca, *a.* frugal.
parche, *n.m.* plaster, sticking plaster; patch.
¡pardiez! *interj.* by Jove!
pardillo, *n.m.* linnet.
pardo, -da, *a.* dark, drab; brown.—*n.m.f.* (*C.A.*) mulatto.
parear, *v.t.* match, pair.
parecer (1) [9], *v.i.* appear.—*v.r.* look alike.
parecer (2), *n.m.* opinion.
parecido, -da, *a.* like, similar.—*n.m.* resemblance.
pared, *n.f.* wall.
paredón, *n.m.* thick wall; (*fig.*) firing squad.
pareja, *n.f.* pair, match, couple.
parejo, -ja, *a.* equal, similar.
parentela, *n.f.* parentage; kinsfolk.
parentesco, *n.m.* relationship.
paréntesis, *n.m. inv.* parenthesis; bracket; ***entre* —,** by the way.
parezco [PARECER].
paridad, *n.f.* parity.
pariente, -ta, *n.m.f.* relative, relation.
parihuela, *n.f.* barrow; stretcher.
parir, *v.t., v.i.* bring forth, give birth (to).
parisiense, *a., n.m.f.* Parisian.
parlamentario, -ria, *a.* parliamentary.—*n.m.f.* member of parliament.
parlamento, *n.m.* parliament; parley; (*theat.*) speech.
parlanchín, -china, *a.* chattering.—*n.m.f.* chatterbox.
parlante, *a.* talking.
parlatorio, *n.m.* parlour; chat.
paro, *n.m.* stoppage, lockout; unemployment; (*orn.*) tit(mouse).
parodia, *n.f.* parody.
paroxismo, *n.m.* paroxysm.
parpadear, *v.i.* blink; wink.
párpado, *n.m.* eyelid.
parque, *n.m.* park.
parquedad, *n.f.* frugality; parsimony.
parra, *n.f.* (trained) vine; honey jar.
párrafo, *n.m.* paragraph; ***echar un* —,** (*fam.*) have a natter *or* chat.
parral, *n.m.* vine arbour.
parranda, *n.f.* revel.
parricida, *n.m.f.* parricide (*person*).
parricidio, *n.m.* parricide (*act*).
parrilla, *n.f.* (*cul.*) grill.
párroco, *n.m.* parish priest.
parroquia, *n.f.* parish; parish church; regular customers, clientele.
parroquial, *a.* parochial.
parroquiano, -na, *a.* parochial.—*n.m.f.* parishioner; regular customer.
parte, *n.f.* part; share; party; direction; (*mus.*) part; (*jur.*) party; ***a* — *de,*** apart from; ***de* — *de,*** on behalf of.—*pl.* parts, talent.
partera, *n.f.* midwife.
partición, *n.f.* partition.
participación, *n.f.* participation; notification.
participante, *a.* notifying; participant.
participar, *v.t.* inform.—*v.i.* participate (***en,*** in); partake (***de,*** of).
partícipe, *a., n.m.f.* participant.
participio, *n.m.* participle.
partícula, *n.f.* particle.
particular, *a.* private; particular; peculiar.—*n.m.* individual; particular subject.
partida, *n.f.* departure; entry (*in accounts*); party; game; certificate.
partidario, -ria, *a., n.m.f.* partisan.
partido, -da, *a.* munificent.—*n.m.* game, match; (*pol.*) party; advantage; protection; district; ***tomar* —,** resolve.
partir, *v.t.* divide; distribute; break; sever, split open.—*v.i.* depart.
parto, *n.m.* childbirth; newborn child.
parturiente, parturienta, *a.* parturient, in childbirth.
parvo, -va, *a.* little, small.
párvulo, -la, *a.* tiny; lowly.—*n.m.f.* child.
pasa, *n.f.* raisin.
pasada, *n.f.* passage; game, trick.
pasadero, -ra, *a.* passable.—*n.f.* stepping-stone; colander.

pasadizo, *n.m.* passage; catwalk.
pasado, -da, *a.* past; out-of-date.—*n.m.* past. —*pl.* ancestors.
pasador, -ra, *a.* smuggling.—*n.m.f.* smuggler.—*n.m.* (door) bolt; pin.
pasaje, *n.m.* passage.
pasajero, -ra, *a.* passing, fleeting; frequented. —*n.m.f.* passenger.
pasamanería, *n.f.* passementerie, lacemaking.
pasamano, *n.m.* lace; (*naut.*) gangway.
pasante, *n.m.* student-teacher; assistant.
pasapasa, *n.m.* legerdemain, hocus-pocus.
pasaporte, *n.m.* passport.
pasar, *v.t.* pass, cross; transfer.—*v.i.* pass, happen; manage, get along; — ***a,*** go on to; — ***de,*** exceed; — ***por,*** pass through; pass as; — ***sin,*** do without.—*v.r.* pass; take an examination.
pasatiempo, *n.m.* pastime.
pascua, *n.f.* Passover; — ***de Resurrección*** or ***florida,*** Easter; — ***de Navidad,*** Christmas; — ***de Espíritu Santo,*** Whitsun.
pascual, *a.* paschal.
pase, *n.m.* pass; feint.
pasear, *v.t.* walk, promenade.—*v.i., v.r.* walk, take a stroll; ***pasearse en bicicleta*** *etc.*, go cycling *etc.*
paseo, *n.m.* walk; stroll, drive; avenue.
pasillo, *n.m.* passage; short step.
pasión, *n.f.* passion.
pasito, *n.m.* short step.—*adv.* gently.
pasividad, *n.f.* passivity.
pasivo, -va, *a.* passive.—*n.m.* (*gram.*) passive; (*com.*) debit side.
pasmar, *v.t.* chill; stun.—*v.i., v.r.* be astounded.
pasmo, *n.m.* amazement; spasm; tetanus.
pasmoso, -sa, *a.* astounding.
paso, -sa, *a.* dried (*fruit*).—*n.m.* pace, step; gait; passage; footprint; pitch (*of screw*); (*theat.*) sketch.—*adv.* gently.
pasquinar, *v.t.* lampoon.
pasta, *n.f.* paste, dough, batter; pulp; pasteboard; pasta.
pastar, *v.t., v.i.* pasture.
pastel, *n.m.* pie; pastel; plot.
pastelería, *n.f.* pastry shop.
pasterizar [C], *v.t.* pasteurize.
pastinaca, *n.f.* (*ichth.*) sting-ray; (*bot.*) parsnip.
pasto, *n.m.* pasture; food.
pastor, *n.m.* shepherd; pastor.
pastora, *n.f.* shepherdess.
pastoso, -sa, *a.* doughy; mellow (*voice*).
pastura, *n.f.* pasture.
pata, *n.f.* paw, foot; (female) duck; ***meter la*** —, put one's foot in it; ***quedar pata(s),*** be a draw.
pataco, -ca, *a.* churlish.—*n.m.f.* churl.—*n.f.* Jerusalem artichoke.
patada, *n.f.* kick.
patagón, -gona, *a., n.m.f.* Patagonian.
patán, -tana, *a.* churlish.—*n.m.f.* churl.
patarata, *n.f.* foolishness; affectation.
patata, *n.f.* potato; bulb, corm; ***patatas fritas,*** potato chips *or* crisps; (*U.S.*) French fries.
patear, *v.t.* trample on.—*v.i.* stamp; (*S.A.*) kick (*of guns*).
patentar, *v.t.* patent.
patente, *a.* patent, evident.—*n.f.* privilege, patent.
patentizar [C], *v.t.* render evident.
paternidad, *n.f.* paternity.
paterno, -na, *a.* paternal.
pateta, *n.f.* (*fam.*) lame person; (*fam.*) Old Nick.
patético, -ca, *a.* pathetic.
patiabierto, -ta, *a.* bow-legged.
patibulario, -ria, *a.* rel. to the scaffold; horrifying.
patíbulo, *n.m.* scaffold, gallows.
patihendido, -da, *a.* cloven-footed.
patilla, *n.f.* small foot; (*esp. pl.*) (side-) whisker; tenon; (*S.A.*) water-melon.
patín, *n.m.* skate (*ice, roller*); runner, skid.
patinadero, *n.m.* skating-rink.
patinaje, *n.m.* skating; skidding.
patinar, *v.i.* skate; skid.
patinazo, *n.m.* skid.
patinete, *n.m.* (child's) scooter.
patio, *n.m.* courtyard, patio; campus; (*theat.*) stalls.
patizambo, -ba, *a.* knock-kneed.
pato, *n.m.* drake, (male) duck.
patochada, *n.f.* (*fam.*) blunder.
patojo, -ja, *a.* waddling.
patología, *n.f.* pathology.
patólogo, *n.m.* pathologist.
patraña, *n.f.* old wives' tale; hoax.
patria, *n.f.* homeland, motherland.
patriarca, *n.m.* patriarch.
patricio, -cia, *a.* patrician; (*S.A.*) American-born.
patrimonio, *n.m.* patrimony.
patrio, -ria, *a.* native, national.
patriota, *n.m.f.* patriot.
patrocinar, *v.t.* favour; sponsor.
patrocinio, *n.m.* patronage.
patrón, -rona, *n.m.f.* patron; protector.—*n.m.* landlord; boss; sample; pattern.—*n.f.* patroness; landlady; mistress.
patronal, *a.* rel. to employers; patronal.
patronato, *n.m.* association of employers; patronage.
patrono, *n.m.* patron; protector; employer.
patrulla, *n.f.* patrol.
patullar, *v.i.* tramp about.
paulatino, -na, *a.* gradual.
paupérrimo, -ma, *a.* (*sup. of* POBRE) very poor.
pausa, *n.f.* pause; (*mus.*) rest.
pausado, -da, *a.* slow; deliberate.
pausar, *v.i.* pause; hesitate.
pauta, *n.f.* guide line; model.
pava, *n.f.* turkey hen; ***pelar la*** —, court.
pavesa, *n.f.* ember.
pavimentar, *v.t.* pave.
pavimento, *n.m.* pavement.
pavo, *n.m.* turkey; — ***real,*** peacock.
pavón, *n.m.* peacock.
pavonear, *v.i.* swagger.
pavor, *n.m.* terror.
pavoroso, -sa, *a.* fearful.
pavura, *n.f.* dread.
payaso, *n.m.* clown.
payés, -yesa, *n.m.f.* Catalan peasant.
payo, paya, *n.m.f.* churl.
payuelas, *n.f.pl.* chicken-pox.
paz, *n.f.* (*pl.* **paces**) peace; ***en*** —, (*fam.*) quits.
pazguato, -ta, *n.m.f.* dolt.
pe, *n.f.* name of letter P; ***de — a pa,*** all through.
pea, *n.f.* drunken binge.
peaje, *n.m.* toll.

peana, *n.f.* pedestal.
peatón, *n.m.* pedestrian.
pebete, *n.m.* joss-stick; stench; (*S.A.*) lad.
peca, *n.f.* freckle.
pecado, *n.m.* sin.
pecador, -ra, *a.* sinning.—*n.m.f.* sinner.
pecaminoso, -sa, *a.* sinful.
pecar [A], *v.i.* sin.
pecarí, *n.m.* (*pl.* **-íes**) peccary.
pecera, *n.f.* goldfish bowl.
pecezuela, *n.f.* small piece.
pecezuelo, *n.m.* small fish.
pecio, *n.m.* flotsam.
pecoso, -sa, *a.* freckled.
peculiar, *a.* peculiar.
pechar, *v.t.* pay as a tax.
pechblenda, *n.f.* pitchblende.
pechero, -ra, *a.* taxable.—*n.m.f.* commoner. —*n.m.* bib.—*n.f.* shirt front; stomacher.
pecho, *n.m.* breast, chest; tax.
pechuga, *n.f.* breast (*of a fowl*).
pedagogía, *n.f.* pedagogy, education.
pedal, *n.m.* pedal.
pedazo, *n.m.* piece.
pedernal, *n.m.* flint.
pedestal, *n.m.* pedestal.
pedestre, *a.* pedestrian.
pedíatra, *n.m.* pediatrician.
pedido, *n.m.* request; (*com.*) order.
pedigüeño, -ña, *a.* importunate.
pedimento, *n.m.* petition.
pedir [8], *v.t.* ask for; beg.
pedregal, *n.m.* stony patch.
pedregoso, -sa, *a.* stony.
pedrera, *n.f.* quarry.
pedrería, *n.f.* jewelry.
pedriscal, *n.m.* stony patch.
pedrisco, *n.m.* hailstorm; shower of stones.
pega, *n.f.* sticking; (*fam.*) trick; snag; (*orn.*) magpie; ***de* —,** fake.
pegadizo, -za, *a.* sticky; sponging; imitation; contagious (*disease*).
pegajoso, -sa, *a.* sticky; catching (*disease*); (*fam.*) mushy.
pegar [B], *v.t.* stick; fasten; transmit (*a disease*); strike.—*v.i.* stick; cling; match; knock; stumble.—*v.r.* fight; stick; be catching.
pegote, *n.m.* sticking plaster; (*fig.*) sore thumb.
peinado, *n.m.* hair-style.
peinador, -ra, *n.m.f.* hairdresser.—*n.m.* dressing-gown.
peinar, *v.t.* comb.—*v.r.* comb one's hair.
peine, *n.m.* comb; instep.
peineta, *n.f.* back-comb.
peladilla, *n.f.* sugared almond; small pebble.
pelado, -da, *a.* bare; barren.
peladura, *n.f.* peeling.
pelapatatas, *n.m.inv.* potato-peeler *or* -scraper.
pelar, *v.t.* pluck; peel; cut (*hair*); fleece; ***pelárselas por,*** crave after.
peldaño, *n.m.* step, tread (*of stairs*).
pelea, *n.f.* fight, struggle.
pelear, *v.i.* fight, struggle.
peletería, *n.f.* furrier's shop; fur trade.
peliagudo, -da, *a.* downy; (*fam.*) tricky.
pelicano, -na, *a.* grey-haired.
pelícano, *n.m.* pelican.
pelicorto, -ta, *a.* short-haired.
película, *n.f.* film.
peliculero, -ra, *a.* rel. to films.—*n.m.* film actor; script writer.—*n.f.* film actress; script writer.
peligro, *n.m.* danger, risk.
peligroso, -sa, *a.* dangerous, perilous.
pelillo, *n.m.* trifle; short hair.
pelirrubio, -bia, *a.* fair-haired.
pelma, *n.m.,* **pelmazo,** *n.m.* (*fam.*) bore.
pelo, *n.m.* hair; down; nap; grain; ***al* —,** (*fam.*) perfectly; ***en* —,** naked; ***tomar el* — *a,*** make fun of.
pelón, -lona, *a.* bald; (*fam.*) broke.
peloso, -sa, *a.* hairy.
pelota, *n.f.* ball; ball game; ***en* —,** naked; penniless.
pelotari, *n.m.* pelota player.
pelotear, *v.t.* audit.—*v.i.* knock a ball around; wrangle.
pelotilla, *n.f.* pellet.
pelotón, *n.m.* large ball; (*mil.*) section, squad.
peltre, *n.m.* pewter.
peluca, *n.f.* wig.
peluche, *n.m.* plush.
peludo, -da, *a.* hairy.
peluquería, *n.f.* hairdresser's shop.
peluquero, -ra, *n.m.f.* hairdresser; wig-maker.
pelusa, *n.f.* down.
pella, *n.f.* pellet; puff-pastry; (*fam.*) unrepaid loan.
pelleja, *n.f.* hide, skin.
pellejo, *n.m.* skin; pelt.
pellizcar [A], *v.t.* pinch, nip.
pellizco, *n.m.* pinch, nip.
pena, *n.f.* punishment; penalty; grief; ***so* — *de,*** on pain of.
penable, *a.* punishable.
penachera, *n.f.,* **penacho,** *n.m.* crest; panache.
penal, *a.* penal.—*n.m.* penitentiary.
penalidad, *n.f.* suffering; penalty.
penar, *v.t.* chastize.—*v.i.* suffer, be tormented.—*v.r.* grieve.
penco, *n.m.,* nag.
pendencia, *n.f.* dispute; quarrel, fight.
pender, *v.i.* hang; depend.
pendiente, *a.* hanging; pending.—*n.m.* pendant; ear-ring; watch-chain.—*n.f.* slope; curve (*of graph*).
péndola, *n.f.* pendulum; quill.
pendón, *n.m.* banner, pennon; (*bot.*) shoot.
péndulo, -la, *a.* pendent.—*n.m.* (*mech.*) pendulum.
penecilina, *n.f.* penicillin.
penetración, *n.f.* penetration; insight.
penetrar, *v.t.* penetrate.
península, *n.f.* peninsula.
peninsular, *a., n.m.f.* peninsular.
penique, *n.m.* penny.
penitencia, *n.f.* penitence, penance.
penitente, *a., n.m.f.* penitent.
penoso, -sa, *a.* difficult; suffering; (*S.A.*) shy.
pensamiento, *n.m.* thought; (*bot.*) pansy.
pensar [I], *v.t.* think; think of; feed (*animals*). —*v.i.* think; ***— de,*** think of (*opinion*); ***— en,*** think of (*direct one's thoughts*).
pensativo, -va, *a.* pensive, thoughtful.
penseque, *n.m.* oversight.
pensión, *n.f.* pension; allowance; boarding house; encumbrance.
pensionar, *v.t.* pension.
pensionista, *n.m.f.* boarder.

pentágono, -na, *a.* pentagonal.—*n.m.* pentagon.
pentagrama, *n.m.* pentagram; (*mus.*) stave.
Pentecostés, *n.m.* Whitsun, Pentecost.
penúltimo, -ma, *a.* penultimate.
peña, *n.f.* boulder; cliff; club.
peñasco, *n.m.* crag; pinnacle.
peñón, *n.m.* rock, crag; ***Peñón de Gibraltar,*** Rock of Gibraltar.
peón, *n.m.* pedestrian; infantryman; pawn; man (*in draughts*); (*S.A.*) farm-hand; labourer.
peonia, *n.f.* (*bot.*) peony.
peonza, *n.f.* (whip-)top.
peor, *a., adv.* worse; worst.
Pepe, *n.m.* Joe.
pepinillo, *n.m.* gherkin.
pepino, *n.m.* cucumber.
pepita, *n.f.* pip.
pepitoria, *n.f.* giblet fricassee; hotchpotch.
pequeñez, *n.f.* (*pl.* **-ñeces**) smallness; trifle.
pequeño, -ña, *a.* small, little, tiny.
pequeñuelo, -la, *a.* tiny.—*n.m.f.* baby, tot.
pera, *n.f.* pear; goatee (*beard*).
peral, *n.m.* pear tree.
perca, *n.f.* (*ichth.*) perch.
percance, *n.m.* misfortune; perquisite.
percatar, *v.i., v.r.* be wary (***de,*** of).
percebe, *n.m.* goose barnacle.
percepción, *n.f.* perception; (tax-)collection.
perceptor, *n.m.* tax-collector.
percibir, *v.t.* perceive; collect; receive (*pay*).
percibo, *n.m.* collection.
percudir, *v.t., v.r.* tarnish.
percusión, *n.f.* percussion.
percusor, *n.m.* firing-pin.
percutir, *v.t.* percuss.
percutor, *n.m.* firing-pin.
percha, *n.f.* perch, pole; clothes-hanger.
perchero, *n.m.* clothes-rack.
perder [2], *v.t.* lose; waste; miss (*a train*).—*v.i.* lose.—*v.r.* lose one's way; get spoiled.
pérdida, *n.f.* loss; waste.
perdigar [B], *v.t.* (*cul.*) brown.
perdigón, *n.m.* young partridge; shot, pellets; (*fam.*) profligate.
perdiguero, *n.m.* pointer, setter.
perdiz, *n.f.* (*pl.* **-ices**) partridge.
perdón, *n.m.* pardon, forgiveness.
perdonable, *a.* pardonable.
perdonar, *v.t.* pardon.
perdulario, -ria, *a.* careless; vicious.
perdurable, *a.* everlasting.
perdurar, *v.i.* last (*a long time*).
perecedero, -ra, *a.* perishable; mortal.
perecer [9], *v.i.* perish; be in want.—*v.r.* pine (***por,*** for, ***de,*** of).
peregrinación, *n.f.* pilgrimage.
peregrino, -na, *a.* wandering; peregrine; strange.—*n.m.f.* pilgrim.
perejil, *n.m.* parsley; (*fam.*) frippery.
perenal, *a.* perennial.
perendengue, *n.m.* trinket; ear-ring.
perengano, -na, *n.m.f.* so-and-so (*after* FULANO).
perenne, *a.* perennial.
pereza, *n.f.* laziness.
perezoso, -sa, *a.* lazy.
perfección, *n.f.* perfection.
perfeccionar, *v.t.* perfect, improve.
perfecto, -ta, *a.* perfect.—*n.m.* (*gram.*) perfect.
perfil, *n.m.* profile, outline; (cross-) section.
perfilar, *v.t.* profile.—*v.r.* stand sideways.
perforar, *v.t.* perforate, drill, punch.
perfume, *n.m.* scent, perfume.
pergamino, *n.m.* parchment.
pérgola, *n.f.* roof garden, arbour.
pericia, *n.f.* skill; practical experience.
pericial, *a.* expert.
perico, *n.m.* parakeet; periwig; mizzen topgallant; chamber-pot.
periferia, *n.f.* periphery.
perifollo, *n.m.* (*bot.*) chervil; (*fam.*) finery.
perífrasis, *n.f. inv.* periphrasis.
perilla, *n.f.* small pear; pommel, knob.
perillán, -llana, *a.* knavish.—*n.m.f.* rascal.
perímetro, *n.m.* perimeter.
periódico, -ca, *a.* periodical.—*n.m.* newspaper.
periodista, *n.m.f.* journalist.
período, *n.m.* period.
peripuesto, -ta, *a.* (*fam.*) very spruce.
periquete, *n.m.* jiffy, trice.
periscopio, *n.m.* periscope.
peritaje, *n.m.* expert's fee; expert work.
perito, -ta, *a.* skilled, expert.—*n.m.f.* expert, technician.
perjudicar [A], *v.t.* harm, impair, prejudice.
perjudicial, *a.* harmful, prejudicial.
perjuicio, *n.m.* harm, injury; prejudice.
perjurar, *v.i., v.r.* commit perjury.
perjuro, -ra, *a.* perjured.—*n.m.f.* perjuror.—*n.m.* perjury.
perla, *n.f.* pearl.
perlesía, *n.f.* palsy.
permanecer [9], *v.i.* stay.
permanencia, *n.f.* permanence; stay; (*esp. pl. educ.*) prep., study hours.
permanente, *a.* permanent.—*n.f.* permanent wave.
permisión, *n.f.* permission; leave.
permiso, *n.m.* permission; permit, licence.
permitir, *v.t.* permit, allow.
pernada, *n.f.* kick.
pernear, *v.i.* kick.
pernera, *n.f.* trouser-leg.
pernicioso, -sa, *a.* pernicious.
pernil, *n.m.* leg (*of trousers, pork*).
pernio, *n.m.* hinge.
pernituerto, -ta, *a.* crooked-legged.
perno, *n.m.* bolt, spike.
pernoctar, *v.i.* pass the night.
pero, *conj.* but.
perogrullada, *n.f.* truism, platitude.
peróxido, *n.m.* peroxide.
perpendicular, *a., n.f.* perpendicular.
perpendículo, *n.m.* plumb-bob; pendulum.
perpetuar, *v.t.* perpetuate.
perpetuo, -tua, *a.* perpetual, for life.—*n.f.* everlasting flower.
perplejo, -ja, *a.* perplexed; anxious.
perra [PERRO].
perrera, *n.f.* kennel, (*U.S.*) doghouse.
perrillo, -lla, *n.m.f.* puppy.—*n.m.* trigger.
perro, -rra, *a.* mean, stingy.—*n.m.* dog; (*mech.*) pawl.—*n.f.* bitch; drunkenness; small coin.
perruno, -na, *a.* canine, dog-like.
persa, *a., n.m.f.* Persian.
persecución, *n.f.* persecution; pursuit.
perseguir [8G], *v.t.* persecute; pursue.
perseverancia, *n.f.* perseverance.

persiano, -na, *a., n.m.f.* Persian.—*n.f.* Venetian blind.
persignar, *v.r.* cross oneself.
persistencia, *n.f.* persistency.
persistente, *a.* persistent.
persistir, *v.i.* persist.
persona, *n.f.* person.
personaje, *n.m.* personage; (*theat.*) character.
personal, *a.* personal.—*n.m.* personnel, staff.
personalidad, *n.f.* personality.
personificar [A], *v.t.* personify.
perspectivo, -va, *a.* perspective.—*n.f.* prospect; perspective.
perspicacia, *n.f.* perspicacity.
perspicaz, *a.* (*pl.* **-aces**) perspicacious.
perspiración, *n.f.* perspiration.
perspirar, *v.i.* perspire.
persuadir, *v.t.* persuade (**a,** to).
persuasible, *a.* credible.
persuasión, *n.f.* persuasion.
persuasivo, -va, *a.* persuasive.
pertenecer [9], *v.i.* belong; pertain.
perteneciente, *a.* pertaining.
pertenencia, *n.f.* property; appurtenance.
pértiga, *n.f.* pole, rod; ***salto con —,*** pole-vault.
pertinaz, *a.* (*pl.* **-aces**) pertinacious.
pertinencia, *n.f.* relevance.
pertrechar, *v.t.* provide, equip.
pertrechos, *n.m.pl.* supplies; tools.
perturbar, *v.t.* perturb; disturb.
el Perú, *n.m.* Peru.
peruano, -na, peruviano, -na, *a., n.m.f.* Peruvian.
perversión, *n.f.* perversion.
perverso, -sa, *a.* perverse; profligate.—*n.m.f.* profligate.
pervertido, -da, *a.* perverted.—*n.m.f.* (*med.*) pervert.
pervertir [6], *v.t.* pervert.
pesa, *n.f.* weight.
pesadez, *n.f.* heaviness, weight; tiresomeness.
pesadilla, *n.f.* nightmare.
pesado, -da, *a.* heavy; tiresome, dull.
pesadumbre, *n.f.* grief; weight.
pésame, *n.m.* condolence.
pesantez, *n.f.* weight, gravity.
pesar (1), *n.m.* sorrow.
pesar (2), *v.t.* weigh;—*v.i.* weigh; be important.
pesca, *n.f.* fishing; catch.
pescada, *n.f.* hake.
pescado, *n.m.* fish.
pescador, -ra, *a.* fishing.—*n.m.* fisherman, angler.
pescante, *n.m.* jib, boom; (*theat.*) trap-door.
pescar [A], *v.t.* fish, catch.
pescuezo, *n.m.* neck; haughtiness.
pesebre, *n.m.* manger; crib; (*S.A.*) crèche.
peseta, *n.f.* peseta.
pesimismo, *n.m.* pessimism.
pésimo, -ma, *a.* very bad, abominable.
peso, *n.m.* weight; gravity; peso (*coin*).
pespunte, *n.m.* backstitch.
pesquero, -ra, *a.* fishing (*industry etc.*).—*n.m.* fishing boat.—*n.f.* fishery.
pesquisa, *n.f.* inquiry.—*n.m.* (*S.A. fam.*) cop.
pesquisar, *v.t.* investigate.
pestaña, *n.f.* eyelash; flange.
pestañear, *v.i.* wink, blink.
pestañeo, *n.m.* blinking.
peste, *n.f.* plague; stench; (*fam.*) abundance.
pestillo, *n.m.* bolt; latch.
pesuña [PEZUÑA].
petaca, *n.f.* tobacco-pouch; leather trunk.
pétalo, *n.m.* petal.
petardo, *n.m.* petard, bomb; firework; swindle.
petate, *n.m.* bedding roll; (*fam.*) baggage.
petición, *n.f.* petition.
petimetre, *n.m.* dandy.
peto, *n.m.* breastplate.
pétreo, -a, *a.* petreous, rocky.
petrificar [A], *v.t., v.r.* petrify.
petróleo, *n.m.* petroleum, crude oil.
petrolero, -ra, *a.* rel. to oil.—*n.m.* oil-dealer; oil tanker; incendiary.
petrología, *n.f.* petrology.
petulancia, *n.f.* pertness.
petulante, *a.* pert, insolent.
peyorativo, -va, *a.* pejorative.
pez (1), *n.m.* (*pl.* **peces**) fish (*live*); ***— espada,*** swordfish.
pez (2), *n.f.* pitch.
pezón, *n.m.* teat, nipple.
pezpita, *n.f.,* **pezpítalo,** *n.m.* pipit.
pezuña, *n.f.* hoof.
pi, *n.f.* (*math.*) pi.
piadoso, -sa, *a.* pious; merciful.
piamontés, -tesa, *a., n.m.f.* Piedmontese.
pianista, *n.m.f.* pianist.
piano, *n.m.* (*mus.*) piano; ***— de cola,*** grand piano.
pianoforte, *n.m.* (*mus.*) pianoforte.
piar [L], *v.i.* chirp.
pica, *n.f.* pike; pica; (*S.A.*) pique.
picado, -da, *a.* perforated; cut (*tobacco*); choppy (*sea*); minced.—*n.m.* mincemeat; (*aer.*) nosedive.—*n.f.* peck; puncture.
picador, *n.m.* (*taur.*) picador.
picadura, *n.f.* bite, prick, sting; puncture; shredded tobacco; (dental) cavity.
picante, *a.* biting; piquant; highly-seasoned.
picaporte, *n.m.* latch; (*S.A.*) door-knocker.
picaposte, *n.m.* (*orn.*) woodpecker.
picar [A], *v.t.* prick; pierce; sting; mince; nibble; (*aer.*) dive.—*v.r.* go sour; get moth-eaten.
picaraza, *n.f.* magpie.
Picardía, *n.f.* Picardy; **picardía,** *n.f.* roguery.
picaresco, -ca, *a.* roguish.—*n.f.* den of thieves.
pícaro, -ra, *a.* roguish.—*n.m.f.* rogue.
picatoste, *n.m.* fried bread.
picazo, -za, *a.* piebald.—*n.m.* jab.—*n.f.* magpie.
pico, *n.m.* beak; spout; nib; (*orn.*) woodpecker; pick; ***las tres y —,*** a little after three.
picoso, -sa, *a.* pock-marked.
picotada, *n.f.,* **picotazo,** *n.m.* peck.
picotear, *v.t.* peck.
pictórico, -ca, *a.* pictorial.
pichel, *n.m.* pewter tankard; pitcher.
pichón, *n.m.* young pigeon.
pie, *n.m.* foot.
piececillo, *n.m.* little foot.
piecezuela, *n.f.* little piece.
piedad, *n.f.* pity; piety.
piedra, *n.f.* stone.
piel, *n.f.* skin; hide; leather; ***— de gallina,*** goose-flesh.
piélago, *n.m.* (*lit.*) ocean.
pienso, *n.m.* feed(ing), fodder.

pierna, *n.f.* leg; shank; ***a — suelta,*** at ease.
pieza, *n.f.* piece; coin; (*mech.*) part; room.
pífano, *n.m.* fife.
pigmento, *n.m.* pigment.
pigmeo, -mea, *a., n.m.f.* pygmy.
pijama, *n.m.* pyjamas, (*U.S.*) pajamas.
pila, *n.f.* basin; trough; font; (*elec.*) pile, battery; ***nombre de —,*** Christian name.
pilar, *n.m.* pillar; basin.
Pilatos, *n.m.* Pilate.
píldora, *n.f.* pill.
pileta, *n.f.* basin.
pilón (1), *n.m.* basin, trough; (pounding) mortar.
pilón (2), *n.m.* pylon.
pilongo, -ga, *a.* lean.
pilotaje, *n.m.* pile-work; pilotage.
pilotar, *v.t.* pilot, drive.
pilote, *n.m.* pile.
pilotear, *v.t.* pilot, drive.
piloto, *n.m.* pilot; navigator, mate.
pillar, *v.t.* pillage.
pillo, -lla, *a.* (*fam.*) roguish.—*n.m.f.* rogue.
pimentón, *n.m.* cayenne pepper; paprika.
pimienta, *n.m.* (black) pepper.
pimiento, *n.m.* capsicum, cayenne pepper.
pimpollo, *n.m.* sprout, sucker.
pinacoteca, *n.f.* picture gallery.
pináculo, *n.m.* pinnacle.
pinar, *n.m.* pine grove.
pincel, *n.m.* brush; beam.
pincelada, *n.f.* brush-stroke.
pinciano, -na, *a.* rel. to Valladolid.
pincha, *n.f.* kitchen-maid.
pinchar, *v.t.* prick; puncture.
pinchazo, *n.m.* puncture; jab.
pincho, *n.m.* prick; thorn.
pingar, *v.i.* drip; jump.
pingo, *n.m.* rag.
pingüe, *a.* oily; rich, plentiful.
pingüino, *n.m.* penguin.
pinguosidad, *n.f.* fatness.
pinito, *n.m.* toddling step.
pino (1), **-na,** *a.* steep.
pino (2), *n.m.* pine (*tree*).
pinocha, *n.f.* pine needle.
pintado, -da, *a.* mottled; (*fam.*) tipsy.—*n.m.f.* guinea fowl.
pintar, *v.t.* paint; (*fam.*) show.
pintarraj(e)ar, *v.t.* daub.
pintiparado, -da, *a.* (*fam.*) perfectly like.
pintor, -ra, *n.m.f.* painter.
pintoresco, -ca, *a.* picturesque.
pintura, *n.f.* painting; paint.
pinza, *n.f.* clothes-peg, (*U.S.*) clothespin; (*esp. pl.*) pincers, tweezers.
pinzón, *n.m.* (*orn.*) chaffinch.
piña, *n.f.* pine-cone; pineapple.
piñón, *n.m.* pine kernel; (*mech.*) pinion.
pío (1), **pía** (1), *a.* pious; merciful.
pío (2), **pía** (2), *a.* pied.
pío (3), *n.m.* chirping.
piojo, *n.m.* louse.
pipa (1), *n.f.* (*tobacco*) pipe; (*wine*) cask; (*mus.*) pipe, reed.
pipa (2), *n.f.* (*orange etc.*) pip.
pipeta, *n.f.* pipette.
pipiar [L], *v.i.* chirp; peep.
pipote, *n.m.* keg.
pique, *n.m.* pique, resentment; (*S.A.*) spade (*at cards*); ***a —,*** steep; ***echar a —,*** sink (*of a ship*); ***a — de,*** on the point of.
piquete, *n.m.* picket.
piquituerto, *n.m.* (*orn.*) crossbill.
piragua, *n.f.* pirogue, canoe, kayak.
pirámide, *n.f.* pyramid.
pirata, *n.m.* pirate.
piratería, *n.f.* piracy.
pirenaico, -ca, pirineo, -nea, *a.* Pyrenean.
los Pirineos, *n.m.pl.* Pyrenees.
pirita, *n.f.* (*min.*) pyrites.
piropear, *v.t.* flatter; compliment.
piropo, *n.m.* compliment; flirtatious remark; garnet.
pisada, *n.f.* tread.
pisapapeles, *n.m. inv.* paperweight.
pisar, *v.t.* trample.
pisaverde, *n.m.* (*fam.*) fop.
piscina, *n.f.* swimming-pool; fishpond; piscina.
piscolabis, *n.m. inv.* (*fam.*) snack.
piso, *n.m.* tread; floor; storey; flat, apartment; ***— bajo,*** ground floor.
pisonadora, *n.f.* steam-roller, road-roller.
pisotear, *v.t.* trample.
pista, *n.f.* track; runway; trail.
pisto, *n.m.* vegetable stew.
pistola, *n.f.* pistol.
pistolera, *n.f.* holster.
pistolero, *n.m.* gunman; gun-operator.
pistón, *n.m.* piston.
pistonear, *v.i.* knock (*cylinder*).
pistonudo, -da, *a.* (*fam.*) smashing.
pitar, *v.i.* blow a whistle.
pitido, *n.m.* whistling.
pitillera, *n.f.* cigarette-case.
pitillo, *n.m.* cigarette.
pito, *n.m.* whistle; fife; car horn; ***no vale un —,*** it's not worth a straw.
pitón (1), *n.m.* python.
pitón (2), *n.m.* nozzle; sprout.
pitonisa, *n.f.* pythoness; sorceress.
pitorra, *n.f.* woodcock.
pituoso, -sa, *a.* tiny, pretty, (*U.S.*) cute.
piular, *v.i.* chirp.
pizarra, *n.f.* slate; shale; blackboard.
pizca, *n.f.* (*fam.*) whit, jot.
placa, *n.f.* plaque, plate.
placer (1), *n.m.* pleasure.—*v.t.* [23] please.
placer (2), *n.m.* sandbank, reef.
plácido, -da, *a.* placid.
plaga (1), *n.f.* plague, scourge.
plaga (2), *n.f.* (compass) point.
plagar [B], *v.t.* plague, infest.
plagiar, *v.t.* plagiarize; (*S.A.*) kidnap.
plagio, *n.m.* plagiarism; (*S.A.*) kidnapping.
plan, *n.m.* plan; plane; (*fam.*) date (*appointment*); ***en — grande,*** on a large scale.
plancha, *n.f.* (flat) iron; sheet (*of metal*); grill-plate; (*fam.*) blunder; gangplank; ***a la —,*** (*cul.*) grilled.
planchar, *v.t.* iron; press.
planeador, *n.m.* (*aer.*) glider.
planear, *v.t.* plane (*wood*).—*v.i.* glide.
planeo, *n.m.* (*aer.*) gliding.
planeta, *n.m.* planet.
planicie, *n.f.* plain.
planificación, *n.f.* planning.
planificar [A], *v.t.* plan.
plano, -na, *a.* plane, smooth, level.—*n.m.* plan; plane; ***de —,*** plainly.—*n.f.* trowel; flat country; ***plana mayor,*** (*mil.*) staff.
planta, *n.f.* (*bot.*) plant; sole (*of foot*); plan; floor plan; storey; stance.

plantar, *v.t.* plant; establish; (*fam.*) jilt.—*v.r.* adopt a stance; stand firm.
planteamiento, *n.m.* planning; framing (*a question*).
plantear, *v.t.* plan; pose (*a question*).
plantilla, *n.f.* insole; template; staff.
plantío, *n.m.* plantation.
plañir [K], *v.t.* lament.—*v.i.* grieve.
plasmar, *v.t.* mould.
plasta, *n.f.* paste, soft mass.
plástico, -ca, *a.* plastic.—*n.m.* plastic (*material*).—*n.f.* modelling.
plata, *n.f.* silver; plate; (*S.A.*) money.
plataforma, *n.f.* platform.
platanero, *n.m.* banana boat.
plátano, *n.m.* banana; plantain; plane tree.
platea, *n.f.* (*theat.*) orchestra stalls.
platear, *v.t.* plate with silver.
platero, *n.m.* silversmith.
plática, *n.f.* talk; chat.
platicar [A], *v.t.* talk over.—*v.i.* chat.
platija, *n.f.* (*ichth.*) plaice.
platillo, *n.m.* plate; saucer; — ***volante,*** flying saucer.
platino, *n.m.* platinum.
plato, *n.m.* dish; plate; course.
Platón, *n.m.* Plato; **platón,** *n.m.* large plate; (*S.A.*) washbowl.
platudo, -da, *a.* (*S.A.*) well-to-do.
plausibilidad, *n.f.* praiseworthiness.
plausible, *a.* praiseworthy, commendable.
playa, *n.f.* beach.
plaza, *n.f.* square, piazza; market place; fortified town; space; employment; (*taur.*) ring.
plazo, *n.m.* term, time; credit; ***comprar a plazos,*** buy on hire-purchase, (*U.S.*) buy on the instalment plan.
pleamar, *n.f.* high tide.
plebe, *n.f.* plebs.
plebeyo, -ya, *a., n.m.f.* plebeian.
plebiscito, *n.m.* plebiscite.
plegadamente, *adv.* confusedly.
plegadizo, -za, *a.* folding.
plegadura, *n.f.*, **plegamiento,** *n.m.* fold; pleat.
plegar [1B], *v.t.* fold; pleat; crease.—*v.r.* yield.
plegaria, *n.f.* prayer.
pleito, *n.m.* lawsuit; dispute; battle.
plenario, -ria, *a.* plenary.
plenilunio, *n.m.* full moon.
plenitud, *n.f.* plenitude.
pleno, -na, *a.* full.
pliego, *n.m.* sheet (*of paper*).
pliegue, *n.m.* fold, crease.
plomar, *v.t.* seal (*with lead*).
plomizo, -za, *a.* leaden.
plomo, *n.m.* lead (*metal*).
plugo [PLACER].
pluma, *n.f.* feather; pen; — ***estilográfica,*** fountain pen.
plumaje, *n.m.* plumage.
plumazo, *n.m.* feather bed.
plural, *a., n.m.* plural.
pluralidad, *n.f.* plurality; majority.
plus, *n.m.* bonus.
pluscuamperfecto, -ta, *a., n.m.* pluperfect.
plusmarca, *n.f.* (sporting) record.
población, *n.f.* population; town, village.
poblado, *n.m.* town, village.
poblar [4], *v.t.* people, populate; colonize, stock.—*v.i.* settle.
pobre, *a.* poor.—*n.m.f.* pauper.
pobrete, -ta, *a.* wretched.
pobreza, *n.f.* poverty.
pocilga, *n.f.* pigsty.
pócima, poción, *n.f.* potion.
poco, -ca, *a.* little.—*pl.* few.—*adv.* little, not at all; — ***a*** —, little by little.—*n.m.* little, bit.
pocho, -cha, *a.* discoloured; rotten; (*fam.*) off colour.
podagra, *n.f.* (*med.*) gout.
podar, *v.t.* prune.
podenco, *n.m.* hound.
poder, *n.m.* power; ***por poderes,*** by proxy.—*v.i.* [24] be able (*to*); can, could etc.; — ***con,*** master, overcome; ***no — menos de,*** not be able to help.
poderío, *n.m.* power, might.
poderoso, -sa, *a.* powerful.
podre, *n.m.* or *f.* pus.
podré [PODER].
podredumbre, *n.f.* corruption; rot.
podrido, -da, *a.* rotten; corrupt.
podrir [PUDRIR].
poema, *n.m.* poem.
poesía, *n.f.* poetry; poem.
poeta, *n.m.* poet.
poético, -ca, *a.* poetic(al).—*n.f.* poetics.
poetisa, *n.f.* poetess.
polaco, -ca, *a.* Polish.—*n.m.f.* Pole.
polaina, *n.f.* legging, puttee.
polea, *n.f.* pulley.
polen, *n.m.* pollen.
policía, *n.f.* police (force); cleanliness.—*n.m.* policeman.
policíaco, -ca, *a.* rel. to the police; detective (*story*).
policopiar, *v.t.* duplicate, cyclostyle.
Polichinela, *n.m.* Punch.
poliedro, *n.m.* polyhedron.
polifacético, -ca, *a.* versatile.
polifonía, *n.f.* polyphony.
poligamia, *n.f.* polygamy.
polígamo, -ma, *a.* polygamous.—*n.m.f.* polygamist.
polígloto, -ta, poligloto, -ta, *a., n.m.f.* polyglot.
polígono, *n.m.* polygon.
polilla, *n.f.* moth; book-worm.
polisón, *n.m.* bustle (*of a dress*).
politeísta, *a.* polytheistic.—*n.m.f.* polytheist.
político, -ca, *a.* political; -in-law; ***padre —,*** father-in-law.—*n.m.f.* politician.—*n.f.* politics; policy.
póliza, *n.f.* policy, contract.
polizón, *n.m.* tramp.
polizonte, *n.m.* (*pej.*) policeman, cop.
polo, *n.m.* pole; polo; Andalusian song.
Polonia, *n.f.* Poland.
poltrón, -rona, *a.* idle; easy.—*n.m.* coward.
poluto, -ta, *a.* dirty, filthy.
polvareda, *n.f.* cloud of dust.
polvera, *n.f.* powder compact.
polvo, *n.m.* dust; (*esp. pl.*) face powder; ***en —,*** powdered; ***hecho —,*** (*fam.*) worn out, exhausted.
pólvora, *n.f.* gunpowder; fireworks.
polvorear, *v.t.* powder.
polvoriento, -ta, *a.* dusty.
polvorizar [C], *v.t.* pulverize.
polvoroso, -sa, *a.* dusty.

pollo, *n.m.* chicken.
polluelo, -la, *n.m.f.* chick.
pomez, *n.m.* pumice.
pomo, *n.m.* pommel; knob.
pompa, *n.f.* pomp; bubble; bulge.
pomposidad, *n.f.* pomposity.
pomposo, -sa, *a.* pompous.
pómulo, *n.m.* cheekbone.
pon [PONER].
ponche, *n.m.* punch (*drink*).
poncho, -cha, *a.* lazy; careless.—*n.m.* poncho.
ponderación, *n.f.* weighing; exaggeration.
ponderar, *v.t.* ponder; exaggerate.
ponderoso, -sa, *a.* ponderous; circumspect.
ponedero, -ra, *a.* laying eggs.—*n.m.* nest-egg.
ponencia, *n.f.* report, paper.
ponente, *n.m.* referee, arbitrator.
poner [25], *v.t.* put, place, lay, set; take (*time*); make, turn; — ***alguien a hacer,*** set s.o. to do; — ***a uno de,*** set s.o. up as a. —*v.r.* set (*of stars*); put on (*dress*); become, get, turn; ***ponerse a hacer,*** set about doing; ***ponerse bien con,*** get in with.
pongo (1), *n.m.* orang-outang.
pongo (2), (*S.A.*) Indian servant; (*S.A.*) gully.
pongo (3) [PONER].
poniente, *n.m.* west; west wind.
ponleví, *n.m.* (*pl.* **-íes**) high heel; high-heeled shoe.
pontífice, *n.m.* pontiff, pontifex.
pontón, *n.m.* pontoon.
ponzoña, *n.f.* poison.
ponzoñoso, -sa, *a.* poisonous.
popa, *n.f.* stern, poop.
popar, *v.t.* scorn; fondle.
popelina, *n.f.* poplin.
populacho, *n.m.* populace, mob.
popular, *a.* popular, people's.
popularizar [C], *v.t.* popularize.
populoso, -sa, *a.* populous.
poquísimo, -ma, *a.* very little; very few.
poquito, -ta, *a.* very little.
por, *prep.* by; (in exchange) for; through; because of; — ***ciento,*** per cent; ***dos — dos,*** two times two; — ***la mañana,*** in the morning; — ***aquí,*** this way; — ***mayor,*** wholesale; ***estar — hacer,*** remain to be done; be about to do; be ready to do; ***¿ — qué?*** why?
porcelana, *n.f.* porcelain.
porcentaje, *n.m.* percentage.
porcino, -na, *a.* rel. to pigs; ***fiebre porcina,*** swine-fever.
porción, *n.f.* portion; lot; allotment.
porcuno, -na, *a.* hoggish.
porche, *n.m.* porch, portico.
pordiosear, *v.i.* go out begging.
pordiosero, -ra, *a.* begging.—*n.m.f.* beggar.
porfía, *n.f.* stubbornness; dispute.
porfiar, *v.i.* contend; persist, insist.
pormenor, *n.m.* detail, particular.
pormenorizar [C], *v.i.* particularize; give a detailed account.
pornografía, *n.f.* pornography.
poro, *n.m.* pore.
porosidad, *n.f.* porosity.
porque, *conj.* because.
porqué, *n.m.* reason why; (*fam.*) wherewithal.
porquería, *n.f.* filth; trifle.
porqueriza, *n.f.* pigsty.
porquer(iz)o, *n.m.* swineherd.
porqueta, *n.f.* woodlouse.
porra, *n.f.* club, bludgeon; (*fam.*) stupid person.
porrón, *n.m.* wine bottle with long spout.
porta, *n.f.* (*naut.*) porthole.
porta(a)viones, *n.m. inv.* aircraft carrier.
portada, *n.f.* porch, façade; title-page; frontispiece.
portador, -ra, *n.m.f.* carrier; bearer.
portaestandarte, *n.m.* standard-bearer.
portal, *n.m.* porch, portico; vestibule.
portalámparas, *n.m. inv.* lamp-holder, socket.
portalón, *n.m.* (*naut.*) gangway; gate.
portaminas, *n.m. inv.* propelling pencil.
portamonedas, *n.m. inv.* purse, (*U.S.*) pocket-book.
portañuela, *n.f.* fly (*of trousers*).
portaplumas, *n.m. inv.* pen-holder, pen.
portar, *v.r.* behave.
portátil, *a.* portable.
portavoz, *n.m.* (*pl.* **-oces**) megaphone; spokesman.
portazgo, *n.m.* toll.
portazo, *n.m.* slam (*of a door*).
porte, *n.m.* freight charge; postage; (*naut.*) tonnage; behaviour; nobility; (*S.A.*) birthday present.
portear, *v.t.* carry, transport.—*v.i.* slam.
portento, *n.m.* prodigy, wonder.
portentoso, -sa, *a.* prodigious, marvellous.
porteño, -ña, *a.* rel. to Buenos Aires.
potería, *n.f.* porter's lodge; (*sport*) goalposts.
portero, -ra, *n.m.f.* doorkeeper.—*n.m.* porter, janitor; (*sport*) goalkeeper.—*n.f.* concierge, janitress.
pórtico, *n.m.* portico.
portilla, *n.f.* (*naut.*) porthole.
portillo, *n.m.* gap, aperture; postern.
portuario, -ria, *a.* rel. to port *or* harbour.
Portugal, *n.m.* Portugal.
portugués, -guesa, *a.*, *n.m.f.* Portuguese.
porvenir, *n.m.* future.
en pos de, *adv. phr.* in pursuit of, after.
posada, *n.f.* inn, small hotel; lodging.
posadero, -ra, *n.m.f.* inn-keeper.—*n.f.* (*esp. pl.*) buttocks.
posar, *v.t.* rest (*a load*).—*v.i.* lodge; perch; pose.—*v.r.* settle (*of lees*); alight.
posdata, *n.f.* postscript.
poseer [N], *v.t.* possess, own; master (*a language*).
posesión, *n.f.* possession.
posesionar, *v.t.* give possession to.—*v.r.* take possession (**de,** of).
posesivo, -va, *a.*, *n.m.* possessive.
poseso, -sa, *a.* possessed.
posfechar, *v.t.* postdate.
posguerra, *n.f.* post-war period.
posibilidad, *n.f.* possibility.
posibilitar, *v.t.* render possible.
posible, *a.* possible.
posición, *n.f.* position, standing.
positivo, -va, *a.*, *n.m.* positive.—*n.f.* (*phot.*) positive.
poso, *n.m.* sediment; repose.
pospelo, *adv.* ***a —,*** against the grain.
posponer [25], *v.t.* subordinate; put off.
posta, *n.f.* post house; stage, relay.
postal, *a.* postal.—*n.f.* post-card.
poste, *n.m.* post, pole; ***dar — a,*** keep waiting.
postema, *n.f.* abscess.

postergar [B], *v.t.* postpone; pass over.
posteridad, *n.f.* posterity.
posterior, *a.* later; posterior, back, rear.
posterioridad, *n.f.* posteriority; ***con — a,*** subsequent to.
postguerra, *n.f.* post-war period.
postigo, *n.m.* postern, wicket.
postilla, *n.f.* scab.
postillón, *n.m.* postilion.
postizo, -za, *a.* false, artificial; detachable.—*n.m.* toupet, switch.
postor, *n.m.* bidder (*at an auction*).
postración, *n.f.* prostration.
postrar, *v.t.* prostrate.
postre, *a.* last; ***al*** or ***a la —,*** in the long run.—*n.m.* dessert.
postremo, -ma, postrero *&* **postrer, -ra, postrimero** *&* **postrimer, -ra,** *a.* last.
postulado, *n.m.* postulate.
postular, *v.t.* postulate; nominate.
póstumo, -ma, *a.* posthumous.
postura, *n.f.* posture; bet; laying; transplanting.
potable, *a.* potable, drinking (*water*).
potación, *n.f.* potation.
potaje, *n.m.* broth, soup: (*mixed*) brew; dried vegetables.
potasa, *n.f.* potash.
potasio, *n.m.* potassium.
pote, *n.m.* pot; flower-pot; ***a —,*** in abundance.
potencia, *n.f.* (*math., phys., pol.*) power.
potencial, *a., n.m.* potential.
potentado, *n.m.* potentate.
potente, *a.* potent, powerful.
potestad, *n.f.* power, dominion.
potra, *n.f.* filly; (*fam.*) hernia.
potro, *n.m.* foal; wooden horse.
pozal, *n.m.* pail, bucket.
pozo, *n.m.* well; deep hole; (*min.*) pit; (*naut.*) hold; ***— negro,*** cesspit.
práctica, *n.f.* practice; habit.
practicable, *a.* feasible.
practicante, *n.m.f.* medical assistant.
practicar [A], *v.t.* practise; cut (*a hole*).
práctico, -ca, *a.* practical.—*n.m.* practitioner; (*naut.*) pilot.
pradera, *n.f.* meadow; prairie.
prado, *n.m.* meadow, pasture; promenade.
pragmático, -ca, *a.* pragmatic(al).—*n.f.* decree, pragmatic.
pravedad, *n.f.* depravity.
pravo, -va, *a.* depraved.
precario, -ria, *a.* precarious.
precaución, *n.f.* precaution; vigilance.
precaver, *v.t.* prevent.—*v.r.* be on one's guard (***contra,*** against).
precedencia, *n.f.* precedence.
precedente, *a., n.m.* precedent.
preceder, *v.t., v.i.* precede.
precepto, *n.m.* precept.
preceptor, -ra, *n.m.f.* teacher.
preces, *n.f.pl.* prayers.
preciar, *v.t.* estimate.—*v.r.* boast (***de,*** of).
precintar, *v.t.* strap; seal.
precinto, *n.m.* strapping; seal.
precio, *n.m.* price; esteem.
preciosidad, *n.f.* value, preciousness; (*fam.*) beautiful thing.
precioso, -a, *a.* precious; (*fam.*) lovely.
precipicio, *n.m.* precipice.
precipitar, *v.t.* precipitate.—*v.r.* hurry.
precipitoso, -sa, *a.* precipitous; rash.
precisamente, *adv.* precisely; just so.
precisar, *v.t.* specify; need; oblige (***a,*** to).—*v.i.* be necessary *or* urgent.
precisión, *n.f.* need; obligation; precision.
preciso, -sa, *a.* necessary; precise.
preclaro, -ra, *a.* illustrious.
precocidad, *n.f.* precociousness, precocity.
preconizar [C], *v.t.* proclaim; praise.
precoz, *a.* (*pl.* **-oces**) precocious.
predecir [17], *v.t.* predict, forecast.
predicción, *n.f.* prediction.
predilección, *n.f.* predilection.
predilecto, -ta, *a.* favourite.
predio, *n.m.* landed property.
predominar, *v.t.* predominate; overlook; prevail.
predominio, *n.m.* superiority; predominance.
preeminente, *a.* pre-eminent.
prefacio, *n.m.* preface.
prefecto, *n.m.* prefect.
preferente, *a.* preferential; preferable.
preferir [6], *v.t.* prefer.
prefijo, *n.m.* (*gram.*) prefix.
pregón, *n.m.* proclamation (*by crier*).
pregonar, *v.t.* proclaim.
pregonero, *n.m.* town-crier; auctioneer.
pregunta, *n.f.* question.
preguntar, *v.t.* ask.—*v.i.* ask, enquire (***por,*** after).—*v.r.* wonder.
prejuicio, *n.m.* prejudice.
prelado, *n.m.* prelate.
preliminar, *a.* preliminary.
preludio, *n.m.* prelude.
prematuro, -ra, *a.* premature.
premeditar, *v.t.* premeditate.
premiar, *v.t.* reward, award a prize to.
premio, *n.m.* prize.
premioso, -sa, *a.* tight; constricting.
premisa, *n.f.* premise.
premura, *n.f.* pressure, urgency.
prenda, *n.f.* pledge; token; garment; article of jewelry; loved one; (*esp. pl.*) talent.
prendar, *v.t.* pawn; charm.—*v.r.* take a fancy (***de,*** to).
prender, *v.t.* seize; pin; capture.—*v.i.* catch on; take root.—*v.r.* dress up.
prensa, *n.f.* press.
prensar, *v.t.* press.
preñado, -da, *a.* pregnant.
preñez, *n.f.* pregnancy.
preocupación, *n.f.* preoccupation; worry; prejudice.
preocupado, -da, *a.* preoccupied; prejudiced.
preocupar, *v.t.* preoccupy.—*v.r.* be worried (***con, por,*** about); be preoccupied; be prejudiced.
preparación, *n.f.* preparation.
preparado, -da, *a.* prepared.—*n.m.* preparation.
preparar, *v.t.* prepare.
preparativo, -va, *a.* preparative.—*n.m.* preparation.
preparatorio, -ria, *a.* preparatory.
preponderancia, *n.f.* preponderance.
preponderante, *a.* preponderant.
preponderar, *v.i.* prevail.
preponer [25], *v.t.* put before, prefer.
preposición, *n.f.* preposition.
preposicional, *a.* prepositional.
prepotente, *a.* very powerful.
prepucio, *n.m.* foreskin, prepuce.
prepuesto [PREPONER].

presa, *n.f.* seizure; prey; dam; claw; — ***de caldo,*** broth.
presbítero, *n.m.* presbyter, priest.
presciencia, *n.f.* prescience, foreknowledge.
prescindible, *a.* dispensable.
prescindir, *v.i.* dispense (***de,*** with).
prescribir [*p.p.* **prescrito**], *v.t., v.i.* prescribe; acquire prescriptive rights over.
prescripción, *n.f.* prescription.
prescripto [PRESCRITO].
presencia, *n.f.* presence; physique.
presenciar, *v.t.* witness.
presentación, *n.f.* presentation.
presentar, *v.t.* present; offer.—*v.r.* offer one's services.
presente, *a.* present, actual, current.—*n.m.* present, gift.
presentemente, *adv.* at present.
presentimiento, *n.m.* presentiment.
presentir [6], *v.t.* have a presentiment of.
preservar, *v.t.* save, guard.
presidencia, *n.f.* presidency; president's residence.
presidente, *n.m.* president; chairman.
presidiario, *n.m.* convict.
presidio, *n.m.* garrison; prison; praesidium.
presidir, *v.t.* preside.
presilla, *n.f.* loop, clip.
presión, *n.f.* pressure.
preso, -sa, *a.* imprisoned.—*n.m.f.* prisoner.
prestación, *n.f.* loan.
prestado, -da, *p.p.* lent; ***dar*** —, lend; ***pedir*** —, borrow.
prestamista, *n.m.f.* money-lender; pawnbroker.
préstamo, *n.m.* loan.
prestar, *v.t.* lend, loan.
presteza, *n.f.* quickness.
prestidigitación, *n.f.* juggling.
prestigiador, -ra, *a.* fascinating; prestige-winning.—*n.m.f.* imposter.
prestigio, *n.m.* prestige; juggling; fascination.
prestigioso, -sa, *a.* spell-binding; renowned.
presto, -ta, *a.* quick; ready.—*adv.* quickly.
presumir, *v.t.* presume.—*v.i.* presume, boast (***de,*** of being).
presunción, *n.f.* presumption.
presuntivo, -va, *a.* presumptive.
presunto, -ta, *a.* presumed, presumptive.
presuntuoso, -sa, *a.* presumptuous.
presuponer [25], *v.t.* presuppose.
presupuesto, *n.m.* motive, pretext; budget, estimate.
presuroso, -sa, *a.* hasty; quick.
pretender, *v.t.* pretend to; claim to; try for.
pretendiente, *n.m.f.* claimant.—*n.m.* suitor.
pretérito, -ta, *a.* past.—*n.m.* (*gram.*) preterit(e).
pretextar, *v.t.* give as a pretext.
pretexto, *n.m.* pretext.
pretil, *n.m.* breastwork, railing.
prevalecer [9], *v.i.* prevail (***sobre,*** against); take root.
prevaler [35], *v.i.* prevail.—*v.r.* take advantage (***de,*** of).
prevaricar [A], *v.i.* play false; prevaricate.
prevención, *n.f.* foresight; warning; preparation; guard-room.
prevenir [36], *v.t.* prepare; forestall; warn.
prever [37], *v.t.* foresee.
previo, -via, *a.* previous.
previsible, *a.* foreseeable.
previsión, *n.f.* prevision, foresight; — ***del tiempo,*** weather forecasting.
previsor, -ra, *a.* provident.
previsto [PREVER].
prez, *n.m.* or *f.* honour, fame.
prieto, -ta, *a.* black; tight.
primacía, *n.f.* primacy.
primado, *n.m.* (*eccl.*) primate.
primario, -ria, *a.* primary.
primate, *n.m.* (*zool.*) primate; worthy.
primavera, *n.f.* spring; (*bot.*) primrose.
primaveral, *a.* rel. to spring.
primer [PRIMERO].
primerizo, -za, *a.* first; firstling.
primero, primer, -ra, *a.* first; prime; raw (*materials*).—*adv.* at first.
primicia, *n.f.* (*esp. pl.*) first fruits.
primitivo, -va, *a.* primitive.
primo, -ma (1), *a.* prime; raw (*materials*).
primo, -ma (2), *n.m.f.* cousin.
primogénito, -ta, *a.* first-born.
primor, *n.m.* elegance; care; skill.
primoroso, -sa, *a.* exquisite; elegant; careful.
princesa, *n.f.* princess.
principado, *n.m.* principality.
principal, *a.* principal, main; notable.—*n.m.* chief, head; main floor, first (***U.S.*** second) floor.
principalidad, *n.f.* nobility.
príncipe, *n.m.* prince.
principiante, -ta, *n.m.f.* beginner.
principiar, *v.t.* begin.
principio, *n.m.* beginning; principle.
pringar [B], *v.t.* dip in grease; meddle.
pringoso, -sa, *a.* greasy.
pringue, *n.m.* or *f.* grease; grease-spot; greasiness.
prior, *a., n.m.* prior.
priora, *n.f.* prioress.
prioridad, *n.f.* priority.
prisa, *n.f.* hurry; speed; ***de*** —, in a hurry; ***darse*** —, hurry; ***tener*** —, be in a hurry.
prisión, *n.f.* seizure; imprisonment.—*pl.* shackles.
prisionero, *n.m.* (*mil.*) prisoner.
prisma, *n.m.* prism.
prístino, -na, *a.* pristine.
privado, -da, *a.* private.—*n.m.* (court-) favourite.—*n.f.* privy.
privanza, *n.f.* favour (*at court*).
privar, *v.t.* deprive; forbid.—*v.i.* be in favour. —*v.r.* deprive oneself (***de,*** of).
privativo, -va, *a.* private; peculiar.
privilegio, *n.m.* privilege; patent.
pro, *n.m.* or *f.* advantage.
proa, *n.f.* bow, prow.
probabilidad, *n.f.* probability.
probable, *a.* probable; provable.
probación, *n.f.* probation.
probanza, *n.f.* proof.
probar [4], *v.t.* try; examine, test; sample; prove.—*v.i.* taste.—*v.r.* try on (*clothes*).
probeta, *n.f.* test specimen; test-glass; pressure gauge.
problema, *n.m.* problem.
probo, -ba, *a.* honest.
procaz, *a.* (*pl.* **-aces**) impudent; bold.
procedencia, *n.f.* origin.
procedente, *a.* originating, coming (***de,*** from).
proceder (1), *n.m.* conduct.
proceder (2), *v.i.* proceed; originate; behave.
procedimiento, *n.m.* proceeding; procedure.

prócer, *a.* lofty.—*n.m.* dignitary.
procesión, *n.f.* procession (*esp. eccl.*).
proceso, *n.m.* law-suit; (*S.A.*) — ***verbal,*** report.
proclamación, *n.f.* proclamation.
proclamar, *v.t.* proclaim; acclaim.
proclive, *a.* inclined.
procreación, *n.f.* procreation.
procrear, *v.t.* procreate.
procuración, *n.f.* careful management; power of attorney.
procurador, *n.m.* solicitor, attorney; proxy.
procurar, *v.t.* strive for; manage.
prodición, *n.f.* treachery.
prodigalidad, *n.f.* prodigality.
prodigar [B], *v.t.* squander.
prodigio, *n.m.* prodigy; portent.
prodigioso, -sa, *a.* prodigious.
pródigo, -ga, *a.* prodigal; lavish.
producción, *n.f.* production.
producir [16], *v.t.* produce.
producto, *n.m.* product.
proemio, *n.m.* introduction, proem.
proeza, *n.f.* prowess.
profanar, *v.t.* profane.
profano, -na, *a.* profane.
profecía, *n.f.* prophecy.
proferir [6], *v.t.* utter.
profesar, *v.t.* profess.
profesión, *n.f.* profession.
profesional, *a.* professional.
profeso, -sa, *a., n.m.f.* (*eccl.*) professed.
profesor, -ra, *n.m.f.* teacher; professor.
profeta, *n.m.* prophet.
profetisa, *n.f.* prophetess.
profetizar [C], *v.t., v.i.* prophesy.
profundidad, *n.f.* profundity; depth.
profundo, -da, *a.* profound; deep.
profusión, *n.f.* profusion.
profuso, -sa, *a.* profuse.
prognosis, *n.f. inv.* prognosis; forecast (*esp.* weather-).
programa, *n.m.* programme; plan.
progresar, *v.i.* progress.
progreso, *n.m.* progress.
prohibir, *v.t.* prohibit.
prohijar, *v.t.* adopt.
prohombre, *n.m.* top man; (*fam.*) big shot.
prójimo, *n.m.* neighbour, fellow man.
prole, *n.f.* progeny, offspring.
proletariado, *n.m.* proletariat.
proletario, -ria, *a.* proletarian.
prolijo, -ja, *a.* prolix.
prólogo, *n.m.* prologue.
prolongar [B], *v.t.* prolong.—*v.r.* extend.
promediar, *v.t.* average.
promedio, *n.m.* average, mean.
promesa, *n.f.* promise.
prometer, *v.t., v.i.* promise.
prometido, -da, *a.* engaged.—*n.m.* fiancé.—*n.f.* fiancée.
prominente, *a.* prominent.
promiscuidad, *n.f.* promiscuity.
promiscuo, -cua, *a.* promiscuous; indiscriminate.
promisión, *n.f.* promise; ***tierra de —,*** promised land.
promoción, *n.f.* promotion; graduation, class.
promontorio, *n.m.* promontory.
promover [5], *v.t.* promote.
promulgar [B], *v.t.* promulgate.
pronombre, *n.m.* pronoun.
pronóstico, *n.m.* prognosis; forecast.
pronto, -ta, *a.* quick; ready; prompt.—*adv.* quickly; soon.
pronunciación, *n.f.* pronunciation.
pronunciamiento, *n.m.* insurrection; decree.
pronunciar, *v.t.* pronounce.—*v.r.* rebel.
propaganda, *n.f.* propaganda; advertising.
propagar [B], *v.t.* propagate, spread.
propender, *v.i.* be inclined.
propiciar, *v.t.* propiate.
propicio, -cia, *a.* propitious.
propiedad, *n.f.* property; ownership.
propietario, -ria, *n.m.* proprietor.—*n.f.* proprietress.
propina, *n.f.* tip.
propinar, *v.t.* treat.
propio, -pia, *a.* proper; peculiar; same; own.
proponer [25], *v.t.* propose; propound.
proporción, *n.f.* proportion.
proporcionar, *v.t.* proportion; furnish, supply.
proposición, *n.f.* proposition.
propósito, *n.m.* aim; intention; subject-matter.
propuesta, *n.f.* proposal.
propuesto [PROPONER].
propulsar, *v.t.* propel.
propulsión, *n.f.* propulsion; ***— a chorro,*** jet propulsion.
propulsor, -ra, *a.* propellent.
prorrumpir, *v.i.* burst forth.
prosa, *n.f.* prose.
prosaico, -ca, *a.* prosaic.
prosapia, *n.f.* ancestry.
proscribir [*p.p.* **proscrito**], *v.t.* proscribe.
proscripción, *n.f.* proscription, outlawing.
proscrito, -ta, *p.p.* [PROSCRIBIR].—*n.m.f.* exile; outlaw.
proseguir [8G], *v.t., v.i.* continue.
prosélito, *n.m.* proselyte.
prosificar [A], *v.t.* turn poetry into prose.
prosista, *n.m.f.* prose-writer.
prosodia, *n.f.* prosody.
prospecto, *n.m.* prospectus.
prosperar, *v.t., v.i.* prosper.
prosperidad, *n.f.* prosperity.
próspero, -ra, *a.* prosperous.
próstata, *n.f.* (*anat.*) prostate gland.
prosternar, *v.r.* prostrate oneself.
prostitución, *n.f.* prostitution.
prostituir [O], *v.t.* prostitute.
prostituta, *n.f.* prostitute.
protagonista, *n.m.f.* protagonist.
protección, *n.f.* protection.
protector, -ra *or* **-triz** (*pl.* **-trices**), *a.* protective.—*n.m.* protector.—*n.f.* protectress.
protectorado, *n.m.* protectorate.
proteger [E], *v.t.* protect.
protegido, -da, *n.m.f.* protegé(e).
proteína, *n.f.* protein.
protesta, *n.f.* protest.
protestante, *a.* protesting; Protestant.—*n.m.f.* Protestant.
protestantismo, *n.m.* Protestantism.
protestar, *v.t.* protest; asseverate.—*v.i.* protest.
protesto, *n.m.* (*com.*) protest.
protocolo, *n.m.* protocol.
protón, *n.m.* (*phys.*) proton.
prototipo, *n.m.* prototype.
protuberancia, *n.f.* protuberance.
provecho, *n.m.* advantage; benefit.

provechoso, -sa, *a.* advantageous.
proveedor, -ra, *n.m.f.* supplier.
proveer [N, *p.p.* **provisto**], *v.t.* provide (*a,* for *de,* with).
proveimiento, *n.m.* provisioning.
provenir [36], *v.i.* come; originate.
Provenza, *n.f.* Provence.
provenzal, *a., n.m.f.* Provençal.
proverbio, *n.m.* proverb.
providencia, *n.f.* providence.
providencial, *a.* providential.
providente, *a.* provident.
provincia, *n.f.* province.
provincial, *a., n.m.f.* provincial.
provisión, *n.f.* provision.
provisto [PROVEER].
provocación, *n.f.* provocation.
provocante, *a.* provocative.
provocar [A], *v.t.* provoke.
proximidad, *n.f.* proximity.
próximo, -ma, *a.* next; near.
proyección, *n.f.* projection.
proyectar, *v.t.* project, cast.
proyectil, *n.m.* projectile, missile; — ***dirigido,*** guided missile; — ***autodirigido,*** homing missile.
proyecto, *n.m.* project, plan; — ***de ley,*** bill.
proyector, *n.m.* projector; searchlight.
prudencia, *n.f.* prudence.
prudente, *a.* prudent.
prueba, *n.f.* proof; sample; test; ***a* —,** on approval; ***a* — *de,*** proof against.
prurito, *n.m.* itch.
Prusia, *n.f.* Prussia.
prúsico, -ca, *a.* prussic.
pseudónimo, *n.m.* pseudonym.
psicoanálisis, *n.m.* or *f.* psychoanalysis.
psicoanalizar [C], *v.t.* psychoanalyze.
psicología, *n.f.* psychology.
psicológico, -ca, *a.* psychological.
psicólogo, *n.m.* psychologist.
psicópata, *n.m.f.* psychopath.
psicosis, *n.f. inv.* psychosis.
psique, *n.f.* cheval glass; psyche.
psiquiatra, psiquíatra, *n.m.f.* psychiatrist.
psiquiatría, *n.f.* psychiatry.
psíquico, -ca, *a.* psychic.
púa, *n.f.* point; prick; tooth (*of comb*); barb.
púbico, -ca, *a.* pubic.
publicación, *n.f.* publication.
publicar [A], *v.t.* publish.
publicidad, *n.f.* publicity; advertising.
publicitario, -ria, *a.* rel. to advertising.
público, -ca, *a., n.m.* public.
puchero, *n.m.* pot; kettle; stew.—*pl.* pouting.
pude [PODER].
pudibundo, -da, *a.* modest; shy.
pudor, *n.m.* modesty.
pudrimiento, *n.m.* rotting.
pudrir [*var. p.p.* **podrido**], *v.t., v.r.* rot.
pueblo, *n.m.* people; town, village.
puente, *n.m.* bridge; deck.
puerco, -ca, *a.* filthy.—*n.m.* hog; — ***espín,*** porcupine.—*n.f.* sow; wood-louse; slug.
pueril, *a.* puerile; childish.
puerro, *n.m.* leek.
puerta, *n.f.* door; gate; (*sport*) goal (*posts*).
puerto, *n.m.* port, harbour.
puertorriqueño, -ña, *a., n.m.f.* Puerto Rican.
pues, *adv.* then, well; yes.—*conj.* for; since; because.—*interj.* well, then!
puesta, *n.f.* stake (*at cards*); setting (*of sun*).
puesto (1) [PONER].
puesto (2), *n.m.* shop, stall; post, employment.
puf (1), *n.m.* pouffe.
¡puf! (2), *interj.* ugh!
pugilato, *n.m.* pugilism, boxing.
pugna, *n.f.* fight, battle; struggle.
pugnar, *v.t.* fight; struggle.
pugnaz, *a.* (*pl.* **-aces**) pugnacious.
pujante, *a.* powerful, puissant.
pujanza, *n.f.* might.
pujar, *v.t.* push ahead.—*v.i.* falter; grope; bid.
pulcritud, *n.f.* neatness, tidiness.
pulcro, -ra, *a.* neat; trim; beautiful.
pulga, *n.f.* flea.
pulgada, *n.f.* inch.
pulgar, *n.m.* thumb.
pulidez, *n.f.* cleanliness; neatness.
pulido, -da, *a.* clean; neat; pretty.
pulir, *v.t.* polish.
pulmón, *n.m.* lung.
pulmonía, *n.f.* pneumonia.
pulpa, *n.f.* pulp.
pulpejo, *n.m.* soft part (*of thumb etc.*).
pulpería, *n.f.* (*S.A.*) grocery store.
púlpito, *n.m.* pulpit.
pulpo, *n.m.* octopus.
pulsación, *n.f.* pulsation.
pulsador, -ra, *a.* pulsating.—*n.m.* push-button.
pulsar, *v.t.* touch lightly; feel the pulse of.—*v.i.* puls(at)e.
pulsera, *n.f.* bracelet; watch-strap.
pulso, *n.m.* pulse; tact.
pulular, *v.i.* pullulate.
pulverizar [C], *v.t.* pulverize.
pulla, *n.f.* cutting *or* obscene remark; innuendo.
¡pum! *interj.* bang!
puma, *n.f.* puma, cougar, panther.
pundonor, *n.m.* point of honour.
pungir [E], *v.t.* prick; sting.
punible, *a.* punishable.
punitivo, -va, *a.* punitive.
punta, *n.f.* point, tip; nail; apex; promontory; tartness; ***de* —,** on tiptoe.
puntada, *n.f.* stitch.
puntapié, *n.m.* kick.
puntear, *v.t.* dot; play (*the guitar*); stitch.—*v.i.* (*naut.*) tack.
puntero, -ra, *a.* sharpshooting.—*n.m.* pointer, hand; chisel.—*n.f.* toe-cap.
puntilla, *n.f.* brad; ***de*** or ***en puntillas,*** on tiptoe.
puntillero, *n.m.* (*taur.*) puntillero, dagger man.
puntillo, *n.m.* small point *or* dot; punctilio.
puntilloso, -sa, *a.* punctilious.
punto, *n.m.* point; dot; full stop, (*U.S.*) period; stitch; — ***y coma,*** semi-colon; — ***muerto,*** (*auto.*) neutral (*gear*); (*pol.*) deadlock; ***dos puntos,*** colon.
puntuación, *n.f.* punctuation; (*educ.*) mark; score.
puntual, *a.* punctual; reliable, certain.
puntualidad, *n.f.* punctuality.
puntuar [M], *v.t., v.i.* punctuate.
puntuoso, -sa, *a.* punctilious.
punzada, *n.f.* prick, sudden pain.
punzante, *a.* pricking; sharp.

punzar [C], *v.t.* prick; punch, bore.—*v.i.* sting.
puñada, *n.f.* punch.
puñal, *n.m.* dagger.
puñalada, *n.f.* stab.
puño, *n.m.* fist; grasp; handful.
pupa, *n.f.* pimple; (*fam.*) hurt.
pupilaje, *n.m.* wardship; board and lodging.
pupilo, -la, *n.m.f.* boarder; ward; pupil.—*n.f.* (*anat.*) pupil.
pupitre, *n.m.* desk.
puré, *n.m.* purée; — ***de patatas,*** mashed potatoes.
pureza, *n.f.* purity.
purga, *n.f.* purge; drainage valve.
purgante, *a.*, *n.m.* purgative.
purgar [B], *v.t.* purge; drain; expiate.—*v.i.* drain; atone.
purgatorio, *n.m.* purgatory.
puridad, *n.f.* purity; secrecy.
purificar [A], *v.t.* purify.
púrpura, *n.f.* purple.
puro, -ra, *a.* pure; sheer.—*n.m.* cigar.
purpurado, -da, purpúreo, -rea, *a.* purple.
purulento, -ta, *a.* purulent.
pus (1), *a.* (*S.A.*) puce.
pus (2), *n.m.* pus.
puse [PONER].
pusilánime, *a.* pusillanimous.
pústula, *n.f.* pustule.
puta, *n.f.* whore, harlot.
putativo, -va, *a.* putative; spurious.
putrefacción, *n.f.* putrefaction.
pútrido, -da, *a.* putrid.
puya, *n.f.* goad.
puyazo, *n.m.* jab.

Q

Q, q, *n.f.* twentieth letter of the Spanish alphabet.
que, *rel. pron.* that, which; who, whom; ***el —,*** that, the one that, he who *etc.*—*adv.* than.—*conj.* that; for.
¿ qué ? *interrog. pron.* what ? which ? ***¿— más da?*** what does it matter ? ***¿ y —?*** so what ?
¡qué! *pron.* what! what a! how! ***¡ — de . . . !*** how much *or* many! what a lot of. . . .!
quebracho, *n.m.* (*bot.*) quebracho.
quebrada, *n.f.* ravine; (*com.*) failure.
quebradero de cabeza, *n.m.* worry, big problem.
quebradizo, -za, *a.* brittle; frail.
quebradura, *n.f.* break; rupture.
quebrajar, *v.t.* split, crack.
quebrantamiento, *n.m.* breaking; break; rupture; fatigue.
quebrantar, *v.t.* crack; break; break open; break out of; crush; diminish; exhaust.—*v.r.* break, get broken.
quebranto, *n.m.* breaking; break; grief; collapse.
quebrar [1], *v.t.* break, smash; crush; break down.—*v.i.* break; collapse; fail.—*v.r.* break; weaken.

quechua [QUICHUA].
queda, *n.f.* curfew.
quedada, *n.f.* stay.
quedar, *v.i.* stay, remain; be left; be; turn out; — ***en,*** agree on *or* to; ***queda por hacer,*** it remains to be done.—*v.r.* stay; ***quedarse con,*** keep.
quedito, *adv.* gently, quietly.
quedo, -da, *a.* still.—*adv.* quietly, gently.
quehacer, *n.m.* task, job.
queja, *n.f.* complaint; moan.
quejar, *v.r.* complain (**de,** of, about); moan.
quejicoso, -sa, *a.* complaining, moaning.
quejido, *n.m.* complaint; groan.
quejoso, -sa, *a.* complaining.
quejumbre, *n.f.* moan.
quejumbroso, -sa, *a.* moaning.
quema, *n.f.* burning; fire; (*fig.*) danger.
quemado, *n.m.* fire, burning.
quemadura, *n.f.* burn; scald; (*agr.*) blight.
quemante, *a.* burning.
quemar, *v.t.* burn; scorch; blight; sell cheaply.—*v.i.* burn; be hot.—*v.r.* burn, be on fire; fret; be warm (*in search*); ***a quema ropa,*** point blank.
quemazón, *n.f.* burning; smarting; itch; (*fam.*) anger; (*fam.*) cutting remark.
quepo [CABER].
querella, *n.f.* complaint; plaint.
querellado, -da, *n.m.f.* (*jur.*) defendant.
querellante, *n.m.f.* (*jur.*) plaintiff.
querellar, *v.r.* complain.
querelloso, -sa, *a.* querulous.
querencia, *n.f.* homing instinct; fondness; haunt.
querer [26], *v.t.* love; want, wish; like.—*v.i.* be willing; be about to; — ***más,*** prefer; ***como quiera,*** anyhow; ***como quiera que,*** whereas; ***cuando quiera,*** any time; ***donde quiera,*** anywhere; ***sin —,*** unwillingly; unintentionally.—*n.m.* love; fondness.
querido, -da, *a.* dear.—*n.m.* lover.—*n.f.* mistress.
queso, *n.m.* cheese.
quetzal, *n.m.* (*orn.*) quetzal.
quevedos, *n.m.pl.* pince-nez.
¡quia! *interj.* (*fam.*) not on your life!
quicial, *n.m.* side-post.
quicio, *n.m.* hook-hinge.
quichua, *a.*, *n.m.f.* Quechua.
quid, *n.m.* gist, main point.
quídam, *n.m.* (*fam.*) who's-it, what's his name; (*fam.*) a nonentity.
quiebra, *n.f.* break; crack; damage; (*com.*) failure, bankruptcy.
quiebro, -bras *etc.* [QUEBRAR].
quien, *rel. pron. sg.* who; whom; he who *etc.*, whoever.
¿ quién ? *interrog. pron.* who ? whom ? whoever ?
quienquiera, *pron.* anybody.—*rel. pron.* whoever.
quiero [QUERER].
quieto, -ta, *a.* still; orderly.
quietud, *n.f.* calm, peace.
quijada, *n.f.* jaw, jawbone.
quijotada, *n.f.* quixotic enterprise.
quijote, *n.m.* Quixote; cuisse; croup.
quijotería, *n.f.* quixotry.
quijotesco, -ca, *a.* quixotic.
quijotismo, *n.m.* quixotism.

quilate, *n.m.* carat; (*fam.*) tiny bit.
quilo- [KILO-].
quilla, *n.f.* keel; breastbone (*of birds*).
quimera, *n.f.* chimera; quarrel.
quimérico, -ca, *a.* chimerical.
quimerista, *n.m.f.* visionary; brawler.
químico, -ca, *a.* chemical; ***productos químicos,*** chemicals.—*n.m.f.* chemist.—*n.f.* chemistry.
quimono, *n.m.* kimono.
quina, *n.f.* Peruvian bark.
quincalla, *n.f.* hardware.
quince, *a., n.m.* fifteen.
quincena, *n.f.* fortnight.
quincenal, *a.* fortnightly.
quinceno, -na, *a., n.m.* fifteenth.
quincuagésima, *n.f.* Quinquagesima.
quingentésimo, -ma, *a.* five-hundredth.
quinientos, -tas, *a., n.m.* five hundred.
quinina, *n.f.* quinine.
quinqué, *n.m.* paraffin lamp; (*fam.*) nous.
quinquenio, *n.m.* quinquennium.
quinta, *n.f.* villa; (*mil.*) draft.
quintacolumnista, *a., n.m.f.* fifth-columnist.
quintaesencia, *n.f.* quintessence.
quintaesenciar, *v.t.* purify.
quintal, *n.m.* hundred-weight (46 *kg.*); ***— métrico,*** 100 kg.
quintar, *v.t.* (*mil.*) draft.
quinteto, *n.m.* quintet.
quintilla, *n.f.* five-lined stanza.
quintillizo, -za, *n.m.f.* quintuplet.
Quintín, *n.m.* Quentin; ***armar la de San —,*** raise a shindy.
quinto, -ta, *a., n.m.f.* fifth.—*n.m.* (*mil.*) conscript; piece of land.
quintuplicar [A], *v.t.* quintuple.
quíntuplo, -la, *a.* fivefold.
quinzavo, -va, *a., n.m.f.* fifteenth.
quiñón, *n.m.* share, portion.
quiñonero, *n.m.* part-owner.
quiosco, *n.m.* kiosk, stand.
quirófano, *n.m.* operating theatre.
quiropodista, *n.m.f.* chiropodist.
quirúrgico, -ca, *a.* surgical.
quise [QUERER].
quisicosa, *n.f.* (*fam.*) stumper, puzzle.
quisquilla, *n.f.* quibble; (*ichth.*) shrimp.
quisquilloso, -sa, *a.* quibbling; touchy.
quiste, *n.m.* cyst.
quisto, -ta, *a.* loved; ***bien —,*** well-liked; ***mal —,*** disliked, unpopular.
quita, *n.f.* (*jur.*) acquittance, discharge.
quitación, *n.f.* salary; (*jur.*) acquittance.
quitamanchas, *n.m. inv.* spot-remover.
quitamiedos, *n.m. inv.* handrail.
quitanieve, *n.m.* snow-plough.
quitanza, *n.f.* (*jur., com.*) quittance.
quitapesares, *n.m. inv.* (*fam.*) comfort; cheering-up; trip.
quitar, *v.t.* take away, remove; save from (*work etc.*); free; parry.—*v.r.* take off (*clothes*); clear off, go away; abstain; get rid of; ***de quita y pon,*** detachable; ***quitarse de encima,*** get rid of, do away with.
quitasol, *n.m.* parasol.
quitasueño, *n.m.* (*fam.*) nagging worry.
quite, *n.m.* hindrance; parry; dodge; (*taur.*) drawing bull away from man in danger.
quito, -ta, *a.* free, exempt; quits.
quizá(s), *adv.* perhaps.
quórum, *n.m. inv.* quorum.

R

R, r, *n.f.* twenty-first letter of the Spanish alphabet.
rábano, *n.m.* radish.
rabear, *v.i.* wag the tail.
rabel, *n.m.* (*mus.*) rebec; (*joc.*) sit-upon.
rabera, *n.f.* tail-end; remains.
rabí, *n.m.* (*pl.* **-íes**) rabbi.
rabia, *n.f.* rage, fury; (*med.*) rabies.
rabiar, *v.i.* rave, rage; long (***por,*** for).
rábido, -da, *a.* rabid.
rabieta, *n.f.* (*fam.*) tantrum.
rabillo, *n.m.* stem; mildew; corner (*of eye*).
rabínico, -ca, *a.* rabbinic(al).
rabino, *n.m.* rabbi.
rabioles, rabiolos, *n.m.pl.* ravioli.
rabioso, -sa, *a.* rabid, furious, wild.
rabo, *n.m.* tail; corner (*of eye*); stalk.
rabosear, *v.t.* fray.
raboso, -sa, *a.* frayed, tattered.
racial, *a.* racial.
racimo, *n.m.* bunch (*of grapes*); cluster.
raciocinio, *n.m.* reason; argument.
ración, *n.f.* portion; allowance; pittance; ration; (*eccl.*) prebend.
racional, *a., n.m.* rational.
racionalidad, *n.f.* rationality.
racionalismo, *n.m.* rationalism.
racionalista, *a., n.m.f.* rationalist.
racionamiento, *n.m.* rationing.
racionar, *v.t.* ration.
racismo, *n.m.* racism, racialism.
racista, *a., n.m.f.* racist, racialist.
racha, *n.f.* gust; run of luck; split; big splinter.
radar, *n.m.* radar
radiación, *n.f.* radiation.
radiactividad, *n.f.* radioactivity.
radiactivo, -va, *a.* radioactive.
radiador, *n.m.* radiator.
radial, *a.* radial.
radiante, *a.* radiant.
radiar, *v.t.* broadcast.—*v.t., v.i.* radiate.
radicación, *n.f.* rooting; situation; established practice.
radical, *a., n.m.f.* radical.
radicalismo, *n.m.* radicalism.
radicar [A], *v.i., v.r.* take root; be situated; settle.
radio, *n.m.* radius; spoke; edge; radium.—*n.f.* radio.
radioact- [RADIACT-].
radioaficionado, -da, *n.m.f.* radio fan, (*fam.*) ham.
radiodifundir, *v.t., v.i.* broadcast.
radiodifusión, *n.f.* broadcasting.
radioemisora, *n.f.* broadcasting station.
radioescucha, *n.m.f.* listener.
radiografía, *n.f.* radiography; X-ray (photograph).
radiografiar, *v.t.* X-ray.
radiogramófono, *n.m.* radiogram.
radioisótopo, *n.m.* radio-isotope.
radiología, *n.f.* radiology.
radiólogo, -ga, *n.m.f.* radiologist.
radio(o)nda, *n.f.* radio-wave.
radiopertubación, *n.f.* (*rad.*) jamming.
radiorreceptor, *n.m.* wireless receiver.

radioso, -sa, *a.* radiant.
radioteléfono, *n.m.* radiotelephone.
radiotelegrafía, *n.f.* radiotelegraphy.
radiotelegrafista, *n.m.f.* wireless operator.
radiotelescopio, *n.m.* radiotelescope.
radioterapia, *n.f.* radiotherapy.
radioyente, *n.m.f.* listener.
raedera, *n.f.* scraper.
raedura, *n.f.* scraping.
raer [27], *v.t.* scrape (off); scratch.—*v.r.* become worn *or* frayed.
ráfaga, *n.f.* gust; flash; burst.
rafia, *n.f.* raffia.
rahez, *a.* (*pl.* **-eces**) low, vile.
raído, -da, *a.* worn, threadbare; cheeky.
raigambre, *n.f.* root-mass; deep-rootedness.
raigón, *n.m.* root.
rail, *n.m.* (*pl.* **raíles**) rail.
raimiento, *n.m.* scraping; barefacedness.
raíz, *n.f.* (*pl.* **raíces**) root; ***a* — *de,*** immediately after.
raja, *n.f.* chink, crack; chip; slice; ***sacar* —,** (*fam.*) gain (***de,*** from, by).
rajar, *v.t.* split, crack; slice.—*v.i.* (*fam.*) boast; (*fam.*) natter, chat—*v.r.* split; (*fam.*) back out, break (*word etc.*).
ralea, *n.f.* kind; (*pej.*) breed; prey (*of hawks etc.*).
ralear, *v.i.* be sparse; reveal one's true nature.
raleza, *n.f.* sparsity.
ralo, -la, *a.* sparse.
rallador, *n.m.* (*cul.*) grater.
rallar, *v.t.* grate; (*fam.*) annoy.
rama, *n.f.* branch; ***en* —,** raw, crude; (*print.*) uncut.
ramada, *n.f.* branches; shed.
ramaje, *n.m.* branches.
ramal, *n.m.* strand; (*rail.*) branch.
rambla, *n.f.* dry ravine; boulevard.
ramera, *n.f.* whore.
ramificación, *n.f.* ramification.
ramificar [A], *v.t.*, *v.r.* ramificate.
ramillete, *n.m.* posy, bouquet; cluster.
ramo, *n.m.* branch; bunch (*of flowers*); line; touch (*of illness*); (***Domingo de***) ***Ramos,*** Palm Sunday.
ramojo, *n.m.* brushwood.
Ramón, *n.m.* Raymond.
rampa, *n.f.* ramp.
rampante, *a.* (*her.*) rampant.
ramplón, -lona, *a.* coarse, vulgar.
ramplonería, *n.f.* vulgarity, crudeness.
rana, *n.f.* frog; ***no ser* —,** (*fam.*) be handy *or* skilled.
rancajada, *n.f.* uprooting.
rancajo, *n.m.* splinter.
ranciar, *v.r.* go rancid.
rancidez, ranciedad, *n.f.* staleness, rancidness.
rancio, -cia, *a.* stale; rancid; old (*wine*).
ranchear, *v.i.*, *v.r.* settle in huts.
ranchería, *n.f.* hut settlement.
ranchero, *n.m.* mess-steward; (*C.A.*) farmer.
rancho, *n.m.* mess; gathering; hut; (*C.A.*) farm; (*naut.*) provisions.
rango, *n.m.* class, rank.
rangua, *n.f.* socket.
ranúnculo, *n.m.* (*bot.*) ranunculus; buttercup.
ranura, *n.f.* groove; ***a* — *y lengüeta,*** tongue and groove.
ranurar, *v.t.* groove.
rapacería, *n.f.* childish prank.
rapacidad, *n.f.* rapacity.
rapagón, *n.m.* stripling, lad.
rapar, *v.t.* crop; shave; steal.
rapaz, *a.* (*pl.* **-aces**) rapacious; thieving.—*n.m.* lad.—*pl.* (*orn.*) raptores.
rapaza, *n.f.* lass.
rape, *n.m.* (*fam.*) scrape, shave; ***al* —,** close-cropped (*hair*).
rapé, *n.m.* snuff.
rapidez, *n.f.* rapidity.
rápido, -da, *a.* rapid.—*n.m.* express (*train*).
rapiña, *n.f.* plundering, rapine; ***ave de* —,** bird of prey.
raposera, *n.f.* fox-hole.
raposería, *n.f.* foxiness.
raposo, -sa, *n.m.f.* fox; foxy person.
rapsodia, *n.f.* rhapsody.
rapsódico, -ca, *a.* rhapsodic(al).
raptar, *v.t.* abduct.
rapto, *n.m.* rapture, swoon; abduction; rape.
raptor, *n.m.* ravisher.
raque, *n.m.* beachcombing.
Raquel, *n.f.* Rachel.
raquero, -ra, *a.* piratical.—*n.m.* beachcomber; dock-thief.
raqueta, *n.f.* racket, racquet; snow-shoe.
raquítico, -ca, *a.* rachitic; rickety.
raquitis, *n.f.*, **raquitismo,** *n.m.* rickets.
rarefacción, *n.f.* rarefaction.
rarefacer [20], *v.t.* rarefy.
rarefacto, -ta, *a.* rarefied.
rareza, *n.f.* rarity, rareness; oddity.
raridad, *n.f.* rarity.
rarificar [A], *v.t.* rarefy; make rare.
raro, -ra, *a.* rare; odd, strange; sparse; ***rara vez*** or ***raras veces,*** rarely.
ras, *n.m.* levelness; ***a* —,** very close (***de,*** to).
rasa, *n.f.* thinness (*in cloth*); plateau.
rasar, *v.t.* level off; graze, skim.—*v.r.* clear.
rascacielos, *n.m. inv.* skyscraper.
rascadera, *n.f.*, **rascador,** *n.m.* scraper.
rascadura, *n.f.* scratch; scraping.
rascar [A], *v.t.* scrape; scratch.—*v.r.* (*S.A.*, *C.A.*) get drunk.
rascatripas, *n.m. inv.* (*pej.*) scraper, fiddler.
rascazón, *n.f.* itch, itching.
rascón, -cona, *a.* sharp, tart.
rasero, *n.m.* strickle; ***medir por un* —,** treat quite impartially.
rasgado, -da, *a.* wide, light (*window*); full, wide (*mouth*); large (*eyes*).—*n.m.* tear, rip.
rasgadura, *n.f.* tearing; tear.
rasgar [B], *v.t.* tear (up); rip apart.—*v.r.* tear; get torn.
rasgo, *n.m.* feature, trait; flourish, dash; feat; flash of wit.
rasgón, *n.m.* rent, rip, tear.
rasguear, *v.t.* strum.
rasgueo, *n.m.* strumming.
rasguñar, *v.t.* scratch; sketch.
rasguño, *n.m.* scratch; outline.
raso, -sa, *a.* smooth, level; flat, plain; clear, open; skimming the ground.—*n.m.* satin; flat land; ***al* —,** in the open air; ***soldado* —,** private.
raspadura, *n.f.* scraping.
raspar, *v.t.* scrape (off); bite, be sharp (on); steal.
raspear, *v.i.* scratch (*pen*).
rastra, *n.f.* sledge; harrow; track; grapnel; string of onions; anything trailing; ***a*** (***la***) **—,** ***a rastras,*** dragging; unwillingly.

rastrear, *v.t.* trail, trace, track; harrow; drag; fathom out; dredge; skim.—*v.i.* fly very low.
rastreo, *n.m.* dredging; trawling.
rastrero, -ra, *a.* trailing; dragging; skimming the ground; low, abject; creeping; grovelling.—*n.m.* slaughterman.
rastrillar, *v.t.* comb, hackle; (*agr.*) rake (up).
rastrillo, *n.m.* (*agr.*) rake; portcullis, grating; (*rail.*) cow-catcher.
rastro, *n.m.* trace; scent, trail; rake, harrow; street market.
rastrojo, *n.m.* stubble.
rasurar, *v.t., v.r.* shave.
rata (1), *n.f.* (*zool.*) rat.—*n.m.* (*fam.*) [RATERO].
rata (2) **por cantidad,** *adv.* pro rata.
rataplán, *n.m.* drum-beat, rub-a-dub.
ratear, *v.t.* share out; lessen; filch.—*v.i.* creep.
ratería, *n.f.* petty larceny; meanness.
ratero, -ra, *a.* trailing; vile; thievish.—*n.m.f.* petty thief, pickpocket.
ratificación, *n.f.* ratification.
ratificar [A] *v.t.* ratify.
rato, *n.m.* while; moment; ***buen —,*** quite a while; ***pasar el —,*** waste one's time; kill time; ***a ratos perdidos,*** during leisure.
ratón, -tona, *n.m.f.* (*zool.*) mouse; ***— de biblioteca,*** (*fam.*) book-worm.
ratonero, -ra, *a.* mousy.—*n.f.* mouse-trap; mouse-hole.
rauco, -ca, (*poet.*) [RONCO].
raudal, *n.m.* torrent; abundance.
raudo, -da, *a.* swift.
raya, *n.f.* stripe; dash; line; scratch; crease, pleat; parting (*of hair*); boundary; (*ichth.*) ray; ***tener a —,*** keep within bounds, keep at bay; ***hacer —,*** be eminent.
rayado, -da, *a.* striped; scratched.—*n.m.* ruling lines.
rayano, -na, *a.* bordering; borderline.
rayar, *v.t.* line; stripe; scratch; cross out; rifle; underline.—*v.i.* border (**en,** on); begin to appear; shine.
rayo, *n.m.* ray, beam; lightning; thunderbolt; sudden havoc; ***echar rayos,*** be fuming with rage; ***rayos alfa, beta, gama,*** alpha, beta, gamma rays; ***rayos infrarrojos*** (***ultravioletas***), infra-red (ultraviolet) rays; ***rayos X,*** X-rays. [RAER].
rayón, *n.m.* rayon.
rayoso, -sa, *a.* striped, rayed.
raza, *n.f.* race; breed; quality; cleft, crack; fault (*in cloth*); ***de —,*** thoroughbred.
rázago, *n.m.* sackcloth.
razón, *n.f.* reason; right; rate; ratio; account, story; ***a — de,*** at the rate of; ***con —,*** rightly; ***dar la — a,*** agree with; ***dar — de,*** give an account of; ***— social,*** (*com.*) firm; ***tener —,*** be right.
razonable, *a.* reasonable.
razonamiento, *n.m.* reasoning.
razonar, *v.t.* reason out, discourse; itemize.
razzia, *n.f.* razzia, raid.
re (1), *n.m.* (*mus.*) (key of) D.
re- (2), *prefix.* **re-** *indicates repetition, as* **releer,** re-read; *prefixed to adjectives & advs.*, very, *as* **rebueno,** very good.
rea, *n.f.* female defendant.
reacción, *n.f.* reaction; ***— en cadena,*** chain reaction; [MOTOR].
reaccionar, *v.i.* react.
reaccionario, -ria, *a., n.m.f.* reactionary.
reacio, -cia, *a.* stubborn.
reactivo, -va, *a.* reactive.—*n.m.* reagent.
reactor, *n.m.* reactor.
reajuste, *n.m.* readjustment.
real, *a.* real; royal; fine, superb.—*n.m.* army camp; real (25 céntimos).
realce, *n.m.* raised work, relief; enhancement; emphasis.
realengo, -ga, *a.* of royal ownership.
realeza, *n.f.* royalty.
realidad, *n.f.* reality; truth.
realismo, *n.m.* royalism; realism.
realista (1), *a.* realistic.—*n.m.f.* realist.
realista (2), *a., n.m.f.* royalist.
realizable, *a.* realizable; saleable.
realización, *n.f.* realization; carrying out; sale; (*cine.*) production.
realizar [C], *v.t.* realize; carry out; perform; (*cine.*) produce.—*v.r.* be fulfilled; happen.
realzar [C], *v.t.* raise; enhance; emphasize, emboss.
reanimar, *v.t., v.r.* revive; cheer up.
reanudar, *v.t.* resume.
reaparecer [9], *v.i.* reappear.
reaparición, *n.f.* reappearance.
rearmar, *v.t., v.r.* rearm.
rearme, *n.m.* rearmament.
reata, *n.f.* tethered line of horses; single file; ***de —,*** in single file; (*fam.*) on a piece of string, round one's little finger.
rebaba, *n.f.* burr, rough edge.
rebaja, *n.f.* rebate, discount; price-cut(ting).
rebajamiento, *n.m.* lowering; discounting; humbling.
rebajar, *v.t.* lower, reduce; tone down; humble.—*v.r.* be humbled; humble oneself, condescend (**a,** to); (*mil.*) be discharged.
rebalsar, *v.t.* dam (*a stream*).—*v.i., v.r.* get blocked up; pile up.
rebanada, *n.f.* slice (*esp. of bread*).
rebanar, *v.t.* slice.
rebañar, *v.t.* clean up, pick clean.
rebaño, *n.m.* flock.
rebasar, *v.t.* go beyond.
rebate, *n.m.* encounter, clash.
rebatimiento, *n.m.* refutation; repulsion.
rebatiña, *n.f.* scramble, grabbing.
rebatir, *v.t.* refute; repel, drive off; deduct.
rebato, *n.m.* (*mil.*) surprise; alarm; great excitement.
rebeco, *n.m.* (*zool.*) chamois.
rebelar, *v.r.* rebel, revolt.
rebelde, *a.* rebellious.—*n.m.* rebel; (*jur.*) defaulter.
rebeldía, *n.f.* rebelliousness; (*jur.*) default.
rebelión, *n.f.* rebellion, revolt.
rebién, *adv.* (*fam.*) very well.
reblandecer [9], *v.t., v.r.* soften.
rebocillo, -ciño, *n.m.* shawl.
rebombar, *v.i.* resound.
rebosadero, *n.m.* overflow.
rebosadura, *n.f.*, **rebosamiento,** *n.m.* overflow, overflowing.
rebosar, *v.t.* overflow with.—*v.i., v.r.* overflow, be bursting (**de, en,** with).
rebotadura, *n.f.* rebounding.
rebotar, *v.t.* repel, reject; bend over; alter; (*fam.*) bother.—*v.i.* rebound, bounce (**en,** off).—*v.r.* alter; (*fam.*) get worried.
rebote, *n.m.* bounce; rebound; ***de —,*** incidentally.

rebozado, -da, *a.* (*cul.*) in batter.
rebozar [C], *v.t.* (*cul.*) batter; disguise; muffle up.—*v.r.* muffle oneself up.
rebozo, *n.m.* disguise; muffler; shawl; ***de* —,** secretly; ***sin* —,** openly.
rebrotar, *v.i.* sprout.
rebrote, *n.m.* (*agr.*) shoot; (*med.*) recurrent attack.
rebufar, *v.i.* blow and snort.
rebujar, *v.t.* jumble up.—*v.r.* wrap oneself up.
rebullir [J], *v.i., v.r.* stir, move.
rebumbar, *v.i.* whistle (*bullet, shell*).
rebusca, *n.f.* careful search; gleaning; remains.
rebuscado, -da, *a.* recherché; affected.
rebuscamiento, *n.m.* searching; affectation.
rebuscar [A], *v.t.* seek; examine; glean.
rebuznar, *v.i.* bray, hee-haw.
rebuzno, *n.m.* bray, hee-haw.
recabar, *v.t.* manage to get.
recadero, -ra, *n.m.f.* messenger, errand-boy *or* girl.
recado, *n.m.* message; errand; gift; outfit; provisions; safety.
recaer [14], *v.i.* fall again; relapse; devolve (***en,*** upon).
recaída, *n.f.* relapse.
recalar, *v.t.* drench.—*v.i.* (*naut.*) sight land.
recalcar [A], *v.t.* press tight; cram; stress.—*v.i.* (*naut.*) list.—*v.r.* sprain; harp on.
recalcitrante, *a.* recalcitrant.
recalcitrar, *v.i.* baulk; resist.
recalentar [1], *v.t.* reheat, warm up; overheat.
recamar, *v.t.* embroider.
recambio, *n.m.* re-exchange; ***de* —,** spare (*part*).
recapacitar, *v.t., v.i.* think out, run over.
recapitulación, *n.f.* recapitulation.
recapitular, *v.t., v.i.* recapitulate.
recarga, *n.f.* recharge, recharging.
recargar [B], *v.t.* reload; recharge; overload; overcharge; increase (*taxes*); overdo.
recargo, *n.m.* new charge *or* load; extra charge; overload; increase.
recatado, -da, *a.* cautious; modest.
recatar, *v.t.* conceal; taste again.—*v.r.* hide; be reserved *or* cautious.
recato, *n.m.* caution, prudence; modesty.
recauchar, *v.t.* retread (*tyres*).
recaudación, *n.f.* tax collecting; tax office.
recaudador, *n.m.* tax-collector.
recaudamiento, *n.m.* tax collecting; tax district.
recaudar, *v.t.* collect, gather; watch over.
recaudo, *n.m.* tax collecting; caution; bail.
recelar, *v.t.* fear, distrust; suspect.—*v.i., v.r.* distrust, be suspicious (***de,*** of).
recelo, *n.m.* fear, foreboding; distrust.
receloso, -sa, *a.* distrustful, fearful.
recensión, *n.f.* review, recension.
recentar [1], *v.t.* leaven.—*v.r.* be renewed.
recepción, *n.f.* reception; admission.
receptáculo, *n.m.* receptacle; refuge.
receptar, *v.t.* (*jur.*) receive (*stolen goods*); welcome; conceal; abet.
receptivo, -va, *a.* receptive; susceptible.
receptor, -ra, *a.* receiving.—*n.m.* (*rad., T.V., tel.*) receiver.
recesivo, -va, *a.* recessive.
receso, *n.m.* recess(ion); deviation.
receta, *n.f.* (*cul.*) recipe; (*med.*) prescription; schedule.
recetar, *v.t.* (*med.*) prescribe.
recibí, *n.m.* receipt.
recibidor, -ra, *n.m.* receiver; ante-room.
recibimiento, *n.m.* reception; hall.
recibir, *v.t.* receive.—*v.r.* be received, be admitted (***de,*** as).
recibo, *n.m.* receipt; salon; reception; at home.
recidiva, *n.f.* relapse.
recién, *adv.* (*only before p.p.s except in S.A.*) recently, newly.
reciente, *a.* recent.
recinto, *n.m.* enclosure.
recio, -cia, *a.* robust, strong; harsh; impetuous.—*adv.* strongly, harshly.
récipe, *n.m.* (*fam.*) prescription; (*fam.*) displeasure.
recipiente, *a.* receiving.—*n.m.* recipient.
reciprocación, *n.f.* reciprocation.
reciprocar [A], *v.t., v.r.* reciprocate.—*v.r.* match.
recíproco, -ca, *a., n.m.f.* reciprocal.
recitación, *n.f.* recitation.
recital, *n.m.* recital.
recitar, *v.t.* recite.
reciura, *n.f.* vigour; rigour.
reclamación, *n.f.* claim; reclamation; objection.
reclamar, *v.t.* claim; reclaim; decoy, lure; call.—*v.i.* cry out.
reclamista, *n.m.f.* publicity agent.
reclamo, *n.m.* decoy, lure; reclamation; call; catch-word; advert(isement), blurb.
reclinar, *v.t., v.r.* recline, lean.
recluir [O], *v.t.* seclude, intern.
reclusión, *n.f.* reclusion, seclusion; imprisonment.
recluso, -sa, *a.* secluded; confined.—*n.m.f.* prisoner; recluse.
recluta, *n.f.* recruiting.—*n.m.* recruit.
reclutamiento, *n.m.* recruitment; recruiting.
reclutar, *v.t.* recruit; (*S.A.*) round up.
recobrar, *v.t., v.r.* recover.
recobro, *n.m.* recovery.
recodar, *v.i., v.r.* lean (*on elbow*); twist and turn.
recodo, *n.m.* bend, turn.
recogedero, *n.m.* gatherer; gathering area.
recogedor, -ra, *n.m.f.* gatherer, collector.—*n.m.* rake; gatherer; box.
recoger [E], *v.t.* pick up; gather; pull *or* take in; welcome; shelter.—*v.r.* take shelter; withdraw; go home; cut spending.
recogido, -da, *a.* secluded, cloistered; modest.—*n.m.f.* inmate.—*n.f.* gathering; withdrawal.
recogimiento, *n.m.* gathering, collection; retreat; shelter.
recolección, *n.f.* summary, compilation; collection; meditation; retreat; harvest.
recolectar, *v.t.* harvest.
recoleto, -ta, *a., n.m.f.* (*eccl.*) said of strict orders.
recomendable, *a.* commendable.
recomendación, *n.f.* recommendation; (*fam.*) piece of advice *or* of one's mind.
recomendar [1], *v.t.* recommend.
recompensa, *n.f.* recompense, reward.
recompensar, *v.t.* recompense, reward.
recomponer [25], *v.t.* repair; recompose.

reconcentrar, *v.t.* gather, concentrate; conceal.—*v.r.* assemble, gather; concentrate.
reconciliable, *a.* reconcilable.
reconciliación, *n.f.* reconciliation.
reconciliar, *v.t.* reconcile; confess (*s.o.*); reconsecrate.—*v.r.* be reconciled.
reconditez, *n.f.* mystery.
recóndito, -ta, *a.* recondite.
reconocedor, -ra, *n.m.f.* inspector.
reconocer [9], *v.t.* recognize; inspect; reconnoitre; admit.—*v.r.* confess; be plain *or* clear.
reconocido, -da, *a.* grateful, obliged.
reconocimiento, *n.m.* recognition; gratitude; inspection; reconnaissance; (*med.*) examination.
reconquista, *n.m.f.* reconquest.
reconquistar, *v.t.* reconquer; recover.
reconstruir [O], *v.t.* reconstruct.
recontar [4], *v.t.* recount, relate.
reconvención, *n.f.* expostulation, charge.
reconvenir [36], *v.t.* reproach, charge.
recopilación, *n.f.* compendium, digest, compilation.
recopilar, *v.t.* compile.
record, *n.m.* (*pl.* **-ds**) record; ***batir*** or ***establecer un* —,** break *or* set up a record.
recordable, *a.* memorable.
recordar [4], *v.t.* remember; remind.—*v.i.* remember; wake; come round.
recorrer, *v.t.* cross, travel through; look over, run over.
recorrido, *n.m.* run, path; refit; mileage; (*mech.*) stroke.
recortado, *n.m.* cut-out (*figure*).
recortadura, *n.f.* cutting, clipping.
recortar, *v.t.* cut off; trim; cut out; outline. —*v.r.* stand out.
recorte, *n.m.* cutting.
recostar [4], *v.t.*, *v.r.* recline, lean.
recoveco, *n.m.* turn, bend; trick.
recreación, *n.f.* recreation.
recrear, *v.t.* re-create; amuse, relax.—*v.r.* relax, amuse oneself.
recreativo, -va, *a.* recreative.
recrecer [9], *v.t.*, *v.i.* increase.—*v.i.* recur.—*v.r.* recover one's spirits.
recreo, *n.m.* recreation; place of amusement.
recriminación, *n.f.* recrimination.
recriminar, *v.t.*, *v.i.* recriminate.
recrudecer [9], *v.i.*, *v.r.* recur; get worse.
recrude(s)cencia, *n.f.* **recrudecimiento,** *n.m.* recrudescence.
rectangular, *a.* rectangular.
rectángulo, *n.m.* rectangle.
rectificación, *n.f.* rectification.
rectificar [A], *v.t.* rectify.
rectilíneo, -nea, *a.* rectilinear.
rectitud, *n.f.* rectitude.
recto, -ta, *a.* straight; right; upright; basic. —*n.m.* rectum.—*adv.* straight ahead.
rector, -ra, *a.* governing.—*n.m.f.* principal. —*n.m.* rector.
recua, *n.f.* drove; multitude.
recubrir [*p.p.* **recubierto**], *v.t.* cover; recover.
recudir, *v.t.* pay (*due*).—*v.i.* revert.
recuento, *n.m.* count; re-count.
recuerdo, *n.m.* memory; souvenir.—*pl.* regards; [RECORDAR].
recuero, *n.m.* drover.
recuesta, *n.f.* request.
recuestar, *v.t.* request, require.
reculada, *n.f.* recoil; backing.
recular, *v.i.* fall back; recoil.
recuperable, *a.* recoverable.
recuperación, *n.f.* recuperation.
recuperar, *v.t.*, *v.r.* recuperate, recover.
recurrir, *v.i.* resort; revert.
recurso, *n.m.* resource; recourse; petition.
recusar, *v.t.* decline; (*jur.*) challenge.
rechazamiento, *n.m.* repulsion; rejection.
rechazar [C], *v.t.* repulse; reject; repel.
rechazo, *n.m.* rebound, recoil; rejection.
rechiflar, *v.t.* boo, hiss, deride.
rechinador, -ra, rechinante, *a.* squeaking creaking.
rechinar, *v.i.* creak, squeak, grate.
rechistar, *v.i.* ***sin* —,** without a word without protest.
rechoncho, -cha, *a.* (*fam.*) chubby.
de rechupete, *a. phr.* (*fam.*) super, smashing.
red, *n.f.* net; net-work; netting; (*fig.*) trap.
redacción, *n.f.* editing; editorial office.
redactar, *v.t.* edit; draw up, compose.
redactor, *n.m.f.* editor.—*n.m.f.* compiler.
redar, *v.t.* net, haul.
redargüir [I], *v.t.* refute; impugn.
redecilla, *n.f.* netting; hair-net.
rededor, *n.m.* surroundings; ***al*** or ***en* — (*de*),** around.
redención, *n.f.* redemption, salvation.
redentor, -ra, *a.* redeeming.—*n.m.* redeemer.
redición, *n.f.* reiteration.
redil, *n.m.* sheepfold.
redimir, *v.t.* redeem; ransom; rescue.
rédito, *n.m.* (*com.*) yield.
redituar [M], *v.t.* (*com.*) yield.
redivivo, -va, *a.* resuscitated.—*n.m.f.* ghost one back from the dead.
redobladura, *n.f.*, **redoblamiento,** *n.m.* redoubling; doubling.
redoblar, *v.t.* double; redouble; bend over; do again.—*v.i.* roll (*drums*).
redoble, *n.m.* [REDOBLAMIENTO]; roll (*of drums*).
redoblón, *n.m.* rivet.
redolor, *n.m.* after-pain, dull ache.
redoma, *n.f.* phial, flask.
redonda, *n.f.* district; pasture; ***a la* —** roundabout.
redondel, *n.m.* circle; bull-ring.
redondez, *n.f.* roundness.
redondo, -da, *a.* round; clear; decided; (*print.*) roman.—*n.m.* circle, ring; (*fam.*) cash; ***caer* —,** fall senseless.
redopelo, *n.m.* scuffle, scrap; ***al* —,** against the grain; without rhyme or reason.
redro, *adv.* (*fam.*) back(wards).
redropelo [REDOPELO].
reducción, *n.f.* reduction.
reducido, -da, *a.* reduced; small; narrow, close.
reducir [15], *v.t.* reduce.—*v.r.* get into order; come, amount (***a***, to).
reducto, *n.m.* redoubt.
reductor, -ra, *a.* reducing.—*n.m.* reducer.
redundancia, *n.f.* redundancy.
redundante, *a.* redundant.
redundar, *v.i.* overflow; redound (***en***, to).
reduplicar [A], *v.t.* redouble, reduplicate.
reduzco [REDUCIR].
reeditar, *v.t.* reprint, republish.

re(e)mbarcar [A], *v.t.* re-embark.
re(e)mbarco, *n.m.* re-embarkation.
re(e)mbolsar, *v.t.* refund, reimburse.
re(e)mbolso, *n.m.* refund; reimbursement; ***contra* —,** cash on delivery.
re(e)mplazante, *n.m.f.* substitute (*person*).
re(e)mplazar [C], *v.t.* replace, substitute.
reencarnación, *n.f.* reincarnation.
re(e)ncuentro, *n.m.* clash.
re(e)nganchar, *v.t.* re-enlist; recouple.
re(e)nviar [L], *v.t.* forward, send on.
re(e)xpedir [8], *v.t.* forward, send on.
refacción, *n.f.* refreshment; (*fam.*) extra; (*S.A.*) upkeep.
refección, *n.f.* refreshment; repairs.
refectorio, *n.m.* refectory.
referencia, *n.f.* reference; narrative; report.
referéndum, *n.m.* (*pl.* **-ms**) referendum.
referente, *a.* referring.
referido, -da, *a., n.m.f.* aforesaid.
referir [6], *v.t.* refer; relate, report.—*v.r.* refer.
refertero, -ra, *a.* quarrelsome.
de refilón, *adv. phr.* askance; in passing.
refinación, *n.f.* refinement; refining.
refinado, -da, *a.* refined; sharp, artful.
refinamiento, *n.m.* refinement; refining.
refinar, *v.t.* refine; polish, improve.
refinería, *n.f.* refinery.
refirmar, *v.t.* ratify.
refitolero, -ra, *n.m.f.* refectioner; (*fam.*) busybody.
reflectar, *v.t.* (*phys.*) reflect.
reflector, -ra, *a.* reflecting.—*n.m.* reflector; (*mil.*) searchlight; head-light.
reflejar, *v.t.* reflect; mirror; show.—*v.r.* be reflected.
reflejo, -ja, *a.* reflected; reflexive.—*n.m.* reflex; reflection; glare, glow.
reflexión, *n.f.* reflection.
reflexionar, *v.t.* think over.—*v.i.* reflect (***en, sobre,*** on).
reflexivo, -va, *a.* reflexive.
reflujo, *n.m.* reflux, ebb.
refocilar, *v.t.* exhilarate; cheer.—*v.r.* frolic; find new vigour.
reforma, *n.f.* reform; (*eccl.*) Reformation.
reformación, *n.f.* reformation.
reformador, -ra, *n.m.f.* reformer.
reformar, *v.t.* reform; re-form; revise; mend.—*v.r.* reform.
reformativo, -va, *a.* reformative.
reformatorio, -ria, *a., n.m.* reformatory.
reformista, *n.m.f.* reformist.
reforzar [4C], *v.t.* reinforce; strengthen; boost; cheer.
refracción, *n.f.* refraction.
refractar, *v.t.* refract.
refractario, -ria, *a.* refractive; stubborn, rebellious.
refractivo, -va, *a.* refractive.
refractor, -ra, *a.* refractive.—*n.m.* refractor.
refrán, *n.m.* proverb.
refranero, *n.m.* collection of proverbs.
refregar [1B], *v.t.* rub; (*fam.*) tell off.
refregón, *n.m.* rub, rubbing.
refreír [28, *p.p.* **refrito**], *v.t.* re-fry; fry well; (*fam.*) bore to tears.
refrenar, *v.t.* restrain, curb.
refrescante, *a.* refreshing; cooling.
refrescar [A], *v.t.* refresh; cool.
refresco, *n.m.* refreshment; cold drink.
refriega, *n.f.* skirmish, affray.
refrigeración, *n.f.* refrigeration; cooling.
refrigerador, *n.m.* refrigerator.
refrigerante, *a.* cooling, refrigerating.
refrigerar, *v.t.* cool; refrigerate.
refrigerio, *n.m.* coolness; refreshment; comfort.
refringir [E], *v.t.* refract.
refrito, -ta, *p.p.* [REFREÍR].—*n.m.* rehash.
refuerzo, *n.m.* reinforcement.
refugiado, -da, *n.m.f.* refugee.
refugiar, *v.t.* shelter.—*v.r.* take refuge.
refugio, *n.m.* refuge; shelter; asylum.
refulgencia, *n.f.* refulgence.
refulgente, *a.* refulgent.
refulgir [E], *v.i.* shine, gleam.
refundición, *n.f.* adaptation; remelting.
refundir, *v.t.* recast; adapt.
refunfuñar, *v.i.* grumble.
refutación, *n.f.* refutation.
refutar, *v.t.* refute.
regadera, *n.f.* watering-can; sprinkler; ditch.
regadío, -ía, *a.* irrigable.—*n.m.* irrigated land.
regajal, regajo, *n.m.* puddle; trickle.
regala, *n.f.* (*naut.*) gunwale.
regalado, -da, *a.* delightful; delicate.
regalar, *v.t.* give; regale; fondle.—*v.r.* live sumptuously.
regalía, *n.f.* privilege; bonus.—*pl.* regalia.
regaliz, *n.m.,* **regaliza,** *n.f.* licorice.
regalo, *n.m.* present; gift; pleasure; luxury.
regalón, -lona, *a.* (*fam.*) easy, comfortable.
regante, *n.m.* irrigator.
a regañadientes, *adv. phr.* grumblingly, reluctantly.
regañar, *v.t.* (*fam.*) scold.—*v.i.* growl; quarrel.
regaño, *n.m.* snarl; scolding.
regar [1B], *v.t.* water; sprinkle.
regata, *n.f.* regatta; water-course.
regatear, *v.t.* haggle over; sell retail; (*fam.*) duck (*evade*).—*v.i.* haggle.
regateo, *n.m.* haggling.
regatería, *n.f.* retailer's.
regatero, -ra, *a.* retailing; (*fam.*) haggling.—*n.m.f.* retailer.
regatonear, *v.i.* trade retail.
regazar [C], *v.t.* tuck up.
regazo, *n.m.* lap.
regencia, *n.f.* regency.
regeneración, *n.f.* regeneration.
regenerar, *v.t.* regenerate.
regenta, *n.f.* wife of regent *or* professor *etc.*
regentar, *v.t.* govern, rule, boss.
regente, *a.* ruling.—*n.m.f.* regent.—*n.m.* manager; foreman; professor.
regicida, *n.m.f.* regicide (*person*).
regicidio, *n.m.* regicide (*act*).
regidor, *n.m.* alderman; prefect.
régimen, *n.m.* (*pl.* **regímenes**) regime; regimen; system; rules; normality; (*med.*) regimen, diet; (*gram.*) government.
regimentación, *n.f.* regimentation.
regimental, *a.* regimental.
regimentar [1], *v.t.* regiment.
regimiento, *n.m.* rule, government; council; regiment.
regio, -gia, *a.* royal, regal.
región, *n.f.* region.
regional, *a.* regional.
regir [8E], *v.t.* rule; govern; direct; steer.—*v.i.* be in force.

registrador, -ra, *a.* registering.—*n.m.f.* registrar, recorder.—*n.f.* till.
registrar, *v.t.* register; record; inspect, search.—*v.r.* register.
registro, *n.m.* register; search, inspection; record; (*mus.*) organ stop; (*med.*) period; pitch.
regla, *n.f.* rule, order; ruler; ***por — general,*** as a general rule; ***— de cálculo,*** slide-rule.
reglado, -da, *a.* moderate.
reglamentar, *v.t.* regulate.
reglamentario, -ria, *a.* statutory, regulation.
reglamento, *n.m.* regulation; regulations.
reglar, *a.* (*eccl.*) regular.—*v.t.* line, rule; regulate; guide.
regocijar, *v.t.* gladden, exhilarate.—*v.r.* rejoice.
regocijo, *n.m.* joy, rejoicing.
regodear, *v.r.* (*fam.*) have fun.
regodeo, *n.m.* (*fam.*) fun.
regoldar [10], *v.i.* (*low*) belch.
regraciar, *v.t.* be grateful for.
regresar, *v.i.* return.
regresión, *n.f.* regression.
regresivo, -va, *a.* regressive.
regreso, *n.m.* return.
regüeldo, *n.m.* (*low*) belch.
regulación, *n.f.* control, regulation.
regular, *a.* regular; (*fam.*) so-so, not bad.—*v.t.* control, regulate.
regularidad, *n.f.* regularity.
regularizar [C], *v.t.* regularize.
regurgitación, *n.f.* regurgitation.
regurgitar, *v.i.* regurgitate.
rehabilitación, *n.f.* rehabilitation.
rehabilitar, *v.t.* rehabilitate, restore.
rehacer [20], *v.t.* remake; re-do; repair.—*v.r.* recover.
rehacimiento, *n.m.* remaking; repair; recovery.
rehecho, -cha, *a.* dumpy.—*p.p.* [REHACER].
rehén, *n.m.* hostage.
reherir [6], *v.t.* repel.
rehervir [6], *v.t.* reboil.—*v.i.* boil again; seethe.—*v.r.* ferment.
rehilar, *v.i.* quiver; whiz.
rehuír [O], *v.t.* flee, shun.
rehusar, *v.t.* refuse.
reidero, -ra, *a.* (*fam.*) laughable.—*n.f.pl.* laughing fit.
reimpresión, *n.f.* reprint.
reimprimir [*p.p.* **reimpreso** *or* **reimprimido**], *v.t.* reprint.
reina, *n.f.* queen.
reinado, *n.m.* reign.
reinante, *a.* reigning, prevailing.
reinar, *v.i.* reign; prevail.
reincidencia, *n.f.* relapse.
reincidir, *v.i.* relapse, fall back.
reino, *n.m.* kingdom, realm.
reintegrar, *v.t.* reintegrate; restore.—*v.r.* recover; return (***a***, to).
reír [28], *v.t.* laugh at.—*v.i.*, *v.r.* laugh (***de***, at); (*fam.*) tear, split.
reiteración, *n.f.* reiteration.
reiterar, *v.t.* reiterate.
reiterativo, -va, *a.* reiterative.
reja, *n.f.* grating, grille; ploughshare.
rejería, *n.f.* ironwork.
rejilla, *n.f.* lattice; screen, grating; (*elec.*) grid.
rejo, *n.m.* goad; vigour.
rejón, *n.m.* dagger; spear.
rejoneador, *n.m.* mounted bullfighter.
rejonear, *v.t.* (*taur.*) fight bulls while mounted.
rejuvenecer [9], *v.t.*, *v.i.*, *v.r.* rejuvenate.
rejuvenecimiento, *n.m.* rejuvenation.
relación, *n.f.* relation; tale; report.
relacionar, *v.t.* relate.—*v.r.* be related.
relajación, *n.f.* relaxation, release, slackening; laxity; rupture.
relajante, *a.* relaxing, slackening.
relajar, *v.t.* relax; hand over; debauch.—*v.r.* relax; become lax; get ruptured.
relamer, *v.t.* lick again.—*v.r.* lick one's lips; relish; glory; use make-up.
relamido, -da, *a.* affected, prim.
relámpago, *n.m.* lightning flash.
relampaguear, *v.i.* flash; lighten.
relampagueo, *n.m.* flashing; lightning.
relance, *n.m.* chance.
relapso, -sa, *a.* relapsed.—*n.m.f.* backslider.
relatar, *v.t.* relate, tell, report.
relatividad, *n.f.* relativity.
relativismo, *n.m.* relativism.
relativo, -va, *a.* relative.
relato, *n.m.* story; report.
relator, -ra, *n.m.f.* narrator; reporter.
relegación, *n.f.* relegation; exile.
relegar [B], *v.t.* relegate.
relevación, *n.f.* relief; (*jur.*) remission.
relevante, *a.* outstanding, excellent.
relevar, *v.t.* bring into relief; relieve; release; replace.—*v.i.* stand out.
relevo, *n.m.* (*mil.*) relief.
relicario, *n.m.* reliquary, shrine.
relicto, -ta, *a.* (*jur.*) bequeathed.
relieve, *n.m.* relief; relievo; ***bajo —,*** bas-relief; ***poner de —,*** emphasize.—*pl.* leavings, offal.
religión, *n.f.* religion.
religioso, -sa, *a.* religious.—*n.m.* monk.—*n.f.* nun.
relinchar, *v.i.* neigh.
relinch(id)o, *n.m.* neigh.
reliquia, *n.f.* relic; vestige; heirloom.
reloj, *n.m.* watch, clock; meter.
relojería, *n.f.* watchmaker's; watchmaking.
relojero, *n.m.* watchmaker.
reluciente, *a.* shining.
relucir [9], *v.i.* shine.
relumbrante, *a.* dazzling, brilliant.
relumbrar, *v.i.* shine, dazzle, glare.
relumbre, *n.m.* flash, blaze, glare.
relumbrón, *n.m.* flash, bright light; tinsel.
rellanar, *v.t.* level out.—*v.r.* fall flat.
rellano, *n.m.* landing (*stair*); flat place.
rellenar, *v.t.* refill; fill up; stuff.
relleno, -na, *a.* very full, packed tight; stuffed.—*n.m.* stuffing; padding.
remachar, *v.t.* rivet; stress.
remanecer [9], *v.i.* appear suddenly.
remanente, *n.m.* residue, remnant.
remansar, *v.r.* slow, eddy.
remanso, *n.m.* backwater, eddy; slowness.
remar, *v.i.* row (*boat*); toil.
rematar, *v.t.* finish off.—*v.i.* end.—*v.r.* come to an end; ***loco rematado,*** raving mad.
remate, *n.m.* end; top, crown; ***de —,*** utterly; ***por —,*** in the end.
remedar, *v.t.* imitate, mimic.
remediable, *a.* remediable.
remediar, *v.t.* remedy; save; aid.

remedio, *n.m.* remedy; aid; amendment; (*jur.*) action; ***no hay (más) —,*** it can't be helped.
remedo, *n.m.* copy, imitation.
remellado, -da, *a.* dented; jagged.
remembrar, rememorar, *v.t.* recollect, recall.
remendar [1], *v.t.* patch (up).
remendón, -dona, *a.* mending.—*n.m.f.* mender.
rementir [6], *v.i., v.r.* tell many lies.
remero, -ra, *n.m.f.* rower.—*n.m.* oarsman.
remesar, *v.t.* remit; ship; tear.
remezón, *n.m.* (*S.A.*) earth tremor.
remiendo, *n.m.* patch, repair; mending.
remilgado, -da, *a.* prudish, fussy, affected.
remilgo, *n.m.* primness, affectation, fussiness.
reminiscencia, *n.f.* reminiscence.
remirado, -da, *a.* watchful, careful.
remirar, *v.t.* look at again *or* closely.—*v.r.* delight in watching; take pains (***en,*** to).
remisión, *n.f.* remission; remitting; reference.
remiso, -sa, *a.* remiss, lazy.
remisor, -ra, *n.m.f.* (*S.A.*) sender.
remitente, *n.m.f.* sender.
remitir, *v.t.* remit, send; refer.—*v.r.* slacken; refer (***a,*** to); submit.
remo, *n.m.* oar; rowing; limb; hard labour.
remoción, *n.f.* removal.
remojar, *v.t.* soak; (*fam.*) drink to.
remojo, *n.m.* soaking.
remolacha, *n.f.* (*bot.*) beet; sugar-beet.
remolcador, *n.m.* (*naut.*) tug; tower.
remolcar [A], *v.t.* tow.
remoler [5], *v.t.* grind up.
remolin(e)ar, *v.t., v.i., v.r.* whirl about.
remolino, *n.m.* whirl, whirlwind, whirlpool; eddy; throng.
remolón, -lona, *a.* shirking.—*n.m.f.* shirker.
remolque, *n.m.* tow, tow-rope, towing; trailer.
remonta, *n.f.* remount; repair.
remontar, *v.t.* scare off; mend; go up; raise. —*v.r.* rise, soar; go back.
remonte, *n.m.* remounting; repair; soaring.
remoquete, *n.m.* punch; gibe; nickname; (*fam.*) flirting.
rémora, *n.f.* hindrance; (*ichth.*) remora.
remorder [5], *v.t.* bite again; prick.—*v.r.* show one's feelings.
remordimiento, *n.m.* remorse; ***remordimientos de conciencia,*** prick(s) of conscience.
remoto, -ta, *a.* remote; vague.
remover [5], *v.t.* remove; upset; stir, shake. —*v.r.* move away.
remozar [C], *v.t., v.r.* rejuvenate.
rempujar, *v.t.* (*fam.*) jostle; shove.
rempujo, rempujón, *n.m.* (*fam.*) shove.
remudar, *v.t.* change, replace.
remuneración, *n.f.* remuneration.
remunerar, *v.t.* remunerate.
remunerativo, -va, *a.* remunerative.
remusgar [B], *v.t.* suspect.
renacentista, *a.* rel. to Renaissance.—*n.m.f.* Renaissance scholar.
renacer [9], *v.i.* be reborn; recover.
renaciente, *a.* renascent.
renacimiento, *n.m.* rebirth; Renaissance.
renacuajo, *n.m.* tadpole.
renal, *a.* renal.
rencilla, *n.f.* quarrel, bickering.
rencilloso, -sa, *a.* bickering.
rencor, *n.m.* rancour.
rencoroso, -sa, *a.* rancorous.
rencuentro, *n.m.* encounter, clash.
rendajo, *n.m.* (*orn.*) jay.
rendición, *n.f.* surrender; exhaustion.
rendido, -da, *a.* weary; abject.
rendija, *n.f.* crack, crevice.
rendimiento, *n.m.* submission; exhaustion; yield, output.
rendir [8], *v.t.* overcome; yield, produce; render; hand over.—*v.i.* yield.—*v.r.* surrender; become weary.
rene, *n.f.* kidney.
renegado, -da, *a., n.m.f.* renegade.
renegar [1B], *v.t.* deny; detest.—*v.i.* curse; apostatize; deny (***de***).
renegrido, -da, *a.* black-and-blue.
renglera, *n.f.* rank, row.
renglón, *n.m.* line (*print, writing*).
reniego, *n.m.* curse.
renitente, *a.* reluctant.
reno, *n.m.* reindeer.
renombrado, -da, *a.* renowned.
renombre, *n.m.* renown; surname.
renovable, *a.* renewable.
renovación, *n.f.* renewal; renovation.
renovador, -ra, *n.m.f.* renovator.
renovar [4], *v.t.* renew; renovate.
renquear, *v.i.* limp, hobble.
renta, *n.f.* income; — ***vitalicia,*** life annuity.
rentabilidad, *n.f.* (*com.*) yield.
rentado, -da, *a.* having an income.
rentar, *v.t.* produce, yield.
rentista, *n.m.f.* financier; receiver of income.
renuente, *a.* reluctant.
renuevo, *n.m.* renewal; new shoot.
renuncia, *n.f.* renunciation; resignation.
renunciación, *n.f.* renunciation.
renunciamiento, *n.f.* renouncement.
renunciar, *v.t.* renounce; resign; abandon; give (***a,*** up).
renuncio, *n.m.* error, slip; (*fam.*) fib.
reñido, -da, *a.* at variance; bitter.
reñir [8K], *v.t.* scold; argue about.—*v.i., v.r.* quarrel, fall out.
reo, rea, *a.* guilty.—*n.m.f.* criminal, offender.
de reojo, *adv. phr.* askance.
reorganizar [C], *v.t., v.r.* reorganize.
reparable, *a.* reparable; remarkable.
reparación, *n.f.* repair; reparation.
reparar, *v.t.* repair; remedy; observe; stop. —*v.i.* halt; spot, take note (***en,*** of).—*v.r.* stop; refrain.
reparo, *n.m.* repair; remark; objection, doubt; shelter; parry.
repartición, *n.f.* dealing; distribution.
repartimiento, *n.m.* distribution; assessment, allotment.
repartir, *v.t.* distribute; allot.
reparto, *n.m.* distribution; (*theat.*) cast.
repasar, *v.t.* retrace; revise; mend.
repaso, *n.m.* review; (*fam.*) scolding.
repatriación, *n.f.* repatriation.
repatriado, -da, *n.m.f.* repatriate.
repatriar [L], *v.t.* repatriate.
repecho, *n.m.* incline.
repelente, *a.* repellent.
repeler, *v.t.* repel.
repelo, *n.m.* twist, irregularity; (*fam.*) squabble; aversion.
repelón, *n.m.* tug, snatch; spurt.
repente, *n.m.* sudden start; ***de —,*** suddenly.

repentino, -na, *a.* sudden.
repentista, *n.m.f.* improviser; (*mus.*) sight-reader.
repercusión, *n.f.* repercussion; reflection.
repercutir, *v.i.* rebound; reverberate; have repercussions (***en,*** on).
repertorio, *n.m.* repertoire; repertory.
repetición, *n.f.* repetition.
repetir [8], *v.t.* repeat.
repicar [A], *v.t.* hash, mince; ring.—*v.i.* resound.—*v.r.* boast.
repinar, *v.r.* rise.
repipi, *a., n.m.f.* (*fam.*) show-off, know-all.
repique, *n.m.* mincing; ringing; (*fam.*) squabble.
repiquete, *n.m.*, peal; rapping; clash.
repiquetear, *v.t.* ring, chime; rap on.—*v.i.* peal; clatter.—*v.r.* (*fam.*) wrangle.
repisa, *n.f.* shelf; sill; mantelpiece.
repisar, *v.t.* trample on; fix in one's mind.
repizcar [A], *v.t.* pinch.
replegar [1B], *v.t.* fold back.—*v.r.* fall back.
repleto, -ta, *a.* replete, packed, full.
réplica, *n.f.* reply, retort; replica.
replicar [A], *v.t.* reply to.—*v.i.* retort.
repliegue, *n.m.* fold; falling back.
repoblación, *n.f.* repopulation; restocking.
repoblar [4], *v.t.* repopulate, restock.
repollo, *n.m.* white cabbage.
reponer [25], *v.t.* replace; restore; reply.—*v.r.* recover; become calm.
reportaje, *n.m.* report, reporting.
repórter, *n.m.* reporter.
reporterismo, *n.m.* newspaper reporting.
reportero, -ra, *n.m.f.* reporter.
reposado, -da, *a.* restful; solemn.
reposar, *v.i., v.r.* rest.
reposición, *n.f.* replacement; recovery.
reposo, *n.m.* repose, rest.
reposteria, *n.f.* pastry-shop; pantry.
repostero, *n.m.* pastry-cook; royal butler.
repregunta, *n.f.* cross-examination.
repreguntar, *v.t.* cross-examine.
reprender, *v.t.* reprehend.
reprensible, *a.* reprehensible.
reprensión, *n.f.* censure.
reprensor, -ra, *a.* reproving.—*n.m.f.* reproacher.
represa, *n.f.* dyke; recapture; check.
represalia, *n.f.* reprisal.
represaliar, *v.t.* retaliate against.
represar, *v.t.* dyke; check; recapture.
representación, *n.f.* performance; representation; dignity.
representanta, *n.f.* actress.
representante, *n.m.f.* representative, agent; actor.
representar, *v.t.* represent; show; perform; declare.—*v.r.* imagine.
representativo, -va, *a.* representative.
represión, *n.f.* repression.
represivo, -va, *a.* repressive.
represor, -ra, *n.m.f.* represser.
reprimenda, *n.f.* reprimand.
reprimir, *v.t* repress.
reprobar [4], *v.t.* reprove.
réprobo, -ba, *a., n.m.f.* reprobate.
reprochar, *v.t.* reproach.
reproche, *n.m.* reproach.
reproducción, *n.f.* reproduction.
reproducir [16], *v.t., v.r.* reproduce.
reproductivo, -va, reproductor, -ra, *a.* reproductive.
reptar, *v.i.* crawl.
reptil, *a., n.m.* reptile.
república, *n.f.* republic; ***República Arabe Unida,*** United Arab Republic.
republicanismo, *n.m.* republicanism.
republicano, -na, *a., n.m.f.* republican.
repudiación, *n.f.* repudiation.
repudiar, *v.t.* repudiate.
repuesto, -ta, *a.* secluded.—*n.m.* spare; ***de —,*** spare.—*p.p.* [REPONER].
repugnancia, *n.f.* repugnance.
repugnante, *a.* repugnant.
repugnar, *v.t.* contradict; avoid.—*v.i.* repel.
repulgo, *n.m.* hem; (*fig.*) silly scruple.
repulir, *v.t.* polish highly.—*v.t., v.r.* doll up.
repulsa, *n.f.* refusal, rejection.
repulsar, *v.t.* reject.
repulsión, *n.f.* repulsion; rejection.
repulsivo, -va, *a.* repulsive.
repullo, *n.m.* bound, start.
repuntar, *v.i.* move (*tide*).—*v.r.* go sour; (*fam.*) have a tiff.
repuse [REPONER].
reputación, *n.f.* reputation.
reputar, *v.t.* repute; appraise.
requebrar [1], *v.t.* flatter; flirt with; re-break.
requemazón, *n.f.* pungency; burn.
requerimiento, *n.m.* request; summons.
requerir [6], *v.t.* require; examine; woo; notify.
requesón, *n.m.* curds.
requetebién, *adv.* (*fam.*) fine, well.
requiebro, *n.m.* flattery; flirting; compliment.
réquiem, *n.m.* (*pl.* **-ms**) requiem.
requilorios, *n.m.pl.* (*fam.*) messing-about.
requisa, *n.f.* inspection; (*mil.*) requisition.
requisar, *v.t.* inspect; (*mil.*) requisition.
requisición, *n.f.* requisition.
requisito, -ta, *a., n.m.* requisite; ***— previo,*** prerequisite.
res, *n.f.* head of cattle, beast.
resaber [30], *v.t.* know completely.
resabiar, *v.t.* lead into evil ways.—*v.r.* contract vices; relish; leave aftertaste.
resabido, -da, *a.* well-known; pedantic.
resabio, *n.m.* nasty aftertaste; vice.
resaca, *n.f.* surge; backwash; (*fam.*) hang-over.
resalir [31], *v.i.* jut out.
resaltar, *v.i.* rebound; stand out.
resalte, *n.m.* projection.
resalto, *n.m.* rebound; projection.
resaludar, *v.t.* return the greeting of.
resarcir [D], *v.t.* compensate.
resbaladero,-ra, *n.m.f.* chute, slide; slipp(er)y place.
resbaladizo, -za, *a.* slipp(er)y.
resbaladura, *n.f.* slip *or* skid mark.
resbalar, *v.i.* slide; skid.—*v.r.* slip.
resbalón, *n.m.* slip.
rescatar, *v.t.* redeem; ransom; rescue.
rescate, *n.m.* ransom; rescue.
rescindir, *v.t.* rescind.
rescoldo, *n.m.* embers; smouldering; scruple.
rescontrar [4], *v.t.* (*com.*) offset.
resé [RESABER].
resecar [A], *v.t., v.r.* dry thoroughly.
reseco, -ca, *a.* very dry; skinny.
resellar, *v.t.* re-stamp; reseal.—*v.r.* turncoat.

resentido, -da, *a.* resentful.
resentimiento, *n.m.* resentment; grudge.
resentir [6], *v.r.* resent (***por***); weaken; suffer (***de,*** from).
reseña, *n.f.* review; outline.
reseñar, *v.t.* review; outline.
resequido, -da, *a.* dried up.
resero, *n.m.* stockman, rancher.
reserva, *n.f.* reserve, reservation.
reservación, *n.f.* reservation.
reservar, *v.t.* reserve; defer; conceal; exempt.—*v.r.* be wary.
reservista, *n.m.* (*mil.*) reservist.
reservón, -vona, *a.* (*fam.*) distant, reserved.
reservorio, *n.m.* reservoir.
resfriado, *n.m.* (*med.*) chill, cold.
resfriante, *a.* cooling.—*n.m.* cooler.
resfriar [L], *v.t., v.i.* cool.—*v.r.* cool off; catch cold.
resfrío, *n.m.* cold.
resguardar, *v.t.* protect, shield.
resguardo, *n.m.* shield, guard, protection; (*com.*) surety.
residencia, *n.f.* residence; hostel; (*jur.*) impeachment.
residencial, *a.* residential.
residenciar, *v.t.* impeach.
residente, *a., n.m.f.* resident.
residir, *v.i.* reside.
residual, *a.* residual, residuary.
residuo, *n.m.* residue; residuum.—*pl.* by-products.
resignación, *n.f.* resignation.
resignar, *v.t.* resign.
resina, *n.f.* resin, rosin.
resinoso, -sa, *a.* resinous.
resistencia, *n.m.f.* resistance; stamina.
resistente, *a.* resistant.
resistir, *v.t.* resist, withstand.—*v.i., v.r.* resist; refuse (***a,*** to).
resistor, *n.m.* (*elec.*) resistor.
resma, *n.f.* ream.
resolución, *n.f.* resolution.
resoluto, -ta, *a.* resolute; skilled; brief.
resolver [5, *p.p.* **resuelto**], *v.t.* decide on; solve; resolve.—*v.r.* resolve (***a,*** to); turn, dissolve (***en,*** into); decide (***por,*** on).
resollar [4], *v.i.* pant; take a rest; ***no —,*** not breathe a word.
resonancia, *n.f.* resonance; (*fig.*) repercussion.
resonante, *a.* resonant.
resonar [4], *v.i.* resound.
resoplar, *v.i.* puff; snort.
resopl(id)o, *n.m.* panting, puff.
resorte, *n.m.* (*mech.*) spring; motive; means; springiness; (*S.A.*) field, province.
respaldar, *n.m.* back (*of seat*).—*v.t.* endorse; back.—*v.r.* lean.
respaldo, *n.m.* back (*of seat*).
respectar, *v.t.* concern.
respectivo, -va, *a.* respective.
respecto, *n.m.* respect, reference; ***— a,*** with regard to.
respetabilidad, *n.f.* respectability.
respetable, *a.* respectable; (*fam.*) audience, spectators.
respetador, -ra, *a.* respectful.
respetar, *v.t.* respect.
respeto, *n.m.* respect, veneration; ***campar por su —,*** be one's own master; ***de —,*** spare; on ceremony.
respetuoso, -sa, *a.* respectful; awesome.
respigar [B], *v.t.* glean.
respingado, -da, *a.* turned-up (*nose*).
respingar [B], *v.i.* kick, baulk; fit badly.
respiración, *n.f.* respiration, breathing.
respiradero, *n.m.* vent.
respirador, *n.m.* respirator.
respirar, *v.t., v.i.* breathe; breathe again; feel respite; smell (***a,*** of).
respiratorio, -ria, *a.* respiratory.
respiro, *n.m.* breathing; respite.
resplandecer [9], *v.i.* shine.
resplandeciente, *a.* brilliant, gleaming.
resplandor, *n.m.* brilliance, radiance.
responder, *v.t.* answer; reply to.—*v.i.* answer (***de,*** for); harmonize; respond.
responsabilidad, *n.f.* responsibility.
responsable, *a.* responsible (***de,*** for).
responsivo, -va, *a.* responsive.
responso, *n.m.* (*eccl.*) response; (*fam.*) telling-off.
respuesta, *n.f.* answer, reply.
resquebra(ja)dura, *n.f.* split, cleft.
resquebrajadizo, -za, *a.* brittle.
resquebrajar, *v.t., v.r.* split.
resquebrar [1], *v.t., v.r.* crack.
resquemar, *v.t.* sting, parch, bite.
resquemazón, *n.f.* bite, sting; burn.
resquemor, *n.m.* anguish; sting.
resquicio, *n.m.* chink, crack; chance.
resta, *n.f.* subtraction; remainder.
restablecer [9], *v.t.* re-establish, restore.—*v.r.* recover.
restablecimiento, *n.m.* re-establishment, restoration; recovery.
restallar, *v.i.* crack, smack.
restante, *a.* remaining.—*n.m.* remainder, rest.
restañar, *v.t.* stanch; re-tin.
restar, *v.t.* subtract.—*v.i.* be left.
restauración, *n.f.* restoration.
restaurán, *n.m.* restaurant.
restaurante, *a.* restoring.—*n.m.* restaurant.
restaurar, *v.t.* restore.
restaurativo, -va, *a.* restorative.
restitución, *n.f.* restitution.
restituir [O], *v.t.* return, restore.
resto, *n.m.* rest, remainder.—*pl.* remains.
restorán, restorante, *n.m.* restaurant.
restregar [1B], *v.t.* scrub.
restricción, *n.f.* restriction; reservation.
restrictivo, -va, *a.* restrictive.
restringir [E], *v.t.* restrict; limit.
restriñir, *v.t.* restrain; bind.
resucitación, *n.f.* resuscitation.
resucitar, *v.t.* resurrect, resuscitate.—*v.i.* rise from the dead, revive.
resudar, *v.i.* sweat; seep; dry out.
resuelto, -ta, *a.* resolute; swift.—*p.p.* [RESOLVER].
resuello, *n.m.* heavy breathing.
resulta, *n.m.* outcome, effect; vacancy.
resultado, *n.m.* result.
resultando, *n.m.* (*jur.*) finding.
resultar, *v.i.* result (***en,*** in); turn out to be.
resumen, *n.m.* résumé; ***en —,*** in short.
resumidamente, *adv.* in short.
resumir, *v.t.* sum up.—*v.r.* be converted (***en,*** into).
resurgimiento, *n.m.* resurgence.
resurgir, *v.i.* re-arise; revive.
resurrección, *n.f.* resurrection.
resurtir, *v.i.* rebound.

retablo, *n.m.* (*eccl.*) altar-piece.
retaguardia, *n.f.* (*mil.*) rearguard.
retahila, *n.f.* file, line.
retama, *n.f.* (*bot.*) broom; furze.
retar, *v.t.* challenge.
retardar, *v.t.* retard.
retardo, *n.m.* delay.
retazo, *n.m.* scrap, piece.
retén, *n.m.*, store; reserve.
retención, *n.f.* retention.
retener [33], *v.t.* retain; detain.
retentivo, -va, *a.* retentive.—*n.f.* memory.
retina, *n.f.* (*anat.*) retina.
retintín, *n.m.* jingle, ringing.
retiñir [K], *v.i.* jingle, ring.
retirada, *n.f.* withdrawal, retreat.
retirar, *v.t.*, *v.r.* retire; withdraw.
retiro, *n.m.* retreat (*place*).
reto, *n.m.* challenge; threat.
retocar [A], *v.t.* retouch, touch up.
retoño, *n.m.* shoot, sprout.
retoque, *n.m.* retouching, touching-up.
retorcer [5D], *v.t.* twist; wring.—*v.r.* twist, writhe.
retórico, -ca, *a.* rhetorical.—*n.f.* rhetoric.
retornar, *v.t.*, *v.i.*, *v.r.* return.
retorno, *n.m.* return; reward; barter.
retortero, *n.m.* turn, twist.
retortijar, *v.t.* twist, curl.
retortijón, *n.m.* stomach-pain.
retozar [C], *v.i.* frolic; seethe.
retozón, -zona, *a.* frisky.
retracción, *n.f.* retraction.
retractación, *n.f.* retractation.
retractar, *v.t.* retract.
retráctil, *a.* retractile.
retraer [34], *v.t.* bring back; withdraw.—*v.r.* withdraw (***de,*** from).
retrasar, *v.t.* delay; put back (*clock*).—*v.i.* be late *or* behind.—*v.r.* delay; be behind; be late.
retraso, *n.m.* delay; lateness.
retratar, *v.t.* portray; copy; photograph.
retrato, *n.m.* portrait; copy; photograph.
retrechero, -ra, *a.* (*fam.*) cunning.
retreta, *n.f.* (*mil.*) retreat; tattoo.
retrete, *n.m.* closet; lavatory.
retribución, *n.f.* payment, fee.
retribuir [O], *v.t.* reward, pay for.
retroceder, *v.i.* recede; recoil.
retroceso, *n.m.* backing; recoil (*of gun*); retrocession.
retrógrado, -da, *a.*, *n.m.f.* retrograde; reactionary.
retrogressión, *n.f.* retrogression.
retropropulsión, *n.f.* jet-propulsion.
retrospección, *n.f.* retrospect(ion).
retrospectivo, -va, *a.* retrospective.
retrovisor, *n.m.* (*auto.*) driving-mirror.
retruécano, *n.m.* pun.
retumbante, *a.* high-flown; resounding.
retumbar, *v.i.* resound, re-echo.
reuma, *n.m.* rheumatism.—*n.m.* or *f.* (*med.*) rheum.
reumático, -ca, *a.* rheumatic.
reumatismo, *n.m.* rheumatism.
reunión, *n.f.* meeting, reunion.
reunir [P], *v.t.* assemble; unite; reunite.—*v.r.* meet, assemble.
revalidar, *v.t.* confirm, ratify.
revaloración, *n.f.* revaluation.
revalorar, revalorizar [C], *v.t.* revalue.
revancha, *n.f.* revenge, (*fam.*) evening the score.
revejecer [9], *v.i.*, *v.r.* age prematurely.
revelación, *n.f.* revelation.
revelar, *v.t.* reveal; (*phot.*) develop.
revenir [36], *v.i.* come back.—*v.r.* turn sour; shrivel; cave in; weaken.
reventar [1], *v.t.* smash up *or* open; burst; work to death; annoy.—*v.i.* burst; (*fam.*) peg out, die.—*v.r.* burst, explode.
reventón, *n.m.* burst; toil; steep hill.
rever [37], *v.t.* review, revise.
reverberar, *v.i.* reverberate.
reverbero, *n.m.* reverberation; reflector; street lamp; (*S.A.*) spirit stove.
reverdecer [9], *v.t.*, *v.i.* turn green again; rejuvenate.
reverencia, *n.f.* reverence; bow, curtsy.
reverenciar, *v.t.* revere.—*v.i.* bow, curtsy.
reverendo, -da, *a.* reverend.—*n.f.pl.* great qualities.
reverente, *a.* reverent.
reversible, *a.* reversible.
reversión, *n.f.* reversion.
reverso, *n.m.* reverse, back.
revés, *n.m.* reverse; back; setback; ***al —,*** the wrong way round; upside down; quite the opposite.
revesado, -da, *a.* complicated; wayward.
revestir [8], *v.t.* coat, cover; don; assume (*an air*); bedeck; invest (***con, de,*** with).
revezar [C], *v.i.* work in shifts.
revezo, *n.m.* shift, turn.
revisar, *v.t.* revise, review, look over.
revisión, *n.f.* revision, revisal.
revisor, -ra, *a.* revisory.—*n.m.f.* reviser; (*rail.*) ticket inspector.
revista, *n.f.* inspection; (*mil.*) review; (*theat.*) revue; magazine; ***pasar —,*** inspect, review.
revivificar [C], *v.t.* revive, revivify.
revivir, *v.i.* revive; be renewed.
revocar [A], *v.t.* revoke; whitewash.
revolar [4], *v.i.* fly about.
revolcar [4A], *v.t.* overturn, knock down.—*v.r.* overturn; wallow.
revolcón, *n.m.* (*fam.*) upset.
revol(ot)ear, *v.t.* fling up.—*v.i.* flutter.
revoltijo, revoltillo, *n.m.* mess, jumble.
revoltoso, -sa, *a.* rebellious; trouble-making; involved; winding.—*n.m.f.* rebel; trouble-maker.
revolución, *n.f.* revolution.
revolucionar, *v.t.* revolutionize; incite to rebellion.—*v.r.* rebel.
revolucionario, -ria, *a.*, *n.m.f.* revolutionary.
revolver [5, *p.p.* **revuelto**], *v.t.* turn over; shake; revolve; retrace.—*v.i.* retrace one's steps.—*v.r.* turn; toss and turn.
revólver, *n.m.* revolver.
revolvimiento, *n.m.* revolving; upset(ting); commotion.
revuelco, *n.m.* upset; wallowing.
revuelo, *n.m.* (second) flight; upset.
revuelto, -ta, *a.* complex; messy; naughty; changeable; boisterous.—*n.f.* return; revolt; fight; change; upset.—*p.p.* [REVOLVER].
rey, *n.m.* king; ***— de zarza,*** (*orn.*) wren; ***Reyes Magos,*** the Three Wise Men (*in Spain, the equivalent of Santa Claus*); (***Día de***) ***Reyes,*** Epiphany.

reyerta, *n.f.* wrangle.
reyezuelo, *n.m.* petty king; (*orn.*) goldcrest.
rezagado, -da, *a.* laggardly.—*n.m.f.* laggard, straggler.
rezagar [B], *v.t.* leave behind, outstrip; postpone.—*v.r.* lag behind.
rezar [C], *v.t.* pray; say.—*v.i.* pray; (*fam.*) have to do (**con**, with).
rezo, *n.m.* prayer; devotions.
rezongar [B], *v.i.* grumble.
rezumar, *v.t.*, *v.i.*, *v.r.* ooze, seep.
ría, *n.f.* inlet, estuary; fjord.
riachuelo, *n.m.* brook, rivulet.
riada, *n.f.* flood.
ribaldo, -da, *a.* (*obs.*) knavish.
ribazo, *n.m.* embankment.
ribera, *n.f.* bank, shore; riverside.
ribero, *n.m.* dyke.
ribete, *n.m.* trimming; sign.
ribetear, *v.t.* trim.
ricacho, -cha, *a.* (*fam.*) very rich.
Ricardo, *n.m.* Richard.
rico, -ca, *a.* rich; (*fam.*) superb; (*pej.*) cheeky. —*n.m.* rich man; ***nuevo* —,** nouveau riche. —*n.m.f.* love, dear.
ridiculez, *n.f.* ridiculousness.
ridiculizar [C], *v.t.* ridicule.
ridículo, -la, *a.* ridiculous; touchy.—*n.m.* ridicule; ***poner en* —,** make a fool of.
riego, *n.m.* irrigation; watering.
riel, *n.m.* rail; ingot.
rienda, *n.f.* rein.
riente, *a.* laughing, cheerful.
riesgo, *n.m.* risk, peril.
rifa, *n.f.* wrangle, fight; raffle.
rifar, *v.t.* raffle.
rifle, *n.m.* rifle.
rigidez, *n.f.* rigidity.
rígido, -da, *a.* rigid.
rigor, *n.m.* rigour; ***ser de* —,** be indispensable; ***en* —,** to be precise.
rigorista, *n.m.f.* stickler, rigorist.
rigoroso, riguroso, -sa, *a.* rigorous.
rija, *n.f.* squabble.
rima, *n.f.* rhyme; pile.
rimar, *v.t.*, *v.i.* rhyme.
rimbombante, *a.* high-flown; resounding.
rimbombar, *v.i.* resound.
rimero, *n.m.* pile.
Rin, *n.m.* Rhine.
rincón, *n.f.* corner, nook; patch.
rinconada, *n.f.* corner.
ringla, ringlera, *n.f.* row, tier.
ringorrango, *n.m.* (*fam.*) fancy flourish; frippery.
rinoceronte, *n.m.* (*zool.*) rhinoceros.
riña, *n.f.* quarrel; scuffle, fight.
riñon, *n.m.* (*anat.*) kidney.—*pl.* back; loins.
río, *n.m.* river.
rioplatense, *a.*, *n.m.f.* rel. to *or* native of River Plate area.
ripio, *n.m.* debris, rubble; doggerel; padding; (*fam.*) chance.
iqueza, *n.f.* riches, wealth; richness.
isa, *n.f.* laugh; laughter.
isco, *n.m.* crag, cliff.
iscoso, -sa, *a.* craggy, rugged.
isible, *a.* laughable.
isica, risilla, risita, *n.f.* giggle, titter.
isotada, *n.f.* guffaw.
isotear, *v.i.* guffaw.

ristra, *n.f.* string, line; lance-rest.
risueño, -ña, *a.* smiling.
rítmico, -ca, *a.* rhythmic(al).
ritmo, *n.m.* rhythm.
rito, *n.m.* rite.
ritual, *a.*, *n.m.* ritual.
rival, *a.*, *n.m.f.* rival.
rivalidad, *n.f.* rivalry.
rivalizar [C], *v.i.* vie, rival.
rizado, -da, *a.* curly.
rizar [C], *v.t.*, *v.r.* curl; frizzle.
rizo, -za, *a.* curly.—*n.m.* curl; (*aer.*) loop.
rizoma, *n.f.* rhizome.
rizoso, *a.* curly.
robar, *v.t.* rob; steal; carry off.
roble, *n.m.* oak.
robledal, robledo, *n.m.* oak-wood *or* forest.
roblón, *n.m.* rivet; tile-ridge.
roborar, *v.t.* reinforce; corroborate.
robot, *n.m.* robot.
robustecer [9], *v.t.*, *v.r.* strengthen.
robustez(a), *n.f.* robustness.
robusto, -ta, *a.* robust.
roca, *n.f.* rock.
rocalla, *n.f.* pebbles, gravel.
roce, *n.m.* rubbing; social contact.
rociada, *n.f.* sprinkling; spray; dew.
rociar [L], *v.t.* sprinkle, spray; dew.—*v.i.* drizzle.
rocín, *n.m.* nag; work-horse.
rocío, *n.m.* dew; drizzle.
rococó, *a.*, *n.m.* rococo.
rocoso, -sa, *a.* rocky.
rodaje, *n.m.* making (*of film*); wheels; ***en* —,** (*auto.*) running-in.
rodamiento, *n.m.* (*mech.*) bearing; tyre-tread.
Ródano, *n.m.* Rhone.
rodante, *a.* rolling.
rodar [4] *v.t.* roll, rotate; make (*a film*); film. —*v.i.* roll; roam; ***echar a* —,** ruin.
rodear, *v.t.* surround; go round.—*v.i.* wander about.—*v.r.* twist about.
rodeo, *n.m.* winding; roundabout way; round-up, rodeo.
rodera, *n.f.* rut, track.
rodilla, *n.f.* knee; ***de rodillas,*** kneeling down.
rodillo, *n.m.* roller; rolling-pin.
Rodrigo, *n.m.* Roderick.
roedor, -ra, *a.* gnawing.—*a.*, *n.m.* (*zool.*) rodent.
roer [29], *v.t.* gnaw; gnaw away.
rogación, *n.f.* petition; rogation.
rogar [4B], *v.t.*, *v.i.* request; beg; plead.
rogativo, -va, *a.* supplicatory.—*n.f.* rogation.
roído, -da, *a.* (*fam.*) stingy. [ROER].
rojear, *v.i.* redden.
rojete, *n.m.* rouge (*make-up*).
rojizo, -za, *a.* reddish.
rojo, -ja, *a.*, *n.m.* red; (*pol.*) Red.
rol, *n.m.* roll, list.
Rolando, Roldán, *n.m.* Roland.
rollar, *v.t.* roll up.
rollizo, -za, *a.* chubby; sturdy; round.
rollo, *n.m.* roll; scroll; roller; log; (*fam.*) mess; (*fam.*) bore.
Roma, *n.f.* Rome.
romana, *n.f.* steelyard; (*fig.*) balance.
romance, *a.* Romance.—*n.m.* Romance; Spanish; traditional ballad; (*fig.*) plain language.—*pl.* romancing.

romancear, *v.t.* translate.
romancero, *a.* romancing.—*n.m.* corpus *or* collection of ballads.
romanesco, -ca, *a.* novelesque; Roman.
románico, -ca, *a.*, *n.m.* Romanic; Romanesque; Romance.
romanilla, *n.f.* (*print.*) roman.
romanizar [C], *v.t.*, *v.r.* Romanize.
romano, -na, *a.*, *n.m.f.* Roman.
romanticismo, *n.m.* romanticism; Romanticism.
romántico, -ca, *a.*, *n.m.f.* romantic; Romantic.
romería, *n.f.* pilgrimage.
romero (1), **-ra,** *n.m.f.* pilgrim.
romero (2), *n.m.* (*bot.*) rosemary.
romo, -ma, *a.* dull, blunt.
rompecabezas, *n.m. inv.* puzzle.
rompehielos, *n.m. inv.* ice-breaker.
rompeolas, *n.m. inv.* breakwater.
romper [*p.p.* **roto**], *v.t.* *v.i.* break; **— *a*,** begin suddenly to.
rompimiento, *n.m.* break; breakage.
Rómulo, *n.m.* Romulus.
ron, *n.m.* rum.
ronca, *n.f.* (*fam.*) menace, bullying.
roncar [A], *v.i.* snore; roar.
roncear, *v.i.* dawdle; wheedle.
ronco, -ca, *a.* hoarse; raucous; husky.
ronchar, *v.t.*, *v.i.* crunch.
ronda, *n.f.* night-patrol; (*fam.*) round (*of drinks*); serenaders.
rondalla, *n.f.* yarn, tale.
rondar, *v.t.* go round; menace; patrol; roam (*esp. at night*).
de rondón, *adv. phr.* rashly, brashly.
ronquedad, *n.f.* hoarseness.
ronquido, *n.m.* snore; harsh sound.
ronronear, *v.i.* purr.
roña, *n.f.* manginess; filth.
roñería, *n.f.* stinginess.
roñoso, -sa, *a.* mangy; filthy; mingy, stingy.
ropa, *n.f.* clothes, clothing.
ropaje, *n.m.* garment(s); adornment.
ropavejero, -ra, *n.m.f.* old-clothes dealer.
ropero, -ra, *n.m.f.* clothier.—*n.m.* wardrobe.
roque, *n.m.* rook (*chess*).
rorro, *n.m.* (*fam.*) baby.
rosa, *n.f.* rose.
rosada, *n.f.* frost, rime.
rosado, -da, *a.* rose, rosy, pink; rosé (*wine*).
rosal, *n.m.* rose-bush.
rosario, *n.m.* rosary.
rosbif, *n.m.* roast-beef.
rosca, *n.f.* spiral; screw-thread.
roscar [A], *v.t.* thread, spiral.
rosco, *n.m.* bun.
róseo, -sea, *a.* rosy.
roseta, *n.f.* red spot; rose (*of pipe*); rosette.—*pl.* pop-corn.
rosicler, *n.m.* dawn-pink.
rosmarino, -na, *a.* pink.—*n.m.* rosemary.
rosquilla, *n.f.* dough-nut.
rostro, *n.m.* face; beak; ***hacer* — *a*,** face up to.
rostropálido, -da, *a.*, *n.m.f.* pale-face (*white man*).
rota, *n.f.* rout; course, route.
rotación, *n.f.* rotation.
rotativo, -va, rotatorio, -ria, *a.* rotary.
roto, -ta, *a.* broken; dissolute; torn.—*p.p.* [ROMPER].
rotular, *v.t.* label.
rótulo, *n.m.* label; poster.
rotundo, -da, *a.* rotund.
rozagante, *a.* showy; sweeping (*dress*).
rozar [C], *v.t.* clear, clean; rub down; graze.—*v.i.* brush (***con,*** against).—*v.r.* rub shoulders; falter.
rubéola, *n.f.* German measles.
rubí, *n.m.* (*pl.* **-íes**) ruby.
rubicundo, -da, *a.* rubicund.
rubio, -bia, *a.* blond(e), fair.—*n.m.f.* blond(e).
rublo, *n.m.* rouble.
rubor, *n.m.* redness; blush; shame.
ruborizar [C], *v.r.* redden.
rúbrica, *n.f.* rubric; heading; flourish.
rubricar [A], *v.t.* sign and seal; endorse.
rubro, -ra, *a.* red.—*n.m.* (*S.A.*) title.
rucio, -cia, *a.* gray, hoary.
rudeza, *n.f.* coarseness; roughness.
rudimentario, -ria, *a.* rudimentary.
rudimento, *n.m.* rudiment.
rudo, -da, *a.* rough; crude; harsh.
rueca, *n.f.* distaff; turn, twist.
rueda, *n.f.* wheel; ring; ***hacer la* —,** flatter; ***— de presos,*** identification parade.
ruedo, *n.m.* bull-ring; turn; circle; arena.
ruego, *n.m.* request, petition.
rufián, *n.m.* pimp; thug.
rugido, *n.m.* roar, bellow.
rugir [E], *v.i.* roar; leak out.
rugoso, -sa, *a.* wrinkled; corrugated.
ruibarbo, *n.m.* rhubarb.
ruido, *n.m.* noise.
ruidoso, -sa, *a.* noisy.
ruin, *a.* vile; wretched; nasty.—*n.m.* rogue.
ruina, *n.f.* ruin; ruination.
ruindad, *n.f.* vileness; pettiness; nastiness.
ruinoso, -sa, *a.* ruinous; harmful; collapsing.
ruiseñor, *n.m.* nightingale.
ruleta, *n.f.* roulette.
Rumania, *n.f.* Romania.
rumano, -na, *a.*, *n.m.f.* Romanian.
rumba, *n.f.* rumba.
rumbático, -ca, *a.* showy, flashy.
rumbo, *n.m.* course; (*fam.*) flashiness.
rumboso, -sa, *a.* flashy, showy; (*fam.*) generous.
rumiante, *a.*, *n.m.* (*zool.*) ruminant.
rumiar, *v.i.* ruminate; muse; fret.
rumor, *n.m.* rumour; murmur.
rumorear, *v.t.* rumour.—*v.i.* murmur.
runrún, *n.m.* (*fam.*) murmur; rumour; noise.
rupestre, *a.* rock, cave (*paintings etc.*).
rupia, *n.f.* rupee.
ruptura, *n.f.* break; rupture; crack.
rural, *a.* rural.
Rusia, *n.f.* Russia.
ruso, -sa, *a.*, *n.m.f.* Russian.
rústico, -ca, *a.*, *n.m.f.* rustic; ***en rústica,*** paper-bound (*book*).
rustiquez(a), **rusticidad,** *n.f.* rusticity.
Rut, *n.f.* Ruth.
ruta, *n.f.* route.
rutilar, *v.i.* (*poet.*) shine.
rutina, *n.f.* routine.
rutinario, -ria, rutinero, -ra, *a.* routine.—*n.m.f.* slave of routine; routinist.

S

S, s, *n.f.* twenty-second letter of the Spanish alphabet.
sábado, *n.m.* Saturday.
sabana, *n.f.* savanna(h).
sábana, *n.f.* sheet.
sabandija, *n.f.* vermin; bug.
sabañón, *n.m.* chilblain.
sabático, -ca, *a.* sabbatical.
sabatino, -na, *a.* rel. to Saturday.
sabedor, -ra, *a.* well-informed.
sabelotodo, *n.m.f. inv.* know-all.
saber, *n.m.* knowledge.—*v.t., v.i.* [30] know; taste (*a,* of); know how to; *a* —, to wit, namely; — *de,* know of; hear from.—(*S.A.*) [SOLER].
sabidillo, -lla, *a., n.m.f.* (*pej.*) know-all.
sabiduría, *n.f.* wisdom, learning.
a sabiendas, *adv. phr.* knowingly.
sabihondo, -da, *a., n.m.f.* know-all.
sabio, -bia, *a.* wise, learned.—*n.m.f.* wise person, sage; scholar; scientist.
sablazo, *n.m.* sabre blow *or* wound; (*fam.*) sponging, touch.
sable, *n.m.* sabre, cutlass; (*her.*) sable.
sabor, *n.m.* flavour; *a* —, to one's liking.
saborear, *v.t.* savour; flavour; entice.—*v.r.* relish, savour, delight (*con,* in).
sabotaje, *n.m.* sabotage.
saboteador, -ra, *n.m.f.* saboteur.
sabotear, *v.t.* sabotage.
sabroso, -sa, *a.* delicious, tasty; (*fam.*) salty.
sabuco, sabugo, *n.m.* (*bot.*) elder.
sabueso, *n.m.* bloodhound.
saca, *n.f.* extraction; draft.
sacabocado(s), *n.m.* ticket-punch.
sacacorchos, *n.m. inv.* corkscrew.
sacacuartos, sacadinero(s), *n.m. inv.* (*fam.*) catch-penny.
sacaliña, *n.f.* goad; cunning.
sacamanchas, *n.m. inv.* stain-remover.
sacamuelas, *n.m. inv.* (*fam.*) dentist, tuggem.
sacaperras, *n.m. inv.* (*fam.*) one-armed bandit, catch-penny.
sacapuntas, *n.m. inv.* pencil sharpener.
sacar [A], *v.t.* take *or* pull *or* draw out; remove; bring out; solve; (*phot.*) take; get, win; book (*tickets*); — *a luz,* publish.
sacarina, *n.f.* saccharine.
sacerdocio, *n.m.* priesthood.
sacerdotal, *a.* priestly.
sacerdote, *n.m.* priest.
saciar, *v.t.* satiate.
saciedad, *n.f.* satiety.
saco, *n.m.* sack, bag; pillage, sacking.
sacramental, *a., n.m.f.* sacramental.
sacramentar, *v.t.* administer the sacrament to.
sacramento, *n.m.* sacrament.
sacratísimo, *sup. of* SACRO.
sacrificar [A], *v.t.* sacrifice.
sacrificio, *n.m.* sacrifice.
sacrilegio, *n.m.* sacrilege.
sacrílego, -ga, *a.* sacrilegious.
sacrista, sacristán, *n.m.* sacristan, sexton.
sacristía, *n.f.* sacristy.
sacro, -ra, *a.* sacred, holy.
sacrosanto, -ta, *a.* sacrosanct.
sacudido, -da, *a.* determined; indocile.—*n.f.* jolt, shake.
sacudir, *v.t.* shake, jar; beat.
sádico, -ca, *a.* sadistic.
sadismo, *n.m.* sadism.
saeta, *n.f.* arrow; finger (*of clock*); song to the Virgin.
saetera, *n.f.* loophole.
saetero, *n.m.* bowman, archer.
saetilla, *n.f.* finger (*of clock*); magnetic needle.
safari, *n.m.* safari.
sáfico, -ca, *a.* Sapphic.
sagacidad, *n.f.* sagacity.
sagaz, *a.* (*pl.* **-aces**) sagacious; sharp, keen.
sagrado, -da, *a.* sacred.—*n.m.* asylum sanctuary.
sagú, *n.m.* (*pl.* **-úes**) sago.
sahorno, *n.m.* scratch, graze.
sahumar, *v.t.* smoke, incense.
saín, *n.m.* grease, fat, oil.
sainete, *n.m.* one-act farce; zest; tit-bit.
sajar, *v.t.* cut, tap.
sajón, -jona, *a., n.m.f.* Saxon.
sal, *n.f.* salt; wit; charm.
sala, *n.f.* hall, drawing-room; court; room.
salacidad, *n.f.* salacity.
saladar, *n.m.* salt-marsh.
salado, -da, *a.* salt, salty; briny; witty; charming; (*S.A.*) dear, high.
salamandra, *n.f.* (*zool.*) salamander; newt.
salar, *v.t.* salt.
salariar, *v.t.* salary.
salario, *n.m.* salary, pay.
salaz, *a.* (*pl.* **-aces**) salacious.
salazón, *n.f.* salting, curing; salted meat.
salchicha, *n.f.* sausage.
saldar, *v.t.* settle, liquidate; sell out.
saldo, *n.m.* liquidation, settlement; sale.
saldré [SALIR].
saledizo, -za, *a.* projecting.—*n.m.* projection.
salero, *n.m.* salt-cellar; salt-mine; wit charm.
salgo [SALIR].
sálico, -ca, *a.* Salic.
salida, *n.f.* exit; departure; result; sally; outlet; success.
salidizo, *n.m.* projection.
salido, -da, *a.* projecting.
saliente, *a.* projecting; outstanding; rising (*sun*).
salino, -na, *a.* saline.—*n.f.* salt-mine; salt-pit.
salir [31], *v.i.* go *or* come out; leave, depart; appear; start; turn out; — *con bien,* succeed; *salirse con la suya,* have one's way.
salitre, *n.m.* saltpetre.
saliva, *n.f.* saliva.
salmantino, -na, *a., n.m.f.* rel. to *or* native of Salamanca.
salmo, *n.m.* psalm.
salmodia, *n.f.* psalmody; (*fam.*) singsong.
salmón, *n.m.* salmon.
salmuera, *n.f.* brine.
salobre, *a.* brackish.
saloma, *n.f.* (*naut.*) shanty.
Salomón, *n.m.* Solomon.
salón, *n.m.* saloon; hall, room.
salpicadura, *n.f.* splash, spatter.
salpicar [A], *v.t.* splash, splatter; skimp.
salpicón, *n.m.* splash; mince, hodge-podge.

salpimentar [I], *v.t.* salt and pepper; (*fam.*) sugar the pill.
salpresar, *v.t.* salt, cure.
salpreso, -sa, *a.* salt, cured.
salpullido, *n.m.* rash.
salsa, *n.f.* sauce; — ***de San Bernado,*** (*fam.*) hunger.
saltabanco(s), *n.m. inv.* mountebank.
saltadizo, -za, *a.* brittle.
saltamontes, *n.m. inv.* grasshopper.
saltar, *v.t., v.i.* jump.—*v.i.* leap, bound, spurt; — ***a la vista,*** be obvious.—*v.r.* skip, omit.
saltarín, -rina, *n.m.f.* dancer; restless person.
salteador, *n.m.* highwayman.
saltear, *v.t.* hold up, waylay; take by surprise; skip through.
salterio, *n.m.* psaltery; Psalter.
saltimbanco [SALTABANCO].
salto, *n.m.* leap, jump; jolt, sudden change; skipping; dive.
saltón, -tona, *a.* jumping.—*n.m.* grasshopper; worm.
salubre, *a.* salubrious.
salud, *n.f.* health; salvation; welfare.—*interj.* good health!
saludable, *a.* salutary, wholesome.
saludar, *v.t.* greet; salute.
saludo, *n.m.* greeting; salute.
salutación, *n.f.* salutation.
salva, *n.f.* salvo; great applause; greeting.
salvación, *n.f.* salvation.
salvado, *n.m.* bran.
el Salvador, *n.m.* the Saviour; **salvador, -ra,** *n.m.f.* saver; saviour.
salvaguardar, *v.t.* safeguard.
salvaguardia, *n.m.* guard.—*n.f.* safeguard; safe-conduct.
salvajada, *n.f.* savagery.
salvaje, *a.* savage; wild.—*n.m.f.* savage.
salvajería, *n.f.*, **salvajismo,** *n.m.* savagery.
a salvamano, *adv. phr.* without risk.
salvam(i)ento, *n.m.* saving; salvage.
salvar, *v.t.* save; salvage; overcome, get round; jump over.—*v.r.* be saved.
salvavidas, *n.m. inv.* life-buoy; guard; (*rail.*) cow-catcher.
salvedad, *n.f.* reservation.
salvo, -va, *a.* safe; excepted.—*prep.* except for, save; — ***que,*** unless; ***a*** —, safe (*de,* from); ***en*** —, safe; at liberty.
salvoconducto, *n.m.* safe-conduct.
samaritano, -na, *a., n.m.f.* Samaritan.
sambenito, *n.m.* sanbenito; infamy.
samblaje, *n.m.* joint; joinery.
San, *n.m.* (*contraction of* SANTO) Saint (*used before masc. names, except those beginning with* **To-** *or* **Do-**).
sanar, *v.t., v.i.* heal.
sanatorio, *n.m.* sanatorium.
sanción, *n.f.* sanction.
sancionar, *v.t.* sanction.
sandalia, *n.f.* sandal.
sandez, *n.f.* (*pl.* **-eces**) folly, nonsense.
sandía, *n.f.* water-melon.
sandio, -dia, *a.* silly, foolish.
sanear, *v.t.* indemnify; guarantee; drain.
sangradura, *n.f.* (*med.*) bleeding; outlet.
sangrante, *a.* bleeding.
sangrar, *v.t.* bleed; drain; indent.—*v.i.* bleed; be new *or* evident.
sangre, *n.f.* blood; — ***azul*** or ***goda,*** blue blood; — ***fría,*** sang-froid, presence of mind.
sangría, *n.f.* (*med.*) bleeding, blood-letting; drain, tap; (*cul.*) wine-cup.
sangriento, -ta, *a.* bloody.
sanguijuela, *n.f.* (*zool.*) leech.
sanguinario, -ria, *a.* sanguinary.
sanguíneo, -nea, *a.* sanguineous; sanguine.
sanguino, -na, *a.* sanguine; sanguineous.
sanidad, *n.f.* health, healthiness; sanitation.
sano, -na, *a.* healthy; sound; safe; — ***y salvo,*** safe and sound.
sánscrito, -ta, *a., n.m.* Sanskrit.
sanseacabó, *interj.* (*fam.*) that's it! all done!
Sansón, *n.m.* Samson.
santabárbara, *n.f.* (*naut.*) magazine.
santanderino, -na, *a., n.m.f.* rel. to *or* native of Santander.
santero, -ra, *a.* devoted to saints.—*n.m.* sexton; beggar.
Santiago, *n.m.* St. James.
santiamén, *n.m.* (*fam.*) jiffy.
santidad, *n.f.* holiness.
santiguar [H], *v.t.* bless, cross.—*v.r.* cross oneself.
Santo, -ta, *prefix* Saint; **santo, -ta,** *a.* holy, blessed, sacred; saintly; (*fam.*) simple.—*n.m.f.* saint.—*n.m.* (*mil.*) password; (*fam.*) onomastic day.
santón, *n.m.* dervish; hypocrite.
santoral, *n.m.* saints' calendar.
santuario, *n.m.* sanctuary.
santurrón, -rrona, *a.* sanctimonious.
saña, *n.f.* fury; — ***vieja,*** old score, vendetta.
sañoso, -sa, sañudo, -da, *a.* furious; irascible.
Sapiencia, *n.f.* (*Bib.*) Wisdom; **sapiencia,** *n.f.* sapience, wisdom
sapiente, *a.* sapient.
sapo, *n.m.* (*zool.*) toad.
saquear, *v.t.* loot, plunder, sack.
saqueo, *n.m.* plundering, sacking.
sarampión, *n.m.* (*med.*) measles.
sarao, *n.m.* soirée.
sarcasmo, *n.m.* sarcasm.
sarcástico, -ca, *a.* sarcastic.
sarcia, *n.f.* burden.
sarcófago, *n.m.* sarcophagus.
sardana, *n.f.* sardana (*Catalan dance*).
sardina, *n.f.* (*ichth.*) sardine.
sardo, -da, *a., n.m.f.* Sardinian.
sardónico, -ca, *a.* sardonic.
sargento, *n.m.* sergeant.
sarmiento, *n.m.* vine shoot.
sarna, *n.f.* mange, itch.
sarnoso, -sa, *a.* mangy.
sarraceno, -na, *a., n.m.f.* Saracen.
sarracina, *n.f.* scuffle, fight.
sarro, *n.m.* sediment; tartar; crust.
sarta, *n.f.* string (*of beads*); file, line.
sartal, *n.m.* string (*of beads*).
sartén, *n.m.* frying-pan.
sastre, *n.m.* tailor.
Satán, Satanás, *n.m.* Satan.
satánico, -ca, *a.* satanic, devilish.
satélite, *n.m.* satellite; (*fam.*) henchman.
sátira, *n.f.* satire.
satírico, -ca, *a.* satirical.—*n.m.f.* satirist.
satirizar [C], *v.t.* satirize.
sátiro, *n.m.* satyr.
satisfacción, *n.f.* satisfaction.

satisfacer [20], *v.t.* satisfy.—*v.r.* be satisfied (*de*, with).
satisfactorio, -ria, *a.* satisfactory.
satisfecho, -cha, *a.* conceited.—*p.p.* [SATISFACER].
sativo, -va, *a.* tilled (*land*).
saturación, *n.f.* saturation.
saturar, *v.t.* saturate; glut.
saturnal, *n.f.* Saturnalia.
Saturno, *n.m.* Saturn.
sauce, *n.m.* (*bot.*) willow.
saúco, *n.m.* (*bot.*) elder.
Saúl, *n.m.* Saul.
savia, *n.f.* sap.
saxófono, *n.m.* saxophone.
saya, *n.f.* petticoat; skirt; tunic.
sayal, *n.m.* sackcloth, serge.
sayo, *n.m.* smock.
sayón, *n.m.* executioner; lout.
sazón, *n.f.* season; time; ripeness; ***a la* —,** at that time; ***en* —,** in season, ripe.
sazonar, *v.t.* ripen; season.
se, *inv. pron. m. & f.* himself; herself; itself; yourself; themselves; *also renders the English passive:* — ***dice,*** it is said; ***aquí* — *habla español,*** Spanish (is) spoken here. —*pron. dat.* (*replaces* LE, LES, *when these are followed by another pronoun*).
sé [SABER].
sebo, *n.m.* tallow.
seca, *n.f.* drought.
secano, -na, *a.* dry, waterless.—*n.m.* dry, arid land.
secante, *a.* drying.—*n.m.* blotting paper.—*n.f.* secant.
secar [A], *v.t.* dry, dry out; bore, annoy.—*v.r.* dry out, dry up.
sección, *n.f.* section; (*mil.*) platoon.
seccionar, *v.t.* section.
secesión, *n.f.* secession.
secesionismo, *n.m.* secessionism.
seco, -ca, *a.* dry, dried up, dried out; lean, meagre; hard; ***en* —,** high and dry; for no reason; suddenly.
secreción, *n.f.* secretion; segregation.
secretaría, *n.f.* secretary's office; secretariat.
secretario, -ria, *n.m.f.* secretary.
secretear, *v.i.* (*fam.*) whisper.
secreto, -ta, *a.* secret; secretive.—*n.m.* secret; — ***a voces,*** open secret.
secta, *n.f.* sect.
sectario, -ria, *a.*, *n.m.f.* sectarian.
sector, *n.m.* sector.
secuaz, *a.* (*pl.* **-aces**) following, attendant. —*n.m.f.* follower.
secuela, *n.f.* sequel, result.
secuestrar, *v.t.* kidnap; sequestrate.
secuestro, *n.m.* kidnapping; sequestration.
secular, *a.* secular; century-long.
secularismo, *n.m.* secularism.
secularizar [C], *v.t.*, *v.r.* secularize.
secundar, *v.t.* second.
secundario, -ria, *a.* secondary.
sed, *n.f.* thirst; ***tener* —,** be thirsty (***de***, for).
seda, *n.f.* silk.
sedal, *n.m.* fishing-line.
sedán, *n.m.* sedan.
sedante, *a.*, *n.m.* sedative.
sedar, *v.t.* allay, soothe.
sede, *n.f.* (*eccl.*) see; seat; (*com.*) head office.
sedentario, -ria, *a.* sedentary.
sedicente, *a.* self-styled.
sedición, *n.f.* sedition.
sedicioso, -sa, *a.* seditious.
sediento, -ta, *a.* thirsty.
sedimentar, *v.t.*, *v.r.* sediment.
sedimento, *n.m.* sediment.
sedoso, -sa, *a.* silken, silky.
seducción, *n.f.* attraction, charm; enticement; seduction.
seducir [15], *v.t.* deceive; captivate; seduce.
seductor, -ra, *a.* captivating; attractive.—*n.m.f.* seducer; enticer.
seduje, seduzco [SEDUCIR].
sefardí, *a.* (*pl.* **-íes**) Sephardic.—*n.m.f.* Sephardi.
segador, -ra, *a.* harvesting.—*n.m.f.* harvester.
segar [1B], *v.t.* mow, reap; mow down.
seglar, *a.* lay; secular.—*n.m.* layman.—*n.f.* laywoman.
segmento, *n.m.* segment.
segregación, *n.f.* segregation; secretion.
segregar [B], *v.t.* segregate; secrete.
seguida, *n.f.* continuation; ***en* —,** at once.
seguidamente, *adv.* successively; at once.
seguidilla, *n.f.* Spanish metre and tune.
seguido, -da, *a.* continuous, successive; direct; running in a row.
seguidor, -ra, *n.m.f.* follower.
seguir [8G], *v.t.* follow; pursue; carry on, continue.—*v.i.* carry on, go on.—*v.r.* ensue; follow, issue.
según, *adv.* it depends.—*prep.* according to.—*conj.* according to what.
segundo, -da, *a.* second; ***de segunda mano,*** second-hand.—*n.m.* second (*time*).
segur, *n.f.* axe, sickle.
seguridad, *n.f.* security; surety, certainty; safety.
seguro, -ra, *a.* sure, certain; safe, secure; steady.—*n.m.* safe place; insurance; ***de* —,** assuredly; ***sobre* —,** without risk.
seis, *a.*, *n.m.* six.
seisavo, -va, *a.*, *n.m.* sixth; hexagon(al).
seísm- [SISM-].
selección, *n.f.* selection.
seleccionar, *v.t.* select.
selectivo, -va, *a.* selective.
selecto, -ta, *a.* select.
selector, -ra, *a.* selecting.—*n.m.* selector.
selva, *n.f.* forest; jungle.
selvicultura, *n.f.* forestry.
selvoso, -sa, *a.* wooded.
sellar, *v.t.* seal; stamp.
sello, *n.m.* seal; stamp.
semáforo, *n.m.* semaphore; traffic-lights.
semana, *n.f.* week; ***entre* —,** during midweek.
semanal, *a.* weekly.
semanario, -ria, *a.*, *n.m.* weekly.
semántico, -ca, *a.* semantic.—*n.f.* semantics.
semblante, *n.m.* face, mien; look, aspect; ***hacer* — *de*,** feign.
sembrado, *n.m.* corn-field, (*U.S.*) grainfield.
sembrar [1], *v.t.* sow; scatter.
semejante, *a.* similar, like, alike.—*n.m.* fellow, equal; likeness.
semejanza, *n.f.* likeness, resemblance; ***a* — *de*,** like.
semejar, *v.i.*, *v.r.* be alike; **— (*a*),** be like, resemble.
semen, *n.m.* semen.
sementar [1], *v.t.* sow, seed.
sementera, *n.f.* seed-bed; sowing; hot-bed.

semestre, ***n.m.*** six months; semester.
semicírculo, ***n.m.*** semicircle.
semiconsciente, ***a.*** semiconscious.
semidiós, ***n.m.*** demigod.
semidormido, -da, ***a.*** half-asleep.
semilla, ***n.f.*** seed.
semillero, ***n.m.*** seed-bed.
seminal, ***a.*** seminal.
seminario, ***n.m.*** seminary; seed-bed; seminar.
seminarista, ***n.m.*** seminarist.
semita, ***a.*** Semitic.—***n.m.f.*** Semite.
semítico, -ca, ***a.*** Semitic.
semivivo, -va, ***a.*** half-alive.
sémola, ***n.f.*** semolina.
sempiterno, -na, ***a.*** everlasting, sempiternal.
Sena, ***n.f.*** Seine; **sena,** ***n.f.*** senna.
senado, ***n.m.*** senate.
senador, ***n.m.*** senator.
sencillez, ***n.f.*** simplicity.
sencillo, -lla, ***a.*** simple.
senda, ***n.f.,*** **sendero,** ***n.m.*** path.
sendos, -das, ***a.*** one each, sundry; (*fam.*) great.
senectud, ***n.f.*** old age.
el Senegal, ***n.m.*** Senegal.
senegalés, -lesa, ***a., n.m.f.*** Senegalese.
senil, ***a.*** senile.
senilidad, ***n.f.*** senility.
senilismo, ***n.m.*** senile decay.
seno, ***n.m.*** bosom; lap; bay; (*math.*) sine.
sensación, ***n.f.*** sensation.
sensacional, ***a.*** sensational.
sensacionalismo, ***n.m.*** sensationalism.
sensatez, ***n.f.*** (good) sense.
sensato, -ta, ***a.*** sensible, wise.
sensibilidad, ***n.f.*** sensitiveness, sensibility.
sensibilizar [C], ***v.t.*** sensitize.
sensible, ***a.*** perceptible; sensitive; grievous.
sensiblería, ***n.f.*** sentimentality.
sensiblero, -ra, ***a.*** sentimental, mawkish.
sensitivo, -va, ***a.*** sensitive; sensual.
sensorio, -ria, ***a.*** sensory.
sensual, ***a.*** sensuous, sensual.
sensualidad, ***n.f.*** sensuality.
sensualismo, ***n.m.*** sensualism.
sentada, ***n.f.*** sitting.
sentadero, ***n.m.*** place to sit.
sentado, -da, ***a.*** settled, stable; grave, sedate; ***dar por* —,** take for granted.
sentar [I], ***v.t.*** seat; fit, suit; settle; set down. —***v.r.*** sit down; mark.
sentencia, ***n.f.*** sentence.
sentenciar, ***v.t.*** sentence.
sentencioso, -sa, ***a.*** sententious.
sentido, -da, ***a.*** felt; feeling; touchy.—***p.p.*** [SENTIR].—***n.m.*** sense; meaning; ***sin* —,** senseless.
sentimental, ***a.*** sentimental.
sentimiento, ***n.m.*** feeling; sentiment; sorrow.
sentina, ***n.f.*** bilge; den of vice.
sentir, ***n.m.*** feeling; opinion.—***v.t.*** [6] feel; regret; be sorry about; perceive; hear.—***v.r.*** feel; complain; have a pain (***de,*** in, from); split; decay.
seña, ***n.f.*** sign, mark, token; vestige; password.—***pl.*** address; ***señas mortales,*** clear indication.
señá, ***n.f.*** (*fam.*) [SEÑORA].
señal, ***n.f.*** sign, token; signal; marker; scar; trace; road-sign; traffic lights; symptom; pledge; ***en — de,*** as a token of.—***pl.*** ***señales acústicas,*** (*auto.*) horn.
señalado, -da, ***a.*** noted.
señalar, ***v.t.*** point out, indicate; mark; designate.—***v.r.*** excel.
el Señor, ***n.m.*** the Lord; **señor, -ra,** ***a.*** master; (*fam.*) fine, great.—***n.m.*** sir (*in voc.*); mister, Mr.; lord; owner, master.—***n.f.*** lady; mistress; Mrs.; madam (*in voc.*); wife; ***nuestra Señora,*** Our Lady.
señorear, ***v.t.*** rule, lord, control; tower above.—***v.r.*** lord it; take control (***de,*** of).
señorío, ***n.m.*** mastery; dominion, rule; gentry; manor; gravity.
señorita, ***n.f.*** Miss; young lady.
señorito, ***n.m.*** Master; young master; (*fam.*) dandy; (*pej.*) whippersnapper.
señuelo, ***n.m.*** decoy, lure.
sepa [SABER].
separación, ***n.f.*** separation.
separado, -da, ***a.*** separate; ***por* —,** separately.
separar, ***v.t., v.r.*** separate.
separata, ***n.f.*** off-print.
separatismo, ***n.m.*** separatism.
separatista, ***a., n.m.f.*** separatist.
sepia, ***n.f.*** (*zool.*) sepia.—***n.m.*** sepia (*colour*).
septentrional, ***a.*** northern.
séptico, -ca, ***a.*** septic.
septiembre, ***n.m.*** September.
séptimo, -ma, ***a., n.m.*** seventh.
sepulcro, ***n.m.*** tomb, sepulchre.
sepultar, ***v.t.*** bury, inter; hide.
sepultura, ***n.f.*** burial; grave.
sequedad, ***n.f.*** dryness, aridity.
sequero, ***n.m.*** arid land, dry place.
sequía, ***n.f.*** drought.
séquito, ***n.m.*** retinue, suite; following.
ser, ***n.m.*** being; essence.—***v.i.*** [32] be; belong (***de,*** to); become (***de,*** of); ***es de,*** it is to be; ***a no — por,*** but for; ***a no — que,*** unless; ***o sea,*** that is; ***— para,*** suit; be fit for.
serafín, ***n.m.*** seraph.
serenar, ***v.t.*** calm.—***v.i., v.r.*** calm down, clear up, settle.
serenata, ***n.f.*** serenade.
serenidad, ***n.f.*** serenity.
sereno, -na, ***a.*** calm, serene, cloudless.—***n.m.*** night watchman; evening dew; ***al* —,** in the night air.
serie, ***n.f.*** series; ***en* —,** in series; mass (*production*).
seriedad, ***n.f.*** seriousness, gravity; sincerity.
serio, -ria, ***a.*** serious; grave; reliable; solemn; ***en* —,** seriously; in earnest.
sermón, ***n.m.*** sermon.
sermonear, ***v.t., v.i.*** sermonize.
seroja, ***n.f.,*** **serojo,** ***n.m.*** firewood; dry leaves.
serpentear, ***v.i.*** wind, meander, twist; wriggle.
serpenteo, ***n.m.*** winding, twisting; wriggling.
serpiente, ***n.f.*** snake, serpent.
serranil, ***n.m.*** knife.
serrano, -na, ***a.*** highland, mountain; ***jamón* —,** smoked ham.—***n.m.f.*** highlander.
serrar [I], ***v.t.*** saw.
serrín, ***n.m.*** sawdust.
servible, ***a.*** serviceable.
servicio, ***n.m.*** service.
servidero, -ra, ***a.*** serviceable; demanding.
servidor, -ra, ***n.m.f.*** servant.
servidumbre, ***n.f.*** servants; servitude (*jur.*) right.

servil, *a.* servile.
servilleta, *n.f.* napkin, serviette.
Servia, *n.f.* Serbia; **servio, -via,** *a., n.m.f.* Serbian.
servir [8], *v.t.* serve; wait on.—*v.i.* be of use; serve (***de,*** as, for).—*v.r.* serve oneself; be pleased to; make use (***de,*** of); ***sírvase . . .,*** please. . . .
servocroata, *a., n.m.f.* Serbo-Croat.
sesear, *v.i.* pronounce *z* and *c* as *s* in Spanish.
sesenta, *a., n.m.* sixty.
sesentón, -tona, *n.m.f.* (*fam.*) sexagenarian.
sesgar, *v.t.* slant.
sesgo, -ga, *a.* slanting; oblique.—*n.m.* slope, slant; bevel; means; ***al* —,** aslant.
sesión, *n.f.* session.
seso, *n.m.* brain; brains; sense, wisdom.
sesquipedal, *a.* sesquipedalian.
sestear, *v.i.* take a siesta.
sesudo, -da, *a.* wise, prudent.
seta, *n.f.* edible fungus; bristle.
setecientos, -tas, *a., n.m.pl.* seven hundred.
setenta, *a., n.m.* seventy.
setentón, -tona, *a., n.m.f.* (*fam.*) seventy-year-old.
setiembre [SEPTIEMBRE].
seto, *n.m.* fence; **—** ***vivo,*** hedge.
seudómino, *n.m.* pseudonym.
severidad, *n.f.* severity.
severo, -ra, *a.* severe; strict.
sexo, *n.m.* sex.
sextante, *n.m.* sextant.
sexto, -ta, *a., n.m.* sixth.
sexual, *a.* sexual.
si (1), *conj.* if; whether; ***por* — *acaso,*** just in case.
si (2), *n.m.* (*mus.*) (key of) B.
sí (1), *adv.* yes; indeed.
sí (2), *r. pron.* (*used after preps.*) himself; herself; oneself; yourself; itself; themselves.
siamés, -mesa, *a., n.m.f.* Siamese.
sibarita, *a., n.m.f.* sybarite.
siberiano, -na, *a.* Siberian.
sibilante, *a., n.f.* sibilant.
Sicilia, *n.f.* Sicily.
siciliano, -na, *a., n.m.f.* Sicilian.
sico- [PSICO-].
sicómoro, *n.m.* sycamore.
siderurgia, *n.f.* siderurgy; iron and steel manufacture.
siderúrgico, -ca, *a.* siderurgical; rel. to iron and steel manufacture.
sidra, *n.f.* cider.
siembra, *n.f.* sowing; sown land.
siempre, *adv.* always; ***de* —,** usual; **—** ***que,*** whenever; provided that.
sien, *n.f.* (*anat.*) temple.
sienta, -te, -to [SENTAR, SENTIR].
sierpe, *n.f.* snake, serpent.
sierra, *n.f.* jagged mountain range; saw.
siervo, -va, *n.m.f.* slave; servant; serf.
siesta, *n.f.* siesta, nap; hottest part of day.
siete, *a., n.m.* seven.
sífilis, *n.f.* syphilis.
sifón, *n.m.* soda-syphon; soda-water; syphon.
sigilo, *n.m.* seal, signet; secrecy, concealment.
sigiloso, -sa, *a.* silent, tight-lipped.
sigla, *n.f.* abbreviation, symbol.
siglo, *n.m.* century; age; the world.
signar, *v.t.* sign; cross; mark.
signatura, *n.f.* sign; reference number; signature.
significación, *n.f.* significance, import.
significado, -da, *a.* well-known, important.—*n.m.* meaning.
significar [A], *v.t.* mean, signify; make known.—*v.i.* matter.
significativo, -va, *a.* significant.
signo, *n.m.* sign; cross; destiny.
siguiente, *a.* following, next.
sílaba, *n.f.* syllable.
silábico, -ca, *a.* syllabic.
silbante, *a.* whistling.
silbar, *v.t., v.i.* whistle; hiss, boo.
silbato, silbido, silbo, *n.m.* whistle; hiss.
silenciador, *n.m.* silencer; suppressor.
silenciar, *v.t.* silence; keep quiet, not reveal.
silencio, *n.m.* silence.
silencioso, -sa, *a.* silent, quiet.
silero, *n.m.* (*agr.*) silo.
sílice, *n.f.* silica.
silicio, *n.m.* silicon.
silo, *n.m.* (*agr.*) silo; cavern.
silogismo, *n.m.* syllogism.
silueta, *n.f.* silhouette.
silvestre, *a.* wild.
silvicultura, *n.f.* forestry.
silla, *n.f.* chair; saddle.
sillín, *n.m.* light saddle; cycle saddle.
sillón, *n.m.* arm-chair.
simbiosis, *n.f.* symbiosis.
simbólico, -ca, *a.* symbolic(al).
simbolismo, *n.m.* symbolism.
simbolizar [C], *v.t.* symbolize.
símbolo, *n.m.* symbol; emblem, device; (*eccl.*) creed.
simetría, *n.f.* symmetry.
simétrico, -ca, *a.* symmetrical.
simiente, *n.f.* seed, germ; semen.
símil, *a.* similar.—*n.m.* similarity; simile.
similar, *a.* similar.
similitud, *n.f.* similitude.
simonía, *n.f.* simony.
simpatía, *n.f.* liking, fellow-feeling; sympathy; ***tener* — *por,*** like (*s.o.*) very much.
simpático, -ca, *a.* nice, likeable, pleasant; sympathetic.
simpatizar [C], *v.i.* get on well (***con,*** with).
simple, *a.* simple; mere; ***a* — *vista,*** at first sight.
simpleza, simplicidad, *n.f.* simplicity.
simpli(ci)sta, *a., n.m.f.* simpliste.
simplificar [A], *v.t.* simplify.
simposio, *n.m.* symposium.
simulación, *n.f.* simulation.
simulacro, *n.m.* simulacrum; sham.
simular, *v.t.* simulate, feign.
simultáneo, -nea, *a.* simultaneous.
sin, *prep.* without.
sinagoga, *n.f.* synagogue.
sinalefa, *n.f.* synal(o)epha.
sinapismo, *n.m.* mustard-plaster; (*fam.*) bore.
sincerar, *v.t.* vindicate, justify.
sinceridad, *n.f.* sincerity.
sincero, -ra, *a.* sincere; ingenuous.
sincopar, *v.t.* syncopate.
síncope, *n.m.* syncope; (*med.*) faint, swoon.
sincronizar [C], *v.t.* synchronize.
sindical, *a.* syndical; trade unionist.
sindicalismo, *n.m.* trade unionism.

sindicato, *n.m.* trade union; syndicate.
sinecura, *n.f.* sinecure.
sinéresis, *n.f.* synaeresis.
sinfín, *n.m.* great number.
sinfonía, *n.f.* symphony.
singlar, *v.i.* (*naut.*) follow a course.
singular, *a.*, *n.m.* singular.
singularidad, *n.f.* singularity.
singularizar [C], *v.t.* distinguish, singularize.
singulto, *n.m.* sob; hiccup.
siniestro, -ra, *a.* sinister; left.—*n.m.* malice; disaster.
sinnúmero, *n.m.* endless number.
sino (1), *n.m.* destiny, fate.
sino (2), *conj.* but, if not; ***no . . . —***, not . . . but.
sínodo, *n.m.* synod.
sinonimia, *n.f.* synonymy.
sinónimo, -ma, *a.* synonymous.—*n.m.* synonym.
sinóptico, -ca, *a.* synoptic(al).
sinrazón, *n.f.* wrong, injustice.
sinsabor, *n.m.* displeasure; sorrow.
sintáctico, -ca, *a.* syntactic(al).
sintaxis, *n.f.* syntax.
síntesis, *n.f. inv.* synthesis.
sintético, -ca, *a.* synthetic(al).
sintetizar [C], *v.t.* synthesize.
síntoma, *n.m.* symptom.
sintomático, -ca, *a.* symptomatic.
sintonizar [C], *v.t.*, *v.i.* (*rad.*) tune (in).
sinuoso, -sa, *a.* sinuous, twisting.
sinvergüenza, *a.* (*fam.*) brazen.—*n.m.f.* (*fam.*) shameless rogue.
sionismo, *n.m.* Zionism.
siqu- [PSIQU-].
siquiera, *adv.* even.—*conj.* even though.
sirena, *n.f.* siren.
sirga, *n.f.* tow-rope.
Siria, *n.f.* Syria.
sirio, -ria, *a.*, *n.m.f.* Syrian.
sirle, *n.m.* dung.
siroco, *n.m.* sirocco.
sirte, *n.f.* sandbank, rock; peril.
sirvienta, *n.f.* servant.
sirviente, *a.* serving.—*n.m.* servant.
sisa, *n.f.* pilfering; (*obs.*) excise.
sisar, *v.t.* filch.
sisear, *v.t.*, *v.i.* hiss; boo.
siseo, *n.m.* hiss; sizzle.
sísmico, -ca, *a.* seismic.
sismografía, *n.f.* seismography.
sismómetro, *n.m.* seismometer.
sisón, *n.m.* filcher; (*orn.*) little bustard.
sistema, *n.m.* system.
sistemático, -ca, *a.* systematic(al).
sistematizar [C], *v.t.* systematize.
sitiar, *v.t.* besiege.
sitio, *n.m.* place, spot; siege.
sito, -ta, *a.* situate.
situación, *n.f.* situation.
situar [M], *v.t.* situate, place.
smoking, *n.m.* (*pl.* **-gs**) dinner-jacket.
so, *n.m.* (*mus.*) (key of) G.
sobaco, *n.m.* armpit.
sobajar, *v.t.* crumple; (*S.A.*) humble.
sobar, *v.t.* knead, pummel; paw.
sobarbada, *n.f.* jerk; reprimand.
sobarcar [A], *v.t.* tuck under the arm.
soberanía, *n.f.* sovereignty; dominion.
soberano, -na, *a.*, *n.m.f.* sovereign.
soberbio, -bia, *a.* vain, proud; superb.—*n.f.* pride.
sobordo, *n.m.* (*naut.*) cargo list.
sobornar, *v.t.* bribe.
soborno, *n.m.* bribe; bribery.
sobra, *n.f.* excess; ***de —***, in excess; left over; superfluous.—*pl.* left-overs.
sobrado, -da, *a.* overmuch, too many; daring; rich.—*n.m.* attic.
sobrancero, -ra, *a.* unemployed.
sobrante, *a.*, *n.m.* surplus.
sobrar, *v.t.* surpass.—*v.i.* be left over; be too much *or* many.
sobre, *n.m.* envelope.—*prep.* on, upon, above, over.—*prefix* over-, super-.
sobreaguar [H], *v.t.*, *v.i.* float (*on*).
sobrecama, *n.f.* bedspread.
sobrecarga, *n.f.* overload; further trouble; surcharge.
sobrecargar [B], *v.t.* overload; surcharge.
sobreceja, *n.f.* brow.
sobrecejo, *n.m.* frown.
sobrecoger [E], *v.t.* surprise, take aback.
sobrecomida, *n.f.* dessert.
sobrecomprimir, *v.t.* (*aer.*) pressurize.
sobrecubierta, *n.f.* wrapper; (*naut.*) upper deck.
sobredicho, -cha, *a.* above-mentioned.
sobredorar, *v.t.* gild; gloss over.
sobreen- [SOBREN-].
sobreexponer [25], *v.t.* over-expose.
sobrefaz, *n.f.* (*pl.* **-aces**) surface.
sobrehombre, *n.m.* superman.
sobrehueso, *n.m.* bother, bore.
sobrehumano, -na, *a.* superhuman.
sobreintendencia, *n.f.* superintendance.
sobrellevar, *v.t.* bear; ease, share; overlook.
sobremanera, *adv.* exceedingly.
sobremesa, *n.f.* table cloth; dessert; ***de —***, after dinner.
sobremodo, *adv.* exceedingly.
sobremundano, -na, *a.* supermundane; other-worldly.
sobrenadar, *v.i.* float.
sobrenatural, *a.* supernatural.
sobrenombre, *n.m.* added name, epithet.
sobrentender [2], *v.t.* gather, read between the lines.
sobrepaga, *n.f.* pay-increase.
sobreparto, *n.m.* (*med.*) confinement.
sobrepasar, *v.t.* surpass.
sobrepelliz, *n.f.* (*pl.* **-ices**) surplice.
sobreponer [25], *v.t.* super(im)pose.—*v.r.* overcome (***a***).
sobrepujar, *v.t.* surpass, exceed.
sobrero, -ra, *a.* extra; spare.
sobresaliente, *a.* outstanding; (*educ.*) excellent, First Class.—*n.m.f.* understudy.
sobresalir [31], *v.i.* stand out, excel.
sobresaltar, *v.t.* assail; startle.—*v.i.* stand out, be noticeable.
sobresalto, *n.m.* sudden attack; start, fright.
sobresanar, *v.t.* heal superficially; cover up, conceal (*defects*).
sobresano, *adv.* feignedly.
sobrescribir, *v.t.* superscribe.
sobrescrito, *n.m.* superscript(ion).
sobreseer [N], *v.t.*, *v.i.* stay.
sobreseguro, *adv.* without risk.
sobrestadía, *n.f.* (*naut.*) extra lay days.
sobrestante, *n.m.* foreman, supervisor.
sobretarde, *n.f.* late evening.

sobretodo, *n.m.* overcoat.—*adv.* above all.
sobrevenida, *n.f.* surprise coming.
sobrevenir [36], *v.i.* happen, supervene.
sobrevienta, *n.f.* gust; onslaught; surprise.
sobreviento, *n.m.* gust of wind.
sobreviviente, *a.* surviving.—*n.m.f.* survivor.
sobrevivir, *v.i.* survive (*a*).
sobrexceder, *v.t.* exceed.
sobrexcitar, *v.t.* overexcite.
sobriedad, *n.f.* sobriety, frugality.
sobrino, -na, *n.m.* nephew.—*n.f.* niece.
sobrio, -ria, *a.* sober, moderate.
socaire, *n.m.* (*naut.*) lee; (*fam.*) safety.
socaliña, *n.f.* swindle.
socaliñar, *v.t.* swindle out of.
socapa, *n.f.* pretext, pretence.
socarrar, *v.t.* scorch.
socarrén, *n.m.* eaves.
socarrena, *n.f.* cavity.
socarrón, -rrona, *a.* crafty, sly.
socarronería, *n.f.* slyness.
socavar, *v.t.* undermine.
sociabilidad, *n.f.* sociability.
sociable, *a.* sociable.
social, *a.* social; rel. to a firm.
socialismo, *n.m.* socialism.
socialista, *a., n.m.f.* socialist.
socializar [C], *v.t.* socialize.
sociedad, *n.f.* society; (*com.*) company, firm.
societario, -ria, *a.* rel. to union(s).—*n.m.f.* member.
socio, -cia, *n.m.f.* member; partner; (*pej.*) person.
sociología, *n.f.* sociology.
sociológico, -ca, *a.* sociological.
sociólogo, -ga, *n.m.f.* sociologist.
socolor, *n.m.* pretext, cover.
socorrer, *v.t.* aid, succour.
socorrido, -da, *a.* helpful; well-stocked; trite.
socorro, *n.m.* help, aid; part payment.—*interj.* help!
soda, *n.f.* soda.
sódico, -ca, *a.* rel. to sodium.
sodio, *n.m.* sodium.
soez, *a.* (*pl.* **soeces**) vile, crude.
sofá, *n.m.* (*pl.* **sofás**) sofa.
sofión, *n.m.* snort; blunderbuss.
sofisma, sofismo, *n.m.* sophism.
sofista, *a.* sophistic(al).—*n.m.f.* sophist.
sofistería, *n.f.* sophistry.
sofisticar [A], *v.t.* falsify.
sofístico, -ca, *a.* sophistic(al).
soflama, *n.f.* glow; blush; cheating; speech.
soflamar, *v.t.* make blush; cheat; char.
soflamero, -ra, *a., n.m.f.* hypocrite.
sofocación, *n.f.* suffocation.
sofocar [A], *v.t.* choke; stifle; smother; embarrass.
sofoco, *n.m.* anguish; embarrassment.
sofocón, *n.m.*, **sofoquina,** *n.f.* (*fam.*) disappointment.
sofrenada, *n.f.* restraint; check(ing).
sofrenar, *v.t.* check; restrain.
soga, *n.f.* rope; (*fam.*) mocking; ***hacer —,*** linger, lag.
soguero, *n.m.* rope-maker.
soguilla, *n.f.* cord; braid.—*n.m.* errand-boy.
soja, *n.f.* soya bean.
sojuzgar [B], *v.t.* conquer, subdue.
sol (1), *n.m.* sun; sunshine; ***hace —,*** it is sunny.
sol (2), *n.m.* (*mus.*) (key of) G.
solana, *n.f.* sunny place; sun-porch *or* -room.
solanera, *n.f.* sunburn; sunny place.
solapa, *n.f.* lapel; pretext, cover.
solapado, -da, *a.* under-hand, sly.
solapar, *v.t.* overlap; conceal, cloak.
solape, solapo, *n.m.* lapel; pretext.
solar, *a.* solar, sun.—*n.m.* plot of ground; family seat, mansion.—*v.t.* [4] pave; sole.
solariego, -ga, *a.* ancestral.
solazar [C], *v.t.* amuse, divert.
solazo, *n.m.* (*fam.*) burning sun.
soldadesco, -ca, *a.* soldierly, soldiers'.—*n.f.* soldiery.
soldado, *n.m.* soldier; ***— raso,*** private.
soldador, *n.m.* solderer; welder; soldering iron.
soldadura, *n.f.* solder(ing); weld(ing).
soldán, *n.m.* sultan.
soldar [4], *v.t.* solder; weld; join; repair.
solear, *v.t.* sun.
soledad, *n.f.* solitude; loneliness; wilderness.
solemne, *a.* solemn; (*fam.*) downright.
solemnidad, *n.f.* solemnity.
solemnizar, *v.t.* solemnize.
soler [5, *only pres. & imperf. indic.*], *v.t.* be used to, be accustomed to; ***suele venir hoy,*** he usually comes today.
solera, *n.f.* beam; floor, bottom; mother-wine; ***de —,*** fine, long-established.
solevamiento, *n.m.* upheaval.
solev(ant)ar, *v.t.* raise; incite.—*v.r.* rise up; rebel.
solfa, *n.f.* (*mus.*) sol-fa; notation; (*fam.*) beating; ***poner en —,*** make fun of.
solfear, *v.t.* (*mus.*) sol-fa; sight-read; (*fam.*) thrash.
solfeo, *n.m.* (*mus.*) sol-fa; sight-reading; (*fam.*) thrashing.
solicitación, *n.f.* request; wooing.
solicitante, *n.m.f.* applicant; petitioner.
solicitar, *v.t.* request; attract; court; see to.
solícito, -ta, *a.* diligent; (*fam.*) affectionate.
solicitud, *n.f.* request; application; care.
solidar, *v.t.* make firm; prove.
solidaridad, *n.f.* solidarity.
solidario, -ria, *a.* solidary; joint; integral.
solidarizar, *v.r.* unite, join resources.
solidez, *n.f.* solidity.
solidificación, *n.f.* solidification.
solidificar [A], *v.t., v.r.* solidify.
sólido, -da, *a., n.m.* solid.
soliloquio, *n.m.* soliloquy.
solista, *n.m.f.* soloist.
solitario, -ria, *a.* solitary.—*n.m.f.* recluse.
sólito, -ta, *a.* wont.
soliviantar, *v.t.* incite, stir up.
soliviar, *v.t.* lift, raise slightly.
solo, -la, *a.* alone; lonely; sole, only; ***a (sus) solas,*** on his own.—*n.m.* solo.
sólo, *adv.* only, solely.
solom(ill)o, *n.m.* sirloin.
solsticio, *n.m.* solstice.
soltar [4], *v.t.* release; let go (of); let out; explain.—*v.i.* begin, burst out (*a*).—*v.r.* come loose *or* off; come undone; loosen up.
soltero, -ra, *n.m.* bachelor.—*n.f.* spinster.
solterón, -rona, (*fam.*) *n.m.* confirmed bachelor.—*n.f.* old maid.
soltura, *n.f.* ease; freedom; release; fluency.
solubilidad, *n.f.* solubility.
soluble, *a.* soluble.

solución, *n.f.* solution.
solucionar, *v.t.* solve; settle.
solvencia, *n.f.* settlement; solvency.
solventar, *v.t.* settle (*debts*); solve.
solvente, *a., n.m.* solvent.
sollamar, *v.t.* singe.
sollastre, *n.m.* scullion.
sollozar [C], *v.i.* sob.
sollozo, *n.m.* sob.
somalí, *a., n.m.f.* Somali.
la Somalía, *n.f.* Somalia.
somatén, *n.m.* vigilantes; (*fam.*) hubbub.
sombra, *n.f.* shade, shadow; (*fam.*) luck; wit.
sombr(e)ar, *v.t.* shade.
sombrerero, -ra, *n.m.* hatter.—*n.f.* milliner.
sombrero, *n.m.* hat.
sombrilla, *n.f.* shade; sun-shade.
sombrío, -ría, *a.* gloomy, sombre, sullen.
sombroso, -sa, *a.* shadowy.
somero, -ra, *a.* superficial, shallow.
someter, *v.t.* subdue.—*v.t., v.r.* submit.
sometido, -da, *a.* submissive.
sometimiento, *n.m.* submission.
somnambulismo, *n.m.* somnambulism.
somnámbulo, -la, *a., n.m.f.* somnambulist.
somnolencia, *n.f.* somnolence.
de somonte, *a. phr.* rough, coarse.
somorgujar, *v.t., v.i., v.r.* dive, duck.
somorgujo, *n.m.* (*orn.*) dabchick, grebe; ***a*** (*lo*) —, under water; on the quiet.
somos [SER].
son, *n.m.* sound; news; pretext; reason. [SER].
sonadero, *n.m.* [PAÑUELO].
sonado, -da, *a.* famous; talked-about.
sonaja, *n.f.* jingle; timbrel.
sonajero, *n.m.* baby's rattle.
sonam- [SOMNAM-].
sonante, *a.* sounding; jingling.
sonar [4], *v.t.* sound; ring; blow (*nose*).—*v.i.* sound; jingle; sound familiar *or* right; be rumoured.—*v.r.* blow one's nose.
sonata, *n.f.* sonata.
sonda, *n.f.* sounding; plummet; borer.
sond(e)ar, *v.t.* sound (out); fathom.
soneto, *n.m.* sonnet.
sónico, -ca, *a.* sonic.
sonido, *n.m.* sound; literal meaning; rumour.
sonochada, *n.f.* late evening; sunset watch.
sonoro, -ra, *a.* sonorous; sounding.
sonreír [28], *v.i., v.r.* smile.
sonriente, *a.* smiling.
sonrisa, *n.f.* smile.
sonroj(e)ar, *v.t.* make blush.—*v.r.* blush.
sonrojo, *n.m.* blush.
sonrosado, -da, *a.* rosy.
sonros(e)ar [SONROJEAR].
sonsaca, *n.f.* pilfering; wheedling.
sonsacar [A], *v.t.* pilfer; wheedle.
sonsonete, *n.m.* sing-song tone; tapping.
soñador, -ra, *a.* dreaming.—*n.m.f.* dreamer.
soñar [4], *v.t., v.i.* dream (***con, en,*** about).
soñ(arr)era, *n.f.* sleepiness.
soñolencia, *n.f.* somnolence.
soñoliento, -ta, *a.* sleepy, drowsy.
sopa, *n.f.* soup; sops.
sopapo, *n.m.* chuck under the chin; slap.
sop(e)ar, *v.t.* steep; trample on.
sopero, -ra, *n.m.* soup-dish.—*n.f.* tureen.
sopesar, *v.t.* try the weight of.
sopetón, *n.m.* slap; ***de*** —, suddenly, in a flash.
sopista, *n.m.f.* person living on charity.
soplar, *v.t.* blow, blow away *or* up; pinch, steal; (*fam.*) split *or* squeal on; tip off; whisper.—*v.i.* blow.—*v.r.* get puffed-up *or* vain.
soplete, *n.m.* blow-pipe; torch.
soplido, *n.m.* blast, puff.
soplo, *n.m.* blast, blowing; breath; (*fam.*) tip-off; squeal, give-away.
soplón, -lona, *n.m.f.* (*fam.*) splitter, squealer.
soponcio, *n.m.* swoon, faint.
sopor, *n.m.* stupor, drowsiness.
soporífero, -ra, soporífico, -ca, *a., n.m.* soporific.
soportable, *a.* bearable.
soportar, *v.t.* bear; endure.
soporte, *n.m.* support, stand.
soprano, *n.m.f.* soprano.
Sor, *n.f.* Sister . . . (*nun*).
sorber, *v.t.* sip; soak up.—*v.r.* swallow.
sorbete, *n.m.* sherbet.
sorbo, *n.m.* sip; gulp.
Sorbona, *n.f.* Sorbonne.
sordera, *n.f.* deafness.
sordidez, *n.f.* sordidity, sordidness.
sórdido, -da, *a.* sordid.
sordo, -da, *a.* deaf; silent; dull.
sordomudo, -da, *a., n.m.f.* deaf-mute.
sorna, *n.f.* sloth; malice.
soroche, *n.m.* (*S.A.*) mountain sickness.
sóror, *n.f.* (*eccl.*) sister.
sorprendente, *a.* surprising.
sorprender, *v.t.* surprise.—*v.r.* be surprised.
sorpresa, *n.f.* surprise.
sortear, *v.t.* raffle off; cast lots for; evade; (*taur.*) fight well.
sorteo, *n.m.* raffle, draw; evasion.
sortero, -ra, *n.m.f.* fortune-teller.
sortija, *n.f.* ring; curl.
sortilegio, *n.m.* sorcery.
sosa, *n.f.* soda.
sosegado, -da, *a.* peaceful, calm.
sosegar [1B], *v.t.* calm.—*v.i., v.r.* calm down.
sosera, sosería, *n.f.* insipidity; dullness; inanity.
sosiego, *n.m.* calm, peace.
soslayar, *v.t.* slant; evade; ward off.
soslayo, -ya, *a.* slanting; ***de*** —, askance; aslant.
soso, -sa, *a.* insipid; dull; inane.
sospecha, *n.f.* suspicion.
sospechable, *a.* suspect.
sospechar, *v.t.* suspect; be suspicious (***de,*** of).
sospechoso, -sa, *a.* suspicious.—*n.m.f.* suspect.
sostén, *n.m.* support.
sostener [33], *v.t.* sustain.
sostenido, *n.m.* (*mus.*) sharp.
sostenimiento, *n.m.* sustenance; support.
sota, *n.f.* jack (*cards*); hussy.
sotabarba, *n.f.* fringe-beard.
sotana, *n.f.* cassock; (*fam.*) beating.
sótano, *n.m.* cellar; basement.
sotavento, *n.m.* leeward.
soterraño, -ña, *a.* underground.
soterrar [1], *v.t.* bury.
sotileza, *n.f.* fishing gut.
soto, *n.m.* copse; thicket.
sotreta, *n.f.* (*S.A.*) broken-down horse.
sotrozo, *n.m.* linch- *or* axle-pin.
soviético, -ca, *a.* soviet.
soy [SER].

su, *poss. pron.* his, its, their, your.
suave, *a.* suave, smooth, gentle.
suavidad, *n.f.* suavity; gentleness.
suavizar [C], *v.t.* smooth; sweeten; mellow; strop.
sub-, *prefix.* sub- under-.
subacuático, -ca, *a.* underwater.
subalterno, -na, *a., n.m.f.* subordinate.
subarrendar [I], *v.t.* sub-let.
subasta, *n.f.* auction.
subastar, *v.t.* auction.
subconsciencia, *n.f.* subconscious(ness).
subconsciente, *a., n.m.* subconscious.
subcontratista, *n.m.f.* subcontractor.
súbdito, -ta, *a., n.m.f.* (*pol.*) subject.
subentender [SOBRENTENDER].
subida, *n.f.* ascent; rise.
subido, -da, *a.* high; strong; bright.
subir, *v.t.* bring *or* take up; lift; go up; raise. —*v.i.* go *or* come up; rise.—*v.r.* rise.
subitáneo, -nea, *a.* sudden.
súbito, -ta, *a.* sudden.—*adv.* suddenly.
subjetividad, *n.f.* subjectivity.
subjetivo, -va, *a.* subjective.
subjuntivo, -va, *a., n.m.* subjunctive.
sublevación, *n.f.* revolt, uprising.
sublevar, *v.t.* incite.—*v.r.* revolt.
sublimación, *n.f.* sublimation.
sublimar, *v.t.* sublimate, exalt.
sublime, *a.* sublime.
sublimidad, *n.f.* sublimity.
subliminar, *a.* subliminal.
submarino, -na, *a., n.m.* submarine.
subordinado, -da, *a., n.m.* subordinate.
subordinar, *v.t.* subordinate.
subrayar, *v.t.* underline; stress.
subrogar [B], *v.t.* subrogate, substitute.
subsanar, *v.t.* excuse; amend.
subscribir [*p.p.* **subscrito**], *v.t., v.r.* subscribe.
subscripción, *n.f.* subscription.
subsecuente, *a.* subsequent.
subseguir [8G], *v.i., v.r.* follow next.
subsidiar, *v.t.* subsidize.
subsidiario, -ria, *a.* subsidiary.
subsidio, *n.m.* subsidy; pension; relief.
subsistencia, *n.f.* subsistence.
subsistir, *v.i.* subsist.
substancia, *n.f.* substance.
substancial, *a.* substantial.
substanciar, *v.t.* condense; (*jur.*) try.
substancioso, -sa, *a.* substantial.
substantivo, -va, *a.* substantival.—*n.m.* noun.
substitución, *n.f.* substitution.
substituir [O], *v.t.* substitute.
substituto, -ta, *n.m.f.* substitute.
substracción, *n.f.* subtraction.
substraer [34], *v.t.* withhold; subtract.—*v.r.* withdraw (*a*, from).
substrato, *n.m.* substratum.
subsuelo, *n.m.* subsoil.
subteniente, *n.m.* second lieutenant.
subterfugio, *n.m.* subterfuge.
subterráneo, -nea, *a.* subterranean.
suburbano, -na, *a.* suburban.—*n.m.f.* suburbanite.
suburbio, *n.m.* suburb; slum.
subvención, *n.f.* subsidy.
subvencionar, *v.t.* subsidize.
subvenir [36], *v.t.* defray; provide.
subversión, *n.f.* subversion.
subversivo, -va, *a.* subversive.
subyugación, *n.f.* subjugation.
subyugar [B], *v.t.* subjugate.
succión, *n.f.* suction.
succionar, *v.t.* (*mech.*) suck.
suceder, *v.t.* succeed, follow.—*v.i.* happen.
sucesión, *n.f.* succession; estate.
sucesivo, -va, *a.* successive; ***en lo —***, henceforth; ***y así sucesivamente***, and so on *or* forth.
suceso, *n.m.* event, incident; (*obs.*) outcome; lapse.
sucesor, -ra, *n.m.f.* successor.
suciedad, *n.f.* filth, dirt.
sucinto, -ta, *a.* succint.
sucio, -cia, *a.* dirty, filthy, foul.—*adv.* unfairly.
suco, *n.m.* juice.
sucucho, *n.m.* nook.
suculento, -ta, *a.* succulent.
sucumbir, *v.i.* succumb.
sucursal, *a., n.f.* (*com.*) branch.
Sudáfrica, *n.f.* South Africa.
sudafricano, -na, *a., n.m.f.* South African.
Sudamérica, *n.f.* South America.
sudamericano, -na, *a., n.m.f.* South American.
Sudán, *n.m.* Sudan.
sudanés, -nesa, *a., n.m.f.* Sudanese.
sudante, *a.* sweating.
sudar, *v.t., v.i.* sweat; ooze.
sudario, *n.m.* shroud.
sudeste, *n.m.* south-east.
sudoeste, *n.m.* south-west.
sudor, *n.m.* sweat.
sudoriento, -ta, sud(or)oso, -sa, *a.* sweaty, sweating.
sudueste [SUDOESTE].
Suecia, *n.f.* Sweden.
sueco, -ca, *a., n.m.* Swedish.—*n.m.f.* Swede; ***hacer(se) el —***, pretend not to notice.
suegro, -ra, *n.m.* father-in-law.—*n.f.* mother-in-law; crust.
suela, *n.f.* sole; ***de siete suelas***, (*fam.*) downright.
sueldo, *n.m.* pay, salary; [SOLDAR].
suelo, *n.m.* ground; land; soil; floor; ***medir el —***, fall flat; [SOLER].
suelto, -ta, *a.* loose; free; odd, single; fluent, agile.—*n.m.* small change; item of news; chapbook.—*n.f.* release; fetters, tie.
sueño, *n.m.* dream; sleep; ***en(tre) sueños***, while dreaming; ***tener —***, be sleepy.
suero, *n.m.* whey; serum.
suerte, *n.f.* chance; fortune, luck; fate; sort; feat; way; ***de — que***, so that; ***echar suertes***, cast lots.
suficiencia, *n.f.* sufficiency, adequacy.
suficiente, *a.* sufficient, enough; competent.
sufijo, -ja, *a.* suffixed.—*n.m.* suffix.
sufragáneo, -nea, *a., n.m.* suffragan.
sufragar [B], *v.t.* aid; defray.—*v.i.* (*S.A.*) vote (***por***, for).
sufragio, *n.m.* suffrage.
sufragista, *n.m.* suffragist.—*n.f.* suffragette.
sufrible, *a.* sufferable.
sufridero, -ra, *a.* sufferable.
sufrido, -da, *a.* long-suffering.
sufridor, -ra, *a.* suffering.—*n.m.f.* sufferer.
sufriente, *a.* suffering.
sufrimiento, *n.m.* suffering; sufferance.
sufrir, *v.t., v.i.* suffer; undergo.

sugerencia, *n.f.* suggestion.
sugerente, *a.* suggestive.
sugerir [6], *v.t.* suggest.
sugestión, *n.f.* suggestion, hint; influence.
sugestionable, *a.* easily suggested *or* influenced.
sugestionar, *v.t.* influence; inveigle.
sugestivo, -va, *a.* suggestive.
suicida, *a.* suicidal.—*n.m.f.* suicide (*person*).
suicidar, *v.r.* commit suicide.
suicidio, *n.m.* suicide (*act*).
Suiza, *n.f.* Switzerland.
suizo, -za, *a., n.m.f.* Swiss.—*n.m.* bun.—*n.f.* brawl.
sujeción, *n.f.* subjection.
sujetar, *v.t.* hold firm, fasten; subject.
sujeto, -ta, *a.* subject, liable; firm, fastened.—*n.m.* (*pej.*) fellow, individual; (*gram.*) subject.
sulfato, *n.m.* sulphate.
sulfurar, *v.t.* sulphurize; enrage.
sulfúreo, -rea, sulfúrico, -ca, *a.* sulphuric.
sulfuro, *n.m.* sulphur.
sulfuroso, -sa, *a.* sulphurous.
sultán, *n.m.* sultan.
suma, *n.f.* sum; total; addition; compendium; summa; ***en* —**, in short.
sumamente, *adv.* extremely.
sumar, *v.t.* add up; amount to.—*v.r.* add up (**a**, to); adhere.
sumario, -ria, *a., n.m.* summary.—*n.m.* (*jur.*) indictment.
sumergible, *a.* submersible.—*n.m.* submarine.
sumergir [E], *v.t., v.r.* submerge.
sumersión, *n.f.* submersion.
sumidad, *n.f.* apex, summit.
sumidero, *n.m.* drain; sump.
suministración, *n.f.* supply.
suministrar, *v.t.* supply.
suministro, *n.m.* provision, supply.
sumir, *v.t., v.r.* sink.—*v.t.* (*eccl.*) receive (*Holy Communion*).
sumisión, *n.f.* submission.
sumiso, -sa, *a.* submissive; humble.
sumo, -ma, *a.* highest, greatest, supreme.
suntuosidad, *n.f.* sumptuousness.
suntuoso, -sa, *a.* sumptuous, gorgeous.
supe [SABER].
supeditar, *v.t.* oppress; subject.
super-, *prefix.* super-, over-.
superable, *a.* superable.
superar, *v.t.* surpass; overcome.
superávit, *n.m.* surplus, residue.
supercheria, *n.f.* fraud, swindle.
superchero, -ra, *a.* deceitful.
superentender [2], *v.t.* superintend.
superestructura, *n.f.* superstructure.
superficial, *a.* superficial.
superficie, *n.f.* surface; exterior.
superfluo, -lua, *a.* superfluous.
superhombre, *n.m.* superhuman.
superintendencia, *n.f.* superintendence.
superintendente, *n.m.f.* superintendent.
superior, *a.* superior; upper.—*n.m.* superior.
superiora, *n.f.* mother superior.
superioridad, *n.f.* superiority.
superlativo, -va, *a., n.m.* superlative.
supernumerario, -ria, *a., n.m.f.* supernumerary.
superponer [25], *v.t.* superpose.
supersensible, *a.* hypersensitive.
supersónico, -ca, *a.* supersonic.
superstición, *n.f.* superstition.
supersticioso, -sa, *a.* superstitious.
supérstite, *a., n.m.f.* (*jur.*) survivor.
supervenir [SOBREVENIR].
supervisión, *n.f.* supervision.
supervivencia, *n.f.* survival.
superviviente, *a.* surviving.
supino, -na, *a., n.m.* supine.
súpito, -ta [SÚBITO].
suplantar, *v.t.* supplant; falsify.
supleausencias, *n.m.f. inv.* substitute.
suplefaltas, *n.m.f. inv.* scapegoat.
suplementario, -ria, *a.* supplementary.
suplemento, *n.m.* supplement.
súplica, *n.f.* petition, request.
suplicación, *n.f.* supplication; cone wafer.
suplicante, *a., n.m.f.* suppli(c)ant.
suplicar [A], *v.t.* implore; (*jur.*) appeal.
suplicio, *n.m.* torture; execution, death penalty.
suplir, *v.t.* supply, furnish; make up for; substitute; excuse; (*gram.*) understand.
suponer, *n.m.* (*fam.*) conjecture.—*v.t.* [25] suppose; imply.—*v.i.* matter.
suposición, *n.f.* surmise supposition; authority; imposture.
supositivo, -va, *a.* suppositional.
supradicho [SOBREDICHO].
supremacía, *n.f.* supremacy.
supremo, -ma, *a.* supreme.
supresión, *n.f.* suppression.
supresor, -ra, *n.m.f.* suppressor.
suprimir, *v.t.* suppress; omit.
supuesto, -ta, *a.* supposed; so-called.—*n.m.* assumption; — ***que***, since; ***por* —**, of course.
supurar, *v.i.* suppurate.
supuse [SUPONER].
suputar, *v.t.* compute.
sur, *n.m.* south.
surcar [A], *v.t.* plough, furrow.
surco, *n.m.* furrow; groove.
surgir [E], *v.i.* spurt; arise; anchor.
suripanta, *n.f.* hussy.
suroeste [SUDOESTE].
surrealismo, *n.m.* surrealism.
surrealista, *a., n.m.f.* surrealist.
surtidero, *n.m.* outlet; jet.
surtido, *n.m.* stock, supply; jet; ***de* —**, stock.
surtidor, -ra, *n.m.f.* supplier.—*n.m.* spout; fountain; pump (*petrol etc.*).
surtir, *v.t.* supply, provide.—*v.i.* spout.
¡sus! *interj.* hurry! cheer up!
sus- [SUBS-].
susceptible, susceptivo, -va, *a.* susceptible.
suscitar, *v.t.* provoke.
susidio, *n.m.* anxiety.
susodicho, -cha, *a.* above-mentioned.
suspender, *v.t.* suspend; astound; (*educ.*) fail.
suspendido, *a.* (*educ.*) fail(ed).
suspense, *n.m.* suspense.
suspensión, *n.f.* suspension; amazement; (*educ.*) failure.
suspensivo, -va, *a.* suspensive.
suspenso, -sa, *a.* suspended; astounded; baffled.
suspensores, *n.m. pl.* (*S.A.*) braces, (*U.S.*) suspenders.
suspicacia, *n.f.* suspicion.

suspicaz, *a.* (*pl.* **-aces**) suspicious.
suspirar, *v.i.* sigh (***por,*** for).
suspiro, *n.m.* sigh; (*cul.*) meringue.
sustentáculo, *n.m.* prop, support.
sustentar, *v.t.* sustain, maintain.
sustento, *n.m.* sustenance.
susto, *n.m.* scare, fright.
susurrar, *v.i.* whisper, murmur.—*v.r.* be rumoured.
susurr(id)o, *n.m.* murmur, whisper.
sutil, *a.* subtle; fine.
sutileza, *n.f.* subtlety; dexterity.
sutilizar [C], *v.t.* make subtle *or* fine.—*v.i.* quibble.
suyo, -ya, *a. poss. & pron.* his, hers, its, yours, theirs; ***de* —,** of his (her *etc.*) accord; ***salirse con la suya,*** have one's way.

T

T, t, *n.f.* twenty-third letter of the Spanish alphabet.
tabacalero, -ra, *a.* tobacco.—*n.m.* tobacconist.—*n.f.* tobacco works *or* firm *or* shop.
tabaco, *n.m.* tobacco.
tabalear, *v.t., v.r.* rock.—*v.i.* drum.
tábano, *n.m.* gadfly.
tabaola, *n.f.* uproar.
taberna, *n.f.* tavern.
tabernáculo, *n.m.* tabernacle.
tabernario, -ria, *a.* vulgar, low.
tabernero, *n.m.* innkeeper.
tabica, *n.f.* panel.
tabicar [A], *v.t.* wall up.
tabique, *n.m.* partition, partition-wall.
tabla, *n.f.* board, plank; table, list; plate, sheet; strip of land; ski; ***a raja* —,** sweeping all before.—*pl.* boards, stage; ***hacer tablas,*** reach a deadlock.
tablado, *n.m.* stage; scaffold; flooring; boarding.
tablaje, *n.m.* planking.
tablazón, *n.f.* boarding; deck.
tablear, *v.t.* saw up (*timber*); lay out.
tablero, *n.m.* panel; board; gambling table; chess-board.
tableta, *n.f.* plank; tablet; lozenge; clapper.
tabletear, *v.i.* rattle.
tablilla, *n.f.* lath; notice-board.
tablón, *n.m.* beam, board; ***coger un* —,** (*fam.*) get tipsy.
tabú, *n.m.* taboo.
tabuco, *n.m.* hovel.
tabular, *a.* tabular.—*v.t.* tabulate.
taburete, *n.m.* stool.
tac, *n.m.* tick (*sound*).
tacaño, -ña, *a.* stingy, mean.—*n.m.f.* miser.
tacar [A], *v.t.* mark, scar.
tacita, *n.f.* small cup.
tácito, -ta, *a.* tacit.
taciturno, -na, *a.* taciturn.
taco, *n.m.* plug, wad, bung; billiard-cue; pad; (*fam.*) curse; (*fam.*) bite, snack; sip.
tacón, *n.m.* heel (*of shoe*).
taconear, *v.i.* drum the heels.
táctico, -ca, *a.* tactical.—*n.m.* tactician.—*n.f.* tactics.
tacto, *n.m.* touch; tact.
tacha, *n.f.* flaw; tack.
tachadura, *n.f.* erasure.
tachar, *v.t.* cross out; accuse, blame.
tacho, *n.m.* (*S.A.*) bin; pan; pot.
tachón, *n.m.* erasure; gilded tack.
tafetán, *n.m.* taffeta.—*pl.* colours, flag.
tafilete, *n.m.* morocco leather.
tagarote, *n.m.* (*orn.*) hawk; (*fam.*) has-been.
taheño, -ña, *a.* red (*hair*).
tahona, *n.f.* bakery; mill.
tahur, -ra, *n.m.f.* gambler; cheat.
taifa, *n.f.* faction; (*fam.*) gang.
Tailandia, *n.f.* Thailand.
tailandés, -desa, *a., n.m.f.* Thai.
taimado, -da, *a.* sly, crafty.
taita, *n.m.* (*fam.*) daddy, poppa.
taja, *n.f.* cut; tally.
tajado, -da, *a.* steep, sheer.—*n.f.* slice; cut.
tajante, *a.* cutting, sharp; utter.
tajar, *v.t.* cut, slice; sharpen.
Tajo, *n.m.* Tagus; **tajo,** *n.m.* cut; drop; trench; block; work.
tal, *a.* such, such a.—*pron.* such a one *or* thing.—*adv.* thus, so; ***con* — *que,*** provided that; ***¿qué* —?** how goes it? ***un*—,** a certain.
tala, *n.f.* felling; havoc; tip-cat.
taladrar, *v.t.* drill, bore; pierce.
taladro, *n.m.* drill; bit, auger; hole.
tálamo, *n.m.* bridal bed; thalamus.
talán, *n.m.* ding-dong.
talanquera, *n.f.* parapet; (*fig.*) safety.
talante, *n.m.* mien; mode; will.
talar (1), *a.* full-length (*robe*).
talar (2), *v.t.* fell; lay waste.
talco, *n.m.* talc, talcum; tinsel.
talcual, talcualillo, -lla, *a.* (*fam.*) so-so, middling.
talego, -ga, *n.m.f.* bag, sack.
talento, *n.m.* talent.
talentoso, -sa, talentudo, -da, *a.* talented.
talismán, *n.m.* talisman.
talón, *n.m.* heel; counterfoil, coupon.
talla, *n.f.* carving; size; stature; reward.
tallado, -da, *a.* shaped.
tallar, *n.m.* timber-land(s).—*v.t.* carve; cut; measure.
talle, *n.m.* figure, shape; size; waist; outline.
taller, *n.m.* workshop; studio.
tallo, *n.m.* stalk; shoot.—*pl.* (*S.A.*) (*cul.*) greens.
tallón, *n.m.* reward.
talludo, -da, *a.* lanky; ageing.
tamaño, -ña, *a.* so big; such a big.—*n.m.* size.
tambalear, *v.i., v.r.* totter.
tambaleo, *n.m.* tottering.
también, *adv.* also, too, as well.
tambo, *n.m.* (*S.A.*) inn; cow-shed.
tambor, *n.m.* drum.
tamborear, *v.i.* drum.
tamboril, *n.m.* timbrel.
tamborilear, *v.t.* extol.—*v.i.* drum.
Támesis, *n.m.* the Thames.
tamiz, *n.m.* (*pl.* **-ices**) sieve.
tamizar [C], *v.t.* sift.
tamo, *n.m.* fluff, dust.
tampoco, *adv.* neither, not either.
tan, *adv.* so.

tanda, *n.f.* turn; relay, shift; batch; series; task; match.
en tanganillas, *a., adv. phr.* wobbly.
tanganillo, *n.m.* prop.
tangente, *a., n.f.* tangent.
Tánger, *n.f.* Tangier.
tangerino, -na, *a., n.m.f.* Tangerine.—*n.f.* tangerine (*fruit*).
tangible, *a.* tangible.
tango, *n.m.* tango.
tanque, *n.m.* tank.
tantán, *n.m.* ding-dong.
tantarantán, *n.m.* beating of drum.
tantear, *v.t.* size up, test; outline; score.—*v.i.* feel one's way.
tanteo, *n.m.* trial and error; sizing-up; score.
tanto, -ta, *a.* so much, as much.—*pl.* so many, as many.—*n.m.* copy; goal, score.—*adv.* so much, so often; ***algún* —,** somewhat; ***al* — *de*,** because of; aware of; ***en*(*tre*) —,** meanwhile; ***por* (*lo*) —,** therefore; — ***mejor*,** so much the better; ***treinta y tantos*,** thirty odd.
tañer [K], *v.t., v.i.* play; ring.
tapa, *n.f.* lid, cover, cap; book cover; titbit, snack.
tapadera, *n.f.* cover, lid.
tapadero, *n.m.* stopper.
tapador, *n.m.* cover; stopper.
tapaporos, *n.m. inv.* filler, primer.
tapar, *v.t.* cover; plug; conceal; stop up.
taparrabo, *n.m.* loincloth; trunks.
tapete, *n.m.* rug, carpet; ***sobre el* —,** (*fig.*) under discussion.
tapia, *n.f.,* **tapial,** *n.m.* (*S.A.*) mud *or* adobe wall; garden wall.
tapiar, *v.t.* wall up *or* in; block.
tapicería, *n.f.* upholstery; tapestries.
tapiz, *n.m.* (*pl.* **-ices**) tapestry.
tapizar [C], *v.t.* upholster; carpet; tapestry.
tapón, *n.m.* cork, stopper; plug; cap.
taponar, *v.t.* plug; stopper.
tapujo, *n.m.* muffler; cover.
taque, *n.m.* click, rap.
taquigrafía, *n.f.* shorthand.
taquígrafo, -fa, *n.m.f.* stenographer.
taquimecanógrafo, -fa, *n.m.f.* shorthand-typist.
taquilla, *n.f.* ticket- *or* box-office; rack, file.
tara, *n.f.* tare; tally; (*fam.*) exaggeration.
tarabilla, *n.f.* clapper; latch.
taracea, *n.f.* marquetry.
tarántula, *n.f.* (*zool.*) tarantula.
tarara, tarará, *n.f.* trumpet-sound.
tararear, *v.t., v.i.* hum.
tarasca, *n.f.* huge dragon carried in Corpus Christi processions; (*fam.*) slut.
tarascar [A], *v.t.* bite (*dogs*).
tarazar [C], *v.t.* bite; bother.
tarazón, *n.m.* chunk.
tardanza, *n.f.* tardiness, delay.
tardar, *v.i.* be late *or* long (***en***, in); ***a más* —,** at the latest.
tarde, *n.f.* afternoon, evening.—*adv.* (too) late.
tardecer [9], *v.i.* get late, go dark.
tardío, -día, *a.* late; slow.
tardo, -da, *a.* late; slow, backward.
tarea, *n.f.* job, task; toil.
tarifa, *n.f.* tariff; price-list; fare.
tarja, *n.f.* buckler; tally; ***sobre* —,** (*fam.*) on tick.
tarjeta, *n.f.* card; tablet; legend (*of maps*).
tarquín, *n.m.* mud, silt.
tarro, *n.m.* jar; (*S.A.*) top hat.
tarta, *n.f.* tart, gâteau.
tártago, *n.m.* (*bot.*) spurge; (*fam.*) tough luck; (*fam.*) mean joke.
tartajoso, -sa, *a.* stuttering.
tartalear, *v.i.* stagger.
tartamudear, *v.i.* stammer.
tartamudez, *n.f.* stutter, stammer.
tartamudo, -da, *a.* stammering.—*n.m.f.* stutterer.
tártaro, -ra, *a., n.m.f.* Tartar.—*n.m.* tartar.
tartufo, *n.m.* hypocrite.
tarugo, *n.m.* wooden peg *or* block.
tarumba, *a. inv.* (*fam.*) rattled.
tasa, *n.f.* rate; valuation; standard.
tasador, -ra, *n.m.f.* (*com.*) valuer.
tasar, *v.t.* value; appraise; grant within limits.
tasca, *n.f.* (*fam.*) pub, bar.
tascar [B], *v.t.* champ, nibble.
tasquera, *n.f.* (*fam.*) scuffle, row.
tasquil, *n.m.* flake, chip.
tasto, *n.m.* tang, bad taste.
tata, *n.f.* (*fam.*) nanny; (*S.A.*) sis.—*n.m.* (*S.A.*) poppa.
tatar(a)-, *prefix.* great-great- (*relative*); ***tatarabuelo*,** great-great-grandfather.
¡tate! *interj.* look out! I see!
tato, -ta, *a.* stuttering.
tatuaje, *n.m.* tattoo(ing).
tatuar [M], *v.t.* tattoo.
taumaturgo, -ga, *n.m.f.* miracle-worker.
taurino, -na, *a.* rel. to bulls *or* bull-fighting.
taurófilo, -la, *n.m.f.* bull-fighting fan.
tauromaquia, *n.f.* bull-fighting.
taxear, *v.i.* (*aer.*) taxi.
taxi, *n.m.* (*pl.* **taxis**) taxi.
taxidermia, *n.f.* taxidermy.
taxímetro, *n.m.* taximeter; taxi.
taxista, *n.m.f.* taxi-driver.
taz a taz, *adv.* without making charges.
taza, *n.f.* cup; basin.
tazar [C], *v.t.* fray.
te (1), *n.f.* name of letter T.
te (2), *pron. fam.* you, to you (thee).
té, *n.m.* tea.
tea, *n.f.* firebrand, torch.
teatral, *a.* theatrical.
teatro, *n.m.* theatre.
teca (1), *n.f.* teak.
teca (2), *n.f.* locket.
tecla, *n.f.* key (*piano, typing etc.*); delicate matter.
teclado, *n.m.* keyboard.
teclear, *v.t.* (*fam.*) feel one's way to.—*v.i.* strum the keys; type; drum.
tecleo, *n.m.* fingering; clatter (*of typing*).
técnica, *n.f.* technique; technic(s).
tecnicidad, *n.f.* technicality.
tecnicismo, *n.m.* technical term.
técnico, -ca, *a.* technical.—*n.m.f.* technician.
tecnicolor, *n.m.* Technicolor (*reg. trade mark*).
tecnología, *n.f.* technology.
tecnológico, -ca, *a.* technological.
tecnólogo, -ga, *n.m.f.* technologist.
techado, *n.m.* roof.
techar, *v.t.* roof.
techo, *n.m.* roof; ceiling; ***bajo* —,** indoors.
techumbre, *n.f.* roofing; ceiling.
tediar, *v.t.* loathe.
tedio, *n.m.* tedium; loathing.

tedioso, -sa, *a.* tedious.
teísta, *a., n.m.f.* theist.
teja, *n.f.* roof-tile.
tejado, *n.m.* roof.
tejar, *v.t.* tile.
tejaroz, *n.m.* eaves.
tejedor, -ra, *n.m.f.*, **tejedera,** *n.f.* weaver.
tejer, *v.t., v.i.* weave; **— *y destejer*,** chop and change.
tejido, *n.m.* fabric, textile; weave, tissue.
tejo (1), *n.m.* quoit.
tejo (2), *n.m.* (*bot.*) yew.
tejón, *n.m.* (*zool.*) badger; [TEJO].
tela, *n.f.* cloth; skin; subject, matter; (*art*) canvas; ***poner en — de juicio*,** question, doubt; **— *metálica*,** wire netting.
telar, *n.m.* loom; frame.
telaraña, *n.f.* cobweb.
tele-, *prefix.* tele-, remote.
telecomunicación, *n.f.* telecommunication.
telecontrol, *n.m.* remote control.
teledifundir, *v.t.* televise; telecast.
telefonazo, *n.m.* (*fam.*) telephone-call.
telefon(e)ar, *v.t., v.i.* telephone.
telefonema, *n.m.* telephone message.
telefonía, *n.f.* telephony.
telefónico, -ca, *a.* telephonic.
telefonista, *n.m.f.* telephonist.
teléfono, *n.m.* telephone.
telegrafía, *n.f.* telegraphy.
telegrafiar [L], *v.t.* telegraph.
telégrafo, *n.m.* telegraph; (*fam.*) sign.
telegrama, *n.m.* telegram.
teleguiado, -da, *a.* remote-controlled, guided.
teleobjetivo, *n.m.* telephoto lens.
telepatía, *n.f.* telepathy.
telerreceptor, *n.m.* T.V. set.
telescopar, *v.t., v.r.* telescope.
telescópico, -ca, *a.* telescopic.
telescopio, *n.m.* telescope.
teleta, *n.f.* blotting-paper.
teletipia, teletipiadora, *n.f.*, **teletipo,** *n.m.* teletype.
teletubo, *n.m.* (T.V.) tube.
televidente, *n.m.f.* television viewer.
televisar, *v.t.* televise.
televisión, *n.f.* television.
televisor, -ra, *a.* rel. to television.—*n.m.* T.V. set.—*n.f.* T.V. transmitter.
telón, *n.m.* (*theat.*) curtain; **— *de acero*,** Iron Curtain.
telliza, *n.f.* quilt.
tema, *n.m.* subject, theme; exercise; (*gram.*) stem.—*n.m.* or *f.* mania; obstinacy; grudge.
temático, -ca, *a.* thematic; obsessed.
tembladero, -ra, *a.* quaking.—*n.m.* quagmire.
temblador, -ra, *n.m.f.* trembler; (*relig.*) Quaker.
temblante, *a.* trembling.—*n.m.* bracelet.
temblar [1], *v.i.* tremble, quake, quiver; shiver.
temblón, -lona, *a.* quaking, shaking.
temblor, *n.m.* tremor; shiver; trembling.
tembl(or)oso, -sa, *a.* tremulous; quivering.
temedero, -ra, *a.* dread.
temer, *v.t.* fear, be afraid of.
temerario, -ria, *a.* rash.
temeridad, *n.f.* temerity, rashness.
temeroso, -sa, *a.* timid; fearful.
temible, *a.* terrible, dreaded.
temor, *n.m.* fear, dread.
témpano, *n.m.* flitch; drum; iceberg.
temperamento, *n.m.* temperament; climate; compromise.
temperar [TEMPLAR].
temperatura, *n.f.* temperature.
temperie, *n.f.* weather.
tempestad, *n.f.* storm.
tempestear, *v.i.* storm.
tempestivo, -va, *a.* timely.
tempestuoso, -sa, *a.* stormy.
templado, -da, *a.* temperate; medium; firm.
templanza, *n.f.* temperance; mildness.
templar, *v.t.* temper, moderate; cool, calm; tune.—*v.r.* be moderate.
temple, *n.m.* weather; temper; humour; tuning.
templo, *n.m.* temple.
temporada, *n.f.* season; space of time.
temporal, *a.* temporal; temporary.—*n.m.* storm; (bad) weather.
temporáneo, -nea, temporario, -ria, *a.* temporary.
témporas, *n.f.pl.* Ember Days.
temporero, -ra, *a., n.m.f.* temporary.
temporizar [C], *v.i.* temporize.
temprano, -na, *a., adv.* early.
tenacidad, *n.f.* tenacity.
tenacillas, *n.f.pl.* tongs; tweezers.
tenaz, *a.* (*pl.* **-aces**) tenacious.
tenazas, *n.f.pl.* tongs; pliers, pincers.
tenca, *n.f.* (*ichth.*) tench.
tención, *n.f.* possession.
tendal, *n.m.* awning; tent.
tendejón, *n.m.* tiny shop; shed.
tendencia, *n.f.* tendency.
tendencioso, -sa, *a.* tendentious.
tender [2], *v.t.* spread (out); tender, offer; extend; hang out; set (*traps*).—*v.i.* tend (***a***, to).—*v.r.* lie down; slacken; stretch.
ténder, *n.m.* (*rail.*) tender.
tendero, -ra, *n.m.f.* shopkeeper.
tendido, *n.m.* batch; laying; coat; slope.
tendón, *n.m.* tendon.
tendré [TENER].
tenducho, -cha, *n.m.f.* shabby shop.
tenebrosidad, *n.f.* darkness, gloom.
tenebroso, -sa, *a.* dark, gloomy.
tenedor, *n.m.* fork; holder.
teneduría, *n.f.* book-keeping.
tenencia, *n.f.* tenure; holding; lieutenancy.
tener [33], *v.t.* have, own; hold; consider; detain; **— *por*,** consider to be; **— *que*,** have to.—*v.r.* hold back; hold oneself.
tenería, *n.f.* tannery.
tengo [TENER].
tenida, *n.f.* session.
teniente, *a.* having, holding; mean; deafish.—*n.m.* lieutenant.
tenis, *n.m.* tennis.
tenisista, *n.m.f.* tennis-player.
tenor, *n.m.* tenor; purport; kind; (*mus.*) tenor.
tenorio, *n.m.* lady-killer.
tensión, *n.f.* tension.
tenso, -sa, *a.* taut, tense.
tentación, *n.f.* temptation.
tentáculo, *n.m.* tentacle.
tentador, -ra, *a.* tempting.—*n.m.* tempter.—*n.f.* temptress.
tentalear, *v.t.* (*fam.*) feel over.
tentar [2], *v.t.* tempt; touch, feel; try.
tentativo, -va, *a.* tentative.—*n.f.* attempt.
a tente bonete, *adv. phr.* (*fam.*) doggedly.

tentemozo, *n.m.* prop; tumbler (*toy*).
tentempié, *n.m.* (*fam.*) snack.
tenue, *a.* slight; fine, light.
tenuidad, *n.f.* tenuousness; triviality.
teñido, *n.m.*, **teñidura,** *n.f.* dyeing.
teñir [8K], *v.t.* dye; stain.
teocrático, -ca, *a.* theocratic.
teodolito, *n.m.* theodolite.
teología, *n.f.* theology.
teológico, -ca, *a.* theological.
teólogo, *n.m.* theologian.
teorema, *n.m.* theorem.
teoría, *n.f.* theory; (*lit.*) band.
teórico, -ca, *a.* theoretic(al).—*n.m.f.* theorist. —*n.f.* theory.
teorizar [C], *v.t., v.i.* theorize (on).
teosofía, *n.f.* theosophy.
tequila, *n.f.* tequila (*drink*).
terapéutico, -ca, *a.* therapeutic(al).
terapia, *n.f.* therapy.
tercena, *n.f.* state tobacco store.
tercer, *a.m. contracted form of* TERCERO *before n.m.sg.*
tercería, *n.f.* mediation.
tercero, -ra, *a., n.m.f.* third.—*n.m.f.* mediator; bawd; umpire; middleman.
terciado, *n.m.* cutlass.
terciana, *n.f.* tertian ague.
terciar, *v.t.* slant; divide into three.—*v.i.* mediate; take part.—*v.r.* be all right.
tercio, -cia, *a., n.m.* third.—*n.m.* troop, corps, regiment; turn, favour.—*pl.* strong limbs.
terciopelo, *n.m.* velvet.
terco, -ca, *a.* stubborn; hard.
tergiversar, *v.t.* falsify, twist.
terma, *n.f.* power station.
termal, *a.* thermal.
termas, *n.f.pl.* hot baths.
térmico, -ca, *a.* thermic.
terminable, *a.* terminable.
terminación, *n.f.* termination.
terminal, *a., n.m.* (*elec.*) terminal.
terminante, *a.* final, definite.
terminar, *v.t., v.i., v.r.* finish, end.
término, *n.m.* end; boundary; aim; district; manner; term, word; terminus; — ***medio,*** average; compromise.
terminología, *n.f.* terminology.
termio, *n.m.* therm.
termo-, *prefix.* thermo-; [TERMOS].
termómetro, *n.m.* thermometer.
termonuclear, *a.* thermonuclear.
termos, *n.m. inv.* thermos.
termóstato, *n.m.* thermostat.
terna, *n.f.* set of three.
terne, *a., n.m.f.* (*fam.*) tough.
ternero, -ra, *n.m.f.* calf.
ternerón, -rona, *a.* soppy, mawkish.
terneza, *n.f.* tenderness.
ternilla, *n.f.* gristle.
terno, *n.m.* suit; set of three; curse; — ***seco,*** (*fam.*) windfall.
ternura, *n.f.* tenderness.
terquedad, *n.f.* stubbornness.
Terranova, *n.f.* Newfoundland.
terraplén, *n.m.* embankment.
terrateniente, *n.m.f.* land-owner.
terraza, *n.f.* terrace; pitcher.
terremoto, *n.m.* earthquake.
terrenal, *a.* earthly.
terreno, -na, *a.* worldly.—*n.m.* ground, land, field.
terrero, -ra, *a.* earthly; humble.—*n.m.* mound; dump; terrace; target.—*n.f.* steep land; (*orn.*) lark.
terrestre, *a.* terrestrial.
terrible, *a.* terrible.
territorial, *a.* territorial; regional.
territorio, *n.m.* territory.
terrón, *n.m.* clod; lump.—*pl.* farmland.
terror, *n.m.* terror.
terr(or)ífico, -ca, *a.* terrifying.
terrorismo, *n.m.* terrorism.
terrorista, *a., n.m.f.* terrorist.
terroso, -sa, *a.* earthy.
terruño, *n.m.* field; native region.
tersar, *v.t.* polish, smooth.
terso, -sa, *a.* smooth, polished.
tersura, *n.f.* smoothness, polish.
tertulia, *n.f.* party; meeting.
tertuliano, -na, tertuliante, *n.m.f.* party-goer; habitué; member.
tesauro, *n.m.* thesaurus.
tesis, *n.f. inv.* thesis.
tesitura, *n.f.* attitude.
teso, -sa, *a.* taut.—*n.m.* lump.
tesón, *n.m.* grit, tenacity.
tesonería, *n.f.* obstinacy.
tesorería, *n.f.* treasury.
tesorero, -ra, *n.m.f.* treasurer.
tesoro, *n.m.* treasure.
testa, *n.f.* head; (*fam.*) nous.
testado, -da, *a.* testate.
testaférrea, testaferro, *n.m.* figurehead, front-man.
testamentario, -ria, *a.* testamentary.—*n.m.f.* executor.
testamento, *n.m.* will; testament.
testar, *v.i.* make a will.
testarada, *n.f.* butt; pig-headedness.
testarudo, -da, *a.* pig-headed.
testificar [A], *v.t., v.i.* testify.
testigo, -ga, *n.m.f.* witness.
testimoniar, *v.t.* attest, vouch for.
testimoniero, -ra, *a.* bearing false witness.
testimonio, *n.m.* testimony; false witness.
teta, *n.f.* teat; breast.
tétano(s), *n.m.* (*med.*) tetanus.
tetar, *v.t.* suckle.
tetera, *n.f.* tea-pot; kettle.
tetilla, *n.f.* nipple.
tetrarca, *n.m.* tetrarch.
tétrico, -ca, *a.* dismal, gloomy.
teutón, -tona, *a., n.m.f.* Teuton.
teutónico, -ca, *a., n.m.* Teutonic.
textil, *a., n.m.* textile.
texto, *n.m.* text; ***fuera de —,*** full-page (*illustration*).
textual, *a.* textual.
textura, *n.f.* texture.
tez, *n.f.* complexion.
ti, *pron.* (*used after preps.*) you, thee.
tía, *n.f.* aunt(ie); (*fam.*) whore; ***no hay tu —,*** (*fam.*) you've had it.
Tíber, *n.m.* Tiber.
tiberio, *n.m.* (*fam.*) racket, uproar.
tibetano, -na, *a., n.m.f.* Tibetan.
tibieza, *n.f.* lukewarmness.
tibio, -bia (1), *a.* lukewarm.
tibia (2), *n.f.* (*anat.*) tibia.
tiburón, *n.m.* shark.
tic, *n.m.* (*pl.* **tiques**) (*med.*) tic.

tictac, *n.m.* tick-tack.
tiemblo, *n.m.* (*bot.*) aspen.
tiempo, *n.m.* time; weather; (*gram.*) tense; tempo; (*mus.*) movement; (*sport*) half; ***hace buen (mal) —,*** the weather is fine (bad).
tienda, *n.f.* shop; tent, awning.
tienta, *n.f.* probe; cunning; ***andar a tientas,*** grope.
tiento, *n.m.* touch; blind-man's stick; care; try-out.
tierno, -na, *a.* tender; weepy.
tierra, *n.f.* earth; land, soil; country; ***echar por —,*** destroy, ruin; ***echar — a,*** (*fig.*) hush up; ***— adentro,*** inland.
tieso, -sa, *a.* taut, tight; stiff.
tiesto, *n.m.* flowerpot; crack.
tífico, -ca, *a.* rel. to typhus.
tifo (1), **-fa,** *a.* (*fam.*) fed-up, sated.
tifo (2), *n.m.* (*med.*) typhus.
tifoideo, -ea, *a.* typhoid.
tifón, *n.m.* typhoon.
tifus, *n.m.* typhus; ***de —,*** (*S.A., low*) buckshee.
tigra, *n.f.* (*S.A.*) jaguar.
tigre, *n.m.* tiger; jaguar.
tigresa, *n.f.* tigress.
tijera, *n.f.* scissors (*usually* **tijeras**); (*fam.*) gossip; big eater.
tijereta, *n.f.* earwig.
tijeretear, *v.t.* snip; meddle in.
tila, *n.f.* (*bot.*) linden blossom; ***infusión de —,*** tisane.
tildar, *v.t.* put a tilde on; brand.
tilde, *n.m.* or *f.* tilde (˜); jot, tittle; flaw.
tilín, *n.m.* ting-a-ling; (*fam.*) trice; winsomeness.
tilo, *n.m.* linden, lime-tree.
tillado, *n.m.* plank floor.
timar, *v.t.* swindle; (*fam.*) ogle.
timba, *n.f.* (*fam.*) gamble.
timbal, *n.m.* kettle-drum.—*pl.* (*mus.*) tympani.
timbre, *n.m.* stamp; (door-)bell, buzzer; timbre.
timidez, *n.f.* timidity.
tímido, -da, *a.* timid.
timo, *n.m.* (*fam.*) swindle.
timón, *n.m.* rudder, helm.
timonel, *n.m.* helmsman.
timorato, -ta, *a.* God-fearing; timid.
tímpano, *n.m.* timpano; tympanum.
tina, *n.f.* large jar; vat, tub.
tinglado, *n.m.* shed; boarding; trick.
tiniebla(s), *n.f.* (*pl.*) darkness.
tino (1), *n.m.* knack; good sense; good aim; ***a buen —,*** at a guess.
tino (2), *n.m.* vat.
tinta, *n.f.* ink; hue; ***de buena —,*** on good authority.
tintar, *v.t.* tinge.
tinte, *n.m.* colour, dye; tint; dyeing; dry cleaner's.
tinterillo, *n.m.* (*fam.*) pen-pusher; (*S.A.*) pettifogger.
tintero, *n.m.* inkwell; ***dejar en el —,*** (*fam.*) forget about.
tintín, *n.m.* clink; tinkle.
tintirintín, *n.m.* tarara (*trumpeting*).
tinto, -ta, *a.* red.—*n.m.* red wine.
tintorero, -ra, *n.m.f.* dyer.
tintura, *n.f.* tincture; make-up; dyeing.
tiña, *n.f.* ringworm; (*fam.*) meanness.
tiñe [TEÑIR].
tiñoso, -sa, *a.* mangy; (*fam.*) mingy.
tío, *n.m.* uncle; (*fam.*) bloke.
tiovivo, *n.m.* merry-go-round.
tipiadora, *n.f.* (*S.A.*) typewriter; typist.
tipiar, *v.t., v.i.* (*S.A.*) type.
típico, -ca, *a.* typical.
tiple, *n.m.f.* treble.
tipo, *n.m.* type; (*fam.*) chap.
tipografía, *n.f.* typography.
tiquismiquis, *n.m.pl.* (*fam.*) faddiness; bowing and scraping.
tira, *n.f.* strip.
tirabuzón, *n.m.* corkscrew.
tirada, *n.f.* throw; pull; issue, edition; period; distance; ***— aparte,*** off-print, separate.
tirado, -da, *a.* dirt-cheap; long; tall.—*n.m.* pulling, drawing.
tirador, -ra, *n.m.f.* puller; good shot.—*n.m.* knob, chain, cord (*to be pulled*).
tiranía, *n.f.* tyranny.
tiránico, -ca, *a.* tyrannical.
tiranizar [C], *v.t., v.i.* tyrannize.
tirano, -na, *a.* tyrannous.—*n.m.f.* tyrant.
tirante, *a.* tight, strained.—*n.m.* brace, tie.—*pl.* braces, (*U.S.*) suspenders.
tirantez, *n.f.* strain, tension; full-length.
tirar, *v.t.* throw (away); fire, shoot; stretch; draw; pull; waste; attract; print.—*v.i.* last; be appealing; shoot; tend; boast; turn.—*v.r.* rush; lie down; ***a todo (más) —,*** the utmost; ***— a,*** shoot at; turn to; aspire to.
tiritar, *v.i.* shiver.
tiritón, *n.m.* shiver.
tiro, *n.m.* throw; shot; charge; length; stretch; range; shooting; theft; depth; ***a —,*** within range *or* reach; ***al —,*** at once; ***de tiros largos,*** all dressed-up.
tirón, *n.m.* tug; novice.
tirotear, *v.t., v.i.* snipe (at).
tiroteo, *n.m.* sniping; shooting.
tirria, *n.f.* (*fam.*) dislike.
tísico, -ca, *a., n.m.f.* consumptive.
tisis, *n.f.* (*med.*) consumption.
tisú, *n.m.* (*pl.* **tisúes**) tissue (*gold, silver*).
Titán, *n.m.* Titan; **titán,** *n.m.* titan.
titánico, -ca, *a.* titanic.
títere, *n.m.* puppet.
titilación, *n.f.* titillation; twinkling.
titilar, *v.t.* titillate.—*v.i.* twinkle.
titiritar, *v.i.* shiver.
titiritero, *n.m.* puppeteer; juggler.
titubeante, *a.* hesitant; tottering.
titubear, *v.i.* waver.
titubeo, *n.m.* tottering; hesitation.
titular, *a.* titulary.—*v.t.* title, call.
título, *n.m.* title; diploma; degree; right; reason; ***¿a qué —?*** what for? with what right? ***a — de,*** by way of, as; ***a — personal,*** speaking for oneself.
tiza, *n.f.* chalk.
tizna, *n.f.* blacking; grime.
tiznadura, *n.f.* (*fam.* **tiznajo,** *n.m.*) smudge, smut.
tiznar, *v.t.* smudge; mark; blacken.—*v.r.* get smudged; (*S.A.*) get drunk.
tizne, *n.m.* smudge; smut, soot.
tizón, *n.m.* firebrand; (*fig.*) disgrace.
tizonear, *v.t.* stir (*fire*).
tizonero, *n.m.* poker.
toalla, *n.f.* towel.

toar, *v.t.* tow.
tobillo, *n.m.* ankle.
toca, *n.f.* coif, hood, wimple.
tocadiscos, *n.m. inv.* record-player.
tocado, *n.m.* coiffure, hair-do.
tocador, -ra, *n.m.f.* (*mus.*) player.—*n.m.* dressing-table; boudoir.
tocante, *a.* touching; concerning (***a***).
tocar [A], *v.t.* touch; feel; (*mus.*) play; do up (*hair*).—*v.i.* touch; concern (***a***); be the turn (***a***, of); knock; fall to; be close.—*v.r.* touch; be related; put on one's hat; (*fam.*) be touched (*daft*).
tocayo, -ya, *n.m.f.* namesake.
tocino, *n.m.* bacon; salt-pork.
tocón, *n.m.* stump.
tocho, -cha, *a.* uncouth.—*n.m.* ingot; brick.
todavía, *adv.* still, yet.
todo, -da, *a.* all; whole; any; every.—*n.m.* everything; all; ***con* —,** all the same; ***del* —,** quite; ***sobre* —,** above all.—*pl.* everybody, all.
todopoderoso, -sa, *a.* almighty.
toga, *n.f.* toga; (*educ., jur.*) gown.
toisón (de oro), *n.m.* Golden Fleece.
tojo, *n.m.* (*bot.*) furze.
toldar, *v.t.* cover with awning.
toldo, *n.m.* awning; pride, pomp.
tole, *n.m.* uproar; outcry.
toledano, -na, *a., n.m.f.* Toledan.
tolerable, *a.* tolerable.
tolerancia, *n.f.* tolerance, toleration.
tolerante, *a.* tolerant.
tolerar, *v.t.* tolerate.
tolondro, -dra, *a., n.m.f.* fool.—*n.m.* lump, bump.
tolva, *n.f.* chute.
tolvanera, *n.f.* dust-storm.
toma, *n.f.* taking; (*elec.*) main; outlet.
tomada, *n.f.* conquest.
tomar, *v.t.* take; grip; catch; get.—*v.r.* rust; **— *a bien* (*mal*),** take well (badly); **— *prestado*,** borrow.
Tomás, *n.m.* Thomas.
tomate, *n.m.* tomato.
tomavistas, *n.m. inv.* camera.
tómbola, *n.f.* raffle.
tomillo, *n.m.* (*bot.*) thyme.
tomo, *n.m.* volume, tome; bulk, importance.
tonada, *n.f.* tune, air.
tonel, *n.m.* barrel.
tonelada, *n.f.* ton.
tonga(da), *n.f.* layer, coat.
tónico, -ca, *a., n.m.* tonic.
tonificar [A], *v.t.* tone up.
tonillo, *n.m.* lilt.
tono, *n.m.* tone; (*fam.*) airs; style; (*mus.*) pitch, key.
tonsura, *n.f.* tonsure; shearing.
tontada, *n.f.* silliness.
tontear, *v.i.* fool about.
tontería, *n.f.* (piece of) foolery, stupidity; worthless object.
tonto, -ta, *a.* silly, stupid.—*n.m.f.* fool, numskull; ***hacer el* —,** play the fool.
topar, *v.t.* butt, run into; **— *con*,** bump into; come across.—*v.i.* crop up; succeed.
tope, *n.m.* butt; collision; buffer; encounter; clash; snag; top, brim.
topetada, *n.f.*, **topetón, topetazo,** *n.m.* butt, bump.
tópico, -ca, *a.* topical.—*n.m.* topic.
topinada, *n.f.* blunder(ing).
top(in)era, *n.f.* mole-hill.
topo, *n.m.* (*zool.*) mole; (*fam.*) blunderer.
topográfico, -ca, *a.* topographic(al).
toponimia, *n.f.* toponymy.
topónimo, *n.m.* place-name.
toque, *n.m.* touch; contact; ring, knock; check, try; beat; tap; gist; (*naut.*) call; **— *de queda*,** curfew (*bell*); ***dar un* — *a*,** try out, sound out; (*fam.*) pump.
torbellino, *n.m.* whirlwind.
torca, *n.f.* cavern.
torcaz, -za, *n.m.f.* woodpigeon.
torcedura, *n.f.* twist; sprain.
torcer [5D], *v.t.* twist; turn; hurt.—*v.i.* turn.—*v.r.* warp; twist; turn; go wrong.
torcido, -da, *a.* twisted; crooked; bent; on bad terms; cross (*eyes*).—*n.m.* twist.
torcimiento, *n.m.* twist(ing); wordiness.
tordo, *a.* dappled.—*n.m.* (*orn.*) thrush; starling.
torear, *v.t., v.i.* fight (*bulls*); tease.
toreo, *n.m.* bull-fighting.
torero, -ra, rel. to bull-fighting.—*n.m.* bull-fighter.
torete, *n.m.* puzzle, baffling thing; current topic.
toril, *n.m.* bull-pen.
tormenta, *n.f.* storm, tempest; turmoil; adversity.
tormento, *n.m.* torture; torment, anguish.
tormentoso, -sa, *a.* stormy.
torna, *n.f.* return; sluice.
tornada, *n.f.* return; (*poet.*) envoi.
tornadizo, -za, *a., n.m.f.* turncoat.
tornado, *n.m.* tornado.
tornar, *v.t., v.i.* return.—*v.r.* turn, become; **— *a hacer*,** do again.
tornasol, *n.m.* sunflower; litmus.
tornasolar, *v.t.* iridesce.
tornátil, *a.* fickle; lathe-turned.
tornear, *v.t.* turn (*on lathe*).—*v.i.* turn round; joust; muse.
torneo, *n.m.* tournament, tourney.
tornillero, *n.m.* (*mil.*) deserter.
tornillo, *n.m.* screw; vice, clamp.
torniquete, *n.m.* tourniquet; swivel; turnstile.
torno, *n.m.* turn; lathe; winch; spindle; wheel; ***en* — *de*,** around.
toro, *n.m.* bull; **— *corrido*,** wily experienced person; **— *de lidia* or *de muerte*,** fighting bull.—*pl.* bull-fight(ing).
toronja, *n.f.* grapefruit.
toroso, -sa, *a.* robust.
torpe, *a.* heavy, clumsy, stupid; crude, lewd; foul.
torpedear, *v.t.* torpedo.
torpedero, *n.m.* torpedo-boat.
torpedo, *n.m.* torpedo.
torpeza, *n.f.* heaviness, clumsiness, stupidity, crudeness, foulness.
torrar, *v.t.* toast.
torre, *n.f.* tower; turret; rook (*chess*).
torrencial, *a.* torrential.
torrente, *n.m.* torrent.
torrentera, *n.f.* ravine, gully.
torreón, *n.m.* turret.
torrezno, *n.m.* bacon rasher.
tórrido, -da, *a.* torrid.
torsión, *n.f.* torsion, sprain.
torso, *n.m.* trunk, torso.

torta, *n.f.* tart, pie; (*fam.*) biff, blow.
tortilla, *n.f.* omelet; flop.
tórtola, *n.f.* turtle-dove.
tortuga, *n.f.* tortoise; turtle.
tortuoso, -sa, *a.* tortuous.
tortura, *n.f.* twist; torture.
torturar, *v.t.* put to torture.
torvo, -va, *a.* grim, stern.
tos, *n.f.* cough.
Toscana, *n.f.* Tuscany.
toscano, -na, *a., n.m.f.* Tuscan.
tosco, -ca, *a.* rough, crude.
toser, *v.t.* (*fam.*) defy, beat.—*v.i.* cough.
tósigo, *n.m.* poison; grief.
tosquedad, *n.f.* coarseness.
tostada, *n.f.* toast.
tostado, *n.m.* toasting.
tostar [4], *v.t., v.r.* toast; roast; tan.
tostón, *n.m.* roast piglet; toast.
total, *a., n.m.* total.—*adv.* in a word.
totalidad, *n.f.* totality; whole.
totalitario, -ria, *a.* totalitarian.
totalitarismo, *n.m.* totalitarianism.
totalizar [C], *v.t.* total, add up.—*v.r.* total (*en*).
tótem, *n.m.* (*pl.* **-ms**) totem.
totuma, *n.f.* (*S.A.*) calabash.
toxicar [A], *v.t.* poison.
tóxico, -ca, *a.* toxic.
toxicomanía, *n.f.* drug-addiction.
toxicómano, -na, *n.m.f.* drug-addict.
toxina, *n.f.* toxin.
tozudo, -da, *a.* stubborn.
traba, *n.f.* bond; trammel.
trabacuenta, *n.f.* mistake; quarrel.
trabajado, -da, *a.* laboured; weary.
trabajador, -ra, *a.* hard-working.—*n.m.f.* worker.
trabajar, *v.t.* work; till; harass.—*v.i.* work; labour; strain.—*v.i., v.r.* strive (***en, por,*** to).
trabajo, *n.m.* work, labour; travail.—*pl.* tribulations; ***trabajos forzados,*** (*jur.*) hard labour.
trabajoso, -sa, *a.* laborious; ailing; laboured.
trabalenguas, *n.m. inv.* tongue-twister.
trabar, *v.t.* join; tie; grasp; shackle; begin.—*v.r.* tangle; get stuck.
trabazón, *n.f.* bond, connexion.
trabuca, *n.f.* fire-cracker.
trabucar [A], *v.t.* upset; mix up.
trabuco, *n.m.* blunderbuss.
tracción, *n.f.* traction; drive.
tracista, *n.m.f.* designer.
tracto, *n.m.* tract.
tractor, *n.m.* tractor.
tradición, *n.f.* tradition.
tradicional, *a.* traditional.
traducción, *n.f.* translation.
traducir [16], *v.t.* translate.
traductor, -ra, *n.m.f.* translator.
traer [34], *v.t.* bring; draw; be wearing; have (***consigo,*** on one).
traeres, *n.m.pl.* finery.
tráfago, *n.m.* traffic; drudgery.
traficante, *n.m.f.* dealer.
traficar [A], *v.i.* travel; deal, trade.
tráfico, *n.m.* traffic.
tragaderas, *n.f.pl.* gullet; ***tener buenas —,*** be credulous.
tragadero, *n.m.* abyss; pit; throat.
tragaluz, *n.f.* (*pl.* **-uces**) skylight.
tragaperras, *n.m. inv.* slot-machine.
tragar [B], *v.t.* swallow; omit.
tragazón, *n.f.* (*fam.*) gluttony.
tragedia, *n.f.* tragedy.
trágico, -ca, *a.* tragic(al).—*n.m.* tragedian.
tragicomedia, *n.f.* tragicomedy.
trago, *n.m.* swallow; bad luck; ***a tragos,*** slowly.
tragón, -gona, *a.* gluttonous.—*n.m.f.* glutton.
traición, *n.f.* betrayal; treachery; treason.
traicionar, *v.t.* betray.
traicionero, -ra, traidor, -ra, *a.* treacherous; treasonous.—*n.m.f.* traitor; villain; betrayer.
traigo [TRAER].
traílla, *n.f.* lead, leash; scraper.
traje, *n.m.* suit; costume. [TRAER].
trajín, *n.m.* carrying, fetching; coming and going.
trama, *n.f.* weft, woof; plot.
tramar, *v.t.* weave; plot, contrive.
tramitación, *n.f.* procedure; transaction.
tramitar, *v.t.* transact.
trámite, *n.m.* transit; procedure; step.
tramo, *n.m.* tract, parcel; flight (*stairs*); span; piece.
tramontar, *v.t.* pass *or* sink behind mountains.—*v.r.* flee, escape.
tramoya, *n.f.* stage machinery; artifice.
trampa, *n.f.* trap; trap-door; pitfall; cheating, fraud.
trampantojo, *n.m.* deception, sleight.
trampear, (*fam.*) *v.t., v.i.* cheat; manage somehow.
trampolín, *n.m.* spring-board.
tramposo, -sa, *a.* cheating.—*n.m.f.* cheat; trickster.
tranca, *n.f.* bar; club; ***coger una —,*** (*fam.*) get canned *or* drunk.
trancada, *n.m.* huge stride; (*fam.*) trice.
trancar, *v.t.* bar.—*v.i.* stride along.
trancazo, *n.m.* club-blow; (*fam.*) flu.
trance, *n.m.* critical moment; (*jur.*) seizure for debt; ***a todo —,*** at any price; ***en — de muerte,*** at death's door.
tranco, *n.m.* big stride; threshold; ***a trancos,*** in a dash.
tranquilidad, *n.f.* tranquillity, peace.
tranquilizar [C], *v.t., v.r.* calm.
tranquilo, -la, *a.* calm; (*fam.*) in peace.
tranquilla, *n.f.* pin, bar; trick question.
trans-, *prefix.* trans- [TRAS].
transacción, *n.f.* settlement; transaction.
transaéreo, *n.m.* air-liner.
transar, *v.i.* (*S.A.*) compromise.
transatlántico, -ca, *a.* transatlantic.—*n.m.* liner; steamer.
transbordador, *n.m.* ferry.
transbordar, *v.t.* trans-ship, transfer.
transbordo, *n.m.* trans-shipment, transfer.
transcendencia, *n.f.* importance, consequence; acumen; transcendence.
transcendental, *a.* far-reaching, highly important; transcendental.
transcendente, *a.* acute; vital; transcendent.
transcender [2], *v.t.* analyse, sift.—*v.i.* spread; leak out; smell sweet.
transcribir [*p.p.* **transcri(p)to**], *v.t.* transcribe.
transcripción, *n.f.* transcription.
transcriptor, -ra, *n.m.f.* transcriber.
transcurrir, *v.i.* elapse.

transcurso, *n.m.* passage, course (*time*).
transeúnte, *a.* transient.—*n.m.f.* passer-by; temporary guest.
transferencia, *n.f.* transfer(ence).
transferir [6], *v.t.* transfer; convey; postpone.
transfiguración, *n.f.* transfiguration.
transfigurar, *v.t.* transfigure.—*v.r.* become transfigured.
transfijo, -ja, *a.* transfixed.
transformación, *n.f.* transformation.
transformador, *n.m.* (*elec.*) transformer.
transformar, *v.t.* transform.
transfretano, -na, *a.* across the straits.
transfretar, *v.t.* cross (*seas*).—*v.i.* spread.
tránsfuga, *n.m.f.*, **tránsfugo,** *n.m.* fugitive; turncoat.
transfundir, *v.t.* transmit; transfuse.
transfusión, *n.f.* transfusion.
transgredir [Q], *v.t.* transgress.
transgresión, *n.f.* transgression.
transgresor, -ra, *a.* transgressing.—*n.m.f.* transgressor.
transición, *n.f.* transition.
transido, -da, *a.* worn out; mean.
transigir [E], *v.t.*, *v.i.* compromise, settle (*en, con*).
transistor, *n.m.* (*elec.*) transistor; (*fam.*) transistor radio.
transitable, *a.* passable.
transitar, *v.i.* journey.
transitivo, -va, *a.* transitive.
tránsito, *n.m.* transit; stop; passing-on (*of saints*); transfer; *de* —, on the way; passing through.
translucidez, *n.f.* translucence.
translúcido, -da, *a.* translucent.
transmisión, *n.f.* transmission.
transmisor, -ra, *n.m.f.* transmitter.
transmitir, *v.t.*, *v.i.* transmit.
transmutación, *n.f.* transmutation.
transmutar, *v.t.*, *v.r.* transmute.
transparencia, *n.f.* transparency; (*photo.*) slide.
transparentar, *v.r.* be(come) transparent; show through.
transparente, *a.* transparent.—*n.m.* stained-glass window.
transpirar, *v.t.*, *v.i.* perspire.
transponer [25], *v.t.* transpose; turn, go round (*corner*); transfer.—*v.r.* get sleepy; set (*sun*).
transportación, *n.f.* transport(ation).
transportamiento, *n.m.* (*lit. fig.*) transport.
transportar, *v.t.* transport; transfer.—*v.r.* go into ecstasies.
transporte, *n.m.* transport.
transpu- [TRANSPONER].
transversal, *a.* transversal, crossing.—*n.f.* side-street.
tranvía, *n.m.* tram, (*U.S.*) streetcar.
tranviario, -ria, *a.* rel. to trams.—*n.m.f.* tram-worker.
tranzar [C], *v.t.* truncate.
trapa, *n.f.* tramping; uproar; (*naut.*) line.
trapacear, *v.i.* cheat.
trapacero, -ra, *n.m.f.* cheat.
trapajo, *n.m.* tatter.
trápala, *n.f.* stamping, tramping; clopping; (*fam.*) swindle.—*n.m.f.* (*fam.*) twister, cheat.
trapaza, *n.f.* swindle, fraud.
trapecio, *n.m.* trapezium; trapeze.
trapense, *a.*, *n.m.f.* Trappist.
trapero, *n.m.* rag-and-bone man.
trapío, *n.m.* spirit, mettle; (*fam.*) nerve, cheek.
trapisonda, *n.f.* (*fam.*) din, clatter; deception.
trapista, *a.*, *n.m.f.* Trappist; (*S.A.*) [TRAPERO].
trapo, *n.m.* rag; sails; (*taur.*) red cape.—*pl.* (*fam.*) rags, togs.
traque, *n.m.* bang; crack; fuse, touch-paper.
traquear, *v.t.* shake; (*fam.*) mess with.—*v.t.*, *v.i.* rattle; bang.
traquido, *n.m.* bang, crack.
tras, *prep.* after, behind.—*n.m.* rap knock. [TRANS].
trascendido, -da, *a.* keen, acute.
trascocina, *n.f.* back kitchen.
trascuenta, *n.f.* mistake.
trasegar [1B], *v.t.* upset; decant.
trasero, -ra, *a.* rear, hind.—*n.m.* rump.—*pl.* (*fam.*) ancestors.—*n.f.* back (part).
transfondo, *n.m.* background.
trasgo, *n.m.* imp; goblin.
trashoguero, -ra, *a.*, *n.m.f.* stay-at-home, idler.—*n.m.* log.
trashojar, *v.t.* glance through (*a book*).
trashumante, *a.* seasonally nomadic (*shepherds and flocks*).
trashumar, *v.t.*, *v.i.* move to seasonal pastures.
trasiego, *n.m.* removal; upset; decanting.
traslación, *n.f.* transfer, move; deferment; copy.
trasladar, *v.t.* (re)move; copy; postpone; transfer.—*v.r.* move (*house, from job etc.*).
traslado, *n.m.* copy, transcript; transfer.
traslapar, *v.t.*, *v.i.* overlap.
traslaticio, -cia, *a.* figurative.
traslucir [9], *v.t.* infer.—*v.r.* leak out; be translucent.
traslumbrar, *v.t.* dazzle.—*v.r.* vanish.
trasluz, *n.m.* reflected light; *a(l)* —, against the light.
trasmano, *n.m.* second hand (*at cards*); *a* —, out of reach; off the beaten track.
trasmañanar, *v.t.* leave for the morrow.
trasmatar, *v.t.* (*fam.*) bury (*consider dead*).
trasminar, *v.t.* undermine.—*v.r.* seep.
trasnochado, -da, *a.* stale; haggard; trite.—*n.f.* sleepless night; last night; night attack.
trasnochar, *v.t.* sleep on (*a problem*).—*v.i.* stay up all night.
trasoñar [4], *v.t.* dream up, muddle.
traspapelar, *v.t.* mislay.—*v.r.* get mislaid.
traspasar, *v.t.* cross (over); transfer; transfix, run through; break (*law*); pain.—*v.r.* overstep the mark.
traspaso, *n.m.* transfer; trespass; anguish.
traspié, *n.m.* stumble, tripping.
trasplantar, *v.t.* transplant.
traspuesta, *n.f.* removal; nook; disappearance; flight.
traspunte, *n.m.* (*theat.*) prompter.
trasquila, *n.f.* shearing.
trasquilar, *v.t.* shear; crop; (*fam.*) lop off.
traste, *n.m.* (*mus.*) fret; ***dar al* — *con,*** spoil; give up as a bad job; ***sin trastes,*** (*fam.*) messily, messy.
trastera, *n.f.* lumber-room.
trastienda, *n.f.* back-room (*of shop*); (*fam.*) wariness.

trasto, *n.m.* piece, thing, luggage.—*pl.* gear tackle.
trastornar, *v.t.* upset; overturn.
trastorno, *n.m.* upset; disorder.
trastrocar [4A], *v.t.* interchange; reverse.
trastulo, *n.m.* plaything; fun.
trasunto, *n.m.* copy, transcript.
trata, *n.f.* — ***de negros,*** slave-trade; — ***de blancas,*** white slave-trade.
tratable, *a.* tractable, sociable.
tratado, *n.m.* treatise; treaty.
tratamiento, *n.m.* treatment; title.
tratante, *n.m.* dealer.
tratar, *v.t.* treat; deal with; address (***de,*** as); —*v.i.* try (***de,*** to); deal.—*v.r.* deal; behave; be a matter (***de,*** of).
trato, *n.m.* treatment, conduct; usage; address; pact; trade; social intercourse.
trauma, *n.m.* trauma.
traumático, -ca, *a.* traumatic.
través, *n.m.* slant; reverse; ***a(l) — de,*** through, across; ***dar al — con,*** do away with.
travesano, *n.m.* cross-bar; bolster.
travesar [1], *v.t.* cross.
travesía, *n.f.* crossing.
travestido, -da, *a.* disguised.
travesura, *n.f.* prank, mischief.
travieso, -sa, *a.* cross; sharp; naughty; lewd.—*n.f.* crossing; cross-beam; (*rail.*) sleeper.
trayecto, *n.m.* journey, distance.
trayectoria, *n.f.* trajectory.
traza, *n.f.* design; looks; mode; sign.
trazado, -da, *a.* outlined; formed.—*n.m.* plan, design; sketch; route.
trazar [C], *v.t.* design; outline; draw; trace.
trazo, *n.m.* outline; tracing; stroke.
trebejo, *n.m.* plaything; chess piece.—*pl.* implements.
trébol, *n.m.* (*bot.*) clover; (*cards*) club.
trece, *a., n.m.* thirteen; ***seguir en sus —,*** (*fam.*) not budge in one's ideas.
treceno, -na, *a.* thirteenth.
trecho, *n.m.* space, stretch; while, time.
tregua, *n.f.* truce; respite.
treinta, *a., n.m.* thirty.
tremebundo, -da, *a.* dreadful.
tremedal, *n.m.* quagmire.
tremendo, -da, *a.* tremendous.
tremer, *v.i.* tremble.
tremolar, *v.t., v.i.* wave.
tremolina, *n.f.* rustling; (*fam.*) fuss.
tremor, *n.m.* tremor.
trémulo, -la, *a.* quivering.
tren, *n.m.* train; retinue; (*sport*) pace; pomp; (*mech.*) gears; — ***de aterrizaje,*** undercarriage.
trencilla, *n.f.* braid, plait.
treno, *n.m.* dirge.
trenza, *n.f.* plait; tress.
trenzar [C], *v.t.* plait.—*v.i.* caper.
trepa, *n.f.* climb(ing); drill(ing); (*fam.*) fraud; (*fam.*) flogging.
trepadora, *n.f.* climbing plant; rambler.
trepanar, *v.t.* (*med.*) trepan.
trepar, *v.t.* climb; drill.—*v.i.* climb (***por,*** up).
trepe, *n.m.* (*fam.*) telling-off.
trepidar, *v.i.* shake, tremble.
tres, *a., n.m.* three.
trescientos, -tas, *a., n.m.pl.* three hundred.
tresillo, *n.m.* ombre (*cards*); set of three; settee.
treta, *n.f.* trick; feint.
triángulo, *n.m.* triangle.
triar [L], *v.t.* sort, select.
trib(u)al, *a.* tribal.
tribu, *n.f.* tribe.
tribulación, *n.f.* tribulation.
tribuna, *n.f.* tribune; rostrum.
tribunal, *n.m.* tribunal, court; board.
tributación, *n.f.* taxation; tribute.
tributar, *v.t.* pay (*taxes, homage*).
tributario, -ria, *a., n.m.f.* tributary; taxpayer.
tributo, *n.m.* tax; contribution; tribute.
tricolor, *a.* tricolour.
tricornio, -nia, *a.* three-cornered *or* -horned. —*n.m.* three-cornered hat.
tridente, *a., n.m.* trident.
trienio, *n.m.* triennium.
trigo, *n.m.* wheat; (*low*) loot, money.
trigonometría, *n.f.* trigonometry.
trilátero, -ra, *a.* trilateral.
trilingüe, *a.* trilingual.
trilogía, *n.f.* trilogy.
trillado, -da, *a.* trite, stale; beaten (*track*).
trillar, *v.t.* thresh; frequent.
trillón, *n.m.* trillion (10^{18}), (*U.S.*) quintillion.
trimestral, *a.* quarterly.
trimestre, *n.m.* term; quarter.
trinar, *v.i.* trill; (*fam.*) rave.
trincar [A], *v.t.* tie, bind; smash; (*fam.*) do in, kill.—*v.i.* (*fam.*) have a drink.
trinchante, *n.m.* carving-knife; carver.
trinchar, *v.t.* carve; (*fam.*) settle.
trinchera, *n.f.* trench.
trineo, *n.m.* sledge, sleigh.
Trinidad, *n.f.* Trinity.
trino, -na, *a.* trinal.—*n.m.* trill.
trinquete, *n.m.* (*mech.*) pawl, ratchet; foresail.
trinquis, *n.m. inv.* (*fam.*) drop, drink.
trío, *n.m.* trio.
tripa, *n.f.* bowel, gut; belly; ***hacer de tripas corazón,*** pluck up courage.
tripartito, -ta, *a.* tripartite.
tripicallos, *n.m.pl.* (*cul.*) tripe.
triple, *a., n.m.* triple, treble.
triplicado, *a.* triplicate.
triplicar [A], *v.t., v.r.* treble.
tríplice, *a.* triple.
tríptico, *n.m.* triptych.
tripudo, -da, *a.* pot-bellied.
tripulación, *n.f.* crew.
tripulante, *n.m.* member of crew.
tripular, *v.t.* man, fit out.
trique, *n.m.* crack, snap.
triquiñuela, *n.f.* hoodwinking.
triquitraque, *n.m.* crack; clatter; cracker.
tris, *n.m.* tinkle, crack; instant; ***en un —,*** within an ace.
triscar [A], *v.t.* mingle; set.—*v.i.* stamp; frisk.
trisecar [A], *v.t.* trisect.
triste, *a.* sad; gloomy; wretched.
tristeza, *n.f.* sadness.
triturar, *v.t.* triturate; crush.
triunfal, *a.* triumphal.
triunfante, *a.* triumphant.
triunfar, *v.i.* triumph (***de,*** over); trump.
triunfo, *n.m.* triumph; trump.
trivial, *a.* ordinary; well-trodden; trivial.

trivialidad, *n.f.* triviality.
triza, *n.f.* fragment, smithereen.
a lo trocado, *adv. phr.* in exchange; in the opposite way.
trocamiento, *n.m.* (ex)change.
trocar [4A], *v.t.* exchange, barter; change; confuse.—*v.r.* change over.
trocatinta, *n.f.* (*fam.*) mix-up.
trocla, tróclea, *n.f.* pulley.
trocha, *n f.* path, trail.
a trochemoche, *adv. phr.* pell-mell.
trofeo, *n.m.* trophy.
troglodita, *a., n.m.f.* troglodyte; (*fig.*) brute.
troj(e), *n.f.* granary, barn.
trola, *n.f.* (*fam.*) fib.
trolebús, *n.m.* trolley-bus.
tromba, *n.f.* whirl, water-spout.
trombón, *n.m.* trombone.
trombosis, *n.f.* thrombosis.
trompa, *n.f.* (*mus.*) horn; trunk, proboscis; (*anat.*) tube.
trompazo, *n.m.* horn-blast; hard bump.
trompeta, *n.f.* trumpet.—*n.m.* trumpeter.
trompetazo, *n.m.* trumpet-call; (*fam.*) silly remark.
trompetero, *n.m.* trumpeter.
trompicar [A], *v.t.* trip; (*fam.*) promote over s.o.'s head.—*v.i.* stumble.
trompicón, *n.m.* stumble; ***a trompicones,*** stumbling(ly).
trompo, *n.m.* top (*toy*); chess-man.
trompón, *n.m.* bump; (*bot.*) daffodil.
tronada, *n.f.* thunder-storm.
tronante, *a.* thunderous.
tronar [4], *v.i.* thunder; (*fam.*) flop; (*fam.*) quarrel (***con,*** with).
troncar [A], *v.t.* truncate.
tronco, *n.m.* (*bot., anat.*) trunk; log.
troncha, *n.f.* (*S.A.*) slice.
tronchar, *v.t.* split.
troncho, *n.m.* stem.
tronera, *n.f.* port-hole; embrasure.
tronido, *n.m.* thunder-clap.
trono, *n.m.* throne.
tronzar [C], *v.t.* shatter, smash.
tropa, *n.f.* troop, crowd.—*pl.* (*mil.*) troops.
tropel, *n.m.* tumult; rush.
tropelía, *n.f.* mad rush; outrage.
tropezar [C], *v.i.* stumble (***con, en,*** on).
tropezón, -zona, *a.* stumbling.—*n.m.* trip, stumble; obstacle; tit-bit.
tropical, *a.* tropic(al).
trópico, *n.m.* tropic.
tropiezo, *n.m.* stumble; slip; hitch.
troquel, *n.m.* die, stamp.
troqueo, *n.m.* trochee.
trotaconventos, *n.f. inv.* procuress.
trotamundos, *n.m.f. inv.* globe-trotter.
trotar, *v.i.* trot.
trote, *n.m.* trot; ***al —,*** on the trot.
trotón, -tona, *a.* trotting.—*n.f.* chaperone.
trova, *n.f.* lay, lyric; (*S.A.*) fib.
trovador, -ra, *a., n.m.* troubadour.
trovar, *v.t.* parody.—*v.i.* write verse.
Troya, *n.f.* Troy.
troyano, -na, *a., n.m.f.* Trojan.
trozo, *n.m.* piece; extract; log.
truco, *n.m.* trick; (*fam.*) wrinkle, knack.
truculento, -ta, *a.* truculent.
trucha, *n.f.* trout.
truchimán, -mana, *a.* shrewd, slick.—*n.m.f.* interpreter.
trueco [TRUEQUE, TROCAR].
trueno, *n.m.* thunder; bang; harum-scarum; scandal.
trueque, *n.m.* barter, exchange; ***a — de,*** in exchange for.
trufa, *n.f.* truffle; lie.
trufar, *v.i.* stuff with truffles; fib.
truhán, -hana, *n.m.f.* crook; buffoon.
truísmo, *n.m.* truism.
trujimán, -mana, *n.m.f.* interpreter.
trulla, *n.f.* trowel; hurly-burly.
truncar [A], *v.t.* truncate; maim; cut short.
tu, *a. poss.* thy, your.
tú, *pron. pers.* thou, you; ***tratar de — a,*** [TUTEAR].
tuáutem, *n.m.f. inv.* (*fam.*) king pin; vital factor.
tubérculo, *n.m.* tubercle.
tuberculosis, *n.f.* tuberculosis.
tuberculoso, -sa, *a.* tuberculous, tubercular. —*n.m.f.* tuberculosis sufferer.
tubería, *n.f.* piping, pipes.
tubo, *n.m.* pipe; tube; gun-barrel.
tubular, *a.* tubular.
tudesco, -ca, *a., n.m.f.* German.
tueco, *n.m.* stump; worm-hole.
tuerca, *n.f.* (*mech.*) nut.
tuerce, *n.m.* twist; sprain.
tuerto, -ta, *a.* twisted; one-eyed.—*n.m.* wrong, tort.
tuétano, *n.m.* marrow; pith.
tufo, *n.m.* vapour, fume; stench.—*pl.* airs, graces.
tufoso, -sa, *a.* foul; cocky, vain.
tugurio, *n.m.* hut.
tuitivo, -va, *a.* protective.
tul, *n.m.* tulle.
tulipán, *n.m.* (*bot.*) tulip.
tullido, -da, *a.* crippled.—*n.m.f.* cripple.
tullir [J], *v.t.* cripple; harm.
tumba, *n.f.* grave, tomb.
tumbar, *v.t.* knock down; (*fam.*) knock out. —*v.i.* fall down.—*v.r.* (*fam.*) lie down; give up.
tumbo, *n.m.* tumble, fall; rumble; important matter; ***— de dado,*** imminent peril.
tumbón, -bona, *a.* (*fam.*) sly; lazy.—*n.m.f.* idler.—*n.f.* air-bed.
tumefacer [20], *v.t., v.r.* swell.
tumescente, *a.* tumescent.
túmido, -da, *a.* tumid.
tumor, *n.m.* tumour.
túmulo, *n.m.* tumulus.
tumulto, *n.m.* tumult.
tumultuoso, -sa, *a.* tumultuous.
tuna (1), *n.f.* (*bot.*) prickly pear.
tuna (2), *n.f.* band of serenaders; (*fam.*) loose living.
tunante, *a.* crafty, dishonest.—*n.m.f.* (*also* **tunanta**) crook; idler.
tunda, *n.f.* (*fam.*) beating.
tundente, *a.* blunt, bruising.
tunecino, -na, *a., n.m.f.* Tunisian.
túnel, *n.m.* tunnel.
Túnez, *n.f.* Tunis; Tunisia.
tungsteno, *n.m.* tungsten.
túnica, *n.f.* tunic.
tuno, -na, *a.* crooked.—*n.m.f.* crook; serenader.
al (buen) tuntún, *adv. phr.* (*fam.*) out of one's hat.
tupa, *n.f.* stuffing.

tupé, *n.m.* toupee; (*fam.*) cheek.
tupido, -da, *a.* dense, thick; blocked.
tupir, *v.t.* block up; press close.—*v.r.* over-eat.
turba, *n.f.* crowd; peat.
turbamulta, *n.f.* rabble.
turbante, *n.m.* turban.
turbar, *v.t.* disturb.
turbieza, *n.f.* obscurity; bewilderment.
turbina, *n.f.* turbine.
turbio, -bia, *a.* muddy, clouded; obscure.
turbión, *n.m.* squall; storm; rush.
turborreactor, *n.m.* turbo-jet.
turbulencia, *n.f.* turbulence.
turbulento, -ta, *a.* turbulent.
turco, -ca, *a.* Turkish.—*n.m.f.* Turk; ***coger una turca,*** (*fam.*) get canned *or* drunk.
turgente, *a.* turgid.
turismo, *n.m.* tourism; (*auto.*) tourer.
turista, *a., n.m.f.* tourist.
turístico, -ca, *a.* tourist.
turnar, *v.i.* take turns.
turnio, -nia, *a.* cross-eyed.
turno, *n.m.* turn; shift; ***de —,*** on duty.
turquesa, *n.f.* turquoise.
Turquía, *n.f.* Turkey.
turrar, *v.t.* roast.
turrón, *n.m.* nut-brittle, nougat.
turulato, -ta, *a.* (*fam.*) staggered.
turuta, *n.f.* (*fam.*) [TURCA].
tus, *interj.* ***sin decir — ni mus,*** (*fam.*) keeping mum.
tutear, *v.t.* speak to familiarly [TÚ]; be on intimate terms with.
tutela, *n.f.* tutelage; guardianship.
tuteo, *n.m.* act of TUTEAR.
a tutiplén, *adv. phr.* (*fam.*) more than enough.
tutor, -tora (*f. also* **-triz**), *n.m.f.* guardian.
tuve [TENER].
tuyo, -ya, *poss. a., pron.* thine, yours.

U

U, u, *n.f.* twenty-fourth letter of the Spanish alphabet.
U. [USTED].
u, *conj.* or (*before following* o). [O].
ubérrimo, -ma, *a. sup.* very fruitful; abundant.
ubicar [A], *v.t.* (*S.A.*) situate, place.—*v.i., v.r.* be situated.
ubicuo, -cua, *a.* ubiquitous.
ubre, *n.f.* udder.
Ucrania, *n.f.* Ukraine.
ucranio, -nia, *a., n.m.f.* Ukrainian.
ues- [OES-].
¡uf! *interj.* ugh!
ufanar, *v.r.* pride oneself (***de, con,*** on).
ufanía, *n.f.* pride; mastery.
ufano, -na, *a.* proud; vain; masterly.
ufo, *adv.* ***a —,*** [DE GORRA].
ujier, *n.m.* usher.
úlcera, *n.f.* ulcer; sore.
ulcerar, *v.t., v.r.* ulcerate.
ulceroso, -sa, *a.* ulcerous.
Ulises, *n.m.* Ulysses.
ulterior, *a.* farther; subsequent.
ultimamente, *adv.* finally; recently.
ultimar, *v.t.* terminate, finish.
ultimátum, *n.m.* ultimatum; final word.
ultimidad, *n.f.* finality; recentness.
último, -ma, *a.* final, last; latest, (most) recent; furthest; best; ***por —,*** finally; ***a últimos de,*** towards the end of.
ultra, *prep., adv.* besides, beyond.
ultra- *prefix.* ultra-, extra-.
ultrajar, *v.t.* offend against, insult.
ultraje, *n.m.* insult, offence, outrage.
ultrajoso, -sa, *a.* outrageous, offensive.
ultramar, *n.m.* overseas.
ultramarino, -na, *a.* overseas.—*n.m.* ultramarine (blue).—*pl.* imported groceries.
ultranza, *adv.* ***a —,*** to death; at any cost.
ultrarrojo, -ja, *a.* infra-red.
ultrasónico, -ca, *a.* supersonic.
ultratumba, *adv.* beyond the grave.
ultraviolado, -da, ultravioleta, *a.* ultraviolet.
úlula, *n.f.* (*orn.*) tawny owl.
ulular, *v.i.* hoot, shriek.
ululato, *n.m.* hoot, shriek.
umbral, *n.m.* threshold (*often pl.*).
umbrío, -ría, *a.* shady.—*n.f.* shady place.
umbro, -ra, *a., n.m.f.* Umbrian.
umbroso, -sa, *a.* shady.
un, una, *indef. art.* a, an.
unánime, *a.* unanimous.
unanimidad, *n.f.* unanimity.
unción, *n.f.* unction.
uncir [D], *v.t.* yoke.
undécimo, -ma, *a., n.m.* eleventh.
undoso, -sa, *a.* wavy, undulating.
undular [ONDULAR].
ungir [E], *v.t.* anoint.
ungüento, *n.m.* ointment, salve.
únicamente, *adv.* solely, only.
único, -ca, *a.* sole, single, only; unique.
unicornio, *n.m.* unicorn.
unidad, *n.f.* unity; unit.
unidireccional, *a.* one-way.
unificación, *n.f.* unification.
unificar [A], *v.t.* unify.—*v.r.* unite.
uniformar, *v.t.* uniform; make uniform.
uniforme, *a., n.m.* uniform.
uniformidad, *n.f.* uniformity.
unigénito, -ta, *a.* only-begotten.
unilateral, *a.* unilateral.
unión, *n.f.* union; ***Unión de Repúblicas Socialistas Soviéticas,*** Union of Soviet Socialist Republics.
unionista, *a., n.m.f.* unionist.
unir, *v.t., v.r.* unite.
unisón, *n.m.* (*mus.*) unison.
unisonancia, *n.f.* monotony.
unísono, -na, *a.* in unison; ***al —,*** unanimously.
unitario, -ria, *a., n.m.f.* unitarian.
universal, *a., n.m.* universal.
universidad, *n.f.* university.
universitario, -ria, *a.* university.—*n.m.f.* university teacher *or* student.
universo, -sa, *a.* universal.—*n.m.* universe.

uno, una, *a., pron.* one. — ***y otro,*** both; —*pl.* some; ***uno — (s) a otro(s),*** each *or* one another; — ***que otro, unos cuantos,*** a few; [UN].
untar, *v.t.* grease; anoint; smear; (*fam.*) bribe.
unto, *n.m.* grease; ointment; polish; bribe.
unt(u)oso, -sa, *a.* greasy; unctuous.
untura, *n.f.* anointing; ointment; greasing.
uña, *n.f.* (*anat.*) nail; talon, claw; hoof; thorn; ***a — de caballo,*** at full speed; ***ser — y carne,*** be very close, intimate; ***ser largo de uñas,*** be light-fingered.
uña(ra)da, *n.f.*, **uñetazo,** *n.m.* scratch.
uñero, *n.m.* ingrown nail.
uñoso, -sa, *a.* long-nailed.
¡upa! *interj.* hoop-la! up!
uranio, *n.m.* uranium.
urbanidad, *n.f.* urbanity, courtesy.
urbanismo, *n.m.* town-planning.
urbanista, *n.m.f.* town-planner.
urbanización, *n.f.* urbanization.
urbanizar [C], *v.t.* urbanize.
urbano, -na, *a.* urbano; urbane.
urbe, *n.f.* metropolis.
urdimbre, *n.f.* warp.
urdir, *v.t.* warp (*yarn*); (*fig.*) plot, contrive.
urea, *n.f.* urea.
urgencia, *n.f.* emergency; urgency.
urgente, *a.* urgent; express (*mail*).
urgir [E], *v.i.* be urgent.
urinal, urinario, *n.m.* urinal.
urraca, *n.f.* (*orn.*) magpie.
el Uruguay, *n.m.* Uruguay.
uruguayo, -ya, *a., n.m.f.* Uruguayan.
usado, -da, *a.* used; second-hand; worn; usual.
usagre, *n.m.* (*med.*) impetigo; distemper.
usanza, *n.f.* usage, custom.
usar, *v.t.* use; wear; enjoy; follow (*profession*). —*v.i.* make use (***de,*** of), employ; be accustomed.—*v.r.* be in use *or* the custom.
usarcé (*obs.*), [USTED].
usgo, *n.m.* loathing.
usía, *pron., m.f.* your excellency.
usina, *n.f.* (*S.A.*) factory; power-station.
uso, *n.m.* use; custom; wear; practice; condition; ***al —,*** according to custom.
uste [OXTE].
usted, *pron. pers.* you (*polite form*; *pl.* **ustedes**).
usual, *a.* usual; usable; sociable.
usufructo, *n.m.* usufruct.
usura, *n.f.* usury; profit; interest; profiteering.
usurear, *v.i.* profiteer.
usurero, -ra, *n.m.f.* usurer; profiteer.
usurpar, *v.t.* usurp.
utensilio, *n.m.* utensil; tool.
útil, *a.* useful; (*jur.*) legal (*day*).—*n.m.* use.—*pl.* tools.
utilidad, *n.f.* usefulness; use; profit.
utilitario, -ria, *a.* utilitarian.
utilizar [C], *v.t.* use, utilize; employ.
utillería, *n.f.* equipment; tools.
utopia, utopía, *n.f.* utopia.
utópico, -ca, *a.* utopian.
UU. [USTEDES].
uva, *n.f.* grape; grapes; — ***espina,*** gooseberry; — ***pasa,*** raisin; ***hecho una —,*** drunk as a lord; ***uvas verdes,*** (*fig.*) sour grapes.

V

V, v, *n.f.* twenty-fifth letter of the Spanish alphabet.
va [IR].
vaca, *n.f.* cow; beef.
vacación, *n.f.* vacation; vacancy.—*pl.* holiday(s); vacation.
vacancia, *n.f.* vacancy.
vacante, *a.* vacant.—*n.f.* vacation; vacancy.
vacar [A], *v.i.* be vacant *or* idle; lack (***de***); attend (***a,*** to).
vaciado, *n.m.* cast; excavation.
vaciante, *n.m.* ebb-tide.
vaciar [L], *v.t., v.i.* empty; drain; hollow out; cast.
vaciedad, *n.f.* frothy nonsense.
vacilación, *n.f.* vacillation.
vacilar, *v.i.* vacillate; waver (***en,*** to).
vacío, -cía, *a.* hollow, empty.—*n.m.* emptiness; hollow; void; ***en —,*** in vacuo.
vacuidad, *n.f.* vacuity.
vacuna, *n.f.* vaccine.
vacunación, *n.f.* vaccination.
vacunar, *v.t.* vaccinate.
vacuno, -na, *a.* bovine.
vacuo, -cua, *a.* empty.—*n.m.* vacuum.
vadear, *v.t.* ford; sound out; overcome.—*v.r.* behave.
vado, *n.m.* ford; way out, solution.
vagabundear, vagamundear, *v.i.* roam; idle.
vagabundo, -da, vagamundo, -da, *a., n.m.f.* vagabond.
vagancia, *n.f.* vagrancy.
vagar, *n.m.* leisure.—*v.i.* [B] wander, roam; idle.
vagaroso, -sa, *a.* wandering.
vago, -ga, *a.* vagrant; lazy; vague; wavering. —*n.m.* loafer.
vagón, *n.m.* wagon; (*rail.*) coach.
vaguear, *v.i.* roam; loaf.
vaguedad, *n.f.* vagueness.
vaguido, -da, *a.* dizzy.—*n.f.* dizziness.
vah(e)ar, *v.i.* emit vapour, exhale.
vahído, *n.m.* dizziness, giddiness.
vaho, *n.m.* fume, vapour; breath.
vaina, *n.f.* sheath; pod; (*S.A.*) bother.
vainilla, *n.f.* vanilla.
vais [IR].
vaivén, *n.m.* seesawing, wavering; risk.
vajilla, *n.f.* crockery, ware.
val [VALLE].
valdré [VALER].
vale, *n.m.* voucher; adieu; receipt; (*S.A. low*) mate, chum.
valedero, -ra, *a.* valid.
valedor, -ra, *n.m.f.* protector; (*S.A.*) chum.
valenciano, -na, *a., n.m.f.* Valencian.
valentía, *n.f.* valour; exploit; boast.
Valentín, *n.m.* Valentine.
valentón, -tona, *a., n.m.f.* braggart.
valentona(da), *n.f.* bragging.
valer, *n.m.* worth.—*v.t.* [36] be worth; avail; produce.—*v.i.* be valuable; be valid; prevail; matter.—*v.r.* make use of, avail oneself of (***de***); ***mas vale . . . ,*** it is better to . . . ; — ***para,*** serve to; — ***por,*** be as good as, equal.

valeroso, -sa, *a.* valiant; effective.
valgo [VALER].
valía, *n.f.* worth, value; credit; faction.
validar, *v.t.* validate.
validez, *n.f.* validity; efficacy.
valido, -da, *a.* valued.—*n.m.* favourite, minister.
válido, -da, *a.* valid; sound.
valiente, *a.* brave; superb; strong.—*n.m.* brave man; bully.
valija, *n.f.* valise; mail-bag.
valimiento, *n.m.* protection; (*pol.*) favouritism.
valioso, -sa, *a.* valuable; wealthy.
valón, -lona, *a., n.m.f.* Walloon.—*n.m. pl.* bloomers.—*n.f.* vandyke collar.
valor, *n.m.* value, worth; valour; validity; import(ance).—*pl.* securities, bonds.
valoración, *n.f.* valuation.
valor(e)ar, *v.t.* value, evaluate.
valoría, *n.f.* worth.
valorizar [C], *v.t.* value.
vals, *n.m.* waltz.
vals(e)ar, *v.i.* waltz.
valuación, *n.f.* valuation.
válvula, *n.f.* valve.
valla, *n.f.* barricade; hurdle; barrier.
valladar, vallado, *n.m.* barrier, fence.
vallar, *v.t.* barricade.
valle, *n.m.* valley; vale.
vallisoletano, -na, *a., n.m.f.* rel. to *or* native of Valladolid.
vamos [IR].
vampiro, *n.m.* vampire.
van [IR].
vanagloria, *n.f.* vainglory.
vanagloriar, *v.r.* boast (*de*, of).
vanaglorioso, -sa, *a.* vainglorious.
vandalismo, *n.m.* vandalism.
vándalo, -la, *a., n.m.f.* Vandal.
vanear, *v.i.* talk rubbish.
vanguardia, *n.f.* vanguard; lead.
vanidad, *n.f.* vanity.
vanidoso, -sa, *a.* vain, conceited.
vanistorio, *n.m.* (*fam.*) stuck-up person.
vano, -na, *a.* vain.—*n.m.* opening.
vapor, *n.m.* steam; mist; vapour; (*naut.*) steamer.
vaporar [EVAPORAR].
vaporizar [C], *v.t.* vaporize.
vaporoso, -sa, *a.* steamy; vaporous.
vapular, *v.t.* flog.
vaquería, *n.f.* dairy; herd.
vaquerizo, -za, *a.* rel. to cattle.—*n.m.* cowman.—*n.f.* cowshed.
vaquero, -ra, *a.* rel. to cattle.—*n.m.* cowherd, cowboy.
vaqueta, *n.f.* leather.
vara, *n.f.* rod; twig; measure of length (2 *ft.* 9 *ins.*); — ***alta,*** authority.
varar, *v.t.* beach (*boats*).—*v.i.* run aground.
varear, *v.t.* knock down; measure; prod.
vareta, *n.f.* twig; stripe; sharp hint.
varga, *n.f.* steep slope.
variable, *a.* variable.
variación, *n.f.* variation.
variante, *a., n.f.* variant.
variar [L], *v.t., v.i.* vary.
várice, *n.f.* varicose vein.
varicoso, -sa, *a.* varicose.
variedad, *n.f.* variety; odd item.
varilla, *n.f.* wand; twig; stem; spoke.
vario, -ria, *a.* various; variegated; fickle.—*pl.* various, several.—*n.m.pl.* miscellanea.
varón, *a., n.m.* male; ***santo*** **—,** simple soul.
varonil, *a.* manly, virile.
Varsovia, *n.f.* Warsaw.
vas [IR].
vasallo, -lla, *a., n.m.f.* vassal.
vasco, -ca, *a., n.m.f.* Basque.
vascongado, -da, *a., n.m.f.* Spanish Basque.
vascuence, *a., n.m.* Basque (*language*).
vaselina, *n.f.* (*reg. trade mark*) Vaseline.
vasija, *n.f.* vessel; dish; cask.
vaso, *n.m.* tumbler, glass; vase.
vástago, *n.m.* shoot; offspring; (*mech.*) rod.
vastedad, *n.f.* vastness.
vasto, -ta, *a.* vast.
vate, *n.m.* bard, poet; seer.
váter, *n.m.* [WATER].
vaticano, -na, *a.* Vatican; ***el Vaticano,*** the Vatican.
vaticinar, *v.t.* foretell, predict.
vatio, *n.m.* (*elec.*) watt.
vaya, *n.f.* scoff.—*v.* [IR.]
Vd., Vds. [USTED(ES)].
ve [IR, VER].
vecero, -ra, *a.* alternating.—*n.m.f.* customer.—*n.f.* herd.
vecinal, *a.* local.
vecindad, *n.f.* neighbourhood.
vecindario, *n.m.* neighbours; population.
vecino, -na, *a.* neighbouring.—*n.m.f.* neighbour; native.
veda, *n.f.* close season; prohibition.
vedado, *n.m.* game reserve.
vedar, *v.t.* forbid; veto; hinder.
vedija, *n.f.* tuft.
veedor, -ra, *a.* prying.
vega, *n.f.* fertile plain.
vegetación, *n.f.* vegetation.
vegetal, *a., n.m.* vegetable.
vegetar, *v.i.* vegetate.
vegetariano, -na, *a., n.m.f.* vegetarian.
vegetativo, -va, *a.* vegetative.
vehemencia, *n.f.* vehemence.
vehemente, *a.* vehement.
vehículo, *n.m.* vehicle.
veía [VER].
veintavo, -va, *a., n.m.* twentieth.
veinte, *a., n.m.* twenty.
veinteno, -na, *a.* twentieth.—*n.f.* score.
veinti- [VEINTE Y -].
vejación, *n.f.* vexation.
vejamen, *n.m.* taunt; vexation.
vejar, *v.t.* annoy, vex; jibe at.
vejestorio, *n.m.* (*fam.*) dotard.
vejez, *n.f.* old age; old story.
vejiga, *n.f.* bladder; blister.
vejigoso, -sa, *a.* blistered.
vela (1), *n.f.* watchfulness, vigil; pilgrimage.
vela (2), *n.f.* candle.
vela (3), *n.f.* sail.
velado, -da, *a.* veiled.—*n.m.* husband.—*n.f.* wife; vigil; soirée.
velador, -ra, *a.* watchful.—*n.m.* watchman.
velaje, velamen, *n.m.* sails.
velar, *a.* velar.—*v.t.* veil; watch (over).—*v.i.* stay awake; work at night; take care; watch (***por, sobre,*** over).—*v.r.* (*phot.*) fog.
velatorio, *n.m.* (*eccl.*) wake.
veleidad, *n.f.* levity; whim; feebleness.
veleidoso, -sa, *a.* fickle, giddy.

velero (1), *n.m.* chandler.
velero (2), *n.m.* sail-maker; sailing boat.
veleta, *n.f.* weather-vane; float; streamer.
velo, *n.m.* veil; (*anat.*) velum.
velocidad, *n.f.* speed, velocity; (*mech.*) gear.
velocímetro, *n.m.* speedometer.
velón, *n.m.* oil-lamp.
velorio, *n.m.* wake; night party; (*eccl.*) taking of the veil.
veloz, *a.* (*pl.* **-oces**) swift, fast, fleet.
vello, *n.m.* down.
vellocino, *n.m.* fleece.
vellón, *n.m.* fleece; copper alloy.
velloso, -sa, *a.* downy.
velludo, -da, *a.* shaggy.—*n.m.* velvet, plush.
ven [VENIR].
vena, *n.f.* vein; dash, streak; inspiration.
venablo, *n.m.* javelin.
venado, *n.m.* deer, stag.
venal, *a.* venal; venous.
venalidad, *n.f.* venality.
venático, -ca, *a.* (*fam.*) cranky.
vencedor, -ra, *n.m.f.* conqueror.
vencejo, *n.m.* band; (*orn.*) swift.
vencer [D], *v.t.* conquer.—*v.i.* mature fall due.
vencible, *a.* superable.
vencimiento, *n.m.* victory, conquest; (*com.*) maturity.
venda, *n.f.* bandage; blindfold.
vendaje, *n.m.* bandaging.
vendar, *v.t.* bandage; blindfold.
vendaval, *n.m.* violent wind.
vendedor, -ra, *n.m.f.* seller.
vendeja, *n.f.* public sale.
vender, *v.t.* sell.—*v.r.* pretend (***por***, to be); ***se vende caro,*** it is dear; it *or* he is rarely seen.
vendible, *a.* sellable, saleable.
vendimia, *n.f.* vintage.
vendimiar, *v.t.* gather (*grapes*); reap unjust benefit; (*fam.*) bump off, kill.
vendré [VENIR].
venduta, *n.f.* (*S.A.*) sale; greengrocer's.
Venecia, *n.f.* Venice; Venetia.
veneciano, -na, *a.* Venetian.
veneno, *n.m.* poison.
venenoso, -sa, *a.* poisonous.
venera, *n.f.* spring; pilgrim's scallop.
venerable, *a.* venerable.
veneración, *n.f.* veneration.
venerando, -da, *a.* reverend.
venerar, *v.t., v.i.* venerate.
venéreo, -rea, *a.* venereal.
venero, *n.m.* spring, source, origin.
venezolano, -na, *a., n.m.f.* Venezuelan.
vengador, -ra, *a.* avenging.—*n.m.f.* avenger.
venganza, *n.f.* revenge, vengeance.
vengar [B], *v.t.* avenge.—*v.r.* take revenge (***de***, for, ***en***, on).
vengativo, -va, *a.* revengeful.
vengo, -ga [VENIR].
venia, *n.f.* forgiveness; leave.
venial, *a.* venial.
venida, *n.f.* coming, arrival; rush.
venidero, -ra, *a.* future, coming.—*n.m.pl.* posterity
venir [36], *v.t.* fit, suit.—*v.i.* come; ***venirse abajo,*** collapse.
venta, *n.f.* sale; inn; ***de*** (***en***) **—,** for (on) sale.
ventada, *n.f.* gust.
ventaja, *n.f.* advantage.
ventajoso, -sa, *a.* advantageous.
ventana, *n.f.* window.
ventanal, *n.m.* church window; large window.
ventanero, -ra, *a.* window-gazing.—*n.m.f.* window-gazer.
ventanilla, *n.f.* window (*ticket-, car- etc.*).
ventanillo, *n.m.* peep-hole.
ventarrón, *n.m.* strong wind.
vent(e)ar, *v.t.* sniff, smell out; air.—*v.i.* blow (*wind*).—*v.r.* split.
ventero, -ra, *n.m.f.* inn-keeper.
ventilación, *n.f.* ventilation.
ventilador, *n.m.* ventilator.
ventilar, *v.t.* ventilate; (*fig.*) air.
ventisco, -ca, *n.m.f.* blizzard; snow-drift.
ventiscar [A], **ventisquear,** *v.i.* snow; drift.
ventisquero, *n.m.* blizzard; snow-drift; glacier; snow-cap.
ventorro, ventorrillo, *n.m.* wretched inn.
ventoso, -sa, *a.* windy; flatulent.
ventrílocuo, -cua, *n.m.f.* ventriloquist.
ventriloquia, *n.f.* ventriloquy, ventriloquism.
ventura, *n.f.* chance, luck; happiness; risk; ***a la* —,** at random.
venturado, -da, *a.* fortunate.
venturero, -ra, *a.* adventurous.—*n.m.f.* adventurer.
venturo, -ra, *a.* coming, future.
venturoso, -sa, *a.* lucky.
venusto, -ta, *a.* beautiful.
veo [VER].
ver, *n.m.* sight; opinion.—*v.t.* [37] see; (*jur.*) try.—*v.r.* find oneself, be; be obvious; ***a mi* —,** to my mind; ***a más* —,** cheerio; ***a* —,** let's see; ***tener que* — *con*,** have to do with; ***ya se ve,*** of course.
vera, *n.f.* edge. [VERAS].
veracidad, *n.f.* veracity.
veranda, *n.f.* veranda.
veraneante, *a.* summering.—*n.m.f.* summer holiday-maker.
veranear, *v.i.* spend the summer.
veraneo, *n.m.* summering; summer holiday.
veraniego, -ga, *a.* summer(y); ailing; slight.
verano, *n.m.* summer
veras, *n.f.pl.* truth; ***de* —,** really; in earnest.
veraz, *a.* (*pl.* **-aces**) veracious.
verbal, *a.* verbal.
verbena, *n.f.* soirée; verbena.
verberación, *n.f.* pounding.
verberar, *v.t.* beat (against).
verbigracia, *adv.* verbi gratia, e.g.
verbo, *n.m.* verb; (*eccl.*) Word.
verborrea, *n.f.* (*fam.*) wordiness.
verbosidad, *n.f.* verbosity.
verboso, -sa, *a.* verbose.
verdad, *n.f.* truth; ***cuatro verdades,*** home truths; ***¿ (no es) —?*** is it not so? ***es* —,** it is true.
verdadero, -ra, *a.* true, real.
verdal, *a.* green.
verde, *a.* green; young; smutty.—*n.m.* green; (*fam.*) fling; ***poner* —,** (*fam.*) tell off strongly.
verdear, *v.i.* look greenish.
verdecer [9], *v.i.* turn green.
verdegal, *n.m.* green field.
verdegay, *a., n.m.* light green.
verdemar, *n.m.* sea-green.
verderón, *n.m.* (*orn.*) greenfinch; (*zool.*) cockle.
verdín, *n.m.* pond-scum; mildew; verdure.

verdinegro, -ra, *a.* dark green.
verdino, -na, *a.* bright green.
verdor, *n.m.* verdure; vigour.
verdoso, -sa, *a.* greenish.
verdugo, *n.m.* shoot, sucker; rod; lash; executioner; (*orn.*) shrike.
verdulero, -ra, *n.m.f.* greengrocer.—*n.f.* vulgar fishwife.
verdura, *n.f.* verdure.—*pl.* greens.
verdusco, -ca, *a.* darkish green.
vereda, *n.f.* path; route; (*S.A.*) pavement, (*U.S.*) sidewalk.
veredicto, *n.m.* verdict.
verga, *n.f.* (*naut.*) yard, boom; penis; bow.
vergel, *n.m.* orchard garden.
vergonzante, *a.* bashful.
vergonzoso, -sa, *a.* shameful; bashful.
verguear, *v.t.* flog.
vergüenza, *n.f.* shame; bashfulness; disgrace; dignity; ***tener* —,** be ashamed (***de,*** of).
verídico, -ca, *a.* truthful.
verificable, *a.* verifiable.
verificación, *n.f.* verification; checking.
verificar [A], *v.t.* verify; check.—*v.r.* prove true; take place.
verisímil [VEROSÍMIL].
verismo, *n.m.* realism; truth.
verja, *n.f.* grill.
verminoso, -sa, *a.* verminous.
vermut, *n.m.* vermouth.
vernáculo, -la, *a.* vernacular.
verónica, *n.f.* (*taur.*) pass with open cape.
verosímil, *a.* likely, probable.
verosimilitud, *n.f.* verisimilitude.
verraco, *n.m.* hog, boar.
verriondo, -da, *a.* rutting; withered.
verruga, *n.f.* wart; (*fam.*) pest.
verrugo, *n.m.* (*fam.*) miser.
versado, -da, *a.* versed (***en,*** in).
versal, *a., n.f.* capital (*letter*).
versalilla, versalita, *n.f.* small capital.
versar, *v.i.* turn; deal with, treat of (***sobre***).—*v.r.* become versed (***en,*** in).
versátil, *a.* versatile, fickle.
versicolor, *a.* many-coloured.
versículo, *n.m.* verse, versicle.
versificar [A], *v.t.* versify.
versión, *n.f.* version; translation.
versista, *n.m.f.* versifier.
verso, *n.m.* verse; line of verse; verso.
vértebra, *n.f.* vertebra.
vertebrado, -da, *a.* vertebrate.
vertebral, *a.* vertebral.
vertedero, *n.m.* dump; weir.
verter [2], *v.t.* pour; spill; dump; translate.
vertible, *a.* changeable.
vertical, *a., n.m.* or *f.* vertical.
vértice, *n.m.* vertex.
vertiente, *n.m.* or *f.* slope; (*S.A., f.*) spring.
vertiginoso, -sa, *a.* vertiginous.
vértigo, *n.m.* vertigo.
vesania, *n.f.* insanity.
vesánico, -ca, *a.* insane.
vesícula, *n.f.* vesicle, sac, cell.
vespertino, -na, *a.* evening.—*n.m.* or *f.* evening class *or* sermon.
vestíbulo, *n.m.* foyer, lobby, vestibule.
vestido, *n.m.* clothing; dress; suit.
vestidura, *n.f.* vestment.
vestigial, *a.* vestigial.
vestigio, *n.m.* vestige.
vestiglo, *n.m.* monster, bogey.
vestimenta, *n.f.* clothes.
vestir [8], *v.t., v.r.* dress (***de,*** in, as); cover.
vestuario, *n.m.* uniform; wardrobe.
Vesubio, *n.m.* Vesuvius.
veta, *n.f.* vein; stripe; seam.
vetar, *v.t.* veto.
vetear, *v.t.* grain.
veterano, -na, *a., n.m.f.* veteran.
veterinario, -ria, *a., n.m.f.* veterinary.
veto, *n.m.* veto.
vetustez, *n.f.* antiquity.
vetusto, -ta, *a.* ancient, age-old.
vez, *n.f.* (*pl.* **veces**) time; turn; herd; ***a la* —,** at once, at the same time; ***a su* —,** in turn; for his part; ***de* — *en cuando,*** from time to time; ***en* — *de,*** instead of; ***tal* —,** perhaps; ***hacer las veces de,*** act for, take the place of.
vezar [C], *v.t.* accustom.
vía, *n.f.* way; route; (*rail.*) track; (*naut.*) leak; **— *muerta,*** (*rail.*) siding.—*prep.* via.
viabilidad, *n.f.* viability.
viable, *a.* viable.
viaducto, *n.m.* viaduct.
viajante, *a.* travelling.—*n.m.* (*com.*) traveller.
viajar, *v.i.* travel.
viajata, *n.f.* (*fam.*) trip.
viaje, *n.m.* journey; voyage; way; load; supply; ***¡buen* — *!*** bon voyage!
viajero, -ra, *n.m.f.* passenger, traveller.
vial, *a.* rel. to roads.
vialidad, *n.f.* highways department.
vianda, *n.f.* viand, victuals.
viandante, *n.m.f.* traveller, tramp.
viático, *n.m.* (*eccl.*) viaticum; travelling expenses.
víbora, *n.f.* (*zool.*) viper.
vibración, *n.f.* vibration.
vibrante, *a.* vibrant.
vibrar, *v.t., v.i.* vibrate.—*v.t.* brandish; hurl; shake.
vicaria, *n.f.* under-abbess.
vicaría, *n.f.* vicarage; vicarship.
vicario, -ria, *a.* vicarious.—*n.m.* vicar.
vice-, *prefix.* vice-, deputy-.
Vicente, *n.m.* Vincent.
viciar, *v.t.* vitiate.
vicio, *n.m.* vice; defect; bad habit; luxuriance; ***de* —,** through habit.
vicioso, -sa, *a.* corrupt(ed); unruly; luxuriant; robust.
vicisitud, *n.f.* vicissitude.
vict- [VIT-].
víctima, *n.f.* victim.
victimar, *v.t.* (*S.A.*) murder.
victo, *n.m.* daily bread.
victoria, *n.f.* victory; victoria (*carriage*).
victorioso, -sa, *a.* victorious.
vicuña, *n.f.* (*zool.*) vicunia.
vid, *n.f.* (*bot.*) vine.
vida, *n.f.* life; living; ***con* —,** alive; ***en la* —,** never; ***hacer* —,** live together; **— *airada*** or ***ancha,*** loose living.
vidente, *a.* seeing.—*n.m.f.* seer.
vidriado, -da, *a.* glazed; brittle.—*n.m.* glazed ware.
vidriar [L], *v.t.* glaze.
vidriera, *n.f.* glass window; (*S.A.*) shop-window.
vidriería, *n.f.* glass-work(s) *or* -shop.
vidriero, *n.m.* glass-worker; glazier.

vidrio, *n.m.* glass.
vidrioso, -sa, *a.* vitreous; glassy; brittle; slippery; peevish.
viejo, -ja, *a.* old.—*n.m.* old man.—*n.f.* old woman.
vienés, -nesa, *a., n.m.f.* Viennese.
vientecillo, *n.m.* breeze.
viento, *n.m.* wind; ***ir — en popa,*** run smoothly.
vientre, *n.m.* belly; womb.
viernes, *n.m.* Friday.
viga, *n.f.* beam; girder.
vigencia, *n.f.* operation, force; vogue.
vigente, *a.* in force, prevailing.
vigesimal, *a.* vigesimal.
vigésimo, -ma, *a., n.m.* twentieth.
vigía, *n.f.* watch.—*n.m.* look-out.
vigilancia, *n.f.* vigilance.
vigilante, *a.* vigilant.—*n.m.* watchman, guard.
vigilar, *v.t., v.i.* watch, guard.
vigilia, *n.f.* vigil, eve; (*mil.*) watch; night-work.
vigor, *n.m.* vigour; ***en —,*** into effect.
vigorizar [C], *v.t.* invigorate.
vigoroso, -sa, *a.* vigorous.
vil, *a.* base, vile, low.
vilano, *n.m.* thistledown.
vileza, *n.f.* vileness; disgrace.
vilipendiar, *v.t.* revile.
vilipendio, *n.m.* scorn.
en vilo, *adv. phr.* suspended, in the air.
vilordo, -da, *a.* slothful.
viltrotera, *n.f.* (*fam.*) gad-about.
villa, *n.f.* town; villa.
Villadiego, ***tomar las de —,*** beat it, run off.
villancete, villancico, *n.m.* carol.
villanchón, -chona, *a.* yokelish.
villanesco, -ca, *a.* rustic; boorish.
villanía, *n.f.* low birth; villainy.
villano, -na, *a.* coarse; wicked.—*n.m.f.* peasant; villain.
villoría, *n.f.* hamlet; farm.
villorio, *n.m.* one-horse town.
vimbre, *n.m.* osier.
vinagre, *n.m.* vinegar.
vinagroso, -sa, *a.* vinegary.
vinajera, *n.f.* (*eccl.*) wine-vessel, cruet.
vinario, -ria, *a.* rel. to wine.
vinatero, *n.m.* vintner.
vincular, *v.t.* (*jur.*) entail; (*fig.*) base; continue.
vindicación, *n.f.* vindication.
vindicar [A], *v.t.* vindicate.
vindicta, *n.f.* vengeance.
vine [VENIR].
vínico, -ca, *a.* vinic, rel. to wine.
vinícola, *a.* vine-growing.—*n.m.f.* vine-grower.
vinicultor, -ra, *n.m.f.* wine-grower.
vinicultura, *n.f.* vine-growing.
vinilo, *n.m.* vinyl.
vino, *n.m.* wine; ***tener mal —,*** be fighting drunk. [VENIR].
vinolento, -ta, *a.* too fond of wine.
vinoso, -sa, *a.* vinous.
viña, *n.f.* vineyard; (*fig.*) gold-mine.
viñador, *n.m.* vine-grower.
viñedo, *n.m.* vineyard.
viñero, -ra, *n.m.f.* owner of vineyard.
viñeta, *n.f.* vignette.
viola (1), *n.f.* (*mus.*) viola.
viola (2), *n.f.* (*bot.*) viola.
violación, *n.f.* violation.
violado, -da, *a., n.m.* violet.
violar, *v.t.* violate.
violencia, *n.f.* violence.
violentar, *v.t.* violate; force; break down.
violento, -ta, *a.* violent; embarrassed.
violeta, *a. inv., n.f.* (*bot.*) violet.—*n.m.* (*colour*) violet.
violín, *n.m.* violin.
violinista, *n.m.f.* violinist.
violón, *n.m.* (*mus.*) double bass.
violonc(h)elo, *n.m.* (violon)cello.
viperino, -na, *a.* viperous.
vira, *n.f.* dart; shoe-welt.
virada, *n.f.* turn, tacking.
virago, *n.f.* virago.
viraje, *n.m.* turn, bend.
virar, *v.t., v.r.* (*naut.*) tack, veer, turn.
virgen, *n.f.* virgin.
Virgilio, *n.m.* Vergil.
virginal, *a., n.m.* virginal.
virginidad, *n.f.* virginity.
vírgula, *n.f.* dash; comma.
viril, *a.* virile; manly.
virilidad, *n.f.* virility.
virolento, -ta, *a.* having small-pox; pock-marked.
virote, *n.m.* dart, bolt; (*fam.*) young blood; stuffed-shirt.
virreinato, *n.m.* viceroyalty.
virrey, *n.m.* viceroy.
virtual, *a.* virtual.
virtud, *n.f.* virtue.
virtuoso, -sa, *a.* virtuous.—*n.m.* virtuoso.
viruela, *n.f.* small-pox; pock-mark.
virulento, -ta, *a.* virulent.
virus, *n.m.inv.* virus.
viruta, *n.f.* shaving, sliver.
visado, *n.m.* visa.
visaje, *n.m.* grimace.
visar, *v.t.* visa; countersign; (*mil.*) sight.
vísceras, *n.f.pl.* viscera.
visco, *n.m.* bird-lime.
viscoso, -sa, *a.* viscous.
visera, *n.f.* visor; cap-peak.
visibilidad, *n.f.* visibility.
visible, *a.* visible; conspicuous.
visigodo, -da, *a., n.m.f.* Visigoth.
visigótico, -ca, *a.* Visigothic.
visillo, *n.m.* window-curtain.
visión, *n.f.* vision.
visionario, -ria, *a., n.m.f.* visionary.
visir, *n.m.* vizier.
visita, *n.f.* visit; visitor; inspection.
visitación, *n.f.* visitation.
visitador, -ra, *n.m.f.* visitor; inspector.
visitante, *a.* visiting.—*n.m.f.* visitor.
visitar, *v.t.* visit; inspect.
visitero, -ra, *n.m.f.* (*fam.*) visitor.
vislumbrar, *v.t.* glimpse.—*v.r.* glimmer.
vislumbre, *n.m.* glimpse; inkling.
viso, *n.m.* sheen, lustre; pretext; semblance; ***de —,*** important; ***a dos visos,*** dual purpose;
visón, *n.m.* mink.
visor, *n.m.* view-finder; bomb-sight.
visorio, -ria, *a.* optic.—*n.m.* expert examination.
víspera, *n.f.* eve.—*pl.* vespers.
vista, *n.f.* sight; view, vista; (*jur.*) trial; loo
vistazo, *n.m.* glance.

vistillas, *n.f.pl.* vantage point.
visto, -ta, *a.* evident; seen; ***bien (mal) —,*** well (ill) regarded; — ***bueno,*** approved; — ***que,*** seeing that. [VER].
vistoso, -sa, *a.* showy; flashy.
visual, *a.* visual.—*n.f.* line of sight.
visualizar [C], *v.t.* visualize.
visura, *n.f.* examination.
vital, *a.* vital; life.
vitalicio, -cia, *a.* life-long.—*n.m.* life policy; life annuity.
vitalidad, *n.f.* vitality.
vitalizar [C], *v.t.* vitalize.
vitamina, *n.f.* vitamin.
vitando, -da, *a.* to be avoided, taboo.
vitela, *n.f.* vellum, calf.
viti- [VINI-].
vito, *n.m.* Andalusian dance.
vítor, *n.m.* triumphal pageant; memorial.—*interj.* hurrah!
vitorear, *v.t.* cheer, acclaim.
vítreo, -trea, *a.* vitreous.
vitrificar [A], *v.t., v.r.* vitrify.
vitrina, *n.f.* glass case.
vitriolo, *n.m.* vitriol.
vitualla, *n.f.* provisions; vegetables.
vituperar, *v.t.* vituperate.
vituperio, *n.m.* vituperation.
viuda, *n.f.* widow.
viudez, *n.f.* widowhood.
viudo, -da, *a.* widowed.—*n.m.* widower.
viva, *n.m.* (*obs.*) huzza.—*interj.* hurrah! long live!
vivacidad, *n.f.* vigour; brilliance.
vivaque, *n.m.* bivouac.
vivar, *n.m.* warren; fish-pond.—*v.t.* (*S.A.*) acclaim.
vivaracho, -cha, *a.* (*fam.*) frisky, lively.
vivaz, *a.* (*pl.* **-aces**) lively; keen; perennial.
víveres, *n.m.pl.* provisions, food.
vivero, *n.m.* nursery; fish-pond; shell-fish beds.
viveza, *n.f.* liveliness; gaiety; ardour; keenness; lustre; thoughtlessness.
vivido, -da, *a.* lived-through.
vívido, -da, *a.* vivid.
vividor, -ra, *a.* living; thrifty.—*n.m.f.* hard-liver; saver; (*fam.*) crook; sponger.
vivienda, *n.f.* dwelling; housing.
viviente, *a.* living.
vivificar [A], *v.t.* vivify.
vivir, *n.m.* life; living.—*v.t., v.i.* live (***de,*** on); ***¿quién vive?*** who goes there?
vivisección, *n.f.* vivisection.
vivo, -va, *a.* alive, living; smart; nimble; quick, raw; acute, keen; expressive.—*n.m.* edge; the quick; ***en lo —,*** to the quick.
vizcaíno, -na, *a., n.m.f.* Biscayan.
Vizcaya, *n.f.* Biscay.
vizconde, *n.m.* viscount.
vocablo, *n.m.* word, term; pun.
vocabulario, *n.m.* vocabulary.
vocación, *n.f.* vocation; dedication.
vocal, *a.* vocal.—*n.m.f.* committee member.—*n.f.* vowel.
vocálico, -ca, *a.* vocalic.
vocalizar [C], *v.t.* vocalize.
vocativo, -va, *a., n.m.* vocative.
vocear, *v.t.* shout; hail.
vocería, *n.f.*, **vocerío,** *n.m.* shouting.
vocero, *n.m.* spokesman.
vociferar, *v.t.* vociferate; boast of.
vocinglero, -ra, *a.* bawling; babbling.—*n.m.f.* bawler; babbler.
volada, *n.f.* short flight.
voladero, -ra, *a.* flying; fleeting.—*n.m.* precipice.
volado, *n.m.* (*cul.*) meringue.
voladura, *n.f.* explosion, blast; flight.
volandero, -ra, *a.* fledgling; dangling; casual chance; unsettled.—*n.f.* (*mech.*) washer.
volante, *a.* flying.—*n.m.* steering-wheel; fly-wheel; shuttlecock; balance wheel; frill.
volantín, -tina, *a.* flying.—*n.m.* fishing-line; (*S.A.*) kite.
volantón, -tona, *a., n.m.f.* fledgling.
volar [4], *v.t.* blow up; flush; enrage.—*v.i.* fly; jut out; vanish; spread rapidly.
volatería, *n.f.* birds; bird hunting; (*fig.*) wool-gathering; ***de —,*** by pure chance.
volátil, *a.* volatile.
volati(li)zar [C], *v.t., v.r.* volatilize, evaporate.
volatín, *n.m.*, **volatinero, -ra,** *n.m.f.* tight-rope walker.
volcán, *n.m.* volcano.
volcánico, -ca, *a.* volcanic.
volcar [4A], *v.t.* upset, overturn; daze; change the mind of; irritate.—*v.i.* capsize.
volea, *n.f.*, **voleo,** *n.m.* volley; punch.
volición, *n.f.* volition.
volitar, *v.i.* flutter.
volquear, *v.r.* roll over.
volquete, *n.m.* tipper, tipping-truck.
voltaje, *n.m.* voltage.
voltario, -ria, *a.* fickle.
voltear, *v.t.* roll; turn upside down; upset.—*v.i.* roll over, tumble.
voltereta, *n.f.* somersault.
volteriano, -na, *a.* Voltairean.
voltio, *n.m.* volt.
voltizo, -za, *a.* twisted; fickle.
voluble, *a.* fickle; voluble.
volumen, *n.m.* volume (*mass, tome*).
voluminoso, -sa, *a.* voluminous.
voluntad, *n.f.* will; free-will; love.
voluntariedad, *n.f.* voluntariness; wilfulness.
voluntario, -ria, *a.* voluntary; wilful.—*n.m.f.* volunteer.
voluntarioso, -sa, *a.* wilful, self-willed; determined.
voluptuoso, -sa, *a.* voluptuous.—*n.m.f.* voluptuary.
voluta, *n.f.* volute.
volver [5, *p.p.* **vuelto**], *v.t.* turn; turn over; send back; close; vomit.—*v.i.* come back, return; turn; — ***a,*** do again; — ***en sí,*** come round; — ***por,*** defend; — ***sobre,*** change (*opinions*); — ***sobre sí,*** retain self-control.—*v.r.* return; turn; become.
vomitar, *v.t., v.i.* vomit, spew.
vómito, *n.m.* vomit.
voracidad, *n.f.* voracity.
vorágine, *n.f.* vortex, whirlpool.
voraz, *a.* (*pl.* **-aces**) voracious; savage.
vórtice, *n.m.* vortex.
vos, *pron. pers. pl.* (*obs., eccl., poet.*) ye, you; (*S.A., fam.*) you, thou (*sing. with pl. v.*); [VOSOTROS, VOS].
vosear, *v.t.* address as VOS; (*S.A.*) [TUTEAR].
voseo, *n.m.* use of VOS; (*S.A.*) [TUTEO].
vosotros, -tras, *pron. pers. m.f.* you (*pl. of* TÚ).
votación, *n.f.* voting; ballot.

votador, -ra, *n.m.f.* voter; swearer.
votante, *n.m.f.* voter.
votar, *v.t.* vote for; vow to; vote on.—*v.i.* vote; vow; swear.
votivo, -va, *a.* votive.
voto, *n.m.* vow; vote; oath.—*pl.* wishes.
voy [IR].
voz, *n.f.* (*pl.* **voces**) voice; word; cry, shout; rumour; ***en — alta,*** aloud; ***dar voces,*** shout.
vuece(le)ncia, *pron. pers.* (*obs.*) [VUESTRA EXCELENCIA].
vuelco, *n.m.* overturning; upset; start, jump.
vuelo, *n.m.* flight; flare, fullness; lace frill; projection; ***al —,*** in flight; quickly; by chance.
vuelta, *n.f.* turn; change; return; reverse; stroll; roll.
vuelto, *n.m.* verso; (*S.A.*) change (*money*). [VOLVER].
vuesamerced, vuesarced, *pers., pron.* (*obs.*) [USTED].
vuestro, -ra, *a., poss. pron.* your, yours.
vulcanita, *n.f.* vulcanite.
vulcanizar [C], *v.t.* vulcanize.
vulgacho, *n.m.* rabble.
vulgar, *a.* vulgar, popular, vernacular.
vulgaridad, *n.f.* vulgarity; commonplace.
vulgarizar [C], *v.t.* vulgarize; popularize.—*v.r.* become vulgar, popular *or* common.
Vulgata, *n.f.* Vulgate.
vulgo, *n.m.* populace, common people, mob.
vulnerable, *a.* vulnerable.
vulnerar, *v.t.* harm, damage.
vulpeja, *n.f.* vixen.

W

W, w, *n.f. this letter does not belong to the Spanish alphabet. It is replaced by* **V, v,** *and pronounced as such.*
wat, *n.m.* (*pl.* **wats**) [VATIO].
wáter, *n.m.* lavatory, toilet, W.C.

X

X, x, *n.f.* twenty-sixth letter of the Spanish alphabet.
xenofobia, *n.f.* xenophobia.
xenófobo, -ba, *a., n.m.f.* xenophobe.
xilófono, *n.m.* xylophone.
xilografía, *n.f.* xylography; wood-cut.

Y

Y, y (1), *n.f.* twenty-seventh letter of the Spanish alphabet.
y (2), *conj.* and. [E].
ya, *adv.* already; now; finally; at once; ***— no,*** no longer; ***— que,*** since, as; ***ya. . . . ya,*** whether . . . or; now . . . . now; ***¡ya ya!*** yes, of course.
yacer [38], *v.i.* lie.
yacija, *n.f.* bed, couch; grave.
yacimiento, *n.m.* (*min.*) deposit, bed.
yaguar [JAGUAR].
yanqui, *a., n.m.f.* Yankee.
yapa, *n.f.* (*S.A.*) extra, bonus.
yarda, *n.f.* yard (*measure*).
yate, *n.m.* yacht.
yedra, *n.f.* ivy.
yegua, *n.f.* mare.
yeísmo, *n.m.* pronunciation of Spanish **ll** as **y.**
yelmo, *n.m.* helmet.
yema, *n.f.* egg-yolk; bud; middle; best.
yendo [IR].
yerba [HIERBA].
yerbajo, *n.m.* weed.
yermar, *v.t.* lay waste; abandon.
yermo, -ma, *a.* waste, deserted.—*n.m.* wilderness, desert.
yerno, *n.m.* son-in-law.
yerro, *n.m.* error, mistake. [ERRAR].
yerto, -ta, *a.* stiff, rigid.
yesca, *n.f.* tinder.
yeso, *n.m.* gypsum; plaster of Paris.
yo, *pron. pers.* I.
yodo, *n.m.* iodine.
yuca, *n.f.* (*bot.*) yucca, cassava.
yugo, *n.m.* yoke.
Yugo(e)slavia, *n.f.* Yu- *or* Jugoslavia.
yugo(e)slavo, -va, *a., n.m.f.* Yu- *or* Jugoslav(ian).
yugular, *a.* jugular.
yunque, *n.m.* anvil; drudge.
yunta, *n.f.* yoke, pair.
yusión, *n.f.* (*jur.*) order; precept.
yute, *n.m.* jute.
yuxtaponer [25], *v.t.* juxtapose.

Z

Z, z, *n.f.* twenty-eighth letter of the Spanish alphabet.
¡za! *interj.* get away! go!
zabordar, *v.i.* (*naut.*) run aground.
zabu- [ZAMBU-].
zabucar [A], *v.t.* shake up.
zacapel(l)a, *n.f.* shindy.
zacear, *v.t.* shoo.—*v.i.* lisp.
zafacoca, *n.f.* (*S.A.*) shindy.
zafrado, -da, *a.* (*S.A.*) cheeky.
zafar (1), *v.t.* deck; adorn.
zafar (2), *v.t.* loosen; clear.—*v.r.* run away; rid oneself.
zafarrancho, *n.m.* (*naut.*) clearing for action; (*fam.*) rumpus.
zafio, -fia, *a.* crude, boorish.
zafir(o), *n.m.* sapphire.
zaga, *n.f.* rear.
zagal (1), *n.m.* youth; swain.
zagal (2), *n.m.* skirt.

zagala, *n.f.* lass; shepherdess.
zaguán, *n.m.* porch, hall.
zaguero, -ra, *a.* hind, rear; loitering.—*n.m.* (*sport*) back.
zahareño, -ña, *a.* wild, haggard.
zaherir [6], *v.t.* reproach.
zahones, *n.m.pl.* chaps, breeches.
zahorí, *n.m.* (*pl.* **-íes**) seer, diviner.
zahurda, *n.f.* pig-sty.
zaino, -na, *a.* chestnut (*horse*); black (*bull*); wicked; ***de* —,** askance.
zalagarda, *n.f.* ambush; trap; shindy.
zalamero, -ra, *a.* wheedling.—*n.m.f.* wheedler.
zamarra, *n.f.* sheepskin jerkin.
zambo, -ba, *a.* knock-kneed.
zambucar [A], *v.t.* hide away.
zambullid(ur)a, *n.f.* dive, plunge.
zambullir [J], *v.t.* duck.—*v.r.* dive.
zampa, *n.f.* pile.
zampar, *v.t.* hide; gobble up.—*v.r.* rush off.
zampoña, *n.f.* shepherd's pipe; rubbish.
zanahoria, *n.f.* carrot.
zanca, *n.f.* shank.
zancada, *n.f.* big stride.
zancadilla, *n.f.* tripping up.
zancajo, *n.m.* heel.
zancajoso, -sa, *a.* pigeon-toed.
zanco, *n.m.* stilt.
zancudo, -da, *a.* long-legged.—*n.f.* (*orn.*) wader.
zanganear, *v.i.* (*fam.*) loaf around.
zángano, -na, *n.m.f.* idler, loafer.—*n.m.* drone.
zangolotino, -na, *a.* babyish (*youth*).
zanguango, -ga, *a.* (*fam.*) shiftless, malingering.
zanja, *n.f.* trench; gully; ***abrir las zanjas,*** lay the foundations.
zanjar, *v.t.* trench; settle.
zanquear, *v.i.* waddle; trot.
zanquituerto, -ta, *a.* bandy-legged.
zapa, *n.f.* spade; trench; shagreen.
zapador, *n.m.* (*mil.*) sapper.
zapapico, *n.m.* pick-axe.
zapar, *v.t.* mine, sap.
zapateado, *n.m.* tap-dance.
zapatería, *n.f.* shoe-maker's shop.
zapatero, *n.m.* shoe-maker, cobbler.
zapatilla, *n.f.* slipper; (*mech.*) soft washer.
zapato, *n.m.* shoe.
zapear, *v.t.* shoo; scare.
zaque, *n.m.* wine-bag; drunk.
zaquizamí, *n.m.* garret.
zar, *n.m.* tsar.
zarabanda, *n.f.* saraband; uproar.
zaragatero, -ra, *a.* rowdy.
Zaragoza, *n.f.* Saragossa.
zaragüelles, *n.m.pl.* breeches.
zarandar, *v.t.* sieve, sift.
zarandillo, *n.m.* sieve; (*fam.*) live wire.
zarapito, *n.m.* (*orn.*) curlew.
zarista, *a., n.m.f.* tsarist.
zarpa, *n.f.* paw; claw; mud-splash.
zarpar, *v.t., v.i.* (*naut.*) weigh anchor.
zarcillo (1), *n.m.* drop earring; tendril.
zarcillo (2), *n.m.* hoe.
zarracatería, *n.f.* (*fam.*) soft soap.
zarramplín, *n.m.* botcher.
zarrapastra, *n.f.* mud-splash.
zarria (1), *n.f.* mud-splash; tatter.
zarria (2), *n.f.* thong.
zarza, *n.f.* bramble.
zarzal, *n.m.* bramble patch.
zarzamora, *n.f.* blackberry.
zarzaparrilla, *n.f.* sarsaparilla.
zarzaperruna, *n.f.* dog-rose.
zarzuela, *n.f.* musical comedy.
¡zas! *interj.* bang!
zascandil, *n.m.* (*fam.*) busybody meddler.
zazo, -za, *a.* stammering.
zedilla, *n.f.* cedilla (ҫ).
Zeland(i)a, *n.f.* Zealand.
zigzag, *n.m.* zigzag.
zigzaguear, *v.i.* zigzag.
zinc, *n.m.* zinc.
¡zis zas! *interj.* bang bang!
ziszás [ZIGZAG].
zócalo, *n.m.* socle; skirting.
zoclo, *n.m.* clog.
zoco, -ca, *a.* (*fam.*) lefty.—*n.m.* clog; Moorish market.
zodíaco, *n.m.* zodiac.
zoilo, *n.m.* carping critic.
zona, *n.f.* zone.
zonzo, -za, *a.* stupid; insipid.
zoología, *n.f.* zoology.
zoológico, -ca, *a.* zoological.
zoólogo, -ga, *n.m.f.* zoologist.
zopenco, -ca, *a.* (*fam.*) doltish.—*n.m.f.* dolt.
zop(it)as, *n.m. inv.* lisper.
zoquete, *n.m.* chunk; dolt.
zorra, *n.f.* vixen, fox; whore; ***pillar una* —,** get tipsy.
zorrero, -ra, *a.* foxy.—*n.f.* fox-hole.
zorrillo, *n.m.* skunk.
zorro, *n.m.* fox; ***hecho un* —,** dog-tired.
zorruno, -na, *a.* foxy.
zorzal, *n.m.* (*orn.*) fieldfare; slyboots; (*S.A.*) clot.
zozobra, *n.f.* upset; worry.
zozobrar, *v.t.* upset.—*v.r.* capsize.
zozobroso, -sa, *a.* anxious.
zuavo, *n.m.* Zouave.
zueco, *n.m.* clog.
zulaque, *n.m.* bitumen; oakum.
zumaque, *n.m.* sumach; (*fam.*) wine.
zumaya, *n.f.* (*orn.*) night-heron; nightjar.
zumba, *n.f.* mule-bell; whistle; ***hacer — a,*** poke fun at.
zumbar, *v.t.* poke fun at; swing (*a blow at*).—*v.i.* buzz, hum.
zumbido, *n.m.* hum, buzz; (*fam.*) slap.
zumbón, -bona, *a.* waggish.—*n.m.f.* wag.
zumo, *n.m.* juice; gain; ***— de cepas*** or ***parras,*** (*fam.*) vine-milk, wine.
zupia, *n.f.* dregs, scum.
zurcir [D], *v.t.* darn; join; (*fam.*) cook up (*lies*).
zurdo, -da, *a.* left(-handed).
zurear, *v.i.* coo.
zureo, *n.m.* cooing.
zurra, *n.f.* drudgery; beating; set-to.
zurrar, *v.t.* tan, curry; flog.—*v.r.* be scared.
zurriaga, *n.f.,* **zurriago,** *n.m.* whip.
zurribanda, *n.f.* (*fam.*) beating; shindy.
zurrir, *v.i.* hum; rattle.
zurrón, *n.m.* shepherd's bag; husk.
zutano, -na, *n.m.f.* (*fam.*) who's-it, so-and-so.
zuzón, *n.f.* (*bot.*) groundsel.

A, a (1) [ei], *n.* primera letra del alfabeto inglés; ***A,*** (*mus.*) la; ***A1,*** de primera clase; ***A-bomb,*** bomba atómica.
a (2) [ə], *art. indef.* un, una; por, cada; — ***pound — month,*** una libra al *o* por mes; — ***penny an ounce,*** un penique la *o* por onza.
aback [ə'bæk], *adv.* (*naut.*) en facha; ***to take —,*** azorar, desconcertar.
abandon [ə'bændən], *n.* abandono.—*v.t.* abandonar.
abase [ə'beis], *v.t.* degradar.
abasement [ə'beismənt], *n.* degradación, *f.*
abash [ə'bæʃ], *v.t.* amilanar; avergonzar.
abate [ə'beit], *v.t.* calmar, disminuir.—*v.i.* decrecer, caer, amainar.
abattoir ['æbətwɑ:], *n.* matadero.
abbacy ['æbəsi], *n.* abadía.
abbess ['æbis], *n.* abadesa.
abbey ['æbi], *n.* abadía.
abbot ['æbət], *n.* abad, *m.*
abbreviate [ə'bri:vieit], *v.t.* abreviar.
abbreviation [əbri:vi'ieʃən], *n.* abreviatura (*signo*); abreviación (*hecho*), *f.*
abdicate ['æbdikeit], *v.t., v.i.* abdicar.
abdomen [æb'doumən], *n.* abdomen, *m.*
abduct [æb'dʌkt], *v.t.* raptar, secuestrar.
abduction [æb'dʌkʃən], *n.* rapto, secuestro; abducción, *f.*
abed [ə'bed], *adv.* (*obs.*) en cama.
aberration [æbə'reiʃən], *n.* aberración, *f.*
abet [ə'bet], *v.t.* instigar; auxiliar.
abettor [ə'betə], *n.* (*jur.*) cómplice, *m.f.*
abeyance [ə'beiəns], *n.* desuetud; cesación, *f.*; ***in —,*** en suspenso.
abhor [əb'hɔ:], *v.t.* abominar, aborrecer.
abhorrent [əb'hɔrənt], *a.* aborrecible.
abide [ə'baid], *v.t.* tolerar, aguantar; ***to — by,*** atenerse a.—*v.i. irr.* (*obs.*) morar.
abiding [ə'baidiŋ], *a.* (*lit.*) eternal, perdurable.
ability [ə'biliti], *n.* capacidad, habilidad, *f.*; talento.
abject ['æbʒekt], *a.* abyecto, abatido.
abjure [əb'dʒuə], *v.t.* abjurar.
ablative ['æblətiv], *a., n.* ablativo.
ablaze [ə'bleiz], *a.* encendido, llameante; en llamas.
able [eibl], *a.* capaz, hábil; ***to be — to,*** poder.
able-bodied ['eibl'bɔdid], *a.* sano, entero; (*naut.*) de primera clase.
ablution [æb'lu:ʃən], *n.* ablución, *f.*
ably ['eibli], *adv.* hábilmente, con acierto.
abnegation [æbni'geiʃən], *n.* abnegación, *f.*
abnormal [æb'nɔ:məl], *a.* anormal; deforme.
abnormality [æbnɔ:'mæliti], *n.* anormalidad; deformidad, *f.*
aboard [ə'bɔ:d], *adv.* (*naut.*) a bordo.—*prep.* al bordo de; en (*trenes*); ***all — !*** ¡al tren!
abode [ə'boud], *n.* (*obs.*) albergue, *m.*, morada. [ABIDE].
abolish [ə'bɔliʃ], *v.t.* anular, abolir, suprimir.
abolition [æbə'liʃən], *n.* anulación, supresión; abolición, *f.*
abominable [æ'bɔminəbl], *a.* abominable.
abominate [æ'bɔmineit], *v.t.* abominar de.
abomination [æbɔmi'neiʃən], *n.* abominación, *f.*
aborigines [æbə'ridʒini:z], *n.pl.* aborígenes, *m.pl.*
abort [ə'bɔ:t], *v.t., v.i.* abortar.
abortion [ə'bɔ:ʃən], *n.* aborto.
abortive [ə'bɔ:tiv], *a.* abortivo.
abound [ə'baund], *v.i.* abundar (***with, in,*** en).
about [ə'baut], *adv.* casi; por aquí, por ahí.—*prep.* alrededor de; cerca de; acerca de; hacia, a eso de; — ***to,*** a punto de; ***what is it — ?*** ¿de qué se trata?
above [ə'bʌv], *adv.* arriba, encima, en lo alto.—*prep.* (por) encima de; superior a; más de *o* que; más alto que; — ***all,*** sobre todo.
above-board [ə'bʌv'bɔ:d], *a.* abierto, franco. — *adv.* abiertamente.
Abraham ['eibrəhæm], *n.* Abrahán, *m.*
abrasion [ə'breiʒən], *n.* abrasión, *f.*
abrasive [ə'breiziv], *a., n.* abrasivo.
abreast [ə'brest], *adv.* de frente; de costado; — ***of,*** al corriente de.
abridge [ə'bridʒ], *v.t.* abreviar, compendiar.
abridg(e)ment [ə'bridʒmənt], *n.* abreviación, *f.*; compendio.
abroad [ə'brɔ:d], *adv.* en el *o* al extranjero; en *o* por todas partes; fuera de casa.
abrogate ['æbrougeit], *v.t.* abrogar.
abrupt [ə'brʌpt], *a.* brusco; repentino; abrupto, escarpado.
abscess ['æbses], *n.* absceso.
abscessed ['æbsest], *a.* apostemado.
abscond [əb'skɔnd], *v.i.* evadirse.
absconder [əb'skɔndə], *n.* prófugo; contumaz, *m.f.*
absence ['æbsəns], *n.* ausencia; falta.
absent ['æbsənt], *a.* ausente.—[æb'sent], *v.r.* ausentarse.
absentee [æbsən'ti:], *n.* ausente; absentista, *m.f.*
absenteeism [æbsən'ti:izm], *n.* absentismo.
absent-minded ['æbsənt'maindid], *a.* distraído.
absinthe ['æbsinθ], *n.* ajenjo; absenta.
absolute ['æbsəlu:t], *a., n.* absoluto.
absolution [æbsə'lu:ʃən], *n.* absolución, *f.*
absolutism ['æbsəlu:tizm], *n.* absolutismo.
absolutist ['æbsəlu:tist], *a., n.* absolutista, *m.f.*
absolve [əb'zɔlv], *v.t.* absolver.
absorb [əb'zɔ:b], *v.t.* absorber.
absorbed [əb'zɔ:bd], *a.* absorto.
absorbent [əb'zɔ:bənt], *a.* absorbente.
absorbing [əb'zɔ:biŋ], *a.* absorbente (*interesante*).
absorption [əb'zɔ:pʃən], *n.* absorción, *f.*
abstain [æb'stein], *v.i.* abstenerse (***from,*** de).
abstainer [æb'steinə], *n.* abstinente.
abstemious [æb'sti:mjəs], *a.* abstemio.
abstention [æb'stenʃən], *n.* abstención, *f.*
abstinence ['æbstinəns], *n.* abstinencia.
abstinent ['æbstinənt], *a.* abstinente.

abstract ['æbstrækt], *a.*, *n.* abstracto.—[æb'strækt], *v.t.* abstraer.
abstraction [æb'strækʃen], *n.* abstracción, *f.*
abstruse [æb'stru:s], *a.* abstruso.
absurd [əb'sə:d], *a.* absurdo.
absurdity [əb'sə:diti], *n.* absurdo; absurdidad, *f.*
abundance [ə'bʌndəns], *n.* abundancia.
abundant [ə'bʌndənt], *a.* abundante.
abuse [ə'bju:s], *n.* abuso; injuria; maltrato.—[ə'bju:z], *v.t.* abusar de; injuriar; maltratar.
abusive [ə'bju:siv], *a.* abusivo; injurioso.
abut [ə'bʌt], *v.t.* lindar con.
abysm [ə'bizm] [ABYSS].
abysmal [ə'bizməl], *a.* abismal.
abyss [ə'bis], *n.* abismo.
acacia [ə'keiʃə], *n.* acacia.
academic [ækə'demik], *a.*, *n.* académico.
academician [əkædə'miʃən], *n.* académico.
academy [ə'kædəmi], *n.* academia.
accede [æk'si:d], *v.i.* acceder.
accelerate [æk'seləreit], *v.t.* acelerar.—*v.i.* -se.
acceleration [æksela'reiʃən], *n.* aceleración, *f.*
accelerator [ak'seləreitə], *n.* acelerador, *m.*
accent ['æksənt], *n.* acento.—[æk'sent], *v.t.* acentuar.
accentuate [æk'sentjueit], *v.t.* acentuar; recalcar.
accept [ək'sept], *v.t.* aceptar.
acceptable [ək'septəbl], *a.* aceptable.
acceptance [ək'septəns], *n.* aceptación, *f.*
acceptation [æksep'teiʃən], *n.* acepción; aceptación, *f.*
access ['ækses], *n.* acceso.
accessible [ək'sesibl], *a.* accesible.
accession [æk'seʃən], *n.* accesión, *f.*; advenimiento; ascenso; adición, *f.*
accessory [æk'sesəri], *a.*, *n.* accesorio.—*n.* (*jur.*) instigador; encubridor, *m.*
accident ['æksidənt], *n.* accidente, *m.*
accidental [æksi'dentəl], *a.* accidental.
acclaim [ə'kleim], *n.* aclamación, *f.*—*v.t.* aclamar, ovacionar.
acclamation [æklə'meiʃən], *n.* aclamación, *f.*
acclimatize [ə'klaimətaiz] (*U.S.* **acclimate** ['æklimeit]), *v.t.* aclimatar.
accolade ['ækəleid], *n.* acolada.
accommodate [ə'kəmədeit], *v.t.* acomodar; alojar.
accommodating [ə'kəmədeitiŋ], *a.* acomodadizo; acomodaticio.
accommodation [əkəmə'deiʃən], *n.* alojamiento; acomodamiento; vivienda.
accompaniment [ə'kʌmpnimənt], *n.* acompañamiento.
accompanist [ə'kʌmpənist], *n.* acompañante, *m.f.*
accompany [ə'kʌmpəni], *v.t.* acompañar.
accomplice [ə'kʌmplis], *n.* cómplice, *m.f.*
accomplish [ə'kʌmpliʃ], *v.t.* realizar, cumplir.
accomplished [ə'kʌmpliʃt], *a.* consumado, acabado; culto.
accomplishment [ə'kʌmpliʃmənt], *n.* consumación, *f.*; talento, prenda.
accord [ə'kɔ:d], *n.* acuerdo; armonía; convenio; ***of his own* —,** de su querer.—*v.t.* acordar; otorgar.—*v.i.* avenirse.
accordance [ə'kɔ:dəns], *n.* conformidad, *f.*; ***in — with,*** de acuerdo con, con arreglo a.
according [ə'kɔ:diŋ], *adv.* según (***to***).
accordingly [ə'kɔ:diŋli], *adv.* en conformidad; en consecuencia.
accordion [ə'kɔ:djən], *n.* acordeón, *m.*
accost [ə'kɔst], *v.t.* abordar.
account [ə'kaunt] *n.* cuenta; monta, importancia; informe, *m.*, narración, *f.*; ***on — of,*** a causa de, por motivo de; ***on no* —,** de ninguna manera, no . . . por lo que sea.—*v.t.* tener por, juzgar; ***to take into* —,** tomar en cuenta; ***to turn to (good)* —,** sacar provecho de.—*v.i.* dar razón de, explicar (***for***).
accountable [ə'kauntəbl], *a.* responsable; explicable.
accountancy [ə'kauntənsi], *n.* contabilidad, *f.*
accountant [ə'kauntənt], *n.* contador, *m.*
accoutre [ə'ku:tə], *v.t.* equipar, aviar.
accoutrements [ə'ku:trəmənts], *n.pl.* equipo, pertrechos, *m.pl.*
accredit [ə'kredit], *v.t.* acreditar.
accretion [ə'kri:ʃən], *n.* acrecimiento; acreción, *f.*
accrue [ə'kru:], *v.i.* resultar; aumentar.
accumulate [ə'kju:mjuleit], *v.t.* acumular.—*v.i.* -se.
accumulation [əkju:mju'leiʃən], *n.* acumulación, *f.*
accumulator [ə'kju:mjuleitə], *n.* acumulador, *m.*
accuracy ['ækjurəsi], *n.* exactitud, corrección, *f.*
accurate ['ækjurit], *a.* exacto, puntual, fiel.
accursed [ə'kə:sid], *a.* maldito, malvado.
accusation [ækju'zeiʃən], *n.* acusación, *f.*
accusative [ə'kju:ʒətiv], *a.*, *n.* acusativo.
accuse [ə'kju:z], *v.t.* acusar, denunciar.
accused [ə'kju:zd], *n.* acusado, procesado.
accuser [ə'kju:zə], *n.* acusador.
accustom [ə'kʌstəm], *v.t.* acostumbrar, avezar.
accustomed [ə'kʌstəmd], *a.* acostumbrado.
ace [eis], *n.* as, *m.*; ***within an — of,*** a dos dedos de.
acetic [ə'si:tik], *a.* acético.
acetone ['æsitoun], *n.* acetona.
acetylene [ə'setili:n], *n.* acetileno.
ache [eik], *n.* dolor, *m.*, pena.—*v.i.* doler.
achieve [ə'tʃi:v], *v.t.* alcanzar, lograr, obtener.
achievement [ə'tʃi:vmənt], *n.* logro, realización, *f.*; proeza.
Achilles [ə'kili:z], *n.* Aquiles, *m.*
aching ['eikiŋ], *a.* dolorido, doliente.—*n.* pena, dolor, *m.*
acid ['æsid], *a.*, *n.* ácido.
acidity [ə'siditi], *n.* acidez, *f.*
ack-ack ['æk'æk], *n.* (*mil.*) artillería antiaérea.
acknowledge [ək'nɔlidʒ], *v.t.* reconocer; acusar (*recibimiento*).
acknowledg(e)ment [ək'nɔlidʒmənt], *n.* reconocimiento; acuse, *m.*
acme ['ækmi], *n.* cumbre, *f.*; (*med.*) acmé, *m.*
acolyte ['ækəlait], *n.* monaguillo, acólito.
aconite ['ækənait], *n.* acónito.
acorn ['eikɔ:n], *n.* bellota.
acoustic [ə'ku:stik], *a.* acústico.—*n.pl.* acústica.
acquaint [ə'kweint], *v.t.* familiarizar; poner al corriente (***with,*** de); ***to be(come) acquainted with,*** conocer; ponerse al corriente de.

acquaintance [ə'kweintəns], *n.* conocimiento; conocido.
acquaintanceship [ə'kweintənsʃip], *n.* conocimiento, relaciones, *f.pl.*, trato.
acquiesce [ækwi'es], *v.i.* consentir, tolerar (*in*).
acquiescence [ækwi'esəns], *n.* consentimiento, transigencia.
acquire [ə'kwaiə], *v.t.* adquirir.
acquirement [ə'kwaiəmənt], *n.* adquisición, *f.*—*pl.* dotes, *m.pl.*, prendas, *f.pl.*
acquisition [ækwi'ziʃən], *n.* adquisición, *f.*
acquisitive [ə'kwizitiv], *a.* adquisidor, codicioso.
acquit [ə'kwit], *v.t.* absolver.—*v.r.* conducirse.
acquittal [ə'kwitəl], *n.* absolución, *f.*
acre ['eikə], *n.* acre, *m.*
acreage ['eikəridʒ], *n.* área.
acrid ['ækrid], *a.* acre, picante.
acrimonious [ækri'mounjəs], *a.* acrimonioso.
acrimony ['ækriməni], *n.* acrimonia.
acrobat ['ækrəbæt], *n.* acróbata, *m.f.*, volatinero.
acrobatic [ækrə'bætik], *a.* acrobático.—*n.pl.* acrobacia.
acropolis [ə'krɔpəlis], *n.* acrópolis, *f.*
across [ə'krɔs], *adv.* a través; al otro lado.—*prep.* a(l) través de; al otro lado de.
acrostic [ə'krɔstik], *a.*, *n.* acróstico.
act [ækt], *n.* acto, obra; acción, *f.*; ***in the —***, en flagrante; (*jur.*) ley, *f.*; (*theat.*) acto, jornada.—*v.t.* (*theat.*) representar; desempeñar (*un papel*); aparentar, simular.—*v.i.* tener efecto; actuar; fingir; comportarse.
acting ['æktiŋ], *a.* interino; teatral.—*n.* histrionismo, arte histriónico; representación, *f.*
action ['ækʃən], *n.* acción, *f.*; expediente, *m.*
actionable ['ækʃənəbl], *a.* (*jur.*) procesable.
active ['æktiv], *a.* activo.
activity [æk'tiviti], *n.* actividad, *f.*
actor ['æktə], *n.* actor, *m.*
actress ['æktris], *n.* actriz, *f.*
actual ['æktjuəl], *a.* efectivo, real; actual.
actuality [æktju'æliti], *n.* realidad; actualidad, *f.*
actually ['æktjuəli], *adv.* verdaderamente, en efecto.
actuary ['æktjuəri], *n.* actuario.
actuate ['æktjueit], *v.t.* poner en acción; impulsar.
acumen [ə'kju:men], *n.* agudeza.
acute [ə'kju:t], *a.* agudo.
acuteness [ə'kju:tnis], *n.* agudeza.
adage ['ædidʒ], *n.* adagio.
Adam ['ædəm], *n.* Adán, *m.*; ***Adam's apple***, nuez (*f.*) de la garganta.
adamant ['ædəmənt], *a.* muy duro; inexorable.
adapt [ə'dæpt], *v.t.* adaptar, ajustar; (*lit.*) refundir.
adaptable [ə'dæptəbl], *a.* adaptable.
adaptation [ædæp'teiʃən], *n.* adaptación, *f.*; (*lit.*) arreglo, refundición, *f.*
add [æd], *v.t.* añadir; sumar, adicionar.—*v.i.* sumar.
addendum [ə'dendəm], *n.* (*pl.* **-da**) addenda, *m.*, adición, *f.*
adder ['ædə], *n.* víbora.
addict ['ædikt], *n.* (en)viciado; adicto; morfinómano. — [ə'dikt], *v.t.* enviciar; entregar.
addiction [ə'dikʃən], *n.* enviciamiento; abandono.
addition [ə'diʃən], *n.* adición, *f.*; suma; ***in — (to)***, además (de).
additional [ə'diʃənəl], *a.* adicional.
addle [ædl], *v.t.* enhuerar.
addled [ædld], *a.* huero.
addle-headed ['ædl'hedid], **addle-brained** ['ædl'breind], *a.* cabeza de chorlito.
address [ə'dres], *n.* dirección, *f.*, señas, *f.pl.*; alocución; destreza; atención, *f.*—*v.t.* dirigirse a; dirigir (*carta*).
addressee [ædre'si:], *n.* destinatario.
adduce [ə'dju:s], *v.t.* aducir.
adept ['ædept], *a.*, *n.* perito; adepto.
adequate ['ædikwit], *a.* suficiente; adecuado.
adhere [əd'hiə], *v.i.* adherir(se).
adherent [əd'hiərənt], *a.*, *n.* adherente, *m.f.*
adhesion [əd'hi:ʒən], *n.* adhesión, *f.*; adherencia.
adhesive [əd'hi:siv], *a.*, *n.* adhesivo.
adieu [ə'dju:], *n.* *interj.* (*lit.*) adiós, *m.*
adjacent [ə'dʒeisənt], *a.* contiguo, adyacente.
adjectival [ædʒik'taivəl], *a.* adjetival.
adjective ['ædʒiktiv], *n.* adjetivo.
adjoin [ə'dʒɔin], *v.t.* lindar con.
adjoining [ə'dʒɔiniŋ], *a.* colindante; contiguo.
adjourn [ə'dʒə:n], *v.t.* prorrogar.—*v.i.* -se.
adjournment [ə'dʒə:nmənt], *n.* suspensión, *f.*, prórroga.
adjudicate [ə'dʒu:dikeit], *v.t.*, *v.i.* juzgar.
adjunct ['ædʒʌŋkt], *a.*, *n.* adjunto.
adjure [ə'dʒuə], *v.t.* juramentar; conjurar.
adjust [ə'dʒʌst], *v.t.* ajustar; tasar; verificar.
adjustable [ə'dʒʌstəbl], *a.* ajustable.
adjustment [ə'dʒʌstmənt], *n.* ajuste, *m.*; arreglo.
adjutant ['ædʒutənt], *n.* ayudante, *m.f.*
ad lib [æd'lib], *v.t.*, *v.i.* (*fam.*) repentizar.
administer [əd'ministə], *v.t.* administrar.
administration [ədminis'treiʃən], *n.* administración, dirección, *f.*
administrator [əd'ministreitə], *n.* administrador, *m.*
admirable ['ædmərəbl], *a.* admirable.
admiral ['ædmərəl], *n.* almirante, *m.*
Admiralty ['ædmərəlti], *n.*, Ministerio de la Marina; **admiralty,** *n.* almirantazgo.
admiration [ædmə'reiʃən], *n.* admiración, *f.*
admire [əd'maiə], *v.t.* admirar.
admirer [əd'maiərə], *n.* admirador, *m.*
admiring [əd'maiəriŋ], *a.* admirativo.
admissible [əd'misibl], *a.* admisible.
admission [əd'miʃən], *n.* admisión; recepción, *f.*; entrada; confesión, *f.*
admit [əd'mit], *v.t.* admitir; confesar.
admittance [əd'mitəns], *n.* admisión, *f.*; entrada; ***no —***, se prohibe entrar.
admixture [əd'mikstʃə], *n.* adición, *f.*
admonish [əd'mɔniʃ], *v.t.* amonestar, prevenir.
admonition [ædmə'niʃən], *n.* admonición, *f.*
ado [ə'du:], *n.* bullicio; ***without more —***, sin más ni más.
adobe [ə'doubi], *n.* adobe, *m.*
adolescence [ædə'lesəns], *n.* adolescencia.
adolescent [ædə'lesənt], *a.*, *n.* adolescente *m.f.*

adopt [ə'dɔpt], *v.t.* adoptar; prohijar.
adoption [ə'dɔpʃən], *n.* adopción, *f.*
adoptive [ə'dɔptiv], *a.* adoptivo.
adorable [ə'dɔ:rəbl], *a.* adorable.
adoration [ædɔ:'reiʃən], *n.* adoración, *f.*
adore [ə'dɔ:], *v.t.* adorar.
adorn [ə'dɔ:n], *v.t.* adornar.
adornment [ə'dɔ:nmənt], *n.* adorno, gala.
Adriatic [eidri'ætik], *a.*, *n.* Adriático.
adrift [ə'drift], *adv.* a la deriva.
adroit [ə'drɔit], *a.* diestro.
adroitness [ə'drɔitnis], *n.* destreza.
adulation [ædju'leiʃən], *n.* adulación, *f.*
adult [ə'dʌlt], *a.*, *n.* adulto.
adulterate [ə'dʌltəreit], *v.t.* adulterar.
adulteration [ədʌltə'reiʃən], *n.* adulteración, *f.*
adulterer [ə'dʌltərə], *n.* adúltero.
adulteress [ə'dʌltəris], *n.* adúltera.
adulterous [ə'dʌltərəs], *a.* adúltero.
adumbrate ['ædʌmbreit], *v.t.* esbozar; presagiar, indicar.
advance [əd'vɑ:ns], *n.* adelanto, avance, *m.*; progreso; — ***payment***, anticipo; ***in*** —, delante; de antemano; por adelantado.—*pl.* requerimientos, *m.pl.*—*v.t.* adelantar; avanzar.—*v.i.* adelantar(se).
advancement [əd'vɑ:nsmənt], *n.* progreso; ascenso; anticipo.
advantage [əd'vɑ:ntidʒ], *n.* ventaja; ***to take — of***, aprovecharse de.—*v.t.* (*obs.*) aventajar.
advantageous [ædvən'teidʒəs], *a.* ventajoso.
Advent ['ædvənt], *n.* (*eccl.*) Adviento; **advent**, *n.* advenimiento.
adventitious [ædvən'tiʃəs], *a.* adventicio.
adventure [əd'ventʃə], *n.* aventura.—*v.t.* aventurar.—*v.i.* -se.
adventurer [əd'ventʃərə], *n.* aventurero.
adventuress [əd'ventʃəris], *n.* aventurera.
adventurous [əd'ventʃərəs], *a.* aventurero, atrevido.
adverb ['ædvə:b], *n.* adverbio.
adverbial [əd'və:bjəl], *a.* adverbial.
adversary ['ædvəsəri], *n.* adversario.
adverse ['ædvə:s], *a.* adverso.
adversity [əd'və:siti], *n.* adversidad, *f.*
advert ['ædvə:t], *n.* (*fam.*) anuncio.
advertise ['ædvətaiz], *v.t.* anunciar; pregonar.
advertisement [əd'və:tizmənt], *n.* anuncio, reclamo.
advertiser ['ædvətaizə], *n.* anunciador, *m.*, anunciante, *m.f.*; diario publicitario.
advertising ['ædvətaiziŋ], *a.* publicitario.—*n.* publicidad, *f.*; anuncios, *m.pl.*
advice [əd'vais], *n.* consejo; aviso.
advisable [əd'vaizəbl], *a.* conveniente, aconsejable.
advise [əd'vaiz], *v.t.* aconsejar; avisar.
advisedly [əd'vaizidli], *adv.* con intención.
adviser, advisor [əd'vaizə], *n.* consejero.
advisory [əd'vaizəri], *a.* consultativo.
advocate ['ædvəkit], *n.* abogado; defensor, *m.* ['ædvəkeit], *v.t.* abogar por.
adze [ædz], *n.* azuela.
Aegean [i'dʒi:ən], *a.* egeo.—*n.* Mar Egeo.
aerate ['ɛəreit], *v.t.* airear; hacer efervescente.
aerial ['ɛəriəl], *a.* aéreo.—*n.* antena.
aerie, aery ['ɛəri, 'iəri], *n.* aguilera.
aerodrome ['ɛərədroum], *n.* aeródromo.
aerodynamic [ɛəroudai'næmik], *a.* aerodinámico.—*n.pl.* aerodinámica.
aeronaut ['ɛərənɔ:t], *n.* aeronauta, *m.f.*
aeronautic [ɛərə'nɔ:tik], *a.* aeronáutico.—*n.pl.* aeronáutica.
aeronautical [ɛərə'nɔ:tikəl], *a.* aeronáutico.
aeroplane ['ɛərəplein], *n.* avión, *m.*; aeroplano.
aesthete ['i:sθi:t], *n.* esteta, *m.f.*
aesthetic [i:s'θetik], *a.* estético.—*n.pl.* estética.
afar [ə'fɑ:], *adv.* lejos; ***from*** —, desde lejos.
affable ['æfəbl], *a.* afable.
affair [ə'fɛə], *n.* negocio, asunto; lance, *m.*; cuestión, *f.*, amorío.
affect [ə'fekt], *v.t.* influir en; afectar; fingir; impresionar.
affectation [æfek'teiʃən], *n.* afectación, *f.*
affected [ə'fektid], *a.* afectado.
affection [ə'fekʃən], *n.* cariño; (*med.*) afección, *f.*
affectionate [ə'fekʃənit], *a.* afectuoso, cariñoso.
affidavit [æfi'deivit], *n.* (*jur.*) declaración jurada.
affiliate [ə'filieit], *v.t.* afiliar.—*v.i.* -se (***with***, a).
affiliation [əfili'eiʃən], *n.* afiliación, *f.*
affinity [ə'finiti], *n.* afinidad, *f.*
affirm [ə'fə:m], *v.t.* afirmar.
affirmation [æfə'meiʃən], *n.* afirmación, *f.*
affirmative [ə'fə:mətiv], *a.* afirmativo.—*n.* afirmativa.
affix [ə'fiks], *v.t.* añadir, poner.
afflict [ə'flikt], *v.t.* afligir.
affliction [ə'flikʃən], *n.* aflicción, *f.*
affluence ['æfluəns], *n.* afluencia.
affluent ['æfluənt], *a.* afluente; opulento (*rico*).
afford [ə'fɔ:d], *v.t.* proporcionar; ***to be able to*** —, poder comprar; tener los medios para; tener con que . . .
afforest [ə'fɔrist], *v.t.* plantar, repoblar.
afforestation [æfɔris'teiʃən], *n.* aforestalación, *f.*
affray [ə'frei], *n.* refriega.
affront [ə'frʌnt], *n.* afrenta.—*v.t.* denostar, afrentar.
Afghan ['æfgæn], *a.*, *n.* afgano.
Afghanistan [æf'gænistæn], *n.* el Afganistán.
afield [ə'fi:ld], *adv.* fuera; ***far*** —, muy lejos.
afire [ə'faiə], *adv.* ardiendo.
aflame [ə'fleim], *adv.* en llamas.
afloat [ə'flout], *adv.* a flote; corriente.
afoot [ə'fut], *adv.* a pie; en movimiento; ***what's — ?*** ¿ qué pasa ?
aforesaid [ə'fɔ:sed], *a.* ya citado, dicho.
aforethought [ə'fɔ:θɔ:t], *a.* ***with malice*** —, con premeditación.
afraid [ə'freid], *a.* medroso, espantado; ***to be*** —, tener miedo (***of, to***, a, de).
afresh [ə'freʃ], *adv.* de nuevo.
Africa ['æfrikə], *n.* África.
African ['æfrikən], *a.*, *n.* africano.
aft [ɑ:ft], *adv.* (*naut.*) a *o* en popa.
after ['ɑ:ftə], *a.* posterior; ***the day*** —, el día siguiente; ***to be*** —, buscar, ir en busca de.—*adv.* después.—*prep.* después de; según; en pos de.—*conj.* después (de) que.
after-birth ['ɑ:ftəbə:θ], *n.* secundinas.
after-care ['ɑ:ʃtəkɛə], *n.* cura postoperatoria.
after-dinner ['ɑ:ftədinə], *a.* de sobremesa.
after-effect ['ɑ:ftəifekt], *n.* efecto posterior.

afterglow ['ɑ:ftəglou], *n.* resplendor crepuscular, *m.*
after-hours ['ɑ:ftərauəz], *n.* horas extraordinarias.—*adv.* después de las horas ordinarias.
after-life ['ɑ:ftəlaif], *n.* resto de la vida; trasmundo.
aftermath ['ɑ:ftəmæθ], *n.* secuela, consecuencia.
aftermost ['ɑ:ftəmoust], *a.* último; trasero.
afternoon [ɑ:ftə'nu:n], *n.* tarde, *f.*
after-taste ['ɑ:ftəteist], *n.* resabio, gustillo.
afterthought ['ɑ:ftəθɔ:t], *n.* idea tardía; idea posterior.
afterwards ['ɑ:ftəwədz], *adv.* después, más tarde.
after-world ['ɑ:ftəwə:ld], *n.* ultramundo.
again [ə'gein], *adv.* de nuevo, otra vez; además; ***now and* —,** de vez en cuando; ***to do* —,** volver a hacer.
against [ə'genst], *prep.* contra; cerca de; tocante.
agape [ə'geip], *a., adv.* con la boca abierta, boquiabierto.
agate ['ægət], *n.* ágata.
agave ['ægeiv], *n.* (*bot.*) pita.
age [eidʒ], *n.* edad; época; vejez *f.*; (*fam.*) eternidad, *f.*; ***of* —,** mayor de edad; ***under* —,** menor de edad. —*pl.* (*fam.*) horas y horas; siglos.—*v.t.* envejecer; madurar.—*v.i.* envejecer(se).
aged [eidʒd], *a.* de la edad de; ['eidʒid] anciano, viejo, envejecido.
ageless ['eidʒlis], *a.* siempre joven.
agency ['eidʒənsi], *n.* agencia; oficio, acción, *f.*
agenda [ə'dʒendə], *n.* agenda.
agent ['eidʒənt], *n.* agente; representante, *m.*
agglomeration [əglɔmə'reiʃən], *n.* aglomeración, *f.*
aggrandizement [ə'grændizmənt], *n.* engrandecimiento.
aggravate ['ægrəveit], *v.t.* agravar; (*fam.*) enfadar.
aggravation [ægrə'veiʃən], *n.* agravamiento; (*fam.*) vejación, *f.*
aggregate ['ægrigit], *a., n.* agregado.—['ægrigeit], *v.t.* agregar, juntar.
aggression [ə'greʃən], *n.* agresión, *f.*
aggressive [ə'gresiv], *a.* agresivo.
aggressor [ə'gresə], *n.* agresor.
aggrieve [ə'gri:v], *v.t.* acongojar, vejar; ofender.
aghast [ə'gɑ:st], *a.* despavorido.
agile ['ædʒail], *a.* ágil, ligero.
agility [ə'dʒiliti], *n.* agilidad, *f.*
agitate ['ædʒiteit], *v.t., v.i.* agitar.
agitation [ædʒi'teiʃən], *n.* agitación, *f.*
agitator ['ædʒiteitə], *n.* agitador; provocador, *m.*
aglow [ə'glou], *a.* encendido.
agnostic [æg'nɔstik], *a., n.* agnóstico.
ago [ə'gou], *adv.* hace, ha; ***two days* —,** hace dos días; ***long* —,** hace mucho.
agog [ə'gɔg], *a., adv.* ansioso; curioso.
agonize ['ægənaiz], *v.t.* atormentar, martirizar.—*v.i.* agonizar.
agony ['ægəni], *n.* agonía; angustia.
agrarian [ə'grɛəriən], *a.* agrario.
agree [ə'gri:], *v.i.* estar de acuerdo; quedar(se) en; concordar; convenir (***to,*** en).
agreeable [ə'gri:əbl], *a.* agradable; dispuesto, conforme.
agreement [ə'gri:mənt], *n.* acuerdo; concordancia.
agricultural [ægri'kʌltʃərəl], *a.* agrícola.
agriculture ['ægrikʌltʃə], *n.* agricultura.
aground [ə'graund], *a., adv.* encallado; ***to run* —,** encallar.
ague ['eigju:], *n.* escalofrío; fiebre.
ahead [ə'hed], *adv.* delante, al frente; por delante; **— *of,*** antes de; ***to get* —,** adelantarse.
ahem! [hm], *interj.* ¡eh! ¡pués!
ahoy! [ə'hɔi], *interj.* (*naut.*) ***ship* —!** ¡ah del barco! **— *there!*** ¡huloa!
aid [eid], *n.* auxilio, ayuda.—*v.t.* ayudar.
aide (-de-camp) ['eid(də'kã)], *n.* (*mil.*) ayudante de campo, edecán, *m.*
ail [eil], *v.t.* doler, afligir.—*v.i.* enfermar, sufrir.
aileron ['eilərɔn], *n.* alerón, *m.*
ailing ['eiliŋ], *a.* enfermizo, doliente.
ailment ['eilmənt], *n.* achaque, *m.*; dolencia.
aim [eim], *n.* hito, blanco; mira; puntería.—*v.t., v.i.* apuntar; ***to* — *to,*** tratar de, mirar a.
aimless ['eimlis], *a.* sin objeto, a la ventura.
ain't [eint], (*dial., low*) [AM NOT; IS NOT; ARE NOT].
air [ɛə], *n.* aire, *m.*; (*fig.*) radio, *f.*—*v.t.* ventilar; **— *force,*** fuerza aérea, ejército del aire; **— *liner,*** transaéreo; **— *mail,*** correo aéreo, correo por avión.
air- [ɛə], *prefix.* aéreo.
airborne ['ɛəbɔ:n], *a.* aéreo, por aire.—*adv.* en vuelo.
air-conditioning ['ɛəkən'diʃəniŋ], *n.* aire acondicionado.
aircraft ['ɛəkrɑ:ft], *n.* avión, *m.*
aircraft-carrier ['ɛəkrɑ:ft'kæriə], *n.* porta(a)viones, *m.inv.*
airfield ['ɛəfi:ld), *n.* campo de aviación.
air-gun ['ɛəgʌn], *n.* escopeta de aire comprimido.
air-hostess ['ɛəhoustes], *n.* azafata.
airing ['ɛəriŋ], *n.* ventilación, *f.*; oreo; paseata.
air-lane ['ɛəlein], *n.* ruta aérea.
air-lift ['ɛəlift], *n.* puente aéreo.
airman ['ɛəmən], *n.* aviador, *m.*; soldado aéreo.
airplane ['ɛəplein], (*U.S.*) [AEROPLANE].
air-pocket ['ɛəpɔkit], *n.* bache aéreo.
airport ['ɛəpɔ:t], *n.* aeropuerto.
air-raid ['ɛəre:d], *n.* bombardeo aéreo; **— *shelter,*** refugio antiaéreo.
airship ['ɛəʃip], *n.* aeronave, *f.*
airstrip ['ɛəstrip], *n.* pista de aterrizaje.
airtight ['ɛətait], *a.* hermético, herméticamente cerrado.
airworthy ['ɛəwə:ði], *a.* en condiciones de vuelo.
airy ['ɛəri], *a.* airoso; alegre.
aisle [ail], *n.* pasillo.
aitch [eitʃ], *n.* H, hache, *f.*
ajar [ə'dʒɑ:], *a., adv.* entornado, entreabierto.
akimbo [ə'kimbou], *a., adv.* ***arms* —,** en jarras.
akin [ə'kin], *a.* semejante; emparentado.
alabaster ['æləbɑ:stə], *a.* alabastrino.—*n.* alabastro.
alacrity [ə'lækriti], *n.* alacridad, *f.*
alarm [ə'lɑ:m], *n.* alarma; rebato.—*v.t.* alarmar.

alarm-clock [ə'lɑ:mklɔk], *n.* despertador, *m.*
alarming [ə'lɑ:miŋ], *a.* alarmante.
alas! [ə'læs], *interj.* ¡ay! ¡guay!
alb [ælb], *n.* (*eccl.*) alba.
Albanian [æl'beinjən], *a.*, *n.* albanés, *m.*
albatross ['ælbətrɔs], *n.* albatros, *m.*
albeit [ɔ:l'bi:it], *conj.* (*lit.*) bien que, aunque.
albino [æl'bi:nou], *a.*, *n.* (*pl.* **-nos**) albino.
Albion ['ælbjən], *n.* Albión, *f.*
album ['ælbəm], *n.* álbum, *n.*
albumen [æl'bju:min], *n.* albúmina; albumen, *m.*
alchemist ['ælkimist], *n.* alquimista.
alchemy ['ælkimi], *n.* alquimia.
alcohol ['ælkəhɔl], *n.* alcohol, *m.*
alcoholic [ælkə'hɔlik], *a.*, *n.* alcohólico, alcoholizado.
alcove ['ælkouv], *n.* nicho, hueco.
alder ['ɔ:ldə], *n.* (*bot.*) aliso.
alderman ['ɔ:ldəmən], *n.* concejal, *m.*
ale [eil], *n.* cerveza.
alert [ə'lə:t], *a.* vigilante, listo, vivo.—*n.* alerta, *m.*; ***on the* —,** alerta, sobre aviso.—*v.t.* alertar.
Alexander [ælig'zɑ:ndə], *n.* Alejandro.
alga ['ælgə], *n.* (*pl.* **algae**) (*bot.*) alga.
algebra ['ældʒibrə], *n.* álgebra.
Algeria [æl'dʒiəriə], *n.* Argelia.
Algerian [æl'dʒiəriən], *a.*, *n.* argelino.
Algiers [æl'dʒiəz], *n.* Argel, *f.*
alias ['eiliəs], *adv.*, *n.* alias, *m.*
alibi ['ælibai], *n.* coartada.
alien ['eiljən], *a.* ajeno, extraño.—*n.* extranjero.
alienate ['eiljəneit], *v.t.* enajenar; malquistar.
alight (1) [ə'lait], *a.* encendido, en llamas.
alight (2) [ə'lait], *v.i.* bajar, apearse; posarse.
align [ə'lain], *v.t.* alinear.
alignment [ə'lainmənt], *n.* alineación, *m.*
alike [ə'laik], *a.* igual, parecido.—*adv.* igualmente, lo mismo.
alimentary [æli'mentəri], *a.* alimenticio.
alimony ['æliməni], *n.* alimentos, *m.pl.*
aline [ALIGN].
alive [ə'laiv], *a.* vivo, con vida; activo; sensible (***to,*** a); hormigueante (***with,*** en).
alkali ['ælkəlai], *n.* (*pl.* **-lis, -lies**) álcali, *m.*
alkaline ['ælkəlain], *a.* alcalino.
all [ɔ:l], *pron.* todo, todos, todo el mundo.—*a.*, *adv.* todo; ***at* —,** de algún modo; ***not at* —,** de ningún modo; de nada; **— *along,*** todo el tiempo; **— *but,*** casi; **— *the better,*** tanto mejor; **— *in,*** todo incluído; (*fam.*) hecho polvo; **— *off,*** (*fam.*) abandonado; **— *over,*** acabado; general; **— *right,*** está bien; regular; **— *told,*** en total; **— *too,*** ya demasiado.
Allah ['ælɑ:], *n.* Alá, *m.*
allay [ə'lei], *v.t.* aliviar, calmar.
allegation [æle'geiʃən], *n.* alegación, *f.*, alegato.
allege [ə'ledʒ], *v.t.* alegar.
allegiance [ə'li:dʒəns], *n.* fidelidad, lealtad, *f.*
allegoric(al) [æli'gɔrik(əl)], *a.* alegórico.
allegory ['æligəri], *n.* alegoría.
alleluia [æli'lu:jə], *n.*, *interj.* aleluya.
allergic [ə'lə:dʒik], *a.* alérgico.
allergy ['ælədʒi], *n.* alergia.
alleviate [ə'li:vieit], *v.t.* aliviar.
alley ['æli], *n.* callejuela; pasadizo.
alley-way ['æliwei], *n.* pasadizo.
All Fools' Day [ɔ:l'fu:lzdei], *n.* día (*m.*) de inocentadas (1 *de abril*).
alliance [ə'laiəns], *n.* alianza.
allied ['ælaid], *a.* afín; aliado.
alligator ['æligeitə], *n.* caimán, *m.*
all-in wrestling ['ɔ:lin'resliŋ], *n.* lucha libre.
alliteration [əlitə'reiʃən], *n.* aliteración, *f.*
allocate ['æləkeit], *v.t.* asignar.
allocation [ælə'keiʃən], *n.* asignación, *f.* cuota.
allot [ə'lɔt], *v.t.* asignar.
allotment [ə'lɔtmənt], *n.* asignación, *f.*; lote, *m.*; porción, *f.*; huerto alquilado.
allow [ə'lau], *v.t.* permitir; admitir, conceder. —*v.i.* (***for***) tener en cuenta.
allowable [ə'lauəbl], *a.* admisible, permisible.
allowance [ə'lauəns], *n.* permiso; ración; rebaja; pensión, *f.*; tolerancia.
alloy ['ælɔi], *n.* liga, aleación, *f.*—[ə'lɔi], *v.t.* ligar, alear; adulterar.
all-powerful ['ɔ:lpauəful], *a.* todopoderoso.
all-round ['ɔ:lraund], *a.* hábil para todo, universal.
allude [ə'l(j)u:d], *v.i.* aludir.
allure [ə'ljuə], *v.t.* halagar, fascinar.
allurement [ə'ljuəmənt], *n.* fascinación, *f.*; halago.
alluring [ə'ljuəriŋ], *a.* seductor, fascinante.
allusion [ə'l(j)u:ʒən], *n.* alusión, *f.*
alluvium [ə'lu:viəm], *n.* (*pl.* **-via**) aluvión, *f.*
ally ['ælai], *n.* aliado.—[ə'lai], *v.t.* aliar.—*v.r.* -se.
almanac(k) ['ɔ:lmənæk], *n.* almanaque, *m.*
Almighty [ɔ:l'maiti], *n.* Todopoderoso; **almighty,** *a.* todopoderoso; (*fam.*) tremendo, gordo, grave.
almond ['ɑ:mənd], *n.* almendra.
almond-tree ['ɑ:mənd'tri:], *n.* almendro.
almoner ['ɑ:mənə], *n.* limosnero.
almost ['ɔ:lmoust], *adv.* casi.
alms [ɑ:mz], *n.inv.* limosna.
almshouse [ɑ:mzhaus], *n.* hospicio, asilo de pobres.
aloe ['ælou], *n.* (*bot.*) áloe(s), *m.*; — *pl.* acíbar, *m.*
aloft [ə'lɔft], *adv.* en alto.
alone [ə'loun], *a.* solo; ***let* —,** sin contar.—*adv.* solamente; ***to let* o *leave* —,** no tocar, no molestar.
along [ə'lɔŋ], *adv.* a lo largo; junto (***with,*** con); adelante.—*prep.* a lo largo de; ***to get* —,** medrar; quedar bien.
alongside [əlɔŋ'said], *adv.* (*naut.*) al costado, bordo con bordo.—*prep.* al costado de.
aloof [ə'lu:f], *a.* apartado; frío.
aloud [ə'laud], *adv.* en voz alta.
alphabet ['ælfəbet], *n.* alfabeto.
alphabetic(al) ['ælfə'betik(əl)], *a.* alfabético.
alpine ['ælpain], *a.* alpino; alpestre.
Alps [ælps], *n.pl.* Alpes, *m.pl.*
already [ɔ:l'redi], *adv.* ya.
also ['ɔ:lsou], *adv.* también.
altar ['ɔ:ltə], *n.* altar, *m.*; ara.
altar-boy ['ɔ:ltəbɔi], *n.* monaguillo.
altar-piece ['ɔ:ltəpi:s], *n.* retablo.
alter ['ɔ:ltə], *v.t.* alterar; cambiar.—*v.i.* -se.
alteration [ɔ:ltə'reiʃən], *n.* cambio, alteración, *f.*
altercation [ɔ:ltə'keiʃən], *n.* altercación, *f.* altercado.

alternate [ɔ:l'tə:nit], *a.* alterno.—['ɔ:ltəneit], *v.t., v.i.* alternar.
alternation [ɔ:ltə:'neiʃən], *n.* alternación, *f.*; alternancia.
alternative [ɔ:l'tə:nətiv], *a.* alternativo.—*n.* alternativa.
although [ɔ:l'ðou], *conj.* aunque.
altimeter ['æltimi:tə], *n.* altímetro.
altitude ['æltitju:d], *n.* altitud, *f.*, altura.
altogether [ɔ:ltə'geðə], *adv.* en conjunto; del todo, totalmente; todos juntos.
altruist ['æltruist], *n.* altruista, *m.f.*
alum ['æləm], *n.* alumbre, *m.*
aluminium [ælju'minjəm], *n.* (*U.S.* **aluminum**) aluminio.
always ['ɔ:lweiz], *adv.* siempre.
am [æm] [BE].
amalgam [ə'mælgəm], *n.* amalgama.
amalgamate [ə'mælgəmeit], *v.t.* amalgamar.—*v.i.* -se.
amanuensis [əmænju'ensis], *n.* (*pl.*-**ses**) amanuense, *m.f.*
amass [ə'mæs], *v.t.* acumular.
amateur ['æmətə], *a., n.* aficionado; chapucero.
amatory ['æmətəri], *a.* amatorio.
amaze [ə'meiz], *v.t.* pasmar, asombrar; ***to be amazed,*** asombrarse (***at, by,*** de).
amazement [ə'meizmənt], *n.* asombro.
amazing [ə'meiziŋ], *a.* asombroso, maravilloso.
Amazon ['æməzən], *n.* Amazonas, *m.sg.*; **amazon,** *n.* amazona.
ambassador [æm'bæsədə], *n.* embajador, *m.*
ambassadress [æm'bæsədris], *n.* embajadora.
amber ['æmbə], *a.* ambarino.—*n.* ambar, *m.*
ambidextrous [æmbi'dekstrəs], *a.* ambidextro; (*fig.*) venal.
ambient ['æmbiənt], *a.* ambiente.
ambiguity [æmbi'gju:iti], *n.* ambigüedad, *f.*
ambiguous [æm'bigjuəs], *a.* ambiguo.
ambit ['æmbit], *n.* ámbito.
ambition [æm'biʃən], *n.* ambición, *f.*
ambitious [æm'biʃəs], *a.* ambicioso.
amble [æmbl], *n.* portante, *m.*; paso de ambladura.—*v.i.* amblar.
ambrosia [æm'brouzjə], *n.* ambrosia.
ambulance ['æmbjuləns], *n.* ambulancia.
ambush ['æmbuʃ], *n.* emboscada.—*v.t.* emboscar, asechar.
ameliorate [ə'mi:ljəreit], *v.t., v.i.* mejorar.
amen ['ɑ:'men,'ei'men], *n., interj.* amén, *m.*
amenable [ə'mi:nəbl], *a.* tratable, dócil.
amend [ə'mend], *v.t.* enmendar; ***to make amends for,*** indemnizar; enmendar.
amendment [ə'mendmənt], *n.* enmienda.
amenity [ə'mi:niti], *n.* amenidad; comodidad, *f.*
America [ə'merikə], *n.* América; Estados Unidos, *m.pl.*
American [ə'merikən], *a., n.* americano; norteamericano, estadounidense, *m.f.*; ***— plan,*** (*U.S.*) pensión completa.
Americanize [ə'merikənaiz], *v.t.* americanizar.
amethyst ['æmiθist], *n.* amatista.
amiable ['eimjəbl], *a.* amigable, amistoso.
amicable ['æmikəbl], *a.* amigable.
amid(st) [ə'mid(st)], *prep.* en medio de.
amiss [ə'mis], *a.* errado, malo.—*adv.* mal, erradamente; ***to take —,*** tomar en mala parte.
amity ['æmiti], *n.* bienquerencia.
ammonia [ə'mounjə], *n.* amoníaco, *m.*
ammunition [æmju'niʃən], *n.* municiones, *f.pl.*
amnesty ['æmnisti], *n.* amnistía.—*v.t.* amnistiar.
amok [AMUCK].
among(st) [ə'mʌŋ(st)], *prep.* entre, en medio de.
amoral [æ'mɔrəl], *a.* amoral.
amorous ['æmərəs], *a.* amoroso.
amount [ə'maunt], *n.* importe, *m.*, cantidad, *f.*—*v.i.* ascender, subir a; ***to — to,*** significar.
amour [ə'muə], *n.* amorio.
amour-propre [ə'muə'prɔpr], *n.* amor propio.
ampere ['æmpɛə], *n.* amperio.
ampersand ['æmpəsænd], *n.* el signo *&*.
amphibian [æm'fibiən], *a., n.* anfibio.
amphibious [æm'fibiəs], *a.* anfibio.
amphitheatre ['æmfiθiətə], *n.* (*U.S.* **amphitheater**) anfiteatro.
amplifier ['æmplifaiə], *n.* amplificador, *m.*
amplify ['æmplifai], *v.t.* amplificar, desarrollar.
amply ['æmpli], *adv.* ampliamente; bastante.
amputate ['æmpjuteit], *v.t.* amputar.
amputation [æmpju'teiʃən], *n.* amputación, *f.*
amuck [ə'mʌk], *adv.* furiosamente; ***to run —,*** correr lleno de furia homicida.
amulet ['æmjulet], *n.* amuleto.
amuse [ə'mju:z], *v.t.* divertir; entretener.
amusement [ə'mju:zmənt], *n.* diversión; recreación, *f.*
amusing [ə'mju:ziŋ], *a.* divertido.
an [æn, ən], *indef. art.* se emplea en lugar de **a** cuando la voz siguiente empieza con vocal o H muda.
anachronism [ə'nækrənizm], *n.* anacronismo.
anaemia [ə'ni:mjə], *n.* anemia.
anaemic [ə'ni:mik], *a.* anémico.
anaesthetic [ænis'θetik], *a., n.* anestético.
anagram ['ænəgræm], *n.* anagrama, *m.*
analogous [ə'næləgəs], *a.* análogo.
analogy [ə'nælədʒi], *n.* analogía.
analyse ['ænəlaiz], *v.t.* analizar.
analysis [ə'næləsis], *n.* analisis, *m.* o *f.*
analyst ['ænəlist], *n.* analista, *m.f.*
analytic(al) [ænə'litik(əl)], *a.* analítico.
anarchic(al) [æ'nɑ:kik(əl)], *a.* anárquico.
anarchist ['ænəkist], *n.* anarquista, *m.f.*
anarchy ['ænəki], *n.* anarquía.
anathema [ə'næθimə], *n.* anatema, *m.* o *f.*
anatomical [ænə'tɔmikəl], *a.* anatómico.
anatomist [ə'nætəmist], *n.* anatómico, anatomista, *m.f.*
anatomy [ə'nætəmi], *n.* anatomía.
ancestor ['ænsestə], *n.* antepasado, antecesor, *m.*
ancestral [æn'sestrəl], *a.* hereditario; solariego (casa).
ancestry ['ænsestri], *n.* prosapia; estirpe, *f.*; abolengo.
anchor ['æŋkə], *n.* ancla, áncora; ***at —,*** anclado.—*v.t.* poner al ancla; sujetar.—*v.i.* anclar.
anchorage ['æŋkəridʒ], *n.* anclaje, *m.*, fondeadero.
anchovy ['æntʃəvi], *n.* anchoa; boquerón, *m.*
ancient ['einʃənt], *a., n.* antiguo.
and [ænd, ənd], *conj.* y, e.

Andalusia [ændə'lu:zjə], *n.* Andalucía.
Andalusian [ændə'lu:zjən], *a., n.* andaluz, *m.*
Andrew ['ændru:], Andrés, *m.*
anecdote ['ænikdout], *n.* anecdota.
anemone [ə'neməni], *n.* anémona.
anew [ə'nju:], *adv.* de nuevo.
angel ['eindʒəl], *n.* ángel, *m.*
angelic [æn'dʒelik], *a.* angélico.
angelus ['ændʒiləs], *n.* ángelus, *m.*
anger ['æŋgə], *n.* ira, cólera, enojo.—*v.t.* enojar, encolerizar.
angle [æŋgl], *n.* ángulo.—*v.t.* inclinar.—*v.i.* pescar con caña (*for*).
angler ['æŋglə], *n.* pescador con caña.
Anglican ['æŋglikən], *a., n.* anglicano.
Anglicism ['æŋglisizm], *n.* anglicismo.
Anglicize ['æŋglisaiz], *v.t.* inglesar.
angling ['æŋgliŋ], *n.* pesca con caña.
Anglo-Saxon ['æŋglou'sæksən], *a., n.* anglosajón, *m.*
angry ['æŋgri], *a.* enojado, encolerizado, colérico; ***to get* —**, enfadarse, enojarse (***at***, de, ***with***, con).
anguish ['æŋgwiʃ], *n.* congoja, angustia.—*v.t.* acongojar.
angular ['æŋgjulə], *a.* angular; anguloso.
anil ['ænil], *n.* añil, *m.*
aniline ['ænili:n, 'ænilain], *n.* anilina.
animal ['æniməl], *a., n.* animal, *m.*
animate ['ænimit], *a.* animado, viviente.—['ænimeit], *v.t.* animar, vivificar.
animation [æni'meiʃən], *n.* animación, *f.*
animosity [æni'mɔsiti], *n.* animosidad, *f.*
anise ['ænis], *n.* anís, *m.*
aniseed ['ænisi:d], *n.* grano de anís.
anisette [æni'zet], *n.* licor (*m.*) de anís.
ankle [æŋkl], *n.* tobillo.
anklet ['æŋklit], *n.* ajorca.
annals ['ænəlz], *n.pl.* anales, *m.pl.*
anneal [ə'ni:l], *v.t.* recocer, templar.
annexe ['æneks], *n.* anexo, anejo; dependencia.—[ə'neks], *v.t.* anexar, anexionar.
annexation [ænek'seiʃən], *n.* anexión, *f.*
annihilate [ə'naiəleit], *v.t.* aniquilar.
annihilation [ənaiə'leiʃən], *n.* aniquilación, *f.*
anniversary [æni'və:səri], *a., n.* aniversario.
anno Domini ['ænou'dɔminai] (*abbrev.* A.D.) *n.* año de Cristo.
annotate ['ænouteit], *v.t.* anotar, glosar.
announce [ə'nauns], *v.t.* anunciar.
announcement [ə'naunsmənt], *n.* aviso, anuncio.
announcer [ə'naunsə], *n.* anunciador; (*rad.*) locutor, *m.*
annoy [ə'nɔi], *v.t.* molestar, enfadar.
annoyance [ə'nɔiəns], *n.* molestia; enfado.
annoying [ə'nɔiiŋ], *a.* molesto.
annual ['ænjuəl], *a.* anual.—*n.* anuario.
annuity [ə'nju:iti], *n.* renta vitalicia, anualidad, *f.*
annul [ə'nʌl], *v.t.* anular, invalidar.
annulment [ə'nʌlmənt], *n.* anulación; revocación, *f.*
annunciation [ənʌnsi'eiʃən], *n.* anunciación, *f.*
anode ['ænoud], *n.* (*elec.*) ánodo.
anoint [ə'nɔint], *v.t.* ungir, untar.
anomalous [ə'nɔmələs], *a.* anómalo.
anomaly [ə'nɔməli], *n.* anomalía.
anon [ə'nɔn], *adv.* (*obs.*) luego, presto.
anonymity [æno'nimiti], *n.* anonimidad, *f.*, anónimo.
anonymous [ə'nɔniməs], *a.* anónimo.
another [ə'nʌðə], *pron.* otro, uno más; ***one* —**, uno(s) a otro(s).—*a.* otro.
answer ['ɑ:nsə], *n.* respuesta, contestación, *f.*—*v.t.* contestar a; resolver (*problemas*); convenir a (*fin*); responder (***for***, de).
answerable ['a:nsərəbl], *a.* contestable; responsable; determinable.
ant [ænt], *n.* hormiga.
antagonism [æn'tægənizm], *n.* antagonismo.
antagonist [æn'tægənist], *n.* antagonista, *m.f.*
antagonistic, [æntægə'nistik], *a.* antagónico.
antagonize [æn'tægənaiz], *v.t.* enemistar; oponerse a.
Antarctic [ænt'ɑ:ktik], *a.* antárctico.—*n.* Antárctica, *f.*
ante- [ænti-], *prefix.* ante-.
antecedent [ænti'si:dənt], *a., n.* antecedente precedente, *m.f.*
antechamber ['æntitʃeimbə], *n.* antecámara.
antedate ['æntideit], *v.t.* antedatar; preceder.
antediluvian [æntidi'lu:vjən], *a.* antediluviano.
antelope ['æntiloup], *n.* antílope, *m.*
antenatal ['æntineitl], *a.* antenatal.
antenna [æn'tenə], *n.* (*pl.* **-nae, -nas**) antena.
antepenultimate [æntipen'ʌltimit], *a., n.* antepenúltimo.
anterior [æn'tiəriə], *a.* anterior.
anteroom ['æntirum], *n.* antecámara.
anthem ['ænθəm], *n.* himno; (*eccl.*) antifona, *f.*, motete, *m.*
anthill ['ænthil], *n.* hormiguero.
anthology [æn'θɔlədʒi], *n.* antología.
anthracite ['ænθrəsait], *n.* antracita.
anthrax ['ænθræks], *n.* ántrax, *m.*
anthropoid ['ænθrəpɔid], *a., n.* antropoide, *m.*
anthropologist [ænθrə'pɔlədʒist], *n.* antropólogo.
anthropology [ænθrə'pɔlədʒi], *n.* antropologia.
anti- ['ænti], *prefix.* anti-, contra.
anti-aircraft [ænti'ɛəkrɑ:ft], *a.* antiaéreo.
antibody ['æntibɔdi], *n.* anticuerpo.
antics ['æntiks], *n. pl.* cabriola, travesura.
Antichrist ['æntikraist], *n.* Anticristo.
anticipate [æn'tisipeit], *v.t.* prever; esperar. prometerse; anticipar(se a).
anticipation [æntisi'peiʃən], *n.* expectación, *f.*; anticipación, *f.*
antidote ['æntidout], *n.* antídoto, contraveneno.
antifreeze ['æntifri:z], *n.* anticongelante, *m.*
Antilles [æn'tili:z], *n.pl.* Antillas, *f.pl.*
antimony ['æntiməni], *n.* antimonio.
antinomy ['æntinəmi], *n.* antinomia.
antipathy [æn'tipəθi], *n.* antipatía; aversión, *f.*
antipodes [æn'tipədi:z], *n.pl.* antípoda, *m.sg.*
antipope ['æntipoup], *n.* antipapa, *m.*
antiquarian [ænti'kwɛəriən], *a. n.* anticuario.
antiquated ['æntikweitid], *a.* anticuado; arcaizante.
antique [æn'ti:k], *a.* antiguo.—*n.* antigualla; ***— dealer***, anticuario.
antiquity [æn'tikwiti], *n.* antigüedad, *f.*
anti-Semitism [ænti'semitizm], *n.* antisemitismo.
antiseptic [ænti'septik], *a., n.* antiséptico.

antisocial [ænti'souʃəl], *a.* antisocial.
antitank [ænti'tæŋk], *a.* antitanque, contracarro.
antithesis [æn'tiθisis], *n.* antítesis, *f.*
antlers ['æntləz], *n. pl.* cornamenta.
Antwerp ['æntwə:p], *n.* Amberes, *f.sg.*
anvil ['ænvil], *n.* yunque, *m.*
anxiety [æŋ'zaiəti], *n.* inquietud, ansiedad, *f.*
anxious ['æŋkʃəs], *a.* inquieto, ansioso.
any ['eni], *a.* cualquier; todo; alguno; ***not — more,*** no . . . más; ya no.
anybody ['enibɔdi], *pron.* alguien, alguno; cualquiera, cualquier persona; todo el mundo; ***not —,*** nadie.
anyhow ['enihau], *adv.* de cualquier modo; como quiera que sea; de todos modos; con todo.
anyone ['eniwʌn] [ANYBODY].
anyplace ['enipleis] (*U.S.*) [ANYWHERE].
anything ['eniθiŋ], *pron.* cualquier cosa; todo lo que; ***not —,*** nada.
anyway ['eniwei] [ANYHOW].
anywhere ['eni(h)wεə], *adv.* dondequiera; en *o* a cualquier parte; ***not —,*** en *o* a ninguna parte.
apace [ə'peis], *adv.*, (*poet.*, *obs.*) aína, presto.
Apache [ə'pætʃi], **apache** [ə'pɑ:ʃ], *n.* apache *m.*
apart [ə'pɑ:t], *adv.* aparte; roto; ***— from,*** aparte de; separado de; ***to take —,*** desmontar, desarmar; ***to tear —,*** despedazar; ***to come —,*** deshacerse, romperse.
apartheid [ə'pɑ:teit, ə'pɑ:taid], *n.* apartheid, *m.*
apartment [ə'pɑ:tmənt], *n.* aposento; (*U.S.*) piso.—*pl.* estancia.
apathetic [æpə'θetik], *a.* apático.
apathy ['æpəθi], *n.* apatía.
ape [eip], *n.* mono, simio.—*v.t.* remedar.
aperient [ə'piəriənt], *a.*, *n.* laxante, *m.*
aperitive [ə'peritiv], *n.* aperitivo.
aperture ['æpətjuə], *n.* abertura; boquete, *m.*; resquicio.
apex ['eipeks], *n.* (*pl.* **apices, apexes**) ápice, *m.*
aphorism ['æfərism], *n.* aforismo.
apiary ['eipjəri], *n.* colmenar, *m.*
apiece [ə'pi:s], *adv.* cada uno; por cabeza.
apish ['eipiʃ], *a.* monesco; fatuo.
aplomb [ə'plɔm], *n.* aplomo, serenidad, *f.*
apocalypse [ə'pɔkəlips], *n.* apocalipsis, *m.*; revelación, *f.*
apocope [ə'pɔkəpi], *n.* apócope, *f.*
apocrypha [ə'pɔkrifə], *n.* libros apócrifos, *m.pl.*
apocryphal [ə'pɔkrifəl], *a.* apócrifo.
apogee ['æpɔdʒi:], *n.* apogeo.
Apollo [ə'pɔlou], *n.* Apolo.
apologetic [əpɔlə'dʒetik], *a.* que pide perdón, arrepentido; apologético.
apologize [ə'pɔlədʒaiz], *v.i.* disculparse (***to,*** con, ***for,*** de).
apology [ə'pɔlədʒi], *n.* excusa, disculpa; apología.
apoplexy ['æpəpleksi], *n.* apoplejía.
apostasy [ə'pɔstəsi], *n.* apostasía.
apostate [ə'pɔstət], *n.* apóstata, *m.f.*, renegado.
apostle [ə'pɔsl], *n.* apóstol, *m.*
apostolic [æpəs'tɔlik], *a.* apostólico.
apostrophe [ə'pɔstrəfi], *n.* (*gram.*) apostrofo ('), apóstrofe, *m.* o *f.*
apothecary [ə'pɔθikəri], *n.* boticario; ***apothecary shop,*** botica.
apotheosis [əpɔθi'ousis], *n.* apoteosis, *f.*
appal [ə'pɔ:l], *v.t.* amendrentar, espantar; arredrar.
appalling [ə'pɔ:liŋ], *a.* espantoso; desconcertante.
apparatus [æpə'reitəs], *n.* aparato.
apparel [ə'pærəl], *n.* (*poet.*, *obs.*) vestidura.
apparent [ə'pærənt], *a.* aparente; evidente, manifiesto.
apparently [ə'pærəntli], *adv.* según parece, por lo visto.
apparition [æpə'riʃən], *n.* aparición, *f.*
appeal [ə'pi:l], *n.* súplica; atracción, *f.*; (*jur.*) apelación, *f.*—*v.i.* suplicar (***to***); atraer (***to***); (*jur.*) apelar.
appealing [ə'pi:liŋ], *a.* suplicante; atractivo.
appear [ə'piə], *v.i.* aparecer; parecer (*impers.*); (*jur.*) comparecer.
appearance [ə'piərəns], *n.* apariencia, aspecto; aparecimiento; (*jur.*) comparecencia.
appease [ə'pi:z], *v.t.* aplacar, apaciguar.
appeasement [ə'pi:zmənt], *n.* aplacamiento, apaciguamiento.
appellant [ə'pelənt], *n.* apelante, *m.f.*
appellation [æpə'leiʃən], *n.* estilo, título, trato.
append [ə'pend], *v.t.* añadir, anexar.
appendage [ə'pendidʒ], *n.* apéndice, *m.*
appendicitis [əpendi'saitis], *n.* apendicitis, *f.*
appendix [ə'pendiks], *n.* (*pl.* **-dices**) apéndice, *m.*
appertain [æpə'tein], *v.i.* atañer, relacionarse con (***to***).
appetite ['æpitait], *n.* apetito.
appetizer ['æpitaizə], *n.* aperitivo, apetite, *m.*
appetizing ['æpitaiziŋ], *a.* apetitoso, tentador.
applaud [ə'plɔ:d], *v.t.*, *v.i.* aplaudir.
applause [ə'plɔ:z], *n.* aplauso(s).
apple [æpl], *n.* manzana; ***— of his eye,*** niña de su ojo; ***in apple-pie order,*** bien regladito.
apple-tree ['æpl'tri:], *n.* manzano.
appliance [ə'plaiəns], *n.* dispositivo, mecanismo; utensilio; aplicación, *f.*
applicable ['æplikəbl, ə'plikəbl], *a.* aplicable.
applicant ['æplikənt], *n.* solicitante, candidato, *m.*
application [æpli'keiʃən], *n.* solicitud, *f.*, candidatura; aplicación, *f.*
apply [ə'plai], *v.t.* aplicar.—*v.i.* aplicarse (***to,*** a); dirigirse; solicitar (***for***).
appoint [ə'pɔint], *v.t.* nombrar, señalar, elegir; establecer; surtir.
appointment [ə'pɔintmənt], *n.* puesto, empleo; nombramiento; cita, compromiso.
apportion [ə'pɔ:ʃən], *v.t.* repartir, prorratear.
apposite ['æpəzit], *a.* conveniente, oportuno.
apposition [æpə'ziʃən], *n.* aposición, *f.*
appraisal [ə'preizəl], *n.* apreciación; valuación, *f.*
appraise [ə'preiz], *v.t.* valorizar, tasar.
appreciable [ə'pri:ʃjəbl], *a.* sensible; apreciable.
appreciate [ə'pri:ʃieit], *v.t.* apreciar; valorizar.—*v.i.* subir en valor.
appreciation [əpri:ʃi'eiʃən], *n.* tasa, valuación, *f.*; aprecio; aumento de precio *o* valor.

appreciative [ə'pri:ʃjətiv], *a.* apreciativo; reconocido.
apprehend [æpri'hend], *v.t.* aprehender; recelar; comprender.
apprehension [æpri'henʃən], *n.* aprehensión, *f.*, captura; aprensión, *f.*, recelo.
apprehensive [æpri'hensiv], *a.* aprensivo, remirado.
apprentice [ə'prentis], *n.* aprendiz, *m.*—*v.t.* poner de aprendiz (*to*, a).
apprenticeship [ə'prentisʃip], *n.* aprendizaje, *m.*
apprise [ə'praiz], *v.t.* informar.
approach [ə'proutʃ], *n.* acercamiento; acceso, entrada; propuesta.—*pl.* (*mil.*) aproches, *m.pl.*—*v.t.* acercarse a; acercar, arrimar; parecerse a.—*v.i.* acercarse, aproximarse.
approachable [ə'proutʃəbl], *a.* abordable, accessible, tratable.
approbation [æprə'beiʃən], *n.* anuencia; aprobación, *f.*
appropriate [ə'prouprieit], *a.* apropiado.—*v.t.* apropiarse; asignar.
approval [ə'pru:vəl], *n.* aprobación, *f.*; ***on* —,** a prueba.
approve [ə'pru:v], *v.t.* aprobar (***of***).
approximate [ə'prɔksimət], *a.* aproximado.—*v.t.* [ə'prɔksimeit] aproximar.—*v.i.* aproximarse (*to*, a).
approximation [əprɔksi'meiʃən], *n.* aproximación, *f.*
appurtenance [ə'pə:tinəns], *n.* pertenencia.
apricot ['eiprikɔt], *n.* albaricoque, *m.*
apricot-tree ['eiprikɔt'tri:], *n.* albaricoquero.
April ['eipril], *n.* abril, *m.*; **— *fool's day,*** el 1° de abril.
apron ['eiprən], *n.* delantal, *m.*; mandil (*blusa*), *m.*; (*arch.*) batiente, *m.* antepecho.
apropos ['æprəpou], *adv.* a propósito (***of***, de).
apse [æps], *n.* ábside, *m.*
apt [æpt], *a.* apto; propenso; capaz.
aptitude ['æptitju:d], *n.* aptitud, *f.*
aptness ['æptnis], *n.* aptitud, *f.*; conveniencia.
aquamarine [ækwəmə'ri:n], *n.* aguamarina.
aquarium [ə'kwɛəriəm], *n.* (*pl.* **-riums, -ria**) acuario.
aquatic [ə'kwætik], *a.* acuático.
aquatint ['ækwətint], *n.* acuatinta.
aqueduct ['ækwidʌkt], *n.* acueducto.
aqueous ['eikwiəs], *a.* ácueo, acuoso.
aquiline ['ækwilain], *a.* aguileño.
Aquinas [ə'kwainæs], *n.* Aquino.
Arab ['ærəb], *a.*, *n.* árabe.
arabesque [ærə'besk], *a.*, *n.* arabesco.
Arabian [ə'reibjən], *a.* árabe, arábigo.—*n.* árabe.
Arabic ['ærəbik], *a.*, *n.* árabe; arábigo.
arable ['ærəbl], *a.* de labrantío, arable.
Aragon ['ærəgən], *n.* Aragón, *m.*
Aragonese [ærəgə'ni:z], *a.*, *n.* aragonés.
arbiter ['ɑ:bitə], *n.* árbitro.
arbitrary ['ɑ:bitrəri], *a.* arbitrario.
arbitrate ['ɑ:bitreit], *v.t.*, *v.i.* arbitrar.
arbitration [ɑ:bi'treiʃən], *n.* arbitraje, *m.*
arbitrator ['ɑ:bitreitə], *n.* árbitro, componedor, *m.*
arbour ['ɑ:bə], *n.* emparrado, glorieta, cenador, *m.*
arbutus [ɑ:'bju:təs], *n.* (*bot.*) madroño.
arc [ɑ:k], *n.* arco.
arcade [ɑ:'keid], *n.* arcada; pasaje, *m.*, galería.
Arcadian [ɑ:'keidjən], *a.*, *n.* árcade, arcadio.
arcane [ɑ:'kein], *a.* arcano.
arcanum [ɑ:'keinəm], *n.* arcano.
arch [ɑ:tʃ], *a.* insigne; socarrón.—*n.* arco.—*v.t.* arquear, combar.—*prefix.* principal.
archaeological [ɑ:kiə'lɔdʒikəl], *a.* arqueológico.
archaeologist [ɑ:ki'ɔlədʒist], *n.* arqueólogo.
archaeology [ɑ:ki'ɔlədʒi], *n.* arqueología.
archaic [ɑ:'keiik], *a.* arcaico, arcaizante.
archaism ['ɑ:keiizm], *n.* arcaísmo.
archangel ['ɑ:keindʒəl], *n.* arcángel, *m.*
archbishop [ɑ:tʃ'biʃəp], *n.* arzobispo.
archdeacon [ɑ:tʃ'di:kən], *n.* arcediano.
archduke [ɑ:tʃ'dju:k], *n.* archiduque, *m.*
archer ['ɑ:tʃə], *n.* arquero, saetero; ballestero.
archery ['ɑ:tʃəri], *n.* tiro de arco; ballestería.
archetype ['ɑ:kitaip], *n.* arquetipo.
archipelago [ɑ:ki'peligou], *n.* archipiélago.
architect ['ɑ:kitekt], *n.* arquitecto.
architecture ['ɑ:kitektʃə], *n.* arquitectura.
archive ['ɑ:kaiv], *n.* archivo.
archway ['ɑ:tʃwei], *n.* arco (*de entrada*), portal, *m.*; arcada.
Arctic ['ɑ:ktik], *n.* el polo ártico; **arctic,** *a.* ártico.
ardent ['ɑ:dənt], *a.* férvido, fogoso.
ardour ['ɑ:də], *n.* fervor, ardor, *m.*, pasión, *f.*
arduous ['ɑ:djuəs], *a.* arduo, dificultoso.
are [ɑ:] [BE].
area ['ɛəriə], *n.* área, superficie; comarca; extensión, *f.*
arena [ə'ri:nə], *n.* arena, liza; ruedo.
aren't [ɑ:nt] [ARE NOT].
argent ['ɑ:dʒənt], *a.* (*poet.*) argento.—*n.* (*her.*) argén, *m.*
Argentina [ɑ:dʒən'ti:nə], *n.* Argentina.
Argentine ['ɑ:dʒəntain], *a.*, *n.* argentino. [ARGENTINA].
argon ['ɑ:gɔn], *n.* argo, argón, *m.*
argosy ['ɑ:gəsi], *n.* bajel rico; cosa de gran valor.
argot ['ɑ:gou], *n.* jerga; argot, *m.*
argue ['ɑ:gju], *v.t.* debatir; argumentar; argüir; disputar; probar.—*v.i.* disputar, discutir.
argument ['ɑ:gjumənt], *n.* argumento; disputa.
argumentative [ɑ:gju'mentətiv], *a.* argumentador; disputador.
aria ['ɑ:riə], *n.* (*mus.*) aria.
arid ['ærid], *a.* árido.
aridness ['æridnis], **aridity** [æ'riditi], *n.* aridez, *f.*
aright [ə'rait], *adv.* justamente, con acierto.
arise [ə'raiz], *v.i.* (*conjug.* like RISE) surgir, provenir; (*obs.*) levantarse.
aristocracy [æris'tɔkrəsi], *n.* aristocracia.
aristocrat ['æristəkræt], *n.* aristócrata, *m.f.*
aristocratic [æristə'krætik], *a.* aristocrático.
Aristotelian [ærisɔ'ti:ljən], *a.* aristotélico.
Aristotle ['æristɔtl], *n.* Aristóteles. *m.*
arithmetic [ə'riθmətik], *n.* aritmética.
ark [ɑ:k], *n.* arca.
arm [ɑ:m], *n.* brazo; (*mil.*) arma.—*v.t.* armar; blindar, acorazar.—*v.i.* armarse.
armament ['ɑ:məmənt], *n.* armamento; ***armaments race,*** carrera armamentista.
armature ['ɑ:mətjuə], *n.* armadura.
armchair [ɑ:m'tʃɛə], *n.* sillón, *m.*

armful ['ɑ:mful], *n.* brazado.
arm-in-arm ['ɑ:min'ɑ:m], *adv.* de bracero.
armistice ['ɑ:mistis], *n.* armisticio.
armless ['ɑ:mlis], *a.* sin brazos *o* armas.
armlet ['ɑ:mlit], *n.* brazal, *m.*
armorial [ɑ:'mɔ:riəl], *a.* héraldico.
armour ['ɑ:mə], *n.* armadura; blindaje, *m.*—*v.t.* blindar.
armourer ['ɑ:mərə], *n.* armero.
armour-plating [ɑ:mə'pleitiŋ], *n.* corazas, *f.pl.*; blindaje, *m.*
armoury ['ɑ:məri], *n.* armería; arsenal, *m.*
armpit ['ɑ:mpit], *n.* sobaco.
army ['ɑ:mi], *a.* castrense.—*n.* ejército.
aroma [ə'roumə], *n.* aroma, *m.*
aromatic [ærou'mætik], *a.* aromático.
around [ə'raund], *adv.* a la redonda; a la vuelta.—*prep.* a la vuelta de; hacia, cerca de; alrededor de. [ROUND].
arouse [ə'rauz], *v.t.* excitar, despertar.
arraign [ə'rein], *v.t.* acusar, denunciar.
arrange [ə'reindʒ], *v.t.* arreglar, ordenar; disponer; refundir.
arrangement [ə'reindʒmənt], *n.* arreglo, orden, *m.*; disposición, *f.*; medida.
arrant ['ærənt], *a.* consumado, de siete suelas.
array [ə'rei], *n.* haz, *m.*, orden (*m.*) de batalla; gala, atavío.—*v.t.* ataviar, engalanar.
arrears [ə'riəz], *n.pl.* atrasos, *m.pl.*
arrest [ə'rest], *n.* detención, *f.*, arresto.—*v.t.* detener, arrestar; impresionar.
arrival [ə'raivəl], *n.* llegada; llegado (*persona*).
arrive [ə'raiv], *v.i.* llegar (***at***, a).
arrogance ['ærəgəns], *n.* arrogancia, altanería.
arrogant ['ærəgənt], *a.* arrogante, altanero.
arrow ['ærou], *n.* flecha, saeta.
arrow-head ['ærouhed], *n.* punta de flecha.
arrow-root ['ærouru:t], *n.* arrurruz, *m.*
arsenal ['ɑ:sinl], *n.* arsenal, *m.*
arsenic ['ɑ:sənik], *a.*, *n.* arsénico.
arson [ɑ:sn], *n.* incendiarismo, delito de incendio.
art (1) [ɑ:t], *n.* arte, *usually f.*
art (2) [ɑ:t], *v.i.*(*obs.*) eres [BE].
arterial [ɑ:'tiəriəl], *a.*, *n.* arterial.
artery ['ɑ:təri], *n.* arteria.
artesian [ɑ:'ti:zjən], *a.* artesiano.
artful ['ɑ:tful], *a.* artero, mañoso.
Arthur ['ɑ:θə], *n.* Arturo, (*obs.*) Artús. *m.*
Arthurian [ɑ:'θjuəriən], *a.* artúrico, de Artús.
artichoke ['ɑ:titʃouk], *n.* alcachofa.
article ['ɑ:tikl], *n.* artículo.
articulate [ɑ:'tikjulit], *a.* articulado; claro, distinto; que sabe hablar.—[ɑ:'tikjuleit], *v.t.* articular.
artifact ['ɑ:rtifækt], *n.* artefacto.
artifice ['ɑ:tifis], *n.* artificio.
artificial [ɑ:ti'fiʃəl], *a.* artificial.
artificiality [ɑ:tifiʃi'æliti], *n.* cosa *o* carácter (*m.*) artificial.
artillery [ɑ:'tiləri], *n.* artillería.
artisan ['ɑ:tizæn], *n.* artesano.
artist ['ɑ:tist], *n.* artista, *m.f.*
artiste [ɑ:'ti:st], *n.* (*theat.*) artista, *m.f.*
artistic [ɑ:'tistik], *a.* artístico.
artistry ['ɑ:tistri], *n.* destreza, maestría; arte, *m.* o *f.*
artless ['ɑ:tləs], *a.* sin arte, chabacano; sincero, sencillo.
Aryan ['ɛəriən], *a.*, *n.* ario.
as [æz, əz], *adv.* tan.—*prep.* como; por.—*conj.* como; ya que; según; a medida que; ***as . . . as,*** tan . . . como; — ***if to,*** como para; — ***for,*** — ***to,*** en cuanto a; — ***well,*** también; — ***well*** —, además de, así como; — ***yet,*** hasta ahora; ***the same*** —, el mismo que.
asbestos [æz'bestɔs], *n.* asbesto.
ascend [ə'send], *v.t.*, *v.i.* ascender, subir.
ascendency [ə'sendənsi], *n.* ascendiente, *m.*; dominio.
ascendent [ə'sendənt], *a.* ascendente.—*n.* ascendiente, *m.*; ***in the*** —, predominante; ganando poder.
Ascension [ə'senʃən], *n.* (*eccl.*) Ascensión, *f.*
ascent [ə'sent], *n.* subida; ascenso.
ascertain [æsə'tein], *v.t.* averiguar.
ascetic [ə'setik], *a.* ascético.—*n.* asceta, *m.f.*
asceticism [ə'setisizm], *n.* ascetismo.
ascribe [əs'kraib], *v.t.* atributir, achacar.
ash (1) [æʃ], *n.* ceniza; ***Ash Wednesday,*** *n.* miércoles de ceniza.
ash (2) [æʃ], *n.* (*bot.*) fresno.
ashamed [ə'ʃeimd], *a.* avergonzado; ***to be*** — (***of***), tener vergüenza (de); avergonzarse (de, por).
ashen [æʃn], *a.* ceniciento; pálido; de fresno.
ashore [ə'ʃɔ:], *adv.* a *o* en tierra; ***to go*** —, desembarcar.
ashtray ['æʃtrei], *n.* cenicero.
ashy ['æʃi], *a.* cenizoso.
Asia ['eiʃə], *n.* Asia.
Asian ['eiʃən], **Asiatic** [eiʃi'ætik], *a.*, *n.* asiático.
aside [ə'said], *n.* aparte, *m.*—*adv.* aparte, a un lado; además (***from,*** de).
asinine ['æsinain], *a.* necio, burro.
ask [ɑ:sk], *v.t.* pedir; preguntar; invitar; ***to — for,*** pedir; ***to — in,*** rogar que entre (*alguien*).
askance [əs'kæns], *adv.* de soslayo; de reojo.
askew [əs'kju:], *a.* de través; al sesgo.
asking ['ɑ:skiŋ], *n.* petición, *f.*; (*eccl.*) amonestación, *f.*; ***for the*** —, con sólo pedirlo.
asleep [ə'sli:p], *a.* dormido; ***to fall*** —, dormirse.
asp [æsp], *n.* áspid, *m.*
asparagus [əs'pærəgəs], *n.* espárrago(s).
aspect ['æspekt], *n.* aspecto.
asperity [æs'periti], *n.* aspereza.
aspersion [əs'pə:ʃən], *n.* calumnia; aspersión, *f.*
asphalt ['æsfælt], *n.* asfalto.—*v.t.*, *v.i.* asfaltar.
asphyxiate [æs'fiksieit], *v.t.* asfixiar.
aspic ['æspik], *n.* áspid, *m.*; jalea de carne *etc.*
aspidistra [æspi'distrə], *n.* aspidistra.
aspirate ['æspəreit], *a.* aspirado.—*v.t.* aspirar.
aspiration [æspə'reiʃən], *n.* aspiración, *f.*
aspire [əs'paiə], *v.i.* aspirar (***to***, a).
aspirin ['æspərin], *n.* aspirina.
ass [æs], *n.* asno.
assail [ə'seil], *v.t.* agredir.
assailant [ə'seilənt], *n.* agresor, asaltador, *m.*
assassin [ə'sæsin], *n.* asesino.
assassinate [ə'sæsineit], *v.t.* asesinar.
assassination [əsæsi'neiʃən], *n.* asesinato.
assault [ə'sɔ:lt], *n.* asalto.—*v.t.* asaltar.
assay [ə'sei], *n.* ensaye, *m.*—*v.t.* ensayar; aquilatar.

assemble [ə'sembl], *v.t.* reunir; (*mech.*) montar.—*v.i.* reunirse.
assembly [ə'sembli], *n.* asamblea; (*mech.*) montaje, *m.*; — ***hall,*** salón (*m*). de sesiones.
assent [ə'sent], *n.* asentimiento, asenso.—*v.i.* asentir (*to*, a).
assert [ə'sə:t], *v.t.* afirmar, hacer valer, aseverar.—*v.r.* imponerse, sostener su dignidad *o* sus derechos.
assertion [ə'sə:ʃən], *n.* afirmación, *f.*, aserto.
assertive [ə'sə:tiv], *a.* asertivo; agresivo.
assess [ə'ses], *v.t.* tasar, fijar; amillarar.
assessment [ə'sesmənt], *n.* prorrateo; fijación, *f.*; tasa.
assessor [ə'sesə], *n.* tasador, *m.*
asset ['æset], *n.* ventaja.—*pl.* (*com.*) activo; bienes, *m.pl.*; haber, *m.*
assiduous [ə'sidjuəs], *a.* asiduo.
assign [ə'sain], *v.t.* asignar; ceder.
assignation [æsig'neiʃən], *n.* asignación, *f.*; cita, compromiso.
assignment [ə'sainmənt], *n.* asignación, cesión, *f.*; tarea.
assimilate [ə'simileit], *v.t.* asimilar(se).
Assisi [ə'si:zi], *n.* Asís, *m.*
assist [ə'sist], *v.t.* asistir, auxiliar.
assistance [ə'sistəns], *n.* ayuda, asistencia.
assistant [ə'sistənt], *n.* ayudante; empleado, dependiente (*tiendas*), *m.f.*
assizes [ə'saiziz], *n.pl.* alto tribunal inglés que suele reunirse dos veces al año en cada condado.
associate [ə'souʃieit], *a.*, *n.* asociado, adjunto.—*v.t.* asociar.—*v.i.* asociarse (***with,*** con).
association [əsousi'eiʃən], *n.* asociación, *f.*
assonance ['æsənəns], *n.* asonancia; asonante, *m.*
assorted [ə'sɔ:tid], *a.* surtido, variado; seleccionado.
assortment [ə'sɔ:tmənt], *n.* surtido; selección variada.
assuage [ə'sweidʒ], *v.t.* suavizar, templar.
assume [ə'sju:m], *v.t.* asumir; arrogarse; suponer, presumir.
assumed [ə'sju:md], *a.* supuesto; fingido, falso.
Assumption [ə'sʌmpʃən], *n.* (*eccl.*) Asunción, *f.*
assumption [ə'sʌmpʃən], *n.* arrogación; adopción; suposición, *f.*
assurance [ə'ʃuərəns], *n.* aseguramiento; confianza, intrepidez, *f.*; (*com.*) seguro.
assure [ə'ʃuə], *v.t.* asegurar.
assured [ə'ʃuəd], *a.* confiado; descarado.
aster ['æstə], *n.* (*bot.*) áster, *m.*
asterisk ['æstərisk], *n.* asterisco (*).
astern [əs'tə:n], *adv.* a *o* en popa.
asteroid ['æstərɔid], *a.*, *n.* asteroide, *m.*
asthma ['æsθmə], *n.* asma.
asthmatic [æs'θmætik], *a.*, *n.* asmático.
astir [ə'stə:], *a.*, *adv.* en movimiento, activo.
astonish [əs'tɔniʃ], *v.t.* pasmar, asombrar.
astonishing [əs'tɔniʃiŋ], *a.* asombroso.
astonishment [əs'tɔniʃmənt], *n.* asombro.
astound [əs'taund], *v.t.* asombrar, aturdir.
astounding [əs'taundiŋ], *a.* pasmoso.
astral ['æstrəl], *a.* astral, sidereal.
astray [əs'trei], *a.*, *adv.* depistado, errado de camino; ***to lead* —,** extraviar.
astride [əs'traid], *adv.* a horcajadas.—*prep.* a horcajadas en.
astringent [əs'trindʒənt], *a.*, *n.* astringente *m.*
astrologer [əs'trɔlədʒə], *n.* astrólogo.
astrology [əs'trɔlədʒi], *n.* astrología.
astronaut ['æstrənɔ:t], *n.* astronauta, *m.*
astronautics [æstrə'nɔ:tiks], *n.* astronáutica.
astronomer [əs'trɔnəmə], *n.* astrónomo.
astronomic(al) [æstrə'nɔmik(əl)], *a.* astronómico.
astronomy [əs'trɔnəmi], *n.* astronomía.
astrophysics [æstrou'fiziks], *n.* astrofísica.
astute [əs'tju:t], *a.* astuto, agudo.
astuteness [əs'tju:tnis], *n.* astucia, sagacidad, *f.*
asunder [ə'sʌndə], *adv.* en dos, en pedazos.
asylum [ə'sailəm], *n.* asilo; ***lunatic* —,** manicomio.
at [æt], *prep.* a, en; **— *X's,*** en casa de **X.**
atavism ['ætəvizm], *n.* atavismo.
ate [et] [EAT].
atheism ['eiθiizm], *n.* ateísmo.
atheist ['eiθiist], *a.*, *n* ateo.
atheistic [eiθi'istik], *a.* ateo.
Athens ['æθinz], *n.* Atenas. *f.sg.*
athlete ['æθli:t], *n.* atleta, *m.f.*
athletic [æθ'letik], *a.* atlético. — ***n.pl.*** atletismo; atlética.
at-home [ət'houm], *n.* recepción, *f.*, guateque, *m.*
Atlantic [ət'læntik], *a.*, *n.* Atlántico.
Atlas ['ætləs], *n.* Atlante, Atlas *m.*; **atlas,** *n.* atlas, *m.*
atmosphere ['ætməsfiə], *n.* atmósfera.
atmospheric [ætməs'ferik], *a.* atmosférico.—*n.pl.* perturbaciones atmosféricas, *f.pl.*
atoll ['ætɔl], *n.* atolón, *m.*
atom ['ætəm], *n.* átomo; — ***bomb,*** bomba atómica.
atomic [ə'tɔmik], *a.* atómico.
atomize ['ætəmaiz], *v.t.* atomizar.
atone [ə'toun], *v.i.* expiar (***for***).
atonement [ə'tounmənt], *n.* expiación; (*eccl.*) redención, *f.*
atrocious [ə'trouʃəs], *a.* atroz.
atrocity [ə'trɔsiti], *n.* atrocidad, *f.*
atrophy ['ætrəfi], *v.t.* atrofiar.—*v.i.* -se.
attach [ə'tætʃ], *v.t.* ligar, pegar, juntar; dar, conceder (*importancia*); (*jur.*) embargar; ***to be attached to,*** tener cariño a.
attaché [ə'tæʃei], *n.* agregado.
attachment [ə'tætʃmənt], *n.* accesorio; unión, *f.*; apego; (*jur.*) embargo.
attack [ə'tæk], *n.* ataque, *m.*—*v.t.*, *v.i.* atacar.
attacker [ə'tækə], *n.* agresor, *m.*
attain [ə'tein], *v.t.* lograr, alcanzar, merecer.
attainment [ə'teinmənt], *n.* consecución, *f.*—*pl.* dotes, *f.pl.*, talento.
attar ['ætə], *n.* esencia fragrante.
attempt [ə'tempt], *n.* tentativa; conato.—*v.t.* intentar.
attend [ə'tend], *v.t.* asistir a; atender; auxiliar; ***to — to,*** atender a.
attendance [ə'tendəns], *n.* asistencia, concurrencia; ***to dance — on,*** bailar el agua delante a.
attendant [ə'tendənt], *a.* concomitante.—*n.* encargado.
attention [ə'tenʃən], *n.* atención, *f.*; ***to call — to,*** hacer presente, destacar.
attentive [ə'tentiv], *a.* atento.
attenuate [ə'tenjueit], *v.t.* atenuar.

attest [ə'test], *v.t.* atestiguar, deponer; ***to — to,*** dar fe de.
attestation [ætes'teiʃən], *n.* atestación, *f.*
attic ['ætik], *n.* desván, *m.*, buharda.
attire [ə'taiə], *n.* atavío, ropaje, *m.—v.t.* ataviar, engalanar.
attitude ['ætitju:d], *n.* actitud, *f.*; ademán, *m.*, postura.
attitudinize [æti'tju:dinaiz], *v.i.* fachendear.
attorney [ə'tə:ni], *n.* procurador, *m.*, apoderado; (*U.S.*) abogado.
attract [ə'trækt], *v.t.* atraer; llamar (*atención*).
attraction [ə'trækʃən], *n.* atracción, *f.*; atractivo, aliciente, *m.*
attractive [ə'træktiv], *a.* atractivo, llamativo.
attribute ['ætribju:t], *n.* atributo.—[ə'tribjut], *v.t.* atribuir.
attribution [ætri'bju:ʃən], *n.* atribución, *f.*
attrition [ə'triʃən], *n.* atrición, *f.*; agotamiento, degaste, *m.*
attune [ə'tju:n], *v.t.* afinar, acordar.
auburn ['ɔ:bən], *a.* castaño, rojizo.
auction ['ɔ:kʃən], *n.* subasta.—*v.t.* subastar.
audacious [ɔ:'deiʃəs], *a.* audaz.
audacity [ɔ:'dæsiti], *n.* audacia.
audible ['ɔ:dibl], *a.* oíble, audible.
audience ['ɔ:diəns], *n.* público, auditorio; audiencia.
audio-visual ['ɔ:diouviʒuəl], *a.* audiovisual.
audit ['ɔ:dit], *n.* intervención, *f.—v.t.* intervenir.
audition [ɔ:'diʃən], *n.* audición, *f.*
auditor ['ɔ:ditə], *n.* interventor, *m.*
auditorium [ɔ:di'tɔ:riəm], *n.* (*pl.* **-ums, -ria**) auditorio; paraninfo.
auger ['ɔ:gə], *n.* barrena.
aught [ɔ:t], *pron.* (*obs.*) algo; nada.
augment [ɔ:g'ment], *v.t., v.i.* aumentar.—*v.i.* aumentarse.
augur ['ɔ:gə], *n.* agorero.—*v.t.* augurar, agorar.
augury ['ɔ:gjuri], *n.* augurio.
August ['ɔ:gəst], *n.* agosto.
august [ɔ:'gʌst], *a.* augusto.
Augustine [ɔ:'gʌstin], **Augustinian** [ɔ:gəs'tiniən], *a., n.* Agustín, agustino.
auk [ɔ:k], *n.* (*orn.*) alca.
aunt [ɑ:nt], *n.* tía.
aunty ['ɑ:nti], tiíta.
aura ['ɔ:rə], *n.* aura.
aurora [ɔ:'rɔ:rə], *n.* aurora.
auspice ['ɔ:spis], *n.* auspicio.
auspicious [ɔ:s'piʃəs], *a.* propicio.
austere [ɔ:s'tiə], *a.* austero.
austerity [ɔ:s'teriti], *n.* austeridad, *f.*
Australian [ɔs'treiliən], *a., n.* australiano.
Austrian ['ɔstriən], *a., n.* austríaco.
authentic [ɔ:'θentik], *a.* auténtico.
authenticate [ɔ:'θentikeit], *v.t.* autenticar.
authenticity [ɔ:θen'tisiti], *n.* autenticidad, *f.*
author ['ɔ:θə], *n.* autor, *m.*
authoress ['ɔ:θəres], *n.* autora.
authoritarian [ɔ:θɔri'tɛəriən], *a.* autoritario.
authoritative [ɔ:'θɔritətiv], *a.* autorizado.
authority [ɔ:'θɔriti], *n.* autoridad; ***to have on good —,*** saber de buena tinta.
authorize ['ɔ:θəraiz], *v.t.* autorizar.
authorship ['ɔ:θəʃip], *n.* paternidad literaria, autoría; profesión (*f.*) de autor.
autobiography [ɔ:toubai'ɔgrəfi], *n.* autobiografía.
autocade ['ɔ:toukeid], *n.* (*U.S.*) desfile (*m.*) de coches.
autocracy [ɔ:'tɔkrəsi], *n.* autocracia.
autograph ['ɔ:təgrɑ:f], *n.* autógrafo.
autogyro [ɔ:tou'dʒairou], *n.* autogiro.
automat ['ɔ:toumæt], *n.* restaurante automático.
automatic [ɔ:tə'mætik], *a.* automático.
automation [ɔ:tə'meiʃən], *n.* automatización, *f.*
automaton [ɔ:'tɔmətən], *n.* autómata, *m.f.*
automobile ['ɔ:təməbi:l], *a., n.* automóvil, *m.*
autonomous [ɔ:'tɔnəməs], *a.* autónomo.
autonomy [ɔ:'tɔnəmi], *n.* autonomía.
autopsy ['ɔ:tɔpsi], *n.* autopsia.
autumn ['ɔ:təm], *n.* otoño.
autumnal [ɔ:'tʌmnəl], *a.*, otoñal, autumnal.
auxiliary [ɔ:g'ziljəri], *a., n.* auxiliar.
avail [ə'veil], *n.* provecho, ventaja.—*v.t.* valer a, aprovechar, beneficiar.—*v.r.* aprovecharse (***of,*** de).
available [ə'veiləbl], *a.* disponible, aprovechable; en venta.
avalanche ['ævəlɑ:nʃ], *n.* alud, *m.*, avalancha.
avarice ['ævəris], *n.* avaricia, codicia.
avaricious [ævə'riʃəs], *a.* avariento.
avenge [ə'vendʒ], *v.t.* vengar.
avenue ['ævənju], *n.* avenida.
aver [ə'və:], *v.t.* afirmar, aseverar.
average ['ævəridʒ], *a.* mediano; ordinario, regular.—*n.* término medio, promedio.—*v.t.* producir *o* recibir por término medio.
averse [ə'və:s], *a.* opuesto, renuente.
aversion [ə'və:ʃən], *n.* aversión, *f.*; antipatía.
avert [ə'və:t], *v.t.* alejar, apartar, evitar.
aviary ['eivjəri], *n.* avería.
aviation [eivi'eiʃən], *n.* aviación, *f.*
aviator ['eivieitə], *n.* aviador, *m.*
avid ['ævid], *a.* ávido, voraz, codicioso.
avidity [ə'viditi], *n.* avidez, *f.*, codicia.
avoid [ə'vɔid], *v.t.* evitar; esquivar, rehuir.
avoidable [ə'vɔidəbl], *a.* evitable.
avoidance [ə'vɔidəns], *n.* evitación, *f.*
avoirdupois [ævədə'pɔiz], *n.* sistema (*m.*) de peso inglés.
avow [ə'vau], *v.t.* confesar, declarar.
await [ə'weit], *v.t.* aguardar, esperar.
awake [ə'weik], *a.* despierto.—*v.t., v.i.* (*conjug. like* WAKE) despertar.
awaken [ə'weikən], *v.t.,v.i.* despertar.
awakening [ə'weikəniŋ], *n.* despertamiento; (*fig.*) alba.
award [ə'wɔ:d], *n.* premio; recompensa.—*v.t.* conceder; conferir.
aware [ə'wɛə], *a.* enterado.
away [ə'wei], *a.* ausente.—*adv.* fuera, lejos; mucho; de en medio.—*interj.* ¡fuera!
awe [ɔ:], *n.* temor, pasmo.—*v.t.* pasmar, atemorizar.
awesome ['ɔ:səm], *a.* pasmoso.
awe-struck ['ɔ:strʌk], *a.* pasmado.
awful ['ɔ:ful], *a.* espantoso, atroz.
awfully ['ɔ:f(u)li], *adv.* (*fam.*) hasta más no poder, muy.
awhile [ə'hwail], *adv.* algún tiempo.
awkward ['ɔ:kwəd], *a.* desmañado; desgarbado; peliagudo.
awl [ɔ:l], *n.* alesna, lezna, subilla.
awning ['ɔ:niŋ], *n.* toldo.
awoke [ə'wouk] [AWAKE].
axe [æks], *n.* hacha; ***an — to grind,*** un fin interesado.

axis ['æksis], *n.* (*pl.* **axes**) eje, *m.*
axle [æksl], *n.* eje, árbol, *m.*
aye (1) [ai], *adv.* (*prov.*) [ai], sí.
aye (2) [ei], *adv.* (*poet.*) siempre.
Aztec ['æztek], *a.*, *n.* azteca, *m.f.*
azure ['æʒjuə], *a.*, *n.* azul, *m.*; (*her.*) blao.

B

B, b [bi:], *n.* segunda letra del alfabeto inglés; **B**, (*mus.*) si.
baa [bɑ:], *n.* balido, be, *m.*—*v.i.* balar.
babble [bæbl], *n.* murmullo; cháchara.—*v.t.* barbotar.—*v.i.* parlotear, murmurar.
babe [beib], *n.* (*poet.*) criatura.
baboon [bə'bu:n], *n.* babuíno.
baby ['beibi], *n.* bebé, nene, *m.* criatura; crío (*animal*).
babyish ['beibiiʃ], *a.* aniñado, pueril.
Babylonian [bæbi'lounjən], *a.*, *n.* babilonio.
Bacchus ['bækəs], *n.* Baco.
bachelor ['bætʃələ], *n.* soltero; (*educ.*) licenciado, bachiller, *m.*
back [bæk], *a.* trasero, posterior; apartado.—*n.* espalda; dorso, reverso, revés, *m.*; lomo espinazo; respaldo; fondo.—*v.t.* apoyar; mover hacia atrás; apostar sobre.—*v.i.* moverse hacia atrás; ***to — out of,*** desdecirse de.—*adv.* de vuelta; re-; hacia atrás, para atrás; hace [AGO]; de nuevo; ***to go*** o ***come —,*** volver; ***to go — on,*** no cumplir.
backbite ['bækbait], *v.t.* (*conjug. like* BITE) cortar un traje a.—*v.i.* chismear.
backbone ['bækboun], *n.* espinazo; (*fig.*) firmeza.
back-door ['bæk'dɔ:], *n.* puerta trasera, postigo.
backer ['bækə], *n.* impulsor; apostador, *m.*
backfire ['bæk'faiə], *n.* petardeo.—*v.i.* petardear; fracasar.
background ['bækgraund], *n.* fondo, último término; educación, *f.*, antecedentes, *m.pl.*
backing ['bækiŋ], *n.* apoyo; refuerzo.
backslide ['bæk'slaid], *v.i.* (*conjug. like* SLIDE) reincidir, apostatar.
backward ['bækwəd], *a.* atrasado; retraído.—*adv.* (also **backwards** ['bækwədz]) atrás, hacia atrás; al revés.
backwardness ['bækwədnis], *n.* atraso; tardanza; timidez, *f.*
backwater ['bækwɔ:tə], *n.* remanso, rebalsa.
backwoods ['bækwudz], *n.pl.* región apartada; monte, *m.*
back-yard [bæk'jɑ:d], *n.* patio, corral, *m.*
bacon ['beikən], *n.* tocino.
bacterium [bæk'ti:riəm], *n.* (*pl.* **-ria**) bateria, microbio.
bad [bæd], *a.* malo; podrido; falso; enfermo.—*n.* mal, *m.*; ***from — to worse,*** de mal en peor; ***not —,*** regular.
bade [bæd, beid] [BID].
badge [bædʒ], *n.* divisa; insignia; señal, *f.*; emblema, *m.*
badger ['bædʒə], *n.* (*zool.*) tejón, *m.*—*v.t.* fastidiar.
badly ['bædli], *adv.* mal; mucho, con urgencia; ***— off,*** maltrecho.
badness ['bædnis], *n.* maldad, *f.*
baffle [bæfl], *v.t.* trabucar.
bag [bæg], *n.* saco; bolsa; caza, piezas cobradas.—*v.t.* ensacar; (*fam.*) cazar, pescar.
baggage ['bægidʒ], *n.* bagaje, *m.*; (*U.S.*) equipaje, *m.*; (*fam.*) descarada.
bagpipe ['bægpaip], *n.* gaita.
bail [beil], *n.* fianza.—*v.t.* salir fiador (***out,*** por); (*naut.*) achicar.
bailiff ['beilif], *n.* corchete; guardián, *m.*
bairn [bɛən], *n.* (*Scot.*) nene, *m.f.*, niño.
bait [beit], *n.* cebo, anzuelo; añagaza.—*v.t.* cebar; hostigar.
baize [beiz], *n.* bayeta.
bake [beik], *v.t.*, *v.i.* cocer al horno.
bakelite ['beikəlait], *n.* baquelita.
baker ['beikə], *n.* panadero; ***baker's dozen,*** docena del fraile (13).
bakery ['beikəri], *n.* panadería.
baking ['beikiŋ], *n.* hornada, cochura; ***— powder,*** levadura química.
balance ['bæləns], *n.* equilibrio, balanza; (*com.*) balance, *m.*; resto.—*v.t.* equilibrar, balancear.—*v.i.* equilibrarse.
balcony ['bælkəni], *n.* balcón, *m.*; (*theat.*) galería.
bald [bɔ:ld], *a.* calvo; directo, escueto.
balderdash ['bɔ:ldədæʃ], *n.* galimatías, *m.sg.*, disparates, *m.pl.*
baldness ['bɔ:ldnis], *n.* calvicie, *f.*
bale [beil], *n.* bala, fardo.—*v.t.* embalar; (*naut.*) [BAIL]; ***to — out,*** (*aer.*) saltar en paracaídas.
baleful ['beilful], *a.* funesto, pernicioso.
balk [bɔ:k], *n.* viga; contratiempo.—*v.t.* frustrar.—*v.i.* rebelarse (***at,*** contra). [BAULK].
ball (1) [bɔ:l], *n.* pelota, balón, *m.*; globo; ovillo; bola; bala (*cañon*); ***— bearings,*** juego de bolas.
ball (2) [bɔ:l], *n.* baile (*danza*), *m.*
ballad ['bæləd], *n.* balada; romance, *m.*
ballast ['bæləst], *n.* lastre, *m.*; (*rail.*) balasto.—*v.t.* lastrar; balastar.
ballerina [bælə'ri:nə], *n.* bailarina.
ballet ['bælei], *n.* ballet, *m.*
ballistics [bə'listiks], *n. pl.* balística.
balloon [bə'lu:n], *n.* globo.
ballot ['bælət], *n.* votación, *f.*; bolita para votar; escrutinio.—*v.i.* votar.
bally ['bæli], *a.* (*fam.*) dichoso, santo.
ballyhoo [bæli'hu:], *n.* bombo; bullanga.
balm [bɑ:m], *n.* bálsamo.
balmy ['bɑ:mi], *a.* balsámico, suave.
balsam ['bɔ:lsəm], *n.* bálsamo.
Baltic ['bɔ:ltik], *a.* báltico.—*n.* Báltico.
balustrade [bæləs'treid], *n.* balaustrada.
bamboo [bæm'bu:], *n.* bambú, *m.*
bamboozle [bæm'bu:zl], *v.t.* (*fam.*) embaucar.
ban [bæn], *n.* prohibición, *f.*; entredicho; bando de destierro.—*v.t.* prohibir, proscribir.
banal [bæ'nɑ:l], *a.* trillado, trivial.
banana [bə'nɑ:nə], *n.* plátano; (*S.A.*) banana; banano (*planta*).
band [bænd], *n.* faja, cinta; lista; banda; cuadrilla; correa.—*v.t.* abanderizar.
bandage ['bændidʒ], *n.* venda.—*v.t.* vendar.

bandit ['bændit], *n.* bandolero, bandido.
banditry ['bænditri], *n.* bandolerismo.
bandy ['bændi], *a.* estevado.—*v.t.* trocar.
bane [bein], *n.* tósigo; (*fig.*) azote, *m.*
baneful ['beinful], *a.* venenoso; nocivo, mortal.
bang [bæŋ], *n.* golpazo; estallido.—*v.t.* golpear con violencia.—*v.i.* saltar, estallar; ***to — the door,*** dar un portazo; ***to — into,*** dar contra, topar con.
bangle [bæŋgl], *n.* ajorca.
banish ['bæniʃ], *v.t.* desterrar; despedir.
banishment ['bæniʃmənt], *n.* destierro.
banister ['bænistə], *n.* baranda, pasamano.
bank [bæŋk], *n.* orilla, ribera (*de un río etc.*); banco, montón (*pila*), *m.*; batería; hilera; (*com.*) banco; cuesta.—*v.t.* amontonar; apresar; depositar en el banco.—*v.i.* tener banco; (*aer.*) ladearse; ***to — on,*** contar con.
banker ['bæŋkə], *n.* banquero.
banking ['bæŋkiŋ], *a.* bancario.—*n.* (*com.*) banca.
bankrupt ['bæŋkrʌpt], *a.* quebrado.—*n.* quebrado; bancarrotero.—*v.t., v.i.* quebrar.
bankruptcy ['bæŋkrʌptsi], *n.* quiebra; bancarrota.
banner ['bænə], *n.* bandera; estandarte, *m.*
banns ['bænz], *n.pl.* (*eccl.*) amonestaciones, *f.pl.*
banquet ['bæŋkwit], *n.* banquete, *m.*—*v.i.* banquetear.
banter ['bæntə], *n.* chanza, vaya.—*v.t.* mofarse de.—*v.i.* chancear.
Bantu ['bæntu:], *a., n.* bantú, *m.f.*
baptism ['bæptizm], *n.* bautizo; bautismo.
Baptist ['bæptist], *n.* baptista (*denominación*), *m.f.*; **baptist,** *n.* bautista, *m.*
baptize [bæp'taiz], *v.t.* bautizar.
bar [bɑ:], *n.* barra; bar (*para bedidas*), mostrador, *f.*; lingote, *m.*; raya; (*jur.*) foro; reja (*en una ventana*).—*v.t.* atrancar; barrear; impedir; exceptuar.—*prep.* excepto.
barb [bɑ:b], *n.* lengüeta, púa.
barbarian [bɑ:'bɛəriən], *a., n.* bárbaro.
barbaric [bɑ:'bærik], *a.* barbárico.
barbarism ['bɑ:bərizm], *n.* barbaridad, *f.*; (*gram.*) barbarismo.
barbarity [bɑ:'bæriti], *n.* barbarie, *f.*
barbarous ['bɑ:bərəs], *a.* bárbaro.
barbecue ['bɑ:bikju:], *n.* (*S.A.*) churrasco, barbacoa.
barbed [bɑ:bd], *a.* armado con lengüetas; ***— wire,*** alambre espinoso *o* de púas.
barbel ['bɑ:bəl], *n.* (*ichth.*) barbo.
barber ['bɑ:bə], *n.* barbero, peluquero.
bard [bɑ:d], *n.* bardo.
bare [bɛə], *a.* desnudo; mero, solo; ***to lay —,*** poner a descubierto.—*v.t.* desnudar; exponer.
barefaced ['bɛəfeisd], *a.* descarado.
barefooted [bɛə'futid], *a.* descalzo.
barely ['bɛəli], *adv.* apenas.
bareness ['bɛənis], *n.* desnudez, *f.*
bargain ['bɑ:gin], *n.* (buen) negocio; ganga; ***into the —,*** de añadidura.—*v.i.* negociar; contratar; regatear.
bargaining ['bɑ:giniŋ], *n.* trato; regateo.
barge [bɑ:dʒ], *n.* barcaza, gabarra.—*v.i.* ***to — in,*** entrar atropelladamente, *o* sin permiso.
baritone ['bæritoun], *n.* barítono.
bark (1) [bɑ:k], *n.* corteza (*árbol*).
bark (2) [bɑ:k], *n.* ladrido.—*v.t.* ladrar (*perros*).
bark (3) [bɑ:k], *n.* (*poet.*) nao, *f.*
barley ['bɑ:li], *n.* cebada.
barmaid ['bɑ:meid], *n.* moza de bar.
barman ['bɑ:mən], *n.* barman, *m.*
barmy ['bɑ:mi], *a.* (*fam.*) guillado, gilí.
barn [bɑ:n], *n.* granero, hórreo; pajar, *m.*
barnacle ['bɑ:nəkl], *n.* (*zool.*) percebe, *m.*
barn-owl ['bɑ:naul], *n.* lechuza.
barometer [bə'rɔmitə], *n.* barómetro.
baron ['bærən], *n.* barón, *m.*
baroness ['bærənes], *n.* baronesa.
baroque [bə'rɔk], *a., n.* barroco.
barrack ['bærək], *v.t.* (*fam.*) silbar, pitar.
barracks ['bærəks], *n.pl.* cuartel, *m.*, caserna.
barrage ['bærɑ:ʒ], *n.* presa; bombardeo.
barrel ['bærəl], *n.* barril, tonel, *m.*; (*mil.*) tubo de cañón.—*v.t.* embarrilar.
barren ['bærən], *a.* yermo; estéril.
barricade [bæri'keid], *n.* empalizada, barricada.—*v.t.* barrear.
barrier ['bæriə], *n.* barrera.
barring ['bɑ:riŋ], *prep.* salvo; amén de.
barrister ['bæristə], *n.* abogado.
barrow ['bærou], *n.* carretilla; túmulo.
barter ['bɑ:tə], *n.* trueque, *m.*, barata.—*v.t.* trocar, baratar.
Bartholomew [bɑ:'θɔləmju:], *n.* Bartolomé, *m.*
base (1) [beis], *a.* vil, bajo; bajo de ley.
base (2) [beis], *n.* base, *f.*, fundamento; (*arch.*) basa.—*v.t.* basar (***on,*** en).
baseball ['beisbɔ:l], *n.* beisbol, *m.*
basement ['beismənt], *n.* sótano.
baseness ['beisnis], *n.* bajeza, vileza.
bash [bæʃ], *v.t.* (*fam.*) golpear.
bashful ['bæʃful], *a.* encogido, tímido, corto.
bashfulness ['bæʃfulnis], *n.* timidez, cortedad, *f.*
basil ['bæz(i)l], *n.* (*bot.*) albahaca.
basilica [bə'zilikə], *n.* basílica.
basin ['beisən], *n.* jofaina; bacía; cuenca (*de un río*); dársena (*puerto*).
basis ['beisis], *n.* (*pl.* **bases**) base, *f.*; fundamento.
bask [bɑ:sk], *v.i.* asolearse; calentarse.
basket ['bɑ:skit], *n.* cesta; cesto (*grande*); canasta.
basket-work ['bɑ:skitwə:k], *n.* cestería.
Basque [bæsk], *a., n.* vasco, vascongado.—*n.* vascuence (*idioma*), *m.*
bas-relief ['bæsrili:f], *n.* bajo relieve, *m.*
bass (1) [beis], *a., n.* (*mus.*) bajo.
bass (2) [bæs], *n.* (*ichth.*) lobina.
bassoon [bə'su:n], *n.* bajón, *m.*
bastard ['bɑ:stəd], *a., n.* bastardo.
bastardy ['bæstədi], *n.* bastardía.
baste [beist], *v.t.,* (*cul.*) pringar, enlardar.
bastion ['bæstiən], *n.* baluarte, bastión, *m.*
bat (1) [bæt], *n.* palo; ladrillo roto.—*v.t.* golpear.—*v.i.* jugar con el palo (*cricket*).
bat (2) [bæt], *n.* (*zool.*) murciélago.
batch [bætʃ], *n.* hornada; grupo.
bath [bɑ:θ], *n.* baño; bañera (*cosa*).—*v.t.* bañar.—*v.i.* ***or to take a —,*** bañarse.
bathe [beið], *n.* baño.—*v.t.* bañar (*herida*).—*v.i.* bañarse (*nadar*).
bather ['beiðə], *n.* bañista, *m.f.*
bathing ['beiðiŋ], *a.* de baño(s), — *n.* baño; ***— costume,*** traje de baño, bañador, *m.*
bathos ['beiθɔs], *n.* anticlímax, *m.*; sensiblería.
bathroom ['bɑ:θrum], *n.* cuarto de baño.
bath-tub ['bɑ:θtʌb], *n.* bañera.

batman ['bætmən], *n.* (*mil.*, *Brit.*) ordenanza, *m.*
baton ['bætən], *n.* (*mus.*) batuta; (*mil.*) bastón, *m.*
batsman ['bætsmən], *n.* el que BATS en CRICKET.
battalion [bə'tæljən], *n.*, (*mil.*) batallón, *m.*
batten [bætn], *n.* (*carp.*) listón, *m.*; tablilla.
batter ['bætə], *n.*, (*cul.*) pasta, batido; (*cul.*) ***in* —**, rebozado en gabardina. — *v.t.* golpear; magullar; ***to* — *down*,** derribar.
battering-ram ['bætəriŋ'ræm], *n.* ariete, *m.*
battery ['bætəri], *n.* (*mil.*, *elec.*) batería; (*elec.*) pila (*para una lámpara eléctrica*); (*jur.*) agresión, *f.*
battle [bætl], *n.* batalla.—*v.i.* batallar.
battle-axe ['bætlæks], *n.* hacha de combate; (*fam.*) marimacho.
battlement ['bætlmənt], *n.* almenas, *f.pl.*
battleship ['bætlʃip], *n.* acorazado.
bauble [bɔ:bl], *n.* friolera.
bauxite ['bɔ:ksait], *n.* bauxita.
Bavarian [bə'vɛəriən], *a.*, *n.* bávaro.
bawd [bɔ:d], *n.* alcahueta.
bawdy ['bɔ:di], *a.* verde, obsceno.
bawl [bɔ:l], *v.t.*, *v.i.* vocear, chillar; (*fam.*) lloriquear.
bay (1) [bei], *n.* bahía (*mar*); ***— window*,** mirador; ventana cimbrada.
bay (2) [bei], *n.* bayo (*caballo*).
bay (3) [bei], *n.* (*bot.*) laurel, *m.*
bay (4) [bei], *v.i.* aullar (*perros*); ***at* —**, acorralado.
bayonet ['beiənit], *n.* bayoneta.—*v.t.* dar un bayonetazo a.
bazaar [bə'zɑ:], *n.* bazar, *m.*
be [bi:], *irreg. v.t.*, *v.i.*, *auxiliary.* ser; estar; ***there is* o *are*,** hay; ***he is to go*,** ha de ir; ***wife to* —**, futura.
beach [bi:tʃ], *n.* playa.—*v.t.* encallar.
beacon ['bi:kən], *n.* faro, fanal, *m.*
bead [bi:d], *n.* abalorio, cuenta; gota; botón, *m.*; puntería.
beadle [bi:dl], *n.* bedel, *m.*
beagle [bi:gl], *n.* sabueso.
beak [bi:k], *n.* pico; (*fam.*) juez, *m.*
beaker ['bi:kə], *n.* vaso, tazón, *m.*
beam [bi:m], *n.* (*carp.*) viga; (*naut.*) bao; rayo. —*v.t.* radiar.—*v.i.* brillar; sonreír.
beaming ['bi:miŋ], *a.* radiante; risueño.
bean [bi:n], *n.* haba (*broad*); habichuela, judía, alubia.
bean-feast ['bi:nfi:st], *n.* comilona.
beano ['bi:nou], *n.* (*fam.*) juerga.
bear (1) [bɛə], *n.* (*zool.*) oso; (*com.*) bajista, *m.f.*
bear (2) [bɛə], *v.t. irr.* llevar; aguantar; permitir; producir; parir.—*v.i.* dirigirse; ***to — out*,** apoyar; ***to — with*,** conllevar; ***to — in mind*,** tener presente *o* en cuenta.
bearable ['bɛərəbl], *a.* soportable.
beard [biəd], *n.* barba.—*v.t.* mesar la barba a, enfrentarse con.
bearded ['biədid], *a.* barbudo.
beardless ['biədlis], *a.* imberbe; afeitado.
bearer ['bɛərə], *n.* portador, *m.*
bear-garden ['bɛəgɑ:dn], *n.* (*fig.*) merienda de negros.
bearing ['bɛəriŋ], *n.* porte, *m.*; paciencia; (*mech.*) cojinete, *m.*; orientación, *f.*; ***to lose one's bearings*,** desorientarse.
beast [bi:st], *n.* bestia.
beastly ['bi:stli], *a.* bestial.
beat [bi:t], *n.* latido; golpe; compás, *m.*; ronda (*patrulla*).—*v.t. irr.* batir; vencer; tocar (*tambor*).—*v.i.* latir.
beatific [bi:ə'tifik], *a.* beatífico.
beating ['bi:tiŋ], *a.* palpitante, latiente.—*n.* paliza; derrota; golpeo; pulsación, *f.*
beau [bou], *n.* (*pl.* **-us** *o* **-ux**) guapo.
beautiful ['bju:təful], *a.* hermoso.
beauty ['bju:ti], *n.* belleza, hermosura, beldad, *f.*; (*fam.*) lo mejor.
beaver ['bi:və], *n.* (*zool.*) castor, *m.*
becalm [bi'kɑ:m], *v.t.* encalmar.
became [bi'keim] [BECOME].
because [bi'kɔz], *conj.* porque; ***— of*,** a causa de.
beckon ['bekən], *v.i.* llamar con señas.
become [bi'kʌm], *v.t.* (*conjug. like* COME) convenir.—*v.i.* hacerse, ponerse, volverse; convertirse en; llegar a ser; ***to — of*,** ser de, hacerse de; ***to — cross*,** enfadarse; ***to — conceited*,** envanecerse *etc.*
becoming [bi'kʌmiŋ], *a.* conveniente.
bed [bed], *n.* cama, lecho; macizo (*jardín*); madre, lecho (*río*); (*min.*) yacimiento.
bedding ['bediŋ], *n.* ropa de cama.
bedevil [bi'devəl], *v.t.* endiablar; obstaculizar.
bedlam ['bedləm], *n.* manicomio.
bedraggle [bi'drægl], *v.t.* hacer cazcarriento.
bedroom ['bedrum], *n.* dormitorio, alcoba.
bedspread ['bedspred], *n.* cubrecama, *m.*, colcha.
bedstead ['bedsted], *n.* cuja.
bee [bi:], *n.* abeja.
beech [bi:tʃ], *n.* haya.
beef [bi:f], *n.* carne (*f.*) de vaca; (*fam.*) carnadura.
beefy ['bi:fi], *a.* (*fam.*) forzudo.
beeline ['bi:lain], *n.* línea recta.
been [bi:n, bin] [BE].
beer [biə], *n.* cerveza.
beet, beetroot ['bi:t(ru:t)], *n.* remolacha.
beetle [bi:tl], *n.* escarabajo.
befall [bi'fɔ:l], *v.t.* (*conjug. like* FALL) ocurrir a, suceder a.—*v.i.* acontecer.
befit [bi'fit], *v.t.* convenir a.
before [bi'fɔ:], *adv.* antes; delante.—*prep.* antes de; delante de.—*conj.* antes (de) que.
beforehand [b:'fɔ:hænd], *adv.* con anticipación, de antemano.
befriend [bi'frend], *v.t.* hacerse amigo de, amparar.
beg [beg], *v.t.* rogar, pedir, mendigar.—*v.i.* mendigar, pordiosear.
beget [bi'get], *v.t. irr.* engendrar.
beggar ['begə], *n.* mendigo, pordiosero; (*fam.*) tío, tipo.—*v.t.* arruinar; imposibilitar.
beggarly ['begəli], *a.* miserable, mezquino.
begin [bi'gin], *v.t.*, *v.i. irr.* empezar, comenzar ***by*,** (por).
beginner [bi'ginə], *n.* principiante; iniciador, *m.*
beginning [bi'giniŋ], *n.* principio; origen, *m.*
begone! [bi'gɔn], *interj.* (*obs.*) ¡fuera!
begot [bi'gɔt] [BEGET].
begrudge [bi'grʌdʒ], *v.t.* escatimar; envidiar; dar de mala gana.
beguile [bi'gail], *v.t.* engañar; engatusar; distraer.
begun [bi'gʌn] [BEGIN].

behalf [bi'hɑ:f], *n.* favor, lugar; ***on — of,*** por cuenta de, a favor de; ***to act on — of,*** hacer las veces de.
behave [bi'heiv], *v.i.* portarse, conducirse; actuar; (*fam.*) portarse bien.
behaviour [bi'heivjə], *n.* conducta; porte, *m.*; operación, *f.*
behead [bi'hed], *v.t.* descabezar.
behind [bi'haind], *n.* (*low.*) trasero, culo.—*adv.* detrás; atrás; con retraso.—*prep.* detrás de.
behindhand [bi'haindhænd], *adv.* atrasado.
behold [bi'hould], *v.t.* (*conjug. like* HOLD) (*obs.*) catar, contemplar.
beholden [bi'houldən], *a.* deudor, obligado.
behove [bi'houv], *v.t.*, (*obs.*) incumbir.
beige [beiʒ], *a.* beige, color (*m.*) de arena. —*n.* sarga.
being ['bi:iŋ], *a.* existente; ***for the time —,*** por el momento.—*n.* ser, *m.*
belabour [bi'leibə], *v.t.* elaborar con afán; apalear.
belated [bi'leitid], *a.* atrasado, tarde.
belch [beltʃ], *n.* eructo.—*v.t.* vomitar.—*v.i.* eructar.
beleaguer [bi'li:gə], *v.t.* sitiar, bloquear.
belfry ['belfri], *n.* campanario.
Belgian ['beldʒən], *a.*, *n.* belga, *m.f.*
Belgium ['beldʒəm], *n.* Bélgica.
belie [bi'lai], *v.t.* desmentir; falsear; calumniar.
belief [bi'li:f], *n.* creencia.
believable [bi'li:vəbl], *a.* creíble.
believe [bi'li:v], *v.t.*, *v.i.* creer (***in,*** en).
believer [bi'li:və], *n.* creyente; (*eccl.*) fiel, *m.f.*
belittle [bi'litl], *v.t.* empequeñecer, achicar.
bell [bel], *n.* campana; timbre, cascabel, *m.*; cencerro.
belladonna [belə'dɔnə], *n.* belladona.
belle [bel], *n.* beldad, mujer bella, *f.*
belles-lettres ['bel'letr], *n.* bellas letras, *f.pl.*
bellhop ['belhɔp], *n.* (*U.S.*) botones, *m.sg.*
bellicose ['belikous], *a.* belicoso.
belligerence [bə'lidʒərəns], *n.* beligerancia.
belligerent [bə'lidʒərənt], *a.*, *n.* beligerante, *m.*
bellow ['belou], *n.* bramido.—*pl.* fuelle, *m.*—*v.t.* vociferar.—*v.i.* bramar.
belly ['beli], *n.* barriga, panza.
belong [bi'lɔŋ], *v.i.* pertenecer (***to,*** a).
belongings [bi'lɔŋiŋz], *n.pl.* pertenencias, *f.pl.*; (*fam.*) bártulo, *m.pl.*
beloved [bi'lʌv(i)d], *a.*, *n.* dilecto, amado.
below [bi'lou], *adv.* abajo.—*prep.* bajo, debajo de.
belt [belt], *n.* cinturón, *m.*; correa; zona.
bemoan [bi'moun], *v.t.* plañir, lamentar.
bemuse [bi'mju:z], *v.t.* pasmar, atontar.
bench [bentʃ], *n.* banco; (*jur.*) tribunal, *m.*
bend [bend], *n.* curva, recodo; inclinación, *f.* —*v.t. irr.* inclinar; torcer; encorvar; dirigir. —*v.i. irr.* encorvarse; inclinarse; doblarse.
beneath [bi'ni:θ], *adv.* debajo, abajo.—*prep.* debajo de.
Benedict ['benidikt], *n.* Benito; Benedicto.
Benedictine [beni'diktin], *a.*, *n.* benedictino.
benediction [beni'dikʃən], *n.* bendición, *f.*; (*eccl.*) Exposición (*f.*) del Santísimo.
benefactor ['benifæktə], *n.* bienhechor, *m.*
benefactress ['benifæktres], *n.* bienhechora.
benefice ['benifis], *n.* (*eccl.*) beneficio.
beneficent [bi'nefisənt], *a.* benéfico.
beneficial [beni'fiʃəl], *a.* beneficioso.
beneficiary [beni'fiʃəri], *n.* beneficiario.
benefit ['benifit], *n.* beneficio.—*v.t.*, *v.i.* aprovechar.
benevolence [bi'nevələns], *n.* benevolencia.
benevolent [bi'nevələnt], *a.* benévolo.
benighted [bi'naitid], *a.* sumido en ignorancia.
benign [bi'nain], *a.* benigno.
bent [bent], *a.* resuelto (***on,*** a).—*n.* propensión *f.*; tendencia. [BEND].
benumb [bi'nʌm], *v.t.* entorpecer.
benzedrine ['benzidri:n], *n.* bencedrina.
benzine ['benzi:n], *n.* bencina.
bequeath [bi'kwi:ð], *v.t.* legar.
bequest [bi'kwest], *n.* legado, manda.
bereave [bi'ri:v], *v.t. irr.* despojar; desolar.
bereavement [bi'ri:vmənt], *n.* privación, *f.*; duelo.
beret ['berei, 'beri], *n.* boina.
Berlin [bə:'lin], *n.* Berlín, *m.*
berry ['beri], *n.* baya; grano.
berserk [bə:'sə:k], *a.* demente, frenético.
berth [bə:θ], *n.* (*naut.*) camarote, *m.*; amarradero.
beseech [bi'si:tʃ], *v.t. irr.* impetrar, instar.
beset [bi'set], *v.t.* (*conjug. like* SET) sitiar, acosar.
beside [bi'said], *adv.* además.—*prep.* al lado de, cerca de; además de; ***— oneself,*** fuera de sí; ***to be — the point,*** no venir al caso.
besides [bi'saidz], *adv.*, *prep.* además (de).
besiege [bi'si:dʒ], *v.t.* sitiar, asediar.
besot [bi'sɔt], *v.t.* embeleñar, entontecer.
bespeak [bis'pi:k], *v.t.* (*conjug. like* SPEAK, *p.p. also* BESPOKE) encomendar, encargar.
best [best], *a.*, *adv. superl. of* GOOD, WELL. mejor; ***the —,*** lo mejor; ***at —,*** a lo más; ***to like —,*** preferir; ***to get the — of,*** vencer, llevar ventaja a.
bestial ['bestjəl], *a.* bestial, embrutecido.
bestir [bis'tə:], *v.t.* mover, incitar.
bestow [bis'tou], *v.t.* otorgar, conceder; dedicar.
bet [bet], *n.* apuesta.—*v.t. irr.* apostar (***on,*** sobre, por); ***I — he comes,*** ¿a que viene?
betake [bi'teik], *v.r.* (*conjug. like* TAKE) acudir, dirigirse.
betide [bi'taid], *v.i.* ***woe — . . . !*** ¡ay de. . . . !
betoken [bi'toukən], *v.t.* presagiar, indicar.
betray [bi'trei], *v.t.* traicionar; descubrir.
betrayal [bi'treiəl], *n.* traición; revelación, *f.*
betroth [bi'trouð], *v.t.* dar en matrimonio.—*v.r.* desposarse.
betrothal [bi'trouðəl], *n.* desposorio, noviazgo.
betrothed [bi'trouðd], *n.* prometido, novio.
better ['betə], *a. compar. of* GOOD, *n.* superior. —*a.*, *adv. compar. of* GOOD, WELL, mejor; ***to be —,*** valer más; estar mejor; ***— half,*** (*fam.*) cara mitad (*mujer*).—*v.t.* mejorar; ***to get —,*** mejorarse; ***to think — of,*** cambiar de idea sobre, cambiar de decisión acerca de.
betterment ['betəmənt], *n.* mejoramiento.
between [bi'twi:n], *adv.* en medio.—*prep.* entre.
betwixt [bi'twikst], *prep.* (*obs.*) entre.
bevel ['bevəl], *n.* bisel, *m.*—*v.t.* biselar.
beverage ['bevəridʒ], *n.* potación, *f.*
bevy ['bevi], *n.* bandada; hato; corrillo.
bewail [bi'weil], *v.t.* lamentar.
beware [bi'wɛə], *v.t.* recatarse (***of,*** de); ***— of. . . . !*** ¡atención a. . . . ! ¡ojo con . . . !

bewilder [bi'wildə], *v.t.* dejar perplejo, aturrullar.
bewilderment [bi'wildəmənt], *n.* aturdimiento.
bewitch [bi'witʃ], *v.t.* embrujar, hechizar.
bewitching [bi'witʃiŋ], *a.* encantador.
beyond [bi'jɔnd], *adv.*, *prep.* más allá (de), fuera (de); ***he is — doing that,*** es incapaz de eso; ***the —,*** el más allá.
bias ['baiəs], *n.* sesgo; prejuicio.—*v.t.* predisponer.
bib [bib], *n.* babero, babador *m.*; pechero.
Bible [baibl], *n.* Biblia.
Biblical ['biblikəl], *a.* bíblico.
bibliography [bibli'ɔgrəfi], *n.* bibliografía.
bibulous ['bibjuləs], *a.* avinado, bebido.
bicarbonate [bai'kɑ:bənit], *n.* bicarbonato.
biceps ['baiseps], *n.pl.* bíceps, *m.pl.*
bicker ['bikə], *v.i.* andarse en cojijos.
bicycle ['baisikl], *n.* bicicleta.
bid (1) [bid], *n.* oferta, puja, postura.—*v.i.* hacer una oferta, pujar.
bid (2) [bid], *v.t. irr.* mandar; dar (*la bienvenida*); decir (*adiós*).
bidder ['bidə], *n.* postor, licitador, *m.*
bidding ['bidiŋ], *n.* mandato; oferta, licitación, *f.*
bide [baid], *v.t.*, *v.i.* aguardar(se); ***to — one's time,*** esparar el momento oportuno.
biennial [bai'eniəl], *a.*, *n.* bienal, *m.*
bier [biə], *n.* féretro.
biff [bif], *n.* (*fam.*) torta, golpe, *m.*—*v.t.* (*fam.*) dar una torta a.
big [big], *a.* grande; abultado; adulto, crecido; ***to talk —,*** (*fam.*) entonarse; decir cosas de gran monta.
bigamist ['bigəmist], *n.* bígamo.
bigamous ['bigəməs], *a.* bígamo.
bigamy ['bigəmi], *n.* bigamia.
big-end ['big'end], *n.* (*mech.*) cabeza de biela.
biggish ['bigiʃ], *a.* grandote, grandecillo.
big-hearted [big'hɑ:tid], *a.* generoso.
bight [bait], *n.* ensenada; recodo.
bigness ['bignis], *n.* grandeza; tamaño.
bigot ['bigət], *n.* beatón, *m.*
bigoted ['bigətid], *a.* fanático.
bike [baik], *n.* (*fam.*) bicicleta.
bile [bail], *n.* bilis, *f.*
bilge [bildʒ], *n.* (*naut.*) pantoque, *m.*; agua de pantoque; (*fam.*) bobería.
bilingual [bai'liŋgwəl], *a.* bilingüe.
bilious ['biljəs], *a.* bilioso; (*fam.*) enfermizo.
bill [bil], *n.* cuenta; (*U.S.*) billete de banco, cartel, *m.*, anuncio; proyecto de ley; (*orn.*) pico; ***— of health,*** patente (*f.*) de sanidad; (*com.*) letra; giro; ***— of exchange,*** letra de cambio; ***— of lading,*** conocimiento de carga; ***— of sale,*** escritura de venta.
billet ['bilit], *n.* (*mil.*) alojamiento; boleta.—*v.t.* (*mil.*) alojar.
billiards ['biljədz], *n.pl.* billar, *m.*
billion ['biljən], *n.* billón, *m.*, (*U.S.*) mil millones.
billow ['bilou], *n.* oleada.—*v.i.* hincharse.
billy-goat ['biligout], *n.* macho cabrío; (*fig.*) bobo.
bin [bin], *n.* hucha; arcón, *m.*
bind [baind], *n.* (*fam.*) pega, lata.—*v.t. irr.* ligar, atar, encuadernar; vendar; obligar.—*v.i. irr.* endurecerse, pegarse.
binding ['baindiŋ], *a.* obligatorio.—*n.* encuadernación, *f.*
bindweed ['baindwi:d], *n.* correhüela, enredadera, *f.*
binge [bindʒ], *n.* (*fam.*) juerga.
binoculars [bi'nɔkjuləz], *n.pl.* prismáticos, *m.pl.*
biographer [bai'ɔgrəfə], *n.* biógrafo.
biography [bai'ɔgrəfi], *n.* biografía.
biological [baiə'lɔdʒikl], *a.* biológico.
biologist [bai'ɔlədʒist], *n.* biólogo.
biology [bai'ɔlədʒi], *n.* biología.
biplane ['baiplein], *n.* biplano.
birch [bə:tʃ], *n.* (*bot.*) abedul, *m.*; palmeta, férula.—*v.t.* (*jur.*) azotar.
bird [bə:d], *n.* pájaro; ave, *f.*; (*fam.*) sujeto.
bird-cage ['bə:dkeidʒ], *n.* jaula.
bird-lime ['bə:dlaim], *n.* liga.
bird's-eye view ['bə:dzai'vju:], *n.* vista de pájaro.
birth [bə:θ], *n.* nacimiento; parto; cuna; alcurnia; origen, *m.*; ***to give — to,*** dar a luz, parir.
birthday ['bə:θdei], *n.* cumpleaños, *m.sg.*
birthplace ['bə:θpleis], *n.* lugar (*m.*) de nacimiento, suelo nativo.
birth-rate ['bə:θreit], *n.* natalidad, *f.*
birthright ['bə:θrait], *n.* primogenitura, mayorazgo; derechos (*m.pl.*) de nacimiento.
biscuit ['biskit], *n.* galleta.
bisect [bai'sekt], *v.t.* dividir en dos partes; bisecar.
bishop ['biʃəp], *n.* obispo; alfil (*ajedrez*), *m.*
bison ['baisən], *n.* (*zool.*) bisonte, *m.*
bit [bit], *n.* trozito, pedacito; ratito; bocado; barrena (*taladro*); ***not a —,*** nada de eso; ***a — tired,*** algo cansado. [BITE].
bitch [bitʃ], *n.* perra; (*low*) zorra.
bite [bait], *n.* mordedura, mordisco; picadura; resquemo; bocado; (*fig.*) impresión, *f.*—*v.t.*, *v.i. irr.* morder; picar; tragar el anzuelo.
biting ['baitiŋ], *a.* mordaz; picante; cáustico.
bitter ['bitə], *a.* amargo; enconado.—*n.* cerveza amarga. —*pl.* bíter, *m.*; ***it is bitterly cold,*** hace un frío criminal *o* cortante.
bitterness ['bitənis], *n.* amargura; amargor, *m.*; encono.
bitumen ['bitjumən], *n.* betún, *m.*
bivouac ['bivuæk], *n.* vivaque, vivac, *m.*—*v.i.* (*past tense and p.p.* **bivouacked**) vivaquear.
bizarre [bi'zɑ:], *a.* estrambótico.
blab [blæb], *n.* lenguaraz, *m.*—*v.t.*, *v.i.* chismear.
black [blæk], *a.*, *n.* negro.—*v.t.* ennegrecer; limpiar (*zapatos*); ***to — out,*** apagar las luces; desmayarse (*persona*).
blackball ['blækbɔ:l], *n.* bola negra.—*v.t.* votar en contra de.
blackberry ['blækbəri], *n.* mora; ***— bush,*** zarzamora.
blackbird ['blækbə:d], *n.* mirlo.
blackboard ['blækbɔ:d], *n.* pizarra.
blacken ['blækən], *v.t.* ennegrecer; difamar, denigrar.
blackguard ['blægɑ:d], *n.* tunante, *m.*
blacklead ['blækled], *n.* grafito, plombagina.
blackleg ['blækleg], *n.* esquirol, *m.*; fullero.
black-letter ['blækletə], *n.* negrilla, negrita; letra gótica.
blackmail ['blækmeil], *n.* chantaje, *m.*—*v.t.* hacer chantaje a.
blackness ['blæknis], *n.* negrura.
black-out ['blækaut], *n.* apagón; síncope, *m.*

blacksmith ['blæksmiθ], *n.* herrero, herrador, *m.*
bladder ['blædə], *n.* vejiga.
blade [bleid], *n.* hoja; brizna, tallo; (*aer.*) aleta; pala.
blame [bleim], *n.* culpa.—*v.t.* culpar, echar la culpa a (*for*, de); ***I am to* —**, yo tengo la culpa.
blameless ['bleimlis], *a.* intachable, inocente.
blameworthy ['bleimwə:ði], *a.* culpable, censurable.
blanch [blɑ:ntʃ], *v.t.* emblanquecer; (*cul.*) blanquear.—*v.i.* palidecer.
blancmange [blə'mɔnʒ], *n.* manjar blanco natillas.
bland [blænd], *a.* blando; lisonjero.
blandishment ['blændiʃmənt], *n.* zalamería, lisonja.
blank [blæŋk], *a.* blanco, en blanco; ciego; vago.—*n.* blanco; (*mil.*) cartucho sin bala.
blanket ['blæŋkit], *n.* manta.
blare [blɛə], *n.* fragor, *m.*—*v.t.* vociferar.—*v.i.* bramar, resonar.
blarney ['blɑ:ni], *n.* zalamería, bola.
blaspheme [blæs'fi:m], *v.i.* blasfemar.
blasphemous ['blæsfəməs], *a.* blásfemo.
blasphemy ['blæsfəmi], *n.* blasfemia.
blast [blɑ:st], *n.* ráfaga; rebufo; explosión, *f.*; (*mus.*) toque, *m.*; ***full* —**, en plena marcha, a pleno tiro.—*v.t.* volar; maldecir.
blast-furnace ['blɑ:stfə:nis], *n.* alto horno.
blatant ['bleitənt], *a.* vocinglero, chillón, llamativo.
blaze [bleiz], *n.* incendio; hoguera; llamarada; señal, *f.*—*v.i.* arder con violencia; ***to* — *a trail*,** abrir un camino.
blazer ['bleizə], *n.* chaqueta de franela.
blazon ['bleizən], *n.* blasón, *m.*—*v.t.* blasonar.
bleach [bli:tʃ], *n.* blanqueo.—*v.t.*, *v.i.* blanquear.
bleak [bli:k], *a.* desabrigado; sombrío.
bleary ['bliəri], *a.* legañoso.
bleed [bli:d], *v.t.*, *v.i. irr.* sangrar; ***to* — *white*,** desangrar.
blemish ['blemiʃ], *n.* tacha, mancilla.—*v.t.* manchar.
blench [blentʃ], *v.i.* palidecer de miedo.
blend [blend], *n.* mezcla, combinación, *f.*—*v.t.* mezclar, combinar, casar.—*v.i.* -se.
bless [bles], *v.t. irr.* bendecir.
blessed ['blesid, blesd], *a.* bendito, bienaventurado; santo.
blessing ['blesiŋ], *n.* bendición, *f.*
blest [blest], *p.p.* [BLESS].
blew [blu:] [BLOW].
blight [blait], *n.* tizón, añublo; pulgón, *m.*; ruina.—*v.t.* atizonar.
blind [blaind], *a.* ciego; — ***alley*,** callejón (*m.*) sin salida.—*n.* velo, venda; pretexto; celosía, persiana.—*v.t.* cegar.
blindfold ['blaindfould], *a.* con los ojos vendados.—*n.* venda.—*v.t.* vendar los ojos a.
blindness ['blaindnis], *n.* ceguera; ceguedad, *f.*
blink [bliŋk], *n.* guiñada.—*v.t.* *v.i.* guiñar; parpadear.
blinker ['bliŋkə], *n.* anteojera.
bliss [blis], *n.* bienaventuranza, beatitud, *f.*; dicha.
blissful ['blisful], *a.* bienaventurado, dichoso.
blister ['blistə], *n.* ampolla.—*v.t.* ampollar.
blithe [blaið], *a.* ledo.
blitz [blits], *n.* bombardeo aéreo.—*v.t.* bombardear.
blizzard ['blizəd], *n.* nevasca, ventisca.
bloat [blout], *v.t.* hinchar.—*v.i.* abotagarse.
bloater ['bloutə], *n.* arenque ahumado.
blob [blɔb], *n.* gota; goterón, *m.*; burujo, gurullo.
block [blɔk], *n.* bloque, *m.*; tajo; (*arch.*) manzana; (*fig.*) obstáculo; cubo de madera.—*v.t.* bloquear; obstruir; parar; tapar.
blockade [blɔ'keid], *n.* bloqueo.—*v.t.* bloquear.
blockage ['blɔkidʒ], *n.* obstáculo; obturación, *f.*
blockhead ['blɔkhed], *n.* zoquete, *m.*, zopenco.
bloke [blouk], *n.* (*low*) tío, fulano.
blond(e) [blɔnd], *a.*, *n.* rubio.
blood [blʌd], *n.* sangre, *f.*; valentón, *m.*; ***blue* —**, sangre azul *o* goda.
bloodcurdling ['blʌdkə:dliŋ], *a.* horripilante.
bloodhound ['blʌdhaund], *n.* sabueso.
bloodless ['blʌdlis], *a.* exangüe; sin derramar sangre.
blood-letting ['blʌdletiŋ], *n.* sangría.
bloodshed ['blʌdʃed], *n.* efusión (*f.*) de sangre; matanza, mortandad, *f.*
blood-sucker ['blʌdsʌkə], *n.* sanguijuela; (*fig.*) usurero.
bloodthirsty ['blʌdθə:sti], *a.* sanguinario sangriento.
bloody ['blʌdi], *a.* sangriento; (*low*) maldito; la mar de, muy.—*v.t.* esangrentar.
bloom [blu:m], *n.* flor, *f.*; florescencia, belleza, lozanía; pelusilla; changote, *m.*—*v.i.* florecer, florar.
bloomer ['blu:mə], *n.*, (*fam.*) gazafatón, *m.*—*pl.* bragas, *f.pl.*
blossom ['blɔsəm], *n.* flor, florescencia; ***in* —**, en cierne, en flor.—*v.i.* [BLOOM].
blot [blɔt], *n.* borrón, *m.*, mancha.—*v.t.* manchar; emborronar; borrar; secar.
blotch [blɔtʃ], *n.* pústula; manchón, *m.*
blotter ['blɔtə], *n.* borrador; papel secante, *m.*
blotting-paper ['blɔtiŋpeipə], *n.* papel secante, *m.*
blouse [blauz], *n.* blusa.
blow [blou], *n.* golpe, choque, revés, *m.*, soplido; ***to come to blows*,** venir a las manos.—*v.t. irr.* soplar; sonar; (*fam.*) maldecir; volar.—*v.i. irr.* soplar; jadear; estallar; ***to* — *up*,** volar; inflar; ***to* — *over*,** pasar, olvidarse.
blow-out ['blouaut], *n.* (*U.S.*) pinchazo, reventón, *m.*; (*fam.*) comilona.
blow-pipe ['bloupaip], *n.* cerbatana; soplete, *m.*
blubber ['blʌbə], *n.* grasa (de ballena).—*v.i.* lloriquear.
bludgeon ['blʌdʒən], *n.* cachiporra.—*v.t.* aporrear.
blue [blu:], *a.* azul; (*fig.*) triste; verde (*obsceno*); ***true* —**, leal.—*n.* azul, *m.*—*pl.* (*fam.*) morriña.
blue-bell ['blu:bel], *n.* (*bot.*) jacinto silvestre.
blue-bottle ['blu:bɔtl], *n.* (*ent.*) moscarda.
bluestocking ['blu:stɔkiŋ], *n.* marisabidilla.
bluff [blʌf], *a.* áspero.—*n.* risco, peñasco; finta, farol, *m.*—*v.i.* farolear, blufar.
blunder ['blʌndə], *n.* desatino, despropósito, patochada.—*v.i.* desatinar; tropezar.
blunderbuss ['blʌndəbʌs], *n.* trabuco.
blunt [blʌnt], *a.* embotado, romo; brusco, directo.—*v.t.* embotar.

blur [blə:], *n.* borrón, *m.*; forma confusa.—*v.t.* hacer borroso.
blurb [blə:b], *n.* reclamo retumbante.
blurred [blə:d], *a.* borroso.
blurt [blə:t], *v.i.* descolgarse (*out,* con).
blush [blʌʃ], *n.* sonrojo; color (*m.*) de rosa.—*v.i.* sonrojarse.
bluster ['blʌstə], *n.* fanfarria; tempestad, *f.*—*v.i.* fanfarrear.
blustering ['blʌstəriŋ], *a.* fanfarrón; tempestuoso.
boa [bouə], *n.* boa.
boar [bɔ:], *n.* (*zool.*) jabalí, *m.*; (*agr.*) verraco.
board [bɔ:d], *n.* tabla; tablero; hospedaje, *m.*, mesa; consejo (*de directores*); cartón, *m.*; — ***and lodging,*** pensión completa; ***on* —,** a bordo; en el vehículo.—*v.t.* hospedar; subir a; (*naut.*) abordar; entablar.
boarder ['bɔ:də], *n.* huésped, *m.*; (*educ.*) interno.
boarding house ['bɔ:diŋhaus], *n.* casa de huéspedes.
boast [boust], *n.* jactancia.—*v.i.* jactarse.
boastful ['boustful], *a.* jactancioso.
boat [bout], *n.* barco; barca.
boating ['boutiŋ], *n.* paseo en barco.
boatman ['boutmən], *n.* barquero.
boatswain [bousn, 'boutswein], *n.* contramaestre, *m.*
bob [bɔb], *n.* balanceo; borla, colgajo; lenteja; (*fam.*) chelín (12 *peniques*), *m.*—*v.t.* desmochar, cortar; (*fam.*) soslayar.—*v.i.* menearse; ***to* — *up,*** aparecer de repente.
bobbin ['bɔbin], *n.* carrete, *m.*; broca.
bobby ['bɔbi], *n.* (*fam.*) polizonte, *m.*
bode [boud], *v.t.*, *v.i.* presagiar, prometer.
bodice ['bɔdis], *n.* corpiño.
bodily ['bɔdili], *a.* corpóreo.—*adv.* todos juntos; el cuerpo entero; en persona.
body ['bɔdi], *n.* (*anat.*) cuerpo; carrocería (*de un coche*); masa; entidad, *f.*; (*fam.*) uno, persona.
bodyguard ['bɔdigɑ:d], *n.* guardia de corps.
Boer [bouə], *a.*, *n.* bóer, *m.f.*
bog [bɔg], *n.* pantano, ciénaga; ***to* — *down,*** atascar; ***to get bogged down,*** atascarse.
bog(e)y ['bougi], *n.* espantajo, duende, *m.*
boggy ['bɔgi], *a.* pantanoso.
bogus ['bougəs], *a.* espurio, fingido.
Bohemian [bou'hi:mjən], *a.*, *n.* bohemio.
boil [bɔil], *n.* hervor, *m.*, cocción, *f.*; (*med.*) grano, divieso.—*v.t.* hacer hervir, calentar.—*v.i.* hervir, cocer.
boiler ['bɔilə], *n.* caldera.
boiler-maker ['bɔiləmeikə], *n.* calderero.
boisterous ['bɔistərəs], *a.* borrascoso, alborotado.
bold [bould], *a.* osado, arrojado; impudente; ***to make* — *to,*** tomar la libertad de.
boldness ['bouldnis], *n.* osadía.
Bolivian [bə'livjən], *a.*, *n.* boliviano.
Bolshevik ['bɔlʃivik], *a.*, *n.* bolchevique, *m.f.*
bolster ['boulstə], *n.* travesaño; soporte, sostén, *m.*—*v.t.* reforzar; sostener; animar.
bolt [boult], *n.* cerrojo, pestillo; cuadrillo; rayo; — ***upright,*** derecho, rígido.—*v.t.* acerrojar; comer vorazmente.—*v.i.* desbocarse; fugarse; lanzarse.
bomb [bɔm], *n.* bomba.—*v.t.* bomb(ard)ear.
bombard [bɔm'bɑ:d], *v.t.* bombardear.
bombast ['bɔmbæst], *n.* bombo, ampulosidad, *f.*
bombastic [bɔm'bæstik], *a.* bombástico, ampuloso.
bomber ['bɔmə], *n.* (*aer.*) bombardero.
bombing ['bɔmiŋ], *n.* bomb(ard)eo.
bombshell ['bɔmʃel], *n.* bomba; (*fig.*) mala sorpresa.
bonanza [bɔ'nænzə], *n.* bonanza.
bond [bɔnd], *n.* lazo; unión, *f.*, vínculo; obligación, *f.*; almacén aduanero; trabazón, *f.*; pagaré, valor, *m.*; divisa.—*pl.* atadura, cadenas, *f.pl.*
bondage ['bɔndidʒ], *n.* servidumbre, *f.*
bondman ['bɔndmən], *n.* esclavo, siervo.
bondsman ['bɔndzmən], *n.* fiador, *m.*
bone [boun], *n.* hueso; espina (*de pez*).—*v.t.* desosar; (*U.S. fam.*) empollar.
bonfire ['bɔnfaiə], *n.* hoguera.
bonhomie ['bɔnɔmi], *n.* afabilidad, *f.*
bonnet ['bɔnit], *n.* toca, sombrero de mujer; capota; (*mech.*) cubierta; (*eccl.*, *educ.*) bonete, *m.*
bonny ['bɔni], *a.* (*dial.*) lindo, bonito; regordete.
bonus ['bounəs], *n.* bonificación, *f.*, adehala.
bony ['bouni], *a.* huesudo; huesoso; descarnado.
boo [bu:], *n.* silba, pitada.—*v.t.*, *v.i.* silbar, pitar.
booby ['bu:bi], *n.* zoquete, *m.*, marmolillo.
booby-prize ['bu:bipraiz], *n.* premio dado con ironía al último.
booby-trap ['bu:bitræp], *n.* armadijo, trampa explosiva.
book [buk], *n.* libro; libreta, librillo; ***to bring to* —,** pedir cuentas a; ***by the* —,** según las reglas.—*v.t.* sacar (*billetes*), reservar; notar; (*fam.*) acusar.
bookbinder ['bukbaində], *n.* encuadernador, *m.*
bookbinding ['bukbaindiŋ], *n.* encuadernación, *f.*
bookcase ['bukkeis], *n.* estantería, armario, *m.*
booking ['bukiŋ], *n.* reservación, *f.*; — ***office,*** taquilla, despacho de billetes.
bookish ['bukiʃ], *a.* libresco.
booklet ['buklit], *n.* folleto, librete, *m.*
bookmaker ['bukmeikə], *n.* corredor (*m.*) de apuestas.
bookmark ['bukmɑ:k], *n.* señal, *f.*
bookseller ['bukselə], *n.* librero.
book-shop ['bukʃɔp], *n.* librería.
bookworm ['bukwə:m], *n.* polilla; (*fam.*) ratón (*m.*) de biblioteca.
boom [bu:m], *n.* trueno; (*mech.*) aguilón, *m.*; (*naut.*) barrera; botalón, *m.*; auge, *m.*; (*com.*) prosperidad repentina.—*v.i.* medrar, prosperar mucho.
boomerang ['bu:məræŋ], *n.* bumerang, *m.*; (*fig.*) repercusión, (*f.*) que causa efecto en el autor de una acción.—*v.i.* repercutir los efectos de una acción en su autor.
boon [bu:n], *n.* favor, *m.*, gracia; dicha, bendición, *f.*; — ***companion,*** buen compañero, compañero inseparable.
boor [buə], *n.* patán, *m.*, pataco.
boorish ['buəriʃ], *a.* chabacano; batueco.
boost [bu:st], *n.* empujón, *m.*; ayuda.—*v.t.* empujar; ayudar; reforzar.
booster ['bu:stə], *n.* (*mech.*) elevador, aumentador, *m.*

boot (1) [bu:t], *n.* bota; (*Brit.*) portaequipaje (*de un coche*), *m.*; —*v.t.* dar un puntapié a.
boot (2) [bu:t], *n.* garancia.
bootblack ['bu:tblæk], *n.* limpiabotas, *m.sg.*
bootee [bu:'ti:], *n.* bota de mujer *o* de niños.
booth [bu:ð], *n.* quiosco, cabina; puesto.
bootlegging ['bu:tlegiŋ], *n.* contrabanda de licores.
boot-licker ['bu:tlikə], *n.* (*fam.*) lameculos, *m.f. inv.*
booty ['bu:ti], *n.* botín, *m.*
booze [bu:z], *n.* (*fam.*) zumo de cepas, bebidas.—*v.i.* (*fam.*) beber mucho, coger una turca.
borax ['bɔ:ræks], *n.* bórax, *m.*
Bordeaux [bɔ:'dou], *n.* Burdeos, *m.*
border ['bɔ:də], *n.* confín, *m.*; frontera; margen, *m.* o *f.*; dobladillo; orla; borde, *m.*; franja; arriata (*jardín*).—*v.t.* orlar, dobladillar.—*v.i.* lindar, confinar (con), rayar en (***on, upon***).
borderline ['bɔ:dəlain], *a.* fronterizo; incierto. —*n.* región fronteriza.
bore [bɔ:], *n.* taladro, barreno; calibre, *m.*; (*fam.*) lata; pelmazo, machacón (*persona*), *m.*—*v.t.* taladrar, barrenar; aburrir, fastidiar. [BEAR].
boredom ['bɔ:dəm], *n.* aburrimiento.
boring ['bɔ:riŋ], *a.* aburrido.
born [bɔ:n], *a.* nacido; nato; ***to be* —**, nacer.
borne [bɔ:n] [BEAR].
borough ['bʌrə], *n.* municipio.
borrow ['bɔrou], *v.t.* prestar, tomar prestado.
bosh [bɔʃ], *n.* (*fam.*) bobada, tontería.
bosom ['buzəm], *n.* seno; **— *friend,*** amigo íntimo.
boss (1) [bɔs], *n.* jefe, *m.*, amo; (*pol.*) cacique, *m.*—*v.t.* dominar, ser muy mandamás.
boss (2) [bɔs], *n.* protuberancia.
bossy ['bɔsi], *a.* mandón.
bo'sun [BOATSWAIN].
botanical [bə'tænikəl], *a.* botánico.
botanist ['bɔtənist], *n.* botánico.
botany ['bɔtəni], *n.* botánica.
botch [bɔtʃ], *n.* chapucería.—*v.t.* chapucear.
both [bouθ], *a.*, *pron.* ambos, los dos; **— . . . *and,*** tanto . . . como.
bother ['bɔðə], *n.* molestia.—*v.t.* molestar.—*v.i.* molestarse (***with, about,*** con).
bothersome ['bɔðəsəm], *a.* molesto.
bottle [bɔtl], *n.* botella.—*v.t.* embotellar.
bottom ['bɔtəm], *n.* fondo; base, *f.*; pie, *m.*; (*fam.*) asentaderas, *f.pl.*; ***at* —**, en el fondo.
bottomless ['bɔtəmlis], *a.* insondable.
boudoir ['bu:dwɑ:], *n.* tocador, gabinete, *m.*
bough [bau], *n.* rama.
bought [bɔ:t] [BUY].
boulder ['bouldə], *n.* canto.
bounce [bauns], *n.* bote, *m.*—*v.t.* hacer botar. —*v.i.* botar; dar saltitos.
bouncing ['baunsiŋ], *a.* rollizo, frescachón.
bound (1) [baund], *a.* forzado, obligado; encuadernado; resuelto; relacionado. [BIND].
bound (2) [baund], *a.* **— *for,*** con rumbo a.
bound (3) [baund], *n.* salto; bote, *m.*—*v.i.* saltar.
bound (4) [baund], *n.* límite, *m.*— *v.t.* confinar.
boundary ['baundəri], *n.* término, límite, confín, *m.*
boundless ['baundlis], *a.* infinito.
bountiful ['bauntiful], *a.* largo, dadivoso; copioso.
bounty ['baunti], *n.* munificencia; prima.
bouquet [bu'kei], *n.* ramillete, *m.*; aroma del vino.
Bourbon ['buəbən], *n.* Borbón, *m.*
bourgeois ['buəʒwɑ:], *a.*, *n. inv.* burgués (*n. m.*).
bourgeoisie [buəʒwɑ:'zi:], *n.* burguesía.
bout [baut], *n.* partida; ataque, *m.*
bovine ['bouvain], *a.* bovino, vacuno.
bow (1) [bou], *n.* arco; nudo, lazo.
bow (2) [bau], *n.* reverencia, cortesía; (*naut.*) proa.—*v.t.* inclinar; someter.—*v.i.* inclinarse; doblarse, ceder.
bowdlerize ['baudləraiz], *v.t.* expurgar.
bowels [bauəlz], *n.pl.* entrañas, *f.pl.*; intestinos, *m.pl.*
bower [bauə], *n.* emparrado, cenador, *m.*
bowl (1) [boul], *n.* escudilla, taza; tazón, *m.*; cuenco. bola (*sport*).—*pl.* bolos (*juego*).—*v.t.* hacer rodar; bolear; ***to* — *over,*** derribar; atropellar; desconcertar.—*v.i.* jugar a los bolos.
bow-legged ['bou'legid], *a.* (pati)estevado.
bowman ['boumən], *n.* arquero.
bowsprit ['bousprit], *n.* bauprés, *m.*
box [bɔks], *n.* caja; (*theat.*) palco; (*bot.*) boj, *m.*; manotada.—*v.t.* encajonar; abofetear.—*v.i.* boxear.
boxer ['bɔksə], *n.* boxeador, *m.*
boxing ['bɔksiŋ], *a.* de boxeo.—*n.* boxeo.
Boxing-day ['bɔksiŋdei], *n.* día (*m.*) de los aguinaldos (*26 de diciembre*).
box-office ['bɔksɔfis], *n.* taquilla; despacho de entradas.
boy [bɔi], *n.* muchacho; chico; niño; mozo; **— *scout,*** explorador, *m.*
boycott ['bɔikɔt], *n.* boicot(eo), *m.*—*v.t.* boicotear.
bra [brɑ:], *n.* (*fam.*) sostén, ajustador, *m.*
brace [breis], *n.* tirante, *m.*; par (*dos*), *m.*; (*carp.*) berbiquí, *m.*; — *pl.* (*Brit.*) tirantes.—*v.t.* arriostrar; asegurar; atesar.—*v.r.* prepararse.
bracelet ['breislit], *n.* pulsera; brazalete, *m.*
bracing ['breisiŋ], *a.* fortificante. [BRACE].
bracken ['brækən], *n.* helecho.
bracket ['brækit], *n.* soporte, *m.*, repisa; (*print.*) corchete, paréntesis, *m.*
brackish ['brækiʃ], *a.* salobre.
bradawl ['brædɔ:l], *n.* (a)lesna, (a)lezna.
brag [bræg], *n.* bravata.—*v.i.* jactarse.
braggart ['brægət], *n.* bravucón, *m.*
bragging ['brægiŋ], *n.* jactancia.
braid [breid], *n.* galón, *m.*; trenza.
brain [brein], *n.* cerebro, seso; — *pl.* inteligencia; (*cul.*) sesos, *m.pl.*; ***to rack one's brains,*** devanarse los sesos.—*v.t.* descalabrar.
brainless ['breinlis], descalabrar.—*a.* lelo, tonto.
brain-wave ['breinweiv], *n.* inspiración genial, *f.*
brainy ['breini], *a.* sesudo, inteligente.
brake [breik], *n.* freno; (*bot.*) helecho; matorral, *m.*—*v.t.* frenar.
bramble [bræmbl], *n.* zarza.
bran [bræn], *n.* salvado.
branch [brɑ:ntʃ], *n.* rama; ramo; (*com.*) sucursal, *f.*; ramal, *m.*—*v.i.* ramificarse; ***to* — *out,*** extenderse.
brand [brænd], *n.* (*com.*) marca; hierro; tizón, *m.*; **— *-new,*** nuevo flamante.—*v.t.* marcar; herrar; tiznar.

brandish ['brændiʃ], *v.t.* blandir, blandear.
brandy ['brændi], *n.* coñac, *m.*
brasier [BRAZIER].
brass [brɑ:s], *n.* latón, *m.*; (*fam.*) parné, *m.*, dinero; (*fam., mil.*) jefotes, *m.pl.*
brass band ['brɑ:s'bænd], *n.* charanga.
brassière ['bræsiɛə], *n.* sostén, ajustador, *m.*
brassy ['brɑ:si], *a.* de latón; descarado; metálico.
brat [bræt], *n.* (*pej.*) mocoso.
bravado [brə'vɑ:dou], *n.* bravata.
brave [breiv], *a.* valiente, valeroso.—*n.* guerrero pelirrojo.—*v.t.* arrostrar; retar.
bravery ['breivəri], *n.* valentía, valor, *m.*
bravo! ['brɑ:vou], *interj.* ¡bravo!
brawl [brɔ:l], *n.* reyerta.—*v.i.* armar camorra.
brawn [brɔ:n], *n.* embutido; fuerza, músculos, *m.pl.*
brawny ['brɔ:ni], *a.* forzudo, fuertote.
bray [brei], *n.* rebuzno.—*v.i.* rebuznar.
brazen ['breizən], *a.* de latón; de bronce; descarado (*persona*).
brazier ['breiziə], *n.* brasero.
Brazil [brə'zil], *n.* Brasil, *m.*
Brazilian [brə'ziljən], *a., n.* brasileño.
breach [bri:tʃ], *n.* brecha, abertura; abuso, violación, *f.*—*v.t.* batir en brecha.
bread [bred], *n.* pan, *m.*
breadth [bredθ], *n.* anchura.
break [breik], *n.* rotura; rompimiento; grieta, raja; interrupción, *f.*; recreo, descanso; ruptura.—*v.t. irr.* quebrar, quebrantar, romper; cortar; comunicar (*noticias*); faltar a (*palabra*); batir (*un 'record'*).—*v.i. irr.* romper(se); quebrar(se); ***to — down,*** analizar; desquiciar; averiarse; deshacerse; ***to — in,*** domar (*caballos*); entrar para robar; forzar; ***to — out,*** declararse, estallar; evadirse.
breakage ['breikidʒ], *n.* rotura; fractura.
breakdown ['breikdaun], *n.* avería; colapso; análisis, *m.sg.*
breakfast ['brekfəst], *n.* desayuno.—*v.i.* desayunar.
break-through ['breikθru:], *n.* brecha; avance sensacional, *m.*
breakwater ['breikwɔ:tə], *n.* rompeolas, *m.sg.*
breast [brest], *n.* pecho; (*orn.*) pechuga; pechera (*ropa*); ***to make a clean — of,*** confesar francamente.
breast-plate ['brestpleit], *n.* peto, coraza.
breastwork ['brestwə:k], *n.* parapeto.
breath [breθ], *n.* aliento, respiración, *f.*; sollo; ***— of wind,*** soplo de viento; ***under one's —,*** en voz baja; ***out of —,*** sin aliento.
breathe [bri:ð], *v.t.* respirar; infundir.—*v.i.* respirar; soplar; ***to — in,*** aspirar; ***to — out,*** espirar.
breather ['bri:ðə], *n.* respiro, descansito.
breathing ['bri:ðiŋ], *n.* respiración, *f.*; ***— space,*** descanso.
breathless ['breθlis], *a.* jadeante; sin aliento.
breath-taking ['breθteikiŋ], *a.* pasmoso.
bred [bred] [BREED].
breech [bri:tʃ], *n.* culata (*fusil*); trasero.—*pl.* calzones, *m.pl.*
breed [bri:d], *n.* raza.—*v.t. irr.* criar.—*v.i. irr.* criarse.
breeder ['bri:də], *n.* criador, *m.*
breeding ['bri:diŋ], *n.* cría; crianza; educación, *f.*; linaje, *m.*
breeze [bri:z], *n.* brisa.
breezy ['bri:zi], *a.* airoso; vivaracho.
brethren ['breðrin], *n.pl.* (*eccl. etc.*) hermanos, *m.pl.*
Breton ['bretən], *a., n.* bretón, *m.*
breve [bri:v], *n.* (*mus.*) breve, *f.*
breviary ['bri:vjəri], *n.* breviario.
brevity ['breviti], *n.* brevedad, *f.*
brew [bru:], *n.* mezcla; infusión, *f.*—*v.t.* bracear (*cerveza*), preparar, hacer (*té etc.*); urdir.—*v.i.* elaborar cerveza; amenazar, urdirse.
brewer [bru:ə], *n.* cervecero.
brewery ['bru:əri], *n.* cervecería.
brewing ['bru:iŋ], *a.* cervecero.
briar [braiə], *n.* rosal silvestre, *m.*; zarza.
bribe [braib], *n.* soborno.—*v.t.* sobornar.
bribery ['braibəri], *n.* cohecho, soborno.
bric-à-brac ['brikəbræk], *n.* fruslerías, curiosidades, *f.pl.*
brick [brik], *n.* ladrillo; (*fam.*) buen tipo.
brickbat ['brikbæt], *n.* pedazo de ladrillo.
bricklayer ['brikleiə], *n.* albañil, *m.*
brickwork ['brikwə:k], *n.* enladrillado.
brickyard ['brikja:d], *n.* ladrillar, *m.*
bridal [braidl], *a.* de novia, nupcial.
bride [braid], *n.* novia.
bridegroom ['braidgrum], *n.* novio.
bridesmaid ['braidzmeid], *n.* madrina de boda.
bridge [bridʒ], *n.* puente, *m.*—*v.t.* pontear; salvar.
bridle [braidl], *n.* brida, freno.—*v.t.* refrenar, embridar.
brief [bri:f], *a.* breve.—*n.* (*jur.*) escrito, causa; (*eccl.*) breve, *m.*—*v.t.* (*jur.*) alegar; dar instrucciones a.
brier [BRIAR].
brig(antine) ['brig(ənti:n)], *n.* bergantín, *m.*
brigade [bri'geid], *n.* brigada.
brigadier [brigə'diə], *n.* general (*m.*) de brigada.
brigand ['brigənd], *n.* bandolero.
bright [brait], *a.* claro, brillante; subido; listo.
brighten [braitn], *v.t.* abrillantar; avivar.—*v.i.* despejarse; avivarse.
brightness ['braitnis], *n.* claridad, brillantez, *f.*; viveza.
brilliance ['briljəns], *n.* brillantez, *f.*, brillo.
brilliant ['briljənt], *a.* brillante.
brim [brim], *n.* orilla; labio (*de vaso*); ala (*de sombrero*).—*v.i.* estar lleno; desbordarse.
brimful ['brimful], *a.* rebosante.
brimstone ['brimstən], *n.* azufre, *m.*
brine [brain], *n.* salmuera.
bring [briŋ], *v.t. irr.* traer; llevar; hacer venir; acarrear; reducir.—*v.r.* resignarse (***to,*** a); ***to — about,*** causar; efectuar; ***to — forth,*** parir; producir; ***to — off,*** lograr; ***to — on,*** ocasionar; acarrear; ***to — out,*** sacar; publicar; ***to — over,*** persuadir; ***to — up,*** subir; educar, criar; ***to — to light,*** descubrir, sacar a luz.
brink [briŋk], *n.* borde, *m.*, margen, *m.* o *f.*; ***on the — of,*** a dos dedos de.
brinkmanship ['briŋkmənʃip], *n.* (*pol.*) política de riesgos calculados.
briny ['braini], *a.* salado, salobre.—*n.* (*fam.*) el mar.
brisk [brisk], *a.* animado; vivo, rápido.
bristle [brisl], *n.* cerda.—*v.i.* erizarse.
bristly ['brisli], *a.* erizado.

Britain ['britən], *n.* Gran Bretaña.
Britannia [bri'tænjə], *n.* dama simbólica de la Gran Bretaña.
British ['britiʃ], *a.* británico; ***the* —,** los britanos.
Briton ['britən], *n.* britano, británico.
Brittany ['britəni], *n.* Bretaña.
brittle [britl], *a.* quebradizo.
broach [broutʃ], *v.t.* encentar; abrir, empezar.
broad [brɔ:d], *a.* ancho; (*fig.*) lato; amplio; claro; indecente; pleno; grosero; fuerte (*dialecto*).
broadcast ['brɔ:dkɑ:st], *n.* (*rad.*) emisión, *f.*—*v.t.* (*conjug. like* CAST) (*rad.*) emitir, radiar; esparciar.
broadcasting ['brɔ:dkɑ:stiŋ], *n.* radio, *f.*
broaden [brɔ:dn], *v.t.* ensanchar.—*v.i.* -se.
broad-minded [brɔ:d'maindid], *a.* de manga ancha, de amplias miras.
broad-shouldered [brɔ:d'ʃouldəd], *a.* ancho de espaldas.
broadsheet ['brɔ:dʃi:t], *n.* pasquín, *m.*
broadside ['brɔ:dsaid], *n.* andanada.
brocade [bro'keid], *n.* brocado.
broccoli ['brɔkəli], *n.* brécol(es), *m.*(*pl.*).
brochure ['brouʃə], *n.* folleto.
brogue [broug], *n.* zapato fuerte; dialecto irlandés.
broil [brɔil], *n.* camorra.—*v.t.* soasar.
broiler ['brɔilə], *n.* pollo para asar.
broke [brouk], *a.* (*fam.*) pelado, sin blanca. [BREAK].
broken [broukn], *a.* roto; accidentado, [BREAK].
broken-down ['broukndaun], *a.* descompuesto; destartalado, desvencijado.
broker ['broukə], *n.* corredor, cambista, *m.*
brokerage ['broukəridʒ], *n.* corretaje, *m.*
brolly ['brɔli], *n.* (*fam.*) paraguas, *m.sg.*
bromine ['broumi:n], *n.* bromo.
bronchitis [brɔŋ'kaitis], *n.* bronquitis, *f.*
bronco ['brɔŋkou], *n.* caballo cerril.
bronze [brɔnz], *n.* bronce, *m.*—*v.t.* broncear.
brooch [broutʃ], *n.* broche, alfiler (*m.*) de pecho.
brood [bru:d], *n.* nidada, camada; casta.—*v.t.* empollar.—*v.i.* enclocar; ***to* — (*over*),** rumiar, meditar melancólicamente.
broody ['bru:di], *a.* clueco; melancólico.—*n.* clueca.
brook [bruk], *n.* arroyo.—*v.t.* tolerar.
brooklet ['bruklit], *n.* arroyuelo.
broom (1) [bru:m], *n.* escoba.
broom (2) [bru:m], *n.* (*bot.*) hiniesta, retama.
broth [brɔθ], *n.* caldo.
brothel [brɔθl], *n.* burdel, *m.*
brother ['brʌðə], *n.* hermano.
brotherhood ['brʌðəhud], *n.* hermandad, *f.*
brother-in-law ['brʌðərinlɔ:], *n.* (*pl.* **brothers-in-law**) cuñado.
brotherly ['brʌðəli], *a.* fraternal.
brought [brɔ:t] [BRING].
browbeat ['braubi:t], *v.t.* (*conjug. like* BEAT) conminar.
brown [braun], *a.* castaño, pardo; moreno; tostado; dorado; — ***bread*,** pan bazo; — ***study*,** ensimismamiento; — ***sugar*,** azúcar moreno.—*v.t.* dorar; tostar.
brownish ['brauniʃ], *a.* pardusco.
browse [brauz], *v.i.* pacer; ramonear; hojear libros.

bruin ['bru:in], *n.* (*fam.*) oso.
bruise [bru:z], *n.* contusión, *f.*, cardenal, *m.*—*v.t.* magullar, contundir; majar.
brunette [bru:'net], *n.* morena.
brunt [brʌnt], *n.* choque, *m.*; (*fig.*) lo más fuerte.
brush [brʌʃ], *n.* cepillo; brocha; (*art.*) pincel, *m.*; escaramuza; roce, *m.*; broza, mata.—*v.t.* cepillar; barrer; ***to* — *against*,** rozar con; ***to* — *up*,** repasar.
brushwood ['brʌʃwud], *n.* broza; matorral, *m.*
brusque [brusk], *a.* rudo, brusco.
Brussels [brʌslz], *n.* Bruselas, *f.sg.*; — ***sprouts*,** bretones, *m.pl.*, coles (*f.pl.*) de Bruselas.
brutal [bru:tl], *a.* brutal, bestial.
brutality [bru:'tæliti], *n.* brutalidad, *f.*
brute [bru:t], *a.*, *n.* bruto.
bubble [bʌbl], *n.* burbuja; ampolla; engañifa. —*v.i.* burbujear; ***to* — *over*,** rebosar.
bubonic plague [bju:'bɔnik'pleig], *n.* peste bubónica.
buccaneer [bʌkə'niə], *n.* filibustero, bucanero.
buck [bʌk], *n.* conejo; ciervo, gamo; macho cabrío; petimetre, *m.*; (*U.S. fam.*) dólar, *m.*—*v.i.* encorvarse; ***to* — *up*,** (*fam.*) animarse.
bucket ['bʌkit], *n.* cubo.
buckle [bʌkl], *n.* hebilla.—*v.t.* abrochar.
bucolic [bju:'kɔlik], *a.* bucólico.—*n.* bucólica.
bud [bʌd], *n.* botón, *m.*; yema; brote, *m.*, pimpollo; ***to nip in the* —,** atajar lo apenas empezado.—*v.i.* brotar.
Buddha ['budə], *n.* Buda, *m.*
buddhist ['budist], *a.*, *n.* budista, *m.f.*
buddy ['bʌdi], *n.* (*U.S.*, *fam.*) compañero.
budge [bʌdʒ], *v.t.* remover.—*v.i.* removerse.
budgerigar ['bʌdʒərigɑ:], *n.* periquito.
budget ['bʌdʒit], *n.* presupuesto.—*v.t.* presuponer.
buff [bʌf], *a.*, *n.* color (*m.*) de ante.
buffalo ['bʌfəlou], *n.* búfalo.
buffer ['bʌfə], *n.* tope, *m.*, paragolpes, *m.sg.*; — ***state*,** estado tapón.
buffet (1) ['bʌfit], *n.* bofetada; alacena.—*v.t.* abofetear; golpear.
buffet (2) ['bufei], *n.* fonda; bar, *m.*; — ***supper*,** cena en frío.
buffoon [bə'fu:n], *n.* bufón, *m.*
buffoonery [bə'fu:nəri], *n.* bufonada.
bug [bʌg], *n.* (*Brit.*) chinche, *m.*; (*U.S.*) bicho, insecto.
bugbear ['bʌgbɛə], *n.* espantajo.
bugle [bju:gl], *n.* corneta.
bugler ['bju:glə], *n.* corneta, *m.*
build [bild], *n.* talle, *m.*—*v.t. irr.* edificar, construir.
builder ['bildə], *n.* constructor, *m.*, maestro de obras.
building ['bildiŋ], *n.* edificio; construcción, *f.*
build-up ['bildʌp], *n.* propaganda preparativa, bombo.
built [bilt], [BUILD].
built-in ['bilt'in], *a.* incorporado; empotrado.
built-up area ['biltʌp'ɛəriə], *n.* aglomeración urbana.
bulb [bʌlb], *n.* (*elec.*) bombilla; (*bot.*) patata, bulbo; ampoll(et)a.
bulbous ['bʌlbəs], *a.* bulboso.
Bulgarian [bʌl'gɛəriən], *a.*, *n.* búlgaro.

bulge [bʌldʒ], *n.* pandeo, comba.—*v.i.* combarse, bombearse.
bulk [bʌlk], *n.* bulto, masa, volumen, *m.*
bulky ['bʌlki], *a.* grueso, abultado.
bull (1) [bul], *n.* toro; (*com.*) alcista, *m.*; (*low*) música celestial.
bull (2) [bul], *n.* (*eccl.*) bula.
bulldog ['buldɔg], *n.* alano inglés, dogo.
bulldozer ['buldouzə], *n.* empujadora.
bullet ['bulit], *n.* bala.
bulletin ['bulitin], *n.* boletín, *m.*; (*U.S.*) anuncio.
bullfight ['bulfait], *n.* corrida de toros.
bullfighter ['bulfaitə], *n.* torero.
bullfighting ['bulfaitiŋ], *n.* toreo, tauromaquia.
bullfinch ['bulfintʃ], *n.* (*orn.*) camachuelo.
bullion ['buljən], *n.* oro *o* plata en lingotes.
bullock ['bulək], *n.* buey, *m.*, novillo.
bull-ring ['bulriŋ], *n.* plaza de toros; ruedo.
bull's-eye ['bulzai], *n.* blanco, centro del blanco.
bully ['buli], *n.* matón, matasiete, *m.*—*v.t.* intimidar, amenazar.
bulrush ['bulrʌʃ], *n.* junco.
bulwark ['bulwək], *n.* baluarte, *m.*
bumble-bee ['bʌmblbi:], *n.* abejarrón, *m.*
bump [bʌmp], *n.* tope, topetón, golpe, *m.*; comba; rebote, *m.*; hinchazón, *f.*—*v.t.* dar contra; golpear.—*v.i.* chocar; dar sacudidas.
bumper ['bʌmpə], *n.* parachoques, *m.sg.*
bumpkin ['bʌmpkin], *n.* patán, *m.*, paleto.
bumptious ['bʌmpʃəs], *a.* fantasmón.
bun [bʌn], *n.* bollo.
bunch [bʌntʃ], *n.* manojo; racimo (*de uvas*); ristra; ramo, ramillete (*de flores*), *m.*, grupo. —*v.t.* juntar.
bundle [bʌndl], *n.* lío; atado; fardo.—*v.t.* liar; mandar.
bung [bʌŋ], *n.* bitoque, tapón, *m.*
bungle [bʌŋgl], *v.t.*, *v.i.* chapucear.
bungler ['bʌŋglə], *n.* chapucero.
bunion ['bʌnjən], *n.* juanete, *m.*
bunk [bʌŋk], *n.* tarima; (*fam.*) música celestial, disparates, *m.pl.*
bunker ['bʌŋkə], *n.* carbonera; fortín, *m.*; hoya.
bunkum ['bʌŋkəm], *n.* (*fam.*) [BUNK].
bunny ['bʌni], *n.* (*fam.*) conejito.
bunsen burner ['bʌnsn'bə:nə], *n.* mechero Bunsen.
bunting (1) ['bʌntiŋ], *n.* banderas (*f.pl.*) de adorno, lanilla.
bunting (2) ['bʌntiŋ], *n.* (*orn.*) escribano.
buoy [bɔi], *n.* boya.
buoyant ['bɔiənt], *a.* boyante; vivaz.
burden [bə:dn], *n.* carga; tema, *m.*; importe, *m.*; estribillo.—*v.t.* cargar; gravar.
bureau [bjuə'rou], *n.* agencia, oficina; escritorio.
bureaucracy [bjuə'rɔkrəsi], *n.* burocracia.
bureaucrat ['bjuəroukræt], *n.* burócrata, *m.f.*
burgess ['bə:dʒis], *n.* ciudadano, burgués, *m.*
burglar ['bə:glə], *n.* ladrón, escalador, *m.*
burglary ['bə:gləri], *n.* robo de una casa.
burgle [bə:gl], *v.t.* robar (*una casa*).
Burgundy ['bə:gəndi], *n.* Borgoña; borgoña (*vino*), *m.*
burial ['beriəl], *n.* entierro.
burlesque [bə:'lesk], *a.* festivo, burlesco.—*n.* parodia.
burly ['bə:li], *a.* fornido.
Burma ['bə:mə], *n.* Birmania.
Burmese ['bə:'mi:z], *a.*, *n.* birmano.
burn [bə:n], *n.* quemadura; (*dial.*) arroyo.—*v.t. irr.* quemar; incendiar.—*v.i. irr.* arder; quemarse; escocer (*dolor*).
burnish ['bə:niʃ], *v.t.* bruñir.
burnt [bə:nt] [BURN].
burrow ['bʌrou], *n.* madriguera.—*v.i.* amadrigarse.
bursar ['bə:sə], *n.* tesorero.
bursary ['bə:səri], *n.* beca; tesorería.
burst [bə:st] *n.* reventón, *m.*; ráfaga.—*v.t. irr.* reventar, quebrar.—*v.i. irr.* reventar (se); arrojarse; romper (***out, into***, a).
bury ['beri], *v.t.* enterrar.
bus [bʌs], *n.* autobús, *m.*
bush [buʃ], *n.* arbusto; matorral, *m.*; mata; (*mech.*) buje, *m.*
bushel [buʃl], *n.* medida de capacidad de unos 36, 35 litros; (*U.S.*) 35, 23 litros.
bushy ['buʃi], *a.* espeso; matoso.
business ['biznis], *n.* negocio(s); comercio; asunto; ***you have no — to do that,*** Vd. no tiene derecho a hacer eso; ***meaning —,*** en serio.
businesslike ['biznislaik], *a.* serio, metódico.
businessman ['biznismən], *n.* hombre (*m.*) de negocios.
buskin ['bʌskin], *n.* borceguí, *m.*
bust [bʌst], *n.* busto; pecho de mujer.
bustle [bʌsl], *n.* bullicio; polisón (*vestido*), *m.*—*v.i.* apresurarse.
busy ['bizi], *a.* ocupado; atareado.—*v.t.* ocupar.
busybody ['bizibɔdi], *n.* bullebulle, *m.*, entremetido.
but [bʌt], *prep.* excepto, sino.—*conj.* pero, mas; (*after neg.*) sino que; ***all —,*** casi; ***nothing —,*** nada más que.
butcher ['butʃə], *n.* carnicero.—*v.t.* matar.
butchery ['butʃəri], *n.* carnicería.
butler ['bʌtlə], *n.* mayordomo, repostero.
butt [bʌt], *n.* blanco, hito; cabezada; hazmerreír; tonel, *m.*; colilla; culata.—*v.t.* top(et)ar; dar cabezadas a.
butter ['bʌtə], *n.* mantequilla.—*v.t.* (*fam.*) lisonjear.
butterfly ['bʌtəflai], *n.* mariposa.
buttocks ['bʌtəks], *n.pl.* nalgas, *f.pl.*
button [bʌtn], *n.* botón, *m.*—*v.t.* abotonar.
button-hole ['bʌtnhoul], *n.* ojal, *m.*—*v.t.* detener (*persona*).
buttress ['bʌtris], *n.* contrafuerte, *m.*; apoyo. —*v.t.* reforzar; apoyar.
buxom ['bʌksəm], *a.f.* regordeta, rolliza.
buy [bai], *n.* (*fam.*) compra.—*v.t. irr.* comprar.
buzz [bʌz], *n.* zumbido.—*v.i.* zumbar; ***— off!*** (*fam.*) ¡lárgate!
buzzard ['bʌzəd], *n.* (*orn.*) ratonero.
buzz saw ['bʌzsɔ:], *n.* (*U.S.*) sierra circular.
by [bai], *adv.* cerca; por aquí *o* ahí.—*prep.* por; de; para (*cierto tiempo*); ***— and —,*** dentro de poco; ***— and large,*** en general; ***— far,*** con mucho.
'bye! [bai], *interj.* ¡hasta luego!
by-election ['baiilekʃn], *n.* (*Brit.*) elección (*f.*) para llenar una vacante parlamentaria.
Byelorussian ['bjelou'rʌʃən], *a.* bielorruso.
bygone ['baigɔn], *a.*, *n.* pasado; ***let bygones be bygones,*** lo pasado pasado.

by-law ['bailɔ:], *n.* ley local, *f.*
by-pass ['baipɑ:s], *n.* desviación, *f.*—*v.t.* evitar.
by-product ['baiprɔdʌkt], *n.* derivado.
bystander ['baistændə], *n.* circunstante, *m.f.*
by-street ['baistri:t], *n.* callejuela.
by-ways ['baiweiz], *n.pl.* andurriales, *m.pl.*
by-word ['baiwə:d], *n.* apodo; oprobio; dicho, refrán, *m.*

C

C, c [si:], *n.* tercera letra del alfabeto inglés; **C,** (*mus.*) do.
cab [kæb], *n.* cabriolé; taxi, *m.*; casilla (*del maquinista*).
cabal [kə'bæl], *n.* cábala.
cabbage ['kæbidʒ], *n.* col, *f.*, berza.
cabby ['kæbi], *n.* (*fam.*) taxista, *m.*
cabin ['kæbin], *n.* cabaña; (*naut.*) camarote, *m.*; (*aer.*) cabina.
cabin-boy ['kæbinbɔi], *n.* mozo de cámara.
cabinet ['kæbinit], *a.* (*pol.*) ministerial.—*n.* gabinete; escaparate, *m.*, vitrina (*de vidrio*); armario.
cabinet-maker ['kæbinit'meikə], *n.* ebanista, *m.*
cable [keibl], *n.* cable; cablegrama, *m.*—*v.t.*, *v.i.* cablegrafiar.
cache [kæʃ], *n.* escondite, *m.*—*v.t.* esconder.
cachet ['kæʃei], *n.* sello particular.
cackle [kækl], *n.* cacareo; cháchara.—*v.i.* cacarear; reírse; chacharear.
cacophonous [kə'kɔfənəs], *a.* cacofónico.
cacophony [kə'kɔfəni], *n.* cacofonía.
cactus ['kæktəs], *n.* cacto.
cad [kæd], *n.* canalla, *m.*; persona mal educada.
cadaverous [kə'dævərəs], *a.* cadavérico.
caddie ['kædi], *n.* muchacho (*golf*).
caddish ['kædiʃ], *a.* mal educado.
caddy ['kædi], *n.* cajita (*para té*).
cadence ['keidəns], *n.* cadencia.
cadet [kə'det], *n.* (*mil.*) cadete, *m.*; (*lit.*) hermano menor.
cadge [kædʒ], *v.t.* (*fam.*) obtener mendigando. —*v.i.* (*fam.*) gorronear.
cadmium ['kædmiəm], *n.* cadmio.
caesura [si'zjuərə], *n.* cesura.
café ['kæfei], *n.* café (*sitio*), *m.*
cafeteria [kæfi'tiəriə], *n.* restaurante, café, *m.*
cafein(e) ['kæfi:n], *n.* cafeína.
cage [keidʒ], *n.* jaula.—*v.t.* enjaular.
cag(e)y ['keidʒi], *a.* (*fam.*) zorro, cauteloso.
Cain [kein] *n.* (*Bib.*) Caín, *m.*
Cairo ['kaiərou], *n.* el Cairo, *m.*
cajole [kə'dʒoul], *v.t.* halagar.
cajolery [kə'dʒouləri], *n.* halago, zalamería.
cake [keik], *n.* bollo, pastel, *m.*; pastilla (*jabón etc.*).—*v.i.* pegarse.
calabash ['kæləbæʃ], *n.* calabaza.
calamitous [kə'læmitəs], *a.* calamitoso.
calamity [kə'læmiti], *n.* calamidad, *f.*
calcium ['kælsiəm], *n.* calcio.
calculate ['kælkjuleit], *v.t.* calcular; ***calculated to,*** aprestado para.
calculation ['kælkju'leiʃən], **calculus** ['kælkjuləs], *n.* cálculo.
caldron [CAULDRON].
Caledonian [kæli'dounjən], *a.* caledonio escocés.
calendar ['kælində], *n.* calendario.
calends ['kælindz], *n.pl.* calendas, *f.pl.*
calf (1) [kɑ:f], *n.* (*pl.* **calves**) ternero; (piel de) becerro; pasta española.
calf (2) [kɑ:f], *n.* (*anat.*) pantorrilla.
calibrate ['kælibreit], *v.t.* calibrar.
calibre ['kælibə], *n.* calibre, *m.*; (*fig.*) calaña.
calico ['kælikou], *n.* calicó.
calipers ['kælipəz], *n.pl.* calibrador, *m.*
caliph ['keilif], *n.* califa, *m.*
caliphate ['kælifeit], *n.* califato.
calix ['keiliks], *n.* (*bot.*) cáliz, *m.*
calk [CAULK].
call [kɔ:l], *n.* llamada; grito; visita; ***on —,*** disponible; de guardia; (*com.*) a solicitud.—*v.t.* llamar; despertar; llamar (por teléfono); ***to — back,*** (*tel.*) volver a llamar; ***to — off,*** aplazar; disuadir; ***to — together,*** convocar; ***to — up,*** reclutar; llamar (por teléfono).—*v.i.* gritar; hacer una visita.
call-boy ['kɔ:lbɔi], *n.* botones, *m.sg.*; (*theat.*) avisador, *m.*
caller ['kɔ:lə], *n.* llamador, *m.*; visita.
calligraphy [kæ'ligrəfi], *n.* caligrafía.
calliper(s) [CALIPERS].
callous ['kæləs], *a.* duro, insensible; calloso.
callousness ['kæləsnis], *n.* (*fig.*) dureza; callosidad, *f.*
callow ['kælou], *a.* joven e inexperto.
callus ['kæləs], *n.* callo.
calm [kɑ:m], *a.* tranquilo, quieto.—*n.* calma; sosiego, serenidad, *f.*—*v.t.* calmar, tranquilizar.—*v.i.* calmarse (***down***).
calmly ['kɑ:mli], *adv.* sosegadamente.
calmness ['kɑ:mnis], *n.* tranquilidad, *f.*
calorie, calory ['kæləri], *n.* caloría.
calumniate [kə'lʌmnieit], *v.t.* calumniar.
calumny ['kæləmni], *n.* calumnia.
Calvary ['kælvəri], *n.* Calvario.
calve ['kɑ:v], *v.t.*, *v.i.* parir (*dícese de la vaca*). —*n.pl.* [CALF].
Calvinist ['kælvinist], *a.*, *n.* calvinista, *m.f.*
calypso [kə'lipsou], *n.* calipso.
calyx [CALIX].
cam [kæm], *n.* leva.
camber ['kæmbə], *n.* comba; convexidad (*del camino*), *f.*
Cambodia [kæm'boudjə], *n.* Camboya.
Cambodian [kæm'boudjən], *a.*, *n.* camboyano.
cambric ['kæmbrik], *n.* batista, holán, *m.*
came [keim] [COME].
camel ['kæməl], *n.* camello.
camellia [kə'mi:ljə], *n.* camelia.
cameo ['kæmiou], *n.* camafeo.
camera ['kæmərə], *n.* máquina (fotográfica); ***in*** — (*jur.*) en secreto.
cameraman ['kæmərəmæn], *n.* (*cin.*) operador.
Cameroons [kæmə'ru:nz], *n.pl.* Camerón, *m.*
camomile ['kæməmail], *n.* manzanilla, camomila.
camouflage ['kæməflɑ:ʒ], *n.* (*mil.*) camuflaje *m.*; enmascaramiento.—*v.t.* camuflar.
camp [kæmp], *n.* campamento; campo.—*v.i.* acampar.
campaign [kæm'pein], *n.* campaña.

camp-follower ['kæmp'fɔlouə], *n.* vivandero.
camphor ['kæmfə], *n.* alcanfor, *m.*
camphorate ['kæmfəreit], *v.t.* alcanforar.
campus ['kæmpəs], *n.* (*esp. U.S.*) recinto (*de la universidad*).
cam-shaft ['kæmʃɑ:ft], *n.* árbol (*m.*) de levas.
can (1) [kæn], *n.* lata, envase, *m.*—*v.t.* enlatar. (TIN).
can (2) [kæn], *v. aux. irr.* poder.
Canaan ['keinən], *n.* (*Bib.*) Tierra de Canaán *o* de promisión.
Canada ['kænədə], *n.* Canadá, *m.*
Canadian [kə'neidjən], *a.*, *n.* canadiense, *m.f.*
canal [kə'næl], *n.* canal, *m.*; acequia (*riego*).
canard [kæ'nɑ:d], *n.* noticia falsa; embuste, *m.*
Canaries [kə'nɛəriz], **Canary Islands** [kə'nɛəri ailəndz], *n.pl.* Canarias, *f.pl.*
canary [kə'nɛəri], *n.* (*orn.*) canario.
cancan ['kænkæn], *n.* cancán, *m.*
cancel ['kænsəl], *v.t.* suprimir; cancelar; matasellar (*correo*).
cancellation [kænsə'leiʃən], *n.* supresión; cancelación, *f.*; matasello (*correo*).
cancer ['kænsə], *n.* cáncer, *m.*; (*astr.*) Cáncer, *m.*
cancerous ['kænsərəs], *a.* canceroso.
candelabrum [kændi'lɑ:brəm], *n.* (*pl.* **-bra**) candelabro.
candid ['kændid], *a.* franco; cándido.
candidate ['kændidit], *n.* candidato.
candidature ['kændiditʃə], *n.* candidatura.
candle [kændl], *n.* vela, bujía, candela.
candlepower ['kændlpauə], *n.* bujía.
candlestick ['kændlstik], *n.* palmatoria; candelero.
candour ['kændə], *n.* franqueza; candor, *m.*
candy ['kændi], *n.* (*esp. U.S.*) dulce, confite, bonbón, *m.*
cane [kein], *n.* bastón, *m.*; caña; mimbre, *m.*—*v.t.* apalear, bastonear.
canine ['keinain], *a.* canino.—*n.* colmillo (*diente*).
canister ['kænistə], *n.* lata, bote, *m.*
canker ['kæŋkə], *n.* (*bot.*) cancro; (*med.*) gangrena; corrosión, *f.*—*v.t.* gangrenar.—*v.i.* -se.
cankerous ['kæŋkərəs], *a.* gangrenoso.
cannery ['kænəri], *n.* fábrica de conservas.
cannibal ['kænibəl], *a.*, *n.* caníbal, *m.f.*, antropófago.
canning ['kæniŋ], *a.* conservero.—*n.* envase (*en latas*), *m.*
cannon ['kænən], *n.* cañón, *m.*
cannon-ball ['kænənbɔ:l], *n.* bala de cañón.
cannon-fodder ['kænən'fɔdə], *n.* carne (*f.*) de cañón.
cannon-shot ['kænən'ʃɔt], *n.* tiro de cañón; alcance (*m.*) de cañón.
cannot ['kænɔt] [CAN NOT].
canny ['kæni], *a.* astuto.
canoe [kə'nu:], *n.* piragua, canoa.
canon ['kænən], *n.* canon (*regla*), *m.*; canónigo (*señor*).
canonical [kə'nɔnikəl], *a.* canónico.
canonize ['kænənaiz], *v.t.* canonizar.
canonry ['kænənri], *n.* canonjía.
can-opener ['kænoupənə], *n.* (*U.S.*) abrelatas, *m.sg.*
canopy ['kænəpi], *n.* dosel, *m.*; (*elec.*) campana.—*v.t.* endoselar.
cant [kænt], *n.* hipocresía; jerga; sesgo.—*v.t.* inclinar.—*v.i.* -se; hablar con hipocresía.
can't [kɑ:nt] [CAN NOT].
cantankerous [kæn'tæŋkərəs], *a.* pendenciero, avieso.
canteen [kæn'ti:n], *n.* cantina; (*mil.*) cantimplora.
canter ['kæntə], *n.* medio galope.—*v.i.* andar (a caballo) a medio galope.
Canterbury ['kæntəbəri], *n.* Cantórbery, *m.*
cantharides [kæn'θæridi:z], *n.pl.* polvo de cantárida.
canticle ['kæntikl], *n.* cántico.
cantilever ['kæntili:və], *n.* viga voladiza; — ***bridge***, puente (*m.*) de contrapeso.
canton ['kæntɔn], *n.* cantón, *m.*
cantonment [kæn'tu:nmənt], *n.* acantonamiento.
cantor ['kæntɔ:], *n.* chantre, *m.*; cantor principal, *m.*
canvas ['kænvəs], *n.* cañamazo, lona; ***under*** —, (*mil.*) en tiendas, (*naut.*) con las velas izadas.
canvass ['kænvəs], *n.* solicitación (*f.*) de votos *o* opiniones; escrutinio.—*v.i.* solicitar votos.
canyon ['kænjən], *n.* cañón, *m.*
cap [kæp], *n.* gorra (*sombrero*); tapa, tapón (*de una lata etc.*), *m.*; bonete (*universidad*), *m.*; cápsula (*percusión*).—*v.t.* poner tapa a; saludar; acabar, rematar.
capability [keipə'biliti], *n.* habilidad, *f.*
capable ['keipəbl], *a.* capaz, hábil.
capacious [kə'peiʃəs], *a.* capaz, espacioso.
capacity [kə'pæsiti], *n.* capacidad; aptitud, *f.*
caparison [kə'pærisn], *n.* caparazón, *m.*, paramento.
cape (1) [keip], *n.* capa, esclavina (*ropa*).
cape (2) [keip], *n.* (*geog.*) cabo; ***Cape Horn***, Cabo de Hornos; ***Cape of Good Hope***, Cabo de Buena Esperanza.
caper (1) ['keipə], *n.* cabriola.—*v.i.* cabriolar.
caper (2) ['keipə], *n.* (*bot.*) alcaparra.
capillary [kə'piləri], *a.* capilar.
capital ['kæpitl], *a.* capital; mayúsculo.—*n.* capital (*dinero*), *m.*; capital (*ciudad*), *f.*
capitalism ['kæpitəlizəm], *n.* capitalismo.
capitalize ['kæpitəlaiz], *v.t.* capitalizar; escribir con mayúscula; aprovechar.
capitol ['kæpitl], *n.* capitolio.
capitulate [kə'pitjuleit], *v.i.* capitular, rendirse.
capon ['keipən], *n.* capón, *m.*
caprice [kə'pri:s], *n.* capricho; veleidad, *f.*
capricious [kə'priʃəs], *a.* caprichoso, antojadizo.
Capricorn ['kæprikɔ:n], *n.* Capricornio.
capsize [kæp'saiz], *v.t.*, *v.i.* volcar.
capstan ['kæpstən], *n.* cabrestante, *m.*
capsule ['kæpsju:l], *n.* cápsula.
captain ['kæptin], *n.* capitán, *m.*
caption ['kæpʃən], *n.* título; subtítulo.—*v.t.* intitular.
captious ['kæpʃəs], *a.* caviloso.
captivate ['kæptiveit], *v.t.* encautivar; fascinar, encantar.
captive ['kæptiv], *a.*, *n.* cautivo.
captivity [kæp'tiviti], *n.* cautiverio.
capture ['kæptʃə], *n.* toma, presa; botín, *m.*—*v.t.* apresar; (*mil.*) tomar.
car [kɑ:], *n.* coche, *m.*; carro.
carafe [kə'ræf], *n.* garafa.
caramel ['kærəməl], *n.* caramelo.
carat ['kærət], *n.* quilate, *m.*

caravan ['kærəvæn], *n.* caravana, recua; remolque, *m.*
caraway ['kærəwei], *n.* alcaravea; carvi, *m.*
carbide ['kɑ:baid], *n.* carburo.
carbine ['kɑ:bain], *n.* carabina.
carbolic [kɑ:'bɔlik], *a.* fénico.—*n.* fenol, *m.*
carbon ['kɑ:bən], *n.* (*chem.*) carbono; (*elec.*) carbón, *m.*; — ***paper,*** papel carbón, *m.*
carbuncle ['kɑ:bʌnkl], *n.* (*med., gem.*) carbunclo.
carburettor [kɑ:bju'retə], *n.* carburador, *m.*
carcass ['kɑ:kəs], *n.* res muerta; (*fig.*) armazón, *m.*
card [kɑ:d], *n.* tarjeta; naipe, *m.*, carta; ficha.
cardboard ['kɑ:dbɔ:d], *n.* cartón, *m.*
cardiac ['kɑ:diæk], *a.* cardíaco.
cardigan ['kɑ:digən], *n.* rebeca.
cardinal ['kɑ:dinəl], *a.* cardinal.—*n.* cardenal, *m.*
care [kɛə], *n.* cuidado; inquietud (*ansiedad*), *f.*; esmero (*atención*); cargo; — ***of Mr. X,*** en casa del Sr. X.—*v.i.* cuidar; tener cuidado; ***to — to,*** tener ganas de; ***to — for something,*** gustar de algo.
career [kə'riə], *n.* carrera.—*v.i.* correr a todo galope.
careful ['kɛəful], *a.* cuidadoso; ansioso; atento.
carefully ['kɛəfuli], *adv.* esmeradamente.
carefulness ['kɛəfulnis], *n.* cuidado.
careless ['kɛəlis], *a.* descuidado; inconsiderado.
carelessness ['kɛəlisnis], *n.* descuido; inconsideración, *f.*
caress [kə'res], *n.* caricia.—*v.t.* acariciar.
caretaker ['kɛəteikə], *n.* conserje, portero; curador, *m.*
cargo ['kɑ:gou], *n.* cargamento, carga.
Caribbean [kæri'bi:ən], *a.* caribe.—*n.* mar Caribe, *m.*
caricature ['kærikətjuə], *n.* caricatura.—*v.t.* ridiculizar.
carillon [kə'riljən], *n.* repique, *m.*; carillón, *m.*
carman ['kɑ:mən], *n.* carretero.
carmine ['kɑ:main], *a.* de carmín.—*n.* carmín, *m.*
carnage ['kɑ:nidʒ], *n.* matanza, mortandad, *f.*
carnal ['kɑ:nəl], *a.* carnal.
carnality [kɑ:'næliti], *n.* carnalidad, *f.*
carnation [kɑ:'neiʃən], *n.* clavel, *m.*
carnival ['kɑ:nivəl], *n.* carnaval, *m.*, carnestolendas, *f.pl.*
carnivorous [kɑ:'nivərəs], *a.* carnívoro.
carob ['kærəb], *n.* algarroba (*judía*); algarrobo (*árbol*).
carol ['kærəl], *n.* villancico.—*v.i.* cantar, gorjear.
carousal [kə'rauzəl], *n.* francachela; jarana.
carouse [kə'rauz], *v.i.* embriagarse, jaranear.
carp (1) [kɑ:p], *n.* (*ichth.*) carpa.
carp (2) [kɑ:p], *v.i.* regañar, cavilar.
carpenter ['kɑ:pintə], *n.* carpintero.
carpentry ['kɑ:pintri], *n.* carpintería.
carpet ['kɑ:pit], *n.* alfombra.—*v.t.* alfombrar; (*fig.*) felpar; — ***sweeper,*** escoba mecánica.
carpet-bagger ['kɑ:pitbægə], *n.* (*U.S.*) politicastro.
carping ['kɑ:piŋ], *a.* caviloso.—*n.* censura inmotivada.
carriage ['kæridʒ], *n.* transporte, *m.*; coche (*vehículo*); porte (*manera de andar etc.*), *m.*; carro (*de una máquina de escribir*); — ***paid,*** porte pagado.
carrier ['kæriə], *n.* portador, *m.*; arriero.
carrion ['kæriən], *n.* carroña.
carrot ['kærət], *n.* zanahoria.
carroty ['kærəti], *a.* (*fam.*) amarillo rojizo.
carry ['kæri], *v.t.* llevar, traer; transportar; incluir; acarrear.—*v.i.* alcanzar, llegar; ***to — off*** o ***away,*** llevarse; ***to — on,*** continuar; ***to — out,*** llevar a cabo; ***to — forward,*** (*com.*) pasar a la vuelta *o* al frente.
cart [kɑ:t], *n.* carro, carreta.—*v.t.* acarrear.
cartage ['kɑ:tidʒ], *n.* acarreo.
carte-blanche ['kɑ:t'blɑ:nʃ], *n.* carta blanca.
cartel [kɑ:'tel], *n.* cartel, *m.*
Carthusian [kɑ:'θju:zjən], *a., n.* cartuj(an)o.
cartilage ['kɑ:tilidʒ], *n.* cartílago.
cartographer [kɑ:'tɔgrəfə], *n.* cartógrafo.
carton ['kɑ:tən], *n.* caja de cartón.
cartoon [kɑ:'tu:n], *n.* caricatura; (*cine.*) dibujo animado; (*art.*) cartón, *m.*
cartridge ['kɑ:tridʒ], *n.* cartucho.
carve [kɑ:v], *v.t.* (*art.*) tallar, esculpir; (*cul.*) trinchar.
carver ['kɑ:və], *n.* tallista, *m.f.*; trinchante (*cuchillo*), *m.*
carving ['kɑ:viŋ], *n.* (obra de) talla, escultura.
cascade [kæs'keid], *n.* cascada.
cascara [kæs'kɑ:rə], *n.* (*med.*) cáscara sagrada.
case [keis], *n.* (*gram., med.*) caso; (*jur.*) causa, pleito; caja; estuche, *m.*, funda; ***(just) in —,*** por si acaso; ***in any —,*** de todos modos.
casement ['keismənt], *n.* ventana a bisagra.
cash [kæʃ], *n.* dinero contante; pago al contado; metálico; (*com.*) caja.—*v.t.* cobrar, hacer efectivo; ***to — in on,*** (*fam.*) aprovechar.
cashbox ['kæʃbɔks], *n.* caja.
cashew [kæ'ʃu:], *n.* anacardo.
cashier [kæ'ʃiə], *n.* cajero, contador, *m.*—*v.t.* (*mil.*) destituir.
Cashmere [kæʃ'miə], *n.* cachemira; casimir, *m.*
cask [kɑ:sk], *n.* barril, tonel, *m.*, pipa.
casket ['kɑ:skit], *n.* cajita (*para joyas*), cofrecito; (*U.S.*) ataúd, *m.*
Caspian ['kæspiən], *a.* caspio.—*n.* mar Caspio.
casserole ['kæsəroul], *n.* cacerola.
cassock ['kæsək], *n.* sotana.
cassowary ['kæsəwɛəri], *n.* (*orn.*) casuario.
cast [kɑ:st], *n.* echada; (*theat.*) reparto, distribución, *f.*; semblante, *m.*—*v.t. irr.* tirar, arrojar, lanzar; echar; fundir; ***to — aside,*** desechar; ***to — down,*** derribar; ***to — forth,*** despedir; ***to — loose,*** soltar; ***to — lots,*** echar a la suerte; ***to — off,*** echar; hacer la última hilera (*de puntadas*); (*naut.*) desmarrar.
castanet [kæstə'net], *n.* castañuela.
castaway ['kɑ:stəwei], *n.* náufrago.
caste [kɑ:st], *n.* casta; grupo privilegiado.
castellated ['kæstileitid], *a.* encastillado.
castigate ['kæstigeit], *v.t.* castigar.
Castile [kæs'ti:l], *n.* Castilla.
Castilian [kəs'tiliən], *a., n.* castellano.
casting ['kɑ:stiŋ], *n.* fundición; pieza fundida; (*theat.*) distribución, *f.*; — ***vote,*** voto de calidad, voto decisivo.
cast-iron ['kɑ:st'aiən], *a.* hecho de hierro colado; fuerte.—*n.* hierro colado.

castle [kɑ:sl], *n.* castillo; torre (*ajedrez*), *f.*—*v.i.* enrocar (*ajedrez*).
castor (1) ['kɑ:stə], *n.* (*zool.*) castor, *m.*
castor (2) ['ka:stə], *n.* rodaja; vinagreras, *f.pl.*
castor-oil ['kɑ:stərɔil], *n.* aceite (*m.*) de ricino.
castrate [kæs'treit], *v.t.* castrar.
casual ['kæʒuəl], *a.* casual, fortuito; informal; poco formal, negligente.
casualness ['kæʒuəlnis], *n.* falta de aplicación *o* de formalidad, despreocupación, *f.*
casualty ['kæʒjuəlti], *n.* (*mil.*) baja; víctima; herido; accidente, *m.*
casuistry ['kæzjuistri], *n.* (*theol.*) casuística; (*fig.*) sofisma, *m.*
cat [kæt], *n.* gato; azote, *m.*
cataclysm ['kætəklizm], *n.* cataclismo.
catacomb ['kætəku:m], *n.* catacumba.
Catalan [kætə'læn], *a.*, *n.* catalán.
catalogue ['kætəlɔg], *n.* catálogo.
Catalonia [kætə'louniə], *n.* Cataluña.
catapult ['kætəpult], *n.* catapulta; honda.
cataract ['kætərækt], *n.* (*geog.*, *med.*) catarata.
catarrh [kə'tɑ:], *n.* (*med.*) catarro.
catastrophe [kə'tæstrəfi], *n.* catástrofe, *m.*
catcall ['kætkɔ:l], *n.* rechifla.
catch [kætʃ], *n.* broche, presa; lo pescado *o* cogido; trampa; buen partido; rondó, *m.*—*v.t.* coger, asir; capturar; alcanzar; enganchar; ***to — cold,*** coger un resfriado; ***to — out,*** cazar; ***to — up,*** alcanzar; ponerse al corriente.
catching ['kætʃiŋ], *a.* contagioso.
catchword ['kætʃwə:d], *n.* (*print.*) reclamo; (*fig.*) lema, *m.*
catechise ['kætəkaiz], *v.t.* catequizar.
catechism ['kætəkizm], *n.* catecismo.
categoric(al) [kæti'gɔrikl], *a.* categórico; terminante.
category ['kætigəri], *n.* categoría.
cater ['keitə], *v.i.* abastecer; ***to — for,*** abastecer.
caterer ['keitərə], *n.* abastecedor, *m.*
caterpillar ['kætəpilə], *n.* oruga, gusano.
catfish ['kætfiʃ], *n.* bagre, *m.*
catgut ['kætgʌt], *n.* cuerda de tripa.
cathedral [kə'θi:drəl], *a.* catedralicio.—*n.* catedral, *f.*
cathode ['kæθoud], *n.* cátodo; ***— ray,*** rayo catódico.
catholic ['kæθəlik], *a.*, *n.* católico.
catholicism [kə'θɔlisizm], *n.* catolicismo.
catholicity [kæθə'lisiti], *n.* catolicidad, *f.*
catkin ['kætkin], *n.* candelilla, amento.
Cato ['keitou], *n.* Catón, *m.*
cat's-paw ['kætspɔ:], *n.* (*fig.*) hombre (*m.*) de paja.
catsup ['kætsʌp], (*U.S.*) [KETCHUP].
cattiness ['kætinis], *n.* chismería; malicia.
cattle [kætl], *n.* ganado, ganado vacuno.
cattleman ['kætlmən], *n.* ganadero; vaquero.
catty ['kæti]. *a.* chismoso; rencoroso; gatuno.
catwalk ['kætwɔ:k], *n.* pasadizo, pasarela.
Caucasian [kɔ:'keiziən], *a.* caucásico; de la raza blanca.
Caucasus ['kɔ:kəsəs], *n.* Cáucaso.
caucus ['kɔ:kəs], *n.* (*esp. U.S.*) camarilla.
caught [cɔ:t] [CATCH].
cauldron ['kɔ:ldrən], *n.* calderón, *m.*
cauliflower ['kɔliflauə], *n.* coliflor, *m.*
caulk [kɔ:k], *v.t.* calafatear.
causal ['kɔ:zəl], *a.* causal.
cause [kɔ:z], *n.* causa; origen, *m.*—*v.t.* causar.
causeway ['kɔ:zwei], *n.* calzada, terraplén, *m.*
caustic ['kɔ:stik], *a.* cáustico; (*fig.*) mordaz.
cauterize ['kɔ:təraiz], *v.t.* cauterizar.
caution ['kɔ:ʃən], *n.* cautela; amonestación, *f.*—*v.t.* amonestar.
cautionary ['kɔ:ʃnəri], *a.* amonestador.
cautious ['kɔ:ʃəs], *a.* cauteloso; prudente.
cautiousness ['kɔ:ʃəsnis], *n.* cautela.
cavalcade [kævəl'keid], *n.* cabalgata.
cavalier [kævə'liə], *a.* altivo.—*n.* caballero; galán, *m.*
cavalry ['kævəlri], *n.* caballería.
cave [keiv], *n.* cueva.—*v.i.* ***to — in,*** derrumbarse.
cavern ['kævən], *n.* caverna.
caviare ['kæviɑ:], *n.* caviar, *m.*
cavil ['kævil], *v.i.* cavilar.
cavity ['kæviti], *n.* cavidad, *f.*, hueco.
caw [kɔ:], *n.* graznido.—*v.i.* graznar.
cease [si:s], *v.t.* parar.—*v.i.* parar, cesar.
ceaseless ['si:slis], *a.* incesante.
cedar ['si:də], *n.* cedro.
cede [si:d], *v.t.* ceder, traspasar.
ceiling ['si:liŋ], *n.* techo, cielo raso.
celandine ['seləndain], *n.* (*bot.*) celidonia.
celebrate ['selibreit], *v.t.*, *v.i.* celebrar.
celebrated ['selibreitid], *a.* célebre.
celebration [seli'breiʃən], *n.* celebración, *f.*, fiesta.
celebrity [si'lebriti], *n.* celebridad, *f.*
celerity [si'leriti], *n.* celeridad, *f.*
celery ['seləri], *n.* apio.
celestial [si'lestjəl], *a.* celestial.
celibacy ['selibəsi], *n.* celibato.
celibate ['selibət], *a.*, *n.* célibe.
cell [sel], *n.* celda; (*elec. etc.*) célula.
cellar ['selə], *n.* sótano; bodega.
cello ['tʃelou], *n.* (violon)celo.
cellophane ['selofein], *n.* celofán, *m.*
cellular ['seljulə], *a.* celular.
celluloid ['seljulɔid], *n.* celuloide, *m.*
cellulose ['seljulouz], *n.* celulosa.
Celt [kelt, selt], *n.* Celta, *m.f.*
Celtiberian [keltai'bi:riən], *a.*, *n.* Celtíbero.
Celtic ['keltik, 'seltik], *a.* céltico.
cement [si'ment], *n.* cemento, argamasa.—*v.t.* unir (con cemento).
cemetery ['semitri], *n.* cementerio, camposanto.
censor ['sensə], *n.* censor, *m.*—*v.t.* censurar.
censorship ['sensəʃip], *n.* censura.
censure ['senʃə], *n.* reprobación, *f.*—*v.t.* criticar, censurar.
census ['sensəs], *n.* censo.
cent [sent], *n.* céntimo, centavo; ***per —,*** por ciento.
centaur ['sentɔ:], *n.* centauro.
centenary [sen'ti:nəri], *n.* centenario.
center (*U.S.*) [CENTRE].
centigrade ['sentigreid], *a.* centígrado.
centigramme ['sentigræm], *n.* centigramo.
centime ['sɑ̃nti:m], *n.* céntimo.
centimetre ['sentimi:tə], *n.* centímetro.
centipede ['sentipi:d], *n.* ciempiés, *m. inv.*
central ['sentrəl], *a.* central, céntrico.—*n.* (*U.S. tel.*) central, *f.*
centralize ['sentrəlaiz], *v.t.* centralizar.
centre ['sentə], *n.* centro.
centrifugal [sen'trifjugəl], *a.* centrífugo.
centripetal [sen'tripitl], *a.* centrípeto.
centurion [sen'tjuəriən], *n.* centurión, *m.*

century ['sentʃuri], *n.* siglo (100 *años*).
ceramic [si'ræmik], *a.* cerámico.—*n.pl.* cerámica.
cereal ['siəriəl], *a.*, *n.* cereal.—*n.* grano, cereal, *m.*
cerebral ['seribrəl], *a.* cerebral.
ceremonial [seri'mounjəl], *a.* ceremonioso, ceremonial.—*n.* ceremonial, *m.*, aparato.
ceremony ['seriməni], *n.* ceremonia.
certain ['sə:tin], *a.* cierto, seguro; *a* **—**, cierto.
certainness ['sə:tinnis], **certainty** ['sə:tinti], *n.* certeza, certidumbre, *f.*
certificate [sə:'tifikeit], *n.* certificado; (*com.*) título; partida.
certify ['sə:tifai], *v.t.* certificar.
certitude ['sə:titju:d], *n.* certidumbre, *f.*
Cesarean [si'zεəriən], *a.* (*med.*) cesáreo.
cessation [se'seiʃən], *n.* cesación, *f.*
cession ['seʃən], *n.* cesión, *f.*, traspaso.
cesspit ['sespit], **cesspool** ['sespu:l], *n.* pozo negro.
Ceylon [si'lɔn], *n.* Ceilán, *m.*
Ceylonese [silə'ni:z], *a.*, *n.inv.* ceilanés, *m.*
chafe [tʃeif], *n.* frotamiento.—*v.t.* frotar; irritar.
chaff [tʃɑ:f], *n.* barcia; paja menuda; chanza. *v.t.* chancear (con), burlarse (de).
chaffinch ['tʃæfintʃ], *n.* pinzón, *m.*
chafing ['tʃeifiŋ], *n.* frotamiento; irritación, *f.*
chagrin ['ʃægrin], *n.* desazón, *m.*; pesadumbre, *f.*—*v.t.* apesadumbrar.
chain [tʃein], *n.* cadena.—*v.t.* encadenar.
chair [tʃεə], *n.* silla; silla de manos; (*educ.*) cátedra.
chairman ['tʃεəmən], *n.* presidente, *m.*
chaise [ʃeiz], *n.* silla volante; calesín, *m.*
chalet ['ʃælei], *n.* chalet, *m.*, casita de campo.
chalice ['tʃælis], *n.* cáliz, *m.*
chalk [tʃɔ:k], *n.* creta; (*educ.*) tiza.—*v.t.* escribir *etc.* con tiza.
chalky ['tʃɔ:ki], *a.* gredoso; pálido.
challenge ['tʃæləndʒ], *n.* desafío; (*mil.*) quién vive, *m.*—*v.t.* desafiar; disputar.
challenger ['tʃælindʒə], *n.* desafiador, *m.*; aspirante, *m.f.*
chamber ['tʃeimbə], *n.* cámara; aposento; **— *pot***, orinal, *m.*
chamberlain ['tʃeimbəlin], *n.* chambelán, *m.*, tesorero, camarlengo.
chamber-maid ['tʃeimbəmeid], *n.* camarera.
chameleon [ke'mi:ljən], *n.* camaleón, *m.*
chamfer ['tʃaemfə], *n.* (*carp.*) chaflán, *m.*—*v.t.* chaflanar.
chamois ['ʃæmwɑ:], *n.* gamuza.
champ [tʃæmp], *n.* mordisco.—*v.t.*, *v.i.* mordiscar.
champagne [ʃæm'pein], *n.* champaña.
champion ['tʃæmpjən], *n.* campeón, *m.*; paladín, *m.*—*v.t.* defender; abogar por.
chance [tʃɑ:ns], *n.* fortuna, accidente, *m.*
chancel ['tʃɑ:nsəl], *n.* (*eccl.*) santuario.
chancellor ['tʃɑ:nsələ], *n.* canciller, *m.*
chancery ['tʃɑ:nsəri], *n.* (*jur.*) cancillería.
chancy ['tʃɑ:nsi], *a.* (*fam.*) arriesgado.
chandelier [ʃændə'liə], *n.* araña de luces.
chandler ['tʃɑ:ndlə], *n.* cerero; abastecedor, *m.*
changeable ['tʃeindʒəbl], *a.* variable, mudable.
changeless ['tʃeindʒlis], *a.* constante, inmutable.
changeling ['tʃeindʒliŋ], *n.* niño cambiado en secreto por otro.
channel ['tʃænəl], *n.* canal, *m.*; acequia; ***English Channel***, Canal de la Mancha.—*v.t.* encauzar.
chant [tʃɑ:nt], *n.* canto; sonsonete, *m.*—*v.t.* *v.i.* cantar.
chantry ['tʃɑ:ntri], *n.* capilla.
chaos ['keiɔs], *n.* caos, *m.sg.*
chaotic [kei'ɔtik], *a.* caótico.
chap (1) [tʃæp], *n.* (*fam.*) tipo, tío.
chap (2) [tʃæp], *n.* grieta.—*v.t.* agrietar, hender.—*v.i.* agrietarse.
chapel ['tʃæpəl], *n.* capilla.
chaperon ['ʃæpəroun], *n.* dueña, señora de compañía.—*v.t.* acompañar, vigilar.
chaplain ['tʃæplin], *n.* capellán, *m.*
chapter ['tʃæptə], *n.* capítulo; categoría; (*eccl.*) cabildo.
char (1) [tʃɑ:], *n.* (*ichth.*) umbra.
char (2) [tʃɑ:], *n.* [CHARWOMAN].—*v.t.* limpiar.
char (3) [tʃɑ:], *v.t.* carbonizar.
character ['kærəktə], *n.* carácter, *m.*; (*theat.*) papel, personaje, *m.*; (*fam.*) original.
characteristic [kærəktə'ristik], *a.* característico, típico.—*n.* rasgo.
characterize ['kærəktəraiz], *v.t.* caracterizar.
charade [ʃə'rɑ:d], *n.* charada.
charcoal ['tʃɑ:koul], *n.* carbón (de leña), *m.*
charge [tʃɑ:dʒ], *n.* carga (*de un fusil, una responsabilidad*), cargo (*responsabilidad*); precio; ***in — of***, a cargo de.—*v.t.* cargar; cobrar; ***to — with***, cargar de, acusar de.
chargé d'affaires [ʃɑ:ʒeidæ'fεə], *n.* encargado de negocios.
charger ['tʃɑ:dʒə], *n.* fuente, *f.*, azafate; caballo de guerra; cargador, *m.*
chariot ['tʃæriət], *n.* carro; carroza.
charioteer [tʃæriə'tiə], *n.* auriga, *m.*
charitable ['tʃæritəbl], *a.* caritativo.
charity ['tʃæriti], *n.* caridad, *f.*
charlatan ['ʃɑ:lətən], *n.* embaidor; curandero.
charm [tʃɑ:m], *n.* encanto; maleficio; amuleto.—*v.t.* encantar; hechizar.
charming ['tʃɑ:miŋ], *a.* encantador.
charnel-house ['tʃɑ:nəlhaus], *n.* carnero.
chart [tʃɑ:t], *n.* carta, mapa, *m.*; cuadro.—*v.t.* trazar en una carta.
charter ['tʃɑ:tə], *n.* carta, fuero; fletamiento. —*v.t.* estatuir; fletar; alquilar (*un avión*).
charwoman ['tʃɑ:wumən], *n.* asistenta.
chary ['tʃεəri], *a.* cauteloso; circunspecto.
chase [tʃeis], *n.* caza; seguimiento; ranura.—*v.t.* cazar; perseguir; grabar.
chasm [kæzm], *n.* abismo, desfiladero.
chaste [tʃeist], *a.* casto.
chasten [tʃeisn], *v.t.* corregir, castigar.
chasteness ['tʃeistnəs], *n.* castidad, *f.*
chastise [tʃæs'taiz], *v.t.* castigar.
chastisement [tʃæs'taizmənt], *n.* castigo.
chastity ['tʃæstiti], *n.* castidad, *f.*
chat [tʃæt], *n.* charla.—*v.i.* charlar, platicar.
chateau ['ʃætou], *n.* casa solariega, castillo.
chatelaine ['ʃætəlein], *n.* castellana; llavero con dijes.
chattels [tʃætlz], *n.pl.* bienes muebles, enseres, *m.pl.*
chatter ['tʃætə], *n.* charla.—*v.i.* charlar; castañetear (*los dientes*).

chatterbox ['tʃætəbɔks], *n.* tarabilla, parlanchín, *m.*
chauffeur ['ʃoufə], *n.* chófer, (*S.A.*) chofer, *m.*
cheap [tʃi:p], *a.* barato; (*fig.*) ordinario; vil, ruin.
cheapen ['tʃi:pən], *v.t.* rebajar, abaratar.—*v.i.* abaratarse.
cheapness ['tʃi:pnis], *n.* baratura.
cheat [tʃi:t], *n.* timador, *m.*; trampa, engaño.—*v.t.* trampear; ***to — someone out of something,*** defraudar algo a alguien.
check [tʃek], *a.* de cuadros.—*n.* resistencia, freno; (*com.*) talón, *m.*; contraseña; (*U.S.*) cuenta; (*U.S.*) cheque; jaque (*ajedrez*), *m.*; comprobación, *f.*, visita.—*v.t.* parar; trabar; facturar; (*U.S.*) depositar (*equipaje*); comprobar, verificar; marcar con cuadros; dar jaque a.—*v.i.* pararse; ***to — in,*** (*U.S.*) llegar (a un hotel); ***to — up,*** verificar.
checker ['tʃekə], *n.* inspector, *m.*; cuadro (*de una tela tejida*); ficha (*damas*).—*pl.* damas, *f.pl.*—*v.t.* cuadricular.
checkerboard ['tʃekəbɔ:d], *n.* (*esp. U.S.*) tablero (de damas).
checkered ['tʃekəd], *a.* (*fig.*) accidentado, irregular.
checkmate ['tʃekmeit], *n.* jaque mate, *m.*—*v.t.* dar mate a.
cheek [tʃi:k], *n.* mejilla, carrillo; (*fam.*) frescura, descaro.
cheeky ['tʃi:ki], *a.* insolente, descarado.
cheep [tʃi:p], *n.* pío.—*v.i.* piar.
cheer [tʃiə], *n.* aplauso; alegría; alimento.—*v.t.* aplaudir, animar.—*v.i.* alegrarse; ***— up!*** ¡ánimo!
cheerful ['tʃiəful], *a.* alegre.
cheerfulness ['tʃiəfulnis], *n.* alegría, buen humor, *m.*
cheerless ['tʃiəlis], *a.* triste.
cheese [tʃi:z], *n.* queso.
cheetah ['tʃi:tə], *n.* (*zool.*) leopardo cazador (de la India).
chef [ʃef], *n.* cocinero; jefe (*m.*) de cocina.
chemical ['kemikəl], *a.* químico.—*n.* producto químico.
chemist ['kemist], *n.* químico; (*Brit.*) boticario, farmacéutico; ***chemist's,*** farmacia.
chemistry ['kemistri], *n.* química.
cheque [tʃek], *n.* cheque, *m.*
cheque-book ['tʃekbuk], *n.* talonario de cheques.
chequered [CHECKERED].
cherish ['tʃeriʃ], *v.t.* acariciar; tratar con ternura; abrigar (*esperanzas*).
cherry ['tʃeri], *n.* cereza, guinda; ***— tree,*** cerezo.
cherub ['tʃerəb], *n.* (*Bib.*) (*pl.* **cherubim**) querubín, *m.*; (*fig.*) (*pl.* **cherubs**) niño angelical.
chess [tʃes], *n.* ajedrez, *m.*
chessboard ['tʃesbɔ:d], *n.* tablero (de ajedrez).
chest [tʃest], *n.* (*anat.*) pecho; arca, cofre (*caja*), *m.*; ***— of drawers,*** cómoda.
chestnut ['tʃesnʌt], *n.* castaña; color de castaño (*árbol*); (*fig.*) chiste viejo.
chevron ['ʃevrən], *n.* (*her.*) cheurón, *m.*; (*mil.*) galón, *m.*
chew [tʃu:], *v.t.* mascar, masticar.
chiaroscuro [kiɑ:rə'skjuərou], *n.* (*art.*) claroscuro.
chic [ʃi:k], *a.* elegante.—*n.* chic, elegancia.
chicanery [ʃi'keinəri], *n.* embuste, *m.*
chick [tʃik], *n.* polluelo.
chicken ['tʃikin], *n.* pollo; gallina, gallo.
chicken-hearted ['tʃikin'hɑ:tid], *a.* cobarde.
chicken-pox ['tʃikinpɔks], *n.* (*med.*) varicela.
chickpea ['tʃikpi:], *n.* garbanzo.
chickweed ['tʃikwi:d], *n.* (*bot.*) morgelina, pamplina.
chicory ['tʃikəri], *n.* (*bot.*) achicoria.
chide [tʃaid], *v.t. irr.* regañar.
chief [tʃi:f], *a.* principal.—*n.* jefe, *m.*, caudillo; cacique, *m.*
chiefly ['tʃi:fli], *adv.* principalmente.
chiffon ['ʃifɔn], *n.* gasa, chifón, *m.*
chilblain ['tʃilblein], *n.* sabañón, *m.*
child [tʃaild], *n.* (*pl.* **children**) niño; descendiente, *m.f.*; ***to be with —,*** estar encinta; ***child's play,*** (*fig.*) cosa facilísima.
childbirth ['tʃaildbə:θ], *n.* parto, alumbramiento.
childhood ['tʃaildhud], *n.* infancia, niñez, *f.*
childish ['tʃaildiʃ], *a.* pueril, infantil.
children ['tʃildrən] [CHILD].
Chile ['tʃili], *n.* Chile, *m.*
Chilean ['tʃiliən], *a.*, *n.* chileno.
chill [tʃil], *a.* frío, glacial.—*n.* frío; resfriado; escalofrío.—*v.t.* helar, enfriar.
chilly ['tʃili], *a.* frío; friolento.
chimera [kai'miərə], *n.* quimera.
chime [tʃaim], *n.* juego de campanas; repique, *m.*—*v.t.*, *v.i.* repicar; ***to — in,*** (*fig.*) hacer coro; entremeterse.
chimerical [ki'merikəl], *a.* quimérico.
chimney ['tʃimni], *n.* chimenea; ***— pot,*** cañón (*m.*) de chimenea; ***— sweep,*** deshollinador, *m.*
chimpanzee [tʃimpæn'zi:], *n.* (*zool.*) chimpancé, *m.*
chin [tʃin], *n.* barbilla, mentón, *m.*
China ['tʃainə], *n.* China; **china**, *n.* porcelana.
Chinese [tʃai'ni:z], *a.*, *n.* chino.
chink [tʃiŋk], *n.* grieta, hendedura; sonido metálico.—*v.i.* sonar metálicamente.
chintz [tʃints], *n.* quimón, *m.*, zaraza.
chip [tʃip], *n.* astilla.—*n.pl.* patatas fritas.—*v.t.* descantillar.—*v.i.* romperse.
chirp [tʃə:p], *v.i.* piar.
chisel ['tʃizəl], *n.* (*carp.*) escoplo; (*art.*, *metal.*) cincel, *m.*
chit (1) [tʃit], *n.* (*fam.*) chiquillo.
chit (2) [tʃit], *n.* (*Brit.*) esquela; vale, *m.*
chit-chat ['tʃittʃæt], *n.* (*fam.*) hablilla, chismes, *m.pl.*
chivalrous ['ʃivəlrəs], *a.* caballeresco; caballeroso.
chivalry ['ʃivəlri], *n.* caballerosidad, *f.*; caballería.
chive [tʃaiv], *n.* (*bot.*) cebollana.
chloral ['klɔ:rəl], *a.* (*chem.*) cloral.
chlorate ['klɔ:reit], *n.* (*chem.*) clorato.
chloride ['klɔ:raid], *n.* (*chem.*) cloruro.
chlorine ['klɔ:ri:n], *n.* (*chem.*) cloro.
chlorinate ['klɔ:rineit], *v.t.* desinfectar con cloro.
chloroform ['klɔrəfɔ:m], *n.* cloroformo.
chlorophyll ['klɔrəfil], *n.* clorofila.
chock [tʃɔk], *n.* cuna.
chock-full ['tʃɔkful], *a.* colmado.
chocolate ['tʃɔklit], *n.* chocolate, *m.*
choice [tʃɔis], *a.* escogido.—*n.* selección, *f.*; preferencia; (cosa) escogida.
choicely ['tʃɔisli], *adv.* primorosamente.
choir [kwaiə], *n.* coro.

choke [tʃouk], *n.* estrangulación, *f.*; (*mech.*) obturador, *m.*—*v.t.* estrangular; atascar.—*v.i.* sofocarse; obstruirse; atragantarse.
cholera ['kɔlərə], *n.* (*med.*) cólera.
choose [tʃu:z], *v.t. irr.* escoger, elegir.—*v.i. irr.* optar.
chop [tʃɔp], *n.* (*cul.*) chuleta; tajada; mejilla.—*v.t.* cortar, tajar.
chopper ['tʃɔpə], *n.* hacha; cuchillo de carnicero.
choppy ['tʃɔpi], *a.* agitado (*mar*).
chopsticks ['tʃɔpstiks] *n.pl.* palitos, *m. pl.*
choral ['kɔ:rəl], *a.* coral.
chord [kɔ:d], *n.* (*mus.*) acorde, *m.*; (*eng.*, *math.*) cuerda.
chore [tʃɔ:], *n.* tarea.
chorus ['kɔ:rəs], *n.* coro (*grupo*); estribillo (*de una canción*); — ***girl,*** corista, *f.*; ***in —,*** en coro, a una voz.
chose(n) ['tʃouʒ(n)], [CHOOSE].
christen [krisn], *v.t.* bautizar.
Christendom ['krisndəm], *n.* cristiandad, *f.*
christening ['krisniŋ], *n.* bautismo, bautizo.
Christian ['kristjən], *a.*, *n.* cristiano;—***name,*** nombre (de pila).
Christianity [kristi'æniti], *n.* cristianismo.
Christmas ['krisməs], *n.* Navidad, *f.*, pascuas de Navidad; — ***box,*** aguinaldo; ***Merry —,*** Felices Pascuas.
chromium ['kroumjəm], *n.* cromo.
chronicle ['krɔnikl], *n.* crónica.
chronology [krə'nɔlədʒi], *n.* cronología.
chrysalis ['krisəlis], *n.* crisálida.
chrysanthemum [kri'zænθəməm], *n.* (*bot.*) cristantemo.
chub [tʃʌb], *n.* (*ichth.*) coto, cacho.
chubby ['tʃʌbi], *a.* gordo, gordiflón.
chuck [tʃʌk], *v.t.* (*fam.*) arrojar.
chuckle [tʃʌkl], *n.* risa ahogada.—*v.i.* reír entre dientes.
chum [tʃʌm], *n.* (*fam.*) compinche, *m.*, compañero.
chump [tʃʌmp], *n.* zoquete, *m.*
chunk [tʃʌŋk], *n.* pedazo grueso.
church [tʃə:tʃ], *n.* iglesia.
churchyard ['tʃə:tʃjɑ:d], *n.* cementerio.
churl [tʃə:l], *n.* palurdo.
churlish ['tʃə:liʃ], *a.* grosero, palurdo.
churn [tʃə:n], *n.* mantequera.—*v.t.* batir (en una mantequera); ***to — out,*** (*fig.*) fabricar en gran serie.
chute [ʃu:t], *n.* conducto.
cicada [si'keidə], *n.* (*ent.*) cigarra.
cider ['saidə], *n.* sidra.
cigar [si'gɑ:], *n.* puro, cigarro (puro).
cigarette [sigə'ret], *n.* cigarrillo, pitillo; — ***holder,*** boquilla; — ***lighter,*** encendedor (*m.*) de cigarrillos, mechero; — ***paper,*** papel (*m.*) de fumar.
cinder ['sində], *n.* ceniza.
Cinderella [sində'relə], *n.* Cenicienta.
cine-camera ['sinikæmərə], *n.* cámara.
cinema ['sinəmɑ:], *n.* cine, *m.*
cinnamon ['sinəmən], *a.* acanelado.—*n.* canela.
cipher ['saifə], *n.* cifra; cero; clave (*de una cifra*), *f.*—*v.t.* cifrar.—*v.i.* calcular.
circa ['sə:kə], *prep.* (*Lat.*) hacia.
circle [sə:kl], *n.* círculo.—*v.t.* dar la vuelta a.—*v.i.* dar vueltas.
circuit ['sə:kit], *n.* circuito.
circuitous [sə'kjuitəs], *a.* tortuoso, indirecto.
circular ['sə:kjulə], *a.* circular, redondo.—*n.* carta circular.
circulate ['sə:kjuleit], *v.t.* diseminar, propagar.—*v.i.* propagarse.
circulation [sə:kju'leiʃən], *n.* circulación, *f.*; tirada.
circumcise ['sə:kʌmsaiz], *v.t.* circuncidar.
circumcision [sə:kəm'siʒən], *n.* circuncisión, *f.*
circumference [sə'kʌmfərəns], *n.* circunferencia, periferia.
circumspect ['sə:kəmspekt], *a.* circunspecto, prudente.
circumstance ['sə:kəmstæns], *n.* circunstancia.
circumstantial [sə:kəm'stænʃl], *a.* circunstanciado; casual.
circumvent [sə:kəm'vent], *v.t.* soslayar.
circumvention [sə:kəm'venʃən], *n.* evitación, *f.*; rodeo.
circus ['sə:kəs], *n.* circo; plaza circular.
Cistercian [sis'tə:ʃən], *a.* cisterciense.
cistern ['sistən], *n.* cisterna, aljibe, *m.*; depósito.
citadel ['sitədəl], *n.* ciudadela.
citation [sai'teiʃən], *n.* citación; (*mil.*) mención, *f.*
cite [sait], *v.t.* citar; (*mil.*) mencionar.
citizen ['sitizən], *n.* ciudadano; súbdito.
citizenship ['sitizənʃip], *n.* ciudadanía; nacionalidad, *f.*
citric ['sitrik], *a.* cítrico.
citron ['sitrən], *n.* cidra, toronja; — ***tree,*** sidro, toronjal, *m.*
citrus ['sitrəs], *a.* auranciáceo; — ***fruits,*** agrios, frutas agrias.
city ['siti], *n.* ciudad, *f.*; — ***council,*** ayuntamiento.
civic ['sivik], *a.* cívico. — *n.pl.* educación política.
civil ['sivəl], *a.* cortés; civil; — ***defence,*** defensa pasiva; — ***servant,*** funcionario.
civilian [si'viljən], *a.*, *n.* (*mil.*) paisano.
civilization [sivilai'zeiʃən], *n.* civilización, *f.*
civilize ['sivilaiz], *v.t.* civilizar.
clad [klæd], *pret.*, *p.p.* (*obs.*) [CLOTHE].
claim [kleim], *n.* demanda; reclamación, *f.*; (*min.*) pertenencia.—*v.t.* reclamar; demandar; declarar; ***to — to be,*** pretender ser.
claimant ['kleimənt], *n.* demandante, *m.f.*
clairvoyant [klɛə'vɔiənt], *a.*, *n.* clarividente, *m.f.*
clam [klæm], *n.* almeja, tellina.
clamber ['klæmbə], *v.i.* subir gateando.
clammy ['klæmi], *a.* frío y húmedo; pegajoso.
clamour ['klæmə], *n.* clamor, *m.*—*v.i.* gritar, clamorear.
clamp [klæmp], *n.* abrazadera.—*v.t.* asegurar; ***to — down on,*** apretar los tornillos a.
clandestine [klæn'destin], *a.* clandestino.
clang [klæŋ], *n.* sonido metálico, tantán, *m.* [CLANK].
clank [klæŋk], *n.* sonido metálico, más profundo que el CLINK y menos resonante que el CLANG.
clap [klæp], *n.* palmoteo.—*v.t.* aplaudir.—*v.i.* dar palmadas; ***to — eyes on,*** (*fam.*) echar la vista a.
claret ['klærət], *n.* vino de Burdeos; clarete, *m.*
clarify ['klærifai], *v.t.* aclarar; clarificar (*azúcar etc.*).

clarinet [klæri'net], *n.* clarinete, *m.*
clarity ['klæriti], *n.* claridad, *f.*
clash [klæʃ], *n.* choque, *m.*; estruendo.—*v.i.* chocar.
clasp [klɑ:sp], *n.* hebilla; agarro.—*v.t.* abrochar; agarrar.
class [klɑ:s], *n.* clase, *f.*—*v.t.* clasificar.
classic ['klæsik], *a.*, *n.* clásico.
classify ['klæsifai], *v.t.* clasificar.
clatter ['klætə], *n.* estruendo; martilleo.—*v.i.* chocar ruidosamente.
clause [klɔ:z], *n.* cláusula; (*gram.*) oración, *f.*
claw [klɔ:], *n.* garra; uña; pinza.—*v.t.* despedazar; arañar.
clay [klei], *n.* arcilla.
clean [kli:n], *a.* limpio.—*adv.* (*fam.*) completamente.—*v.t.* limpiar.
cleaning ['kli:niŋ], *n.* limpieza, limpiadura.
cleanliness ['klenlinis], *n.* limpieza, aseo.
cleanly (1) ['klenli], *a.* habitualmente limpio.
cleanly (2) ['kli:nli], *adv.* limpiamente.
cleanness ['kli:nnis], *n.* limpieza.
cleanse [klenz], *v.t.* limpiar, purificar.
clear [kliə], *a.* claro; completo; evidente; — ***of,*** libre de.—*adv.* completamente.—*v.t.* limpiar; aclarar; clarificar; saltar por encima de; absolver; ***to — away,*** quitar; ***to — one's throat,*** carraspear; ***to — the way,*** abrir camino.—*v.i.* aclararse; despejarse.
clearance ['kliərəns], *n.* espacio libre (*entre dos cosas*), espacio muerto; — ***sale,*** liquidación, *f.*
clearing ['kliəriŋ], *n.* claro (*de un bosque*); vindicación, *f.*
cleave (1) [kli:v], *v.t. irr.* hender; dividir.—*v.i.* henderse.
cleave (2) [kli:v], *v.i.* pegarse; ser fiel.
cleft [kleft], *p.p.*, *a.* hendido.—*n.* grieta.
clematis ['klemətis], *n.* (*bot.*) clemátide, *f.*
clench [klentʃ], *v.t.* apretar; agarrar.
clergy ['klə:dʒi], *n.* clero, clerecía.
clergyman ['klə:dʒimən], *n.* clérigo; cura, *m.*
cleric ['klerik], *n.* clérigo.
clerical ['klerikəl], *a.* eclesiástico, clerical; oficinesco; — ***error,*** error (*m.*) de pluma.
clerk [klɑ:k], *n.* oficinista, *m.f.*; (*U.S.*) dependiente de tienda; eclesiástico; escribiente, *m.*; archivero; escribano.
clever ['klevə], *a.*diestro, mañoso; inteligente, hábil.
cleverness ['klevənis], *n.* destreza; inteligencia.
cliché ['kliʃei], *n.* (*print.*) clisé; (*fig.*) cliché, *m.*
click [klik], *n.* golpecito; tecleo; chasquido.—*v.t.* chascar (*la lengua*).—*v.i.* hacer tictac.
client ['klaiənt], *n.* cliente, *m.f.*, parroquiano.
cliff [klif], *n.* acantilado, escarpa, precipicio.
climate ['klaimət], *n.* clima, *m.*
climax ['klaimæks], *n.* colmo, culminación, *f.*
climb [klaim], *n.* subida.—*v.t.*, *v.i.* trepar, escalar, subir.
climber ['klaimə], *n.* escalador, trepador, *m.*; (*bot.*) trepadora.
clime [klaim], *n.* (*poet.*) clima, *m.*; región, *f.*
clinch [klintʃ], *n.* agarro.—*v.t.* agarrar; resolver decisivamente.—*v.i.* luchar cuerpo a cuerpo.
cling [kliŋ], *v.i. irr.* adherirse, pegarse.
clinic ['klinik], *n.* clínica.
clink [kliŋk], *n.* tintín, *m.*, sonido metálico [CLANK].
clinker ['kliŋkə], *n.* escoria.
clip [klip], *n.* presilla; tijereteo, trasquila; pinza; (*fam.*) golpe seco.—*v.t.* esquilar; recortar.
clipper ['klipə], *n.* (*naut.*) clíper, *m.*—*pl.* tijeras, *f.pl.*; cizalla.
clique [kli:k], *n.* pandilla.
cloak [klouk], *n.* capa; (*fig.*) disimulo.—*v.t.* encubrir.
cloakroom ['kloukrum], *n.* guardarropa.
clock [klɔk], *n.* reloj, *m.*; ***it is four o'clock,*** son las cuatro.
clockwise ['klɔkwaiz], *adv.* en el sentido de las agujas de reloj.
clockwork ['klɔkwə:k], *n.* aparato de relojería; movimiento de reloj.
clod [klɔd], *n.* terrón, *m.*; palurdo.
clog [klɔg], *n.* zueco; (*fig.*) embarazo.—*v.t.* estorbar; atascar.
cloister ['klɔistə], *n.* claustro.
close (1) [klous], *a.* cercano; cerrado.—*n.* recinto.—*adv.* de cerca.
close (2) [klouz], *n.* fin, terminación, *f.*—*v.t.* cerrar; terminar; ***to — in,*** acercarse.
closely ['klousli], *adv.* estrechamente; de cerca.
closet ['klɔzit], *n.* gabinete; retrete, *m.*
closure ['klouʒə], *n.* clausura, fin, *m.*
clot [klɔt], *n.* grumo; cuajarón, *m.*; (*fam.*) imbécil.—*v.i.* engrumecerse, cuajarse.
cloth [klɔθ], *n.* (*pl.* **cloths** [klɔðz]) tela, paño; género.
clothe [klouð], *v.t. irr.* vestir; cubrir.
clothes [klouðz], *n.pl.* ropa, vestidos; ***bed —,*** ropa de cama.
clothes-brush ['klouðzbrʌʃ], *n.* cepillo de ropa.
clothes-hanger ['klouðzhæŋə], *n.* percha.
clothes-horse ['klouðzhɔ:s], *n.* enjugador, *m.*
clothing ['klouðiŋ], *n.* vestidos, ropa.
cloud [klaud], *n.* nube, *f.*—*v.t.* nublar; entristecer.—*v.i.* nublarse; entristecerse.
cloud-burst ['klaudbə:st], *n.* chaparrón, *m.*
cloudy ['klaudi], *a.* nublado; velado; oscuro.
clout [klaut], *n.* (*fam.*) golpe, *m.*; trapo.
clove [klouv], *n.* clavo (*de especia*).
cloven ['klouvən], *p.p.* [CLEAVE].—*a.* hendido.
clover ['klouvə], *n.* trébol, *m.*
clown [klaun], *n.* payaso; palurdo.
cloy [klɔi], *v.t.*, *v.i.* empalagar, hastiar.
club [klʌb], *n.* porra, cachiporra; club, *m.*; círculo; trébol (*naipes*), *m.*—*v.t.* aporrear.—*v.i.* contribuir.
cluck [klʌk], *n.* cloqueo.—*v.i.* cloquear.
clue [klu:], *n.* indicio; guía.
clump [klʌmp], *n.* grupo; pisada fuerte.—*v.i.* andar torpemente.
clumsy ['klʌmzi], *a.* torpe.
clung [klʌŋ] [CLING].
Cluniac ['klu:niæk], *a.* cluniacense.
cluster ['klʌstə], *n.* racimo; grupo.—*v.i.* agruparse, juntarse.
clutch [klʌtʃ], *n.* agarro; nidada; (*aut.*) embrague, *m.*—*v.t.* agarrar, asir.
clutter ['klʌtə], *n.* confusión, *f.*; baraúnda.—*v.t.* poner en desorden.
coach (1) [koutʃ], *n.* coche, *m.*; diligencia
coach (2) [koutʃ], *n.* (*sport*) preparador, entrenador, *m.*; (*educ.*) profesor particular, *m.*—*v.t.* preparar.

coachman ['koutʃmæn], *n.* cochero, mayoral, *m.*
coagulate ['kouægjuleit], *v.i.* coagular, cuajar.
coal [koul], *n.* carbón (*de piedra*), *m.*; ascua, brasa.
coalesce [kouə'les], *v.i.* unirse.
coalition [kouə'liʃən], *n.* coalición, *f.*; alianza.
coal-mine ['koulmain], *n.* mina de carbón, mina hullera.
coal-miner ['koulmainə], *n.* minero, hullero.
coarse [kɔːs], *a.* basto; grueso; soez.
coast [koust], *n.* costa, orilla.—*v.i.* (*naut.*) costear; (*mech.*) andar en punto muerto.
coat [kout], *n.* hábito; chaqueta, americana; abrigo; capa, mano (*de pintura*), *f.*; — ***of arms,*** escudo de armas.—*v.t.*, *v.i.* cubrir.
coax [kouks], *v.t.* halagar, engatusar.
cob (1) [kɔb], *n.* mazorca.
cob (2) [kɔb], *n.* jaca.
cobalt ['koubɔːlt], *n.* cobalto.
cobbler ['kɔblə], *n.* zapatero de viejo.
cobblestone ['kɔbəlstoun], *n.* guijarro.
cob-nut ['kɔbnʌt], *n.* avellana.
cobweb ['kɔbweb], *n.* telaraña.
cocaine [ko'kein], *n.* cocaína.
cochineal [kɔtʃi'niːl], *n.* cochinilla.
cock [kɔk], *n.* gallo; macho (*de una ave*); grifo; veleta.—*v.t.* erguir, levantar.
cockerel ['kɔkərəl], *n.* gallo.
cockle ['kɔkəl], *n.* coquina.
Cockney ['kɔkni], *a.*, *n.* londinense.
cockpit ['kɔkpit], *n.* gallera, valla; (*aer.*) carlinga.
cockroach ['kɔkroutʃ], *n.* cucaracha.
cockscomb ['kɔkskoum], *n.* cresta de gallo; fanfarrón, *m.*
cocktail ['kɔkteil], *n.* cóctel, *m.*, combinado; cualquier mezcla.
cocoa ['koukou], *n.* cacao (*árbol, fruto*); chocolate (*bebida*), *m.*
coconut ['koukənʌt], *n.* coco.
cocoon [kə'kuːn], *n.* capullo.
cod [kɔd], *n.* (*ichth.*) bacalao, abadejo.
code [koud], *n.* código; cifra.
codex ['koudeks], *n.* códice, *m.*
codify ['koudifai], *v.t.* codificar.
coexistence [kouig'zistəns], *n.* coexistencia, convivencia.
coffee ['kɔfi], *n.* café, *m.*; ***black* —,** café solo; ***white* —,** café con leche.
coffee-mill ['kɔfimil], *n.* molinillo.
coffee-pot ['kɔfipɔt], *n.* cafetera.
coffer ['kɔfə], *n.* arca, cofre, *m.*
coffin ['kɔfin], *n.* ataúd, *m.*
cog [kɔg], *n.* diente (*de rueda*), *m.*
cogent ['koudʒənt], *a.* convincente, fuerte.
cogitate ['kɔdʒiteit], *v.i.* meditar.
cognac ['kɔnjæk], *n.* coñac, *m.*
cognate ['kɔgneit], *a.* cognado; análogo.
cognizance ['kɔgnizəns], *n.* conocimiento.
cohabit [kou'hæbit], *v.i.* cohabitar.
co-heir ['kou'ɛə], *n.* coheredero.
coherence [kou'hiərəns], *n.* consecuencia; cohesión, *f.*, coherencia.
coherent [kou'hiərənt], *a.* coherente.
cohesion [kou'hiːʒən], *n.* cohesión, *f.*
cohort ['kouhɔːt], *n.* cohorte, *f.*
coiffure [kwɑ'fjuə], *n.* peinado, tocado.
coil [kɔil], *n.* rollo, espiral, *m.*; (*elec.*) carrete, *m.*; rizo (*de cabellos*).—*v.t.* arrollar.—*v.i.* -se.
coin [kɔin], *n.* moneda; dinero.—*v.t.* acuñar.
coinage ['kɔinidʒ], *n.* sistema monetario, *m.*; acuñación, *f.*
coincide [kouin'said], *v.i.* coincidir.
coincidence [kou'insidəns], *n.* coincidencia, casualidad, *f.*
coincidental [kouinsi'dentl], *a.* coincidente.
coiner ['kɔinə], *n.* acuñador, *m.*; monedero falso.
coke [kouk], *n.* coque, *m.*
colander ['kʌləndə], *n.* colador, pasador, *m.*
cold [kould], *a.* frío.—*n.* frío; resfriado, constipado; ***to catch* —,** constiparse, resfriarse.
cold-chisel [kould'tʃizl], *n.* cortafrío.
coldness ['kouldnis], *n.* frialdad, *f.*
collaborate [kə'læbəreit], *v.i.* colaborar.
collapse [kə'læps], *n.* derrumbamiento; ruina.—*v.i.* derrumbarse; fracasar.
collar ['kɔlə], *n.* cuello; collar (*de perro*), *m.* —*v.t.* (*fam.*) coger.
collar-bone ['kɔləboun], *n.* clavícula.
collate [kə'leit], *v.t.* cotejar, comparar.
collateral [kɔ'lætərəl], *a.* colateral; paralelo. —*n.* (*com.*) resguardo.
collation [kə'leiʃən], *n.* contejo.
colleague ['kɔliːg], *n.* colega, *m.*
collect [kə'lekt], *v.t.* recoger; coleccionar; cobrar; ***to* — *oneself,*** reponerse.
collection [kə'lekʃən], *n.* colección; recaudación, *f.*; (*eccl.*) colecta.
collective [kə'lektiv], *a.* colectivo.
collector [kə'lektə], *n.* coleccionador; recaudador, *m.*
college ['kɔlidʒ], *n.* colegio.
collide ['kə'laid], *v.i.* chocar.
collier ['kɔljə], *n.* hullero, minero; barco carbonero.
colliery ['kɔljəri], *n.* mina de carbón.
collision [kə'liʒən], *n.* colisión, *f.*, choque, *m.*
colloquial [kə'loukwiəl], *a.* familiar.
colloquy ['kɔləkwi], *n.* coloquio.
collusion [kə'luːʒən], *n.* confabulación, conclusión, *f.*
Colombia [kə'lɔmbiə], *n.* Colombia.
Colombian [kə'lɔmbiən], *a.*, *n.* colombiano.
colon (1) ['koulən], *n.* (*anat.*) colon, *m.*
colon (2) ['koulən], *n.*(*gram.*) dos puntos.
colonel ['kəːnəl], *n.* coronel, *m.*
colonial [kə'lounjəl], *a.* colonial.
colonist ['kɔlənist], *n.* colono, colonizador, *m.*
colonization [kɔlənai'zeiʃən], *n.* colonización, *f.*
colonize ['kɔlənaiz], *v.t.* colonizar.
colony ['kɔləni], *n.* colonia.
colossal [kə'lɔsəl], *a.* colosal.
colour ['kʌlə], *n.* color, *m.*—*v.t.* colorar.
coloured ['kʌləd], *a.* colorado; exagerado; de color, de raza negra.
colouring ['kʌləriŋ], *n.* color, *m.*, colorido.
colt [koult], *n.* potro.
columbine ['kɔləmbain], *n.* aguileña.
Columbus [kə'lʌmbəs], *n.* Colón, *m.*
column ['kɔləm], *n.* columna.
comb [koum], *n.* peine, *m.*—*v.t.* peinar.
combat ['kɔmbæt], *n.* combate, *m.*, batalla.
combine (1) ['kɔmbɑin], *n.* monopolio; (*agr.*) segadora, trilladora.
combine (2) [kəm'bain], *v.t.* combinar.—*v.i.* unirse.
combustible [kəm'bʌstəbl], *a.* combustible.
combustion [kəm'bʌstʃən], *n.* combustión, *f.*

come [kʌm], *v.i. irr.* venir; ir; — ***along!*** ¡vamos!; ***coming!*** ¡ya voy! ***to — about,*** suceder; ***to — across,*** encontrar; ***to — between,*** desunir; ***to — by,*** obtener; ***to — off,*** tener lugar; despegarse; ***to — out,*** salir; ***to — to,*** volver en sí; llegar a; ***to — upon,*** encontrar, dar con.
comedian [kə'mi:djən], *n.* cómico.
comedy ['kɔmədi], *n.* comedia.
comeliness ['kʌmlinis], *n.* hermosura; donaire, *m.*
comely ['kʌmli], *a.* gentil, hermoso, bien parecido.
comet ['kɔmit], *n.* cometa, *m.*
comfort ['kʌmfət], *n.* comodidad, *f.*; confort, *m.*, alivio, consuelo.—*v.t.* confortar.
comfortable ['kʌmfətəbl], *a.* cómodo, confortable.
comic ['kɔmik], *a.*, *n.* cómico; gracioso; — (***paper***), tebeo; — ***strip,*** tira cómica.
comical ['kɔmikl], *a.* cómico.
coming ['kʌmiŋ], *n.* venida, llegada, (*eccl.*) advenimiento.
comma ['kɔmə], *n.* coma.
command [kə'mɑ:nd], *n.* mando; orden, *f.*; dominio.—*v.t.*, *v.i.* mandar.
commandant ['kɔməndænt], *n.* comandante, *m.*
commander [kə'mɑ:ndə], *n.* comandante; comendador (*de una orden militar*), *m.*
commander-in-chief [kə'mɑ:ndərintʃi:f], *n.* (*pl.* **commanders-in-chief**) generalísimo, jefe supremo.
commandment [kə'mɑ:ndmənt], *n.* (*Bibl.*) mandamiento.
commemoration [kəmemə'reiʃən], *n.* conmemoración, *f.*
commence [kə'mens], *v.t.*, *v.i.* comenzar, empezar.
commencement [kə'mensmənt], *n.* principio, comienzo; (*U.S.*) graduación, *f.*
commend [kə'mend], *v.t.* recomendar; alabar; encomendar.
commendable [kə'mendəbl], *a.* loable.
comment ['kɔment], *n.* observación, *f.*; comentario.—*v.t.* comentar, glosar (***on***).—*v.i.* comentar.
commerce ['kɔmə:s], *n.* comercio, negocios, *m.pl.*; trato familiar.
commercial [kə'mə:ʃəl], *a.* comercial; — ***traveller,*** viajante, *m.*
commiserate [kə'mizəreit], *v.i.* condolerse (***with,*** de).
commissar [kɔmi'sɑ:], *n.* comisario.
commissariat [kɔmi'sɛəriæt], *n.* comisaría; administración militar, *f.*
commission [kə'miʃən], *n.* comisión, *f.*—*v.t.* comisionar, apoderar, encargar.
commit [kə'mit], *v.t.* cometer; entregar; ***to — oneself,*** comprometerse.
committee [kə'miti], *n.* comité, *m.*
commode [kə'moud], *n.* cómoda; lavabo.
commodious [kə'moudiəs], *a.* espacioso.
commodity [kə'mɔditi], *n.* mercancía, género; comidad, *f.*
commodore ['kɔmədɔ:], *n.* comodoro.
common ['kɔmən], *a.* común; vulgar, ordinario.—*n.* pastos comunes; (*pol.*) ***the Commons,*** la Cámara de los Comunes.
commoner ['kɔmənə], *n.* plebeyo.
commonwealth ['kɔmənwelθ], *n.* república; federación, mancomunidad, *f.*, commonwealth, *m.*
commotion [kə'mouʃən], *n.* alboroto; conmoción, *f.*
communal ['kɔmjunəl], *a.* comunal.
commune ['kɔmju:n], *n.* (*pol.*) comuna.—[kə'mju:n], *v.i.* conversar; comulgar.
communicant [kə'mju:nikənt], *n.* (*eccl.*) comulgante, *m.f.*
communicate [kə'mju:nikeit], *v.t.*, *v.i.* comunicar; (*eccl.*) comulgar.
communication [kəmju:ni'keiʃən], *n.* comunicación, *f.*
communion [kə'mju:njən], *n.* comunión, *f.*
communiqué [kə'mju:nikei], *n.* comunicado, parte, *m.*
communism ['kɔmjunizm], *n.* comunismo.
communist ['kɔmjunist], *n.* comunista, *m.f.*
community [kə'mju:niti], *n.* comunidad, *f.*; vecindario; — ***chest,*** (*U.S.*) caja de beneficencia.
commute [kə'mju:t], *v.t.* conmutar.—*v.i.* viajar cada día entre su lugar de trabajo y el barrio (lejano) en que vive.
commuter [kə'mju:tə], *n.* abonado al ferrocarril que viaja cada día a su lugar de trabajo.
compact [kəm'pækt], *a.* compacto.—['kɔmpækt], *n.* estuche, *m.*; convenio.—*v.t.* comprimir.
companion [kəm'pænjən], *n.* compañero.
companion-way [kəm'pænjənwei], *n.* (*naut.*) escalera de cámara.
company ['kʌmpəni], *n.* (*com.*) compañía, sociedad, *f.*, empresa; (*mil.*) compañía; (*naut.*) tripulación, *f.*; (*fam.*) invitados, *m.pl.*, visitas, *f. pl.*
compare [kəm'pɛə], *v.t.* comparar. — *n.* (*only in*) ***beyond —,*** sin comparación.
comparison [kəm'pærisən], *n.* comparación, *f.*; ***in — with,*** comparado con.
compartment [kəm'pɑ:tmənt], *n.* compartimiento; (*rail.*) departamento.
compass ['kʌmpəs], *n.* (*naut.*) brújula; alcance; ***pair of compasses,*** compás, *m.sg.*—*v.t.* alcanzar; rodear.
compatriot [kəm'peitriət], *n.* compatriota, *m.f.*, paisano.
compel [kəm'pel], *v.t.* compeler, obligar, forzar.
compendium [kəm'pendiəm], *n.* compendio.
compensate ['kɔmpənseit], *v.t.* indemnizar, compensar.—*v.i.* compensarse.
compensation [kɔmpən'seiʃən], *n.* compensación, (*jur.*) indemnización, *f.*
compete [kəm'pi:t], *v.i.* rivalizar; competir concurrir.
competence ['kɔmpitəns], *n.* suficiencia; capacidad, *f.*, competencia.
competent ['kɔmpitənt], *a.* competente.
competition [kɔmpi'tiʃən], *n.* concurrencia; competencia; concurso.
competitive [kəm'petitiv], *a.* de concurso, de oposición.
competitor [kəm'petitə], *n.* concurrente, *m.f.*, competidor, *m.*
compile [kəm'pail], *v.t.* recopilar, compilar.
complacency [kəm'pleisensi], *n.* satisfacción (*f.*) de sí mismo; complacencia.
complacent [kəm'pleisənt], *a.* satisfecho de sí mismo, engreído.
complain [kəm'plein], *v.i.* quejarse.

complaint [kəm'pleint], *n.* queja; querella; enfermedad (*falta de salud*), *f.*
complaisant [kəm'pleizənt], *a.* complaciente.
complement ['kɔmplimənt], *n.* complemento; personal, *m.*
complementary [kɔmpli'mentəri], *a.* complementario.
complete [kəm'pli:t], *a.* completo; cabal.—*v.t.* completar, acabar.
completion [kəm'pli:ʃən], *n.* terminación, *f.*
complex ['kɔmpleks], *a.*, *n.* complejo.
complexion [kəm'plekʃən], *n.* tez (*de la cara*), *f.*; carácter, *m.*
compliance [kəm'plaiəns], *n.* sumisión, *f.*, complacencia; obediencia.
compliant [kəm'plaiənt], *a.* sumiso; obediente.
complicate ['kɔmplikeit], *v.t.* complicar.
complicated ['kɔmplikeitid], *a.* complicado.
complication [kɔmpli'keiʃən], *n.* complicación, *f.*
compliment ['kɔmplimənt], *n.* cumplido, alabanza; saludo.—*v.t.* cumplimentar, felicitar.
complimentary [kɔmpli'mentəri], *a.* de cortesía, gratuito; galante, lisonjero.
complin(e) ['kɔmplin], *n.* completas, *f.pl.*
comply [kəm'plai], *v.i.* conformarse (***with***, con).
component [kəm'pounənt], *a.*, *n.* componente, *m.* o *f.*
compose [kəm'pouz], *v.t.* componer.
composed [kəm'pouzd], *a.* sosegado; compuesto (***of***, de).
composer [kəm'pouzə], *n.* compositor, *m.*
composite ['kɔmpəzit], *a.* compuesto.
composition [kɔmpə'ziʃən], *n.* composición, *f.*
compositor [kəm'pɔzitə], *n.* (*print.*) cajista, *m.*
compost ['kɔmpɔst], *n.* abono compuesto.
composure [kəm'pouʒə], *n.* serenidad, *f.*, calma.
compound ['kɔmpaund], *a.*, *n.* compuesto.—[kəm'paund], *v.t.* componer; (*jur.*) encubrir.
comprehend [kɔmpri'hend], *v.t.* comprender.
comprehension [kɔmpri'henʃən], *n.* comprensión, *f.*
comprehensive [kɔmpri'hensiv], *a.* comprensivo; amplio.
compress ['kɔmpres], *n.* compresa.—[kəm'pres], *v.t.* comprimir.
compressor [kəm'presə], *n.* compresor, *m.*
comprise [kəm'praiz], *v.t.* comprender, constar de.
compromise ['kɔmprəmaiz], *n.* compromiso.—*v.t.* comprometer.—*v.i.* transigir.
comptroller [kən'troulə], *n.* interventor, *m.*
compulsory [kəm'pʌlsəri], *a.* obligatorio.
compute [kəm'pju:t], *v.t.* computar, calcular.
computer [kəm'pju:tə], *n.* calculadora; calculista (*persona*), *m.f.*
comrade ['kɔmrid], *n.* camarada, *m.f.*
comradeship ['kɔmridʃip], *n.* camaradería, compañerismo.
con (1) [kɔn], *n.* contra.
con (2) [kɔn], *v.t.* estudiar, aprender.
concatenate [kən'kætineit], *v.t.* concatenar.
concave ['kɔnkeiv], *a.* cóncavo.
conceal [kən'si:l], *v.t.* ocultar.
concede [kən'si:d], *v.t.* conceder.
conceit [kən'si:t], *n.* presunción, *f.*, engreimiento; concepto.
conceited [kən'si:tid], *a.* vanidoso, engreído.
conceive [kən'si:v], *v.t.* concebir.
concentrate ['kɔnsəntreit], *v.t.* concentrar.—*v.i.* -se.
concentration [kɔnsən'treiʃən], *n.* concentración, *f.*
concentric [kɔn'sentrik], *a.* concéntrico.
concept ['kɔnsept], *n.* concepto.
conception [kən'sepʃən], *n.* concepción, *f.*
concern [kən'sə:n], *n.* empresa, compañía; interés, *m.*; preocupación, inquietud, *f.*—*v.t.* preocupar; atañer, tocar a; interesar; ***as concerns***, respecto a.
concerning [kən'sə:niŋ], *prep.* respecto a; sobre.
concert ['kɔnsət], *n.* concierto.—[kən'sə:t], *v.t.* concertar.
concerto [kən'tʃə:tou], *n.* conc(i)erto.
concession [kən'seʃən], *n.* concesión, *f.*
conch [kɔntʃ], *n.* concha.
concierge [kɔnsi'ɛəʒ], *n.* conserje, *m.*, portero.
conciliate [kən'silieit], *v.t.* conciliar.
concise [kən'sais], *a.* sucinto, conciso.
concision [kən'siʒən], *n.* concisión, *f.*
conclave ['kɔnkleiv], *n.* conclave, *m.*
conclude [kən'klu:d], *v.t.*, *v.i.* concluir.
conclusion [kən'klu:ʒən], *n.* conclusión, *f.*
conclusive [kən'klu:siv], *a.* concluyente.
concoct [kən'kɔkt], *v.t.* confeccionar; forjar, urdir.
concoction [kən'kɔkʃən], *n.* confección, *f.*; forja, trama.
concomitant [kən'kɔmitənt], *a.*, *n.* concomitante, *m.*
concord ['kɔnkɔ:d], *n.* concord(anc)ia.—[kən'kɔ:d], *v.i.* concordar.
concordat [kən'kɔ:dæt], *n.* concordato.
concourse ['kɔnkɔ:s], *n.* concurso; confluencia.
concrete ['kɔnkri:t], *a.* concreto; sólido; de hormigón.—*n.* hormigón, *m.*
concubine ['kɔŋkjubain], *n.* concubina.
concur [kən'kə:], *v.i.* concurrir.
concussion [kən'kʌʃən], *n.* concusión, *f.*
condemn [kən'dem], *v.t.* condenar.
condemnation [kɔndem'neiʃən], *n.* condenación, *f.*
condensation [kɔnden'seiʃən], *n.* condensación, *f.*
condense [kən'dens], *v.t.* condensar.—*v.i.* -se.
condescend [kɔndi'send], *v.i.* dignarse (***to***, a).
condescending [kɔndi'sendiŋ], *a.* arrogante, condescendente.
condescension [kɔndi'senʃən], *n.* aire (*m.*) protector *o* de superioridad.
condiment ['kɔndimənt], *n.* condimento.
condition [kən'diʃən], *n.* condición, *f.* — *v.t.* (a)condicionar.
conditional [kən'diʃənəl], *a.* condicional.
condolence [kən'douləns], *n.* condolencia.
condone [kən'doun], *v.t.* condonar.
condor ['kɔndɔ:], *n.* cóndor, *m.*
conducive [kən'dju:siv], *a.* conducente.
conduct ['kɔndʌkt], *n.* conducta.—[kən'dʌkt], *v.t.*, *v.i.* conducir; (*mus.*) dirigir.
conduction [kən'dʌkʃən], *n.* conducción, *f.*
conductor [kən'dʌktə], *n.* (*elec.*) conductor; (*mus.*) director de orquesta; (*U.S.*, *rail.*) revisor; cobrador (*de autobus*), *m.*
conduit ['kʌndit], *n.* conducto, canal, *m.*

cone [coun], *n.* cono; cucurucho; barquillo (*para helados*).
coney ['kouni], *n.* conejo.
confab ['kɔnfæb], (*fam. abbr.* **confabulation** [kənfæbju'leiʃən]), *n.* confabulación, *f.*
confection [kən'fekʃən], *n.* confite, *m.*; confección, *f.*
confectionery [kən'fekʃənri], *n.* confitería; confites, *n.pl.*
confederate [kən'fedərit], *a.*, *n.* confederado, cómplice, *m.*—[kən'fedəreit], *v.t.* confederar.—*v.i.* -se.
confederation [kənfedə'reiʃən], *n.* confederación, *f.*
confer [kən'fə:], *v.t.* conferir, otorgar.—*v.i.* conferenciar.
conference ['kɔnfərəns], *n.* congreso; conferencia.
confess [kən'fes], *v.t.*, *v.i.* confesar(se).
confessedly [kən'fesidli], *adv.* manifiestamente.
confession [kən'feʃən], *n.* confesión, *f.*
confessional [kən'feʃənl], *n.* confesionario.
confessor [kən'fəsə], *n.* confesor, *m.*; penitente, *m.*
confidant(e) ['kɔnfidænt], *n.m.f.* confidente, confidenta.
confide [kən'faid], *v.t.* confiar.—*v.i.* confiar; *to — in*, decir confidencias a.
confidence ['kɔnfidəns], *n.* confianza; confidencia; *— trickster*, timador, *m.*
confident ['kɔnfidənt], *a.* confiado, seguro.
confidential [kɔnfi'denʃəl], *a.* confidencial, en confianza.
confine ['kɔnfain], *n.* confín, límite, *m.*—[kən'fain], *v.t.* limitar; encerrar; *to be confined*, estar de parto; *to be confined to bed*, guardar la cama.
confinement [kən'fainmənt], *n.* parto; limitación; prisión, *f.*
confirm [kən'fə:m], *v.t.* confirmar.
confirmation [kɔnfə'meiʃən], *n.* confirmación, *f.*
confiscate ['kɔnfiskeit], *v.t.* comisar, confiscar.
conflagration [kɔnflə'greiʃən], *n.* conflagración, *f.*
conflict ['kɔnflikt], *n.* conflicto.—[kən'flikt], *v.i.* contradecirse; chocar; combatir.
conform [kən'fɔ:m], *v.i.* conformarse.
conformist [kən'fɔ:mist], *n.* conformista, *m.f.*
conformity [kən'fɔ:miti], *n.* conformidad, *f.*
confound [kən'faund], *v.t.* confundir; condenar.
confront [kən'frʌnt], *v.t.* arrostrar; confrontar; confrontarse con.
confuse [kən'fju:z], *v.t.* confundir.
confused [kən'fju:zd], *a.* confuso.
confusion [kən'fju:ʒən], *n.* confusión, *f.*
confute [kən'fju:t], *v.t.* confutar.
congeal [kən'dʒi:l], *v.t.* congelar.—*v.i.* -se.
congenial [kən'dʒi:niəl], *a.* congenial, simpático; compatible.
conger eel ['kɔŋgər'i:l], *n.* congrio.
congest [kən'dʒest], *v.t.* apiñar, congestionar.
congestion [kən'dʒestʃən], *n.* congestión, obstrucción, *f.*
conglomerate [kən'glɔməreit], *v.t.* conglomerar.—*v.i.* -se.
conglomeration [kənglɔmə'reiʃən], *n.* conglomeración, *f.*
Congolese [kɔŋgə'li:z], *a.*, *n.* congolés, congoleño.
congratulate [kən'grætjuleit], *v.t.* felicitar.
congratulation [kəngrætju'leiʃən], *n.* felicitación, *f.*
congregate ['kɔŋgrigeit], *v.i.* congregarse.
congregation [kɔŋgri'geiʃən], *n.* congregación, *f.*; (*eccl.*) fieles, *m.pl.*
congress ['kɔŋgres], *n.* congreso.
congressional [kən'greʃənəl], *a.* congresional.
congressman ['kɔŋgresmən], *n.* congresista *m.*; (*U.S.*) diputado.
congruent ['kɔŋgruənt], *a.* congruente.
conical ['kɔnikəl], *a.* cónico.
conifer ['kɔnifə], *n.* conífera.
coniferous [kə'nifərəs], *a.* conífero.
conjecture [kən'dʒektʃə], *n.* conjetura.—*v.t.* conjeturar.
conjoint [kən'dʒɔint], *a.* aliado, conjunto.
conjugal ['kɔndʒugəl], *a.* conyugal.
conjugate ['kɔndʒugeit], *v.t.* conjugar.
conjugation [kɔndʒu'geiʃən], *n.* conjugación, *f.*
conjunction [kən'dʒʌŋkʃən], *n.* conjunción, *f.*
conjuncture [kən'dʒʌŋktʃə], *n.* coyuntura.
conjure [kən'dʒuə], *v.t.* conjurar; ['kʌndʒə], conjurar; realizar por arte mágica; *to — up*, evocar; *to — away*, exorcizar.
conjurer, conjuror ['kʌndʒərə], *n.* prestidigitador, *m.*
connect [kə'nekt], *v.t.* conectar, enlazar.—*v.i.* -se.
connection, connexion [kə'nekʃən], *n.* conexión, *f.*; (*rail.*) combinación, *f.*; enlace; empalme, *m.*
conning-tower ['kɔniŋtauə], *n.* torreta.
connivance [kə'naivəns], *n.* connivencia.
connive [kə'naiv], *v.i.* tolerar, hacer la vista gorda (*at*, a).
connoisseur [kɔni'sə:], *n.* conocedor, perito; catador, *m.*
connotation [kɔnə'teiʃən], *n.* connotación, *m.*
conquer ['kɔŋkə], *v.t.* conquistar; vencer.
conqueror ['kɔŋkərə], *n.* conquistador; vencedor, *m.*
conquest ['kɔŋkwest], *n.* conquista.
conscience ['kɔnʃəns], *n.* conciencia.
conscientious [kɔnʃi'enʃəs], *a.* concienzudo; *— objector*, pacifista, *m.f.*
conscious ['kɔnʃəs], *a.* consciente; *to be — of*, tener conocimiento de.
consciousness ['kɔnʃəsnis], *n.* conciencia; *to lose —*, perder el conocimiento.
conscript ['kɔnskript], *n.* recluta, *m.*, quinto, conscripto.—[kən'skript], *v.t.* reclutar.
conscription [kən'skripʃən], *n.* conscripción, *f.*, reclutamiento.
consecrate ['kɔnsikreit], *v.t.* consagrar.
consecutive [kən'sekjutiv], *a.* consecutivo, seguido.
consensus [kən'sensəs], *n.* consenso.
consent [kən'sent], *n.* consentimiento.—*v.i.* consentir (*to*, en).
consequence ['kɔnsikwəns], *n.* consecuencia.
consequently ['kɔnsikwəntli], *a.* por consiguiente.
conservation [kɔnsə'veiʃən], *n.* conservación, *f.*
conservatism [kən'sə:vətizm], *n.* conservadurismo.

conservative [kən'sə:vətiv], *a.*, *n.* conservativo; (*pol.*) conservador, *m.*
conservatoire [kən'sə:vətwɑ:], *n.* conservatorio.
conservatory [kən'sə:vətəri], *n.* conservatorio; invernáculo.
conserve [kən'sə:v], *n.* conserva.—*v.t.* conservar.
consider [kən'sidə], *v.t.* considerar.
considerable [kən'sidərəbl], *a.* considerable.
considerate [kən'sidərit], *a.* considerado, atento.
consideration [kənsidə'reiʃən], *n.* consideración, *f.*
consign [kən'sain], *v.t.* encomendar; consignar.
consignment [kən'sainmənt], *n.* consignación, *f.*; envío.
consist [kən'sist], *v.i.* consistir en, constar de (*of*).
consistency [kən'sistənsi], *n.* consecuencia; consistencia.
consistent [kən'sistənt], *a.* consistente, consecuente.
consolation [kənsə'leiʃən], *n.* consolación, *f.*, consuelo.
console (1) ['kənsoul], *n.* consola.
console (2) [kən'soul], *v.t.* consolar.
consolidate [kən'səlideit], *v.t.* consolidar.—*v.i.* -se.
consoling [kən'souliŋ], *a.* consolador.
consols ['kənsoulz], *n.pl.* (*com.*) consolidados, *m.pl.*
consonant ['kənsənənt], *a.*, *n.* consonante, *f.*
consort ['kənsɔ:t], *n.* consorte, *m.f.*—[kən'sɔ:t], *v.t.* asociarse.
consortium [kən'sɔ:tjəm], *n.* consorcio.
conspectus [kən'spektəs], *n.* sumario, compendio.
conspicuous [kən'spikjuəs], *a.* conspicuo.
conspiracy [kən'spirəsi], *n.* conjuración, conspiración, *f.*
conspirator [kən'spirətə], *n.* conspirador, *m.*, conjurado.
conspire [kən'spaiə], *v.i.* conspirar, conjurarse, maquinar.
constable ['kʌnstəbl], *n.* condestable, *m.*; policía, *m.*, guardia, *m.*
constabulary [kən'stæbjuləri], *n.* policía regional, *f.*
constancy ['kənstənsi], *n.* constancia.
constant ['kənstənt], *a.* constante.
constellation [kənstə'leiʃən], *n.* constelación, *f.*
consternation [kənstə'neiʃən], *n.* consternación, *f.*
constipate ['kənstipeit], *v.t.* estreñir.
constipation [kənsti'peiʃən], *n.* estreñimiento.
constituency [kən'stitjuənsi], *n.* distrito electoral.
constituent [kən'stitjuənt], *a.*, *n.* constitutivo, constituyente, *m.*; (*pol.*) constituyente; votante, *m.f.*
constitute ['kənstitju:t], *v.t.* constituir.
constitution [kənsti'tju:ʃən], *n.* constitución, *f.*
constitutional [kənsti'tju:ʃənəl], *a.* constitucional.
constitutive [kən'stitjutiv], *a.* constitutivo, constituyente.
constraint [kən'streint], *n.* coacción, *f.*, constreñimiento.
constrict [kən'strikt], *v.t.* estrechar, constreñir.
constriction [kən'strikʃən], *n.* constricción, *f.*
constringent [kən'strindʒənt], *a.* constringente.
construct [kən'strʌkt], *v.t.* construir.
construction [kən'strʌkʃən], *n.* construcción; interpretación, *f.*
constructive [kən'strʌktiv], *a.* constructivo.
constructor [kən'strʌktə], *n.* constructor, *m.*
construe [kən'stru:], *v.t.* construir; interpretar.
consul ['kənsəl], *n.* cónsul, *m.*
consular ['kənsjulə], *a.* consular.
consulate ['kənsjulit], *n.* consulado.
consult [kən'sʌlt], *v.t.*, *v.i.* consultar.
consultant [kən'sʌltənt], *n.* consultor, *m.*; especialista, *m.f.*
consultation [kənsəl'teiʃən], *n.* consulta(ción), *f.*
consultative [kən'sʌltətiv], *a.* consult(at)ivo.
consume [kən'sju:m], *v.t.* consumir.—*v.i.* -se.
consumer [kən'sju:mə], *n.* consumidor, *m.*
consummate [kən'sʌmit], *a.* consumado.—['kənsəmeit], *v.t.* consumar.
consumption [kən'sʌmpʃən], *n.* consumo; (*med.*) consunción, *f.*
consumptive [kən'sʌmptiv], *a.*, *n.* tísico.
contact ['kəntækt], *n.* contacto.—*v.t.* ponerse en contacto con.
contagious [kən'teidʒəs], *a.* contagioso.
contain [kən'tein], *v.t.* contener.
container [kən'teinə], *n.* continente; envase *m.*
contaminate [kən'tæmineit], *v.t.* contaminar.
contamination [kəntæmi'neiʃən], *n.* contaminación, *f.*
contemplate ['kəntəmpleit], *v.t.* contemplar; proponerse.
contemplation [kəntəm'pleiʃən], *n.* contemplación, *f.*
contemplative [kən'templətiv], *a.* contemplativo.
contemporary [kən'tempərəri], *a.*, *n.* contemporáneo, coetáneo.
contempt [kən'tempt], *n.* desprecio; (*jur.*) contumacia.
contemptible [kən'temptibl], *a.* despreciable.
contemptuous [kən'temptjuəs], *a.* despreciativo, desdeñoso, altivo.
contend [kən'tend], *v.t.* sostener.—*v.i.* contender.
contender [kən'tendə], *n.* competidor, *m.*, contendiente, *m.f.*
contending [kən'tendiŋ], *a.* contrario, opuesto.
content [kən'tent], *a.* contento, satisfecho.—['kəntent], *n.* contenido; cabida.—[kən'tent], *v.t.* contentar, satisfacer.
contented [kən'tentid], *a.* contento, satisfecho.
contention [kən'tenʃən], *n.* contención, *f.*; contienda.
contentious [kən'tenʃəs], *a.* contencioso.
contentment [kəntentmənt], *n.* contentamiento.
contest ['kəntest], *n.* contienda, lucha; concurso.—[kən'test], *v.t.* disputar, competir por.

context ['kɔntekst], *n.* contexto.
contiguous [kən'tigjuəs], *a.* contiguo.
continence ['kɔntinəns], *n.* continencia.
continent ['kɔntinənt], *a.*, *n.* continente, *m.*
continental [kɔnti'nentəl], *a.*, *n.* continental, *m.f.*
contingency [kən'tindʒənsi], *n.* contingencia.
contingent [kən'tindʒənt], *a.*, *n.* contingente, *m.*
continual [kən'tinjuəl], *a.* continuo.
continually [kən'tinjuəli], *adv.* continua(da)-mente.
continuation [kəntinju'eiʃən], *n.* continuación, prolongación, *f.*
continue [kən'tinju:], *v.t.*, *v.i.* continuar.
continuity [kɔnti'nju:iti], *n.* continuidad, *f.*
continuous [kən'tinjuəs], *a.* continuo.
contorted [kən'tɔ:tid], *a.* torcido, contorsionado.
contortion [kən'tɔ:ʃən], *n.* contorsión, *f.*
contour ['kɔntuə], *n.* contorno; curva de nivel (*sobre un mapa*).
contraband ['kɔntrəbænd], *n.* contrabando.
contract ['kɔntrækt], *n.* contrato; [kɔn'trækt], *v.t.* contraer.—*v.i.* contraerse.
contraction [kən'trækʃən], *n.* contracción, *f.*
contractor [kən'træktə], *n.* contratista, *m.f.*; empresario.
contradict [kɔntrə'dikt], *v.t.* contradecir.
contradiction [kɔntrə'dikʃən], *n.* contradicción, *f.*
contradictory [kɔntrə'diktəri], *a.* contradictorio.
contralto [kən'træltou], *n.* contralto.
contraption [kən'træpʃən], (*fam.*) cachivache, *m.*, dispositivo, artefacto.
contrary ['kɔntrəri], *a.*, *n.* contrario; ***on the* —**, al contrario; [kən'trɛəri], *a.* terco (*persona*).
contrast ['kɔntrɑ:st], *n.* contraste, *m.* —[kən'trɑ:st], *v.t.* poner en contraste.—*v.i.* contrastar.
contravene [kɔntrə'vi:n], *v.t.* infringir, contravenir.
contribute [kən'tribju:t], *v.t.* contribuir.
contribution [kɔntri'bju:ʃən], *n.* contribución; cooperación, *f.*
contributor [kən'tribjutə], *n.* contribuyente, *m.f.*
contrite ['kɔntrait], *a.* contrito.
contrivance [kən'traivəns], aparato, artefacto; invención, *f.*
contrive [kən'traiv], *v.t.* idear, maquinar, fraguar.—*v.i.* ingeniarse (***to***, para).
control [kən'troul], *n.* gobierno, dirección, *f.*; mando; freno; manejo; dominio; ***under* —**, dominado.—*v.t.* gobernar, mandar; dominar; dirigir; regular; manejar.—*v.r.* dominarse.
controller [kən'troulə], *n.* interventor; regulador, *m.*
controversial [kɔntrə'və:ʃəl], *a.* debatido, batallón.
controversy ['kɔntrəvə:si], *n.* controversia, debate, *m.*
contusion [kən'tju:ʒən], *n.* contusión, *f.*
conundrum [kə'nʌndrəm], *n.* rompecabezas, *m. inv.*
convalesce [kɔnvə'les], *v.i.* reponerse, convalecer.
convalescent [kɔnvə'lesənt], *a.*, *n.* convaleciente, *m.f.*; **— *home***, clínica de reposo.
convection [kən'vekʃən], *n.* convección, *f.*
convene [kən'vi:n], *v.t.* convocar.—*v.i.* reunirse.
convenience [kən'vi:niəns], *n.* comodidad, *f.*; retrete, *m.* (*W.C.*).
convenient [kən'vi:niənt], *a.* cómodo, oportuno, conveniente.
convent ['kɔnvent], *n.* convento (de monjas).
convention [kən'venʃən], *n.* congreso; convención, *f.*, conveniencia.
conventional [kən'venʃənəl] *a.* convencional.
converge [kən'və:dʒ], *v.i.* convergir.
convergence [kan'və:dʒəns], *n.* convergencia.
conversant [kən'və:sənt], *a.* versado(***with,*** en).
conversational [kɔnvə'seiʃənəl], *a.* de la conversación; conversacional.
converse ['kɔnvə:s], *a.*,*n.* inverso, contrario.—[kən'və:s], *v.i.* conversar.
conversion [kən'və:ʃən], *n.* conversión, *f.*
convert ['kɔnvə:t], *n.* convertido, converso.—[kən'və:t], *v.t.* convertir.
convertible [kən'və:təbl], *a.* convertible.—*n.* descapotable (*coche*), *m.*
convex ['kɔnveks], *a.* convexo.
convey [kən'vei], *v.t.* transportar; comunicar, participar; transferir.
conveyance [kən'veiəns], *n.* transporte, *m.*; comunicación, *f.*; vehículo; traspaso.
conveyor [kən'veiə], *n.* conductor, *m.*; (*mech.*) correa transportadora.
convict ['kɔnvikt], *n.* reo, preso, presidiario. —[kən'vikt], *v.t.* sentenciar, condenar.
conviction [kən'vikʃən], *n.* convicción, *f.*; (*jur.*) sentencia, condena.
convince [kən'vins], *v.t.* convencer.
convincing [kən'vinsiŋ], *a.* convincente.
convivial [kən'viviəl], *a.* festivo, jovial.
convocation [kɔnvə'keiʃən], *n.* convocación, *f.*, asamblea.
convoke [kən'vouk], *v.t.* convocar.
convoy ['kɔnvɔi], *n.* convoy, *m.*, escolta.—[kɔn'vɔi], *v.t.* convoyar.
convulse [kən'vʌls], *v.t.* convulsionar, crispar, agitar.
convulsion [kən'vʌlʃən], *n.* convulsión, *f.*, espasmo.
cony ['kouni], *n.* conejuna (*piel*), [CONEY].
coo [ku:], *n.* arrullo.—*v.i.* arrullar.
cook [kuk], *n.* cocinero.—*v.t.* cocinar, cocer; (*fam.*) falsificar; arruinar.—*v.i.* cocer; cocinar, guisar (*persona*).
cookery ['kukəri], *n.* cocina, arte (*f.*) de cocina.
cookie ['kuki], *n.* (*U.S.*) galleta, pastelito.
cool [ku:l], *a.* fresco; sereno.—*n.* fresco.—*v.t.* refrescar, enfriar; calmar.—*v.i.* -se.
cooler ['ku:lə], *n.* enfriadera; (*low*) chirona, cárcel, *f.*
coolie ['ku:li], *n.* culí, *m.*
coolness ['ku:lnis], *n.* fresco; frío; frialdad, *f.*; calma.
coop [ku:p], *n.* gallinero.—*v.t.* encerrar (***up***).
cooper ['ku:pə], *n.* tonelero.
co-operate [kou'ɔpəreit], *v.i.* cooperar (***in***, a).
co-operation [kouɔpə'reiʃən], *n.* cooperación, *f.*
co-operative [kou'ɔpərətiv], *a.* cooperativo. —*n.* cooperativa.
co-operator [kou'ɔpəreitə], *n.* cooperador, *m.*
co-ordinate [kou'ɔ:dineit], *v.t.* coordinar.
coot [ku:t], *n.* focha, foja.
cop [kɔp], *n.* (*fam.*) polizonte, *m.*; detención, *f.* —*v.t.* (*fam.*) pillar.

cope (1) [koup], *n.* capa, capucho.
cope (2) [koup], *v.i.* hacer frente a, manejárselas con (*with*).
coping ['koupiŋ], *n.* albardilla.
copious ['koupiəs], *a.* copioso.
copper ['kɔpə], *n.* cobre, *m.*; (*fam.*) polizonte, *m.*, guindilla, *m.*; vellón (*para monedas*), *m.*; calderilla (*dinero suelto*); caldera (*para hervir*).
coppery ['kɔpəri], *a.* cobrizo; cobreño.
coppice ['kɔpis], **copse** [kɔps], *n.* soto.
copy ['kɔpi], *n.* copia; ejemplar, *m.*, número; (*print.*) manuscrito.—*v.t.* copiar.
copyist ['kɔpiist], *n.* copista, *m.*
copyright ['kɔpirait], *n.* propriedad literaria; — ***reserved***, queda hecho el depósito que marca la ley.
coquette [kɔ'ket], *n.* coqueta.
coquettish [kɔ'ketiʃ], *a.* coqueta, coquetón.
coral ['kɔrəl], *a.* coralino.—*n.* coral, *m.*
cord [kɔ:d], *n.* cuerda, cordel, cordón, *m.*; ***spinal*** —, médula espinal.
cordial ['kɔ:diəl], *a.* cordial.—*n.* cordial, licor tónico, *m.*
cordite ['kɔ:dait], *n.* cordita.
cordon ['kɔ:dən], *n.* (*mil. etc.*) cordón, *m.*
corduroy ['kɔ:djurɔi], *n.* pana.
core [kɔ:], *n.* corazón, *m.*; centro; alma; (*elec.*) núcleo.
coriander [kɔri'ændə], *n.* culantro.
cork [kɔ:k], *n.* corcho; tapón, *m.*—*v.t.* tapar con corcho.
corkscrew ['kɔ:kskru:], *n.* sacacorchos, *m.*
cormorant ['kɔ:mərənt], *n.* corvejón, *m.*
corn [kɔ:n], *n.* grano; trigo; (*U.S.*) maíz, *m.*; (*anat.*) callo; (*U.S.*, *fam.*) lo trillado y cursi. —*v.t.* acecinar.
cornea ['kɔ:niə], *n.* córnea.
corned-beef ['kɔ:nd'bi:f], *n.* carne prensada.
corner ['kɔ:nə], *n.* esquina (*exterior*); rincón (*interior*), *m.*; recodo (*de carretera*); (*com.*) monopolio.—*v.t.* arrinconar; (*com.*) acaparar.
corner-stone ['kɔ:nəstoun], *n.* piedra angular.
cornet ['kɔ:nit], *n.* corneta; cucurucho.
corn-field ['kɔ:nfi:ld], *n.* trigal; (*U.S.*) maizal, *m.*
corn-flour ['kɔ:nflauə], *n.* harina de maiz.
cornflower ['kɔ:nflauə], *n.* aciano.
cornice ['kɔ:nis], *n.* cornisa.
Cornish ['kɔ:niʃ], *a.*, *n.* rel. a, natural de Cornualles.
Cornwall ['kɔ:nwəl], *n.* Cornualles, *m.*
corny ['kɔ:ni], *a.* calloso; (*fam.*) trillado y cursi.
coronary ['kɔrənəri], *a.* coronario.
coronation [kɔrə'neiʃən], *n.* coronación, *f.*
coroner ['kɔrənə], *n.* juez (*m.*) de guardia.
coronet ['kɔrənət], *n.* corona nobiliaria.
corporal ['kɔ:pərəl], *a.* corporal.—*n.* (*mil.*) cabo.
corporate ['kɔ:pərit], *a.* corporativo.
corporation [kɔ:pə'reiʃən], *n.* ayuntamiento; corporación, *f.*
corporeal [kɔ:'pɔ:riəl], *a.* corpóreo.
corps [kɔ:], *n.* (*mil. etc.*) cuerpo.
corpse [kɔ:ps], *n.* cadáver, *m.*
corpulent ['kɔ:pjulənt], *a.* corpulento.
corpuscle ['kɔ:pʌsl], *n.* corpúsculo.
corral [kə'rɑ:l], *n.* corral, *m.*
correct [kə'rekt], *a.* correcto.—*v.t.* corregir.
correction [kə'rekʃən], *n.* corrección, *f.*
corrective [kə'rektiv], *a.*, *n.* correctivo.
correctness [kə'rektnis], *n.* corrección, *f.*
correlate ['kɔrəleit], *v.t.* correlacionar.
correspond [kɔrəs'pɔnd], *v.i.* corresponder; cartearse.
correspondence [kɔrəs'pɔndəns], *n.* correspondencia.
correspondent [kɔrəs'pɔndənt], *n.* correspondiente, corresponsal, *m.f.*
corresponding [kɔrəs'pondiŋ], *a.* correspondiente.
corridor ['kɔridɔ:], *n.* pasillo, corredor, *m.*
corroborate [kə'rɔbəreit], *v.t.* corroborar.
corrode [kə'roud], *v.t.* corroer.
corrosion [kə'rouʒən], *n.* corrosión, *f.*
corrosive [kə'rouziv], *a.*, *n.* corrosivo.
corrugate ['kɔrugeit], *v.t.* arrugar; acanalar; corrugar; ***corrugated iron***, hierro acanalado *o* ondulado.
corrupt [kə'rʌpt], *a.* corrompido.—*v.t.* corromper.
corruption [kə'rʌpʃən], *n.* corrupción, *f.*
corsage [kɔ:'sɑ:ʒ], *n.* corpiño.
corset ['kɔ:sit], *n.* corsé, *m.*
Corsica ['kɔ:sikə], *n.* Córcega.
Corsican ['kɔ:sikən], *a.*, *n.* corso.
Corunna [kə'rʌnə], *n.* La Coruña.
corvette [kɔ:'vet], *n.* (*naut.*) corbeta.
cosmic ['kɔzmik], *a.* cósmico.
cosmopolitan [kɔzmə'pɔlitən], *a.* cosmopolita.
Cossack ['kɔsæk], *a.*, *n.* cosaco.
cosset ['kɔsit], *v.t.* mimar.
cost [kɔst], *n.* costa.—*v.t.*, *v.i.* costar.
Costa Rican ['kɔstə'ri:kən], *a.*, *n.* costarriqueño, costarricense, *m.f.*
costermonger ['kɔstəmʌŋgə], **coster** ['kɔstə], *n.* (*Brit.*) vendedor ambulante (*de frutas etc.*), *m.*
costliness ['kɔstlinis], *n.* suntuosidad, *f.*
costly ['kɔstli], *a.* suntuoso; costoso.
costume ['kɔstju:m], *n.* traje, *m.*, vestido; disfraz, *m.*; — ***jewel(le)ry***, joyas de fantasía.
costumier [kɔs'tju:miə], *n.* sastre (*m.*) de teatro.
cosy ['kouzi], *a.* cómodo, agradable.
cot [kɔt], *n.* cuna; catre, *m.*; choza.
coterie ['koutəri], *n.* pandilla
cottage ['kɔtidʒ], *n.* choza, cabaña; — ***cheese***, requesón, *m.*
cotter ['kɔtə], *n.* chaveta.
cotton [kɔtn], *n.* algodón, *m.*; — ***gin***, desmotadera de algodón; — ***waste***, desperdicios *o* hilacha de algodón; — ***wool***, algodón en rama, guata. — *v.i.* (*fam.*) comprender (***on***).
couch [kautʃ], *n.* canapé, sofá, *m.*; lecho.—*v.t.* expresar.
couch-grass ['ku:tʃgrɑ:s], *n.* (*bot.*) grama.
cough [kɔf], *n.* tos, *f.*—*v.i.* toser; ***to — up***, (*fam.*) pagar.
could [kud] [CAN].
council ['kaunsil], *n.* concilio; ayuntamiento, concejo; — ***of war***, concejo de guerra.
councillor ['kaunsilə], *n.* concejal, *m.*
counsel ['kaunsəl], *n.* consejo; consejero; abogado.—*v.t.* aconsejar.
count (1) [kaunt], *n.* conde, *m.*
count (2) [kaunt], *n.* cálculo, cuenta; (*jur.*) cargo; (*sport*) cuento.—*v.t.* contar; ***to — out***, (*sport*) declarar vencido.—*v.i.* contar; valer; ***to — for***, valer; ***to — on***

someone, contar con alguien; ***to — on doing***, contar hacer; ***to — one's chickens***, hijo no tener y nombre le poner.
countdown ['kauntdaun], *n.* cuenta hacia atrás.
countenance ['kauntinəns], *n.* semblante, *m.*; cara; aspecto.—*v.t.* apoyar; tolerar.
counter (1) ['kauntə], *a.* contrario, opuesto. —*v.t.* oponerse a; contradecir.
counter (2) ['kauntə], *n.* mostrador, *m.*; ficha.
counteract [kauntər'ækt], *v.t.* neutralizar.
counter-attraction ['kauntərətrækʃən], *n.* atracción contraria.
counterbalance [kauntə'bæləns], *v.t.* contrapesar.
counterfeit ['kauntəfi:t], *a.* contrahecho, falso.—*n.* moneda falsa; engaño.—*v.t.* contrahacer; falsificar.
counterfoil ['kauntəfɔil], *n.* talón, *m.*
countermand [kauntə'mɑ:nd], *v.t.* revocar.
counterpane ['kauntəpein], *n.* cubrecama, *m.*, colcha.
counterpart ['kauntəpɑ:t], *n.* contraparte, *f.*; copia, duplicado.
counterplot ['kauntəplɔt], *n.* contratreta.
counterpoint ['kauntəpɔint], *n.* contrapunto.
counterpoise ['kauntəpɔiz], *n.* contrapeso.
Counter-Reformation ['kauntərefɔ:meiʃən], *n.* Contrarreforma.
counter-revolutionary ['kauntərevəlu:ʃənəri], *a.* contrarrevolucionario.
countersign ['kauntəsain], *n.* (*mil.*) contraseña; (*com.*) refrendata.—*v.t.* (*com.*) refrendar.
countess ['kauntis], *n.* condesa.
counting-house ['kauntiŋhaus], *n.* escritorio, contaduría.
countless ['kauntlis], *a.* innumerable.
country ['kʌntri], *n.* país, *m.*, nación, *f.*; campo.
countryman ['kʌntrimən], *n.* (*pl.* **-men**) compatriota, *m. f.*; campesino.
county ['kaunti], *n.* condado, provincia; — ***town***, capital (*f.*) de condado, cabeza de partido.
coup [ku:], *n.* golpe, *m.*
coupé [ku'pei], *n.* cupé, *m.*
couple [kʌpl], *n.* par, *m.*; pareja; ***married —***, matrimonio.—*v.t.* acoplar; unit; casar. —*v.i.* juntarse; casarse, copularse.
couplet ['kʌplit], *n.* dístico, versos pareados; par, *m.*
coupon ['ku:pɔn], *n.* cupón; talón, *m.*; bono.
courage ['kʌridʒ], *n.* ánimo, valor, *m.*
courageous [kə'reidʒəs], *a.* valiente.
courier ['kuriə], *n.* estafeta, *m.*; guía, *m.*
course [kɔ:s], *n.* (*naut.*) rumbo; (*cul.*) plato; campo; curso; cauce (*m.*) de un río; hilera (*de ladrillos*); ***in the — of***, durante; ***of —***, por supuesto.—*v.t.* cazar.—*v.i.* correr.
court [kɔ:t], *n.* (*pol.*) corte, *f.*; (*jur.*) tribunal, *m.*; patio.—*v.t.* cortejar.
courteous ['kə:tjəs], *a.* cortés.
courtesan ['kɔ:tizæn], *n.* cortesana, ramera.
courtesy ['kə:tizi], *n.* cortesía; reverencia.
court-house ['kɔ:thaus], *n.* palacio de justicia.
courtier ['kɔ:tjə], *n.* cortesano, palaciego.
courtly ['kɔ:tli], *a.* cortés, cortesano.
court-martial [kɔ:t'mɑ:ʃəl], *n.* (*pl.* **courts-martial**) consejo de guerra.—*v.t.* someter a consejo de guerra.
courtship ['kɔ:tʃip], *n.* cortejo; noviazgo.
courtyard ['kɔ:tjɑ:d], *n.* patio.
cousin ['kʌzin], *n.* primo.
cove (1) [kouv], *n.* (*geog.*) ensenada.
cove (2) [kouv], *n.* (*fam.*) tío.
covenant ['kʌvənənt], *n.* (*Bibl.*) alianza; pacto.
cover ['kʌvə], *n.* tapa, cubierta; velo, pretexto; cubierto (*en la mesa*); portada (*de una revista*); forro.—*v.t.* cubrir; incluir.
coverage ['kʌvəridʒ], *n.* alcance, *m.*
coverlet ['kʌvəlit], *n.* cubrecama, *m.*, colcha.
covert ['kʌvat], *a.* cubierto; escondido, secreto. —*n.* asilo, guarida.
covet ['kʌvit], *v.t.*, *v.i.* codiciar.
covetous ['kʌvitəs], *a.* codicioso.
covetousness ['kʌvitəsnis], *n.* codicia.
cow [kau], *n.* vaca.—*v.t.* intimidar.
coward [kauəd], *n.* cobarde *m.*
cowardice ['kauədis], *n.* cobardía.
cowardly ['kauədli], *a.* cobarde.
cowbell ['kaubel], *n.* cencerro.
cowboy ['kaubɔi], *n.* vaquero.
cower [kauə], *v.i.* agacharse, acobardarse.
cow-herd ['kauhə:d], *n.* vaquero, pastor de vacas.
cow-hide ['kauhaid], *n.* piel (*f.*) de vaca, cuero.
cowl [kaul], *n.* cogulla; caperuza; caballete, *m.*
cowpox ['kaupɔks], *n.* vacuna.
cowry ['kauri], *n.* cauri, *m.*
cowslip ['kauslip], *n.* (*bot.*) primavera.
coxcomb ['kɔkskoum], *n.* cresta de gallo; mequetrefe, *m.*
coxswain ['kɔksən], *n.* (*naut.*) timonel, *m.*
coy [kɔi], *a.* tímido; coquetón.
crab [kræb], *n.* cangrejo.
crab-apple ['kræbæpl], *n.* manzana silvestre.
crabbed [kræbd], *a.* áspero; enredoso.
crack [kræk], *a.* de primera clase.—*n.* grieta; estallido; chiste, *m.*; (*fam.*) esfuerzo.—*v.t.* agrietar; romper; fraccionar; ***to — up***, alabar.—*v.i.* agrietarse; cascarse (*la voz*); desbaratarse; ***to — up***, perder la salud *o* el ánimo.
crack-brained ['krækbreind], *a.* mentecato.
cracker ['krækə], *n.* (*esp. U.S.*) galleta; petardo.
crackle [krækl], *n.* crepitación, *f.*—*v.i.* crujir.
crackling ['krækliŋ], *n.* crepitación, *f.*; chicharrón, *m.*
cradle [kreidl], *n.* cuna.—*v.t.* acunar, mecer.
craft [krɑ:ft], *n.* oficio; arte, *m.*; treta, astucia; gremio; embarcación, *f.*; avión, *m.*
craftiness ['krɑ:ftinis], *n.* astucia.
craftsman ['krɑ:ftsmən], *n.* artífice, *m.*; artesano.
crafty ['krɑ:fti], *a.* astuto, ladino, taimado.
crag [kræg], *n.* peñasco.
cram [kræm], *v.t.* embutir, rellenar, henchir; cebar.—*v.i.* atracarse (*de comida*); aprender apresuradamente.
cramp [kræmp], *n.* (*med.*) calambre, *m.*; (*eng.*) abrazadera.—*v.t.* engrapar; apretar; ***to — one's style***, cortarle las alas a uno.
cranberry ['krænbəri], *n.* arándano.
crane [krein], *n.* (*orn.*) grulla; (*eng.*) grúa.
cranium ['kreinjəm], *n.* cráneo, casco.
crank [kræŋk], *n.* manivela, manubrio, biela; (*fam.*) chiflado.—*v.t.* (*eng.*) arrancar con la manivela.
crankcase ['kræŋkkeis], *n.* (*eng.*) cárter, *m.*
crankshaft ['kræŋkʃɑ:ft], *n.* (*eng.*) cigüeñal, *m.*
cranky ['kræŋki], *a.* chiflado, excéntrico.

cranny ['kræni], *n.* grieta.
crape [kreip], *n.* crespón negro,
crash [kræʃ], *n.* estallido; desplome, *m.*; fracaso; quiebra.—*v.t.* estrellar.—*v.i.* chocar; desplomarse; quebrar; estrellarse.
crass [kræs], *a.* tosco, basto; torpe.
crate [kreit], *n.* (caja de) embalaje, *m.*, jaula; banasta, cuévano.—*v.t.* embalar con tablas.
crater ['kreitə], *n.* cráter, *m.*
cravat [krə'væt], *n.* corbata.
crave [kreiv], *v.t.* anhelar, ansiar; pedir, suplicar.
craven ['kreivən], *a.* cobarde.
craving ['kreiviŋ], *n.* anhelo.
crawfish ['krɔ:fiʃ], *n.* langostino; cámbaro; cangrejo de río.
crawl [krɔ:l], *n.* reptación, *f.*, gateo; (*natación*) crawl, *m.*, arrastre, *m.*
crayfish ['kreifiʃ], [CRAWFISH].
crayon ['kreiən], *n.* clarión, *m.*; lápiz (*m.*) de color.
craze [kreiz], *n.* manía; moda.—*v.t.* enloquecer; grietar.
craziness ['kreizinis], *n.* locura.
crazy ['kreizi], *a.* loco; desvencijado; — ***bone,*** (*U.S.*) [FUNNY BONE].
creak [kri:k], *n.* chirrido, rechinamiento.—*v.i.* chirriar, rechinar.
cream [kri:m], *n.* nata, crema.—*v.t.* desnatar.
crease [kri:s], *n.* pliegue, *m.*; arruga; doblez, *f.*, raya (*del pantalón*).—*v.t.* plegar; arrugar.
create [kri'eit], *v.t.* crear, producir, causar.
creation [kri'eiʃən], *n.* creación, *f.*
creative [kri'eitiv], *a.* creativo, creador.
creator [kri'eitə], *n.* creador; inventor, *m.*
creature ['kri:tʃə], *n.* criatura.
credential [kri'denʃəl], *a.* credencial.—*n.pl.* (cartas) credenciales, *f.pl.*
credibility [kredi'biliti], *n.* credibilidad, verosimilitud, *f.*
credible ['kredibl], *a.* creíble, verosímil.
credit ['kredit], *n.* crédito; ***on* —,** al fiado, a crédito.—*v.t.* creer; acreditar.
creditable ['kreditəbl], *a.* honorable.
creditor ['kreditə], *n.* acreedor.
credulity [kri'dju:liti], *n.* credulidad, *f.*
credulous ['kredjuləs], *a.* crédulo.
creed [kri:d], *n.* fe, *f.*; credo, símbolo (de la fe).
creek [kri:k], *n.* cala, ensenada; (*U.S.*) arroyo.
creep [kri:p], *n.* arrastramiento.—*pl.* (*fam.*) hormigueo.—*v.i. irr.* arrastrarse, deslizarse; hormiguear.
creeper ['kri:pə], *n.* (planta) trepadora.
creepy ['kri:pi], *a.* hormigueante.
cremate [kri'meit], *v.t.* incinerar.
cremation [kri'meiʃən], *n.* cremación, incineración (*f.*) de cadáveres.
crematorium [kremə'tɔ:riəm], *n.* crematorio.
crenellate ['krenəleit], *v.t.* almenar, dentar.
creole ['kri:oul], *a.*, *n.* criollo; negro criollo.
creosote ['kriəsout], *n.* creosota.—*v.t.* creosotar.
crept [krept], [CREEP].
crepuscular [kri'pʌskjulə], *a.* crepuscular.
crescendo [kri'ʃendou], *n.* crescendo.
crescent ['kresənt], *a.* creciente.—*n.* creciente, (*esp. fig.*) media luna.
cress [kres], *n.* (*bot.*) mastuerzo.
crest [krest], *n.* cresta; (*her.*) cimera, cresta.—*v.t.* coronar.
crestfallen ['krestfɔ:lən], *a.* abatido, cabizbajo.
Cretan ['kri:tən], *a.* cretense.
Crete [kri:t], *n.* Creta.
cretin ['kretin], *n.* cretino.
crevasse [kri'væs], *n.* grieta profunda.
crevice ['krevis], *n.* grieta.
crew [kru:], *n.* tripulación, *f.*; equipo; cuadrilla. [CROW].
crib [krib], *n.* pesebre, *m.*; belén, *m.*; camilla de niño; (*educ.*) chuleta; (*fam.*) plagio.—*v.t.* enjaular; (*educ.*) usar chuletas; (*fam.*) plagiar.
crick [krik], *n.* tortícolis, *f.*
cricket (1) ['krikit], *n.* (*ent.*) grillo.
cricket (2) ['krikit], *n.* (*sport*) cricket, *m.*; (*fig.*) juego limpio.
crikey! ['kraiki], *interj.* (*vulg.*) ¡caray!
crime [kraim], *n.* crimen, *m.*, delito.
criminal ['kriminəl], *a.*, *n.* criminal, reo.
crimson ['krimzən], *a.*, *n.* carmesí, *m.*
cringe [krindʒ], *v.i.* arrastrarse, acobardarse.
cringing ['krindʒiŋ], *a.* vil, rastrero.
crinkle [kriŋkl], *n.* arruga, pliegue, *m.*—*v.t.* arrugar.—*v.i.* -se.
crinoline ['krinəlin], *n.* miriñaque, *m.*
cripple [kripl], *a.*, *n.* estropeado, mutilado.—*v.* estropear, lisiar, mutilar. [COJO; MANCO.]
crisis ['kraisis], *n.* (*pl.* **crises**) crisis, *f.*
crisp [krisp], *a.* quebradizo; tostado; (*fig.*) incisivo; fresco.—*n.pl. or* ***potato crisps,*** patatas fritas (a la inglesa).—*v.t.* hacer quebradizo; rizar.
crisscross ['kriskrɔs], *a.* entrelazado.—*v.t.* marcar con líneas cruzadas.
criterion [krai'tiəriən], *n.* (*pl.* **criteria** [krai'tiəriə]), criterio.
critic ['kritik], *n.* crítico.
critical ['kritikl], *a.* crítico.
criticism ['kritisizm], *n.* crítica; reseña.
criticize ['kritisaiz], *v.t.*, *v.i.* criticar.
croak [krouk], *n.* graznido.—*v.i.* graznar.
crochet ['krouʃei], *v.t.*, *v.i.* hacer ganchillo *o* crochet.
crock [krɔk], *n.* cazuela; tiesto; olla; (*fam.*) cosa agotada *o* estropeada.—*pl.* vajilla.—*v.t.* estropear.
crockery ['krɔkəri], *n.* vajilla.
crocodile ['krɔkədail], *n.* cocodrilo; caimán, *m.*; fila; — ***tears,*** dolor fingido.
crocus ['kroukəs], *n.* croco.
crone [kroun], *n.* (*pej.*) vieja.
crony ['krouni], *n.* compinche, *m.*
crook [kruk], *n.* curva; gancho; cayado; criminal, *m.f.*
crooked ['krukid], *a.* curvado; torcido; deshonesto, criminal.
croon [kru:n], *v.t.*, *v.i.* canturrear.
crop [krɔp], *n.* cosecha, recolección, (*fig.*) colección, *f.*; (*orn.*) buche, *m.*—*pl.* la mies.—*v.t.* cosechar; recortar, rapar; pacer—*v.i.* ***to* — *up,*** parecer, descubrirse.
cropper ['krɔpə], *n.* caída; ***to come a* —,** caer de bruces.
cross [krɔs], *a.* enfadado, enojado; de mal humor; contrario, adverso; ***at* — *purposes,*** involuntariamente en pugna.—*n.* cruz, *f.*; cruce, *m.*—*v.t.* cruzar, atravesar; oponerse a, contrariar; ***to* — *one's mind,*** ocurrírsele a uno; ***to* — *off,*** tachar; ***to* — *swords,*** medir las armas.—*v.i.* cruzar(se); entrecortarse; ***to* — *over,*** pasar al otro lado.—*v.r.* santiguarse, persignarse.

crossbar ['krɔsbɑ:], *n.* travesaño.
crossbow ['krɔsbou], *n.* ballesta.
crossbred ['krɔsbred], *a.* híbrido; mestizo.
cross-examine [krɔsig'zæmin], *v.t.* interrogar.
cross-eyed ['krɔsaid], *a.* bizco.
crossing ['krɔsiŋ], *n.* travesía; cruce, *m.*
crossroads ['krɔsroudz], *n.* encrucijada; (*fig.*) punto crítico.
cross-section ['krɔs'sekʃən], *n.* corte transversal, *m.*
crossword ['krɔswə:d], *n.* crucigrama, *m.*
crotchet ['krɔtʃit], *n.* (*mus.*) negra.
crouch [krautʃ], *n.* posición (*f.*) de agachado.—*v.i.* agacharse, agazaparse.
crow [krou], *n.* (*orn.*) corneja; cacareo, canto del gallo; grito.—*v.i.* cacarear, cantar; (*fig.*) cantar victoria, alardear.
crowbar ['kroubɑ:], *n.* pie (*m.*) de cabra, palanca (*de hierro*).
crowd [kraud], *n.* muchedumbre, *f.*, gentío; público, espectadores, *m. pl.*; vulgo.—*v.i.* apiñarse, agolparse, apretarse.
crown [kraun], *n.* corona; (*anat.*) coronilla; copa (*de sombrero*); cinco chelines.—*v.t.* coronar; (*fig.*) premiar.
crozier ['krouziə], *n.* báculo de obispo.
crucial ['kru:ʃəl], *a.* crucial, decisivo.
crucible ['kru:sibl], *n.* crisol, *m.*
crucifix ['kru:sifiks], *n.* crucifijo, Cristo.
crucifixion [kru:si'fikʃən], *n.* crucifixión, *f.*
cruciform ['kru:sifɔ:m], *a.* cruciforme.
crucify ['kru:sifai], *v.t.* crucificar; (*fig.*) atormentar, mortificar.
crude [kru:d], *a.* crudo; tosco; no refinado; bruto.
crudity ['kru:diti], *n.* crudeza.
cruel [kru:əl], *a.* cruel.
cruelty ['kru:əlti], *n.* crueldad, *f.*
cruet [kru:it], *n.* vinagrera.
cruise [kru:z], *n.* crucero; viaje (*m.*) por mar.—*v.i.* viajar por mar; cruzar.
cruiser ['kru:zə], *n.* crucero.
crumb [krʌm], *n.* miga.
crumble [krʌmbl], *v.t.* desmigajar, desmenuzar.—*v.i.* -se; desmoronarse, derrumbarse.
crumple [krʌmpl], *v.t.* arrugar.—*v.i.* -se.
crunch [krʌntʃ], *v.t.* cascar, ronchar.
crusade [kru:'seid], *n.* cruzada.
crusader [kru:'seidə], *n.* cruzado.
crush [krʌʃ], *n.* apiñamiento, aglomeración, *f.*—*v.t.* aplastar, machacar, triturar.
crust [krʌst], *n.* corteza; mendrugo; costra; capa.
crusty ['krʌsti], *a.* de mal genio, brusco.
crutch [krʌtʃ], *n.* muleta, muletilla.
crux [krʌks], *n.* lo esencial.
cry [krai], *n.* grito; alarido; ***a far — from,*** muy distinto de; ***in full —,*** acosando de cerca.—*v.i.* gritar; llorar; pregonar; ***to — for,*** reclamar; pedir a voces; ***to — off,*** renunciar; ***to — out,*** gritar, exclamar.
crying ['kraiiŋ], *n.* llanto, lloro; pregoneo.
crypt [kript], *n.* cripta.
cryptic ['kriptik], *a.* secreto; con doble intención.
crystallize ['kristəlaiz], *v.t.* cristalizar.—*v.i.* -se.
cub [kʌb], *n.* cachorro.
Cuban ['kju:bən], *a., n.* cubano.
cubbyhole ['kʌbihoul], *n.* chiribitil, chiscón, *m.*
cube [kju:b], *n.* cubo.—*v.t.* (*math.*) cubicar.
cubic(al) ['kju:bik(əl)], *a.* cúbico.
cubicle ['kju:bikl], *n.* cubículo.
cubit ['kju:bit], *n.* codo.
cuckold ['kʌkəld], *n.* marido cornudo.—*v.t.* poner los cuernos a.
cuckoo ['kuku:], *n.* (*orn.*) cuclillo; cucú (*canción*), *m.*
cucumber ['kju:kʌmbə], *n.* pepino, cohombro.
cud [kʌd], *n.* ***to chew the —,*** rumiar.
cuddle [kʌdl], *n.* abrazo cariñoso.—*v.t.* abrazar con cariño.—*v.i.* estar abrazados.
cudgel ['kʌdʒəl], *n.* porra.—*v.t.* aporrear.
cue (1) [kju:], *n.* (*theat.*) apunte, *m.*; señal, *f.*
cue (2) [kju:], *n.* taco (*de billar*).
cuff [kʌf], *n.* puño (*de camisa*); (*U.S.*) vuelta (*de pantalón*); bofetón, *m.*—*v.t.* abofetear.
cuff-links ['kʌfliŋks], *n.pl.* gemelos, *m.pl.*
cuirass [kwir'ræs], *n.* coraza.
cuisine [kwi'zi:n], *n.* cocina, manera de guisar.
culinary ['kʌlinəri], *a.* culinario.
cull [kʌl], *v.t.* escoger, espigar.
culminate ['kʌlmineit], *v.i.* culminar.
culmination [kʌlmi'neiʃən], *n.* culminación, cumbre, *f.*
culpability [kʌlpə'biliti], *n.* culpabilidad, *f.*
culpable ['kʌlpəbl], *a.* culpable.
culprit ['kʌlprit], *n.* reo, culpable, *m.f.*
cult [kʌlt], *n.* culto; secta.
cultivable ['kʌltivəbl], *a.* cultivable.
cultivate ['kʌltiveit], *v.t.* cultivar.
cultivation [kʌlti'veiʃən], *n.* cultivo; cultura.
culture ['kʌltʃə], *n.* cultura.
culvert ['kʌlvət], *n.* alcantarilla.
cumbersome ['kʌmbəsəm], *a.* embarazoso; incómodo.
cumbrous ['kʌmbrəs], *a.* pesado; incómodo.
cumulative ['kju:mjulətiv], *a.* cumulativo.
cunning ['kʌniŋ], *a.* astuto, mañoso; diestro; (*U.S.*) mono, gracioso.—*n.* astucia; (*obs.*) arte, *m.*, sutileza.
cup [kʌp], *n.* taza; jícara; copa.—*v.t.* ahuecar (en forma de taza).
cupboard ['kʌbərd], *n.* armario, alacena aparador, *m.*
cupful ['kʌpful], *n.* taza *o* lo que contiene una taza.
Cupid ['kju:pid], *n.* (*myth.*) Cupido.
cupola ['kju:pələ], *n.* cúpola.
cupreous ['kju:priəs], *a.* cobreño, cobrizo.
cur [kə:], *n.* gozque, (*fig.*) canalla, *m.*
curate ['kjuərət], *n.* cura, *m.*, adjutor, *m.*
curator [kju:'reitə], *n.* director (de museo), conservador, *m.*
curb [kə:b], *n.* barbada (*del freno*); (*fig.*) freno. [KERB].—*v.t.* refrenar. [KERB].
curd [kə:d], *n.* cuajada; requesón, *m.*
curdle [kə:dl], *v.t.*, cuajar, coagular.—*v.i.* -se.
cure [kjuə], *n.* remedio; cura.—*v.t.* curar.—*v.i.* curar; curarse.
curfew ['kə:fju], *n.* queda; toque (*m.*) de queda.
curiosity [kjuri'ɔsiti], *n.* curiosidad, *f.*
curious ['kjuəriəs], *a.* curioso.
curl [kə:l], *n.* rizo, bucle, espiral, *m.*—*v.t.* rizar.—*v.i.* -se.
curlew ['kə:lju], *n.* (*orn.*) zarapito.
curly ['kə:li], *a.* rizado, ondulado.
currant ['kʌrənt], *n.* pasa (de Corinto) grosella.

currency [ˈkʌrənsi], *n.* moneda corriente, divisa; uso corriente; acceptación, *f.*
current [ˈkʌrənt], *a.* corriente; presente, actual.—*n.* corriente, *f.*
currently [ˈkʌrəntli], *adv.* actualmente; por lo general.
curriculum [kəˈrikjuləm], *n.* programa (*m.*) de estudios.
curry (1) [ˈkʌri], *n.* (*cul.*) cari, *m.*
curry (2) [ˈkʌri], *v.t.* almohazar (*caballos*); ***to — favour,*** insinuarse.
curry-comb [ˈkʌrikoum], *n.* almohaza.
curse [kə:s], *n.* maldición, *f.*—*v.t.* maldecir.—*v.i.* echar pestes, maldecir.
cursed [ˈkə:sid], *a.* maldito.
cursive [ˈkə:siv], *a.* cursivo.—*n.* cursiva.
cursory [ˈk:əsəri], *a.* precipitado; superficial.
curt [kə:t], *a.* brusco, áspero.
curtail [kəˈteil], *v.t.* abreviar, reducir.
curtailment [kəˈteilmənt], *n.* reducción, *f.*
curtain [kə:tn], *n.* cortina; (*theat.*) telón, *m.*
curtsy [ˈkə:tsi], *n.* reverencia.—*v.i.* hacer una reverencia.
curve [kə:v], *n.* curva.—*v.i.* encorvarse.
curved [kə:vd], *a.* curvo.
cushion [ˈkuʃən], *n.* cojín, *m.*, almohadilla.—*v.t.* amortiguar.
cuss [kʌs], *n.* (*fam.*) tunante, *m.*; *pronunciación fam. de* CURSE; (*fig.*) higo.
custard [ˈkʌstəd], *n.* natillas, *f.pl.*
custodian [kʌsˈtoudjən], *n.* custodio.
custody [ˈkʌstədi], *n.* custodia; ***in —,*** en prisión, *f.*
custom, [ˈkʌstəm], *n.* costumbre, *f.*; clientela.—*pl.* aduana; derechos (*m.pl.*) de aduana.
customary [ˈkʌstəməri], *a.* acostumbrado.
customer [ˈkʌstəmə], *n.* cliente, *m.*, parroquiano.
cut [kʌt], *a.* cortado; ***— up,*** (*fig.*) turbado.—*n.* corte, *m.*; tajada; atajo; golpe cortante, *m.*; hechura.—*v.t. irr.* cortar, recortar; hender; tallar; (*fig.*) faltar a; negar el saludo a; ***to — down,*** derribar, abatir; rebajar; ***to — off,*** amputar; desheredar; ***to — out,*** omitir, suprimir; ***to — up,*** despedazar.
cute [kju:t], *a.* (*U.S.*) mono; (*fam.*) astuto.
cutlass [ˈkʌtləs], *n.* sable (*m.*) de abordaje; alfanje, *m.*
cutler [ˈkʌtlə], *n.* cuchillero.
cutlery [ˈkʌtləri], *n.* cubiertos; instrumentos cortantes, *m.pl.*
cutlet [ˈkʌtlit], *n.* chuleta.
cut-out [ˈkʌtaut], *n.* válvula de escape; portafusible, *m.*; diseño recortado.
cutter [ˈkʌtə], *n.* cortador, (*naut.*) cúter, *m.*
cut-throat [ˈkʌtθrout], *a.*, *n.* asesino; (*fig.*) rufián, *m.*
cutting [ˈkʌtiŋ], *a.* incisivo, mordaz.
cuttle-fish [ˈkʌtlfiʃ], *n.* jibia.
cyanide [ˈsaiənaid], *n.* cianuro.
cyclamen [ˈsikləmən], *n.* (*bot.*) pamporcino, ciclamino.
cycle [saikl], *n.* ciclo; (*eng.*) tiempo; bicicleta.—*v.i.* ir en bicicleta; practicar el ciclismo.
cycling [ˈsaikliŋ], *n.* ciclismo.
cyclist [ˈsaiklist], *n.* ciclista, *m.f.*
cyclone [ˈsaikloun], *n.* ciclón, *m.*
cygnet [ˈsignit], *n.* pollo del cisne.
cylinder [ˈsilində], *n.* cilindro; ***— head,*** culata.
cymbal [ˈsimbəl], *n.* címbalo.
cynic [ˈsinik], *n.* cínico.
cynical [ˈsinikəl], *a.* cínico.
cynicism [ˈsinisizm], *n.* cinismo.
cypress [ˈsaiprəs], *n.* ciprés, *m.*
Cypriot [ˈsipriət], *a.*, *n.* chipriote, chipriota, *m.f.*
Cyprus [ˈsaiprəs], *n.* Chipre, *f.*
cyst [sist], *n.* (*med.*) quiste, *m.*
czar [zɑ:], *n.* (*hist.*) zar, *m.*
Czech [tʃek], *a.*, *n.* checo.
Czechoslovakia [tʃekouslouˈvækiə], *n.* Checoeslovaquia.

D

D, d, [di:], *n.* cuarta letra del alfabeto inglés; D, (*mus.*) re.
dab [dæb], *n.* golpecito; brochazo.—*v.t.* frotar suavemente, tocar; dar un brochazo a.
dabble [dæbl], *v.i.* chapotear; mangonear; especular.
dactyl [ˈdæktil], *n.* dáctilo.
dad [dæd], **daddy** [ˈdædi], *n.* (*fam.*) papá, *m.*
daffodil [ˈdæfədil], *n.* narciso, trompón, *m.*
daft [dɑ:ft], *a.* chiflado.
dagger [ˈdægə], *n.* puñal, *m.*
daily [ˈdeili], *a.*, *n.* diario.—*adv.* cada día.
dainty [ˈdeinti], *a.* delicado.—*n.* golosina.
dairy [ˈdɛəri], *n.* lechería.
dairy-maid [ˈdɛərimeid], *n.* lechera.
dais [ˈdeiis], *n.* estrado.
daisy [ˈdeizi], *n.* margarita.
dale [deil], *n.* vallecico.
dally [ˈdæli], *v.i.* retozar; holgar; rezagarse.
dam [dæm], *n.* presa; (*zool.*) madre, *f.*—*v.t.* estancar, represar.
damage [ˈdæmidʒ], *n.* daño, perjuicio; avería.—*v.t.* dañar, perjudicar; averiar.
damask [ˈdæməsk], *n.* damasco.
dame [deim], *n.* dama.
damn [dæm], *a.* maldito.—*v.t.* condenar.
damnation [dæmˈneiʃən], *n.* damnación, *f.*
damp [dæmp], *a.* húmedo.—*n.* humedad, *f.*—*v.t.* humedecer; amortiguar.
dampen [ˈdæmpən], *v.t.* humedecer; amortiguar.
dampness [ˈdæmpnis], *n.* humedad, *f.*
damsel [ˈdæmzəl], *n.* damisela.
damson [ˈdæmzən], *n.* ciruela damascena.
dance [dɑ:ns], *n.* baile, *m.*; danza.—*v.t.*, *v.i.* bailar, danzar.
dancer [ˈdɑ:nsə], *n.* bailador; bailarín, *m.*
dandelion [ˈdændilaiən], *n.* diente (*m.*) de león.
dandle [dændl], *v.t.* mecer, mimar.
dandruff [ˈdændrʌf], *n.* caspa.
dandy [ˈdændi], *a.* (*fam.*) de órdago.—*n.* pisaverde, *m.*
Dane [dein], *n.* danés, dinamarqués, *m.*
danger [ˈdeindʒə], *n.* peligro.
dangerous [ˈdeindʒərəs], *a.* peligroso.
dangle [dæŋgl], *v.t.* colgar (delante).
Danish [ˈdeiniʃ], *a.* danés, dinamarqués.
dank [dæŋk], *a.* liento.
dapper [ˈdæpə], *a.* apuesto, gallardo.
dapple [dæpl], *n.* caballo rodado.—*v.t.* motear.

dare [dɛə], *n.* reto.—*v.t.* retar, provocar.—*v.i.* atreverse, osar.
dare-devil [ˈdɛədevl], *n.* atrévelotodo.
daring [ˈdɛəriŋ], *a.* osado, atrevido.—*n.* osadía, atrevimiento.
dark [dɑ:k], *a.* o(b)scuro; moreno.—*n.* o(b)scuridad, *f.*; tinieblas, *f.pl.*; noche, *f.*; ***in the* —,** a oscuras; ***to get* —,** obscurecerse, anochecer.
darken [ˈdɑ:kən], *v.t.* obscurecer.—*v.i.* -se.
darkness [ˈdɑ:knis], *n.* obscuridad, *f.*
darling [ˈdɑ:liŋ], *a.*, *n.* querido.—*interj.* cariño.
darn [dɑ:n], *n.* zurcido.—*v.t.* zurcir; (*fam.*) maldecir.
dart [dɑ:t], *n.* dardo; saeta; (*sport*) rechilete; arranque, *m.*—*v.i.* lanzarse, volar.
dash [dæʃ], *n.* arremetida; brío; gota, rociada; raya; gran prisa.—*v.t.* frustrar; quebrar.—*v.i.* lanzarse, correr aprisa.
dash-board [ˈdæʃbɔ:d], *n.* tablero de instrumentos (*en un coche*).
dashing [ˈdæʃiŋ], *a.* gallardo, bizarro, arrojado.
dastardly [ˈdæstədli], *a.* vil, cobarde.
date (1) [deit], *n.* fecha, data; cita (*encuentro*); ***out of* —,** anticuado; caducado; ***up to* —,** moderno; al corriente.—*v.t.* fechar, datar; citarse con.—*v.i.* datar (***from,*** de).
date (2) [deit], *n.* (*bot.*) dátil, *m.*
dative [ˈdeitiv], *a.*, *n.* dativo.
datum [ˈdeitəm], *n.* (*pl.* **data**) dato.
daub [dɔ:b], *n.* embarradura; pintarrajo.—*v.t.* embadurnar; pintarrajear.
daughter [ˈdɔ:tə], *n.* hija.
daughter-in-law [ˈdɔ:tərinlɔ:], *n.* (*pl.* **daughters-in-law**) nuera.
daughterly [ˈdɔ:təli], *a.* filial, de hija.
daunt [dɔ:nt], *v.t.* acobardar, desmayar, intimidar.
dauntless [ˈdɔ:ntlis], *a.* impávido.
dauphin [ˈdɔ:fin], *n.* delfín, *m.*
Davy Jones's locker [ˈdeivi'dʒounziz'lɔkə], *n.* (*fam.*) el fondo del mar.
daw [dɔ:], *n.* graja.
dawdle [dɔ:dl], *v.i.* haraganear.
dawn [dɔ:n], *n.* alba; amanecer, *m.*—*v.i.* amanecer; ***it dawned on him that* . . .,** se dio cuenta de que . . .
day [dei], *n.* día, *m.*; ***by* —,** de día; **— *in,* — *out,*** día tras día; **— *off,*** día libre; ***the* — *before,*** la víspera; ***to win the* —,** vencer, ganar la palma.
daybreak [ˈdeibreik], *n.* amanecer, *m.*
day-dream [ˈdeidri:m], *n.* ensueño, castillo en el aire.
daylight [ˈdeilait], *n.* luz (*f.*) del día; día, *m.*; ***in broad* —,** en pleno día.
daytime [ˈdeitaim], *n.* día, *m.*; ***in*** o ***during the* —,** de día.
daze [deiz], *n.* aturdimiento.—*v.t.* aturdir, deslumbrar.
dazzle [dæzl], *n.* deslumbramiento.—*v.t.* deslumbrar.
deacon [ˈdi:kən], *n.* diácono.
dead [ded], *a.* muerto; (*fam.*) rendido.—*n.* ***the* — *of winter,*** lo más frío del invierno; ***at* — *of night,*** en el silencio de la noche.—*adv.* (*fam.*) completamente.
dead-beat [ded'bi:t], *a.* (*fam.*) rendido.
deaden [dedn], *v.t.* amortiguar, desvirtuar.
deadline [ˈdedlain], *n.* fin (*m.*) del plazo.
deadlock [ˈdedlɔk], *n.* callejón (*m.*) sin salida, punto muerto.
deadly [ˈdedli], *a.* mortal, mortífero.
deaf [def], *a.* sordo; **— *and dumb,*** sordomudo.
deafen [defn], *v.t.* ensordecer, aturdir.
deaf-mute [ˈdefˈmju:t], *n.* sordomudo.
deafness [ˈdefnis], *n.* sordera.
deal [di:l], *n.* negocio; trato; reparto; (tabla de) pino; ***a good* —,** mucho.—*v.t. irr.* tratar (***with, in,*** de); repartir.—*v.i.* comerciar; tratar; intervenir; comportarse.
dealer [ˈdi:lə], *n.* comerciante; repartidor (*naipes*), *m.*
dealings [ˈdi:liŋz], *n.pl.* relaciones, *f.pl.*; negocios, *m.pl.*
dealt [delt] [DEAL].
dean [di:n], *n.* decano; deán, *m.*
dear [diə], *a.* caro, costoso; querido, amado; **— *Sir,*** Muy señor mío; **— *me!*** ¡Dios mío!
dearth [də:θ], *n.* escasez, *f.*
death [deθ], *n.* muerte, *f.*; **— *penalty,*** pena de muerte; **— *throes,*** agonía (de la muerte).
deathly [ˈdeθli], *a.* mortal; cadavérico.—*adv.* como muerto *o* la muerte.
death-rate [ˈdeθreit], *n.* mortalidad, *f.*
death-rattle [ˈdeθrætl], *n.* estertor, *m.*
death-trap [ˈdeθtræp], *n.* situación peligrosa.
debar [diˈbɑ:], *v.t.* excluir.
debase [diˈbeis], *v.t.* envilecer; falsificar.
debatable [diˈbeitəbl], *a.* discutible.
debate [diˈbeit], *n.* debate, *m.*—*v.t., v.i.* debatir.
debauch [diˈbɔ:tʃ], *n.* lujuria.—*v.t.* corromper.
debauchee [dibɔ:ˈtʃi:], *n.* disoluto, calavera, *m.*
debauchery [diˈbɔ:tʃəri], *n.* libertinaje, *m.*
debenture [diˈbentʃə], *n.* bono, vale, *m.*
debilitate [diˈbiliteit], *v.t.* debilitar.
debility [diˈbiliti], *n.* debilidad, *f.*
debit [ˈdebit], *n.* debe, *m.*, débito.—*v.t.* debitar, adeudar.
debonair [debəˈnɛə], *a.* garboso, urbano.
debris [ˈdebri], *n.* escombros, *m.pl.*
debt [det], *n.* deuda.
debtor [ˈdetə], *n.* deudor, *m.*
début [ˈdeibju:], *n.* estreno; debut, *m.*
débutante [ˈdebju:tɑ̃:t], *n.* debutante, muchacha que se pone de largo.
decade [ˈdekeid], *n.* decenio, década.
decadence [ˈdekədəns], *n.* decadencia.
decadent [ˈdekədənt], *a.* decadente.
decamp [diˈkæmp], *v.i.* decampar.
decant [diˈkænt], *v.t.* decantar.
decanter [diˈkæntə], *n.* garrafa.
decapitate [diˈkæpiteit], *v.t.* decapitar, degollar.
decay [diˈkei], *n.* podredumbre, podre, *f.*—*v.i.* pudrir(se); decaer.
deceased [diˈsi:st], *a.*, *n.* difunto.
deceit [diˈsi:t], *n.* engaño; fraude, *m.*
deceitful [diˈsi:tful], *a.* engañoso, falaz.
deceive [diˈsi:v], *v.t.* engañar; burlar.
December [diˈsembə], *n.* diciembre, *m.*
decency [ˈdi:sənsi], *n.* decencia.
decent [ˈdi:sənt], *a.* decente.
decentralize [di:ˈsentrəlaiz], *v.t.* descentralizar.
deception [diˈsepʃən], *n.* decepción, *f.* engaño.

deceptive [di'septiv], *a.* engañoso.
decide [di'said], *v.t.* decidir.—*v.i.* decidir; decidirse (*to*, a)
decimal ['desimәl], *a.*, *n.* decimal, *m.*
decimate ['desimeit], *v.t.* diezmar.
decipher [di'saifә], *v.t.* descifrar.
decision [di'siʒәn], *n.* decisión, *f.*
decisive [di'saisiv], *a.* decisivo.
deck [dek], *n.* (*naut.*) cubierta; (*U.S.*) baraja (*naipes*).—*v.t.* ataviar.
declaim (di'kleim], *v.t.* declamar.
declaration [deklә'reiʃәn], *n.* declaración, *f.*
declare [di'klɛә], *v.t.* declarar; manifestar.—*v.i.* declararse.
declension [di'klenʃәn], *n.* declinación, *f.*
decline [di'klain], *n.* declinación, *f.*; baja; decaimiento.—*v.t.*, *v.i.* declinar; decaer.
declivity [di'kliviti], *n.* declive, *m.*
declutch ['di:klʌtʃ], *v.t.*, *v.i.* desembragar.
décolleté [deikɔl'tei], *a.* escotado.—*n.* escote, *m.*
decompose [di:kәm'pouz], *v.t.* descomponer.—*v.i.* -se.
decomposition [di:kɔmpә'ziʃәn], *n.* descomposición, *f.*
décor ['deikɔ:], *n.* decorado.
decorate ['dekәreit], *v.t.* decorar; pintar; condecorar (*honor*).
decoration [dekә'reiʃәn], *n.* decoración; condecoración, *f.*
decorative ['dekәrәtiv], *a.* decorativo.
decorator ['dekәreitә], *n.* pintor, decorador, *m.*
decorous ['dekәrәs], *a.* decoroso.
decorum [di'kɔ:rәm], *n.* decoro.
decoy [di'kɔi], *n.* señuelo, reclamo; trampa.—*v.t.* entruchar, atraer con señuelo.
decrease ['di:kri:s], *n.* disminución, *f.*, decremento.—[di'kri:s], *v.t.*, *v.i.* disminuir.—*v.i.* decrecer.
decree [di'kri:], *n.* decreto.—*v.t.* decretar.
decrepit [di'krepit], *a.* decrépito.
decry [di'krai], *v.t.* afear, desacreditar.
dedicate ['dedikeit], *v.t.*dedicar.
dedication [dedi'keiʃәn], *n.* dedicación, *f.*; dedicatoria.
deduce [di'dju:s], *v.t.* deducir.
deduct [di'dʌkt], *v.t.* deducir, restar.
deduction [di'dʌkʃәn], *n.* deducción, *f.*
deed [di:d], *n.* hecho; hazaña; (*jur.*) escritura.
deem [di:m] *v.t.* juzgar, creer.
deep [di:p], *a.* profundo.—*n.* piélago; abismo.
deepen [di:pn], *v.t.* profundizar.
deer [diә], *n.* (*pl.* **deer**) ciervo.
deface [di'feis], *v.t.* desfigurar.
defamation [defә'meiʃәn], *n.* difamación, *f.*
defame [di'feim], *v.t.* difamar.
default [di'fɔ:lt], *n.* falta, incumplimiento.—*v.t.*, *v.i.* faltar, no cumplir.
defeat [di'fi:t], *n.* derrota.—*v.t.* derrotar, vencer.
defeatist [di'fi:tist], *a.*, *n.* derrotista, *m.f.*
defect [di'fekt, 'di:fekt], *n.* defecto.
defective [di'fektiv], *a.* defectuoso; defectivo; deficiente.
defence [di'fens], *n.* defensa.
defend [di'fend], *v.t.* defender.
defendant [di'fendәnt], *n.* acusado; demandado.
defensive [di'fensiv], *a.* defensivo.—*n.* defensiva.
defer [di'fә:], *v.t.* aplazar.
deference ['defәrәns] *n.* deferencia.
deferment [di'fә:mәnt] *n.* aplazamiento.
defiance [di'faiәns], *n.* desafío; desobediencia.
defiant [di'faiәnt], *a.* desafiador; desobediente.
deficiency [di'fiʃәnsi], *n.* deficiencia; insolvencia.
deficient [di'fiʃәnt], *a.* deficiente.
deficit ['defisit], *n.* déficit, *m.*
defile (1) ['di:fail], *n.* desfiladero.
defile (2) [di'fail], *v.t.* profanar, manchar.
define [di'fain], *v.t.* definir.
definite ['definit], *a.* definido, concreto.
definition [defi'niʃәn], *n.* definición, *f.*
definitive [di'finitiv], *a.* definitivo.
deflate [di'fleit], *v.t.* desinflar.
deflation [di'fleiʃәn], *n.* desinflación, *f.*
deflect [di'flekt], *v.t.* desviar.
deflection [di'flekʃәn], *n.* desviación, *f.*
deflower [di:'flauә], *v.t.* desflorar.
deform [di'fɔ:m], *v.t.* deformar.
deformed [di'fɔ:md], *a.* deforme.
deformity [di'fɔ:miti], *n.* deformidad, *f.*
defraud [di'frɔ:d], *v.t.* defraudar, estafar.
defray [di'frei], *v.t.* costear, sufragar.
defrost [di:'frost], *v.t.* deshelar.
deft [deft], *a.* diestro, mañoso.
defunct [di'fʌŋkt], *a.* difunto.
defy [di'fai], *v.t.* desafiar; resistir tercamente.
degeneracy [di'dʒenәrәsi], *n.* degeneración, *f.*
degenerate [di'dʒenәrit], *a.*, *n.* degenerado.—[di'dʒenәreit], *v.i.* degenerar.
degradation [degrә'deiʃәn], *n.* degradación, *f.*
degrade [di'greid], *v.t.* degradar.
degrading [di'greidiŋ], *a.* degradante.
degree [di'gri:], *n.* grado; (*educ.*) título.
dehydrate [di:hai'dreit], *v.t.* deshidratar.
deify ['di:ifai], *v.t.* deificar.
deign [dein], *v.i.* dignarse (*to*).
deity ['di:iti], *n.* deidad, *f.*
deject [di'dʒekt], *v.t.* abatir, desanimar.
dejection [di'dʒekʃәn], *n.* abatimiento.
delay [di'lei], *n.* retraso, tardanza.—*v.t.* retrasar.—*v.i.* tardar (en).
delectable [di'lektәbl], *a.* deleitable.
delegate ['deligit], *n.* delegado.—['deligeit], *v.t.* delegar.
delegation [deli'geiʃәn], *n.* delegación, *f.*
delete [di'li:t], *v.t.* borrar, suprimir.
deleterious [deli'tiәriәs], *a.* perjudicial, nocivo.
deletion [di'li:ʃәn], *n.* borradura, supresión, *f.*
deliberate [di'libәrit], *a.* pensado; cauto; pausado.—[di'libәreit], *v.t.*, *v.i.* deliberar.
deliberation [delibә'reiʃәn], *n.* deliberación, *f.*
delicacy ['delikәsi], *n.* delicadeza; (*cul.*) golosina.
delicate ['delikit], *a.* delicado.
delicious [di'liʃәs], *a.* delicioso.
delight [di'lait], *n.* delicia, gozo; deleite, *m.*—*v.t.* deleitar.—*v.i.* deleitarse (*in*, con, en).
delightful [di'laitful], *a.* deleitoso, encantador.
Delilah [di'lailә], *n.* Dalila.
delimit [di:'limit], *v.t.* delimitar.
delineate [di'linieit], *v.t.* delinear.
delinquency [di'liŋkwәnsi], *n.* delincuencia; delito.

delinquent [di'liŋkwənt], *a.*, *n.* delincuente, *m.f.*
delirious [di'liriəs], *a.* delirante; ***to be —,*** delirar.
delirium [di'liriəm], *n.* delirio.
deliver [di'livə], *v.t.* libertar; entregar; asestar; distribuir (*correo*); pronunciar (*oración*); ***to be delivered of,*** parir.
deliverance [di'livərəns], *n.* liberación, *f.*; rescate, *m.*
delivery [di'livəri], *n.* liberación, *f.*; rescate, *m.*; distribución, *f.*; entrega; modo de expresarse; parto.
dell [del], *n.* vallejuelo.
delta ['deltə], *n.* delta.
delude [di'l(j)u:d], *v.t.* seducir, ilusionar.
deluge ['delju:dʒ], *n.* diluvio.—*v.t.* inundar.
delusion [di'l(j)u:ʒən], *n.* alucinación; decepción, *f.*
delve [delv], *v.t.* (*obs.*) cavar; ***to — into,*** sondear.
demagnetize [di:'mægnitaiz], *v.t.* desiman(t)ar.
demagogue ['deməgɔg], *n.* demagogo.
demand [di'mɑ:nd], *n.* demanda.—*v.t.* exigir; demandar; ***to be in —,*** tener demanda.
demanding [di'mɑ:ndiŋ], *a.* exigente.
demarcate ['di:mɑ:keit], *v.t.* demarcar, deslindar.
demarcation [di:mɑ'keiʃən], *n.* demarcación, *f.*, deslinde, *m.*
demean [di'mi:n], *v.r.* rebajarse, degradarse.
demeanour [di'mi:nə], *n.* conducta; porte, *m.*
demented [di'mentid], *a.* demente.
demigod ['demigɔd], *n.* semidiós, *m.*
demilitarize [di:'militəraiz], *v.t.* desmilitarizar.
demise [di'maiz], *n.* óbito.
demobilize [di:'moubilaiz], (*fam.* **demob** [di'mɔb]), *v.t.* desmovilizar.
democracy [di'mɔkrəsi], *n.* democracia.
democrat ['deməkræt], *n.* demócrata, *m.f.*
democratic [demə'krætik], *a.* democrático.
demolish [di'mɔliʃ], *v.t.* derribar, demoler.
demolition [demə'liʃən], *n.* derribo, demolición, *f.*
demon ['di:mən], *n.* demonio.
demonstrate ['demənstreit], *v.t.* demostrar.
demonstration [demәns'treiʃən], *n.* demostración, *f.*
demonstrative [di'mɔnstrətiv], *a.*, *n.* demostrativo.
demoralize [di'mɔrəlaiz], *v.t.* desmoralizar.
demote [di'mout], *v.t.* (*U.S.*) degradar.
demur [di'mə:], *n.* escrúpulo, titubeo.—*v.i.* vacilar, titubear.
demure [di'mjuə], *a.* sentado, serio; gazmoño.
den [den], *n.* guarida, cubil, *m.*
denial [di'naiəl], *n.* negación, *f.*
denigrate ['denigreit], *v.t.* denigrar.
Denis ['denis], *n.* Dionisio.
denizen ['denizn], *n.* habitante, *m.f.*
Denmark ['denmɑ:k], *n.* Dinamarca.
denote [di'nout], *v.t.* denotar.
dénouement [dei'nu:mã], *n.* desenlace, *m.*
denounce [di'nauns], *v.t.* denunciar.
dense [dens], *a.* denso, espeso.
density ['densiti], *n.* densidad, *f.*
dent [dent], *n.* abolladura.—*v.t.* abollar.—*v.i.* -se.
dental [dentl], *a.*, *n.* dental, *f.*
dentifrice ['dentifris], *n.* dentífrico, pasta de dientes.
dentist ['dentist], *n.* dentista, *m.f.*
denture ['dentʃə], *n.* dentadura.
denude [di'nju:d], *v.t.* desnudar.
deny [di'nai], *v.t.* negar.
deodorant [di:'oudərənt], *a.*, *n.* desodorante, *m.*
depart [di'pɑ:t], *v.i.* partir, salir; divergir, desviarse; fallecer.
departed [di'pɑ:tid], *a.*, *n.* difunto, pasado.
department [di'pɑ:tmənt], *n.* departamento, sección, *f.*; ***— store,*** almacén, *m.*
departure [di'pɑ:tʃə], *n.* salida, partida; divergencia.
depend [di'pend], *v.i.* depender (***on,*** de).
dependable [di'pendəbl], *a.* digno de confianza.
dependant [di'pendənt], *n.* dependiente, *m.f.*
dependence [di'pendəns], **dependency** [di'pendənsi], *n.* dependencia.
dependent [di'pendənt], *a.* dependiente.
depict [di'pikt], *v.t.* retratar, representar.
deplete [di'pli:t], *v.t.* consumir, agotar.
deplore [di'plɔ:], *v.t.* lamentar, deplorar.
deploy [di'plɔi], *v.t.* desplegar.—*v.i.* -se.
depopulate [di:'pɔpjuleit], *v.t.* despoblar.
deport [di'pɔ:t], *v.t.* deportar.
deportment [di'pɔ:tmənt], *n.* porte, *m.*, conducta; postura.
depose [di'pouz], *v.t.* deponer.
deposit [di'pɔzit], *n.* depósito.—*v.t.* depositar. —*v.i.* -se.
depot ['depou], *n.* depósito, almacén, *m.*; (*U.S.*) estación, *f.*
deprave [di'preiv], *v.t.* depravar.
depravity [di'præviti], *n.* depravación, *f.*
deprecate ['deprikeit], *v.t.* desaprobar.
depreciate [di'pri:ʃieit], *v.t.* depreciar; abaratar.—*v.i.* depreciarse.
depredation [depri'deiʃən], *n.* depredación, *f.*
depress [di'pres], *v.t.* abatir, desalentar; deprimir.
depressing [di'presiŋ], *a.* desalentador; deprimente.
depression [di'preʃən], *n.* depresión; (*com.*) crisis, *f.*
deprive [di'praiv], *v.t.* privar.
depth [depθ], *n.* profundidad, *f.*, fondo; ***in the depths of,*** sumido en.
deputation [depju'teiʃən], *n.* diputación; delegación, *f.*
depute [di'pju:t], *v.t.* diputar.
deputize ['depjutaiz], *v.t.* diputar, delegar.—*v.i.* hacer las veces (***for,*** de).
deputy ['depjuti], *n.* diputado; teniente, *m.*
derail [di'reil], *v.t.* hacer descarrilar.
derange [di'reindʒ], *v.t.* desarreglar; trastornar.
derelict ['derilikt], *a.* abandonado; remiso.—*n.* derrelicto.
deride [di'raid], *v.t.* mofarse de.
derision [di'riʒən], *n.* irrisión, *f.*, mofa.
derivation [deri'veiʃən], *n.* derivación, *f.*
derive [di'raiv], *v.t.*, *v.i.* derivar.
derogatory [di'rɔgətəri], *a.* despreciativo.
derrick ['derik], *n.* grúa, cabria; torre (*f.*) de taladrar.
dervish ['də:viʃ], *n.* derviche, *m.*

descant ['deskænt], *n.* discante, *m.*
descend [di'send], *v.t., v.i.* descender, bajar; caer (***on,*** sobre).
descendant [di'sendənt], *n.* descendiente, *m.f.*
descendent [di'sendənt], *a.* descendente.
descent [di'sent], *n.* descenso; descendimiento; descendencia (*linaje*).
describe [dis'kraib], *v.t.* describir.
description [dis'kripʃən], *n.* descripción, *f.*
descriptive [dis'kriptiv], *a.* descriptivo.
descry [dis'krai], *v.t.* divisar.
desecrate ['desikreit], *v.t.* profanar.
desert (1) [di'zə:t], *n.* merecimiento, mérito.
desert (2) [di'zə:t], *v.t.* desertar; abandonar.
desert (3) ['dezət], *a., n.* desierto, yermo.
deserter [di'zə:tə], *n.* desertor, *m.*
desertion [di'zə:ʃən], *n.* deserción, *f.*, abandono.
deserve [di'zə:v], *v.t.* merecer.
design [di'zain], *n.* dibujo, diseño; designio, proyecto; intención, *f.—v.t.* diseñar, dibujar; proyectar, idear; destinar.
designate ['dezignit], *a.* designado.—['dezigneit], *v.t.* señalar; nombrar; designar.
designing [di'zainiŋ], *a.* insidioso, intrigante.
desirable [di'zaiərəbl], *a.* deseable.
desire [di'zaiə], *n.* deseo.—*v.t.* desear.
desirous [di'zaiərəs], *a.* deseoso.
desist [di'zist], *v.i.* desistir.
desk [desk], *n.* escritorio, mesa; pupitre, *m.*
desolate ['desəlit], *a.* desolado, desierto, lúgubre.—['desəleit], *v.t.* desolar.
desolation [desə'leiʃən], *n.* desolación, *f.*; desierto.
despair [dis'pɛə], *n.* desesperación, *f.—v.i.* desesperar(se) (***of,*** de).
desperate ['despərit], *a.* desesperado; violento.
desperation [despə'reiʃən], *n.* desesperación, *f.*
despicable [dis'pikəbl], *a.* despreciable, vil.
despise [dis'paiz], *v.t.* despreciar.
despite [dis'pait], *prep.* a pesar de.
despoil [dis'pɔil], *v.t.* despojar.
despondent [dis'pɔndənt], *a.* desalentado.
despot ['despɔt], *n.* déspota, *m.f.*
despotic [des'pɔtik], *a.* despótico.
dessert [di'zə:t], *n.* postre, *m.*
destination [desti'neiʃən], *n.* destino; destinación, *f.*
destine ['destin], *v.t.* destinar.
destiny ['destini], *n.* destino, sino.
destitute ['destitju:t], *a.* desamparado; desprovisto.
destitution [desti'tju:ʃən], *n.* desamparo.
destroy [dis'trɔi], *v.t.* destruir, destrozar.
destroyer [dis'trɔiə], *n.* destructor (*also naut.*), *m.*
destruction [dis'trʌkʃən], *n.* destrucción, *f.*
destructive [dis'trʌktiv], *a.* destructivo.
desultory ['desəltəri], *a.* inconexo, veleidoso.
detach [di'tætʃ], *v.t.* separar, desprender; (*mil.*) destacar.
detached [di'tætʃt], *a.* imparcial.
detachment [di'tætʃmənt], *n.* desprendimiento; desinterés, *m.*; (*mil.*) destacamento.
detail ['di:teil], *n.* detalle, pormenor, *m.*; (*mil.*) destacamento.—[di'teil], *v.t.* detallar; (*mil.*) destacar.
detain [di'tein], *v.t.* detener.
detect [di'tekt], *v.t.* descubrir; percibir.
detection [di'tekʃən], *n.* averiguación, *f.*, descubrimiento.
detective [di'tektiv], *a.* policíaco (*cuento etc.*). —*n.* detective, *m.*
detention [di'tenʃən], *n.* detención, *f.*
deter [di'tə:], *v.t.* disuadir, refrenar.
detergent [di'tə:dʒənt], *a., n.* detergente, *m.*
deteriorate [di'tiəriəreit], *v.i.* deteriorarse.
deterioration [ditiəriə'reiʃən], *n.* deterioro.
determination [ditə:mi'neiʃən], *n.* determinación, *f.*
determine [di'tə:min], *v.t.* determinar.—*v.i.* -se.
deterrent [di'terənt], *a., n.* deterrente, *m.*
detest [di'test], *v.t.* detestar.
dethrone [di'θroun], *v.t.* destronar.
detonate ['detəneit], *v.t.* hacer detonar.—*v.i.* detonar.
detour ['di:tuə], *n.* desviación, *f.*, desvío, rodeo.
detract [di'trækt], *v.t.* detraer, detractar.
detriment ['detrimənt], *n.* perjuicio.
detrimental [detri'mentl], *a.* perjudicial.
deuce [dju:s], *n.* (*fam.*) dos; ***the —!*** ¡diablos!
deuced [dju:st], *a.* (*fam.*) diabólico.
deucedly ['dju:sidli], *adv.* (*fam.*) formidablemente, muy.
devaluation [di:vælju'eiʃən], *n.* desvalorización, *f.*
devalue [di:'vælju:], *v.t.* desvalor(iz)ar.
devastate ['devəsteit], *v.t.* devastar, asolar.
devastation [devəs'teiʃən], *n.* devastación, *f.*, ruina.
develop [di'veləp], *v.t.* desarrollar; (*phot.*) revelar; (*com.*) explotar.—*v.i.* desarrollarse, evolucionar.
development [di'veləpmənt], *n.* desarrollo; (*com.*) explotación; reconstrucción; evolución, *f.*; suceso reciente.
deviate ['di:vieit], *v.i.* divergir, desviarse.
device [di'vais], *n.* artificio, invento, aparato; ardid; emblema, *m.*, lema, *m.*
devil ['devil], *n.* diablo.—*v.t.*, (*fam.*) estorbar.
devilish ['deviliʃ], *a.* diabólico.
devilment ['devilmənt], *n.* diablura.
devilry ['devilri], *n.* diablura.
devious ['di:viəs], *a.* tortuoso.
devise [di'vaiz], *v.t.* ideal, trazar.
devoid [di'vɔid], *a.* desprovisto, falto.
devote [di'vout], *v.t.* dedicar.
devoted [di'voutəd], *a.* devoto, dedicado.
devotee [devo'ti:], *n.* devoto, dedicado.
devotion [di'vouʃən], *n.* devoción, dedicación, *f.—pl.* (*eccl.*) oraciones, *f.pl.*
devour [di'vauə], *v.t.* devorar.
devout [di'vaut], *a.* devoto, piadoso.
dew [dju:], *n.* rocío.—*v.t.* rociar.
dexterity [deks'teriti], *n.* destreza.
dexterous ['dekstrəs], *a.* diestro.
diabetic [daiə'betik], *a., n.* diabético.
diabolic(al) [daiə'bɔlik(əl)], *a.* diabólico.
diadem ['daiədem], *n.* diadema.
diæresis [dai'iərisis], *n.* (*pl.* **-reses**) diéresis, *f.*
diagnose ['daiəgnouz], *v.t.* diagnosticar.
diagnosis [daiəg'nousis], *n.* (*pl.* **-noses**) diagnosis, *f.*
diagonal [dai'ægənəl], *a., n.* diagonal, *f.*
diagram ['daiəgræm], *n.* diagrama, *m.*, gráfica.

dial ['daiəl], *n.* esfera; cuadrante, *m.*; (*tel.*) disco.—*v.t.*, *v.i.* (*tel.*) marcar.
dialect ['daiəlekt], *n.* dialecto.
dialogue ['daiəlɔg], *n.* diálogo.
diameter [dai'æmitə], *n.* diámetro.
diamond ['daiəmənd], *n.* diamante, brillante, *m.*
diaper ['daiəpə], *n.* lienzo adamascado; (*U.S.*) pañal, *m.*
diaphragm ['daiəfræm], *n.* diafragma, *m.*; (*tel.*, *rad.*) membrana.
diarrhoea [daiə'riə], *n.* diarrea.
diary ['daiəri], *n.* diario, jornal, *m.*; agenda.
diatribe ['daiətraib], *n.* diatriba.
dice [dais], *n.pl.* dados (*sg.* **die,** *q.v.*).—*v.t.* cortar en cubitos.—*v.i.* jugar a los dados.
dickens ['dikinz], *n.*, *interj.* (*fam.*) diantre, *m.*
dictate ['dikteit], *n.* dictado, mandato.—[dik'teit], *v.t.*, *v.i.* dictar; mandar.
dictation [dik'teiʃən], *n.* dictado.
dictator [dik'teitə], *n.* dictador, *m.*
dictatorship [dik'teitəʃip], *n.* dictadura.
diction ['dikʃən], *n.* dicción, *f.*; lenguaje, *m.*
dictionary ['dikʃənri], *n.* diccionario.
did [did], [DO].
diddle [didl], *v.t.* (*fam.*) estafar.
didn't [didnt] [DID NOT].
die (1) [dai], *n.* (*pl.* **dice,** *q.v.*) dado.
die (2) [dai], *n.* (*pl.* **dies**) troquel, *m.*, cuño; cubito.
die (3) [dai], *v.i.* morir; apagarse; ***to be dying to*** o ***for,*** (*fam.*) morirse por.
die-hard ['daihɑ:d], *a.*, *n.* exaltado, intransigente.
diesel-engine ['di:zlendʒin], *n.* motor diesel, *m.*
diesel-oil ['di:zlɔil], *n.* gas-oil, *m.*
diet ['daiət], *n.* régimen, *m.*; dieta.—*v.i.* estar de régimen.
differ ['difə], *v.i.* diferenciar(se), diferir.
difference ['difrəns], *n.* diferencia; disensión, *f.*; ***it makes no —,*** da lo mismo.
different ['difrənt], *a.* diferente, distinto.
differentiate [difə'renʃieit], *v.t.* diferenciar, distinguir.
difficult ['difikəlt], *a.* difícil, dificultoso.
difficulty ['difikəlti], *n.* dificultad, *f.*; apuro.
diffident ['difidənt], *a.* desconfiado, tímido.
diffuse [di'fju:s], *a.* difuso.—[di'fju:z], *v.t.* difundir.—*v.i.* -se.
diffusion [di'fju:ʒən], *n.* difusión, *f.*
dig [dig], *n.* codazo; (*fam.*) pulla, chafaldita.—*pl.* (*fam.*) alojamiento.—*v.t.*, *v.i. irr.* cavar; excavar; ***to — up,*** desenterrar.
digest ['daidʒest], *n.* digesto, recopilación, *f.*—[di'dʒest], *v.t.*, *v.i.* digerir.
digestion [di'dʒestʃən], *n.* digestión, *f.*
digit ['didʒit], *n.* dígito.
digital ['didʒitl], *a.* digital.
dignified ['dignifaid], *a.* grave, majestuoso.
dignitary ['dignitəri], *n.* personalidad, *f.*, alta jerarquía.
dignity ['digniti], *n.* dignidad, *f.*
digress [dai'gres], *v.i.* divagar.
digression [dai'greʃən], *n.* digresión, divagación, *f.*
dike [daik], *n.* dique, *m.*
dilapidated [di'læpideitid], *a.* desmantelado.
dilate [dai'leit], *v.t.* dilatar.—*v.i.* -se.
dilatory ['dilətəri], *a.* lento; dilatorio.
dilemma [di'lemə], *n.* disyuntiva; dilema, *m.*
diligence ['dilidʒəns], *n.* diligencia.
diligent ['dilidʒənt], *a.* diligente, asiduo.
dilly-dally ['dili'dæli], *v.i.* haraganear.
dilute [dai'lju:t], *v.t.* diluir.
dim [dim], *a.* débil; turbio; cegato (*vista*); indistinto; (*fig.*) boto, lerdo.—*v.t.* amortiguar.—*v.i.* nublarse.
dime [daim], *n.* (*U.S.*) moneda de diez centavos.
dimension [di'menʃən], *n.* dimensión, *f.*; tamaño.
diminish [di'miniʃ], *v.t.*, *v.i.* disminuir.
diminutive [di'minjutiv], *a.* diminuto; (*gram.*) diminutivo.—*n.* (*gram.*) diminutivo.
dimple [dimpl], *n.* hoyuelo.
din [din], *n.* estrépito, alboroto.
dine [dain], *v.i.* cenar; comer.
ding-dong ['diŋ'dɔŋ], *n.* dindán, tintín, *m.*
dinghy ['diŋgi], *n.* dinga; bote, *m.*
dingy ['dindʒi], *a.* empañado, negruzco; oscuro.
dining room ['dainiŋrum], *n.* comedor, *m.*
dinner ['dinə], *n.* cena; comida; banquete, *m.*
dint [dint], *n.* [DENT]; ***by — of,*** a fuerza de.
diocese ['daiəsis], *n.* diócesis, *f.*
dip [dip], *n.* zambullida; depresión, *f.*; (*fam.*) baño.—*v.t.* bajar; sumergir; batir (*bandera*).—*v.i.* bajar; sumergirse; inclinarse hacia abajo.
diphtheria [dif'θiəriə], *n.* difteria.
diphthong ['difθɔŋ], *n.* diptongo.
diploma [di'ploumə], *n.* diploma, *m.*
diplomacy [di'plouməsi], *n.* diplomacia.
diplomat ['dipləmæt], *n.* diplomático.
diplomatic [diplə'mætik], *a.* diplomático.
dire [daiə], *a.* horrendo.
direct [di'rekt, dai'rekt], *a.* directo; recto; inmediato; franco.—*v.t.* dirigir; regir; mandar.
direction [di'rekʃən], *n.* dirección, *f.*
director [di'rektə], *n.* director; gerente, *m.*
directory [di'rektəri], *n.* directorio; (*tel.*) guía.
dirge [də:dʒ], *n.* endecha.
dirigible ['diridʒibl], *a.*, *n.* dirigible, *m.*
dirk [də:k], *n.* daga.
dirt [də:t], *n.* barro; tierra; mugre, *f.*; porquería.
dirt-cheap ['də:t'tʃi:p], *a.* (*fam.*) barato, regalado.
dirty ['də:ti], *a.* sucio; vil; obsceno, verde.
disability [disə'biliti], *n.* incapacidad, *f.*
disable [dis'eibl], *v.t.* incapacitar, inhabilitar; mutilar.
disadvantage [disəd'vɑ:ntidʒ], *n.* desventaja.
disaffected [disə'fektid], *a.* desafecto.
disagree [disə'gri:], *v.i.* disentir; desconvenir; desavenirse; no estar de acuerdo; ***to — with,*** sentar mal a (*comida*).
disagreement [disə'gri:mənt], *n.* desacuerdo.
disallow [disə'lau], *v.t.* negar, desaprobar.
disappear [disə'piə], *v.i.* desaparecer.
disappearance [disə'piərəns], *n.* desaparición, *f.*
disappoint [disə'pɔint], *v.t.* decepcionar frustrar, chasquear.
disappointment [disə'pɔintmənt], *n.* desilusión, decepción, *f.*, chasco.
disapproval [disə'pru:vl], *n.* desaprobación, *f.*
disapprove [disə'pru:v], *v.t.*, *v.i.* desaprobar (*of*).
disarm [dis'ɑ:m], *v.t.*, *v.i.* desarmar.

disarmament [dis'ɑ:məmənt], *n.* desarme, *m.*
disarray [disə'rei], *n.* desarreglo, desorden, *m.*—*v.t.* descomponer, desarreglar.
disassociate [disə'souʃieit], *v.t.* disociar, separar.
disaster [di'zɑ:stə], *n.* desastre, *m.*
disastrous [di'zɑ:strəs], *a.* calamitoso, desastroso.
disavow [disə'vau], *v.t.* desconocer, negar.
disband [dis'bænd], *v.t.* licenciar, disolver.—*v.i.* dispersarse.
disbelief [disbi'li:f], *n.* incredulidad, *f.*
disbelieve [disbi'li:v], *v.t.*, *v.i.* no creer, descreer.
disburse [dis'bə:s], *v.t.* desembolsar.
disbursement [dis'bə:smənt], *n.* desembolse, *m.*
disc [disk], *n.* disco.
discard [dis'kɑ:d], *v.t.* descartar.
discern [di'sə:n], *v.t.* percibir, discernir.
discernment [di'sə:nmənt], *n.* discernimiento, perspicacia.
discharge ['distʃɑ:dʒ], *n.* descarga; descargo; liberación, *f.*; cumplimiento; licencia; despedida.—[dis'tʃɑ:dʒ], *v.t.* descargar; cumplir, desempeñar; licenciar; libertar; despedir.—*v.i.* descargar(se).
disciple [di'saipl], *n.* discípulo.
disciplinary ['disiplinəri], *a.* disciplinario.
discipline ['disiplin], *n.* disciplina.—*v.t.* disciplinar.
disclaim [dis'kleim], *v.t.* renunciar; negar.
disclaimer [dis'kleimə], *n.* renuncia, negación, *f.*
disclose [dis'klouz], *v.t.* revelar, descubrir, publicar.
disclosure [dis'klouʒə], *n.* revelación, *f.*, descubrimiento.
discolour [dis'kʌlə], *v.t.* descolorar.
discomfit [dis'kʌmfit], *v.t.* desconcertar.
discomfort [dis'kʌmfət], *n.* incomodidad, *f.* —*v.t.* incomodar.
discompose [diskəm'pouz], *v.t.* inquisitar, descomponer.
disconcert [diskən'sə:t], *v.t.* desconcertar.
disconnect [diskə'nekt], *v.t.* desacoplar, desunir; (*elec.*) desconectar.
disconnected [diskə'nektid], *a.* incoherente.
disconsolate [dis'kɔnsəlit], *a.* desconsolado.
discontent [diskən'tent], *a.*, *n.* descontento.—*v.t.* descontentar.
discontented [diskən'tentid], *a.* descontento.
discontinue [diskən'tinju:], *v.t.* descontinuar.
discord ['diskɔ:d], *n.* discordia; discordancia.
discordant [dis'kɔ:dənt], *a.* discordante.
discount ['diskaunt], *n.* descuento.—[dis'kaunt], *v.t.* descontar.
discourage [dis'kʌridʒ], *v.t.* desanimar, desalentar; disuadir.
discourse ['diskɔ:s], *n.* discurso, plática. —[dis'kɔ:s], *v.i.* discurrir.
discourteous [dis'kə:tjəs], *a.* descortés.
discourtesy [dis'kə:tisi], *n.* descortesía.
discover [dis'kʌvə], *v.t.* descubrir.
discovery [dis'kʌvəri], *n.* descubrimiento.
discredit [dis'kredit], *n.* descrédito.—*v.t.* desacreditar; descreer.
discreditable [dis'kreditəbl], *a.* ignominioso, deslustrador.
discreet [dis'kri:t], *a.* discreto.
discrepancy [dis'krepənsi], *n.* discrepancia.
discretion [dis'kreʃən], *n.* discreción, *f.*
discriminate [dis'krimineit], *v.t.* distinguir. —*v.i.* discriminar, hacer distinciones injustas.
discrimination [diskrimi'neiʃən], *n.* discernimiento; distinción (*f.*) injusta.
discus ['diskəs], *n.* disco.
discuss [dis'kʌs], *v.t.* discutir; hablar de.
discussion [dis'kʌʃən], *n.* discusión, *f.*
disdain [dis'dein], *n.* desdén, *m.*—*v.t.* desdeñar.
disdainful [dis'deinful], *a.* desdeñoso.
disease [di'zi:z], *n.* enfermedad, *f.*
disembark [disim'bɑ:k], *v.t.*, *v.i.* desembarcar.
disembowel [disim'bauəl], *v.t.* desentrañar.
disenchant [disin'tʃɑ:nt], *v.t.* desencantar; desengañar.
disengage [disin'geidʒ], *v.t.* desenredar; desembarazar; soltar.
disentangle [disin'tæŋgl], *v.t.* desenmarañar.
disfavour [dis'feivə:], *n.* disfavor; desaire, *m.* —*v.t.* desfavorecer.
disfigure [dis'figə], *v.t.* desfigurar.
disgorge [dis'gɔ:dʒ], *v.t.* desembuchar; vomitar.
disgrace [dis'greis], *n.* deshonra, vergüenza, afrenta.—*v.t.* deshonrar.
disgraceful [dis'greisful], *a.* afrentoso, deshonroso.
disgruntle [dis'grʌntl], *v.t.* amohinar.
disguise [dis'gaiz], *n.* disfraz, *m.*—*v.t.* disfrazar.
disgust [dis'gʌst], *n.* aversión, *f.*, repugnancia.—*v.t.* repugnar, dar asco a.
disgusting [dis'gʌstiŋ], *a.* repugnante, asqueroso.
dish [diʃ], *n.* plato.—*pl.* vajilla.—*v.t.* — ***up***, (*fam.*) servir en un plato; ofrecer.
dish-cloth [diʃklɔθ], *n.* estropajo; albero.
dishearten [dis'hɑ:tn], *v.t.* descorazonar, desalentar.
dishevel [di'ʃevəl], *v.t.* desgreñar.
dishonest [dis'ɔnist], *a.* fraudulento, ímprobo, deshonrado.
dishonesty [dis'ɔnisti], *n.* improbidad, *f.*; dolo.
dishonour [dis'ɔnə], *n.* deshonor, *m.*; deshonra.—*v.t.* deshonrar; desflorar; (*com.*) aceptar.
disillusion [disi'lu:ʒən], *n.* desilusión, *f.*—*v.t.* desilusionar.
disinclination [disinkli'neiʃən], *n.* aversión, desinclinación, *f.*
disincline [disin'klain], *v.t.* desinclinar.
disinfect [disin'fekt], *v.t.* desinfectar.
disinfectant [disin'fektənt], *n.* antiséptico, desinfectante, *m.*
disinherit [disin'herit], *v.t.* desheredar.
disintegrate [dis'intigreit], *v.t.* disgregar, desintegrar.—*v.i.* -se.
disinter [disin'tə:], *v.t.* desenterrar.
disinterested [dis'intərəstid], *a.* desprendido, imparcial.
disjoint [dis'dʒɔint], *v.t.* descoyuntar, desarticular.
disjointed [dis'dʒɔintid], *a.* (*fig.*) inconexo.
disk [disk], *n.* disco.
dislike [dis'laik], *n.* antipatía, aversión, *f.*—*v.t.* tener aversión a, desaprobar; ***I — cheese***, no me gusta el queso.
dislocate ['dislokeit], *v.t.* dislocar.
dislodge [dis'lɔdʒ], *v.t.* desalojar.

disloyal [dis'lɔiəl], *a.* desleal.
disloyalty [dis'lɔiəlti], *n.* deslealtad, *f.*
dismal ['dizməl], *a.* lúgubre, aciago, funesto.
dismantle [dis'mæntl], *v.t.* desmontar.
dismay [dis'mei], *n.* consternación, *f.*, espanto.—*v.t.* consternar.
dismiss [dis'mis], *v.t.* despedir; licenciar; descartar.
dismissal [dis'misəl], *n.* despedida, despido; destitución, *f.*; licencia(miento).
dismount [dis'maunt], *v.t.*, *v.i.* desmontar.—*v.i.* apearse.
disobedience[diso'bi:djəns], *n.* desobediencia.
disobedient [diso'bi:djənt], *a.* desobediente, inobediente.
disobey [diso'bei], *v.t.*, *v.i.* desobedecer.
disorder [dis'ɔ:də], *n.* desorden, *m.*—*v.t.* desordenar.
disorderly [dis'ɔ:dəli], *a.* desordenado; escandaloso.
disorganize [dis'ɔ:gənaiz], *v.t.* desorganizar.
disown [dis'oun], *v.t.* repudiar.
disparage [dis'pæridʒ], *v.t.* deslustrar, menospreciar.
disparaging [dis'pæridʒiŋ], *a.* menospreciativo.
disparity [dis'pæriti], *n.* desigualdad, *f.*
dispassionate [dis'pæʃənit], *a.* desapasionado.
dispatch [dis'pætʃ], *n.* despacho.—*v.t.* despachar; expedir.
dispel [dis'pel], *v.t.* dispersar.
dispensary [dis'pensəri], *n.* dispensario.
dispersal [dis'pə:səl], *n.* dispersión, *f.*
disperse [dis'pə:s], *v.t.* dispersar.—*v.i.* -se.
dispersion [dis'pə:ʃən], *n.* dispersión, *f.*
dispirit [di'spirit], *v.t.* desanimar.
displace [dis'pleis], *v.t.* desplazar; dislocar; remover.
display [dis'plei], *n.* exhibición, presentación, *f.*; espectáculo.—*v.t.* exhibir; ostentar.
displease [dis'pli:z], *v.t.* desagradar, disgustar.
displeasure [dis'pleʒə], *n.* desplacer, disgusto.
disposal [dis'pouzəl], *n.* disposición; venta; distribución; destrucción, *f.*; ***to have at one's* —,** disponer de.
dispose [dis'pouz], *v.t.* disponer; inducir; arreglar; decidir.—*v.i.* disponer (**of,** de); deshacerse (**of,** de); arreglar, terminar (**of**).
disposition [dispə'ziʃən], *n.* disposición, *f.*; natural, *m.*, índole, *f.*
dispossess [dispə'zes], *v.t.* desposeer, desposesionar.
disproof [dis'pru:f], *n.* refutación, *f.*
disproportionate [disprə'pɔ:ʃənit], *a.* desproporcionado.
disprove [dis'pru:v], *v.t.* refutar, confutar.
dispute [dis'pju:t], *n.* disputa.—*v.t.*, *v.i.* disputar.
disqualify [dis'kwɔlifai], *v.t.* inhabilitar; desclasificar; descalificar.
disquiet [dis'kwaiət], *n.* inquietud, *f.*—*v.t.* inquietar.
disregard [disri'gɑ:d], *n.* desatención, *f.*; desprecio.—*v.t.* desatender; desairar; no hacer caso de, pasar por alto.
disrepair [disri'pɛə], *n.* mal estado, estropeo.
disreputable [dis'repjutəbl], *a.* desdoroso, desacreditado.
disrepute [disri'pju:t], *n.* mala fama, descrédito; ***to bring into* —,** desacreditar.
disrespect [disri'spekt], *n.* desacato.—*v.t.* desacatar.
disrupt [dis'rʌpt], *v.t.* trastornar, desbaratar.
dissatisfaction [disætis'fækʃən], *n.* descontento.
dissatisfied [di'sætisfaid], *a.* malcontento, descontento.
dissatisfy [di'sætisfai], *v.t.* descontentar.
dissect [di'sekt], *v.t.* disecar.
dissection [di'sekʃən], *n.* disección, *f.*
dissemble [di'sembl], *v.t.* disimular, fingir.
disseminate [di'semineit], *v.t.* difundir, propalar.
dissension [di'senʃən], *n.* disensión, *f.*, discordia.
dissent [di'sent], *n.* disidencia; disensión, *f.*—*v.i.* disentir, disidir.
dissenter [di'sentə], *n.* disidente, *m.f.*
disservice [di'sə:vis], *n.* deservicio.
dissident ['disidənt], *a.*, *n.* disidente, *m.f.*
dissimilar [di'similə], *a.* desemejante, desigual.
dissimulate [di'simjuleit], *v.t.* disimular.
dissipate ['disipeit], *v.t.* disipar.
dissociate [di'souʃieit], *v.t.* disociar.
dissolute ['disəlu:t], *a.* disoluto.
dissolution [disə'lu:ʃən], *n.* disolución, *f.*
dissolve [di'zɔlv], *v.t.*, *v.i.* disolver.
dissuade [di'sweid], *v.t.* disuadir.
distaff ['distɑ:f], *n.* rueca; (*fig.*) las mujeres.
distance ['distəns], *n.* distancia; ***in the* —,** a lo lejos.
distant ['distənt], *a.* distante, lejano; frío, esquivo.
distaste [dis'teist], *n.* aversión, *f.*, disgusto.
distasteful [dis'teistful], *a.* desabrido, disgustoso.
distemper [dis'tempə], *n.* temple (*pintura*), *m.*; (*vet.*) moquillo; enfermedad, *f.*—*v.t.* destemplar; pintar al temple.
distend [dis'tend], *v.t.* hinchar.—*v.i.* -se.
distil [dis'til], *v.t.* destilar.
distillation [disti'leiʃən], *n.* destilación, *f.*
distillery [dis'tiləri], *n.* destilería, destilatorio.
distinct [dis'tiŋkt], *a.* distinto; claro, cierto.
distinction [dis'tiŋkʃən], *n.* distinción, *f.*; (*educ.*) sobresaliente, *m.*
distinctive [dis'tiŋktiv], *a.* distintivo.
distinguish [dis'tiŋgwiʃ], *v.t.* distinguir.
distort [dis'tɔ:t], *v.t.* torcer.
distortion [dis'tɔ:ʃən], *n.* torcimiento.
distract [dis'trækt], *v.t.* distraer; enloquecer.
distraction [dis'trækʃən], *n.* distracción, *f.*; locura; frenesí, *m.*
distraught [dis'trɔ:t], *a.* aturdido, atolondrado.
distress [dis'tres], *n.* pena, angustia; apuro, aprieto.—*v.t.* angustiar, penar; apurar.
distressing [dis'tresiŋ], *a.* penoso, congojoso.
distribute [dis'tribju:t], *v.t.* distribuir, repartir.
distribution [distri'bju:ʃən], *n.* distribución, *f.*
district ['distrikt], *n.* región, *f.*, comarca; (*pol.*) distrito.
distrust [dis'trʌst], *n.* desconfianza.—*v.t.* desconfiar de.
disturb [dis'tə:b], *v.t.* perturbar; molestar; desordenar.
disturbance [dis'tə:bəns], *n.* disturbio; desorden, *m.*; molestia.

disuse [dis'ju:s], *n.* desuso.—[dis'ju:z], *v.t.* desusar.
ditch [ditʃ], *n.* zanja; foso.—*v.t.* zanjar; (*fam.*) echar.—*v.i.* (*aer.*) caer en el mar.
dither ['diðə], *n.* tambaleo.—*v.i.* tambalear.
ditto ['ditou], *a., n., adv.* ítem.
ditty ['diti], *n.* cantilena, cancioncilla.
diurnal [dai'ə:nl], *a.* diurno.
divan [di'væn, 'daivæn], *n.* diván, *m.*
dive [daiv], *n.* zambullida, buceo; (*fam., U.S.*) timba; guarida.—*v.i. irr.* tirarse, zambullirse; (*nav.*) bucear; (*aer.*) picar; meterse a prisa.
dive-bomb ['daivbəm], *v.i.* (*aer.*) bombardear en picado.
diver ['daivə], *n.* zambullidor, *m.*; (*nav.*) buzo; (*orn.*) somorgujo.
diverge [dai'və:dʒ], *v.i.* divergir.
divergence [dai'və:dʒəns], **divergency** [dai'və:dʒənsi], *n.* divergencia.
divergent [dai'və:dʒənt], *a.* divergente.
divers ['daivəz], *a.pl.* diversos, varios.
diverse [dai'və:s], *a.* diverso, diferente.
diversion [dai'və:ʃən], *n.* diversión, *f.*, desvío.
diversity [dai'və:siti], *n.* diversidad, *f.*
divert [dai'və:t], *v.t.* desviar, apartar; divertir.
diverting [dai'və:tiŋ], *a.* divertido.
divest [dai'vest], *v.t.* despojar, desposeer.
divide [di'vaid], *v.t.* dividir.—*v.i.* -se.
dividend ['dividend], *n.* dividendo.
divine [di'vain], *a.* divino.—*n.* clérigo, predicador, *m.*—*v.t., v.i.* adivinar, pronosticar.
diving ['daiviŋ], *n.* buceo; **— *suit,*** escafandra.
divinity [di'viniti], *n.* divinidad, *f.*; (*educ.*) teología.
division [di'viʒən], *n.* división, *f.*
divorce [di'vɔ:s], *n.* divorcio.—*v.t.* divorciarse de; divorciar (*dar un divorcio*).—*v.i.* divorciarse.
divulge [di'vʌldʒ], *v.t.* revelar, publicar, divulgar.
dizzy ['dizi], *a.* vertiginoso; ligero, desvanecido; perplejo.
do [du:], *n.*(*fam.*) función, *f.*—*v.t. irr.* hacer; bastar a; (*fam.*) estafar; (*fam.*) matar; (*fam.*) recorrer.—*v.i. irr.* servir, bastar; obrar; hacer; salir; hallarse; ***to — away with,*** destruir, acabar con; ***to — up,*** liar; abrochar; ***to — without,*** pasarse sin; ***to be done for,*** (*fam.*) estar hecho polvo; estar arruinado; ***to have to — with,*** tener que ver con; ***I could — with,*** me iría bien. . . .
docile ['dousail], *a.* dócil, manso, sumiso.
dock (1) [dɔk], *n.* (*naut.*) dique, *m.*; dársena; muelle, *m.*; (*jur.*) banquillo.—*v.t.* (*naut.*) poner en dique.—*v.i.* atracar en el muelle.
dock (2) [dɔk], *n.* (*bot.*) bardana.
dock (3) [dɔk], *v.t.* cercenar.
docker ['dɔkə], *n.* estibador, *m.*
docket ['dɔkit], *n.* tótulo; minuta.
dockyard ['dɔkjɑ:d], *n.* astillero; arsenal, *m.*
doctor ['dɔktə], *n.* doctor, *m.*; (*med.*) médico. —*v.t.* (*fam.*) componer; adulterar.
doctrine ['dɔktrin], *n.* doctrina.
document ['dɔkjumənt], *n.* documento.— ['dɔkjument], *v.t.* documentar.
documentary [dɔkju'mentəri], *a.* documental.
dodder ['dɔdə], *v.i.* chochear.
doddering ['dɔdəriŋ], *a.* chocho.
dodge [dɔdʒ], *n.* regate, *m.*; (*fam.*) esquinazo. —*v.t.* esquivar, evadir.—*v.i.* trampear; meterse.
dodo ['doudou], *n.* (*orn.*) dodo.
doe [dou], *n.* gama, cierva; (*zool.*) hembra.
does [dʌz], [DO].
doff [dɔf], *v.t.* quitar (*el sombrero*).
dog [dɔg], *n.* perro; (*zool.*) macho; ***— Latin,*** latinajo; ***to go to the dogs*** (*fig.*), arruinarse. —*v.t.* perseguir.
dog-ear ['dɔgiə], *n.* orejón (*de una página*), *m.*
dog-fight ['dɔgfait], *n.* refriega.
dogged ['dɔgid], *a.* terco, tozudo, obstinado.
doggerel ['dɔgərəl], *n.* coplas (*f.pl.*) de ciego.
dogma ['dɔgmə], *n.* dogma, *m.*
dogmatic [dɔg'mætik], *a.* dogmático.
dog-tired ['dɔgtaiəd], *a.* (*fam.*) rendido, hecho polvo.
doings ['du:iŋz], *n.pl.* hechos, actividad, *f.*; (*fam.*) cachivache, *m.*
doldrums ['dɔldrəmz], *n.pl.* calma chicha ecuatorial; (*fig.*) murria, desánimo.
dole [doul], *n.* soccorro para los parados; cesantía, paro; limosna; (*lit.*) angustia.—*v.t.* repartir (***out***).
doll [dɔl], *n.* muñeca.—*v.r.* ***to — oneself up*** (*fam.*) empapirotarse.
dollar ['dɔlə], *n.* dólar, *m.*
dolphin ['dɔlfin], *n.* delfín, *m.*
dolt [doult], *n.* zamacuco, zoquete, *m.*
domain [do'mein], *n.* dominio; heredad, *f.*
dome [doum], *n.* cúpola; cimborrio.
Domesday ['du:mzdei], *n.* día (*m.*) del Juicio final.
domestic [də'mestik], *a., n.* doméstico.
domesticate [də'mestikeit], *v.t.* domesticar.
domicile ['dɔmisail], *n.* domicilio.—*v.t.* domiciliar.
dominant ['dɔminənt], *a.* dominante.
dominate ['dɔmineit], *v.t.* dominar.
domination [dɔmi'neiʃən], *n.* dominación, *f.*, dominio.
domineer [dɔmi'niə], *v.t., v.i.* mandonear, dominar mucho.
Dominican [də'minikən], *a., n.* (*geog.*) dominicano; (*eccl.*) dominicano, dominico.
dominion [də'minjən], *n.* dominio.
domino ['dɔminou], *n.* dominó; ficha de dominó.—*n.pl.* dominó.
don [dɔn], *n.* (*educ.*) socio (de colegio); académico, universitario.
donate [dou'neit], *v.t.* donar, contribuir.
donation [dou'neiʃən], *n.* donación, *f.*, donativo.
done [dʌn], *a.* acabado; asado, cocido; (*fam.*) rendido; ***— for,*** (*fam.*) rendido; muerto; arruinado, [DO].
donkey ['dɔŋki], *n.* burro, asno.
donor ['dounə], *n.* donante, donador, *m.*
don't [dount], [DO NOT].
doodle [du:dl], *v.i.* borronear.
doom [du:m], *n.* sino, hado; perdición, *f.*; juicio.—*v.t.* condenar.
doomsday [DOMESDAY].
door [dɔ:], *n.* puerta; portal, *m.*; portezuela (*de vehículo*).
door-keeper ['dɔ:ki:pə], *n.* portero.
door-knocker ['dɔ:nɔkə], *n.* aldaba.
door-man ['dɔ:mən], *n.* portero.
door-mat ['dɔ:mæt], *n.* esterilla.
doorstep ['dɔ:step], *n.* escalón (*de puerta*), *m.*

doorway ['dɔ:wei], *n.* portal, *m.*
dope [doup], *n.* narcótico(s); (*U.S. fam.*) datos, *m.pl.*; (*fam.*) bobo.—*v.t.* narcotizar.
dormant ['dɔ:mənt], *a.* latente; durmiente.
dormitory ['dɔ:mitri], *n.* dormitorio.
dormouse ['dɔ:maus], *n.* (*pl.* **-mice**) lirón, *m.*
dose [dous], *n.* dósis, *f.*—*v.t.* dosificar; medicinar.
dot [dɔt], *n.* punto, puntito.—*v.t.* puntear, motear.
dotage ['doutidʒ], *n.* chochez, *f.*
dotard ['doutəd], *n.* chocho.
dote [dout], *v.i.* chochear; ***to — on,*** idolatrar.
dotty ['dɔti], *a.* (*fam.*) chiflado, gilí.
double [dʌbl], *a., n.* doble, *m.*; ***— bed,*** cama de matrimonio.—*v.t.* doblar.—*v.i.* doblarse.
double-chin [dʌbl'tʃin], *n.* papada.
double-cross [dʌbl'krɔs], *n.* (*fam.*) traición, *f.*—*v.t.* engañar (*a un cómplice*).
double-dealing [dʌbl'di:liŋ], *n.* doblez, *m.*, trato doble.
double-decker [dʌbl'dekə], *n.* autobús (*de dos pisos*), *m.*
double-edged [dʌbl'edʒd], *a.* de dos filos.
double-faced [dʌbl'feist], *a.* doble, falaz.
doubt [daut], *n.* duda; ***no —,*** sin duda.—*v.t., v.i.* dudar.
doubtful ['dautful], *a.* dudoso.
doubtless ['dautlis], *a.* indudable.—*adv.* sin duda.
dough [dou], *n.* masa; pasta; (*fam., U.S.*) parné, *m.*
doughty ['dauti], *a.* valeroso.
dour [duə], *a.* melancólico; (*Scot.*) austero.
douse [daus], *v.t.* zambullir; apagar.
dove [dʌv], *n.* paloma.
dovecote ['dʌvkɔt], *n.* palomar, *m.*
dovetail ['dʌvteil], *n.* (*carp.*) cola de milano. —*v.t.* machihembrar a cola de milano.—*v.i.* cuadrar perfectamente.
dowager ['dauədʒə], *n.* matrona; viuda (*de un hidalgo*).
dowdy ['daudi], *a.* basto, sucio, zafio.
down (1) [daun], *n.* (*geog.*) collado.
down (2) [daun], *n.* (*orn.*) plumón, flojel, *m.*; vello.
down (3) [daun], *n.* (*fam.*) caída, revés, *m.*—*v.t.* (*fam.*) derribar; tragar.—*adv.* abajo.—*prep.* abajo (*follows noun*); ***— and out,*** tronado, que se ha tronado; ***— with . . .!*** ¡abajo. . . .! ***to get — to,*** aplicarse a; llegar a; ***to take —,*** poner por escrito.
downcast ['daunkɑ:st], *a.* abatido.
downfall ['daunfɔ:l], *n.* caída, ruina.
down-hearted [daun'hɑ:tid], *a.* desalentado.
downhill [daun'hil], *adv.* cuesta abajo.
downpour ['daunpɔ:], *n.* aguacero, chaparrón, *m.*
downright ['daunrait], *a.* categórico, total, absoluto; de siete suelas (*pícaro*).—*adv.* del todo, totalmente.
downstairs ['daunstɛəz], *a.* de abajo.—*n.* planta baja.—[daun'stɛəz], *adv.* abajo.
downstream [daun'stri:m], *adv.* río abajo.
downtown ['dauntaun], *a.* (*U.S.*) céntrico.—[daun'taun], *adv.* al *o* en el centro (*de la ciudad*).
downtrodden ['dauntrɔdn], *a.* oprimido, tiranizado.
downward ['daunwəd], *a.* descendente.—*adv.* (*also* **-rds** [-dz]) hacia abajo; en adelante.
dowry ['dauri], *n.* dote, *m.* o *f.*
doze [douz], *n.* dormidita.—*v.i.* dormitar.
dozen [dʌzn], *n.* docena.
dozy ['douzi], *a.* amodorrado; lelo.
drab (1) [dræb], *a.* parduzco, gris.
drab (2) [dræb], *n.* zorra, mujerzuela.
draft [drɑ:ft], *n.* (*com.*) libranza, giro; bosquejo, borrador, plan, *m.*; (*mil., U.S.*) quinta.—*v.t.* bosquejar; redactar; (*mil.*) destacar, (*U.S.*) quintar; (*U.S.*) [DRAUGHT].
draftee [drɑ:f'ti:], *n.* (*U.S.*) quinto.
drag [dræg], *n.* narria (*carretilla*); resistencia; impedimento, traba; rastra.—*v.t.* arrastrar; rastrear.—*v.i.* arrastrarse; ***to — out,*** hacer(se) muy largo.
drag-net ['drægnet], *n.* red barredera.
dragon ['drægən], *n.* dragón, *m.*
dragon-fly ['drægənflai], *n.* libélula.
dragoon [drə'gu:n], *n.* (*mil.*) dragón, *m.*—*v.t.* regimentar.
drain [drein], *n.* desaguadero; desagüe, *m.*—*v.t.* desaguar; desangrar; vaciar.
drake [dreik], *n.* pato.
dram [dræm], *n.* dracma; (*Scot.*) copita, traguito.
drama ['drɑ:mə], *n.* drama, *m.*
dramatic [drə'mætik], *a.* dramático.
dramatist ['dræmətist], *n.* dramaturgo.
drank [dræŋk], [DRINK].
drape [dreip], *n.* colgadura.—*v.t.* entapizar; colgar; vestir.
draper ['dreipə], *n.* pañero, lencero.
drapery ['dreipəri], *n.* paños, *m.pl.*, ropaje, *m.*; (*Brit.*) lencería.
drastic ['dræstik], *n.* drástico, violento.
draught [drɑ:ft], *n.* corriente (*f.*) de aire, trago, pócima; tiro; ***— beer,*** cerveza del barril. — *pl.* juego de damas. [DRAFT].
draughtsman ['drɑ:ftsmən], *n.* dibujante, *m.*
draughty ['drɑ:fti], *a.* airoso, lleno de corrientes.
draw [drɔ:], *n.* (*sport*) empate, *m.*; tiro; sorteo; (*fam.*) exitazo.—*v.t. irr.* dibujar; tirar (*arrastrar*); correr, descorrer (*cortina*); atraer; desenvainar (*espada*); cobrar (*dinero*); sacar; ***to — forth,*** hacer salir, ocasionar; ***to — up,*** redactar; acercar; pararse.—*v.i. irr.* empatar.
drawback ['drɔ:bæk], *n.* inconveniente, *m.*, pega.
drawbridge ['drɔ:bridʒ], *n.* puente levadizo.
drawer [drɔ:], *n.* cajón, *m.*, gaveta.—*pl.* (*vestido*) bragas.
drawing-pin ['drɔ:iŋpin], *n.* chinche, *m.*
drawing-room ['drɔ:iŋrum], *n.* salón, *m.*, sala.
drawl [drɔ:l], *n.* habla lenta.—*v.t., v.i.* hablar muy despacio.
drawn [drɔ:n], [DRAW].
dray-horse ['dreihɔ:s], *n.* caballo de tiro.
dread [dred], *a.* pavoroso.—*n.* pavor, *m.*—*v.t.* temer.
dreadful ['dredful], *a.* espantoso; (*fam.*) malo.
dreadnought ['drednɔ:t], *n.* (*naut.*) gran buque acorazado.
dream [dri:m], *n.* sueño, ensueño.—*v.i. irr.* soñar (***of,*** con).
dreamy ['dri:mi], *a.* soñador; vago.
dreary ['driəri], *a.* pesado, aburrido.
dredge [dredʒ], *n.* draga.—*v.t.* dragar.
dregs [dregz], *n.pl.* heces, *f.pl.*
drench [drentʃ], *v.t.* empapar, calar.

dress [dres], *n.* vestido; traje, *m.*, ropa.—*v.t.* vestir; peinar (*pelo*); (*cul.*) aderezar; curtir (*cuero*); preparar, adobar; (*med.*) curar.—*v.i.* vestir(se); ***to — down,*** (*fam.*) calentar las orejas a; ***to — up,*** vestirse de gala.
dresser ['dresə], *n.* aparador, *m.*; (*U.S.*) cómoda.
dressing ['dresiŋ], *n.* (*cul.*) aliño, salsa; (*med.*) vendaje, *m.*
dressing-gown ['dresiŋgaun], *n.* bata, peinador, *m.*
dressing-table ['dresiŋteibl], *n.* coqueta.
dressmaker ['dresmeikə], *n.* costurera, modista, *f.*
dressy ['dresi], *a.* (*fam.*) vistoso, acicalado.
drew [dru:] [DRAW].
dribble [dribl], *n.* gotita, goteo.—*v.t.* (*sport*) driblar.—*v.i.* gotear, babear.
dried [draid], *a.* paso (*fruta*). [DRY].
drift [drift], *n.* corriente, *f.*; tendencia; sentido, tenor, *m*; deriva; ventisquero.—*v.t.* amontonar; llevar.—*v.i.* ir a la deriva, derivar; flotar; dejarse llevar; amontonarse.
drill [dril], *n.* taladro; (*mil.*) instrucción, *f.*; (*agr.*) surquito para sembrar; rutina; ejercicio.—*v.t.* disciplinar, entrenar; taladrar, barrenar.—*v.i.* hacer ejercicios.
drink [driŋk], *n.* bebida.—*v.t.*, *v.i. irr.* beber; ***to — in*** *o* ***up,*** beberse.
drinking ['driŋkiŋ], *a.* potable (*agua*); para beber.—*n.* beber, *m.*; ***— trough,*** abrevadero.
drip [drip], *n.* gotera.—*v.t.* verter gota a gota. —*v.i.* gotear.
dripping ['dripiŋ], *n.* pringue, *m.* o *f.*; grasa.
drive [draiv], *n.* calzada, avenida; paseo; energía; conducción; impulsión, *f.*—*v.t. irr.* conducir (*coche*); empujar, forzar; clavar; mover; arrojar; ***to — at,*** querer decir; ***to — away*** o ***off,*** ahuyentar; irse (en coche); ***to — back,*** rechazar; ***to — mad,*** volver loco.—*v.i. irr.* ir en coche.
drivel [drivl], *n.* baba; cháchara.—*v.i.* babear.
driven [drivn] [DRIVE].
driver ['draivə], *n.* conductor, *m.*
drizzle [drizl], *n.* llovizna.—*v.i.* lloviznar.
droll [droul], *a.* chancero, chusco.
dromedary ['drʌmədəri], *n.* dromedario.
drone (1) [droun], *n.* (*ent.*, *fig.*) zángano.—*v.i.* zumbar.
drone (2) [droun], *n.* zumbido (*ruido*).
drool [dru:l], *n.* baba.—*v.i.* babear.
droop [dru:p], *n.* caída, inclinación, *f.*—*v.t.* inclinar, bajar.—*v.i.* ir cayéndose; marchitarse; decaer.
drop [drɔp], *n.* caída; baja; pendiente, *f.*; gota.—*v.t.* dejar caer; abandonar; bajar; omitir; soltar.—*v.i.* caer(se); dejarse caer; cesar; ***to — a line,*** (*fam.*) poner una carta; ***to — in,*** visitar de paso; ***to — off,*** decaer; dormirse; ***to — out,*** desaparecer; darse de baja; retirarse.
dropsy ['drɔpsi], *n.* hidropesía.
dross [drɔs], *n.* escoria.
drought [draut], *n.* sequía.
drove [drouv], *n.* manada. [DRIVE].
drown [draun], *v.t.* ahogar, anegar.—*v.i.* -se.
drowse [drauz], *v.i.* adormitarse.
drowsy ['drauzi], *a.* adormecido, amodorrado.
drub [drʌb], *v.t.* tundir, derrotar.
drudge [drʌdʒ], *n.* yunque, *m.*, burro de carga.—*v.i.* afanarse.
drudgery ['drʌdʒəri], *n.* afán, *m.*, trabajo penoso.
drug [drʌg], *n.* droga; narcótico; artículo invendible; ***— addict,*** morfinómano; ***— store,*** (*U.S.*) farmacia.—*v.t.* narcotizar.
druggist ['drʌgist], *n.* (*U.S.*) farmacéutico; droguista, *m.*
drum [drʌm], *n.* tambor, *m.*; (*anat.*) tímpano; bidón, *m.*—*v.i.* tocar el tambor; teclear, tabalear.
drummer ['drʌmə], *n.* tambor; (*U.S.*) viajante, *m.*
drumstick ['drʌmstik], *n.* baqueta, palillo; (*orn.*) muslo.
drunk [drʌŋk], *a.* borracho; ***to get —,*** emborracharse. [DRINK].
drunkard ['drʌŋkəd], *n.* beodo, borrachín, *m.*
drunken ['drʌŋkən], *a.* embriagado, ebrio.
drunkenness ['drʌŋkənnis], *n.* embriaguez, *f.*, borrachera.
dry [drai], *a.* seco; árido; ***— goods,*** (*U.S.*) lencería.—*v.t.* secar.—*v.i.* secarse; ***to — up,*** (*fam.*) callarse.
dry-clean [drai'kli:n], *v.t.* limpiar en seco.
dry-cleaner [drai'kli:nə], *n.* tintorero.
dry-dock [drai'dɔk], *n.* dique seco.
dryness ['drainis], *n.* sequedad, *f.*
dry-rot ['drai'rɔt], *n.* pudrición seca, carcoma.
dual [dju:əl], *a.* dual, binario.
dub [dʌb], *v.t.* apellidar; doblar (*película*); armar caballero.
dubious ['dju:bjəs], *a.* dudoso; equívoco.
ducat ['dʌkit], *n.* ducado.
duchess ['dʌtʃis], *n.* duquesa.
duck [dʌk], *n.* (*orn.*) pato, pata; agachada; dril, *m.*; zambullida; (*fam.*) querido.—*v.t.* evitar; agachar; chapuzar.—*v.i.* agacharse; chapuzar.
duckling ['dʌkliŋ], *n.* patito, anadeja.
duct [dʌkt], *n.* conducto, tubo.
ductile ['dʌktail], *a.* dúctil; dócil.
dud [dʌd], *n.* cosa falsa *o* que no funciona; —*pl.* (*U.S. colloq.*) ropa.
dude [dju:d], *n.* (*U.S.*) caballerete, *m.*
dudgeon ['dʌdʒən], *n.* ojeriza, indignación, *f.*
due [dju:], *a.* debido; esperado; pagadero; derecho, directo.—*n.* merecido; derecho.—*pl.* abono, cuota, subscripción, *f.*; impuestos, *m.pl.*—*adv.* directamente; ***— to,*** debido a.
duel [dju:əl], *n.* duelo.—*v.i.* batirse en duelo.
duellist ['dju:əlist], *n.* duelista, *m.*
duet [dju:'et], *n.* dúo.
duffel [dʌfl], *n.* moletón, *m.*
duffer ['dʌfə], *n.* zamacuco, zote, *m.*
dug [dʌg], [DIG].
dug-out ['dʌgaut], *n.* trinchera, cueva; canoa.
duke [dju:k], *n.* duque, *m.*
dull [dʌl], *a.* obscuro; apagado; romo, embotado; pesado, aburrido; torpe; soso.—*v.t.* embotar; deslucir; empañar; obscurecer.
dullness ['dʌlnis], *n.* pesadez, *f.*; deslustre, *m.*; obscuridad, *f.*
duly ['dju:li], *adv.* debidamente.
dumb [dʌm], *a.* mudo; (*fam.*) estúpido.
dumbfound [dʌm'faund], *v.t.* pasmar, dejar sin habla.
dumbness ['dʌmnis], *n.* mudez; (*fam.*) estupidez, *f.*
dummy ['dʌmi], *a.* falso, postizo.—*n.* maniquí, *m.*; imitación, *f.*, contrafigura; chupete (*de niño*), *m.*

dump [dʌmp], *n.* basurero (*para basura echada*); (*mil.*) depósito.—*v.t.* descargar, echar; inundar el mercado con (artículos invendibles); ***to be down in the dumps***, (*fam.*) tener murria.
dumpling ['dʌmpliŋ], *n.* (*cul.*) bola de pasta cocida en un guisado.
dumpy ['dʌmpi], *a.* rechoncho, rollizo.
dun (1) [dʌn], *a.*, *n.* bruno, pardo.
dun (2) [dʌn], *v.t.* importunar (*deudores*).
dunce [dʌns], *n.* zopenco.
dunderhead ['dʌndəhed], *n.* (*fam.*) tarugo, bolonio.
dune [dju:n], *n.* duna.
dung [dʌŋ], *n.* estiércol, *m.*; excremento.
dungeon ['dʌndʒən], *n.* mazmorra, calabozo.
duodecimo [dju:ou'desimou], *a.* en dozavo.
dupe [dju:p], *n.* primo, papanatas, *m.sg.*—*v.t.* engatusar, embaucar.
duplicate ['dju:plikit], *a.*, *n.* duplicado; ***in —***, por duplicado.—['dju:plikeit], *v.t.* duplicar.
duplicator ['dju:plikeitə], *n.* multicopista, *m.*
duplicity [dju:'plisiti], *n.* doblez, duplicidad, *f.*
durability [djuərə'biliti], *n.* durabilidad, *f.*
durable ['djuərəbl], *a.* duradero, durable.
duration [djuə'reiʃən], *n.* duración, *f.*
duress [djuə'res], *n.* coacción; prisión, *f.*
during ['djuəriŋ], *prep.* durante.
dusk [dʌsk], *n.* anochecer, *m.*, crepúsculo.
dusky ['dʌski], *a.* obscuro; moreno; negruzco.
dust [dʌst], *n.* polvo; cenizas (*restos mortales*), *f.pl.*; (*fam.*) alboroto.—*v.t.* quitar el polvo a, despolvorear; polvorear (*derramar*).
dustbin ['dʌstbin], *n.* receptáculo para basura, cubo de basura.
duster ['dʌstə], *n.* plumero, paño, trapo.
dust-jacket ['dʌstdʒækit], *n.* (sobre)cubierta (*de un libro*).
dustman ['dʌstmən], *n.* basurero.
dusty ['dʌsti], *a.* polvoriento; grisáceo.
Dutch [dʌtʃ], *a.*, *n.* holandés; ***double —***, algarabia, griego; ***go —***, (*fam.*) pagar cada uno su escote.
Dutchman ['dʌtʃmən], *n.* holandés, *m.*
duteous ['dju:tiəs], *a.* rendido, obediente.
dutiful ['dju:tiful], *a.* concienzudo; rendido, obediente.
duty ['dju:ti], *n.* deber, *m.*; tarea; derechos (*m.pl.*) de aduana; ***on —***, de guardia.
dwarf [dwɔ:f], *a.*, *n.* enano.—*v.t.* achicar; impedir el crecimiento de.
dwell [dwel], *v.i. irr.* morar; ***to — on***, hacer hincapié en.
dwelling ['dweliŋ], *n.* morada, vivienda.
dwindle [dwindl], *v.i.* disminuirse, menguar.
dye [dai], *n.* tinte, *m.*, color.—*v.t.* teñir; ***dyed-in-the-wool***, *a.* (*fig.*) intransigente.
dying ['daiiŋ], *a.* moribundo.
dyke [DIKE].
dynamic [dai'næmik], *a.* dinámico.—*n.pl.* dinamica.
dynamo ['dainəmou], *n.* dínamo, *f.* (*S.A. m.*).
dynasty ['dinəsti], *n.* dinastía.
dysentery ['disəntri], *n.* disentería.

E

E, e [i:], *n.* quinta letra del alfabeto inglés; **E,** (*mus.*) mi.

each [i:tʃ], *a.* cada.—*pron.* cada uno, cada cual; ***— other***, el uno al otro.—*adv.* cada uno; por persona.
eager ['i:gə], *a.* ansioso, deseoso; fogoso.
eagerness ['i:gənis], *n.* ansia; anhelo, ahinco.
eagle [i:gl], *n.* águila.
ear [iə], *n.* (*anat.*) oreja; oído; (*bot.*) espiga.
ear-drum ['iədrʌm], *n.* tímpano.
earl [ə:l], *n.* conde, *m.*
early ['ə:li], *a.* temprano; primitivo; próximo.—*adv.* temprano; al principio (***in***, de); anticipadamente; ***— riser***, madrugador, *m.*; ***to rise —***, madrugar.
earmark ['iəmɑ:k], *n.* marca, señal, *f.*—*v.t.* marcar; destinar.
earn [ə:n], *v.t.* ganar; ganarse; merecer.
earnest ['ə:nist], *a.* serio; celoso; atento; ***in —***, en serio.
earnings ['ə:niŋz], *n.pl.* ingresos, *m.pl.*, ganancias, *f.pl.*; sueldo; jornal, *m.*
earring ['iəriŋ], *n.* pendiente, arete, *m.*
earshot ['iəʃɔt], *n.* ***within —***, al alcance del oído.
earth [ə:θ], *n.* tierra; ***down to —***, práctico.
earthenware ['ə:θənwɛə], *n.* loza de barro.
earthly ['ə:θli], *a.* mundano, terrenal.
earthquake ['ə:θkweik], *n.* terremoto.
earthworm ['ə:θwə:m], *n.* lombriz, *f.*
earthy ['ə:θi], *a.* terroso; basto, grosero; mundano.
earwig ['iəwig], *n.* (*ent.*) tijereta.
ease [i:z], *n.* tranquilidad; holgura; facilidad, *f.*; ***at —***, cómodo, a sus anchas; ***to take one's —***, ponerse a sus anchas.—*v.t.* templar, suavizar, aliviar; mover lentamente.
easel ['i:zəl], *n.* caballete, *m.*
easily ['i:zili], *adv.* fácilmente; con mucho.
east [i:st], *a.* oriental, del este.—*n.* este, oriente, Levante (*de España*), *m.*—*adv.* al este.
Easter ['i:stə], *n.* Pascua florida *o* de Resurrección.
easterly ['i:stəli], *a.* oriental.
eastern ['i:stən], *a.* oriental.
easy ['i:zi], *a.* fácil; holgado; ***easy-going,*** de manga ancha; ***— chair***, poltrona, butaca, sillón, *m.*; ***to take it —***, ir despacio; descansar.
eat [i:t], *v.t.*, *v.i. irr.* comer; ***to — up***, comerse; devorar.
eatable ['i:təbl], *a.* comestible.
eaten [i:tn], [EAT].
eau-de-Cologne ['oudəkə'loun], *n.* (agua de) Colonia.
eaves [i:vz], *n.pl.* alero, tejaroz, *m.*
eavesdrop ['i:vzdrɔp], *v.i.* espiar, escuchar, fisgonear.
ebb [eb], *n.* reflujo, menguante.—*v.i.* bajar.
ebony ['ebəni], *a.* de ébano.—*n.* ébano.
eccentric [ek'sentrik], *a.*, *n.* excéntrico.
eccentricity [eksen'trisiti], *n.* excentricidad, *f.*
ecclesiastic [ikli:zi'æstik], *n.* eclesiástico.—(*also* **ecclesiastical**) *a.* eclesiástico.
echo ['ekou], *n.* eco.—*v.t.* repetir.—*v.i.* resonar.
éclat [ei'klɑ:], *n.* esplendor; renombre, *m.*
eclectic [e'klektik], *a.* ecléctico.
eclipse [i'klips], *n.* eclipse, *m.*—*v.t.* eclipsar.
eclogue ['eklɔg], *n.* égloga.
economic(al) [i:kə'nɔmik(əl)], *a.* económico.

economics [i:kə'nɔmiks], *n.* economía política; ciencias económicas.
economist [i:'kɔnəmist], *n.* economista, *m.f.*
economize [i:'kɔnəmaiz], *v.t.*, *v.i.* economizar.
economy [i:'kɔnəmi], *n.* economía; frugalidad, *f.*
ecstasy ['ekstəsi], *n.* éxtasis, *f.*, delirio, rapto.
ecstatic [ek'stætik], *a.* extático.
Ecuador ['ekwədɔ:], *n.* el Ecuador.
Ecuadorian [ekwə'dɔ:riən], *a.*, *n.* ecuatoriano.
eczema ['ekzimə], *n.* eczema.
eddy ['edi], *n.* remolino.—*v.t.*, *v.i.* remolinar.
edge ['edʒ], *n.* margen, *m.* o *f.*, orilla; borde (*de carretera*), *m.*; filo (*cortante*); canto; lado; ribete, *m.*; ***on* —**, (*fig.*) nervioso, de mal humor.—*v.t.* orlar, ribetear (*recortar*); afilar, aguzar; mover un poco.—*v.i.* meterse de lado.
edgeways ['edʒweiz], *adv.* de lado, de canto.
edging ['edʒiŋ], *n.* ribete, orla.
edible ['edibl], *a.* comestible.
edict ['i:dikt], *n.* edicto, decreto.
edifice ['edifis], *n.* edificio; fábrica.
edify ['edifai], *v.t.* edificar (*moralmente*).
Edinburgh ['edinbərə], *n.* Edimburgo.
edit ['edit], *v.t.* redactar; dirigir.
edition [i'diʃən], *n.* edición, *f.*; tirada (*número de copias*).
editor ['editə], *n.* director (*de periódico*); redactor, *m.*
editorial [edi'tɔ:riəl], *a.* editorial.—*n.* artículo de fondo.
educate ['edjukeit], *v.t.* educar.
education [edju'keiʃən], *n.* instrucción; educación, *f.*; enseñanza; pedagogía.
educational [edju'keiʃənəl], *a.* educacional; instructivo.
eel [i:l], *n.* anguila.
e'en [i:n], *adv.* (*poet.*) [EVEN].
e'er [ɛə], *adv.* (*poet.*) [EVER].
eerie, eery ['iəri], *a.* espectral, miedoso.
effect [i'fekt], *n.* efecto; impresión, *f.*; ***in* —**, efectivamente; vigente; ***to the — that***, en el sentido de que; ***to put into* —**, poner en vigor.—*v.t.* efectuar.
effective [i'fektiv], *a.* eficaz; operativo.
effectual [i'fektjuəl], *a.* eficaz.
effeminate [i'feminit], *a.* afeminado.
effervescent [efə'vesənt], *a.* efervescente.
effete [i'fi:t], *a.* gastado, estéril, decadente.
efficacious [efi'keiʃəs], *a.* eficaz.
efficacy ['efikəsi], *n.* eficacia.
efficiency [i'fiʃənsi], *n.* eficacia, eficiencia.
efficient [i'fiʃənt], *a.* eficaz, eficiente.
effigy ['efidʒi], *n.* efigie, *f.*
effort ['efət], *n.* esfuerzo.
effrontery [i'frʌntəri], *n.* descaro, desfachatez, *f.*
effusive [i'fju:siv], *a.* efusivo, derramado.
egg (I) [eg], *n.* huevo; ***— custard***, flan, *m.*; ***— white***, claro (de huevo).
egg (2) [eg], *v.t.* ***to — on***, hurgar, incitar.
eggshell ['egʃel], *n.* cascarón, *m.*
ego ['i:gou], *n.* yo; ego.
egoist ['egouist], *n.* egoísta, *m.f.*
egress ['i:gres], *n.* salida.
Egypt ['i:dʒipt], *n.* Egipto.
Egyptian [i'dʒipʃən], *a.*, *n.* egipcio.
eiderdown ['aidədaun], *n.* edredón, *m.*
eight [eit], *a.*, *n.* ocho.
eighteen [ei'ti:n], *a.*, *n.* dieciocho, diez y ocho.
eighteenth [ei'ti:nθ], *a.*, *n.* décimoctavo, dieciochavo; dieciocho (*en las fechas*).
eighth [eitθ], *a.* octavo.—*n.* octavo; ocho (*en las fechas*).
eightieth ['eitjəθ], *a.*, *n.* octogésimo, ochentavo.
eighty ['eiti], *a.*, *n.* ochenta, *m.*
either ['aiðə, 'i:ðə], *a.* cualquier(a), uno u otro (*de los dos*).—*adv.* tampoco.—*conj.* o; ***— . . . or***, o . . . o.
ejaculate [i'dʒækjuleit], *v.t.* exclamar; (*anat.*) eyacular.
eject [i'dʒekt], *v.t.* expulsar, arrojar.
ejection [i'dʒekʃən], *n.* expulsión, *f.*
eke [i:k], *v.t.* ***to — out***, economizar, escatimar.
elaborate [i'læbərit], *a.* detallado, complicado.—[i'læboreit], *v.t.* elaborar; ampliar.
elapse [i'læps], *v.i.* transcurrir, pasar.
elastic [i'læstik], *a.*, *n.* elástico.
elasticity [ilæs'tisiti], *n.* elasticidad, *f.*
elate [i'leit], *v.t.* exaltar.
elation [i'leiʃən], *n.* exaltación, *f.*
elbow ['elbou], *n.* (*anat.*) codo; recodo (*curva*); ***at one's* —**, a la mano.—*v.t.* dar codazos.
elbow-room ['elbouru:m], *n.* anchura, espacio, libertad, *f.*
elder (I) ['eldə], *a.*, *n.* mayor, *m.f.*
elder (2) ['eldə], *n.* (*bot.*) saúco.
elderly ['eldəli], *a.* anciano, mayor.
eldest ['eldist], *a.* el mayor, el más viejo.
elect [i'lekt], *a.* electo, elegido.—*v.t.* elegir.
election [i'lekʃən], *n.* elección, *f.*
electioneer [ilekʃə'niə], *v.i.* hacer propaganda electoral.
electioneering [ilekʃə'niəriŋ], *n.* campaña electoral.
elector [i'lektə], *n.* elector, *m.*; votante, *m.f.*
electoral [i'lektərəl], *a.* electoral.
electric(al) [i'lektrik(əl)], *a.* eléctrico.
electrician [ilek'triʃən], *n.* electricista, *m.*
electricity [ilek'trisiti], *n.* electricidad, *f.*
electrify [i'lektrifai], *v.t.* electrificar; (*fig.*) electrizar.
electrocute [i'lektrəkju:t], *v.t.* electrocutar.
electrocution [ilektrə'kju:ʃən], *n.* electrocución, *f.*
electrode [i'lektroud], *n.* electrodo.
electron [i'lektrɔn], *n.* electrón, *m.*
electronic [ilek'trɔnik], *a.* electrónico.—*n.pl.* electrónica.
elegance ['eligəns], *n.* elegancia.
elegant ['eligənt], *a.* elegante.
elegy ['elidʒi], *n.* elegía.
element ['elimənt], *n.* elemento.
elementary [eli'mentəri], *a.* elemental.
elephant ['elifənt], *n.* elefante, *m.*
elevate ['eliveit], *v.t.* elevar.
elevation [eli'veiʃən], *n.* elevación, *f.*
elevator ['eliveitə], *n.* (*U.S.*) ascensor, *m.*
eleven [i'levən], *a.*, *n.* once, *m.*
eleventh [i'levənθ], *a.*, *n.* undécimo, onceno; once (*en las fechas*); ***at the — hour***, a última hora.
elf [elf], *n.* (*pl.* **elves**) duende, *m.*, elfo.
elfin ['elfin], **elfish** ['elfiʃ], *a.* elfino, travieso.
elicit [i'lisit], *v.t.* (son)sacar.
elide [i'laid], *v.t.* elidir.
eligible ['elidʒibl], *a.* eligible; admisible; deseable.

eligibility [elidʒi'biliti], *n.* elegibilidad, *f.*; competencia.
eliminate [e'limineit], *v.t.* eliminar.
elision [i'liʒən], *n.* elisión, *f.*
élite [ei'li:t], *n.* la flor y (la) nata.
elixir [i'liksə], *n.* elíxir, *m.*
Elizabeth [i'lizəbəθ], *n.* Isabel, *f.*
elliptical [i'liptikəl], *a.* elíptico.
elm [elm], *n.* (*bot.*) olmo.
elocution [elo'kju:ʃən], *n.* elocución, *f.*
elongate ['i:ləŋgeit], *v.t.* alargar, prolongar, extender.—*v.i.* -se.
elope [i'loup], *v.i.* fugarse con el amante.
elopement [i'loupmənt], *n.* fuga.
eloquence ['eləkwəns], *n.* elocuencia.
eloquent ['eləkwənt], *a.* elocuente.
else [els], *a.* más.—*adv.* de otro modo, de otra manera.
elsewhere ['els'wɛə], *adv.* a *o* en otra parte.
elude [i'lu:d], *v.t.* eludir.
elusive [i'lu:siv], *a.* evasivo.
elves [elvz], *pl.* [ELF.]
emaciate [i'meisieit], *v.t.* enflaquecer, extenuar.
emanate ['eməneit], *v.i.* emanar.
emancipate [i'mænsipeit], *v.t.* emancipar.
emancipation [imænsi'peiʃən], *n.* emancipación, *f.*
embalm [em'bɑ:m], *v.t.* embalsamar.
embankment [em'bæŋkmənt], *n.* terraplén, dique, *m.*
embargo [im'bɑ:gou], *n.* embargo.—*v.t.* embargar.
embark [em'bɑ:k], *v.t.* embarcar.—*v.i.* -se.
embarrass [em'bærəs], *v.t.* sofocar, avergonzar; comprometer.
embarrassing [em'bærəsiŋ], *a.* vergonzoso, desconcertante.
embarrassment [em'bærəsmənt], *n.* sofoco; enredo; desconcierto; embarazo.
embassy ['embəsi], *n.* embajada.
embed [im'bed], *v.t.* encajar, empotrar; clavar.
embellish [im'beliʃ], *v.t.* hermosear; adornar.
ember ['embə], *n.* ascua, ceniza.—*pl.* rescoldo.
embezzle [im'bezl], *v.t.* malversar.
embezzlement [im'bezlmənt], *n.* desfalco, malversación, *f.*
embitter [im'bitə], *v.t.* amargar, agriar.
emblem ['embləm], *n.* emblema, *m.*, divisa.
emblematic [emblə'mætik], *a.* emblemático.
embodiment [im'bɔdimənt], *n.* personificación, encarnación, *f.*
embody [im'bɔdi], *v.t.* incorporar; personificar.
embolden [im'bouldən], *v.t.* envalentonar.
emboss [im'bɔs], *v.t.* labrar en relieve.
embrace [im'breis], *n.* abrazo.—*v.t.* abrazar. —*v.i.* -se.
embroider [im'brɔidə], *v.t.* bordar.
embroil [im'brɔil], *v.t.* enredar, embrollar.
embryo ['embriou], *n.* embrión, *m.*
embryonic [embri'ɔnik], *a.* embrionario.
emend [i'mend], *v.t.* enmendar.
emendation [imən'deiʃən], *n.* enmienda.
emerald ['emərəld], *n.* esmeralda.
emerge [i'mə:dʒ], *v.i.* emerger; salir.
emergency ['imə:dʒənsi], *n.* accidente, *m.*; urgencia, crisis, *f.*, emergencia.
emery ['eməri], *n.* esmeril, *m.*; — ***paper***, papel (*m.*) de lija, lija.
emetic [i'metik], *a.*, *n.* emético.
emigrant ['emigrənt], *a.*, *n.* emigrante, *m.f.*
emigrate ['emigreit], *v.i.* emigrar.
emigration [emi'greiʃən], *n.* emigración, *f.*
emigré ['emigrei], *n.* emigrado.
eminence ['eminəns], *n.* eminencia.
eminent ['eminənt], *a.* eminente.
emir [e'miə], *n.* emir, *m.*
emirate ['emireit], *n.* emirato.
emissary ['emisəri], *n.* emisario.
emit [i'mit], *v.t.* emitir, exhalar.
emmet ['emit], *n.* hormiga.
emolument [i'mɔljumənt], *n.* emolumento.
emotion [i'mouʃən] *n.* emoción, *f.*
emotional [i'mouʃənəl], *a.* emocional.
emperor ['empərə], *n.* emperador, *m.*
emphasis ['emfəsis], *n.* énfasis, *f.*
emphasize ['emfəsaiz], *v.t.* dar énfasis a destacar, poner der relieve, acentuar.
emphatic [im'fætik], *a.* enfático.
empire ['empaiə], *n.* imperio.
empirical [im'pirikəl], *a.* empírico.
employ [im'plɔi], *n.* empleo.—*v.t.* emplear.
employee [emplɔi'i:], *n.* empleado.
employer [im'plɔiə], *n.* patrón, jefe, *m.*
employment [im'plɔimənt], *n.* empleo.
emporium [em'pɔ:riəm], *n.* emporio; bazar, *m.*
empower [im'pauə], *v.t.* facultar, autorizar.
empress ['empris], *n.* emperatriz, *f.*
empty ['empti], *a.* vacío; vano.—*v.t.* vaciar. —*v.i.* -se.
empty-handed ['empti'hændid], *a.* manivacío.
empty-headed ['empti'hedid], *a.* casquivano.
emulate ['emjuleit], *v.t.*, *v.i.* emular.
emulation [emju'leiʃən], *n.* emulación, *f.*
emulsion [i'mʌlʃən], *n.* emulsión, *f.*
enable [i'neibl], *v.t.* permitir, facilitar.
enact [i'nækt], *v.t.* promulgar (*ley*); hacer el papel de; realizar.
enactment [i'næktmənt], *n.* promulgación: representactión, *f.*
enamel [i'næməl], *n.* esmalte, *m.*—*v.t.* esmaltar.
enamour [i'næmə], *v.t.* enamorar.
encamp [in'kæmp], *v.t.*, *v.i.* acampar.
enchant [in'tʃɑ:nt], *v.t.* encantar, hechizar.
enchanting [in'tʃɑ:ntiŋ], *a.* encantador.
enchantment [in'tʃɑ:ntmənt], *n.* encant(amient)o, ensalmo.
encircle [in'sə:kl], *v.t.* cercar, encerrar, rodear.
enclose [in'klouz], *v.t.* incluir; encerrar; adjuntar.
enclosed [in'klouzd], *a.*, *n.* adjunto (*en una carta*).
encompass [in'kʌmpəs], *v.t.* abarcar; cercar.
encore ['ɔŋkɔ:], *n.* propina; bis, *m.*—*v.t.* pedir una repetición de; repetir.—*interj.* ¡bis!
encounter [in'kauntə], *n.* encuentro.—*v.t.* encontrar(se con), dar con.—*v.i.* encontrarse.
encourage [en'kʌridʒ], *v.t.* animar; fomentar.
encouragement [en'kʌridʒmənt], *n.* ánimo, estímulo; fomento.
encroach [in'kroutʃ], *v.i.* pasar los límites (***on***, de).
encumber [in'kʌmbə], *v.t.* impedir, embarazar.
encumbrance [in'kʌmbrəns], *n.* estorbo, impedimento, embarazo.

encyclopedia [ensaiklou'pi:djə], *n.* enciclopedia.
end [end], *n.* fin, cabo, final, *m.*; fin, *m.*, mira, objeto; cabo suelto, pieza; colilla (*de pitillo*); ***in the* —,** al fin y al cabo; ***on* —,** de canto; ***to make both ends meet,*** pasar con lo que uno tiene.—*v.t., v.i.* terminar, acabar; ***to* — *up,*** acabar.
endanger [in'deindʒə], *v.t.* poner en peligro, arriesgar.
endear [en'diə], *v.t.* hacer querer.
endearment [en'diəmənt], *n.* palabra cariñosa; caricia.
endeavour [in'devə], *n.* conato, esfuerzo, empeño.—*v.i.* esforzarse (***to,*** por).
ending ['endiŋ], *n.* fin, *m.* o *f.*, terminación, *f.*; (*gram.*) desinencia; desenlace, *m.*
endive ['endiv], *n.* endibia.
endless ['endlis], *a.* sin fin, interminable.
endorse [in'dɔ:s], *v.t.* endosar; aprobar.
endow [in'dau], *v.t.* dotar (***with,*** de).
endowment [in'daumənt], *n.* dotación; prenda, dote, *f.*
endue [in'dju:], *v.t.* dotar; vestir.
endurance [in'djuərəns], *n.* tolerancia; resistencia; sufrimiento; duración, *f.*
endure [in'djuə], *v.t.* aguantar; sufrir, tolerar.—*v.i.* durar, perdurar.
enemy ['enəmi], *a., n.* enemigo.
energetic [enə'dʒetik], *a.* enérgico.
energy ['enədʒi], *n.* energía.
enervate ['enəveit], *v.t.* enervar.
enfeeble [en'fi:bl], *v.t.* debilitar.
enfilade [enfi'leid], *n.* enfilada.—*v.t.* enfilar.
enfold [en'fould], *v.t.* envolver.
enforce [en'fɔ:s], *v.t.* imponer, poner en vigor.
enfranchise [en'fræntʃaiz], *v.t.* franquear; dar el voto a.
engage [en'geidʒ], *v.t.* ocupar; emplear; alquilar; (*mech.*) engranar con; trabar batalla con.—*v.i.* ocuparse (***in,*** en).
engaged [en'geidʒd], *a.* prometido (*novios*); ocupado.
engagement [en'geidʒmənt], *n.* noviazgo; (*mil.*) combate, *m.*; compromiso, cita.
engaging [en'geidʒiŋ], *a.* insinuante, encantador.
engender [en'dʒendə], *v.t.* engendrar.
engine ['endʒin], *n.* máquina; motor, *m.*; (*rail.*) locomotora; ***two-stroke* —,** motor (*m.*) de dos tiempos.
engine-driver ['endʒindraivə], *n.* maquinista, *m.*
engineer [endʒi'niə], *n.* ingeniero; (*U.S. rail.*) maquinista, *m.*—*v.t.* dirigir; maquinar.
engineering [endʒi'niəriŋ], *n.* ingeniería.
enginery ['endʒinri], *n.* maquinaria.
England ['iŋglənd], *n.* Inglaterra.
English ['iŋgliʃ], *a., n.* inglés; ***the English,*** los ingleses.
Englishman ['iŋgliʃmən], *n.* inglés, *m.*
Englishwoman ['iŋgliʃwumən], *n.* inglesa.
engrain [en'grein], *v.t.* teñir.
engrave [en'greiv], *v.t.* grabar.
engraving [en'greiviŋ], *n.* grabado.
engross [en'grous], *v.t.* absorber.
engulf [en'gʌlf], *v.t.* abismar; inundar.
enhance [en'hɑ:ns], *v.t.* realzar; encarecer.
enigma [e'nigmə], *n.* enigma, *m.*
enigmatic(al) [enig'mætik(əl)], *a.* enigmático.
enjoin [en'dʒɔin], *v.t.* mandar, encargar.
enjoy [en'dʒɔi], *v.t.* gozar; gozar de.—*v.r.* divertirse.
enjoyable [en'dʒɔiəbl], *a.* agradable.
enjoyment [en'dʒɔimənt], *n.* goce, *m.*; gusto, placer.
enlarge [en'lɑ:dʒ], *v.t.* agrandar; ensanchar; ampliar, (*also phot.*)—*v.i.* ampliarse, agrandarse, ensancharse; ***to enlarge on,*** tratar más detalladamente.
enlargement [en'lɑ:dʒmənt], *n.* ampliación, *f.*; ensanchamiento.
enlighten [en'laitn], *v.t.* ilustrar, iluminar.
enlightenment [en'laitnmənt], *n.* ilustración, *f.*
enlist [en'list], *v.t.* conseguir, granjear; (*mil.*) alistar; ***enlisted soldier,*** soldado raso.—*v.i.* alistarse.
enliven [en'laivn], *v.t.* avivar, animar.
enmity ['enmiti], *n.* enemistad, *f.*
ennoble [in'noubl], *v.t.* ennoblecer.
ennui [ã:'nwi], *n.* tedio, aburrimiento.
enormity [i'nɔ:miti], *n.* enormidad, *f.*
enormous [i'nɔ:məs], *a.* enorme.
enough [i'nʌf], *a., adv.* bastante; ***to be* —,** bastar.—*interj.* !basta!
enrage [en'reidʒ], *v.t.* enfurecer, encolerizar.
enrapture [en'ræptʃə], *v.t.* arrebatar, embelesar.
enrich [en'ritʃ], *v.t.* enriquecer.
enrol [en'roul], *v.t.* inscribir, alistar.—*v.i.* -se.
enrolment [en'roulmənt], *n.* inscripción, *f.*
ensconce [en'skɔns], *v.t.* acomodar, resguardar.
enshrine [en'ʃrain], *v.t.* guardar como reliquia.
enshroud [en'ʃraud], *v.t.* amortajar; (*fig.*) entenebrar.
ensign ['enzən, 'ensain], *n.* bandera, pabellón, *m.*; (*mil.*) alférez, *m.*
enslave [en'sleiv], *v.t.* esclavizar.
ensnare [en'snɛə], *v.t.* entrampar.
ensue [en'sju:], *v.i.* seguirse, resultar.
ensuing [en'sju:iŋ], *a.* siguiente.
ensure [en'ʃuə], *v.t.* asegurar; asegurarse de, aceriorarse de.
entail [en'teil], *v.t.* ocasionar, suponer; (*jur.*) vincular.
entangle [en'tæŋgl], *v.t.* enmarañar, enredar.
enter ['entə], *v.t.* entrar en; asentar; matricular; inscribir.—*v.i.* entrar; (*theat.*) salir; ***to* — *into,*** participar en; celebrar; ***to* — *on,*** emprender.
enterprise ['entəpraiz], *n.* empresa; iniciativa; arrojo.
enterprising ['entəpraiziŋ], *a.* emprendedor, enérgico.
entertain [entə'tein], *v.t.* divertir; considerar; abrigar; recibir.—*v.i.* recibir (*visitas*); divertir.
entertainer [entə teinə], *n.* artista, *m.f.*, cómico, músico *etc.*
entertaining [entə'teiniŋ], *a.* divertido, entretenido.
entertainment [entə'teinmənt], *n.* diversión, *f.*; espectáculo; entretenimiento.
enthral [en'θrɔ:l], *v.t.* captivar, esclavizar, encantar.
enthrone [en'θroun], *v.t.* entronizar.
enthronement [en'θrounmənt], *n.* entronización, *f.*

enthusiasm [en'θju:ziæzm], *n.* entusiasmo.
enthusiast [en'θju:ziæst], *n.* entusiasta, *m.f.*
enthusiastic [enθju:zi'æstik], *a.* entusiástico.
entice [en'tais], *v.t.* tentar, seducir, incitar.
enticement [en'taismənt], *n.* tentación, seducción, incitación, *f.*
enticing [en'taisiŋ], *a.* tentador.
entire [en'taiə], *a.* entero.
entirety [en'taiəriti], *n.* entereza, totalidad, *f.*
entitle [en'taitl], *v.t.* intitular; dar derecho a, autorizar.
entity ['entiti], *n.* entidad, *f.*
entomb [en'tu:m], *v.t.* sepultar.
entomology [ento'mɔlədʒi], *n.* entomología.
entrails ['entreilz], *n.pl.* entrañas, *f.pl.*
entrain [en'trein], *v.t.* mandar (en tren).—*v.i.* subir al tren.
entrance (1) ['entrəns], *n.* entrada.
entrance (2) [en'trɑ:ns], *v.t.* hechizar, transportar, fascinar.
entreat [en'tri:t], *v.t.* implorar, suplicar.
entrench [en'trentʃ], *v.t.* atrincherar; establecer con firmeza.
entrust [en'trʌst], *v.t.* confiar (***s.o. with s.th.***, algo a alguien).
entry ['entri], *n.* entrada; artículo (*en un libro*); (*theat.*) salida.
entwine [en'twain], *v.t.* entrelazar, entretejer.
enumerate [e'nju:məreit], *v.t.* enumerar.
envelop [en'veləp], *v.t.* envolver.
envelope ['enviloup], *n.* sobre (*para una carta*), *m.*; envoltura.
envious ['enviəs], *a.* envidioso.
environs [en'vaiərənz], *n.pl.* cercanías, *f.pl.*, contornos, *m.pl.*
environment [en'vaiərənmənt], *n.* medio, ambiente, *m.*
envisage [en'vizidʒ], *v.t.* imaginarse; figurarse.
envoy ['envɔi], *n.* enviado.
envy ['envi], *n.* envidia.—*v.t.* envidiar.
enwrap [en'ræp], *v.t.* envolver.
enzyme ['enzaim], *n.* enzima.
epaulet ['epəlet], *n.* charretera.
ephemeral [i'femərəl], *a.* efímero.
epic ['epik], *a.* épico.—*n.* epopeya; épica.
epicure ['epikjuə], *n.* epicúreo.
epidemic [epi'demik], *a.* epidémico.—*n.* epidemia.
epigram ['epigræm], *n.* epigrama, *m.*
epilepsy ['epilepsi], *n.* epilepsia.
epileptic [epi'leptik], *a.* epiléptico.
epilogue ['epilɔg], *n.* epílogo.
Epiphany [i'pifəni], *n.* Epifanía, día (*m.*) de los Reyes (Magos), Reyes (Magos).
episcopal [i'piskəpəl], *a.* episcopal.
episode ['episoud], *n.* episodio.
epistle [i'pisl], *n.* epístola.
epithet ['epiθet], *n.* epíteto.
epitome [i'pitəmi], *n.* epítome, *m.*
epitomize [i'pitəmaiz], *v.t.* epitomar.
epoch ['i:pɔk], *n.* época.
epoch-making ['i:pɔkmeikiŋ], *a.* trascendental.
equable ['ekwəbl], *a.* uniforme; ecuánime.
equal ['i:kwəl], *a.*, *n.* igual.—*v.t.* igualar; igualarse a; ***to be — to***, (*fig.*) poder con.
equality [i:'kwɔliti], *n.* igualdad, *f.*
equate [i'kweit], *v.t.* igualar.
equation [i'kweiʃən], *n.* ecuación, *f.*
equator [i'kweitə], *n.* ecuador, *m.*
equatorial [ekwə'tɔ:riəl], *a.* ecuatorial.
equestrian [i'kwestriən], *a.* ecuestre.—*n.* jinete, *m.*
equilibrium [i:kwi'libriəm], *n.* equilibrio.
equine ['ekwain], *a.* equino, caballar.
equinox ['i:kwinɔks], *n.* equinoccio.
equip [i'kwip], *v.t.* equipar, aparejar.
equipment [i'kwipmənt], *n.* equipo; pertrechos, *m.pl.*; material, *m.*
equitable ['ekwitəbl], *a.* equitativo.
equity ['ekwiti], *n.* equidad, *f.*
equivalence [i'kwivələns], *n.* equivalencia.
equivalent [i'kwivələnt], *a.*, *n.* equivalente, *m.*
equivocal [i'kwivəkəl], *a.* equívoco.
era ['iərə], *n.* era, época.
eradicate [i'rædikeit], *v.t.* extirpar.
erase [i'reiz], *v.t.* borrar, tachar.
Erasmus [i'ræzməs], *n.* Erasmo.
erasure [i'reiʒə], *n.* borradura, raspadura.
ere [ɛə], (*obs.*) [BEFORE].
erect [i'rekt], *a.* vertical, derecho, erguido.—*v.t.* erigir; montar; construir.
erection [i'rekʃən], *n.* erección; construcción, *f.*
ermine ['ə:min], *n.* armiño; (*fig.*) toga.
erode [i'roud], *v.t.* corroer; erosionar.
erosion [i'rouʒən], *n.* erosión, *f.*
erotic [i'rɔtik], *a.* erótico.
err [ə:], *v.i.* errar, marrar.
errand ['erənd], *n.* recado, mandado.
errant ['erənt], *a.* errante, erróneo; andante (*caballero*).
erratic [i'rætik], *a.* excéntrico, irregular.
erratum [e'rɑ:təm], *n.* (*pl.* **-ata**) errata.
erroneous [i'rounjəs], *a.* erróneo.
error ['erə], *n.* error, *m.*; yerro.
ersatz ['ɛərzæts], *a.* substitutivo.
erstwhile ['ə:stwail], *a.* antiguo.
erudite ['erudait], *a.*, *n.* erudito.
erudition [eru'diʃən], *n.* erudición, *f.*
erupt [i'rʌpt], *v.i.* erumpir, hacer erupción.
eruption [i'rʌpʃən], *n.* erupción, *f.*
escalate ['eskəleit], *v.i.* intensificarse.
escalator ['eskəleitə], *n.* escalera móvil.
escapade ['eskəpeid], *n.* escapada; travesura.
escape [is'keip], *n.* escape, *m.*; evasión, *f.*—*v.t.* escaparse a; escapar; evitar.—*v.i.* salvarse; escaparse (***from***, de).
escarpment [is'kɑ:pmənt], *n.* escarpa(dura).
eschew [is'tʃu:], *v.t.* esquivar, evitar.
escort ['eskɔ:t], *n.* escolta; acompañante, *m.*—[is'kɔ:t], *v.t.* escoltar.
escutcheon [is'kʌtʃən], *n.* escudo, blasón, *m.*
Eskimo ['eskimou], *a.*, *n.* esquimal, *m.f.*
esoteric [eso'terik], *a.* esotérico.
esparto [es'pɑ:tou], *n.* esparto.
especially [is'peʃəli], *adv.* especialmente.
espionage ['espiənɑ:ʒ], *n.* espionaje, *m.*
espousal [is'pauzl], *n.* adherencia (***of***, a).
espouse [is'pauz], *v.t.* adherirse a, sostener; (*obs.*) casarse con.
espy [es'pai], *v.t.* divisar, percibir.
esquire [es'kwaiə], *n.* escudero; (*Brit.*) don (*título*).
essay ['esei], *n.* ensayo.—[e'sei], *v.t.* ensayar.
essence ['esəns], *n.* esencia.
essential [e'senʃəl], *a.*, *n.* esencial, *m.*
establish [is'tæbliʃ], *v.t.* establecer.
establishment [is'tæbliʃmənt], *n.* establecimiento; (*fig.*) la oligarquía.
estate [es'teit], *n.* propiedad, *f.*; herencia; heredad, *f.*, finca; estado.

esteem [es'ti:m], *n.* estima.—*v.t.* estimar, apreciar.
estimate ['estimit], *n.* estimación, *f.*, cálculo; presupuesto; tasa.—['estimeit], *v.t.* estimar, calcular.
estimation [esti'meiʃən], *n.* estimación, *f.*
estrange [es'treindʒ], *v.t.* enajenar, enemistar.
estuary ['estjuəri], *n.* estuario, desembocadura.
et cetera [et'setrə] (*abbrev.* **etc.**), *adv.* etcétera.
etch [etʃ], *v.t.* grabar al agua fuerte.
etching ['etʃiŋ], *n.* aguafuerte, *f.*
eternal [i'tə:nəl], *a.* eterno.
eternity [i'tə:niti], *n.* eternidad, *f.*
ether ['i:θə], *n.* éter, *m.*
ethereal [i'θiəriəl], *a.* etéreo.
ethics ['eθiks], *n.pl.* ética.
ethical ['eθikəl], *a.* ético.
Ethiopia [i:θi:'oupjə], *n.* Etiopía.
Ethiopian [i:θi:'oupjən], *a.*, *n.* etiopio.
ethyl ['eθil, 'i:θil], *n.* etilo.
ethnology [eθ'nɔlədʒi], *n.* etnología.
etiquette ['etiket], *n.* etiqueta.
etymology [eti'mɔlədʒi], *n.* etimología.
Eucharist ['ju:kərist], *n.* Eucaristía.
eulogize ['ju:lədʒaiz], *v.t.* encomiar.
eulogy ['ju:lədʒi], *n.* encomio.
eunuch ['ju:nək], *n.* eunuco.
euphemism ['ju:fəmizm], *n.* eufemismo.
Europe ['ju:rəp], *n.* Europa.
European [juərə'pi:ən], *a.*, *n.* europeo.
euthanasia ['ju:θə'neizjə], *n.* eutanasia.
evacuate [i'vækjueit], *v.t.* evacuar.
evacuation [ivækju'eiʃən], *n.* evacuación, *f.*
evacuee [ivækju'i:], *n.* evacuado.
evade [i'veid], *v.t.* evadir, esquivar.
evaluate [i'væljueit], *v.t.* evaluar.
evangelic(al) [i:væn'dʒelik(əl)], *a.*, *n.* evangélico.
evangelist [i'vændʒəlist], *n.* evangelista, *m.f.*
evaporate [i'væpəreit], *v.t.* evaporar.—*v.i.* -se.
evasion [i'veiʒən], *n.* evasión, *f.*, evasiva.
Eve [i:v], *n.* Eva.
eve [i:v], *n.* víspera; ***on the — of,*** en vísperas de; (*poet.*) tardecita.
even ['i:vən], *a.* igual, llano, liso; par (*número*); constante; ***to get — with,*** desquitarse *or* despicarse con.—*adv.* aún, hasta; mismo. —*v.t.* allanar.
evening ['i:vniŋ], *a.* vespertino; de etiqueta (*traje*).—*n.* tarde, *f.*, anochecer, *m.*
evenness ['i:vənnis], *n.* uniformidad; igualdad, *f.*
evensong ['i:vənsɔŋ], *n.* (*eccl.*) vísperas, *f.pl.*
event [i'vent], *n.* suceso; acto; caso; (*sport*) certamen, *m.*; ***at all events,*** en todo caso; ***in the — of,*** en caso de.
eventful [i'ventful], *a.* accidentado; memorable.
eventual [i'ventjuəl], *a.* último, final; acaecedero.
eventually [i'ventjuəli], *adv.* andando el tiempo, finalmente.
ever ['evə], *adv.* siempre; alguna vez; jamás; ***hardly —,*** casi nunca; ***for — and —,*** por siempre jamás; ***— so,*** (*fam.*) sumamente.
evergreen ['evəgri:n], *a.* siempre verde.—*n.* (*bot.*) siempreviva.
everlasting [evə'lɑ:stiŋ], *a.* sempiterno.
evermore [evə'mɔ:], *adv.* eternamente.
every ['evri], *a.* todo, cada; todos los, *m.pl.*
everybody ['evribɔdi], *pron.* todo el mundo, todos, *m.pl.*
everyday ['evridei], *a.* corriente, ordinario, cotidiano.
everyone ['evriwʌn], *pron.* todo el mundo, todos, *m.pl.*
everything ['evriθiŋ], *pron.* todo.
everywhere ['evriwɛə], *adv.* en *o* por todas partes.
evict [i'vict], *v.t.* desposeer, desahuciar.
eviction [i'vikʃən], *n.* desahucio, despojo.
evidence ['evidəns], *n.* evidencia, prueba; deposición; ***in —,*** visible.
evident ['evidənt], *a.* evidente, patente.
evil ['i:vil], *a.* malo.—*n.* mal, *m.*
evil-doer ['i:vildu:ə], *n.* malhechor, *m.*
evil eye ['i:vil'ai], *n.* aojo.
evoke [i'vouk], *v.t.* evocar.
evolution [i:və'lu:ʃən], *n.* evolución, *f.*
evolutionary [i:və'lu:ʃənəri], *a.* evolucionario; evolutivo.
evolve [i'vɔlv], *v.t.* desarrollar.—*v.i.* evolucionar.
ewe [ju:], *n.* oveja.
ewer [ju:ə], *n.* jarro, aguamanil, *m.*
ex- [eks-], *prefix*–ex., antiguo.
exacerbate [eg'zæsə:beit], *v.t.* exacerbar.
exact [eg'zækt], *a.* exacto, preciso.—*v.t.* exigir.
exacting [eg'zæktiŋ], *a.* exigente.
exactly [eg'zæktli], *adv.* exactamente; en punto (*de la hora*).
exactness [eg'zæktnis], *n.* exactitud, corrección, *f.*
exaggerate [eg'zædʒəreit], *v.t.*, *v.i.* exagerar.
exaggeration [egzædʒə'reiʃən], *n.* exageración, *f.*
exalt [eg'zɔ:lt], *v.t.* exaltar.
exam [eg'zæm], *n.* (*fam.*) examen, *m.*
examination [egzæmi'neiʃən], *n.* examen, *m.*; (*med.*) reconocimiento.
examine [eg'zæmin], *v.t.* examinar; reconocer; registrar.
example [eg'zɑ:mpl], *n.* ejemplo.
exasperate [eg'zɑ:spəreit], *v.t.* exasperar.
exasperation [egzɑ:spə'reiʃən], *n.* exasperación, *f.*
excavate ['ekskəveit], *v.t.* excavar.
excavation [ekskə'veiʃən], *n.* excavación, *f.*
exceed [ek'si:d], *v.t.* exceder, sobrepasar.
exceedingly [ek'si:diŋli], *adv.* sumamente.
excel [ek'sel], *v.t.* sobrepujar, avantajar.—*v.i.* sobresalir.
excellence ['eksələns], *n.* excelencia.
excellency ['eksələnsi], *n.* excelencia (*título*).
excellent ['eksələnt], *a.* excelente.
except [ek'sept], *prep.* excepto, a excepción de. —*v.t.* exceptuar.
exception [ek'sepʃən], *n.* excepción, *f.*; ofensa.
exceptionable [ek'sepʃənəbl], *a.* ofensivo, recusable.
exceptional [ek'sepʃənəl], *a.* excepcional.
excerpt ['eksə:pt], *n.* trozo, selección, *f.*, cita.
excess [ek'ses], *n.* exceso, demasía.
excessive [ek'sesiv], *a.* excesivo.
exchange [eks'tʃeindʒ], *n.* cambio, canje, *m.*; (*tel.*) central, *f.*; (*com.*) bolsa.—*v.t.* canjear, cambiar.
exchequer [eks'tʃekə], *n.* fisco, tesorería; (*Brit.*) Hacienda.

excise ['eksaiz], *n.* impuesto sobre consumos. —[ek'saiz], *v.t.* extirpar.
excitable [ek'saitəbl], *a.* excitable.
excite [ek'sait], *v.t.* emocionar; excitar.
excitement [ek'saitmənt], *n.* emoción, agitación; excitación, *f.*
exciting [ek'saitiŋ], *a.* emocionante; excitante.
exclaim [eks'kleim], *v.t., v.i.* exclamar.
exclamation [eksklə'meiʃən], *n.* exclamación, *f.*; — ***mark***, punto de admiración (¡!).
exclude [eks'klu:d], *v.t.* excluir.
exclusion [eks'klu:ʒən], *n.* exclusión, *f.*
exclusive [eks'klu:siv], *a.* exclusivo; — ***of***, sin contar.
excommunicate [ekskə'mju:nikeit], *v.t.* descomulgar.
excommunication [ekskəmju:ni'keiʃən], *n.* excommunión, descomunión, *f.*
excrement ['ekskrimənt], *n.* excremento.
excrete [eks'kri:t], *v.t.* excretar.
excruciating [eks'kru:ʃieitiŋ], *a.* atroz, agudísimo.
excursion [eks'kə:ʃən], *n.* excursión.
excusable [eks'kju:zəbl], *a.* perdonable, excusable.
excuse [eks'kju:s], *n.* disculpa, excusa.—[eks'kju:z], *v.t.* perdonar, excusar, dispensar; — ***me***, dispense, Vd. perdone.
execute ['eksikju:t], *v.t.* ejecutar; ajusticiar.
execution [eksi'kju:ʃən], *n.* ejecución, *f.*
executioner [eksi'kju:ʃənə], *n.* verdugo.
executive [ig'zekjutiv], *a.* ejecutivo.—*n.* administrador, gerente, *m.*; autoridad suprema, gobierno.
exegesis [eksi'dʒi:sis], *n.* exégesis, *f.*
exemplary [ig'zempləri], *a.* ejemplar.
exemplify [ig'zemplifai], *v.t.* ejemplificar.
exempt [ig'zempt], *a.* exento.—*v.t.* eximir, exentar.
exemption [eg'zempʃən], *n.* exención, *f.*, dispensa.
exercise ['eksəsaiz], *n.* ejercicio.—*v.t.* ejercitar; ejercer.
exert [eg'zə:t], *v.t.* desplegar; ejercer.—*v.r.* esforzarse.
exertion [eg'zə:ʃən], *n.* esfuerzo.
exhale [eks'heil], *v.t.* exhalar, emitir.—*v.i.* espirar.
exhaust [eg'zɔ:st], *n.* escape, *m.*—*v.t.* agotar.
exhaustion [eg'zɔ:stʃən], *n.* agotamiento.
exhaustive [eg'zɔ:stiv], *a.* exhaustivo, minucioso.
exhibit [eg'zibit], *n.* artículo exhibido.—*v.t.* exhibir.
exhibition [egzi'biʃən], *n.* exposición, *f.*; (*educ.*) beca.
exhibitor [eg'zibitə], *n.* expositor, *m.*
exhilarate [eg'ziləreit], *v.t.* alegrar, emocionar.
exhilaration [egzilə'reiʃən], *n.* regocijo, excitación, *f.*
exhort [eg'zɔ:t], *v.t.* exhortar.
exile ['egzail], *n.* destierro; desterrado.—*v.t.* desterrar.
exist [eg'zist], *v.i.* existir.
existence [eg'zistəns], *n.* existencia.
exit ['egzit], *n.* salida; (*stage direction*) vase.
ex-officio [eksɔ'fiʃiou], *a., adv.* en virtud de autoridad.
exonerate [eg'zɔnəreit], *v.t.* exonerar; disculpar.
exorbitant [eg'zɔ:bitənt], *a.* excesivo, enorme.
exorcism ['eksɔ:sizəm], *n.* exorcismo.
exotic [eg'zɔtik], *a.* exótico.
expand [eks'pænd], *v.t.* extender; ensanchar. —*v.i.* -se.
expanse [eks'pæns], *n.* extensión, *f.*
expansion [eks'pænʃən], *n.* expansión, *f.*; desarrollo.
expatiate [eks'peiʃieit], *v.i.* espaciarse.
expatriate [eks'pætriət], *a., n.* expatriado.—[eks'pætrieit], *v.t.* expatriar.
expect [eks'pekt], *v.t.* esperar, suponerse, prometerse.
expectancy [eks'pektənsi], *n.* expectación, *f.* expectativa.
expectant [eks'pektənt], *a.* expectante; encinta (*mujer*).
expectation [ekspek'teiʃən], *n.* expectación, *f.*
expedient [eks'pi:diənt], *a.* conveniente; oportuno; ventajoso.—*n.* expediente, *m.*
expedite ['ekspədait], *v.t.* despachar, gestionar, expedir.
expedition [ekspi'diʃən], *n.* expedición, *f.*
expel [eks'pel], *v.t.* expulsar.
expend [eks'pend], *v.t.* invertir, gastar, consumir.
expendable [eks'pendəbl], *a.* gastable.
expenditure [eks'penditʃə], *n.* desembolso, gasto.
expense [eks'pens], *n.* gasto; costa.—*pl.* expensas.
expensive [eks'pensiv], *a.* costoso, caro.
experience [eks'piəriəns], *n.* experiencia.—*v.t.* experimentar.
experiment [eks'perimənt], *n.* experiencia, experimento.
expert ['ekspə:t], *a., n.* perito, experto.
expertise [ekspə:'ti:z], *n.* pericia.
expiate ['ekspieit], *v.t.* expiar.
expire [eks'paiə], *v.i.* caducar; expirar.
expiry [eks'paiəri], *n.* expiración, *f.*; fin (*m.*) de plazo.
explain [eks'plein], *v.t., v.i.* explicar.
explanation [eksplə'neiʃən], *n.* explicación, *f.*
expletive [eks'pli:tiv], *n.* reniego; interjección, *f.*; taco.
explicit [eks'plisit], *a.* explícito.
explode [eks'ploud], *v.t.* volar, hacer saltar; refutar.—*v.i.* estallar.
exploit ['eksplɔit], *n.* hazaña.—[eks'plɔit], *v.t.* explotar.
exploitation [eksplɔi'teiʃən], *n.* explotación, *f.*
exploration [eksplə'reiʃən], *n.* exploración, *f.*
explore [eks'plɔ:], *v.t., v.i.* explorar.
explorer [eks'plɔrə], *n.* explorador, *m.*
explosion [eks'plouʒən], *n.* explosion, *f.*
explosive [eks'plouziv], *a., n.* explosivo.
exponent [eks'pounənt], *n.* expositor; exponente, *m.*; adicto.
export ['ekspɔ:t], *n.* exportación, *f.*—[eks'pɔ:t], *v.t.* exportar.
expose [eks'pouz], *v.t.* exponer; desenmascarar.
expostulate [eks'pɔstjuleit], *v.i.* protestar.
exposure [eks'pouʒə], *n.* exposición, *f.*; desenmascaramiento.
expound [eks'paund], *v.t.* exponer.
express [eks'pres], *a., n.* expreso; (*rail.*) rápido.—*v.t.* expresar.—*adv.* expresamente.
expression [eks'preʃən], *n.* expressión, *f.*
expressive [eks'presiv], *a.* expresivo.

expressly [eks'presli], *adv.* expresamente; adrede.
expulsion [eks'pʌlʃən], *n.* expulsión, *f.*
expunge [eks'pʌndʒ], *v.t.* cancelar, borrar.
expurgate ['ekspə:geit], *v.t.* expurgar.
exquisite [eks'kwizit], *a.* exquisito.
ex-serviceman [eks'se:visman], *n.* excombatiente, *m.*
extant [eks'tænt], *a.* existente.
extempore [eks'tempəri], *a.* improvisado.—*adv.* de improviso.
extemporize [eks'tempəraiz], *v.i.* improvisar.
extend [eks'tend], *v.t.* extender; prolongar; alargar; ofrecer.—*v.i.* extenderse.
extension [eks'tenʃən], *n.* extensión, *f.*; (*com.*) prórroga.
extensive [eks'tensiv], *a.* extensivo, extenso.
extent [eks'tent], *n.* extensión, *f.*; punto, grado; ***to a certain* —,** hasta cierto punto; ***to a great* —,** en su mayor parte.
extenuate [eks'tenjueit], *v.t.* atenuar; extenuar; ***extenuating circumstances,*** circunstancias atenuantes, *f.pl.*
exterior [eks'tiəriə], *a.* exterior, externo.—*n.* exterior, *m.*
exterminate [eks'tə:mineit], *v.t.* exterminar.
external [eks'tə:nl], *a.* externo.
extinct [eks'tiŋkt], *a.* extinto.
extinction [eks'tiŋkʃən], *n.* extinción, *f.*
extinguish [eks'tiŋgwiʃ], *v.t.* extinguir; apagar.
extirpate ['ekstə:peit], *v.t.* extirpar.
extol [eks'toul], *v.t.* ensalzar.
extort [eks'tɔ:t], *v.t.* arrancar, sacar por fuerza.
extortion [eks'tɔ:ʃən], *n.* extorción, *f.*
extra ['ekstrə], *a.* adicional; de repuesto; extra.—*n.* extra, *m.*
extract ['ekstrækt], *n.* extracto.—[eks'trækt] *v.t.* extraer, sacar.
extraction [eks'trækʃən], *n.* extracción, *f.*
extradition [ekstrə'diʃən], *n.* extradición, *f.*
extraneous [eks'treinjəs], *a.* externo, ajeno.
extraordinary [eks'trɔ:dnəri], *a.* extraordinario.
extravagance [eks'trævəgəns], *n.* extravagancia; prodigalidad, *f.*
extravagant [eks'trævəgənt], *a.* extravagante; despilfarrado.
extreme [eks'tri:m], *a.* extremo; extremado.—*n.* extremo, extremidad, *f.*; ***in the* —,** en sumo grado.
extremist [eks'tri:mist], *a., n.* extremista, *m.f.*
extremity [eks'tremiti], *n.* extremidad, *f.*
extricate ['ekstrikeit], *v.t.* desenredar, librar.
extrovert ['ekstrovə:t], *a., n.* extrovertido.
extrude [eks'tru:d], *v.t.* empujar.—*v.i.* resaltar.
exuberance [eg'zju:bərəns], *n.* exuberancia.
exuberant [eg'zju:bərənt], *a.* exuberante.
exude [eg'zju:d], *v.t.* exudar, rezumar.
exult [eg'zʌlt], *v.i.* exultar.
exultation [egzʌl'teiʃən], *n.* exultación, *f.*
eye [ai], *n.* ojo; ***with an* — *to,*** con la idea de; ***in the eyes of,*** a los ojos de.—*v.t.* ojear; ***to catch one's* —,** llamar la atención a; ***to see* — *to* —,** estar de acuerdo; ***to make eyes,*** hacer guiños; ***to shut one's* —*s to,*** hacer la vista gorda a.
eye-ball ['aibɔ:l], *n.* globo del ojo.
eyebrow ['aibrau], *n.* ceja.
eyelash ['ailæʃ], *n.* pestaña.
eye-lid ['ailid], *n.* párpado.
eyesight ['aisait], *n.* vista.
eyesore ['aisɔ:], *n.* mácula, fealdad, *f.*
eyewash ['aiwɔʃ], *n.* (*fam.*) lisonja engañosa.
eye-witness ['aiwitnis], *n.* testigo ocular.
eyrie *or* **eyry** ['aiəri *or* 'ɛəri], *n.* aguilera, nido de ave rapaz.

F

F, f [ef], *n.* sexta letra del alfabeto inglés; ***F,*** (*mus.*) fa.
fable [feibl], *n.* fábula.
fabric ['fæbrik], *n.* tela, tejido; fábrica.
fabricate ['fæbrikeit], *v.t.* fabricar, forjar.
fabrication [fæbri'keiʃən], *n.* fabricación, *f.*; mentira.
fabulous ['fæbjuləs], *a.* fabuloso.
façade [fə'sɑ:d], *n.* fachada.
face [feis], *n.* cara; haz (*de encima*); faz (*del mundo*), *f.*; mueca; (*print.*) caracter, *m.*; ***to save* —,** salvar las apariencias.—*v.t.* encararse con, enfrentar; mirar hacia; estar en frente de; alisar, acabar; ***to* — *the music,*** (*fam.*) aceptar las consecuencias.—*v.i.* carear; ***to* — *about,*** volver la cara; ***to* — *up to,*** arrostrar.
facet ['fæsit], *n.* faceta.
facetious [fə'si:ʃəs], *a.* patoso, chistoso.
facile ['fæsail], *a.* fácil; dócil.
facilitate [fə'siliteit], *v.t.* facilitar.
facility [fə'siliti], *n.* facilidad, *f.*
facing ['feisiŋ], *n.* cubierta; paramento.—*prep.* enfrente de; (de) cara a.
facsimile [fæk'simili], *n.* facsímil(e), *m.*
fact [fækt], *n.* hecho; ***in* —,** en realidad.
faction ['fækʃən], *n.* facción, *f.*; tumulto.
factor ['fæktə], *n.* factor, *m.*
factory ['fæktəri], *n.* fábrica.
factual ['fæktjuəl], *a.* objetivo.
faculty ['fækəlti], *n.* facultad, *f.*
fad [fæd], *n.* guilladura; novedad, *f.*, capricho.
faddy ['fædi], *a.* quisquilloso.
fade [feid], *v.t.* desteñir.—*v.i.* marchitarse; desteñirse; ***to* — *away,*** desvanecerse.
fag [fæg], *n.* lata, afán, *m.*; (*Brit. educ.*) alumno sirviente; burro de carga, yunque, *m.*; (*fam.*) pitillo.—*v.t.* afanar, fatigar.
fag-end ['fægend], *n.* colilla (*de pitillo*); desperdicio (*trozo inútil*); retal (*trozo de tela*).
faggot ['fægət], *n.* haz, *m.*; (*fam.*) bruja, vieja.
fail [feil], *n.* ***without* —,** sin falta.—*v.t.* faltar a; (*educ.*) suspender; ser suspendido en (*un examen*).—*v.i.* fracasar; (*com.*) quebrar; ser suspendido; decaer, menguar; ***not to* — *to,*** no dejar de.
failing ['feiliŋ], *a.* decadente.—*n.* falta; fracaso; debilidad, *f.*—*prep.* a falta de.
failure ['feiljə], *n.* fracaso, malogro; (*com.*) quiebra; fracasado (*persona*); suspensión (*en un examen*), *f.*
faint [feint], *a.* débil; desmayado.—*n.* desmayo.—*v.i.* desmayarse.
faint-hearted ['feint'hɑ:tid], *a.* medroso, cobarde.

fair [fɛə], *a.* justo, imparcial; legal; propicio; rubio; blanco; hermoso, bueno (*tiempo*); admisible; (*fam.*) regular; — ***play,*** juego limpio, proceder leal, *m.*; — ***sex,*** sexo bello. —*n.* verbena; feria.
fairy ['fɛəri], *a.* de hadas.—*n.* hada; — ***tale*** *o* ***story,*** cuento de hadas; (*fig.*) patraña.
faith [feiθ], *n.* fe, *f.*; (*fig.*) palabra.
faithful ['feiθful], *a.* fiel, leal; ***the*** —, los creyentes.
faithfulness ['feiθfulnis], *n.* fidelidad, *f.*
faithless ['feiθlis], *a.* infiel, desleal.
fake [feik], *a.* (*fam.*) falso, fingido.—*n.* falsificación, *f.*; impostor (*persona*), *m.*—*v.t.* falsificar.
falcon ['fɔ:lkən], *n.* halcón, *m.*
falconry ['fɔ:lkənri], *n.* cetrería.
fall [fɔ:l], *n.* caída; baja; salto de agua; (*U.S.*) otoño.—*irr. v.i.* caer(se); ponerse (*enfermo, triste, etc.*); ***to — back,*** replegarse; ***to — back on,*** recurrir a; ***to — behind,*** quedarse atrás; ***to — for,*** (*fam.*) tragar; chiflarse por; ***to — out,*** desavenirse; ***to — through,*** fracasar, salir mal.
fallacious [fə'leiʃəs], *a.* falaz; erróneo.
fallacy ['fæləsi], *n.* falsedad, *f.*, error, *m.*; falacia.
fallen ['fɔ:lən], *n.pl.* los caídos (*de guerra*), *m.pl.* [FALL].
fallible ['fælibl], *a.* falible.
fall-out ['fɔ:laut], *n.* desperdicios nucleares, *m.pl.*
fallow ['fælou], *a.* barbechado; flavo.—*n.* barbecho.
fallow-deer ['fælou'diə], *n.* gamo.
false [fɔ:ls], *a.* falso; postizo.
false-hearted ['fɔ:ls'hɑ:tid], *a.* traicionero, pérfido.
falsehood ['fɔ:lshud], *n.* falsedad, *f.*, mentira.
falsetto [fɔ:l'setou], *n.* falsete, *m.*; falsetista, *m.f.*
falsify ['fɔ:lsifai], *v.t.* falsificar.
falsity ['fɔ:lsiti], *n.* falsedad, *f.*
falter ['fɔ:ltə], *n.* titubeo.—*v.i.* titubear, vacilar; balbucear.
fame [feim], *n.* fama.
familiar [fə'miljə], *a.*, *n.* familiar, *m.f.*; — ***with,*** familiarizado con; al tanto de.
familiarize [fə'miljəraiz], *v.t.* familiarizar.
family ['fæmili], *a.* familiar.—*n.* familia.
famine ['fæmin], *n.* hambre, *f.*, carestía.
famished ['fæmiʃt], *a.* hambriento.
famous ['feiməs], *a.* famoso, célebre.
fan [fæn], *n.* abanico; (*mech.*) ventilador, *m.*; (*fam.*) aficionado.—*v.t.* abanicar; avivar.
fanatic [fə'nætik], *a.*, *n.* fanático.
fanaticism [fə'nætisizm], *n.* fanatismo.
fancied ['fænsid], *a.* imaginario; favorecido.
fancier ['fænsiə], *n.* aficionado.
fanciful ['fænsiful], *a.* antojadizo, fantástico.
fancy ['fænsi], *a.* de fantasía; fantástico; extravagante; caprichoso; — ***dress,*** traje (*m.*) de fantasía.—*n.* fantasía; afición, *f.*; antajo.—*v.t.* imaginar; prendarse de; ***what do you —?*** ¿qué le apetece?
fanfare ['fænfɛə], *n.* toque (*m.*) de trompetas; fanfarria.
fang [fæŋ], *n.* colmillo, diente, *m.*
fanlight ['fænlait], *n.* tragaluz, *m.*, abanico.
fantastic [fæn'tæstik], *a.* fantástico.
fantasy ['fæntəsi], *n.* fantasía.

far [fɑ:], *a.* lejano, remoto.—*adv.* lejos; muy; ***as — as,*** hasta; en cuanto que (*with subj.*); tan lejos como; ***by —,*** con mucho; ***so —,*** hasta ahora *o* aquí; — ***off,*** lejano; a lo lejos.
far-away [fɑ:rə'wei], *a.* lejano.
farce [fɑ:s], *n.* farsa.
farcical ['fɑ:sikəl], *a.* ridículo.
fare [fɛə], *n.* tarifa, pasaje, *m.*; vianda, comida. —*v.i.* pasarlo, acontecer; (*poet.*) andar.
farewell [fɛə'wel], *n.* despedida.—*interj.* ¡adiós!
far-fetched ['fɑ:'fetʃt], *a.* forzado, improbable.
farm [fɑ:m], *n.* granja; (*S.A.*) estancia.—*v.t.* cultivar; arrendar.
farmer ['fɑ:mə], *n.* granjero; labrador, *m.*
farmhouse ['fɑ:mhaus], *n.* granja, cortijo, alquería.
farmyard ['fɑ:mjɑ:d], *n.* corral, *m.*
far-reaching ['fɑ:ri:tʃiŋ], *a.* de gran alcance.
farther ['fɑ:ðə], *a.* más lejano.—*adv.* más lejos.
farthest ['fɑ:ðist], *a.* más lejano.—*adv.* lo más lejos.
farthing ['fɑ:ðiŋ], *n.* cuarto de penique.
fascinate ['fæsineit], *v.t.* fascinar.
fascinating ['fæsineitiŋ], *a.* fascinador.
fascination [fæsi'neiʃən], *n.* fascinación, *f.*
fascism ['fæʃizm], *n.* fascismo.
fascist ['fæʃist], *a.*, *n.* fascista, *m.f.*
fashion ['fæʃən], *n.* moda; estilo; manera; elegancia; ***after a —,*** en cierto modo.—*v.t.* forjar, formar.
fashionable ['fæʃnəbl], *a.* de moda; de buen tono, elegante.
fast (1) [fɑ:st], *a.* rápido; adelantado (*reloj*); disoluto, ligero.—*adv.* rapidamente, aprisa.
fast (2) [fɑ:st], *n.* ayuno.—*v.i.* ayunar.
fast (3) [fɑ:st], *a.* fijo, constante; ***to make—,*** (*naut.*) amarrar.—*adv.* firmemente; profundamente.
fasten [fɑ:sn], *v.t.* atar; cerrar; fijar; abrochar.—*v.i.* fijarse; cerrarse; ***to — on,*** asirse de.
fastener ['fɑ:snə], *n.* cierre, *m.*, asilla.
fastidious [fæs'tidiəs], *a.* melindroso, quisquilloso.
fasting ['fɑ:stiŋ], *n.* ayuno.
fastness ['fɑ:stnis], *n.* rapidez, *f.*; fijeza, firmeza; plaza fuerte; ligereza.
fat [fæt], *a.* gordo, grueso; pingüe; ***to get —,*** engordar.—*n.* grasa, sebo; ***to live off the — of the land,*** vivir a cuerpo del rey.
fatal [feitl], *a.* fatal; mortal.
fate [feit], *n.* hado, sino; suerte, *f.*
fated ['feitid], *a.* fatal; predestinado (a la muerte).
father ['fɑ:ðə], *n.* padre, *m.*—*v.t.* engendrar; prohijar; originar; atribuir.
father-in-law ['fɑ:ðərinlɔ:], *n.* (*pl.* ***fathers-in-law***) suegro.
fatherland ['fɑ:ðəlænd], *n.* patria.
fatherly ['fɑ:ðəli], *a.* paternal.
fathom ['fæðəm], *n.* (*naut.*) braza.—*v.t* sondear; profundizar; (*fig.*) entender.
fatigue [fə'ti:g], *n.* fatiga; (*mil.*) faena.—*v.t* fatigar.
fatten [fætn], *v.t.* engordar, cebar.
fatty ['fæti], *a.* graso, grasoso; (*fam.*) gordinflón.
fatuous ['fætjuəs], *a.* fatuo; ilusorio; necio.
faucet ['fɔ:sit], *n.* (*U.S.*) [TAP].

fault [fɔ:lt], *n.* culpa; defecto; falta; (*geol.*) falla; (*elec.*) avería; ***at* —,** culpable; ***it is John's* —,** Juan tiene la culpa.—*v.t.* hallar una falta.
fault-finder ['fɔ:ltfaində], *n.* criticón, *m.*
faultless ['fɔ:ltlis], *a.* perfecto; cabal; sin falta.
faulty ['fɔ:lti], *a.* defectuoso.
favour ['feivə], *n.* favor, *m.*; (*com.*) grata, atenta (*carta*); ***in* — *of,*** a favor de; ***to be in* — *of,*** estar por; ser partidario de.—*v.t.* favorecer.
favourable ['feivərəbl], *a.* favorable.
favourite ['feivrit], *a.* favorito, predilecto. —*n.* favorito.
fawn (1) [fɔ:n], *a.* color de cervato.—*n.* cervato.
fawn (2) [fɔ:n], *v.i.* adular, bailar el agua delante (***on,*** a).
fear [fiə], *n.* miedo, temor, *m.*—*v.t., v.i.* temer.
fearful ['fiəful], *a.* temeroso; espantoso.
fearless ['fiəlis], *a.* intrépido, audaz.
fearsome ['fiəsəm], *a.* miedoso; terrible.
feasible ['fi:zibl], *a.* factible, hacedero; dable.
feast [fi:st], *n.* festín, banquete, *m.*; (*eccl.*) fiesta; abundancia.—*v.t.* banquetear, regalar.—*v.i.* festejarse.
feat [fi:t], *n.* hazaña, proeza.
feather ['feðə], *n.* pluma; (*fig.*) humor, *m.*; clase, *f.*; ***white* —,** cobardía.—*v.t.* ***to* — *one's nest,*** hacer su agosto.
feather-brained ['feðəbreind], *a.* casquivano.
featherweight ['feðəweit], *a.* ligero como una pluma; (*sport*) peso pluma.
feature ['fi:tʃə], *n.* facción (*cara*), *f.*; rasgo, característica; parte principal, *f.*—*pl.* facciones, *f.pl.*—*v.t.* destacar; ofrecer; presentar.
February ['februəri], *n.* febrero.
fecundity [fə'kʌnditi], *n.* fecundidad, *f.*
fed [fed], [FEED].—*a.* — ***up,*** (*fam.*) harto (***with,*** de).
federal ['fedərəl], *a.* federal.
federate ['fedəreit], *v.t.* federar.
federation [fedə'reiʃən], *n.* federación, *f.*
fee [fi:], *n.* honorario; derechos, *m.pl.*; (*jur.*) herencia.
feeble [fi:bl], *a.* débil; flaco; enfermizo.
feed [fi:d], *n.* alimentación, *f.*; pienso; (*fam.*) comilona.—*v.t. irr.* alimentar; dar de comer a.—*v.i. irr.* comer; alimentarse (***on,*** de).
feel [fi:l], *n.* tacto; sensación, *f.*—*v.t. irr.* sentir; tocar, tentar, palpar; sondear; tomar (*el pulso*).—*v.i. irr.* sentirse; ser al tacto; estar; ***to* — *for,*** buscar a tientas; condolerse de; ***to* — *cold, hot, hungry, thirsty,*** tener frío, calor, hambre, sed; ***to* — *like,*** tener ganas de; ***to* — *sorry,*** sentirlo; compadecerse (***for,*** de).
feeler ['fi:lə], *n.* (*ent.*) antena, palpo; (*zool.*) tentáculo; (*fig.*) tentativa, tanteo.
feeling ['fi:liŋ], *n.* sensación, *f.*; sentimiento; parecer, *m.*—*pl.* sensibilidad, *f.*
feet [fi:t], [FOOT].
feign [fein], *v.t.* fingir, aparentar, simular.
felicitation [filisi'teiʃən], *n.* felicitación, *f.*
felicitous [fi'lisitəs], *a.* feliz, oportuno.
felicity [fi'lisiti], *n.* felicidad, *f.*; ocurrencia oportuna.
feline ['fi:lain], *a., n.* felino.
fell [fel], *v.t.* talar (*árbol*); derribar. [FALL].
fellow ['felou], *a.* *Spanish uses prefix* con-; — ***countryman,*** compatriota, *m.f.*—*n.* socio; miembro; compañero; igual, *m.*; (*fam.*) tío, sujeto.
fellow-creature ['felou'kri:tʃə], *n.* semejante, *m.f.*
fellow-feeling ['felou'fi:liŋ], *n.* compañerismo.
fellow-man ['felou'mæn], *n.* prójimo.
fellowship ['felouʃip], *n.* compañerismo; (*educ.*) pensión, *f.*, beca.
fellow-soldier ['felou'souldʒə], *n.* conmilitón, *m.*
fellow-traveller ['felou'trævələ], *n.* (*fig.*) comunistoide, *m.f.*; compañero de viaje.
felon ['felən], *n.* reo, criminal.
felony ['feləni], *n.* delito de mayor cuantía.
felt (1) [felt], *n.* fieltro.
felt (2) [felt] [FEEL].
female ['fi:meil], *a.* hembra, femenino.—*n.* hembra.
feminine ['feminin], *a.* femenino; mujeril.
fen [fen], *n.* pantano, laguna.
fence [fens], *n.* cerca, seto; traficante (*m.*) en objetos robados; ***to sit on the* —,** estar a ver venir; no participar, no comprometerse. —*v.t.* cercar, defender.—*v.i.* esgrimir.
fencing ['fensiŋ], *n.* esgrima; cercas, *f.pl.* materiales (*m.pl.*) para cercas.
fend [fend], *v.t.* parar, resguardar.—*v.i.* defenderse (***for oneself***).
fender ['fendə], *n.* guardafuegos, *m.sg.*; (*U.S.*) guardabarros, *m.sg.*
fennel ['fenəl], *n.* hinojo.
ferment ['fə:ment], *n.* fermento, fermentación, *f.*—*v.t., v.i.* [fə'ment], fermentar.
fern [fə:n], *n.*(*bot.*) helecho.
ferocious [fə'rouʃəs], *a.* feroz.
ferocity [fə'rɔsiti], *n.* ferocidad, *f.*
ferret ['ferit], *n.* (*zool.*) hurón, *m.*—*v.t.* huronear (***out***).
ferry ['feri], *n.* barco para pasar un río; trasbordador, *m.*; balsadero.—*v.t.* balsear (*río*); llevar a la otra orilla, trasbordar.
fertile ['fə:tail], *a.* fértil, fecundo.
fertility [fə:'tiliti], *n.* fertilidad, fecundidad, *f.*
fertilize ['fə:tilaiz], *v.t.* fertilizar; fecundar; abonar.
fertilizer ['fə:tilaizə], *n.* (*agr.*) abono, fertilizante, *m.*
fervent ['fə:vənt], *a.* fervoroso.
fervour ['fə:və], *n.* fervor, *m.*
fester ['festə], *v.t.* enconar.—*v.i.* enconarse; pudrir.
festival ['festivəl], *n.* fiesta; festival, *m.*
festive ['festiv], *a.* festivo.
festivity [fes'tiviti], *n.* festividad, *f.*
festoon [fes'tu:n], *n.* festón, *m.*—*v.t.* festonear.
fetch [fetʃ], *v.t.* traer, ir por; hacer venir; producir; (*fam.*) pegar (*golpe*); captar, atraer.
fetching ['fetʃiŋ], *a.* atractivo, llamativo.
fête [feit], *n.* fiesta.—*v.t.* festejar.
fetid ['fetid], *a.* fétido, hediondo.
fetish ['fetiʃ], *n.* fetiche, *m.*
fetter ['fetə], *n.* grillo, hierro.—*v.t.* engrillar.
feud [fju:d], *n.* saña vieja; enemistad (*f.*) tradicional entre dos familias.—*v.i.* luchar, oponerse con saña.
feudal ['fju:dəl], *a.* feudal.
fever ['fi:və], *n.* fiebre, *f.*, calentura.
feverish ['fi:vriʃ], *a.* febril, calenturiento.

few [fju:], *a.pl.*, pocos; ***a* —,** unos cuantos; ***the* —,** la minoría.
fiancé(e) [fi'ɔ:nsei], *n.* novio, novia, prometido, prometida.
fiasco [fi'æskou], *n.* fiasco.
fib [fib], *n.* trola, trápala, mentira.—*v.i.* embustear, mentir.
fibre ['faibə], *n.* fibra, hebra.
fibreglass ['faibəglɑ:s], *n.* vidrio fibroso.
fibrous ['faibrəs], *a.* fibroso.
fickle [fikl], *a.* veleidoso, inconstante.
fiction ['fikʃən], *n.* ficción, *f.*; literatura novelesca.
fictional ['fikʃənəl], *a.* ficcionario; novelesco.
ficitious [fik'tiʃəs], *a.* ficticio; fingido.
fiddle [fidl], *n.* (*fam.*) violín, *m.*; engañifa; ***fit as a* —,** en buena salud.—*v.t.* falsear, estafar.—*v.i.* tocar el violín; embustear; ***to* — *with*,** manosear, perder tiempo en; ***to play second* —,** estar subordinado (***to*,** a).
fiddler ['fidlə] *n.* (*fam.*) violinista, *m.f.*; embustero.
fiddlesticks! ['fidlstiks], *interj.* ¡tonterías! ¡qué va!
fiddling ['fidliŋ], *a.* trivial.
fidelity [fi'deliti], *n.* fidelidad, *f.*
fidget ['fidʒit], *n.* persona inquieta.—*v.i.* inquietarse, azogarse.
field [fi:ld], *n.* campo; (*sport*) participantes, *m.pl.*
field-day ['fi:lddei], *n.* día (*m.*) de mucha actividad.
field-glasses ['fi:ldglɑ:siz], *n.pl.* gemelos, prismáticos, *m.pl.*
field-marshal ['fi:ld'ma:ʃəl], *n.* mariscal, *m.*
fiend [fi:nd], *n.* demonio, diablo; fiero.
fiendish ['fi:ndiʃ], *a.* diabólico.
fierce [fiəs], *a.* feroz, fiero; furioso, violento.
fiery ['faiəri], *a.* ardiente, fogoso.
fife [faif], *n.* pífano.
fifteen [fif'ti:n], *a.*, *n.* quince, *m.*
fifteenth [fif'ti:nθ], *a.*, *n.* décimoquinto, quinceno; quince (*en las fechas*).
fifth [fifθ], *a.* quinto.—*n.* quinto; cinco (*en las fechas*); (*mus.*) quinta.
fifth-columnist ['fifθ'kɔləmist], quintacolumnista, *m.f.*
fiftieth ['fiftiəθ], *a.*, *n.* quincuagésimo.
fifty ['fifti], *a.*, *n.* cincuenta, *m.*
fifty-fifty ['fifti'fifti], *a.*, *adv.* (*fam.*) mitad y mitad, a medias.
fig [fig], *n.* higo; **— *tree*,** higuera; ***I don't give a* — *for it*,** no me importa un bledo *o* higo.
fight [fait], *n.* pelea, lucha; pujanza.—*v.t. irr.* combatir, pelearse con, luchar con *o* contra. —*v.t. irr.* pelear, lidiar, luchar (***for*,** por); ***to pick a* — *with*,** meterse con; ***to* — *it out*,** decidirlo luchando; ***to* — *shy of*,** evadir.
fighter ['faitə], *n.* combatiente, luchador; (*aer.*) caza, *m.*
fighting ['faitiŋ], *n.* combate, *m.*, lucha, batalla; **— *chance*,** posibilidad (*f.*) de éxito pero con riesgos.
figment ['figmənt], *n.* ficción, invención, *f.*
figurative ['figjurətiv], *a.* figurativo, figurado.
figure ['figə], *n.* figura; (*anat.*) talle, *m.*, tipo, línea; precio; cifra.—*v.t.* figurar; calcular; ***to* — *out*,** descifrar.—*v.i.* figurar(se); ***to* — *on*,** contar con.
figurehead ['figəhed], *n.* figurón, *m.*
filch [filtʃ], *v.t.* sisar, birlar.
file (1) [fail], *n.* carpeta, fichero.—*v.t.* archivar; registrar.
file (2) [fail], *n.* lima (*herramienta*).—*v.t.* limar.
file (3) [fail], *n.* fila.—*v.i.* desfilar.
filibuster ['filibʌstə], *n.* filibustero.—*v.t.*, *v.i.* (*U.S. pol.*) impedir la aprobación de una ley *etc.*
filigree ['filigri:], *n.* filigrana.
filing cabinet ['failiŋkæbinət], *n.* archivador *m.*; fichero.
filing-card ['failiŋkɑ:d], *n.* ficha.
filings ['failiŋz], *n.pl.* limalla.
Filipino [fili'pi:nou], *a.*, *n.* filipino.
fill [fil], *n.* terraplén, *m.*; hartazgo; ***to have one's* — *of*,** hartarse de.—*v.t.* llenar; tapar; ***to* — *in*,** rellenar, completar.—*v.i.* llenarse; bañarse (*de lágrimas*); hartarse; ***to* — *in*,** terciar, hacer las veces (***for*,** de).
fillet ['filit], *n.* filete, *m.*
filling ['filiŋ], *n.* relleno; empastadura (*de dientes*); **— *station*,** (*U.S.*) [SERVICE STATION].
fillip ['filip], *n.* capirotazo; estímulo.—*v.t.* dar un capirotazo a; estimular.
filly ['fili], *n.* potra; (*fam.*) retozona.
film [film], *n.* película; capa (*polvo*).—*v.t.* rodar, filmar.
film-star ['filmstɑ:], *n.* estrella del cine.
filmy ['filmi], *a.* pelicular; diáfano.
filter ['filtə], *n.* filtro.—*v.t.* filtrar.
filter-tipped ['filtə'tipt], *a.* con filtro, emboquillado.
filth [filθ], *n.* mugre, suciedad; obscenidad, *f.*
filthy ['filθi], *a.* mugriento, sucio; obsceno.
fin [fin], *n.* aleta.
final [fainl], *a.* final; último; terminante.—*n.* final, *m.* o *f.*
finale [fi'nɑ:li], *n.* final, *m.*
finance ['fainæns], *n.* finanzas, *f.pl.*, hacienda. —*v.t.* financiar.
financial [fai'nænʃəl], *a.* financiero.
financier [fai'nænsiə], *n.* financiero.
finch [fintʃ], *n.* (*orn.*) pinzón, *m.*
find [faind], *n.* hallazgo.—*v.t. irr.* hallar, encontrar.—*v.i. irr.* fallar, pronunciar un fallo; ***to* — *out*,** averiguar, descubrir.
finding ['faindiŋ], *n.* (*jur.*) fallo, resultando.
fine (1) [fain], *a.* fino; excelente; bueno (*tiempo*); delicado; (*fam.*) magnífico; **— *arts*,** bellas artes.
fine (2) [fain], *n.* multa (*castigo*).—*v.t.* multar.
fineness ['fainnis], *n.* fineza; finura.
finery ['fainəri], *n.* galas, *f.pl.*, atavíos, *m.pl.*
finesse [fi'nes], *n.* sutileza, tino.
finger ['fiŋgə], *n.* dedo; manecilla (*de reloj*); ***to have at one's* — *tips*,** saber al dedillo; ***to twist round one's little* —,** saber manejar completamenta a (*una persona*).—*v.t.* manosear; (*mus.*) pulsar, teclear.
finger-nail ['fiŋgəneil], *n.* uña.
finger-print ['fiŋgəprint], *n.* huella digital.
finicky ['finiki], *a.* melindroso, remilgado.
finish ['finiʃ], *n.* final, remate, *m.*; acabamiento.—*v.t.* acabar, terminar; pulir; (*fam.*) matar, arruinar.—*v.i.* acabar; ***to* — *off*,** rematar; matar; acabar con; ***to* — *with*,** acabar con, romper con.
Finland ['finlənd], *n.* Finlandia.

Finn [fin], **Finnish** ['finiʃ], *a.*, *n.* finlandés, finés, *m.*
fir [fə:], *n.* (*bot.*) abeto.
fire [faiə], *n.* fuego; incendio; ***to be on —,*** arder, estar ardiendo; ***to catch —,*** encenderse; ***to miss —,*** hacer fogonazo, fallar; ***to set on —,*** pegar fuego a; ***under —,*** (*mil.*) expuesto al fuego.—*v.t.* disparar (*armas*); encender; incendiar; lanzar (*proyectil*); cocer (*en el horno*); hacer explotar (*cargas*); (*fam.*) despedir, dar pasaporte a.—*v.i.* hacer fuego, disparar; encenderse.
fire-arm ['faiərɑ:m], *n.* arma de fuego.
fire-brigade ['faiəbrigeid], *n.* cuerpo de bomberos.
fire-engine ['faiərendʒin], *n.* bomba de incendios.
fire-escape ['faiəreskeip], *n.* escalera de incendios.
fireman ['faiəmən], *n.* bombero; (*rail.*) fogonero.
fireplace ['faiəpleis], *n.* chiminea, hogar, *m.*
fireside ['faiəsaid], *n.* hogar, *m.*
firewood ['faiəwud], *n.* leña.
fireworks ['faiəwə:ks], *n.* fuegos artificiales, *m.pl.*; (*fam.*) berrinche, *m.*; jarana.
firing-squad ['fairiŋskwəd], *n.* pelotón (*m.*) de fusilamiento.
firm (1) [fə:m], *a.* firme.
firm (2) [fə:m], *n.* (*com.*) razón (*f.*) social, empresa, firma.
firmament ['fə:məmənt], *n.* firmamento.
firmness ['fə:mnis], *n.* firmeza.
first [fə:st], *a.*, *n.*, *adv.* primero; ***— of all,*** ante todo; ***at —,*** al principio, en primer lugar; ***— aid,*** cura de urgencia, primeros auxilios; ***— floor,*** (*Brit.*) piso principal, piso segundo; (*U.S.*) planta baja.
firstborn ['fə:stbɔ:n], *a.*, *n.* primogénito.
first-class [fə:st'klɑ:s], *a.* de primera clase.
first-hand [fə:st'hænd], *a.*, *adv.* de primera mano.
first-rate [fə:st'reit], *a.* de primera categoría, excelente.
firth [fə:θ], *n.* estuario, ría.
fiscal ['fiskəl], *a.*, *n.* fiscal, *m.*
fish [fiʃ], *n.* (*ichth.*) pez, *m.*; (*cul.*) pescado.—*v.t.*, *v.i.* pescar; ***to — for,*** (*fig.*) buscar.
fishbone ['fiʃboun], *n.* espina, raspa.
fisherman ['fiʃəmən], *n.* pescador, *m.*
fishing ['fiʃiŋ], *a.* pesquero.—*n.* pesca; ***— rod,*** caña de pescar.
fishmonger ['fiʃmʌŋgə], *n.* pescadero.
fish-pond ['fiʃpənd], *n.* vivero.
fishwife ['fiʃwaif], *n.* pescadera; (*fig.*) marimacho.
fishy ['fiʃi], *a.* que huele *o* sabe a pescado; (*fam.*) sospechoso, dudoso, inverosímil.
fission ['fiʃən], *n.* fisión; escisión, *f.*
fissure ['fiʃə], *n.* grieta; fisura.—*v.t.* hender.—*v.i.* henderse.
fist [fist], *n.* puño; (*print.*) manecilla.
fisticuff ['fistikʌf], *n.* puñetazo.
fit (1) [fit], *a.* apto; conveniente; sano; decente; digno.—*n.* ajuste, encaje, *m.*—*v.t.* sentar; ajustar, encajar; cuadrar con; equipar.—*v.i.* encajar; sentar.
fit (2) [fit], *n.* (*med.*) acceso; ataque; arranque.
fitful ['fitful], *a.* espasmódico.
fitness ['fitnis], *n.* conveniencia; aptitud; buena salud, *f.*
fitting ['fitiŋ], *a.* propio, conveniente; justo.—*n.* prueba; ajuste, *m.*—*pl.* accesorios, *m.pl.*
five [faiv], *a.*, *n.* cinco.
five-year plan ['faivjiə'plæn], *n.* plan quinquenal, *m.*
fix [fiks], *n.* (*fam.*) apuro, aprieto.—*v.t.* fijar; arreglar; ***to — up,*** (*fam.*) componer; organizar; ***to — on,*** clavar en; elegir.
fixation [fik'seiʃən], *n.* fijación, *f.*
fixed [fikst], *a.* fijo.
fixture ['fikstjə], *n.* mueble fijo, *m.*; accesorio; instalación (*f.*) fija; soporte, *m.*—*pl.* habilitaciones, guarniciones, *f.pl.*
fizz [fiz], *n.* efervescencia.—*v.i.* chisporrotear.
flabbergast ['flæbəgɑ:st], *v.t.* (*fam.*) pasmar, aturdir.
flabby ['flæbi], *a.* lacio, flojo.
flag (1) [flæg], *n.* bandera. —*v.t.* hacer señales con una bandera a.
flag (2) [flæg], *v.i.* flaquear, flojear, aflojar.
flag (3) [flæg], *n.* losa.—*v.t.* enlosar.
flag (4) [flæg], *n.* (*bot.*) lirio.
flagon ['flægən], *n.* jarro, frasco.
flag-pole ['flægpoul], *n.* asta.
flagrant ['fleigrənt], *a.* escandaloso, notorio.
flag-ship ['flægʃip], *n.* (*naut.*) capitana, buque (*m.*) insignia.
flail [fleil], *n.* mayal, *m.*—*v.t.* azotar, golpear.
flair [flɛə], *n.* don especial, *m.*, instinto.
flak [flæk], *n.* fuego antiaéreo.
flake [fleik], *n.* copo (*de nieve*); escama, hojuela.—*v.t.* hacer escamas.—*v.i.* deshacerse en escamas.
flamboyant [flæm'bɔiənt], *a.* flameante; ampuloso.
flame [fleim], *n.* llama.—*v.i.* llamear; inflamarse.
flamingo [flə'miŋgou], *n.* flamenco.
flange [flændʒ], *n.* pestaña; realce, *m.*
flank [flæŋk], *n.* lado; costado; flanco.—*v.t.* flanquear.
flannel ['flænəl], *n.* franela.
flap [flæp], *n.* faldeta; hoja plegadiza; aletazo; (*fam.*) trastorno.—*v.t.* batir, sacudir, golpear.—*v.i.* aletear.
flare [flɛə], *n.* llamarada; cohete (*m.*) de señales; destello.—*v.i.* destellar; ***to — up,*** encolerizarse; recrudecer.
flash [flæʃ], *n.* destello, relámpago; rayo; instante (*phot.*) flash, *m.*—*v.t.* hacer brillar; lanzar; transmitir rápidamente.—*v.i.* relampaguear.
flashlight ['flæʃlait], *n.* linterna eléctrica.
flashy ['flæʃi], *a.* chillón, charro, ostentoso.
flask [flɑ:sk], *n.* frasco, redoma.
flat [flæt], *a.* plano; llano; raso; liso; chato (*nariz*); mate, flojo; insípido; terminante.—*n.* piso; llano; pantano; (*mus.*) bemol, *m.*; (*U.S.*) pneumático desinflado; pinchazo.
flatten [flætn], *v.t.* allanar; desazonar.—*v.i.* allanarse.
flatter ['flætə], *v.t.* lisonjear; sentar bien a.—*v.r.* hacerse la ilusión (***that,*** de que).
flatterer ['flætərə], *n.* lisonjero.
flattery ['flætəri], *n.* lisonja, adulación, *f.*
flaunt [flɔ:nt], *v.t.* ostentar, hacer alarde de.
flavour ['fleivə], *n.* sabor, *m.*; gustillo; (*cul.*) condimento.—*v.t.* sazonar, condimentar.
flaw [flɔ:], *n.* defecto, tacha.—*v.t.* agrietar, afear.
flawless ['flɔ:lis], *a.* sin tacha, entero.
flax [flæks], *n.* lino.
flay [flei], *v.t.* desollar; despellejar.

flea [fli:], *n.* pulga.
flea-bite ['fli:bait], *n.* picadura de pulga; nonada.
fleck [flek], *n.* punto, veta.—*v.t.* puntear, vetear.
fled [fled], [FLEE].
fledg(e)ling ['fledʒliŋ], *n.* volantón, *m.*; novato.
flee [fli:], *v.t.*, *v.i. irr.* huir.
fleece [fli:s], *n.* vellón, *m.*; lana.—*v.t.* esquilar; (*fam.*) pelar.
fleet [fli:t], *a.* raudo, veloz.—*n.* (*aer.*, *naut.*) flota; (*naut.*) armada.—*v.i.* volar, pasar rápidamente.
fleeting ['fli:tiŋ], *a.* fugaz; transitorio.
Fleming ['flemiŋ], *n.* flamenco.
Flemish ['flemɪʃ], *a.*, *n.* flamenco.
flesh [fleʃ], *n.* carne, *f.*; (*fig.*) familia; ***in the* —,** en persona; vivo; **— *and blood,*** carne y hueso.
flesh-pots ['fleʃpɔts], *n.pl.* (*fig.*) vida regalona.
fleshy ['fleʃi], *a.* carnoso; carnal; gordo.
flew [flu:], [FLY].
flex [fleks], *n.* (*elec.*) cordón, *m.*—*v.t.* doblar.
flexible ['fleksibl], *a.* flexible.
flick [flik], *n.* golpecito rápido.—*pl.* (*fam.*) el cine.—*v.t.* dar un golpecito a; tirar; chasquear.
flicker ['flikə], *n.* llama *o* luz (*f.*) vacilante; temblor, *m.*—*v.i.* temblar; oscilar.
flight [flait], *n.* huída, fuga; vuelo; tramo (*escalera*); ***to take* —,** alzar el vuelo; huir.
flighty ['flaiti], *a.* caprichoso, frívolo.
flimsy ['flimzi], *a.* débil, endeble; fútil.
flinch [flintʃ], *v.i.* encogerse, apocarse.
fling [fliŋ], *n.* tiro violento; baile escocés, *m.*—*v.t. irr.* arrojar; ***to have one's* —,** correrla, echar una cana al aire.
flint [flint], *n.* pedernal, *m.*
flip [flip], *n.* capirotazo.—*v.t.* dar un capirotazo a.
flippant ['flipənt], *a.* frívolo, impertinente.
flirt [flə:t], *n.* coqueta, coquetón, *m.*, flirt, *m.f.*; tirón, *m.*—*v.t.* tirar, lanzar, mover rápidamente.—*v.i.* flirtear, galantear, coquetear (***with,*** con); jugar (***with,*** con).
flirtatious [flə:'teiʃəs], *a.* coqueta, coquetón.
flit [flit], *v.i.* revolotear; (*fam.*) mudar de casa.
float [flout], *n.* veleta (*pesca*); boya; carro.—*v.t.* (*com.*) lanzar; emitir; (*naut.*) poner a flote.—*v.i.* flotar.
floating['floutiŋ], *a.* flotante, boyante; a flote; de tránsito.
flock (1) [flɔk], *n.* rebaño; bandada (*pájaros*).
flock (2) [flɔk], *n.* borra.—*v.i.* congregarse; venir de tropel.
floe [flou], *n.* témpano.
flog [flɔg], *v.t.* azotar; (*low*) vender.
flood [flʌd], *n.* inundación, *f.*, diluvio; (*fig.*) torrente, *m.*—*v.t.* inundar.—*v.i.* desbordar.
floor [flɔ:], *n.* suelo, piso; fondo; ***to take the* —,** tomar la palabra.—*v.t.* derribar.
flop [flɔp], *n.* (*fam.*) birria, fracaso; ruido sordo.—*v.i.* agitarse; caer pesadamente; (*fam.*) salir calabaza, fracasar.
floral ['flɔ:rəl], *a.* floral.
florid ['flɔrid], *a.* florido; encarnado (*cara*).
florin ['flɔrin], *n.* florín (*dos chelines*), *m.*
florist ['flɔrist], *n.* florero, florista.
flotilla [flou'tilə], *n.* flotilla.
flotsam ['flɔtsəm], *n.* pecio(s).
flounce (1) [flauns], *n.* volante (*costura*), *m.*
flounce (2) [flauns], *v.i.* saltar de enojo.
flounder (1) ['flaundə], *n.* (*ichth.*) platija.
flounder (2), *v.i.* forcejear, revolcarse.
flour [flauə], *n.* harina.
flourish ['flʌriʃ], *n.* floreo; molinete, *m.*, rúbrica; rasgo.—*v.t.* blandir, menear.—*v.i.* florecer, medrar.
flout [flaut], *v.t.* mofarse de.
flow [flou], *n.* flujo.—*v.i.* fluir; manar.
flower [flauə], *n.* flor, *f.*; (*fig.*) la flor y la nata.—*v.i.* florecer.
flower-bed ['flauəbed], *n.* macizo, cuadro.
flowering ['flauəriŋ], *a.* floreciente; florido. —*n.* florecimiento; floración, *f.*
flower-pot ['flauəpɔt], *n.* maceta, tiesto.
flowery ['flauəri], *a.* florido.
flowing ['flouiŋ], *a.* corriente; ondeante.
flown [floun], [FLY].
'flu [flu], *n.* (*fam.*) gripe, *f.*
fluctuate ['flʌktjueit], *v.i.* fluctuar.
flue [flu:], *n.* humero; tamo.
fluency ['flu:ənsi], *n.* fluidez, *f.*
fluent ['flu:ənt], *a.* flúido.
fluently ['flu:əntli], *adv.* corrientemente.
fluff [flʌf], *n.* pelusa, borra, plumón, *m.*
fluffy ['flʌfi], *a.* fofo; mullido; velloso.
fluid [flu:id], *a.*, *n.* flúido.
fluke [flu:k], *n.* chiripa.
flung [flʌŋ], [FLING].
fluorescent [fluə'resənt], *a.* fluorescente.
flurry ['flʌri], *n.* ráfaga, racha.—*v.t.* aturrullar.
flush (1) [flʌʃ], *a.* copioso; próspero; robusto. —*n.* rubor, *m.*; bochorno; abundancia; ataque febril, *m.*; floración, *f.*—*v.t.* abochornar; animar; limpiar con un chorro de agua.—*v.i.* abochornarse.
flush (2) [flʌʃ], *a.* rasante, enrasado.—*v.t.* nivelar.
flush (3) [flʌʃ], *v.t.* (*hunt.*) levantar.—*v.i.* fluir precipitadamente.
flush (4) [flʌʃ], *n.* flux, *m.*
fluster ['flʌstə], *n.* aturdimiento.—*v.t.* aturrullar.
flute [flu:t], *n.* flauta.—*v.t.* estriar.
flutter ['flʌtə], *n.* aleteo; agitación, *f.*—*v.t.* sacudir.—*v.i.* aletear.
flux [flʌks], *n.* flujo; mudanza frecuente.
fly [flai], *n.* (*pl.* **flies**) (*ent.*) mosca; bragueta (*de pantalones*); telar, *m.*—*pl.* (*theat.*) bambalina.—*v.t. irr.* (*aer.*) dirigir; hacer volar.—*v.i. irr.* volar; ***to* — *over,*** trasvolar; ***to* — *open,*** abrirse de repente.
flying ['flaiiŋ], *a.* volante.—*n.* aviación, *f.*; ***with* — *colours,*** con banderas desplegadas.
fly-leaf ['flaili:f], *n.* hoja de guarda.
flyover ['flaiouvə], *n.* viaducto.
foal [foul], *n.* potro.—*v.i.* parir.
foam [foum], *n.* espuma.—*v.i.* espumar.
focus ['foukəs], *n.* enfoque, *m.*; foco.—*v.t.* enfocar.
fodder ['fɔdə], *n.* forraje, *m.*
foe [fou], *n.* enemigo.
fog [fɔg], *n.* niebla.—*v.t.* empañar, velar.—*v.i.* obscurecer; velarse.
fog-horn ['fɔghɔ:n], *n.* sirena de niebla.
foggy ['fɔgi], *a.* nebuloso, brumoso.
foible [fɔibl], *n.* lado flaco, flaqueza.
foil (1) [fɔil], *n.* hojuela; contraste.
foil (2) [fɔil], *n.* florete, *m.*—*v.t.* frustrar.

foist [fɔist], *v.t.* vender *o* hacer aceptar algo con engaño (***on,*** a).
fold [fould], *n.* pliegue; redil, *m.*—*v.t.* plegar, doblar.—*v.i.* plegarse, doblarse; ***to — up,*** doblar; doblarse; (*fam.*) fracasar.
folder ['fouldə], *n.* carpeta.
folding ['fouldiŋ], *a.* plegadizo.
foliage ['fouliidʒ], *n.* follaje, *m.*
folio ['fouliou], *a.* en folio.—*n.* folio.
folk [fouk], *n.* gente, *f.*; pueblo.
folk-dance ['foukdɑ:ns], *n.* baile popular, *m.*
folklore ['fouklɔ:], *n.* folklore, *m.*
folk-song ['fouksɔŋ], *n.* canción popular, *f.*
follow ['fɔlou], *v.t.* seguir.—*v.i.* seguir(se); ***to — on,*** seguir; continuar; ***to — up,*** reforzar; seguir; ***as follows,*** como sigue.
follower ['fɔlouə], *n.* secuaz, *m.f.*, seguidor, *m.*
following ['fɔlouiŋ], *a.* siguiente.—*n.* secuaces, *m.pl.*, séquito; aficionados, *m.pl.*
folly ['fɔli], *n.* locura, desatino.
foment [fou'ment], *v.t.* fomentar.
fond [fɔnd], *a.* cariñoso; (*obs.*) tonto; ***— of,*** aficionado a; encariñado de.
fondle [fɔndl], *v.t.* acariciar.
font [fɔnt], *n.* (*eccl.*) pila.
food [fu:d], *n.* alimento.
food-stuffs ['fu:dstʌfs], *n.pl.* productos alimenticios, *m.pl.*
fool [fu:l], *a.* (*fam.*) tonto, loco.—*n.* tonto, bobo; bufón, *m.*; ***fool's errand,*** caza de grillos.—*v.t.* embaucar.—*v.i.* tontear; ***to make a — of,*** poner en ridículo; ***to play the —,*** hacer el tonto; ***to — with,*** frangollar; jugar con.
foolhardy ['fu:lhɑ:di], *a.* temerario; arriesgado.
foolish ['fu:liʃ], *a.* tonto, bobo.
fool-proof ['fu:lpru:f], *a.* a prueba de impericia; cierto, seguro.
foot [fut], *n.* (*pl.* **feet**) pie, *m.*; (*mil.*) infantería; ***on —,*** de *o* a pie; ***to put one's — down,*** (*fam.*) imponer la disciplina; ***to put one's — in it,*** (*fam.*) meter la pata.—*v.t.* pagar (*cuenta*).—*v.i.* (*fam.*) ir a pie.
football ['futbɔ:l], *n.* futbol, balompié; balón, *m.*, pelota.
foothold ['futhould], *n.* posición segura, arraigo, pie, *m.*
footing ['futiŋ], *n.* posición segura, arraigo; ***on an equal —,*** en condiciones iguales; ***on a war —,*** en pie de guerra.
footlights ['futlaits], *n.* (*theat.*) candilejas.
footman ['futmən], *n.* lacayo.
footmark ['futmɑ:k], *n.* huella.
footnote ['futnout], *n.* nota al pie de la página; (*fig.*) glosa, apéndice, *m.*
footpath ['futpɑ:θ], *n.* senda, vereda.
foot-print ['futprint], *n.* huella, pisada.
footsore ['futsɔ:], *a.* despeado.
footstep ['futstep], *n.* paso.
footwear ['futwɛə], *n.* calzado.
fop [fɔp], *n.* currutaco, pisaverde, *m.*
for [fɔ:], *prep.* para; por; a; de; como; a pesar de.—*conj.* pues, puesto que; ***as —,*** en cuanto a; ***O — . . !*** ¡ quién tuviera. . . . !
forage ['fɔridʒ], *n.* forraje, *m.*—*v.t.*, *v.i.* forrajear.
foray ['fɔrei], *n.* correría.—*v.t.* saquear.
forbade [fɔ:'beid *or* -'bæd], [FORBID].
forbear (1) [FOREBEAR].
forbear (2) [fɔ:'bɛə], *v.t.*, *v.i. irr.* abstenerse, detenerse (de).
forbearance [fɔ:'bɛərəns], *n.* paciencia, abstención, *f.*
forbid [fɔ:'bid], *v.t. irr.* vedar, prohibir.
forbidding [fɔ:'bidiŋ], *a.* adusto; repugnante.
force [fɔ:s], *n.* fuerza; ***in —,*** en grandes números; vigente.—*v.t.* forzar.
forceful ['fɔ:sful], *a.* potente, eficaz.
forceps ['fɔ:seps], *n.pl.* fórceps, *m.sg.*, pinzas, *f.pl.*
forcible ['fɔ:sibl], *a.* violento; eficaz.
ford [fɔ:d], *n.* vado.—*v.t.* vadear.
fore [fɔ:], *a.* delantero.—*n.* delantera, cabeza. —*prefix.* pre-, ante-.
forearm ['fɔ:rɑ:m], *n.* antebrazo.
forebear ['fɔ:bɛə], *n.* antepasado.
forebode [fɔ:'boud], *v.t.* presagiar.
foreboding [fɔ:'boudiŋ], *n.* presentimiento; presagio.
forecast ['fɔ:kɑ:st], *n.* pronóstico.—*v.t.*, *v.i. irr.* (*conjug. like* CAST) pronosticar; prever.
forecastle [fouksl], *n.*(*naut.*) castillo de proa.
forefather ['fɔ:fɑ:ðə], *n.* antepasado.
forefinger ['fɔ:fiŋgə], *n.* dedo índice.
forego [fɔ:'gou], *v.t. irr.* (*conjug. like* GO) preceder.
foregoing ['fɔ:gouiŋ], *a.*, *n.* precedente, anterior.
foregone ['fɔ:gɔn], *a.* inevitable (*conclusión*); [FOREGO].
foreground ['fɔ:graund], *n.* primer término.
forehead ['fɔrid], *n.* frente, *f.*
foreign ['fɔrin], *a.* extranjero; ajeno; extraño; ***— affairs,*** asuntos exteriores; ***Foreign Office,*** ministerio de asuntos exteriores.
foreigner ['fɔrinə], *n.* extranjero.
forelock ['fɔ:lɔk], *n.* copete, mechón, *m.*
foreman ['fɔ:mən], *n.* capataz; (*jur.*) presidente, *m.*
foremost ['fɔ:moust], *a.* (más) delantero; primero, principal.—*adv.* primero.
forensic [fɔ'rensik], *a.* forense.
forerunner ['fɔ:rʌnə], *n.* precursor, *m.*
foresee [fɔ:'si:], *v.t. irr.* (*conjug. like* SEE) prever.
foreshadow [fɔ:'ʃædou], *v.t.* presagiar.
foresight ['fɔ:sait], *n.* previsión, *f.*, providencia.
forest ['fɔrist], *a.* forestal.—*n.* bosque, *m.*, selva.
forestall [fɔ:'stɔ:l], *v.t.* prevenir; acopiar, acaparar.
forestry ['fɔristri], *n.* silvicultura, ingeniería forestal.
foretaste ['fɔ:teist], *n.* goce anticipado; muestra.
foretell [fɔ:'tel], *v.t. irr.* (*conjug. like* TELL) predecir.
forethought ['fɔ:θɔ:t], *n.* premeditación; consideración, *f.*, prudencia.
forever [fɔr'evə], *adv.* (*U.S.*) [FOR EVER].
foreword ['fɔ:wə:d], *n.* prefacio, prólogo.
forfeit ['fɔ:fit], *n.* multa, pena; prenda.—*v.t.* perder el derecho a.
forgave [fɔ:geiv] [FORGIVE].
forge [fɔ:dʒ], *n.* fragua; herrería.—*v.t.* fraguar, forjar; falsificar; ***to — ahead,*** ir avanzando.
forgery ['fɔ:dʒəri], *n.* falsificación, *f.*
forget [fɔ:'get], *v.t. irr.* olvidar, olvidarse de.

forgetful [fɔ:'getful], *a.* olvidadizo.
forget-me-not [fɔ:'getminɔt], *n.* (*bot.*) nomeolvides, *m.sg.*
forgive [fɔ:'giv], *v.t. irr.* (*conjug. like* GIVE) perdonar.
forgiveness [fɔ:'givnis], *n.* perdón, *m.*
forgo [fɔ:'gou], *v.t. irr.* (*conjug. like* GO) privarse de.
forgot(ten) [fɔ:'gɔt(n)] [FORGET].
fork [fɔ:k], *n.* (*cul.*) tenedor, *m.*; horca, horquilla; (*rail.*) ramal, *m.*; bifurcación, *f.*—*v.t.* ahorquillar.—*v.i.* bifurcarse.
forlorn [fɔ:'lɔ:n], *a.* desamparado, desesperado.
form [fɔ:m], *n.* forma; impreso, papeleta cédula; (*educ.*) clase, *f.*, grado.—*v.t.* formar. —*v.i.* formarse.
formal ['fɔ:məl], *a.* formal; solemne.
formality [fɔ:'mæliti], *n.* etiqueta; formalidad, *f.*; pormenor, *m.*
formation [fɔ:'meiʃən], *n.* formación, *f.*
former ['fɔ:mə], *a.* anterior; antiguo; ***the* —,** aquél.
formidable ['fɔ:midəbl], *a.* formidable.
formula ['fɔ:mjulə], *n.* fórmula.
forsake [fɔ:'seik], *v.t. irr.* abandonar, dejar.
forsaken [fɔ:'seikən], **forsook** [fɔ:'suk] [FORSAKE].
fort [fɔ:t], *n.* fortaleza, fortín, *m.*
forth [fɔ:θ], *adv.* adelante; fuera; en adelante; ***and so* —,** y así sucesivamente.
forthcoming [fɔ:θ'kʌmiŋ], *a.* próximo; dispuesto.
forthwith [fɔ:θ'wiθ], *adv.* sin dilación, *f.*
fortieth ['fɔ:tiəθ], *a.*, *n.* cuadragésimo; cuarentavo.
fortification [fɔ:tifi'keiʃən], *n.* fortificación, *f.*
fortify ['fɔ:tifai], *v.t.* fortificar; fortalecer.
fortitude ['fɔ:titju:d], *n.* fortaleza, firmeza.
fortnight ['fɔ:tnait], *n.* quincena, quince días.
fortress ['fɔ:tris], *n.* fortaleza.
fortuitous [fɔ:'tju:itəs], *a.* fortuito.
fortunate ['fɔ:tjunit], *a.* afortunado.
fortune ['fɔ:tju:n], *n.* fortuna.
fortune-teller ['fɔ:tju:n'telə], *n.* adivino sortílego.
forty ['fɔ:ti], *a.*, *n.* cuarenta, *m.*
forum ['fɔ:rəm], *n.* foro, plaza; juzgado.
forward ['fɔ:wəd], *a.* delantero; precoz; adelantado; atrevido.—*n.* delantero.—*v.t.* hacer seguir (*carta*); promover.—*adv.* adelante; en adelante.
forwards ['fɔ:wədz], *adv.* (hacia) adelante.
fossil ['fɔsil], *a.*, *n.* fósil, *m.*
foster ['fɔstə], *a.* adoptivo.—*v.t.* criar; fomentar.
fought [fɔ:t], [FIGHT].
foul [faul], *a.* sucio, asqueroso; obsceno; fétido; vil; atroz; obstruído; **— *play*,** traición, *f.*, juego sucio.—*n.* falta, juego sucio.—*v.t.* enredar; obstruir; ensuciar; ***to fall* — *of*,** enredarse con *o* en.
foul-mouthed ['faulmauðd], *a.* deslenguado.
found (1) [faund], *v.t.* fundar.
found (2) [faund], *v.t.* (*metal*) fundir.
found (3) [faund], [FIND].
foundation [faun'deiʃən], *n.* fundamento; cimiento; fundación, *f.*
foundling ['faundliŋ], *n.* expósito.
foundry ['faundri], *n.* fundición, *f.*, fundería.
fount [faunt] (*poet.*), **fountain** ['fauntin], *n.* fuente, *f.*
fountain-pen ['fauntin'pen], *n.* pluma estilográfica.
four [fɔ:], *a.*, *n.* cuatro; ***on all fours*,** a gatas.
fourteen [fɔ:'ti:n], *a.*, *n.* catorce, *m.*
fourteenth [fɔ:'ti:nθ], *a.*, *n.* décimo-cuarto, catorzavo; catorce (*en las fechas*).
fourth [fɔ:θ], *a.* cuarto.—*n.* cuarto; cuatro (*en las fechas*); (*mus.*) cuarta.
fowl [faul], *n.* ave, *f.*; gallina, gallo.—*n.pl.* aves en general.
fox [fɔks], *n.* (*zool.*, *fig.*) zorro.—*v.t.* confundir.
foxglove ['fɔksglʌv], *n.* (*bot.*) dedalera.
foxy ['fɔksi], *a.* zorruno; taimado.
foyer ['fɔiei], *n.* salón de entrada *o* descanso, zaguán, *m.*
fracas ['frækɑ:], *n.* riña, gresca.
fraction ['frækʃən], *n.* fracción, *f.*, quebrado.
fracture ['fræktʃə], *n.* fractura, rotura.—*v.t.* fracturar.—*v.i.* -se.
fragile ['frædʒail], *a.* frágil.
fragment ['frægmənt], *n.* fragmento.
fragrance ['freigrəns], *n.* fragancia.
fragrant ['freigrənt], *a.* fragante.
frail [freil], *a.* frágil, delicado, débil.
frailty ['freilti], *n.* debilidad, *f.*
frame [freim], *n.* marco; armazón, *f.*; armadura; talle, *m.*; estado; sistema, *m.*—*v.t.* formar, fraguar; enmarcar, colocar en marco; servir de marco a; (*fam.*) incriminar (*a un inocente*).
framework ['freimwə:k], *n.* armadura, armazón, *f.*
franc [fræŋk], *n.* franco.
France [frɑ:ns], *n.* Francia.
franchise ['fræntʃaiz], *n.* sufragio; franquicia.
Francis ['frɑ:nsis], *n.* Francisco.
Franciscan [fræn'siskən], *a.*, *n.* franciscano.
frank [fræŋk], *a.* franco.—*v.t.* franquear.
frankincense ['fræŋkinsens], *n.* olíbano incienso.
frankness ['fræŋknis], *n.* franqueza.
frantic ['fræntik], *a.* frenético.
fraternal [frə'tə:nl], *a.* fraternal.
fraternize ['frætənaiz], *v.i.* fraternizar.
fraud [frɔ:d], *n.* fraude, *m.*, timo; (*fam.*) tramposo.
fraudulent ['frɔ:djulənt], *a.* fraudulento.
fraught [frɔ:t], *a.* cargado, lleno (***with*,** de).
fray (1) [frei], *n.* contienda.
fray (2) [frei], *v.t.* raer, rozar.—*v.i.* raerse; deshilacharse.
freak [fri:k], *a.* monstruoso; extraordinario.—*n.* rareza, fenómeno, monstruosidad, *f.*
freakish ['fri:kiʃ], *a.* raro, monstruoso.
freckle [frekl], *n.* peca.—*v.t.* motear.
freckly ['frekli], *a.* pecoso.
free [fri:], *a.* libre; gratis; liberal; **— *and easy*,** desenvuelto; **— *rein*,** rienda suelta. —*adv.* gratis; libremente.—*v.t.* libertar, librar; exentar.
freebooter ['fri:bu:tə], *n.* pirata, *m.*; filibustero.
freedom ['fri:dəm], *n.* libertad, *f.*
free-for-all ['fri:fɔ:r'ɔ:l], *n.* sarracina.
freehold ['fri:hould], *n.* (*jur.*) feudo franco.
freelance ['fri:lɑ:ns], *a.* independiente.—*n.* mercenario.
Freemason ['fri:meisən], *n.* francmasón, *m.*

freeze [fri:z], *n.* helada.—*v.t. irr.* helar; congelar.—*v.i. irr.* helarse.
freight [freit], *n.* carga; flete, *m.*; mercancías, *f.pl.*
French [frentʃ], *a.*, *n.* francés; — ***bean,*** judía verde; — ***window(s),*** ventana con puerta.
Frenchman ['frentʃmən], *n.* francés, *m.*
Frenchwoman ['frentʃwumən], *n.* francesa.
frenzy ['frenzi], *n.* frenesí, *m.*
frequency ['fri:kwənsi], *n.* frecuencia.
frequent ['fri:kwənt], *a.* frecuente.—[fri'kwent], *v.t.* frecuentar.
fresh [freʃ], *a.* fresco; nuevo; dulce (*agua*); puro; novicio; (*fam.*) fresco, atrevido.
freshen [freʃn], *v.t.* refrescar.—*v.i.* -se.
freshness ['freʃnis], *n.* pureza; frescura.
fret (1) [fret], *n.* calado; (*mus.*) traste, *m.*—*v.t.* recamar; adornar con calados.
fret (2) [fret], *n.* roce, *m*; enfado.—*v.t.* rozar; raer.—*v.i.* apurarse, incomodarse; raerse.
fretful ['fretful], *a.* mohino, descontentadizo.
fretwork ['fretwə:k], *n.* calado.
friar [fraiə], *n.* fraile, *m.*
friary ['fraiəri], *n.* convento de frailes.
friction ['frikʃən], *n.* fricción, *f.*; rozamiento.
Friday ['fraidei], *n.* viernes, *m.sg.*
fried [fraid], *a.* frito.
friend [frend], *n.* amigo.—*interj.* (*mil.*) gente (*f.*) de paz.
friendly ['frendli], *a.* amistoso, amigable; benévolo.
friendship ['frendʃip], *n.* amistad, *f.*
frieze [fri:z], *n.* (*arch.*) friso.
frigate ['frigət], *n.* fragata.
fright [frait], *n.* susto.
frighten [fraitn], *v.t.* asustar; espantar; ***to be frightened,*** tener miedo.
frightful ['fraitful], *a.* espantoso.
frigid ['fridʒid], *a.* frío.
frill [fril], *n.* escarola, lechuga; (*fam.*) ringorrango.—*v.t.* escarolar.
fringe [frindʒ], *n.* orla, franja; borde, *m.*—*v.t.* orlar.
frisk [frisk], *v.t.* (*fam.*) cachear.—*v.i.* retozar.
fritter ['fritə], *n.* frisuelo, buñuelo.—*v.t.* malgastar, desperdiciar (***away***).
frivolous ['frivələs], *a.* frívolo.
frock [frɔk], *n.* vestido.
frock-coat ['frɔk'kout], *n.* levita.
frog [frɔg], *n.* rana; — ***in the throat,*** carraspera.
frogman ['frɔgmən], *n.* hombre-rana, *m.*
frolic ['frɔlik], *n.* travesura, retozo; jaleo.—*v.i.* retozar, loquear.
from [frɔm], *prep.* de; desde; por; de parte de; según.
front [frʌnt], *a.* delantero; ***in* —,** delante, en frente (***of,*** de); — ***door,*** puerta principal, puerta de la calle.—*n.* frente, *m.* o *f.*; fachada; principio; delantera; pechera (*de vestido*); (*mil.*) frente, *m.*; apariencia falsa.
frontier ['frʌntjə], *a.* fronterizo.—*n.* frontera.
frost [frɔst], *n.* helada, escarcha.—*v.t.* escarchar.
froth [frɔθ], *n.* espuma.—*v.i.* espum(aje)ar.
frown [fraun], *n.* ceño.—*v.i.* fruncir el entrecejo, ponerse ceñudo; ***to* — *at*** o ***on,*** mirar con ceño.
froze(n) [frouz(n)] [FREEZE].
frugal ['fru:gəl], *a.* frugal, sobrio.
fruit [fru:t], *n.* fruta; frutas, *f.pl.*; (*fig.*) fruto.—*v.i.* dar fruto.
fruitful ['fru:tful], *a.* fructuoso, provechoso.
fruition [fru:'iʃən], *n.* fruición, *f.*, goce, *m.*; cumplimiento.
fruitless ['fru:tlis], *a.* infructuoso, vano.
frumpish ['frʌmpiʃ], *a.* desaliñado.
frustrate [frʌs'treit], *v.t.* frustrar.
frustration [frʌs'treiʃən], *n.* frustración, *f.*; desengaño.
fry [frai], *n.* fritada; pececillo(s).—*v.t.* freír.
frying-pan ['fraiiŋpæn], *n.* sartén, *f.*
fuel ['fjuəl], *n.* combustible, *m.*; (*fig.*) pábulo.—*v.t.* proveer de combustible.
fugitive ['fju:dʒitiv], *a.*, *n.* fugitivo; prófugo.
fugue [fju:g], *n.* fuga.
fulcrum ['fʌlkrəm], *n.* (*pl.* **-crums** *o* **-cra**) fulcro.
fulfil [ful'fil], *v.t.* cumplir; llenar; colmar; realizar.
fulfilment [ful'filmənt], *n.* cumplimiento; realización, *f.*
full [ful], *a.* lleno; amplio; completo (*vehículo*); pleno; fuerte; ***in* —,** por completo; ***to the* —,** enteramente; — ***well,*** muy bien; — ***dress,*** traje (*m.*) de etiqueta; uniforme (*m.*) de gala.
full-grown ['fulgroun], *n.* maduro.
fulness ['fulnis], *n.* plenitud, *f.*, hartura.
fulsome ['fulsəm], *a.* insincero; craso; repugnante.
fumble [fʌmbl], *v.i.* titubear; obrar con desmaña; buscar con las manos.
fume [fju:m], *n.* vaho; tufo.—*v.i.* vahear; humear; (*fig.*) encolerizarse.
fumigate ['fju:migeit], *v.t.* fumigar.
fun [fʌn], *n.* broma, diversión, *f.*, chacota, burla; ***for* o *in* —,** por gusto; en broma, de burlas; ***to have* —,** divertirse; ***to make* — *of,*** burlarse de.
function ['fʌŋkʃən], *n.* función, *f.*—*v.i.* funcionar.
fund [fʌnd], *n.* fondo.
fundamental [fʌndə'mentl], *a.* fundamental.—*n.pl.* fundamentos, *m.pl.*
funeral ['fju:nərəl], *a.* funerario.—*n.* funeral(es), *m.pl.*
funereal [fju:'niəriəl], *a.* fúnebre.
fungus ['fʌŋgəs], *n.* (*pl.* **fungi**) hongo.
funk [fʌŋk], *n.* (*fam.*) jindama.—*v.t.*, *v.i.* perder *o* evitar por cobardía.
funnel [fʌnl], *n.* embudo; (*naut.*) chimenea.
funny ['fʌni], *a.* divertido, gracioso, cómico; (*fam.*) raro;— ***bone,*** hueso de la alegriá; ***to be* —,** tener gracia; ***to seem* —,** hacer gracia (***to,*** a).
fur [fə:], *n.* piel, *f.*; (*fig.*) sarro.
furious ['fju:riəs], *a.* furioso.
furlong ['fə:lɔŋ], *n.* estadio.
furlough ['fə:lou], *n.* (*U.S. mil.*) licencia.
furnace ['fə:nis], *n.* horno.
furnish ['fə:niʃ], *v.t.* amueblar; proporcionar.
furniture ['fə:nitʃə], *n.* muebles, *m.pl.*; mueblaje, *m.*
furrow ['fʌrou], *n.* surco.—*v.t.* surcar.
further ['fə:ðə], *a.* adicional; más lejano.—*v.t.* fomentar, promover.—*adv.* más lejos; además.
furthermore [fə:ðə'mɔ:], *adv.* además.
furthermost ['fə:ðəmoust], **furthest** ['fə:ðist], *a.*, *adv.* más lejano.
furtive ['fə:tiv], *a.* furtivo.

fury ['fju:ri], *n.* furia.
furze [fə:z], *n.* aulaga; retama.
fuse [fju:z], *n.* mecha; (*elec.*) fundible, *m.*—*v.t.* fundir.—*v.i.* fundirse.
fuselage ['fju:zilɑ:ʒ], *n.* fuselaje, *m.*
fusilier [fju:zi'liə], *n.* fusilero.
fusion ['fju:ʒən], *n.* fusión, *f.*
fuss [fʌs], *n.* bulla, ajetreo; alharaca, hazañería.—*v.t.* mimar; molestar.—*v.i.* zangolotear, hacer alharacas; ***to make a* —,** armar un alboroto; hacer fiestas (***of***, a).
fussy ['fʌsi], *a.* remilgado, melindroso; exigente; molesto.
fusty ['fʌsti], *a.* mohoso, rancio.
futile ['fju:tail], *a.* vano, inútil; fútil, frívolo.
future ['fju:tʃə], *a.* venidero, futuro.—*n.* provenir, *m.*, futuro.
fuzzy ['fʌzi], *a.* borroso, velloso.

G

G, g [dʒi:], *n.* séptima letra del alfabeto inglés; **G,** (*mus.*) so.
gab [gæb], *n.* ***the gift of the* —,** (*fam.*) labia, facundia.
gabardine ['gæbədi:n], *n.* gabardina.
gabble [gæbl], *n.* cotorreo.—*v.i.* picotear.
gable [geibl], *n.* faldón, gablete, *m.*
gad [gæd], *v.i.* pindonguear.
gadabout ['gædəbaut], *n.* corretón, cantonero.
gadfly ['gædflai], *n.* tábano.
gadget ['gædʒit], *n.* (*fam.*) adminículo, dispositivo.
gag [gæg], *n.* mordaza; (*fam., U.S.*) chiste, *m.* —*v.t.* amordazar.
gage [geidʒ], *n.* prenda. [GAUGE].
gaiety ['geiiti], *n.* alegría.
gaily ['geili], *adv.* alegremente.
gain [gein], *n.* ganancia; provecho; aumento, incremento.—*v.t.* ganar.—*v.i.* ganar, avanzar; adelantarse (*reloj*); ***to* — *on*,** alcanzar.
gainsay [gein'sei], *v.t. irr.* (*conjug. like* SAY) contradecir.
gait [geit], *n.* paso, modo de andar.
gaiter ['geitə], *n.* botina; polaina.
gala ['gɑ:lə], *n.* fiesta, gala.
galaxy ['gæləksi], *n.* galaxia; grupo brillante.
gale [geil], *n.* ventarrón, *m.*
Galician [gə'liʃiən], *a., n.* gallego; galiciano.
Galilean [gæli'li:ən], *a., n.* galileo.
gall (1) [gɔ:l], *n.* hiel, *f.*; (*fig.*) rencor, *m.*, encono.
gall (2) [gɔ:l], *n.* (*bot.*) agalla; rozadura; (*fig.*) descaro. —*v.t.* irritar; amargar.
gallant ['gælənt], *a.* galante, cortés; gallardo, valiente.—*n.* galán, *m.*
gallantry ['gæləntri], *n.* gallardía; galantería; valentía.
galleon ['gæljən], *n.* galeón, *m.*
gallery ['gæləri], *n.* galería; pasadizo; balcón, *m.*
galley ['gæli], *n.* (*print., naut.*) galera.
galley-slave ['gæli'sleiv], *n.* galeote, *m.*; esclavo.
Gallicism ['gælisizəm], *n.* galicismo.
Gallicize ['gælisaiz], *v.t.* afrancesar.
galling ['gɔ:liŋ], *a.* molesto, irritante.
gallon ['gælən], *n.* galón, *m.*
gallop ['gæləp], *n.* galope, *m.*—*v.i.* galopar.
gallows ['gælouz], *n. pl.* horca.
galore [gə'lɔ:], *adv.* en abundancia.
galvanize ['gælvənaiz], *v.t.* galvanizar.
gambit ['gæmbit], *n.* gambito; táctica.
gamble [gæmbl], *n.* juego; riesgo.—*v.t.* jugar, aventurar.—*v.i.* jugar; especular.
gambler ['gæmblə], *n.* jugador, tahur, *m.*
gambling [gæmbliŋ], *n.* juego; especulación, *f.*
gambol ['gæmbəl], *n.* cabriola.—*v.i.* cabriolar, brincar.
game [geim], *a.* [GAMMY]; listo, animoso.—*n.* juego; (*sport*) partido; caza; ***big* —,** caza mayor.—*pl.* deportes, *m.pl.*
game-keeper ['geimki:pə], *n.* guardamonte, *m.*
gammon ['gæmən], *n.* jamón, *m.*
gammy ['gæmi], *a.* (*fam.*) cojo.
gamp [gæmp], *n.* (*fam.*) paraguas, *m.sg.*
gamut ['gæmət], *n.* gama.
gander ['gændə], *n.* ganso; (*fam.*) mirada, ojeada.
gang [gæŋ], *n.* pandilla; cuadrilla.—*v.i.* apandillar; acometer (***up on***, en pandilla).
gangster ['gæŋstə], *n.* pandillero, gángster, *m.*
gangway ['gæŋwei], *n.* pasarela, pasamano.
gaol [dʒeil], *n.* cárcel, *f.*—*v.t.* encarcelar.
gaoler ['dʒeilə], *n.* carcelero.
gap [gæp], *n.* laguna; buco, buquete, *m.*
gape [geip], *v.i.* boquear; abrirse mucho; embobarse (***at***, de).
garage ['gærɑ:ʒ], *n.* garaje, *m.*—*v.t.* poner en el garaje.
garb [gɑ:b], *n.* vestidura.
garbage ['gɑ:bidʒ], *n.* (*U.S.*) basura; **—** ***can***, (*U.S.*) [DUSTBIN].
garble [gɑ:bl], *v.t.* mutilar, pervertir.
garden [gɑ:dn], *n.* jardín (*flores*), *m.*; huerto (*legumbres*); huerta (*área fértil*); ***common or* —,** ordinario, corriente.—*v.t.*, *v.i.* cultivar.
gardener ['gɑ:dnə], *n.* jardinero; hortelano.
gardening ['gɑ:dniŋ], *n.* jardinería; horticultura.
gargle ['gɑ:gəl], *n.* gargarismo.—*v.i.* gargarizar.
garish ['gɛəriʃ], *a.* charro, ostentoso.
garland ['gɑ:lənd], *n.* guirnalda.
garlic ['gɑ:lik], *n.* ajo.
garment ['gɑ:mənt], *n.* prenda de vestir.
garner ['gɑ:nə], *v.t.* entrojar; acopiar.
garnet ['gɑ:nit], *n.* granate, *m.*
garnish ['gɑ:niʃ], *v.t.* adornar.
garret ['gærit], *n.* buharda, desván, *m.*
garrison ['gærisən], *n.* guarnición, *f.*—*v.t.* guarnicionar.
garrulous ['gæruləs], *a.* gárrulo.
garter ['gɑ:tə], *n.* liga; (*her.*) jarretera.
gas [gæs], *n.* gas, *m.*; (*U.S.*) gasolina; (*fam.*) parloteo; — ***station***, (*U.S.*) [SERVICE STATION]. —*v.t.* atacar *o* matar con gas.—*v.i.* (*fam.*) parlotear.
gas-bag ['gæsbæg], *n.* (*fam.*) churrullero.
gaseous ['geisiəs], *a.* gaseoso.
gas-fitter ['gæs'fitə], *n.* gasista, *m.*
gash [gæʃ], *n.* herida, cuchillada.—*v.t.* herir, acuchillar.
gas-holder ['gæs'houldə], *n.* gasómetro.
gas-mask ['gæsmɑ:sk], *n.* careta antigás.

gas-meter ['gæsmi:tə], *n.* contador (*m.*) de gas.
gasolene, gasoline ['gæsəli:n], *n.* (*U.S.*) gasolina.
gasometer [gæ'sɔmitə], *n.* gasómetro.
gasp [gɑ:sp], *n.* boqueada; grito sofocado; anhelo entrecortado.—*v.i.* boquear, sofocarse.
gas-stove ['gæs'stouv], *n.* cocina de gas.
gastric ['gæstrik], *a.* gástrico.
gas-works ['gæswə:ks], *n.* fábrica de gas.
gate [geit], *n.* puerta, portillo, entrada; cancela; (*sport*) entrada, concurrencia.
gateway ['geitwei], *n.* (*fig.*) entrada.
gather ['gæðə], *v.t.* recoger; coger; cobrar; colegir; fruncir (*costura*).—*v.i.* reunirse; acumularse.
gathering ['gæðəriŋ], *n.* reunión; acumulación, *f.*
gaudy ['gɔ:di], *a.* chillón, cursi.
gauge [geidʒ], *n.* calibrador, calibre *m.*; tamaño; norma; (*rail.*) ancho de la vía.—*v.t.* calibrar; aforar; graduar; calcular.
Gaul [gɔ:l], *n.* galo (*persona*); Galia (*país*).
gaunt [gɔ:nt], *a.* desvaído, descarnado; sombrío.
gauntlet ['gɔ:ntlit], *n.* guantelete, *m.*; ***to run the —,*** correr (las) baquetas.
gauze [gɔ:z], *n.* gasa; cendal, *m.*
gave [geiv] [GIVE].
gawk [gɔ:k], *n.* (*fam.*) papamoscas, *m.sg.*—*v.i.* (*fam.*) papar moscas.
gawky ['gɔ:ki], *a.* desgarbado; tonto.
gay [gei], *a.* alegre, festivo; ligero.
gaze [geiz], *n.* mirada fija.—*v.i.* mirar con fijeza (***at***).
gazelle [gə'zel], *n.* gacela.
gazette [gə'zet], *n.* gaceta.
gazetteer [gæze'tiə], *n.* gacetero; diccionario geográfico.
gear [giə], *n.* (*mech.*) engranaje, *m.*; marcha; aparejo, pertrechos, *m.pl.*; rueda dentada. *v.t.*—engranar; encajar.
gear-box ['giəbɔks], *n.* caja de engranajes, cárter, *m.*; caja de velocidades.
gear-change ['giətʃeindʒ], *n.* cambio de marchas.
gear-lever ['giə'li:və], *n.* palanca de cambio.
geese [gi:s] [GOOSE].
gelatine ['dʒeləti:n], *n.* gelatina.
gem [dʒem], *n.* alhaja, joya, gema.
gender ['dʒendə], *n.* género; sexo.
gene [dʒi:n], *n.* gen, *m.*
genealogy [dʒi:ni'ælədʒi], *n.* genealogía.
general ['dʒenərəl], *a.*, *n.* general, *m.*
generalize ['dʒenrəlaiz], *v.t.*, *v.i.* generalizar.
generate ['dʒenəreit], *a.* generar; engendrar.
generation [dʒenə'reiʃən], *n.* generación, *f.*
generator ['dʒenəreitə], *n.* generador, *m.*
generic [dʒə'nerik], *a.* genérico.
generosity [dʒenə'rɔsiti], *n.* generosidad, *f.*
generous ['dʒenərəs], *a.* generoso; amplio.
genesis ['dʒenisis], *n.* génesis, *m.*
genetic [dʒə'netik], *a.* genético.—*n.pl.* genética.
Geneva [dʒi'ni:və], *n.* Ginebra.
genial ['dʒi:njəl], *a.* afable, cordial.
genital ['dʒenitl], *a.*, *n.* genital, *m.*
genitive ['dʒenitiv], *a.*, *n.* genitivo.
genius ['dʒi:niəs], *n.* genio.
genre [ʒɑ̃:r], *n.* (*lit.*) género.
genteel [dʒen'ti:l], *a.* señoril, gentil.
gentile ['dʒentail], *a.*, *n.* gentil, pagano.
gentle [dʒentl], *a.* dulce, suave; blando, benévolo; ligero.
gentlefolk ['dʒentlfouk], *n.* gente bien nacida.
gentleman ['dʒentlmən], *n.* caballero.
gentlemanly ['dʒentlmənli], *a.* caballeroso.
gentleness ['dʒentlnis], *n.* dulzura, suavidad, *f.*
gentry ['dʒentri], *n.* gente bien nacida; (*fam.*) gente, *f.*
genuine ['dʒenjuin], *a.* genuino; sincero; auténtico.
genus ['dʒi:nəs], *n.* (*pl.* **genera** ['dʒenərə]) género.
geographer [dʒi'ɔgrəfə], *n.* geógrafo.
geographic(al) [dʒiou'græfik(əl)], *a.* geográfico.
geography [dʒi'ɔgrəfi], *n.* geografía.
geological [dʒiou'lɔdʒikəl], *a.* geológico.
geologist [dʒi'ɔlədʒist], *n.* geólogo.
geology [dʒi'ɔlədʒi], *n.* geología.
geometry [dʒi'ɔmətri], *n.* geometría.
geometric [dʒiou'metrik], *a.* geométrico.
George [dʒɔ:dʒ], *n.* Jorge, *m.*
germ [dʒə:m], *n.* germen, *m.*; ***— warfare,*** guerra bacteriológica.
German ['dʒə:mən], *a.*, *n.* alemán, *m.*; ***— measles,*** rubéola.
german ['dʒə:mən], *a.* carnal.
germane [dʒə:'mein], *a.* afín, relacionado.
Germany ['dʒə:məni], *n.* Alemania.
germinate ['dʒə:mineit], *v.i.* germinar.
gesticulate [dʒes'tikjuleit], *v.i.* accionar, hacer ademanes.
gesture ['dʒestʃə], *n.* gesto, ademán, *m.*; seña; muestra.
get [get], *v.t. irr.* obtener, lograr; ir por, traer; hacer; (*fam.*) comprender.—*v.i.* hacerse, ponerse; (*fam.*) largarse; lograr pasar (***by, over, through***); ***to — about,*** divulgarse; reponerse y levantarse; ***to — along,*** largarse; ir tirando; portarse; congeniar (***with,*** con); ***to — at,*** llegar a; (*fam.*) meterse con; ***to — away,*** escapar(se); partir; ***to — back,*** regresar, volver; ***to — better,*** mejorar(se); ***to — by,*** (*fam.*) arreglárselas; ***to — down,*** bajar; ***to — in,*** entrar en; meter; llegar; ***to — off,*** bajar (de); irse, escapar; ***to — on,*** subir (a); progresar; congeniar (***with,*** con); ***to — out,*** salir, salir lograr; dejar (***of***); publicar(se); sacar; ***to — over,*** pasar por encima de; recobrarse de; vencer; ***to — to,*** hacer, persuadir a; ***to — up,*** levantarse, montar, armar; ***to have got,*** tener, poseer; ***to have got to,*** tener que; ***to — angry, dark, tired*** *etc.*, enfadarse, obscurecer, cansarse *etc.*
get-away ['getəwei], *n.* escapatoria; arranque, *m.*
get-together ['gettə'geðə], *n.* reunión, *f.*, tertulia.
gewgaw ['gju:gɔ:], *n.* chuchería.
geyser ['gi:zə], *n.* géiser, *m.*
ghastly ['gɑ:stli], *a.* cadavérico; horrible.
gherkin ['gə:kin], *n.* pepinillo.
ghost ['goust], *n.* fantasma, *m.*; espectro.
ghost-writer ['goustraitə], *n.* colaborador anónimo.
giant ['dʒaiənt], *a.* gigantesco.—*n.* gigante, *m.*
gibberish ['dʒibəriʃ], *n.* jerigonza.
gibbet ['dʒibit], *n.* horca, patíbulo.

gibe [dʒaib], *n.* pulla, mofa.—*v.i.* mofarse (*at*, de).
giblets ['dʒiblits], *n.pl.* menudillos, *m.pl.*
giddiness ['gidinis], *n.* vértigo; veleidad, *f.*
giddy ['gidi], *a.* vertiginoso; casquivano.
gift [gift], *n.* regalo; (*fig.*) dote, *f.*; prenda.
gifted ['giftid], *a.* talentoso; dotado (***with***, de).
gigantic [dʒai'gæntik], *a.* gigantesco.
giggle [gigl], *n.* risilla tonta.—*v.i.* reírse tontamente.
gild [gild], *v.t.* dorar.
gill (1) [gil], *n.* (*ichth.*) agalla.
gill (2) [dʒil], *n.* cuarto de pinta líquida.
gilt [gilt], *a.*, *n.* dorado.
gimlet ['gimlit], *n.* barrena de mano.
gin (1) [dʒin], *n.* ginebra (*bebida*).
gin (2) [dʒin], *n.* desmotadora.
ginger ['dʒindʒə], *n.* jengibre, *m.*
gingerly ['dʒindʒəli], *a.* cauteloso.—*adv.* con cautela.
gin-trap ['dʒintræp], *n.* trampa.
gipsy ['dʒipsi], *a.*, *n.* gitano.
gird [gə:d], *v.t.* ceñir.
girder ['gə:də], *n.* viga de acero.
girdle [gə:dl], *n.* ceñidor; faja, corsé, *m.*—*v.t.* ceñir.
girl [gə:l], *n.* chica; niña; (*fam.*) novia.
girth [gə:θ], *n.* cincha; circunferencia.
gist [dʒist], *n.* substancia, enjundia.
give [giv], *v.t. irr.* dar; pronunciar (*oración*); otorgar, conceder; ofrecer; ocasionar; dedicar; ***to — away***, regalar; tracionar, revelar; ***to — back***, devolver; ***to give in***, entregar; ***to — out***, divulgar; ***to — up***, entregar; abandonar.—*v.i. irr.* dar de sí; ***to — in***, rendirse, ceder; hundirse; ***to — out***, agotarse; ***to — up***, rendirse.
give-and-take ['givənd'teik], *n.* tolerancia mutua.
given [givn] [GIVE]
gizzard ['gizəd], *n.* molleja.
glacial ['gleiʃjəl], *a.* glacial.
glacier ['glæsiə], *n.* glaciar, *m.*, helero.
glad [glæd], *a.* alegre, gozoso, contento.
gladden [glædn], *v.t.* alegrar.
glade [gleid], *n.* claro (*en un bosque*).
gladiator ['glædieitə], *n.* gladiador, *m.*
gladly ['glædli], *adv.* con mucho gusto.
glamorous ['glæmərəs], *a.* bello, lindo.
glamour ['glæmə], *n.* belleza, encanto.
glance [glɑ:ns], *n.* ojeada, vistazo.—*v.i.* echar un vistazo (***at***, a); ojear (***at***); desviarse (*golpes*) de soslayo.
gland [glænd], *n.* glándula.
glare [glɛə], *n.* brillo, fulgor, resplandor, *m.*; deslumbramiento; mirada indignada.—*v.i.* relumbrar; echar miradas de indignación.
glass [glɑ:s], *n.* vidrio; vaso, copa (*vasija*); cristal (*ventana*), *m.*; lente, *m.* o *f.*; espejo; ***— case***, vitrina.—*pl.* gafas, *f.pl.*, anteojos, *m.pl.*
glass-house ['glɑ:shaus], *n.* invernáculo; (*mil.*) cárcel, *f.*
glassy ['glɑ:si], *a.* vidrioso.
glaze [gleiz], *n.* barniz, esmalte, lustre, *m.*—*v.t.* vidriar; esmaltar.
glazier ['gleiziə], *n.* vidriero.
gleam [gli:m], *n.* destello, centelleo; rayo.—*v.i.* lucir, brillar tenuemente.
glean [gli:n], *v.t.* espigar.
glee [gli:], *n.* júbilo, gozo, alegría.
gleeful ['gli:ful], *a.* jubiloso, gozoso, alegre.
glen [glen], *n.* hocino, vallecito.
glib [glib], *a.* voluble, locuaz; engañoso.
glide [glaid], *n.* deslizamiento; (*aer.*) planeo.—*v.i.* deslizarse; (*aer.*) planear.
glider ['glaidə], *n.* (*aer.*) planeador, *m.*
glimmer ['glimə], *n.* vislumbre, *m.*; luz débil, *f.*—*v.i.* brillar tenuemente.
glimpse [glimps], *n.* vislumbre, *m.*; apariencia ligera.—*v.t.* vislumbrar.
glint [glint], *n.* destello, relumbrón, *m.*—*v.i.* brillar, reflejar.
glitter ['glitə], *n.* resplandor; oropel, *m.*—*v.i.* centellear, relucir.
gloat [glout], *v.i.* relamerse, deleitarse (***over***, en).
global ['gloubəl], *a.* global.
globe [gloub], *n.* globo.
globe-trotter ['gloubtrɔtə], *n.* trotamundos, *m.sg.*
globule ['glɔbju:l], *n.* glóbulo.
gloom ['glu:m], *n.* tinieblas, *f.pl.*, lobreguez, *f.*; tristeza.
gloomy ['glu:mi], *a.* tenebroso, lóbrego; triste, tétrico.
glorify ['glɔ:rifai], *v.t.* glorificar.
glorious ['glɔ:riəs], *a.* glorioso.
glory ['glɔ:ri], *n.* gloria.—*v.i.* gloriarse (***in***, de).
gloss [glɔs], *n.* lustre, barniz, *m.*; glosa.—*v.t.* satinar, lustrar; paliar; glosar; ***to — over***, encubrir, paliar.
glossary ['glɔsəri], *n.* glosario.
glossy ['glɔsi], *a.* lustroso, satinado; especioso.
glove [glʌv], *n.* guante, *m.*; ***to be hand in — with***, ser uña y carne, ser compinches.
glow [glou], *n.* vivo; resplandor, *m.*, brillo; viveza.—*v.i.* relucir, brillar, arder.
glow-worm ['glouwə:m], *n.* luciérnaga.
glucose ['glu:kous], *n.* glucosa.
glue [glu:], *n.* cola.—*v.t.* encolar, pegar.
glum [glʌm], *a.* moroso, tétrico, hosco.
glut [glʌt], *n.* exceso, plétora.—*v.t.* hartar, saturar; inundar (*mercado*).
glutton [glʌtn], *n.* glotón, *m.*
gluttonous ['glʌtnəs], *a.* glotón.
gluttony ['glʌtəni], *n.* glotonería; gula (*pecado*).
glycerine ['glisəri:n], *n.* glicerina.
gnarled [nɑ:ld], *a.* nudoso, retorcido.
gnash [næʃ], *v.t.*, *v.i.* rechinar.
gnat [næt], *n.* (*ent.*) jenjén, *m.*
gnaw [nɔ:], *v.t.* roer.
gnome [noum], *n.* trasgo, gnomo.
go [gou], *n.* empuje, *m.*, energía; ida; jugada; (*fam.*) moda; ensayo.—*v.i. irr.* ir, irse; marchar; funcionar; pasar; andar; volverse; desaparecer; caer, sentar; decirse; ***to — away***, irse, marcharse; ***to — by***, seguir; pasar por; ***to — in***, entrar en; ***to — in for***, interesarse en; ***to — into***, entrar en; investigar; ***to — off***, irse, alejarse; estallar; tener lugar; ***to — on***, continuar; ***to — out***; salir; apagarse; ***to — over***, pasar por encima de; revisar; ***to — with***, hacer juego con; ***to — without***, dejar; pasarse sin; privarse de.
goad [goud], *n.* aguijón, *m.*—*v.t.* aguijonear.
goal [goul], *n.* meta; (*sport*) meta, portería; tanto, gol, *m.*
goal-keeper ['goulki:pə], *n.* portero, guardameta, *m.*
goat [gout], *n.* cabra.

gobble [gɔbl], *n.* gluglú, *m.*—*v.t.* engullir.—*v.i.* gluglutear.
go-between ['goubitwi:n], *n.* medianero; alcahuete, *m.*
goblet ['gɔblit], *n.* copa.
goblin ['gɔblin], *n.* trasgo, duende, *m.*
God [gɔd], *n.* Dios; **god,** *n.* dios, *m.*
godchild ['gɔdtʃaild], *n.* ahijado.
goddess ['gɔdis] *n.* diosa.
godfather ['gɔdfɑ:ðə], *n.* padrino.
godless ['gɔdlis], *a.* infiel, descreído, ateo.
godmother [gɔdmʌðə], *n.* madrina.
godsend ['gɔdsend], *n.* divina merced; buena suerte, *f.*
godson ['gɔdsʌn], *n.* ahijado.
goggle [gɔgl], *n.pl.* anteojos de camino.—*v.i.* mirar pasmado (***at***), abrir los ojos mucho.
going ['gouiŋ], *a.* en marcha; próspero.—*n.* ida; estado del camino.
goings-on ['gouiŋz'ɔn], *n.pl.* (*fam*). andanzas, *f.pl.*; jarana.
gold ['gould], *n.* oro; ***Gold Coast,*** Costa de Oro.
golden ['gouldən], *a.* de oro, dorado.
goldfinch ['gouldfintʃ], *n.* jilguero.
goldfish ['gouldfiʃ] *n.* carpa dorada.
goldsmith ['gouldsmiθ], *n.* orfebre, orífice, *m.*
golf [gɔlf], *n.* golf, *m.*
gondola ['gɔndələ], *n.* góndola; (*aer.*) barquilla.
gone [gɔn], *a.* ido, pasado; arruinado; muerto; (*fam.*) chiflado (***on,*** por).—*p.p.* [GO].
gong [gɔŋ], *n.* batintín, *m.*, gongo.
good [gud], *a.* bueno; — ***day,*** ¡buenos dias! — ***morning,*** ¡buenos días! — ***afternoon,*** — ***evening,*** ¡buenas tardes! — ***night,*** ¡buenas noches!; ***as — as,*** tanto como, casi; ***for —,*** para siempre; ***Good Friday,*** Viernes Santo.—*n.* bien, *m.*—*pl.* mercancías, *f.pl.*
good-bye! [gud'bai], *interj.* ¡adiós!
good-for-nothing ['gudfənʌθiŋ] *a., n.* perdido, dejado de la mano de Dios.
good-looking [gud'lukiŋ], *a.* guapo.
good-natured [gud'neitʃəd], *a.* benévolo, afable, bonachón.
goodness ['gudnis], *n.* bondad, *f.*—*interj.* ¡Diós mío!
goofy ['gu:fi], *a.* (*fam.*) gilí.
goose [gu:s], *n.* (*pl.* **geese**) oca; ganso (*male & generic*).
gooseberry ['gu:zbəri], *n.* uva espina, grosella.
goose-flesh ['gu:sfleʃ], **goose-pimples** ['gu:spimplz], *n.* carne de gallina.
gore [gɔ:], *n.* sangre, *f.*, crúor, *m.*—*v.t.* acornear, coger.
gorge [gɔ:dʒ], *n.* garganta; barranco.—*v.t., v.i.* engullir, traguar; hartar(se) (***on,*** de).
gorgeous ['gɔ:dʒəs], *a.* brillante, espléndido, bellísimo.
gorilla [gə'rilə], *n.* gorila, *m.*
gorse [gɔ:s], *n.* tojo, árgoma, aulaga.
gory ['gɔ:ri], *a.* ensangrentado.
gosling ['gɔzliŋ], *n.* ansarino.
gospel ['gɔspəl], *n.* evangelio; (*fig.*) verdad pura.
gossamer ['gɔsəmə], *n.* telaraña finísima; gasa.
gossip ['gɔsip], *n.* chismes, *m.pl.*, chismería; chismoso.—*v.i.* chismear.
got [gɔt], [GET].
Goth [gɔθ], *n.* godo.
Gothic ['gɔθik], *a.* gótico.
gouge [gaudʒ], *n.* gubia.—*v.t.* excavar; sacar; arrancar.
gourd [guəd], *n.* calabaza.
gourmand [gur'mã], *n.* goloso.
gourmet ['gurmei], *n.* gastrónomo.
gout [gaut], *n.* gota, podagra.
govern ['gʌvən], *v.t., v.i.* gobernar; (*gram.*) regir.
governess ['gʌvənis], *n.* institutriz, *f.*, aya.
government ['gʌvənmənt], *n.* gobierno.
governor ['gʌvənə], *n.* gobernador; (*fam.*) jefe, *m.*
gown [gaun], *n.* (*educ., jur.*) toga; vestido talar; bata.
grab [græb], *n.* gancho; arrebatina; agarro.—*v.t.* agarrar; arrebatar.
grace [greis], *n.* gracia; favor, *m.*; discreción, *f.*; talante, *m.*; ***to say —,*** bendecir la mesa.—*v.t.* ilustrar, favorecer, hermosear.
graceful ['greisful], *a.* gracioso, agraciado.
graceless ['greislis], *a.* desgraciado; desgarbado.
gracious ['greiʃəs], *a.* gracioso; cortés; benigno.—*interj.* ¡válgame Dios!
grade [greid], *n.* grado; clase *f.*; cuesta; (*U.S. educ.*) clase (*f.*) de escuela;—***crossing,*** (*U.S. rail.*) cruce (*m.*) a nivel.—*v.t.* clasificar, graduar.
gradient ['greidiənt], *n.* pendiente, *f.*
gradual ['grædjuəl], *a.* gradual; graduado.
gradually ['grædjuəli], *adv.* poco a poco.
graduate ['grædjuit], *a., n.* graduado.—['grædjueit], *v.t.* graduar.—*v.i.* -se.
graduation [grædju'eiʃən], *n.* graduación, *f.*
graft (1) [grɑ:ft], *n.* injerto.
graft (2) [grɑ:ft], *n.* (*U.S.*) soborno político.
graft (3) [grɑ:ft], *n.* (*fam.*) trabajo fuerte, aplicación, *f.*
Grail [greil], *n.* Grial, *m.*
grain [grein], *n.* grano, granos, *m.pl.*; cereal, *m.*; fibra, veta, trepa; ***against the —,*** (*fig.*) a contra pelo, cuesta arriba.—*v.t.* granular; vetear.
gram [græm], [GRAMME].
grammar ['græmə], *n.* gramática.
grammarian [grə'meəriən], *n.* gramático.
grammatical [grə'mætikəl], *a.* gramático.
gramme [græm], *n.* gramo.
gramophone ['græməfoun], *n.* gramófono, tocadiscos, *m. inv.*
granary ['grænəri], *n.* granero, hórreo.
grand [grænd], *a.* grandioso; principal; excelente; grande.
grandchild ['græntʃaild], *n.* nieto.
granddaughter ['grændɔ:tə], *n.* nieta.
grandee [græn'di:], *n.* grande (de España), *m.*
grandeur ['grændjə], *n.* grandeza, esplendor, *m.*
grandfather ['grændfɑ:ðə], *n.* abuelo.
grandiose ['grændious], *a.* grandioso; hinchado.
grandmother ['grændmʌðə], *n.* abuela.
grandson ['grændsʌn], *n.* nieto.
grand-stand ['grændstænd], *n.* tribuna.
granite ['grænit], *n.* granito.
grant [grɑ:nt], *n.* concesión; subvención, *f.*—*v.t.* conceder, otorgar; ***to take for granted,*** dar por supuesto; no apreciar debidamente.
grape [greip], *n.* uva.
grapefruit ['greipfru:t], *n.* toronja, pomelo.

grape-shot ['greipʃɔt], *n.* metralla.
grape-vine ['greipvain], *n.* vid, *f.*; parra; (*fig., fam.*) las vías por donde corren rumores y por donde se llega a saber cosas secretas.
graph [grɑ:f], *n.* gráfica; curva.
graphic ['græfik], *a.* gráfico.
graphite ['græfait], *n.* grafito.
grapnel ['græpnəl], *n.* garabato; anclote, *m.*
grapple ['grapəl], *v.t.* agarrar.—*v.i.* luchar (***with,*** con).
grasp [grɑ:sp], *n.* asimiento; alcance, *m.*; agarro; (*fig.*) poder, entendimiento.—*v.t.* agarrar, empuñar; entender.
grasping ['grɑ:spiŋ], *a.* codicioso, avaro.
grass [grɑ:s], *n.* hierba; césped, *m.*
grasshopper ['grɑ:shɔpə], *n.* saltamontes, *m.sg.*
grate (1) [greit], *n.* reja; parrilla; hogar, *m.*
grate (2) [greit], *v.t.* rallar; rechinar.—*v.i.* rechinar.
grateful ['greitful], *a.* agradecido.
gratify ['grætifai], *v.t.* satisfacer, complacer.
grating (1) ['greitiŋ], *a.* irritante.
grating (2) ['greitiŋ], *n.* reja; rejilla.
gratis ['greitis], *a.* gratuito.—*adv.* gratis.
gratitude ['grætitju:d], *n.* gratitud, *f.*, agradecimiento.
gratuitous [grə'tju:itəs], *a.* gratuito.
gratuity [grə'tju:iti], *n.* gratificación, *f.*
grave (1) [greiv], *a.* serio, grave.
grave (2) [greiv], *n.* sepultura, sepulcro, tumba. —*v.t.* grabar; ***graven image,*** ídolo.
gravel ['grævil], *n.* grava, guijo.
grave-yard ['greivjɑ:d], *n.* cementerio.
gravitate ['græviteit], *v.i.* gravitar.
gravity ['græviti], *n.* gravedad; (*phys.*) gravitación, *f.*
gravy ['greivi], *n.* salsa, jugo.
gray (*U.S.*) [GREY].
graze [greiz], *n.* arañazo.—*v.t.* rozar; rasguñar.—*v.i.* pacer.
grease [gri:s], *n.* grasa.—*v.t.* engrasar.
greasy ['gri:si], *a.* grasiento.
great [greit], *a.* grande; ***A. the —,*** A. Magno.
great- [greit], *prefix.* — ***great-grandfather,*** bisabuelo; ***great-great-grandfather,*** tatarabuelo; ***great-uncle,*** tío abuelo.
greatness ['greitnis], *n.* grandeza.
Greece [gri:s], *n.* Grecia.
greed [gri:d], *n.* codicia, avaricia; gula.
greedy ['gri:di], *a.* voraz, goloso; avaro.
Greek [gri:k], *a., n.* griego.
green [gri:n], *a.* verde; novato; tierno, joven. —*n.* verde, *m.*—*pl.* verduras, *f.pl.*
greenery ['gri:nəri], *n.* verdura.
greengrocer ['gri:n'grousə], *n.* verdulero.
greenhouse ['gri:nhaus], *n.* invernáculo.
greenish ['gri:niʃ], *a.* verdoso.
greet [gri:t], *v.t.* saludar; presentarse a.
greeting ['gri:tiŋ], *n.* saludo.
gregarious [grə'gɛəriəs], *a.* gregario.
gremlin ['gremlin], *n.* duende, *m.*
grenade [grə'neid], *n.* granada.
grew [gru:], [GROW].
grey [grei], *a.* gris, grisáceo; — ***hairs,*** canas, *f.pl.*—*n.* gris, *m.*
greyhound ['greihaund], *n.* galgo.
grid [grid], *n.* rejilla; cuadriculado.
grief [gri:f], *n.* pena, quebranto, congoja.
grievance ['gri:vəns], *n.* pesar, *m.*; agravio.
grieve [gri:v], *v.t.* apenar, afligir.—*v.i.* afligirse, penar.
grill [gril], *n.* parrilla.—*v.t.* asar en parrilla; (*fam.*) interrogar.
grille [gril], *n.* rejilla.
grim [grim], *a.* fiero, severo, ceñudo.
grimace [gri'meis], *n.* mueca; visaje, *m.*—*v.i.* hacer muecas.
grime [graim], *n.* tiznado, mugre, *f.*—*v.t.* tiznar.
grimy ['graimi], *a.* tiznado, mugriento.
grin [grin], *n.* sonrisa burlona; mueca.—*v.i.* sonreír mostrando los dientes.
grind [graind], *n.* (*fam.*) zurra.—*v.t. irr.* moler; afilar; agobiar.—*v.i. irr.* rechinar.
grindstone ['graindstoun], *n.* muela; ***nose to the —,*** con afán, con ahinco.
grip [grip], *n.* apretón, *m.*; agarro; (*U.S.*) saco de mano.—*v.t.* asir, apretar; (*fig.*) cautivar.
grisly ['grizli], *a.* horroroso.
grist [grist], *n.* molienda; (*fig.*) provecho.
gristle [grisl], *n.* cartílago, ternilla.
grit [grit], *n.* arena, grava; (*fig.*) tesón, *m.*—*v.t.* apretar (*los dientes*).
grizzly ['grizli], *a.* grisáceo, cano; — ***bear,*** oso gris.
groan [groun], *n.* gemido.—*v.i.* gemir; crujir.
grocer ['grousə], *n.* especiero; (*S.A.*) abarrotero.
groceries ['grousəriz], *n.pl.* ultramarinos; (*S.A.*) abarrotes, *m.pl.*
groggy ['grɔgi], *a.* calamocano; inseguro.
groin [grɔin], *n.* ingle, *f.*
groom [gru:m], *n.* novio; caballerizo.—*v.t.* almohazar; asear; preparar.
groove [gru:v], *n.* surco; ranura; rodada; (*fam.*) rutina.
grope [group], *v.i.* ir a tientas; ***to — for,*** buscar a tientas.
gross [grous], *a.* craso; total; grueso; grosero. —*n.* gruesa (*144*).
grotesque [grou'tesk], *a.* grotesco.
grotto ['grɔtou], *n.* gruta.
ground (1) [graund], *n.* tierra; suelo; terreno; fundamento; motivo; campo.—*pl.* parque, *m.*, jardines, *m.pl.*; heces, *f.pl.*, posos, *m.pl.* —*v.t.* (*aer.*) vedar que vuele.
ground (2) [graund] [GRIND].
ground-floor ['graund'flɔ:], *n.* piso bajo, planta baja.
groundless ['graundlis], *a.* infundado.
ground-nut ['graundnʌt], *n.* cacahuete, *m.*
group [gru:p], *n.* grupo.—*v.t.* agrupar.
grouse (1) [graus], *n.* (*orn.*) lagópedo.
grouse (2) [graus], *n.* (*fam.*) rezongo.—*v.i.* rezongar.
grove [grouv], *n.* arboleda, soto.
grovel ['grɔvəl], *v.i.* arrastrarse; envilecerse.
grow [grou], *v.t. irr.* cultivar; dejarse crecer (*barba*).—*v.i. irr.* crecer; aumentarse; ponerse; ***to — old,*** envejecerse.
grower [grouə], *n.* cultivador, agricultor, *m.*
growing ['grouiŋ], *a.* creciente.—*n.* cultivo.
growl [graul], *n.* gruñido.—*v.i.* gruñir.
grown [groun], *a.* crecido; adulto.—*p.p.* [GROW].
grown-up ['groun'ʌp], *a., n.* adulto, mayor.
growth [grouθ], *n.* crecimiento; (*med.*) tumor, *m.*; aumento.
grub [grʌb], *n.* gusano, gorgojo; (*fam.*) manduca.—*v.i.* hozar; cavar; escarbar.
grubby ['grʌbi], *a.* sucio.

grudge [grʌdʒ], *n.* rencor, *m.*, ojeriza.—*v.t.* envidiar; escatimar.
grudgingly ['grʌdʒiŋli], *adv.* de mala gana.
gruel [gru:əl], *n.* avenate, *m.*, gachas, *f.pl.*
gruelling ['gru:əliŋ], *a.* afanoso, agotador.
gruesome ['gru:səm], *a.* horrendo, horripilante.
gruff [grʌf], *a.* áspero, arisco.
grumble [grʌmbl], *n.* queja.—*v.i.* quejarse, refunfuñar.
grumpy ['grʌmpi], *a.* (*fam.*) rezongón, gruñón.
grunt [grʌnt], *n.* gruñido.—*v.i.* gruñir.
guarantee [gærən'ti:], *n.* garantía.—*v.t.* garantizar.
guard [gɑ:d], *n.* guardia (*cuerpo*); guardia (*señor*), *m.*; guarda; (*fig.*) prevención, *f.*, cautela; ***on one's —,*** sobre aviso, prevenido. —*v.t.* guardar, proteger. — *v.i.* ***to — against,*** guardarse de.
guarded ['gɑ:did], *a.* cauteloso.
guardian [gɑ:diən], *n.* guardián; tutor, *m.*
Guatemalan [gwæti'mɑlən], *a.*, *n.* guatemalteco.
guerrilla [gə'rilə], *n.* guerrillero.
guess [ges], *n.* conjetura.—*v.t.* suponer; adivinar.
guest [gest], *n.* huésped, *m.f.*, convidado.
guffaw [gʌ'fɔ:], *n.* carcajada. —*v.i.* reírse a carcajadas.
guidance ['gaidəns], *n.* guía, dirección, *f.*, gobierno.
guide [gaid], *n.* guía (*cosa*); guía (*señor*), *m.* —*v.t.* guiar; ***guided missile,*** proyectil dirigido.
guild [gild], *n.* gremio.
guile [gail], *n.* maña, dolo.
guillotine ['gilǝti:n], *n.* guillotina.—*v.t.* guillotinar.
guilt [gilt], *n.* culpa.
guiltless ['giltlis], *a.* inocente.
guilty ['gilti], *a.* culpable; reo.
guinea ['gini], *n.* guinea.
guinea-fowl ['ginifaul], *n.* gallina de Guinea *o* pintada.
Guinean ['giniən], *a.*, *n.* guineo.
guinea-pig ['ginipig], *n.* conejillo de Indias, cobayo.
guise [gaiz], *n.* modo; color, *m.*, pretexto; apariencia; (*obs.*) guisa.
guitar [gi'ta:], *n.* guitarra.
gulch [gʌltʃ], *n.* (*U.S.*) quebrada, rambla.
gulf [gʌlf], *n.* golfo.
gull [gʌl], *n.* (*orn.*) gaviota; bobo.
gullet ['gʌlit], *n.* gaznate, *m.*
gully ['gʌli], *n.* cárcava, arroyada, barranca; badén, *m.*
gulp [gʌlp], *n.* trago.—*v.i.* tragar (***down***).
gum [gʌm], *n.* goma; (*anat.*) encía.—*v.t.* engomar.
gumption ['gʌmpʃən], *n.* (*fam.*) caletre, *m.*
gun [gʌn], *n.* fusil, *m.*; pistola; cañón, *m.*
gun-boat ['gʌnbout], *n.* cañonero.
gun-fire ['gʌnfaiə], *n.* tiroteo; fuego.
gun-man ['gʌnmən], *n.* pistolero.
gunner ['gʌnə], *n.* artillero.
gunnery ['gʌnəri], *n.* artillería.
gunpowder ['gʌnpaudə], *n.* pólvora.
gunwale ['gʌnəl], *n.* borda, regala.
gurgle [gə:gl], *n.* gorgoteo; murmullo.—*v.i.* gorgotear.
gush [gʌʃ], *n.* chorro.—*v.i.* brotar, chorrear; ser extremoso.
gushing ['gʌʃiŋ], *a.* surgente; extremoso.
gust [gʌst], *n.* ráfaga; arrebato.
gusto ['gʌstou], *n.* placer, *m.*, gusto, brío.
gusty ['gʌsti], *a.* tempestuoso, borrascoso.
gut [gʌt], *n.* tripa.—*pl.* (*fam.*) valor, *m.*, valentía.
gutter ['gʌtə], *n.* gotera, canal, *m.*; arroyo.—*v.i.* gotear.
guttural ['gʌtərəl], *a.*, *n.* gutural, *f.*
guy [gai], *n.* tirante, *m.*; (*U.S. fam.*) tío, individuo.
guzzle [guzl], *v.t.* engullir.
Guyanan [gai'ɑ:nən], **Guyanese** [gaiə'ni:z], *a.*, *n.* guayanés, *m.*
gymnasium [dʒim'neiziəm], *n.* gimnasio.
gymnastics [dʒim'nastiks], *n.pl.* gimnasia.
gypsum ['dʒipsəm], *n.* yeso.
gyrate [dʒaiə'reit], *v.i.* girar.
gypsy ['dʒipsi], *a.*, *n.* gitano.
gyroscope ['dʒaiərəskoup], *n.* giroscopio.

H

H, h [eitʃ], *n.* octava letra del alfabeto inglés.
haberdasher ['hæbədæʃə], *n.* mercero, camisero.
haberdashery ['hæbədæʃəri], *n.* mercerías, *f.*pl.
habit ['hæbit], *n.* costumbre, *f.*, hábito; traje, *m.*, hábito (*vestido*); ***to be in the — of,*** soler, acostumbrar.
habitat ['hæbitæt], **habitation** [hæbi'teiʃən], *n.* habitación, *f.*
habitual [hə'bitjuəl], *a.* habitual.
habituate [hə'bitjueit], *v.t.* habituar.
hack (1) [hæk], *n.* hachazo; tos seca. —*v.t.* machetear, mellar.
hack (2) [hæk], *n.* rocín, *m.*; escritor mercenario.
hackney ['hækni], *n.* coche de alquiler; rocín, *m.*—*v.t.* gastar, vulgarizar.
hackneyed ['hæknid], *a.* trillado.
hacksaw ['hæksɔ:], *n.* sierra para metal.
had [hæd], [HAVE].
haddock ['hædək], *n.* (*ichth.*) merluza, róbalo.
haemorrhage ['hemərid3], *n.* hemorragia.
haft [hɑ:ft], *n.* mango, asa, puño.
hag [hæg], *n.* bruja; vejarrona.
haggard ['hægəd], *a.* macilento; zahareño.
haggle [hægl], *v.i.* regatear.
The Hague [heig], *n.* La Haya.
hail (1) [heil], *n.* granizo.—*v.i.* granizar.
hail (2) [heil], *n.* saludo; llamada.—*v.t.* saludar; vocear; llamar.—*v.i.* proceder (***from,*** de).
hailstone ['heilstoun], *n.* piedra de granizo.
hair [hɛə], *n.* pelo, cabello; pelillo; ***to split hairs,*** andar en quisquillas.
hairbrush ['hɛəbrʌʃ], *n.* cepillo de cabeza.
haircut ['hɛəkʌt], *n.* corte (*m.*) de pelo.
hairdresser ['hɛədresə], *n.* peluquero.
hairpin ['hɛəpin], *n.* horquilla.
hairless ['hɛəlis], *a.* pelón, pelado.
hairy ['hɛəri], *a.* peludo, peloso; velloso.
Haiti ['heiti], *n.* Haití, *m.*

Haitian ['heiʃən], *a.*, *n.* haitiano.
hake [heik], *n.* (*ichth.*) merluza.
hale (1) [heil], *a.* sano, fuerte.
hale (2) [heil], *v.t.* arrastrar.
half [hɑ:f], *a.*, *adv.* medio.—*n.* (*pl.* **halves**) mitad, *f.*; — ***past***, y media (*hora*); — ***and*** —, a medias; mitad y mitad.
half-breed ['hɑ:f'bri:d], **half-caste** ['hɑ:f'kɑ:st], *a.*, *n.* mestizo.
half-crown ['hɑ:f'kraun], *n.* (*Brit.*) dos chelines con seis peniques, media corona.
half-hearted ['hɑ:f'hɑ:tid], *a.* sin ánimo, flojo, frío.
half-pay ['hɑ:f'pei], *n.* medio sueldo.
halfpenny ['heipni], *n.* medio penique.
half-truth ['hɑ:f'tru:θ], *n.* verdad (*f.*) a medias.
half-way ['hɑ:f'wei], *a.*, *adv.* a mitad de; a medio camino.
half-witted ['hɑ:f'witid], *a.* imbécil, necio.
half-yearly ['hɑ:f'jiəli], *a.*, *adv.* semestral(mente).
hall [hɔ:l], *n.* vestíbulo, recibimiento, zaguán, *m.*; sala; edificio público; casa solariega.
hallelujah [hæli'lu:jə], *n.*, *interj.* aleluya.
hallmark ['hɔ:lmɑ:k], *n.* marca de ley; (*fig.*) sello.
hallo! [hə'lou], *interj.* ¡hola!
hallow ['hælou], *v.t.* santificar.
hallucination [həlu:si'neiʃən], *n.* alucinación, *f.*
halo ['heilou], *n.* halo; aureola.
halt [hɔ:lt], *a.* (*obs.*) cojo.—*n.* parada, alto.—*v.t.* parar.—*v.i.* hacer alto; vacilar.
halter ['hɔ:ltə], *n.* cabestro, ronzal, *m.*
halting ['hɔ:ltiŋ], *a.* vacilante; imperfecto.
halve [hɑ:v], *v.t.* partir en dos; demediar; reducir por la mitad.—*n.pl.* [HALF].
ham [hæm], *n.* jamón; pernil, *m.*; (*fam.*) aficionado a la radio; (*fam.*) comicastro.
hamlet ['hæmlit], *n.* aldea; caserío.
hammer ['hæmə], *n.* martillo.—*v.t.* martillar; machacar; golpear.—*v.i.* martillar; repiquetear.
hammock ['hæmək], *n.* hamaca.
hamper (1) ['hæmpə], *n.* excusabaraja; cesto, cuévano.
hamper (2) ['hæmpə], *v.t.* estorbar.
hamstring ['hæmstriŋ], *v.t.* *irr.* (*conjug. like* STRING) desjarretar.
hand [hænd], *n.* mano, *f.*; mano de obra; obrero; letra; ayuda; (*U.S.*) aplauso; ***by*** —, a mano; ***in*** —, entre manos; dominado; de sobra, como reserva; ***on*** —, a la mano; disponible; ***on the other*** —, por otra parte; ***out of*** —, rebelón, desbocado; en seguida; — ***to*** —, cuerpo a cuerpo; — ***in glove***, uña y carne; ***to lend a*** —, prestar ayuda; ***to shake hands***, estrechar la mano (***with***, a).—*v.t.* entregar (***over***).
hand-bag ['hændbæg], *n.* bolso de mano.
hand-book ['hændbuk], *n.* manual, *m.*; guía.
hand-cart ['hændkɑ:t], *n.* carretilla de mano.
handcuff ['hændkʌf], *n.pl.* esposas, *f.pl.*—*v.t.* poner esposas a.
handful ['hændful], *n.* puñado; (*fig.*) persona *o* cosa difícil.
hand-grenade ['hændgrineid], *n.* granada (de mano).
handicap ['hændikæp], *n.* obstáculo, desventaja.—*v.t.* impedir; perjudicar.
handiwork ['hændiwə:k], *n.* obra manual.
handkerchief ['hæŋkətʃif], *n.* pañuelo.
handle [hændl], *n.* asa; mango, asidero; tirador, *m.*—*v.t.* manejar; manosear; gobernar; comerciar en.
handshake ['hændʃeik], *n.* apretón (*m.*) de manos.
handsome ['hænsəm], *a.* hermoso, guapo; generoso.
handwriting ['hændraitiŋ], *n.* letra, escritura; puño y letra.
handy ['hændi], *a.* útil; hábil; a la mano.
hang [haeŋ], *n.* caída, modo de colgar; (*fam.*) idea general; maña; bledo.—*v.t.* *irr.* colgar; ***to — out***, tender; (*jur.*) ahorcar (*regular in this sense*).—*v.i.* colgar, pender; ***to — back***, quedar por indeciso; ***to — about***, haraganear; ***to — fire***, suspender el fuego; ***to — on***, agarrarse; esperar; ***to — out***, (*fam.*) habitar.
hangar ['hæŋə], *n.* hangar, *m.*
hanger ['hæŋə], *n.* percha, colgadero.
hanger-on ['hæŋər'ɔn], *n.* mogollón, pegote; secuaz, *m.*
hanging ['hæŋiŋ], *a.* colgante.—*n.* colgadura; (*jur.*) muerte (*f.*) en la horca.
hangman ['hæŋmən], *n.* verdugo.
hang-over ['hæŋouvə], *n.* (*fig.*, *fam.*) resaca.
hanker ['hæŋkə], *v.i.* pasar anhelo (***after***, por).
haphazard ['hæp'hæzəd], *a.* casual, fortuito; sin pies ni cabeza.—*adv.* al azar, al acaso.
hapless ['hæplis], *a.* desventurado.
happen ['hæpən], *v.i.* suceder, acontecer, pasar, ocurrir; ***to — to do***, hacer por casualidad.
happening ['hæpəniŋ], *n.* suceso acontecimiento.
happiness ['hæpinis], *n.* felicidad, *f.*
happy ['hæpi], *a.* feliz, contento; ***to be — to***, tener el gusto **de**; alegrarse de.
happy-go-lucky ['hæpigou'lʌki], *a.* irresponsable, a la buena de Dios.
harangue [hə'ræŋ], *n.* arenga.—*v.t.* arengar.
harass ['hærəs], *v.t.* hostigar, vejar.
harbinger ['hɑ:bindʒə], *n.* precursor, *m.*; presagio.
harbour ['hɑ:bə], *n.* puerto.—*v.t.* albergar; abrigar.
hard [hɑ:d], *a.* duro; difícil; penoso; — ***and fast***, riguroso.—*adv.* fuerte; duro; con ahinco; mucho.
harden ['hɑ:dən], *v.t.* endurecer.—*v.i.* -se.
hard-fought ['hɑ:dfɔ:t], *a.* reñido.
hard-hearted ['hɑ:d'hɑ:tid], *a.* duro, empedernido.
hardly ['hɑ:dli], *adv.* apenas; casi no.
hardness ['hɑ:dnis], *n.* dureza.
hardship ['hɑ:dʃip], *n.* fatiga, apuro; privación, *f.*
hard-up ['hɑ:d'ʌp], *a.* pelón, sin blanca.
hardware ['hɑ:dwɛə], *n.* quincalla; — ***stores***, ferretería.
hardy ['hɑ:di], *a.* robusto; (*bot.*) resistente.
hare [hɛə], *n.* (*zool.*) liebre, *f.*
hare-lipped ['hɛəlipd], *a.* labihendido.
haricot bean ['hærikou'bi:n], *n.* judía blanca.
hark [hɑ:k], *v.t.*, *v.i.* (*obs.*) escuchar.
harlequin ['hɑ:likwin], *n.* arlequín, *m.*
harlot ['hɑ:lət], *n.* ramera.
harm [hɑ:m], *n.* daño, mal, *m.*, perjuicio.—*v.t.* dañar.

harmful ['hɑ:mful], *a.* dañoso, nocivo, perjudicial.
harmless ['hɑ:mləs], *a.* inocuo, inofensivo.
harmonious [hɑ:'mounjəs], *a.* armonioso.
harmony ['hɑ:məni], *n.* armonía.
harness ['hɑ:nis], *n.* arneses, *m.pl.*, jaeces, *m.pl.*, arreos, *m.pl.*; guarniciones, *f.pl.* —*v.t.* enjaezar; explotar, captar (*energía*).
harp [hɑ:p], *n.* arpa.—*v.i.* ***to — on,*** porfiar en, machacar.
harpoon [hɑ:'pu:n], *n.* arpón, *m.*—*v.t.* arponear.
harridan ['hæridən], *n.* bruja, regañona.
harrow ['hærou], *n.* (*agr.*) grada, rastro.—*v.t.* gradar; (*fig.*) atormentar.
Harry ['hæri], *n.* Enrique, *m.*
harry ['hæri], *v.t.* acosar, perseguir.
harsh [hɑ:ʃ], *a.* áspero, acerbo; cruel.
hart [hɑ:t], *n.* (*zool., poet.*) ciervo.
harum-scarum ['hɛərəm'skɛərəm], *n.* tarambana, *m.f.*—*adv.* a troche y moche.
harvest ['hɑ:vist], *n.* cosecha.—*v.t., v.i.* cosechar, recoger.
has [hæz], [HAVE].
has-been ['hæzbi:n], *n.* (*fam.*) tagarote, *m.*
hash [hæʃ], *n.* picadillo; embrollo.—*v.t.* picar; embrollar.
hasp [hæsp], *n.* broche, *m.*, manecilla.
haste [heist], *n.* prisa; ***to make —,*** apresurarse.
hasten [heisn], *v.t.* apresurar, precipitar.—*v.i.* apresurarse.
hasty ['heisti], *a.* precipitado, apresurado.
hat [hæt], *n.* sombrero.
hatch [hætʃ], *n.* nidada; portezuela, trampa; (*naut.*) escotilla.—*v.t.* empollar; (*fig.*) tramar.—*v.i.* salir del cascarón (***out***).
hatchet ['hætʃit], *n.* hacha, destral, *m.*; ***to bury the —,*** hacer la paz *o* (las) paces.
hatchway ['hætʃwei], *n.* escotillón, *m.*, escotilla.
hate [heit], *n.* odio, aborrecimiento.—*v.t.* aborrecer, odiar.
hateful ['heitful], *a.* odioso; malévolo.
hatred ['heitrid], *n.* odio.
hatter ['hætə], *n.* sombrerero.
haughty ['hɔ:ti], *a.* altivo, altanero.
haul [hɔ:l], *n.* tirón; arrastre, *m.*; redada; trayecto.—*v.t.* arrastrar; trasportar; (*naut.*) virar.
haulage ['hɔ:lidʒ], *n.* trasporte, *m.*, acarreo.
haunch [hɔ:ntʃ], *n.* anca, cadera; pierna.
haunt [hɔ:nt], *n.* guarida, querencia.—*v.t.* frecuentar; vagar por; obsesionar; ***haunted,*** que tiene fantasmas.
Havana [hə'vænə], *n.* la Habana; habano, puro (*cigarro*).
have [hæv], *v.t. irr.* tener; traer; tomar; sentir; (*fam.*) estafar.—*auxiliary v.* haber; ***to — made,*** hacer hacer; mandar hacer; ***to — to,*** tener que; haber de; ***the have-nots,*** los desposeídos.
haven [heivn], *n.* asilo, abrigo; puerto.
haversack ['hævəsæk], *n.* mochila.
havoc ['hævək], *n.* estrago(s).
hawk [hɔ:k], *n.* (*orn.*) azor, *m.*—*v.t.* pregonar. —*v.i.* cazar con azores; buhonear.
hawker ['hɔ:kə], *n.* buhonero; cetrero.
hawk-eyed ['hɔ:kaid], *a.* de ojo avisor.
hawking ['hɔ:kiŋ], *n.* cetrería.
hawser ['hɔ:zə], *n.* (*naut.*) cable, *m.*, guindaleza.
hawthorn ['hɔ:θɔ:n], *n.* (*bot.*) espino blanco.
hay [hei], *n.* heno; ***— fever,*** alergia del heno; romadizo; ***to make — while the sun shines,*** machacar en caliente.
hayrick ['heirik], **haystack** ['heistæk], *n.* almiar, *m.*
haywire ['heiwaiə], *a.* (*fam., esp. U.S.*) desarreglado; gilí.—*adv.* desbaratadamente.
hazard ['hæzəd], *n.* riesgo, peligro; azar, *m.*—*v.t.* aventurar; arriesgar.
hazardous ['hæzədəs], *a.* arriesgado, peligroso.
haze [heiz], *n.* calina, niebla.
hazel ['heizəl], *n.* avellano.
hazel-nut ['heizəlnʌt], *n.* avellana.
hazy ['heizi], *a.* calinoso, anieblado; confuso vago.
H-bomb ['eitʃbɔm], *n.* bomba-H.
he [hi:], *a.* macho.—*pron.* él.
head [hed], *a.* principal; delantero.—*n.* cabeza; jefe, *m.*; cabecera (*cama*); res (*de ganado*), *f.*; (*educ.*) director, *m.*; crisis, *f.*; ***on his —,*** a su responsibilidad; —*pl.* cara (*de moneda*).—*v.t.* acaudillar; ser el primero de; encabezar; conducir.—*v.i.* dirigirse (***for, towards,*** a, hacia); ***to come to a —,*** llegar a una crisis final, madurar; ***to go to one's —,*** subir a la cabeza; ***to lose one's —,*** perder el equilibrio por pánico; ***to — off,*** interceptar.
headache ['hedeik], *n.* dolor (*m.*) de cabeza.
head-dress ['heddres], *n.* tocado.
head-first ['hed'fə:st], *adv.* de cabeza.
heading ['hediŋ], *n.* encabezamiento, título.
headland ['hedlənd], *n.* promontorio.
head-light ['hedlait], *n.* faro; linterna.
headline ['hedlain], *n.* cabecera, título.
headlong ['hedlɔŋ], *a.* precipitado.—*adv.* de cabeza, de bruces.
headmaster [hed'mɑ:stə], *n.* director, *m.*
headmistress [hed'mistris], *n.* directora.
head-on ['hed'ɔn], *a., adv.* de frente.
headphone ['hedfoun], *n.* auricular, *m.*
headquarters [hed'kwɔ:təz], *n.* jefatura (*mil.*) cuartel general, *m.*
headstrong ['hedstrɔŋ], *a.* testarudo, reacio.
headway ['hedwei], *n.* progreso, avance, *m.*
heady ['hedi], *a.* impetuoso; encabezado (*vino*).
heal [hi:l], *v.t.* sanar, curar.—*v.i.* sanar.
health [helθ], *n.* salud; sanidad (*pública etc.*), *f.*
healthy ['helθi], *a.* sano.
heap [hi:p], *n.* montón, *m.*—*v.t.* amontonar; colmar.
hear [hiə], *v.t. irr.* oír; (*jur.*) ver; ***to — about,*** oír hablar de; ***to — from,*** tener noticias de, saber algo de; ***to — of,*** oír hablar de; ***to — that,*** oír decir que.
heard [hə:d], [HEAR].
hearing ['hiəriŋ], *n.* oído; audición, *f.*; (*jur.*) examen (*m.*) de testigos; ***— aid,*** audífono.
hearsay ['hiəsei], *n.* rumor, *m.*, fama, voz común, *f.*; ***by —,*** de *o* por oídas.
hearse [hə:s], *n.* coche fúnebre, *m.*
heart [hɑ:t], *n.* corazón, *m.*; (*fig.*) gusto; ***at —,*** en el fondo; ***by —,*** de memoria; ***— and soul,*** con toda el alma; ***to lose —,*** perder ánimo.
heartache ['hɑ:teik], *n.* congoja, cordojo, pena.
heartbreak ['hɑ:tbreik], *n.* angustia, congoja.

hearten [hɑ:tn], *v.t.* alentar.
heartfelt ['hɑ:tfelt], *a.* sincero, cordial.
hearth [hɑ:θ], *n.* hogar, *m.*
heartless ['hɑ:tlis], *a.* desalmado; apocado.
heart-to-heart ['hɑ:ttu'hɑ:t], *a.* franco, íntimo.
hearty ['hɑ:ti], *a.* cordial; robusto; alegre; voraz.
heat [hi:t], *n.* calor, *m.*; (*sport*) carrera, corrida; (*zool.*) celo.—*v.t.* calentar; calefaccionar; acalorar.
heater ['hi:tə], *n.* calentador, *m.*; estufa.
heath [hi:θ], *n.* (*bot.*) brezo; brezal, *m.*
heathen ['hi:ðən], *a.*, *n.* pagano.
heather ['heðə], *n.* brezo.
heating ['hi:tiŋ], *n.* calefacción, *f.*
heave [hi:v], *n.* esfuerzo, alzadura; tirón, *m.*—*v.t.* alzar; lanzar con un esfuerzo; exhalar (*suspiro*).—*v.i.* ir subiendo y bajando; palpitar; vomitar; jadear; ***to — to***, (*naut.*) (*irregular in this sense*) ponerse al pairo.
heaven ['hevən], *n.* cielo; paraíso.
heavenly ['hevənli], *a.* celestial; (*astr.*) celeste.
heavy ['hevi], *a.* pesado; grueso; denso; fuerte; difícil; abundante; grave; triste; cansado.—*adv.* pesadamente.
heavy-weight ['heviweit], *a.* de gran peso; de gran importancia.—*n.* (*sport*) peso fuerte.
Hebrew ['hi:bru:], *a.*, *n.* hebreo.
heckle [hekl], *v.t.* importunar, interrumpir (*a un orador*).
hectic ['hektik], *a.* agitado, febril; (*med.*) hético.
hedge [hedʒ], *n.* seto vivo.—*v.t.* cercar; rodear; encerrar.—*v.i.* no comprometerse; esconderse; evitar una respuesta.
hedgehog ['hedʒhɔg], *n.* erizo.
heed [hi:d], *n.* atención, *f.*—*v.t.* hacer caso de.
heedless ['hi:dlis], *a.* desatento; incauto.
heel [hi:l], *n.* talón; calcañar; tacón, *m.*; ***head over heels,*** patas arriba; ***to take to one's heels,*** poner pies en polvorosa.
hefty ['hefti], *a.* (*fam.*) morrocotudo.
heifer ['hefə], *n.* vaquilla, novilla.
height [hait], *n.* altura; lo alto; colmo.
heighten [haitn], *v.t.* realzar.
heinous ['heinəs], *a.* nefando.
heir [ɛə], *n.* heredero.
heiress ['ɛəris], *n.* heredera.
heirloom ['ɛəlu:m], *n.* herencia, reliquia.
held [held], [HOLD].
helicopter ['helikɔptə], *n.* helicóptero.
hell [hel], *n.* infierno.
hellish ['heliʃ], *a.* infernal.
hello! [he'lou], *interj.* ¡ola!
helm [helm], *n.* caña del timón, timón, *m.*
helmet ['helmit], *n.* casco, yelmo.
helmsman ['helmzmən], *n.* timonel, *m.*
help [help], *n.* ayuda, socorro; remedio; ayudante, *m.f.*; obrero.—*v.t.* ayudar, socorrer; adelantar; servir; remediar; ***it can't be helped,*** no hay más remedio; ***— yourself,*** sírvase; ***they can't — doing it,*** no pueden menos de hacerlo.
helper ['helpə], *n.* ayudante, *m.f.*
helpful ['helpful], *a.* útil; provechoso.
helpless ['helplis], *a.* desvalido; desmañado; irremediable.
helter-skelter ['heltə-'skeltə], *adv.* a trochemoche, al tuntún.
hem [hem], *n.* dobladillo, bastilla.—*interj.* ¡eh!—*v.t.* bastillar; ***to — in,*** cercar y encerrar.
hemisphere ['hemisfiə], *n.* hemisferio.
hemlock ['hemlɔk], *n.* cicuta.
hemorrhage ['hemərid3], *n.* hemorragia.
hemp [hemp], *n.* cáñamo.
hen [hen], *n.* gallina; (*orn.*) hembra.
hence [hens], *adv.* de(sde) aquí; por lo tanto; ***two years —,*** de aquí a dos años.
henceforth [hens'fɔ:θ], **henceforward** [hens'fɔ:wəd], *adv.* de aquí en adelante.
henchman ['hentʃmən], *n.* secuaz, muñidor, compinche, *m.*
hen-coop ['henku:p], *n.* gallinero.
henpeck ['henpek], *v.t.* dominar (*a un marido*); ***henpecked husband,*** bragazas, *m.sg.*
Henry ['henri], *n.* Enrique, *m.*
her [hə:], *pron.* la; ella.—*poss. a.* su, de ella.
herald ['herəld], *n.* heraldo; precursor, *m.*—*v.t.* anunciar.
heraldry ['herəldri], *n.* blasonería, heráldica.
herb [hə:b], *n.* hierba (aromática); hortaliza.
herbalist ['hə:bəlist], *n.* herbolario, simplista, *m.*
Herculean [hə:kju'li:ən], *a.* hercúleo.
herd [hə:d], *n.* hato, manada, ganado; chusma, vulgo.—*v.t.* reunir, juntar.—*v.i.* juntarse, formar manada.
herdsman ['hə:dzmən], *n.* manadero, vaquero.
here [hiə], *adv.* aquí; acá; ***— and there;*** acá y acullá; ***— is*** (***are***), he aquí . . . por aquí.
hereabouts [hiərə'bauts], *adv.* por aquí.
hereafter [hiər'ɑ:ftə], *n.* la vida de más allá.—*adv.* de aquí en adelante.
hereby ['hiəbai], *adv.* por esto medio; (*jur.*) por la presente, por éstas.
hereditary [hi'reditəri], *a.* hereditario; heredero.
heredity [hi'rediti], *n.* herencia.
herein ['hiə'rin], *adv.* aquí dentro; adjunto.
hereon ['hiə'rɔn], *adv.* en *o* sobre esto.
heresy ['herəsi], *n.* herejía.
heretic ['herətik], *a.* herético.—*n.* hereje, *m.f.*
heretical [hə'retikəl], *a.* herético.
hereupon ['hiərə'pɔn], *adv.* en esto, a esto.
heritage ['heritid3], *n.* herencia.
hermetic [hə:'metik], *a.* hermético.
hermit ['hə:mit], *n.* ermitaño.
hermitage['hə:mitid3], *n.* ermita.
hero ['hiərou], *n.* héroe, *m.*
heroic [hi'rouik], *a.* heroico.—*n.pl.* temeridad, *f.*; extravagancia.
heroin ['herouin], *n.* (*med.*) heroína.
heroine ['herouin], *n.* heroína.
heroism ['herouizm], *n.* heroísmo.
heron ['herən], *n.* garza.
herring ['heriŋ], *n.* arenque, *m.*; ***red —,*** (*fig.*) distracción, *f.*
hers [hə:z], *poss. pron.* suyo, de ella; el suyo *etc.*
herself [hə:'self], *pron. r.* sí misma; se; ella misma.
hesitant ['hezitənt], *a.* vacilante, indeciso.
hesitate ['heziteit], *v.i.* vacilar (*to*, en).
hesitation [hezi'teiʃən], *n.* hesitación, vacilación, *f.*
heterodox ['hetərodɔks], *a.* heterodoxo.
heterodoxy ['hetərodɔksi], *n.* heterodoxia.
hew [hju:], *v.t. irr.* desbastar, hachear, dolar.
hewn [hju:n] [HEW].

heyday ['heidei], *n.* apogeo, época de grandeza.
hiatus [hai'eitəs], *n.* laguna; (*gram.*) hiato.
hibernate ['haibəneit], *v.i.* invernar; hibernar.
hibernation [haibə'neiʃən], *n.* invernación, *f.*
hiccough, hiccup ['hikʌp], *n.* hipo.—*v.i.* hipar.
hick [hik], *a.*, *n.* (*U.S.*) palurdo.
hid, hidden [hid, hidn], [HIDE (2)].
hide (1) [haid], *n.* cuero, pellejo, piel, *f.*; (*fam. fig.*) badana.
hide (2) [haid], *n.* escondite, *m.*, escondrijo.—*v.t. irr.* esconder, ocultar.—*v.i. irr.* -se.
hide-and-seek ['haidən'si:k], *n.* escondite, *m.*
hidebound ['haidbaund], *a.* fanático, reaccionario.
hideous ['hidiəs], *a.* horrendo, monstruoso.
hide-out ['haidaut], *n.* escondrijo.
hiding ['haidiŋ], *n.* ocultación, *f.*; retiro, escondrijo; (*fam.*) zurra; — ***place,*** escondrijo.
hierarchy ['haiərɑ:ki], *n.* jerarquía.
hieroglyph [haiəro'glif], *n.* jeroglífico.
hieroglyphic [haiəro'glifik], *a.*, *n.* jeroglífico.
high [hai], *a.* alto; arrogante; fuerte; sublime; subido; crecido; mayor (*misa*); — ***and dry,*** en seco; — ***and low,*** por todas partes;— ***and mighty,*** altanero.—*adv.* altamente, alto; arriba; ***it is — time to . . .,*** ya es hora de . . .
high-born ['haibɔ:n], *a.* linajudo.
highbrow ['haibrau], *a.*, *n.* erudito, culto.
high-flown ['haiflaun], *a.* retumbante, ampuloso.
high-handed ['haihændid], *a.* despótico.
highland ['hailənd], *a.* serrano, montañés.—*n.* sierra, meseta, montaña.
highlight ['hailait], *n.* punto más notable.—*v.t.* destacar.
highly ['haili], *adv.* altamente; sumamente; con aprecio; ***to think — of,*** tener gran concepto de.
highness ['hainis], *n.* altura; alteza (*título*).
high-spirited ['hai'spiritid], *a.* animoso, fogoso.
high-water ['hai'wɔ:tə], *n.* pleamar, *f.*, marea alta.
highway ['haiwei], *n.* camino real; carretera.
highwayman ['haiweimən], *n.* salteador, *m.*, bandolero.
hike [haik], *n.* caminata.—*v.i.* caminar por el campo.
hilarious [hi'lɛəriəs], *a.* regocijado, bullicioso.
hilarity [hi'læriti], *n.* regocijo, hilaridad, *f.*
hill [hil], *n.* colina, cuesta, cerro, collado.
hillock ['hilək], *n.* cerrejón, *m.*, montecillo.
hillside ['hilsaid], *n.* ladera.
hilly ['hili], *a.* montuoso.
hilt [hilt], *n.* puño; ***up to the —,*** totalmente.
him [him], *pron.* le, lo; él.
himself [him'self], *pron.* sí mismo; él mismo; se.
hind (1) [haind], *a.* trasero.
hind (2) [haind], *n.* (*zool.*) cierva.
hinder ['hində], *v.t.* estorbar, dificultar.
hindmost ['haindmoust], *a.* postrero.
hindrance ['hindrəns], *n.* obstáculo, estorbo.
hinge [hindʒ], *n.* bisagra; gozne, *m.*; charnela; (*also fig.*) quicio.—*v.t.* engoznar, enquiciar.—*v.i.* depender (***on,*** de).
hint [hint], *n.* indirecta; indicación, *f.*; consejo.—*v.t.* insinuar, indicar.—*v.i.* aludir (***at,*** a); pescar (***at***).
hinterland ['hintəlænd], *n.* interior, *m.*
hip (1) [hip], *n.* cadera (*de persona*).
hip (2) [hip], *n.* (*bot.*) agavanzo.
hip-bone ['hipboun], *n.* cía.
hippopotamus [hipə'pɔtəməs], *n.* hipopótamo.
hire [haiə], *n.* alquiler, *m.*, sueldo.—*v.t.* alquilar; (*U.S.*) ajornalar.
hireling ['haiəliŋ], *n.* alquilón, *m.*, alquiladizo.
his [hiz], *poss. pron.* su; de él; suyo; el suyo.
Hispanic [his'pænik], *a.* hispánico.
Hispanist ['hispənist], *n.* hispanista, *m.f.*
hiss [his], *n.* silbido, siseo.—*v.t.*, *v.i.* silbar sisear.
historian [his'tɔ:riən], *n.* historiador, *m.*
historic(al) [his'tɔrik(əl)], *a.* histórico.
history ['histəri], *n.* historia.
histrionic [histri:'ɔnik], *a.* histriónico, teatral.
hit [hit], *n.* golpe, *m.*; tiro; acierto; (*fam*). éxito.—*v.t. irr.* golpear, pegar; dar; acertar; dar en; dar con.—*v.i. irr.* tocar, chocar; ***to — on,*** dar con, encontrar.
hitch [hitʃ], *n.* parada, dificultad, *f.*, avería; tirón, *m.*; nudo.—*v.t.* acoplar, atar, amarrar; tirar; (*fam.*) casar.
hitch-hike ['hitʃhaik], *v.i.* hacer autostop.
hitch-hiking ['hitʃhaikiŋ], *n.* autostop, *m.*
hither ['hiðə], *adv.* (hacia) acá; — ***and thither,*** acá y allá.
hitherto [hiðə'tu:], *adv.* hasta ahora.
hive [haiv], *n.* colmena; (*fig.*) enjambre, *m.*
hoard [hɔ:d], *n.* repuesto, cúmulo, tesoro oculto.—*v.t.* amontonar, atesorar, acaparar.
hoarding ['hɔ:diŋ], *n.* amontonamiento; tablado de avisos; cerca provisional.
hoarfrost ['hɔ:frɔst], *n.* escarcha.
hoarse [hɔ:s], *a.* ronco, enronquecido.
hoary ['hɔ:ri], *a.* cano, canoso.
hoax [houks], *n.* pajarota(da), burla.—*v.t.* mistificar, burlar.
hobble [hɔbl], *n.* traba; cojera.—*v.t.* maniatar.—*v.i.* cojear.
hobby ['hɔbi], *n.* pasatiempo; comidilla; afición, *f.*
hobby-horse ['hɔbihɔ:s], *n.* caballito (*juguete*); (*fig.*) manía, tema predilecto.
hobnail ['hɔbneil], *n.* tachuela.
hobnob ['hɔbnɔb], *v.i.* codearse (***with,*** con).
hobo ['houbou], *n.* (*U.S.*) vagabundo.
hock (1) [hɔk], *n.* vino del Rin.
hock (2) [hɔk], *n.* corva, jarrete, *m.*—*v.t.* (*fam.*) empeñar.
hocus-pocus ['houkəs'poukəs], *n.* birlibirloque, *m.*, engaño.
hodge-podge ['hɔdʒpɔdʒ], *n.* baturrillo.
hod [hɔd], *n.* esparavel, *m.*; cubo (*para e carbón*).
hoe [hou], *n.* azadón, *m.*—*v.t.* sachar.
hog [hɔg], *n.* cerdo.—*v.t.* (*fam.*) tomar demasiado.
hoist [hɔist], *n.* cabria, grúa.—*v.t.* izar; alzar.
hold [hould], *n.* agarro; dominio; mango; (*naut.*) bodega.—*v.t. irr.* tener; sujetar; agarrar, coger; contener; sostener; celebrar; considerar.—*v.i. irr.* valer; quedar firme; pegarse; ***to — forth,*** perorar; ***to — one's own,*** defenderse; ***to — out,*** ofrecer; defenderse; durar; ***how many does***

***this car* —?** cuántos caben en este coche?
holder ['houldə], *n.* tenedor, posesor, *m.*; boquilla (*de pitillo*); titular (*de un documento*), *m.f.*; ***letterholder,*** portacartas, *m.sg.*
holding ['houldiŋ], *n.* tenencia, posesión, *f.*
hole [houl], *n.* agujero; hoyo; (*fam.*) casucha; (*fam.*) aprieto.—*v.t.* agujerear; cavar; taladrar; ***to — up,*** esconderse.
holiday ['hɔlidei], *n.* fiesta; vacación, *f.*; ***on —,*** de vacaciones; de veraneo; ***— maker,*** veraneante, *m.f.*
holiness ['houlinis], *n.* santidad, *f.*
Holland ['hɔlənd], *n.* Holanda.
hollow ['hɔlou], *a.* hueco, ahuecado; insincero. —*n.* hueco, cavidad, *f.*—*v.t.* ahuecar.
holly ['hɔli], *n.* (*bot.*) acebo.
holy ['houli], *n.* santo, sagrado.
homage ['hɔmidʒ], *n.* homenaje, *m.*
home [houm], *a.* doméstico, casero; natal, nacional.—*n.* casa, hogar, *m.*; asilo, hospicio; patria; ***at —,*** en casa; recepción (*fiesta*), *f.*—*v.i.* dirigirse, guiarse (***on,*** hacia).—*adv.* a casa; en casa; (*fig.*) en el blanco.
homely ['houmli], *a.* casero, llano, acogedor; (*U.S.*) feo.
home-made ['houm'meid], *a.* de fabricación casera, casero.
homesick ['houmsik], *a.* nostálgico.
homesickness [houm'siknis], *n.* morriña de la tierra, añoranza.
homestead ['houmsted], *n.* finca solariega; (*U.S.*) granja.
homeward(s) ['houmwəd(z)], *adv.* hacia casa.
home-work ['houmwə:k], *n.* (*educ.*) deber, *m.*
homicide ['hɔmisaid], *n.* homicida (*persona*), *m.f.*; homicidio (*crimen*).
homing missile ['houmiŋ'misail], *n.* proyectil autodirigido.
homogeneous [hɔmɔ'dʒi:njəs], *a.* homogéneo.
Honduran [hɔn'dju:rən], *a.*, *n.* hondureño.
Honduras [hɔn'dju:rəs], *n.* Honduras, *f.sg.*
honest ['ɔnist], *a.* honrado, recto, probo; sincero; fiel.
honesty ['ɔnisti], *n.* honradez, rectitud; sinceridad, *f.*
honey ['hʌni], *n.* miel, *f.*
honeycomb ['hʌnikoum], *n.* panal, *m.*—*v.t.* perforar, apanalar.
honeyed ['hʌnid], *a.* meloso; enmelado.
honeymoon ['hʌnimu:n], *n.* luna de miel.
honeysuckle ['hʌnisʌkl], *n.* madreselva.
honorary ['ɔnərəri], *a.* honorario.
honour ['ɔnə], *n.* honor, *m.*; honra.—*v.t.* honrar; aceptar.
honourable ['ɔnərəbl], *a.* honrado; honorable.
hood [hud], *n.* capucha, capriote, *m.*, caperuza; cubierta (*de coche*).—*v.t.* encapirotar.
hoodlum ['hu:dləm], *n.* (*U.S. fam.*) maleante, *m.*
hoodwink ['hudwiŋk], *v.t.* emprimar, engañar.
hoof [hu:f], *n.* (*pl.* **hooves**) casco, pezuña.
hook [huk], *n.* gancho; anzuelo (*para pescar*); corchete, *m.*; ***by — or by crook,*** a buenas o a malas, a todo trance.—*v.t.* enganchar; coger, pescar.—*v.i.* doblarse.
hooked [hukt], *a.* ganchudo; aguileña (*nariz*).
hooky ['huki], *n.* (*U.S.*) ***to play —,*** hacer novillos.
hooligan ['hu:ligən], *n.* gamberro.
hoop [hu:p], *n.* aro; collar, *m.*—*v.t.* enarcar.
hooray! [hu'rei], *interj.* ¡viva! ¡bravo!
hoot [hu:t], *n.* ululato; grito.—*v.t.* sisear; sonar.—*v.i.* ulular; reír a carcajadas.
hooter ['hu:tə], *n.* bocina.
hooves [hu:vz], [HOOF].
hop (1) [hɔp], *n.* brinco, saltito.—*v.i.* brincar; andar a saltitos; (*fam.*) viajar.
hop (2) [hɔp], *n.* (*bot.*) lúpulo, hombrecillo.
hope [houp], *n.* esperanza.—*v.t.*, *v.i.* esperar.
hopeful ['houpful], *a.* esperanzado; alentador; prometedor.
hopeless ['houplis], *a.* desesperado; desesperanzado.
horde [hɔ:d], *n.* horda.
horizon [hə'raizn], *n.* horizonte, *m.*
horizontal [hɔri'zɔntl], *a.*, *n.* horizontal, *f.*
hormone ['hɔ:moun], *n.* hormona, *f.*, hormón, *m.*
horn [hɔ:n], *n.* cuerno; (*mus.*) trompa.
hornet ['hɔ:nit], *n.* avispón, *m.*
horny ['hɔ:ni], *a.* córneo; calloso.
horoscope ['hɔrəskoup], *n.* horóscopo.
horrible ['hɔribl], *a.* horrible.
horrid ['hɔrid], *a.* horroroso; malísimo.
horrify ['hɔrifai], *v.t.* horripilar, horrorizar.
horror ['hɔrə], *n.* horror, *m.*
hors d'oeuvres ['ɔ:'də:vrə], *n.pl.* entremeses, *m.pl.*
horse [hɔ:s], *n.* caballo; (*mil.*) caballería; (*carp. etc.*) caballete, burro; potro; ***dark —,*** persona misteriosa *o* desconocida; ***to ride the high —,*** ser evanecido y mandón.
horseback ['hɔ:sbæk], *a.*, *adv.* ***on —,*** a caballo.
horse-chestnut ['hɔ:s'tʃesnʌt], *n.* castaño de Indias (*árbol*); castaña de Indias (*fruta*).
horse-dealer ['hɔ:s'di:lə], *n.* chalán, caballista, *m.*
horse-laugh ['hɔ:slɑ:f], *n.* carcajada.
horseman ['hɔ:smən], *n.* jinete, *m.*
horseplay ['hɔ:splei], *n.* payasada.
horsepower ['hɔ:spauə], *n.* caballo de vapor *o* de fuerza.
horseshoe ['hɔ:sʃu:], *n.* herradura.
horsewhip ['hɔ:shwip], *n.* látigo.—*v.t.* azotar, zurriagar.
horsewoman ['hɔ:swumən], *n.* amazona.
hors(e)y ['hɔ:si], *a.* caballuno; caballar.
horticulture ['hɔ:tikʌltʃə], *n.* horticultura.
hose [houz], *n.* manga, manguera (*para el agua*); calzas, *f.pl.*, calceta (*ropa*).
hosiery ['houzjəri], *n.* medias; calcetería.
hospitable ['hɔspitəbl], *a.* hospitalario.
hospital ['hɔspitl], *n.* hospital, *m.*, clínica.
hospitality [hɔspi'tæliti], *n.* hospitalidad, *f.*
host (1) [houst], *n.* huésped, *m.*; mesonero; anfitrión, *m.*
host (2) [houst], *n.* hueste (*multitud*), *f.*
hostage ['hɔstidʒ], *n.* rehén, *m.*
hostel ['hɔstəl], *n.* parador, *m.*; residencia.
hostess ['houstis], *n.* huéspeda; patrona; (*aer.*) azafata.
hostile ['hɔstail], *a.* hostil, enemigo.
hostility [hɔs'tiliti], *n.* hostilidad, *f.*
hot [hɔt], *a.* caliente; cálido (*clima*); caluroso (*tiempo*); ardiente, apasionado; (*cul.*) picante; (*fam.*) insoportable; ***to be —,*** hacer calor (*tiempo*), tener calor (*persona*) ***— air,*** palabrería; ***— water,*** (*fam.*) apuro, aprieto.

hotbed ['hɔtbed], *n.* (*agr.*) almajara; (*fig.*) sementera.
hotel [(h)ou'tel], *n.* hotel, *m.*
hotelier [(h)ou'teliə], *n.* hotelero.
hothead ['hɔthed], *n.* alborotador, *m.*, temerario.
hotheaded ['hɔthedid], *a.* temerario.
hothouse ['hɔthaus], *n.* invernáculo.
hound [haund], *n.* podenco, sabueso.—*pl.* jauría.
hour [auə], *n.* hora.
houri ['huəri], *n.* hurí, *f.*
hourly ['auəli], *a.*, *adv.* (a) cada hora; por horas.
house [haus], *n.* casa; (*pol.*) cámara; (*fig.*) público, entrada; — ***arrest,*** arresto domiciliario; — ***coat,*** bata; ***House of Commons,*** Cámara de los Comunes.— [hauz], *v.t.* dar casa a, alojar; (*mech.*) encajar.
house-breaking ['hausbreikiŋ], *n.* escalo.
household ['haushould], *a.* casero, familiar.—*n.* casa, familia.
housekeeper ['hauski:pə], *n.* ama de llaves; mujer (*f.*) de casa.
housekeeping ['hauski:piŋ], *n.* gobierno doméstico.
housemaid ['hausmeid], *n.* criada.
house-warming ['hauswɔ:miŋ], *n.* estreno (de una casa).
housewife ['hauswaif], *n.* madre de familia, mujer casera.
house-work ['hauswə:k], *n.* quehaceres domésticos, limpieza.
housing ['hauziŋ], *n.* vivienda; casas; (*mech.*) caja, encaje, *m.*
hove [houv], [HEAVE].
hovel ['hɔvəl], *n.* casucha, choza mala.
hover ['hɔvə], *v.i.* cernerse; rondar; colgar.
hovercraft ['hɔvəkrɑ:ft], *n.* aereodeslizador, *m.*
how [hau], *adv.*, *conj.* como, de qué modo; cuán, cuanto;— ***many,*** cuantos; — ***much,*** cuanto.—*interj.* ¡cómo! ¡qué!—*interrog.* ¿cómo? ¿cuánto? — ***far is it to X?*** ¿cuánto hay de aquí a X?
however [hau'evə], *adv.* sin embargo; como quiera; — ***big it is,*** por grande que sea.
howitzer ['hauitsə], *n.* obús, *m.*
howl [haul], *n.* aullido, alarido.—*v.i.* aullar, chillar; soltar carcajadas.
howler ['haulə], *n.* (*fam.*) patochada, gazapo.
hoyden [hɔidn], *n.* tunantuela.
hub [hʌb], *n.* (*mech.*) cubo; (*fig.*) eje, *m.*
hubbub ['hʌbʌb], *n.* alboroto, bulla.
huckster ['hʌkstə], *n.* (*U.S.*) buhonero.
huddle [hʌdl], *n.* tropel, *m.*; (*fam.*) conchabanza.—*v.i.* acurrucarse; arracimarse.
hue (1) [hju:], *n.* matiz, tinte, *m.*
hue (2) [hju:], *n.* — ***and cry,*** vocería, alarma.
huff [hʌf], *n.* enfado súbito.—*v.t.* enojar; soplar (*juego de damas*).
hug [hʌg], *n.* apretón, abrazo fuerte, *m.*—*v.t.* abrazar, apretar; navegar muy cerca de.
huge [hju:dʒ], *a.* enorme, inmenso.
hulk [hʌlk], *n.* casco; carraca; masa.
hulking ['hʌlkiŋ], *a.* grueso, pesado, enorme.
hull [hʌl], *n.* casco; armazón, *f.*
hullabaloo [hʌləbə'lu:], *n.* baraúnda, bulla.
hum [hʌm], *n.* zumbido; tarareo.—*v.t.* canturrear, tararear.—*v.i.* canturrear; zumbar.
human ['hju:mən], *a.*, *n.* humano.
humane [hju:'mein], *a.* humanitario.
humanist ['hju:mənist], *n.* humanista, *m.f.*
humanitarian [hju:mæni'tɛəriən], *a.*, *n.* humanitario.
humanity [hju:'mæniti], *n.* humanidad, *f.*
humble [hʌmbl], *a.* humilde.—*v.t.* humillar; ***to eat — pie,*** desdecirse, someterse.
humbleness ['hʌmblnəs], *a.* humilidad, *f.*
humbug ['hʌmbʌg], *n.* bambolla; patraña; farsante (*persona*), *m.f.*
humdrum ['hʌmdrʌm], *a.* monótono, pesado, rutinario.
humid ['hju:mid], *a.* húmedo.
humidity [hju:'miditi], *n.* humedad, *f.*
humiliate [hju:'milieit], *v.t.* humillar, degradar.
humiliation [hju:mili'eiʃən], *n.* humillación, *f.*
humility [hju:'militi], *n.* humilidad, *f.*
humming-bird ['hʌmiŋbə:d], *n.* (*orn.*) colibrí, picaflor, *m.*
humorist ['hju:mərist], *n.* humorista, *m.f.*
humorous ['hju:mərəs], *a.* humorístico, chistoso.
humour ['hju:mə], *n.* humor, *m.*—*v.t.* seguir el humor de, acomodarse a.
hump [hʌmp], *n.* joroba, corcova.—*v.t.* encorvar.
humpback ['hʌmpbæk], *n.* joroba; jorobado (*persona*).
Hun [hʌn], *n.* huno; (*pej.*) alemán, *m.*
hunch [hʌntʃ], *n.* joroba; (*fam.*) corazonada.—*v.t.* encorvar.
hunchback ['hʌntʃbæk], *n.* joroba; jorobado (*persona*).
hunchbacked ['hʌntʃbækt], *a.* jorobado.
hundred ['hʌndrəd], *a.* cien; ciento.—*n.* ciento; centenar.
hundredth ['hʌndrədθ], *a.*, *n.* centésimo.
hundredweight ['hʌndrədweit], *n.* quintal (50·8 *kgs.*), *m.*
hung [hʌŋ] [HANG].
Hungarian [hʌŋ'gɛəriən], *a.*, *n.* húngaro.
Hungary ['hʌŋgəri], *n.* Hungría.
hunger ['hʌŋgə], *n.* hambre, *f.*—*v.i.* hambrear; anhelar (***for***).
hungry ['hʌŋgri], *a.* hambriento (***for,*** de); ***to be —,*** tener hambre.
hunt [hʌnt], *n.* caza; cacería; busca.—*v.t.* cazar; buscar.—*v.i.* cazar, buscar (***for***).
hunter ['hʌntə], *n.* cazador, *m.*; perro *o* caballo de caza.
hunting ['hʌntiŋ], *a.* de caza; cazador.—*n.* caza; cacería, montería.
huntsman ['hʌntsmən], *n.* cazador, *m.*; montero.
hurdle [hə:dl], *n.* zarzo; (*also sport*) valla; (*fig.*) obstáculo.—*v.t.* saltar, vencer; cercar con vallas.
hurdy-gurdy ['hə:di'gə:di], *n.* (*mus.*) organillo, zanfonía.
hurl ['hə:l], *v.t.* lanzar, arrojar.
hurly-burly ['hə:li'bə:li], *n.* trulla, alboroto.
hurrah! [hu:'rɑ:], **hurray!** [hu:'rei], *interj.* ¡viva!
hurricane ['hʌrikən], *n.* huracán, *m.*
hurry ['hʌri], *n.* prisa.—*v.t.* dar prisa a, apresurar; hacer con prisa.—*v.i.* or **hurry up,** darse prisa, apresurarse.
hurt [hə:t], *n.* daño; herida; dolor; mal, *m.*—*v.t. irr.* dañar; doler; lastimar; herir.—*v.i. irr.* doler, hacer daño.

hurtful ['hə:tful], *a.* dañoso; malicioso.
hurtle [hə:tl], *v.t.* arrojar.—*v.i.* arrojarse; chocar.
husband ['hʌzbənd], *n.* marido, esposo.—*v.t.* dirigir; economizar; cultivar.
husbandry ['hʌzbəndri], *n.* labranza, granjería; buen gobierno, economía.
hush [hʌʃ], *n.* silencio, quietud, *f.*—*v.t.* callar. —*v.i.* callar(se); ***to — up,*** echar tierra a (*escándalo etc.*).—*interj.* ¡chitón! ¡chito!
hush-hush ['hʌʃ'hʌʃ], *a.* muy secreto.
husk [hʌsk], *n.* cáscara, vaina, hollejo.—*v.t.* pelar, mondar.
husky ['hʌski], *a.* ronco, rauco (*voz*); (*fam.*) fortachón.—*n.* (*zool.*) perro esquimal.
hussy ['hʌsi, 'hʌzi], *n.* tunanta, descarada.
hustle [hʌsl], *n.* prisa; bulla.—*v.t.* empujar; dar prisa a.—*v.i.* darse prisa; patullar.
hut [hʌt], *n.* cabaña, choza, cobertizo.
hutch [hʌtʃ], *n.* conejera; arca; cabaña.
hyacinth ['haiəsinθ], *n.* jacinto.
hybrid ['haibrid], *a.*, *n.* híbrido.
hydrant ['haidrənt], *n.* boca de riego.
hydraulic [hai'drɔ:lik], *a.* hidráulico.
hydrochloric [haidro'klɔrik], *a.* clorhídrico.
hydroelectric [haidroi'lektrik], *a.* hidroeléctrico.
hydrogen ['haidrədʒən], *n.* hidrógeno; ***— bomb,*** bomba de hidrógeno.
hyena [hai'i:na], *n.* hiena.
hygiene ['haidʒi:n], *n.* higiene, *f.*
hygienic [hai'dʒi:nik], *a.* higiénico.
hymn [him], *n.* himno.
hyper- ['haipə], *prefix.* hiper-, excesivamente.
hyperbole [hai'pə:bəli], *n.* hipérbole, *f.*
hyphen ['haifən], *n.* guión, *m.*
hyphenate ['haifəneit], *v.t.* escribir con guión, insertar un guión.
hypnosis [hip'nousis], *n.* hipnosis, *f.*
hypnotic [hip'nɔtik], *a.*, *n.* hipnótico.
hypnotism ['hipnətizm], *n.* hipnotismo.
hypnotize ['hipnətaiz], *v.t.* hipnotizar.
hypochondriac [haipo'kɔndriæk], *a.*, *n.* hipocondríaco.
hypocrisy [hi'pɔkrisi], *n.* hipocresía.
hypocrite ['hipəkrit], *n.* hipócrita, *m.f.*
hypocritical [hipə'critikəl], *a.* hipocrítico.
hypodermic [haipo'də:mik], *a.* hipodérmico.—*n.* (jeringa) hipodérmica.
hypothesis [hai'pɔθisis], *n.* hipótesis, *f.*
hypothetical [haipo'θetikəl], *a.* hipotético.
hysteria [his'tiəriə], *n.* histeria, histerismo.
hysteric(al) [his'terik(əl)], *a.* histérico.
hysterics [his'teriks], *n.pl.* histerismo, paroxismo histérico.

I

I, (1) **i** [ai], *n.* novena letra del alfabeto inglés.
I (2) [ai], *pron.* yo.
Iberian [ai'biəriən], *a.* ibérico.—*n.* íbero.
ibex ['aibeks], *n.* íbice, *m.*, cabra montés.
ice [ais], *n.* hielo; helado; (*cul.*) garapiña.—*v.t.* helar; poner hielo en; garapiñar.—*v.i.* helarse.
iceberg ['aisbə:g], *n.* iceberg, *m.*, témpano de hielo.
icebox ['aisbɔks], *n.* (*U.S.*) nevera.
ice-cream ['ais'kri:m], *n.* helado.
Iceland ['aislənd], *n.* Islandia.
Icelander ['aislændə], *n.* islandés (*persona*), *m.*
Icelandic [ais'lændik], *a.* islandés.—*n.* islandés (*idioma*), *m.*
icicle ['aisikl], *n.* carámbano, canelón, *m.*
icing ['aisiŋ], *n.* garapiña, costra de azúcar; (*aer.*) helamiento.
iconoclast [ai'kɔnoklæst, ai'kɔnoklɑ:st], *n.* iconoclasta, *m.f.*
icy ['aisi], *a.* helado, frío.
I'd [aid] [I WOULD, I SHOULD, I HAD].
idea [ai'diə], *n.* idea.
ideal [ai'diəl], *a.*, *n.* ideal, *m.*
idealist [ai'diəlist], *n.* idealista, *m.f.*
idealistic [aidiə'listik], *a.* idealista.
idealize [ai'diəlaiz], *v.t.* idealizar.
identical [ai'dentikəl], *a.* idéntico.
identify [ai'dentifai], *v.t.* identificar.
identity [ai'dentiti], *n.* identidad, *f.*
ideology [aidi'ələdʒi], *n.* ideología.
idiocy ['idiəsi], *n.* idiotez, necedad, *f.*
idiom ['idjəm], *n.* modismo, idiotismo; lenguaje, *m.*; estilo.
idiot ['idiət], *n.* idiota, *m.f.*
idiotic [idi'ɔtik], *a.* idiota.
idle [aidl], *a.* ocioso; perezoso; vano (*inútil*). —*v.t.* ***to — away,*** malgastar (*tiempo*).—*v.i.* holgazanear; marchar despacio.
idleness ['aidlnis], *n.* ociosidad; pereza; paro.
idler ['aidlə], *n.* holgazán, haragán, *m.*
idol [aidl], *n.* ídolo.
idolater [ai'dɔlətə], *n.* idólatra, *m.*
idolatress [ai'dɔlətris], *n.* idólatra, *f.*
idolatry [ai'dɔlətri], *n.* idolatría.
idolize ['aidəlaiz], *v.t.* idolatrar.
idyll ['idil], *n.* idilio.
if [if], *conj.* si; ***— so,*** si es así.—*n.* (*fam.*) pero, duda.
igloo ['iglu:], *n.* iglú, *m.*
ignite [ig'nait], *v.t.* encender.—*v.i.* -se.
ignition [ig'niʃən], *n.* encendido, ignición, *f.*
ignoble [ig'noubl], *a.* innoble; infame.
ignominious [ignə'miniəs], *a.* ignominioso.
ignominy ['ignəmini], *n.* ignominia.
ignoramus [ignə'reiməs], *n.* ignorante, *m.f.*
ignorance ['ignərəns], *n.* ignorancia.
ignorant ['ignərənt], *a.* ignorante; indocto; ***to be — of,*** ignorar, desconocer.
ignore [ig'nɔ:], *v.t.* no hacer caso de, desconocer, desairar; rechazar.
I'll [ail] [I WILL, I SHALL].
ill [il], *a.* enfermo, malo.—*n.* mal, *m.*; ***to take —,*** tomar a mal.—*adv.* mal; poco.
ill- [il], *prefix.* mal-, des-.
illegal [i'li:gəl], *a.* ilegal.
illegitimacy [ili'dʒitiməsi], *n.* ilegitimidad, *f.*
illegitimate [ili'dʒitimit], *a.* ilegítimo.
ill-fated [il'feitid], *a.* malogrado.
ill-gotten [il'gotən], *a.* mal adquirido.
illicit [i'lisit], *a.* ilícito.
illiteracy [i'litərəsi], *n.* analfabetismo; incultura.
illiterate [i'litərit], *a.* analfabeto; iliterato.
ill-mannered [il'mænəd], *a.* malcriado, mal educado, descortés.
illness ['ilnis], *n.* enfermedad, *f.*
illogical [i'lɔdʒikəl], *a.* ilógico.

illogicality [ilɔdʒi'kæliti], *n.* falta de lógica.
ill-tempered [il'tempəd], *a.* desabrido, de mal genio.
ill-timed [il'taimd], *a.* inoportuno.
illuminate [i'lju:mineit], *v.t.* iluminar; alumbrar.
illumination [ilju:mi'neiʃən], *n.* iluminación, *f.*; alumbrado.
illumine [i'lju:min], *v.t.* iluminar, alumbrar.
ill-use [il'ju:z], *v.t.* maltratar.
illusion [i'lju:ʒən], *n.* ilusión, *f.*
illustrate ['iləstreit], *v.t.* ilustrar.
illustration [iləs'treiʃən], *n.* ilustración, *f.*; grabado, lámina.
illustrious [i'lʌstriəs], *a.* ilustre, preclaro.
I'm [aim] [I AM].
image ['imidʒ], *n.* imagen, *f.*; (*gram.*) metáfora.
imaginary [i'mædʒinəri], *a.* imaginario.
imagination [imædʒi'neiʃən], *n.* imaginación, *f.*
imagine [i'mædʒin], *v.t.*, *v.i.* imaginar(se).
imbecile ['imbisi:l], *a.*, *n.* imbécil, *m.f.*
imbed [im'bed], *v.t.* enclavar, encajar.
imbibe [im'baib], *v.t.* beber, embeber(se en *o* de), empapar(se de).
imbroglio [im'brouliou], *n.* embrollo, enredo.
imbue [im'bju:], *v.t.* imbuir (***with,*** de, en).
imitate ['imiteit], *v.t.* imitar, remedar.
imitation [imi'teiʃən], *n.* imitación, *f.*
imitator ['imiteitə], *n.* imitador, *m.*
immaculate [i'mækjulit], *a.* inmaculado.
immaterial [imə'tiəriəl], *a.* sin importancia; inmaterial.
immature [imə'tjuə], *a.* inmaturo, verde.
immaturity [imə'tjuəriti], *n.* inmadurez, *f.*
immediate [i'mi:djət], *a.* inmediato.
immediately [i'mi:djətli], *adv.* en seguida, inmediatamente.
immense [i'mens], *a.* inmenso, vasto.
immigrant ['imigrənt], *a.*, *n.* inmigrante, *m.f.*
immigration [imi'greiʃən], *n.* inmigración, *f.*
imminent ['iminənt], *a.* inminente.
immobilize [i'moubilaiz], *v.t.* inmovilizar.
immoderate [i'mɔdərit], *a.* inmoderado.
immodest [i'mɔdist], *a.* inmodesto, impúdico.
immodesty [i'mɔdisti], *n.* inmodestia, impudicia.
immoral [i'mɔrəl], *a.* inmoral.
immorality [imə'ræliti], *n.* inmoralidad, *f.*
immortal [i'mɔ:təl], *a.* inmortal.
immortality [imɔ:'tæliti], *n.* inmortalidad, *f.*
immortalize [i'mɔ:təlaiz], *v.t.* inmortalizar.
immune [i'mju:n], *a.* inmune (***to,*** contra).
immunize ['imjunaiz], *v.t.* inmunizar.
imp [imp], *n.* diablillo, duende, *m.*
impact ['impækt], *n.* choque, *m.*, impacto.
impair [im'pɛə], *v.t.* empeorar, perjudicar.
impale [im'peil], *v.t.* empalar, atravesar.
impart [im'pɑ:t], *v.t.* comunicar; hacer saber.
impartial [im'pɑ:ʃəl], *a.* imparcial.
impassable [im'pɑ:səbl], *a.* intransitable.
impasse [im'pɑ:s], *n.* callejón (*m.*) sin salida.
impassive [im'pæsiv], *a.* impasible.
impatience [im'peiʃəns], *n.* impaciencia.
impatient [im'peiʃənt], *a.* impaciente.
impeach [im'pi:tʃ], *v.t.* acusar, encausar, denunciar.
impeccable [im'pekəbl], *a.* impecable.
impede [im'pi:d], *v.t.* dificultar, impedir.
impediment [im'pedimənt], *n.* impedimento.
impel [im'pel], *v.t.* impeler, impulsar.
impend [im'pend], *v.i.* amenazar; pender; ser inminente.
impenitent [im'penitənt], *a.*, *n.* impenitente.
imperative [im'peritiv], *a.* imperativo, imperioso.—*n.* (*gram.*) imperativo.
imperfect [im'pə:fikt], *a.*, *n.* imperfecto.
imperfection [impə'fekʃən], *n.* imperfección, *f.*; defecto.
imperforate [im'pə:fərit], *a.* sin dentar (*sello*).
imperial [im'piəriəl], *a.* imperial.
imperialism [im'piəriəlizm], *n.* imperialismo.
impersonal [im'pə:sənəl], *a.* impersonal.
impersonate [im'pə:səneit], *v.t.* imitar, fingir ser; personificar.
impertinent [im'pə:tinənt], *a.* impertinente.
impervious [im'pə:vjəs], *a.* impermeable; impersuasible.
impetuous [im'petjuəs], *a.* impetuoso.
impetus ['impitəs], *n.* ímpetu, *m.*
impinge [im'pindʒ], *v.i.* tocar, incidir (***on,*** en).
impious ['impiəs], *a.* impío.
implacable [im'plækəbl], *a.* implacable.
implant [im'plɑ:nt], *v.t.* (im)plantar.
implement ['implimənt], *n.* herramienta, utensilio.—['impliment], *v.t.* poner en ejecución.
implicate ['implikeit], *v.t.* implicar, enredar.
implication [impli'keiʃən], *n.* insinuación; implicación, *f.*
implicit [im'plisit], *a.* implícito; absoluto.
implied [im'plaid], *a.* implícito (***by,*** en).
implore [im'plɔ:], *v.t.* suplicar, implorar.
imply [im'plai], *v.t.* implicar, suponer; insinuar, dar a entender.
impolite [impə'lait], *a.* descortés.
import ['impɔ:t], *n.* importación, *f.*; importancia; tenor, *m.*, sentido.—[im'pɔ:t], *v.t.* importar.
importance [im'pɔ:təns], *n.* importancia.
important [im'pɔ:tənt], *a.* importante.
importune [im'pɔ:tju:n], *v.t.* importunar.
impose [im'pouz], *v.t.* imponer; abusar (***on,*** de).
imposing [im'pouziŋ], *a.* imponente.
imposition [impə'ziʃən], *n.* imposición, *f.*; abuso; (*educ.*) tarea extraordinaria.
impossibility [impɔsi'biliti], *n.* imposibilidad, *f.*
impossible [im'pɔsibl], *a.* imposible.
impostor [im'pɔstə], *n.* impostor, *m.*
impotence ['impətəns], *n.* impotencia.
impotent ['impətənt], *a.* impotente.
impoverish [im'pɔvəriʃ], *v.t.* empobrecer.
impracticable [im'præktikəbl], *a.* impracticable, infactible.
impractical [im'præktikəl], *a.* irrealizable; poco práctico.
impregnable [im'pregnəbl], *a.* inexpugnable.
impregnate [im'pregneit], *v.t.* impregnar.
impresario [impre'sɑ:riou], *n.* empresario.
impress [im'pres], *v.t.* imprimir; impresionar; inculcar.
impression [im'preʃən], *n.* impresión, *f.*
impressive [im'presiv], *a.* impresionante.

imprint ['imprint], *n.* pie (*m.*) de imprenta; marca.—[im'print], *v.t.* estampar, imprimir, grabar.
imprison [im'prizən], *v.t.* encarcelar.
imprisonment [im'prizənmənt], *n.* encarcelamiento.
improbable [im'prɔbəbl], *a.* improbable.
impromptu [im'prɔmptju:], *a.* impremeditado, de improviso.—*n.* improvisación, *f.* —*adv.* improvisando.
improper [im'prɔpə], *a.* indecoroso; impropio.
impropriety [imprə'praiəti], *n.* indecencia; impropiedad, *f.*
improve [im'pru:v], *v.t.* mejorar; perfeccionar (*on*).—*v.i.* mejorar(se); perfeccionarse.
improvement [im'pru:vmənt], *n.* mejoramiento; mejoría; mejora.
improvise ['imprəvaiz], *v.t.*, *v.i.* improvisar.
imprudent [im'pru:dənt], *a.* imprudente.
impudence ['impjudəns], *n.* impudencia, desfachatez, *f.*
impudent ['impjudənt], *a.* impudente, desfachatado.
impugn [im'pju:n], *v.t.* impugnar, poner en tela de juicio.
impulse ['impʌls], *n.* impulso.
impulsive [im'pʌlsiv], *a.* impulsivo.
impunity [im'pju:niti], *n.* impunidad, *f.*
impure [im'pjuə], *a.* impuro.
impurity [im'pjuəriti], *n.* impureza; impuridad, *f.*
impute [im'pju:t], *v.t.* imputar.
in [in], *prep.* en; dentro de; de; con.—*adv.* en casa; dentro.
in- [in-], *prefix.* in-, des-.
inability [inə'biliti], *n.* inhabilidad; incapacidad, *f.*
inaccessible [inæk'sesibl], *a.* inasequible; inaccesible.
inaccuracy [in'ækjurisi], *n.* incorreción, inexactitud, *f.*
inaccurate [in'ækjurit], *a.* incorrecto, inexacto.
inactive [in'æktiv], *a.* inactivo.
inadequate [in'ædikwit], *a.* inadecuado, insuficiente.
inadvertent [inəd'və:tənt], *a.* inadvertido.
inadvisable [inəd'vaizəbl], *a.* no aconsejable, imprudente.
inane [in'ein], *a.* vano, inane, sandio.
inanimate [in'ænimit], *a.* inanimado.
inapplicable [in'æplikəbl], *a.* inaplicable.
inappropriate [inə'proupriit], *a.* poco apropriado, inadecuado.
inarticulate [inɑ:'tikjulit], *a.* inarticulado; incapaz de expresarse.
inasmuch as [inəz'mʌtʃəz], *conj.* visto que; en cuanto.
inattentive [inə'tentiv], *a.* desatento.
inaudible [in'ɔ:dibl], *a.* inaudible.
inaugurate [in'ɔ:gjureit], *v.t.* inaugurar.
inauspicious [inɔ:'spiʃəs], *a.* desfavorable, poco propicio.
inborn ['inbɔ:n], *a.* innato.
inbreed ['in'bri:d], *v.t. irr.* (*conjug. like* BREED) engendrar dentro de la misma estirpe; dotar de . . . al nacer.
Inca ['iŋkə], *a.* incaico.—*n.* inca, *m.f.*
incantation [inkæn'teiʃən], *n.* conjuro.
incapable [in'keipəbl], *a.* incapaz.
incapacitate [inkə'pæsiteit], *v.t.* incapacitar.
incarcerate [in'kɑ:səreit], *v.t.* encarcelar, aprisionar.
incarnate [in'kɑ:nit], *a.* encarnado.—['inkɑ:neit], *v.t.* encarnar.
incarnation [inkɑ:'neiʃən], *n.* encarnación, *f.*
incautious [in'kɔ:ʃəs], *a.* incauto, descuidado.
incendiary [in'sendjəri], *a.*, *n.* incendiario.
incense (1) ['insens], *n.* incienso.—*v.t.* incensar.
incense (2) [in'sens], *v.t.* encolerizar, exasperar.
incentive [in'sentiv], *a.* incentivo.—*n.* incentivo, aliciente, *m.*
inception [in'sepʃən], *n.* comienzo, estreno.
incessant [in'sesənt], *a.* incesante, sin cesar.
incest ['insest], *n.* incesto.
inch [intʃ], *n.* pulgada; ***within an — of***, a dos dedos de.—*v.t.*, *v.i.* mover(se) poco a poco.
incident ['insidənt], *a.*, *n.* incidente, *m.*
incidental [insi'dentl], *a.* incidental.
incinerate [in'sinəreit], *v.t.* incinerar.
incipient [in'sipiənt], *a.* incipiente.
incision [in'siʒən], *n.* incisión, *f.*
incite [in'sait], *v.t.* incitar, instigar.
inclement [in'klemənt], *a.* inclemente.
inclination [inkli'neiʃən], *n.* inclinación, *f.*
incline ['inklain], *n.* declive, *m.*—[in'klain], *v.t.* inclinar.—*v.i.* inclinarse (**to**, a).
include [in'klu:d], *v.t.* incluir.
inclusive [in'klu:siv], *a.* inclusivo.
incognito [in'kɔgnitou], *a.* incógnito.—*adv.* de incógnito.
incoherent [inkou'hiərənt], *a.* incoherente.
income ['inkəm], *n.* renta, ingresos, *m.pl.* rédito.
income-tax ['inkəmtæks], *n.* impuesto de utilidades, impuesto sobre renta.
incommode [inkə'moud], *v.t.* incomodar.
incompatible [inkəm'pætibl], *a.* incompatible.
incompetence [in'kəmpitəns], *n.* incompetencia.
incompetent [in'kəmpitənt], *a.* incompetente.
incomplete [inkəm'pli:t], *a.* incompleto.
incomprehensible [inkəmpri'hensibl], *a.* incomprensible.
inconceivable [inkən'si:vəbl], *a.* inconcebible.
inconclusive [inkən'klu:siv], *a.* inconcluyente, indeciso.
incongruity [inkɔŋ'gru:iti], *n.* incongruencia.
incongruous [in'kɔŋgruəs], *a.* incongruo.
inconsequent [in'kɔnsikwənt], *a.* inconsecuente.
inconsequential [inkɔnsi'kwenʃəl], *a.* inconsecuente; sin importancia.
inconsiderable [inkən'sidərəbl], *a.* insignificante.
inconsiderate [inkən'sidərit], *a.* desconsiderado.
inconsistent [inkən'sistənt], *a.* inconsistente, inconsecuente.
inconstant [in'kɔnstənt], *a.* inconstante.
incontinent [in'kɔntinənt], *a.* incontinente.
inconvenience [inkən'vi:niəns], *n.* incomodidad, *f.*; inconveniente, *m.*, molestia.—*v.t.* incomodar.
inconvenient [inkən'vi:niənt], *a.* inconveniente, incómodo molesto.

incorporate [in'kɔ:pəreit], *v.t.* incorporar; formar una sociedad anónima.
incorrect [inkə'rekt], *a.* incorrecto.
incorrigible [in'kɔridʒibl], *a.* incorregible.
increase ['inkri:s], *n.* aumento; ganancia; progenie, *f.*—[in'kri:s], *v.t., v.i.* aumentar.
increasingly [in'kri:siŋli], *adv.* cada vez más, con creces.
incredible [in'kredibl], *a.* increíble.
incredulous [in'kredjuləs], *a.* incrédulo.
increment ['inkrimənt], *n.* incremento, aumento.
incriminate [in'krimineit], *v.t.* acriminar, incriminar.
incubate ['inkjubeit], *v.t., v.i.* incubar.
incubator ['inkjubeitə], *n.* incubadora.
inculcate ['inkʌlkeit], *v.t.* inculcar.
incumbent [in'kʌmbənt], *a.* incumbente.—*n.* (*eccl.*) beneficiado; ***to be — on,*** incumbir a.
incur [in'kə:], *v.t.* contraer, incurrir en; causarse.
incurable [in'kjuərəbl], *a.* incurable.
incursion [in'kə:ʃən], *n.* incursión, *f.*, correría.
indebted [in'detid], *a.* adeudado; obligado.
indecency [in'di:sənsi], *n.* indecencia.
indecent [in'di:sənt], *a.* indecente.
indecision [indi'siʒən], *n.* indecisión, *f.*
indecisive [indi'saisiv], *a.* indeciso.
indecorous [indi'kɔ:rəs], *a.* indecoroso.
indeed [in'di:d], *adv.* de veras, por cierto.
indefinite [in'definit], *a.* indefinido.
indelible [in'delibl], *a.* indeleble.
indemnify [in'demnifai], *v.t.* indemnizar.
indemnity [in'demniti], *n.* indemnización, indemnidad, *f.*
indent [in'dent], *v.t.* mellar; (*print.*) sangrar.
indenture [in'dentʃə], *n.* contrato (de aprendizaje).
independence [indi'pendəns], *n.* independencia.
independent [indi'pendənt], *a.* independiente.
indescribable [indis'kraibəbl], *a.* indescriptible.
index ['indeks], *n.* (*pl.* **-dexes, -dices**) índice, *m.*
India ['indjə], *n.* la India.
Indian ['indjən], *a., n.* indio; ***— ink,*** tinta china.
india-rubber ['indjərʌbə], *n.* goma.
indicate ['indikeit], *v.t.* indicar.
indication [indi'keiʃən], *n.* indicación, *f.*
indicative [in'dikətiv], *a., n.* indicativo.
indicator ['indikeitə], *n.* indicador, *m.*
indict [in'dait], *v.t.* (*jur.*) acusar, procesar.
indictment [in'daitmənt], *n.* (auto de) acusación, *f.*
indifference [in'difrəns], *n.* indiferencia.
indifferent [in'difrənt], *a.* indiferente; pasadero, regular.
indigenous [in'didʒinəs], *a.* indígena, natural.
indigent ['indidʒənt], *a.* indigente.
indigestion [indi'dʒestʃən], *n.* indigestión, *f.*
indignant [in'dignənt], *a.* indignado.
indignation [indig'neiʃən], *n.* indignación, *f.*
indignity [in'digniti], *n.* indignidad, *f.*
indigo ['indigou], *n.* índigo; añil, *m.*
indirect [indi'rekt], *a.* indirecto.
indiscreet [indis'kri:t], *a.* indiscreto.
indiscretion [indis'kreʃən], *n.* indiscreción, *f.*
indiscriminate [indis'kriminit], *a.* promiscuo; indistinto.
indispensable [indis'pensəbl], *a.* indispensable, imprescindible.
indisposed [indis'pouzd], *a.* indispuesto, maldispuesto.
indisposition [indispə'ziʃən], *n.* indisposición, *f.*
indisputable [indis'pju:təbl], *a.* indisputable, irrebatible.
indistinct [indis'tiŋkt], *a.* indistinto, confuso.
indistinguishable [indis'tiŋgwiʃəbl], *a.* indistinguible.
individual [indi'vidjuəl], *a.* individual.—*n.* individuo.
Indo-China [indou'tʃainə], *n.* la Indochina.
indoctrinate [in'dɔktrineit], *v.t.* adoctrinar, catequizar.
Indo-European [indoujuərə'piən], *a., n.* indoeuropeo.
indolence ['indələns], *n.* indolencia.
indomitable [in'dɔmitəbl], *a.* indómito, indomable.
Indonesian [ində'ni:zjən], *a., n.* indonesio.
indoor ['indɔ:], *a.* de puertas adentro; interior.
indoors [in'dɔ:z], *adv.* en casa, dentro.
indorse [in'dɔ:s], *v.t.* endosar; respaldar.
induce [in'dju:s], *v.t.* inducir; ocasionar.
inducement [in'dju:smənt], *n.* aliciente, *m.*, incentivo.
indulge [in'dʌldʒ], *v.t.* gratificar; mimar.—*v.i.* entregarse (***in,*** a), gozar.
indulgence [in'dʌldʒəns], *n.* (*eccl.*) indulgencia; mimo; abandono.
indulgent [in'dʌldʒənt], *a.* indulgente.
industrial [in'dʌstriəl], *a.* industrial.
industrialist [in'dʌstriəlist], *n.* industrial, *m.*
industrialize [in'dʌstriəlaiz], *v.t.* industrializar.
industrious [in'dʌstriəs], *a.* industrioso, aplicado.
industry ['indəstri], *n.* industria.
inebriate [i'ni:brieit], *v.t.* embriagar.
inedible [i'nedibl], *a.* no comestible.
ineffable [i'nefəbl], *a.* inefable.
ineffective [ini'fektiv], *a.* ineficaz.
ineffectual [ini'fektjuəl], *a.* ineficaz.
inefficiency [ini'fiʃənsi], *n.* ineficacia.
inefficient [ini'fiʃənt], *a.* ineficaz; ineficiente.
inept [i'nept], *a.* inepto.
inequality [ini'kwɔliti], *n.* desigualdad, *f.*
inert [i'nə:t], *a.* inerte.
inertia [i'nə:ʃə], *n.* inercia; desidia.
inescapable [inis'keipəbl], *a.* ineludible.
inevitable [i'nevitəbl], *a.* inevitable.
inexact [inig'zækt], *a.* inexacto.
inexhaustible [inig'zɔ:stibl], *a.* inagotable.
inexpedient [iniks'pi:djənt], *a.* impropio, inoportuno, imprudente.
inexpensive [iniks'pensiv], *a.* barato.
inexperienced [iniks'piəriənst], *a.* inexperto.
inexpert [ineks'pə:t], *a.* imperito.
inexplicable [i'neksplikəbl], *a.* inexplicable.
infallible [in'fælibl], *a.* infalible.
infamous ['infəməs], *a.* infame.
infamy ['infəmi], *n.* infamia.
infancy ['infənsi], *n.* infancia.
infant ['infənt], *a.* infantil.—*n.* niño; infante, *m.*; (*educ.*) párvulo; (*jur.*) menor, *m.f.*
infantile ['infəntail], *a.* infantil; aniñado.
infantry ['infəntri], *n.* infantería.

infatuate [in'fætjueit], *v.t.* amartelar, apasionar; engreír.
infatuation [infætju'eiʃən], *n.* encaprichamiento, apasionamiento.
infect [in'fekt], *v.t.* inficionar, infectar, contagiar.
infection [in'fekʃən], *n.* infección. *f.*
infectious [in'fekʃəs], *a.* contagioso, infeccioso.
infer [in'fə:], *v.t.* inferir; (*fam.*) dar a entender.
inferior [in'fiəriə], *a.*, *n.* inferior, *m.*
inferiority [infiəri'ɔriti], *n.* inferioridad, *f.*
infernal [in'fə:nəl], *a.* infernal.
inferno [in'fə:nou], *n.* infierno.
infertile [in'fə:tail], *a.* estéril, infecundo.
infest [in'fest], *v.t.* infestar; apestar; plagar.
infidel ['infidəl], *a.*, *n.* infiel, *m.f.*
infidelity [infi'deliti], *n.* infidelidad, deslealtad, *f.*
infiltrate ['infiltreit], *v.t.* infiltrar; infiltrarse en.
infinite ['infinit], *a.*, *n.* infinito.
infinitive [in'finitiv], *a.*, *n.* infinitivo.
infinity [in'finiti], *n.* infinidad, *f.*; (*math.*) infinito.
infirm [in'fə:m], *a.* enfermizo, doliente; débil; inestable.
infirmary [in'fə:məri], *n.* enfermería; hospital, *m.*
infirmity [in'fə:miti], *n.* dolencia, achaque, *m.*; inestabilidad, *f.*
inflame [in'fleim], *v.t.* inflamar, encender.—*v.i.* inflamarse.
inflammable [in'flæməbl], *a.* inflamable.
inflammation [inflə'meiʃən], *n.* inflamación, *f.*
inflate [in'fleit], *v.t.* inflar, hinchar.—*v.i.* inflarse.
inflation [in'fleiʃən], *n.* inflación, *f.*; (*fig.*) hinchazón, *f.*
inflect [in'flekt], *v.t.* dar (las) inflexión(es) a.
inflection, inflexion [in'flekʃən], *n.* inflexión.
inflict [in'flikt], *v.t.* infligir (***on,*** a).
influence ['influəns], *n.* influencia, influjo.—*v.t.* influenciar, influir sobre *o* en.
influenza [influ'enzə], *n.* gripe, *f.*
influx ['inflʌks], *n.* afluencia.
inform [in'fɔ:m], *v.t.* informar.
informal [in'fɔ:məl], *a.* familiar; (*pej.*) informal (*impolite*).
informality [infɔ:'mæliti], *n.* sencillez, *f.*, falta de ceremonia; informalidad, *f.*
informant [in'fɔ:mənt], *n.* informante, *m.f.*, informador, *m.*
information [infə'meiʃən], *n.* informes, *m.pl.*, información, *f.*
informer [in'fɔ:mə], *n.* delator, soplón, *m.*
infraction [in'frækʃən], *n.* infracción, *f.*
infrequent [in'fri:kwənt], *a.* infrecuente.
infringe [in'frindʒ], *v.t.* violar, infringir.
infuriate [in'fjuərieit], *v.t.* enfurecer.
infuse [in'fju:z], *v.t.* infundir.
ingenious [in'dʒi:niəs], *a.* ingenioso, genial.
ingenuity [indʒi'nju:iti], *n.* ingeniosidad, *f.*
ingenuous [in'dʒenjuəs], *a.* ingenuo.
inglorious [in'glɔ:riəs], *a.* obscuro; deshonroso.
ingot ['iŋgət], *n.* lingote, *m.*
ingrained [in'greind], *a.* muy pegado *o* arraigado.
ingratiate [in'greiʃieit], *v.r.* insinuarse (***with,*** con).
ingratitude [in'grætitju:d], *n.* ingratitud, *f.* desagradecimiento.
ingredient [in'gri:diənt], *n.* ingrediente, *m.*
inhabit [in'hæbit], *v.t.* habitar.
inhabitant [in'hæbitənt], *n.* habitante, *m.f.*
inhale [in'heil], *v.t.*, *v.i.* aspirar.
inherent [in'hiərənt], *a.* inherente; innato.
inherit [in'herit], *v.t.* heredar.
inheritance [in'heritəns], *n.* herencia.
inhibit [in'hibit], *v.t.* inhibir.
inhibition [inhi'biʃən], *n.* inhibición, *f.*
inhospitable [inhɔs'pitəbl], *a.* inhospitalario, inhospedable.
inhuman [in'hju:mən], *a.* inhumano, desalmado.
inimitable [i'nimitəbl], *a.* inimitable.
iniquitous [i'nikwitəs], *a.* inicuo, malvado.
iniquity [i'nikwiti], *n.* iniquidad, *f.*
initial [i'niʃəl], *a.*, *n.* inicial, *f.*—*v.t.* rubricar; marcar.
initiate [i'niʃieit], *n.* iniciado.—*v.t.* iniciar.
initiative [i'niʃiətiv], *n.* iniciativa.
inject [in'dʒekt], *v.t.* inyectar.
injection [in'dʒekʃən], *n.* inyección, *f.*
injunction [in'dʒʌŋkʃən], *n.* mandato; entredicho.
injure ['indʒə], *v.t.* dañar; herir; injuriar.
injurious [in'dʒuəriəs], *a.* dañoso; injurioso.
injury ['indʒəri], *n.* lesión, *f.*, herida; daño.
injustice [in'dʒʌstis], *n.* injusticia.
ink [iŋk], *n.* tinta.—*v.t.* entintar.
inkling ['iŋkliŋ], *n.* noción, *f.*, sospecha.
inkwell ['iŋkwel], *n.* tintero.
inky ['iŋki], *a.* negro; manchado de tinta.
inlaid ['inleid], *a.* embutido.
inland ['inlənd] *a.* interior.—[in'lænd], *adv.* tierra adentro.
inlet ['inlet], *n.* abra, ensenada, cala.
inmate ['inmeit], *n.* residente, *m.f.*; asilado; preso.
inmost ['inmoust], *a.* el más íntimo *o* recóndito.
inn [in], *n.* posada, mesón, *m.*, fonda.
innate [i'neit], *a.* innato, ingénito.
inner ['inə], *a.* interior; — ***tube,*** cámara de aire.
innermost [INMOST].
innings ['iniŋz], *n.sg.* (*sport*) turno; (*fig.*) turno, goce, *m.*
innkeeper ['inki:pə], *n.* posadero, mesonero.
innocence ['inəsəns], *n.* inocencia.
innocent ['inəsənt], *a.* inocente.
innovate ['inoveit], *v.t.* innovar.
innovation [ino'veiʃən], *n.* innovación, *f.*
innuendo [inju'endou], *n.* indirecta, insinuación, *f.*
innumerable [i'nju:mərəbl], *a.* innumerable.
inoculate [i'nɔkjuleit], *v.t.* inocular.
inoffensive [inə'fensiv], *a.* inofensivo.
inopportune [i'nɔpətju:n], *a.* inoportuno; intempestivo.
inordinate [i'nɔ:dinit], *a.* excesivo, desordenado.
inorganic [inɔ:'gænik], *a.* inorgánico.
input ['input], *n.* gasto; energía invertida; lo que se invierte.
inquest ['iŋkwest], *n.* indagación judicial, *f.*
inquire [in'kwaiə], *v.i.* preguntar (***about, after,*** por; ***of,*** a); investigar (***into***).

inquiry [in'kwaiəri], *n.* pesquisa, investigación, *f.*; pregunta.
inquisition [inkwi'ziʃən], *n.* inquisición, *f.*
inquisitive [in'kwizitiv], *a.* curioso, preguntón.
inquisitor [in'kwizitə], *n.* inquisidor, *m.*
inroad ['inroud], *n.* incursión, *f.*; desgaste, *m.*
insane [in'sein], *a.* loco, demente, insano.
insanity [in'sæniti], *n.* locura, insania, demencia.
insatiable [in'seiʃəbl], *a.* insaciable.
inscribe [in'skraib], *v.t.* inscribir; grabar.
inscription [in'skripʃən], *n.* inscripción, *f.*
inscrutable [in'skru:təbl], *a.* inescrutable, insondable.
insect ['insekt], *n.* insecto.
insecticide [in'sektisaid], *n.* insecticida, *m.*
insecure [insi'kjuə], *a.* inseguro; precario.
insecurity [insi'kjuəriti], *n.* inseguridad, *f.*
insensible [in'sensibl], *a.* insensible; inconsciente.
inseparable [in'sepərəbl], *a.* inseparable.
insert [in'sə:t], *v.t.* insertar.
inside ['insaid], *a.*, *n.* interior, *m.*; **— *information,*** informes secretos; **— *out,*** al revés. — [in'saidz], *n.pl.* (*fam.*) entrañas, *f.pl.*— [in'said], *adv.* dentro, hacia dentro.—*prep.* dentro de.
insight ['insait], *n.* perspicacia, penetración, *f.*
insignia [in'signiə], *n.pl.* insignias, *f.pl.*
insignificant [insig'nifikənt], *a.* insignificante.
insincere [insin'siə], *a.* insincero.
insinuate [in'sinjueit], *v.t.* insinuar.
insipid [in'sipid], *a.* insípido, soso.
insipidity [insi'piditi], *n.* insipidez, *f.*
insist [in'sist], *v.i.* insistir (***on,*** en).
insistence [in'sistəns], *n.* insistencia.
insistent [in'sistənt], *a.* insistente.
insolence ['insələns], *n.* descaro, insolencia.
insolent ['insələnt], *a.* descarado, insolente.
insoluble [in'sɔljubl], *a.* in(di)soluble.
insolvent [in'sɔlvənt], *a.* insolvente.
insomnia [in'sɔmniə], *a.* insomnio.
inspect [in'spekt], *v.t.* inspeccionar.
inspection [in'spekʃən], *n.* inspección, *f.*
inspector [in'spektə], *n.* inspector, *m.*
inspiration [inspi'reiʃən], *n.* inspiración, *f.*
inspire [in'spaiə], *v.t.* inspirar; ***to be inspired by,*** inspirarse en.
inspiring [ins'paiəriŋ], *a.* inspirador, inspirante.
instability [instə'biliti], *n.* inestabilidad, *f.*
install [in'stɔ:l], *v.t.* instalar.
installation [instə'leiʃən], *n.* instalación *f.*
instalment [in'stɔ:lmənt], *n.* entrega; plazo (*pago*).
instance ['instəns], *n.* ejemplo, caso; instancia; ***for —,*** por ejemplo.
instant ['instənt], *a.* inmediato; corriente.—*n.* instante; mes corriente, *m.*
instantaneous [instən'teinjəs], *a.* instantáneo.
instantly ['instəntli], *a.* al instante.
instead [in'sted], *adv.* en su lugar.—*prep.* en lugar, en vez (***of,*** de).
instep ['instep], *n.* empeine, *m.*
instigate ['instigeit], *v.t.* instigar.
instil [in'stil], *v.t.* instilar.
instinct ['instiŋkt], *n.* instinto.
instinctive [in'stiŋktiv], *a.* instintivo.
institute ['institju:t], *n.* instituto.—*v.t.* instituir.
institution [insti'tju:ʃən], *n.* institución, *f.*; uso establecido.
instruct [in'strʌkt], *v.t.* instruir; mandar.
instruction [in'strʌkʃən], *n.* instrucción; indicación, *f.*
instructive [in'strʌktiv], *a.* instructivo.
instructor [in'strʌktə], *n.* instructor, *m.*
instrument ['instrumənt], *n.* instrumento.
instrumental [instru'mentl], *a.* instrumental.
insubordinate [insə'bɔ:dinit], *a.* insubordinado.
insubordination [insəbɔ:di'neiʃən], *n.* insubordinación, *f.*
insufferable [in'sʌfərəbl], *a.* insufrible, inaguantable.
insufficient [insə'fiʃənt], *a.* insuficiente.
insular ['insjulə], *a.* insular; estrecho de miras.
insulate ['insjuleit], *v.t.* aislar.
insulation [insju'leiʃən], *n.* aislamiento.
insulator ['insjuleitə], *n.* aislador, *m.*
insult ['insʌlt] *n.* insulto.—[in'sʌlt], *v.t.* insultar.
insulting [in'sʌltiŋ], *a.* insultante.
insuperable [in'sju:pərəbl], *a.* insuperable.
insurance [in'ʃuərəns, in'ʃɔ:rəns], *n.* seguro.
insure [in'ʃuə, in'ʃɔ:], *v.t.* asegurar.
insurgent [in'sə:dʒənt], *a.*, *n.* insurrecto, insurgente.
insurrection [insə'rekʃən], *n.* insurrección, *f.*
intact [in'tækt], *a.* intacto, íntegro, incólume.
intake ['inteik], *n.* admisión; entrada.
intangible [in'tændʒibl], *a.* intangible.
integer ['intidʒə], *n.* (*math.*) entero.
integral ['intigrəl], *a.* íntegro; integral; solidario.
integrate ['intigreit], *v.t.* integrar.
integration [inti'greiʃən], *n.* integración, *f.*
integrity [in'tegriti], *n.* integridad, *f.*; entereza.
intellect ['intilekt], *n.* intelecto.
intellectual [inti'lektjuəl], *a.*, *n.* intelectual.
intelligence [in'telidʒəns], *n.* inteligencia; información, *f.*
intelligent [in'telidʒənt], *a.* inteligente.
intelligible [in'telidʒibl], *a.* inteligible.
intemperance [in'tempərəns], *n.* intemperancia; exceso.
intemperate [in'tempərit], *a.* intemperante; inclemente.
intend [in'tend], *v.t.* proponerse, pensar.
intended [in'tendid], *n.* (*fam.*) prometido, prometida.
intense [in'tens], *a.* intenso.
intensify [in'tensifai], *v.t.* intensificar.—*v.i.* -se.
intensity [in'tensiti], *n.* intensidad, *f.*
intensive [in'tensiv], *a.* intensivo.
intent [in'tent], *a.* atentísimo; resuelto (***on,*** a); ***to be — on,*** pensar sólo en.—*n.* intento; intención, *f.*; sentido; ***to all intents and purposes,*** prácticamente; virtualmente.
intention [in'tenʃən], *n.* intención, *f.*; fin, *m.*
intentional [in'tenʃənəl], *a.* intencional, intencionado.
inter [in'tə:], *v.t.* enterrar.
inter ['intə], *prefix.* entre-.

intercede [intə'si:d], *v.i.* interceder.
intercept [intə'sept], *v.t.* interceptar, atajar.
interchange [intə'tʃeindʒ], *n.* intercambio.—*v.t.* intercambiar.—*v.i.* -se.
intercommunicate [intəkə'mju:nikeit], *v.i.* comunicarse.
intercourse ['intəkɔ:s], *n.* trato, intercambio; comercio; coito.
interdict ['intədikt], *n.* interdicto, entredicho.
interest ['intərəst], *n.* interés, *m* —*v.t.* interesar.
interesting ['intərəstiŋ], *a* interesante.
interfere [intə'fiə], *v.i.* meterse (*in*, en); estorbar (*with*).
interference [intə'fiərəns], *n.* intrusión, *f.*; estorbo; (*rad.*) interferencia.
interim ['intərim], *a.* interino; *in the —*, ínterin, entre tanto.
interleave [intə'li:v], *v.t.* interfoliar.
interlock [intə'lɔk], *v.t.* trabar, engargantar. —*v.i.* -se.
interloper ['intəloupə], *n.* intruso.
interlude ['intəlju:d], *n.* intermedio, intervalo.
intermediary [intə'mi:djəri], *a.*, *n.* intermediario.
intermediate [intə'mi:djət], *a.* intermedi(ari)o.
interment [in'tə:mənt], *n.* entierro.
interminable [in'tə:minəbl], *a.* interminable.
intermingle [intə'miŋgl], *v.t.* entreverar, entremezclar.—*v.i.* -se.
intermittent [intə'mitənt], *a.* intermitente.
intern [in'tə:n], *v.t.* internar, encerrar.
internal [in'tə:nəl], *a.* interno, interior.
international [intə'næʃənəl], *a.* internacional.
internment [in'tə:nmənt], *n.* internación, *f.*
interpolate [in'tə:pəleit], *v.t.* interpolar.
interpret [in'tə:prit], *v.t.* interpretar.
interpretation [intə:pri'teiʃən], *n.* interpretación *f.*
interpreter [in'tə:pritə], *n.* intérprete, *m.*
interrogate [in'terəgeit], *v.t.* interrogar.
interrogation [interə'geiʃən], *n.* interrogación, *f.*; — *mark*, punto de interrogación.
interrogative [intə'rɔgətiv], *a.*, *n.* interrogativo.
interrogator [in'terəgeitə], *n.* interrogante, *m.f.*
interrupt [intə'rʌpt], *v.t.* interrumpir.
interruption [intə'rʌpʃən], *n.* interrupción, *f.*
interval ['intəvəl], *n.* intervalo; intermedio, descanso.
intervene [intə'vi:n], *v.i.* intervenir; mediar; ocurrir.
intervention [intə'venʃən], *n.* intervención, *f.*
interview ['intəvju], *n.* entrevista.—*v.t.* entrevistar.
interweave [intə'wi:v], *v.t. irr.* (*conjug. like* WEAVE) entretejer.
intestate [in'testeit], *a.* (ab)intestado.
intestine [in'testin], *n.* intestino.
intimacy ['intiməsi], *n.* intimidad, *f.*
intimate (1) ['intimit], *a.* íntimo.
intimate (2) ['intimeit], *v.t.* intimar; indicar.
intimidate [in'timideit], *v.t.* intimidar.
into ['intu], *prep.* en, hacia el interior de.
intolerable [in'tɔlərəbl], *a.* intolerable.
intolerance [in'tɔlərəns], *n.* intolerancia.
intolerant [in'tɔlərənt], *a.* intolerante.
intonation [intə'neiʃən], *n.* entonación, *f.*
intone [in'toun], *v.t.* entonar; salmodiar.
intoxicate [in'tɔksikeit], *v.t.* embriagar.
intoxicating [in'tɔksikeitiŋ], *a.* embriagante.
intransigent [in'trænsidʒənt], *a.* intransigente.
intransitive [in'trɑ:nsitiv], *a.* intransitivo.
intrepid [in'trepid], *a.* intrépido.
intricacy ['intrikəsi], *n.* intrincación, *f.*
intricate ['intrikit], *a.* intrincado.
intrigue ['intri:g], *n.* intriga.—[in'tri:g], *v.t.* fascinar.—*v.i.* intrigar.
intriguer [in'tri:gə], *n.* intrigante, *m.f.*
intriguing [in'tri:giŋ], *a.* intrigante; fascinador.
intrinsic [in'trinsik], *a.* intrínseco.
introduce [intrə'dju:s], *v.t.* introducir; presentar (*gente*).
introduction [intrə'dʌkʃən], *n.* introducción; presentación, *f.*
introductory [intrə'dʌktəri], *a.* introductivo; proemial.
intrude [in'tru:d], *v.i.* estorbar, entremeterse.
intruder [in'tru:də], *n.* intruso; entremetido.
intrusion [in'tru:ʒən], *n.* intrusión, *f.*
intrust [in'trʌst], *v.t.* confiar.
intuition [intju:'iʃən], *n.* intuición, *f.*
intuitive [in'tju:itiv], *a.* intuitivo.
inundate ['inʌndeit], *v.t.* inundar.
inure [i'njuə], *v.t.* avezar, endurecer.
invade [in'veid], *v.t.* invadir.
invader [in'veidə], *n.* invasor, *m.*
invading [in'veidiŋ], *a.* invasor.
invalid (1) [in'vælid], *a.* inválido, nulo.
invalid (2) ['invəlid], *a.*, *n.* inválido, enfermo.
invalidate [in'vælideit], *v.t.* invalidar.
invaluable [in'væljuəbl], *a.* inestimable, precioso.
invariable [in'vɛəriəbl], *a.* invariable.
invasion [in'veiʒən], *n.* invasión, *f.*
invective [in'vektiv], *n.* invectiva.
inveigh [in'vei], *v.i.* prorrumpir en invectivas.
inveigle [in'vi:gl, in'veigl], *v.t.* seducir, engatusar.
invent [in'vent], *v.t.* inventar.
invention [in'venʃən], *n.* invención, *f.*, hallazgo; invento.
inventor [in'ventə], *n.* inventor, *m.*
inventory ['invəntəri], *n.* inventario, catálogo.
inversion [in'və:ʃən], *n.* inversión, *f.*
invert [in'və:t], *v.t.* invertir, transponer.
invertebrate [in'və:tibreit], *a.*, *n.* invertebrado.
invest [in'vest], *v.t.* invertir (*dinero*); (*mil.*) sitiar; investir (*honor*).
investigate [in'vestigeit], *v.t.* investigar.
investigation [investi'geiʃən], *n.* investigación, *f.*
investment [in'vestmənt], *n.* inversión; (*mil.*) cerco.
investor [in'vestə], *n.* inversionista, *m.f.*
inveterate [in'vetərit], *a.* inveterado, habitual.
invidious [in'vidjəs], *a.* detestable, odioso; injusto.
invigorate [in'vigəreit], *v.t.* vigorizar.
invincible [in'vinsibl], *a.* invencible.
inviolate [in'vaiəlit], *a.* inviolado.
invisible [in'vizibl], *a.* invisible.

invitation [invi'teiʃən], *n.* invitación, *f.*, convite, *m.*
invite [in'vait], *v.t.* invitar, convidar.
inviting [in'vaitiŋ], *a.* seductor, halagante, provocativo.
invoice ['invɔis], *n.* factura.—*v.t.* facturar.
invoke [in'vouk], *v.t.* invocar.
involuntary [in'vɔləntri], *a.* involuntario.
involve [in'vɔlv], *v.t.* implicar; envolver; enredar.
invulnerable [in'vʌlnərəbl], *a.* invulnerable.
inward ['inwəd], *a.* interior.
inwards ['inədz], *n.pl.* (*fam.*) tripas, entrañas, *f.pl.*—['inwədz], *adv.* hacia dentro.
iodine ['aiədi:n], *n.* yodo.
iota [ai'outə], *n.* iota; (*fig.*) jota, tilde, *f.*
Iran [i'rɑ:n], *n.* Irán, *m.*
Iranian [i'reinjən], *a.*, *n.* iranés, *m.*, iranio.
Iraq [i'rɑ:k], *n.* Irak, *m.*
Iraqi [i'rɑ:ki], *a.*, *n.* iraquiano, iraqués, *m.*
irascible [i'ræsibl], *a.* irascible, colérico.
irate [ai'reit], *a.* airado.
ire [aiə], *n.* (*poet.*) ira.
Ireland ['aiələnd], *n.* Irlanda.
iris ['aiəris], *n.* (*anat.*) iris, *m.*; (*bot.*) lirio.
Irish ['aiəriʃ], *a.* irlandés.—*n.* irlandés (*idioma*), *m.*
Irishman ['aiəriʃmən], *n.* irlandés, *m.*
irksome ['ə:ksəm], *a.* cargante, molesto.
iron [aiən], *n.* hierro; plancha (*para vestidos*); ***iron curtain***, telón (*m.*) de acero.—*v.t.* planchar; ***to iron out***, allanar (*problemas*).
ironclad ['aiənklæd], *a.*, *n.* acorazado.
ironic(al) [aiə'rɔnik(əl)], *a.* irónico.
ironmonger ['aiənmʌŋgə], *n.* ferretero, quincallero.
ironmongery ['aiənmʌŋgəri], *n.* ferretería, quincalla.
irony ['aiərəni], *n.* ironía.
irrational [i'ræʃənəl], *a.* irracional.
irregular [i'regjulə], *a.* irregular.
irregularity [iregju'læriti], *n.* irregularidad, *f.*
irrelevance [i'reləvəns], *n.* inaplicabilidad, *f.*
irrelevant [i'reləvənt], *a.* inaplicable, fuera de propósito.
irreligion [iri'lidʒən], *n.* irreligión, *f.*
irreligious [iri'lidʒəs], *a.* irreligioso.
irreparable [i'repərəbl], *a.* irreparable.
irrepressible [iri'presibl], *a.* incontenible.
irresistible [iri'zistibl], *a.* irresistible.
irresolute [i'rezəlju:t], *a.* irresoluto.
irrespective [iris'pektiv], *a.* independiente; aparte, sin hacer caso (***of***, de).
irresponsible [iris'pɔnsibl], *a.* irresponsable.
irreverence [i'revərəns], *n.* irreverencia.
irreverent [i'revərənt], *a.* irreverente.
irrevocable [i'revəkəbl], *a.* irrevocable.
irrigate ['irigeit], *v.t.* regar, irrigar.
irrigation [iri'geiʃən], *n.* riego, irrigación, *f.*
irritable ['iritəbl], *a.* irritable, enfadadizo.
irritate ['iriteit], *v.t.* irritar.
is [iz], [BE].
Islam [iz'lɑ:m], *n.* el Islam.
Islamic [iz'læmik], *a.* islámico.
island ['ailənd], *n.* isla.
islander ['ailəndə], *n.* isleño.
isle [ail], *n.* (*poet.*) isla.
isn't [iznt], [IS NOT].
isolate ['aisəleit], *v.t.* aislar.
isolation [aisə'leiʃən], *n.* aislamiento.
Israel ['izreil], *n.* Israel, *m.*
Israeli [iz'reili], *a.*, *n.* israelí, *m.f.*
Israelite ['izriəlait], *n.* (*Bibl.*) israelita, *m.f.*
issue ['iʃju:], *n.* tirada; emisión, *f.*; número (*de una revista*); resultado; asunto discutido; progenie, *f.*; ***at* —**, en disputa.—*v.t.* emitir; publicar.—*v.i.* salir; provenir; ***to join* —**, disputar.
isthmus ['isməs], *n.* istmo.
it [it], *pron.* ello; lo, la; le.
Italian [i'tæljən], *a.*, *n.* italiano.
italic [i'tælik], *a.* itálico, bastardillo.—*n.pl.* bastardilla, cursiva.
italicize [i'tælisaiz], *v.t.* subrayar.
Italy ['itəli], *n.* Italia.
itch [itʃ], *n.* picazón, comezón, *f.*; prurito.—*v.i.* comer, picar; sentir prurito (***to***, de).
itchy ['itʃi], *a.* hormigoso.
item ['aitəm], *n.* ítem, *m.*, párrafo, artículo; detalle, *m.*
itemize ['aitəmaiz], *v.t.* detallar.
itinerant [ai'tinərənt], *a.* ambulante viandante.
itinerary [ai'tinərəri], *n.* itinerario.
its [its], *poss. a.* su; suyo.
itself [it'self], *pron.* sí (mismo); se.
ivory ['aivəri], *n.* marfil, *m*; ***Ivory Coast***, Costa de Marfil.
ivy ['aivi], *n.* hiedra.

J

J, j [dʒei], *n.* décima letra del alfabeto inglés.
jab [dʒæb], *n.* hurgonazo, pinchazo; codazo.—*v.t.* pinchar; dar un codazo a.
jabber ['dʒæbə], *n.* chapurreo.—*v.t.*, *v.i.* chapurrear.
jack [dʒæk], *n.* (*mech.*) gato, cric, *m.*; (*zool.*) macho; (*fam.*) mozo; marinero; sota (*naipes*); burro; sacabotas, *m.sg.*
jackal ['dʒækɔ:l], *n.* chacal, *m.*
jackass ['dʒækæs], *n.* burro; (*orn.*) martín, *m.*
jack-boot ['dʒækbu:t], *n.* bota alta.
jack-in-office ['djækin'ɔfis], *n.* oficial engreído.
jack-in-the-box ['djækinðə'bɔks], *n.* caja de sorpresa.
jack-knife ['dʒæknaif], *n.* navaja (sevillana *o* de Albacete).
jack-of-all-trades ['djækəvɔ:l'treidz], *n.* dije, factótum, *m.*
Jack Tar ['djæk'tɑ:], *n.* lobo de mar.
jade (1) [dʒeid], *a.* verde.—*n.* (*min.*) jade, *m.*
jade (2) [dʒeid], *n.* picarona, mujerzuela; rocín, *m.*—*v.t.* cansar.
jaded ['dʒeidid], *a.* cansado, ahito.
jagged ['dʒægid], *a.* mellado, aserrado.
jaguar ['dʒægjuə], *n.* jaguar, *m.*
jail [dʒeil], *n.* cárcel, *f.*
jailer ['dʒeilə], *n.* carcelero.
jalopy [dʒə'lɔpi], *n.* (*fam.*) coche ruinoso.
jam [dʒæm], *n.* conserva, mermelada; agolpamiento, apiñadura; (*fam.*) aprieto.—*v.t.* apiñar; estrechar; atorar; (*rad.*) perturbar.—*v.i.* apiñarse; trabarse; atascarse.

Jamaican [dʒə'meikən], *a.*, *n.* jamaicano.
James [dʒeimz], *n.* Jaime, Diego, Santiago.
jamming ['dʒæmiŋ], *n.* (*rad.*) perturbación, *f.*
Jane [dʒein], *n.* Juana.
jangle [dʒæŋgl], *n.* cencerreo; riña.—*v.t.* hacer cencerrear.—*v.i.* cencerrear; reñir.
janitor ['dʒænitə], *n.* (*U.S.*) portero, conserje, *m.*
January ['dʒænjuəri], *n.* enero.
Japan [dʒə'pæn], *n.* Japón, *m.*; **japan,** *n.* laca.
Japanese [dʒæpə'ni:z], *a.*, *n.* japonés.
jar (1) [dʒɑ:], *n.* vaso, tarro, orza, jarro.
jar (2) [dʒɑ:], *n.* sacudida.—*v.t.* sacudir; bazucar; irritar.—*v.i.* sacudirse; chirriar.
jargon ['dʒɑ:gən], *n.* jerga.
jasmine ['dʒæzmin], *n.* jazmín, *m.*
jasper ['dʒæspə], *n.* jaspe, *m.*
jaundice ['dʒɔ:ndis], *n.* (*med.*) ictericia; (*fig.*) envidia.—*v.t.* amargar.
jaunt [dʒɔ:nt], *n.* (*fam.*) caminata, excursión, *f.*
jaunty ['dʒɔ:nti], *a.* airoso, garboso.
javelin ['dʒævəlin], *n.* jabalina.
jaw [dʒɔ:], *n.* quijada; (*fam.*) cháchara.—*pl.* (*fig.*) garras, *f.pl.*
jay [dʒei], *n.* (*orn.*) arrendajo.
jaywalker ['dʒeiwɔ:kə], *n.* peatón imprudente, *m.*
jazz [dʒæz], *n.* jazz, *m.*
jealous ['dʒeləs], *a.* celoso.
jealousy ['dʒeləsi], *n.* celos, *m.pl.*
jeep [dʒi:p], *n.* coche (*m.*) militar pequeño.
jeer [dʒiə], *n.* mofa, befa.—*v.i.* mofarse (***at,*** de).
jelly ['dʒeli], *n.* jalea, gelatina.
jelly-fish ['dʒelifiʃ], *n.* medusa, aguamar, *m.*
jemmy ['dʒemi], *n.* palanqueta.
jeopardize ['dʒepədaiz], *v.t.* arriesgar, poner en peligro.
jeopardy ['dʒepədi], *n.* riesgo, peligro.
jerk (1) [dʒə:k], *n.* tirón, arranque; tic, *m.*; (*pej.*) tío.—*v.t.* sacudir.—*v.i.* moverse a tirones; sacudir(se).
jerk (2) [dʒə:k], *v.t.* tasajear (*carne*).
jerry-built ['dʒeribilt], *a.* mal construido.
Jerusalem [dʒə'ru:sələm], *n.* Jerusalén, *f.*
jest [dʒest], *n.* chanza, broma.—*v.i.* chancear.
jester ['dʒestə], *n.* bufón, *m.*; bromista, *m.f.*
Jesuit ['dʒezjuit], *a.*, *n.* jesuita, *m.*
Jesus ['dʒi:zəs], *n.* Jesús;—***Christ,*** Jesucristo.
jet (1) [dʒet], *n.* chorro; surtidor; mechero.
jet (2) [dʒet], *n.* (*min.*) azabache, *m.*
jet-aeroplane ['dʒet'ɛərəplein], *n.* avion (*m.*) de chorro *o* de reacción.
jet-engine ['dʒet'endʒin], *n.* motor (*m.*) a chorro.
jetsam ['dʒetsəm], *n.* echazón, *f.*, pecio.
jettison ['dʒetisən], *v.t.* echar a la mar; desechar.
jetty ['dʒeti], *n.* malecón, muelle, *m.*
Jew [dʒu:], *n.* judío.
jewel [dʒu:əl], *n.* joya, alhaja.
jeweller ['dʒu:ələ], *n.* joyero.
jewel(le)ry ['dʒu:əlri], *n.* joyas, *f.pl.*; joyería.
Jewess [dʒu:'es], *n.* judía.
Jewish ['dʒu:iʃ], *a.* judío.
Jewry ['dʒuəri], *n.* judería.
jib (1) [dʒib], *n.* aguilín, pescante (*de una grúa*); (*naut.*) foque, *m.*—*v.i.* virar.
jib (2) [dʒib], *v.i.* negarse, resistirse (***at,*** a).
jibe [dʒaib], *n.* befa, pulla.—*v.i.* mofarse (***at,*** de).
jiffy ['dʒifi], *n.* (*fam.*) santiamén, *m.*
jig [dʒig], *n.* giga (*baile*); (*mech.*) gálibo; criba.
jigger ['dʒigə], *n.* criba; criba de vaivén; (*naut.*) palo de mesana.—*v.t.* (*fam.*) pasmar.
jig-saw ['dʒigsɔ:], *n.* sierra de vaivén; rompecabezas (*juguete*), *m.sg.*
jilt [dʒilt], *v.t.* plantar, dejar colgado, dar calabazas a.
Jim(my) ['dʒim(i)], *n.* Jaimito.
jimmy ['dʒimi], (*U.S.*) [JEMMY].
jingle [dʒingl], *n.* cascabeleo; rima pueril, aleluya.—*v.t.* hacer sonar.—*v.i.* cascabelear.
jingoism ['dʒiŋgouizm], *n.* jingoísmo.
jinx [dʒinks], *n.* cenizo, gafe, *m.*
jitters ['dʒitəz], *n.pl.* (*fam.*) jindama, miedo.
Joan [dʒoun], *n.* Juana; — ***of Arc,*** Juana de Arco.
job [dʒɔb], *n.* tarea; empleo, oficio; destajo; agiotaje, *m.*; negocio; (*print.*) remiendo; — ***lot,*** lote, *m.*, saldo; ***odd* —,** tarea pequeña.
jobber ['dʒɔbə], *n.* corredor; agiotista, *m.*
jockey ['dʒɔki], *n.* jockey, *m.*—*v.t.* maniobrar.
jocular ['dʒɔkjulə], *a.* jocoso.
jocund ['dʒɔkənd], *a.* jocundo, jovial.
Joe [dʒou], *n.* Pepe, *m.*
jog [dʒɔg], *n.* empujoncito; trote, *m.*; — ***trot,*** trote de perro.—*v.t.* empujar; refrescar (*la memoria*).—*v.i.* seguir adelante, irse defendiendo.
John [dʒɔn], *n.* Juan, *m.*; — ***Bull,*** el inglés típico, Inglaterra.
join [dʒɔin], *n.* juntura.—*v.t.* juntar, unir, ensamblar; ingresar en; asociarse a; librar (*batalla*); unirse con.—*v.i.* juntarse.
joiner ['dʒɔinə], *n.* ebanista, *m.*; carpintero.
joinery ['dʒɔinəri], *n.* ebanistería.
joint [dʒɔint], *a.* común, mutuo; unido, solidario.—*prefix.* co-.—*n.* juntura, unión; (*anat.*) coyuntura, articulación, *f.*; (*U.S.*; *fam.*) sitio de reunión; tabernucho; (*cul.*) pedazo, tajada (*de carne*); ***to put out of* —,** descoyuntar. —*v.t.* articular; juntar; ensamblar.
joint-stock company ['dʒɔint'stɔk'kʌmpəni], *n.* sociedad anónima.
joist [dʒɔist], *n.* viga, vigueta.
joke [dʒouk], *n.* chiste, *m.*, broma; ***joking aside,*** sin broma, en serio.—*v.i.* chancear; hablar en broma.
joker ['dʒoukə], *n.* bromista, *m.f.*; comodín (*naipes*), *m.*
jolly ['dʒɔli], *a.* festivo, jovial, alegre; (*fam.*) agradable; ***Jolly Roger,*** bandera negra de los piratas.—*adv.* (*fam.*) muy.
jolt [dʒoult], *n.* sacudión, *m.*; salto.—*v.t.* sacudir.—*v.i.* traquear.
Jonah ['dʒounə], *n.* Jonás, *m.*; (*fam.*) gafe, *m.*, cenizo.
Jordan [dʒɔ:dn], *n.* Jordán (*río*), *m.*; Jordania (*país*).
Jordanian [dʒɔ:'deinjən], *a.*, *n.* jordano.
Joseph ['dʒousif], *n.* José, *m.*
jostle [dʒɔsl], *v.t.* codear, empujar.
jot [dʒɔt], *n.* jota, tilde, *f.*—*v.t.* apuntar (***down***).
journal [dʒə:nl], *n.* diario; revista.
journal-bearing ['dʒə:nl'bɛəriŋ], *n.* cojinete, *m.*, chumacera.
journalism ['dʒə:nəlizm], *n.* periodismo.
journalist ['dʒə:nəlist], *n.* periodista, *m.f.*
journey ['dʒə:ni], *n.* viaje, *m.*—*v.i.* viajar.
joust [dʒaust], *n.* torneo, justa.—*v.i.* justar.

jovial ['dʒouvjəl], *a.* jovial, alegre.
jowl [dʒaul], *n.* carrillo; quijada.
joy [dʒɔi], *n.* alegría, gozo.
joyful ['dʒɔiful], *a.* alegre, gozoso.
joy-ride ['dʒɔiraid], *n.* paseo de placer en coche.
joy-stick ['dʒɔistik], *n.* (*aer.*) palanca de mando.
jubilant ['dʒu:bilənt], *a.* jubiloso.
jubilation [dʒu:bi'leiʃən], *n.* júbilo.
jubilee ['dʒu:bili:], *n.* jubileo; bodas (*f.pl.*) de oro.
judge [dʒʌdʒ], *n.* juez, *m.* (*of*, en).—*v.t.*, *v.i.* juzgar (*by*, por).
judg(e)ment ['dʒʌdʒmənt], *n.* juicio; discreción, *f.*; sentencia.
judicial [dʒu'diʃəl], *a.* judicial.
judiciary [dʒu'diʃiəri], *n.* judicatura.
judicious [dʒu'diʃəs], *a.* juicioso, cuerdo.
jug [dʒʌg], *n.* jarra, jarro; (*fam.*) cárcel, *f.*, banasto.
juggle [dʒʌgl], *v.t.* escamotear; ***to — with,*** falsear.—*v.i.* hacer juegos malabares.
juggler ['dʒʌglə], *n.* malabarista, *m.f.*
jugular ['dʒʌgjulə], *a.* yugular.
juice [dʒu:s], *n.* zumo, jugo; (*fam.*) electricidad, *f.*; gasolina.
juicy ['dʒu:si], *a.* jugoso; (*fam.*) picante.
July [dʒu'lai], *n.* julio.
jumble [dʒʌmbl], *n.* enredo, revoltijo. —*v.t.* emburujar, revolver.
jumble-sale ['dʒʌmblseil], *n.* venta de trastos.
jumbo ['dʒʌmbou], *n.* (*fam.*) elefante, *m.*
jump [dʒʌmp], *n.* salto.—*v.t.*, *v.i.* saltar; ***to — at,*** aceptar, coger en seguida; ***to — to,*** darse prisa; deducir sin reflexión.
jumper (1) ['dʒʌmpə], *n.* saltador, *m.*
jumper (2) ['dʒʌmpə], jersey, *m.*
jumpy ['dʒʌmpi], *a.* asustadizo.
junction ['dʒʌŋkʃən], *n.* juntura; empalme (*ferrocarril*), *m.*
juncture ['dʒʌŋktʃə], *n.* juntura; ocasión, *f.*; coyuntura.
June [dʒu:n], *n.* junio.
jungle [dʒʌŋgl], *n.* jungla, selva.
junior ['dʒu:njə], *a.* menor, más joven; juvenil; hijo (*nombre*).—*n.* menor, *m.f.*
junk (1) [dʒʌŋk], *n.* trastos, chatarra.
junk (2) [dʒʌŋk], *n.* (*naut.*) junco.
junketing ['dʒʌŋkitiŋ], *n.* festín, *m.*
jurisdiction [dʒuəriz'dikʃən], *n.* jurisdicción, *f.*
jurist ['dʒuərist], *n.* jurista, *m.f.*
juror ['dʒuərə], *n.* jurado.
jury ['dʒuəri], *n.* jurado.
jury-box ['dʒuəribɔks], *n.* tribuna del jurado.
jury-mast ['dʒuərimɑ:st], *n.* (*naut.*) bandola.
just [dʒʌst], *a.* justo.—*adv.* justamente; apenas, casi; hace muy poco; sólo; (*fam.*) muy; ***to have —,*** acabar de; ***— now,*** hace poco; ahora mismo.
justice ['dʒʌstis], *n.* justicia; juez, *m.*
justify ['dʒʌstifai], *v.t.* justificar.
jut [dʒʌt], *n.* saledizo.—*v.i.* proyectarse (***out***).
jute [dʒu:t], *n.* yute, *m.*
juvenile ['dʒu:vinail], *a.* juvenil.—*n.* joven, menor, *m.f.*
juxtapose [dʒʌkstə'pouz], *v.t.* yuxtaponer.

K

K, k [kei], *n.* undécima letra del alfabeto inglés.
kaf(f)ir ['kæfiə], *a.*, *n.* (*pej.*) cafre, *m.f.*
kale [keil], *n.* col, *f.*
kaleidoscope [kə'laidəskoup], *n.* cal(e)idoscopio.
kangaroo [kæŋgə'ru:], *n.* canguro.
keel [ki:l], *n.* quilla.
keen [ki:n], *a.* agudo; afilado; ansioso, entusiasmado; aficionado (***on,*** a).
keep [ki:p], *n.* mantenimiento; (*fort.*) torre, *f.*; ***for keeps,*** (*fam.*) para siempre.—*v.t. irr.* guardar, quedarse con; criar (*un ganado*); cumplir (*una promesa*); mantener; detener; celebrar.—*v.i. irr.* quedar; mantenerse; no dañarse; ***to — away,*** tener alejado; mantenerse alejado; no acercarse; ***to — back,*** retener; no acercarse; ***to — down,*** sujetar; ***to — on,*** no quitarse; seguir, continuar; ***to — quiet,*** estarse callado.
keeper ['ki:pə], *n.* encargado; guardia, *m.f.*, custodio.
keeping ['ki:piŋ], *n.* custodia; celebración, *f.*; ***in — with,*** de acuerdo con; ***in safe —,*** en buenas manos.
keg [keg], *n.* cuñete, *m.*, barrilito.
ken [ken], *n.* alcance mental, *m.*
kennel [kenl], *n.* perrera.
kept [kept] [KEEP].
kerb [kə:b], *n.* bordillo de acera, adoquín, *m.* [CURB].
kernel [kə:nl], *n.* almendra; (*fig.*) meollo.
kestrel ['kestrəl], *n.* (*orn.*) cernícalo.
kettle [ketl], *n.* caldero; tetera.
kettledrum ['ketldrʌm], *n.* timbal, *m.*
key [ki:], *a.* clave.—*n.* llave, *f.*; tecla (*de piano*); (*fig.*) clave, *f.*; (*mus.*) tono.
key-hole ['ki:houl], *n.* ojo de la llave.
key-note ['ki:nout], *n.* nota tónica; (*fig.*) idea básica.
keystone ['ki:stoun], *n.* piedra clave.
khaki ['kɑ:ki], *a.*, *n.* caqui, *m.*
kick [kik], *n.* coz, *f.*, puntapié, *m.*; culatazo (*de un fusil*); (*fam.*) gusto vivo.—*v.t.*, *v.i.* cocear, dar puntapiés (a); patalear.
kid [kid], *n.* cabrito; (*fam.*) nene, *m.*, niño. —*v.t.* (*fam.*) embromar.
kid-gloves ['kid'glʌvz], *n.pl.* guantes (*m.pl.*) de cabritilla; (*fig.*) blandura, delicadeza.
kidnap ['kidnæp], *v.t.* secuestrar, raptar.
kidnapping ['kidnæpiŋ], *n.* secuestro, rapto.
kidney ['kidni], *n.* riñón, *m.*
kidney-bean ['kidni'bi:n], *n.* judía pinta *o* verde.
kill [kil], *n.* muerte, *f.*, matanza.—*v.t.* matar.
killer ['kilə], *n.* matador, *m.*, asesino.
killing ['kiliŋ], *a.* (*fam.*) agobiante; (*hum.*) ridículo.—*n.* matanza; asesinato.
kill-joy ['kildʒɔi], *n.* aguafiestas, *m.sg.*
kiln [kiln], *n.* horno; ladrillera.
kilo ['ki:lou], *n.* kilo, kilogramo.
kilogram(me) ['kilougræm], *n.* kilogramo.
kilometre ['kiloumi:tə], *n.* kilómetro.
kilt [kilt], *n.* falda escocesa.
kin [kin], *n.* deudos; ***next of —,*** parientes próximos.

kind [kaind], *a.* bondadoso; afectuoso (*recuerdos*).—*n.* clase, *f.*, género, especie, *f.*; ***in* —,** de la misma moneda; en mercancías (*en vez de dinero*); **— *of,*** (*fam.*) algo.
kindergarten ['kindəgɑ:tn], *n.* jardín (*m.*) de la infancia.
kind-hearted [kaind'hɑ:tid], *a.* bondadoso.
kindle [kindl], *v.t.* encender.—*v.i.* -se.
kindly ['kaindli], *a.* benigno.—*adv.* bondadosamente; ***not to take* — *to,*** aceptar de mala gana.
kindness ['kaindnis], *n.* bondad, *f.*
kindred ['kindrid], *a.* semejante; allegado.—*n.* parentela, parientes, *m.pl.*
king [kiŋ], *n.* rey, *m.*
kingdom ['kiŋdəm], *n.* reino.
kingfisher ['kiŋfiʃə], *n.* martín **pescador,** *m.*
kingly ['kiŋli], *a.* regio, real.
king-pin ['kiŋpin], *n.* pivote central, *m.*; bolo central.
kink [kiŋk], *n.* enroscadura; arruga; (*fam.*) capricho, manía.
kinsfolk ['kinzfouk], *n.* parientes, deudos, *m.pl.*
kinsman ['kinzmən], *n.* deudo, pariente, *m.*
kiosk ['ki:ɔsk], *n.* quiosco.
kipper ['kipə], *n.* arenque (*m.*) ahumado.
kirk [kə:k], *n.* (*Scot.*) iglesia.
kiss [kis], *n.* beso.—*v.t.*, *v.i.* besar(se).
kit [kit], *n.* avíos, *m.pl.*, equipo, pertrechos, *m.pl.*
kitchen ['kitʃin], *n.* cocina; **— *garden,*** huerto.
kite [kait], *n.* cometa; (*orn.*) milano.
kith and kin ['kiθənd'kin], *n.* parientes y amigos.
kitten [kitn], *n.* gatito.
kitty (1) ['kiti], *n.* (*fam.*) minino (*gatito*).
kitty (2) ['kiti], *n.* puesta (*polla*).
knack [næk], *n.* tranquillo, truco.
knapsack ['næpsæk], *n.* mochila, barjuleta.
knave [neiv], *n.* bribón, *m.*; sota (*naipes*); (*obs.*) villano; mozo.
knavery ['neivəri], *n.* bellaquería.
knead [ni:d], *v.t.* amasar.
knee [ni:], *n.* rodilla; (*fig.*) codo; ***on his knees,*** de rodillas.
knee-cap ['ni:kæp], *n.* rótula.
knee-deep ['ni:'di:p], *a.* metido hasta las rodillas.
knee-high ['ni:'hai], *a.* hasta las rodillas (de alto).
kneel [ni:l], *v.i. irr.* arrodillarse.
knell [nel], *n.* doble, *m.*, toque (*m.*) de difuntos; mal agüero.
knelt [nelt] [KNEEL].
knew [nju:] [KNOW].
knickers ['nikəz], *n.* bragas, *f.pl.*, cucos, *m.pl.*
knick-knack ['niknæk], *n.* chuchería, bujería.
knife [naif], *n.* (*pl.* **knives**) cuchillo.—*v.t.* acuchillar; apuñalar.
knight [nait], *n.* caballero; **— *errant,*** caballero andante.—*v.t.* armar caballero.
knighthood ['naithud], *n.* caballería.
knit [nit], *v.t. irr.* hacer de punto; unir; fruncir (*la frente*).—*v.i. irr.* hacer punto; hacer calceta; unirse, trabarse.
knitting ['nitiŋ], *n.* labor (*m.*) de punto.
knives [naivz] [KNIFE].
knob [nɔb], *n.* botón, *m.*; protuberancia.
knock [nɔk], *n.* golpe, *m.*; llamada, aldabonazo (*a la puerta*).—*v.t.* golpear; ***to* — *about,*** estar *o* ir por ahí; ***to* — *down,*** derribar; atropellar (*coche*); ***to* — *out,*** sacar a golpes; dejar sin sentido (con un puñetazo).—*v.i.* llamar (*a la puerta*); pistonear (*motor*).
knocker ['nɔkə], *n.* aldaba (*de la puerta*).
knock-kneed ['nɔkni:d], *a.* zambo, patizambo.
knock-out ['nɔkaut], *a.* decisivo; final.—*n.* fuera (*m.*) de combate, knock-out, *m.*
knoll [noul], *n.* otero, loma.
knot [nɔt], *n.* nudo; lazo.—*v.t.* anudar.—*v.i.* -se.
knotty ['nɔti], *a.* nudoso; (*fig.*) espinoso.
know [nou], *v.t.*, *v.i. irr.* saber (*un hecho*); conocer (*por los sentidos*); ***in the* —,** (*fam.*) enterado; ***to* — *best,*** saber lo que más conviene; ***to* — *how to,*** saber; ***to* — *what's what,*** saber cuántas son cinco.
know-all ['nouɔ:l], *n.* (*fam.*) sabelotodo.
know-how ['nouhau], *n.* (*fam.*) conocimiento técnico; tranquillo.
knowingly ['nouiŋli], *adv.* a sabiendas.
knowledge ['nɔlidʒ], *n.* conocimiento(s); erudición, *f.*; ciencia; ***to my* —,** que yo sepa.
known [noun] [KNOW].
knuckle [nʌkl], *n.* nudillo, artejo; codillo, jarrete (*carne*), *m.*—*v.i.* ***to* — *down,*** ponerse (***to it,*** al trabajo); someterse; ***to* — *under,*** someterse.
Koran [kə'rɑ:n], *n.* Alcorán, Corán, *m.*
Korea [kə'riə], *n.* Corea.
Korean [kə'riən], *a.*, *n.* coreano.
Kuwait [ku'weit], *n.* Estado del Kuwait.

L

L, l [el], *n.* **duodécima letra del alfabeto inglés.**
lab [læb], *n.* (*fam.*) [LABORATORY].
label [leibl], *n.* etiqueta, rótula, letrero; rotuelo (*de un libro*); (*fam.*) nombre, *m.*—*v.t.* rotular; apodar.
laboratory [lə'bɔrətəri], *n.* laboratorio.
laborious [lə'bɔ:riəs], *a.* laborioso, penoso.
labour ['leibə], *n.* trabajo; obreros, *m.pl.*, mano (*f.*) de obra; (*med.*) parto; ***Labour Party,*** (*pol.*) partido laborista.—*v.t.* macear, machacar; trillar.—*v.i.* trabajar, forcejar; padecer, sufrir (***under***).
laboured ['leibəd], *a.* penoso; forzado.
labourer ['leibərə], *n.* peón, *m.*, bracero, jornalero.
laburnum [lə'bə:nəm], *n.* (*bot.*) codeso, laburno.
labyrinth ['læbirinθ], *n.* laberinto.
lace [leis], *n.* encaje; cordón (*de un zapato*), *m.*—*v.t.* atar (*un zapato*); añadir licor a.
lacerate ['læsəreit], *v.t.* lacerar.
lack [læk], *n.* falta, carencia, escasez, *f.*—*v.t.* carecer de; necesitar.—*v.i.* faltar.
lackadaisical [lækə'deizikəl], *a.* cachazudo.
lackey ['læki], *n.* lacayo.
lacking ['lækiŋ], *a.* falto, carente (***in,*** de).
laconic [lə'kɔnik], *a.* lacónico.

lacquer ['lækə], *n.* laca, barniz, *m.*—*v.t.* laquear.
lad [læd], *n.* chaval, *m.*
ladder ['lædə], *n.* escalera (de mano); carrera (*en una media*).
laden [leidn], *a.* cargado.
ladle [leidl], *n.* cucharón, *m.*
lady ['leidi], *n.* dama, señora.
lady-in-waiting ['leidiin'weitiŋ], *n.* dama de servicio.
lady-killer ['leidikilə], *n.* (*fam.*) tenorio.
ladyship ['leidiʃip], *n.* señoría (*título*).
lag (1) [læg], *n.* retraso.—*v.i.* rezagarse.
lag (2) [læg], *v.t.* proteger con fieltro (*tubos*).
lag (3) [læg], *n.* (*fam.*) preso.
laggard ['lægəd], *a.*, *n.* rezagado.
lagoon [lə'gu:n], *n.* laguna.
laid [leid], *a.*, *p.p.* [LAY]; — ***up***, fuera de servicio; enfermo.
lain [lein], [LIE].
lair [lɛə], *n.* cubil, *m.*, guarida.
laird [lɛəd], *n.* (*Scot.*) señor hacendado.
laity ['leiiti], *n.* los legos.
lake [leik], *n.* lago; laca (*color*).
lamb [læm], *n.* cordero.
lame [leim], *a.* cojo; flojo.—*v.t.* encojar.
lameness ['leimnis], *n.* cojera; defecto; flojedad, *f.*
lament [læ'ment], *n.* lamento.—*v.t.*, *v.i.* lamentar(se).
lamentable ['læməntəbl], *a.* lamentable.
lamentation [læmən'teiʃən], *n.* lamentación, *f.*
lamina ['læminə], *n.* lámina.
lamp [læmp], *n.* lámpara; farol, *m.*
lampoon [læm'pu:n], *n.* pasquín, *m.*—*v.t.* pasquinar.
lamp-post ['læmppoust], *n.* pie *o* poste (*m.*) de farol.
lance [lɑ:ns], *n.* lanza; (*med.*) lanceta; — ***corporal***, (*mil.*) cabo menor.—*v.t.* abrir con lanceta.
lancer ['lɑ:nsə], *n.* lancero.
lancet ['lɑ:nsit], *n.* lanceta.
land [lænd], *n.* tierra; terreno.—*v.t.* desembarcar; poner en tierra; sacar a la tierra.—*v.i.* desembarcar; (*aer.*) aterrizar; ir a parar.
landed ['lændid], *a.* hacendado.
landing ['lændiŋ], *n.* desembarco; desembarcadero (*sitio*); (*aer.*) aterrizaje, *m.*; descanso (*de la escalera*).
landlady ['lændleidi], *n.* mesonera; patrona.
landlord ['lændlɔ:d], *n.* mesonero; patrón, *m.*
land-lubber ['lændlʌbə], *n.* marinero de agua dulce.
landmark ['lændmɑ:k], *n.* mojón, *m.*; marca; punto culminante *o* de referencia.
land-owner ['lændounə], *n.* terrateniente, *m.f.*
landscape ['lændskeip], *n.* paisaje, *m.*
landslide ['lændslaid], *n.* derrumbe, *m.*, argayo, desprendimiento de tierra; (*pol.*) victoria aplastante.
lane [lein], *n.* senda, vereda, callejuela; (*aer.*, *naut.*) ruta, derrotero.
language ['læŋgwidʒ], *n.* lenguaje (*estilo*), *m.*; lengua, idioma, *m.*
languid ['læŋgwid], *a.* lánguido, flojo.
languish ['læŋgwiʃ], *v.i.* languidecer, penar.
languor ['læŋgə], *n.* languidez, *f.*
lank [læŋk], *a.* flaco; lacio; descarnado.
lanky ['læŋki], *a.* (*fam.*) larguirucho.
lantern ['læntən], *n.* linterna.
Laos [laus], *n.* Laos, *m.*
Laotian ['lauʃən], *a.*, *n.* laocio, laosiano.
lap (1) [læp], *n.* regazo; (*sport*) etapa; doblez, *f.*, traslapo.—*v.t.* traslapar.—*v.i.* -se.
lap (2) [læp], *n.* chapaleteo (*de agua*).—*v.t.* lamer; beber a lengüetadas.—*v.i.* lamer.
lap-dog ['læpdɔg], *n.* perrillo faldero.
lapel [lə'pel], *n.* solapa.
Lapland ['læplænd], *n.* Laponia.
Lapp [læp], *n.* lapón (*persona*), *m.*
Lappish ['læpiʃ], *a.* lapón.—*n.* lapón (*idioma*), *m.*
lapse [læps], *n.* lapso; yerro; transcurso (*período*); caducidad, *f.*—*v.i.* recaer; caducar.
lapwing ['læpwiŋ], *n.* (*orn.*) avefría.
larceny ['lɑ:səni], *n.* hurto, latrocinio.
larch [lɑ:tʃ], *n.* (*bot.*) alerce, *m.*
lard [lɑ:d], *n.* manteca (de cerdo).—*v.t.* (*cul.*) mechar; (*fig.*) entreverar.
larder ['lɑ:də], *n.* despensa.
large [lɑ:dʒ], *n.* grande, grueso; ***at*** —, en general; en libertad.
largess ['lɑ:dʒes], *n.* largueza.
lariat ['læriət], *n.* lazo.
lark (1) [lɑ:k], *n.* (*orn.*) alondra.
lark (2) [lɑ:k], *n.* (*fam.*) calaverada, parranda.—*v.i.* bromear.
larynx ['læriŋks], *n.* laringe, *f.*
lascivious [lə'siviəs], *a.* lascivo.
lash [læʃ], *n.* látigo; latigazo; (*anat.*) pestaña.—*v.t.* azotar; atar.
lashing ['læʃiŋ], *n.* azotamiento; atadura, ligadura.—*pl.* gran cantidad. *f.*
lass [læs], *n.* chavala.
lasso [læ'su:], *n.* lazo.—*v.t.* lazar.
last (1) [lɑ:st], *a.* último; postr(im)ero; pasado; — ***night***, anoche; — ***straw***, colmo, acabóse, *m.*; — ***week***, la semana pasada. —*n.* el último.—*adv.* la última vez; por último; ***at*** —, por fin.
last (2) [lɑ:st], *n.* horma (*para los zapatos*).—*v.i.* durar, continuar, seguir; conservarse.
lasting ['lɑ:stiŋ], *a.* duradero.
latch [lætʃ], *n.* cerrojo, picaporte, *m.*—*v.t.* cerrar con picaporte.
latchkey ['lætʃki:], *n.* llavín, *m.*
late [leit], *a.* tardío; reciente; avanzado (*hora*); difunto, lamentado; — ***lamented***, fallecido.—*adv.* tarde; ***to be*** —, ser tarde; llevar un retraso; ***of*** —, recientemente.
late-comer ['leitkʌmə], *n.* rezagado.
lately ['leitli], *adv.* estos días, últimamente.
latent ['leitənt], *a.* latente.
lateral ['lætərəl], *a.* lateral.
latex ['leiteks], *n.* látex, *m.*
lath [lɑ:θ], *n.* listón, *m.*
lathe [leið], *n.* torno.
lather ['lɑ:ðə], *n.* espuma de jabón.
Latin ['lætin], *a.*, *n.* latino; latín (*idioma*), *m.*; — ***America***, la América Latina, Hispanoamérica.
latitude ['lætitju:d], *n.* latitud, *f.*
latrine [lə'tri:n], *n.* letrina.
latter ['lætə], *a.* posterior, moderno; ***the*** —, éste.
lattice ['lætis], *n.* celosía, enrejado.—*v.t.* enrejar.
laud [lɔ:d], *n.* loa.—*v.t.* loar.
laudable ['lɔ:dəbl], *a.* laudable, loable.

laugh [lɑ:f], *n.* risa.—*v.i.* reír(se); ***to — at,*** reírse de; ***to — off,*** tomar a risa.
laughable ['lɑ:fəbl], *a.* risible.
laughing ['lɑ:fiŋ], *a.* risueño.—*n.* risa.
laughingly ['lɑ:fiŋli], *adv.* entre risas; risiblemente.
laughing-stock ['lɑ:fiŋstɔk], *n.* hazmerreír, *m.*
laughter ['lɑ:ftə], *n.* risa.
launch [lɔ:ntʃ], *n.* lancha.—*v.t.* lanzar; botar (*un navío*).—*v.i.* lanzarse.
lauching-pad ['lɔ:ntʃiŋpæd], *n.* plataforma de lanzamiento.
launder ['lɔ:ndə], *v.t.* lavar y planchar.
laundress ['lɔ:ndris], *n.* lavandera.
laundry ['lɔ:ndri], *n.* lavadero; ropa lavada.
laureate ['lɔ:rieit], *a., n.* laureado.
laurel ['lɔrəl], *n.* laurel, lauro, *m.*
lava ['lɑ:və], *n.* lava.
lavatory ['lævətəri], *n.* lavabo, retrete, *m.*
lavender ['lævində], *n.* espliego, alhucema.
lavish ['læviʃ], *a.* pródigo.—*v.t.* prodigar, desparramar.
law [lɔ:], *n.* ley, *f.*; derecho (*asignatura*); — ***and order,*** paz pública.
law-abiding ['lɔ:əbaidiŋ], *a.* pacífico, formal, probo.
law-breaker ['lɔ:breikə], *n.* transgresor, *m.*, criminal, *m.f.*
law-court ['lɔ:kɔ:t], *n.* tribunal (*m.*) de justica.
lawful ['lɔ:ful], *a.* legal, lícito, legítimo.
law-giver ['lɔ:givə], *n.* legislador, *m.*
lawless ['lɔ:lis], *a.* desaforado.
lawn [lɔ:n], *n.* césped, *m.*
lawn-mower ['lɔ:nmouə], *n.* segadora de césped.
law-suit ['lɔ:sju:t], *n.* pleito.
lawyer ['lɔ:jə], *n.* abogado.
lax [læks], *a.* laxo, vago; negligente.
laxative ['læksətiv], *a.* laxativo.—*n.* laxante, *m.*
laxity ['læksiti], *n.* laxitud, flojedad, *f.*; descuido, dejadez, *f.*
lay (1) [lei], *a.* seglar, lego, profano.
lay (2) [lei], *n.* caída, orientación, *f.*; balada.—*v.t. irr.* poner, colocar; echar, tender; matar (*polvo etc.*); poner (*huevos, la mesa*); calmar; conjurar (*aparecido*); achacar; trazar (*proyectos*); ***to — aside,*** poner a un lado; ***to — down,*** declarar, sentar; rendir (*armas*); dar (*vida*); ***to — waste,*** asolar, devastar.—*v.i. irr.* poner (*gallinas*); apostar; ***to — oneself open to,*** exponerse a.
layer [leiə], *n.* capa, cama, lecho; estrato.
layette [lei'et], *n.* canastilla.
layman ['leimən], *n.* lego; (*fig.*) profano.
lay-out ['leiaut], *n.* disposición, *f.*; plan, *m.*
laze [leiz], *v.i.* holgazanear.
laziness ['leizinis], *n.* pereza.
lazy ['leizi], *a.* perezoso.
lazy-bones ['leizibounz], *n.* (*fam.*) gandul, *m.* vago.
lea [li:], *n.* (*poet.*) prado.
lead (1) [led], *n.* plomo.
lead (2) [li:d], *n.* delantera; primacía; dirección, *f.*; (*theat.*) papel principal, *m.*; (*elec.*) conductor, *m.*—*v.t. irr.* conducir; acaudillar; dirigir; llevar.—*v.i. irr.* ser el primero; conducir; mandar; ***to — up to,*** resultar en, conducir a.
leaden [ledn], *a.* plomizo; muy pesado; de plomo.
leader ['li:də], *n.* caudillo; líder; director, *m.*; artículo de fondo (*en un periódico*).
leadership ['li:dəʃip], *n.* jefatura, mando; dotes (*m.pl.*) de mando.
leading ['li:diŋ], *a.* principal; eminente; director; — ***lady,*** dama; — ***man,*** primer galán, *m.*
leaf [li:f], *n.* (*pl.* **leaves**) hoja.—*v.i.* echar hojas; ***to — through,*** hojear.
leaflet ['li:flit], *n.* hojuela; hoja volante.
leafy ['li:fi], *a.* frondoso.
league [li:g], *n.* liga.
leak [li:k], *n.* gotera; escape, *m.*; (*naut.*) vía de agua.—*v.i.* hacer agua; escaparse, salirse; ***to — out,*** trascender.
leaky ['li:ki], *a.* llovedizo; que hace agua.
lean [li:n], *a.* magro; flaco; pobre.—*n.* molla, carne mollar, *f.*—*v.t. irr.* apoyar, arrimar.—*v.i. irr.* apoyarse, arrimarse; inclinarse; ***to — out,*** asomarse (***of,*** a).
leaning ['li:niŋ], *a.* inclinado.—*n.* propensión, *f.*, tendencia.
lean-to ['li:ntu:], *a., n.* colgadizo.
leap [li:p], *n.* salto; — ***year,*** año bisiesto.—*v.t., v.i. irr.* saltar.
learn [lə:n], *v.t., v.i. irr.* aprender; ***to — of,*** saber.
learned ['lə:nid], *a.* docto, erudito.
learner ['lə:nə], *n.* principiante, aprendiz, *m.*
learning ['lə:niŋ], *n.* erudición, *f.*, ciencia.
lease [li:s], *n.* arriendo.—*v.t.* arrendar.
leasehold ['li:should], *n.* censo.
leash [li:ʃ], *n.* traílla.
least [li:st], *a.* el menor, el más pequeño.—*adv.* menos; lo menos; ***at —,*** al menos, por lo menos.
leather ['leðə], *n.* cuero.
leathery ['leðəri], *a.* correoso.
leave [li:v], *n.* permiso; (*mil.*) licencia.—*v.t. irr.* dejar; (*jur.*) legar; salir de.—*v.i. irr.* salir; irse; ***to — alone,*** dejar en paz; ***to — out,*** omitir; ***to take one's — of,*** despedirse de.
leaven [levn], *n.* levadura.—*v.t.* leudar.
leaves [li:vz] [LEAF].
leave-taking ['li:vteikiŋ], *n.* despedida.
leavings ['li:viŋz], *n.pl.* sobras, *f.pl.*; desechos, *m.pl.*
Lebanese [lebə'ni:z], *a., n.inv.* libanés, *m.*
Lebanon ['lebənən], *n.* el Líbano.
lecher ['letʃə], *n.* lujurioso.
lecherous ['letʃərəs], *a.* lujurioso.
lechery ['letʃəri], *n.* lujuria.
lectern ['lektə:n], *n.* atril, facistol, *m.*
lecture ['lektʃə], *n.* conferencia; — ***theatre,*** aula, anfiteatro.—*v.t.* sermonear.—*v.i.* dar conferencias.
lecturer ['lektʃərə], *n.* conferenciante, *m.f.*, profesor universitario.
led [led], [LEAD].
ledge [ledʒ], *n.* anaquel, *m.*; tonga; repisa.
ledger ['ledʒə], *n.* libro mayor.
lee [li:], *n.* (*naut.*) sotavento, socaire, *m.*
leech [li:tʃ], *n.* sanguijuela; (*obs.*) médico.
leek [li:k], *n.* puerro.
leer [liə], *n.* mirada lasciva, mirada de reojo.—*v.i.* mirar con lascivia, mirar de reojo (***at***).
lees [li:z], *n.pl.* heces, *f.pl.*
leeward ['lu:əd], *a.* de sotavento.
leeway ['li:wei], *n.* (*naut.*) deriva; tardanza; libertad, *f.*
left [left], *a.* izquierdo.—*n.* izquierda.

left-handed ['left'hændid], *a.* zurdo.
left-overs ['leftouvəz], *n.pl.* sobras.
left-wing ['left'wiŋ], *a.* izquierdista.
leg [leg], *n.* pierna; pata; etapa; ***to pull someone's —***, tomar el pelo a; ***on one's last legs,*** a la muerte, de capa caída.
legacy ['legəsi], *n.* legado.
legal ['li:gəl], *a.* legal.
legate ['legit], *n.* legado.
legation [li'geiʃən], *n.* legación, *f.*
legend ['ledʒənd], *n.* leyenda.
legendary ['ledʒəndri], *a.* legendario.
legible ['ledʒibl], *a.* legible.
legion ['li:dʒən], *n.* legión, *f.*
legislate ['ledʒisleit], *v.t., v.i.* legislar.
legislation [ledʒis'leiʃən], *n.* legislación, *f.*
legitimate [li'dʒitimit], *a.* legítimo.
leg-up ['legʌp], *n.* (*fam.*) ayuda.
leisure ['leʒə], *n.* ocio, ratos libres, *m.pl.*
leisurely ['leʒəli], *a.* pausado.
lemon ['lemən], *n.* limón, *m.*
lemonade [lemə'neid], *n.* limonada.
lend [lend], *v.t. irr.* prestar.
length [leŋθ], *n.* largura, largo; ***at —***, por fin; ***to go to any length(s),*** hacer todo lo posible.
lengthen ['leŋθən], *v.t.* alargar.
lengthy ['leŋθi], *a.* prolongado, largo.
lenient ['li:njənt], *a.* clemente.
lens [lenz], *n.* lente, *m.* o *f.*
Lent [lent], *n.* Cuaresma.
lent [lent] [LEND].
lentil ['lentil], *n.* lenteja.
leopard ['lepəd], *n.* leopardo.
leper ['lepə], *n.* leproso.
leprosy ['leprəsi], *n.* lepra.
lese-majesty [li:z'mædʒisti], *n.* lesa majestad, *f.*
less [les], *a.* menor.—*adv.* menos; ***— and —,*** cada vez menos.
lessen [lesn], *v.t.* minorar, disminuir.—*v.i.* disminuirse; amainar (*viento*).
lesson [lesn], *n.* lección; clase, *f.*; ***to be a — to,*** escarmentar.
lest [lest], *conj.* para que no, de miedo que.
let (1) [let], *v.t. irr.* dejar; alquilar; ***to — by,*** dejar pasar; ***to — down,*** bajar; desilusionar, dejar colgado; ***to — go,*** soltar; ***to — know,*** hacer saber, avisar; ***to — off,*** disparar; perdonar; ***— him come,*** que venga; ***— us say,*** digamos.
let (2) [let], *n.* ***without —***, sin estorbo.
lethal ['li:θəl], *a.* letal.
lethargic [lə'θɑ:dʒik], *a.* letárgico.
let's [lets] [LET US].
letter ['letə], *n.* carta (*correo*); letra (*del alfabeto*).—*pl.* letras (*literatura*).
letter-box ['letəbɔks], *n.* buzón, *m.*
lettuce ['letis], *n.* lechuga.
Levant [lə'vænt], *n.* Levante, *m.*
level ['levəl], *a.* nivelado, llano, raso; cuerdo; ***to do one's — best,*** hacer su posible.—*n.* nivel, *m.*; llano.—*v.t.* allanar, anivelar; apuntar.
level-crossing ['levəl'krɔsiŋ], *n.* paso a nivel.
level-headed ['levəl'hedid], *a.* sensato.
lever ['li:və], *n.* palanca.
leveret ['levərit], *n.* lebratillo.
leviathan [lə'vaiəθən], *n.* leviatán, *m.*
levity ['leviti], *n.* ligereza, veleidad, *f.*
levy ['levi], *n.* (*mil.*) leva; exacción, recaudación, *f.*—*v.t.* (*mil.*) reclutar; recaudar.
lewd [lju:d], *a.* salaz, lascivo.
lexical ['leksikəl], *a.* léxico.
lexicon ['leksikən], *n.* léxico.
liability [laiə'biliti], *n.* responsibilidad, *f.*; desventaja.
liable ['laiəbl], *a.* responsable; sujeto, expuesto; propenso.
liaison [li'eizən], *n.* coordinación, *f.*, enlace, *m.*; amorío.
liar [laiə], *n.* mentiroso.
libel ['laibəl], *n.* calumnia.—*v.t.* calumniar.
liberal ['libərəl], *a., n.* liberal, *m.f.*
liberate ['libəreit], *v.t.* liber(t)ar.
liberation [libə'reiʃən], *n.* liberación, *f.*
liberator ['libəreitə], *n.* liber(t)ador, *m.*
Liberian [lai'biərjən], *a., n.* liberiano.
libertine ['libəti:n], *a., n.* libertino.
liberty ['libəti], *n.* libertad, *f.*
librarian [lai'brɛəriən], *n.* bibliotecario.
library ['laibrəri], *n.* biblioteca.
Libya ['libjə], *n.* la Libia.
Libyan ['libjən], *a., n.* libio.
lice [lais] [LOUSE].
licence ['laisəns], *n.* (*U.S.* **license**) licencia; permiso; libertinaje, *m.*; ***driving —,*** permiso de conducir; ***— number,*** (número de) matrícula.—*v.t.* licenciar; autorizar.
licentious [lai'senʃəs], *a.* licencioso.
lichen ['laikən, 'litʃin], *n.* liquen, *m.*
licit ['lisit], *a.* lícito.
lick [lik], *n.* lamedura.—*v.t.* lamer; (*fam.*) tundear; vencer.
licorice ['likəris], *n.* regaliz, *m.*
lid [lid], *n.* tapa, tapadera, cobertera.
lie (1) [lai], *n.* mentira.—*v.t., v.i.* mentir; ***to give the — to,*** desmentir.
lie (2) [lai], *n.* situación, *f.*—*v.i. irr.* yacer; echarse; hallarse; ***to — down,*** acostarse.
liege [li:dʒ], *a.* feudal.—*n.* vasallo; señor, *m.*
lieu [lju:], *n.* ***in — of,*** en vez de.
lieutenant [lef'tenənt], *n.* lugarteniente; (*mil.*) teniente, *m.*
life [laif], *a.* vital; vitalicio; perpetuo.—*n.* (*pl.* **lives**) vida; vivacidad, *f.*; ***— insurance,*** seguro de vida.
life-boat ['laifbout], *n.* lancha salvavidas.
lifeless ['laiflis], *a.* muerto; exánime; flojo.
lifelike ['laiflaik], *a.* vivo, natural.
lifelong ['laiflɔŋ], *a.* de toda la vida.
lifetime ['laiftaim], *n.* curso de la vida, vida.
lift [lift], *n.* alzamiento; (*Brit.*) ascensor, *m.*; (*fam.*) invitación (*f.*) para subir a un coche.—*v.t.* levantar, elevar, alzar; reanimar; (*fam.*) sisar, hurtar.
light [lait], *a.* ligero; leve; claro (*color*); rubio.—*n.* luz; lumbre, *f.*, fuego.—*pl.* bofes, *m.pl.*—*v.t. irr.* encender; alumbrar, iluminar (***up***).
lighten [laitn], *v.t.* aligerar; alegrar.—*v.i.* relampaguear.
lighter (1) ['laitə], *n.* mechero.
lighter (2) ['laitə], *n.* (*naut.*) barcaza, gabarra.
light-fingered [lait'fiŋgəd], *a.* largo de uñas.
light-headed [lait'hedid], *a.* casquivano; mareado.
light-hearted [lait'hɑ:tid], *a.* alegre, festivo.
lighthouse ['laithaus], *n.* faro.
lighting ['laitiŋ], *n.* alumbrado; encendido.
lightning ['laitniŋ], *n.* relámpago, relampagueo, rayo.
light-ship ['laitʃip], *n.* buque faro.

like (1) [laik], *a.* semejante; probable.—*n.* semejante, *m.*—*prep.* como, igual que; ***to look* —,** parecerse a.
like (2) [laik], *n.* gusto.—*v.t.* gustar de; ***I* — *this,*** esto me gusta; ***when you* —,** cuando Vd. quiera.
likelihood ['laiklihud], *n.* probabilidad, *f.*
likely ['laikli], *a.* probable.
liken ['laikən], *v.t.* comparar, asemejar.
likewise ['laikwaiz], *adv.* también, igualmente.
liking ['laikiŋ], *n.* gusto, afición, *f.*
lilac ['lailək], *n.* lila.
lilt [lilt], *n.* ritmo, paso alegre.
lily ['lili], *n.* azucena, lirio.
limb [lim], *n.* miembro; brazo; rama (*árbol*).
limbo ['limbou], *n.* limbo.
lime (1) [laim], *n.* cal, *f.*
lime (2) [laim], *n.* lima (*fruta*).
lime (3) [laim], *n.* (*bot.*) tilo.
lime-kiln ['laimkiln], *n.* calera.
lime-light ['laimlait], *n.* (*theat.*) luz (*f.*) del proyector; (*fig.*) luz (*f.*) de la publicidad.
limerick ['limərik], *n.* copla jocosa.
limestone ['laimstoun], *n.* piedra caliza.
limit ['limit], *n.* límite, *m.*; (*fam.*) colmo.—*v.t.* limitar.
limitation [limi'teiʃən], *n.* limitación, *f.*
limited ['limitid], *a.* limitado; ***— company,*** sociedad anónima.
limp [limp], *a.* flojo, blando.—*n.* cojera.—*v.i.* cojear.
limpet ['limpit], *n.* lapa, lápade, *f.*
limpid ['limpid], *a.* cristalino.
linden ['lindən], *n.* (*bot.*) tilo.
line [lain], *n.* línea; renglón, *m.*; cuerda; raya; (*rail.*) vía; descendencia; (*com.*) ramo; especialidad, *f.*; ***in — with,*** de acuerdo con; ***hard lines,*** (*fam.*) lástima, mala suerte.— *v.t.* poner en fila *o* línea; forrar.—*v.i.* ***to — up,*** hacer cola.
lineage ['liniidʒ], *n.* linaje, *m.*
lineal ['liniəl], **linear** ['liniə], *a.* lineal.
linen ['linin], *n.* lino, lienzo.
liner ['lainə], *n.* transatlántico.
linger ['liŋgə], *v.i.* tardar, demorarse.
lingerie ['lɛ̃ʒri:], *n.* ropa blanca de mujer.
lingo ['liŋgou], *n.* (*fam.*) jerga.
linguist ['liŋgwist], *n.* lingüista, *m.f.*
linguistic [liŋ'gwistik], *a.* lingüístico.
lining ['lainiŋ], *n.* forro; rayado.
link (1) [liŋk], *n.* eslabón, *m.*—*v.t.* eslabonar, juntar.
link (2) [liŋk], *n.* (*pl.*) campo de golf.
linnet ['linit], *n.* pardillo.
linoleum [lin'ouljəm], *n.* linóleo.
linseed ['linsi:d], *n.* linaza.
lint [lint], *n.* hilas.
lion ['laiən], *n.* león, *m.*; ***lion's share,*** parte (*f.*) del león.
lioness ['laiənis], *n.* leona.
lip [lip], *n.* labio; (*low*) descaro.
lip-service ['lipsə:vis], *n.* jarabe (*m.*) de pico.
lipstick ['lipstik], *n.* barra *o* lápiz (*m.*) de labios.
liquefy ['likwifai], *v.t.* liquidar.—*v.i.* -se.
liqueur [li'kjuə], *n.* licor, *m.*
liquid ['likwid], *a.*, *n.* líquido.
liquidate ['likwideit], *v.t.* liquidar.
liquor ['likə], *n.* licor, *m.*; (*U.S.*) bebidas alcohólicas, *f.pl.*
liquorice [LICORICE].
Lisbon ['lizbən], *n.* Lisboa.
lisp [lisp], *n.* ceceo.—*v.i.* cecear.
list (1) [list], *n.* lista.—*v.t.* hacer una lista de.
list (2) [list], *n.* (*naut.*) ladeo, escora.—*v.i.* (*naut.*) ir a la banda, escorar.
listen [lisn], *v.i.* escuchar (*to*).
listener ['lisnə], *n.* oyente, *m.*, *f.*
listless ['listlis], *a.* apático, indiferente.
lit [lit] [LIGHT].
litany ['litəni], *n.* letanía.
literal ['litərəl], *a.* literal.
literary ['litərəri], *a.* literario.
literate ['litərit], *a.* que sabe leer y escribir; literato.
literature ['litərətʃə], *n.* literatura.
lithe [laið], *a.* ágil, cimbreño.
lithograph ['liθogrɑ:f *or* -græf], *n.* litografía.
litigant ['litigənt], *n.* litigante, *m.f.*
litigate ['litigeit], *v.i.* litigar.
litigation [liti'geiʃən], *n.* litigación, *f.*
litmus ['litməs], *n.* (*chem.*) tornasol, *m.*
litre ['li:tə], *n.* litro.
litter ['litə], *n.* basura, desechos; litera camilla; paja; ventregada, camada.—*v.t.* esparcir, echar basura en; desordenar.
little [litl], *a.* pequeño; poco; ***— finger,*** dedo meñique.—*adv.* poco; ***a —,*** un poco (de); algún tanto; ***— by —,*** poco a poco; ***to think — of,*** tener en poco.
liturgical [li'tə:dʒikl], *a.* litúrgico.
liturgy ['litədʒi], *n.* liturgia.
live (1) [liv], *v.t.* llevar (*una vida*); vivir; ***to — down,*** borrar (el recuerdo de).—*v.i.* vivir; ***to — up to,*** cumplir, honrar.
live (2) [laiv], *a.* vivo; cargado (*elec.*, *munición*); ardiente; natural.
livelihood ['laivlihud], *n.* vida, subsistencia.
lively ['laivli], *a.* vivo, vivaz, brioso.
liver ['livə], *n.* (*anat.*) hígado.
livery ['livəri], *n.* librea; de alquiler.
lives [laivz] [LIFE].
livestock ['laivstɔk], *n.* ganado.
livid ['livid], *a.* lívido; (*fam.*) negro.
living ['liviŋ], *a.* vivo, viviente.—*n.* vida; modo de ganar la vida; (*eccl.*) beneficio.
living-room ['liviŋrum], *n.* sala de estar.
lizard ['lizəd], *n.* lagarto, lagartija.
load [loud], *n.* carga.—*pl.* (*fam.*) una barbaridad de.—*v.t.* cargar.
loadstone [LODESTONE].
loaf [louf], *n.* (*pl.* **loaves**) pan, *m.*; hogaza.—*v.i.* gandulear.
loafer ['loufə], *n.* haragán, gandul, *m.*
loam [loum], *n.* marga.
loan [loun], *n.* préstamo; empréstito.—*v.t.* prestar.
loath [louθ], *a.* poco dispuesto.
loathe [louð], *v.t.* detestar, abominar.
loathing ['louðiŋ], *n.* detestación, *f.*, asco.
loathsome ['louðsəm], *a.* asqueroso, nauseabundo.
loaves [louvz] [LOAF].
lobby ['lɔbi], *n.* vestíbulo; (*pol.*) cabilderos, *m.pl.*—*v.t.* cabildear.
lobe [loub], *n.* lóbulo.
lobster ['lɔbstə], *n.* langosta.
local ['loukəl], *a.* local.
localize ['loukəlaiz], *v.t.* localizar.
locate [lou'keit], *v.t.* situar; localizar.
loch [lɔk, lɔx], *n.* (*Scot.*) ría; lago.

lock [lɔk], *n.* cerradura; esclusa (*de canal*); bucle (*pelo*), *m.*; (*mech.*) cámara (*aire*); ***under — and key,*** debajo de llave; —, ***stock and barrel,*** todo; del todo.—*v.t.* cerrar con llave; trabar; ***to — up,*** (*fam.*) encarcelar. —*v.i.* cerrarse; trabarse.
lock-jaw ['lɔkdʒɔ:], *n.* trismo, tétano.
lock-out ['lɔkaut], *n.* (*com., pol.*) cierre, *m.*; paro forzoso.
locksmith ['lɔksmiθ], *n.* cerrajero.
lock-up ['lɔkʌp], *n.* (*fam.*) calabozo.
locomotive [loukə'moutiv], *n.* locomotora.
locust ['loukəst], *n.* (*ent.*) langosta.
lode [loud], *n.* (*min.*) venero, veta.
lodestone ['loudstoun], *n.* piedra imán.
lodge [lɔdʒ], *n.* casita; pabellón, *m.*; portería; logia.—*v.t.* alojar; hospedar; fijar, plantar; presentar (*una queja*).—*v.i.* alojarse.
lodger ['lɔdʒə], *n.* huésped, *m.*, inquilino.
lodging ['lɔdʒiŋ], *n.* alojamiento.—*pl.* pensión, *f.*, cuartos alquilados, *m.pl.*
loft [lɔft], *n.* desván; pajar, *m.*
lofty ['lɔfti], *a.* encumbrado; excelso; altivo.
log [lɔg], *n.* tronco, leño; (*naut., aer.*) diario de navegación *o* de vuelo; (*fam.*) logaritmo.
logarithm ['lɔgəriðəm], *n.* logaritmo.
log-book ['lɔgbuk], *n.* (*naut.*) cuaderno de bitácora; (*aer.*) diario de vuelo.
loggerheads ['lɔgəhedz], *n.pl.* ***to be at —,*** estar reñidos, venir a las manos.
logic ['lɔdʒik], *n.* lógica.
logical ['lɔdʒikəl], *a.* lógico.
logwood ['lɔgwud], *n.* campeche, *m.*
loin [lɔin], *n.* (*anat.*) ijada; lomo.
loiter ['lɔitə], *v.i.* haraganear, tardar.
loiterer ['lɔitərə], *n.* vago, haragán, *m.*
loll [lɔl], *v.i.* colgar, repantigarse.
lollipop ['lɔlipɔp], *n.* paleta, dulce (*m.*) en palito.
London ['lʌndən], *n.* Londres, *m.*
Londoner ['lʌndənə], *n.* londinense, *m.f.*
lone [loun], *a.* solo, solitario.
loneliness ['lounlinis], *n.* soledad, *f.*
lonely ['lounli], *a.* (*U.S.* **lonesome**) solo, solitario, triste.
long [lɔŋ], *a.* largo.—*adv.* mucho tiempo, mucho; ***as — as,*** mientras que; con tal que; ***how —,*** cuanto tiempo; ***— ago,*** hace mucho tiempo; ***so — !*** (*fam.*) ¡hasta luego! — *v.i.* morirse, anhelar (***for,*** por); ansiar; ***to be — in,*** tardar en.
long-distance ['lɔŋ'distəns], *a., adv.* (*tel.*) interurbano.
longhand ['lɔŋhænd], *n.* escritura ordinaria.
longing ['lɔŋiŋ], *n.* anhelo, ansia.
longitude ['lɔndʒitju:d], *n.* longitud, *f.*
long-lived ['lɔŋlivd], *a.* de larga vida, duradero.
longshoreman ['lɔŋʃɔ:mən], *n.* estibador, *m.*
long-standing ['lɔŋstændiŋ], *a.* que existe desde hace mucho tiempo.
long-winded [lɔŋ'windid], *a.* palabrero, interminable.
look [luk], *n.* mirada; aspecto, aire, *m.*—*v.i.* parecer; ***to — after,*** cuidar; ***to — at,*** mirar; ***to — for,*** buscar; ***to — into,*** investigar; ***to — like,*** parecerse a; ***to — on,*** juzgar, tener (***as,*** por); ***to — out,*** tener cuidado; ***to — out for,*** aguardar; guardarse de; ***to — up,*** buscar; (*fam.*) mejorar; (*fam.*) visitar; ***to — (out) on(to),*** dar a.
looker-on [lukə'rɔn], *n.* (*pl.* **lookers-on**) espectador, mirón, *m.*
looking-glass ['lukiŋglɑ:s], *n.* espejo.
look-out ['lukaut], *n.* atalaya (*sitio*), *f.*; atalaya (*hombre*), *m.*; ***on the — for,*** a la mira de.
loom (1) [lu:m], *n.* telar, *m.*
loom (2) [lu:m], *v.i.* asomar; amenazar.
loony ['lu:ni], *a.* (*fam.*) chiflado.
loop [lu:p], *n.* lazo; recodo. vuelta; recoveco; presilla; (*aer.*) rizo.—*v.t.* enlazar; doblar; atar.—*v.i.* formar lazo(s); recodar; ***to — the —,*** rizar el rizo.
loophole ['lu:phoul], *n.* abertura; (*mil.*) aspillera; (*fig.*) escapatoria.
loose [lu:s], *a.* suelto; flojo; disoluto; vago; ***to set —,*** libertar; soltar; ***to come —,*** desprenderse.—*v.t.* soltar; desatar.
loosen [lu:sn], *v.t.* aflojar; desatar.
loot [lu:t], *n.* botín, *m.*—*v.t.* saquear, pillar.
lop [lɔp], *v.t.* desmochar, podar (***off***).
lope [loup], *n.* zancada, paso largo.
lop-sided [lɔp'saidid], *a.* al sesgo, desequilibrado.
loquacious [lou'kweiʃəs], *a.* locuaz.
lord [lɔ:d], *n.* señor; (*Brit.*) lord; ***Our Lord,*** Nuestro Señor; ***House of Lords,*** Cámara de los Lores; ***Lord Chamberlain,*** Camarero Mayor; ***Lord's Prayer,*** padrenuestro.—*v.i.* ***to — it over,*** señorear altivamente.
lore [lɔ:], *n.* saber popular, *m.*
lorry ['lɔri], *n.* (*Brit.*) camión, *m.*
lose [lu:z], *v.t., v.i. irr.* perder.
loss [lɔs], *n.* pérdida; ***at a —,*** perplejo.
lost [lɔst] [LOSE].
lot [lɔt], *n.* mucho, gran cantidad; suerte, *f.*, sino; partija, lote, *m.*, solar (*sitio para construir casas etc.*), *m.*; ***to draw lots,*** echar suertes.
loth [LOATH].
lotion ['louʃən], *n.* loción, *f.*
lottery ['lɔtəri], *n.* lotería.
lotus ['loutəs], *n.* loto.
loud [laud], *a.* alto, fuerte, ruidoso; (*fam.*) vistoso, chillón; cursi.
loud-speaker [laud'spi:kə], *n.* (*rad. etc.*) altavoz, *m.*
lounge [laundʒ], *n.* salón, *m.*; gandulería.—*v.i.* recostarse, repantigarse; haraganear.
louse [laus], *n.* (*pl.* **lice**) piojo.
lousy ['lauzi], *a.* piojoso; (*fam.*) malísimo, sucio; (*fam.*) colmado (*de dinero*).
love [lʌv], *n.* amor, *m.*; cariño; (*sport*) cero; ***in —,*** enamorado (***with,*** de).—*v.t.* querer, amar; (*fam.*) gustarle muchísimo.
love affair ['lʌvə'fɛə], *n.* amores, *m.pl.*; (*pej.*) amorío.
lovely ['lʌvli], *a.* hermoso; precioso.
lover ['lʌvə], *n.* amante; querido.
loving ['lʌviŋ], *a.* cariñoso.
low (1) [lou], *a.* bajo; desanimado; ruin.—*adv.* bajo; ***Low Countries,*** Países Bajos; ***— water*** o ***tide,*** marea baja, bajamar, *f.*; ***— gear,*** primera marcha.—*adv.* bajo; ***to lie —,*** tenerse escondido.
low (2) [lou], *v.i.* mugir (*vacas*).
low-brow ['loubrau], *a.* (*fam.*) poco culto.
lower [louə], *v.t., v.i.* bajar.—*compar. of* LOW.
lowly ['louli], *a.* humilde.
loyal ['lɔiəl], *a.* leal, fiel.
loyalty ['lɔiəlti], *n.* lealtad, *f.*
lozenge ['lɔzindʒ], *n.* pastilla; (*geom., her.*) losange, *m.*

lubricant ['lu:brikənt], *a.*, *n.* lubricante, *m.*
lubricate ['lu:brikeit], *v.t.* lubricar.
lucid ['lju:sid], *a.* luciente; lúcido.
luck [lʌk], *n.* suerte, *f.*
lucky ['lʌki], *a.* afortunado, dichoso; ***to be* —**, tener (buena) suerte.
lucrative ['lu:krətiv], *a.* lucrativo.
lucre ['lu:kə], *n.* lucro, el vil metal.
ludicrous ['lu:dikrəs], *a.* absurdo, ridículo.
luggage ['lʌgidʒ], *n.* equipaje, *m.*
lugubrious [lu'gju:briəs], *a.* lóbrego, funesto.
lukewarm ['lu:kwɔ:m], *a.* tibio.
lull [lʌl], *n.* momento de calma, tregua.—*v.t.* calmar, adormecer.—*v.i.* calmarse; amainar.
lullaby ['lʌləbai], *n.* canción (*f.*) de cuna, nana.
lumbago [lʌm'beigou], *n.* lumbago.
lumber ['lʌmbə], *n.* maderaje, *m.*, madera; trastos, *m.pl.*
lumbering ['lʌmbəriŋ], *a.* pesado, torpe, desmañado.
lumberjack ['lʌmbədʒæk], *n.* hachero, leñador, *m.*
lumber-room ['lʌmbərum], *n.* leonera, trastera.
lumber-yard ['lʌmbəya:d], *n.* madería.
luminous ['lju:minəs], *a.* luminoso.
lump [lʌmp], *n.* pedazo; bulto; borujo; chichón, *m.*; — ***sugar***, azúcar (*m.*) en terrón; — ***sum***, pago *o* suma total.—*v.t.* aterronar; juntar; (*fam.*) aguantar.—*v.i.* aterronarse.
lumpy ['lʌmpi], *a.* borujoso, aterronado.
lunacy ['lu:nəsi], *n.* locura, demencia.
lunatic ['lu:nətik], *a.*, *n.* loco; — ***asylum***, manicomio.
lunch [lʌntʃ], *n.* almuerzo.—*v.i.* almorzar.
luncheon ['lʌntʃən], *n.* almuerzo de ceremonia.
lung [lʌŋ], *n.* pulmón, *m.*
lunge [lʌndʒ], *n.* estocada; arremetida.—*v.i.* dar una estocada (***at***, a); arremetir.
lupin(e) ['lu:pin], *n.* lupino, altramuz, *m.*
lurch [lə:tʃ], *n.* sacudida; guiñada, bandazo; ***to leave in the* —**, dejar en las astas del toro. — *v.i.* dar una sacudida; tambalearse; (*naut.*) guiñar, dar un bandazo.
lure [ljuə], *n.* señuelo, añagaza.—*v.t.* atraer con señuelo; seducir, entruchar.
lurid ['ljuərid], *a.* ominoso, espeluznante.
lurk [lə:k], *v.i.* acechar.
luscious ['lʌʃəs], *a.* exquisito, rico.
lush [lʌʃ], *a.* lozano.
lust [lʌst], *n.* lujuria; codicia; deseo vehemente.—*v.i.* codiciar (***after***); lujuriar.
lustful ['lʌstful], *a.* lujurioso.
lustre ['lʌstə], *n.* lustre, *m.*, brillo.
lusty ['lʌsti], *a.* recio, robusto, forzudo.
lute [lju:t], *n.* laúd, *m.*
Luther ['lu:θə], *n.* Lutero.
Lutheran ['lu:θərən], *a.*, *n.* luterano.
Luxemb(o)urg ['lʌksəmbə:g], *n.* Luxemburgo.
Luxemburger ['lʌksəm'bə:gə], *n.* luxemburgués.
Luxemburgian ['lʌksəm'bə:gjən], *a.* luxemburgués.
luxuriant [lʌg'zjuəriənt], *a.* lujuriante.
luxuriate [lʌg'zjuərieit], *v.i.* crecer con lozanía; lozanear; abundar.
luxurious [lʌg'zjuəriəs], *a.* lujoso.
luxury ['lʌkʃəri], *n.* lujo.
lying (1) ['laiiŋ], *a.* mentiroso.—*n.* mentiras, *f.pl.*
lying (2) ['laiiŋ] [LIE (2)].
lynch [lintʃ], *v.t.* linchar.
lynx [liŋks], *n.* lince, *m.*
lyre [laiə], *n.* lira.
lyric ['lirik], *a.* lírico.—*n.* lírica; letra (*de una canción*).
lyrical ['lirikəl], *a.* lírico.

M

M, m [em], *n.* letra decimotercera del alfabeto inglés.
ma'am [ma:m] [MADAM].
macabre [mə'ka:br], *a.* macabro.
macaroni [mækə'rouni], *n.* macarrones, *m.pl.*
mace (1) [meis], *n.* maza (*ceremonial*).
mace (2) [meis], *n.* macia (*especia*).
Machiavelli [mækiə'veli], *n.* Maquiavelo.
Machiavellian [mækiə'veliən], *a.* maquiavélico.—*n.* maquiavelista, *m.f.*
machination [mæki'neiʃən], *n.* maquinación, *f.*
machine [mə'ʃi:n], *n.* máquina.—*v.t.* hacer a máquina.
machinery [mə'ʃi:nəri], *n.* maquinaria.
machine-gun [mə'ʃi:ngʌn], *n.* ametralladora.
mackerel ['mækərəl], *n.* (*pl.* **mackerel**) caballa.
mackintosh ['mækintɔʃ], *n.* impermeable, *m.*, gabardina.
mad [mæd], *a.* loco; enojado; ***to go* —**, volverse loco.
madam ['mædəm], *n.* señora; (*fam.*) descarada.
madcap ['mædkæp], *n.* botarate, *m.*
madden [mædn], *v.t.* enloquecer; enojar.
made [meid], *a.* hecho; próspero. [MAKE].
made-up ['meid'ʌp], *a.* falso, ficticio; hecho; compuesto; pintado.
madhouse ['mædhaus], *n.* manicomio.
madman ['mædmən], *n.* loco.
madness ['mædnis], *n.* locura.
magazine [mægə'zi:n], *n.* revista; recámara (*de un fusil*); almacén; polvorín, *m.*; (*naut.*) santabárbara.
maggot ['mægət], *n.* cresa.
magic ['mædʒik], *a.* mágico.—*n.* magia; brujería.
magician [mə'dʒiʃən], *n.* mágico; brujo.
magistrate ['mædʒistreit], *n.* magistrado, juez, *m.*
magnanimous [mæg'næniməs], *a.* magnánimo.
magnate ['mægneit], *n.* magnate, *m.*
magnesium [mæg'ni:zjəm], *n.* magnesio.
magnet ['mægnit], *n.* imán, *m.*
magnetic [mæg'netik], *a.* magnético.
magnetism ['mægnitizm], *n.* magnetismo.
magnetize ['mægnitaiz], *v.t.* magnetizar.
magnificence [mæg'nifisəns], *n.* magnificencia.
magnificent [mæg'nifisənt], *a.* magnífico.

magnify ['mægnifai], *v.t.* magnificar.
magnifying glass ['mægnifaiiŋ'glɑ:s], *n.* lupa.
magnitude ['mægnitju:d], *n.* magnitud, *f.*
magpie ['mægpai], *n.* (*orn.*) urraca, picaza.
mahogany [mə'hɔgəni], *n.* caoba.
Mahomet, *n.* [mə'hɔmit] [MOHAMMED].
maid [meid], *n.* criada; doncella; virgen, *f.*
maiden [meidn], *a.* primero, de estreno; virginal.—*n.* doncella.
mail (1) [meil], *n.* correo; cartas, *f.pl.* — ***man,*** (*U.S.*) cartero.—*v.t.* (*U.S.*) echar al correo, mandar por correo.
mail (2) [meil], *n.* malla.
mail-bag ['meilbæg], *n.* valija.
mail-train ['meiltrein], *n.* tren correo.
maim [meim], *v.t.* mutilar.
main [mein], *a.* principal; mayor (*calle*); maestro.—*n.* robustez, *f.*; (*poet.*) océano; cañería maestra; cable maestro; ***in the —,*** principalmente.
mainland ['meinlænd], *n.* continente, *m.*, tierra firme.
maintain [mein'tein], *v.t.* mantener.
maintenance ['meintinəns], *n.* mantenimiento; conservación, *f.*
maize [meiz], *n.* maíz, *m.*
majestic [mə'dʒestik], *a.* majestuoso.
majesty ['mædʒisti], *n.* majestad, *f.*
major ['meidʒə], *a.* principal; mayor.—*n.* mayor (*m.f.*) de edad; (*mil.*) comandante, mayor, *m.*; — ***general,*** general (*m.*) de división.
Majorca [mə'dʒɔ:kə], *n.* Mallorca.
Majorcan [mə'dʒɔ:kən], *a.*, *n.* mallorquín, *m.*
majordomo ['meidʒə'doumou], *n.* mayordomo.
majority [mə'dʒɔriti], *n.* mayoría.
make [meik], *n.* marca, fabricación, *f.*; hechura.—*v.t. irr.* hacer; producir; fabricar; ganar (*dinero*); pronunciar (*una oración*); forzar, obligar; calcular; ***to — after,*** correr en pos de; ***to — as if to,*** hacer como que, fingir; ***to — away with,*** llevarse; matar; ***to — fast,*** amarrar; ***to — good,*** reparar; indemnizar; tener éxito; ***to — off,*** escaparse; ***to — out,*** descifrar; explicar; ***to — up,*** inventar; recompensar (*for*); formar; reconciliar(se); pintarse; maquillar(se); ***to — up one's mind,*** decidirse; ***to — sense,*** tener sentido; ***to — way,*** abrir paso.
make-believe ['meikbili:v], *a.* fingido.—*n.* artificio, simulación, *f.*
Maker ['meikə], *n.* Creador, *m.*; **maker,** *n.* fabricante, *m.*
makeshift ['meikʃift], *a.* provisional.—*n.* suplente; expediente, *m.*
make-up ['meikʌp], *n.* cosméticos, *m.pl.*; composición, *f.*; (*theat.*) maquillaje, *m.*
makeweight ['meikweit], *n.* contrapeso; suplente, *m.*
making ['meikiŋ], *n.* fabricación, *f.*; hechura; éxito.
mal- [mæl], *prefix.* mal-, des-.
maladjusted [mælə'dʒʌstid], *a.* inadaptado, mal adaptado.
malady ['mælədi], *n.* dolencia, enfermedad, *f.*
malaria [mə'lɛəriə], *n.* paludismo.
Malaysian [mə'leiʒən], *a.*, *n.* malaysia.
malcontent ['mælkəntent], *a.*, *n.* malcontento.
male [meil], *a.*, *n.* macho (*animales*); varón (*personas*), *m.*
malediction [mæli'dikʃən], *n.* maldición, *f.*
malefactor ['mælifæktə], *n.* malhechor, maleante, *m.*
malevolence [mə'levələns], *n.* malevolencia.
malevolent [mə'levələnt], *a.* malévolo.
malformed [mæl'fɔ:md], *a.* deformado.
malice ['mælis], *n.* malicia; rencor, *m.*
malicious [mə'liʃəs], *a.* malicioso.
malign [mə'lain], *a.* maligno.—*v.t.* calumniar.
malignant [mə'lignənt], *a.* maligno.
malinger [mə'liŋgə], *v.i.* fingirse enfermo.
malingerer [mə'liŋgərə], *n.* enfermo fingido.
mallard ['mæləd], *n.* (*orn.*) pato silvestre, lavanco.
malleable ['mæliəbl], *a.* maleable.
mallet ['mælit], *n.* mazo.
mallow ['mælou], *n.* (*bot.*) malva.
malmsey ['mɑ:mzi], *n.* malvasía.
malnutrition [mælnju(:)'triʃən], *n.* desnutrición, *f.*
malpractice [mæl'præktis], *n.* abuso, procedimientos ilegales, *m.pl.*
malt [mɔ:lt], *n.* malta.
Maltese [mɔ:l'ti:z], *a.*, *n.* maltés, *m.*
maltreat [mæl'tri:t], *v.t.* maltratar.
maltreatment [mæl'tri:tmənt], *n.* maltrato.
mammal ['mæməl], *a.*, *n.* mamífero.
mammoth ['mæməθ], *a.* gigantesco.—*n.* mamut, *m.*
man [mæn], *n.* (*pl.* **men**) hombre; varón, *m.*; criado; pieza (*ajedrez etc.*); ***no —,*** nadie; ***to a —,*** todos; unánimemente; ***— and boy,*** desde la mocedad.—*v.t.* guarnecer, (*naut.*) tripular.
manacle ['mænəkl], *n.* manilla, esposas, *f.pl.*—*v.t.* maniatar, poner esposas a.
manage ['mænidʒ], *v.t.* manejar; (*com.*) dirigir.—*v.i.* arreglárselas; conseguir (*to*).
management ['mænidʒmənt], *n.* manejo; gerencia, dirección, *f.*
manager ['mænidʒə], *n.* gerente, director, *m.*; apoderado; empresario; ahorrador, *m.*
manageress [mænidʒə'res], *n.* directora.
mandarin ['mændərin], *n.* mandarín, *m.*; mandarina (*fruta*).
mandate ['mændeit], *n.* mandato.
mandolin ['mændəlin], *n.* mandolina.
mane [mein], *n.* crin (*de caballo*), *f.*; melena (*de león*).
man-eater ['mæni:tə], *n.* caníbal, *m.f.*, antropófago.
maneuver [mən'u:və], (*U.S.*) [MANOEUVRE].
manfully ['mænfuli], *adv.* valientemente.
manganese [mæŋgə'ni:z], *n.* manganeso.
mange [meindʒ], *n.* sarna.
manger ['meindʒə], *n.* pesebre, *m.*
mangle [mæŋgl], *n.* calandria; exprimidor, *m.*—*v.t.* pasar por el exprimidor; mutilar, despedazar.
mangy ['meindʒi], *a.* sarnoso.
manhole ['mænhoul], *n.* pozo de registro, buzón, *m.*
manhood ['mænhud], *n.* virilidad, *f.*; los hombres; edad viril, *f.*
mania ['meinjə], *n.* manía.
maniac ['meiniæk], *a.*, *n.* maniático.
manicure ['mænikjuə], *n.* manicura.
manifest ['mænifest], *a.*, *n.* manifiesto.—*v.t.* manifestar.
manifesto [mæni'festou], *n.* manifiesto.
manifold ['mænifould], *a.* múltiple.

manikin ['mænikin], *n.* maniquí, *m.*
manipulate [mə'nipjuleit], *v.t.* manipular.
mankind [mæn'kaind], *n.* humanidad, *f.*, el género humano; los hombres.
manliness ['mænlinis], *n.* virilidad, *f.*
manly ['mænli], *a.* viril; varonil.
manna ['mænə], *n.* maná, *m.*
mannequin ['mænikin], *n.* modelo, *f.*
manner ['mænə], *n.* manera.—*pl.* costumbres, *f.pl.*, modales, *m.pl.*
mannered ['mænəd], *a.* amanerado; educado.
mannerism ['mænərizm], *n.* hábito; amaneramiento.
mannerly ['mænəli], *a.* cortés, urbano.
mannish ['mæniʃ], *a.* hombruno.
manoeuvre [mə'nu:və], *n.* maniobra.—*v.t.* hacer maniobrar.—*v.i.* maniobrar.
man-of-war ['mænəv'wɔ:], *n.* (*pl.* **men-of-war**) buque (*m.*) de guerra.
manor ['mænə], *n.* casa señorial, finca solariega; feudo.
mansion ['mænʃən], *n.* palacio, casa señorial.
manslaughter ['mænslɔ:tə], *n.* homicidio accidental *o* no premeditado.
mantel [mæntl], *n.* manto.
mantelpiece ['mæntlpi:s], *n.* repisa de chimenea.
mantilla [mæn'tilə], *n.* mantilla.
mantle [mæntl], *n.* manto, capa; manguito (*gas*).—*v.t.* tapar, cubrir.
manual ['mænjuəl], *a.*, *n.* manual, *m.*
manufacture [mænju'fæktʃə], *n.* fabricación, *f.*—*v.t.* fabricar, manufacturar.
manufacturer [mænju'fæktʃərə], *n.* fabricante, *m.*
manure [mə'njuə], *n.* estiércol, *m.*—*v.t.* abonar, estercolar.
manuscript ['mænjuskript], *a.*, *n.* manuscrito.
many ['meni], *a.*, *pron.* muchos; gran número (de); ***a good*** o ***great* —**, muchísimos; ***how* —**, cuantos; ***so* —**, tantos; ***too* —**, demasiados; de sobra.
many-coloured ['meni'kʌləd], *a.* multicolor.
many-sided ['meni'saidid], *a.* multilátero; versátil, polifacético.
map [mæp], *n.* mapa, *m.*, plan, *m.*—*v.t.* planear, trazar el mapa de (***out***).
maple [meipl], *n.* arce, *m.*
mar [mɑ:], *v.t.* echar a perder, desfigurar.
maraud [mə'rɔ:d], *v.t.* merodear por.
marauder [mə'rɔ:də], *n.* merodeador, *m.*
marauding [mə'rɔ:diŋ], *a.* merodeante.—*n.* merodeo.
marble [mɑ:bl], *n.* mármol, *m.*; bolita, canica (*juguete*).—*v.t.* marmolizar.
March [mɑ:tʃ], *n.* marzo.
march (1) [mɑ:tʃ], *n.* marcha.—*v.t.* hacer marchar.—*v.i.* marchar.
march (2) [ma:tʃ], *n.* marca (*frontería*).
marchioness ['mɑ:ʃənis], *n.* marquesa.
march-past ['mɑ:tʃ'pɑ:st], *n.* desfile, *m.*
mare [mεə], *n.* yegua; ***mare's nest***, parto de los montes.
Margaret ['mɑ:gərit], *n.* Margarita.
margarine, [mɑ:dʒə'ri:n, mɑ:gə'ri:n], *n.* margarina.
margin ['mɑ:dʒin], *n.* margen (*de un papel*), *m.* o *f.*; reserva.
marginal ['mɑ:dʒinəl], *a.* marginal.
marigold ['mærigould], *n.* (*bot.*) maravilla; clavelón, *m.*
marijuana [mæri'hwɑ:nə], *n.* mariguana.
marine [mə'ri:n], *a.* marítimo, marino.—*n.* marina; soldado de la marina.
mariner ['mærinə], *n.* marinero.
marital ['mæritəl], *a.* marital.
maritime ['mæritaim], *a.* marítimo.
mark [mɑ:k], *n.* marca, señal, *f.*; indicio; traza, vestigio; nota, calificación (*en un examen*), *f.*; blanco (*tiro*); signo; rango; marco (*moneda*).—*v.t.* marcar; notar; señalar; anotar.
market ['mɑ:kit], *n.* mercado.—*v.t.* vender; comerciar en.
market-garden ['mɑ:kit'gɑ:dn], *n.* huerta, granja.
marksman ['ma:ksmən], *n.* tirador, *m.*, buen tiro.
marksmanship ['mɑ:ksmənʃip], *n.* buena puntería.
marmalade ['mɑ:məleid], *n.* mermelada.
maroon (1) [mə'ru:n], *a.*, *n.* marrón, *m.*
maroon (2) [mə'ru:n], *v.t.* abandonar, aislar.
marquee [mɑ:'ki:], *n.* tienda grande.
marquess, marquis ['mɑ:kwis], *n.* marqués, *m.*
marriage ['mæridʒ], *n.* matrimonio; casamiento; (*fig.*) maridaje, *m.*
marriageable ['mæridʒəbl], *a.* casadero.
marriage-licence ['mæridʒ'laisəns], *n.* dispensa de amonestación.
married ['mærid], *a.* casado; conyugal.
marrow ['mærou], *n.* médula, meollo; (*bot.*) calabaza.
marry ['mæri], *v.t.* casar; casarse con; (*fig.*) maridar.—*v.i.* casarse.
Mars [mɑ:z], *n.* Marte, *m.*
Marseilles [mɑ:'seilz], *n.* Marsella.
marsh [mɑ:ʃ], *n.* pantano; marisma.
marshal ['mɑ:ʃəl], *n.* mariscal, *m.*—*v.t.* ordenar, regimentar.
marshy ['mɑ:ʃi], *a.* pantanoso, palustre.
mart [mɑ:t], *n.* mercado, emporio.
marten ['mɑ:tin], *n.* marta, garduña.
martial ['mɑ:ʃəl], *a.* marcial, bélico. [COURT-MARTIAL].
martin ['mɑ:tin], *n.* (*orn.*) avión, *m.*
martyr ['mɑ:tə], *n.* mártir, *m.f.*—*v.t.* martirizar.
martyrdom ['mɑ:tədəm], *n.* martirio.
marvel ['mɑ:vəl], *n.* maravilla.—*v.i.* maravillarse (***at***, de).
marvellous ['mɑ:viləs], *a.* maravilloso.
Marxism ['mɑ:ksizm], *n.* marxismo.
Marxist ['mɑ:ksist], *a.*, *n.* marxista, *m.f.*
Mary ['mεəri], *n.* María.
marzipan ['mɑ:zipæn], *n.* mazapán, *m.*
mascot ['mæskɔt], *n.* mascota.
masculine ['mæskjulin], *a.* masculino.
mash [mæʃ], *n.* masa; amasijo.—*v.t.* magullar majar, aplastar.
mask [mɑ:sk], *n.* máscara.—*v.t.* enmascarar.
mason [meisn], *n.* albañil; (franco)masón, *m.*
masonic [mə'sɔnik], *a.* masónico.
masonry ['meisnri], *n.* albañilería; mampostería, ladrillos, piedras *etc.*; masonería.
masquerade [mæskə'reid], *n.* mascarada; farsa.—*v.i.* enmascararse; hacer una farsa; hacerse pasar (***as***, por).
mass (1) [mæs], *n.* masa; multitud. *f.*; bulto.—*v.t.* amasar; juntar en masa.—*v.i.* juntarse en masa.
mass (2) [mæs, mɑ:s], *n.* (*eccl.*) misa.

massacre ['mæsəkə], *n.* matanza, carnicería. —*v.t.* degollar, destrozar.
massage ['mæsɑ:dʒ], *n.* masaje, *m.*—[mə'sɑ:dʒ], *v.t.* masar, sobar.
masseur [mæ'sə:], *n.* masajista, *m.*
masseuse [mæ'sə:z], *n.* masajista.
massive ['mæsiv], *a.* macizo, enorme.
mass-meeting ['mæs'mi:tiŋ], *n.* mitín popular, *m.*
mass-production ['mæsprə'dʌkʃən], *n.* fabricación (*f.*) en serie.
mast [mɑ:st], *n.* (*naut.*) mástil, *m.*, palo; (*rad.*) torre, *f.*
master ['mɑ:stə], *a.* maestro.—*n.* maestro; patrón; dueño; (*educ.*) profesor, *m.*; perito; amo.—*v.t.* dominar.
masterful ['mɑ:stəful], *a.* imperioso; perito.
masterly ['mɑ:stəli], *a.* magistral.
masterpiece ['mɑ:stəpi:s], *n.* obra maestra.
mastery ['mɑ:stəri], *n.* dominio; maestría.
masthead ['mɑ:sthed], *n.* tope, *m.*
masticate ['mæstikeit], *v.t.* masticar.
mastiff ['mæstif], *n.* mastín, *m.*, alano.
mat (1) [mæt], *n.* estera; greña.—*v.t.* esterar; enredar.—*v.i.* enredarse.
mat (2) [mæt], *a.* mate.
match (1) [mætʃ], *n.* igual; pareja; boda; (*sport*) partido.—*v.t.* hacer juego con; igualar.
match (2) [mætʃ], *n.* cerilla, fósforo.
match-box ['mætʃbɔks], *n.* cajetilla.
match-maker ['mætʃmeikə], *n.* casamentero (*entre novios*).
mate (1) [meit], *n.* compañero; (*naut.*) contramaestre, *m.*; (*fam.*) camarada, amigo.—*v.i.* acoplarse.
mate (2) [meit], *n.* (*chess*) mate, *m.*—*v.t.* (*chess*) dar mate a.
material [mə'tiəriəl], *a.* material; importante. —*n.* material, *m.*; materia; tela, género.
materialism [mə'tiəriəlizm], *n.* materialismo.
materialist [mə'tiəriəlist], *n.* materialista, *m.f.*
materialistic [mətiəriə'listik], *a.* materialista.
materialize [mə'tiəriəlaiz], *v.t.* realizar; dar cuerpo a.—*v.i.* realizarse; tomar cuerpo.
maternal [mə'tə:nəl], *a.* materno; maternal.
maternity [mə'tə:niti], *n.* maternidad, *f.*
mathematical [mæθə'mætikəl], *a.* matemático.
mathematician [mæθəmə'tiʃən], *n.* matemático.
mathematics [mæθə'mætiks], *n.* matemáticas, *f.pl.*
matinée ['mætinei], *n.* función (*f.*) de tarde.
matins ['mætinz], *n.pl.* maitines, *m.pl.*
matriculate [mə'trikjuleit], *v.t.* matricular.—*v.i.* -se.
matriculation [mətrikju'ləiʃən], *n.* matrícula.
matrimonial [mætri'mounjəl], *a.* matrimonial, conyugal.
matrimony ['mætriməni], *n.* matrimonio.
matrix ['mætriks], *n.* (*pl.* **matrices**) matriz, *f.*
matron ['meitrən], *n.* matrona.
matter ['mætə], *n.* materia; asunto; motivo; importancia; (*med.*) pus, *m.*; ***as a — of fact,*** en realidad; ***a — of,*** cosa de; ***no —,*** no importa.—*v.i.* importar; supurar; ***to be the — with,*** pasar a.
matter-of-fact ['mætərəv'fækt], *a.* prosaico.
Matthew ['mæθju:], *n.* Mateo.
mattress ['mætris], *n.* colchón, *m.*
mature [mə'tjuə], *a.* maduro; (*com.*) pagadero.—*v.t.*, *v.i.* madurar; (*com.*) vencer.
maturity [mə'tjuəriti], *n.* madurez, *f.*; (*com.*) vencimiento.
maudlin ['mɔ:dlin], *a.* sensiblero; calamocano.
maul [mɔ:l], *v.t.* sobar; maltratar; destrozar.
Maundy Thursday ['mɔ:ndi'θə:zdei], *n.* jueves santo.
mausoleum [mɔ:sə'liəm], *n.* mausoleo.
mauve [mouv], *a.* color (*m.*) de malva.—*n.* malva.
mawkish ['mɔ:kiʃ], *a.* sensiblero, ñoño.
maxim ['mæksim], *n.* máxima.
maximum ['mæksiməm], *a.* máximo.—*n.* máximum, *m.*
May [mei], *n.* mayo.
may [mei], *v. aux. irr.* poder; tener permiso; ***it — be,*** puede ser.
maybe ['meibi, mei'bi:], *adv.* acaso, tal vez.
mayor [mɛə], *n.* alcalde, *m.*
mayoress ['mɛəres], *n.* alcaldesa.
maze [meiz], *n.* laberinto.
me [mi:], *pron.* me; mí; ***with —,*** conmigo.
meadow ['medou], *n.* prado, pradera.
meagre ['mi:gə], *a.* escaso; flaco.
meal (1) [mi:l], *n.* comida.
meal (2) [mi:l], *n.* harina.
mealy-mouthed ['mi:li'mauðd], *a.* meloso, mojigato.
mean (1) [mi:n], *a.* tacaño; ruin; malintencionado.
mean (2) [mi:n], *a.* medio, mediano (*ordinario*).—*n.* medio, promedio.—*pl.* medios; manera; recursos, dinero; ***by all means,*** no faltaba más; ***by no means,*** de ninguna manera; ***by some means,*** de alguna manera.
mean (3) [mi:n], *v.t. irr.* querer decir, significar.—*v.i. irr.* proponerse, pensar.
meander [mi'ændə], *n.* meandro.—*v.i.* serpentear.
meaning ['mi:niŋ], *n.* significado, sentido.
meaningful ['mi:niŋful], *a.* significativo.
meaningless ['mi:niŋlis], *a.* sin sentido.
meanness ['mi:nnis], *n.* mezquindad, *f.*, tacañería; ruindad, *f.*
meant [ment] [MEAN].
meantime ['mi:ntaim], *n.* interín, *m.*; ***in the —,*** entretanto.
meanwhile ['mi:n'hwail], *adv.* entretanto.
measles [mi:zlz], *n.* sarampión, *m.*
measure ['meʒə], *n.* medida; (*mus.*) compás, *m.*; medio, gestión, *f.*; (*jur.*) proyecto de ley.—*v.t.*, *v.i.* medir.
measured ['meʒəd], *a.* deliberado; mesurado; rítmico.
measurement ['meʒəmənt], *n.* medida; mensuración, *f.*
meat [mi:t], *n.* carne, *f.*; ***cold —,*** fiambre, *m.*; ***minced —,*** picadillo.
meaty ['mi:ti], *a.* carnoso; (*fig.*) jugoso, substancial.
Mecca ['mekə], *n.* la Meca.
mechanic [mə'kænik], *n.* mecánico.—*pl.* mecánica.
mechanical [mə'kænikəl], *a.* mecánico; maquinal.

mechanism ['mekənizm], *n.* mecanismo.
mechanize ['mekənaiz], *v.t.* mecanizar.
medal [medl], *n.* medalla.
medallion [mə'dæljən], *n.* medallón, *m.*
meddle [medl], *v.i.* entremeterse.
meddler ['medlə], *n.* entremetido, intruso.
meddlesome ['medlsəm], *a.* entremetido.
meddling ['medliŋ], *a.* entremetido.—*n.* oficiosidad, *f.*
mediaeval [MEDIEVAL].
mediate ['mi:dieit], *v.t., v.i.* mediar.
medical ['medikəl], *a.* médico, de medicina.
medicament ['medikəmənt], *n.* medicamento.
medicinal [me'disinl], *a.* medicinal.
medicine [medsn], *n.* medicina.
medicine-man ['medsnmæn], *n.* curandero.
medieval [medi'i:vəl], *a.* medieval.
mediocre ['mi:dioukə], *a.* mediocre, mediano.
mediocrity [mi:di'ɔkriti], *n.* mediocridad, *f.*
meditate ['mediteit], *v.i.* meditar.
meditation [medi'teiʃən], *n.* meditación, *f.*
Mediterranean [meditə'reinjən], *a., n.* Mediterráneo.
medium ['mi:djəm], *a.* mediano.—*n.* (*pl.* **-ums** *o* **-a**) medio.
medley ['medli], *n.* mescolanza, fárrago.
meek [mi:k], *a.* manso, dócil.
meet [mi:t], *n.* (*sport*) concurso.—*v.t. irr.* encontrar; encontrarse con; recibir; honrar; cumplir.—*v.i. irr.* encontrarse (***with,*** con).
meeting ['mi:tiŋ], *n.* reunión, *f.*; (*pol.*) mitin, *m.*; encuentro.
megacycle ['megəsaikl], *n.* megaciclo.
megalomaniac [megəlou'meiniæk], *a., n.* megalómano.
megaphone ['megəfoun], *n.* portavoz, *m.*, megáfono.
melancholia [melən'kouljə], *n.* melancolía.
melancholic [melən'kɔlik], *a., n.* melancólico.
melancholy ['melənkəli], *a.* melancólico.—*n.* melancolía.
mêlée ['melei], *n.* refriega.
mellow ['melou], *a.* suave, meloso; maduro. —*v.t.* suavizar.—*v.i.* suavizarse.
melodious [mi'loudjəs], *a.* melodioso.
melodrama ['melədrɑ:mə], *n.* melodrama, *m.*
melodramatic [meloudrə'mætik], *a.* melodramático.
melody ['melədi], *n.* melodía.
melon ['melən], *n.* melón, *m.*
melt [melt], *v.t.* fundir, derretir.—*v.i.* fundirse, derretirse; deshacerse.
melting pot ['meltiŋpɔt], *n.* crisol, *m.*
member ['membə], *n.* miembro; socio; vocal (*de un comité*), *m.*
membership ['membəʃip], *n.* personal, *m.*, socios, *m.pl.*; el ser miembro *o* socio.
membrane ['membrein], *n.* membrana.
memo ['memou], *n.* (*fam.*) apunte, *m.*
memoir ['memwɑ:], *n.* memoria.
memorandum [memə'rændəm], *n.* (*pl.* **-da**) memorándum, *m.*
memorial [mə'mɔ:rjəl], *a.* conmemorativo.—*n.* monumento.
memorize ['meməraiz], *v.t.* aprender de memoria.
memory ['meməri], *n.* memoria; recuerdo.
men [men] [MAN].
menace ['menis], *n.* amenaza.—*v.t., v.i.* amenazar.

menagerie [mi'nædʒəri], *n.* colección (*f.*) de fieras, zoo, *m.*
mend [mend], *n.* remiendo.—*v.t.* remendar, componer, reparar.
mendicant ['mendikənt], *a., n.* mendicante, *m.*
menfolk ['menfouk], *n.pl.* hombres, *m.pl.*
menial ['mi:njəl], *a.* servil.—*n.* lacayo.
mental ['mentəl], *a.* mental.
mentality [men'tæliti], *n.* mentalidad, *f.*
menthol ['menθəl], *n.* mentol, *m.*
mention ['menʃən], *n.* mención, *f.*—*v.t.* mencionar.
menu ['menju:], *n.* menú, *m.*, minuta.
mercantile ['mə:kəntail], *a.* mercantil.
mercenary ['mə:sinri], *a., n.* mercenario.
merchandise ['mə:tʃəndaiz], *n.* mercancías, *f.pl.*, mercadería.
merchant ['mə:tʃənt], *a.* mercante.—*n.* mercader, comerciante, *m.*
merciful ['mə:siful], *a.* clemente, misericordioso.
merciless ['mə:silis], *a.* desapiadado, desalmado.
mercury ['mə:kjuri], *n.* mercurio.
mercy ['mə:si], *n.* misericordia, clemencia; gracia; ***at the — of,*** a la merced de.
mere (1) [miə], *a.* mero, solo.
mere (2) [miə], *n.* (*poet.*) lago.
meretricious [meri'triʃəs], *a.* de oropel, charro.
merge [mə:dʒ], *v.t.* combinar, fusionar.—*v.i.* fusionarse; convertirse (***into,*** en).
merger ['mə:dʒə], *n.* (*com.*) fusión (*f.*) de empresas.
meridian [mə'ridiən], *a., n.* meridiano.
meringue [mə'ræŋ], *n.* merengue, *m.*
merit ['merit], *n.* mérito, merecimiento.—*v.t., v.i.* merecer.
meritorious [meri'tɔ:rjəs], *a.* meritorio.
mermaid ['mə:meid], *n.* sirena.
merriment ['merimənt], *n.* regocijo, alegría.
merry ['meri], *a.* alegre.
merry-go-round ['merigouraund], *n.* tiovivo.
merry-maker ['merimeikə], *n.* parrandista, *m.f.*, juerguista, *m.f.*
mesh [meʃ], *n.* malla, red, *f.*
mesmerize ['mezməraiz], *v.t.* hipnotizar.
mess (1) [mes], *n.* desorden, *m.*, enredo; bazofia.—*v.t.* ensuciar; desordenar.—*v.i.* ***— about,*** perder el tiempo.
mess (2) [mes], *n.* (*mil. etc.*) rancho.—*v.i.* hacer rancho.
message ['mesidʒ], *n.* mensaje, *m.*, recado.
messenger ['mesindʒə], *n.* mensajero.
Messiah [mə'saiə], *n.* Mesías, *m.sg.*
messy ['mesi], *a.* sucio; desordenado.
mestizo [mes'ti:zou], *a., n.* mestizo.
metal [metl], *a.* metálico.—*n.* metal, *m.*; grava (*de caminos*).
metallic [mə'tælik], *a.* metálico.
metaphor ['metəfə], *n.* metáfora.
metaphorical [metə'fɔrikəl], *a.* metafórico.
metaphysical [metə'fizikəl], *a.* metafísico.
metaphysics [metə'fiziks], *n.* metafísica.
meteor ['mi:tjɔ:], *n.* estrella fugaz, bólido; meteoro (*tiempo*).
meteorite ['mi:tjərait], *n.* meteorito.
meteorology [mi:tjə'rɔlədʒi], *n.* meteorología.

meter ['mi:tə], *n.* contador, *m.*; (*U.S.*) metro. —*v.t.* medir.
methane ['meθein], *n.* metano.
method ['meθəd], *n.* método.
methodic(al) [mə'θɔdik(əl)], *a.* metódico.
methyl ['meθil], *n.* metilo.
meticulous [mə'tikjuləs], *a.* meticuloso, minucioso.
métier ['meitiei], *n.* oficio, aptitud, *f.*
metre ['mi:tə], *n.* metro.
metric ['metrik], *a.* métrico.
metronome ['metrənoum], *n.* metrónomo.
metropolis [mi'trɔpəlis], *n.* metrópoli, *f.*
metropolitan [metrə'pɔlitən], *a.*, *n.* metropolitano.
mettle [metl], *n.* brío, vigor, *m.*; ***to be on one's* —**, estar dispuesto a hacer lo mejor posible; ***to put on one's* —**, estimular.
mew (1) [mju:], *n.* maullido.—*v.i.* maullar, miar (*gatos*).
mew (2) [mju:], *n.* (*orn.*) gaviota.
mews [mju:z], *n.pl.* caballeriza; callejuela (*en Londres*).
Mexican ['meksikən], *a.*, *n.* mejicano.
Mexico ['meksikou], *n.* Méjico.
miaow [mi'au], *n.* miau, *m.*, maullido.—*v.i.* maullar.
Michael ['maikəl], *n.* Miguel, *m.*
microbe ['maikroub], *n.* microbio.
microfilm ['maikroufilm], *n.* microfilm, *m.*
microphone ['maikrəfoun], *n.* micrófono.
microscope ['maikrəskoup], *n.* microscopio.
microscopic [maikrə'skɔpik], *a.* microscópico.
mid [mid], *a.* medio; ***in mid-air***, en el aire; ***in mid-winter*** o ***mid-summer***, en pleno invierno *o* verano.
midday ['mid'dei], *n.* mediodía, *m.*
middle [midl], *a.* medio, central; ***— finger***, dedo del corazón; ***Middle Ages***, Edad Media; ***Middle East***, Oriente Medio.—*n.* centro, medio, mitad, *f.*; mediados (*m.pl.*) del mes; promedio.
middle-aged ['midl'eidʒd], *a.* de mediana edad.
middle-class ['midl'klɑ:s], *a.* de la clase media.
middleman ['midlmæn], *n.* (*com.*) corredor, *m.*, intermediario.
middling ['midliŋ], *a.* regular, mediano.
midge [midʒ], *n.* mosquito.
midget ['midʒit], *a.*, *n.* enano.
midland ['midlənd], *a.* del centro, del interior.—*n. pl.* ***the Midlands***, región (*f.*) central de Inglaterra.
midnight ['midnait], *n.* medianoche, *f.*
midriff ['midrif], *n.* diafragma, *m.*
midshipman ['midʃipmən], *n.* guardia marina, *m.*
midst [midst], *n.* centro.—*prep.* (*poet.*) entre; ***in the — of***, en medio de.
midway ['mid'wei], *adv.* a (la) mitad del camino.
midwife ['midwaif], *n.* (*pl.* **midwives**) partera, comadrona.
mien [mi:n], *n.* semblante, *m.*
might [mait], *n.* poderío, poder, *m.*, fuerza. [MAY].
mighty ['maiti], *a.* poderoso; (*fam.*) muy.
migraine ['mi:grein], *n.* jaqueca.
migrant ['maigrənt], *a.* migratorio.
migrate [mai'greit], *v.i.* emigrar.
migration [mai'greiʃən], *n.* migración, *f.*
Mike [maik], *n.* Miguelito.
mike [maik], *n.* (*fam.*) micrófono.
milch [miltʃ], *a.f.* (*obs.*) lechera (*vaca*).
mild [maild], *a.* suave, templado, ligero.
mildew ['mildju:], *n.* mildeu, *m.*, moho.
mile [mail], *n.* milla.
mileage ['mailidʒ], *n.* kilometraje, *m.*
milestone ['mailstoun], *n.* piedra miliar; (*fig.*) hito.
milieu ['mi:ljə:], *n.* ambiente, *m.*
militant ['militənt], *a.* militante.
militarism ['militərizm], *n.* militarismo.
military ['militəri], *a.* militar.—*n.* milicia, militares, *m.pl.*
militate ['militeit], *v.i.* militar.
militia [mi'liʃə], *n.* milicia.
milk [milk], *n.* leche, *f.*—*v.t.* ordeñar.
milkmaid ['milkmeid], *n.* lechera.
milkman ['milkmən], *n.* lechero.
milksop ['milksɔp], *n.* marica, *m.*
milky ['milki], *a.* lechoso; ***Milky Way***, Vía Láctea.
mill [mil], *n.* molino; fábrica; ***to go through the* —**, pasarlo mal.—*v.t.* moler; fabricar; acordonar (*monedas*).—*v.i.* hormiguear.
millennium [mi'lenjəm], *n.* milenio, milenario.
miller ['milə], *n.* molinero; fabricante, *m.*
millet ['milit], *n.* mijo.
millibar ['milibɑ:], *n.* milibar, *m.*
milligram(me) ['miligræm], *n.* miligramo.
millimetre ['milimi:tə], *n.* milímetro.
milliner ['milinə], *n.* sombrerero.
million ['miljən], *n.* millón, *m.*
millionaire [miljə'nɛə], *n.* millonario.
millionth ['miljənθ], *a.*, *n.* millonésimo.
mill-pond ['milpɔnd], *n.* alberca, represa.
mill-race ['milreis], *n.* caz, *m.*
millstone ['milstoun], *n.* muela de molino.
mime [maim], *n.* mimo.—*v.t.* remedar.
mimic ['mimik], *a.* mímico.—*n.* mimo, remedador, *m.*—*v.t.* remedar.
mimicry ['mimikri], *n.* mímica, remedo.
minaret ['minəret], *n.* alminar, *m.*
mince [mins], *n.* picadillo.—*v.t.* picar, desmenuzar; (*fig.*) medir (*palabras*).
mincemeat ['minsmi:t], *n.* carne picada, cuajado.
mincing ['minsiŋ], *a.* remilgado.
mind [maind], *n.* mente, *f.*; juicio; ánimo; parecer, *m.*; intención, *f.*, deseo; ***to bear in* —**, tener presente *o* en cuenta; ***to change one's* —**, cambiar de opinión; ***to make up one's* —**, decidirse.—*v.t.* cuidar; tener en cuenta; ***to — one's own business***, no meterse en lo que no le toca a uno.—*v.i.* molestar a; ***do you — ?*** ¿le molesta? ***never* —**, no se preocupe.
mindful ['maindful], *a.* atento (*of*, a).
mine (1) [main], *poss. pron.* mío, el mío.
mine (2) [main], *n.* mina.—*v.t.* minar.
miner ['mainə], *n.* minero; (*mil.*) minador, *m.*
mineral ['minərəl], *a.*, *n.* mineral, *m.*; (*Brit.*) gaseosa.
mine-sweeper ['mainswi:pə], *n.* dragaminas, *m.sg.*
mingle [miŋgl], *v.t.* mezclar.—*v.i.* -se.
miniature ['minətʃə], *a.* en miniatura.—*n.* miniatura.
minimal ['miniməl], *a.* mínimo.
minimize ['minimaiz], *v.t.* reducir al mínimo.

minimum ['miniməm], *a.*, *n.* mínimo.
mining ['mainiŋ], *n.* minería; (*mil.*) minado.
minion ['minjən], *n.* paniaguado.
minister ['ministə], *n.* ministro.—*v.t.*, *v.i.* ministrar.
ministerial [mini'stiəriəl], *a.* ministerial.
ministry ['ministri], *n.* ministerio.
mink [miŋk], *n.* visón, *m.*
minnow ['minou], *n.* pececillo, foxino.
minor ['mainə], *a.*, *n.* menor, *m.f.*
minority [mai'nɔriti], *n.* minoría.
minster ['minstə], *n.* basílica, catedral, *f.*
minstrel ['minstrəl], *n.* juglar, *m.*
mint (1) [mint], *a.* sin usar.—*n.* casa de moneda.—*v.t.* acuñar.
mint (2) [mint], *n.* (*bot.*) menta, yerbabuena.
minus ['mainəs], *a.*, *n.*, *prep.* menos.
minute (1) [mai'nju:t], *a.* diminuto.
minute (2) ['minit], *n.* minuto.—*pl.* actas.
minute-hand ['minit'hænd], *n.* minutero.
minuteness [mai'nju:tnis], *n.* menudencia.
minutiae [mai'nju:ʃii:], *n.pl.* minucias, *f. pl.*
minx [miŋks], *n.* (*zool.*) marta; descarada.
miracle ['mirikl], *n.* milagro.
miraculous [mi'rækjuləs], *a.* milagroso.
mirage [mi'rɑ:ʒ], *n.* espejismo.
mire [maiə], *n.* fango, lodo.
mirror ['mirə], *n.* espejo.—*v.t.* reflejar.
mirth [mə:θ], *n.* regocijo, júbilo.
miry ['maiəri], *a.* fangoso, cenagoso.
mis- [mis], *prefix.* des-, mal-.
misadventure [misəd'ventʃə], *n.* infortunio, contratiempo.
misanthrope ['misənθroup], *n.* misántropo.
misapprehension [misæpri'henʃən], *n.* equivocación, *f.*
misbegotten [misbi'gɔtn], *a.* bastardo.
misbehave [misbi'heiv], *v.i.* portarse mal.
misbehaviour [misbi'heiviə], *n.* mala conducta; desmán, *m.*
miscarriage [mis'kæridʒ], *n.* aborto, malogro.
miscarry [mis'kæri], *v.i.* malparir, abortar; salir mal.
miscellaneous [misə'leiniəs], *a.* misceláneo.
miscellany [mi'seləni], *n.* miscelánea.
mischief ['mistʃi:f], *n.* daño; diablura, travesura; ***to make* —**, sembrar cizaña.
mischievous ['mistʃivəs], *a.* travieso; dañoso, malicioso.
misconception [miskən'sepʃən], *n.* concepto erróneo.
misconduct [mis'kɔndʌkt], *n.* mala conducta, mal porte, *m.*
misconstrue [miskən'stru:], *v.t.* interpretar mal.
miscreant ['miskriənt], *a.*, *n.* malvado, maleante, *m.*
misdeed [mis'di:d], *n.* malhecho.
misdemeanour [misdi'mi:nə], *n.* delito, fechoría.
misdirect [misdi'rekt], *v.t.* dirigir mal.
miser ['maizə], *n.* avaro.
miserable ['mizərəbl], *a.* desgraciado, miserable.
miserly ['maizəli], *a.* avariento, tacaño.
misery ['mizəri], *n.* miseria; pena, dolor, *m.*
misfire [mis'faiə], *v.i.* fallar.
misfit ['misfit], *n.* lo que no cae bien; persona desequilibrada.
misfortune [mis'fɔ:tʃən], *n.* desventura.
misgiving [mis'giviŋ], *n.* recelo, duda, desconfianza.
misguided [mis'gaidid], *a.* equivocado, descarriado.
mishap [mis'hæp], *n.* percance, *m.*, contratiempo.
misinform [misin'fɔ:m], *v.t.* informar mal.
misinterpret [misin'tə:prit], *v.t.* interpretar mal.
mislay [mis'lei], *v.t. irr.* (*conjug. like* LAY) extraviar, traspapelar.
mislead [mis'li:d], *v.t. irr.* (*conjug. like* LEAD) despistar, engañar.
misleading [mis'li:diŋ], *a.* engañoso.
misnomer [mis'noumə], *n.* nombre inapropriado.
misogyny [mi'sɔdʒini], *n.* misoginia.
misplace [mis'pleis], *v.t.* colocar mal; prestar (*fe*) a quien no la merece.
misprint ['misprint], *n.* errata (de imprenta).
misrepresent [misrepri'zent], *v.t.* falsificar, pervertir.
misrule [mis'ru:l], *n.* desgobierno.
Miss [mis], *n.* Señorita.
miss [mis], *n.* falta; fracaso, malogro; tiro errado.—*v.t.* echar de menos (*gente, cosas*); perder (*el tren*); no hallar; omitir; errar (*el blanco*); pasar por alto.—*v.i.* errar el blanco; malograr; ***to just* —**, por poco no coger.
missal ['misəl], *n.* misal, *m.*
missel thrush ['misəl θrʌʃ], *n.* charla, zorzal, *m.*
misshapen [mis'ʃeipən], *a.* deforme.
missile ['misail], *n.* proyectil, *m.*; ***guided* —**, proyectil teleguiado.
missing ['misiŋ], *a.* desaparecido; ***to be* —**, faltar.
mission ['miʃən], *n.* misión, *f.*; acometido.
missionary ['miʃənri], *a.*, *n.* misionario, misionero.
misspell [mis'spel], *v.t. irr.* (*conjug. like* SPELL) deletrear mal.
misspelling [mis'speliŋ], *n.* falta ortográfica.
mist [mist], *n.* neblina; (*U.S.*) llovizna.
mistake [mis'teik], *n.* error, *m.*; malentendido; falta.—*v.t. irr.* (*conjug. like* TAKE) comprender mal; tomar (***for***, por).
mistaken [mis'teikən], *a.* equivocado, errado, erróneo; ***to be* —**, equivocarse, engañarse.
Mister ['mistə], *n.* (el) señor, *m.*
mistletoe ['misəltou], *n.* (*bot.*) muérdago.
mistook [mis'tuk] [MISTAKE].
Mistress, Mrs. ['misiz], *n.* (la) señora, Sra. (de); **mistress** ['mistris], *n.* señora; (*educ.*) maestra, profesora, *n.*; (*pej.*) querida.
mistrust [mis'trʌst], *n.* desconfianza.—*v.t.*, *v.i.* desconfiar (de).
misty ['misti], *a.* nebuloso.
misunderstand [misʌndə'stænd], *v.t. irr.* (*conjug. like* STAND) entender mal.
misunderstanding [misʌndə'stændiŋ], *n.* malentendido.
misuse [mis'ju:s], *n.* mal uso.—[mis'ju:z], *v.t.* usar mal de; emplear mal.
mite (1) [mait], *n.* pizca; blanca (*moneda*).
mite (2) [mait], *n.* (*zool.*) ácaro; chiquitín, *m.*
mitigate ['mitigeit], *v.t.* atenuar, mitigar.
mitre ['maitə], *n.* (*eccl.*) mitra; (*carp.*) inglete, *m.*
mitt, mitten [mit, mitn], *n.* mitón, *m.*, manopla.

mix [miks], *n.* mezcla.—*v.t.* mezclar.—*v.i.* mezclarse; ***to* —*up*,** confundir.
mixed [mikst], *a.* mezclado; mixto (*matrimonio, sexos etc.*); ***to get* — *up in*,** enredarse en.
mixer ['miksə], *n.* mezclador, *m.*; ***to be a good mixer*,** (*fam.*) tener don de gentes.
mixture ['mikstʃə], *n.* mezcla, mixtura.
mix-up ['miksʌp], *n.* (*fam.*) lío, enredo.
mizzen ['mizən], *n.* (*naut.*) mesana.
moan [moun], *n.* gemido.—*v.i.* gemir.
moat [mout], *n.* foso.
mob [mɔb], *n.* populacho, gentuza, gentío.—*v.t.* festejar, atropellar.
mobile ['moubail], *a.* móvil.
mobilize ['moubilaiz], *v.t.* movilizar.
mock [mɔk], *a.* simulado, fingido.—*n.* mofa, burla.—*v.t., v.i.* mofarse, burlarse (*de*).
mockery ['mɔkəri], *n.* mofa, escarnio; irrisión, *f.*; remedo.
mock-up ['mɔkʌp], *n.* maqueta, modelo.
mode [moud], *n.* modo; moda.
model ['mɔdəl], *a.* modelo, *inv.*—*n.* modelo; modelo (*moda*), *f.*—*v.t., v.i.* modelar.
moderate ['mɔdərit], *a.* moderado.—['mɔdəreit], *v.t.* moderar.
moderation [mɔdə'reiʃən], *n.* moderación, *f.*
modern [mɔdn], *a.* moderno.
modernistic [mɔdə'nistik], *a.* modernista.
modernize ['mɔdənaiz], *v.t.* modernizar.—*v.i.* -se.
modest ['mɔdist], *a.* humilde; modesto; moderado.
modesty ['mɔdisti], *n.* humildad, *f.*, recato; modestia.
modicum ['mɔdikəm], *n.* pitanza.
modification [mɔdifi'keiʃən], *n.* modificación, *f.*
modify ['mɔdifai], *v.t.* modificar.
modulate ['mɔdjuleit], *v.t.* modular.
Mohammed [mou'hæmid], *n.* Mahoma, *m.*
Mohammedan [mou'hæmidən], *a., n.* mohametano.
moist [mɔist], *a.* húmedo.
moisten [mɔisn], *v.t.* humedecer, mojar.—*v.i.* -se.
moisture ['mɔistʃə], *n.* humedad, *f.*
molar ['moulə], *a.* molar.—*n.* molar, *m.*, muela.
molasses [mɔ'læsiz], *n.* melaza.
mold (*U.S.*) [MOULD].
mole (1) [moul], *n.* (*zool.*) topo.
mole (2) [moul], *n.* (*anat.*) lunar, *m.*
mole (3) [moul], *n.* (*naut.*) malecón, *m.*
molecular [mɔ'lekjulə], *a.* molecular.
molecule ['mɔlikju:l], *n.* molécula.
molest [mɔ'lest], *v.t.* incomodar; vejar.
mollify ['mɔlifai], *v.t.* mitigar, suavizar; apaciguar.
mollusc, mollusk ['mɔlʌsk], *n.* molusco; (*cul.*) marisco.
molten ['moultən], *a.* fundido, derretido.
moment ['moumənt], *n.* momento; (*fig.*) importancia.
momentary ['mouməntəri], *a.* momentáneo.
momentous [mou'mentəs], *a.* trascendental.
momentum [mou'mentəm], *n.* ímpetu, *m.*
monarch ['mɔnək], *n.* monarca, *m.*
monarchist ['mɔnəkist], *a., n.* monarquista, *m.f.*, monárquico.
monarchy ['mɔnəki], *n.* monarquía.
monastery ['mɔnəstri], *n.* monasterio, convento.
monastic [mə'næstik], *a.* monástico.
Monday ['mʌndei], *n.* lunes, *m.sg.*
monetary ['mʌnitəri], *a.* monetario.
money ['mʌni], *n.* dinero.
money-bag ['mʌnibæg], *n.* talega, bolso.
money-bags ['mʌnibægz], *n.* (*fam.*) ricacho.
money-box ['mnʌiboks], *n.* hucha.
money-lender ['mʌnilendə], *n.* prestamista, *m.f.*
monger ['mʌŋgə], *n.* traficante, tratante, *m.*
Mongol ['mɔŋgəl], *a., n.* mongol, *m.f.*
Mongolia [mɔŋ'gouljə], *n.* la Mogolia.
Mongolian [mɔŋ'gouljən], *a., n.* mogol, *m.*
mongrel ['mʌŋgrəl], *a., n.* mestizo.
monitor ['mɔnitə], *n.* monitor, *m.*—*v.t.* controlar.
monk [mʌŋk], *n.* monje, *m.*
monkey ['mʌŋki], *n.* mono.—*v.i.* tontear, hacer monadas.
monocle ['mɔnəkl], *n.* monóculo.
monogamy [mɔ'nɔgəmi], *n.* monogamia.
monogram ['mɔnəgræm], *n.* monograma, *m.*
monologue ['mɔnəlɔg], *n.* monólogo.
monopolize [mə'nɔpəlaiz], *v.t.* monopolizar, acaparrar.
monopoly [mə'nɔpəli], *n.* monopolio.
monorail ['mɔnoureil], *n.* monorriel, *m.*
monosyllable ['mɔnəsiləbl], *n.* monosílabo.
monotheism ['mɔnouθi:izm], *n.* monoteísmo.
monotonous [mə'nɔtənəs], *a.* monótono.
monotony [mə'nɔtəni], *n.* monotonía.
monsignor [mɔn'si:njɔ:], *n.* monseñor *m.*
monsoon [mɔn'su:n], *n.* monzón, *m.*
monster ['mɔnstə], *n.* monstruo.
monstrance ['mɔnstrəns], *n.* (*eccl.*) custodia.
monstrosity [mɔns'trɔsiti], *n.* monstruosidad, *f.*
monstrous ['mɔnstrəs], *a.* monstruoso.
month [mʌnθ], *n.* mes, *m.sg.*
monthly ['mʌnθli], *a.* mensual.—*adv.* mensualmente.
monument ['mɔnjumənt], *n.* monumento.
monumental [mɔnju'mentl], *a.* monumental.
moo [mu:], *n.* mugido.—*v.i.* mugir.
mood [mu:d], *n.* genio, humor, talante, *m.*; mal humor, *m.*
moody ['mu:di], *a.* irritable, tosco; caviloso; caprichoso.
moon [mu:n], *n.* luna.
moonbeam ['mu:nbi:m], *n.* rayo lunar.
moonlight ['mu:nlait], *n.* luna, luz (*f.*) de la luna.
moonshine ['mu:nʃain], *n.* sueños dorados, *m.pl.*, ilusión, *f.*
moonstruck ['mu:nstrʌk], *a.* aturdido; lunático.
Moor [muə], *n.* moro.
moor (1) [muə], páramo, brezal, *m.*
moor (2) [muə], *v.t.* amarrar.
Moorish ['muəriʃ], *a.* moro.
moorland ['muəlænd], *n.* brezal, *m.*, páramo.
moose [mu:s], *n.* alce, *m.*, mosa.
moot [mu:t], *a.* batallona (*cuestión*).—*n.* junta.
mop [mɔp], *n.* estropajo, aljofifa; mueca; mechón, *m.*
mope [moup], *v.i.* estar abatido.

moral ['mɔrəl], *a.* moral.—*n.* moraleja.—*pl.* moral, *f.*
morale [mə'rɑ:l], *n.* moral, *f.*
morality [mə'ræliti], *n.* moralidad, *f.*
moralize ['mɔrəlaiz], *v.t., v.i.* moralizar.
moratorium [mɔrə'tɔ:riəm], *n.* moratoria.
morbid ['mɔ:bid], *a.* morboso, malsano.
more [mɔ:], *a., n., adv.* más; ***no —,*** no ya; no más; ***the — . . . the —,*** cuanto más . . . tanto más.
moreover [mɔ:'rouvə], *adv.* además, por otra parte.
morgue [mɔ:g], *n.* depósito de cadáveres.
moribund ['mɔribʌnd], *a.* moribundo.
morn [mɔ:n], *n.* (*poet.*) mañana.
morning ['mɔ:niŋ], *n.* mañana; ***early —,*** madrugada.
Moroccan [mə'rɔkən], *a., n.* marroquí, *m.f.*
Morocco [mə'rɔkou], *n.* Marruecos, *m.sg.*
morose [mə'rous], *a.* bronco, lóbrego.
morphia ['mɔ:fjə], **morphine** ['mɔ:fi:n], *n.* morfina.
morphology [mɔ:'fɔlədʒi], *n.* morfología.
morrow ['mɔrou], *n.* (*obs.*) mañana, el día siguiente.
morsel ['mɔ:səl], *n.* bocado; manjar.
mortal ['mɔ:təl], *a., n.* mortal, *m.f.*
mortality [mɔ:'tæliti], *n.* mortalidad; mortandad, *f.*
mortar ['mɔ:tə], *n.* mortero; (*arch.*) argamasa.
mortgage ['mɔ:gidʒ], *n.* hipoteca.—*v.t.* hipotecar.
mortician [mɔ:'tiʃən], *n.* (*U.S.*) director (*m.*) de pompas fúnebres.
mortify ['mɔ:tifai], *v.t.* mortificar; (*fig.*) humillar.
mortise ['mɔ:tis], *n.* mortaja, muesca; ***— and tenon joint,*** ensambladura de caja y espiga.
mortuary ['mɔ:tjuəri], *n.* depósito de cadáveres.
Mosaic [mou'zeiik], *a.* mosaico.
mosaic [mou'zeik], *a., n.* mosaico.
Moscow ['mɔskou], *n.* Moscú, *f.*
Moses ['mouziz], *n.* Moisés, *m.sg.*
Moslem ['mɔzləm] [MUSLIM].
mosque [mɔsk], *n.* mezquita.
mosquito [mɔs'ki:tou], *n.* mosquito.
moss [mɔs], *n.* musgo.
mossy ['mɔsi], *a.* musgoso.
most [moust], *a.* más; la mayoría de.—*n.* lo más; la mayoría.—*adv.* más; lo más; ***to make the — of,*** sacar el mayor partido de.
mostly ['moustli], *adv.* principalmente, en su mayor parte.
mote [mout], *n.* mota.
moth [mɔθ], *n.* (*ent.*) mariposa nocturna; polilla (*en tela*).
moth-eaten ['mɔθi:tn], *a.* apolillado.
mother ['mʌðə], *n.* madre, *f.*; ***— tongue,*** lengua materna.—*v.t.* servir de madre a; mimar.
motherhood ['mʌðəhud], *n.* maternidad, *f.*
mother-in-law ['mʌðərinlɔ:], *n.* (*pl.* **mothers-in-law**) suegra.
motherly ['mʌðəli], *a.* maternal.
motif [mou'ti:f], *n.* motivo, tema, *m.*
motion ['mouʃən], *n.* movimiento; señal, *f.*; moción (*en un debate*), *f.*; ***in —,*** en marcha; ***— picture,*** (*U.S. cine.*) película; ***to carry a motion,*** adoptar una moción.—*v.t.* señalar, indicar.
motionless ['mouʃənlis], *a.* inmoble, inmóvil.
motivate ['moutiveit], *v.t.* motivar.
motivation [mouti'veiʃən], *n.* motivación, *f.*
motive ['moutiv], *a., n.* motivo.
motley ['mɔtli], *a.* abigarrado.—*n.* mezcla, abigarrada.
motor ['moutə], *a.* de motor.—*n.* motor, *m.* —*v.i.* pasear en coche, recorrer en coche.
motor-bike ['moutəbaik], *n.* (*fam.*) moto, *f.*
motor-boat ['moutəbout], *n.* canoa automóvil; gasolinera.
motor-car ['moutəkɑ:], *n.* coche, *m.*, automóvil, *m.*
motor-cycle ['moutəsaikl], *n.* motocicleta.
motor-cyclist ['moutəsaiklist], *n.* motociclista, *m.f.*
motoring ['moutəriŋ], *n.* automovilismo.
motorist ['moutərist], *n.* automovilista, *m.f.*
motorize ['moutəraiz], *v.t.* motorizar.
motorway ['moutəwei], *n.* autopista.
mottle ['mɔtl], *n.* veta, mancha.—*v.t.* motear, jaspear.
motto ['mɔtou], *n.* lema, *m.*
mould (1) [mould], *n.* (*bot.*) moho.—*v.t.* enmohecer.—*v.i.* enmohecerse.
mould (2) [mould], *n.* molde, *m.*; índole, *f.*—*v.t.* moldear, amoldar.
moulder ['mouldə], *v.i.* enmohecerse, desmoronarse.
moulding ['mouldiŋ], *n.* moldura; formación, *f.*
mouldy ['mouldi], *a.* mohoso, enmohecido.
moult [moult], *n.* muda.—*v.t., v.i.* mudar (*la pluma*).
mound [maund], *n.* montón, *m.*, terrero; terraplén, *m.*; dique, *m.*
mount [maunt], *n.* monte, *m.*; montura, cabalgadura; montaje, *m.*—*v.t., v.i.* montar.
mountain ['mauntin], *a.* montañoso, montañés.—*n.* montaña; ***to make a — out of a molehill,*** hacer de una pulga un elefante.
mountain-climbing ['mauntin'klaimiŋ], *n.* alpinismo.
mountaineer [maunti'niə], *n.* montañés; alpinista, *m.f.*
mountainous ['mauntinəs], *a.* montañoso.
mountain-range ['mauntin'reindʒ], *n.* cordillera; sierra.
mountebank ['mauntibæŋk], *n.* saltimbanqui, *m.*
mounting ['mauntiŋ], *n.* montaje; engaste *m.*
mourn [mɔ:n], *v.t.* llorar, lamentar.—*v.i* lamentarse; estar de luto.
mourner ['mɔ:nə], *n.* enlutado; afligido ***paid —,*** plañidera.
mourning ['mɔ:niŋ], *n.* luto; ***in —,*** de luto.
mouse [maus], *n.* (*pl.* **mice**) ratón, *m.*
mouse-hole ['maushoul], *n.* ratonera.
mouse-trap ['maustræp], *n.* ratonera, trampa
moustache [məs'tɑ:ʃ], *n.* bigote, *m.*
mouth ['mauθ], *n.* boca; orificio; desembocadura (*de un río*); ***down in the —*** cariacontecido; ***to make one's — water*** hacerse agua la boca.—[mauð], *v.t.* articular pronunciar; meter en la boca.
mouth-organ ['mauθɔ:gən], *n.* armónica (de boca).

mouth-piece ['mauθpi:s], *n.* boquilla; (*fig.*) portavoz, *m.*
movable ['mu:vəbl], *a.* móvil, movible.—*n.pl.* bienes muebles, *m.pl.*
move [mu:v], *n.* movimiento; paso; jugada, turno; ***it's your* —,** le toca a Vd.—*v.t.* mover; trasladar; conmover (*emoción*).—*v.i.* moverse; mudar de casa; avanzar; ***to* — *in*,** tomar posesión (de); entrar en acción; ***to* — *away*,** apartar(se).
movement ['mu:vmənt], *n.* movimiento.
movie ['mu:vi], *n.* (*U.S. fam.*) película.—*pl.* cine, *m.*
moving ['mu:viŋ], *a.* motor, motriz; conmovedor, emocionante.—*n.* traslado; cambio; mudanza.
mow [mou], *v.t.* (*p.p. also* **mown**) segar.
mower [mouə], *n.* segador, *m.*; segadora (*máquina*).
much [mʌtʃ], *a.*, *n.*, *adv.* mucho; ***as* —,** tanto; ***how* —,** cuanto; ***too* —,** demasiado; ***so* —,** tanto; **— *of a muchness*,** (*fam.*) otro que tal, casi lo mismo.
muck [mʌk], *n.* estiércol, *m.*; (*fig.*) porquería.—*v.t.* (*fam.*) ensuciar, estropear (***up***).
muck-raker ['mʌkreikə], *n.* buscavidas, *m.sg.*
mucky ['mʌki], *a.* (*fam.*) puerco, sucio.
mud [mʌd], *n.* barro, lodo, fango; ***to sling* — *at*,** llenar de fango.
muddle [mʌdl], *n.* lío, enredo, embrollo.—*v.t.* confundir, embrollar; aturdir.—*v.i.* ***to* — *along*,** ir a la buena de Dios, obrar confusamente.
muddy ['mʌdi], *a.* barroso, fangoso; turbio.—*v.t.* enturbiar.
mudguard ['mʌdgɑ:d], *n.* guardabarros, *m.sg.*
muezzin [mu'ezin], *n.* almuédano.
muff (1) [mʌf], *n.* manguito.
muff (2) [mʌf], *n.* (*fam.*) chapucería.—*v.t.* (*fam.*) chapucear, frangollar.
muffin ['mʌfin], *n.* mollete, *m.*, bollo.
muffle [mʌfl], *n.* mufla; funda.—*v.t.* amortiguar; embozar.
muffler ['mʌflə], *n.* bufanda; (*U.S. mech.*) silenciador, *m.*
mufti ['mʌfti], *n.* traje paisano; mufti, *m.*
mug [mʌg], *n.* cubilete, pichel, *m.*; (*low*) jeta; (*fam.*) primo, ganso.
muggy ['mʌgi], *a.* sofocante, bochornoso.
mulatto [mju'lætou], *a.*, *n.* mulato.
mulberry ['mʌlbəri], *n.* (*bot.*) morera (*árbol*); mora (*fruta*).
mule [mju:l], *n.* mulo, mula.
multilateral [mʌlti'lætərəl], *a.* multilátero.
multiple ['mʌltipl], *a.* múltiplc.—*n.* múltiplo.
multiplication [mʌltipli'keiʃən], *n.* multiplicación, *f.*
multiply ['mʌltiplai], *v.t.* multiplicar.—*v.i.* -se.
multitude ['mʌltitju:d], *n.* multitud, *f.*
mum [mʌm], *a.* (*fam.*) callado.—*n.* (*fam.*) mamá, *f.*
mumble [mʌmbl], *n.* mascullada.—*v.t.*, *v.i.* mascullar, farfullar.
mumbo-jumbo ['mʌmbou'dʒʌmbou], *n.* fetiche, *m.*; música celestial.
mummy (1) ['mʌmi], *n.* momia.
mummy (2) ['mʌmi], *n.* (*fam.*) mamá, *f.*
mumps [mʌmps], *n.* parótidas, *f.pl.*, lamparones, *m.pl.*
munch [mʌntʃ], *v.t.*, *v.i.* masticar, ronchar.
mundane ['mʌndein], *a.* mundano.
municipal [mju:'nisipəl], *a.* municipal.
municipality [mju:nisi'pæliti], *n.* municipio.
munificent [mju:'nifisənt], *a.* munífico.
munitions [mju:'niʃənz], *n.pl.* municiones, *f.pl.*
mural ['mjuərəl], *a.* mural.—*n.* pintura mural.
murder ['mə:də], *n.* asesinato, homicidio.—*v.t.* asesinar; (*fig.*) destripar.
murderer ['mə:dərə], *n.* asesino.
murderess ['mə:dəris], *n.* asesina.
murderous ['mə:dərəs], *a.* asesino.
murk [mə:k], *n.* tinieblas *f.pl.*; cerrazón, *f.*
murky ['mə:ki], *a.* lóbrego, tenebroso; borrascoso.
murmur ['mə:mə], *n.* murmullo.—*v.t.*, *v.i.* murmurar.
muscle [mʌsl], *n.* músculo.
muscular ['mʌskjulə], *a.* muscular; musculoso.
muse [mju:z], *n.* musa.—*v.i.* meditar.
museum [mju:'zi:əm], *n.* museo.
mushroom ['mʌʃrum], *n.* champiñón, *m.*, seta.—*v.i.* aparecer de la noche a la mañana.
mushy ['mʌʃi], *a.* (*fam.*) pulposo; sensiblero.
music ['mju:zik], *n.* música.
musical ['mju:zikəl], *a.* músico, musical.
musician [mju:'ziʃən], *n.* músico.
musk [mʌsk], *n.* almizcle, *m.*
musket ['mʌskit], *n.* mosquete, *m.*
musketeer [mʌski'tiə], *n.* mosquetero.
Muslim ['mʌzlim], *a.*, *n.* musulmán, *m.*
muslin ['mʌzlin], *n.* muselina.
mussel [mʌsl], *n.* mejillón, *m.*, almeja.
must [mʌst], *n.* moho; zumo, mosto.—*v. aux. irr.* (*existe solamente en el tiempo presente*) deber, tener que; deber de.
mustard ['mʌstəd], *n.* mostaza.
muster ['mʌstə], *n.* asemblea, reunión, *f.*; revista, alarde, *f.*, lista; ***to pass* —,** ser aceptable.—*v.t.* reunir, juntar; cobrar (*ánimo*).
musty ['mʌsti], *a.* mohoso, rancio.
mutant ['mju:tənt], *a.*, *n.* mutante, *m.*
mutation [mju:'teiʃən], *n.* mutación, *f.*
mute [mju:t], *a.*, *n.* mudo.—*v.t.* poner sordina a.
mutilate ['mju:tileit], *v.t.* mutilar.
mutineer [mju:ti'niə], *n.* amotinado, sedicioso.
mutiny ['mju:tini], *n.* motín, *m.*, sublevación, *f.*—*v.i.* amotinarse.
mutter ['mʌtə], *v.t.*, *v.i.* murmurar, refunfuñar.
mutton [mʌtn], *n.* carnero (*carne*).
mutual ['mju:tjuəl], *a.* mutuo.
muzzle [mʌzl], *n.* bozal, *m.*, mordaza; boca (*de un fusil*).—*v.t.* amordazar, embozar.
my [mai], *poss. pron.* mi.
myopic [mai'ɔpik], *a.* miope.
myrrh [mə:], *n.* mirra.
myrtle [mə:tl], *n.* mirto, arrayán, *m.*
myself [mai'self], *pron.* yo mismo; me, a mí mismo.
mysterious [mis'tiəriəs], *a.* misterioso.
mystery ['mistəri], *n.* misterio.
mystic ['mistik], *a.*, *n.* místico.
mysticism ['mistisizm], *n.* misticismo.
mystify ['mistifai], *v.t.* dejar perplejo, mistificar.

myth [miθ], *n.* mito, leyenda.
mythical ['miθikəl], *a.* mítico.
mythology [mi'θələdʒi], *n.* mitología.

N

N, n [en], *n.* décimocuarta letra del alfabeto inglés.
nab [næb], *v.t.* (*fam.*) agarrar.
nadir ['neidiə], *n.* nadir, *m.*
nag (1) [næg], *n.* jaca.
nag (2) [næg], *n.* (*fam.*) regañona.—*v.t.*, *v.i.* regañar, jeringar.
nail [neil], *n.* clavo; (*anat.*) uña.—*v.t.* clavar.
naive [nai'i:v], *a.* ingenuo, cándido.
naiveté [nai'i:vtei], *n.* ingenuidad, candidez, *f.*
naked ['neikid], *a.* desnudo; ***with the — eye,*** a simple vista.
name [neim], *n.* nombre, *m.*; ***by —,*** de nombre; ***to call names,*** poner motes (a); ***what is your —?*** ¿cómo se llama Vd.? —*v.t.* nombrar; bautizar; apodar.
nameless ['neimlis], *a.* sin nombre; desconocido.
namely ['neimli], *adv.* a saber.
name-plate ['neimpleit], *n.* placa.
namesake ['neimseik], *n.* tocayo.
nanny ['næni], *n.* (*fam.*) niñera.
nanny-goat ['nænigout], *n.* cabra.
nap (1) [næp], *n.* duermevela, *m.*, siestecita.—*v.i.* echar una siestecita; ***to catch napping,*** coger desprevenido.
nap (2) [næp], *n.* lanilla (*de tela*).
nape [neip], *n.* nuca.
naphtha ['næfθə], *n.* nafta.
napkin ['næpkin], *n.* servilleta; pañal (*para un niño*), *m.*
Naples [neiplz], *n.* Nápoles, *m.*
Napoleon [nə'pouljən], *n.* Napoleón, *m.*
Napoleonic [nəpouli'ɔnik], *a.* napoleónico.
narcissus [nɑ:'sisəs], *n.* narciso.
narcotic [nɑ:'kɔtik], *a.*, *n.* narcótico.
narrate [næ'reit], *v.t.* narrar, relatar.
narration [næ'reiʃən], *n.* narración, *f.*
narrative ['nærətiv], *a.* narrativo.—*n.* narrativa.
narrow ['nærou], *a.* estrecho, angosto; intolerante.—*n.pl.* angostura.—*v.t.* enangostar, estrechar.—*v.i.* -se.
narrow-minded ['nærou'maindid], *a.* intolerante, mojigato.
narrowness ['nærounis], *n.* estrechez, *f.*
nasal ['neizəl], *a.* nasal.
nastiness ['nɑ:stinis], *n.* suciedad, *f.*; horror, *m.*; ruindad, *f.*
nasty ['nɑ:sti], *a.* sucio, puerco; indecente; intratable; odioso.
natal ['neitəl], *a.* natal.
nation ['neiʃən], *n.* nación, *f.*
national ['næʃənəl], *a.*, *n.* nacional, *m.f.*
nationalist ['næʃnəlist], *a.*, *n.* nacionalista, *m.f.*
nationality [næʃə'næliti], *n.* nacionalidad, *f.*
nationalize ['næʃnəlaiz], *v.t.* nacionalizar.
native ['neitiv], *a.* nativo, indígena.—*n.* natural, indígena, *m.f.*
nativity [nə'tiviti], *n.* nacimiento, natividad, *f.*
natty ['næti], *a.* garboso, majo, elegante.
natural ['nætʃurəl], *a.* natural.
naturalize ['nætʃurəlaiz], *v.t.* naturalizar.
nature ['neitʃə], *n.* naturaleza.
naught [nɔ:t], *n.* nada, cero; ***to come to —,*** frustrarse.
naughty ['nɔ:ti], *a.* travieso, desobediente; pícaro.
nausea ['nɔ:siə], *n.* náusea.
nauseate ['nɔ:sieit], *v.t.* dar asco (a).
nauseating ['nɔ:sieitiŋ], *a.* asqueroso, nauseabundo.
nautical ['nɔ:tikəl], *a.* náutico; ***— mile,*** milla marina.
naval ['neivəl], *a.* naval.
Navarre [nə'vɑ:], *n.* Navarra.
Navarrese [nævə'ri:z], *a.*, *n.* navarro.
nave [neiv], *n.* (*arch.*) nave, *f.*
navel ['neivəl], *n.* (*anat.*) ombligo.
navigable ['nævigəbl], *a.* navegable marinero (*barco*).
navigate ['nævigeit], *v.t.*, *v.i.* navegar.
navigation [nævi'geiʃən], *n.* navegación, *f.*
navvy ['nævi], *n.* bracero, peón, *m.*
navy ['neivi], *n.* marina.
navy-blue ['neivi'blu:], *a.*, *n.* azul marino.
nay [nei], *adv.* (*obs.*, *dial.*) no.
Nazi ['nɑ:tsi], *a.*, *n.* nazi, nacista, *m.f.*
Nazi(i)sm ['nɑ:ts(i:)izm], *n.* nazismo.
neap-tide ['ni:p'taid], *n.* marea muerta, bajamar, *f.*
near [niə], *a.* cercano; próximo; ***— at hand,*** a mano.—*adv.* cerca.—*prep.* cerca de.—*v.t.* acercarse a.
nearby ['niəbai], *a.* cercano, vecino.—['niə'bai], *adv.* cerca.
nearly ['niəli], *adv.* casi; por poco.
near-sighted ['niə'saitid], *a.* miope.
neat [ni:t], *a.* aseado; esmerado; sin mezcla.
'neath [ni:θ], *prep.* (*poet.*) so, bajo.
neatness ['ni:tnis], *n.* aseo; pulidez, *f.*, primor, *m.*
nebula ['nebjulə], *n.* nebulosa.
nebulous ['nebjuləs], *a.* nebuloso.
necessary ['nesisəri], *a.* necesario.—*n.* lo necesario.
necessitate [nə'sesiteit], *v.t.* necesitar, requerir.
necessity [nə'sesiti], *n.* necesidad, *f.*
neck [nek], *n.* cuello; gollete (*de una botella*), *m.*; (*geog.*) península; ***— and —,*** parejos; ***— or nothing,*** todo o nada.
neckerchief ['nekətʃi:f], *n.* pañuelo de cuello.
necklace ['neklis], *n.* collar, *m.*
necropolis [ne'krɔpəlis], *n.* necrópolis, *f.*
nectar ['nektə], *n.* nectar, *m.*
née [nei], *a.f.* nacida; ***Anne Smith — Brown,*** Anne Brown de Smith.
need [ni:d], *n.* necesidad, *f.*; ***in —,*** necesitado.—*v.t.* necesitar, hacer falta a; ***if need(s) be,*** si fuera necesario.
needful ['ni:dful], *a.* necesario.
needle [ni:dl], *n.* aguja.
needless ['ni:dlis], *a.* innecesario.
needlework ['ni:dlwə:k], *n.* labor, *f.*, costura.
needs [ni:dz], *adv.* necesariamente, forzosamente.
needy ['ni:di], *a.* necesitado, menesteroso.

ne'er [nɛə], *adv.* (*poet.*) nunca.
ne'er-do-well ['nɛədu:wel], *n.* dejado de la mano de Dios.
negation [ni'geiʃən], *n.* negación, *f.*, negativa.
negative ['negətiv], *a.* negativo.—*n.* (*gram.*) negación, *f.*; (*phot.*) negativo; negativa (*repulsa*).
neglect [ni'glekt], *n.* descuido, negligencia.—*v.t.* abandonar, descuidar, desatender.—*v.i.* dejar, olvidarse (*to*, de).
neglectful [ni'glektful], *a.* negligente.
negligence ['neglidʒəns], *n.* negligencia.
negligent ['neglidʒənt], *a.* negligente.
negligible ['neglidʒəbl], *a.* sin importancia, insignificante.
negotiable [ni'gouʃəbl], *a.* negociable; transitable.
negotiate [ni'gouʃieit], *v.t.* negociar; salvar, transitar.—*v.i.* negociar.
negotiation [nigouʃi'eiʃən], *n.* negociación, *f.*
Negress ['ni:gris], *n.* negra.
Negro ['ni:grou], *a.*, *n.* negro.
neigh [nei], *n.* relincho.—*v.i.* relinchar.
neighbour ['neibə], *n.* vecino; (*fig.*) prójimo.
neighbourhood ['neibəhud], *n.* vecindad, *f.*
neighbouring ['neibəriŋ], *a.* vecino.
neighbourly ['neibəli], *a.* buen vecino, amigable.
neither ['naiðə, 'ni:ðə], *a.* ninguno (de los dos).—*adv.* tampoco.—*conj.* **— . . . nor,** ni . . . ni.
neon ['ni:ɔn], *n.* neón, *m.*
Nepal [ni'pɔ:l], *n.* el Nepal.
Nepalese [nepə'li:z], *a.*, *n. inv.* nepalés, *m.*
nephew ['nefju:], *n.* sobrino.
nepotism ['nepətizm], *n.* nepotismo.
Nero ['niərou], *n.* Nerón, *m.*
nerve [nə:v], *n.* nervio; (*fam.*) descaro; ***to get on one's nerves,*** irritar, fastidiar, exasperar.
nerve-racking ['nə:vrækiŋ], *a.* exasperante, agobiante.
nervous ['nə:vəs], *a.* nervioso; tímido; ***— breakdown,*** crisis nerviosa.
nest [nest], *n.* nido.—*v.i.* anidar; buscar nidos.
nest-egg ['nesteg], *n.* hucha, peculio.
nestle [nesl], *v.t.* arrimar, abrigar.—*v.i.* arrimarse, abrigarse.
net (1) [net], *n.* red, *f.*—*v.t.* coger (en red); ganar.
net (2) [net], *a.* neto.
nether ['neðə], *a.* inferior.
Netherlands ['neðələndz], **The,** *n.pl.* los Países Bajos.
netting ['netiŋ], *n.* malla, red, *f.*, redes, *f.pl.*
nettle [netl], *n.* ortiga.—*v.t.* picar, irritar.
network ['netwə:k], *n.* red, *f.*
neurotic [njuə'rɔtik], *a.*, *n.* neurótico.
neuter ['nju:tə], *a.*, *n.* neutro.
neutral ['nju:trəl], *a.* neutral; neutro.
neutrality [nju:'træliti], *n.* neutralidad, *f.*
never ['nevə], *adv.* nunca, (no) jamás.
nevertheless [nevəðə'les], *adv.* no obstante, a pesar de eso.
new [nju:], *a.* nuevo; ***New World,*** Nuevo Mundo; ***New York,*** Nueva York; ***New Zealand,*** Nueva Zelandia; ***New Zealander,*** neocelandés, *m.*
new-comer ['nju:kʌmə], *n.* recién venido.
new-fangled [nju:'fæŋgld], *a.* inventado por novedad, nuevo.
newly ['nju:li], *adv.* nuevamente; (*before p.p.*) recién.
newly-wed ['nju:li'wed], *a.*, *n.* recién casado.
newness ['nju:nis], *n.* novedad, *f.*; inexperiencia.
news [nju:z], *n.sg.* noticias; ***piece of —,*** noticia; ***—reel,*** (*cine.*) actualidades, *f.pl.*
newscast ['nju:zkɑ:st], *n.* (*U.S.*) noticiario.
newspaper ['nju:zpeipə], *n.* periódico; ***— reporter*** o ***— man,*** periodista, *m.*
newt [nju:t], *n.* tritón, *m.*
next [nekst], *a.* próximo; que viene; ***— day,*** el día siguiente; ***— door,*** la casa de al lado.—*adv.* luego, después; la próxima vez; ***what —?*** y luego ¿ qué ?—*prep.* junto (*to*, a), al lado (*to*, de); casi (*to*).
nib [nib], *n.* punta (*de pluma*).
nibble [nibl], *v.t.* mordiscar, picar.
Nicaraguan [nikə'rægjuən], *a.*, *n.* nicaragüense, *m.f.*, nicaragüeño.
nice [nais], *a.* fino; preciso; (*fam.*) simpático, agradable, amable; decente.
nicely ['naisli], *adv.* con exactitud; finamente; amablemente.
nicety ['naisəti], *n.* sutileza; precisión, *f.*
niche [nitʃ], *n.* nicho.
Nick [nik], *n.* ***Old Nick,*** patillas, *m.sg.*, el Diablo.
nick [nik], *n.* muesca, mella; ***in the — of time,*** a pelo, al momento preciso.—*v.t.* hacer muescas en, cortar; (*low*) robar.
nickel ['nikəl], *n.* níquel, *m.*
nick-nack ['niknæk], *n.* fruslería, friolera.
nickname ['nikneim], *n.* apodo.—*v.t.* motejar, apodar.
nicotine ['nikəti:n], *n.* nicotina.
niece [ni:s], *n.* sobrina.
nifty ['nifti], *a.* (*fam.*) guapo, de órdago.
Niger ['naidʒə], *n.* colonia del Níger (*país*); Níger (*río*).
niggardly ['nigədli], *a.*, *adv.*, tacaño.
nigger ['nigə], *n.* (*pej.*) negro.
nigh [nai], *adv.*, *prep.* (*poet.*) [NEAR].
night [nait], *n.* noche, *f.*; ***at*** o ***by —,*** de noche; ***first —,*** (*theat.*, *cine.*) estreno.
night-dress ['naitdres], *n.* camisón, *m.* camisa de dormir.
nightfall ['naitfɔ:l], *n.* anochecer, *m.*
nightingale ['naitiŋgeil], *n.* ruiseñor, *m.*
nightly ['naitli], *a.* nocturno.—*adv.* cada noche.
nightmare ['naitmɛə], *n.* pesadilla.
night-watchman [nait'wɔtʃmən], *n.* sereno; vigilante, *m.*
nihilist ['naiilist], *a.*, *n.* nihilista, *m.f.*
nil [nil], *n.* cero, nada.
the Nile [nail], *n.* el Nilo.
nimble [nimbl], *a.* ágil, listo.
nincompoop ['ninkəmpu:p], *n.* badulaque, *m.*, majadero.
nine [nain], *a.*, *n.* nueve, *m.*
ninepins ['nainpinz], *n.* juego de bolos.
nineteen [nain'ti:n], *a.*, *n.* diecinueve, diez y nueve, *m.*
nineteenth [nain'ti:nθ], *a.*, *n.* décimonono, diecinueveavo; diecinueve (*en las fechas*).
ninetieth ['naintiəθ], *a.*, *n.* nonagésimo, noventavo.
ninety ['nainti], *a.*, *n.* noventa, *m.*
ninth [nainθ], *a.*, *n.* noveno, nono.
nip [nip], *n.* mordisco; pellizco; quemadura; traguito.—*v.t.* mordiscar; pellizcar; cortar.

nipper ['nipə], *n.* (*fam.*) chaval, *m.*—*pl.* tenazas, pinzas.
nipple [nipl], *n.* pezón, *m.*; tetilla.
nit [nit], *n.* liendre, *f.*
nitrate ['naitreit], *n.* nitrato.
nitre ['naitə], *n.* nitro.
nitric ['naitrik], *a.* nítrico.
nitrogen ['naitrədʒən], *n.* nitrógeno.
nitwit ['nitwit], *n.* (*fam.*) bobatel, *m.*
no [nou], *a.* ninguno; — ***good,*** inútil, sin valor; ***to be — use (for anything),*** no servir para nada.—*adv.* no.
Noah [nouə], *n.* Noé, *m.*
nobility [nou'biliti], *n.* nobleza.
noble [noubl], *a., n.* noble, *m.f.*
nobleman ['noublmən], *n.* noble, *m.*
nobody ['noubədi], *pron.* nadie.—*n.* persona insignificante.
nocturnal [nɔk'tə:nəl], *a.* nocturno.
nod [nɔd], *n.* seña afirmativa hecha con la cabeza; cabezada.—*v.t.* inclinar (la cabeza). —*v.i.* cabecear; inclinar la cabeza.
node [noud], *n.* nudo.
noise [nɔiz], *n.* ruido. ***to — abroad,— v.t.*** divulgar.
noiseless ['nɔizlis], *a.* silencioso.
noisy ['nɔizi], *a.* ruidoso.
nomad ['noumæd], *n.* nómada, *m.f.*
nomadic [nou'mædik], *a.* nómada.
nominal ['nɔminəl], *a.* nominal.
nominate ['nɔmineit], *v.t.* nombrar, nominar.
nominative ['nɔminətiv], *a., n.* nominativo.
nominee [nɔmi'ni:], *n.* propuesto, candidato nombrado.
non- [nɔn], *prefix.* des-, no, falta de . . .
nonage ['nɔnidʒ], *n.* minoría, infancia.
nonagenarian [nɔnədʒi'nɛəriən], *a., n.* noventón, *m.*, nonagenario.
nonchalant ['nɔnʃələnt], *a.* descuidado, dejado, desidioso.
non-commissioned officer ['nɔnkəmiʃənd 'ɔfisə], *n.* suboficial, *m.*, cabo, sargento.
non-committal [nɔnkə'mitl], *a.* evasivo.
nonconformist [nɔnkən'fɔ:mist], *a., n.* disidente, *m.f.*
nondescript ['nɔndiskript], *a.* indefinible, indeterminable.
none [nʌn], *pron.* ninguno; nada; nadie; — ***the less,*** a pesar de eso, sin embargo.
nonentity [nɔ'nentiti], *n.* nada, ficción, *f.*; persona insignificante, nulidad, *f.*
nones [nounz], *n.pl.* (*eccl.*) nona.
nonplus ['nɔn'plʌs], *v.t.* confundir, dejar perplejo.
non-profitmaking [nɔn'prɔfitmeikiŋ], *a.* no comercial.
nonsense ['nɔnsəns], *n.* tontería, disparate, *m.*; estupidez, *f.*
nonsensical [nɔn'sensikəl], *a.* disparatado, desatinado.
non-stop ['nɔn'stɔp], *a., adv.* sin parar.
noodle (1) [nu:dl], *n.* tallarín, *m.*, fideo.
noodle (2) [nu:dl], *n.* (*fam.*) simplon, *m.*
nook [nuk], *n.* rincón, *m.*, ángulo.
noon [nu:n], *n.* mediodía, *m.*
noose [nu:s], *n.* lazo, corredizo; trampa; dogal (*para ahorcar a un criminal*), *m.*
nor [nɔ:], *conj.* ni. [NEITHER].
norm [nɔ:m], *n.* norma.
normal ['nɔ:məl], *a.* normal.—*n.* estado normal.
normalcy ['nɔ:məlsi] (*U.S.*), **normality** [nɔ:'mæliti], *n.* normalidad, *f.*
Norman ['nɔ:mən], *a., n.* normando.
Norse [nɔ:s], *a., n.* nórdico, noruego (*idioma*).
north [nɔ:θ], *a.* septentrional.—*n.* norte, *m.*; ***North America,*** Norteamérica.
northeast [nɔ:θ'i:st], *a., n.* nordeste, *m.*
northerly ['nɔ:ðəli], *a.* que viene del norte, boreal.
northern ['nɔ:ðən], *a.* septentrional, norteño; del norte; ***Northern Lights,*** aurora boreal.
northerner ['nɔ:ðənə], *n.* norteño.
northwest [nɔ:θ'west], *a., n.* noroeste, *m.*
Norway ['nɔ:wei], *n.* Noruega.
Norwegian [nɔ:'wi:dʒən], *a., n.* noruego.
nose [nouz], *n.* nariz, *f.*; hocico (*de animales*); olfato; ***to blow one's —,*** sonarse las narices; ***to talk through one's —,*** ganguear; ***to turn up one's — at,*** menospreciar desdeñar.
nose-dive ['nouzdaiv], *n.* descenso en picado.
nosegay ['nouzgei], *n.* ramillete, *m.*
nostalgia [nɔs'tældʒə], *n.* nostalgia, añoranza.
nostalgic [nɔs'tældʒik], *a.* nostálgico.
nostril ['nɔstril], *n.* nariz, *f.*, ventana de la nariz.
nostrum ['nɔstrəm], *n.* panacea.
nosy ['nouzi], *a.* (*fam.*) curioso, entremetido
not [nɔt], *adv.* no.
notable ['noutəbl], *a.* notable.
notary ['noutəri], *n.* notario.
notch [nɔtʃ], *n.* mella, muesca.—*v.t.* mellar
note [nout], *n.* nota; billete (*dinero*), *m.* apunte, *m.*; ***of —,*** notable.—*v.t.* notar apuntar.
note-book ['noutbuk], *n.* cuaderno.
noted ['noutid], *a.* conocido, eminente.
noteworthy ['noutwə:ði], *a.* digno de atención, notable.
nothing ['nʌθiŋ], *n., pron.* nada; cero; ***for —*** gratis; ***to be good for —,*** no servir para nada; ***to have — to do with,*** no tener que ver con; ***to make — of,*** no comprender ***to think — of,*** tener en poco.
nothingness ['nʌθiŋnis], *n.* nada, *f.*
notice ['noutis], *n.* aviso; letrero; anuncio cartel, *m.*; despedida; atención, reseña notificación, *f.*; ***at short —,*** a corto plazo.—*v.t.* observar, notar, fijarse en.
noticeable ['noutisəbl], *a.* perceptible.
notice-board ['noutisbɔ:d], *n.* tablón (*m.*) tablero de avisos.
notify ['noutifai], *v.t.* avisar, notificar.
notion ['nouʃən], *n.* noción, *f.*—*pl.* (*U.S* [HABERDASHERY].
notoriety [noutə'raiəti], *n.* notoriedad, *f.*
notorious [nou'tɔ:riəs], *a.* notorio; de mala fama.
notwithstanding [nɔtwiθ'stændiŋ], *prep.* pesar de.—*adv.* no obstante.
nougat ['nu:gɑ:], *n.* turrón, *m.*
nought [nɔ:t], *n.* nada; cero. [NAUGHT.]
noun [naun], *n.* sustantivo, nombre, *m.*
nourish ['nʌriʃ], *v.t.* alimentar, nutrir; (*fig.*) abrigar.
nourishing ['nʌriʃiŋ], *a.* nutritivo.
nourishment ['nʌriʃmənt], *n.* nutrimento
novel ['nɔvəl], *a.* nuevo, insólito.—*n.* novela
novelist ['nɔvəlist], *n.* novelista, *m.f.*
novelty ['nɔvəlti], *n.* novedad, innovación,
November [nou'vembə], *n.* noviembre, *m.*
novice ['nɔvis], *a., n.* novicio.

now [nau], *adv.* ahora, ya; — ***and then,*** de vez en cuando; — . . . —, ora . . . ora, ya . . . ya; ***just*** —, hace poco.
nowadays ['nauədeiz], *adv.* hoy día.
nowhere ['nouwεə], *adv.* en ninguna parte.
noxious ['nɔkʃəs], *a.* nocivo, dañoso.
nozzle [nɔzl], *n.* boquerel, *m.*, boquilla.
nuance ['nu:ɑ:ns], *n.* matiz, *m.*
nuclear [nju:kliə], *a.* nuclear.
nucleus ['nju:kliəs], *n.* núcleo.
nude [nju:d], *a.* desnudo; ***in the*** —, desnudo, en cueros.
nudge [nʌdʒ], *n.* codacito.—*v.t.* dar un codacito a.
nudist ['nju:dist], nudista, *m.f.*
nugget ['nʌgit], *n.* pepita (*de oro etc.*).
nuisance ['nju:səns], *n.* molestia, incomodidad, fastidio; ***what a — !*** ¡qué lata!
null [nʌl], *a.* nulo.
nullify ['nʌlifai], *v.t.* anular.
nullity ['nʌliti], *n.* nulidad, *f.*
numb [nʌm], *a.* entumecido.—*v.t.* entumecer.
number ['nʌmbə], *n.* número; ***to look after — one,*** barrer hacia dentro; — ***one,*** (*fam.*) mingas.—*v.t.* numerar; ***to be numbered among,*** considerarse uno de.
numeral ['nju:mərəl], *a.* numeral.—*n.* número.
numerical [nju:'merikəl], *a.* numérico.
numerous ['nju:mərəs], *a.* numeroso.
numskull ['nʌmskʌl], *n.* bobo, zote, bodoque, *m.*
nun [nʌn], *n.* religiosa, monja.
nuncio ['nʌnsiou], *n.* nuncio.
nunnery ['nʌnəri], *n.* convento de monjas.
nuptial ['nʌpʃəl], *a.* nupcial.—*n.pl.* nupcias, *f.pl.*
nurse [nə:s], *n.* enfermera; niñera.—*v.t.* criar, alimentar; cuidar; amamantar; fomentar.
nursemaid ['nə:smeid], *n.* niñera.
nursery ['nə:səri], *n.* cuarto de los niños; (*agr.*) semillero, plantel, *m.*; — ***rhyme,*** copla infantil.
nursing ['nə:siŋ], *n.* oficio de enfermera; amamantamiento.
nursing-home ['nə:siŋhoum], *n.* clínica de reposo; clínica de maternidad.
nurture ['nə:tʃə], *v.t.* educar; criar; (*fig.*) cebar (*pasión*).
nut [nʌt], *n.* nuez, *f.*; tuerca (*de tornillo*); (*fam.*) calamorra, cabeza; (*fam.*) estrafalario, loco.
nutcrackers ['nʌtkrækəz], *n.pl.* cascanueces, *m. inv.*
nutmeg ['nʌtmeg], *n.* nuez moscada.
nutriment ['nju:trimənt], *n.* nutrimento.
nutrition [nju:'triʃən], *n.* nutrición, *f.*
nutritious [nju:'triʃəs], *a.* nutritivo.
nutshell ['nʌtʃel], *n.* cáscara de nuez; ***in a***—, (*fig.*) en una palabra.
nuzzle [nʌzl], *v.t.* hozar.—*v.i.* arrimarse.
nymph [nimf], *n.* ninfa.

O

O (1), **o** [ou], *n.* decimoquinta letra del alfabeto inglés.
O (2), **oh** [ou], *interj.* ¡o! — ***if only it were,*** ¡ojalá que fuera!
o' [ə] [OF].
oaf [ouf], *n.* tonto, zoquete, *m.*
oak [ouk], *n.* roble, *m.*; — ***apple,*** agalla.
oar [ɔ:], *n.* remo; remero.
oarsman ['ɔ:zmən], *n.* remero.
oasis [ou'eisis], *n.* (*pl.* **oases**) oasis, *m.*
oath [ouθ], *n.* juramento, blasfemia, taco.
oatmeal ['outmi:l], *n.* harina de avena; gachas, *f.pl.*
oats [outs], *n.pl.* avena.
obedience [ə'bi:djəns], *n.* obediencia.
obedient [ə'bi:djənt], *a.* obediente.
obeisance [ə'beisəns], *n.* reverencia; homenaje, *m.*
obelisk ['ɔbilisk], *n.* obelisco.
obese [ou'bi:s], *a.* obeso, gordo.
obey [ou'bei], *v.t., v.i.* obedecer.
obituary [ə'bitjuəri], *a.* necrológico.—*n.* necrología.
object ['ɔbdʒikt], *n.* objeto.—[əb'dʒekt], *v.t., v.i.* objetar.
objection [əb'dʒekʃən], *n.* objeción, *f.*; inconveniente, *m.*
objectionable [əb'dʒekʃənəbl], *a.* inadmisible; desagradable.
objective [ɔb'dʒektiv], *a., n.* objetivo.
objectivity [ɔbdʒek'tiviti], *n.* objetividad, *f.*
objector [əb'dʒektə], *n.* objetante, *m.f.*
obligation [ɔbli'geiʃən], *n.* obligación, *f.*; precepto.
obligatory [ə'bligətri], *a.* obligatorio.
oblige [ə'blaidʒ], *v.t.* obligar, constreñir; complacer, favorecer; ***to be obliged for,*** estar agradecido por; ***to be obliged to,*** estar obligado a.
obliging [ə'blaidʒiŋ], *a.* servicial.
oblique [ə'bli:k], *a.* oblicuo; sesgado; indirecto.
obliterate [ə'blitəreit], *v.t.* borrar, destruir.
obliteration [əblitə'reiʃən], *n.* borradura, destrucción, *f.*
oblivion [ə'bliviən], *n.* olvido.
oblivious [ə'bliviəs], *a.* absorto; olvidadizo.
oblong ['ɔblɔŋ], *a.* oblongo, apaisado.—*n.* cuadrilongo.
obnoxious [əb'nɔkʃəs], *a.* odioso, detestable.
oboe ['oubou], *n.* oboe, *m.*
obscene [əb'si:n], *a.* obsceno.
obscenity [əb'seniti], *n.* obscenidad, *f.*
obscure [əb'skjuə], *a.* oscuro.—*v.t.* oscurecer.
obscurity [əb'skjuəriti], *n.* oscuridad, *f.*
obsequies ['ɔbsikwiz], *n.pl.* exequias, *f.pl.*
obsequious [əb'si:kwiəs], *a.* servil, zalamero.
observatory [əb'zə:vətri], *n.* observatorio.
observe [əb'zə:v], *v.t.* observar; guardar.
obsess [əb'ses], *v.t.* obsesionar.
obsession [əb'seʃən], *n.* obsesión, *f.*
obsidian [ɔb'sidiən], *n.* (*min.*) obsidiana.
obsolescent [ɔbsə'lesənt], *a.* algo anticuado.
obsolete ['ɔbsəli:t], *a.* anticuado, desusado.
obstacle ['ɔbstikəl], *n.* obstáculo.
obstetrician [ɔbste'triʃən], *n.* obstétrico, médico partero.
obstinacy ['ɔbstinəsi], *n.* testarudez, obstinación, *f.*; porfía.
obstinate ['ɔbstinit], *a.* obstinado, testarudo; porfiado.
obstreperous [əb'strepərəs], *a.* turbulento, desmandado.
obstruct [əb'strʌkt], *v.t.* obstruir, estorbar.

obstruction [ɔb'strʌkʃən], *n.* obstrucción, *f.*; obstáculo, estorbo.
obtain [ɔb'tein], *v.t.* obtener.—*v.i.* prevalecer.
obtrude [ɔb'tru:d], *v.t.* imponer.—*v.i.* entremeterse.
obtrusion [ɔb'tru:ʒən], *n.* imposición, *f.*
obtuse [ɔb'tju:s], *a.* obtuso; torpe.
obtuseness [ɔb'tju:snis], *n.* terquedad, *f.*; falta de inteligencia, torpeza.
obverse ['ɔbvə:s], *n.* anverso.
obviate ['ɔbvieit], *v.t.* evitar, apartar, obviar.
obvious ['ɔbviəs], *a.* evidente, manifiesto, obvio.
occasion [ə'keiʒən], *n.* ocasión, *f.*—*v.t.* ocasionar.
occasional [ə'keiʒənəl], *a.* poco frecuente; de circunstancia.
occasionally [ə'keiʒnəl], *adv.* de vez en cuando.
occident ['ɔksidənt], *n.* occidente, *m.*
occidental [ɔksi'dentl], *a.*, *n.* occidental, *m.f.*
occiput ['ɔksipʌt], *n.* occipucio, colodrillo.
occult [ɔ'kʌlt], *a.* oculto; mágico.
occupancy ['ɔkjupənsi], *n.* tenencia, ocupación, *f.*
occupant ['ɔkjupənt], *n.* inquilino; ocupante, *m.f.*
occupation [ɔkju'peiʃən], *n.* ocupación, *f.*; inquilinato; profesión, *f.*
occupational [ɔkju'peiʃənəl], *a.* profesional.
occupier ['ɔkjupaiə], *n.* inquilino.
occupy ['ɔkjupai], *v.t.* ocupar; habitar.
occur [ə'kə:], *v.i.* acontecer, suceder; encontrarse; ocurrir, venir a la mente.
occurrence [ə'kʌrəns], *n.* acontecimiento, suceso; ocurrencia.
ocean ['ouʃən], *n.* océano; ***oceans of,*** (*fam.*) la mar de.
Oceania [ouʃi'einjə], *n.* (*geog.*) Oceanía.
ocelot ['ousələt], *n.* (*zool.*) ocelote, *m.*
ochre ['oukə], *n.* ocre, *m.*
o'clock [ə'klɔk] [CLOCK].
octagon ['ɔktəgən], *n.* octágono.
octagonal [ɔk'tægənəl], *a.* octágono.
octane ['ɔktein], *n.* octano.
octave ['ɔktiv], *n.* (*mus.*, *eccl.*) octava.
octavo [ɔk'teivou], *a.* en octavo.
October [ɔk'toubə], *n.* octubre, *m.*
octopus ['ɔktəpəs], *n.* pulpo.
octosyllabic [ɔktousi'læbik], *a.* octosílabo.
ocular ['ɔkjulə], *a.* ocular, visual.
odd [ɔd], *a.* impar (*número*); extraño, raro; sobrante; ***three hundred —,*** trescientos y pico.
odds [ɔdz], *n.pl.* ventaja, puntos de ventaja; ***it makes no —,*** lo mismo da; ***to be at —,*** estar de punta; ***— and ends,*** cabos sueltos, trocitos.
ode [oud], *n.* oda.
odious ['oudjəs], *a.* detestable.
odium ['oudjəm], *n.* odio, oprobio.
odorous ['oudərəs], *a.* fragrante, oloroso.
odour ['oudə], *n.* olor, perfume, *m.*
odourless ['oudəlis], *a.* inodoro.
Odysseus [o'disju:s], *n.* (*myth.*) Odiseo.
Odyssey ['ɔdisi], *n.* (*myth.*) Odisea.
Œdipus ['i:dipəs], *n.* (*myth.*) Edipo.
of [ɔv, əv], *prep.* de.
off [ɔf], *a.* malo; errado; libre; podrido; (*elec.*) cortado.—*adv.* lejos; ***— and on,*** por intervalos.—*prep.* de, desde, fuera de.
offal ['ɔfəl], *n.* menudillos, *m.pl.*; desperdicio.
offence [ə'fens], *n.* ofensa, agravio; crimen, *m.*
offend [ə'fend], *v.t.*, *v.i.* ofender; transgresar.
offender [ə'fendə], *n.* delincuente, *m.f.*; ofensor, *m.*
offensive [ə'fensiv], *a.* ofensivo, desagradable. —*n.* ofensiva, ataque, *m.*
offer ['ɔfə], *n.* oferta.—*v.t.* ofrecer; proponer. —*v.i.* ofrecerse.
offering ['ɔfəriŋ], *n.* ofrenda; sacrificio.
off-hand ['ɔf'hænd], *a.* descomedido, informal; improvisado.
office ['ɔfis], *n.* oficina; oficio, cargo; despacho; (*U.S.*) consultorio.
officer ['ɔfisə], *n.* oficial, *m.*; funcionario; agente (*m.*) de policía.
official [ə'fiʃəl], *a.* oficial.—*n.* funcionario; encargado.
officialdom [ə'fiʃəldəm], *n.* burocracia.
officially [ə'fiʃəli], *adv.* oficialmente, de oficio.
officiate [ə'fiʃieit], *v.i.* oficiar (***as,*** de).
officious [ə'fiʃəs], *a.* entremetido, oficioso.
offing ['ɔfiŋ], *n.* (*naut.*) largo; ***in the —,*** inminente.
off-peak ['ɔf'pi:k], *a.* de las horas de menos carga; ***— heater,*** termos (*m.sg.*) de acumulación.
offprint ['ɔfprint], *n.* separata.
offset ['ɔfset], *v.t.* compensar, equivaler.
offshoot ['ɔfʃu:t], *n.* vástago; retoño.
offside [ɔf'said], *a.*, *adv.* fuera de juego.
offspring ['ɔfspriŋ], *n.* vástago, descendiente, *m.*; descendencia.
often [ɔfn], *adv.* a menudo, muchas veces; ***how —?*** ¿cuántas veces?
ogive ['oudʒaiv], *n.* (*arch.*) ojiva.
ogle [ougl], *v.t.* guiñar, ojear.
ogre ['ougə], *n.* ogro, monstruo.
oh [O].
ohm [oum], *n.* (*elec.*) ohmio.
oho! [ou'hou], *interj.* ¡ajá!
oil [ɔil], *n.* aceite, *m.*; petróleo; (*art.*) óleo; ***— pipe-line,*** oleoducto.—*v.t.* engrasar, aceitar.
oil-can ['ɔilkæn], *n.* aceitera.
oilcloth ['ɔilklɔθ], *n.* hule, *m.*; linóleo.
oilskin ['ɔilskin], *n.* hule, *m.*, encerado.
oil-stove ['ɔilstouv], *n.* estufa de aceite *o* petróleo.
oil-tanker ['ɔiltæŋkə], *n.* (buque) petrolero.
oily ['ɔili], *a.* aceitoso, grasiento; (*fig.*) zalamero.
ointment ['ɔintmənt], *n.* ungüento, pomada.
O.K. ['ou'kei], *a.*, *interj.* (*fam.*) muy bien, está bien.
old [ould], *a.* viejo; antiguo; añejo; ***how — are you?*** ¿cuántos años tiene Vd.? ***of —,*** antiguamente, antaño; ***— fogey,*** vejarrón, vejete.
olden ['ouldən], *a.* (*poet.*) antiguo.
old-fashioned [ould'faʃənd], *a.* chapado a lo antiguo.
oldish ['ouldiʃ], *a.* algo viejo.
old maid [ould'meid], *n.* solterona.
Old Testament [ould 'testəmənt], *n.* Antiguo Testamento.
old-world ['ouldwə:ld], *a.* antañón, de antaño; del Mundo Antiguo.
oleander [ouli'ændə], *n.* adelfa, baladre, *m.*
olfactory [ɔl'fæktəri], *a.* olfactorio.
oligarch ['ɔligɑ:k], *n.* oligarca, *m.*

oligarchy ['ɔligɑ:ki], *n.* oligarquía.
olive ['ɔliv], *a.* aceitunado.—*n.* (*bot.*) olivo, aceituno (*árbol*); aceituna (*fruta*); oliva (*color*); — ***oil,*** aceite de olivo.
Olympian [ɔ'limpiən],**Olympic** [ɔ'limpik], *a.* olímpico.—*n.pl.* ***the Olympics,*** los Olímpicos (*Juegos olímpicos*).
Olympus [ɔ'limpəs], (*myth., geog.*) Olimpo.
omelette ['ɔmlit], *n.* tortilla (de huevos).
omen ['oumen], *n.* agüero, presagio.
ominous ['ɔminəs], *a.* ominoso, de mal agüero.
omission [o'miʃen], *n.* omisión, *f.*
omit [o'mit], *v.t.* omitir, excluir.
omnibus ['ɔmnibʌs], *a.* general.—*n.* autobús, *m.*
omnipotence [ɔm'nipotəns], *n.* omnipotencia.
omnipotent [ɔm'nipotənt], *a.* omnipotente.
omniscient [ɔm'nisiənt], *a.* omnisciente, omniscio.
on [ɔn], *prep.* sobre, en, encima de; respecto a; — ***account of,*** a causa de; — ***arriving,*** al llegar; — ***board,*** a bordo (de); — ***condition that,*** con tal que; — ***the right,*** a la derecha.—*adv.* ***the light is —,*** la luz está encendida; ***he has his hat —,*** lleva el sombrero puesto; — ***and off,*** de vez en cuando; ***and so —,*** y así sucesivamente; — ***and —,*** continuamente, sin parar.
once [wʌns], *adv.* una vez; ***at —,*** en seguida; — ***upon a time there was . . .,*** érase una vez . . .—*conj.* una vez que.
one [wʌn], *a.* uno; cierto; ***it's all —,*** lo mismo da.—*pron.* uno; ***any —,*** cualquiera; ***every —,*** cada uno; — ***by —,*** uno a uno; ***no —,*** nadie; ***some —,*** [SOMEONE]; ***that's the —,*** ése es.
one-eyed ['wʌnaid], *a.* tuerto.
one-handed ['wʌn'hændid], *a.* manco.
one-horse ['wʌnhɔ:s], *a.* (*fam.*) de poca monta.
oneness ['wʌnnis], *n.* unidad, *f.*
onerous ['ɔnərəs], *a.* oneroso.
oneself [wʌn'self], *pron.* sí, sí mismo; uno mismo.
one-sided ['wʌn'saidid], *a.* parcial.
one-way ['wʌn'wei], *a.* de dirección única.
onion ['ʌnjən], *n.* cebolla.
on-looker ['ɔnlukə], *n.* testigo, espectador.
only ['ounli], *a.* único, solo.—*adv.* sólo, solamente.—*conj.* sólo que; ***if — . . .*** ¡ojalá . . .!
only-begotten ['ounlibi'gɔtn], *a.* unigénito.
onomatopœia [ɔnɔmætə'pi:ə], *n.* onomatopeya.
onrush ['ɔnrʌʃ], *n.* embestida.
onset ['ɔnset], *n.* primer ataque, *m.*, acceso.
onslaught ['ɔnslɔ:t], *n.* ataque violento, *m.*
onto ['ɔntu:], *prep.* en, sobre, encima de; a.
onus ['ounəs], *n.* carga.
onward ['ɔnwəd], *a.* avanzado.—*adv.* (also **onwards** ['ɔnwədz]) (en) adelante.
onyx ['ɔniks], *n.* ónice, *m.*
ooze [u:z], *n.* cieno, limo; rezumo.—*v.t.* manar, sudar, rezumar.—*v.i.* rezumar(se), manar.
opal ['oupəl], *n.* ópalo.
opaque [ou'peik], *a.* opaco, oscuro.
ope [oup], *v.t., v.i.* (*poet.*) [OPEN].
open ['oupən], *a.* abierto; — ***sea,*** alta mar; — ***secret,*** secreto a voces.—*n.* ***in the —,*** al aire libre.—*v.t.* abrir.—*v.i.* abrirse; ***to — on,*** dar a.
opening ['oupəniŋ], *n.* abertura; (*theat.*) estreno; inauguración, *f.*
open-minded [oupən'maindid], *a.* receptivo, imparcial.
opera ['ɔpərə], *n.* ópera.
operate ['ɔpəreit], *v.t.* actuar; dirigir.—*v.i.* funcionar; operar; ser vigente; ***to — on,*** (*med.*) operar.
operatic [ɔpə'rætik], *a.* operístico, de ópera.
operating-theatre ['ɔpəreitiŋθiətə], *n.* quirófano.
operation [ɔpə'reiʃən], *n.* operación, *f.*; funcionamiento; (*med.*) intervención quirúrgica.
operative ['ɔpərətiv], *a.* operativo; vigente.—*n.* operario.
operator ['ɔpəreitə], *n.* telefonista, *m.f.*
ophthalmic [ɔf'θælmik], *a.* oftálmico.
opiate ['oupieit], *n.* opiata, narcótico.
opine [ou'pain], *v.t., v.i.* (*obs.*) opinar.
opinion [ou'pinjən], *n.* opinión, *f.*, parecer, *m.*
opinionated [ou'pinjəneitid], *a.* dogmático, presuntuoso.
opium ['oupiəm], *n.* opio.
opossum [ou'pɔsəm], *n.* (*zool.*) zarigüeya.
opponent [ɔ'pounənt], *n.* adversario; contrincante, *m.f.*
opportune ['ɔpətju:n], *a.* oportuno.
opportunist [ɔpə'tju:nist], *a., n.* oportunista, *m.f.*
opportunity [ɔpə'tju:niti], *n.* ocasión; oportunidad, *f.*
oppose [ɔ'pouz], *v.t.* oponer(se a).
opposing [ɔ'pouziŋ], *a.* opuesto; contrario.
opposition [ɔpə'ziʃən], *n.* oposición, *f.*
oppress [ɔ'pres], *v.t.* oprimir, gravar.
oppression [ɔ'preʃən], *n.* opresión, *f.*
oppressive [ɔ'presiv], *a.* opresivo.
oppressor [ɔ'presə], *n.* opresor, *m.*
opt [ɔpt], *v.i.* optar (***for,*** a, por).
optician [ɔp'tiʃən], *n.* óptico; oculista, *m.f.*
optics ['ɔptiks], *n.* óptica.
optimism ['ɔptimizm], *n.* optimismo.
optimist ['ɔptimist], *n.* optimista, *m.f.*
optimistic [ɔpti'mistik], *a.* optimista.
optimum ['ɔptiməm], *a.* óptimo.—*n.* grado óptimo.
option ['ɔpʃən], *n.* opción, *f.*
optional ['ɔpʃənəl], *a.* facultativo, optativo.
opulence ['ɔpjuləns], *n.* opulencia.
opulent ['ɔpjulənt], *a.* opulento.
opus ['oupəs], *n.* opus, *m.*; obras completas, *f.pl.*
or [ɔ:], *conj.* o; o sea.
oracle ['ɔrəkl], *n.* oráculo.
oral ['ɔ:rəl], *a.* oral.
orange ['ɔrindʒ], *a.* anaranjado.—*n.* naranja (*fruta*), naranjo (*árbol*).
oration [ɔ'reiʃən], *n.* discurso, oración, *f.*
orator ['ɔrətə], *n.* orador, *m.*
oratory ['ɔrətri], *n.* oratoria; (*eccl.*) oratorio.
orb [ɔ:b], *n.* orbe, *m.*
orbit ['ɔ:bit], *n.* órbita.—*v.t., v.i.* orbitar.
orchard ['ɔ:tʃəd], *n.* huerto, vergel, *m.*
orchestra ['ɔ:kistrə], *n.* orquesta.
orchid ['ɔ:kid], *n.* orquídea.
ordain [ɔ:'dein], *v.t.* ordenar (*eccl.* ***as*** (priest etc.), de).
ordeal [ɔ:'diəl], *n.* (*hist.*) ordalías, *f.pl.*; aprieto.

order ['ɔ:də], *n.* orden, *m.*; (*eccl.*, *mil.*) orden, *f.*; (*com.*) pedido; ***in — to,*** para; ***in — that,*** para que; ***out of —,*** desarreglado; no funciona.—*v.t.* mandar, ordenar; (*com.*) pedir; encargar.
orderly ['ɔ:dəli], *a.* ordenado, en orden.—*n.* (*mil.*) ordenanza, *m.*; (*med.*) practicante, *m.f.*
ordinal ['ɔ:dinəl], *a.* ordinal.
ordinance ['ɔ:dinəns], *n.* ordenanza.
ordinary ['ɔ:dinəri], *a.* ordinario, regular.
ordination [ɔ:di'neiʃən], *n.* ordenación, *f.*
ordnance ['ɔ:dnəns], *n.* municiones, *f.pl.*
ore [ɔ:], *n.* mena; óxido.
organ ['ɔ:gən], *n.* órgano.
organic [ɔ:'gænik], *a.* orgánico.
organism ['ɔ:gənizm], *n.* organismo.
organization [ɔ:gənai'zeiʃən], *n.* organización, *f.*
organize ['ɔ:gənaiz], *v.t.* organizar.—*v.i.* -se.
orgy ['ɔ:dʒi], *n.* orgía.
Orient ['ɔ:riənt], *n.* oriente, *m.*—[ɔ:ri'ent], *v.t.* orientar.
oriental [ɔ:ri'entəl], *a.*, *n.* oriental, *m.f.*
orientate ['ɔ:rienteit], *v.t.* orientar.—*v.i.* -se.
orientation [ɔ:rien'teiʃen], *n.* orientación, *f.*
orifice ['ɔrifis], *n.* orificio.
origin ['ɔridʒin], *n.* origen, *m.*
original [ɔ'ridʒinəl], *a.* original.
originality [ɔridʒi'næliti], *n.* originalidad, *f.*
originate [ɔ'ridʒineit], *v.t.* originar.—*v.i.* -se.
originator [ɔ'ridʒineitə], *n.* inventor, *m.*
ornament ['ɔ:nəmənt], *n.* adorno, ornamento.—*v.t.* ornamentar.
ornamental [ɔ:nə'mentl], *a.* ornamental.
ornate [ɔ:'neit], *a.* florido, ornado.
ornithology [ɔ:ni'θɔlədʒi], *n.* ornitología.
orphan ['ɔ:fən], *a.*, *n.* huérfano.—*v.t.* dejar huérfano a.
orphanage ['ɔ:fənidʒ], *n.* orfanato.
orthodox ['ɔ:θodɔks], *a.* ortodoxo.
orthodoxy ['ɔ:θodɔksi], *n.* ortodoxia.
orthography [ɔ:'θɔgrəfi], *n.* ortografía.
orthopaedic [ɔ:θou'pi:dik], *a.* ortopédico.
oscillate ['ɔsileit], *v.i.* oscilar.
oscillation [ɔsi'leiʃən], *n.* oscilación, *f.*
osier ['ouziə], *n.* (*bot.*) mimbrera, sauce, *m.*
ostensible [ɔs'tensibl], *a.* ostensible, supuesto.
ostentation [ɔsten'teiʃən], *n.* ostentación, *f.*, pompa.
ostentatious [ɔsten'teiʃəs], *a.* ostentoso; vanaglorioso.
ostler ['ɔslə], *n.* establero, mozo de cuadra.
ostracize ['ɔstrəsaiz], *v.t.* desterrar; negar el trato social a.
ostrich ['ɔstritʃ], *n.* avestruz, *m.*
other ['ʌðə], *a.* otro; ***every — day,*** un día sí y otro no.—*adv.* ***— than,*** además de, aparte de.
otherwise ['ʌðəwaiz], *adv.* de otro modo, si no.
otter ['ɔtə], *n.* nutria.
Ottoman ['ɔtoumən], *a.*, *n.* otomano; **ottoman,** *n.* sofá, *m.*, otomana.
ouch! [autʃ], *interj.* ¡aj! ¡ay!
ought [ɔ:t], *pron.* (*obs.*) algo; nada [AUGHT].—*v. irr.* ***you — to,*** Vd. debiera *or* debería.
ounce [auns], *n.* onza.
our [auə], *a.* nuestro.
ours [auəz], *pron.* el nuestro.
ourselves [auə'selvz], *pron. pl.* nosotros mismos.
oust [aust], *v.t.* desalojar, expulsar.

out [aut], *adv.* fuera; ***— of,*** de; fuera de; sin; ***— to,*** con intención de; ***it is —,*** se acaba de publicar; se sabe ya.—*prefix.* sobre-, vencer.
out-and-out ['autənd'aut], *adv.* de siete suelas.
outbid [aut'bid], *v.t. irr.* (*conjug. like* BID) mejorar, sobrepujar.
outbreak ['autbreik], *n.* estallido, arranque, *m.*
outburst ['autbə:st], *n.* arranque *m.*
outcast ['autcɑ:st], *n.* paria, *m.f.*
outclass [aut'clɑ:s], *v.t.* aventajar.
outcome ['autkʌm], *n.* resultado.
outcry ['autcrai], *n.* vocería, alboroto.
outdate [aut'deit], *v.t.* anticuar.
outdid [aut'did] [OUTDO].
outdistance [aut'distəns], *v.t.* rezagar, dejar atrás.
outdo [aut'du:], *v.t. irr.* (*conjug. like* DO) exceder, sobrepujar.
outdoor [aut'dɔ:], *a.* al aire libre.
outer ['autə], *a.* exterior.
outermost ['autəmoust], *a.* extremo, más exterior.
outface [aut'feis], *v.t.* desafiar, arrostrar.
outfall ['autfɔ:l], *n.* desembocadero.
outfit ['autfit], *n.* equipo; juego (*colección*); traje (*vestido*), *m.*; cuerpo, grupo.—*v.t.* equipar.
outflank [aut'flæŋk], *v.t.* flanquear.
outgoing ['autgouiŋ], *a.* saliente.—*n.* salida.—*pl.* gastos, *m.pl.*
outgrow [aut'grou], *v.t.* crecer más que; ser ya grande para; dejar (*vestidos de niños, etc.*).
outhouse ['authaus], *n.* accesoria, tejadillo.
outing ['autiŋ], *n.* excursión, *f.*, caminata.
outlandish [aut'lændiʃ], *a.* estrambótico, estrafalario.
outlast [aut'lɑ:st], *v.t.* sobrevivir a, durar más que.
outlaw ['autlɔ:], *n.* forajido, proscrito.—*v.t.* proscribir.
outlay ['autlei], *n.* desembolso inicial.
outlet ['autlet], *n.* salida; desaguadero.
outline ['autlain], *n.* contorno; esbozo.—*v.t.* esbozar.
outlive [aut'liv], *v.t.* sobrevivir a.
outlook ['autluk], *n.* perspectiva.
outlying ['autlaiiŋ], *a.* remoto, de las cercanías.
outmoded [aut'moudid], *a.* fuera de moda.
outnumber [aut'nʌmbə], *v.t.* exceder en número.
out-of-date [autəv'deit], *a.* anticuado.
out-of-doors [autəv'dɔ:z], *adv.* al aire libre.
outpace [aut'peis], *v.t.* dejar atrás.
out-patient ['autpeiʃənt], *n.* enfermo no hospitalizado.
outpost ['autpoust], *n.* avanzada.
outpour ['autpɔ:], *n.* chorreo, derrame, *m.*
output ['autput], *n.* rendimiento, producción, *f.*
outrage ['autreidʒ], *n.* atrocidad, *f.*, atropello.—*v.t.* violar; violentar; enojar mucho.
outrageous [aut'reidʒəs], *a.* atroz.
outrank [aut'ræŋk], *v.t.* aventajar, exceder en grado.
outright ['autrait], *a.* cabal, rotundo.—[aut'rait], *adv.* sin reserva; al instante; de una vez.

outrun [aut'rʌn], *v.t.* dejar atrás corriendo; pasar el límite de.
outsell [aut'sel], *v.t.* vender más que.
outset ['autset], *n.* principio, comienzo.
outshine [aut'ʃain], *v.t.* eclipsar, brillar más que.
outside [aut'said], *n.* exterior, *m.*; ***at the —,*** a más tirar.—*adv.* fuera.—['autsaid], *a.* exterior, externo.—*prep.* fuera de.
outsider [aut'saidə], *n.* forastero; intruso; (*sport*) caballo desconocido en una carrera, caballo no favorito.
outsize ['autsaiz], *a.* de tamaño extraordinario.
outskirts ['autskə:ts], *n.pl.* afueras, cercanías, *f.pl.*, arrabales, *m.pl.*
outspoken [aut'spoukən], *a.* franco, boquifresco.
outstanding [aut'stændiŋ], *a.* sobresaliente; destacado; (*com.*) pendiente.
outstretch [aut'stretʃ], *v.t.* extender, alargar.
outstrip [aut'strip], *v.t.* sobrepujar, vencer, adelantarse a.
outward ['autwəd], *a.* exterior, externo.—*adv.* (also **outwards** ['autwədz]) hacia fuera.
outwardly ['autwədli], *adv.* fuera, de fuera; al parecer.
outweigh [aut'wei], *v.t.* preponderar.
outwit [aut'wit], *v.t.* burlar(se de), ser más listo que.
outworn [aut'wɔ:n], *a.* gastado.
oval ['ouvəl], *a.* oval(ado).—*n.* óvalo.
ovary ['ouvəri], *n.* ovario.
ovation [ou'veiʃən], *n.* ovación, *f.*
oven ['ʌvən], *n.* horno, hornillo.
over ['ouvə], *adv.* (por) encima; al otro lado; demasiado; (*U.S.*) de nuevo, otra vez; patas arriba; durante; allá; ***all —,*** por todas partes; ***it is all —,*** se acabó ya; ***— and — again,*** repetidas veces; ***please turn — (P.T.O.),*** a la vuelta.—*prep.* sobre; (por) encima de; a través de; más de; ***— and above,*** además de.—*prefix.* sobre-, demasiado (*e.g.* ***—active,*** demasiado activo.)
overall ['ouvərɔ:l], *a.* general, cabal, total.—*n.* delantal, mandil, *m.*—*n.pl.* zafones, *m.pl.*, mono.
overawe [ouver'ɔ:], *v.t.* intimidar.
overbalance [ouvə'bæləns], *v.t.* hacer perder el equilibrio; volcar, derribar.—*v.i.* caerse, perder el equilibrio.
overbearing [ouvə'bɛəriŋ], *a.* imperioso, altanero.
overboard ['ouvəbɔ:d], *a.* al agua.
overcast [ouvə'kɑ:st], *a.* anublado.
overcharge [ouvə'tʃɑ:dʒ], *v.t.* hacer pagar demasiado; (*mech. etc.*) sobrecargar.
overcloud [ouvə'klaud], *v.t.* anublar.
overcoat ['ouvəkout], *n.* abrigo, sobretodo, gabán, *m.*
overcome [ouvə'kʌm], *v.t. irr.* (*conjug. like* COME) superar, domar.
overcrowded [ouvə'kraudid], *a.* atestado.
overdo [ouvə'du:], *v.t. irr.* (*conjug. like* DO) exagerar; hacer demasiado.
overdose ['ouvədous], *n.* dosis excesiva.
overdraft ['ouvədrɑ:ft], *n.* sobregiro, giro en descubierto.
overdraw [ouvə'drɔ:], *v.i.* exceder el crédito.
overdrive ['ouvədraiv], *n.* sobremarcha (*coche*).
overdue [ouvə'dju:], *a.* atrasado; vencido y no pagado.
overeat [ouvə'i:t], *v.i.* comer demasiado.
overflow ['ouvəflou], *n.* reboso; diluvio; rebosadero.—[ouvə'flou], *v.i.* desbordarse, rebosar.
overflowing [ouvəflouiŋ], *a.* abundante, desbordante.
overgrown [ouvə'groun], *a.* entapizado; demasiado grande.
overhang ['ouvəhæŋ], *n.* alero (*techo*); proyección, *f.*—[ouvə'hæŋ], *v.t. irr.* (*conjug. like* HANG) colgar sobre; amenazar.
overhaul ['ouvəhɔ:l], *n.* recorrido, reparación, *f.*—[ouvə'hɔ:l], *v.t.* componer, repasar, registrar.
overhead ['ouvəhed], *a.* de arriba; elevado.—*n.* (*usually pl.*) gastos generales.—[ouvə'hed], *adv.* arriba, en lo alto; (por) encima.
overhear [ouvə'hi:ə], *v.t. irr.* (*conjug. like* HEAR) oír por casualidad.
overjoyed [ouvə'dʒɔid], *a.* encantadísimo.
overland ['ouvəlænd], *a.*, *adv.* por tierra, por vía terrestre.
overlap ['ouvəlæp], *n.* solapo, solapadura.—[ouvə'læp], *v.t.* solapar.—*v.i.* solaparse; coincidir.
overlook [ouvə'luk], *v.t.* pasar por alto; traspapelar; dar a, dar en.
overlord ['ouvəlɔ:d], *n.* jefe supremo.
overnight [ouvə'nait], *adv.* durante la noche; toda la noche.
overpass ['ouvəpɑ:s], *n.* (*U.S.*) [FLYOVER].
overpopulation [ouvəpɔpju'leiʃən], *n.* exceso de población.
overpower [ouvə'pauə], *v.t.* supeditar, subyugar; colmar, abrumar.
overrate [ouvə'reit], *v.t.* apreciar con exceso.
overreach [ouvə'ri:tʃ], *v.t.* exceder.
override [ouvə'raid], *v.t. irr.* (*conjug. like* RIDE) rechazar; fatigar.
overrule [ouvə'ru:l], *v.t.* rechazar; anular; desechar.
overrun [ouvə'rʌn], *v.t. irr.* (*conjug. like* RUN) invadir; plagar, infestar; exceder.
overseas [ouvə'si:z], *a.* de ultramar.—*adv.* en ultramar.
overseer ['ouvəsi:ə], *n.* capataz, *m.*
overshadow [ouvə'ʃædou], *v.t.* sombrear; (*fig.*) eclipsar.
overshoot [ouvə'ʃu:t], *v.t.* pasar la raya.
oversight ['ouvəsait], *n.* descuido, inadvertencia.
overstate [ouvə'steit], *v.t.* exagerar.
overstatement [ouvə'steitmənt], *n.* exageración, *f.*
overstep [ouvə'step], *v.t.* traspasar.
overstrung [ouvə'strʌŋ], *a.* demasiado excitable.
overt ['ouvət], *a.* manifiesto, patente.
overtake [ouvə'teik], *v.t. irr.* (*conjug. like* TAKE) alcanzar y pasar, adelantarse a; sorprender.
overtax [ouvə'tæks], *v.t.* agobiar.
overthrow ['ouvəθrou], *n.* derrocamiento, derribo.—[ouvə'θrou], *v.t. irr.* (*conjug. like* THROW) derrocar, derribar.
overtime ['ouvətaim], *n.* horas extraordinarias, *f.pl.*
overture ['ouvətjuə], *n.* obertura.
overturn [ouvə'tə:n], *v.t.* volcar, trastornar.
overvalue [ouvə'vælju:], *v.t.* apreciar demasiado.

overweening [ouvə'wi:niŋ], *a.* engreído, presuntuoso.
overweight [ouvə'weit], *a.* gordo con exceso.
overwhelm [ouvə'hwelm], *v.t.* abrumar; engolfar; colmar.
overwhelming [ouvə'hwelmiŋ], *a.* abrumador; irresistible.
overwrought [ouvə'rɔ:t], *a.* sobreexcitado, agotado por un exceso de trabajo *o* de pena.
Ovid ['ɔvid], *n.* Ovidio.
owe [ou], *v.t.* deber.—*v.i.* tener deudas.
owing ['ouiŋ], *a.* debido; — *to,* a causa de.
owl [aul], *n.* lechuza, buho, mochuelo.
own [oun], *a.* propio.—*v.t.* poseer, tener; reconocer, confesar; ***to — up,*** (*fam.*) confesar.
owner ['ounə], *n.* propietario, dueño.
ownerless ['ounəlis], *a.* sin dueño; mostrenco.
ownership ['ounəʃip], *n.* propiedad, posesión, *f.*
ox [ɔks], *n.* (*pl.* **oxen** ['ɔksən]) buey, *m.*
oxide ['ɔksaid], *n.* óxido.
oxidize ['ɔksidaiz], *v.t.* oxidar.
oxygen ['ɔksidʒən], *n.* oxígeno.
oyez! ['oujez], *interj.* ¡oíd!
oyster ['ɔistə], *n.* ostra.
ozone ['ouzoun], *n.* ozono.

P

P, p [pi:], *n.* décimosexta letra del alfabeto inglés; ***to mind one's p's and q's,*** ir con pies de plomo.
pace [peis], *n.* paso; marcha, andadura; velocidad, *f.*; ***to keep — with,*** ir al mismo paso que; mantenerse al corriente de.—*v.t.* recorrer; marcar el paso para; ***to — out,*** medir a pasos.—*v.i.* pasear(se); ambular; ***to — up and down,*** dar vueltas.
pacific [pə'sifik], *a.* pacífico; sosegado; ***the Pacific (Ocean),*** el Océano Pacífico.
pacification [pæsifi'keiʃən], *n.* pacificación, *f.*
pacifism ['pæsifizm], *n.* pacifismo.
pacifist ['pæsifist], *a., n.* pacifista, *m.f.*
pacify ['pæsifai], *v.t.* pacificar; tranquilizar; conciliar.
pack [pæk], *n.* fardo; lío; carga; paquete, *m.*; manada; jauría; ***— of cards,*** baraja de naipes; ***— of lies,*** sarta de mentiras; ***— of thieves,*** cuadrilla de malhechores.—*v.t.* embalar; empaquetar; apretar; atestar; llenar.—*v.i.* hacer la maleta; ***to — up,*** (*fam.*) liar el hato; ***to send packing,*** (*fam.*) dar calabazas a, mandar a la porra.
package ['pækidʒ], *n.* paquete, *m.*; fardo.—*v.t.* empaquetar.
packer ['pækə], *n.* embalador, *m.*
packet ['pækit], *n.* paquete, *m.*; cajetilla; (*mar.*) paquebote, *m.*; ***to make one's —,*** (*fam.*) hacer su pacotilla; ***to cost a —,*** (*fam.*) costar un dineral.
pack-horse ['pæk'hɔ:s], *n.* caballo de carga.
packing ['pækiŋ], *n.* embalaje, *m.*; ***to do one's —,*** hacer la maleta.
packing-case ['pækiŋkeis], *n.* caja de embalaje.
pack-saddle ['pæksædl], *n.* albarda.
pact [pækt], *n.* pacto; ***to make a —,*** pactar.
pad [pæd], *n.* almohadilla, cojinete, *m.*; (*sport*) espinillera.—*v.t.* almohadillar; rellenar, forrar; meter paja en.
padding ['pædiŋ], *n.* borra, algodón, *m.*; almohadilla; (*fig.*) paja.
paddle [pædl], *n.* canalete, *m.*, zagual, *m.*; paleta.—*v.t.* remar.—*v.i.* chapotear.
paddle-steamer ['pædlsti:mə], *n.* vapor (*m.*) de paletas.
paddock ['pædək], *n.* prado; parque, *m.*; picadero.
padlock ['pædlɔk], *n.* candado.—*v.t.* cerrar con candado.
padre ['pɑ:dri], *n.* cura castrense, *m.*
pagan ['peigən], *a., n.* pagano.
paganism ['peigənizm], *n.* paganismo.
page (1) [peidʒ], *n.* paje, *m.*, escudero (*muchacho*).—*v.t.* hacer llamar por el paje.
page (2) [peidʒ], *n.* página, hoja (*de un libro*).—*v.t.* paginar.
pageant ['pædʒənt], *n.* espectáculo, procesión *f.*; pompa.
pageantry ['pædʒəntri], *n.* pompa, aparato; ostentación, *f.*
paid [peid], *pret., p.p.* [PAY].
paid-up share ['peidʌp'ʃɛə], *n.* acción liberada.
pail [peil], *n.* cubo, pozal, *m.*
pain [pein], *n.* dolor, *m.*; sufrimiento; tormento; ***labour pains,*** dolores (*m.pl.*) de parto; ***on — of death,*** so pena de muerte; ***to take pains,*** tomarse trabajo, esforzarse; ***to be in —,*** sufrir.—*v.t.* doler; afligir; atormentar.
pained [peind], *a.* dolorido; afligido.
painful ['peinful], *a.* doloroso; angustioso; molesto; arduo.
painless ['peinlis], *a.* sin dolor.
painstaking ['peinzteikiŋ], *a.* cuidadoso; diligente; concienzudo.
paint [peint], *n.* pintura.—*v.t., v.i.* pintar; ***to — the town red,*** hacer una boda de negros.
paint-box ['peintbɔks], *n.* caja de pinturas.
paint-brush ['peintbrʌʃ], *n.* pincel, *m.*; brocha.
painter ['peintə], *n.* pintor, *m.*; (*naut.*) boza.
painting ['peintiŋ], *n.* pintura; cuadro.
pair [pɛə], *n.* par, *m.*; pareja.—*v.t.* parear; emparejar; aparear; casar.—*v.i.* parearse; aparearse; casarse; ***to — off,*** formar pareja.
Pakistan [pɑ:kis'tɑ:n], *n.* el Paquistán.
Pakistani [pɑ:kis'tɑ:ni], *a., n.* pakistano, pakistaní, *m.f.*
pal [pæl], *n.* (*fam.*) amigo, compañero.
palace ['pælis], *n.* palacio.
palatable ['pælətəbl], *a.* sabroso, apetitoso; aceptable.
palate ['pælit], *n.* paladar, *m.*
palatial [pə'leiʃəl], *a.* palaciego; suntuoso.
pale (1) [peil], *a.* pálido; descolorido; claro (*color*); tenue (*luz*); ***to grow —,*** palidecer.
pale (2) [peil], *n.* estaca; límite, *m.*
paleness ['peilnis], *n.* palidez, *f.*
palette ['pælit], *n.* paleta.
palette-knife ['pælitnaif], *n.* espátula.
paling ['peiliŋ], *n.* palizada, estacada.
palisade [pæli'seid], *n.* palizada, estacada.

pall (1) [pɔ:l], *n.* palio; manto; paño mortuorio.
pall (2) [pɔ:l], *v.i.* perder el sabor.
pall-bearer ['pɔ:lbɛərə], *n.* doliente, *m.*
palliate ['pælieit], *v.t.* paliar, mitigar; excusar, disculpar.
palliative ['pæljətiv], *a.*, *n.* paliativo.
pallid ['pælid], *a.* pálido, descolorido.
pallor ['pælə], *n.* palidez, *f.*
palm [pɑ:m], *n.* palma; — ***tree,*** palmera; ***Palm Sunday,*** Domingo de Ramos.—*v.t.* enpalmar; ***to — off,*** defraudar con; (*fam.*) dar gato por liebre.
palmist ['pɑ:mist], *n.* quiromántica, *m.f.*
palmistry ['pɑ:mistri], *n.* quiromancia.
palm-oil ['pɑ:mɔil], *n.* aceite (*m.*) de palma.
palmy ['pɑ:mi], *a.* palmar; floreciente; próspero.
palpable ['pælpəbl], *a.* palpable.
palpitate ['pælpiteit], *v.i.* palpitar.
palpitating ['pælpiteitiŋ], *a.* palpitante.
palpitation [pælpi'teiʃən], *n.* palpitación, *f.*
palsied ['pɔ:lzid], *a.* paralizado, paralítico.
palsy ['pɔ:lzi], *n.* parálisis, *f.*—*v.t.* paralizar.
paltriness ['pɔ:ltrinis], *n.* mezquindad, *f.*
paltry ['pɔ:ltri], *a.* mezquino; despreciable.
pamper ['pæmpə], *v.t.* mimar.
pamphlet ['pæmflit], *n.* folleto.
pamphleteer [pæmfli'tiə], *n.* folletista, *m.f.*
pan [pæn], *n.* cazuela; cacerola; cazoleta (*de fusil*); ***flash in the —,*** fuego de paja.—*v.t.* separar (el oro en una gamella).
panacea [pænə'siə], *n.* panacea.
panache [pə'næʃ], *n.* penacho.
Panama [pænə'mɑ:], *n.* Panamá, *m.*; ***panama hat,*** sombrero de jipijapa.
Panamanian [pænə'meinjən], *a.*, *n.* panameño.
pancake ['pænkeik], *n.* hojuela, fruta de sartén; — ***landing,*** (*aer.*) aterrizaje brusco; ***Pancake (Tues)day,*** martes (*m.*) de Carnaval.
panda ['pændə], *n.* panda, *m. f.*
pandemonium [pændi'mounjəm], *n.* pandemonio; estrépito.
pander ['pændə], *n.* alcahuete, *m.*—*v.i.* alcahuetear; ***to — to,*** mimar; prestarse a.
pane [pein], *n.* (hoja de) vidrio; cristal, *m.*; cuadro.
panegyric [pæni'dʒirik], *a.*, *n.* panegírico.
panel [pænl], *n.* entrepaño; artesón, *m.*; tabla; registro; jurado; — ***doctor,*** médico de seguros.—*v.t.* labrar a entrepaños; (*arch.*) artesonar.
panelled ['pænəld], *a.* entrepañado; artesonado.
panelling ['pænəliŋ], *n.* entrepaños, *m.pl.*; artesonado.
pang [pæŋ], *n.* punzada, dolor agudo; remordimiento, congoja.
panic ['pænik], *n.* pánico; espanto, terror, *m.* —*v.i.* espantarse.
panic-stricken ['pænikstrikən], *a.* aterrorizado, despavorido.
pannier ['pæniə], *n.* alforja.
panoply ['pænəpli], *n.* panoplia.
panorama [pænə'rɑ:mə], *n.* panorama, *m.*
panoramic [pænə'ræmik], *a.* panorámico.
pansy ['pænzi], *n.* pensamiento, trinitaria; (*fam.*) maricón, *m.*
pant [pænt], *n.* jadeo; palpitación, *f.*—*v.i.* jadear; palpitar; hipar (*perro*).
pantechnicon [pæn'teknikən], *n.* carro de mudanzas.
pantheism ['pænθiizm], *n.* panteísmo.
pantheon ['pænθiən], *n.* panteón, *m.*
panther ['pænθə], *n.* pantera.
panties ['pæntiz], *n.pl.* pantalones (*de mujer*), *m.pl.*; bragas, *f.pl.*
panting ['pæntiŋ], *a.* jadeante.—*n.* jadeo; resuello; palpitación, *f.*
pantomime ['pæntəmaim], *n.* pantomima; revista; mímica; ***in —,*** por gestos *o* señas.
pantry ['pæntri], *n.* despensa.
pants [pænts], *n.pl.* (*fam.*) calzoncillos; pantalones, *m.pl.*
Panzer division ['pænzədi'viʒən], *n.* división (*f.*) motorizada.
pap [pæp], *n.* teta; pezón, *m.*; papilla.
papacy ['peipəsi], *n.* papado, pontificado.
papal ['peipəl], *a.* papal, pontificio; — ***bull,*** bula pontificia; — ***see,*** sede apostólica.
paper ['peipə], *a.* de papel.—*n.* papel, *m.*; hoja de papel; documento; disertación, *f.*; conferencia; periódico; examen escrito; — ***bag,*** saco de papel.—***pl.*** credenciales, *m.pl.* —*v.t.* empapelar.
paper-chase ['peipətʃeis], *n.* rally-paper, *m.*
paper-clip ['peipəklip], *n.* clip, *m.*
paper-hanger ['peipəhæŋə], *n.* empapelador, *m.*
paper-hanging ['peipəhæŋiŋ], *n.* empapelado.
papering ['peipəriŋ], *n.* empapelado.
paper-knife ['peipənaif], *n.* cortapapeles, *m.sg.*
paper-mill ['peipəmil], *n.* fábrica de papel.
paper-money ['peipə'mʌni], *n.* papel moneda, *m.*
paper-weight ['peipəweit], *n.* pisapapeles, *m.sg.*
papier-mâché ['pæpjei'mɑ:ʃei], *n.* cartón piedra, *m.*
papist ['peipist], *a.*, *n.* papista, *m.f.*
papoose [pə'pu:s], *n.* niño indio.
papyrus [pə'paiərəs], *n.* papiro.
par [pɑ:], *n.* par, *f.*; ***above —,*** a premio; ***at —,*** a la par; ***below —,*** a descuento; ***to be on a — with,*** estar al nivel de, ser igual a.
parable ['pærəbl], *n.* parábola.
parachute ['pærəʃu:t], *n.* paracaídas, *m.sg.*; — ***troops,*** cuerpo de paracaidistas.—*v.i.* lanzarse en paracaídas.
parachutist ['pærəʃu:tist], *n.* paracaidista, *m.f.*
parade [pə'reid], *n.* procesión, *f.*; desfile, *m.*, revista; paseo; alarde, *m.*, pompa; — ***ground,*** campo de instrucción; plaza de armas.—*v.t.* hacer alarde de; pasar revista a. —*v.i.* desfilar; pasearse.
paradise ['pærədais], *n.* paraíso; (*fig.*) jauja; ***bird of —,*** ave (*f.*) del paraíso.
paradox ['pærədɔks], *n.* paradoja.
paradoxical [pærə'dɔksikəl], *a.* paradójico.
paraffin ['pærəfin], *n.* parafina, kerosina.
paragon ['pærəgən], *n.* dechado.
paragraph ['pærəgrɑ:f], *n.* párrafo; suelto; ***new —,*** punto y aparte.
Paraguay ['pærəgwai], *n.* el Paraguay.
Paraguayan [pærə'gwaiən], *a.*, *n.* paraguayo.
parakeet ['pærəki:t], *n.* perico.

parallel ['pærəlel], *a.* paralelo; igual; semejante, análogo; — ***bars,*** paralelas.—*n.* paralelo, línea paralela; semejanza; cotejo; (*mil.*) paralela; ***without* —,** sin ejemplo.—*v.t.* poner en paralelo; cotejar, comparar.
parallelism ['pærəlelizm], *n.* paralelismo.
parallelogram [pærə'leləgræm], *n.* paralelogramo.
paralyse ['pærəlaiz], *v.t.* paralizar.
paralysis [pə'rælisis], *n.* parálisis; (*fig.*) paralización, *f.*
paralytic [pærə'litik], *a.*, *n.* paralítico.
paramount ['pærəmaunt], *a.* supremo, sumo.
paramour ['pærəmuə], *n.* amante, *m.*; querida.
paranoia [pærə'nɔiə], *n.* paranoia.
parapet ['pærəpit], *n.* parapeto.
paraphernalia [pærəfə'neiljə], *n.* (*jur.*) bienes parafernales, *m.pl.*; atavíos, *m.pl.*; pertrechos, *m.pl.*
paraphrase ['pærəfreiz], *n.* paráfrasis, *f.*—*v.t.* parafrasear.
parasite ['pærəsait], *n.* parásito.
parasitic [pærə'sitik], *a.* parásito; (*med.*) parasítico.
parasol [pærə'sɔl], *n.* quitasol, *m.*; sombrilla.
paratroops ['pærətru:ps], *n.pl.* paracaidistas, *m.pl.*
parcel [pɑ:sl], *n.* paquete, *m.*, bulto; parcela (*de tierra*).—*v.t.* empaquetar, envolver; ***to* — *out,*** repartir.
parch [pɑ:tʃ], *v.t.* secar; abrasar.—*v.i.* secarse.
parched [pɑ:tʃt], *a.* sediento, seco; — ***with thirst,*** muerto de sed.
parchedness ['pɑ:tʃidnis], *n.* aridez, sequedad, *f.*
parchment ['pɑ:tʃmənt], *n.* pergamino; parche (*de un tambor*), *m.*
pardon [pɑ:dn], *n.* perdón, *m.*; absolución, *f.*; amnistía; ***to beg* —,** pedir perdón, disculparse; **—?** ¿cómo?—*v.t.* perdonar; absolver; amnistiar.
pardonable ['pɑ:dnəbl], *a.* perdonable, disculpable, excusable.
pardoner ['pɑ:dnə], *n.* vendedor (*m.*) de indulgencias; perdonador, *m.*
pare [pɛə], *v.t.* cortar; pelar; reducir.
parent ['pɛərənt], *n.* padre, *m.*; madre, *f.*; antepasado.—*pl.* padres, *m.pl.*
parentage ['pɛərəntidʒ], *n.* parentela; linaje, *m.*; familia, alcurnia; extracción, *f.*, origen, *m.*
parental [pə'rentəl], *a.* paternal; maternal.
parenthesis [pə'renθisis], *n.* (*pl.* **-theses**) paréntesis, *m.*
parenthetical [pærən'θetikəl], *a.* entre paréntesis.
parenthood ['pɛərənthud], *n.* paternidad; maternidad, *f.*
paring ['pɛəriŋ], *n.* raedura, peladura; corteza, cortadura; desecho, desperdicio.
paring-knife ['pɛəriŋnaif], *n.* trinchete, *m.*
Paris ['pæris], *n.* París, *m.*
parish ['pæriʃ], *a.* parroquial.—*n.* parroquia; — ***church,*** parroquia; — ***clerk,*** sacristán, *m.*; — ***priest,*** cura, *m.*
parishioner [pə'riʃənə], *n.* parroquiano; feligrés, *m.*
Parisian [pə'rizjən], *a.*, *n.* parisiense, *m.f.*
parity ['pæriti], *n.* paridad, *f.*
park [pɑ:k], *n.* parque, *m.*; jardín (público), *m.*; ***car* —,** parque de automóviles.—*v.t.* estacionar; aparcar.—*v.i.* estacionarse, aparcarse.
parking ['pɑ:kiŋ], *n.* estacionamiento; — ***lights,*** luces (*f.pl.*) de estacionamiento; — ***place,*** parque (*m.*) de estacionamiento; ***no* —,** ¡prohibido estacionarse!
park-keeper ['pɑ:kki:pə], *n.* guardián, *m.*
parlance ['pɑ:ləns], *n.* lenguaje, *m.*
parley ['pɑ:li], *n.* (*mil.*) parlamento.—*v.i.* parlamentar.
parliament ['pɑ:ləmənt], *n.* parlamento; cortes, *f.pl.*
parliamentary [pɑ:lə'mentəri], *a.* parlamentario; — ***immunity,*** inviolabilidad (*f.*) parlamentaria.
parlour ['pɑ:lə], *n.* sala de recibo; locutorio; — ***games,*** juegos, (*m.pl.*) de prendas.
Parnassus [pɑ:'næsəs], *n.* Parnaso.
parochial [pə'roukiəl], *a.* parroquial, parroquiano; (*fig.*) provincial.
parodist ['pærədist], *n.* parodista, *m.f.*
parody ['pærədi], *n.* parodia.—*v.t.* parodiar.
parole [pə'roul], *n.* promesa de honor.—*v.t.* poner en libertad bajo palabra.
paroxysm ['pærəksizm], *n.* paroxismo; acceso.
parricide ['pærisaid], *n.* parricidio (*crimen*); parricida (*persona*), *m.f.*
parrot ['pærət], *n.* papagayo, loro.
parry ['pæri], *n.* parada; quite, *m.*—*v.t.*, *v.i.* parar; evitar.
parse [pɑ:z], *v.t.* analizar.
parsimonious [pɑ:si'mounjəs], *a.* parsimonioso.
parsimony ['pɑ:siməni], *n.* parsimonia.
parsing ['pɑ:ziŋ], *n.* análisis, *m.* o *f.*
parsley ['pɑ:sli], *n.* perejil, *m.*
parsnip ['pɑ:snip], *n.* chirivía.
parson [pɑ:sn], *n.* clérigo; cura anglicano, *m.*
parsonage ['pɑ:sənidʒ], *n.* rectoría.
part [pɑ:t], *n.* parte, *f.*; porción, *f.*; trozo; pieza; región, *f.*; lugar, *m.*; papel (*de un actor*), *m.*; (*mus.*) voz, *f.*;—*pl.* prendas, dotes, partes, *f.pl.*, ***for my* —,** por mi parte; ***foreign parts,*** el extranjero ***in* —,** en parte; ***in parts,*** por entregas; ***spare* —,** pieza de recambio; — ***owner,*** conpropietario; ***to take* — *in,*** tomar parte en; ***to take in good* —,** tomar bien; ***to play a* —,** desempeñar un papel; ***to take a person's* —,** ser partidario de alguien.—*v.t.* distribuir, repartir; abrir; ***to* — *one's hair,*** hacerse la raya.—*v.i.* partir, despedirse; ***to* — *from,*** despedirse de; separarse de; ***to* — *with,*** deshacerse de.
partake [pɑ:'teik], *v.t. irr.* (*conjug. like* TAKE) participar de; tomar parte en.—*v.i.* tomar algo; ***to* — *of,*** comer de; beber de.
partial ['pɑ:ʃəl], *a.* parcial; aficionado.
partiality [pɑ:ʃi'æliti], *n.* parcialidad, *f.*; preferencia.
participant [pɑ:'tisipənt], *n.* participante, *m.f.*
participate [pɑ:'tisipeit], *v.i.* participar (de); tomar parte (en).
participation [pɑ:tisi'peiʃən], *n.* participación, *f.*
participle ['pɑ:tisipl], *n.* participio.
particle ['pɑ:tikl], *n.* partícula; átomo, pizca.

particular [pə'tikjulə], *a.* particular; especial; individual; exacto; escrupuloso; ***in* —,** en particular; ***to be — about,*** ser exigente en cuanto a.—*n.* particular, pormenor, *m.*; circunstancia.—*pl.* detalles, *m.pl.*
particularize [pə'tikjuləraiz], *v.t.* particularizar; especificar.
parting ['pɑ:tiŋ], *n.* despedida; separación, *f.*; raya; bifurcación, *f.*; ***the — of the ways,*** el punto decisivo.
partisan [pɑ:ti'zæn], *a.* partidario.—*n.* partidario; guerrillero.
partition [pɑ:'tiʃən], *n.* partición; división; pared, *f.*, tabique, *m.*—*v.t.* partir, dividir.
partly ['pɑ:tli], *adv.* en parte.
partner ['pɑ:tnə], *n.* socio, asociado; compañero; pareja; consorte, *m.f.*
partnership ['pɑ:tnəʃip], *n.* asociación; sociedad, *f.*, compañía; ***to take into* —,** tomar como socio; ***to go into* —,** asociarse.
partook [pɑ:'tuk] [PARTAKE].
partridge ['pɑ:tridʒ], *n.* perdiz, *f.*
party ['pɑ:ti], *n.* partido; grupo; reunión; (*jur.*) parte, *f.*; interesado; ***to be a — to,*** ser cómplice en.
parvenu ['pɑ:vənju:], *a.*, *n.* advenedizo.
pass [pɑ:s], *n.* paso; desfiladero; salvoconducto; permiso, licencia; crisis, *f.*; (*sport*) pase, *m.*; estocada (*esgrima*); aprobación (*examen*), *f.*; ***free* —,** billete (*m.*) de favor. —*v.t.* pasar; alargar; aventajar; tolerar; aprobar (*un examen*); evacuar; ***to — sentence,*** pronunciar sentencia; (*fam.*) ***to — the buck,*** echar la carga.—*v.i.* pasar; cesar, desaparecer; ***to — away,*** fallecer, morir; ***to — by,*** pasar cerca de; (*fig.*) pasar por; ***to — for,*** pasar por; ***to — on,*** seguir andando; fallecer; ***to — out,*** salir; (*fig.*) desmayarse; ***to — over,*** atravesar; excusar; pasar por; ***to — through,*** atravesar; traspasar; (*fig.*) experimentar; ***to bring to* —,** ocasionar; ***to come to* —,** suceder.
passable ['pɑ:səbl], *a.* transitable; tolerable; regular.
passage ['pæsidʒ], *n.* pasaje, *m.*; travesía; viaje, *m.*; tránsito; entrada; pasillo; callejón, *m.*
pass-book ['pɑ:sbuk], *n.* libreta de banco.
passenger ['pæsindʒə], *n.* pasajero, viajero; peatón, *m.*
pass-key ['pɑ:ski:], *n.* llave maestra, *f.*
passer-by ['pɑ:sə'bai], *n.* (*pl.* **passers-by**) transeúnte, paseante, *m.f.*
passing ['pɑ:siŋ], *a.* pasajero, fugaz, momentáneo; ***in* —,** de paso.—*n.* paso, pasada; muerte, *f.*, fallecimiento; aprobación, *f.*—*adv.* (*poet.*) sumamente.
passion ['pæʃən], *n.* pasión, *f.*; ira; ardor, *m.*; ***Passion Sunday,*** Domingo de Pasión; ***to fly into a* —,** montar en cólera.
passionate ['pæʃənit], *a.* apasionado; irascible; ardiente; impetuoso.
passion-flower ['pæʃənflauə], *n.* pasionaria.
passive ['pæsiv], *a.* pasivo.—*n.* voz pasiva.
Passover ['pɑ:souvə], *n.* Pascua.
passport ['pɑ:spɔ:t], *n.* pasaporte, *m.*
password ['pɑ:swə:d], *n.* contraseña.
past [pɑ:st], *a.* pasado; terminado; antiguo; ***— president,*** ex-presidente, *m.*—*n.* pasado; historia; pretérito; (*fam.*) ***to have a* —,** tener malos antecedentes.—*adv.* más allá.—*prep.* después de; más allá de; sin; fuera de; incapaz de; ***— belief,*** increíble; ***he is — caring,*** no le importa ya; ***it is ten — six,*** son las seis y diez.
paste [peist], *a.* imitado.—*n.* pasta; engrudo. —*v.t.* pegar; engrudar.
pasteboard ['peistbɔ:d], *a.* de cartón.—*n.* cartón, *m.*
pastel ['pæstəl], *n.* (*art.*) pastel, *m.*
pasteurization [pɑ:stərai'zeiʃən], *n.* pasteurización, *f.*
pasteurize ['pɑ:stəraiz], *v.t.* pasteurizar.
pastille ['pæsti:l], *n.* pastilla.
pastime ['pɑ:staim], *n.* pasatiempo.
past-master ['pɑ:st'mɑ:stə], *n.* maestro consumado.
pastor ['pɑ:stə], *n.* pastor, *m.*
pastoral ['pɑ:stərəl], *a.* pastoril.—*a.*, *n.* (*eccl.*) pastoral, *f.*
pastry ['peistri], *n.* pasta; pastel, *m.*; pastelería.
pastry-cook ['peistrikuk], *n.* pastelero.
pasture ['pɑ:stʃə], *n.* pasto; prado, pradera.—*v.t.* pastar, apacentar.—*v.i.* pastar, pacer.
pasty ['peisti], *a.* pálido; pastoso.—*n.* ['pæsti], empanada.
pat (1) [pæt], *n.* golpecito; caricia; (*fig.*) ***— on the back,*** elogio.—*adv.* a propósito; fácilmente.—*v.t.* dar golpecitos; acariciar.
pat (2) [pæt], *n.* ***— of butter,*** pedacito de mantequilla.
patch [pætʃ], *n.* remiendo; parche, *m.*; pedazo; lunar postizo; mancha; (*fam.*) ***not to be a — on,*** no llegar a los zancajos de.—*v.t.* remendar; (*fam.*) chafallar; (*fig.*) ***to — up,*** hacer las paces.
patchy ['pætʃi], *a.* cubierto de parches; (*fig.*) desigual.
paten ['pætən], *n.* (*eccl.*) patena.
patent ['peitənt], *a.* patente; evidente; ***— leather,*** charol, *m.*; ***— medicine,*** específico farmacéutico.—*n.* patente, *f.*; ***— of nobility,*** carta de hidalguía; ***— applied for,*** patente solicitada.—*v.t.* obtener una patente; conceder una patente.
paternal [pə'tə:nl], *a.* paterno, paternal.
paternity [pə'tə:niti], *n.* paternidad, *f.*
path [pɑ:θ], *n.* senda, sendero; camino; trayectoia.
pathetic [pə'θetik], *a.* patético.
pathological [pæθə'lɔdʒikəl], *a.* patológico.
pathologist [pə'θɔlədʒist], *n.* patólogo.
pathology [pə'θɔlədʒi], *n.* patología.
pathos ['peiθɔs], *n.* lo patético.
pathway ['pɑ:θwei], *n.* senda, sendero.
patience ['peiʃəns], *n.* paciencia; ***to play* —,** hacer solitarios (*naipes*); ***to lose* —,** perder la paciencia, impacientarse.
patient ['peiʃənt], *a.* paciente.—*n.* paciente, *m.f.*; enfermo.
patois ['pætwɑ:], *n.* dialecto.
patriarch ['peitriɑ:k], *n.* patriarca, *m.*
patriarchal [peitri'ɑ:kəl], *a.* patriarcal.
patrician [pə'triʃən], *a.*, *n.* patricio.
patrimony ['pætriməni], *n.* patrimonio.
patriot ['pætriət], *n.* patriota, *m.f.*
patriotic [pætri'ɔtik], *a.* patriótico.
patriotism ['pætriətizm], *n.* patriotismo.
patrol [pə'troul], *n.* patrulla; ronda.—*v.t.*, *v.i.* patrullar; rondar.

patron ['peitrən], *n.* mecenas, *m.sg.*; protector, *m.*; patrono; cliente, *m.f.*; — ***saint,*** santo patrón, santa patrona.
patronage ['pætrənidʒ], *n.* patronato; patrocinio; clientela; superioridad, *f.*
patroness ['peitrənes], *n.* protectora; patrona.
patronize ['pætrənaiz], *v.t.* patrocinar; proteger; ser parroquiano de; tratar con arrogancia.
patronizing ['pætrənaiziŋ], *a.* que patrocina; altivo.
patter ['pætə], *n.* ruido; golpecitos, *m.pl.*; parladuría.—*v.i.* patear; hacer ruido.
pattern ['pætən], *n.* modelo; muestra; patrón, *m.*; norma.
paunch [pɔ:ntʃ], *n.* panza, barriga.
pauper ['pɔ:pə], *n.* pobre, *m.f.*
pause [pɔ:z], *n.* pausa; cesación, *f.*—*v.i.* pausar; detenerse.
pave [peiv], *v.t.* empedrar, enlosar; (*fig.*) ***to — the way for,*** facilitar el camino para.
pavement ['peivmənt], *n.* pavimento; pavimentado; acera.
pavilion [pə'viljən], *n.* pabellón, *m.*; tienda; quiosco.
paving ['peiviŋ], *n.* empedrado, pavimento.
paving-stone ['peiviŋstoun], *n.* losa, adoquín, *m.*
paw [pɔ:], *n.* pata; garra.—*v.t.* arañar; manosear.—*v.i.* piafar.
pawn (1) [pɔ:n], *n.* empeño; (*fig.*) prenda; ***in —,*** empeñado; — ***ticket,*** papeleta de empeño.—*v.t.* empeñar; dar en prenda.
pawn (2) [pɔ:n], *n.* peón (*ajedrez*), *m.*
pawnbroker ['pɔ:nbroukə], *n.* prestamista, *m.f.*
pawnshop ['pɔ:nʃɔp], *n.* casa de préstamos, monte (*m.*) de piedad.
pay [pei], *n.* paga; salario; sueldo; jornal, *m.*, recompensa; (*mil.*) soldada.—*v.t.* (*pret., p.p.* **paid**) pagar; recompensar; satisfacer; gastar; presentar; ***to — attention,*** prestar atención; ***to — back,*** devolver; (*fig.*) pagar en la misma moneda; ***to — by instalments,*** pagar a plazos; ***to — in full,*** saldar; ***to — a call,*** hacer una visita; ***to — off,*** pagar y despedir; redimir; ***to — out,*** largar, arriar (*cordel*).—*v.i.* pagar; ser provechoso; sufrir un castigo; ***to — through the nose,*** costar un ojo de la cara; ***to — for it,*** (*fig.*) pagarlas.
payable ['peiəbl], *a.* pagadero.
pay-day ['peidei], *n.* día (*m.*) de pago.
payee [pei'i:], *n.* (*com.*) portador, *m.*
payer [peiə], *n.* pagador, *m.*
paymaster ['peimɑ:stə], *n.* pagador, *m.*; (*mil.*) habilitado.
Paymaster-General ['peimɑ:stə'dʒenərəl], *n.* ordenador (*m.*) de pagos.
payment ['peimənt], *n.* pago, paga; (*fig.*) recompensa; premio; ***cash —,*** pago en especie; ***on — of,*** mediante el pago de; — ***in advance,*** pago adelantado.
pay-roll ['peiroul], *n.* nómina.
pea [pi:], *n.* guisante, *m.*
peace [pi:s], *n.* paz; quietud; tranquilidad, *f.*; sosiego; ***to hold one's —,*** callarse; ***to make —,*** hacer las paces.
peaceable ['pi:səbl], *a.* pacífico; apacible.
peaceful ['pi:sful], *a.* tranquilo; pacífico.
peace-loving ['pi:slʌviŋ], *a.* pacífico.
peace-maker ['pi:smeikə], *n.* conciliador, *m.*
peace-offering ['pi:sɔfəriŋ], *n.* sacrificio propiciatorio.
peach [pi:tʃ], *n.* melocotón, *m.*
peacock ['pi:kɔk], *n.* pavón, *m.*, pavo real.
peahen ['pi:hen], *n.* pava real.
peak [pi:k], *n.* pico; cumbre, *f.*; punta; visera; (*fig.*) apogeo, auge, *m.*; — ***hours,*** horas de mayor tráfico.
peaked [pi:kt], *a.* puntiagudo; con visera; (*fam.*) enfermizo.
peal [pi:l], *n.* repique (*de campanas*), *m.*; estruendo; sonido; — ***of laughter,*** carcajada.—*v.t.* tañer.—*v.i.* repicar; sonar.
peanut ['pi:nʌt], *n.* cacahuete, *m.*
pear [pɛə], *n.* pera; — ***tree,*** peral, *m.*
pearl [pə:l], *n.* perla.
pearl-barley ['pə:l'bɑ:li], *n.* cebada perlada.
pearl-grey ['pə:l'grei], *a.* gris de perla.
pearly ['pə:li], *a.* perlino.
peasant ['pezənt], *n.* campesino.
peasantry ['pezəntri], *n.* campesinos, *m.pl.*
pea-shooter ['pi:ʃu:tə], *n.* cerbatana.
peat [pi:t], *n.* turba.
peat-bog ['pi:tbɔg], *n.* turbera.
peaty ['pi:ti], *a.* turboso.
pebble [pebl], *n.* guijarro, guija.
pebbly ['pebli], *a.* guijarroso, guijoso.
peccadillo [pekə'dilou], *n.* pecadillo.
peck [pek], *n.* picotazo; besito.—*v.t.* picotear; rozar con los labios.
peculiar [pi'kju:ljə], *a.* peculiar, particular; característico; extraño.
peculiarity [pikju:li'æriti], *n.* peculiaridad, particularidad, *f.*
pecuniary [pi'kju:njəri], *a.* pecuniario.
pedagogic [pedə'gɔdʒik], *a.* pedagógico.
pedagogue ['pedəgɔg], *n.* pedagogo.
pedagogy ['pedəgɔdʒi], *n.* pedagogía.
pedal [pedl], *n.* pedal, *m.*—*v.i.* pedalear.
pedant ['pedənt], *n.* pedante, *m.f.*
pedantic [pə'dæntik], *a.* pedante.
pedantry ['pedəntri], *n.* pedantería.
peddle [pedl], *v.t.* revender.—*v.i.* ser buhonero.
peddling ['pedliŋ], *n.* buhonería.
pedestal ['pedistl], *n.* pedestal, *m.*
pedestrian [pə'destriən], *a.* pedestre; (*fig.*) trillado, prosaico.—*n.* peatón, *m.*; — ***crossing,*** cruce (*m.*) de peatones.
pedigree ['pedigri:], *a.* de raza, de casta.—*n.* genealogía; raza.
pediment ['pedimənt], *n.* (*arch.*) frontón, *m.*
pedlar ['pedlə], *n.* buhonero.
peel [pi:l], *n.* corteza, hollejo, piel, *f.*—*v.t.* pelar.—*v.i.* pelarse; desconcharse (*pintura*).
peeling ['pi:liŋ], *n.* peladura; desconchadura.
peep (1) [pi:p], *n.* ojeada; vista.—*v.i.* atisbar; mostrarse.
peep (2) [pi:p], *n.* pío.—*v.i.* piar.
peep-hole ['pi:phoul], *n.* mirilla.
peep-show ['pi:pʃou], *n.* óptica.
peer (1) [piə], *n.* par, *m.*; igual; noble, *m.f.*
peer (2) [piə], *v.i.* escudriñar.
peerage ['piəridʒ], *n.* dignidad (*f.*) de par; aristocracia.
peeress ['piəres], *n.* paresa.
peerless ['piəlis], *a.* sin par, incomparable.
peevish ['pi:viʃ], *a.* enojadizo; displicente.
peevishness ['pi:viʃnis], *n.* mal humor, *m.* displicencia.

peg [peg], *n.* clavija; estaca; colgadero; pinza; ***to take down a* —**, bajar los humos a.—*v.t.* enclavijar, clavar.—*v.i.* ***to* — *away,*** batirse el cobre.
pejorative ['pi:dʒərətiv, pə'dʒərətiv], *a.* peyorativo.
pelican ['pelikən], *n.* pelicano.
pellet ['pelit], *n.* pelotilla; píldora; bolita.
pell-mell ['pel'mel], *adv.* a trochemoche; atropelladamente.
pelt (1) [pelt], *n.* piel, *f.*; pellejo.
pelt (2) [pelt], *n.* golpe, *m.*—*v.t.* arrojar, apedrear, azotar.—*v.i.* llover.
pelvis ['pelvis], *n.* pelvis, *f.*
pen (1) [pen], *n.* pluma.—*v.t.* escribir.
pen (2) [pen], *n.* corral, *m.*; pollera.—*v.t.* acorralar, encerrar.
penal ['pi:nəl], *a.* penal; **— *servitude,*** trabajos forzados, *m.pl.*
penalize ['pi:nəlaiz], *v.t.* penar, castigar.
penalty ['penəlti], *n.* pena, castigo; multa; (*sport*) penalty, *m.*
penance ['penəns], *n.* penitencia.
pence [pens] [PENNY].
pencil ['pensil], *n.* lápiz, *m.*—*v.t.* escribir, dibujar, marcar con lápiz.
pendant ['pendənt], *n.* pendiente; gallardete, *m.*
pending ['pendiŋ], *a.* pendiente.—*prep.* hasta, en espera de.
pendulum ['pendjuləm], *n.* péndulo, péndola.
penetrability [penitrə'biliti], *n.* penetrabilidad, *f.*
penetrable ['penitrəbl], *a.* penetrable.
penetrate ['penitreit], *v.t., v.i.* penetrar.
penetrating ['penitreitiŋ], *a.* penetrante.
penetration [peni'treiʃən], *n.* penetración, *f.*
penguin ['peŋgwin], *n.* pingüino.
penicillin [peni'silin], *n.* penicilina.
peninsula [pi'ninsjulə], *n.* península.
peninsular [pi'ninsjulə], *a.* peninsular.
penis ['pi:nis], *n.* pene, *m.*
penitence ['penitəns], *n.* penitencia.
penitent ['penitənt], *a., n.* penitente, *m.f.*
penitential [peni'tenʃəl], *a.* penitencial.
penitentiary [peni'tenʃəri], *a.* penitenciario. —*n.* casa de corrección; presidio.
penknife ['pennaif], *n.* cortaplumas *m.sg.*
penmanship ['penmənʃip], *n.* caligrafía.
pen-name ['penneim], *n.* seudónimo.
penniless ['penilis], *a.* sin dinero, sin blanca; indigente.
penny ['peni], *n.* (*pl.* **pennies** *o* **pence**) penique, *m.*; (*fam.*) dinero.
pennyworth ['peniwə:θ], *n.* valor (*m.*) de un penique.
pension ['penʃən], *n.* pensión, *f.*; beca; retiro;—*v.t.* pensionar; ***to* — *off,*** jubilar.
pensioner ['penʃənə], *n.* pensionista, *m.f.*; inválido.
pensive ['pensiv], *a.* pensativo, meditabundo; cabizbajo.
pentagon ['pentəgən], *n.* pentágono.
pentameter [pen'tæmitə], *n.* pentámetro.
Pentecost ['pentikəst], *n.* Pentecostés, *m.*
pent-up ['pentʌp], *a.* encerrado; enjaulado; (*fig.*) reprimido.
penultimate [pen'ʌltimit], *a.* penúltimo.
penurious [pi'njuəriəs], *a.* indigente, muy pobre; escaso; tacaño.
penury ['penjuri], *n.* penuria.
peony ['piəni], *n.* peonia.
people [pi:pl], *n.* pueblo; nación, *f.*; gente, *f.*; personas, *f.pl.*; vulgo; súbditos, *m.pl.*; familia; ***common* —**, gentuza; **— *say,*** se dice.—*v.t.* poblar.
pepper ['pepə], *n.* pimienta; pimiento.—*v.t.* sazonar con pimienta; acribillar; salpimentar.
peppermint ['pepəmint], *n.* menta; pastilla de menta.
peppery ['pepəri], *a.* picante; (*fig.*) irascible.
per [pə:], *prep.* por; **— *annum,*** al año; **— *cent,*** por ciento; **— *hour,*** por hora.
perambulate [pə'ræmbjuleit], *v.t., v.i.* recorrer.
perambulator [pə'ræmbjuleitə], *n.* coche (*m.*) de niño.
perceive [pə'si:v], *v.t.* percibir; darse cuenta de, comprender; discernir.
percentage [pə'sentidʒ], *n.* porcentaje, *m.*
perceptible [pə'septibl], *a.* perceptible; sensible.
perception [pə'sepʃən], *n.* percepción; sensibilidad, *f.*
perceptive [pə'septiv], *a.* perceptivo.
perch (1) [pə:tʃ], *n.* (*ichth.*) perca.
perch (2) [pə:tʃ], *n.* percha; pértica.—*v.t.* posar.—*v.i.* posarse.
percolate ['pə:kəleit], *v.t.* colar, filtrar.—*v.i.* colarse, filtrarse.
percolator ['pə:kəleitə], *n.* filtro, colador, *m.*
percussion [pə'kʌʃən], *n.* percusión, *f.*; choque, *m.*
perdition [pə'diʃən], *n.* perdición, *f.*; ruina.
peremptory ['perəmptəri], *a.* perentorio; imperioso.
perennial [pə'renjəl], *a.* perenne, perpetuo. —*n.* planta vivaz.
perfect ['pə:fikt], *a.* perfecto; acabado.—[pə'fekt], *v.t.* perfeccionar.
perfectible [pə'fektəbl], *a.* perfectible.
perfection [pə'fekʃən], *n.* perfección, *f.*; ***to* —**, a la perfección.
perfectionist [pə'fekʃənist], *n.* perfeccionista, *m.f.*
perfidious [pə'fidjəs], *a.* pérfido.
perfidy ['pə:fidi], *n.* perfidia.
perforate ['pə:fəreit], *v.t.* perforar, agujerear.
perforation [pə:fə'reiʃən], *n.* perforación, *f.*; agujero.
perform [pə'fɔ:m], *v.t.* ejecutar; desempeñar; representar.—*v.i.* representar, desempeñar un papel; tocar; cantar; hacer trucos.
performance [pə'fɔ:məns], *n.* ejecución, realización, *f.*; desempeño; representación, *f.*; ***first* —**, estreno.
performer [pə'fɔ:mə], *n.* ejecutante, *m.f.*; actor, *m.*; actriz, *f.*; artista, *m.f.*
perfume ['pə:fju:m], *n.* perfume, *m.*; aroma, fragancia.—[pə:'fju:m], *v.t.* perfumar; aromatizar, embalsamar.
perfumer [pə:'fju:mə], *n.* perfumista, *m.f.*
perfunctoriness [pə'fʌŋktərinis], *n.* descuido; superficialidad, *f.*
perfunctory [pə'fʌŋktəri], *a.* perfunctorio; superficial; negligente.
perhaps [pə'hæps], *adv.* quizá, quizás, tal vez.
peril ['peril], *n.* peligro; riesgo.
perilous ['periləs], *a.* peligroso, arriesgado.
perimeter [pə'rimitə], *n.* perímetro.

period ['piəriəd], *n.* período; edad, *f.*, tiempo; época; término, plazo; (*U.S.*) punto final; (*med.*) menstruación, *f.*, regla; — ***costume***, vestido de época.
periodic [piəri'ɔdik], *a.* periódico.
periodical [piəri'ɔdikəl], *a.* periódico.—*n.* revista.
peripheral [pə'rifərəl], *a.* periférico.
periphery [pə'rifəri], *n.* periferia.
periphrastic [peri'fræstik], *a.* perifrástico.
periscope ['periskoup], *n.* periscopio.
perish ['periʃ], *v.i.* perecer; marchitarse; acabar, fenecer.
perishable ['periʃəbl], *a.* perecedero.
perjure ['pə:dʒə], *v.t.* perjurar; ***to — oneself***, perjurarse.
perjurer ['pə:dʒərə], *n.* perjuro, perjurador, *m.*
perjury ['pə:dʒəri], *n.* perjurio; ***to commit —***, jurar en falso.
perk [pə:k], *v.i.* levantar la cabeza; ***to — up***, (*fam.*) reponerse; cobrar ánimo.
perky ['pə:ki], *a.* desenvuelto, gallardo; alegre.
permanence ['pə:mənəns], *n.* permanencia; estabilidad, *f.*
permanent ['pə:mənənt], *a.* permanente; estable; fijo; — ***wave***, ondulación permanente, *f.*
permeate ['pə:mieit], *v.t.* impregnar; infiltrar.
permissible [pə'misəbl], *a.* permisible, admisible.
permission [pə'miʃən], *n.* permiso, licencia.
permissive [pə'misiv], *a.* permisivo, tolerado.
permit ['pə:mit], *n.* permiso; licencia; pase, *m.*—[pə'mit], *v.t.* permitir; tolerar.
permutation [pə:mju:'teiʃən], *n.* permutación, *f.*
pernicious [pə'niʃəs], *a.* pernicioso.
peroration [perə'reiʃən], *n.* peroración, *f.*
peroxide [pə'rɔksaid], *n.* peróxido.
perpendicular [pə:pən'dikjulə], *a.*, *n.* perpendicular, *f.*
perpetrate ['pə:pitreit], *v.t.* perpetrar, cometer.
perpetration [pə:pi'treiʃən], *n.* perpetración, comisión, *f.*
perpetrator ['pə:pitreitə], *n.* perpetrador; autor, *m.*
perpetual [pə'petjuəl], *a.* perpetuo; continuo, incesante; eterno.
perpetuate [pə'petjueit], *v.t.* perpetuar, eternizar; inmortalizar.
perpetuity [pə:pi'tjuiti], *n.* perpetuidad, *f.*; ***in —***, para siempre.
perplex [pə'pleks], *v.t.* confundir, aturdir, embrollar.
perplexed [pə'plekst], *a.* perplejo, confuso.
perplexing [pə'pleksiŋ], *a.* inquietante; confuso, intricado.
perplexity [pə'pleksiti], *n.* perplejidad, confusión, *f.*
persecute ['pə:sikju:t], *v.t.* perseguir; molestar.
persecution [pə:si'kju:ʃən], *n.* persecución, *f.*
persecutor ['pə:sikju:tə], *n.* perseguidor, *m.*
perseverance [pə:si'viərəns], *n.* perseverancia.
persevere [pə:si'viə], *v.i.* perseverar.
persevering [pə:si'viəriŋ], *a.* perseverante.
Persia ['pə:ʃə], *n.* Persia.
Persian ['pə:ʃən], *a.* persa.—*n.* persa, *m.f.*
persist [pə'sist], *v.i.* persistir; empeñarse; permanecer.
persistence [pə'sistəns], *n.* persistencia.
persistent [pə'sistənt], *a.* persistente.
person [pə:sn], *n.* persona; ***in —***, en persona.
personable ['pə:snəbl], *a.* bien parecido.
personage ['pə:sənidʒ], *n.* personaje, *m.*
personal ['pə:snəl], *a.* personal; particular; íntimo; en persona.
personality [pə:sə'næliti], *n.* personalidad, *f.*
personification [pə:sɔnifi'keiʃən], *n.* personificación, *f.*
personify [pə:'sɔnifai], *v.t.* personificar.
personnel [pə:sə'nel], *n.* personal, *m.*
perspective [pə'spektiv], *n.* perspectiva.
perspicacious [pə:spi'keiʃəs], *a.* perspicaz.
perspicacity [pə:spi'kæsiti], *n.* perspicacia.
perspicuity [pə:spi'kjuiti], *n.* perspicuidad, *f.*
perspiration [pə:spə'reiʃən], *n.* transpiración, *f.*, sudor, *m.*
perspire [pə'spaiə], *v.i.* transpirar, sudar.
persuade [pə'sweid], *v.t.* persuadir; inducir, mover.
persuader [pə'sweidə], *n.* persuasor, *m.*
persuasion [pə'sweiʒən], *n.* persuasión; opinión, *f.*; secta.
persuasive [pə'sweiziv], *a.* persuasivo.
persuasiveness [pə'sweizivnis], *n.* persuasiva.
pert [pə:t], *a.* listo; desenvuelto, fresco.
pertain [pə'tein], *v.i.* pertenecer; tocar; referirse.
pertinacious [pə:ti'neiʃəs], *a.* pertinaz.
pertinacity [pə:ti'næsiti], *n.* pertinacia, tenacidad, *f.*
pertinence ['pə:tinəns], *n.* pertinencia.
pertinent ['pə:tinənt], *a.* pertinente, atinado.
pertness ['pə:tnis], *n.* viveza; desenvoltura, frescura.
perturb [pə'tə:b], *v.t.* perturbar, inquietar, agitar.
perturbation [pə:tə'beiʃən], *n.* perturbación, *f.*
Peru [pə'ru:], *n.* el Perú.
perusal [pə'ru:zəl], *n.* lectura; escudriño.
peruse [pə'ru:z], *v.t.* leer con cuidado; escudriñar.
Peruvian [pə'ru:vjən], *a.*, *n.* peruano.
pervade [pə:'veid], *v.t.* penetrar; llenar; difundirse por.
pervasive [pə:'veiziv], *a.* penetrante.
perverse [pə'və:s], *a.* perverso, depravado; obstinado; petulante.
perverseness [pə'və:snis], *n.* perversidad; obstinación, *f.*
perversion [pə'və:ʃən], *n.* perversión, *f.*
pervert ['pə:və:t], *n.* pervertido; renegado.—[pə'və:t], *v.t.* pervertir, corromper; falsificar.
pervious ['pə:vjəs], *a.* penetrable; permeable.
pessary ['pesəri], *n.* pesario.
pessimism ['pesimizm], *n.* pesimismo.
pessimist ['pesimist], *n.* pesimista, *m.f.*
pessimistic [pesi'mistik], *a.* pesimista.
pest [pest], *n.* insecto nocivo; peste, *f.*; (*fig.*) plaga; mosca.
pester ['pestə], *v.t.* molestar, importunar.
pestilence ['pestiləns], *n.* pestilencia, peste, *f.*
pestilential [pesti'lenʃəl], *a.* pestífero, pestilente.
pestle [pesl], *n.* pistadero, mano (*f.*) de mortero.

pet (1) [pet], *n.* animal doméstico; favorito; niño mimado; (*fam.*) querido, querida.—*v.t.* mimar; acariciar.
pet (2) [pet], *n.* despecho, mal humor, *m.*
petal [petl], *n.* pétalo.
peter ['pi:tə], *v.i.* ***to — out,*** agotarse; desaparecer.
petition [pi'tiʃən], *n.* petición, *f.*; memorial, *m.*; súplica; instancia.—*v.t.* pedir; suplicar; dirigir un memorial.
petitioner [pi'tiʃənə], *n.* peticionario.
petrify ['petrifai], *v.t.* petrificar.—*v.i.* petrificarse.
petrol ['petrəl], *n.* gasolina; — ***pump,*** surtidor (*m.*) de gasolina; —***station,*** puesto de gasolina.
petroleum [pi'trouljəm], *n.* petróleo.
petticoat ['petikout], *n.* engua.
pettifogger ['petifɔgə], *n.* picapleitos, *m. inv.*; sofista, *m.f.*
pettiness ['petinis], *n.* pequeñez; mezquindad, *f.*; insignificancia.
petty ['peti], *a.* pequeño; mezquino; insignificante; — ***cash,*** gastos menores; — ***larceny,*** hurto menor; — ***officer,*** suboficial, *m.*; — ***thief,*** ratero.
petulance ['petjuləns], *n.* displicencia, mal humor, *m.*
petulant ['petjulənt], *a.* displicente, mal humorado.
pew [pju:], *n.* banco de iglesia.
pewter ['pju:tə], *a.* de peltre.—*n.* peltre, *m.*
phalanx ['fælæŋks], *n.* falange, *f.*
phallic ['fælik], *a.* fálico.
phantasmagoria [fæntæzmə'gɔ:rjə], *n.* fantasmagoría.
phantom ['fæntəm], *n.* fantasma, *m.*, espectro, sombra.
pharisaic [færi'seiik], *a.* farisaico.
Pharisee ['færisi:], *n.* fariseo.
pharmaceutical [fɑ:mə'sju:tikəl], *a.* farmacéutico.
pharmacist ['fɑ:məsist], *n.* farmacéutico.
pharmacy ['fɑ:məsi], *n.* farmacia.
phase [feiz], *n.* fase, *f.*; aspecto.
pheasant ['fezənt], *n.* faisán, *m.*
phenomenal [fi'nɔminəl], *a.* fenomenal.
phenomenon [fi'nɔminən], *n.* (*pl.* **phenomena** [fi'nɔminə]) fenómeno.
phial ['faiəl], *n.* redoma.
philander ['filændə], *v.i.* galantear.
philanderer [fi'lændərə], *n.* tenorio, galanteador, *m.*
philandering [fi'lændəriŋ], *n.* galanteo.
philanthropic [filən'θrɔpik], *a.* filantrópico.
philanthropist [fi'lænθrəpist], *n.* filántropo.
philanthropy [fi'lænθrəpi], *n.* filantropía.
philatelic [filə'telik], *a.* filatélico.
philatelist [fi'lætəlist], *n.* filatelista, *m.f.*
philately [fi'lætəli], *n.* filatelia.
philharmonic [filhɑ:'mɔnik], *a.* filarmónico.
Philippine ['filipi:n], *a.* filipino.—*n.pl.* Filipinas (*islas*).
Philistine ['filistain], *a.*, *n.* filisteo.
philologist [fi'lɔləd3ist], *n.* filólogo.
philology [fi'lɔləd3i], *n.* filología.
philosopher [fi'lɔsəfə], *n.* filósofo; ***philosopher's stone,*** piedra filosofal.
philosophical [filə'sɔfikəl], *a.* filosófico.
philosophize [fi'lɔsəfaiz], *v.i.* filosofar.
philosophy [fi'lɔsəfi], *n.* filosofía.
philtre ['filtə], *n.* filtro.
phlebitis [fli'baitis], *n.* flebitis, *f.*
phlegm [flem], *n.* flema.
phlegmatic [fleg'mætik], *a.* flemático.
Phoenician [fi'ni:ʃən], *a.*, *n.* fenicio.
phoenix ['fi:niks], *n.* fénix, *f.*
phonetic [fə'netik], *a.* fonético.—*n.pl.* fonética.
phoney ['founi], *a.* falso; espurio.
phonograph ['founəgrɑ:f], *n.* fonógrafo.
phonology [fə'nɔləd3i], *n.* fonología.
phosphate ['fɔsfeit], *n.* fosfato.
phosphorescent [fɔsfə'resənt], *a.* fosforescente.
phosphorus ['fɔsfərəs], *n.* fósforo.
photogenic [foutə'd3enik], *a.* fotogénico.
photograph ['foutəgrɑ:f], *n.* fotografía, foto, *f.*—*v.t.* fotografiar.
photographer [fə'tɔgrəfə], *n.* fotógrafo.
photographic [foutə'græfik], *a.* fotográfico.
photography [fə'tɔgrəfi], *n.* fotografía.
photogravure [foutəgrə'vjuə], *n.* fotograbado.
photostat ['foutoustæt], *n.* fotostato.
phrase [freiz], *n.* frase, *f.*—*v.t.* frasear, expresar, redactar.
phrase-book ['freizbuk], *n.* libro de frases.
phraseology [freizi'ɔləd3i], *n.* fraseología.
phrenetic [fri'netik], *a.* frenético.
physical ['fizikəl], *a.* físico.
physician [fi'ziʃən], *n.* médico.
physicist ['fizisist], *n.* físico.
physics ['fiziks], *n.* física.
physiognomy [fizi'ɔnəmi], *n.* fisonomía.
physiological [fiziə'lɔd3ikəl], *a.* fisiológico.
physiologist [fizi'ɔləd3ist], *n.* fisiólogo.
physiology [fizi'ɔləd3i], *n.* fisiología.
physiotherapy [fiziə'θerəpi], *n.* fisioterapia.
physique [fi'zi:k], *n.* físico, presencia.
pianist ['pi:ənist], *n.* pianista, *m.f.*
piano ['pjænou], *n.* piano; ***grand —,*** piano de cola; ***baby grand (—),*** piano de media cola; ***upright —,*** piano vertical; — ***stool,*** taburete (*m.*) de piano; — ***tuner,*** afinador (*m.*) de pianos; ***to play the —,*** tocar el piano.
piccolo ['pikəlou], *n.* flautín, *m.*
pick (1) [pik], *n.* escogimiento; lo mejor. —*v.t.* escoger, elegir; picar; limpiar, mondar; abrir con ganzúa; ***to — a bone,*** roer un hueso; (*fig.*) ajustar cuentas; ***to — and choose,*** vacilar; ***to — a quarrel,*** buscar camorra; ***to — someone's pocket,*** limpiar la faltriquera a; ***to — off,*** arrancar; fusilar; ***to — out,*** escoger; distinguir, reconocer; ***to — up,*** recoger, coger; levantar; adquirir; trabar amistad con; aprender; interceptar.—*v.i.* comer poco; escoger; ***to — up,*** recobrar la salud, reponerse.
pick (2) [pik], *n.* pico.
pick-axe ['pikæks], *n.* zapapico.
picket ['pikit], *n.* estaca; piquete, *m.*—*v.t.* cercar con estacas; poner piquetes.
picking ['pikiŋ], *n.* recolección, *f.*; escogimiento; robo.—*pl.* desperdicios, *m.pl.*; ganancias, *f.pl.*
pickle [pikl], *n.* escabeche, *m.*; encurtido; (*fam.*) apuro.—*v.t.* escabechar, encurtir.
picklock ['piklɔk], *n.* ganzúa.
pick-me-up ['pikmi:ʌp], *n.* tónico; trinquis, *m.*
pickpocket ['pikpɔkit], *n.* ratero.

picnic ['piknik], *n.* partida de campo, picnic, *m.*—*v.i.* hacer un picnic.
pictorial [pik'tɔ:riəl], *a.* pictórico, gráfico.
picture ['piktʃə], *n.* cuadro; retrato; ilustración, *f.*; imagen, *f.*; grabado; fotografía; película; — ***book,*** libro de estampas; — ***frame,*** marco; ***to go to the pictures,*** ir al cine.
picturesque [piktʃə'resk], *a.* pintoresco.
pie [pai], *n.* pastel, *m.*, empanada; ***to have a finger in the*** —, meter cuchara; ***to eat humble*** —, bajar las orejas.
piece [pi:s], *n.* pedazo; trozo; porción, *f.*; pieza; — ***of paper,*** papelito, hoja de papel; — ***of ground,*** parcela de tierra; — ***of furniture,*** mueble, *m.*; — ***of news,*** noticia; ***to come to pieces,*** deshacerse; ***to cut to pieces,*** destrozar; ***to go to pieces,*** hacerse pedazos; ***to pull to pieces,*** despedezar; ***to take to pieces,*** desmontar.—*v.t.* unir; remendar.
piecemeal ['pi:smi:l], *adv.* en pedazos; por partes.
piece-work ['pi:swə:k], *n.* trabajo a destajo.
pied [paid], *a.* pío; abigarrado.
pier [piə], *n.* embarcadero; malecón, *m.*; pila.
pierce [piəs], *v.t.* penetrar; agujerear; traspasar.—*v.i.* penetrar.
piercing ['piəsiŋ], *a.* penetrante; cortante.
piety ['paiəti], *n.* piedad, devoción, *f.*
piffle [pifl], *n.* disparates, *m.pl.*, patrañas, *f.pl.*
pig [pig], *n.* puerco, cerdo; lingote, *m.*; ***guinea*** —, conejillo de Indias; ***to buy a — in a poke,*** comprar a ciegas.—*v.i.* ***to — it,*** (*fam.*) vivir como cochinos.
pigeon (1) ['pidʒin], *n.* pichón, *m.*, paloma; ***carrier*** —, paloma mensajera.
pigeon (2) ['pidʒin], *n.* ***that's his*** —, (*fam.*) con su pan se lo coma.
pigeon-hole ['pidʒinhoul], *n.* casilla.—*v.t.* encasillar.
pigeon-toed ['pidʒin'toud], *a.* patituerto.
pigheaded ['pig'hedid], *a.* cabezudo, terco.
pig-iron ['pigaiən], *n.* lingote (*m.*) de fundición.
piglet ['piglit], *n.* cerdito.
pigment ['pigmənt], *n.* pigmento.—*v.t.* pigmentar.
pigmy ['pigmi], *n.* pigmeo.
pigskin ['pigskin], *n.* piel (*f.*) de cerdo.
pigsty ['pigstai], *n.* pocilga.
pigtail ['pigteil], *n.* coleta, trenza.
pike (1) [paik], *n.* sollo; pica, chuzo.
pike (2) [paik], *n.* (*ichth.*) lucio.
pikestaff ['paikstɑ:f], *n.* asta de pica; ***as plain as a*** —, a bola vista.
pile (1) [pail], *n.* pila, montón, *m.*; pira; mole, *f.*, edificio grande; ***atomic*** —, pila atómica; ***to make one's*** —, (*fig.*) hacer su pacotilla. —*v.t.* apilar, amontonar.—*v.i.* ***to — up,*** amontonarse.
pile (2) [pail], *n.* pilote, *m.*, estaca.—*v.t.* clavar estacas.
pile (3) [pail], *n.* pelo.
piles [pailz], *n.pl.* (*med.*) hemorroides, *f.pl.*
pilfer ['pilfə], *v.t.* hurtar, ratear, sisar.
pilfering ['pilfəriŋ], *n.* ratería, sisa.
pilgrim ['pilgrim], *n.* peregrino, romero.
pilgrimage ['pilgrimidʒ], *n.* peregrinación, *f.*, romería.
pill [pil], *n.* píldora.
pillage ['pilidʒ], *n.* saqueo.—*v.t.* saquear, pillar.
pillager ['pilidʒə], *n.* saqueador, *m.*
pillar ['pilə], *n.* pilar, *m.*, columna; (*fig.*) sostén, *m.*; ***from — to post,*** de Ceca en Meca; — ***of strength,*** (*fam.*) roca.
pillar-box ['piləbɔks], *n.* buzón, *m.*
pillion ['piljən], *n.* grupa; grupera; ***to ride*** —, ir a la grupa.
pillory ['piləri], *n.* picota.—*v.t.* empicotar.
pillow ['pilou], *n.* almohada.—*v.t.* apoyar.
pillow-case ['piloukeis], *n.* funda de almohada.
pilot ['pailət], *n.* piloto.—*v.t.* pilotar, pilotear; guiar.
pilotage ['pailətidʒ], *n.* pilotaje; (*naut.*) practicaje, *m.*
pimp [pimp], *n.* alcahuete, *m.*—*v.i.* alcahuetear.
pimpernel ['pimpənel], *n.* pimpinela.
pimple [pimpl], *n.* grano.
pin [pin], *n.* alfiler, *m.*; clavija; clavo; prendedor, *m.*; ***pins and needles,*** agujetas, *f.pl.*, aguijones, *m.pl.*—*v.t.* prender con alfileres; enclavijar; sujetar.
pinafore ['pinəfɔ:], *n.* delantal, *m.*
pince-nez ['pɛ̃snei], *n.* quevedos, *m.pl.*
pincers ['pinsəz], *n.pl.* tenazas; pinzas, *f.pl.*
pinch [pintʃ], *n.* pellizco; pulgarada; polvo; apuro; dolor, *m.*; ***at a*** —, en caso de apuro. —*v.t.* pellizcar; apretar; hurtar, birlar; coger, prender.—*v.i.* pellizcar; apretar; economizar.
pincushion ['pinkuʃən], *n.* acerico.
pine (1) [pain], *n.* pino; madera de pino.
pine (2) [pain], *v.i.* languidecer, consumirse; ***to — for,*** suspirar por; ***to — away,*** languidecer, morirse de pena.
pineapple ['painæpl], *n.* piña; ananás, *m.sg.*
pine-cone ['painkoun], *n.* piña.
pine-needle ['painni:dl], *n.* pinocha.
ping-pong ['piŋpɔŋ], *n.* 'ping-pong', *m.*, tenis (*m.*) de mesa.
pin-head ['pinhed], *n.* cabeza de alfiler.
pinion ['pinjən], *n.* piñón, *m.*; ala; alón, *m.*; —*v.t.* atar las alas; maniatar; trincar.
pink (1) [piŋk], *a.* rosado.—*n.* clavel, *m.*; color (*m.*) de rosa; casaquín (*m.*) de caza; modelo; ***in the*** —, en sana salud.
pink (2) [piŋk], *v.i.* picar.
pinking ['piŋkiŋ], *n.* picadura.
pin-money ['pinmʌni], *n.* alfileres, *m.pl.*
pinnace ['pinis], *n.* pinaza.
pinnacle ['pinəkl], *n.* pináculo; cumbre, *f.*
pin-point ['pinpɔint], *n.* punta de alfiler.
pint [paint], *n.* pinta.
pioneer [paiə'niə], *n.* explorador; iniciador; (*mil.*) zapador, *m.*—*v.t.* explorar; introducir.
pious [paiəs], *a.* piadoso, pío, devoto.
pip [pip], *n.* pepita; moquillo; punto.
pipe [paip], *n.* pipa; cañón, *m.*, tubo; trino; (*mus.*) caramillo; (*naut.*) silbo; ***waste*** —, tubo de relleno, desaguadero; ***water*** —, cañería; — ***clay,*** blanquizal, *m.*—*v.t.* tocar; silbar; conducir con cañerías.—*v.i.* tocar la gaita; silbar; trinar.
pipe-cleaner ['paipkli:nə], *n.* limpiapipas, *m.sg.*
pipe-line ['paiplain], *n.* cañería; oleoducto.
piper ['paipə], *n.* flautista, *m.f.*; gaitero.
piping ['paipiŋ], *n.* cañería; cordoncillo; trino; — ***hot,*** hirviente.

pock-marked ['pɔkma:kd], *a.* picado de viruelas.
pod [pɔd], *n.* vaina.
poem ['pouim], *n.* poema, *m.*, poesía.
poet ['pouit], *n.* poeta, *m.*
poetaster [poui'tæstə], *n.* poetastro.
poetess ['pouitis], *n.* poetisa.
poetic [pou'etik], *a.* poético.
poetics [pou'etiks], *n.sg.* poética.
poetry ['pouitri], *n.* poesía.
pogrom ['pɔgrəm], *n.* pogrom, *m.*
poignancy ['pɔinjənsi], *n.* patetismo; acerbidad, *f.*; fuerza.
poignant ['pɔinjənt], *a.* conmovedor; patético; agudo.
point [pɔint], *n.* punto; punta; (*geog.*) cabo; (*rail.*) aguja; agudeza; cuestión, *f.*; detalle; fin, *m.*; peculiaridad, *f.*; (*com.*) entero; ***to be on the — of,*** estar a punto de; ***to come to the —,*** venir al caso; ***to score a —,*** ganar un tanto; ***in — of,*** tocante a; ***on all points,*** de todos lados; ***in —,*** a propósito; ***in — of fact,*** en efecto; ***— of view,*** punto de vista; ***— of order,*** cuestión (*f.*) de orden.—*v.t.* afilar, puntuar; rejuntar; ***to — out,*** señalar; ***to — a moral,*** inculcar una moral.—*v.i.* señalar; mostrar la caza; ***to — at,*** señalar con el dedo; ***to — to,*** indicar.
point-blank ['pɔint'blæŋk], *a.*, *adv.* de punto en blanco.
pointed ['pɔintid], *a.* afilado, puntiagudo; (*arch.*) ojival; (*fig.*) directo; intencionado.
pointer ['pɔintə], *n.* puntero; perro perdiguero; aguja; (*fig.*) índice, *m.*
pointing ['pɔintiŋ], *n.* puntería; relleno de juntas.
pointless ['pɔintlis], *a.* sin punta; fútil.
poise [pɔiz], *n.* equilibrio; aplomo; porte, *m.*—*v.t.* balancear; pesar.—*v.i.* estar suspendido.
poison [pɔizn], *n.* veneno.—*v.t.* envenenar.
poisoner ['pɔiznə], *n.* envenenador.
poisonous ['pɔiznəs], *a.* venenoso.
poke [pouk], *n.* empujón, *m.*—*v.t.*, *v.i.* hurgar; atizar (*fuego*); empujar; ***to — one's nose in,*** meterse en todo; ***to — fun at,*** burlarse de.
poker (1) ['poukə], *n.* hurgón; atizador, *m.*
poker (2) ['poukə], *n.* poker, *m.*
poky ['pouki], *a.* pequeño; miserable.
Poland ['poulənd], *n.* Polonia.
polar ['poulə], *a.* polar; ***— bear,*** oso blanco.
polarize ['pouləraiz], *v.t.* polarizar.
Pole [poul], *n.* polaco.
pole [poul], *n.* (*geog.*, *geom.*) polo; (*sport*) pértiga; palo; mástil.
poleaxe ['poulæks], *n.* hachuela de mano.—*v.t.* aturdir.
polecat ['poulkæt], *n.* mofeta.
polemic [pə'lemik], *n.* polémica.
police [pə'li:s], *n.* policía; ***— constable,*** agente (*m.*) de policía; ***— force,*** policía; ***— station,*** comisaría.—*v.t.* mantener el orden público en; administrar.
policeman [pə'li:smən], *n.* policía, *m.*
policewoman [pə'li:swumən], *n.* agente femenino de policía.
policy ['pɔlisi], *n.* política; sistema, *m.*; curso de acción; póliza de seguro.
poliomyelitis [pouliomaiə'laitis], *n.* poliomielitis, *f.*
Polish ['pouliʃ], *a.* polaco, polonés.
polish ['pɔliʃ], *n.* pulimento; cera; barniz, *m.*; tersura; (*fig.*) urbanidad, *f.*—*v.t.* pulir; dar brillo; (*fig.*) civilizar; ***to — off,*** (*fam.*) terminar; acabar con; engullir.
polished ['pɔliʃt], *a.* pulido; culto; cortés.
polisher ['pɔliʃə], *n.* pulidor, *m.*; ***French —,*** barnizador, *m.*
polite [pə'lait], *a.* cortés, bien educado.
politeness [pə'laitnis], *n.* cortesía.
politic ['pɔlitik], *a.* político.
political [pə'litikəl], *a.* político.
politician [pɔli'tiʃən], *n.* político.
politics ['pɔlitiks], *n.pl.* política; ciencias políticas, *f.pl.*
polka ['pɔlkə], *n.* polca.
polka-dotted ['pɔlkə'dɔtid], *a.* de *o* con lunares.
poll [poul], *n.* lista electoral; escrutinio; cabeza; votación, *f.*; colegio electoral.—*v.t.* descabezar; podar; descornar; escrutar; dar voto; recoger (*votos*).
pollen ['pɔlin], *n.* polen, *m.*
polling ['pouliŋ], *n.* votación, *f.*
pollute [pə'lu:t], *v.t.* ensuciar; contaminar; profanar.
pollution [pə'lu:ʃən], *n.* contaminación; profanación; corrupción, *f.*
polygamous [pəligəməs], *a.* polígamo.
polygamy [pə'ligəmi], *n.* poligamia.
polyglot ['pɔliglɔt], *a.*, *n.* poligloto.
polygon ['pɔligən], *n.* polígono.
Polynesian [pɔli'ni:zjən], *a.*, *n.* polinesio.
polysyllabic ['pɔlisi'læbik], *a.* polisílabo.
polytechnic [pɔli'teknik], *a.* politécnico.
polytheism ['pɔliθi:izm], *n.* politeísmo.
pomade [pə'meid], *n.* pomada.
pomegranate ['pɔmigrænit], *n.* granada.
pommel [pʌml], *n.* pomo.—*v.t.* aporrear.
pomp [pɔmp], *n.* pompa, fausto.
pompom ['pɔmpɔm], *n.* pompón, *m.*
pomposity [pɔm'pɔsiti], *n.* pomposidad, *f.*
pompous ['pɔmpəs], *a.* pomposo.
pond [pɔnd], *n.* estanque, *m.*, charca.
ponder ['pɔndə], *v.t.* ponderar, pesar, estudiar.—*v.i.* meditar.
ponderous ['pɔndərəs], *a.* abultado; pesado.
pontiff ['pɔntif], *n.* pontífice, *m.*
pontifical [pɔn'tifikəl], *a.* pontificio.
pontificate [pɔn'tifikit], *n.* pontificado.—[pɔn'tifikeit], *v.t.* pontificar.
pontoon [pɔn'tu:n], *n.* pontón, *m.*
pony ['pouni], *n.* jaca.
poodle [pu:dl], *n.* perro de lanas.
pooh-pooh [pu:'pu:], *v.t.* tratar con desprecio.
pool [pu:l], *n.* estanque, *m.*; charco; rebalsa; polla (*en el juego*); conjunto; ***football pool(s),*** quiniela(s).—*v.t.* combinar.
poop [pu:p], *n.* popa.
poor [puə], *a.* pobre; infeliz; malo; ***the —,*** los pobres.
poor-box ['puəbɔks], *n.* cepillo de pobres.
poor-house ['puəhaus], *n.* casa de caridad.
pop (1) [pɔp], *n.* detonación, *f.*; taponazo; (*fam.*) gaseosa.—*v.t.* meter de repente; disparar; hacer saltar.—*v.i.* saltar; dar un chasquido; ***to — in,*** (*fam.*) visitar; entrar de repente; ***to — off,*** (*fam.*) marcharse; estirar la pata; ***to — out,*** (*fam.*) salir.—*interj.* ¡pum!
pop (2) [pɔp], *n.* (*fam.*) música yeyé.
Pope [poup], *n.* papa, *m.*
popery ['poupəri], *n.* papismo.
poplar ['pɔplə], *n.* álamo.
poplin ['pɔplin], *n.* popelina.

poppy ['pɔpi], *n.* amapola, adormidera.
populace ['pɔpjuləs], *n.* pueblo; populacho.
popular ['pɔpjulə], *a.* popular.
popularity [pɔpju'læriti], *n.* popularidad, *f.*
popularize ['pɔpjuləraiz], *v.t.* popularizar, vulgarizar.
populate ['pɔpjuleit], *v.t.* poblar.
population [pɔpju'leiʃən], *n.* población, *f.*
populous ['pɔpjuləs], *a.* populoso.
porcelain ['pɔ:slin], *n.* porcelana.
porch [pɔ:tʃ], *n.* pórtico; vestíbulo.
porcupine ['pɔ:kjupain], *n.* puerco espín.
pore (1) [pɔ:], *n.* poro.
pore (2) [pɔ:], *v.i.* **to — over,** leer con mucha atención.
pork [pɔ:k], *n.* carne (*f.*) de cerdo.
pornographic [pɔ:nə'græfik], *a.* pornográfico.
pornography [pɔ:'nɔgrəfi], *n.* pornografía.
porous ['pɔ:rəs], *a.* poroso.
porpoise ['pɔ:pəs], *n.* marsopa.
porridge ['pɔridʒ], *n.* puches, *m.pl.*
port (1) [pɔ:t], *n.* puerto; porta.
port (2) [pɔ:t], *n.* vino de Oporto.
port (3) [pɔ:t], *n.* (*naut.*) babor (*costado izquierdo*), *m.*
portable ['pɔ:təbl], *a.* portátil.
portal [pɔ:tl], *n.* portal, *m.*
portcullis [pɔ:t'kʌlis], *n.* rastrillo.
portend [pɔ:'tend], *v.t.* presagiar.
portent ['pɔ:tent], *n.* augurio, presagio.
portentous [pɔ:'tentəs], *a.* portentoso, ominoso.
porter ['pɔ:tə], *n.* portero, mozo; conserje, *m.*; cerveza negra.
portfolio [pɔ:t'fouljou], *n.* cartera; carpeta; (*pol.*) ministerio.
porthole ['pɔ:thoul], *n.* porta.
portion ['pɔ:ʃən], *n.* porción, parte, *f.*; dote, *m.* o *f.*
portly ['pɔ:tli], *a.* corpulento.
portmanteau [pɔ:t'mæntou], *n.* maleta.
portrait ['pɔ:treit], *n.* retrato.
portraiture ['pɔ:tritʃə], *n.* retrato; pintura.
portray [pɔ:'trei], *v.t.* retratar; describir.
portrayal [pɔ:'treiəl], *n.* representación, *f.*; pintura.
Portugal ['pɔ:tjugəl], *n.* Portugal, *m.*
Portuguese [pɔ:tju'gi:z], *a.*, *n.* portugués, *m.*
pose [pouz], *n.* actitud, postura; afectación, *f.*—*v.t.* plantear; colocar.—*v.i.* colocarse; adoptar posturas; **to — as,** dárselas de, hacerse pasar por.
poser ['pouzə], *n.* problema, *m.*; pregunta difícil.
position [pə'ziʃən], *n.* posición; situación, condición; actitud, *f.*; puesto; **in a — to,** en estado de.
positive ['pɔzətiv], *a.* positivo; categórico.—*n.* (*phot.*) (prueba) positiva; (*elec.*) positivo.
possess [pə'zes], *v.t.* poseer, tener; gozar de; dominar.
possession [pə'zeʃən], *n.* posesión, *f.*; **to take — of,** apoderarse de; entrar en.
possessive [pə'zesiv], *a.* posesivo.
possessor [pə'zesə], *n.* poseedor, *m.*
possibility [pɔsi'biliti], *n.* posibilidad, *f.*
possible ['pɔsibl], *a.* posible; **as soon as —,** cuanto antes.
post (1) [poust], *n.* correo; poste, *m.*; puesto; **by return of —,** a vuelta de correo; **— office,** casa de correos.—*v.t.* echar al correo; fijar; colocar; tener al corriente.
post (2) [poust], *prefix.* después de; **— mortem,** autopsia; **— war,** (de la) postguerra.
postage ['poustidʒ], *n.* porte, *m.*, franqueo; **— stamp,** sello.
postal ['poustəl], *a.* postal; **— order,** giro postal.
postcard ['poustka:d], *n.* tarjeta postal.
poster ['poustə], *n.* cartel, *m.*
posterior [pɔs'tiəriə], *a.* posterior.—*n.* trasero.
posterity [pɔs'teriti], *n.* posteridad, *f.*
postern ['poustə:n], *n.* posterna.
post-haste ['poust'heist], *a.* apresurado; a toda prisa.
posthumous ['pɔstjuməs], *a.* póstumo.
postman ['poustmən], *n.* (*pl.* **-men**) cartero.
postmark ['poustma:k], *n.* matasellos, *m.sg.*
postmaster ['poustma:stə], *n.* administrador (*m.*) de correos.
post-paid ['poust'peid], *a.* franco.
postpone [pous'poun], *v.t.* aplazar.
postponement [pous'pounmənt], *n.* aplazamiento.
postscript ['pous(t)skript], *n.* posdata.
postulate ['pɔstjuleit], *n.* postulado.—*v.t.* postular.
posture ['pɔstʃə], *n.* postura, actitud; situación, *f.*
posy ['pouzi], *n.* ramillete, *m.*
pot [pɔt], *n.* olla, marmita; orinal, *m.*—*v.t.* preservar; plantar en tiestos.
potage [pɔ'ta:ʒ], *n.* potaje, *m.*
potash ['pɔtæʃ], *n.* potasa.
potassium [pə'tæsjəm], *n.* potasio.
potato [pə'teitou], *n.* patata; **sweet —,** batata.
pot-belly ['pɔt'beli], *n.* panza; **pot-bellied,** panzudo.
pot-boiler ['pɔtbɔilə], *n.* obra hecha de prisa para ganarse la vida.
potency ['poutənsi], *n.* potencia, fuerza.
potent ['poutənt], *a.* potente, fuerte.
potentate ['poutənteit], *n.* potentado.
potential [pə'tenʃəl], *a.* potencial; virtual.
potentiality [pətenʃi'æliti], *n.* potencialidad, *f.*
pothole ['pɔthoul], *n.* bache, *m.*
pothook ['pɔthuk], *n.* garabato; palote, *m.*
potion ['pouʃən], *n.* poción, *f.*
pot-luck ['pɔt'lʌk], *n.* fortuna del puchero.
potman ['pɔtmən], *n.* mozo de taberna.
pot-pourri ['poupu'ri:], *n.* (*mus.*) popurrí, *m.*; (*fig.*) baturillo.
pot-shot ['pɔt'ʃɔt], *n.* tiro al azar.
potter (1) ['pɔtə], *n.* alfarero.
potter (2) ['pɔtə], *v.i.* andar de vagar.
pottery ['pɔtəri], *n.* alfarería.
pouch [pautʃ], *n.* bolsa; tabaquera, petaca.
poultice ['poultis], *n.* emplasto.—*v.t.* bizmar.
poultry ['poultri], *n.* volatería.
poultry-farming ['poultri'fa:ming], *n.* avicultura.
pounce [pauns], *n.* calada.—*v.i.* calarse.
pound (1) [paund], *n.* libra.
pound (2) [paund], *n.* corral (*m.*) de concejo.
pound (3) [paund], *v.t.* golpear.
pour [pɔ:], *v.t.* verter; vaciar; derramar.—*v.i.* fluir; **to — with rain,** diluviar, llover a cántaros.
pouring ['pɔ:riŋ], *a.* torrencial.
pout [paut], *n.* pucherito.—*v.i.* hacer pucheritos.

pouting ['pautiŋ], *n.* pucheritos, *m.pl.*
poverty ['pɔvəti], *n.* pobreza.
powder ['paudə], *n.* polvo; pólvora.—*v.t.* pulverizar; polvorear.—*v.i.* pulverizarse; ponerse polvos.
powdery ['paudəri], *a.* polvoriento.
power [pauə], *n.* poder, *m.*; fuerza; facultad, *f.*; potencia; — ***of attorney,*** (*jur.*) procuración, *f.*; ***the Great Powers,*** las grandes potencias; ***the powers that be,*** los que mandan.
powerful ['pauəful], *a.* poderoso, potente; fuerte; eficaz.
powerless ['pauəlis], *a.* impotente; ineficaz.
power-station ['pauəsteiʃən], *n.* terma, central (*f.*) de energía eléctrica.
pox [pɔks], *n.* viruelas, *f.pl.*; sífilis, *f.*
practicable ['præktikəbl], *a.* practicable, factible.
practical ['præktikəl], *a.* práctico; — ***joke,*** broma.
practice ['præktis], *n.* práctica; costumbre, *f.*; experiencia; profesión, *f.*; clientela; ejercicio; ***to put into*** —, poner en obra; ***out of*** —, desentrenado.
practise ['præktis], *v.t.* practicar; ejercer; entrenarse en.—*v.i.* practicar; estudiar.
practised ['præktist], *a.* experimentado.
practitioner [præk'tiʃənə], *n.* practicante, *m.*; médico.
pragmatic [præg'mætik], *a.* pragmático, práctico.
prairie ['prɛəri], *n.* pradera; pampa.
praise [preiz], *n.* elogio; alabanza.—*v.t.* elogiar, alabar.
praiseworthy ['preizwəːði], *a.* digno de alabanza, loable.
pram [præm], *n.* (*fam.*) [PERAMBULATOR].
prance [prɑːns], *n.* cabriola.—*v.i.* cabriolar, encabritarse.
prank [præŋk], *n.* travesura.
prate [preit], *v.i.* chacharear.
prattle [prætl], *n.* cháchara.—*v.t.* balbucear. —*v.i.* chacharear.
prawn [prɔːn], *n.* gamba.
pray [prei], *v.t., v.i.* rezar; suplicar; implorar.
prayer [prɛə], *n.* oración, *f.*; plegaria; súplica; — ***book,*** devocionario.
praying ['preiiŋ], *n.* rezo; suplicación, *f.*
preach [priːtʃ], *v.t., v.i.* predicar.
preacher ['priːtʃə], *n.* predicador, *m.*
preaching ['priːtʃiŋ], *n.* predicación, *f.*
preamble [priː'æmbl], *n.* preámbulo.
prearrange [priːə'reindʒ], *v.t.* arreglar de antemano, predisponer.
prebendary ['prebəndəri], *n.* prebendado.
precarious [pri'kɛərjəs], *a.* precario; incierto, inseguro.
precariousness [pri'kɛərjəsnis], *n.* estado precario, condición (*f.*) incierta; incertidumbre, inseguridad, *f.*
precaution [pri'kɔːʃən], *n.* precaución, *f.*
precautionary [pri'kɔːʃənəri], *a.* preventivo.
precede [pri'siːd], *v.t.* preceder, anteceder; exceder en importancia.—*v.i.* tener la primacia; ir delante.
precedence [pri'siːdəns], *n.* prioridad; superioridad, *f.*; precedencia.
precedent ['presidənt], *n.* precedente, *m.*
preceding [pri'siːdiŋ], *a.* precedente.
precept ['priːsept], *n.* precepto.
preceptor [pri'septə], *n.* preceptor, *m.*
precinct ['priːsiŋkt], *n.* recinto; barrio.—*pl.* recinto.
precious ['preʃəs], *a.* precioso; de gran valor; querido.—*adv.* (*fam.*) — ***little,*** muy poco.
precipice ['presipis], *n.* precipicio.
precipitant [pri'sipitənt], *a.* precipitado.
precipitate [pri'sipiteit], *v.t.* precipitar.—*v.i.* precipitarse.
precipitation [prisipi'teiʃən], *n.* precipitación, *f.*; (*chem.*) precipitado.
precipitous [pri'sipitəs], *a.* precipitoso, escarpado.
precise [pri'sais], *a.* preciso; exacto; justo; escrupuloso; puntual; (*fam.*) pedante, ceremonioso.
precision [pri'siʒən], *n.* precisión; exactitud; escrupulosidad, *f.*
preclude [pri'kluːd], *v.t.* impedir; excluir.
precocious [pri'kouʃəs], *a.* precoz.
preconceive [priːkən'siːv], *v.t.* preconcebir.
preconception [priːkən'sepʃən], *n.* opinión (*f.*) preconcebida; prejuicio.
precursor [pri'kəːsə], *n.* precursor, *m.*
predatory ['predətəri], *a.* rapaz; voraz.
predecessor ['priːdisesə], *n.* predecesor, *m.*; antepasado.
predestination [priːdesti'neiʃən], *n.* predestinación, *f.*
predestine [priː'destin], *v.t.* predestinar.
predetermine [priːdi'təːmin], *v.t.* predeterminar.
predicament [pri'dikəmənt], *n.* apuro; (*phil.*) predicamento.
predicate ['predikit], *n.* predicado.—['predikeit], *v.t.* afirmar.
predict [pri'dikt], *v.t.*—predecir, pronosticar.
prediction [pri'dikʃən], *n.* predicción, *f.*; pronóstico.
predilection [priːdi'lekʃən], *n.* predilección, *f.*
predispose [priːdis'pouz], *v.t.* predisponer.
predisposition [priːdispə'ziʃən], *n.* predisposición, *f.*
predominance [pri'dɔminəns], *n.* predominio.
predominant [pri'dɔminənt], *a.* predominante.
predominate [pri'dɔmineit], *v.i.* predominar.
pre-eminence [priː'eminəns], *n.* preeminencia; primacia.
pre-eminent [priː'eminənt], *a.* preeminente; extraordinario.
preen [priːn], *v.i.* limpiar las plumas; ***to — oneself,*** jactarse.
preface ['prefis], *n.* prólogo; (*eccl.*) prefacio. —*v.t.* poner un prólogo.
prefatory ['prefətəri], *a.* preliminar.
prefect ['priːfekt], *n.* prefecto.
prefecture ['priːfektjuə], *n.* prefectura.
prefer [pri'fəː], *v.t.* preferir; ascender; presentar.
preferable ['prefərəbl], *a.* preferible.
preference ['prefərəns], *n.* preferencia.
preferential [prefə'renʃəl], *a.* preferente.
preferment [pri'fəːmənt], *n.* promoción, *f.* ascenso; puesto eminente.
prefix ['priːfiks], *n.* prefijo.—*v.t.* prefijar.
pregnancy ['pregnənsi], *n.* embarazo, preñez *f.*
pregnant ['pregnənt], *a.* embarazada, preñada, encinta; (*fig.*) fértil.
prehensile [pri'hensail], *a.* prensil.
prehistoric [priːhis'tɔrik], *a.* prehistórico.

prejudge [pri:'dʒʌdʒ], *v.t.* prejuzgar.
prejudice ['predʒjudis], *n.* prejuicio; (*jur.*) perjuicio.—*v.t.* perjudicar; influir.
prejudicial [predʒju'diʃəl], *a.* perjudicial.
prelate ['prelit], *n.* prelado.
preliminary [pri'liminəri], *a.*, *n.* preliminar, *m.*
prelude ['prelju:d], *n.* preludio; presagio.—*v.t.*, *v.i.* preludiar.
premature [premə'tjuə], *a.* prematuro.
premeditate [pri:'mediteit], *v.t.* premeditar.
premeditation [pri:medi'teiʃən], *n.* premeditación, *f.*
premier ['premiə], *a.* primero, principal.—*n.* primer ministro; presidente (*m.*) del consejo.
première ['premiɛə], *n.* estreno.
premise ['premis], *n.* prémisa.—*pl.* recinto; local, *m.*; tierras, *f.pl.*
premium ['pri:mjəm], *n.* premio; (*com.*) prima; ***at a* —,** a prima; (*fig.*) en gran demanda.
premonition [pri:mə'niʃən], *n.* presentimiento.
preoccupation [pri:ɔkju'peiʃən], *n.* preocupación, *f.*
preoccupied [pri:'ɔkjupaid], *a.* preocupado; absorto.
preoccupy [pri:'ɔkjupai], *v.t.* preocupar.
preordain [pri:ɔ:'dein], *v.t.* preordenar; predestinar.
prepaid [pri:'peid], *a.* porte pagado. [PREPAY].
preparation [prepə'reiʃən], *n.* preparación; disposición, *f.*; (*med.*) preparado.
preparatory [pri'pærətəri], *a.* preparatorio; preliminar.
prepare [pri'pɛə], *v.t.* preparar; equipar; aderezar.—*v.i.* prepararse.
preparedness [pri'pɛədnis], *n.* estado de preparación.
prepay [pri:'pei], *v.t.* (*conjug. like* PAY) pagar por adelantado.
preponderance [pri'pɔndərəns], *n.* preponderancia.
preposition [prepə'ziʃən], *n.* preposición, *f.*
prepossessing [pri:pə'zesiŋ], *a.* atractivo.
preposterous [pri'pɔstərəs], *a.* absurdo, ridículo.
prerequisite [pri:'rekwizit], *a.*, *n.* requisito.
prerogative [pri'rɔgətiv], *n.* prerrogativa.
presage ['presidʒ], *n.* presagio.—[pri'seidʒ], *v.t.* presagiar.
presbyterian [prezbi'tiəriən], *a.*, *n.* presbiteriano.
presbytery ['prezbitəri], *n.* presbiterio.
prescient ['pri:ʃiant], *a.* presciente.
prescribe [pris'kraib], *v.t.*, *v.i.* prescribir; (*med.*) recetar; (*jur.*) dar leyes.
prescription [pris'kripʃən], *n.* prescripción, *f.*; (*med.*) receta.
presence ['prezəns], *n.* presencia; aparición, *f.*; **— *of mind*,** presencia de ánimo.
present (1) ['prezənt], *a.* presente; actual; ***to be* — *at*,** asistir a.—*n.* presente, *m.*; actualidad, *f.*
present (2) [pri'zent], *v.t.* presentar; regalar, dar; manifestar.—['prezənt], *n.* regalo, presente, *m.*
presentable [pri'zentəbl], *a.* presentable.
presentation [prezən'teiʃən], *n.* presentación, *f.*; **— *copy*,** ejemplar (*m.*) de regalo.
present-day ['prezənt'dei], *a.* actual.
presentiment [pri'zentimənt], *n.* presentimiento.
presently ['prezəntli], *adv.* luego, dentro de poco; (*obs.*, *U.S.*) al presente.
preservation [prezə'veiʃən], *n.* preservación; conservación, *f.*
preservative [pri'zə:vətiv], *a.*, *n.* preservativo.
preserve [pri'zə:v], *n.* conserva; compota; coto.—*v.t.* preservar; conservar; proteger; garantizar.
preside [pri'zaid], *v.i.* presidir; ***to* — *over*,** presidir.
presidency ['prezidənsi], *n.* presidencia.
president ['prezidənt], *n.* presidente, *m.*; presidenta.
presidential [prezi'denʃəl], *a.* presidencial.
presiding [pri'zaidiŋ], *a.* que preside; tutelar.
press (1) [pres], *n.* urgencia; apretón, *m.*; armario; muchedumbre, *f.*; imprenta; prensa; ***in the* —,** en prensa; **— *agent*,** agente (*m.*) de publicidad; **— *box*,** tribuna de la prensa.—*v.t.* apretar; prensar; exprimir; abrumar; oprimir; obligar; apremiar; acosar; planchar; insistir.—*v.i.* ***to* — *on*,** avanzar; apretar el paso; ***to* — *for*,** exigir.
press (2) [pres], *n.* leva forzada.—*v.t.* hacer levas.
press-gang ['pres'gæŋ], *n.* ronda de matrícula.
pressing ['presiŋ], *a.* urgente, importuno, apremiante.—*n.* presión, *f.*; prensadura; expresión (*f.*) (de zumo); planchado.
press-stud ['presstʌd], *n.* botón automático.
pressman ['presmən], *n.* tirador, *m.*; periodista, *m.f.*
pressure ['preʃə], *n.* presión; opresión, *f.*; peso; apremio; impulso; apretón, *m.*
pressure-cooker ['preʃə'kukə], *n.* olla exprés, autoclave, *f.*
pressure-gauge ['preʃə'geidʒ], *n.* manómetro.
prestige [pres'ti:ʒ], *n.* prestigio.
presumable [pri'zju:məbl], *a.* presumible.
presume [pri'zju:m], *v.t.* presumir; suponer.—*v.i.* presumir; jactarse; abusar.
presumption [pri'zʌmpʃən], *n.* suposición, presunción, *f.*; insolencia.
presumptive [pri'zʌmptiv], *a.* presunto; presuntivo.
presumptuous [pri'zʌmptjuəs], *a.* presuntuoso, presumido.
presuppose [pri:sə'pouz], *v.t.* presuponer.
pretence [pri'tens], *n.* pretexto; afectación, *f.*; fingimiento; pretensión, *f.*; ***false pretences*,** apariencias fingidas, *f.pl.*; ***under* — *of*,** so pretexto de.
pretend [pri'tend], *v.t.* fingir.—*v.i.* fingir; pretender.
pretender [pri'tendə], *n.* pretendiente, *m.*; hipócrita, *m.f.*
pretension [pri'tenʃən], *n.* pretensión, *f.*; simulación, *f.*
pretentious [pri'tenʃəs], *a.* presumido; hinchado.
pretentiousness [pri'tenʃəsnis], *n.* hinchazón, *m.*
preterite ['pretərit], *n.* pretérito.
pretext ['pri:tekst], *n.* pretexto.
prettiness ['pritinis], *n.* lo bonito; gracia.

pretty ['priti], *a.* bonito; guapo, lindo; mono.—*adv.* bastante; muy; casi.
prevail [pri'veil], *v.i.* prevalecer, predominar; vencer; ***to — upon,*** persuadir.
prevailing [pri'veiliŋ], *a.* predominante; general; común.
prevalence ['prevələns], *n.* predominio.
prevalent ['prevələnt], *a.* prevaleciente; predominante; general; común.
prevaricate [pri'værikeit], *v.i.* tergiversar.
prevarication [priværi'keiʃən], *n.* tergiversación, *f.*
prevent [pri'vent], *v.t.* prevenir, impedir; evitar.
preventable [pri'ventəbl], *a.* evitable.
prevention [pri'venʃən], *n.* prevención, *f.*; estorbo.
preventive [pri'ventiv], *a.* preventivo.—*n.* preservativo.
preview ['pri:vju:], *n.* representación privada; vista de antemano.
previous ['pri:vjəs], *a.* previo, anterior.
prey [prei], *n.* presa; víctima; ***bird of —,*** ave (*f.*) de rapiña.—*v.i.* ***to — on,*** devorar; hacer presa; oprimir.
price [prais], *n.* precio; valor, *m.*; premio; ***— list,*** tarifa; ***at any —,*** cueste lo que cueste; ***not at any —,*** por nada del mundo.—*v.t.* evaluar; fijar el precio de.
priceless ['praislis], *a.* sin precio; (*fam.*) divertidísimo.
prick [prik], *n.* aguijón, *m.*; picadura; alfilerazo; pinchazo; remordimiento.—*v.t.* picar; punzar; atormentar; avivar.
prickle [prikl], *n.* espina; escozor, *m.*
prickly ['prikli], *a.* espinoso; ***— pear,*** higo chumbo.
pride [praid], *n.* soberbia; orgullo; aparato, pompa; ***to take — in,*** estar orgulloso de.—*v.r.* ***to — oneself on,*** jactarse de.
priest [pri:st], *n.* sacerdote; cura, *m.*
priestess ['pri:stis], *n.* sacerdotisa.
priesthood ['pri:sthud], *n.* sacerdocio.
priestly ['pri:stli], *a.* sacerdotal.
prig [prig], *n.* fatuo.
priggish ['prigiʃ], *a.* fatuo.
prim [prim], *a.* etiquetero, almidonado.
primacy ['praiməsi], *n.* primacía.
primary ['praiməri], *a.* primario.
primate ['praimit], *n.* (*eccl.*) primado.
prime [praim], *a.* primero; de primera clase; excelente; principal.—*n.* aurora; principio; (*fig.*) flor, *f.*, nata; (*eccl.*) prima; (*math.*) número primo.—*v.t.* cebar (*las armas*); preparar.
primer ['praimə], *n.* abecedario; libro escolar; cebador, *m.*
primeval [prai'mi:vəl], *a.* primitivo.
priming ['praimiŋ], *n.* cebo (*de armas*); preparación; imprimación; instrucción, *f.*
primitive ['primitiv], *a.* primitivo; anticuado.
primness ['primnis], *n.* gravedad afectada; escrupulosidad, *f.*
primogeniture [praimou'dʒenitʃə], *n.* primogenitura.
primordial [prai'mɔ:djəl], *a.* primordial.
primrose ['primrouz], *a.* de color amarillo claro.—*n.* primavera.
prince [prins], *n.* príncipe, *m.*
princely ['prinsli], *a.* principesco; magnífico.
princess [prin'ses], *n.* princesa.
principal ['prinsəpəl], *a.* principal.—*n.* principal; director; rector; (*jur.*) causante, *m.*
principality [prinsi'pæliti], *n.* principado.
principle ['prinsəpl], *n.* principio.
print [print], *n.* impresión, *f.*; imprenta; grabado; prueba positiva; molde, *m.*; huella; estampado; ***in —,*** en letra de molde; impreso; ***out of —,*** agotado.—*v.t.* imprimir; estampar; tirar; publicar; (*fig.*) grabar; (*phot.*) tirar una prueba.
printed ['printid], *a.* impreso; ***— fabric,*** (tejido) estampado; ***— matter,*** impresos, *m.pl.*
printer ['printə], *n.* impresor, *m.*; tipógrafo.
printing ['printiŋ], *n.* imprenta; tipografía; impresión; estampación, *f.*; ***— house,*** imprenta; ***— press,*** prensa tipográfica.
prior [praiə], *a.* anterior.—*n.* prior, *m.*
prioress ['praiəris], *n.* priora.
priority [prai'ɔriti], *n.* prioridad, *f.*
priory ['praiəri], *n.* priorato.
prise [praiz], *v.t.* ***to — open,*** abrir a la fuerza.
prism [prizm], *n.* prisma, *m.*
prison [prizn], *n.* cárcel, *f.*; prisión, *f.*; ***— camp,*** campamento de prisioneros.
prisoner ['priznə], *n.* prisionero; preso; ***to take —,*** prender.
privacy ['praivəsi, 'privəsi], *n.* soledad, *f.*, retiro; secreto.
private ['praivit], *a.* particular, personal; privado; secreto; confidencial; ***in —,*** confidencialmente; en secreto; ***— individual,*** particular, *m.f.*; ***— parts,*** vergüenzas, *f.pl.* —*n.* soldado raso.
privateer [praivə'tiə], *n.* corsario.
privation [prai'veiʃən], *n.* privación, *f.*; carencia.
privet ['privit], *n.* alheña.
privilege ['privilidʒ], *n.* privilegio; exención, *f.*—*v.t.* privilegiar.
privy ['privi], *a.* privado; cómplice; enterado; ***Privy Council,*** Consejo Privado.—*n.* retrete, *m.*
prize [praiz], *n.* premio; ***first —,*** premio mayor; premio gordo (*de lotería*).—*v.t.* estimar, apreciar.
prize-fight ['praiz'fait], *n.* partido de boxeo.
prize-fighter ['praiz'faitə], *n.* boxeador, *m.*
probability [prɔbə'biliti], *n.* probabilidad, *f.*
probable ['prɔbəbl], *a.* probable.
probate ['proubeit], *n.* verificación (*f.*) (*de testamentos*).
probation [prə'beiʃən], *n.* probación, *f.*; (*jur.*) libertad vigilada.
probationary [prə'beiʃnəri], *a.* de probación.
probationer [prə'beiʃnə], *n.* novicio, aprendiz, *m.*
probe [proub], *n.* tienta, sonda; (*fig.*) investigación, *f.*—*v.t.* tentar; escudriñar.
probity ['proubiti], *n.* probidad, *f.*
problem ['prɔbləm], *n.* problema, *m.*
problematic [prɔbli'mætik], *a.* problemático.
procedure [prə'si:dʒə], *n.* procedimiento.
proceed [prə'si:d], *v.i.* proceder; seguir adelante; ***to — against,*** armar un pleito contra.
proceeding [prə'si:diŋ], *n.* procedimiento; conducta; transacción, *f.*—*pl.* actas, *f.pl.*; proceso.
proceeds ['prousi:dz], *n.pl.* producto; ganancias, *f.pl.*

process ['prouses], *n.* proceso; procedimiento; método; curso.—*v.t.* procesar; esterilizar.
procession [prə'seʃən], *n.* (*eccl.*) procesión, *f.*; (*mil.*) desfile, *m.*; cortejo.
proclaim [prə'kleim], *v.t.* proclamar; publicar.
proclamation [prɔklə'meiʃən], *n.* proclamación; publicación, *f.*; edicto.
proclivity [prə'kliviti], *n.* proclividad, *f.*
procrastinate [prou'kræstineit], *v.i.* dilatar; vacilar.
procrastination [proukræsti'neiʃən], *n.* dilación; vacilación, *f.*
procreate ['proukrieit], *v.t.* procrear.
procreation [proukri'eiʃən], *n.* procreación, *f.*
proctor ['prɔktə], *n.* procurador; censor (de una universidad), *m.*
procure [prə'kjuə], *v.t.* conseguir, obtener; alcahuetear.
procurer [prə'kjuərə], *n.* alcahuete, *m.*
procuress ['prɔkjuəris], *n.* alcahueta.
prod [prɔd], *n.* punzada; pinchazo.—*v.t.* punzar; pinchar.
prodigal ['prɔdigəl], *a.*, *n.* pródigo.
prodigality [prɔdi'gæliti], *n.* prodigalidad, *f.*
prodigious [prə'didʒəs], *a.* prodigioso.
prodigy ['prɔdidʒi], *n.* prodigio.
produce ['prɔdju:s], *n.* producto; provisiones, *f.pl.*—[prə'dju:s], *v.t.* producir; causar; mostrar; (*geom.*) prolongar; fabricar; (*theat.*) poner en escena; (*com.*) rendir.
producer [prə'dju:sə], *n.* productor, *m.*; (*theat.*) director (*m.*) de escena.
product ['prɔdʌkt], *n.* producto; resultado.
production [prə'dʌkʃən], *n.* producción, *f.*; producto; (*theat.*) dirección (escénica), *f.*
productive [prə'dʌktiv], *a.* productivo.
productivity [prɔdʌk'tiviti], *n.* productividad, *f.*
profanation [prɔfə'neiʃən], *n.* profanación, *f.*
profane [prə'fein], *a.* profano.—*v.t.* profanar.
profanity [prə'fæniti], *n.* profanidad, *f.*
profess [prə'fes], *v.t.* profesar; afirmar; declarar; fingir.
professed [prə'fest], *a.* declarado; profeso; fingido.
profession [prə'feʃən], *n.* profesión, declaración, *f.*
professional [prə'feʃənl], *a.*, *n.* profesional, *m.f.*
professor [prə'fesə], *n.* catedrático; profesor, *m.*
professorial [prɔfə'sɔ:rjəl], *a.* de un catedrático; profesorial.
professorship [prə'fesəʃip], *n.* cátedra.
proffer ['prɔfə], *v.t.* ofrecer; proponer.
proficiency [prə'fiʃənsi], *n.* habilidad, *f.*, pericia.
proficient [prə'fiʃənt], *a.* experto, perito.
profile ['proufail], *n.* perfil, *m.*; ***in* —,** de perfil.—*v.t.* perfilar.
profit ['prɔfit], *n.* provecho; utilidad, *f.*; ventaja; (*com.*) ganancia.—*v.t.* aprovechar.—*v.i.* ganar; (*com.*) sacar ganancia; ***to* — *by*,** aprovechar.
profitable ['prɔfitəbl], *a.* provechoso, útil; lucrativo.
profiteer [prɔfi'tiə], *n.* estraperlista, *m.f.*—*v.i.* usurear.
profitless ['prɔfitlis], *a.* infructuoso.
profligacy ['prɔfligəsi], *n.* libertinaje, *m.*
profligate ['prɔfligit], *a.*, *n.* libertino.
profound [prə'faund], *a.* profundo.
profundity [prə'fʌnditi], *n.* profundidad, *f.*
profuse [prə'fju:s], *a.* profuso; pródigo.
profusion [prə'fju:ʒən], *n.* profusión; prodigalidad, *f.*
progenitor [prou'dʒenitə], *n.* progenitor, *m.*
progeny ['prɔdʒini], *n.* prole, *f.*
prognosis [prɔg'nousis], *n.* pronóstico; prognosis, *f.*
prognosticate [prɔg'nɔstikeit], *v.t.* pronosticar.
prognostication [prɔgnɔsti'keiʃən], *n.* pronosticación, *f.*
programme ['prougræm], *n.* programa, *m.*; ***programmed learning*,** instrucción programada.
progress ['prougres], *n.* progreso; desarrollo; curso; ***to make* —,** hacer progresos.—[prə'gres], *v.i.* progresar; avanzar.
progression [prə'greʃən], *n.* progresión, *f.*
progressive [prə'gresiv], *a.* progresivo.
prohibit [prə'hibit], *v.t.* prohibir; impedir.
prohibition [proui'biʃən], *n.* prohibición, *f.*; prohibicionismo (*de bebidas alcohólicas*).
prohibitive [prə'hibitiv], *a.* prohibitivo.
project ['prɔdʒekt], *n.* proyecto, plan, *m.*—[prə'dʒekt], *v.t.* proyectar.—*v.i.* sobresalir; destacarse.
projectile [prə'dʒektail], *a.* arrojadizo.—*n.* proyectil, *m.*
projecting [prə'dʒektiŋ], *a.* saliente; saltón (*ojos, dientes, etc.*).
projection [prə'dʒekʃən], *n.* proyección, *f.*; lanzamiento.
proletarian [prouli'tɛərjən], *a.*, *n.* proletario.
proletariat [prouli'tɛərjət], *n.* proletariado.
prolific [prə'lifik], *a.* prolífico; fecundo.
prolix ['prouliks], *a.* prolijo.
prolixity [prou'liksiti], *n.* prolijidad, *f.*
prologue ['proulɔg], *n.* prólogo.—*v.t.* prologar.
prolong [prə'lɔŋ], *v.t.* prolongar.
prolongation [proulɔŋ'geiʃən], *n.* prolongación, *f.*
promenade [prɔmi'nɑ:d], *n.* paseo; bulevar, *m.*—*v.i.* pasearse.
prominence ['prɔminəns], *n.* prominencia; protuberancia; eminencia.
prominent ['prɔminənt], *a.* prominente; eminente; saltón (*ojos, dientes etc.*).
promiscuous [prə'miskjuəs], *a.* promiscuo.
promiscuousness [prə'miskjuəsnis], **promiscuity** [prɔmis'kju:iti], *n.* promiscuidad, *f.*
promise ['prɔmis], *n.* promesa; esperanza; ***to break one's* —,** faltar a su palabra; ***to keep one's* —,** cumplir su palabra; ***a man of* —,** un hombre de porvenir.—*v.t.*, *v.i.* prometer.
promising ['prɔmisiŋ], *a.* prometedor, que promete.
promissory ['prɔmisəri], *a.* promisorio; **— *note*,** pagaré, *m.*
promontory ['prɔməntri], *n.* promontorio.
promote [prə'mout], *v.t.* promover, fomentar; ascender; (*com.*) negociar.
promoter [prə'moutə], *n.* promotor, *m.*; empresario.
promotion [prə'mouʃən], *n.* promoción, *f.*; ascenso; fomento.

prompt [prɔmpt], *a.* pronto; puntual; diligente; rápido; en punto (*de la hora*).
prompter ['prɔmptə], *n.* apuntador, *m.*
prompting ['prɔmptiŋ], *n.* sugestión, *f.*—*pl.* dictados, *m.pl.*
promulgate ['prɔməlgeit], *v.t.* promulgar; publicar.
promulgation [prɔməl'geiʃən], *n.* promulgación; publicación, *f.*
prone [proun], *a.* postrado; propenso.
proneness ['prounnis], *n.* postración; propensión, *f.*
prong [prɔŋ], *n.* horquilla; diente, *m.*; punta.
pronged [prɔŋd], *a.* dentado; provisto de púas.
pronoun ['prounaun], *n.* pronombre, *m.*
pronounce [prə'nauns], *v.t.* pronunciar.
pronounced [prə'naunst], *a.* marcado.
pronouncement [prə'naunsmənt], *n.* pronunciamiento.
pronunciation [prənʌnsi'eiʃən], *n.* pronunciación, *f.*
proof [pru:f], *a.* impenetrable.—*n.* prueba; demostración, *f.*; ensayo.—*v.t.* impermeabilizar.
prop [prɔp], *n.* apoyo, puntal, *m.*; rodrigón, *m.*; (*min.*) entibo.—*v.t.* apoyar; ahorquillar; acodalar; apuntalar.
propaganda [prɔpə'gændə], *n.* propaganda.
propagandist [prɔpə'gændist], *n.* propagandista, *m.f.*
propagate ['prɔpəgeit], *v.t.* propagar.—*v.i.* propagarse.
propagation [prɔpə'geiʃən], *n.* propagación, *f.*
propel [prə'pel], *v.t.* propulsar.
propeller [prə'pelə], *n.* propulsor, *m.*; hélice, *f.*
propensity [prə'pensiti], *n.* propensión, *f.*, tendencia.
proper ['prɔpə], *a.* propio; particular; apropiado; decoroso; exacto.
property ['prɔpəti], *n.* propiedad, *f.*; bienes, *m.pl.*; hacienda.—*pl.* (*theat.*) accesorios, *m.pl.*
prophecy ['prɔfisi], *n.* profecía.
prophesy ['prɔfisai], *v.t.*, *v.i.* profetizar.
prophet ['prɔfit], *n.* profeta, *m.*
prophetess ['prɔfitis], *n.* profetisa.
prophetic [prə'fetik], *a.* profético.
propitiate [prə'piʃieit], *v.t.* propiciar; apaciguar.
propitiation [prəpiʃi'eiʃən], *n.* propiciación, *f.*
propitiatory [prə'piʃjətəri], *a.* propiciatorio.
propitious [prə'piʃəs], *a.* propicio, favorable.
proportion [prə'pɔ:ʃən], *n.* proporción; porción, *f.*; ***in — as***, a medida que; ***out of —***, desproporcionado.
proportional [prə'pɔ:ʃənəl], *a.* proporcional, en proporción.
proportionate [prə'pɔ:ʃnit], *a.* proporcionado.
proposal [prə'pouzəl], *n.* proposición, *f.*; propósito; oferta; declaración, *f.*
propose [prə'pouz], *v.t.* proponer; brindar.—*v.i.* tener la intención de; declararse.
proposer [prə'pouzə], *n.* proponente, *m.f.*
proposition [prɔpə'ziʃən], *n.* proposición, *f.*; propósito, proyecto.
propound [prə'paund], *v.t.* proponer; presentar.
proprietary [prə'praiətəri], *a.* propietario.
proprietor [prə'praiətə], *n.* propietario, dueño.
proprietress [prə'praiətris], *n.* propietaria, dueña.
propriety [prə'praiəti], *n.* decoro; corrección, *f.*
propulsion [prə'pʌlʃən], *n.* propulsión, *f.*
prorogue [prə'roug], *v.t.* prorrogar; suspender.
prosaic [prou'zeiik], *a.* prosaico.
proscribe [prou'skraib], *v.t.* proscribir.
proscription [prou'skripʃən], *n.* proscripción, *f.*
prose [prouz], *a.* en prosa.—*n.* prosa; ***— writer***, prosista, *m.f.*
prosecute ['prɔsikju:t], *v.t.* proseguir; (*jur.*) procesar.
prosecution [prɔsi'kju:ʃən], *n.* prosecución; (*jur.*) acusación; parte actora.
prosecutor ['prɔsikju:tə], *n.* demandante, actor, *m.*
proselyte ['prɔsilait], *n.* prosélito.
prosody ['prɔsədi], *n.* prosodia.
prospect ['prɔspekt], *n.* perspectiva; esperanza; probabilidad, *f.*; ***to have good prospects***, tener porvenir.—[prə'spekt], *v.t.*, *v.i.* explorar.
prospective [prə'spektiv], *a.* previsor; en perspectiva.
prospector [prə'spektə], *n.* explorador, operador, *m.*
prospectus [prə'spektəs], *n.* prospecto, programa, *m.*
prosper ['prɔspə], *v.t.*, *v.i.* prosperar.
prosperity [prɔs'periti], *n.* prosperidad, *f.*
prosperous ['prɔspərəs], *a.* próspero; adinerado.
prostitute ['prɔstitju:t], *n.* prostituta, ramera. —*v.t.* prostituir.
prostitution [prɔsti'tju:ʃən], *n.* prostitución, *f.*
prostrate ['prɔstreit], *a.* postrado; tendido. —[prɔs'treit], *v.t.* postrar; derribar; rendir. —*v.i.* postrarse.
prostration [prɔs'treiʃən], *n.* postración, *f.*; abatimiento.
protect [prə'tekt], *v.t.* proteger, amparar.
protection [prə'tekʃən], *n.* protección, *f.*, amparo; salvoconducto; (*pol.*) proteccionismo.
protective [prə'tektiv], *a.* protector.
protector [prə'tektə], *n.* protector, *m.*
protectorate [prə'tektərit], *n.* protectorado.
protein ['prouti:n], *n.* proteína.
protest ['proutest], *n.* protesta.—[prə'test], *v.t.* protestar.—*v.i.* protestar; quejar(se).
Protestant ['prɔtistənt], *a.*, *n.* protestante, *m.f.*
Protestantism ['prɔtistəntizm], *n.* protestantismo.
protestation [prɔtes'teiʃən], *n.* protesta, protestación, *f.*
protocol ['proutəkɔl], *n.* protocolo.
protoplasm ['proutəplæzm], *n.* protoplasma, *m.*
prototype ['proutətaip], *n.* prototipo.
protract [prə'trækt], *v.t.* prolongar, dilatar.
protractor [prə'træktə], *n.* (*math.*) transportador, *m.*
protrude [prə'tru:d], *v.t.* sacar fuera.—*v.i.* salir fuera; sobresalir.

protuberance [prə'tju:bərəns], *n.* protuberancia.
protuberant [prə'tju:bərənt], *a.* prominente.
proud [praud], *a.* orgulloso; noble; soberbio; arrogante; espléndido.
prove [pru:v], *v.t.* probar; demostrar; (*jur.*) verificar.—*v.i.* resultar.
provenance ['prɔvinəns], *n.* origen, *m.*
proverb ['prɔvə:b], *n.* refrán, *m.*, proverbio.
proverbial [prə'və:bjəl], *a.* proverbial.
provide [prə'vaid], *v.t.* proveer; proporcionar.—*v.i.* abastecer, proveer lo necesario; ***provided that,*** con tal que.
providence ['prɔvidəns], *n.* providencia.
provident ['prɔvidənt], *a.* próvido.
providential [prɔvi'denʃəl], *a.* providencial.
provider [prə'vaidə], *n.* proveedor, *m.*
province ['prɔvins], *n.* provincia; (*fig.*) esfera.
provincial [prə'vinʃəl], *a.* provincial.—*n.* provinciano.
provision [prə'viʒən], *n.* provisión; estipulación, *f.*—*pl.* víveres, *m.pl.*—*v.t.* aprovisionar.
provisional [prə'viʒənl], *a.* provisional.
proviso [prə'vaizou], *n.* condición, estipulación, *f.*
provocation [prɔvə'keiʃən], *n.* provocación, *f.*
provocative [prə'vɔkətiv], *a.* provocativo, provocador.
provoke [prə'vouk], *v.t.* provocar; encolerizar; inducir.
provoking [prə'voukiŋ], *a.* provocativo.
provost ['prɔvəst], *n.* preboste; director de colegio; (*Scot.*) alcalde, *m.*
prow [prau], *n.* proa.
prowess ['prauis], *n.* proeza.
prowl [praul], *v.t.*, *v.i.* rondar.
prowler ['praulə], *n.* rondador, *m.*
proximity [prɔk'simiti], *n.* proximidad, *f.*
proxy ['prɔksi], *n.* poder, *m.*; apoderado; delegado; ***by —,*** por poderes.
prude [pru:d], *n.* mojigata.
prudence ['pru:dəns], *n.* prudencia.
prudent ['pru:dənt], *a.* prudente.
prudery ['pru:dəri], *n.* mojigatería.
prudish ['pru:diʃ], *a.* mojigato.
prune (1) [pru:n], *n.* ciruela pasa.
prune (2) [pru:n], *v.t.* podar.
pruning ['pru:niŋ], *n.* poda.
pruning-knife ['pru:niŋnaif], *n.* podadera.
prurient ['pruəriənt], *a.* lascivo, salaz.
Prussian ['prʌʃən], *a.*, *n.* prusiano.
pry (1) [prai], *v.i.* espiar; fisgonear, entremeterse.
pry (2) [prai], *v.t.* (*mech.*) alzaprimar.
prying ['praiiŋ], *a.* fisgón, curioso.—*n.* fisgoneo; curiosidad, *f.*
psalm [sɑ:m], *n.* salmo.
psalmist ['sɑ:mist], *n.* salmista, *m.*
psalter ['sɔ:ltə], *n.* salterio.
pseudo ['sju:dou], *a.* seudo.
pseudonym ['sju:dənim], *n.* seudónimo.
psychiatrist [sai'kaiətrist], *n.* (p)siquiatra, *m.f.*
psychiatry [sai'kaiətri], *n.* (p)siquiatría.
psychic ['saikik], *a.* (p)síquico.
psycho-analyse [saikou'ænəlaiz], *v.t.* (p)sicoanalizar.
psycho-analysis [saikouə'næləsis], *n.* (p)sicoanálisis, *m.* o *f.*
psycho-analyst [saikou'ænəlist], *n.* (p)sicoanalista, *m.f.*
psychological [saikə'lɔdʒikəl], *a.* (p)sicológico.
psychologist [sai'kɔlədʒist], *n.* (p)sicólogo.
psychology [sai'kɔlədʒi], *n.* (p)sicología.
psychopathic [saikou'pæθik], *a.* (p)sicopático.
pub [pʌb], *n.* (*fam.*) taberna.
puberty ['pju:bəti], *n.* pubertad, *f.*
pubic ['pju:bik], *a.* púbico.
public ['pʌblik], *a.*, *n.* público; ***— house,*** taberna.
publican ['pʌblikən], *n.* tabernero.
publication [pʌbli'keiʃən], *n.* publicación, *f.*
publicity [pʌb'lisiti], *n.* publicidad, *f.*
public-spirited ['pʌblik'spiritid], *a.* patriótico.
publish ['pʌbliʃ], *v.t.* publicar.
publisher ['pʌbliʃə], *n.* editor, *m.*
puce [pju:s], *a.* color de pulga.
puck [pʌk], *n.* duende, *m.*; trasgo.
pucker ['pʌkə], *n.* arruga; fruncido.—*v.t.* arrugar; fruncir.
pudding ['pudiŋ], *n.* pudín, *m*; ***black —,*** morcilla.
puddle [pʌdl], *n.* charco.
puerile ['pjuərail], *a.* pueril.
puff [pʌf], *n.* soplo; resoplido; bocanada (*de humo*); borla (*para polvos*); jactancia; bollo. —*v.t.*, *v.i.* hinchar; soplar.
puffy ['pʌfi], *a.* hinchado; jadeante.
pugilism ['pju:dʒilizm], *n.* pugilato.
pugilist ['pju:dʒilist], *n.* boxeador, *m.*
pugnacious [pʌg'neiʃəs], *a.* pugnaz.
pugnacity [pʌg'næsiti], *n.* pugnacidad, *f.*
pull [pul], *n.* tirón, *m.*; sacudida; tirador (*de puerta*), *m.*; (*fam.*) influencia; ventaja; atracción, *f.*; fuerza.—*v.t.* tirar; arrastrar; sacar; remar; chupar; ***to — away,*** arrancar; quitar con violencia; ***to — back,*** retirar hacia atrás; retener; ***to — down,*** derribar; humillar; ***to — off,*** quitarse (*vestidos*); (*fam.*) conseguir; ***to — one's leg,*** (*fam.*) tomar el pelo a uno; ***to — out,*** sacar; ***to — to pieces,*** hacer pedazos; ***to — up,*** desarraigar.—*v.i.* tirar; remar; ***to — in*** o ***up,*** enfrenar; parar; ***to — round,*** (*fam.*) reponerse; ***to — through,*** salir de apuros; reponerse.
pulley ['puli], *n.* polea; (*naut.*) garrucha.
pulmonary ['pʌlmənəri], *a.* pulmonar.
pulp [pʌlp], *n.* pulpa; carne (*de fruta*), *f.*; pasta (*para hacer papel*).—*v.t.* reducir a pulpa.
pulpit ['pulpit], *n.* púlpito.
pulsate [pʌl'seit], *v.i.* pulsar.
pulse [pʌls], *n.* pulso; pulsación, *f.*; latido; (*fig.*) ritmo; ***to feel the —,*** tomar el pulso. —*v.i.* pulsar, latir.
pulverize ['pʌlvəraiz], *v.t.* pulverizar.
pumice ['pʌmis], *n.* piedra pómez.
pump [pʌmp], *n.* bomba; escarpín; surtidor, *m.*—*v.t.* bombear; (*fig.*) sondear; ***to — up,*** inflar.
pumpkin ['pʌmpkin], *n.* calabaza, calabacera.
pun [pʌn], *n.* retruécano, juego de palabras.
Punch [pʌntʃ], *n.* Polichinela, *m.*
punch [pʌntʃ], *n.* puñetazo; punzón, *m.*; taladro; ponche (*bebida*), *m.*—*v.t.* punzar; dar puñetazos.
punctilious [pʌŋk'tiljəs], *a.* puntilloso, escrupuloso.

punctiliousness [pʌŋk'tiljəsnis], *n.* puntualidad, *f.*
punctual ['pʌŋktjuəl], *a.* puntual.
punctuality [pʌŋktju'æliti], *n.* puntualidad, *f.*
punctuate ['pʌŋktjueit], *v.t.* puntuar; (*fig.*) interponer.
punctuation [pʌŋktju'eiʃən], *n.* puntuación, *f.*
puncture ['pʌŋktʃə], *n.* pinchazo; perforación, *f.*; picada.—*v.t.* pinchar; perforar; picar.
pungency ['pʌndʒənsi], *n.* naturaleza picante; mordacidad, *f.*
pungent ['pʌndʒənt], *a.* picante; mordaz.
punish ['pʌniʃ], *v.t.* castigar.
punishable ['pʌniʃəbl], *a.* punible.
punishment ['pʌniʃmənt], *n.* castigo; pena.
punitive ['pju:nitiv], *a.* punitivo.
punt [pʌnt], *n.* batea.
punter (1) ['pʌntə], *n.* el que va en una batea.
punter (2) ['pʌntə], *n.* pelete, apostador, *m.*
puny ['pju:ni], *a.* delicado, encanijado; pequeño.
pup [pʌp], *n.* cachorro.—*v.i.* parir.
pupil (1) [pju:pl], *n.* (*anat.*) pupila, niña del ojo.
pupil (2) [pju:pl], *n.* discípulo, alumno.
puppet ['pʌpit], *n.* títere, *m.*; muñeca; (*fig.*) maniquí, *m.*
puppy ['pʌpi], *n.* perrillo; cachorro.
purchase ['pə:tʃəs], *n.* compra; adquisición, *f.*; palanca.—*v.t.* comprar; adquirir.
pure [pjuə], *a.* puro.
purgation [pə:'geiʃən], *n.* purgación, *f.*
purgative ['pə:gətiv], *a.* purgativo.—*n.* purga.
purgatory ['pə:gətəri], *n.* purgatorio.
purge [pə:dʒ], *n.* purga; purgación; depuración , *f.*—*v.t.* purgar; depurar.
purification [pjuərifi'keiʃən], *n.* purificación, *f.*
purify ['pjuərifai], *v.t.* purificar; refinar; depurar.
purist ['pjuərist], *n.* purista, *m.f.*
puritan ['pjuəritən], *a.*, *n.* puritano.
puritanical [pjuəri'tænikəl], *a.* puritano.
purity ['pjuəriti], *n.* pureza.
purloin [pə:'lɔin], *v.t.* robar, hurtar.
purple [pə:pl], *a.* purpúreo.—*n.* púrpura, violeta.
purport ['pə:pət], *n.* sentido; objeto.—[pə:'pɔ:t], *v.t.* significar; indicar; pretender.
purpose ['pə:pəs], *n.* intención, *f.*; objeto; utilidad, *f.*; propósito; ***to no* —,** inútilmente; ***to the* —,** al propósito; ***on* —,** adrede.—*v.t.*, *v.i.* proponerse.
purposeful ['pə:pəsful], *a.* resuelto.
purposeless ['pə:pəslis], *a.* vago; sin objeto.
purposely ['pə:pəsli], *adv.* expresamente, adrede.
purr [pə:], *n.* ronroneo.—*v.i.* ronronear.
purse [pə:s], *n.* bolsa.—*v.t.* embolsar; apretar (*los labios*).
purser ['pə:sə], *n.* contador, *m.*
pursue [pə'sju:], *v.t.* seguir; continuar; perseguir.
pursuer [pə'sju:ə], *n.* perseguidor, *m.*
pursuit [pə'sju:t], *n.* perseguimiento; busca; prosecución; ocupación, *f.*
purvey [pə:'vei], *v.t.* proveer; abastecer.
purveyor [pə:'veiə], *n.* abastecedor, proveedor, *m.*
push [puʃ], *n.* empujón, *m.*; impulso; empuje; ataque, *m.*; esfuerzo; momento crítico; ***at a* —,** (*fam.*) en caso de necesdiad.—*v.t.* empujar; impeler; apretar; importunar; ayudar; insistir en; ***to* — *back,*** hacer retroceder a; ***to* — *off,*** desatracar; ***to* — *down,*** derribar.—*v.i.* empujar; dar un empujón; ***to* — *back,*** retroceder; ***to* — *off,*** (*fam.*) coger la calle; ***to* — *in,*** entremeterse.
pushing ['puʃiŋ], *a.* enérgico; agresivo.
pusillanimous [pju:si'læniməs], *a.* pusilánime.
put [put], *v.t. irr.* poner, meter; colocar; expresar; lanzar; presentar; hacer (*una pregunta*); ***to* — *away,*** apartar; repudiar; ahorrar; (*fam.*) comerse; ***to* — *back,*** atrasar; devolver; ***to* — *by,*** poner de lado; ahorrar; ***to* — *down,*** deponer; humillar; apuntar; ***to* — *forth,*** publicar; brotar; ***to* — *forward,*** adelantar; exponer; ***to* — *in,*** meter, introducir; entrar en un puerto; ***to* — *in for,*** solicitar; ***to* — *in mind,*** recordar; ***to* — *into practice,*** poner en uso; ***to* — *in writing,*** poner por escrito; ***to* — *off,*** dilatar; aplazar; quitarse; desilusionar; ***to* — *on,*** ponerse; fingir; imponer; ***to* — *out,*** echar fuera; brotar; dislocar; apagar; publicar; irritar; ***to* — *over,*** sobreponer; diferir; exponer; ***to* — *an end to,*** acabar con; ***to* — *a stop to,*** poner coto a; ***to* — *to,*** añadir; exponer; ***to* — *to bed,*** acostar; ***to* — *to death,*** dar la muerte; ***to* — *to flight,*** ahuyentar; ***to* — *to the vote,*** poner a votación; ***to* — *together,*** juntar, reunir; ***to* — *up,*** poner en venta; aumentar; edificar; proponer; poner (*dinero*); presentarse como candidato; alojar; ***to* — *up with,*** aguantar; ***to* — *upon,*** poner en; persuadir; oprimir.
putrefaction [pju:tri'fækʃən], *n.* putrefacción, *f.*
putrefy ['pju:trifai], *v.t.* pudrir.—*v.i.* -se.
putrid ['pju:trid], *a.* podrido, pútrido.
putty ['pʌti], *n.* masilla.—*v.t.* poner masilla.
puzzle [pʌzl], *n.* enigma, *m.*; rompecabezas, *m.inv.*; problema, *m.*; perpejidad. *f.*—*v.t.* traer perplejo; desconcertar; confundir; embrollar.—*v.i.* estar perplejo.
puzzling ['pʌzliŋ], *a.* extraño.
pygmy ['pigmi], *n.* pigmeo.
pyjamas [pə'dʒɑ:məz], *n.pl.* pijama, *m.*
pylon ['pailən], *n.* pilón; poste, *m.*
pyramid ['pirəmid], *n.* pirámide, *f.*
pyre [paiə], *n.* pira.
the Pyrenees [pirə'ni:z], *n.pl.* los Pirineos.
pyrotechnic [pairou'teknik], *a.* pirotécnico.—*n. pl.* pirotécnica.
python ['paiθən], *n.* pitón, *m.*

Q

Q, q [kju:], *n.* decimoséptima letra del alfabeto inglés.
quack [kwæk], *n.* graznido (*del pato*); (*fam.*) matasanos, *m.inv.*—*v.i.* graznar (*un pato*), parpar.

quackery ['kwækəri], *n.* charlatanismo.
quadrangle ['kwɔdræŋgl], *n.* cuadrángulo; (*arch.*) patio; (*abbr.* **quad** [kwɔd]) patio (*de colegio*).
quadruped ['kwɔdruped], *n.* cuadrúpedo.
quadruplet ['kwɔdruplit] (*abbr.* **quad** [kwɔd]), *n.* cuatrillizo, cuadrúpleto.
quaff [kwɔf], *v.t.* beber de un trago.
quagmire ['kwægmaiə], *n.* cenagal, *m.*
quail (1) [kweil], *n.* (*orn.*) codorniz, *f.*
quail (2) [kweil], *v.i.* acobardarse, temblar.
quaint [kweint], *a.* curioso, pintoresco.
quake [kweik], *n.* terremoto.—*v.i.* estremecerse, temblar.
Quaker ['kweikə], *a., n.* cuáquero.
qualification [kwɔlifi'keiʃən], *n.* calificación, *f.*; requisito; atenuación, *f.*—*pl.* competencia, capacitación, *f.*
qualified ['kwɔlifaid], *a.* competente; calificado.
qualify ['kwɔlifai], *v.t.* calificar; capacitar, habilitar.—*v.i.* capacitarse; tener derecho (***for***, a).
quality ['kwɔliti], *n.* calidad, *f.*
qualm [kwa:m], *n.* escrúpulo; basca.
quandary ['kwɔndəri], *n.* atolladero, perplejidad, *f.*
quantity ['kwɔntiti], *n.* cantidad, *f.*
quantum ['kwɔntəm], *a.* cuántico.—*n.* cuanto, cuántum, *m.*
quarantine ['kwɔrənti:n], *n.* cuarentena.—*v.t.* poner en cuarentena.
quarrel ['kwɔrəl], *n.* riña, disputa.—*v.i.* reñirse.
quarrelsome ['kwɔrəlsəm], *a.* pendenciero.
quarry (1) ['kwɔri], *n.* cantera.—*v.t.* explotar una cantera.
quarry (2) ['kwɔri], *n.* ralea, presa (*víctima*).
quart [kwɔ:t], *n.* cuarto de galón.
quarter ['kwɔ:tə], *n.* cuarto; barrio; parte; piedad, *f.*; ***to give no —***, no dar cuartel. —*pl.* vivienda, alojamiento; (*mil.*) cuartel, *m.*; ***at close quarters***, (de) muy cerca.—*v.t.* cuartear, descuartizar; alojar.
quarterly ['kwɔ:təli], *a.* trimestral.
quartermaster ['kwɔ:təma:stə], *n.* (*mil.*) comisario.
quartet [kwɔ:'tet], *n.* cuarteto.
quarto ['kwɔ:tou], *a.* en cuarto 4°.
quartz [kwɔ:ts], *n.* cuarzo.
quash [kwɔʃ], *v.t.* anular.
quatrain ['kwɔtrein], *n.* cuarteto.
quaver ['kweivə], *n.* temblor, *m.*; (*mus.*) trémolo; corchea (*nota*).—*v.i.* temblar; (*mus.*) trinar.
quay [ki:], *n.* muelle, *m.*
queasy ['kwi:zi], *a.* bascoso; remilgado.
queen [kwi:n], *n.* reina; dama (*naipes*).—*v.i.* ***to — it***, darse tono, hacerse la reina.
queenly ['kwi:nli], *a.* de reina, como reina.
queer [kwi:ə], *a.* curioso, raro; (*fam.*) malucho; (*low*) maricón; ***in — street***, pelado, apurado.—*v.t.* ***to — the pitch***, poner chinitas.
quell [kwel], *v.t.* reprimir, sofocar; sosegar.
quench [kwentʃ], *v.t.* apagar (*fuego, sed*).
query ['kwi:əri], *n.* pregunta, duda; (*U.S.*) punto de interrogación (?).—*v.t.* dudar; poner en tela de juicio.
quest [kwest], *n.* demanda, búsqueda.
question ['kwestʃən], *n.* pregunta; cuestión (*asunto*), *f*; ***beyond —***, fuera de duda; ***out of the —***, imposible; ***to be in —***, tratarse de; ***there is no —***, no cabe duda; ***— mark***, punto de interrogación.—*v.t.* interrogar; poner en duda; desconfiar de.
questionable ['kwestʃənəbl], *a.* cuestionable; dudoso; sospechoso.
questionnaire [kwestʃə'nεə], *n.* cuestionario.
queue [kju:], *n.* cola.—*v.i.* hacer cola.
quibble [kwibl], *n.* sutileza.—*v.i.* sutilizar.
quibbler ['kwiblə], *n.* pleitista, *m.f.*
quick [kwik], *a.* rápido; listo; vivo.—*n.* carne viva, lo vivo; ***the —***, los vivos; ***to cut to the —***, herir en lo vivo.—*adv.* aprisa, pronto.
quicken ['kwikən], *v.t.* avivar.—*v.i.* -se.
quicklime ['kwiklaim], *n.* cal viva.
quickly ['kwikli], *adv.* rápidamente, pronto.
quicksand ['kwiksænd], *n.* arena movediza.
quicksilver ['kwiksilvə], *n.* azogue, *m.*
quickstep ['kwikstep], *n.* pasacalle, *m.*
quid (1) [kwid], *n.* mascasa de tabaco.
quid (2) [kwid], *n.* (*Brit. fam.*) libra esterlina.
quiescent [kwi'esənt], *a.* tranquilo; quiescente.
quiet ['kwaiət], *a.* callado, silencioso; quieto; ***to be —***, callar.—*n.* silencio.—*v.t.* tranquilizar, acallar.
quill [kwil], *n.* cañón (*m.*) de pluma; púa.
quilt [kwilt], *n.* colcha.—*v.t.* acolchar.
quince [kwins], *n.* membrillo.
quinine [kwi'ni:n], *n.* quinina.
quinquennium [kwin'kweniəm], *n.* quinquenio.
quintessence [kwin'tesəns], *n*. quintaesencia.
quintuplet ['kwintjuplit] (*abbr.* **quin** ['kwin]), *n.* quintillizo, quintúpleto.
quip [kwip], *n.* pulla, agudeza.—*v.i.* echar pullas.
quire [kwaiə], *n.* mano (*f.*) de papel.
quirk [kwə:k], *n.* rareza, capricho.
quit [kwit], *v.t. irr.* (*U.S.*) abandonar.—*v.i.* rendirse; marcharse; rajarse.
quite [kwait], *adv.* del todo, completamente.
quits [kwits], *adv.* (*fam.*) ***to be —***, estar desquitado(s), quedar en paz.
quitter ['kwitə], *n.* (*U.S.*) dejado, remolón, *m.*
quiver ['kwivə], *n.* aljaba, carcaj; tremor, *m.* —*v.i.* temblar.
Quixote ['kwiksət], *n.* Quijote, *m.*
quixotic [kwik'sɔtik], *a.* quijotesco.
quiz [kwiz], *n.* (*pl.* **quizzes**) examen, *m.*; interrogatorio.—*v.t.* (*fam.*) interrogar.
quizzical ['kwizikəl], *a.* curioso, raro; guasо.
quoit [k(w)ɔit], *n.* tejo, herrón, *m.*
quorum ['kwɔ:rəm], *n.* cuórum, *m.*
quota ['kwoutə], *n.* cuota, cupo.
quotation [kwou'teiʃən], *n.* cita; (*com.*) cotización, *f.*; ***— marks***, comillas, *f.pl.*
quote [kwout], *n.* cita.—*pl.* (*U.S.*) comillas, *f.pl.*—*v.t.* citar; (*com.*) cotizar.
quotient ['kwouʃənt], *n.* cociente, *m.*

R

R, r [a:], *n.* decimoctava letra del alfabeto inglés; ***the three Rs***, las primeras letras.

rabbi ['ræbai], *n.* rabino.
rabbit ['ræbit], *n.* conejo; (*fig.*) novicio.
rabble [ræbl], *n.* gentuza, populacho.
rapid ['ræbid], *a.* rabioso.
rabies ['reibi:z], *n.* rabia.
race (1) [reis], *n.* (*sport*) carrera; corriente (*f.*) de agua.—*v.t.* competir en una carrera con; acelerar demasiado.—*v.i.* correr en una carrera; ir de prisa; acelerarse demasiado.
race (2) [reis], *n.* raza; ***human* —,** género humano.
race-track ['reistræk], *n.* hipódromo.
racial ['reiʃəl], *a.* racial.
racing ['reisiŋ], *n.* carreras (*de caballos*), *f.pl.*
rack (1) [ræk], *n.* estante, *m.*; percha; (*rail.*) red, *f.*; tormento; caballete, *m.*—*v.t.* torturar; ***to — one's brains,*** devanarse los sesos.
rack (2) [ræk], *n.* ***— and ruin,*** ruina total.
racket ['rækit], *n.* (*fam.*) jaleo (*ruido*); (*fam.*) estafa.
racketeer [ræki'tiə], *n.* trapacista, *m.*
racquet ['rækit], *n.* raqueta (*para tenis*).
racy ['reisi], *a.* picante, chispeante.
radar ['reidɑ:], *n.* radar, *m.*
radiant ['reidjənt], *a.* radiante, brillante.
radiate ['reidieit], *v.t.* radiar.—*v.i.* irradiar.
radiation [reidi'eiʃən], *n.* radiación, *f.*
radiator ['reidieitə], *n.* radiador, *m.*
radical ['rædikəl], *a.*, *n.* radical, *m.f.*
radio ['reidjou], *n.* radio, *f.* [WIRELESS].
radioactive [reidjou'æktiv], *a.* radiactivo.
radioactivity [reidjouæk'tiviti], *n.* radiactividad, *f.*
radish ['rædiʃ], *n.* rábano.
radium ['reidjəm], *n.* radio.
radius ['reidjəs], *n.* radio.
raffle [ræfl], *n.* sorteo, rifa, tómbola.—*v.t.* rifar.
raft [rɑ:ft], *n.* balsa.
rafter ['rɑ:ftə], *n.* viga, cabrio.
rag [ræg], *n.* trapo, harapo; (*fam.*) jolgorio, fisga.—*v.t.* (*fam.*) tomar el pelo a.
ragamuffin ['rægəmʌfin], *n.* pelagatos, *m.sg.*
rage [reidʒ], *n.* rabia, furia; (*fam.*) furor, *m.*, boga.—*v.i.* encolerizarse, rabiar; bramar.
ragged ['rægid], *a.* harapiento; áspero; desigual.
raging ['reidʒiŋ], *a.* violento; bramador.
raid [reid], *n.* correría; ataque, *m.*—*v.t.* invadir, atacar.
rail (1) [reil], *a.* ferroviario.—*n.* carril, riel, *m.*; barra; barandilla; ***by —,*** por ferrocarril; ***to go off the rails,*** descarrilarse.—*v.t.* cercar.
rail (2) [reil], *v.i.* injuriar (***at***), mofarse (***at***, de).
railing ['reiliŋ], *n.* barandilla, antepecho.
raillery ['reiləri], *n.* escarnio, burla.
railroad ['reilroud], *n.* (*U.S.*) ferrocarril, *m.*
railway ['reilwei], *a.* ferroviario.—*n.* ferrocarril, *m.*
railway-carriage ['reilwei'kæridʒ], *n.* vagón, coche, *m.*
railwayman ['reilweimən], *n.* ferroviario.
raiment ['reimənt], *n.* indumento.
rain [rein], *n.* lluvia.—*v.t.*, *v.i.* llover; ***— or shine,*** llueva o no.
rainbow ['reinbou], *n.* arco iris.
raincoat ['reinkout], *n.* impermeable, *m.*, gabardina.
rainfall ['reinfɔ:l], *n.* lluvia, precipitación, *f.*
rainstorm ['reinstɔ:m], *n.* aguacero, chubasco.
rainy ['reini], *a.* lluvioso; ***— day,*** (*fig.*) necesidad futura.
raise [reiz], *n.* (*U.S.*) subida, aumento.—*v.t.* alzar, levantar; subir; reunir (*dinero*); criar (*animales etc.*); cultivar; armar (*un lío*); suscitar (*observaciones*).
raiser ['reizə], *n.* cultivador, *m.*; ganadero.
raisin ['reizin], *n.* pasa, uva pasa.
raja(h) ['rɑ:dʒə], *n.* rajá, *m.*
rake (1) [reik], *n.* rastrillo.—*v.t.* rastrillar; atizar (*fuego*); escudriñar; (*mil.*) barrer.
rake (2) [reik], *n.* (*fig.*) libertino.
rakish ['reikiʃ], *a.* airoso, elegante; libertino.
rally ['ræli], *n.* reunión, *f.*; concurso.—*v.t.* reunir; recobrar.—*v.i.* reunirse; recobrar las fuerzas.
ram [ræm], *n.* carnero; (*mil.*) ariete, *m.*—*v.t.* chocar con; atacar con espolón.
ramble [ræmbl], *n.* paseo, escursión, *f.*—*v.i.* pasearse; vagar, serpentear; divagar.
rambling ['ræmbliŋ], *a.* errante; incoherente; enorme.—*n.* divagación, *f.*
ramp [ræmp], *n.* rampa.
rampant ['ræmpənt], *a.* desenfrenado; (*her.*) rampante.
rampart ['ræmpɑ:t], *n.* baluarte, *m.*, muralla.
ramshackle ['ræmʃækl], *a.* desvencijado.
ran [ræn] [RUN].
ranch [rɑ:ntʃ], *n.* hacienda, ganadería, rancho.
rancid ['rænsid], *a.* rancio.
rancour ['ræŋkə], *n.* rencor, *m.*, encono.
random ['rændəm], *a.* casual, al azar; ***at —,*** al azar, a troche y moche.
rang [ræŋ] [RING].
range [reindʒ], *n.* serie, *f.*; alcance, *m.*; terrenos (*m.pl.*) de pasto; hornillo; duración, *f.*—*v.t.* colocar, poner en fila, ordenar.—*v.i.* extenderse; variar; vagar.
ranger ['reindʒə], *n.* guardia, *m.*; guardabosque, *m.*
rank (1) [ræŋk], *a.* notorio; violento; lozano.
rank (2) [ræŋk], *n.* rango; grado; (*mil.*) fila (*línea*).—*pl.* (*mil.*) soldados rasos, *m.pl.*—*v.t.* colocar; ordenar.—*v.i.* ocupar un puesto.
rankle [ræŋkl], *v.t.* irritar, inflamar.—*v.i.* enconarse.
ransack ['rænsæk], *v.t.* saquear, rebuscar.
ransom ['rænsəm], *n.* rescate, *m.*—*v.t.* rescatar.
rant [rænt], *v.i.* desvariar, delirar.
rap [ræp], *n.* golpe seco; (*fig.*) bledo.—*v.t.*, *v.i.* dar un golpecito seco (a), tocar.
rapacious [rə'peiʃəs], *a.* rapaz.
rape [reip], *n.* estupro.—*v.t.* violar.
rapid ['ræpid], *a.* rápido.—*n.pl.* rabión, *m.*
rapidity [rə'piditi], *n.* rapidez, *f.*
rapier ['reipiə], *n.* espadín, estoque, *m.*
rapt [ræpt], *a.* arrebatado, absorto.
rapture ['ræptʃə], *n.* éxtasis, *m.*
rare [rɛə], *a.* raro; sobresaliente, poco común; (*cul.*) medio asado.
rarefy ['rɛərifai], *v.t.* rarificar.
rarity ['rɛəriti], *n.* rareza.
rascal ['rɑ:skəl], *n.* bribón, tunante, *m.*
rase [reiz] [RAZE].
rash (1) [ræʃ], *a.* temerario, arrojado.
rash (2) [ræʃ], *n.* erupción, *f.*, brote, *m.*
rasher (1) ['ræʃə], *n.* torrezno, lonja.
rasher (2) ['ræʃə], *compar.* [RASH] (1).
rashness ['ræʃnis], *n.* temeridad, *f.*
rasp [rɑ:sp], *n.* escofina, raspa; sonido estridente.—*v.t.* raspar.

raspberry ['rɑ:zbəri], *n.* frambuesa (*fruta*); frambueso (*planta*).
rasping ['rɑ:spiŋ], *a.* áspero, ronco.
rat [ræt], *n.* (*zool.*) rata; (*pej.*) canalla, *m.f.*; ***to smell a —,*** (*fam.*) tener sus malicias.—*v.i.* ***to — on,*** delatar, soplar.
ratable [RATEABLE].
ratchet ['rætʃit], *n.* trinquete, *m.*
rate (1) [reit], *n.* razón, *f.*; (*com.*) tasa, tipo; velocidad, *f.*; modo; calidad, *f.*; ***at any —,*** de todos modos; ***at the — of,*** a razón de.—*pl.* (*Brit.*) impuestos locales sobre propiedad inmueble.—*v.t.* estimar, valuar.—*v.i.* ser considerado.
rate (2) [reit], *v.t.* regañar.
rateable ['reitəbl], *a.* sujeto a contribución.
ratepayer ['reitpeiə], *n.* contribuyente, *m.f.*
rather ['rɑ:ðə], *adv.* algo, bastante; más bien; ***I had*** o ***would —,*** preferiría.
ratification [rætifi'keiʃən], *n.* ratificación, *f.*
ratify ['rætifai], *v.t.* ratificar.
rating ['reitiŋ], *n.* valuación, capacidad, *f.*; (*Brit.*) marinero.
ratio ['reiʃiou], *n.* razón, *f.*
ration ['ræʃən], *n.* ración, *f.*—*v.t.* racionar.
rational ['ræʃənəl], *a.* racional.
rationalize ['ræʃənəlaiz], *v.t.* hacer racional, racionalizar.
rationing ['ræʃəniŋ], *n.* racionamiento.
rattle [rætl], *n.* carraca; sonajero; traqueteo; ***death —,*** estertor, *m.*, agonía.—*v.t.*, *v.i.* traquetear; (*fam.*) meter miedo.
rattle-snake ['rætlsneik], *n.* crótalo, serpiente (*f.*) de cascabel.
raucous ['rɔ:kəs], *a.* ronco.
ravage ['rævidʒ], *n.* estrago.—*v.t.* estragar.
rave [reiv], *v.i.* delirar; ***to — about,*** estar loco por.
ravel ['rævəl], *v.t.* deshilar, desenredar; (*obs.*) enredar.
raven ['reivən], *a.* negro, lustroso.—*n.* cuervo.
ravenous ['rævinəs], *a.* voraz, hambriento.
ravine [ræ'vi:n], *n.* hondonada, barranco.
ravish ['ræviʃ], *v.t.* violar; arrebatar.
ravishing ['ræviʃiŋ], *a.* encantador.
raw [rɔ:], *a.* crudo; verde; bisoño, novato; ***— deal,*** (*fam.*) mala pasada; ***— materials,*** materias primas.
ray (1) [rei], *n.* rayo.
ray (2) [rei], *n.* (*ichth.*) raya.
rayon ['reijən], *n.* rayón, *m.*
raze [reiz], *v.t.* arrasar.
razor ['reizə], *n.* navaja; ***safety —,*** maquinilla de afeitar; ***— blade,*** hoj(it)a de afeitar, cuchilla.
re (1) [rei, ri:], *prep.* (*jur.*, *com.*) concerniente a.
re (2) [ri:], *prefix.* re-; de nuevo, otra vez, volver a.
reach [ri:tʃ], *n.* alcance, *m.*; extensión, *f.*—*v.t.* alcanzar, llegar a; alargar.—*v.i.* extenderse; alcanzar; ***to — for,*** intentar, alcanzar; alargar la mano para coger.
react [ri:'ækt], *v.i.* reaccionar.
reaction [ri:'ækʃən], *n.* reacción, *f.*
reactionary [ri:'ækʃənəri], *a.*, *n.* reaccionario.
reactor [ri:'æktə], *n.* reactor, *m.*
read [ri:d], *v.t. irr.* leer; recitar; ***to — out,*** leer en voz alta; ***to — through,*** repasar.—*v.i. irr.* leer; rezar.—[red], *p.p. and past of* [READ].
readable ['ri:dəbl], *a.* leíble; legible.
reader ['ri:də], *n.* lector, *m.*; (*educ.*, *Brit.*) catedrático auxiliar, catedrático asociado.
readily ['redili], *adv.* de buena gana; pronto; fácilmente.
readiness ['redinis], *n.* preparación; expedición; disponibilidad, *f.*; agudeza.
reading ['ri:diŋ], *n.* lectura.
reading-room ['ri:diŋ'rum], *n.* sala de lectura.
ready ['redi], *a.* listo, preparado; dispuesto; contante (*dinero*).
re-afforestation [ri:əfɔris'teiʃən], *n.* repoblación (*f.*) de montes.
reagent [ri:'eidʒənt], *n.* reactivo.
real ['ri:əl], *a.* real; auténtico, verdadero; (*jur.*, *U.S.*) inmueble; ***— estate,*** (*U.S.*) bienes raíces, *m.pl.*
realism ['ri:əlizm], *n.* realismo.
realist ['ri:əlist], *n.* realista, *m.f.*
realistic [ri:ə'listik], *a.* realista.
reality [ri'æliti], *n.* realidad, *f.*
realization [riəlai'zeiʃən], *n.* realización; comprensión, *f.*
realize ['riəlaiz], *v.t.* darse cuenta de; (*com. etc.*) realizar.
realm [relm], *n.* reino.
ream [ri:m], *n.* resma.
reap [ri:p], *v.t.* cosechar, segar.
rear (1) [riə], *a.* posterior; trasero; último.—*n.* parte posterior, *f.*; zaga; fondo; cola.
rear (2) [riə], *v.t.* levantar, elevar.—*v.i.* empinarse, encabritarse (*caballo*).
rear-admiral ['riə'ædmirəl], *n.* contraalmirante, *m.*
rearguard ['riəgɑ:d], *n.* retaguardia.
rearm [ri:'ɑ:m], *v.t.* rearmar.—*v.i.* -se.
rearmanent [ri:'ɑ:məmənt], *n.* rearme, *m.*
rearmost ['riəmoust], *a.* postrero, último.
reason ['ri:zən], *n.* razón, *f.*; ***by — of,*** a causa de; ***there is no — to,*** no hay para qué; ***within —,*** dentro de lo razonable; ***to stand to —,*** ser razonable.—*v.t.*, *v.i.* razonar.
reasonable ['ri:zənəbl], *a.* razonable.
reasoning ['ri:zəniŋ], *n.* razonamiento.
reassurance [ri:ə'ʃɔ:rəns], *n.* certeza restablecida.
reassure [ri:ə'ʃɔ:], *v.t.* asegurar, tranquilizar.
reassuring [ri:ə'ʃɔ:riŋ], *a.* tranquilizador.
rebate ['ri:beit], *n.* descuento, rebaja.—*v.t.* rebajar.
rebel ['rebəl], *a.*, *n.* rebelde, *m.f.*—[ri'bel], *v.i.* rebelarse.
rebellion [ri'beljən], *n.* rebelión, *f.*
rebellious [ri'beljəs], *a.* rebelde, revoltoso.
rebirth [ri:'bə:θ], *n.* renacimiento.
rebound ['ri:baund], *n.* rebote, *m.*—[ri'baund], *v.i.* rebotar.
rebuff [ri'bʌf], *v.t.* desairar.—*n.* repulsa.
rebuild [ri:'bild], *v.t. irr.* (*conjug. like* BUILD) reconstruir.
rebuke [ri'bju:k], *v.t.* censurar, reprender.
rebut [ri'bʌt], *v.t.* refutar.
rebuttal [ri'bʌtəl], *n.* refutación, *f.*
recall [ri'kɔ:l], *v.t.* recordar; llamar, hacer volver.
recant [ri'kænt], *v.i.* retractarse.
recapitulate [ri:kə'pitjuleit], *v.t.*, *v.i.* recapitular.
recapture [ri:'kæptʃə], *n.* recobro.—*v.t.* recobrar; represar.
recast [ri:'kɑ:st], *v.t.* refundir.

recede [ri'si:d], *v.i.* retirarse, retroceder.
receipt [ri'si:t], *n.* recibo.—*pl.* entradas, *f.pl.*
receive [ri'si:v], *v.t.* recibir; (*jur.*) receptar.
receiver [ri:'si:və], *n.* receptor, *m.*; (*jur.*) síndico; receptador (*de objetos robados*), *m.*
recent ['ri:sənt], *a.* reciente; próximo (*historia*).
recently ['ri:səntli], *adv.* recientemente; (*before p.p.*) recién.
receptacle [ri'septəkl], *n.* receptáculo, recipiente, *m.*
reception [ri'sepʃən], *n.* recepción, *f.*; acogida.
recess [ri'ses], *n.* descanso, vacaciones, *f.pl.*; nicho.
recipe ['resipi], *n.* receta.
recipient [ri'sipjənt], *n.* recibidor, *m.*
reciprocal [ri'siprəkəl], *a.* recíproco.
reciprocate [ri'siprəkeit], *v.t.* reciprocar.
recital [ri'saitl], *n.* recital, *m.*
recitation [resi'teiʃən], *n.* recitación, *f.*
recite [ri'sait], *v.t.* recitar.
reckless ['reklis], *a.* precipitado, temerario.
reckon ['rekən], *v.t.* calcular; ***to — on,*** contar con; ***to — up,*** adicionar.
reckoning ['rekəniŋ], *n.* cálculo; ajuste (*m.*) de cuentas; juicio final.
reclaim [ri'kleim], *v.t.* reclamar.
reclamation [reklə'meiʃən], *n.* reclamación, *f.*
recline [ri'klain], *v.t.* reclinar.—*v.i.* -se.
recluse [ri'klu:s], *n.* hermitaño; persona retirada.
recognition [rekəg'niʃən], *n.* reconocimiento.
recognize ['rekəgnaiz], *v.t.* reconocer.
recoil [ri'kɔil], *n.* reculada, retroceso.—*v.i.* recular.
recollect [rekə'lekt], *v.t.* recordar.
recollection [rekə'lekʃən], *n.* recuerdo.
recommend [rekə'mend], *v.t.* recomendar.
recommendation [rekəmen'deiʃən], *n.* recomendación, *f.*
recompense ['rekəmpens], *n.* recompensa.—*v.t.* recompensar.
reconcile ['rekənsail], *v.t.* reconciliar.—*v.r.* resignarse; ***to become reconciled,*** reconciliarse.
reconciliation [rekənsili'eiʃən], *n.* reconciliación, *f.*
reconnaissance [ri'kɔnisəns], *n.* reconocimiento.
reconnoitre [rekə'nɔitə], *v.t.*, *v.i.* reconocer.
reconquer [ri:'kɔŋkə], *v.t.* reconquistar.
reconsider [ri:kən'sidə], *v.t.* reconsiderar.
reconstruct [ri:kən'strʌkt], *v.t.* reconstruir.
record ['rekɔ:d], *n.* historia personal, antecedentes, *m.pl.*; (*mus.*) disco; registro; (*sport*) record, *m.*, marca.—*pl.* anales, *m.pl.*; archivo.—[ri'kɔ:d], *v.t.* registrar, anotar; grabar (*sonidos*).
recorder [ri'kɔ:də], *n.* juez municipal, *m.*; (*mus.*) caramillo.
recount [ri'kaunt], *v.t.* recontar; narrar (*un cuento*).
recoup [ri'ku:p], *v.t.* recobrar, desquitar.—*v.i.* recobrarse.
recourse [ri'kɔ:s], *n.* recurso; ***to have — to,*** recurrir a.
recover [ri'kʌvə], *v.t.* recobrar, recuperar.—*v.i.* reponerse; resarcirse.
recovery [ri'kʌvəri], *n.* recobro, recuperación, *f.*
recreation [rekri'eiʃən], *n.* recreo.
recriminate [ri'krimineit], *v.t.*, *v.i.* recriminar.
recrimination [rikrimi'neiʃən], *n.* recriminación, reconvención, *f.*
recruit [ri'kru:t], *n.* recluta, *m.*, quinto.—*v.t.* reclutar.
recruiting [ri'kru:tiŋ], *n.* reclutamiento.
rectangle ['rektæŋgl], *n.* rectángulo.
rectangular [rek'tæŋgjulə], *a.* rectangular.
rectify ['rektifai], *v.t.* rectificar.
rectitude ['rektitju:d], *n.* rectitud, probidad, *f.*
rector ['rektə], *n.* rector, *m.*; cura anglicano.
recumbent [ri'kʌmbənt], *a.* reclinado.
recuperate [ri'k(j)u:pəreit], *v.t.* recobrar, recuperar.—*v.i.* recuperarse.
recur [ri'kə:], *v.i.* repetirse.
recurrent [ri'kʌrənt], *a.* periódico; recurrente.
red [red], *a.* rojo, colorado; (*pol.*) rojo; tinto (*vino*); ***— letter day,*** día señalado; ***— tape,*** (*fam.*) burocratismo; papeleo.—*n.* rojo; (*pol.*) rojo.
red-cap ['redkæp], *n.* (*fam.*) policía militar, *m.*; (*U.S.*) [PORTER].
redcoat ['redkout], *n.* (*fam.*, *hist.*) soldado inglés.
redden [redn], *v.t.* enrojecer.—*v.i.* enrojecerse; ponerse colorado.
reddish ['rediʃ], *a.* rojizo.
redeem [ri'di:m], *v.t.* redimir, rescatar; (*com.*) cumplir; amortizar.
redeemer [ri'di:mə], *n.* redentor, *m.*
redemption [ri'dempʃən], *n.* redención, *f.*
redhead ['redhed], *n.* pelirrojo.
red-hot ['red'hɔt], *a.* calentado al rojo, cadente.
redness ['rednis], *n.* rojez, *f.*
redolent ['redələnt], *a.* fragante; reminiscente.
redouble [ri'dʌbl], *v.t.* redoblar.
redoubt [ri'daut], *n.* reducto.
redound [ri'daund], *v.i.* redundar (***to,*** en).
redress [ri'dres], *n.* reparación; compensación, *f.*; remedio.—*v.t.* reparar; remediar.
redskin ['redskin], *n.* piel roja, *m.*
reduce [ri'dju:s], *v.t.* reducir.—*v.i.* reducirse; ***to be reduced to,*** verse obligado a.
reduction [ri'dʌkʃən], *n.* reducción, *f.*; (*com.*) descuento.
redundancy [ri'dʌndənsi], *n.* redundancia; sobra.
redundant [ri'dʌndənt], *a.* redundante, de sobra.
re-echo [ri:'ekou], *v.t.* repetir como eco, retumbar.
reed [ri:d], *n.* (*bot.*) cañavera, carrizo; (*mus.*) lengüeta.
reef [ri:f], *n.* arrecife, *m.*
reefer ['ri:fə], *n.* pitillo de mariguana.
reek [ri:k], *n.* tufo, vaho.—*v.i.* vahear; oler (***of,*** a).
reel (1) [ri:l], *n.* carrete, *m.*; devanadera.—*v.i.* ***to — off,*** soltar con facilidad, decir sin dificultad alguna una serie de.
reel (2) [ri:l], *v.i.* tambalear.
reel (3) [ri:l], *n.* baile escocés, *m.*
re-enter [ri:'entə], *v.t.* volver a entrar (en).
re-entry [ri:'entri], *n.* nueva entrada.
refectory [ri'fektəri], *n.* refectorio.
refer [ri'fə:], *v.t.* referir.—*v.i.* referirse, aludir (***to,*** a).
referee [refə'ri:], *n.* árbitro; garante, *m.*

reference ['refərəns], *n.* referencia; alusión, *f.*; consulta.
referendum [refə'rendəm], *n.* referéndum, *m.*, plebiscito.
refill ['ri:fil], *n.* relleno, recambio.
refine [ri'fain], *v.t.* refinar.
refined [ri'faind], *a.* refinado; fino; pulido.
refinement [ri'fainmənt], *n.* refinamiento; sutileza; elegancia.
refinery [ri'fainəri], *n.* refinería.
refit ['ri:fit], *n.* reparación, *f.*, recorrido.—[ri:'fit], *v.t.* reparar, componer.
reflect [ri'flekt], *v.t.* reflejar.—*v.i.* reflexionar.
reflection [ri'flekʃən], *n.* reflejo; reflexión, *f.*; reproche, *m.*
reflective [ri'flektiv], *a.* reflexivo.
reflector [ri'flektə], *n.* reflector, *m.*
reflex ['ri:fleks], *n.* reflejo.
reflexive [ri'fleksiv], *a.* reflexivo.
refloat [ri:'flout], *v.t.* poner a flote de nuevo, desvarar.
reforestation [ri:fəris'teiʃən], *n.* (*U.S.*) [RE-AFFORESTATION].
reform [ri'fɔ:m], *n.* reforma.—*v.t.* reformar. —*v.i.* -se.
Reformation [refɔ:'meiʃən], *n.* (*hist.*) Reforma.
reformatory [ri'fɔ:mətəri], *n.* casa de corrección.
refraction [ri'frækʃən], *n.* refracción, *f.*
refresh [ri'freʃ], *v.t.* refrescar.
refreshing [ri'freʃiŋ], *a.* refrescante.
refreshment [ri'freʃmənt], *n.* refresco.
refrigeration [rifridʒə'reiʃən], *n.* refrigeración, *f.*
refrigerator [ri'fridʒəreitə], *n.* nevera, frigorífico.
refuge ['refju:dʒ], *n.* refugio; asilo; ***to take —,*** refugiarse.
refugee [refju:'dʒi:], *n.* refugiado.
refusal [ri'fju:zəl], *n.* negación, *f.*, negativa.
refuse (1) ['refju:s], *n.* basura, desechos, *m. pl.*
refuse (2) [ri'fju:z], *v.t.* rechazar; ***to — to,*** negarse a.
refute [ri'fju:t], *v.t.* refutar.
regain [ri'gein], *v.t.* recobrar.
regal ['ri:gəl], *a.* real, regio.
regale [ri'geil], *v.t.* regalar, agasajar.
regalia [ri'geiliə], *n.pl.* regalías; insignias reales, *f.pl.*
regard [ri'gɑ:d], *n.* mirada; miramiento, consideración, *f.*; respecto, concepto, motivo; ***out of — for,*** por respeto a; ***to pay — to,*** tener miramientos por; ***with — to,*** respecto a; ***without — for,*** sin hacer caso de.—*pl.* recuerdos, saludos.—*v.t.* considerar; tocar a; ***as regards,*** en cuanto a.
regarding [ri'gɑ:diŋ], *prep.* tocante a.
regardless [ri'gɑ:dlis], *a.* desatento.—*adv.* cueste lo que cueste; ***—of,*** sin reparar en.
regatta [ri'gætə], *n.* regata.
regency ['ri:dʒənsi], *n.* regencia.
regenerate [ri'dʒenərit], *a.* regenerado.—[ri:'dʒenəreit], *v.t.* regenerar.
regent ['ri:dʒənt], *n.* regente, *m.*
regicide ['redʒisaid], *n.* regicida (*persona*), *m.f.*, regicidio (*crimen*).
regime [rei'ʒi:m], *n.* régimen, *m.*
regiment ['redʒimənt], *n.* regimiento.—['redʒiment], *v.t.* regimentar.
region ['ri:dʒən], *n.* región, *f.*
regional ['ri:dʒənəl], *a.* regional.
register ['redʒistə], *n.* registro; matrícula; lista; contador, *m.*—*v.t.* registrar, inscribir, matricular.—*v.i.* inscribirse, registrarse.
registrar [redʒis'trɑ:], *n.* registrador, *m.*, archivero.
registry ['redʒistri], *n.* archivo, registro.
regress [ri'gres], *v.i.* retroceder.
regression [ri'greʃən], *n.* regresión, *f.*
regret [ri'gret], *n.* pesadumbre, *f.*, pesar, *m.* —*pl.* excusas, *f.pl.*—*v.t.* sentir; arrepentirse de.
regrettable [ri'gretəbl], *a.* lamentable.
regular ['regjulə], *a.*, *n.* regular, *m.f.*
regularity [regju'læriti], *a.*, *n.* regularidad, *f.*
regularize ['regjuləraiz], *v.t.* regularizar.
regulate ['regjuleit], *v.t.* regular.
regulation [regju'leiʃən], *n.* ordenanza, regla, reglamento; regulación, *f.*
regurgitate [ri'gə:dʒiteit], *v.t.* expeler vomitar.—*v.i.* regurgitar.
rehabilitate [ri:hæ'biliteit], *v.t.* rehabilitar.
rehash ['ri:hæʃ], *n.* refundición, *f.*, refrito.—[ri:'hæʃ], *v.t.* rehacer, refundir.
rehearsal [ri'hə:səl], *n.* ensayo.
rehearse [ri'hə:s], *v.t.* ensayar.
reign [rein], *n.* reinado.—*v.i.* reinar.
reimburse [ri:im'bə:s], *v.t.* reembolsar.
rein [rein], *n.* rienda; ***free —,*** rienda suelta. —*v.t.* gobernar, refrenar.
reindeer ['reindiə], *n.* reno.
reinforce [ri:in'fɔ:s], *v.t.* reforzar; ***reinforced concrete,*** hormigón armado.
reinforcement [ri:in'fɔ:smənt], *n.* refuerzo.
reinstate [ri:in'steit], *v.t.* reinstalar.
reiterate [ri:'itəreit], *v.t.* reiterar.
reject [ri'dʒekt], *v.t.* rechazar.
rejection [ri'dʒekʃən], *n.* rechazamiento.
rejoice [ri'dʒɔis], *v.i.* regocijarse; celebrar (***at***).
rejoicing [ri'dʒɔisiŋ], *n.* regocijo.
rejoin [ri'dʒɔin], *v.t.* reunirse con.—*v.i.* contestar (*hablar*).
rejoinder [ri'dʒɔində], *n.* réplica, contrarréplica.
rejuvenate [ri'dʒu:vəneit], *v.t.* rejuvenecer.
relaid [ri:'leid] [RELAY (2)].
relapse [ri'læps], *n.* recaída, reincidiva.—*v.i.* recaer, reincidir.
relate [ri'leit], *v.t.* referir, narrar; relacionar. —*v.i.* relacionarse con, tocar a (***to***).
related [ri'leitid], *a.* emparentado.
relation [ri'leiʃən], *n.* pariente, *m.f.*; parentesco; relación, *f.*; ***in — to,*** respecto a.
relationship [ri'leiʃənʃip], *n.* relación, *f.*; parentesco; afinidad, *f.*
relative ['relətiv], *a.* relativo.—*n.* pariente, *m.f.*
relativity [relə'tiviti], *n.* relatividad, *f.*
relax [ri'læks], *v.t.* relajar; aliviar.—*v.i.* calmarse, descansar.
relaxation [rilæk'seiʃən], *n.* relajación, *f.*; descanso, recreo.
relay (1) ['ri:lei], *n.* relevo; (*elec.*) relé, *m.*—[ri:'lei], *v.t.* relevar; retransmitir; llevar.
relay (2) [ri:'lei], *v.t.* recolocar.
relay-race ['ri:lei'reis], *n.* carrera de relevos.
release [ri'li:s], *n.* liberación; producción; cesión, *f.*; escape, *m.*—*v.t.* libertar; publicar; soltar; aliviar.
relegate ['reləgeit], *v.t.* relegar.
relent [ri'lent], *v.i.* aplacarse, desenojarse.

relentless [ri'lentlis], *a.* implacable; empedernido.
relevant ['reləvənt], *a.* pertinente.
reliable [ri'laiəbl], *a.* fidedigno; seguro.
relic ['relik], *n.* reliquia.
relief [ri'li:f], *n.* alivio; relieve, *m.*; (*mil.*) relevo; socorro.
relieve [ri'li:v], *v.t.* relevar; aliviar; socorrer.
religion [ri'lidʒən], *n.* religión, *f.*
religious [ri'lidʒəs], *a.*, *n.* religioso.
relinquish [ri'liŋkwiʃ], *v.t.* abandonar, ceder.
relish ['reliʃ], *n.* saborcillo; condimento; goce, *m.*—*v.t.* paladear, saborear; gozar de.
reluctance [ri'lʌktəns], *n.* aversión, *f.*, desgana.
reluctant [ri'lʌktənt], *a.* renuente, mal dispuesto.
rely [ri'lai], *v.i.* confiar (*on*, en), contar (*on*, con).
remain [ri'mein], *v.i.* quedar, quedarse; ***it remains to be done,*** queda por hacer.
remainder [ri'meində], *n.* residuo, restante, *m.*, resto.
remains [ri'meinz], *n.pl.* restos, *m.pl.*
remand [ri'mɑ:nd], *v.t.* reencarcelar; — ***home,*** casa de corrección.
remark [ri'mɑ:k], *n.* observación, *f.*—*v.t.*, *v.i.* observar, notar; ***to — on,*** comentar.
remarkable [ri'mɑ:kəbl], *a.* notable, singular.
remedy ['remidi], *n.* remedio.—*v.t.* remediar.
remember [ri'membə], *v.t.* recordar, acordarse de.
remembrance [ri'membrəns], *n.* memoria, recuerdo solemne.
remind [ri'maind], *v.t.* recordar (*of*).
reminder [ri'maində], *n.* recordatorio.
reminisce [remi'nis], *v.i.* entregarse a los recuerdos.
reminiscent [remi'nisənt], *a.* evocador (*of*, de).
remiss [ri'mis], *a.* negligente.
remission [ri'miʃən], *n.* remisión, *f.*
remit [ri'mit], *v.t.* remitir; trasladar.
remittance [ri'mitəns], *n.* giro, remesa.
remnant ['remnənt], *n.* residuo; retazo, retal, *m.*; resto.
remorse [ri'mɔ:s], *n.* remordimiento.
remorseless [ri'mɔ:slis], *a.* implacable.
remote [ri'mout], *a.* remoto; — ***control,*** telecontrol, *m.*, mando a distancia.
removal [ri'mu:vəl], *n.* traslado; eliminación, *f.*
remove [ri'mu:v], *n.* grado; traslado.—*v.t.* quitar, sacar; trasladar.
remunerate [ri'mju:nəreit], *v.t.* remunerar.
Renaissance [rə'neisəns], *n.* Renacimiento.
renascence [ri'næsəns], *n.* renacimiento.
rend [rend], *v.t. irr.* desgarrar; hender.
render ['rendə], *v.t.* rendir; dar, prestar; hacer, poner; verter; interpretar; ***to — down,*** derretir.
rendezvous ['rɔ:ndeivu:], *n.sg.* cita, lugar (*m.*) de cita.
renegade ['renigeid], *a.*, *n.* renegado, apóstata, *m.f.*
renew [ri'nju:], *v.t.* renovar.—*v.i.* renovarse.
renewal [ri'nju:əl], *n.* renovación, *f.*; prórroga.
renounce [ri'nauns], *v.t.* renunciar.
renovate ['renouveit], *v.t.* renovar.
renown [ri'naun], *n.* renombre, *m.*
renowned [ri'naund], *a.* renombrado.
rent (1) [rent], *n.* alquiler, *m.* renta.—*v.t.* alquilar.
rent (2) [rent], *n.* desgarro, raja.
rental ['rentəl], *n.* arriendo.
renunciation [rinʌnsi'eiʃən], *n.* renunciación, *f.*
repair [ri'pɛə], *n.* remiendo, reparación, *f.*; ***in good —,*** en buen estado.—*v.t.* reparar, remendar; remontar (*zapatos*).—*v.i.* dirigirse.
reparation [repə'reiʃən], *n.* reparación, *f.*
repartee [repɑ:'ti:], *n.* réplica, respuesta aguda.
repast [ri'pɑ:st], *n.* yantar, *f.*
repatriate [ri:'pætrieit], *v.t.* repatriar.
repay [ri'pei], *v.t.* (*conjug. like* PAY) recompensar, reembolsar.
repeal [ri'pi:l], *v.t.* revocar.
repeat [ri'pi:t], *n.* repetición, *f.*—*v.t.*, *v.i.* repetir.
repel [ri'pel], *v.t.* repugnar; rechazar.
repellent [ri'pelənt], *a.* repulsivo, repelente.
repent [ri'pent], *v.i.* arrepentirse (de).
repentance [ri'pentəns], *n.* arrepentimiento.
repentant [ri'pentənt], *a.*, *n.* arrepentido.
repercussion [ri:pə'kʌʃən], *n.* repercusión, *f.*
repertoire ['repətwɑ:], *n.* repertorio.
repetition [repi'tiʃən], *n.* repetición, *f.*
rephrase [ri:'freiz], *v.t.* reformular.
replace [ri'pleis], *v.t.* reemplazar; reponer.
replacement [ri'pleismənt], *n.* reemplazo; reposición, *f.*; (*mech. etc.*) repuesto, pieza de repuesto.
replenish [ri'pleniʃ], *v.t.* rellenar, resarcir.
replete [ri'pli:t], *a.* repleto.
replica ['replikə], *n.* réplica, duplicado.
reply [ri'plai], *n.* respuesta, contestación, *f.*—*v.i.* responder, contestar.
report [ri'pɔ:t], *n.* informe, reportaje, *m.*; voz, *f.*; estallido.—*v.t.* relatar, dar parte de; denunciar.—*v.i.* presentarse.
reporter [ri'pɔ:tə], *n.* reportero.
repose [ri'pouz], *n.* reposo.—*v.i.* reposar.
reprehend [repri'hend], *v.t.* reprender, censurar.
reprehensible [repri'hensibl], *a.* reprensible, censurable.
represent [repri'zent], *v.t.* representar.
representative [repri'zentətiv], *a.* representativo.—*n.* representante, *m.f.*
repress [ri'pres], *v.t.* reprimir.
repression [ri'preʃən], *n.* represión, *f.*
reprieve [ri'pri:v], *n.* suspensión (*f.*) de castigo.—*v.t.* suspender el castigo de; aliviar.
reprimand ['reprimɑ:nd], *n.* reprimenda reprensión, *f.*—*v.t.* reprender, censurar.
reprint ['ri:print], *n.* tirada aparte; reimpresión, *f.*—[ri:'print], *v.t.* reimprimir.
reprisal [ri'praizəl], *n.* represalia.
reproach [ri'proutʃ], *n.* reproche, *m.*—*v.t.* reprochar.
reprobate ['reproubeit], *a.*, *n.* réprobo.
reproduce [ri:prə'dju:s], *v.t.* reproducir.—*v.i.* -se.
reproduction [ri:prə'dʌkʃən], *n.* reproducción, *f.*
reproof [ri'pru:f], *n.* reprobación, *f.*, reproche, *m.*
reprove [ri'pru:v], *v.t.* reprobar, censurar.
reptile ['reptail], *a.*, *n.* reptil, *m.*

republic [ri'pʌblik], *n.* república.
republican [ri'pʌblikən], *a.*, *n.* republicano.
repudiate [ri'pju:dieit], *v.t.* repudiar.
repugnance [ri'pʌgnəns], *n.* repugnancia.
repugnant [ri'pʌgnənt], *a.* repugnante.
repulse [ri'pʌls], *n.* repulsa.—*v.t.* repulsar, repeler.
repulsion [ri'pʌlʃən], *n.* repulsión, aversión, *f.*
repulsive [ri'pʌlsiv], *a.* repulsivo, repelente.
reputable ['repjutəbl], *a.* respetable, fidedigno.
reputation [repju:'teiʃən], *n.* reputación, *f.*, nombre, *m.*
repute [ri'pju:t], *n.* reputación, *f.*—*v.t.* reputar; ***to be reputed to be,*** tener fama de.
reputedly [ri'pju:tidli], *adv.* según dicen.
request [ri'kwest], *n.* petición, solicitud, *f.*; ***on* —,** a pedido.—*v.t.* rogar, suplicar, pedir.
requiem ['rekwiem], *n.* réquiem, *m.*
require [ri'kwaiə], *v.t.* necesitar; exigir.
requirement [ri'kwaiəmənt], *n.* requisito, necesidad, *f.*
requisite ['rekwizit], *a.* necesario, debido.—*n.* requisito.
requisition [rekwi'ziʃən], *n.* requisición, *f.*—*v.t.* requisar.
requite [ri'kwait], *v.t.* corresponder a.
reredos ['riərədɔs], *n.* (*eccl.*) retablo.
rescind [ri'sind], *v.t.* rescindir, abrogar.
rescue ['reskju:], *n.* rescate, *m.*; salvamento, liberación, *f.*; socorro.—*v.t.* salvar, rescatar, libertar.
research [ri'sə:tʃ], *n.* investigación, *f.*—*v.i.* investigar.
resemblance [ri'zembləns], *n.* semejanza, parecido.
resemble [ri'zembl], *v.t.* parecerse a.
resent [ri'zent], *v.t.* resentirse de.
resentful [ri'zentful], *a.* resentido.
resentment [ri'zentmənt], *n.* resentimiento.
reservation [rezə'veiʃən] *n.* reservación, *f.*; reserva; salvedad, *f.*
reserve [ri'zə:v], *n.* reserva.—*v.t.* reservar.
reservist [ri'zə:vist], *a.*, *n.* reservista, *m.f.*
reservoir ['rezəvwɑ:], *n.* embalse, *m.*, depósito; pantano; (*fig.*) mina.
reshape [ri:'ʃeip], *v.t.* reformar.
reside [ri'zaid], *v.i.* residir, morar.
residence ['rezidəns], *n.* residencia.
resident ['rezidənt], *a.*, *n.* residente, *m.f.*
residential [rezi'denʃəl], *a.* residencial.
residual [ri'zidjuəl], *a.* residual.
residue ['rezidju:], *n.* residuo, resto.
resign [ri'zain], *v.t.* resignar.—*v.i.* dimitir; resignarse.
resignation [rezig'neiʃən], *n.* dimisión; resignación, *f.*
resilient [ri'ziljənt], *a.* elástico, resaltante; vivo, activo.
resin ['rezin], *n.* resina.
resist [ri'zist], *v.t.* resistir a.—*v.i.* resistirse.
resistance [ri'zistəns], *n.* resistencia.
resistant [ri'zistənt], *a.* resistente.
resolute ['rezəlju:t], *a.* resuelto.
resolution [rezə'lju:ʃən], *n.* resolución, *f.*
resolve [ri'zɔlv], *n.* resolución, determinación, *f.*—*v.t.* resolver.—*v.i.* resolverse (***to,*** a).
resonant ['rezənənt], *a.* resonante.
resort [ri'zɔ:t], *n.* recurso; estación, *f.*, lugar (*m.*) de veraneo; concurso.—*v.i.* recurrir (***to,*** a).
resound [ri'zaund], *v.t.* hacer resonar.—*v.i.* resonar.
resource [ri'sɔ:s], *n.* recurso.
resourceful [ri'sɔ:sful], *a.* ingenioso, avisado.
respect [ri'spekt], *n.* respeto, estimación, *f.*; respecto; ***in — of, with — to,*** respecto a.—*pl.* saludos, *m.pl.*—*v.t.* respetar, acatar.
respectability [rispektə'biliti], *n.* respetabilidad, *f.*
respectable [ris'pektəbl], *a.* respetable.
respectful [ris'pektful], *a.* respetuoso.
respecting [ris'pektiŋ], *prep.* (con) respecto a.
respective [ris'pektiv], *a.*, respectivo; sendo.
respiration [respi'reiʃən], *n.* respiración, *f.*
respite ['respait, 'respit], *n.* tregua, respiro; plazo.
resplendent [ris'plendənt], *a.* resplandeciente.
respond [ris'pɔnd], *v.i.* responder.
response [ris'pɔns], *n.* respuesta.
responsibility [rispɔnsi'biliti], *n.* responsabilidad, *f.*
responsible [ris'pɔnsibl], *a.* responsable.
responsive [ris'pɔnsiv], *a.* sensible, responsivo.
rest (1) [rest], *n.* descanso; reposo; estribo; pausa; ***at* —,** en reposo; en paz.—*v.t.* descansar, apoyar, colocar.—*v.i.* descansar; ***to — with,*** tocar a, correr a cuenta de.
rest (2) [rest], *n.* resto; ***the* —,** lo demás; los demás.—*v.i.* verse, hallarse, estar; ***to — assured,*** estar seguro.
restaurant ['restərənt, 'restrã], *n.* restaurante, restóran, *m.*
restful ['restful], *a.* tranquilo, sosegado.
restitution [resti'tju:ʃən], *n.* restitución, *f.*
restive ['restiv], *a.* inquieto.
restless ['restlis], *a.* inquieto, impaciente; insomne.
restlessness ['restlisnis], *n.* desasosiego; insomnio.
restoration [restɔ:'reiʃən], *n.* restauración, *f.*
restore [ri'stɔ:], *v.t.* restaurar; restituir.
restrain [ri'strein], *v.t.* refrenar; encerrar.
restraint [ri'streint], *n.* mesura, comedimiento; freno; restricción, *f.*
restrict [ri'strikt], *v.t.* restringir.
restriction [ri'strikʃən], *n.* restricción, *f.*
restrictive [ri'striktiv], *a.* restrictivo.
result [ri'zʌlt], *n.* resultado; resulta.—*v.i.* resultar; ***to — in,*** acabar por, terminar en.
resultant [ri'zʌltənt], *a.*, *n.* resultante, *m.*
resume [ri'zju:m], *v.t.* reasumir; reanudar; volver a ocupar (*un asiento*).—*v.i.* seguir, recomenzar.
résumé [rezju:mei], *n.* resumen, *m.*, sumario.
resumption [ri'zʌmpʃən], *n.* reasunción *f.*,
resurgence [ri'sə:dʒəns], *n.* resurgimiento.
resurrect [rezə'rekt], *v.t.*, *v.i.* resuscitar.
resurrection [rezə'rekʃən], *n.* resurrección, *f.*
resuscitate [ri'sʌsiteit], *v.t.* resuscitar.
retail ['ri:teil], *a.*, *adv.* al por menor.—*n.* venta al por menor, reventa.—[ri'teil], *v.t.* vender al por menor; repetir, contar.
retailer ['ri:teilə], *n.* tendero, vendedor al por menor, *m.*
retain [ri'tein], *v.t.* retener; contratar.
retainer [ri'teinə], *n.* partidario, criado; honorario (*pago*).
retaliate [ri'tælieit], *v.i.* desquitarse, vengarse.

retaliation [ritæli'eiʃən], *n.* desquite, *m.*, represalias, *f. pl.*
retard [ri'tɑ:d], *v.t.* atrasar.
retch [retʃ], *v.i.* arquear, tener bascas.
retention [ri'tenʃən], *n.* retención, *f.*
retentive [ri'tentiv], *a.* retentivo.
reticence ['retisəns], *n.* reticencia, reserva.
reticent ['retisənt], *a.* reservado.
retina ['retinə], *n.* retina.
retinue ['retinju:], *n.* séquito, comitiva.
retire [ri'taiə], *v.t.* retirar; jubilar.—*v.i.* retirarse; jubilarse; acostarse.
retirement [ri'taiəmənt], *n.* jubilación, *f.*; retiro; — ***pension***, pensión vitalicia.
retiring [ri'taiəriŋ], *a.* tímido, retraído; dimitente.
retort [ri'tɔ:t], *n.* réplica; retorta.—*v.i.* replicar.
retouch [ri:'tʌtʃ], *v.t.* retocar.
retrace [ri'treis], *v.t.* desandar; repasar.
retract [ri'trækt], *v.t.* retractar.—*v.i.* -se.
retraction [ri'trækʃən], *n.* retracción, *f.*
retreat [ri'tri:t], *n.* retiro (*lugar*); retirada (*hecho*).—*v.i.* retirarse.
retribution [retri'bju:ʃən], *n.* retribución, *f.*, castigo.
retrieve [ri'tri:v], *v.t.* cobrar; resarcirse de.
retriever [ri'tri:və], *n.* perro cobrador, sabueso.
retrograde ['retrougreid], *a.* retrógrado.
retrospective [retrou'spektiv], *a.* retrospectivo.
retroussé [ri'tru:sei], *a.* respingado.
return [ri'tə:n], *n.* vuelta; devolución, *f.*; correspondencia; (*pol.*) resultado; (*com.*) rédito; — ***ticket,*** billete (*m*). de ida y vuelta; ***in —,*** en cambio; en recompensa; ***many happy returns,*** feliz cumpleaños, felicidades.—*v.t.* devolver; rendir; dar; elegir; corresponder a (*un favor*).—*v.t.* volver; regresar.
reunion [ri:'ju:njən], *n.* reunión, *f.*
reunite [ri:ju:'nait], *v.t.* reunir; reconciliar.—*v.i.* -se.
reveal [ri'vi:l], *v.t.* revelar.
reveille [ri'væli], *n.* (*mil.*) diana.
revel ['revəl], *n.* jerga, francachela.—*v.i.* ir de parranda; gozarse (***in,*** de).
revelation [revə'leiʃən], *n.* revelación, *f.*; (*Bib.*) Apocalipsis, *m.*
reveller ['revələ], *n.* juerguista, *m.f.*
revelry ['revəlri], *n.* jarana, juerga.
revenge [ri'vendʒ], *n.* venganza.—*v.t.* vengar, vengarse de.—*v.i.* vengarse.
revengeful [ri'vendʒful], *a.* vengativo.
revenue ['revənju:], *n.* rentas públicas, *f.pl*; (*com.*) rédito; ingresos, *m.pl.*; aduana.
reverberate [ri'və:bəreit], *v.t.* reflejar.—*v.i.* resonar, retumbar.
reverberation [rivə:bə'reiʃən], *n.* retumbo; reverberación, *f.*
revere [ri'viə], *v.t.* reverenciar, venerar.
reverence ['revərəns], *n.* reverencia.
reverend ['revərənd], *a.*, *n.* reverendo.
reverent ['revərənt], *a.* reverente.
reverie ['revəri:], *n.* ensueño.
reversal [ri'və:səl], *n.* reversión, *f.*, cambio; revocación, *f.*
reverse [ri'və:s], *a.* contrario.—*n.* revés, *m.*; reverso; contratiempo.—*v.t.* invertir; revocar; ***to — the charges,*** (*tel.*) cobrar al número llamado.—*v.i.* invertirse; ir hacia atrás.
reversible [ri'və:sibl], *a.* reversible; a dos caras.
reversion [ri'və:ʃən], *n.* reversión, *f.*
revert [ri'və:t], *v.i.* recudir; (*jur.*) revertir; saltar atrás.
review [ri'vju:], *n.* revista; (*lit.*) reseña.—*v.t.* repasar; (*lit.*) reseñar; (*mil.*) revistar, pasar en revista.
revile [ri'vail], *v.t.* ultrajar, injuriar.
revise [ri'vaiz], *v.t.* revisar; repasar; corregir.
revision [ri'viʒən], *n.* revisión, *f.*; repaso; corrección. *f.*
revival [ri'vaivəl], *n.* renacimiento; restauración; (*rel.*) despertamiento; (*theat.*) reestreno.
revive [ri'vaiv], *v.t.* resuscitar; restaurar; reanimar; (*theat*). reestrenar.—*v.i.* resuscitar; reanimarse; volver en sí.
revoke [ri'vouk], *v.t.* revocar.
revolt [ri'voult], *n.* sublevación, rebelión, *f.*—*v.t.* dar asco a, repugnar.—*v.i.* rebelarse; sentir repulsión.
revolting [ri'voultiŋ], *a.* repugnante.
revolution [revə'lu:ʃən], *n.* revolución, *f.*
revolutionary [revə'lu:ʃənəri], *a.*, *n.* revolucionario.
revolutionize [revə'lu:ʃənaiz], *v.t.* revolucionar.
revolve [ri'vəlv], *v.t.* hacer girar; ponderar. —*v.i.* girar.
revolver [ri'vəolvə], *n.* revólver, *m.*
revolving [ri'vəlviŋ], *a.* giratorio.
revue [ri'vju:], *n.* (*theat.*) revista.
revulsion [ri'vʌlʃən], *n.* revulsión; reacción, *f.*
reward [ri'wɔ:d], *n.* premio, recompensa; retribución, *f.*—*v.t.* recompensar, premiar.
rewarding [ri'wɔ:diŋ], *a.* provechoso; satisfaciente.
reword [ri:'wə:d], *v.t.* expresar *o* formular de otra manera.
rhapsody ['ræpsədi], *n.* rapsodia.
rhetoric ['retərik], *n.* retórica.
rhetorical [ri'tərikəl], *a.* retórico.
rheum [ru:m], *n.* reuma.
rheumatic [ru'mætik], *a.* reumático.—*n.pl.* (*fam.*) reumatismo.
rheumatism ['ru:mətizm], *n.* reumatismo.
Rhine [rain], *n.* Rin, *m.*
rhinocerous [rai'nəsərəs], (*fam.* **rhino** ['rainou]), *n.* rinoceronte, *m.*
rhizome ['raizoum], *n.* rizoma, *m.*
Rhodesia [rou'di:zjə], *n.* la Rodesia.
rhododendron [roudə'dendrən], *n.* rododendro.
Rhône [roun], *n.* Ródano.
rhubarb ['ru:bɑ:b], *n.* ruibarbo.
rhyme [raim], *n.* rima; ***without — or reason,*** sin ton ni son.—*v.t.*, *v.i.* rimar.
rhymester ['raimstə], *n.* poetastro, rimador, *m.*
rhythm [riðm], *n.* ritmo.
rhythmic ['riðmik], *a.* rítmico.
rib [rib], *n.* costilla; varilla (*de un abanico, etc.*); nervadura.—*v.t.* (*fam.*) tomar el pelo a.
ribald ['ribəld], *a.* grosero, escabroso.
ribaldry ['ribəldri], *n.* grosería, escabrosidad, *f.*
riband ['ribənd], *n.* cinta; listón, *m.*
ribbing ['ribiŋ], *n.* costillaje, *m.*; nervadura; burlas, *f.pl.*
ribbon ['ribən], *n.* cinta.

rice [rais], *n.* arroz, *m.*; — ***pudding,*** arroz con leche.
rich [ritʃ], *a.* rico; (*fig.*) rico; (*fam.*) divertido y ridículo.—*n.pl.* —***es*** ['ritʃiz], riquezas, *f.pl.*
Richard ['ritʃəd], *n.* Ricardo.
rick [rik], *n.* almiar, *m.*
rickets ['rikits], *n. pl.* raquitis, *f.*, raquitismo.
rickety ['rikiti], *a.* raquítico; (*fig.*) desvencijado.
rickshaw ['rikʃɔ:], *n.* riksha, *m.*
ricochet ['rikəʃei], *n.* rebote, *m.*—*v.i.* rebotar.
rid [rid], *v.t.* desembarazar, librar; ***to get — of,*** quitar de en medio, deshacerse de.
riddance ['ridəns], *n.* ***good —!*** ¡adiós, gracias! ¡de buena me he librado!
ridden [ridn], [RIDE].
riddle (1) [ridl], *n.* enigma, *m.*, acertijo.
riddle (2) [ridl], *n.* garbillo, criba.—*v.t.* cribar (*tamizar*); acribillar (*con agujeros, balas*).
ride [raid], *n.* paseo.—*v.t.* montar; surcar (*el mar*); tiranizar.—*v.i.* cabalgar, montar; pasear; flotar.
rider ['raidə], *n.* caballero, jinete, *m.*; pasajero; añadidura.
ridge [ridʒ], *n.* espinazo, lomo; caballete, *m.*
ridicule ['ridikju:l], *n.* ridículo, irrisión, *f.*—*v.t.* poner en ridículo, ridiculizar.
ridiculous [ri'dikjuləs], *a.* ridículo.
riding ['raidiŋ], *a.* de montar.—*n.* equitación, *f.*
rife [raif], *a.* abundante, corriente; lleno (***with,*** de).
riff-raff ['rifræf], *n.* bahorrina, gentuza.
rifle (1) [raifl], *n.* rifle, fusil, *m.*—*v.t.* rayar (*fusil*).
rifle (2) [raifl], *v.t.* pillar.
rifleman ['raiflmən], *n.* fusilero.
rift [rift], *n.* raja, hendedura; desavenencia.
rig (1) [rig], *n.* aparejo, jarcias, *f.pl.*; (*fam.*) traje, *m.*—*v.t.* enjarciar; aparejar; (*fam.*) emperifollar.
rig (2) [rig], *v.t.* (*fam.*) manipular, falsificar.
rigging (1) ['rigiŋ], *n.* aparejos, *m.pl.*, jarcias, *f.pl.*
rigging (2) ['rigiŋ], *n.* manipulación, *f.*, forcejeos, *m.pl.*
right [rait], *a.* correcto; derecho; ***to be —,*** tener razón; — ***angle,*** ángulo recto; ***in his — mind,*** en sus cabales.—*n.* derecho; título; derecha (*lado*); ***by —,*** en derecho.—*v.t.* rectificar; enderezar.—*adv.* correctamente; en buen estado; mismo; bien; ***all —,*** muy bien; — ***away,*** en seguida; — ***or wrong,*** a tuertas o a derechas; ***to put —,*** enderezar, corregir; encaminar, orientar.
righteous ['raitʃəs], *a.* justo, virtuoso.
righteousness ['raitʃəsnis], *n.* virtud, *f.*, justicia.
rightful ['raitful], *a.* legítimo, justo.
rigid ['ridʒid], *a.* rígido, tieso; riguroso, rigoroso.
rigidity [ri'dʒiditi], *n.* rigidez, *f.*
rigor mortis ['rigə'mɔ:tis], *n.* rigor (*m.*) de la muerte.
rigorous ['rigərəs], *a.* riguroso, rigoroso.
rigour ['rigə], *n.* rigor, *m.*
rile [rail], *v.t.* (*fam.*) picar, exasperar.
rim [rim], *n.* canto, borde, *m.*; llanta (*de una rueda*).—*v.t.* cercar.
rime (1) [raim], *n.* escarcha.
rime (2) [raim] [RHYME].
rind [raind], *n.* corteza.
ring (1) [riŋ], *n.* sortija, anillo; círculo; plaza, ruedo; corro (*gente*).—*v.t.* cercar, rodear; anillar.
ring (2) [riŋ], *n.* (*tel.*) llamada; repique, *m.*, campaneo.—*v.t. irr.* sonar; tocar; (*tel.*) llamar.—*v.i. irr.* sonar; resonar, zumbar; ***to — up,*** llamar por teléfono.
ringleader ['riŋli:də], *n.* cabecilla, *m.*
rink [riŋk], *n.* pista de patinar.
rinse [rins], *n.* enjuague, *m.*—*v.t.* enjuagar.
riot ['raiət], *n.* tumulto, alboroto, motín, *m.*; orgía; ***to run —,*** desenfrenarse.—*v.i.* amotinarse, alborotarse.
riotous ['raiətəs], *a.* alborotado, amotinado.
rip [rip], *n.* rasgón, *m.*, rasgadura; (*fam.*) gamberro, pícaro.—*v.t.* descoser; rasgar; arrancar.—*v.i.* rasgarse; correr.
ripe [raip], *a.* maduro.
ripen ['raipən], *v.t., v.i.* madurar.
ripeness ['raipnis], *n.* madurez, *f.*
riposte [ri'pɔst], *n.* réplica aguda.
ripping ['ripiŋ], *a.* (*fam.*) de órdago.
ripple [ripl], *n.* rizo, oleadita.—*v.i.* rizarse.
rise [raiz], *n.* subida; cuesta; aumento; salida; origen, *m.*; ***to give — to,*** ocasionar, motivar.—*v.i. irr.* levantarse; subir; salir; surgir; nacer, brotar.
risen [rizn] [RISE].
rising ['raiziŋ], *a.* saliente (*sol*); asciendiente; que sube.—*n.* sublevación, *f.*
risk [risk], *n.* riesgo.—*v.t.* arriesgar; arriesgarse a.
risky ['riski], *a.* arriesgado.
risqué ['riskei], *a.* escabroso, picante.
rissole ['risoul], *n.* risol, *m.*
rite [rait], *n.* rito.
ritual ['ritjuəl], *a., n.* ritual, *m.*
ritualist ['ritjuəlist], *a., n.* ritualista, *m.f.*
rival ['raivəl], *a., n.* rival, *m.f.*—*v.t.* rivalizar con.
rivalry ['raivəlri], *n.* rivalidad, *f.*
river ['rivə], *a.* fluvial.—*n.* río; — ***bed,*** cauce, *m.*
riverside ['rivəsaid], *n.* ribera.
rivet ['rivit], *n.* remache, *m.*—*v.t.* remachar; clavar (*los ojos en*).
rivulet ['rivjulit], *n.* riachuelo, arroyo.
roach (1) [routʃ], *n.* (*ichth.*) leucisco.
roach (2) [routʃ], *n.* (*ent.*) cucaracha.
road [roud], *n.* camino; carretera; (*naut.*) rada; — ***map,*** mapa itinerario.
road-block ['roudblɔk], *n.* barricada.
roadside ['roudsaid], *n.* borde, *m.*
roam [roum], *v.t.* vagar por.—*v.i.* vagar vagabundear.
roan [roun], *a., n.* roano.
roar [rɔ:], *n.* bramido, rugido.—*v.i.* rugir, bramar; estallar.
roast [roust], *a., n.* asado.—*v.t.* asar; tostar.—*v.i.* -se.
roastbeef ['roust'bi:f], *n.* rosbif, *m.*
rob [rɔb], *v.t.* robar.
robber ['rɔbə], *n.* ladrón, *m.*
robbery ['rɔbəri], *n.* robo.
robe [roub], *n.* túnica; traje talar, *m.*—*v.t.* vestir, ataviar.—*v.i.* vestirse, ataviarse de ceremonia.
robin ['rɔbin], *n.* (*orn.*) petirrojo.
robot ['roubət], *n.* robot, *m.*
robust [rou'bʌst], *a.* robusto; fornido membrudo.

rock (1) [rɔk], *n.* roca; peñón, *m.*; (*fam.*) ***on the rocks,*** pelado, en un apuro.
rock (2) [rɔk], *v.t.* mecer; sacudir.—*v.i.* bambolear; mecerse.
rocker ['rɔkə], *n.* mecedora; balancín, *m.*
rocket ['rɔkit], *n.* cohete, *m.*—*v.i.* subir hasta las nubes.
rocking-chair ['rɔkiŋtʃɛə], *n.* mecedora.
rocky ['rɔki], *a.* rocoso, roqueño; poco firme; ***Rockies*** o ***Rocky Mountains,*** Montañas Rocosas, *f.pl.*
rococo [rə'koukou], *a.*, *n.* rococó, *m.*
rod [rɔd], *n.* varilla; caña de pescar; pértica; jalón, *m.*; vástago; (*fam.*, *U.S.*) pistola; ***to rule with a — of iron,*** governar con mano de hierro; ***to spare the —,*** no castigar (*a un niño travieso*).
rode [roud], [RIDE].
rodent ['roudənt], *a.*, *n.* roedor, *m.*
rodeo ['roudiou, rou'deiou], *n.* rodeo, circo.
roe (1) [rou], *n.* (*ichth.*) hueva.
roe (2) [rou], *n.* (*zool.*) corzo.
rogation [rou'geiʃən], *n.* rogación, *f.*, rogativa.
rogue [roug], *n.* bribón, *m.*, bellaco.
roguery ['rougəri], *n.* picardía, bellaquería; travesura.
role [roul], *n.* papel, *m.*
roll [roul], *n.* rollo; registro, rol, *m.*; panecillo; balanceo; retumbo del trueno; oleaje, *m.*; ***to call the —,*** pasar lista.—*v.t.* hacer rodar; arrollar; liar (*cigarrillo*); mover; vibrar; redoblar (*tambor*).—*v.i.* rodar; balancearse; dar vueltas; retumbar; ***to — up,*** arrollar; (*fam.*) llegar; ***to — up one's sleeves,*** arremangarse; ***to — in money,*** nadar en dinero.
roller ['roulə], *n.* rodador, *m.*; ruedecilla; ola grande; ***— bearing,*** cojinete (*m.*) de rodillos; ***— skate,*** patín (*m.*) de ruedas; ***— towel,*** toalla sin fin.
rollicking ['rɔlikiŋ], *a.* turbulento, retozón.
rolling-pin ['rouliŋpin], *n.* rodillo, hataca.
rolling-stock ['rouliŋstɔk], *n.* (*rail.*) material móvil, *m.*
rolling stone ['rouliŋ'stoun], *n.* (*fig.*) persona veleidosa.
roly-poly ['rouli'pouli], *a.* rechoncho.—*n.* pudín (*m.*) en forma de rollo.
Roman ['roumən], *a.*, *n.* romano; ***— nose,*** nariz aguileña; **roman,** *n.* (*print.*) redondo.
Romance [rou'mæns], *a.* románico.—*n.* romance, *m.*
romance [rou'mæns], *n.* romance, *m.*; romanticismo; amor, *m.*; ficción, *f.*—*v.i.* fingir fábulas.
Romanesque [roumə'nesk], *a.* románico.
Romania [rou'meiniə] [RUMANIA].
Romanian [rou'meiniən] [RUMANIAN].
romantic [rou'mæntik], *a.*, *n.* romántico.
romanticism [rou'mæntisizm], *n.* romanticismo.
romp [rɔmp], *n.* retozo, juego animado.—*v.i.* retozar, triscar, juguetear.
rompers ['rɔmpəz], *n.pl.* traje (*m.*) de juego; ***in —,*** en pañales.
rood [ru:d], *n.* crucifijo; la Cruz.
roof [ru:f], *n.* tejado, techo; paladar (*boca*), *m.*
roofing ['ru:fiŋ], *n.* material (*m.*) para techos.
rook [ruk], *n.* grajo, cuervo merendero; roque (*ajedrez*), *m.*—*v.t.* (*fam.*) estafar.
rookery ['rukəri], *n.* colonia de grajos.
rookie ['ru:ki], *n.* (*U.S. fam.*) bisoño.
room [ru:m], *n.* cuarto, habitación, *f.*; sitio, espacio; oportunidad, *f.*; ***there is — for,*** cabe(n).
rooming house ['ru:miŋhaus], *n.* (*U.S.*) casa de cuartos alquilados.
roomy ['ru:mi], *a.* holgado, espacioso.
roost [ru:st], *n.* percha; gallinero; ***to rule the —,*** mandar, tener vara alta.—*v.i.* posar.
rooster ['ru:stə], *n.* gallo.
root [ru:t], *n.* ráiz, *f.*; (*fig.*) origen, *m.*; ***to take —,*** arraigarse, echar raíces.—*v.i.* desarraigar (***up*** o ***out***); hocicar; echar raíces.
rope [roup], *n.* cuerda, soga; ***to know the ropes,*** saber cuántas son cinco.—*v.t.* atar; coger con lazo.—*v.i.* ***to — in,*** (*fam.*) implicar; (*U.S.*) embaucar.
ropy ['roupi], *a.* pegajosa, fibroso; (*fam.*) inseguro, débil.
rosary ['rouzəri], *n.* (*eccl.*) rosario; jardín (*m.*) de rosales.
rose (1) [rouz], *a.* rosado; ***to see everything through rose-coloured spectacles,*** verlo todo color de rosa.—*n.* rosa; rosal (*mata*), *m.*; roseta (*de una manguera*); ***under the —,*** bajo cuerda.
rose (2) [rouz], [RISE].
rosebush ['rouzbuʃ], *n.* rosal, *m.*
rosemary ['rouzməri], *n.* romero.
rosette [rou'zet], *n.* rosa.
rosewood ['rouzwud], *n.* palisandro.
rosin ['rɔzin], *n.* resina.
roster ['rɔstə], *n.* lista de turnos; horario.
rostrum ['rɔstrəm], *n.* tribuna.
rosy ['rouzi], *a.* rosado, color (*m.*) de rosa; (*fam.*) feliz, alegre.
rot [rɔt], *n.* podre, podredumbre, *f.*; (*fam.*) tontería, disparate, *m.*—*v.t.* pudrir.—*v.i.* pudrirse.
rotary ['routəri], *a.* rotativo.
rotate [rou'teit], *v.t.* hacer girar.—*v.i.* girar; alternar.
rotation [rou'teiʃən], *n.* rotación; ***in —,*** por turnos.
rote [rout], *n.* rutina maquinal; ***by —,*** de memoria.
rotten [rɔtn], *a.* podrido; corrompido; (*fam.*) ruin.
rotter ['rɔtə], *n.* (*fam.*) calavera, *m.*, sinvergüenza, *m.*
rouble [ru:bl], *n.* rublo.
roué ['ru:ei], *n.* libertino.
rouge [ru:ʒ], *n.* arrebol, colorete, *m.*
rough [rʌf], *a.* áspero; tosco; borrascoso; aproximado; turbulento; bruto; ***— diamond,*** (*fig.*) persona inculta pero de buen fondo; ***— draft,*** borrador, *m.*—*v.t.* hacer áspero; bosquejar; ***to — it,*** vivir sin comodidades.
rough-and-ready ['rʌfənd'redi], *a.* tosco pero eficaz.
roughen [rʌfn], *v.t.* poner tosco *or* áspero. —*v.i.* ponerse áspero.
roughness ['rʌfnis], *n.* aspereza, rudeza, tosquedad, *f.*; borrasca; rigor, *m.*; agitación, *f.*
roughshod ['rʌfʃɔd], *adv.* ***to ride — over,*** imponerse con arrogancia a.
roulette [ru:'let], *n.* ruleta.
Roumania [RUMANIA].
Roumanian [RUMANIAN].

round [raund], *a.* redondo; rotundo.—*n.* círculo; ronda; giro; tiro, bala; recorrido.—*v.t.* arredondar, redondear; volver.—*v.i.* redondearse; volverse; ***to — off,*** redondear; rematar; ***to — up,*** encerrar, recoger.—*adv.* alrededor; por ahí; por todas partes; ***to go —,*** rodear, pasar dando un rodeo; ser bastante; dar vueltas; ***to come —,*** rodear; venir por; volver en sí; ***to stand —,*** rodear; circundar.—*prep.* al rededor de; a la vuelta de (*una esquina*).
roundabout ['raundəbaut], *a.* indirecto.—*n.* tío vivo; glorieta, redondel (*de carreteras*), *m.*
roundhand ['raundhænd], *n.* letra redonda.
round-shouldered ['raund'ʃouldəd], *a.* cargado de espaldas.
round-up ['raundʌp], *n.* encierro, rodeo.
rouse [rauz], *v.t.* despertar; animar; levantar.
rousing ['rauziŋ], *a.* emocionante, conmovedor.
rout [raut], *n.* derrota, fuga.—*v.t.* derrotar.
route [ru:t], *n.* ruta.
routine [ru:'ti:n], *a.* rutinario.—*n.* rutina.
rove [rouv], *v.t.* vagar por; torcer.—*v.i.* vagar.
rover ['rouvə], *n.* vagabundo; pirata, *m.*; (*fam.*) perro.
row (1) [rou], *n.* fila; hilera; remadura; paseo en barca.—*v.t., v.i.* remar.
row (2) [rau], *n.* pendencia, camorra; alboroto.—*v.i.* armar camorra, reñirse.
rowdy ['raudi], *a., n.* pendenciero, gamberro.
rowing ['rouiŋ], *n.* remo.
rowlock ['rʌlək], *n.* chumacera.
royal ['rɔiəl], *a.* real.
royalism ['rɔiəlizm], *n.* realismo.
royalty ['rɔiəlti], *n.* realeza; familia real. —*pl.* derechos de autor.
rub [rʌb], *n.* roce, *m.*; (*fig.*) pega.—*v.t.* frotar; fregar; (*fig.*) molestar.—*v.i.* frotar; ***to — out,*** borrar.
rubber ['rʌbə], *n.* goma, caucho; goma de borrar; ***— band,*** liga de goma.
rubberneck ['rʌbənek], *n.* (*U.S. fam.*) turista boquiabierto.
rubber-stamp ['rʌbə'stæmp], *n.* estampillo. —*v.i.* firmar por rutina.
rubbery ['rʌbəri], *a.* elástico.
rubbish ['rʌbiʃ], *n.* basura; necedad, *f.*
rubble [rʌbl], *n.* ripios, escombros, *m.pl.*
rubicund ['ru:bikʌnd], *a.* rubicundo.
rubric ['ru:brik], *n.* rúbrica.
ruby ['ru:bi], *n.* rubí, *m.*
rucksack ['ruksæk], *n.* mochila, barjuleta.
rudder ['rʌdə], *n.* timón, gobernalle, *m.*
ruddy ['rʌdi], *a.* rojizo; rubicundo; (*low*) puñetero.
rude [ru:d], *a.* tosco; descortés, informal; insolente.
rudeness ['ru:dnis], *n.* descortesía, insolencia; rudeza.
rudiment ['ru:dimənt], *n.* rudimento.
rudimentary [ru:di'mentəri], *a.* rudimentario.
rue [ru:], *v.t.* sentir, arrepentirse de.
rueful ['ru:ful], *a.* lastimoso, lamentable.
ruff [rʌf], *n.* lechuguilla (*collar*), golilla; collarín; (*orn.*) combatiente, *m.*
ruffian ['rʌfiən], *n.* tunante, bergante, bribón, *m.*
ruffle [rʌfl], *v.t.* arrugar; rizar; desaliñar; vejar.
rug [rʌg], *n.* alfombra, tapete, *m.*; manta.
rugged ['rʌgid], *a.* recio; escabroso.
ruin ['ru:in], *n.* ruina.—*v.t.* arruinar.
ruination [ru:i'neiʃən], *n.* ruina, perdición, *f.*
ruinous ['ru:inəs], *a.* ruinoso.
rule [ru:l], *n.* regla; autoridad, gobierno; ***as a —,*** generalmente, por regla general; ***to be the —,*** ser de regla; ***to make it a — to,*** imponerse la regla de.—*v.t.* gobernar, mandar; regir; determinar, disponer; ***to — out,*** excluir, no admitir; ***to — over,*** gobernar.—*v.i.* regir, señorear; prevalecer, ser vigente.
ruler ['ru:lə], *n.* gobernante, *m.*; regla.
ruling ['ru:liŋ], *n.* rayado; (*jur. etc.*) fallo.
rum (1) [rʌm], *a.* (*fam.*) raro, sospechoso.
rum (2) [rʌm], *n.* ron, *m.*
Rumania [ru:'meiniə], *n.* Romania.
Rumanian [ru:'meiniən], *a., n.* rumano.
rumba ['rʌmbə], *n.* rumba.
rumble (1) [rʌmbl], *n.* retumbo, rumor bajo. —*v.i.* retumbar, rugir.
rumble (2) [rʌmbl], *v.t.* (*fam.*) cazar, descubrir.
ruminant ['ru:minənt], *a., n.* rumiante, *m.f.*
ruminate ['ru:mineit], *v.t., v.i.* rumiar; ponderar.
rummage ['rʌmidʒ], *n.* trastos viejos, *m.pl.*—*v.t., v.i.* escudriñar, buscar desordenadamente.
rumour ['ru:mə], *n.* rumor, chisme, *m.* —*v.t.* ***it is rumoured that,*** corre la voz de que.
rump [rʌmp], *n.* nalga, anca; resto.
rumple [rʌmpl], *v.t.* arrugar, desaliñar.
rumpus ['rʌmpəs], *n.* batahola.
run [rʌn], *n.* corrida, curso, carrera; viajecito; serie; duración, *f.*; tanto (*de cricket*); ***in the long —,*** a la larga; ***on the —,*** en fuga; escapado.—*v.t. irr.* dirigir; pasar; correr; presentar.—*v.i. irr.* correr; manar; viajar; correrse; funcionar; ser candidato; ***to — across,*** tropezar con; cruzar corriendo; ***to — after,*** perseguir; ***to — away,*** fugarse, escaparse; ***to — down,*** gotear; agotarse; cazar y matar; atropellar; desprestigiar; ***to — in,*** entrar corriendo; (*fam.*) detener; ***to — dry,*** secarse; ***to — foul of,*** incurrir el enojo de; ***to — off,*** salvarse, huir; ***to — out,*** salir corriendo; agotarse; expirar, caducar; ***to — out of,*** no tener más; ***to — over,*** repasar; atropellar; rebosar.
runaway ['rʌnəwei], *a., n.* fugitivo, tránsfuga, *m.f.*
rung (1) [rʌŋ], *n.* escalón, *m.*
rung (2) [rʌŋ] [RING].
runner ['rʌnə], *n.* corredor; contrabandista, *m.*; (*bot.*) sarmiento.
runner-bean ['rʌnə'bi:n], *n.* judía verde.
runner-up ['rʌnər'ʌp], *n.* subcampeón, *m.*
running ['rʌniŋ], *a.* corriente; corredizo; seguido; en marcha; ***— in,*** en rodaje.—*n.* carrera, corrida; marcha; dirección, *f.*; ***in the —,*** con esperanzas todavía; ***— costs,*** gastos corrientes.
running-board ['rʌniŋbɔ:d], *n.* estribo.
runt [rʌnt], *n.* redrojo.
runway ['rʌnwei], *n.* pista de aterrizaje.
rupee [ru:'pi:], *n.* rupia.
rupture ['rʌptʃə], *n.* ruptura; hernia.—*v.t.* romper; causar una hernia.—*v.i.* romperse.
rural ['ruərəl], *a.* rural.

ruse [ru:z], *n.* ardid, *f.*, artimaña.
rush (1) [rʌʃ], *n.* acometida; tropel, *m.*; prisa; demanda extraordinaria; (*U.S.*) lucha estudiantil; — ***hour,*** hora de tráfico intenso.—*v.t.* llevar con gran prisa; hacer con gran prisa; atacar con prisa, sorprender.—*v.i.* ir de prisa; hacer con prisa.
rush (2) [rʌʃ], *n.* (*bot.*) junco.
rusk [rʌsk], *n.* galleta, rosca.
russet ['rʌsit], *a.* rojizo, bermejizo.
Russia ['rʌʃə], *n.* Rusia.
Russian ['rʌʃən], *a.*, *n.* ruso.
rust [rʌst], *n.* orín, herrín, *m.*, moho; (*bot.*) tizón, *m.*, roña.—*v.t.* enmohecer, aherrumbrar.—*v.i.* -se, oxidarse.
rustic ['rʌstik], *a.*, *n.* rústico; campesino.
rusticate ['rʌstikeit], *v.t.* desterrar al campo; (*educ.*) expulsar temporalmente.—*v.i.* rusticar.
rustle [rʌsl], *n.* crujido, susurro.—*v.t.* hacer crujir; robar ganado.—*v.i.* crujir, susurrar; (*U.S.*) patear, pernear; ***to — up,*** (*fam.*) improvisar.
rustler ['rʌslə], *n.* ladrón (*m.*) de ganado.
rusty ['rʌsti], *a.* herrumbroso, mohoso, oxidado; (*fig.*) casi olvidado por falta de práctica.
rut (1) [rʌt], *n.* bache, *m.*, rodada, surco.—*v.t.* hacer rodadas en.
rut (2) [rʌt], *n.* (*zool.*) celo.—*v.i.* bramar; estar en celo.
ruthless ['ru:θlis], *a.* desalmado, despiadado.
rye [rai], *n.* centeno; (*U.S.*) whisky (*m.*) de centeno.

S

S, s [es], *n.* décimonona letra del alfabeto inglés.
Sabbath ['sæbəθ], *n.* sábado (*judío*); domingo (*cristiano*).
sable [seibl], *a.* sable; negro.—*n.* marta.
sabotage ['sæbətɑ:ʒ], *n.* sabotaje, *m.*—*v.t.* sabotear.
saboteur [sæbə'tə:], *n.* saboteador, *m.*
sabre ['seibə], *n.* sable, *m.*
saccharine ['sækərin], *n.* sacarina.
sack (1) [sæk], *n.* saco; ***to give the —,*** despedir; ***to get the —,*** ser despedido.—*v.t.* meter en un saco; despedir.
sack (2) [sæk], *n.* (*mil.*) saqueo.—*v.t.* saquear.
sack (3) [sæk], *n.* (*obs.*) vino.
sackcloth ['sækkloθ], *n.* harpillera; (*eccl.*) cilicio.
sacrament ['sækrəmənt], *n.* sacramento.
sacramental [sækrə'mentl], *a.* sacramental.
sacred ['seikrid], *a.* sagrado; consagrado.
sacrifice ['sækrifais], *n.* sacrificio.—*v.t.*, *v.i.* sacrificar.
sacrificial [sækri'fiʃəl], *a.* del sacrificio.
sacrilege ['sækrilidʒ], *n.* sacrilegio.
sacrilegious [sækri'lidʒəs], *a.* sacrílego.
sacristan ['sækristən], *n.* sacristán, *m.*
sacristy ['sækristi], *n.* sacristía.
sad [sæd], *a.* triste; pensativo; funesto; (*fig.*) travieso.
sadden [sædn], *v.t.* entristecer.
saddle [sædl], *n.* silla de montar; (*mec.*) silla.—*v.t.* ensillar; cargar.
saddle-bag ['sædlbæg], *n.* alforja.
sadism ['sædizm, 'seidizm], *n.* sadismo.
sadist ['sædist, 'seidist], *n.* sadista, *m.f.*
sadistic [sæ'distik], *a.* sadista.
sadness ['sædnis], *n.* tristeza.
safe [seif], *a.* seguro; incólume, salvo; intacto; cierto; digno de confianza; — ***and sound,*** sano y salvo.—*n.* caja fuerte *o* de caudales; alacena.
safe-conduct ['seif'kəndʌkt], *n.* salvoconducto.
safeguard ['seifgɑ:d], *n.* protección; precaución, *f.*—*v.t.* proteger.
safety ['seifti], *n.* seguridad; — ***belt,*** salvavidas, *m.sg.*; — ***catch,*** fiador, *m.*; — ***pin,*** imperdible, *m.*
safety-valve ['seiftivælv], *n.* válvula de seguridad.
saffron ['sæfrən], *a.* azafranado.—*n.* azafrán, *m.*
sag [sæg], *v.i.* ceder, doblegarse; flaquear.
saga ['sɑ:gə], *n.* saga; epopeya.
sagacious [sə'geiʃəs], *a.* sagaz; sutil.
sagacity [sə'gæsiti], *n.* sagacidad, *f.*
sage (1) [seidʒ], *a.* sabio; sagaz.—*n.* sabio.
sage (2) [seidʒ], *n.* (*bot.*) salvia.
said [sed], *a.* dicho; citado. [SAY].
sail [seil], *n.* vela; paseo en barco; aspa (*de molino*); ***under full —,*** a toda vela; ***to set —,*** hacerse a la vela; zarpar.—*v.t.* gobernar (*un barco*); navegar por.—*v.i.* navegar; zarpar; flotar.
sailcloth ['seilkloθ], *n.* lona.
sailing ['seiliŋ], *n.* navegación, *f.*; ***plain —,*** (*fig.*) progreso fácil.
sailing-boat ['seiliŋbout], *n.* barco de vela.
sailor ['seilə], *n.* marinero; (*mil.*) marino.
saint [seint], *a.* San, *m.*; Santo (*before male names beginning with Do- or To*)-; Santa; ***St. Bernard,*** perro de San Bernardo.—*n.* santo; santa; (*fig.*) ángel, *m.*
saintliness ['seintlinis], *n.* santidad, *f.*
sake [seik], *n.* causa; amor, *m.*; ***for the — of,*** por amor de; ***for your —,*** por Vd.; por su propio bien.
salacious [sə'leiʃəs], *a.* salaz.
salad ['sæləd], *n.* ensalada.
salad-bowl ['sælədboul], *n.* ensaladera.
salad-dressing ['sæləd'dresiŋ], *n.* mayonesa.
salaried ['sælərid], *a.* asalariado.
salary ['sæləri], *n.* salario, sueldo.
sale [seil], *n.* venta; subasta; demanda; ***for —, on —,*** de *o* en venta.
salesman ['seilzmən], *n.* dependiente (*de tienda*); viajante, *m.*
saleswoman ['seilzwumən], *n.* dependienta (*de tienda*).
salient ['seiljənt], *a.* saliente; conspicuo.—*n.* saliente, *m.*
saliva [sə'laivə], *n.* saliva.
sallow ['sælou], *a.* cetrino.
sallowness ['sælounis], *n.* amarillez, *f.*
sally ['sæli], *n.* salida.—*v.i.* hacer una salida.
salmon ['sæmən], *a.* (*also* **salmon-pink**) de color (*m.*) de salmón.—*n.* salmón, *m.*
saloon [sə'lu:n], *n.* sala; salón, *m.*; cámara (*de un vapor*); (*U.S.*) taberna.

salt [sɔ:lt], *a.* salado; salobre.—*n.* sal, *f.*; sabor, *m.*; ***old* —,** lobo de mar; **— *cellar*,** salero; ***he is not worth his* —,** no vale el pan que come; ***to take with a pinch of* —,** creer con cierta reserva.—*v.t.* salar; salpimentar.
saltpetre [sɔ:lt'pi:tə], *n.* salitre, *m.*
salty ['sɔ:lti], *a.* salado; salobre.
salubrious [sə'lju:briəs], *a.* salubre, saludable.
salutary ['sæljutəri], *a.* saludable.
salutation [sælju'teiʃən], *n.* salutación, *f.*, saludo.
salute [sə'lju:t], *n.* saludo; salva.—*v.t.*, *v.i.* saludar.
Salvador(i)an [sælvə'dɔ:r(i)ən], *a.*, *n.* salvadoreño.
salvage ['sælvidʒ], *n.* salvamento.—*v.t.* salvar.
salvation [sæl'veiʃən], *n.* salvación, *f.*
salve [sɑ:v, sælv], *n.* pomada; remedio.—*v.t.* curar; remediar; tranquilizar; salvar.
salver ['sælvə], *n.* bandeja.
Samaritan [sə'mæritn], *a.*, *n.* samaritano.
same [seim], *a.* mismo; idéntico; igual; ***much the* — *as*,** casi como; ***it is all the* — *to me*,** me es igual, me da lo mismo; ***all the* —,** sin embargo.
sameness ['seimnis], *n.* identidad, *f.*; parecido.
sample [sɑ:mpl], *n.* muestra.—*v.t.* probar.
sanatorium [sænə'tɔ:riəm], *n.* sanatorio.
sanctify ['sæŋktifai], *v.t.* santificar.
sanctimonious [sæŋkti'mounjəs], *a.* beato, mojigato.
sanction ['sæŋkʃən], *n.* sanción, *f.*—*v.t.* sancionar, autorizar.
sanctity ['sæŋktiti], *n.* santidad; inviolabilidad, *f.*
sanctuary ['sæŋktjuəri], *n.* santuario; asilo; ***to take* —,** acogerse a sagrado.
sand [sænd], *n.* arena; **— *dune*,** duna.—*pl.* playa.
sandal [sændl], *n.* sandalia; alpargata.
sandalwood ['sændlwud], *n.* sándalo.
sand-paper ['sændpeipə], *n.* papel (*m.*) de lija.
sand-pit ['sændpit], *n.* arenal, *m.*
sandstone ['sændstoun], *n.* arenisca.
sandwich ['sændwidʒ], *n.* sandwich, *m.*, bocadillo.—*v.t.* insertar.
sandy ['sændi], *a.* arenoso; rufo (*de pelo*).
sane [sein], *a.* cuerdo; prudente.
sang [sæŋ] [SING].
sanguinary ['sæŋgwinəri], *a.* sanguinario.
sanguine ['sæŋgwin], *a.* confiado, optimista; sanguíneo.
sanitary ['sænitəri], *a.* sanitario.
sanitation [sæni'teiʃən], *n.* higiene, *f.*; sanidad pública, *f.*; instalación sanitaria, *f.*
sanity ['sæniti], *n.* cordura; sentido común; prudencia.
Santa Claus ['sæntə'klɔ:z], *n.* Papá Noel, *m.*; los Reyes Magos.
sap (1) [sæp], *n.* savia; (*fam.*) necio.
sap (2) [sæp], *v.t.* zapar; (*fig.*) agotar, debilitar.
sapling ['sæpliŋ], *n.* árbol joven, *m.*
sapper ['sæpə], *n.* zapador, *m.*
sapphire ['sæfaiə], *n.* zafiro.—*a.* de color (*m.*) de zafiro.
sarcasm ['sɑ:kæzm], *n.* sarcasmo.
sarcastic [sɑ:'kæstik], *a.* sarcástico.
sardine [sɑ:'di:n], *n.* sardina.
sardonic [sɑ:'dɔnik], *a.* sardónico.
sash (1) [sæʃ], *n.* faja; cinturón, *m.*
sash (2) [sæʃ], *n.* marco (*de ventana*); **— *window*,** ventana de guillotina.
sat [sæt] [SIT].
Satan ['seitən], *n.* Satanás, *m.*
satanic [sə'tænik], *a.* satánico.
satchel ['sætʃəl], *n.* cartapacio; cartera.
sate [seit], *v.t.* hartar, saciar.
satellite ['sætəlait], *a.*, *n.* satélite, *m.*
satiate ['seiʃieit], *v.t.* hartar, saciar; satisfacer.
satiety [sə'taiəti], *n.* hartura, saciedad, *f.*
satin ['sætin], *n.* raso.
satiny ['sætini], *a.* arrasado.
satire ['sætaiə], *n.* sátira.
satirical [sə'tirikəl], *a.* satírico.
satirist ['sætirist], *n.* escritor (*m.*) satírico.
satirize ['sætiraiz], *v.t.* satirizar.
satisfaction [sætis'fækʃən], *n.* satisfacción, *f.*; contento; recompensa; pago (*de una deuda*).
satisfactory [sætis'fæktəri], *a.* satisfactorio; expiatorio.
satisfy ['sætisfai], *v.t.* satisfacer; convencer; pagar; apagar (*la sed*).
saturate ['sætʃəreit], *v.t.* saturar; (*fig.*) imbuir.
saturation [sætʃə'reiʃən], *n.* saturación, *f.*
Saturday ['sætədei], *n.* sábado.
satyr ['sætə], *n.* sátiro.
sauce [sɔ:s], *n.* salsa; compota; (*fam.*) insolencia.
sauce-boat ['sɔ:sbout], *n.* salsera.
saucepan ['sɔ:spən], *n.* cacerola.
saucer ['sɔ:sə], *n.* platillo; ***flying* —,** platillo volante.
saucy ['sɔ:si], *a.* respondón, impudente.
Saudi Arabia ['saudiə'reibjə], *n.* la Arabia Saudita.
saunter ['sɔ:ntə], *n.* paseo, vuelta.—*v.i.* vagar, pasearse.
sausage ['sɔsidʒ], *n.* salchicha; chorizo.
savage ['sævidʒ], *a.* salvaje; feroz; cruel.—*n.* salvaje, *m.f.*
savagery ['sævidʒri], *n.* salvajismo; ferocidad; crueldad, *f.*
save [seiv], *v.t.* salvar; ahorrar (*dinero*); conservar; evitar.—*v.i.* ahorrar.—*prep.* salvo, excepto.—*conj.* sino, a menos que.
saving ['seiviŋ], *a.* económico, frugal; calificativo.—*n.* ahorro; salvedad, *f.*—*pl.* ahorros; ***savings bank*,** caja de ahorros. —*prep.* salvo, excepto.
saviour ['seivjə], *n.* salvador, *m.*
savour ['seivə], *n.* sabor, *m.*, gusto, dejo.—*v.t.* saborear; sazonar.—*v.i.* saber, oler (***of***, a).
savoury ['seivəri], *a.* sabroso, apetitoso; agradable.—*n.* entremés salado.
saw (1) [sɔ:], *n.* (*carp.*) sierra.—*v.t.* aserrar. —*v.i.* usar una sierra.
saw (2) [sɔ:], *n.* refrán, *m.*
saw (3) [sɔ:] [SEE].
sawdust ['sɔ:dʌst], *n.* serrín, *m.*
sawmill ['sɔ:mil], *n.* molino de aserrar, aserradero.
Saxon ['sæksən], *a.*, *n.* sajón.
saxophone ['sæksəfoun], *n.* saxófono.
say [sei], *n.* ***to have a* — *in the matter*,** entrar en el asunto.—*v.t. irr.* decir; recitar; ***no sooner said than done*,** dicho y hecho. —*v.i.* decir; ***you don't* —!** ¿de veras? ***that is to* —,** es decir.

saying ['seiiŋ], *n.* dicho; refrán, *m.*, proverbio; ***as the — is*** o ***goes,*** como se dice.
scab [skæb], *n.* costra; escabro; (*fam.*) esquirol, *m.*
scabbard ['skæbəd], *n.* vaina.
scabby ['skæbi], *a.* costroso; roñoso; (*fig.*) despreciable.
scaffold ['skæfəld], *n.* andamio; cadalso.
scaffolding ['skæfəldiŋ], *n.* andamiaje, *m.*
scald [skɔ:ld], *n.* escaldadura.—*v.t.* escaldar.
scale (1) [skeil], *n.* platillo de balanza; (*math.*, *mus.*) escala; ***on a large —,*** en gran escala; ***on a small —,*** en pequeña escala; ***to —,*** a escala.—*pl.* balanza.—*v.t.* escalar; ***to — down,*** reducir.
scale (2) [skeil], *n.* (*zool.*) escama; laminita. —*v.t.* escamar.
scallop ['skɔləp], *n.* venera; (*sew.*) festón, *m.*
scalp [skælp], *n.* pericráneo; cuero cabelludo. —*v.t.* quitar la cabellera.
scalpel ['skælpəl], *n.* escalpelo.
scaly ['skeili], *a.* escamoso; incrustado.
scamp [skæmp], *n.* bribón, *m.*
scamper ['skæmpə], *v.i.* escaparse, escabullirse.
scan [skæn], *v.t.* escudriñar; escandir (*versos*).
scandal [skændl], *n.* escándalo; difamación, *f.*
scandalize ['skændəlaiz], *v.t.* escandalizar.
scandalous ['skændələs], *a.* escandaloso; vergonzoso; calumnioso.
Scandinavia [skændi'neivjə], *n.* Escandinavia.
Scandinavian [skændi'neivjən], *a.*, *n.* escandinavo.
scansion ['skænʃən], *n.* escansión, *f.*
scant [skænt], **scanty** ['skænti], *a.* escaso; insuficiente.
scapegoat ['skeipgout], *n.* cabeza de turco, víctima propiciatoria.
scar [skɑ:], *n.* cicatriz, *f.*—*v.t.* marcar con una cicatriz.
scarce [skɛəs], *a.* escaso; raro; ***to make oneself —,*** largarse.
scarcely ['skɛəsli], *adv.* apenas; no bien; con dificultad.
scarcity ['skɛəsiti], *n.* escasez, *f.*; rareza; carestía.
scare [skɛə], *n.* susto; alarma.—*v.t.* asustar; intimidar; ***to — away,*** ahuyentar.
scarecrow ['skɛəkrou], *n.* espantajo.
scarf [skɑ:f], *n.* bufanda; pañuelo.
scarlet ['skɑ:lit], *a.* de color escarlata.—*n.* escarlata; ***— fever,*** escarlatina.
scathing ['skeiðiŋ], *a.* mordaz, cáustico.
scatter ['skætə], *v.t.* esparcir; derramar; dispersar.—*v.i.* dispersarse; disiparse.
scatter-brained ['skætəbreind], *a.* atolondrado.
scattered ['skætəd], *a.* disperso.
scavenge ['skævindʒ], *v.t.* recoger la basura.
scavenger ['skævindʒə], *n.* basurero; animal (*m.*) que se alimenta de carroña.
scenario [si'nɑ:riou], *n.* escenario; guión, *m.*
scene [si:n], *n.* escena; vista; lugar, *m.*; escándalo; ***behind the scenes,*** entre bastidores; ***to come on the —,*** entrar en escena.
scene-painter ['si:npeintə], *n.* escenógrafo.
scenery ['si:nəri], *n.* decorado; paisaje, *m.*
scene-shifter ['si:nʃiftə], *n.* tramoyista, *m.f.*
scenic ['si:nik], *a.* escénico; pintoresco.
scent [sent], *n.* olor, *m.*; fragancia; perfume, *m.*; pista; ***to throw off the —,*** despistar.—*v.t.* husmear; perfumar; sospechar.
sceptic ['skeptik], *n.* escéptico.
sceptical ['skeptikəl], *a.* escéptico.
scepticism ['skeptisizm], *n.* escepticismo.
sceptre ['septə], *n.* cetro.
schedule ['ʃedju:l], *n.* lista; horario; programa, *m.*—*v.t.* inventariar; ***to be scheduled to*** o ***for,*** haber de, deber.
scheme [ski:m], *n.* plan, *m.*, proyecto; diagrama, *m.*; esquema, *m.*; ardid, *m.*; ***colour —,*** combinación (*f.*) de colores.—*v.i.* formar planes; intrigar.
schemer ['ski:mə], *n.* proyectista, *m.f.*; intrigante, *m.f.*
schism [sizm], *n.* cisma, *m.* o *f.*
scholar ['skɔlə], *n.* alumno; estudiante, *m.f.*; erudito; becario.
scholarly ['skɔləli], *a.* de estudiante; erudito.
scholarship ['skɔləʃip], *n.* erudición, *f.*; beca.
scholastic [skə'læstik], *a.* escolástico; pedantesco.
school [sku:l], *n.* escuela; colegio (*particular*); instituto (*del estado*); facultad, *f.*; departamento (*de universidad*); (*ichth.*) banco; ***boarding —,*** colegio de internos; ***— book,*** libro de clase; ***in —,*** en clase.—*v.t.* instruir, enseñar; disciplinar.
schoolboy ['sku:lbɔi], *n.* alumno.
schooling ['sku:liŋ], *n.* enseñanza, educación; formación, *f.*
schoolmaster ['sku:lmɑ:stə], *n.* maestro de escuela; profesor, *m.*
schoolmistress ['sku:lmistris], *n.* maestra; profesora.
schooner ['sku:nə], *n.* goleta; vaso, copa.
science ['saiəns], *n.* ciencia.
scientific [saiən'tifik], *a.* científico; sistemático.
scientist ['saiəntist], *n.* hombre (*m.*) de ciencia, científico.
scintillate ['sintileit], *v.i.* chispear, centellear.
scissors ['sizəz], *n.pl.* tijeras, *f.pl.*
scoff [skɔf], *n.* mofa, burla.—*v.i.* mofarse, burlarse (***at,*** de).
scoffer ['skɔfə], *n.* mofador, *m.*
scold [skould], *v.t.* reñir, reprender.
scolding ['skouldiŋ], *n.* regaño, reprensión, *f.*
scoop [sku:p], *n.* pala de mano; cucharón (*m.*) de draga; ganancia; reportaje sensacional, *m.*—*v.t.* sacar con pala *o* cuchara; vaciar; ganar; ***to — out,*** excavar.
scooter ['sku:tə], *n.* patinete (*de niño*); scúter, *m.*
scope [skoup], *n.* alcance, *m.*; esfera de acción; plan, *m.*
scorch [skɔ:tʃ], *v.t.* chamuscar; tostar; abrasar, agostar (*el sol*).
scorching ['skɔ:tʃiŋ], *a.* ardiente, abrasador; (*fig.*) mordaz.
score [skɔ:], *n.* muesca; (*sport*) tanteo; señal, *f.*; motivo; raya; veintena (*20*); (*mus.*) partitura; ***to pay off old scores,*** saldar cuentas viejas.—*v.t.* rayar, marcar; tachar; apuntar; (*mus.*) orquestar; (*sport*) ganar (*puntos*); marcar (*un gol*).—*v.i.* llevar ventaja (***over,*** a).
scorn [skɔ:n], *n.* desdén, *m.*, desprecio.—*v.t.* despreciar, desdeñar; burlarse de.
scornful ['skɔ:nful], *a.* desdeñoso.
scorpion ['skɔ:pjən], *n.* escorpión, *m.*
Scot [skɔt], *n.* escocés, *m.*

scotch [skɔtʃ], *n.* whisky, *m.*
Scotland ['skɔtlənd], *n.* Escocia.
Scots [skɔts], *a.* escocés.
Scotsman ['skɔtsmən] [SCOT].
Scotswoman ['skɔtswumən], *n.* escocesa.
Scottish ['skɔtiʃ] [SCOTS].
scoundrel ['skaundrəl], *n.* canalla, *m.*
scour [skauə], *v.t.*, *v.i.* fregar; limpiar; recorrer.
scourge [skə:dʒ], *n.* azote, *m.*; (*fig.*) plaga.—*v.t.* azotar; castigar.
scout [skaut], *n.* (*mil.*) explorador, *m.*—*v.i.* explorar, reconocer.
scowl [skaul], *n.* ceño.—*v.i.* ponerse ceñudo; ***to — at,*** mirar con ceño.
scowling ['skauliŋ], *a.* ceñudo.—*n.* ceño.
scraggy ['skrægi], *a.* descarnado, flaco.
scramble [skræmbl], *n.* trepa; contienda.—*v.t.* revolver (*huevos*).—*v.i.* trepar; andar a la rebatiña; ***scrambled eggs,*** huevos revueltos, *m.pl.*
scrap [skræp], *n.* pedacito; fragmento; riña, camorra.—*pl.* desperdicios; sobras.—*v.t.* echar a la basura.—*v.i.* reñise.
scrap-book ['skræpbuk], *n.* album (*m.*) de recortes.
scrape [skreip], *n.* acción *o* efecto *o* ruido de raspar; lío; dificultad, *f.*—*v.t.* raspar, rascar; restregar (*los pies*); ***to — together,*** amontonar poco a poco.—*v.i.* ***to — through,*** aprobar por milagro.
scratch [skrætʃ], *n.* arañazo, rasguño; borradura; línea de partida.—*v.t.* rascar; hacer un rasguño; arañar; cavar; retirar de una carrera.—*v.i.* arañar; retirarse.
scrawl [skrɔ:l], *n.* garabato.—*v.t.* garabatear.
scrawny ['skrɔ:ni], *a.* esquelético.
scream [skri:m], *n.* chillido.—*v.t.*, *v.i.* chillar, gritar.
screech [skri:tʃ], *n.* chillido.—*v.t.*, *v.i.* chillar.
screen [skri:n], *n.* biombo; mampara; (*eccl.*) cáncel, *m.*; pantalla (*de cine*); (*mil.*) cortina; abrigo.—*v.t.* abrigar; esconder; proteger; cribar; proyectar (*una película*).
screw [skru:], *n.* tornillo; rosca; (*aer.*, *naut.*) hélice, *f.*; (*fam.*) tacaño; (*fam.*) salario.—*v.t.* atornillar; oprimir; torcer; apretar.—*v.i.* dar vueltas; ***to — down,*** fijar con tornillo; ***to — in,*** atornillar; ***to — up,*** cerrar con tornillo; ***to — up one's courage,*** tomar coraje.
screwdriver ['skru:draivə], *n.* destornillador, *m.*
scribble [skribl], *n.* garrapatos, *m.pl.*—*v.t.* escribir de prisa.—*v.i.* garrapatear.
script [skript], *n.* escritura; letra cursiva; (*print.*) plumilla; texto; manuscrito; guión, *m.*
scriptural ['skriptʃərəl], *a.* bíblico.
Scripture ['skriptʃə], *n.* Sagrada Escritura.
scroll [skroul], *n.* rollo; voluta; rúbrica.
scrub [skrʌb], *n.* fregado; matorral, *m.*—*v.t.* fregar; restregar.
scrubbing ['skrʌbiŋ], *n.* fregado.
scrubbing-brush ['skrʌbiŋbrʌʃ], *n.* cepillo de fregar.
scruff [skrʌf], *n.* nuca.
scruffy ['skrʌfi], *a.* (*fam.*) desaliñado, ruin.
scrum [skrʌm], *n.* mêlée, *f.*
scruple [skru:pl], *n.* escrúpulo.—*v.i.* tener escrúpulos.
scrupulous ['skru:pjuləs], *a.* escrupuloso; temoroso; exacto.
scrupulousness ['skru:pjuləsnis], *n.* escrupulosidad; meticulosidad, *f.*
scrutineer [skru:ti'niə], *n.* escrutador, *m.*
scrutinize ['skru:tinaiz], *v.t.* escudriñar; escrutar.
scrutiny ['skru:tini], *n.* escrutinio.
scuffle [skʌfl], *n.* pelea, sarracina.—*v.i.* pelear, forcejear.
scull [skʌl], *n.* remo.—*v.t.* remar.
scullery ['skʌləri], *n.* fregadero, trascocina.
sculptor ['skʌlptə], *n.* escultor, *m.*
sculptress ['skʌlptris], *n.* escultora.
sculptural ['skʌlptʃərəl], *a.* escultural.
sculpture ['skʌlptʃə], *n.* escultura.—*v.t.* esculpir.
scum [skʌm], *n.* espuma; hez, *f.*; (*fig.*) canalla.
scurf [skə:f], *n.* caspa.
scurrility [skʌ'riliti], *n.* grosería.
scurrilous ['skʌriləs], *a.* grosero.
scurry ['skʌri], *n.* fuga precipitada; remolino.—*v.i.* escabullirse.
scurvy ['skə:vi], *a.* vil, ruin.—*n.* escorbuto.
scuttle (1) [skʌtl], *n.* escotillón, *m.*—*v.t.* (*naut.*) echar a pique.—*v.i.* apretar a correr, escabullirse.
scuttle (2) [skʌtl], *n.* fuga precipitada.
scuttle (3) [skʌtl], *n.* cubo.
scythe [saið], *n.* guadaña.—*v.t.* guadañar.
sea [si:], *n.* mar, *m.* o *f.*; (*fig.*) abundancia; ***— level,*** nivel (*m.*) del mar; ***— water,*** agua salada; ***at —,*** en el mar; (*fig.*) perplejo; ***high —,*** alta mar; ***to put to —,*** hacerse a la vela, zarpar.
seafarer ['si:fɛərə], *n.* marinero.
seafaring ['si:fɛəriŋ], *a.* marino.—*n.* vida del marinero.
sea-green ['si:'gri:n], *a.* verdemar.
seagull ['si:gʌl], *n.* gaviota.
sea-horse ['si:hɔ:s], *n.* caballo marino.
seal (1) [si:l], *n.* sello; timbre, *m.*—*v.t.* sellar; estampar; cerrar (*cartas*); confirmar; ***to — up,*** cerrar.
seal (2) [si:l], *n.* (*zool.*) foca.
sealing-wax ['si:liŋwæks], *n.* lacre, *m.*
sealskin ['si:lskin], *n.* piel (*f.*) de foca.
seam [si:m], *n.* costura; (*med.*) sutura; arruga; cicatriz, *f.*; (*geol.*, *min.*) filón, *m.*, veta, capa.
seaman ['si:mən], *n.* marinero.
seamanship ['si:mənʃip], *n.* náutica, marinería.
seamstress ['si:mstris], *n.* costurera.
séance ['seiã:ns], *n.* sesión (*f.*) de espiritistas.
seaplane ['si:plein], *n.* hidroavión, *m.*
seaport ['si:pɔ:t], *n.* puerto de mar.
sear [siə], *v.t.* chamuscar; cauterizar.
search [sə:tʃ], *n.* registro; busca; examen, *m.*—*v.t.* registrar; investigar.—*v.i.* buscar (*for*).
searching ['sə:tʃiŋ], *a.* penetrante, escrutador.
searchlight ['sə:tʃlait], *n.* reflector, *m.*
search-warrant ['sə:tʃwɔrənt], *n.* auto de registro.
sea-shore ['si:ʃɔ:], *n.* playa.
seasick ['si:sik], *a.* mareado; ***to be —,*** marearse.
seasickness ['si:siknis], *n.* mareo.

season [si:zn], *n.* estación (*del año*); sazón, *f.*; tiempo; temporada; — ***ticket,*** billete (*m.*) de abono; ***in —,*** en sazón; del tiempo; ***out of —,*** fuera de estación; ***close —,*** veda.—*v.t.* sazonar; acostumbrar; templar; imbuir.—*v.i.* madurarse.
seasonable ['si:znəbl], *a.* oportuno, tempestivo; de estación.
seasoning ['si:zniŋ], *n.* condimento; salsa; madurez; aclimatación, *f.*
seat [si:t], *n.* asiento; banco; silla; fondillos (*de los pantalones*), *m.pl.*; sitio, puesto; mansión; (*theat.*) localidad, *f.*; (*pol.*) escaño; ***to hold a — in Parliament,*** ser diputado a Cortes.—*v.t.* sentar; tener asientos para.
sea-wall ['si:wɔ:l], *n.* dique, *m.*
seaweed ['si:wi:d], *n.* alga marina.
seaworthy ['si:wə:ði], *a.* en buen estado.
secede [si'si:d], *v.i.* separarse.
secession [si'seʃən], *n.* secesión, *f.*
secessionist [si'seʃənist], *n.* separatista, *m.f.*, secesionista, *m.f.*
secluded [si'klu:did], *a.* apartado, solitario.
seclusion [si'klu:ʒən], *n.* reclusión, *f.*; apartamiento; soledad, *f.*
second ['sekənd], *a.* segundo; inferior; igual, otro; — ***class*** o ***rate,*** de segunda clase; — ***lieutenant,*** alférez, *m.*; — ***sight,*** doble vista; — ***to none,*** inferior a nadie; ***on — thoughts,*** después de pensarlo bien; — ***fiddle,*** papel secundario; — ***nature,*** otra naturaleza; ***to come off — best,*** llevar lo peor.—*n.* segundo; dos (*en las fechas*), *m.*; padrino; (*mus.*) segunda; momento.—*pl.* mercancías (*f.pl.*) de calidad inferior.—*v.t.* apoyar; secundar; ayudar.
secondary ['sekəndri], *a.* secundario; subordinado; accesorio.
second-hand ['sekənd'hænd], *a.*, *adv.* de segunda mano.
secondly ['sekəndli], *adv.* en segundo lugar.
secrecy ['si:krəsi], *n.* secreto, reserva; misterio.
secret ['si:krit], *a.*, *n.* secreto; — ***service,*** servicio de espionaje.
secretarial [sekrə'tɛəriəl], *a.* de secretario.
secretariat [sekrə'tɛəriət], *n.* secretaría.
secretary ['sekrətəri], *n.* secretario; secretaria; (*pol.*) ministro.
secrete [si'kri:t], *v.t.* esconder, ocultar; (*med.*) secretar.
secretion [si'kri:ʃən], *n.* escondimiento; (*anat.*) secreción, *f.*
secretive [si'kri:tiv], *a.* callado, reservado.
sect [sekt], *n.* secta.
sectarian [sek'tɛəriən], *a.*, *n.* sectario.
section ['sekʃən], *n.* sección; porción; subdivisión, *f.*; (*mil.*) pelotón, *m.*
sectional ['sekʃənəl], *a.* seccionario; hecho de secciones.
sector ['sektə], *n.* sector, *m.*
secular ['sekjulə], *a.* seglar, profano.
secularize ['sekjuləraiz], *v.t.* secularizar.
secure [si'kjuə], *a.* seguro; cierto; firme.—*v.t.* asegurar; adquirir.
security [si'kjuəriti], *n.* seguridad, *f.*; fiador, *m.*; ***to stand — for,*** salir fiador por.—*pl.* (*com.*) valores, *m.pl.*, títulos, *m.pl.*
sedate [si'deit], *a.* formal, serio; sosegado.
sedative ['sedətiv], *a.*, *n.* sedativo.
sedentary ['sedəntəri], *a.* sedentario.
sediment ['sedimənt], *n.* sedimento.
sedimentary [sedi'mentəri], *a.* sedimentario.
sedition [si'diʃən], *n.* sedición, *f.*
seditious [si'diʃəs], *a.* sedicioso.
seduce [si'dju:s], *v.t.* seducir.
seducer [si'dju:sə], *n.* seductor, *m.*
seduction [si'dʌkʃən], *n.* seducción, *f.*
seductive [si'dʌktiv], *a.* seductivo; persuasivo.
sedulous ['sedjuləs], *a.* asiduo.
see (1) [si:], *n.* sede, *f.*; ***Holy See,*** Santa Sede.
see (2) [si:], *v.t.*, *v.i. irr.* ver; mirar; comprender; visitar; recibir visitas; acompañar; ***to — about,*** hacerse cargo de; ***to — into,*** examinar a fondo; ***to — the point,*** caer en la cuenta; ***let's —,*** vamos a ver; ***to — the sights,*** visitar los monumentos; — ***you tomorrow,*** hasta mañana.
seed [si:d], *n.* semilla, simiente, *f.*; pepita (*de fruta*); (*fig.*) germen, *m.*; progenie, *f.*; ***to run to —,*** granar.—*v.t.* sembrar; despepitar.—*v.i.* granar.
seedy ['si:di], *a.* granado; (*fam.*) andrajoso; indispuesto.
seeing ['si:iŋ], *n.* vista; visión, *f.*; — ***is believing,*** ver y creer.—*conj.* — ***that,*** visto que.
seek [si:k], *v.t. irr.* buscar; procurar; pretender, solicitar; pedir; ***to — after*** o ***for,*** buscar; ***to — out,*** buscar por todos lados.
seem [si:m], *v.i.* parecer.
seeming ['si:miŋ], *a.* aparente.
seemingly ['si:miŋli], *adv.* al parecer.
seemliness ['si:mlinis], *n.* decoro.
seemly ['si:mli], *a.* decente, decoroso.
seen [si:n] [SEE].
seep [si:p], *v.i.* rezumarse.
seer [siə], *n.* profeta, *m.*; vidente; veedor, *m.*
seesaw ['si:sɔ:], *n.* columpio (*de niños*); vaivén, *m.*—*v.i.* balancear; columpiarse.
seethe [si:ð], *v.i.* hervir; (*fig.*) bullir.
segment ['segmənt], *n.* segmento.
segregate ['segrigeit], *v.t.* segregar.—*v.i.* -se.
segregation [segri'geiʃən], *n.* segregación, *f.*
seize [si:z], *v.t.* asir, coger; (*jur.*) secuestrar; prender; apoderarse de; (*fig.*) comprender; ***to — up,*** (*mech.*) atascarse.
seizure ['si:ʒə], *n.* asimiento; captura; (*med.*) ataque, *m.*; (*jur.*) secuestro.
seldom ['seldəm], *adv.* rara vez.
select [si'lekt], *a.* selecto, escogido; exclusivo.—*v.t.* escoger.
selection [si'lekʃən], *n.* selección, *f.*; ***to make a —,*** escoger.
selective [si'lektiv], *a.* selectivo.
self [self], *a.* mismo; propio.—*n.* (*pl.* **selves**) personalidad, *f.*; el yo.—*pron.* se, sí mismo.
self-acting ['self'æktiŋ], *a.* automático.
self-centred ['self'sentəd], *a.* egocéntrico.
self-confidence ['self'kɔnfidəns], *n.* confianza en sí mismo.
self-conscious ['self'kɔnʃəs], *a.* apocado.
self-consciousness ['self'kɔnʃəsnis], *n.* timidez, *f.*
self-contained ['selfkən'teind], *a.* reservado; completo; independiente.
self-control ['selfkən'troul], *n.* dominio de sí mismo.
self-defence ['selfdi'fens], *n.* defensa propia.
self-denial ['selfdi'naiəl], *n.* abnegación, *f.*
self-esteem ['selfes'ti:m], *n.* amor propio.
self-evident ['self'evidənt], *a.* patente.

self-government ['self'gʌvənmənt], *n.* autonomía.
self-importance ['selfim'pɔ:təns], *n.* altivez, *f.*, orgullo.
self-interest ['self'intərəst], *n.* propio interés.
selfish ['selfiʃ], *a.* interesado, egoísta.
selfishness ['selfiʃnis], *n.* egoísmo.
selfless ['selflis], *a.* desinteresado.
self-love ['self'lʌv], *n.* amor propio.
self-made ['self'meid], *a.* levantado por sus propios esfuerzos.
self-portrait ['self'pɔ:treit], *n.* autorretrato.
self-preservation ['selfprezə'veiʃən], *n.* defensa de sí mismo.
self-reliant ['selfri'laiənt], *a.* confiado en sí mismo.
self-respect ['selfri'spekt], *n.* respecto de sí mismo; dignidad, *f.*
self-sacrifice ['self'sækrifais], *n.* abnegación, *f.*
self-satisfied ['self'sætisfaid], *a.* satisfecho de sí mismo.
self-starter ['self'stɑ:tə], *n.* arranque automático.
self-styled ['self'staild], *a.* que se llama a sí mismo.
self-sufficient ['selfsə'fiʃənt], *a.* que basta a sí mismo.
self-supporting ['selfsə'pɔ:tiŋ], *a.* independiente.
sell [sel], *v.t.*, *v.i. irr.* vender; ***to — for cash,*** vender al contado; ***to — off,*** saldar; ***to — on credit,*** vender al fiado.
seller ['selə], *n.* vendedor, *m.*
selves [selvz] [SELF].
semaphore ['seməfɔ:], *n.* semáforo.
semblance ['sembləns], *n.* apariencia; máscara.
semen ['si:men], *n.* semen, *m.*
semi- ['semi], *prefix.* semi; medio.
semicircle ['semisə:kl], *n.* semicírculo.
semicircular [semi'sə:kjulə], *a.* semicircular.
semicolon ['semikoulən], *n.* punto y coma.
seminar ['seminɑ:], *n.* seminario.
seminary ['seminəri], *n.* seminario; colegio.
semiquaver ['semikweivə], *n.* semicorchea.
Semitic [si'mitik], *a.* semítico.
semitone ['semitoun], *n.* semitono.
senate ['senit], *n.* senado.
senator ['senətə], *n.* senador, *m.*
send [send], *v.t. irr.* enviar, mandar; remitir; arrojar; conceder; infligir; volver (*loco*, *etc.*); ***to — away,*** despedir; ***to — back,*** devolver, mandar volver; ***to — down,*** hacer bajar; (*fam.*) suspender; ***to — for,*** enviar a buscar; ***to — in,*** hacer entrar; introducir; ***to — off,*** expedir; despedir; ***to — out,*** hacer salir; enviar; emitir; ***to — up,*** hacer subir; lanzar; (*fam.*) parodiar; (*fam.*) enviar a la cárcel; ***to — word,*** mandar aviso.
sender ['sendə], *n.* remitente, *m.f.*
send-off ['sendɔf], *n.* despedida.
senile ['si:nail], *a.* senil.
senility [si'niliti], *n.* senilidad, *f.*
senior ['si:njə], *a.* mayor, de mayor edad; superior en grado; más antiguo; padre.
seniority [si:ni'ɔriti], *n.* ancianidad, *f.*; precedencia.
sensation [sen'seiʃən], *n.* sensación, *f.*
sensational [sen'seiʃənl], *a.* sensacional.
sense [sens], *n.* sentido; juicio; ***to be out of one's senses,*** haber perdido el juicio; ***common —,*** sentido común; ***to come to one's senses,*** volver en sí; recobrar el sentido común.
senseless ['senslis], *a.* sin sentido; disparatado, absurdo.
sensibility [sensi'biliti], *n.* sensibilidad, *f.*
sensible ['sensibl], *a.* cuerdo, sensato; sensible; consciente (de); perceptible.
sensitive ['sensitiv], *a.* sensitivo; sensible; impresionable; delicado.
sensitivity [sensi'tiviti], *n.* sensibilidad, *f.*; delicadeza.
sensitize ['sensitaiz], *v.t.* sensibilizar.
sensory ['sensəri], *a.* sensorio.
sensual ['sensjuəl], *a.* sensual; voluptuoso.
sensualism ['sensjuəlizm], *n.* sensualismo.
sensualist ['sensjuəlist], *n.* sensualista, *m.f.*
sensuality [sensju'æliti], *n.* sensualidad, *f.*
sensuous ['sensjuəs], *a.* sensorio.
sensuousness ['sensjuəsnis], *n.* sensualidad, *f.*
sent [sent] [SEND].
sentence ['sentəns], *n.* (*gram.*) frase, oración, *f.*; (*jur.*) sentencia; máxima.—*v.t.* sentenciar, condenar.
sententious [sen'tenʃəs], *a.* sentencioso.
sentient ['senʃənt], *a.* sensible.
sentiment ['sentimənt], *n.* sentimiento; opinión, *f.*
sentimental [senti'mentl], *a.* sentimental; tierno.
sentimentality [sentimen'tæliti], *n.* sentimentalismo; sensiblería.
sentinel ['sentinl], **sentry** ['sentri], *n.* centinela, *m.f.*
sentry-box ['sentribɔks], *n.* garita de centinela.
separable ['sepərəbl], *a.* separable.
separate ['sepərit], *a.* separado, distinto; segregado.—['sepəreit], *v.t.* separar, dividir. —*v.i.* separarse.
separation [sepə'reiʃən], *n.* separación, *f.*
separatist ['sepərətist], *a.*, *n.* separatista, *m.f.*
sepia ['si:pjə], *n.* sepia.
September [səp'tembə], *n.* se(p)tiembre, *m.*
septic ['septik], *a.* séptico.
sepulchral [si'pʌlkrəl], *a.* sepulcral.
sepulchre ['sepəlkə], *n.* sepulcro.
sequel ['si:kwəl], *n.* resultado; consecuencia; continuación, *f.*
sequence ['si:kwəns], *n.* serie; sucesión, *f.*; consecuencia.
sequestered [si'kwestəd], *a.* aislado, remoto.
sequin ['si:kwin], *n.* lentejuela.
seraph ['serəf], *n.* serafín, *m.*
seraphic [sə'ræfik], *a.* seráfico.
serenade [seri'neid], *n.* serenata.—*v.t.* dar una serenata.
serene [si'ri:n], *a.* sereno.
serenity [si'reniti], *n.* serenidad, *f.*
serf [sə:f], *n.* siervo.
serfdom ['sə:fdəm], *n.* servidumbre, *f.*
serge [sə:dʒ], *n.* estameña.
sergeant ['sɑ:dʒənt], *n.* sargento.
sergeant-major ['sɑ:dʒənt'meidʒə], *n.* sargento instructor.
serial ['siəriəl], *a.* de *o* en serie; por entregas. —*n.* novela por entregas; drama por episodios.
series ['siəri:z], *n.* serie, *f.*
serious ['siəriəs], *a.* serio; grave; sincero; importante.

seriously ['siəriəsli], *adv.* ***to take* —,** tomar en serio.
seriousness ['siəriəsnis], *n.* seriedad; gravedad, *f.*
sermon ['sə:mən], *n.* sermón, *m.*
sermonize ['sə:mənaiz], *v.t., v.i.* predicar, sermonear.
serpent ['sə:pənt], *n.* serpiente, *f.*; (*mus.*) serpentón, *m.*
serrated [se'reitid], *a.* dentellado; serrado.
serried ['serid], *a.* apretado, apiñado.
serum ['siərəm], *n.* suero.
servant ['sə:vənt], *n.* criado; criada; servidor, *m.*; empleado.
serve [sə:v], *v.t.* servir; ser útil a; manejar; (*jur.*) entregar (*una citación etc.*); cumplir (*una condena*); tratar.—*v.i.* servir (*as*, de); bastar; ***to* — *for*,** servir para; ***to* — *time*,** cumplir una condena; ***to* — *one's time*,** terminar el aprendizaje; ***to* — *one's turn*,** bastar; ***it serves you right*,** lo tienes merecido.
server ['sə:və], *n.* servidor, *m.*; (*eccl.*) acólito; bandeja.
service ['sə:vis], *n.* servicio; servicio de mesa; (*eccl.*) oficio; (*sport*) saque, *m.*; ***at your* —,** a la disposición de Vd.; ***out of* —,** desacomodado, 'no funciona'; ***to be of* — *to*,** ser útil a; ***coffee* —,** juego de café; ***diplomatic* —,** cuerpo diplomático; ***on active* —,** en acto de servicio; en el campo de batalla.
serviceable ['sə:visəbl], *a.* servible, útil; duradero; servicial.
service-station ['sə:vissteiʃən], *n.* (estación) gasolinera.
servile ['sə:vail], *a.* servil; adulador.
servility [sə:'viliti], *n.* servilismo.
serving ['sə:viŋ], *a.* sirviente.
serving-maid ['sə:viŋmeid], *n.* criada.
servitude ['sə:vitju:d], *n.* servidumbre, esclavitud, *f.*; ***penal* —,** trabajos forzados.
session ['seʃən], *n.* sesión, *f.*; junta; curso académico; ***petty sessions*,** tribunal (*m.*) de primera instancia.
set [set], *a.* obstinado, terco; establecido, prescrito; ajustado; inmóvil, fijo; engastado; forzado.—*n.* aparato (*de radio*); (*theat.*) decoración, *f.*; juego; clase, colección, *f.*; grupo; posición, *f.*; movimiento; tendencia; porte, *m.*; triscamiento (*de una sierra*); juego (*de herramientas etc.*); inclinación, *f.*; partido (*de tenis*).—*v.t. irr.* fijar; poner; plantar; establecer, instalar; preparar; (*print.*) componer; engastar, montar (*joyas*); (*mus.*) poner en música; (*med.*) reducir; encasar (*un hueso roto*); (*naut.*) desplegar (*velas*); tender (*lazos*); regular (*un reloj*).—*v.i.* ponerse (*el sol*); cuajarse (*un liquido*); fluir (*una corriente*); ***to* — *about doing something*,** ponerse a hacer una cosa; ***to* — *about each other*,** venir a las manos; ***to* — *against*,** oponer; ***to be* — *against*,** detestar; ***to* — *aside*,** poner a un lado; abrogar; ***to* — *at*,** estimar en; ***to* — *at rest*,** poner en reposo; ***to* — *back*,** hacer retroceder; ***to* — *before*,** presentar; ***to* — *down*,** imputar; poner por tierra; poner por escrito; ***to* — *fire to*,** pegar fuego a; ***to* — *forth*,** exponer; avanzar; ponerse en camino; ***to* — *free*,** poner en libertad; ***to* — *in motion*,** poner en movimiento; ***to* — *off*,** adornar; poner en relieve; salir; ***to* — *one's heart on*,** tener ilusión por; ***to* — *one's teeth on edge*,** dar dentera; ***to* — *out*,** ponerse en camino; hacer ver; ***to* — *to rights*,** rectificar; ***to* — *on*,** atacar; ***to* — *to work*,** poner(se) a; trabajar; ***to* — *up*,** exaltar; fundar; establecerse; montar; ***to* — *upon*,** asaltar.
setback ['setbæk], *n.* revés, *m.*, contrariedad, *f.*
settee [se'ti:], *n.* canapé, sofá, *m.*
setting ['setiŋ], *n.* fondo; puesta (*del sol*); engaste (*de joyas*); (*naut.*) dirección, *f.*; fraguado (*del cemento*); (*theat.*) decorado; (*mus.*) arreglo; marco; aliño (*de huesos*).
settle [setl], *v.t.* colocar; establecer; sosegar; poblar, colonizar; poner fin a; clarificar; resolver; afirmar, asegurar; saldar; satisfacer; arreglar; ***to* — *accounts*,** ajustar cuentas; ***to* — *on*,** escoger; señalar (*una pensión etc.*).—*v.i.* establecerse; calmarse; hacer sedimento; decidirse; clarificarse; ***to* — *down*,** establecerse; calmarse; asentarse; ponerse (***to***, a).
settled [setld], *a.* fijo; establecido; determinado; poblado; sereno.
settlement ['setlmənt], *n.* establecimiento; colonia; colonización, *f.*; ajuste, *m.*; solución, *f.*; (*com.*) saldo, liquidación, *f.*; (*jur.*) dote, *m.*; traspaso.
settler ['setlə], *n.* colono.
seven [sevn], *a., n.* siete, *m.*
seventeen [sevn'ti:n], *a., n.* diecisiete, diez y siete, *m.*
seventeenth [sevn'ti:nθ], *a., n.* décimoséptimo; diez y siete (*en las fechas*), *m.*
seventh [sevnθ], *a.* séptimo.—*n.* séptimo; séptima parte; siete (*en las fechas*), *m.*; (*mus.*) séptima.
seventieth ['sevntiəθ], *a., n.* septuagésimo.
seventy ['sevnti], *a., n.* setenta, *m.*
sever ['sevə], *v.t.* separar; romper.
several ['sevərəl], *a.* varios; distinto respectivo.
severance ['sevərəns], *n.* separación, *f.*
severe [si'viə], *a.* severo; riguroso; duro; austero; fuerte; grave.
severity [si'veriti], *n.* severidad; gravedad, *f.*; inclemencia (*del tiempo*).
sew [sou], *v.t., v.i. irr.* coser.
sewage ['sju:idʒ], *n.* aguas (*f.pl.*) de albañal; alcantarillado.
sewer [sjuə], *n.* albañal, *m.*, alcantarilla, cloaca.
sewing ['souiŋ], *n.* costura.
sewing-machine ['souiŋmə'ʃi:n], *n.* máquina de coser.
sex [seks], *n.* sexo; ***the fair* —,** el bello sexo.
sexless ['sekslis], *a.* neutro; frío.
sexton ['sekstən], *n.* sacristán, *m.*; sepulturero.
sexual ['seksjuəl], *a.* sexual.
sexuality [seksju'æliti], *n.* sexualidad, *f.*
shabby ['ʃæbi], *a.* raído; andrajoso; pobre; ruin; mezquino.
shack [ʃæk], *n.* choza.
shackle [ʃækl], *n.* grillo, esposa; traba.—*v.t.* encadenar, poner esposas; estorbar.
shade [ʃeid], *n.* sombra; matiz, *m.*; pantalla (*de lámpara*); visera; espectro; toldo.—*v.t.* sombrear; esfumar; amparar.
shading ['ʃeidiŋ], *n.* sombreado, degradación, *f.*

shadow [ˈʃædou], *n.* sombra; (*art*) toque (*m.*) de obscuro.—*v.t.* obscurecer, sombrear; seguir de cerca.
shadowy [ˈʃædoui], *a.* umbroso; vago.
shady [ˈʃeidi], *a.* sombreado; sombrío; (*fig.*) sospechoso.
shaft [ʃɑːft], *n.* flecha; asta, mango (*de un arma etc.*); (*mech.*) eje, *m.*; vara (*de un carro*); pozo (*de mina, de ascensor*); rayo (*de luz*).
shaggy [ˈʃægi], *a.* velludo, peludo; lanudo.
shake [ʃeik], *n.* meneo; sacudida; apretón (*m.*) de manos; temblor; (*fam.*) periquete, *m.* —*v.t. irr.* sacudir; menear; agitar; hacer temblar; desalentar; debilitar; estrechar (*la mano*); ***to — one's head,*** mover la cabeza; ***to — off,*** librarse de; sacudir; despistar; ***to — up,*** sacudir, remover.—*v.i.* estremecerse; trepidar; dar un apretón de manos.
shaking [ˈʃeikiŋ], *a.* tembloroso.—*n.* sacudimiento; meneo; temblor, *m.*
shaky [ˈʃeiki], *a.* trémulo; poco firme; dudoso.
shall [ʃæl], *v.i. aux. irr.* tener que; (*when it simply indicates the future, the future tense is used in Spanish*).
shallow [ˈʃælou], *a.* somero, poco profundo; (*fig.*) superficial.—*n.* bajío.
sham [ʃæm], *a.* fingido; falso.—*n.* impostura, farsa.—*v.t., v.i.* simular, fingir.
shamble [ʃæmbl], *n.* paso pesado y lento.—*pl.* matadero; (*fig.*) carnicería.—*v.i.* andar arrastrando los pies.
shambling [ˈʃæmbliŋ], *a.* pesado, lento.
shame [ʃeim], *n.* vergüenza; ignominia; afrenta; lástima; ***to put to —,*** avergonzar.—*v.t.* avergonzar; afrentar.
shamefaced [ˈʃeimˈfeist], *a.* tímido, vergonzoso; avergonzado.
shameful [ˈʃeimful], *a.* vergonzoso, escandaloso; indecente.
shameless [ˈʃeimlis], *a.* desvergonzado; indecente.
shamelessness [ˈʃeimlisnis], *n.* desvergüenza; impudicia.
shampoo [ʃæmˈpuː], *n.* champú, *m.*—*v.t.* dar un champú a.
shamrock [ˈʃæmrɔk], *n.* trébol blanco.
shank [ʃæŋk], *n.* zanca; (*mech.*) asta.
shape [ʃeip], *n.* forma; bulto; talle; molde; fantasma, *m.*; ***to put into —,*** dar forma a. —*v.t.* formar, dar forma; ordenar; modificar; concebir; tallar.
shapeless [ˈʃeiplis], *a.* informe; disforme.
shapelessness [ˈʃeiplisnis], *n.* informidad; deformidad, *f.*
shapely [ˈʃeipli], *a.* simétrico; bien formado.
share (1) [ʃɛə], *n.* parte, porción, *f.*; cuota; (*com.*) acción, *f.*; interés, *m.*—*v.t.* dividir; compartir; tomar parte en; distribuir; ***to — out,*** repartir.—*v.i.* participar; tomar parte (en).
share (2) [ʃɛə], *n.* reja (*del arado*).
shareholder [ˈʃɛəhouldə], *n.* accionista, *m.f.*
shark [ʃɑːk], *n.* tiburón; (*fam.*) caimán, *m.*
sharp [ʃɑːp], *a.* agudo; astuto; vivo; cortante; repentino; afilado; penetrante; áspero; picante; mordaz; fino (*de oído*); severo; violento; listo; bien definido; (*mus.*) sostenido.—*adv.* en punto; puntualmente.—*n.* (*mus.*) sostenido.
sharp-edged [ˈʃɑːpˈedʒd], *a.* aguzado.
sharpen [ˈʃɑːpən], *v.t.* afilar; aguzar; amolar.
sharpener [ˈʃɑːpənə], *n.* amolador, afilador, *m.*; ***pencil —,*** cortalápiz, *m.*; ***knife —,*** chaira.
sharper [ˈʃɑːpə], *n.* fullero; timador, *m.*
sharp-eyed [ˈʃɑːpˈaid], *a.* de vista penetrante.
sharp-featured [ˈʃɑːpˈfiːtʃəd], *a.* cariaguileño.
sharpness [ˈʃɑːpnis], *n.* agudeza; aspereza.
sharp-witted [ˈʃɑːpˈwitid], *a.* perspicaz.
shatter [ˈʃætə], *v.t.* hacer pedazos; romper; frustrar (*esperanzas*).—*v.i.* hacerse pedazos; romperse.
shave [ʃeiv], *n.* afeitada; ***to have a close —,*** (*fig.*) escapar por un pelo.—*v.t.* afeitar; acepillar; rozar.—*v.i.* afeitarse.
shaving [ˈʃeiviŋ], *n.* afeitada; acepilladura.
shaving-brush [ˈʃeiviŋbrʌʃ], *n.* brocha de afeitar.
shaving-soap [ˈʃeiviŋsoup], *n.* jabón (*m.*) de afeitar.
shawl [ʃɔːl], *n.* chal, *m.*
she [ʃiː], *pron.* ella; la; hembra.
sheaf [ʃiːf], *n.* (*pl.* **sheaves**) gavilla; haz (*de flechas*), *m.*; lío, paquete (*de papeles*), *m.*
shear [ʃiə], *v.t. irr.* tonsurar; esquilar (*ovejas*); cortar; tundir (*tela*).
shears [ʃiəz], *n.* tijeras grandes, *f.pl.*; (*mech.*) cizallas, *f.pl.*
sheath [ʃiːθ], *n.* vaina.
sheathe [ʃiːð], *v.t.* envainar; (*naut.*) aforrar.
sheaves [ʃiːvz] [SHEAF].
she-cat [ˈʃiːkæt], *n.* gata.
she-devil [ˈʃiːdevil], *n.* diabla.
shed (1) [ʃed], *n.* cabaña; cobertizo.
shed (2) [ʃed], *v.t. irr.* quitarse *or* desprenderse de; mudar, derramar.
sheen [ʃiːn], *n.* brillo, lustre, *m.*
sheep [ʃiːp], *n.* (*pl.* **sheep**) oveja; carnero; ***black —,*** (*fig.*) garbanzo negro; ***to make sheep's eyes at,*** lanzar miradas de carnero degollado.
sheep-dip [ˈʃiːpdip], *n.* desinfectante (*m.*) para ganado.
sheep-dog [ˈʃiːpdɔg], *n.* perro de pastor.
sheepfold [ˈʃiːpfould], *n.* majada.
sheepish [ˈʃiːpiʃ], *a.* vergonzoso, tímido.
sheep-shearing [ˈʃiːpˈʃiəriŋ], *n.* esquileo.
sheer (1) [ʃiə], *a.* puro; transparente; acantilado.—*adv.* de un golpe; a pico.
sheer (2) [ʃiə], *v.t., v.i.* desviar.
sheet [ʃiːt], *n.* hoja, plancha; sábana; mortaja; extensión (*de agua*), *f.*; (*naut.*) escota; ***— anchor,*** ancla de la esperanza.
sheikh [ʃeik], *n.* jeque, *m.*
shekel [ʃekl], *n.* siclo; (*fam.*) cuarto.
shelf [ʃelf], *n.* (*pl.* **shelves**) anaquel, estante, *m.*; banco de arena; ***to be left on the —,*** (*fig.*) quedarse para tía.
shell [ʃel], *n.* casco; cáscara; concha; coraza; caparazón, *m.*; cubierta; (*mil.*) granada; ***tortoise —,*** carey, *m.*—*v.t.* desvainar; descascarar; (*mil.*) bombardear.
shellfish [ˈʃelfiʃ], *n.* marisco.
shelling [ˈʃeliŋ], *n.* bombardeo.
shelter [ˈʃeltə], *n.* amparo, abrigo; asilo; refugio.—*v.t.* abrigar; amparar; ocultar.—*v.i.* refugiarse, abrigarse.
sheltered [ˈʃeltəd], *a.* abrigado; retirado.
shelve (1) [ʃelv], *v.t.* poner sobre un estante; proveer de estantes; (*fig.*) aplazar indefinidamente.
shelve (2) [ʃelv], *v.i.* inclinarse.

shelves [ʃelvz] [SHELF].
shelving [ˈʃelviŋ], *a.* inclinado, en declive.—*n.* estantería; declive, *m.*
shepherd [ˈʃepəd], *n.* pastor, *m.*—*v.t.* guiar.
shepherdess [ˈʃepədis], *n.* pastora.
sherry [ˈʃeri], *n.* vino de Jerez.
shield [ʃi:ld], *n.* escudo; (*fig.*) amparo, defensa.—*v.t.* amparar.
shield-bearer [ˈʃi:ldbɛərə], *n.* escudero.
shift [ʃift], *n.* cambio; expediente, *m.*; artificio; camisa; tanda, turno (*de obreros*).—*v.t.* trasladar; mover; quitar.—*v.i.* moverse; cambiar(se); variar.
shiftless [ˈʃiftlis], *a.* incapaz; perezoso.
shifty [ˈʃifti], *a.* astuto; falso; furtivo.
shilling [ˈʃiliŋ], *n.* chelín, *m.*
shimmer [ˈʃimə], *n.* luz trémula; resplandor, *m.*—*v.i.* rielar.
shin [ʃin], *n.* espinilla.—*v.t.* ***to — up,*** trepar.
shine [ʃain], *n.* brillo.—*v.t. irr.* pulir; dar lustre a (*los zapatos*).—*v.i.* relucir, resplandecer, brillar; distinguirse.
shining [ˈʃainiŋ], *a.* brillante, radiante, resplandeciente.
shiny [ˈʃaini], *a.* brillante, lustroso.
ship [ʃip], *n.* buque, *m.*, barco.—*v.t.* embarcar; (*com.*) expedir; armar (*remos etc.*).
shipbuilder [ˈʃipbildə], *n.* constructor (*m.*) de buques.
shipbuilding [ˈʃipbildiŋ], *n.* construcción naval, *f.*
shipment [ˈʃipmənt], *n.* embarque, *m.*; remesa.
shipper [ˈʃipə], *n.* remitente; importador; exportador, *m.*
shipping [ˈʃipiŋ], *n.* barcos, buques, *m.pl.*; (*com.*) embarque, *m.*
shipshape [ˈʃipʃeip], *a.* en buen orden; bien arreglado.
shipwreck [ˈʃiprek], *n.* naufragio.—*v.t.* hacer naufragar; ***to be shipwrecked,*** naufragar.
shipyard [ˈʃipjɑ:d], *n.* astillero.
shire [ʃaiə], *n.* condado.
shirk [ʃə:k], *v.t.* evitar, esquivar; faltar a.
shirt [ʃə:t], *n.* camisa; ***in one's shirt-sleeves,*** en mangas de camisa.
shirt-front [ˈʃə:tfrʌnt], *n.* pechera.
shiver [ˈʃivə], *n.* estremecimiento, escalofrío; fragmento.—*v.t.* romper, hacer pedazos.—*v.i.* tiritar, temblar.
shivery [ˈʃivəri], *a.* tembloroso; friolero.
shoal [ʃoul], *n.* banco (*de arena, de peces*); muchedumbre, *f.*
shock [ʃɔk], *n.* choque, *m.*; susto; (*med.*) postración nerviosa, *f.*; (*elec.*) sacudida.—*v.t.* sacudir; chocar; escandalizar.
shocking [ˈʃɔkiŋ], *a.* espantoso; ofensivo; escandaloso.
shod [ʃɔd] [SHOE].
shoddy [ˈʃɔdi], *a.* de pacotilla; espurio.—*n.* lana regenerada.
shoe [ʃu:], *n.* zapato; herradura (*de caballo*); (*mech.*) zapata; ***to be in someone's shoes,*** estar en el pellejo de uno.—*v.t. irr.* herrar.
shoe-horn [ˈʃu:hɔ:n], *n.* calzador, *m.*
shoe-lace [ˈʃu:leis], *n.* lazo.
shoemaker [ˈʃu:meikə], *n.* zapatero.
shoe-shop [ˈʃu:ʃɔp], *n.* zapatería.
shone [ʃɔn] [SHINE].
shook [ʃuk] [SHAKE].
shoot [ʃu:t], *n.* retoño; partida de caza.—*v.t. irr.* disparar, tirar; lanzar; vaciar; fusilar; pegar un tiro (a); empujar; hacer (*una película*).—*v.i.* tirar, disparar; brotar; lanzarse; latir (*un dolor*); caer (*una estrella*); ***to — off,*** tirar; llevarse; ***to — up,*** espigarse (*plantas, niños etc.*); subir rápidamente.
shooting [ˈʃu:tiŋ], *n.* caza con escopeta; tiro; tiroteo.—*a.* ***— star,*** estrella fugaz.
shooting-range [ˈʃu:tiŋreindʒ], *n.* campo de tiro.
shooting-stick [ˈʃu:tiŋstik], *n.* bastón asiento.
shop [ʃɔp], *n.* tienda; ***to talk —,*** hablar de negocios.—*v.i.* (*also* ***to go shopping***) ir de compras.
shopkeeper [ˈʃɔpki:pə], *n.* tendero.
shoplifter [ˈʃɔpliftə], *n.* ladrón (*m.*) de tiendas.
shopping [ˈʃɔpiŋ], *n.* compras, *f.pl.*;***— centre,*** barrio de tiendas.
shop-window [ˈʃɔpˈwindou], *n.* escaparate, *m.*
shore (1) [ʃɔ:], *n.* costa; playa; orilla (*de un río*).
shore (2) [ʃɔ:], *v.t.* ***to — (up),*** apuntalar.
shorn [ʃɔ:n] [SHEAR].
short [ʃɔ:t], *a.* corto; bajo; breve; escaso; insuficiente; brusco; (*com.*) alcanzado; ***in —,*** en suma; ***to fall — of,*** no llegar a; ser inferior a; ***to be — of,*** carecer de; ***— of,*** fuera de, menos; ***to cut —,*** interrumpir bruscamente; ***to run —,*** faltar; ***— cut,*** atajo.—*n.pl.* calzones cortos, *m.pl.*—*adv.* brevemente; bruscamente.
shortage [ˈʃɔ:tidʒ], *n.* falta; carestía.
short-circuit [ˈʃɔ:tˈsə:kit], *n.* corto circuito.
shortcoming [ʃɔ:tˈkʌmiŋ], *n.* defecto.
shorten [ʃɔ:tn], *v.t.* acortar.—*v.i.* acortarse.
shorthand [ˈʃɔ:thænd], *n.* taquigrafía, estenografía.
short-handed [ˈʃɔ:tˈhændid], *a.* falto de mano de obra.
shortly [ˈʃɔ:tli], *adv.* pronto; brevemente; bruscamente.
shortness [ˈʃɔ:tnis], *n.* cortedad, *f.*
short-sighted [ˈʃɔ:tˈsaitid], *a.* miope; (*fig.*) poco perspicaz.
short-sightedness [ˈʃɔ:tˈsaitidnis], *n.* miopia; (*fig.*) falta de perspicacia.
shot [ʃɔt], *a.* tornasolado.—*n.* perdigón, *m.*; bala; tiro; tirador, *m.*; tirada; (*min.*) barreno; (*fam.*) ensayo. [SHOOT].
shotgun [ˈʃɔtgʌn], *n.* escopeta.
should [ʃud] [SHALL].
shoulder [ˈʃouldə], *n.* hombro; espalda.—*v.t.* echarse a la espalda; (*fig.*) cargar con; codear; ***— arms!*** ¡armas al hombro!
shoulder-blade [ˈʃouldəbleid], *n.* omoplato.
shoulder-stap [ˈʃouldəstræp], *n.* tirante, *m.*
shout [ʃaut], *n.* grito.—*v.t., v.i.* gritar.
shouting [ˈʃautiŋ], *n.* gritos, *m.pl.*, aclamación, *f.*
shove [ʃʌv], *n.* empujón, *m.*—*v.t., v.i.* empujar.
shovel [ʃʌvl], *n.* pala.—*v.t.* traspalar.
show [ʃou], *n.* exposición, *f.*; espectáculo; función, *f.*; pompa, aparato; seña; apariencia; negocio; ***to make a — of,*** hacer gala de.—*v.t. irr.* indicar; mostrar; hacer ver; demostrar; descubrir, exponer; explicar; conducir; ***to — off,*** exhibir; lucir (*vestidos*); ***to — out,*** acompañar a la puerta; ***to — up,*** hacer subir; exponer (*un fraude*).—*v.i.* parecer; mostrarse; ***to — off,*** pavonearse; ***to — up,*** presentarse.
show-case [ˈʃoukeis], *n.* vitrina.

shower [ʃauə], *n.* chubasco; (*fig.*) lluvia; abundancia; — ***bath,*** ducha; ***to take a —,*** ducharse.—*v.t.* derramar.—*v.i.* llover.
showery ['ʃauəri], *a.* lluvioso.
showiness ['ʃouinis], *n.* ostentación, *f.*
shown [ʃoun] [SHOW].
showy ['ʃoui], *a.* vistoso, ostentoso.
shrank [ʃræŋk] [SHRINK].
shred [ʃred], *n.* harapo; fragmento; pizca.—*v.t.* desmenuzar.
shrew [ʃru:], *n.* (*zool.*) musaraña; (*fig.*) fiera.
shrewd [ʃru:d], *a.* sagaz, perspicaz; sutil.
shrewdness ['ʃru:dnis], *n.* sagacidad, *f.*, perspicacia; sutileza.
shriek [ʃri:k], *n.* chillido, grito agudo.—*v.i.* chillar; gritar.
shrill [ʃril], *a.* agudo, estridente.
shrimp [ʃrimp], *n.* camarón, *m.*; quisquilla; (*fam.*) hombrecillo.
shrine [ʃrain], *n.* relicario; sepulcro de santo; capilla.
shrink [ʃriŋk], *v.t. irr.* encoger; reducir.—*v.i.* encogerse; contraerse; disminuir; (*fig.*) temblar; retirarse; ***to — from,*** huir de.
shrinkage ['ʃriŋkidʒ], *n.* encogimiento; contracción; reducción, *f.*
shrinking ['ʃriŋkiŋ], *a.* tímido.
shrivel ['ʃrivəl], *v.t.* arrugar; marchitar.—*v.i.* arrugarse; marchitarse; avellanarse.
shroud [ʃraud], *n.* mortaja.—*pl.* (*naut.*) obenques, *m.pl.*—*v.t.* amortajar; velar.
Shrove Tuesday [ʃrouv'tju:zd(e)i], *n.* martes (*m.*) de carnaval.
shrub [ʃrʌb], *n.* arbusto.
shrubbery ['ʃrʌbəri], *n.* arbustos, *m.pl.*
shrug [ʃrʌg], *n.* encogimiento de hombros.—*v.i.* encogerse de hombros.
shrunk [ʃrʌŋk], **shrunken** ['ʃrʌŋkən] [SHRINK].
shudder ['ʃʌdə], *n.* estremecimiento; vibración, *f.*—*v.i.* estremecerse; vibrar.
shuffle [ʃʌfl], *n.* barajadura; embuste, *m.*—*v.t.* mezclar (*papeles*); barajar (*naipes*); arrastrar (*los pies*); ***to — off,*** esquivar; largarse arrastrando los pies.
shun [ʃʌn], *v.t.* rehuir, evitar, esquivar; apartarse de.
shunt [ʃʌnt], *v.t.* apartar; (*rail.*) desviar.
shunting ['ʃʌntiŋ], *n.* (*rail.*) maniobras, *f.pl.*
shut [ʃʌt], *v.t. irr.* cerrar.—*v.i.* cerrarse; juntarse; ***to — down,*** cerrar; parar (*fábrica*); ***to — in,*** encerrar; rodear; ***to — off,*** cortar; ***to — out,*** excluir; ***to — up,*** cerrar; encerrar; (*fam.*) hacer callar; callarse.
shutter ['ʃʌtə], *n.* postigo; persiana; contraventana; (*phot.*) obturador, *m.*
shuttle [ʃʌtl], *n.* lanzadera.
shuttle-cock ['ʃʌtlkɔk], *n.* volante, *m.*
shy (1) [ʃai], *a.* tímido.—*n.* respingo.—*v.i.* respingar; asustarse.
shy (2) [ʃai], *n.* lanzamiento; prueba.—*v.t.* lanzar.
shyness ['ʃainis], *n.* timidez, *f.*
Siamese [saiə'mi:z], *a.*, *n.* siamés.
Sicilian [si'siljən], *a.*, *n.* siciliano.
Sicily ['sisili], *n.* Sicilia.
sick [sik], *a.* nauseado, mareado; enfermo; ***to be — of,*** estar harto de; ***to be —,*** estar enfermo; vomitar.
sick-bed ['sikbed], *n.* lecho de enfermo.
sicken [sikn], *v.t.* marear; dar asco a; hartar.—*v.i.* enfermar(se), caer enfermo; marearse.
sickening ['sikniŋ], *a.* nauseabundo; repugnante; fastidioso.
sickle [sikl], *n.* hoz, *f.*
sickly ['sikli], *a.* enfermizo; nauseabundo; — ***sweet,*** empalagoso.
sickness ['siknis], *n.* enfermedad, *f.*; náusea.
side [said], *n.* lado; margen, *m.*, orilla; falda (*de colina*); partido; (*sport*) equipo; costado; ijada (*de animal*); ***to be on the — of,*** estar por; ***on all sides,*** por todas partes; ***wrong — out,*** al revés.—*v.i.* ***to — with,*** declararse por.
sideboard ['saidbɔ:d], *n.* aparador, *m.*
side-car ['saidkɑ:], *n.* sidecar, *m.*
side-glance ['saidglɑ:ns], *n.* mirada de soslayo.
side-light ['saidlait], *n.* luz lateral, *f.*
sidelong ['saidlɔŋ], *a.* lateral, oblicuo.—*adv.* de lado; de soslayo.
side-show ['saidʃou], *n.* función secundaria.
side-street ['saidstri:t], *n.* callejuela.
side-track ['saidtræk], *n.* apartadero; desvío.
sideways ['saidweiz], *adv.* de lado; oblicuamente; de soslayo.
side-whiskers ['saidhwiskəz], *n.pl.* patillas, *f.pl.*
siding ['saidiŋ], *n.* apartadero.
sidle [saidl], *v.i.* ir de lado; ***to — up to,*** acercarse furtivamente a.
siege [si:dʒ], *n.* sitio, asedio; ***to lay —,*** poner, sitio.
sieve [siv], *n.* tamiz, *m.*, cedazo.—*v.t.* tamizar, cerner.
sift [sift], *v.t.* cerner; escudriñar; separar.
sigh [sai], *n.* suspiro.—*v.i.* suspirar; ***to — for,*** anhelar.
sight [sait], *n.* vista; visión, *f.*; aspecto; espectáculo; mira (*de fusil*); ***to come into —,*** asomarse; ***in —,*** a la vista; ***out of —,*** perdido de vista; ***to catch — of,*** vislumbrar; ***to lose — of,*** perder de vista; ***to know by —,*** conocer de vista.—*v.t.* avistar; ver; apuntar.
sightseeing ['saitsi:iŋ], *n.* visita de los monumentos.
sightseer ['saitsi:ə], *n.* turista, *m.f.*
sign [sain], *n.* señal, *f.*; signo (*del zodíaco*); marca; síntoma, *m.*; seña; muestra; huella.—*v.t.* firmar; (*eccl.*) persignar; señalar.
signal ['signəl], *a.* insigne, notable.—*n.* señal, *f.*—*v.t.*, *v.i.* hacer señas, señalar.
signal-box ['signəlbɔks], *n.* garita de señales.
signatory ['signətəri], *n.* signatario.
signature ['signitʃə], *n.* firma.
signboard ['sainbɔ:d], *n.* muestra, letrero.
significance [sig'nifikəns], *n.* significación, *f.*; importancia.
significant [sig'nifikənt], *a.* significativo.
signify ['signifai], *v.t.* significar; expresar; importar.
signpost ['sainpoust], *n.* indicador (*m.*) de dirección.
silence ['sailəns], *n.* silencio.—*interj.* ¡silencio!—*v.t.* imponer silencio a; mandar callar; silenciar.
silencer ['sailənsə], *n.* silenciador, *m.*
silent ['sailənt], *a.* silencioso; ***to remain —,*** guardar silencio.
silhouette [silu'et], *n.* silueta.—*v.t.* destacar.
silk [silk], *n.* seda; ***shot —,*** seda tornasolada.
silkworm ['silkwə:m], *n.* gusano de seda.
silky ['silki], *a.* sedoso; (*fig.*) suave.

sill ['sil], *n.* umbral (*de puerta*), *m.*; antepecho, repisa (*de ventana*).
silliness ['silinis], *n.* simpleza; tontería.
silly ['sili], *a.* tonto, imbécil; disparatado.
silt [silt], *n.* aluvión, *m.*
silver ['silvə], *a.* de plata; argentino; — ***birch,*** abedul, *m.*; — ***paper,*** papel (*m.*) de estaño; — ***plate,*** vajilla de plata; — ***wedding,*** bodas, (*f.pl.*) de plata.—*n.* plata; monedas (*f.pl.*) de plata (*dinero*); vajilla de plata.—*v.t.* platear; azogar; blanquear.
silversmith ['silvəsmiθ], *n.* platero.
silvery ['silvəri], *a.* plateado; argentino.
similar ['similə], *a.* semejante, parecido.
similarity [simi'læriti], *n.* semejanza.
simile ['simili], *n.* símil, *m.*
simmer ['simə], *v.i.* hervir a fuego lento; ***to — down,*** (*fig.*) moderarse poco a poco.
simper ['simpə], *v.i.* sonreírse afectadamente.
simple [simpl], *a.* sencillo; simple; ingenuo; mero; necio.
simple-minded ['simpl'maindid], *a.* ingenuo.
simpleton ['simpltən], *n.* papanatas, *m.sg.*
simplicity [sim'plisiti], *n.* sencillez; simplicidad, *f.*
simplification [simplifi'keiʃən], *n.* simplificación, *f.*
simplify ['simplifai], *v.t.* simplificar.
simulate ['simjuleit], *v.t.* simular, fingir.
simulation [simju'leiʃən], *n.* simulación, *f.*, fingimiento.
simultaneous [siməl'teinjəs], *a.* simultáneo.
sin [sin], *n.* pecado.—*v.i.* pecar.
since [sins], *adv.* desde; desde entonces; ***long —,*** hace mucho.—*conj.* ya que, puesto que; desde que.—*prep.* desde.
sincere [sin'siə], *a.* sincero.
sincerity [sin'seriti], *n.* sinceridad, *f.*
sinew ['sinju:], *n.* tendón, *m.*; (*fig.*) fuerza.
sinewy ['sinju:i], *a.* fibroso; fuerte.
sinful ['sinful], *a.* pecador (*persona*); pecaminoso (*hecho*).
sinfulness ['sinfulnis], *n.* pecado; perversidad, *f.*
sing [siŋ], *v.t. irr.* cantar; elogiar.—*v.i.* cantar; zumbar (*los oídos*).
singe [sindʒ], *v.t.* chamuscar.
singer ['siŋə], *n.* cantante, *m.f.*; cantor, *m.*
singing ['siŋiŋ], *a.* cantante.—*n.* canto; zumbido (*de los oídos*).
single [siŋgl], *a.* único; sencillo; solo; individual; soltero (*no casado*); — ***file,*** fila india; — ***combat,*** combate singular, *m.*; — ***ticket,*** billete sencillo, *m.*—*v.t.* ***to — out,*** escoger.
single-breasted ['siŋgl'brestid], *a.* recto.
single-handed ['siŋgl'hændid], *a.* solo, sin ayuda.
single-minded ['siŋgl'maindid], *a.* sin doblez; de una sola idea.
singlet ['siŋglit], *n.* camiseta.
singly ['siŋgli], *adv.* a solas; separadamente, uno a uno.
singular ['siŋgjulə], *a.*, *n.* singular, *m.*
singularity [siŋgju'læriti], *n.* singularidad, *f.*
sinister ['sinistə], *a.* siniestro.
sink [siŋk], *n.* fregadero, pila; sumidero; (*fig.*) sentina.—*v.t. irr.* hundir, sumergir, echar a pique; excavar; bajar, disminuir; hacer caer; invertir; ocultar; grabar.—*v.i.* hundirse, sumergirse; grabarse (*en la memoria*); caer; penetrar; bajar, disminuir; irse a pique; debilitarse; ***to — to one's knees,*** caer de rodillas.
sinner ['sinə], *n.* pecador, *m.*
sinuous ['sinjuəs], *a.* sinuoso, tortuoso.
sinus ['sainəs], *n.* seno.
sip [sip], *n.* sorbo.—*v.t.* sorber, beber a sorbos; saborear.
siphon ['saifən], *n.* sifón, *m.*—*v.t.* sacar con sifón.
sir [sə:], *n.* señor, *m.*; caballero.
sirloin ['sə:lɔin], *n.* solomillo.
sister ['sistə], *n.* hermana; (*eccl.*) sor, *f.*
sister-in-law ['sistərinlɔ:], *n.* (*pl.* **sisters-in-law**) cuñada.
sisterly ['sistəli], *a.* de hermana.
sit [sit], *v.t.* ***to — an examination,*** examinarse.—*v.t.*, *v.i.* sentarse; posarse; empollar; celebrar sesión; formar parte (***on,*** de); sentar; montar (*a caballo*); servir de modelo; ***to — by,*** sentarse al lado de; ***to — down,*** sentarse; ***to — up,*** incorporarse; velar.
site [sait], *n.* sitio; solar, *m.*
sitting ['sitiŋ], *n.* asentada; empolladura; nidada (*de pajarillos*); sesión, *f.*
sitting-room ['sitiŋrum], *n.* sala de estar.
situated ['sitjueitid], *a.* situado.
situation [sitju'eiʃən], *n.* situación, *f.*; empleo.
six [siks], *a.*, *n.* seis, *m.*; ***at sixes and sevens,*** en estado de desorden.
sixpence ['sikspəns], *n.* (moneda de) seis peniques, *m.pl.*
sixteen [siks'ti:n], *a.*, *n.* diez y seis, dieciséis, *m.*
sixteenth [siks'ti:nθ], *a.*, *n.* décimosexto; dieciseisavo; diez y seis (*en las fechas*), *m.*
sixth [siksθ], *a.* sexto.—*n.* sexta parte, *f.*; seis (*en las fechas*), *m.*; (*mus.*) sexta.
sixtieth ['sikstiəθ], *a.* sexagésimo; sesenta.—*n.* sexagésima parte, *f.*
sixty ['siksti], *a.*, *n.* sesenta, *m.*
sizable ['saizəbl], *a.* bastante grande.
size (1) [saiz], *n.* tamaño; medida; talle *m.*; dimensión, *f.*; diámetro; corpulencia; número (*de zapatos etc.*); cola.—*v.t.* medir; clasificar según el tamaño; encolar; ***to — up,*** tomar las medidas a; considerar.
size (2) [saiz], *n.* cola.—*v.t.* encolar.
sizzle [sizl], *n.* chisporroteo.—*v.i.* chisporrotear.
skate (1) [skeit], *n.* patín, *m.*
skate (2) [skeit], *n.* (*ichth.*) raya.
skater ['skeitə], *n.* patinador, *m.*
skating ['skeitiŋ], *n.* patinaje, *m.*
skating-rink ['skeitiŋriŋk], *n.* pista de patinar.
skein [skein], *n.* madeja.
skeleton ['skelitn], *n.* esqueleto; armadura; esbozo; — ***key,*** llave maestra.
sketch [sketʃ], *n.* esbozo; croquis, *m.*; (*theat.*) entremés, *m.*—*v.t.* esbozar; dibujar.
sketchy ['sketʃi], *a.* bosquejado; incompleto.
skewer ['skju:ə], *n.* broqueta.—*v.t.* espetar.
ski [ski:], *n.* esquí, *m.*—*v.i.* esquiar.
skid [skid], *n.* (*aut.*) patinazo.—*v.i.* patinar.
skidding ['skidiŋ], *n.* patinaje, *m.*
ski-ing ['ski:iŋ], *n.* el esquiar.
skilful ['skilful], *a.* hábil.
skill [skil], *n.* habilidad, *f.*
skilled [skild], *a.* hábil, diestro.
skim [skim], *v.t.* desnatar (*la leche*); espumar; rozar; leer superficialmente.

skimp [skimp], *v.t.* escatimar; frangollar.—*v.i.* ser tacaño.
skin [skin], *n.* piel, *f.*; cutis, *m.*; cáscara, pellejo (*de fruta*); odre (*para vino*), *m.*; ***soaked to the —***, calado hasta los huesos. —*v.t.* despellejar; pelar; (*fam.*) desollar.
skin-deep ['skin'di:p], *a.* superficial.
skinflint ['skinflint], *n.* avaro.
skinny ['skini], *a.* flaco, descarnado.
skip [skip], *n.* brinco.—*v.t.* pasar por alto; omitir.—*v.i.* brincar; saltar a la comba; escaparse.
skipping ['skipiŋ], *n.* acción (*f.*) de saltar; comba.
skipping-rope ['skipiŋroup], *n.* comba.
skirmish ['skə:miʃ], *n.* escaramuza.—*v.i.* escaramuzar.
skirt [skə:t], *n.* falda; faldón (*de chaqueta*), *m.*; margen, *m.*; (*fam.*) chica.—*v.t.* ladear.
skirting ['skə:tiŋ], *n.* zócalo.
skit [skit], *n.* parodia.
skittle [skitl], *n.* bolo.—*pl.* juego de bolos.
skull [skʌl], *n.* cráneo; calavera.
skull-cap ['skʌlkæp], *n.* casquete *m.*
skunk [skʌŋk], *n.* mofeta.
sky [skai], *n.* cielo.
sky-blue ['skai'blu:], *a.*, *n.* azul celeste, *m.*
sky-high [skai'hai], *a.*, *adv.* hasta las nubes.
skylark ['skailɑ:k], *n.* alondra.
skylight ['skailait], *n.* claraboya.
sky-line ['skailain], *n.* horizonte, *m.*
sky-scraper ['skaiskreipə], *n.* rascacielos, *m.inv.*
slab [slæb], *n.* plancha; losa.
slack [slæk], *a.* flojo; débil; negligente; perezoso; lento; (*com.*) encalmado.
slacken ['slækən], *v.t.*, *v.i.* aflojar; relajar; amainar (*el viento*); reducir.
slacker ['slækə], *n.* gandul, *m.*
slackness ['slæknis], *n.* flojedad, *f.*; descuido; pereza; desanimación, *f.*
slacks [slæks], *n.pl.* pantalones, *m.pl.*
slag [slæg], *n.* escoria.
slag-heap ['slæghi:p], *n.* escorial, *m.*
slain [slein], [SLAY].
slake [sleik], *v.t.* apagar (*la sed*); satisfacer.
slam (1) [slæm], *n.* portazo.—*v.t.* cerrar de golpe.—*v.i.* cerrarse de golpe.
slam (2) [slæm], *n.* capote (*naipes*), *m.*
slander ['slɑ:ndə], *n.* calumnia.—*v.t.* calumniar.
slanderer ['slɑ:ndərə], *n.* calumniador, *m.*
slanderous ['slɑ:ndərəs], *a.* calumnioso.
slang [slæŋ], *n.* argot, *m.*, jerga.
slant [slɑ:nt], *n.* inclinación; oblicuidad, *f.*; ***on the —***, inclinado; oblicuo.—*v.t.* inclinar.—*v.i.* inclinarse.
slanting ['slɑ:ntiŋ], *a.* oblicuo; inclinado.
slap [slæp], *n.* bofetada.—*v.t.* pegar; golpear.
slapdash ['slæpdæʃ], *a.* descuidado; chapucero.
slash [slæʃ], *n.* cuchillada; latigazo; corte, *m.* —*v.t.* acuchillar; azotar; cortar.
slate [sleit], *n.* pizarra; — ***quarry***, pizarral, *m.*—*v.t.* empizarrar; (*fam.*) censurar.
slate-coloured ['sleitkʌləd], *a.* apizarrado.
slaughter ['slɔ:tə], *n.* matanza; carnicería.—*v.t.* matar.
slaughter-house ['slɔ:təhaus], *n.* matadero.
Slav [slɑ:v], *a.*, *n.* eslavo.
slave [sleiv], *n.* esclavo.—*v.i.* trabajar como un negro.
slave-driver ['sleivdraivə], *n.* capataz (*m.*) de esclavos.
slaver (1) ['sleivə], *n.* negrero.
slaver (2) ['slævə], *n.* baba.—*v.i.* babosear.
slavery ['sleivəri], *n.* esclavitud, *f.*
slave-trade ['sleiv'treid], *n.* trata de esclavos; ***white —***, trata de blancas.
slavish ['sleiviʃ], *a.* servil.
Slavonic [slə'vɔnik], *a.* eslavo.
slay [slei], *v.t. irr.* matar.
slayer [sleiə], *n.* matador, *m.*
sledge [sledʒ], *n.* trineo.
sledge-hammer ['sledʒhæmə], *n.* acotillo.
sleek [sli:k], *a.* liso, lustroso; pulcro; obsequioso.—*v.t.* alisar.
sleekness ['sli:knis], *n.* lisura; gordura.
sleep [sli:p], *n.* sueño; ***to put to —***, adormecer; ***to go to —***, dormirse.—*v.i. irr.* dormir; ***to — on***, consultar con la almohada; seguir durmiendo; ***to — like a top***, dormir como un lirón; ***to — it off***, dormirla.
sleeper ['sli:pə], *n.* durmiente, *m.f.*; (*rail.*) traviesa; coche-cama, *m.*
sleepiness ['sli:pinis], *n.* somnolencia; letargo.
sleeping ['sli:piŋ], *a.* durmiente; (*com.*) — ***partner***, socio comanditario.
sleeping-car ['sli:piŋkɑ:], *n.* coche-cama, *m.*
sleepless ['sli:plis], *a.* insomne; ***a — night***, una noche blanca.
sleep-walker ['sli:pwɔ:kə], *n.* somnámbulo.
sleep-walking ['sli:pwɔ:kiŋ], *n.* somnambulismo.
sleepy ['sli:pi], *a.* soñoliento; letárgico; ***to be —***, tener sueño.
sleet [sli:t], *n.* aguanieve, *f.*—*v.i.* caer aguanieve.
sleeve [sli:v], *n.* manga; (*mech.*) manguito.
sleeveless ['sli:vlis], *a.* sin manga.
sleigh [slei], *n.* trineo.
sleight [slait], *n.* — ***of hand***, juego de manos, prestidigitación, *f.*
slender ['slendə], *a.* delgado, tenue, esbelto; escaso; pequeño; — ***hope***, esperanza remota; — ***means***, renta corta.
slenderness ['slendənis], *n.* delgadez, esbeltez; pequeñez; escasez, *f.*
slept [slept] [SLEEP].
slew [slu:] [SLAY].
slice [slais], *n.* rebanada (*de pan*); lonja, tajada; pala (*para pescado*).—*v.t.* cortar en lonjas, *etc.*; tajar; cortar.
slicer ['slaisə], *n.* rebanador, *m.*
slick [slik], *a.* (*fam.*) mañoso.
slide [slaid], *n.* (*photo.*) diapositiva; resbalón, *m.*; portaobjetos (*para el microscopio*), *m.inv.*; encaje (*de un bastidor*), *m.*; desprendimiento (*de rocas*); (*mus.*) ligado; (*mech.*) guía; pasador (*para el pelo*), *m.*—*v.i. irr.* resbalar, deslizarse; pecar; ***to — over***, pasar por alto; ***to let things —***, dejar rodar la bola.
slide-rule ['slaidru:l], *n.* regla de cálculo.
sliding ['slaidiŋ], *a.* corredizo; resbaladizo.—*n.* deslizamiento.
sliding-door ['slaidiŋ'dɔ:], *n.* puerta corrediza.
sliding-scale ['slaidiŋ'skeil], *n.* escala graduada.
slight [slait], *a.* ligero; escaso; pequeño; débil; insignificante.—*n.* desaire, *m.*, desprecio.—*v.t.* despreciar, desairar.
slighting ['slaitiŋ], *a.* despreciativo.

slim [slim], *a.* delgado; tenue; escaso.—*v.i.* adelgazarse.
slime [slaim], *n.* cieno; baba.
slimming ['slimiŋ], *n.* adelgazamiento.
slimy ['slaimi], *a.* viscoso, limoso; (*fig.*) servil.
sling [sliŋ], *n.* honda; (*med.*) cabestrillo.—*v.t.* tirar; suspender.
slink [sliŋk], *v.i. irr.* escabullirse.
slip [slip], *n.* resbalón; tropezón; desliz, *m.*; equivocación, *f.*; tira (*de papel*); combinación (*de mujer*), *f.*; funda (*de almohada*); (*bot.*) vástago; escapada; ***to give someone the—,*** escaparse de alguien.—*v.t.* deslizar; soltar; dislocar (*un hueso*).—*v.i.* deslizarse, resbalar; salirse (*de su sitio*); escurrirse; equivocarse; cometer un desliz; correr; ***to — away,*** escabullirse; ***to — into,*** introducirse en; vestirse; ***to — off,*** quitarse; ***to let the opportunity —,*** perder la ocasión.
slipper ['slipə], *n.* pantuflo; zapatilla.
slippery ['slipəri], *a.* resbaladizo; escurridizo; poco firme; sin escrúpulos.
slipshod ['slipʃɔd], *a.* descuidado, chapucero.
slit [slit], *n.* resquicio; cortadura.—*v.t. irr.* hender; cortar; ***to — the throat,*** degollar.
sliver ['slivə], *n.* astilla.
slobber ['slɔbə], *n.* baba.—*v.i.* babosear.
sloe [slou], *n.* endrina (*fruta*); endrino (*árbol*).
slogan ['slougən], *n.* grito de combate; mote, slogan, *m.*
slop [slɔp], *n.* charco.—*pl.* agua sucia.—*v.t.* derramar.—*v.i.* derramarse.
slope [sloup], *n.* inclinación, *f.*; falda (*de colina*).—*v.i.* inclinarse, estar en declive.
sloping ['sloupiŋ], *a.* inclinado, en declive.
sloppy ['slɔpi], *a.* aguoso; lodoso; chapucero.
slot [slɔt], *n.* muesca, ranura.
slot-machine ['slɔtməʃi:n], *n.* tragaperras, *m.sg.*
slouch [slautʃ], *n.* inclinación (*f.*) del cuerpo.—*v.i.* ir cabizbajo.
slovenly ['slʌvnli], *a.* desaseado; sucio; descuidado.
slow [slou], *a.* lento; tardo; torpe; pesado; ***the clock is five minutes —,*** el reloj lleva cinco minutos de atraso.—*v.t.*, *v.i.* ***to — down,*** ir más despacio; retrasar.
slowcoach ['sloukoutʃ], *n.* perezoso.
slowly ['slouli], *adv.* despacio.
slow-motion ['slou'mouʃən], *n.* velocidad reducida, *f.*
slowness ['slounis], *n.* lentitud, *f.*; tardanza; torpeza.
slow-witted ['slou'witid], *a.* torpe.
sludge [slʌdʒ], *n.* cieno, lodo.
slug [slʌg], *n.* (*zool.*) babosa; bala (*munición*).—*v.t.* (*fam.* aporrear, golpear).
sluggish ['slʌgiʃ], *a.* perezoso; lento; flojo.
sluice [slu:s], *n.* esclusa; canal, *m.* —*v.t.* ***to — down,*** lavar; regar.
sluice-gate ['slu:sgeit], *n.* compuerta.
slum [slʌm], *n.* barrio pobre, suburbio.
slumber ['slʌmbə], *n.* sueño.—*v.i.* dormitar.
slump [slʌmp], *n.* baja.—*v.i.* caerse; bajar.
slung [slʌŋ] [SLING].
slunk [slʌŋk] [SLINK].
slur [slə:], *n.* estigma, *m.*; (*mus.*) ligado.—*v.t.* comerse palabras; ligar; manchar; ***to — over,*** pasar por encima de.
slush [slʌʃ], *n.* aguanieve, *f.*; cieno; (*fig.*) ñoñería.
slushy ['slʌʃi], *a.* fangoso; (*fig.*) ñoño.
slut [slʌt], *n.* pazpuerca; ramera.
sly [slai], *a.* astuto, taimado; disimulado; ***on the —,*** a hurtadillas.
slyness ['slainis], *n.* astucia; disimulo.
smack (1) [smæk], *n.* sabor, *m.*; dejo.—*v.i.* saber (**of,** a).
smack (2) [smæk], *n.* beso sonado y fuerte; bofetada, cachete, *m.*; chasquido (*de látigo*).—*v.t.* dar una bofetada *o* un cachete.
smack (3) [smæk], *n.* lancha de pescar.
small [smɔ:l], *a.* pequeño; menudo; corto; bajo (*de estatura*); mezquino; poco; de poca importancia; ***— change,*** (dinero) suelto; ***— fry,*** pececillos, *m.pl.*; gente menuda *o* de poca importancia; ***— hours,*** altas horas de la noche; ***— print,*** carácter (*m.*) de letra menuda; ***— talk,*** trivialidades, *f.pl.*
smallish ['smɔ:liʃ], *a.* bastante pequeño.
smallness ['smɔ:lnis], *n.* pequeñez, *f.*; insignificancia.
smallpox ['smɔ:lpɔks], *n.* viruelas, *f.pl.*
smart [smɑ:t], *a.* vivo; listo; elegante.—*n.* escozor, dolor, *m.*—*v.i.* picar, escocer; dolerse.
smarten [smɑ:tn], *v.t.* embellecer.
smartness ['smɑ:tnis], *n.* viveza; habilidad, *f.*; elegancia.
smash [smæʃ], *n.* rotura; fracaso; ruina, quiebra; accidente, *m.*; ***— and grab raid,*** robo violento.—*v.t.* romper, quebrar; aplastar, destrozar.—*v.i.* romperse; quebrarse; hacer bancarrota; ***to — up,*** quebrar.
smattering ['smætəriŋ], *n.* tintura; conocimiento superficial.
smear [smiə], *n.* mancha; calumnia.—*v.t.* untar; manchar, ensuciar; (*fig.*) calumniar.
smell [smel], *n.* olfato; olor, *m.*—*v.t. irr.* oler; (*fig.*) percibir; ***to — a rat,*** (*fig.*) oler el poste.—*v.i.* oler (***of,*** a); oler mal.
smelling ['smeliŋ], *a.* ***foul —,*** hediondo; ***sweet —,*** oloroso.—*n.* acción (*f.*) de oler.
smelling-salts ['smeliŋsɔlts], *n.pl.* sales inglesas, *f.pl.*
smelt (1) [smelt], *v.t.* fundir.
smelt (2) [smelt] [SMELL].
smelting ['smeltiŋ], *n.* fundición, *f.*
smile [smail], *n.* sonrisa.—*v.i.* sonreír(se); (*fig.*) ser propicio.
smiling ['smailiŋ], *a.* risueño, sonriente.
smirk [smə:k], *n.* sonrisa afectada.—*v.i.* sonreír afectadamente.
smite [smait], *v.t. irr.* herir; golpear; castigar; encantar; doler.
smith [smiθ], *n.* herrero.
smithereens [smiðə'ri:nz], *n.pl.* añicos, *m.pl.*
smithy ['smiði], *n.* fragua.
smitten ['smitn] [SMITE].
smock [smɔk], *n.* blusa.
smoke [smouk], *n.* humo.—*v.t.* fumar; ahumar; ennegrecer.—*v.i.* humear; fumar.
smokeless ['smouklis], *a.* sin humo.
smoker ['smoukə], *n.* fumador, *m.*; (*rail.*) coche (*m.*) para fumadores.
smoke-screen ['smoukskri:n], *n.* cortina de humo.
smoke-signal ['smouksignəl], *n.* ahumada.
smoking ['smoukiŋ], *a.* humeante.—*n.* el fumar, *m.*; ***no —,*** se prohibe fumar.
smoking-jacket ['smoukiŋdʒækit], *n.* batín, *m.*
smoky ['smouki], *a.* humeante; ahumado.

smooth [smu:ð], *a.* liso; suave; manso (*del agua*); uniforme; igual; lisonjero; afable.—*v.t.* allanar; alisar; igualar; acepillar; calmar; ***to — over,*** exculpar.
smoothness ['smu:ðnis], *n.* lisura; igualdad; suavidad; afabilidad, *f.*
smooth-tongued ['smu:ð'tʌŋd], *a.* lisonjero, obsequioso.
smote [smout] [SMITE].
smother ['smʌðə], *v.t.* ahogar, sofocar; suprimir; apagar.
smoulder ['smouldə], *v.i.* arder sin llama; (*fig.*) arder; estar latente.
smouldering ['smouldəriŋ], *a.* que arde lentamente; latente.
smudge [smʌdʒ], *n.* mancha.—*v.t.* tiznar; manchar.
smug [smʌg], *a.* presumido; farisaico.
smuggle [smʌgl], *v.t.* pasar de contrabando. —*v.i.* contrabandear.
smuggler ['smʌglə], *n.* contrabandista, *m.f.*
smuggling ['smʌgliŋ], *n.* contrabando.
smugness ['smʌgnis], *n.* satisfacción (*f.*) de sí mismo.
smut [smʌt], *n.* mancha (*de hollín*); (*fig.*) indecencia.
smutty ['smʌti], *a.* tiznado; (*fig.*) verde.
snack [snæk], *n.* tentempié, *m.*, merienda.
snag [snæg], *n.* pega, tropiezo; nudo.
snail [sneil], *n.* caracol, *m.*; ***snail's pace,*** paso de tortuga.
snake [sneik], *n.* culebra, serpiente, *f.*
snap [snæp], *a.* repentino, inesperado.—*n.* chasquido; castañeteo (*con los dedos*); mordedura; cierre (*de resorte*); vigor, *m.*; período corto (*de frío*); (*photo.*) instantánea. —*v.t.* morder; chasquear; romper; cerrar de golpe; castañetear (*los dedos*); sacar una instantánea.—*v.i.* chasquear; partirse; romperse; hablar bruscamente; ***to — at,*** tratar de morder; ***to — off,*** romper(se); ***to — up,*** coger.
snappy ['snæpi], *a.* irritable; vigoroso.
snare [snɛə], *n.* lazo, trampa; red, *f.*—*v.t.* enredar.
snarl [snɑ:l], *n.* regaño, gruñido.—*v.i.* regañar, gruñir.
snatch [snætʃ], *n.* agarro; ratito; fragmento. —*v.t.* agarrar; disfrutar.
sneak [sni:k], *n.* mandilón, *m.*, chivato.—*v.i.* colarse (en); acusar; chismear.
sneaking ['sni:kiŋ], *a.* vil; furtivo; secreto.
sneer [sniə], *n.* sonrisa de desprecio; mofa.—*v.i.* mirar *o* hablar con desprecio; ***to — at,*** mofarse de.
sneeze [sni:z], *n.* estornudo.—*v.i.* estornudar.
sniff [snif], *v.t.* olfatear.—*v.i.* resollar.
snigger ['snigə], *n.* risa disimulada.—*v.i.* reírse disimuladamente.
snip [snip], *n.* tijeretada; recorte (*de paño*), *m.* —*v.t.* tijeretear.
sniper ['snaipə], *n.* paco, tirador apostado, *m.*
snivel [snivl], *v.i.* moquear; lloriquear.
snivelling ['snivliŋ], *a.* mocoso; llorón.
snob [snɔb], *n.* esnob, *m.f.*
snobbish ['snɔbiʃ], *a.* esnob.
snoop [snu:p], *v.i.* espiar, curiosear.
snooze [snu:z], *n.* siesta.—*v.i.* dormitar.
snore [snɔ:], *n.* ronquido.—*v.i.* roncar.
snoring ['snɔ:riŋ], *n.* ronquido.
snort [snɔ:t], *n.* bufido, resoplido.—*v.i.* bufar. resoplar.
snout [snaut], *n.* hocico.
snow [snou], *n.* nieve, *f.*—*v.i.* nevar; ***to — up,*** aprisionar con nieve.
snowball ['snoubɔ:l], *n.* bola de nieve.
snow-bound ['snoubaund], *a.* aprisionado por la nieve.
snow-capped ['snoukæpt], *a.* coronado de nieve.
snowdrift ['snoudrift], *n.* acumulación (*f.*) de nieve.
snowdrop ['snoudrɔp], *n.* campanilla de invierno.
snowfall ['snoufɔ:l], *n.* nevada.
snowflake ['snoufleik], *n.* copo de nieve.
snowman ['snoumæn], *n.* figura de nieve.
snow-plough ['snouplau], *n.* quitanieves, *m.sg.*
snow-shoe ['snouʃu:], *n.* raqueta de nieve.
snowstorm ['snoustɔ:m], *n.* ventisca.
snow-white ['snou'hwait], *a.* blanco como la nieve.
snowy ['snoui], *a.* nevoso.
snub [snʌb], *n.* repulsa; desaire, *m.*; nariz chata.—*v.t.* desairar; repulsar; tratar con desdén.
snub-nosed ['snʌb'nouzd], *a.* chato.
snuff [snʌf], *n.* moco (*de candela*); rapé, *m.* —*v.t.* oler; despabilar (*una candela*).
snuff-box ['snʌfbɔks], *n.* tabaquera.
snug [snʌg], *a.* cómodo; caliente; escondido.
snuggle [snʌgl], *v.i.* acomodarse; ***to — up to,*** arrimarse a.
so [sou], *adv.* así; de este modo; tan; tanto; de igual modo; también; por tanto; aproximadamente; ***— as to,*** para; a fin de que; ***— on and — forth,*** etcétera; ***— that,*** de modo que, para que; ***— much,*** tanto; ***— be it,*** así sea; ***— far,*** hasta aquí; ***— to speak,*** por decirlo así.
soak [souk], *n.* remojo; (*fam.*) borrachín, *m.*—*v.t.* remojar; ***to — up,*** empapar.—*v.i.* estar en remojo.
so-and-so ['souənd'sou], *n.* fulano (de tal).
soap [soup], *n.* jabón, *m.*—*v.t.* jabonar.
soap-dish ['soupdiʃ], *n.* jabonera.
soap-suds ['soupsʌdz], *n.pl.* jabonaduras, *f.pl.*
soapy ['soupi], *a.* jabonoso.
soar [sɔ:], *v.i.* remontarse, encumbrarse.
sob [sɔb], *n.* sollozo.—*v.i.* sollozar.
sober ['soubə], *a.* sobrio; sereno; modesto; obscuro; ***to — up,*** desemborrachar; calmar. —*v.i.* ***to — up,*** volverse sobrio.
sober-minded ['soubəmaindid], *a.* grave.
sobriety [sou'braiəti], *n.* sobriedad; moderación; seriedad, *f.*
so-called ['sou'kɔ:ld], *a.* llamado, supuesto.
soccer ['sɔkə], *n.* fútbol, *m.*
sociable ['souʃəbl], *a.* sociable.
social ['souʃəl], *a.* social; sociable.—*n.* velada.
socialism ['souʃəlizm], *n.* socialismo.
socialist ['souʃəlist], *a.*, *n.* socialista, *m.f.*
society [sə'saiəti], *n.* sociedad, *f.*; mundo elegante; compañía.
sociological [sousiə'lɔdʒikəl], *a.* sociólogo.
sociologist [sousi'ɔlədʒist], *n.* sociólogo.
sociology [sousi'ɔlədʒi], *n.* sociología.
sock (1) [sɔk], *n.* calcetín, *m.*
sock (2) [sɔk], *n.* (*fam.*) puñetazo.—*v.t.* (*fam.*) pegar.

socket ['sɔkit], *n.* hueco; (*mech.*) cubo, caja; cuenca (*del ojo*); fosa (*de un hueso*); (*elec.*) enchufe, *m.*; alvéolo (*de un diente*).
sod [sɔd], *n.* césped, *m.*
soda ['soudə], *n.* sosa, soda.
soda-water ['soudə'wɔ:tə], *n.* (agua de) seltz *o* sifón, *m.*
sodden [sɔdn], *a.* saturado.
sodomy ['sɔdəmi], *n.* sodomía.
sofa ['soufə], *n.* sofá, *m.*
soft [sɔft], *a.* suave; blando; dulce; tonto; — ***drinks,*** bebidas no alcohólicas.
soften [sɔfn], *v.t.* ablandar; enternecer; suavizar.—*v.i.* ablandarse; enternecerse.
softening ['sɔfniŋ], *n.* ablandamiento; enternecimiento.
softness ['sɔftnis], *n.* blandura; suavidad, *f.*; dulzura; debilidad (*f.*) de carácter.
soggy ['sɔgi], *a.* empapado, saturado.
soil [sɔil], *n.* tierra.—*v.t.* ensuciar.
soiled [sɔild], *a.* sucio.
soirée ['swɑ:rei], *n.* velada.
sojourn ['sɔdʒə:n], *n.* residencia.—*v.i.* residir.
solace ['sɔləs], *n.* solaz, *m.*, consuelo.—*v.t.* solazar; consolar.
solar ['soulə], *a.* solar.
sold [sould] [SELL].
solder ['sɔldə], *n.* soldadura.—*v.t.* soldar.
soldering ['sɔldəriŋ], *n.* soldadura.
soldering-iron ['sɔldəriŋ'aiən], *n.* soldador, *m.*
soldier ['souldʒə], *n.* soldado; militar, *m.*
sole (1) [soul], *a.* único, solo; exclusivo.
sole (2) [soul], *n.* (*anat.*) planta; suela (*del zapato*).—*v.t.* solar (*zapatos*).
sole (3) [soul], *n.* (*ichth.*) lenguado.
solemn ['sɔləm], *a.* solemne, grave.
solemnity [sə'lemniti], *n.* solemnidad, *f.*
solemnize ['sɔləmnaiz], *v.t.* solemnizar.
solicit [sə'lisit], *v.t.* solicitar; rogar, implorar.
solicitor [sə'lisitə], *n.* abogado.
solicitous [sə'lisitəs], *a.* solícito; deseoso; inquieto.
solicitude [sə'lisitju:d], *n.* solicitud, *f.*; cuidado; preocupación, *f.*
solid ['sɔlid], *a.* sólido; macizo; serio; unánime.—*n.* sólido.
solidarity [sɔli'dæriti], *n.* solidaridad, *f.*
solidify [sə'lidifai], *v.t.* solidificar.—*v.i.* solidificarse.
solidity [sə'liditi], *n.* solidez; unanimidad, *f.*
soliloquy [sə'liləkwi], *n.* soliloquio.
solitaire [sɔli'tɛə], *n.* solitario.
solitary ['sɔlitəri], *a.* solitario; solo, único; ***in — confinement,*** incomunicado.
solitude ['sɔlitju:d], *n.* soledad, *f.*
solo ['soulou], *n.* solo.—*a.* — ***flight,*** vuelo a solas.
soloist ['soulouist], *n.* solista, *m.f.*
soluble ['sɔljubl], *a.* soluble.
solution [sə'lu:ʃən], *n.* solución, *f.*
solve [sɔlv], *v.t.* resolver.
solvency ['sɔlvənsi], *n.* solvencia.
solvent ['sɔlvənt], *a.* disolvente; (*com.*) solvente.—*n.* disolvente, *m.*
sombre ['sɔmbə], *a.* sombrío.
some [sʌm], *a.* un poco de, algo de; alguno; algunos, unos.—*pron.* algo; algunos; algunas.
someone ['sʌmwʌn], **somebody** ['sʌmbədi], *pron.* alguien, *m.f.*; — ***else,*** otro, otra persona; ***to be —,*** ser un personaje.
somehow ['sʌmhau], *adv.* de alguna manera.
somersault ['sʌməsɔ:lt], *n.* salto mortal.—*v.i.* dar un salto mortal.
something ['sʌmθiŋ], *pron.* alguna cosa, algo; — ***else,*** otra cosa; ***to have — to do,*** tener que hacer.—*adv.* algún tanto.
sometime ['sʌmtaim], *adv.* algún día; en algún tiempo; — ***last week,*** durante la semana pasada; — ***or other,*** tarde o temprano; — ***soon,*** dentro de poco.
sometimes ['sʌmtaimz], *adv.* algunas veces, a veces.
somewhat ['sʌmwɔt], *adv.* algo, algún tanto.
somewhere ['sʌmwɛə], *adv.* en alguna parte; — ***else,*** en otra parte.
somnolence ['sɔmnələns], *n.* somnolencia.
somnolent ['sɔmnələnt], *a.* soñoliento; soporífero.
son [sʌn], *n.* hijo.
sonata [sə'nɑ:tə], *n.* sonata.
song [sɔŋ], *n.* canción, *f.*; canto; poesía; (*fig.*) bagatela; ***Song of Songs,*** el Cantar de los Cantares; ***drinking —,*** canción báquica; ***to sell for a —,*** vender por un pedazo de pan.
song-bird ['sɔŋbə:d], *n.* ave cantora.
song-book ['sɔŋbuk], *n.* cancionero.
songster ['sɔŋstə], *n.* cantor, *m.*; ave cantora.
son-in-law ['sʌninlɔ:], *n.* (*pl.* **sons-in-law**) yerno.
sonnet ['sɔnit], *n.* soneto.
sonorous ['sɔnərəs], *a.* sonoro.
soon [su:n], *adv.* pronto; dentro de poco; ***as — as,*** luego que; ***as — as possible,*** cuanto antes; — ***after,*** poco después.
sooner ['su:nə], *adv., compar. of* SOON; más pronto; antes; ***I would — die,*** antes la muerte; ***the — the better,*** cuanto antes mejor; — ***or later,*** tarde o temprano; ***no — said than done,*** dicho y hecho; ***no — had he come than . . .,*** apenas había venido cuando . . .; ***I would — go,*** preferiría ir.
soot [sut], *n.* hollín, *m.*
soothe [su:ð], *v.t.* calmar; aliviar.
soothing ['su:ðiŋ], *a.* calmante; consolador.
soothsayer ['su:θseiə], *n.* adivino.
sooty ['suti], *a.* cubierto de hollín; negro; obscurecido.
sop [sɔp], *n.* sopa; soborno.
sophisticated [sə'fistikeitid], *a.* mundano; culto; elegante.
sophistication [səfisti'keiʃən], *n.* mundanería; cultura.
sophistry ['sɔfistri], *n.* sofistería.
soporific [sɔpə'rifik], *a.* soporífero.
sopping ['sɔpiŋ], *a.* calado, empapado.
soppy ['sɔpi], *a.* (*fam.*) afeminado.
soprano [sə'prɑ:nou], *n.* soprano, tiple, *m.f.*
sorcerer ['sɔ:sərə], *n.* mago, brujo.
sorceress ['sɔ:səris], *n.* bruja.
sorcery ['sɔ:səri], *n.* hechicería, sortilegio.
sordid ['sɔ:did], *a.* sórdido; bajo.
sordidness ['sɔ:didnis], *n.* sordidez, *f.*; bajeza.
sore [sɔ:], *a.* doloroso; violento; extremo; enojado; — ***throat,*** mal (*m.*) de garganta.—*n.* llaga; úlcera.
soreness ['sɔ:nis], *n.* dolor, *m.*; (*fig.*) amargura.
sorrow ['sɔrou], *n.* pesar, *m.*, pesadumbre, *f.* tristeza; duelo.

sorrowful ['sɔrəful], *a.* afligido; triste.
sorrowing ['sɔrouiŋ], *a.* afligido.—*n.* aflicción, *f.*
sorry ['sɔri], *a.* arrepentido; afligido; despreciable; ***I am —,*** lo siento.
sort [sɔ:t], *n.* clase, especie, *f.*; ***all sorts of people,*** toda clase de gente; ***nothing of the —,*** nada de eso; ***out of sorts,*** indispuesto; ***a good —,*** (*fam.*) buen tipo.—*v.t.* separar; clasificar; ***to — out,*** escoger y arreglar.
so-so ['sousou], *a.* regular.
sot [sɔt], *n.* zaque, *m.*
sought [sɔ:t] [SEEK].
soul [soul], *n.* alma; espíritu, *m.*; ánima; ser; corazón, *m.*; ***All Souls' Day,*** Día de los Difuntos; ***— in purgatory,*** alma en pena.
soulful ['soulful], *a.* conmovedor; espiritual.
soulfulness ['soulfulnis], *n.* sensibilidad; espiritualidad, *f.*
soulless ['soullis], *a.* sin alma; despreciable.
sound (1) [saund], *a.* sano; entero; (*com.*) solvente; seguro; profundo; sólido; válido.—*adv.* bien.
sound (2) [saund], *n.* estrecho (*de mar*).
sound (3) [saund], *n.* sonido; son; ruido; sonda.—*v.t.* tocar; sonar; anunciar, publicar, celebrar.—*v.i.* sonar, hacer ruido; resonar.
sound (4) [saund], *v.t.* (*med.*) sondar, tentar; (*naut.*) sondear.
sound-barrier ['saund'bæriə], *n.* barrera del sonido.
sounding ['saundiŋ], *a.* sonoro.—*n.* sondeo.—*pl.* sondas, *f.pl.*
soundness ['saundnis], *n.* salud, *f.*; fuerza, validez, solidez, *f.*
sound-proof ['saundpru:f], *a.* aislado de todo sonido.
sound-track ['saundtræk], *n.* guía sonora.
sound-wave ['saundweiv], *n.* onda sonora.
soup [su:p], *n.* sopa; ***clear —,*** consommé, *m.*; ***thick —,*** puré, *m.*; ***in the —,*** (*fam.*) en apuros.
soup-plate ['su:p'pleit], *n.* plato sopero.
soup-tureen ['su:ptju'ri:n], *n.* sopera.
sour [sauə], *a.* agrio, ácido; áspero; ***— grapes!*** ¡están verdes!—*v.t.* agriar.
source [sɔ:s], *n.* fuente, *f.*; nacimiento (*de un río*); foco; ***to have from a good —,*** saber de buena tinta.
sourness ['sauənis], *n.* acidez, *f.*, agrura; aspereza.
south [sauθ], *a.* meridional, del sur; ***South American,*** sudamericano; ***South African,*** sudafricano.—*n.* mediodía, sur, *m.*
south-east ['sauθ'i:st], *n.* sudeste, *m.*
south-easterly ['sauθ'i:stəli], *a.* hacia el sudeste; del sudeste.
south-eastern ['sauθ'i:stən], *a.* del sudeste.
southerly ['sʌðəli], *a.* meridional; hacia el sur.
southern ['sʌðən], *a.* del sur, meridional.
southward ['sauθwəd], *a.* del sur.—*adv.* hacia el sur.
south-west ['sauθ'west], *n.* sudoeste, *m.*
south-westerly ['sauθ'westəli], *a.* hacia el sudoeste; del sudoeste.
south-western ['sauθ'westən], *a.* del sudoeste.
souvenir ['su:vəniə], *n.* recuerdo.
sovereign ['sɔvrin], *a.*, *n.* soberano.
Soviet ['souvjet], *a.* soviético.—*n.* soviet, *m.*
sow (1) [sau], *n.* puerca, cerda; jabalina.
sow (2) [sou], *v.t.*, *v.i. irr.* sembrar; esparcir; ***to — one's wild oats,*** (*fig.*) correr sus mocedades.
sower [souə], *n.* sembrador, *m.*
sowing ['souiŋ], *n.* siembra; sembradura.
sown [soun] [SOW (2)].
spa [spɑ:], *n.* balneario.
space [speis], *n.* espacio; intervalo; período.—*v.t.* espaciar.
spacious ['speiʃəs], *a.* espacioso; amplio.
spaciousness ['speiʃəsnis], *n.* espaciosidad; amplitud, *f.*
spaceman ['speismæn], *n.* astronauta, *m.*; hombre (*m.*) del espacio.
space-ship ['speisʃip], *n.* astronave, *f.*
space-suit ['speissju:t], *n.* escafandra espacial.
spade [speid], *n.* pala; espada (*naipes*); ***to call a — a —,*** llamar al pan pan y al vino vino.
Spain [spein], *n.* España.
span [spæn], *n.* palmo; espacio; vano (*de puente*); envergadura (*de alas*).—*v.t.* medir a palmos; cruzar; extenderse sobre.
spangle [spæŋgl], *n.* lentejuela.—*v.t.* adornar con lentejuelas; sembrar.
Spaniard ['spænjəd], *n.* español, *m.*
spaniel ['spænjəl], *n.* perro de aguas.
Spanish ['spæniʃ], *a.*, *n.* español, *m.*
Spanish-American ['spæniʃə'merikən], *a.*, *n.* hispanoamericano.
spank [spæŋk], *n.* nalgada.—*v.t.* zurrar.
spanking ['spæŋkiŋ], *a.* veloz.—*n.* zurra.
spanner ['spænə], *n.* llave (inglesa), *f.*
spar (1) [spɑ:], *n.* (*min.*) espato.
spar (2) [spɑ:], *n.* (*naut.*) percha.
spar (3) [spɑ:], *n.* boxeo; riña.—*v.i.* boxear.
spare [spɛə], *a.* disponible, de sobra; de repuesto; escaso; enjuto; ***— part,*** pieza de repuesto; ***— time,*** tiempo desocupado; ***— wheel,*** rueda de recambio.—*v.t.* ahorrar; escatimar; pasarse sin; evitar; perdonar; hacer gracia de; dedicar (*el tiempo*); ***to have to —,*** tener de sobra.
sparing ['spɛəriŋ], *a.* escaso; frugal.
spark [spɑ:k], *n.* chispa; (*fam.*) pisaverde, *m.*—*v.t.* ***to — off,*** instigar.—*v.i.* chispear.
sparking-plug ['spɑ:kiŋplʌg], *n.* bujía (de encendido).
sparkle [spɑ:kl], *n.* centelleo; brillo.—*v.i.* centellear; brillar; ser espumoso (*de ciertos vinos*).
sparkling ['spɑ:kliŋ], *a.* centelleante; brillante; espumante (*vino*).
sparrow ['spærou], *n.* gorrión, *m.*
sparrow-hawk ['spærouhɔ:k], *n.* gavilán, *m.*
sparse [spɑ:s], *a.* esparcido, claro.
Spartan ['spɑ:tən], *a.*, *n.* espartano.
spasm [spæzm], *n.* espasmo; ataque, *m.*
spasmodic [spæz'mɔdik], *a.* espasmódico.
spastic ['spæstik], *a.* (*med.*) espasmódico.
spat (1) [spæt], *n.* polaina (*para los pies*).
spat (2) [spæt] [SPIT].
spate [speit], *n.* crecida; (*fig.*) torrente, *m.*
spatial ['speiʃəl], *a.* espacial.
spatter ['spætə], *n.* salpicadura; rociada.—*v.t.* salpicar; regar; manchar.—*v.i.* rociar.
spawn [spɔ:n], *n.* freza; producto.—*v.t.*, *v.i.* desovar; engendrar.
speak [spi:k], *v.t.*, *v.i. irr.* hablar; decir; pronunciar; ***to — for itself,*** (*fig.*) ser manifiesto; ***to — one's mind,*** decir lo que se piensa; ***to — out,*** hablar claro; ***to — up,*** elevar la voz, hablar más alto; ***to — up for,*** hablar por; ***so to —,*** por decirlo así.

Speaker ['spi:kə], *n.* (*Brit.*) Presidente (*m.*) de la Cámara de los Comunes.
speaker ['spi:kə], *n.* el que habla; orador, *m.*
speaking ['spi:kiŋ], *a.* hablante; para hablar. —*n.* habla, discurso; — ***trumpet,*** portavoz, *m.*; — ***tube,*** tubo acústico; ***they are not on — terms,*** no se hablan.
spear [spiə], *n.* lanza; venablo; arpón (*de pesca*), *m.*—*v.t.* alancear; arponear.
spear-head ['spiəhed], *n.* punta de lanza.
special ['speʃəl], *a.* especial; extraordinario; particular.
specialist ['speʃəlist], *n.* especialista, *m.f.*
speciality [speʃi'æliti], *n.* especialidad; peculiaridad, *f.*
specialize ['speʃəlaiz], *v.t.* especializar.—*v.i.* -se.
species ['spi:ʃi:z], *n.* (*pl.* **species**) especie, *f.*
specific [spi'sifik], *a., n.* específico; — ***gravity,*** peso específico.
specification [spesifi'keiʃən], *n.* especificación, *f.*
specify ['spesifai], *v.t.* especificar.
specimen ['spesimin], *n.* espécimen, *m.*; ejemplo.
specious ['spi:ʃəs], *a.* especioso.
speck [spek], **speckle** [spekl], *n.* manchita; punto, átomo.—*v.t.* manchar.
spectacle ['spektəkl], *n.* espectáculo; exposición, *f.*; escena.—*pl.* gafas, *f.pl.*
spectacular [spek'tækjulə], *a.* espectacular.
spectator [spek'teitə], *n.* espectador, *m.*
spectral ['spektrəl], *a.* espectral.
spectre ['spektə], *n.* espectro, fantasma, *m.*
spectrum ['spektrəm], *n.* espectro.
speculate ['spekjuleit], *v.i.* especular.
speculation [spekju'leiʃən], *n.* especulación, *f.*
speculative ['spekjulətiv], *a.* especulativo.
speculator ['spekjuleitə], *n.* especulador, *m.*
sped [sped] [SPEED].
speech [spi:tʃ], *n.* palabra; lenguaje, *m.*; habla, discurso; idioma, *m.*
speechless ['spi:tʃlis], *a.* mudo; sin habla; desconcertado.
speed [spi:d], *n.* rapidez; velocidad, *f.*; presteza; prisa; ***at full —,*** a toda velocidad; ***with all —,*** a toda prisa.—*v.t. irr.* ayudar; despedir; acelerar; hacer salir bien. —*v.i. irr.* correr; darse prisa; marchar con velocidad excesiva.
speed-boat ['spi:dbout], *n.* lancha de carrera.
speedily ['spi:dili], *adv.* aprisa; prontamente.
speediness ['spi:dinis], *n.* celeridad, rapidez, *f.*; prisa.
speed-limit ['spi:dlimit], *n.* velocidad máxima.
speed-way ['spi:dwei], *n.* pista de ceniza.
speedy ['spi:di], *a.* rápido; pronto.
spell (1) [spel], *n.* hechizo, encanto.—*v.t. irr.* deletrear; significar; ***how do you — . . .?*** ¿cómo se escribe . . . ?
spell (2) [spel], *n.* turno; rato; temporada.
spellbound ['spelbaund], *a.* fascinado, encantado.
spelling ['speliŋ], *n.* deletreo, ortografía.
spelt [spelt] [SPELL].
spend [spend], *v.t. irr.* gastar; consumir; agotar; pasar (*tiempo*).—*v.i. irr.* hacer gastos.
spendthrift ['spendθrift], *n.* pródigo, manirroto.
spent [spent] [SPEND].
sperm [spə:m], *n.* esperma.
sperm-whale ['spə:m'hweil], *n.* cachalote, *m.*
sphere [sfiə], *n.* esfera; — ***of influence,*** zona de influencia.
spherical ['sferikəl], *a.* esférico.
sphinx [sfiŋks], *n.* esfinge, *f.*
spice [spais], *n.* especia; (*fig.*) sabor, *m.*; dejo.—*v.t.* especiar.
spick-and-span ['spikənd'spæn], *a.* más limpio que una patena; flamante (*nuevo*).
spicy ['spaisi], *a.* especiado; aromático; (*fig.*) picante.
spider ['spaidə], *n.* araña; ***spider's web,*** telaraña.
spidery ['spaidəri], *a.* parecido a una araña.
spigot ['spigət], *n.* espiche, *m.*
spike [spaik], *n.* clavo; (*bot.*) espiga; espliego. —*v.t.* clavar (*un cañón*).
spill (1) [spil], *n.* vuelco.—*v.t. irr.* derramar; volcar; ***to — the beans,*** soltar el gato.
spill (2) [spil], *n.* astilla.
spin [spin], *n.* vuelta; paseo.—*v.t. irr.* hilar; hacer girar; ***to — out,*** prolongar; ***to — a yarn,*** contar un cuento.—*v.i. irr.* hilar; girar; dar vueltas (*vértigo*).
spinach ['spinidʒ], *n.* espinaca(s).
spinal [spainl], *a.* espinal; — ***column,*** columna vertebral.
spindle [spindl], *n.* huso; (*mech.*) eje, *m.*
spine [spain], *n.* (*anat.*) espinazo; (*bot.*) espina; (*zool.*) púa.
spinner ['spinə], *n.* hilandero.
spinney ['spini], *n.* arboleda.
spinning ['spiniŋ], *n.* hilado.
spinning-top ['spiniŋtɔp], *n.* trompo.
spinning-wheel ['spiniŋhwi:l], *n.* torno de hilar.
spinster ['spinstə], *n.* soltera.
spiny ['spaini], *a.* espinoso.
spiral [spaiərəl], *a., n.* espiral, *f.*; — ***staircase,*** escalera en caracol.
spire (1) [spaiə], *n.* aguja (*de iglesia*).
spire (2) [spaiə], *n.* espira.
spirit ['spirit], *n.* espíritu, *m.*; alma; ánimo; energía; agudeza; espectro; temperamento; ingenio; alcohol, *m.*—*pl.* licores, *m.pl.*; ***low spirits,*** abatamiento; ***high spirits,*** alegría; ***to keep up one's spirits,*** mantener el valor.
spirited ['spiritid], *a.* fogoso; animoso.
spirit-level ['spiritlevəl], *n.* nivel (*m.*) de aire.
spiritual ['spiritjuəl], *a.* espiritual.
spiritualism ['spiritjuəlizm], *n.* espiritismo.
spit (1) [spit], *n.* asador, espetón (*para cocer*), *m.*—*v.t.* espetar.
spit (2) [spit], *n.* saliva.—*v.t., v.i. irr.* escupir (***out***).
spit (3) [spit], *n.* lengua de tierra.
spite [spait], *n.* rencor, *m.*, ojeriza, malevolencia; ***in — of,*** a pesar de.—*v.t.* dar pesar a.
spiteful ['spaitful], *a.* rencoroso, malévolo.
spitefulness ['spaitfulnis], *n.* malevolencia.
spittle [spitl], *n.* saliva.
spittoon [spi'tu:n], *n.* escupidera.
splash [splæʃ], *n.* chapoteo; (*fam.*) sensación, *f.*—*v.t.* salpicar; (*fam.*) tratar sensacionalmente.—*v.i.* chapotear.
splay-footed ['spleifutid], *a.* zancajoso.
spleen [spli:n], *n.* (*anat.*) bazo; rencor, *m.*; esplín, *m.*
splendid ['splendid], *a.* espléndido, magnífico, glorioso.

splendour ['splendə], *n.* resplandor, *m.*; esplendor, *m.*; magnificencia.
splice [splais], *n.* empalme, *m.*—*v.t.* empalmar; juntar; (*fam.*) casar
splint [splint], *n.* tablilla.
splinter ['splintə], *n.* astilla.—*v.t.* astillar. —*v.i.* romperse en astillas.
split [split], *n.* hendidura, grieta; división, *f.*, cisma.—*v.t.* *irr.* hender; dividir; (*fig.*) desunir.—*v.i.* *irr.* henderse; dividirse; partirse; ***to — on,*** (*fam.*) denunciar.
splutter ['splʌtə], *n.* chisporroteo; balbuceo; —*v.t.*, *v.i.* chisporrotear; balbucir.
spoil [spɔil], *n.* botín, *m.*—*v.t.* *irr.* estropear; corromper; mimar; saquear.—*v.i.* estropearse.
spoilt [spɔilt] [SPOIL].
spoke (1) [spouk], *n.* rayo; peldaño.
spoke (2) [spouk], **spoken** ['spoukən] [SPEAK].
spokesman ['spouksmən], *n.* portavoz, *m.*
sponge [spʌndʒ], *n.* esponja; ***— cake,*** bizcocho; ***to throw up the —,*** (*fig.*) darse por vencido.—*v.t.* limpiar con esponja.—*v.i.* (*fig.*) vivir de gorra.
sponger ['spʌndʒə], *n.* gorrista, *m.f.*
spongy ['spʌndʒi], *a.* esponjoso.
sponsor ['spɔnsə], *n.* fiador, *m.*; padrino; madrina.
spontaneity [spɔntə'ni:iti], *n.* espontaneidad, *f.*
spontaneous [spɔn'teinjəs], *a.* espontáneo.
spool [spu:l], *n.* canilla, carrete, *m.*
spoon [spu:n], *n.* cuchara.—*v.t.* sacar con cuchara.
spoonful ['spu:nful], *n.* cucharada.
sporadic [spə'rædik], *a.* esporádico.
spore [spɔ:], *n.* espora.
sport [spɔ:t], *n.* deporte, *m.*; pasatiempo; broma; objeto de broma; ***to make — of,*** burlarse de.—*pl.* concurso de atletismo.—*v.t.* lucir, ostentar.—*v.i.* divertirse, jugar.
sporting ['spɔ:tiŋ], *a.* deportivo; de buena disposición; ***— chance,*** posibilidad (*f.*) de éxito.
sportive ['spɔ:tiv], *a.* juguetón.
sportsman ['spɔ:tsmən], **sportswoman** ['spɔ:tswumən], *n.* deportista, *m.f.*
spot [spɔt], *n.* sitio, lugar, *m.*; mancilla; mancha; gota (*de lluvia*); grano; poco; ***on the —,*** en al acto.—*v.t.* motear, manchar; observar.
spotless ['spɔtlis], *a.* limpio, sin mancha, inmaculado.
spotlight ['spɔtlait], *n.* proyector, *m.*; luz (*f.*) del proyector.—*v.t.* señalar.
spotted ['spɔtid], *a.* manchado; con manchas; con lunares (*diseño*).
spotty ['spɔti], *a.* lleno de manchas.
spouse [spauz], *n.* esposo; esposa.
spout [spaut], *n.* tubo, cañería; canalón, *m.*; cuello (*de vasija*); pico (*de tetera etc.*); chorro.—*v.t.* arrojar; echar; recitar.—*v.i.* brotar, chorrear; (*fam.*) hablar.
sprain [sprein], *n.* torcedura.—*v.t.* torcer.
sprang [spræŋ] [SPRING].
sprat [spræt], *n.* sardineta.
sprawl [sprɔ:l], *v.i.* extenderse; recostarse (en).
spray [sprei], *n.* rocío (*de agua*); espuma (*del mar*); pulverizador, *m.*; ramita.—*v.t.* rociar, pulverizar.
spread [spred], *n.* extensión; propagación, *f.*; colcha (*de cama*); (*fam.*) banquete, *m.*—*v.t.* *irr.* tender, extender; desplegar; difundir; divulgar; diseminar; poner.—*v.i.* *irr.* extenderse; desplegarse; propagarse; difundirse.
spree [spri:], *n.* parranda; ***to go on a —,*** ir de parranda.
sprig [sprig], *n.* ramita; espiga.
sprightly ['spraitli], *a.* alegre, despierto.
spring [spriŋ], *a.* primaveral.—*n.* primavera; muelle, resorte, *m.*; brinco, salto; elasticidad, *f.*; manantial, *m.*, fuente, *f.*—*v.t.* *irr.* soltar; dar de golpe; ***to — a leak,*** hacer agua.—*v.i.* *irr.* brincar, saltar; brotar; originarse; ***to — back,*** saltar hacia atrás; ***to — up,*** brotar: surgir.
springtime ['spriŋtaim], *n.* primavera.
springy ['spriŋi], *a.* elástico.
sprinkle [spriŋkl], *v.t.* rociar; salpicar.
sprinkling ['spriŋkliŋ], *n.* rociadura; pequeño número, poco.
sprint [sprint], *n.* sprint, *m.*—*v.i.* sprintar.
sprout [spraut], *n.* retoño.—*pl.* bretones, coles (*f.pl.*) de Bruselas.—*v.i.* germinar; retoñar.
sprung [sprʌŋ] [SPRING].
spun [spʌn] [SPIN].
spur [spə:], *n.* espuela; espolón (*de gallo*), *m.*; (*fig.*) estímulo; ***on the — of the moment,*** de sopetón.—*v.t.* espolear; poner(se) espuelas; (*fig.*) estimular.
spurious ['spjuəriəs], *a.* espurio; falso.
spurn [spə:n], *v.t.* despreciar; rechazar.
spurt [spə:t], *n.* chorro; esfuerzo repentino.—*v.t.* hacer chorrear; lanzar.—*v.i.* chorrear; brotar; hacer un esfuerzo supremo.
spy [spai], *n.* espía, *m.f.*;—*v.t.* divisar; observar; ***to — out,*** explorar.—*v.i.* ser espía.
spy-glass ['spaiglɑ:s], *n.* catalejo.
spying ['spaiiŋ], *n.* espionaje, *m.*
squabble [skwɔbl], *n.* riña, disputa.—*v.i.* reñir, disputar.
squad [skwɔd], *n.* escuadra; pelotón, *m.*
squadron ['skwɔdrən], *n.* (*aer.*) escuadrilla; (*naut.*) escuadra; (*mil.*) escuadrón, *m.*
squadron-leader ['skwɔdrən'li:də], *n.* comandante, *m.*
squalid ['skwɔlid], *a.* escuálido; mezquino.
squall [skwɔ:l], *n.* chillido; ráfaga; (*fig.*) tempestad, *f.*—*v.i.* chillar.
squally ['skwɔ:li], *a.* tempestuoso; violento.
squalor ['skwɔlə], *n.* escualidez, *f.*
squander ['skwɔndə], *v.t.* malgastar; desperdiciar; derrochar.
square [skwɛə], *a.* cuadrado; justo; honrado; categórico; (*fam.*) fuera de moda; ***— deal,*** trato honrado; ***— root,*** raíz cuadrada. —*n.* (*geom.*) cuadrado; casilla, escaque (*de ajedrez*), *m.*; plaza; (*mil.*) cuadro. — *v.t.* cuadrar; escuadrar; ajustar; sobornar; ***to — the account,*** saldar la cuenta.—*v.i.* cuadrar; conformarse, ajustarse.
squareness ['skwɛənis], *n.* cuadratura; honradez, *f.*
squash [skwɔʃ], *n.* aplastamiento; apiñamiento (*gentío*); limonada; pulpa (*de fruta*). —*v.t.* aplastar.—*v.i.* -se.
squashy ['skwɔʃi], *a.* blando.
squat [skwɔt], *a.* rechoncho.—*v.i.* agacharse, agazaparse; ocupar sin derecho.
squatter ['skwɔtə], *n.* intruso, colono usurpador.
squawk [skwɔ:k], *n.* graznido.—*v.i.* graznar.

squeak [skwi:k], *n.* chillido; chirrido; ***to have a narrow* —,** escapar por milagro.—*v.i.* chillar; chirriar; crujir.
squeal [skwi:l], *n.* chillido, grito agudo.—*v.i.* chillar; (*fam.*) cantar.
squeamish ['skwi:miʃ], *a.* delicado; remilgado; asqueado.
squeeze [skwi:z], *n.* estrujón; apretón, *m.*; ***tight* —,** (*fig.*) aprieto.—*v.t.* estrujar; apretar; sacar; arrancar; ***to* — *in,*** hacer sitio para.—*v.i.* ***to* — *through,*** pasar por fuerza; ***to* — *in,*** entrar con dificultad.
squelch [skweltʃ], *v.t.* despachurrar.—*v.i.* chapotear.
squib [skwib], *n.* buscapiés, *m.sg.*, petardo; pasquinada (*sátira*).
squid [skwid], *n.* calamar, *m.*
squint [skwint], *n.* estrabismo; mirada furtiva; (*fam.*) vistazo.—*v.i.* bizcar.
squint-eyed ['skwintaid], *a.* bizco.
squire [skwaiə], *n.* escudero; hacendado.
squirm [skwə:m], *n.* retorcimiento.—*v.i.* retorcerse.
squirrel ['skwirəl], *n.* ardilla.
squirt [skwə:t], *n.* chorro; jeringa; (*fam.*) majadero.—*v.t.* lanzar.—*v.i.* chorrear.
stab [stæb], *n.* puñalada; (*fig.*) punzada.—*v.t.* apuñalar.
stability [stə'biliti], *n.* estabilidad, *f.*; firmeza.
stable (1) [steibl], *a.* estable; firme.
stable (2) [steibl], *n.* cuadra; establo (*para vacas*).—*v.t.* poner en la cuadra.
stack [stæk], *n.* niara (*de heno*); montón; pabellón (*de fusiles*); cañón (*de chimenea*), *m.*; (*fam.*) abundancia.—*v.t.* hacinar; amontonar.
stadium ['steidjəm], *n.* estadio.
staff [stɑ:f], *n.* báculo; palo; bordón (*de peregrino*), *m.*; vara; asta (*de bandera*); personal, *m.*; (*mil.*) estado mayor; (*mus.*) pentagrama, *m.*
stag [stæg], *n.* ciervo.
stage [steidʒ], *n.* tablas, *f.pl.*; escena; andamio, etapa; estado; — ***hand,*** tramoyista, *m.*; — ***manager,*** director (*m.*) de escena; ***by easy stages,*** poco a poco; a pequeñas etapas; ***to go on the* —,** hacerse actor; ***to put on the* —,** poner en escena.—*v.t.* poner en escena; organizar.
stage-coach ['steidʒkoutʃ], *n.* diligencia.
stage-fright ['steidʒfrait], *n.* miedo al público.
stagger ['stægə], *n.* tambaleo.—*v.t.* desconcertar; escalonar (*horas etc.*).—*v.i.* tambalear.
staggering ['stægəriŋ], *a.* tambaleante; (*fig.*) asombroso.
stagnant ['stægnənt], *a.* estancado; paralizado.
stagnate [stæg'neit], *v.i.* estancarse.
stagnation [stæg'neiʃən], *n.* estancación; paralización, *f.*
stag-party ['stægpɑ:ti], *n.* reunión (*f.*) de hombres solos.
staid [steid], *a.* serio, formal.
stain [stein], *n.* mancha; descoloración, *f.*; tinte, *m.*—*v.t.* manchar; teñir; descolorar; ***stained glass,*** vidrio de color.
stainless ['steinlis], *a.* sin mancha; inmaculado; inoxidable (*acero*).
stair [stɛə], *n.* escalón, *m.*, peldaño.—*pl.* escalera.
staircase ['stɛəkeis], *n.* escalera.
stake [steik], *n.* estaca; (*agr.*) rodrigón; (*com.*) interés, *m.*; apuesta (*en los juegos*).—*v.t.* estacar; apostar; ***to* — *a claim,*** hacer una reclamación.
stalactite ['stæləktait], *n.* estalactita.
stalagmite ['stæləgmait], *n.* estalagmita.
stale [steil], *a.* viejo; pasado; cansado.
stalemate ['steilmeit], *n.* tablas, *f.pl.* (*ajedrez*); empate, *m.*
staleness ['steilnis], *n.* rancidez; vejez, *f.*
stalk (1) [stɔ:k], *n.* (*bot.*) tallo; pie (*de copa*), *m.*
stalk (2) [stɔ:k], *n.* paso majestuoso.—*v.t.* cazar al acecho.—*v.i.* andar con paso majestuoso.
stall (1) [stɔ:l], *n.* puesto (*de establo*); (*theat.*) butaca; sitial (*de coro*), *m.*; barraca.
stall (2) [stɔ:l], *v.t.* cortar (*máquina*).—*v.i.* pararse; dilatar, poner obstáculos.
stallion ['stæljən], *n.* garañón, *m.*
stalwart ['stɔ:lwət], *a.*, *n.* fornido; leal, *m.*
stamina ['stæminə], *n.* vigor, *m.*
stammer ['stæmə], *n.* tartamudeo; balbuceo.—*v.i.* tartamudear; balbucir.
stamp [stæmp], *n.* sello; timbre, *m.*, marca; estampilla; cuño; mano de mortero; (*fig.*) temple, *m.*, clase, *f.*; patada.—*v.t.* estampar; imprimir; sellar; timbrar; fijar el sello; acuñar; patear; apisonar; estigmatizar.—*v.i.* patear.
stampede [stæm'pi:d], *n.* estampida; pánico.—*v.t.* ahuyentar; dispersar en pánico.—*v.i.* salir de estampía; huir con pavor.
stanch [stɑ:ntʃ], *v.t.* restañar.
stand [stænd], *n.* posición, *f.*; tribuna; sostén, *m.*; puesto; (*mus.*) atril, *m.*; parada (*de taxis*); resistencia; ***to make a* — *against,*** oponerse a.—*v.t. irr.* poner de pie; poner; tolerar; resistir; convidar.—*v.i. irr.* estar; ser; estar de pie; ponerse en pie; sostenerse; parar(se); quedar(se); estancarse; presentarse como candidato; durar; estar vigente; ***to* — *against,*** oponerse a; ***to* — *aloof,*** mantenerse separado; ***to* — *aside,*** dejar pasar; mantenerse separado; ***to* — *back,*** recular; ***to* — *by,*** sostener; ser espectador; atenerse a; estar listo; ***to* — *for,*** representar; significar; presentarse como candidato para; tolerar; ***to* — *in for,*** sustituir; ***to* — *in need of,*** necesitar; ***to* — *in the way of,*** cerrar el paso a; impedir; ***to* — *on end,*** erizarse (*el pelo*); ***to* — *out,*** resistir; destacarse; ***to* — *up,*** ponerse en pie; ***to* — *up for,*** defender; volver por.
standard ['stændəd], *a.* normal; clásico; — ***work,*** obra clásica.—*n.* marco; norma; nivel, *m.*; ley (*del oro*), *f.*; (*mech.*) poste; pie; estandarte, *m.*, bandera; ***gold* —,** patrón (*m.*) de oro.
standardize ['stændədaiz], *v.t.* hacer uniforme; controlar.
standing ['stændiŋ], *a.* derecho, de pie; constante; permanente, fijo; vigente; — ***army,*** ejército permanente.—*n.* posición; reputación; duración; antigüedad, *f.*; — ***room,*** sitio para estar de pie (*en un teatro etc.*)
stand-offish [stænd'ɔfiʃ], *a.* altanero.
standpoint ['stændpɔint], *n.* punto de vista.
standstill ['stændstil], *n.* parada; pausa completa.
stank [stæŋk] [STINK].
stanza ['stænzə], *n.* estrofa.

staple (1) [steipl], *a.* corriente; principal.—*n.* producto principal (*de un país*); fibra; materia prima.
staple (2) [steipl], *n.* grapa, picolete, *m.*
star [stɑ:], *n.* estrella; asterisco; ***Stars and Stripes,*** las barras y las estrellas.—*v.t.* estrellar; (*theat.*) presentar como estrella; señalar con asterisco.—*v.i.* ser estrella.
starch [stɑ:tʃ], *n.* almidón, *m.*—*v.t.* almidonar.
starchy ['stɑ:tʃi], *a.* almidonado; (*med.*) feculoso; (*fig.*) tieso.
stare [stɛə], *n.* mirada fija.—*v.i.* abrir grandes ojos; mirar fijamente; ***to — in the face,*** saltar a la vista.
starfish ['stɑ:fiʃ], *n.* estrella de mar.
staring ['stɛəriŋ], *a.* que mira fijamente; llamativo.
stark [stɑ:k], *a.* rígido; árido; completo; ***— naked,*** en cueros.
starlight ['stɑ:laⁱt], *n.* luz (*f.*) de las estrellas.
starling ['stɑ:liŋ], *n.* estornino.
starlit ['stɑ:lit], **starry** ['stɑ:ri], *a.* estrellado.
star-spangled ['stɑ:spæŋgld], *a.* sembrado de estrellas.
start [stɑ:t], *n.* sobresalto; comienzo, principio; salida, partida; arranque, *m.*; ventaja.—*v.t.* empezar; poner en marcha; espantar (*caza*); dar la señal de partida; provocar; iniciar; abrir.—*v.i.* asustarse; dar un salto; ponerse en marcha; salir (*un tren*); arrancar (*un coche*); comenzar; combarse (*madera*); ***to — back,*** saltar hacia atrás; emprender el viaje de regreso; ***to — out,*** salir; ***to — up,*** ponerse en marcha.
starter ['stɑ:tə], *n.* iniciador; (*sport*) stárter; (*aut.*) arranque, *m.*
startle [stɑ:tl], *v.t.* asustar; alarmar.
starvation [stɑ:'veiʃən], *n.* hambre; inanición, *f.*
starve [stɑ:v], *v.t.* matar de hambre.—*v.i.* morir de hambre.
state [steit], *a.* de estado, estatal; público; de gala.—*n.* estado; dignidad, *f.*; pompa; ***in —,*** con gran pompa; ***in a —,*** (*fam.*) agitado.—*v.t.* exponer; decir; proponer (*un problema*).
statecraft ['steitkrɑ:ft], *n.* arte (*m.*) de gobernar.
stately ['steitli], *a.* imponente, majestuoso.
statement ['steitmənt], *n.* declaración; exposición, *f.*; resumen, *m.*; (*com.*) estado de cuenta.
statesman ['steitsmən], *n.* estadista, *m.*
statesmanlike ['steitsmənlaik], *a.* propio de un estadista.
statesmanship ['steitsmənʃip], *n.* arte (*m.*) de gobernar.
static ['stætik], *a.* estático.—*n.* perturbación atmosférica *o* eléctrica.
statics ['stætiks], *n.* estática.
station ['steiʃən], *n.* puesto; condición social; (*rail.*) estación, *f.*; (*rad.*) emisora; ***— master,*** jefe (*m.*) de estación.—*v.t.* colocar.
stationary ['steiʃənəri], *a.* estacionario, inmóvil.
stationery ['steiʃənəri], *n.* papelería.
statistical [stə'tistikl], *a.* estadístico.
statistics [stə'tistiks], *n. pl.* estadística.
statue ['stætju:], *n.* estatua.
statuesque [stætju'esk], *a.* escultural.
statuette [stætju'et], *n.* figurilla.
stature ['stætʃə], *n.* estatura.
status ['steitəs], *n.* estado; posición; reputación, *f.*
statute ['stætju:t], *n.* estatuto, ley, *f.*
statutory ['stætjutəri], *a.* establecido; estatuario.
staunch [stɔ:ntʃ], *a.* firme; leal; constante.
stave [steiv], *n.* duela; (*mus.*) pentagrama, *m.*—*v.t. irr.* ***to — in,*** abrir boquete en; quebrar; ***to — off,*** diferir; evitar; apartar.
stay (1) [stei], *n.* estancia; residencia; suspensión, *f.*; parada; freno.—*v.t.* detener; posponer.—*v.i.* permanecer, quedar(se); detenerse; hospedarse; ***to — in,*** quedarse en casa; ***to — on,*** permanecer; ***to — up,*** no acostarse.
stay (2) [stei], *n.* puntal; sostén; (*naut.*) estay, *m.*—*pl.* corsé, *m.*
stead [sted], *n.* lugar, *m.*; ***to stand in good —,*** ser útil.
steadfast ['stedfɑ:st], *a.* constante; firme; leal.
steady ['stedi], *a.* firme; fijo; seguro; formal; constante; uniforme.—*v.t.* hacer firme; estabilizar; calmar.
steak [steik], *n.* filete; biftec, *m.*
steal [sti:l], *v.t.*, *v.i. irr.* robar, hurtar; ***to — away,*** escabullirse; ***to — in,*** entrar furtivamente.
stealth [stelθ], *n.* astucia; cautela; ***by —,*** a hurtadillas.
stealthy ['stelθi], *a.* furtivo; cauteloso.
steam [sti:m], *n.* vapor, *m.*—*v.t.* saturar; cocer al baño María; empañar (*ventanas*).—*v.i.* echar vapor.
steamboat ['sti:mbout] [STEAMSHIP].
steam-engine ['sti:mendʒin], *n.* máquina de vapor.
steamer ['sti:mə] [STEAMSHIP].
steam-hammer ['sti:m'hæmə], *n.* maza de fragua.
steam-roller ['sti:mroulə], *n.* apisonadura.
steamship ['sti:mʃip], *n.* vapor, *m.*
steel [sti:l], *a.* de acero.—*n.* acero; afilón, *m.*; ***cold —,*** arma blanca; ***stainless —,*** acero inoxidable.—*v.t.* acerar; endurecer.
steep (1) [sti:p], *a.* escarpado; acantilado; empinado (*de escaleras*); exorbitante (*de precios*).—*n.* despeñadero.
steep (2) [sti:p], *n.* remojo.—*v.t.* empapar; remojar.
steeple [sti:pl], *n.* aguja.
steeplechase ['sti:pltʃeis], *n.* carrera de obstáculos.
steeplejack ['sti:pldʒæk], *n.* reparador (*m.*) de campanarios.
steepness ['sti:pnis], *n.* carácter escarpado.
steer (1) [stiə], *v.t.* gobernar; conducir.—*v.i.* navegar; timonear; conducirse; ***to — clear of,*** evitar.
steer (2) [stiə], *n.* novillo.
steering ['stiəriŋ], *n.* gobierno; (mecanismo de) dirección, *f.*
steering-wheel ['stiəriŋhwi:l], *n.* volante, *m.*
stem (1) [stem], *n.* (*bot.*) tallo; tronco; pie (*de copa*), *m.*; (*gram.*) raíz, *f.*; tubo (*de pipa*); ***from — to stern,*** de proa a popa.
stem (2) [stem], *v.t.* ir contra; resistir; contener; estancar.
stench [stentʃ], *n.* hedor, *m.*; tufo.
stencil [stensl], *n.* patrón (*m.*) para estarcir; estarcido; cliché (*duplicador*), *m.*—*v.t.* estarcir.

stenographer [ste'nɔgrəfə], *n.* estenógrafo.
step [step], *n.* paso; escalón, *m.*; grado; huella; (*mus.*) intervalo; — ***ladder,*** escalera de tijera; ***in —,*** a compás; ***to keep in —,*** llevar el paso; ***watch your —!*** ¡tenga cuidado! ***to retrace one's steps,*** volver sobre sus pasos; ***to take steps,*** tomar medidas.—*v.i. irr.* dar un paso; pisar; caminar; ***to — aside,*** desviarse; ***to — back,*** retroceder; ***to — down,*** bajar; ***to — in,*** entrar; ***to — on,*** pisar; ***to — out,*** salir; apearse; dar pasos grandes; ***to — over,*** atravesar; ***to — up,*** subir; aumentar.
stepbrother ['stepbrʌðə], *n.* hermanastro.
stepdaughter ['stepdɔ:tə], *n.* hijastra.
stepfather ['stepfɑ:ðə], *n.* padrastro.
stepmother ['stepmʌðə], *n.* madrastra.
stepsister ['stepsistə], *n.* hermanastra.
stepson ['stepsʌn], *n.* hijastro.
stereophonic [stiəriə'fɔnik], *a.* estereofónico.
stereoscopic [stiəriəs'kɔpik], *a.* estereoscópico.
stereotype ['stiəriətaip], *n.* estereotipia.—*v.t.* estereotipar.
sterile ['sterail], *a.* estéril; árido.
sterility [ste'riliti], *n.* esterilidad; aridez, *f.*
sterilization [sterilai'zeiʃən], *n.* esterilización, *f.*
sterilize ['sterilaiz], *v.t.* esterilizar.
sterilizer ['sterilaizə], *n.* esterilizador, *m.*
sterling ['stə:liŋ], *a.* esterlina; (*fig.*) genuino.
stern (1) [stə:n], *a.* austero; rígido; áspero.
stern (2) [stə:n], *a.* (*naut.*) de popa.—*n.* popa.
sternness ['stə:nnis], *n.* austeridad, severidad, *f.*
stethoscope ['steθəskoup], *n.* estetoscopio.
stevedore ['sti:vədɔ:], *n.* estibador, *m.*
stew [stju:], *n.* estofado; (*fig.*) agitación, *f.*—*v.t.* estofar; hervir; cocer (*fruta*).
steward ['stju:əd], *n.* administrador, *m.*; mayordomo; despensero; camarero (*en los vapores*).
stewpan ['stju:pæn], **stewpot** ['stju:pɔt], *n.* cazuela, olla.
stick (1) [stik], *n.* palo; estaca; leña; vara; bastón, *m.*; (*mus.*) batuta; barra; tallo; (*fig.*) ***in a cleft —,*** entre la espada y la pared.
stick (2) [stik], *v.t. irr.* hundir; clavar; meter; fijar; picar; pegar; tolerar; ***to — out,*** sacar.—*v.i. irr.* estar clavado; clavarse; pegarse; quedar; detenerse; atascarse; encallarse; perseverar; ***to — at,*** persistir en; detenerse ante; tener escrúpulos sobre; ***to — at nothing,*** no tener escrúpulos; ***to — by,*** sostener; ***to — close,*** mantenerse juntos; ***to — out,*** sobresalir; proyectar; ***to — to,*** pegarse a; mantener; perseverar en; ***to — up for,*** defender.
stickiness ['stikinis], *n.* viscosidad, *f.*
sticking-plaster ['stikiŋplɑ:stə], *n.* esparadrapo.
stickler ['stiklə], *n.* rigorista, *m.f.*
sticky ['stiki], *a.* pegajoso, viscoso; (*fig.*) difícil.
stiff [stif], *a.* tieso; duro; inflexible; espeso; almidonado; severo, difícil; frío; alto (*precio*); fuerte (*brisa*); — ***neck,*** torticolis, *m.*
stiffen [stifn], *v.t.* atiesar; endurecer; reforzar; espesar; aterir (*de frío*).—*v.i.* atiesarse; endurecerse; robustecerse; obstinarse; enderezarse; aterirse; refrescar (*el viento*).
stiffener ['stifnə], *n.* contrafuerte, *m.*
stiffness ['stifnis], *n.* tiesura; rigidez; severidad; obstinación; dificultad, *f.*
stifle [staifl], *v.t.* ahogar; apagar; suprimir.—*v.i.* ahogarse.
stigma ['stigmə], *n.* estigma, *m.*
stigmatize ['stigmətaiz], *v.t.* estigmatizar.
still (1) [stil], *a.* inmóvil; quedo, tranquilo; no espumoso (*vino*); — ***life,*** naturaleza muerta; ***to keep —,*** no moverse.—*adv.* todavía, aún; no obstante; siempre.—*n.* silencio; (*cine.*) retrato de propaganda.—*v.t.* hacer callar; calmar; detener.
still (2) [stil], *n.* alambique, *m.*
still-born ['stilbɔ:n], *a.* nacido muerto.
stillness ['stilnis], *n.* silencio; quietud tranquilidad, *f.*
stilt [stilt], *n.* zanco.
stilted ['stiltid], *a.* hinchado, pomposo.
stimulant ['stimjulənt], *a., n.* estimulante, *m.*
stimulate ['stimjuleit], *v.t.* estimular, excitar.
stimulating ['stimjuleitiŋ], *a.* estimulante; inspirador.
stimulation [stimju'leiʃən], *n.* estímulo; excitación, *f.*
stimulus ['stimjuləs], *n.* estímulo; incentivo.
sting [stiŋ], *n.* aguijón (*de insecto*), *m.*; mordedura (*de culebra*); estímulo; (*bot.*) púa.—*v.t., v.i. irr.* picar; morder, estimular; atormentar.
stinginess ['stindʒinis], *n.* tacañería.
stingy ['stindʒi], *a.* tacaño; pequeño.
stink [stiŋk], *n.* hedor, *m.*—*v.i. irr.* heder apestar.
stinking ['stiŋkiŋ], *a.* hediondo.
stint [stint], *n.* tarea; límite, *m.*—*v.t.* limitar; escatimar.
stipend ['staipend], *n.* estipendio, salario.
stipendiary [stai'pendjəri], *a., n.* estipendiario.
stipulate ['stipjuleit], *v.t.* estipular.
stipulation [stipju'leiʃən], *n.* estipulación; condición, *f.*
stir [stə:], *n.* movimiento; conmoción, *f.*; bullicio.—*v.t.* agitar; mover; revolver; conmover; inspirar; atizar; ***to — up,*** despertar, fomentar.—*v.i.* moverse; levantarse (*de la cama*).
stirring ['stə:riŋ], *a.* conmovedor, emocionante.—*n.* movimiento; el revolver.
stirrup ['stirəp], *n.* estribo.
stitch [stitʃ], *n.* puntada; punto; punzada (*dolor*).—*v.t., v.i.* coser; (*med.*) suturar; ***to — up,*** remendar; suturar.
stoat [stout], *n.* armiño.
stock [stɔk], *a.* corriente; del repertorio; — ***phrase,*** frase hecha.—*n.* tronco; injerto; estirpe (*de familia*), *f.*; (*com.*) valores, *m.pl.*; capital, *m.*; surtido (*de mercancías*); caldo; provisión, *f.*; reserva; ganado; (*bot.*) alhelí, *m.*; culata (*de fusil*); alzacuello; ***to take —,*** hacer inventario; ***Stock Exchange,*** Bolsa.—*pl.* cepo.—*v.t.* abastecer; proveer.
stockade [stɔ'keid], *n.* estacada, empalizada.—*v.t.* empalizar.
stockbroker ['stɔkbroukə], *n.* corredor (*m.*) de valores, bolsista, *m.*
stockholder ['stɔkhouldə], *n.* accionista, *m.f.*
stocking ['stɔkiŋ], *n.* media.
stocktaking ['stɔkteikiŋ], *n.* inventario.
stocky ['stɔki], *a.* rechoncho.
stoic ['stouik], *a., n.* estoico.

stoicism ['stouisizm], *n.* estoicismo.
stoke [stouk], *v.t.* alimentar; echar carbón.
stoke-hold ['stoukhould], **stoke-room** ['stoukrum], *n.* cuarto de calderas.
stoker ['stoukə], *n.* fogonero.
stole (1) [stoul], *n.* estola.
stole (2) [stoul], **stolen** ['stoulən] [STEAL].
stolid ['stɔlid], *a.* estólido; impasible.
stolidity [stɔ'liditi], *n.* estolidez; impasibilidad, *f.*
stomach ['stʌmək], *n.* estómago; vientre, *m.*; (*fig.*) apetito; valor, *m.*—*v.t.* digerir; (*fig.*) aguantar.
stone [stoun], *a.* de piedra.—*n.* piedra; hueso, pepita (*de fruta*); ***to leave no — unturned,*** (*fig.*) hacer todo lo posible.—*v.t.* apedrear; deshuesar (*la fruta*); revestir de piedras.
stone-cold ['stoun'kould], *a.* frío como la piedra.
stone-deaf ['stoun'def], *a.* completamente sordo.
stone-quarry ['stounkwɔri], *n.* pedrera.
stony ['stouni], *a.* pedregoso; (*fig.*) empedernido, duro, insensible.
stood [stud] [STAND].
stool [stu:l], *n.* taburete, *m.*
stool-pigeon ['stu:lpidʒən], *n.* soplón, *m.*
stoop [stu:p], *n.* inclinación, *f.*; cargazón (*f.*) de espaldas.—*v.i.* inclinarse; ser cargado de espaldas; rebajarse, humillarse.
stooping ['stu:piŋ], *a.* inclinado; cargado (*de espaldas*).—*n.* inclinación, *f.*
stop [stɔp], *n.* parada; cesación; detención; interrupción; suspensión, *f.*; (*mus.*) registro; ***full —,*** punto; ***to make a —,*** detenerse; ***to put a — to,*** poner coto a. —*v.t.* detener, parar; cortar; reprimir; suspender; poner fin a; obstruir; tapar; restañar; cesar (de); evitar; ***to — up,*** tapar.—*v.i.* parar(se), detenerse; cesar; quedarse; terminar; ***to — at nothing,*** no tener escrúpulos.
stop-cock ['stɔpkɔk], *n.* llave (*f.*) de agua.
stop-gap ['stɔpgæp], *n.* tapagujeres, *m.sg.*
stoppage ['stɔpidʒ], *n.* cesación; interrupción; obstrucción, *f.*; parada.
stopper ['stɔpə], *n.* tapón, *m.*
stop-press ['stɔp'pres], *n.* noticias (*f.pl.*) de última hora.
stop-watch ['stɔpwɔtʃ] *n.* cronógrafo.
storage ['stɔ:ridʒ], *n.* almacenaje, *m.*; ***— battery,*** (*U.S.*) [ACCUMULATOR].
store [stɔ:], *n.* abundancia; provisión, *f.*; depósito, almacén, *m.*; tienda; ***to set — by,*** estimar en mucho.—*pl.* pertrechos, *m.pl.*; provisiones, *f.pl.*—*v.t.* proveer; acumular; tener en reserva; almacenar.
storeroom ['stɔ:rum], *n.* despensa.
storey ['stɔ:ri] [STORY (2)].
stork [stɔ:k], *n.* cigüeña.
storm [stɔ:m], *n.* tempestad, *f.*, tormenta; tumulto; (*mil.*) asalto; ***to take by —,*** tomar por asalto; ***— in a teacup,*** tempestad (*f.*) en un vaso de agua.—*v.t.* asaltar.—*v.i.* bramar de cólera.
stormy ['stɔ:mi], *a.* tempestuoso; turbulento.
story (1) ['stɔ:ri], *n.* historia; cuento; anécdota; argumento.
story (2), **storey** ['stɔ:ri], *n.* piso; ***a four-story house,*** casa de cuatro pisos.
stout (1) [staut], *a.* fornido; corpulento; fuerte; firme; resuelto; intrépido.
stout (2) [staut], *n.* cerveza negra.
stoutness ['stautnis], *n.* corpulencia; solidez, *f.*; fuerza; valor, *m.*
stove (1) [stouv], *n.* horno, estufa.
stove (2) [stouv] [STAVE].
stow [stou], *v.t.* colocar; esconder; (*naut.*) estibar.—*v.i.* ***to — away,*** embarcarse clandestinamente.
stowaway ['stouəwei], *n.* polizón, *m.*
straddle [strædl], *v.t.*, *v.i.* montar a horcajadas.
strafe [strɑ:f], *v.t.* bombardear intensamente.
straggle [strægl], *v.i.* rezagarse; dispersarse; extenderse.
straggler ['stræglə], *n.* rezagado.
straggling ['stræglin], *a.* rezagado; disperso; desordenado.
straight [streit], *a.* derecho; recto, directo; lacio (*pelo*); ordenado; justo; honrado; franco; ***— face,*** cara seria.—*adv.* derecho; en línea directa; directamente; ***— away,*** en seguida.
straighten [streitn], *v.t.* poner derecho; enderezar; poner en orden, arreglar; ***to — out,*** poner en orden.—*v.i.* ***to — up,*** erguirse.
straightforward [streit'fɔ:wəd], *a.* honrado; sincero; sencillo; directo.
strain (1) [strein], *n.* tensión; tirantez, *f.*; esfuerzo; torcedura; estilo; exceso; (*mus.*) melodía.—*v.t.* estirar; forzar; esforzar; torcer (*un músculo*); forzar (*la vista*); aguzar (*el oído*); obligar demasiado; abusar de; filtrar; colar.
strain (2) [strein], *n.* raza; (*biol.*) cepa; vena; disposición heredada.
strainer ['streinə], *n.* coladero.
strait [streit], *n.* estrecho; apuro.
straiten [streitn], *v.t.* estrechar; limitar.
strait-jacket ['streitdʒækit], *n.* camisa de fuerza.
strait-laced [streit'leist], *a.* (*fig.*) mojigato.
strand (1) [strænd], *n.* playa; ribera.—*v.t.*, *v.i.* encallar; ***to be stranded,*** quedarse abandonado; (*fig.*) quedarse colgado.
strand (2) [strænd], *n.* hebra; hilo, sarta; cabo, ramal.
strange [streindʒ], *a.* extraño, singular; extraordinario; desconocido.
strangeness ['streindʒnis], *n.* rareza; novedad, *f.*
stranger ['streindʒə], *n.* desconocido; forastero; extranjero.
strangle [strængl], *v.t.* estrangular; ahogar.
strangler ['strænglə], *n.* estrangulador, *m.*
strangulation [strængju'leiʃən], *n.* estrangulación, *f.*
strap [stræp], *n.* correa.—*v.t.* atar con correas.
strapping ['stræpiŋ], *a.* robusto.
stratagem ['strætədʒəm], *n.* estratagema, ardid, *m.*
strategic [strə'ti:dʒik], *a.* estratégico.
strategist ['strætidʒist], *n.* estratego.
strategy ['strætidʒi], *n.* estrategia.
stratosphere ['strætəsfiə], *n.* estratosfera.
stratum ['strɑ:təm], *n.* estrato.
straw [strɔ:], *n.* paja; ***to be the last —,*** ser el colmo.
strawberry ['strɔ:bəri], *n.* fresa.
straw-coloured ['strɔ:kʌləd], *a.* pajizo.
stray [strei], *a.* perdido, descarriado.—*n.* animal perdido.—*v.i.* descarriarse, perder el camino; errar.

streak [stri:k], *n.* raya; rayo (*de luz*); vena; — ***of lightning,*** relámpago.—*v.t.* rayar.
streaky ['stri:ki], *a.* rayado.
stream [stri:m], *n.* corriente, *f.*; arroyo; torrente, *m.*; chorro.—*v.i.* correr, manar, brotar, fluir; chorrear.
streamer ['stri:mə], *n.* gallardete, *m.*
street [stri:t], *n.* calle, *f.*; ***the man in the —,*** el hombre medio; el ciudadano típico.
street-walker ['stri:twɔ:kə], *n.* prostituta.
strength [streŋθ], *n.* fuerza; validez; intensidad, *f.*
strengthen ['streŋθən], *v.t.* fortificar; reforzar; confirmar.—*v.i.* fortificarse; reforzarse.
strenuous ['strenjuəs], *a.* enérgico; arduo.
stress [stres], *n.* importancia; tensión, compulsión, *f.*; acento; (*mech.*) esfuerzo; ***to lay great — on,*** insistir en; dar mucha importancia a.—*v.t.* insistir en; dar énfasis a; acentuar.
stretch [stretʃ], *n.* tensión, *f.*; estirón, *m.*; esfuerzo; extensión, *f.*—*v.t.* extender; alargar; estirar; dilatar; ensanchar; exagerar; ***to — a point,*** hacer una concesión.—*v.i.* extenderse; dar de sí; estirarse; desperezarse; ***to — out,*** extenderse.
stretcher ['stretʃə], *n.* camilla.
stretcher-bearer ['streʃəbɛərə], *n.* camillero.
strew [stru:], *v.t. irr.* esparcir, derramar.
strewn [stru:n] [STREW].
stricken ['strikən], *a.* herido; afligido.
strict [strikt], *a.* estricto; exacto; severo.
strictly ['striktli], *adv.* ***strictly speaking,*** en rigor.
strictness ['striktnis], *n.* rigor, *m.*; severidad, *f.*
stride [straid], *n.* paso largo, tranco.—*v.t. irr.* cruzar a grandes trancos; montar a horcajadas.—*v.i.* andar a pasos largos.
strident ['straidənt], *a.* estridente; (*fig.*) chillón.
strife [straif], *n.* disputa, lucha; rivalidad, *f.*
strike [straik], *n.* golpe, *m.*; huelga; (*min.*) descubrimiento de un filón.—*v.t. irr.* golpear; pegar; herir; tocar, chocar contra; encender (*un fósforo*); acuñar (*moneda*); cerrar (*un trato*); dar (*la hora*); parecer; dar una impresión; ocurrírsele a uno (*una idea*); descubrir, encontrar; adoptar (*una postura*); arriar (*una bandera*); hacer (*un balance*); nivelar; desmontar (*una tienda*); ***to — against,*** chocar contra; ***to — down,*** derribar; acometer; ***to — off,*** borrar; ***to — out,*** borrar, tachar; ***to — up,*** trabar (*amistad*); ***it strikes me,*** me parece; ***how does it — you?*** ¿qué te parece?—*v.i. irr.* golpear; (*naut.*) encallar; declararse en huelga; sonar; arraigar; dar la hora; estallar; ***to — back,*** dar golpe por golpe; ***to — home,*** dar en el vivo; ***to — out,*** asesar un puñetazo; arrojarse; ***to — up,*** empezar a tocar.
striker ['straikə], *n.* huelguista, *m.f.*
striking ['straikiŋ], *a.* sorprendente, notable; impresionante; fuerte.
string [striŋ], *n.* bramante, *m.*; ristra (*de cebollas*); cinta; cuerda (*de un arco*); hilera; (*mus.*) cuerda; (*fig.*) sarta, serie, *f.*; — ***beans,*** judías verdes; ***to pull strings,*** (*fig.*) manejar los hilos.—*v.t. irr.* (*mus.*) encordar; ensartar; quitar las fibras; ***to — out,*** extender en fila; ***to — up,*** ahorcar.
stringed [striŋd], *a.* encordado; — ***instrument,*** instrumento de cuerda.
stringency ['strindʒənsi], *n.* aprieto; estrechez, severidad, *f.*
stringent ['strindʒənt], *a.* estricto, severo.
stringy ['striŋi], *a.* fibroso; correoso.
strip [strip], *n.* tira; listón (*de madera*), *m.*—*v.t.* desnudar; despojar; robar; descortezar.—*v.i.* desnudarse.
stripe [straip], *n.* raya, lista; azote; (*mil.*) galón, *m.*—*v.t.* rayar.
strive [straiv], *v.i. irr.* esforzarse; contender; pugnar.
strode [stroud] [STRIDE].
stroke [strouk], *n.* golpe, *m.*; (*mech.*) golpe del émbolo; plumada; pincelada; campanada (*de un reloj*); tacada (*en el billar*); (*med.*) ataque, *m.*; caricia con la mano; ***not a —,*** absolutamente nada; — ***of genius,*** rasgo ingenioso; — ***of luck,*** golpe de fortuna.—*v.t.* acariciar.
stroll [stroul], *n.* paseo.—*v.i.* pasearse, vagar.
stroller ['stroulə], *n.* paseante, *m.f.*
strong [strɔŋ], *a.* fuerte, vigoroso, robusto; poderoso; concentrado; firme; enérgico; resuelto; vivo; pronunciado; ***ten thousand —,*** de diez mil hombres.
strong-box ['strɔŋbɔks], *n.* caja de caudales.
stronghold ['strɔŋhould], *n.* fortaleza; (*fig.*) refugio.
strong-minded ['strɔŋ'maindid], *a.* resuelto; de firmes creencias.
strove [strouv] [STRIVE].
struck [strʌk] [STRIKE].
structural ['strʌktʃərəl], *a.* estructural.
structure ['strʌktʃə], *n.* construcción, *f.*; edificio; estructura.
struggle [strʌgl], *n.* lucha, disputa, conflicto.—*v.i.* luchar; esforzarse; contender.
strum [strʌm], *v.t.* rasgar (*la guitarra etc.*).
strung [strʌŋ] [STRING].
strut (1) [strʌt], *n.* pavonada.—*v.i.* pavonearse.
strut (2) [strʌt], *n.* (*carp.*) jabalcón, *m.*
stub [stʌb], *n.* cabo; talón (*de cheque*), *m.*; colilla (*de pitillo*); fragmento.—*v.t.* apagar (***out***).
stubble [stʌbl], *n.* rastrojo; barba.
stubborn ['stʌbən], *a.* terco; inquebrantable; persistente.
stubbornness ['stʌbənnis], *n.* obstinación, terquedad, *f.*
stuck [stʌk] [STICK].
stud (1) [stʌd], *n.* tachón, *m.*; botón (*m.*) de camisa.—*v.t.* tachonar; (*fig.*) adornar.
stud (2) [stʌd], *n.* caballeriza.
student ['stju:dənt], *a.* estudiantil.—*n.* estudiante, *m.f.*
studio ['stju:diou], *n.* estudio.
studious ['stju:djəs], *a.* estudioso, aplicado; solícito.
study ['stʌdi], *n.* estudio; gabinete, *m.*; meditación, *f.*—*v.t., v.i.* estudiar.
stuff [stʌf], *n.* materia; esencia; cachivaches, *m.pl.*; tela, estofa.—*v.t.* henchir; llenar; rellenar; apretar.
stuffing ['stʌfiŋ], *n.* rehenchimiento; relleno.
stuffy ['stʌfi], *a.* mal ventilado; (*fig.*) hinchado.
stultify ['stʌltifai], *v.t.* embrutecer; invalidar.
stumble [stʌmbl], *n.* traspié, tropezón, *m.*—*v.i.* tropezar; ***to — across,*** hallar casualmente, tropezar con.

stumbling-block ['stʌmbliŋblɔk], *n.* tropiezo; impedimento.
stump [stʌmp], *n.* tocón (*de árbol*), *m.*; troncho (*de col*); muñón (*de brazo etc.*); raigón (*de muela*); poste, *m.*—*v.t.* dejar perplejo.
stun [stʌn], *v.t.* aturdir con un golpe; pasmar; atolondrar.
stung [stʌŋ] [STING].
stunk [stʌŋk] [STINK].
stunning ['stʌniŋ], *a.* aturdidor; (*fam.*) estupendo.
stunt (1) [stʌnt], *n.* reclamo llamativo; ejercicio de proeza.
stunt (2) [stʌnt], *v.t.* impedir el crecimiento de.
stupefy ['stju:pifai], *v.t.* causar estupor; atontar; pasmar.
stupendous [stju:'pendəs], *a.* estupendo.
stupid ['stju:pid], *a.* estúpido; estupefacto.
stupidity [stju:'piditi], *n.* estupidez, *f.*; tontería.
stupor ['stju:pə], *n.* estupor, *m.*
sturdiness ['stə:dinis], *n.* robustez; tenacidad, *f.*
sturdy ['stə:di], *a.* robusto; tenaz.
sturgeon ['stə:dʒən], *n.* esturión, *m.*
stutter ['stʌtə], *n.* tartamudeo.—*v.i.* tartamudear.
stuttering ['stʌtəriŋ], *a.* tartamudo.—*n.* tartamudeo.
sty (1) [stai], *n.* pocilga.
sty (2), **stye** [stai], *n.* (*med.*) orzuelo.
style [stail], *n.* estilo; manera de obrar; moda; modelo; tratamiento; tono; clase, *f.*—*v.t.* nombrar.
stylish ['stailiʃ], *a.* elegante; a la moda.
stylize ['stailaiz], *v.t.* estilizar.
suave [swɑ:v], *a.* urbano, tratable.
suavity ['swɑ:viti], *n.* urbanidad, *f.*
subaltern ['sʌbəltən], *n.* subalterno.
subcommittee ['sʌbkəmiti], *n.* subcomisión, *f.*
subconscious [sʌb'kɔnʃəs], *a.* subconsciente.—*n.* subconsciencia.
subdivide [sʌbdi'vaid], *v.t.* subdividir.
subdivision ['sʌbdiviʒən], *n.* subdivisión, *f.*
subdue [səb'dju:], *v.t.* sojuzgar, reprimir; dominar; amansar; suavizar.
sub-editor ['sʌbeditə], *n.* subdirector, *m.*
subject ['sʌbdʒikt], *a.* sujeto; sometido.—*n.* (*pol.*) súbdito; tema, *m.*, asunto; (*educ.*) asignatura.—[səb'dʒekt], *v.t.* sujetar, someter, subyugar.
subjection [səb'dʒekʃən], *n.* sujeción, *f.*, sometimiento.
subjective [səb'dʒektiv], *a.* subjetivo.
subjugate ['sʌbdʒugeit], *v.t.* subyugar, someter.
subjugation [sʌbdʒu'geiʃən], *n.* subyugación, *f.*
subjunctive [səb'dʒʌŋktiv], *a.*, *n.* subjuntivo.
sublimate ['sʌblimeit], *v.t.* sublimar.
sublimation [sʌbli'meiʃən], *n.* sublimación, *f.*
sublime [sə'blaim], *a.* sublime; supremo; ***the* —**, lo sublime.
sublimity [sə'blimiti], *n.* sublimidad, *f.*
submarine ['sʌbməri:n], *a.*, *n.* submarino.
submerge [səb'mə:dʒ], *v.t.* sumergir; ahogar.—*v.i.* sumergirse.
submersion [səb'mə:ʃən], *n.* sumersión, *f.*
submission [səb'miʃən], *n.* sumisión; rendición, *f.*
submissive [səb'misiv], *a.* sumiso.
submit [səb'mit], *v.t.* someter; presentar.—*v.i.* someterse; rendirse.
subnormal [sʌb'nɔ:məl], *a.* subnormal.
subordinate [sə'bɔ:dinit], *a.*, *n.* subordinado.—[sə'bɔ:dineit], *v.t.* subordinar.
subscribe [səb'skraib], *v.t.*, *v.i.* subscribir; abonarse.
subscriber [səb'skraibə], *n.* subscriptor, *m.*; abonado.
subscription [səb'skripʃən], *n.* subscripción, *f.*; cuota; abono.
subsequent ['sʌbsikwənt], *a.* subsiguiente.
subservient [səb'sə:vjənt], *a.* útil; servil; subordinado.
subside [səb'said], *v.i.* calmarse; callarse; cesar; bajar (*el agua*); hundirse; disminuir.
subsidence [səb'saidəns], *n.* hundimiento; desplome, *m.*; bajada; poso; (*fig.*) apaciguamiento.
subsidiary [səb'sidjəri], *a.* subsidiario.
subsidize ['sʌbsidaiz], *v.t.* subvencionar.
subsidy ['sʌbsidi], *n.* subvención, *f.*
subsist [səb'sist], *v.i.* subsistir.
subsistence [səb'sistəns], *n.* subsistencia.
subsoil ['sʌbsɔil], *n.* subsuelo.
substance ['sʌbstəns], *n.* substancia.
substantial [səb'stænʃəl], *a.* substancial, sólido; verdadero.
substantiate [səb'stænʃieit], *v.t.* verificar; justificar; substanciar.
substantive ['sʌbstəntiv], *a.*, *n.* substantivo.
substitute ['sʌbstitju:t], *n.* substituto.—*v.t.* substituir.
substitution [sʌbsti'tju:ʃən], *n.* substitución, *f.*
substratum [sʌb'strɑ:təm], *n.* (*pl.* **substrata**) substrato.
subterfuge ['sʌbtəfju:dʒ], *n.* subterfugio; evasión, *f.*
subterranean [sʌbtə'reinjən], *a.* subterráneo.
subtle [sʌtl], *a.* sutil; penetrante; hábil; astuto.
subtlety ['sʌtlti], *n.* sutileza; agudeza; astucia.
subtract [səb'trækt], *v.t.* substraer, restar.
subtraction [səb'trækʃən], *n.* substracción, *f.*, resta.
suburb ['sʌbə:b], *n.* suburbio.—*pl.* afueras, *f.pl.*
suburban [sə'bə:bən], *a.* suburbano.
subversion [səb'və:ʃən], *n.* subversión, *f.*
subversive [səb'və:siv], *a.* subversivo.
subvert [səb'və:t], *v.t.* subvertir.
subway ['sʌbwei], *n.* pasaje subterráneo, *m.*; (*U.S.*) metro.
succeed [sək'si:d], *v.t.* suceder (a); seguir (a).—*v.i.* tener éxito; ser el sucesor; ***to* — *in***, lograr, conseguir.
succeeding [sək'si:diŋ], *a.* subsiguiente, futuro.
success [sək'ses], *n.* éxito.
successful [sək'sesful], *a.* próspero, afortunado; ***to be* —**, tener éxito.
succession [sək'seʃən], *n.* sucesión, *f.*; ***in* —**, sucesivamente.
successor [sək'sesə], *n.* sucesor, *m.*; heredero.
succinct [sək'siŋkt], *a.* sucinto, conciso.
succour ['sʌkə], *n.* socorro, auxilio.—*v.t.* socorrer.
succulent ['sʌkjulənt], *a.* suculento.
succumb [sə'kʌm], *v.i.* sucumbir; rendirse.
such [sʌtʃ], *a.* tal; semejante, parecido.—*adv.* tan.—*pron.* tal; el (la, lo, los, las) que.

suchlike ['sʌtʃlaik], *a.* semejante, tal; de esta clase.
suck [sʌk], *n.* succión, *f.*; chupada; ***to give —***, (*obs.*) amamantar.—*v.t.* chupar; mamar.
sucker ['sʌkə], *n.* lechón, chupador, *m.*; (*bot.*) retoño; (*zool.*) ventosa; (*fam.*) primo.
sucking-pig ['sʌkiŋpig], *n.* lechoncito, cochinillo.
suckle [sʌkl], *v.t.* amamantar.
suction ['sʌkʃən], *n.* succión, *f.*
suction-pump ['sʌkʃən'pʌmp], *n.* bomba aspirante.
Sudan [su'dɑ:n], *n.* el Sudán.
Sudanese [sudə'ni:z], *a.*, *n.* sudanés, *m.*
sudden [sʌdn], *a.* imprevisto, impensado; súbito; precipitado; ***all of a —***, de repente.
suddenly ['sʌdnli], *adv.* de repente, súbitamente.
suddenness ['sʌdnnis], *n.* calidad repentina, brusquedad, *f.*
suds [sʌdz], *n.pl.* jabonaduras, *f.pl.*, espuma.
sue [sju:], *v.t.* demandar, pedir en juicio; ***to — for,*** pedir; ***to — for damages,*** demandar por daños y perjuicios.
suède [sweid], *a.* de ante.—*n.* ante, *m.*
suet ['s(j)u:it], *n.* sebo.
suffer ['sʌfə], *v.t.* sufrir, padecer; tolerar, aguantar; permitir.—*v.i.* sufrir.
sufferance ['sʌfərəns], *n.* tolerancia.
sufferer ['sʌfərə], *n.* sufridor, *m.*; enfermo; víctima.
suffering ['sʌfəriŋ], *a.* doliente, sufriente.—*n.* sufrimiento, dolor, *m.*
suffice [sə'fais], *v.t.* satisfacer.—*v.i.* bastar.
sufficiency [sə'fiʃənsi], *n.* suficiencia.
sufficient [sə'fiʃənt], *a.* suficiente, bastante.
suffix ['sʌfiks], *n.* sufijo.
suffocate ['sʌfəkeit], *v.t.* sofocar, ahogar; apagar.—*v.i.* sofocarse, ahogarse.
suffocation [sʌfə'keiʃən], *n.* sofocación, *f.*, ahogo.
suffrage ['sʌfridʒ], *n.* sufragio.
suffuse [sə'fju:z], *v.t.* bañar, cubrir; extender.
sugar ['ʃugə], *n.* azúcar, *m.*—*v.t.* azucarar; ***to — the pill,*** (*fig.*) dorar la píldora.
sugar-beet ['ʃugəbi:t], *n.* remolacha.
sugar-bowl ['ʃugəboul], *n.* azucarero.
sugar-cane ['ʃugəkein], *n.* caña de azucar.
sugar-coated ['ʃugəkoutid], *a.* confitado.
sugar-tongs ['ʃugətɔŋz], *n.pl.* tenacillas, *f.pl.*
sugary ['ʃugəri], *a.* azucarado; (*fig.*) meloso.
suggest [sə'dʒest], *v.t.* sugerir; insinuar; indicar; aconsejar; evocar.—*v.r.* ocurrirse (*una idea*).
suggestion [sə'dʒestʃən], *n.* sugestión; insinuación, *f.*
suggestive [sə'dʒestiv], *a.* sugestivo; picante.
suicidal [sjui'saidl], *a.* suicida.
suicide ['sjuisaid], *n.* suicidio (*hecho*); suicida (*persona*), *m.f.*; ***to commit —,*** suicidarse.
suit [sju:t], *n.* petición, *f.*; cortejo; pleito; traje, *m.*; palo (*naipes*); serie, *f.*; ***to follow —,*** jugar el mismo palo; (*fig.*) seguir el ejemplo.—*v.t.* convenir; ir bien, sentar; agradar.
suitability [sju:tə'biliti], *n.* conveniencia; aptitud, *f.*
suitable ['sju:təbl], *a.* apropiado, apto, a propósito, conveniente.
suitcase ['sju:tkeis], *n.* maleta.
suite [swi:t], *n.* juego (*de muebles etc.*); serie, *f.*; séquito.
suitor ['sju:tə], *n.* pretendiente, *m.*; (*jur.*) demandante, *m.f.*
sulk [sʌlk], *n.* mohina.—*v.i.* ponerse mohino.
sulky ['sʌlki], *a.* mohino, malhumorado.
sullen ['sʌlən], *a.* hosco, taciturno; sombrío.
sullenness ['sʌlənnis], *n.* hosquedad, taciturnidad, *f.*, mal humor, *m.*
sully ['sʌli], *v.t.* manchar, empañar; desdorar.
sulphur ['sʌlfə], *n.* azufre, *m.*
sulphurous ['sʌlfərəs] *a.* sulfuroso.
sultan ['sʌltən], *n.* sultán, *m.*
sultana [sʌl'tɑ:nə], *n.* sultana.
sultry ['sʌltri], *a.* bochornoso, sofocante.
sum [sʌm], *n.* (*math.*) suma; problema, *m.*; total, *m.*; (*com.*) cantidad, *f.*; resumen, *m.*—*v.t.* sumar; ***to — up,*** recapitular; resumir.
summarize ['sʌməraiz], *v.t.* resumir, compendiar.
summary ['sʌməri], *a.* sumario; somero.—*n.* sumario, resumen, *m.*
summer ['sʌmə], *a.* estival, de verano.—*n.* verano, estío.
summer-house ['sʌməhaus], *n.* cenador, *m.*
summit ['sʌmit], *n.* cima, cumbre, *f.*
summon ['sʌmən], *v.t.* citar; mandar; llamar; invocar; ***to — up,*** animar.
summons ['sʌmənz], *n.* citación, *f.*; requerimiento.
sumptuous ['sʌmptjuəs], *a.* suntuoso, magnífico.
sumptuousness ['sʌmptjuəsnis], *n.* suntuosidad, *f.*, magnificencia.
sun [sʌn], *n.* sol, *m.*—*v.r.* tomar el sol.
sun-bathing ['sʌnbeiðiŋ], *n.* baño de sol.
sunbeam ['sʌnbi:m], *n.* rayo de sol.
sun-blind ['sʌnblaind], *n.* toldo para el sol.
sunburn ['sʌnbə:n], *n.* quemadura del sol; bronceado.
sunburnt ['sʌnbə:nt], *a.* moreno, tostado por el sol, bronceado.
Sunday ['sʌnd(e)i], *a.* dominical.—*n.* domingo.
sunder ['sʌndə], *v.t.* separar, hender.
sun-dial ['sʌndaiəl], *n.* reloj (*m.*) de sol.
sundown ['sʌndaun], *n.* puesta del sol.
sundry ['sʌndri], *a.* varios.—*n.pl.* **sundries,** artículos diversos, *m.pl.*
sunflower ['sʌnflauə], *n.* girasol, *m.*
sung [sʌŋ] [SING].
sun-glasses ['sʌnglɑ:siz], *n.pl.* gafas (*f.pl.*) de sol.
sunk [sʌŋk] [SINK].
sunken ['sʌŋkən], *a.* hundido.
sunlight ['sʌnlait], *n.* luz (*f.*) del sol.
sunny ['sʌni], *a.* expuesto al sol, asoleado; (*fig.*) risueño; alegre; ***to be —,*** hacer sol.
sunrise ['sʌnraiz], *n.* salida del sol; ***from — to sunset,*** de sol a sol.
sunset ['sʌnset], *n.* puesta del sol.
sunshade ['sʌnʃeid], *n.* quitasol, *m.*
sunshine ['sʌnʃain], *n.* luz (*f.*) del sol; ***in the —,*** al sol.
sunstroke ['sʌnstrouk], *n.* insolación, *f.*
sup [sʌp], *n.* sorbo.—*v.t.* sorber, beber.—*v.i.* (*obs.*) cenar.
superabundance [sju:pərə'bʌndəns], *n.* superabundancia.
superabundant [sju:pərə'bʌndənt], *a.* superabundante.
superannuated [sju:pər'ænjueitid], *a.* jubilado; anticuado.

superb [sju'pə:b], *a.* soberbio; espléndido.
supercilious [sju:pə'siljəs], *a.* desdeñoso, altivo.
superficial [sju:pə'fiʃəl], *a.* superficial.
superficiality [sju:pəfiʃi'æliti], *n.* superficialidad, *f.*
superfluity [sju:pə'flu:iti], *n.* superfluidad, *f.*, sobra.
superfluous [sju:'pə:fluəs], *a.* superfluo.
superhuman [sju:pə'hju:mən], *a.* sobrehumano.
superimpose [sju:pərim'pouz], *v.t.* sobreponer.
superintend [sju:prin'tend], *v.t.* dirigir, vigilar, superentender.
superintendent [sju:prin'tendənt]. *n.* superintendente, *m.f.*
superior [sju'piərjə], *a.* superior; altivo.—*n.* superior, *m.*; ***Mother Superior***, superiora.
superiority [sjupiəri'ɔriti], *n.* superioridad, *f.*
superlative [sju'pə:lətiv], *a.*, *n.* superlativo.
superman ['sju:pəmæn], *n.* superhombre, *m.*
supernatural [sju:pə'nætʃrəl], *a.* sobrenatural.
supersede [sju:pə'si:d], *v.t.* reemplazar, suplantar.
superstition [sju:pə'stiʃən], *n.* superstición, *f.*
superstitious [sju:pə'stiʃəs], *a.* supersticioso.
supervene [sju:pə'vi:n], *v.i.* sobrevenir.
supervise ['sju:pəvaiz], *v.t.* superentender, vigilar, dirigir.
supervision [sju:pə'viʒən], *n.* superintendencia, dirección, *f.*, vigilancia.
supervisor ['sju:pəvaizə], *n.* superintendente, *m.f.*
supper ['sʌpə], *n.* cena; ***to have —***, cenar.
supplant [sə'plɑ:nt], *v.t.* suplantar.
supple [sʌpl], *a.* flexible; ágil; dócil; servil, lisonjero.
supplement ['sʌplimənt], *n.* suplemento; apéndice, *m.*—[sʌpli'ment], *v.t.* suplementar, complementar.
supplementary [sʌpli'mentəri], *a.* suplementario, adicional.
suppliant ['sʌpljənt], *a.*, *n.* suplicante, *m.f.*
supplicate ['sʌplikeit], *v.t.* suplicar.
supplication [sʌpli'keiʃən], *n.* súplica, suplicación, *f.*
supplier [sə'plaiə], *n.* suministrador, proveedor, *m.*
supply [sə'plai], *n.* suministro, provisión, *f.*; cantidad suficiente, *f.*; substituto; (*com.*) oferta; ***— and demand***, oferta y demanda. —*pl.* **supplies**, pertrechos, *m.pl.*; provisiones, *f.pl.*—*v.t.* proveer; suministrar; proporcionar; suplir, reemplazar.
support [sə'pɔ:t], *n.* sostén, *m.*; apoyo; ***in — of***, en favor de.—*v.t.* sostener, apoyar; mantener; aguantar; defender; vindicar; ***to — oneself***, ganarse la vida.
supporter [sə'pɔ:tə], *n.* defensor, *m.*; partidario.
suppose [sə'pouz], *v.t.* suponer; figurarse; creer.
supposition [sʌpə'ziʃən], *n.* suposición, hipótesis, *f.*
suppress [sə'pres], *v.t.* suprimir; reprimir; ocultar; contener.
suppression [sə'preʃən], *n.* supresión; represión, *f.*
supremacy [sju'preməsi], *n.* supremacía.
supreme [sju'pri:m], *a.* supremo; sumo.
surcharge ['sə:tʃɑ:dʒ], *n.* sobrecarga.
sure [ʃuə], *a.* seguro, cierto; ***to be —***, seguramente; estar seguro; ***to make — of***, asegurarse de.—*adv.* seguramente, ciertamente.
sure-footed ['ʃuə'futid], *a.* de pie firme.
sureness ['ʃuənis], *n.* seguridad, *f.*, certeza.
surety ['ʃuəti], *n.* garante, *m.f.*; garantía.
surf [sə:f], *n.* rompiente, *m.*, resaca.
surface ['sə:fis], *a.* superficial.—*n.* superficie, *f.*—*v.t.* allanar.—*v.i.* salir a la superficie.
surfeit ['sə:fit], *n.* ahito; (*fig.*) empalago.—*v.t.* saciar.
surf-riding ['sə:fraidiŋ], *n.* patinaje (*m.*) sobre las olas.
surge [sə:dʒ], *n.* oleada.—*v.i.* agitarse, bullir; embravecerse (*el mar*); romper (*las olas*).
surgeon ['sə:dʒən], *n.* cirujano.
surgery ['sə:dʒəri], *n.* cirugía; consultorio.
surgical ['sə:dʒikəl], *a.* quirúrgico.
surliness ['sə:linis], *n.* acedía, mal genio; taciturnidad, *f.*
surloin [SIRLOIN].
surly ['sə:li], *a.* agrio, malhumorado; taciturno.
surmise ['sə:maiz], *n.* conjetura, suposición, *f.*—[sə:'maiz], *v.t.* conjeturar; suponer.
surmount [sə:'maunt], *v.t.* vencer, superar; coronar.
surname ['sə:neim], *n.* apellido.—*v.t.* nombrar, llamar.
surpass [sə:'pɑ:s], *v.t.* superar; exceder.
surpassing [sə:'pɑ:siŋ], *a.* incomparable.
surplice ['sə:plis], *n.* sobrepelliz, *f.*
surplus ['sə:pləs], *a.* sobrante.—*n.* sobras, *f.pl.*, sobrante, *m.*, exceso; (*com.*) superávit, *m.*
surprise [sə'praiz], *n.* sorpresa, asombro.—*v.t.* sorprender, asombrar; coger de improviso.
surprising [sə'praiziŋ], *a.* sorprendente.
surrealism [sə'riəlizm], *n.* surrealismo.
surrender [sə'rendə], *n.* rendición, *f.*, entrega; sumisión, *f.*; (*jur.*) cesión, *f.*—*v.t.* rendir, entregar; ceder; renunciar a.—*v.i.* entregarse, rendirse.
surreptitious [sʌrəp'tiʃəs], *a.* subrepticio.
surround [sə'raund], *n.* borde, *m.*—*v.t.* rodear, cercar; sitiar.
surrounding [sə'raundiŋ], *a.* vecino; alrededor, *inv.*—*n.pl.* alrededores, *m.pl.*, cercanías, *f.pl.*; ambiente, *m.*
survey ['sə:vei], *n.* apeo; vista; inspección, *f.*, examen, *m.*—[sə:'vei], *v.t.* apear (*tierras*); inspeccionar (*casas*); mirar; examinar.
surveying [sə'veiiŋ], *n.* agrimensura.
surveyor [sə:'veiə], *n.* agrimensor; inspector, *m.*
survival [sə'vaivəl], *n.* supervivencia; reliquia.
survive [sə'vaiv], *v.t.*, *v.i.* sobrevivir; subsistir.
survivor [sə'vaivə], *n.* sobreviviente, *m.f.*
susceptibility [səsepti'biliti], *n.* susceptibilidad; propensión, *f.*
susceptible [sə'septibl], *a.* susceptible; sensible; impresionable; enamoradizo.
suspect ['sʌspekt], *a.*, *n.* sospechoso.—[səs'pekt], *v.t.* sospechar; conjeturar; dudar. —*v.i.* tener sospechas.
suspend [səs'pend], *v.t.* suspender.

suspenders [səs'pendəz], *n.pl.* ligas, *f.pl.*; (*U.S.*) tirantes (*m.pl.*) del pantalón.
suspense [səs'pens], *n.* incertidumbre, *f.*
suspension [səs'penʃən], *n.* suspensión, *f.*
suspension-bridge [səs'penʃənbridʒ], *n.* puente colgante, *m.*
suspicion [səs'piʃən], *n.* sospecha; conjetura; pizca, dejo.
suspicious [səs'piʃəs], *a.* sospechoso; suspicaz.
sustain [səs'tein], *v.t.* sostener, sustentar, mantener; apoyar; confirmar; (*mus.*) prolongar; ***to — a loss,*** sufrir una pérdida.
sustenance ['sʌstinəns], *n.* mantenimiento; sustento, alimentos, *m.pl.*
swab [swɔb], *n.* fregajo; (*med.*) torunda; (*naut.*) lampazo.—*v.t.* fregar; (*naut.*) lampacear.
swagger ['swægə], *n.* fanfarria; pavoneo.—*v.i.* fanfarrear; pavonearse.
swaggering ['swægəriŋ], *a.* fanfarrón, majo.
swallow (1) ['swɔlou], *n.* trago.—*v.t.* tragar, engullir; retractar.
swallow (2) ['swɔlou], *n.* (*orn.*) golondrina.
swam [swæm] [SWIM].
swamp [swɔmp], *n.* pantano.—*v.t.* sumergir, echar a pique; mojar; (*fig.*) hundir.
swampy ['swɔmpi], *a.* pantanoso.
swan [swɔn], *n.* cisne, *m.*
swank [swæŋk], *n.* farolero; farolería.—*v.i.* fanfarrear; darse tono.
swap [swɔp], *n.* cambio, trueque, *m.*—*v.t.* cambiar, trocar.
swarm [swɔ:m], *n.* enjambre, *m.*; caterva, multitud, *f.*—*v.i.* enjambrar; pulular, hormiguear; abundar.
swarthy ['swɔ:ði], *a.* moreno.
swashbuckler ['swɔʃbʌklə], *n.* matasiete, *m.*
swat [swɔt], *v.t.* matar (*moscas*).
swathe [sweið], *v.t.* fajar, envolver; vendar.
sway [swei], *n.* ascendiente, *m.*, influencia; poder, *m.*, imperio; vaivén, *m.*, balanceo, oscilación, *f.*; bamboleo; ***to hold —,*** gobernar.—*v.t.* inclinar; influir; cimbrar; dominar, gobernar; mecer, oscilar.—*v.i.* inclinarse; oscilar; bambolearse, tambalearse.
swear [swɛə], *v.t. irr.* jurar; declarar bajo juramento; ***to — in,*** hacer prestar juramento a.—*v.i. irr.* jurar; blasfemar; hacer votos; ***to — by,*** (*fam.*) poner confianza implícita en; ***to — to,*** atestiguar.
sweat [swet], *n.* sudor, *m.*; (*fig.*) trabajo duro.—*v.t.* hacer sudar.—*v.i.* sudar.
sweating ['swetiŋ], *n.* transpiración; explotación, *f.*
sweaty ['sweti], *a.* sudoroso.
Swede [swi:d], *n.* sueco.
swede [swi:d], *n.* (*bot.*) nabo sueco.
Sweden [swi:dn], *n.* Suecia.
Swedish ['swi:diʃ], *a.*, *n.* sueco.
sweep [swi:p], *n.* barredura; extensión, *f.*; alcance, *m.*; curva; envergadura (*de alas*); gesto.—*v.t. irr.* barrer; deshollinar; pasar por; arrebatar; examinar (*con la mirada*); ***to — along,*** arrastrar; ***to — aside,*** apartar con un gesto desdeñoso; ***to — away,*** barrer; llevar; ***to — up,*** barrer; ***to be swept off one's feet,*** ser arrebatado.—*v.i. irr.* barrer; pasar rápidamente por; marchar majestuosamente; extenderse; ***to — along,*** pasar majestuosamente; ***to — on,*** seguir su marcha.
sweeper ['swi:pə], *n.* barrendero.
sweeping ['swi:piŋ], *a.* comprehensivo; demasiado amplio *o* general; ***— changes,*** cambios radicales.
sweepstake ['swi:psteik], *n.* lotería.
sweet [swi:t] *a.* dulce; oloroso; melodioso; encantador; amable; bonito.—*n.* dulzura: dulce, bombón, *m.*; persona querida.
sweet-corn ['swi:tkɔ:n], *n.* mazorca.
sweeten [swi:tn], *v.t.* endulzar, azucarar.
sweetheart ['swi:thɑ:t], *n.* enamorada, novia; enamorado, novio.
sweetness ['swi:tnis], *n.* dulzura; bondad, *f.*; fragancia.
sweet-pea ['swi:t'pi:], *n.* guisante (*m.*) de olor.
sweet-smelling ['swi:t'smeliŋ], *a.* fragante.
sweet-toothed ['swi:t'tu:θd], *a.* goloso.
sweet-william ['swi:t'wiljəm], *n.* clavel barbado.
swell [swel], *n.* oleada, oleaje, *m.*; hinchazón, *f.*; ondulación (*del terreno*), *f.*; (*mus.*) crescendo; aumento; (*fam.*) petimetre, *m.*—*v.t. irr.* hinchar; aumentar; envanecer.—*v.i. irr.* hincharse; entumecerse (*el mar*); crecer; envanecerse.
swelling ['sweliŋ], *n.* hinchazón, *f.*; (*med.*) tumefacción, *f.*
swelter ['sweltə], *v.i.* abrasarse; sudar la gota gorda.
swept [swept] [SWEEP].
swerve [swə:v], *n.* desviación, *f.*—*v.i.* torcerse; desviarse.
swift [swift], *a.* veloz, rápido; pronto; repentino.—*n.* (*orn.*) vencejo.
swiftness ['swiftnis], *n.* velocidad, rapidez; prontitud, *f.*
swim [swim], *n.* nadada, baño; ***to be in the —,*** estar al corriente.—*v.t. irr.* pasar a nado; hacer flotar; mojar.—*v.i. irr.* nadar; flotar; resbalar; inundarse; abundar; ***my head swims,*** se me va la cabeza.
swimmer ['swimə], *n.* nadador, *m.*
swimming ['swimiŋ], *n.* natación, *f.*; (*med.*) vértigo.
swimming-costume ['swimiŋ'kɔstju:m], *n.* traje (*m.*) de baño.
swimming-pool ['swimiŋpu:l], *n.* piscina.
swindle [swindl], *n.* estafa, timo.—*v.t.* estafar, timar.
swindler ['swindlə], *n.* estafador, *m.*
swine [swain], *n.* (*inv.*) puerco, cerdo; (*fig.*) cochino.
swing [swiŋ], *n.* oscilación, *f.*, balanceo; vaivén, *m.*; ritmo; columpio; alcance, *m.*; ***in full —,*** en plena operación.—*v.t. irr.* columpiar; mecer; hacer oscilar; blandir.—*v.i. irr.* oscilar; columpiarse; balancearse; dar vueltas; (*naut.*) bornear; (*fam.*) ser ahorcado.
swinging ['swiŋiŋ], *a.* oscilante; rítmico.—*n.* oscilación, *f.*; balanceo; vaivén, *m.*
swish [swiʃ], *n.* silbo; crujido; susurro.—*v.t.* blandir; agitar, menear; azotar.—*v.i.* silbar; susurrar; crujir.
Swiss [swis], *a.*, *n.* suizo.
switch [switʃ], *n.* varilla; látigo; cabellera postiza; (*rail.*) apartadero; aguja; (*elec.*) conmutador, interruptor, *m.*—*v.t.* azotar; (*elec.*) interrumpir; trasladar; ***to — off,*** (*elec.*) desconectar, cortar; ***to — on,*** (*elec.*) conectar, encender.

switchboard ['switʃbɔ:d], *n.* cuadro de distribución.
Switzerland ['switsələnd], *n.* Suiza.
swivel [swivl], *n.* alacrán, torniquete, *m.*—*v.i.* girar sobre un eje.
swollen ['swoulən] [SWELL].
swoon [swu:n], *n.* desmayo.—*v.i.* desmayarse.
swoop [swu:p], *n.* calada.—*v.i.* abatirse, abalanzarse.
sword [sɔ:d], *n.* espada; ***to put to the —,*** pasar a cuchillo.
sword-belt ['sɔ:dbelt], *n.* talabarte, *m.*
sword-fish ['sɔ:dfiʃ], *n.* pez espada, *m.*
sword-play ['sɔ:dplei], *n.* esgrima.
swordsman ['sɔ:dzmən], *n.* espadachín, *m.*
swore [swɔ:], **[sworn]** [swɔ:n] [SWEAR].
swum [swʌm] [SWIM].
swung [swʌŋ] [SWING].
sycamore ['sikəmɔ:], *n.* sicómoro.
sycophant ['sikəfənt], *n.* adulador, *m.*
sycophantic [sikə'fæntik], *a.* adulatorio.
syllabic [si'læbik], *a.* silábico.
syllable ['siləbl], *n.* sílaba.
syllabus ['siləbəs], *n.* programa, *m.*
syllogism ['silədʒizm], *n.* silogismo.
symbol ['simbəl], *n.* símbolo.
symbolic [sim'bɔlik], *a.* simbólico.
symbolism ['simbəlizm], *n.* simbolismo.
symbolist ['simbəlist], *n.* simbolista, *m.f.*
symbolize ['simbəlaiz], *v.t.* simbolizar.
symmetrical [si'metrikəl], *a.* simétrico.
symmetry ['simitri], *n.* simetría.
sympathetic [simpə'θetik], *a.* compasivo; simpático.
sympathize ['simpəθaiz], *v.i.* simpatizar; compadecerse.
sympathizer ['simpəθaizə], *n.* partidario.
sympathy ['simpəθi], *n.* compasión, *f.*; simpatía.
symphonic [sim'fɔnik], *a.* sinfónico.
symphony ['simfəni], *n.* sinfonía.
symptom ['simptəm], *n.* síntoma, *m.*; indicio.
symptomatic [simpto'mætik], *a.* sintomático.
synagogue ['sinəgɔg], *n.* sinagoga.
synchronize ['siŋkrənaiz], *v.t.* sincronizar.—*v.i.* sincronizarse; coincidir.
syncopation [siŋko'peiʃən], *n.* síncopa.
syndicate ['sindikit], *n.* sindicato.—['sindikeit], *v.t.* sindicar.
synonym ['sinənim], *n.* sinónimo.
synonymous [si'nɔniməs], *a.* sinónimo.
synopsis [si'nɔpsis], *n.* sinopsis, *f.*
syntactic [sin'tæktik], *a.* sintático.
syntax ['sintæks], *n.* sintaxis, *f.*
synthesis ['sinθisis], *n.* síntesis, *f.*
synthesize ['sinθisaiz], *v.t.* sintetizar.
synthetic [sin'θetik], *a.* sintético.
syphillis ['sifilis], *n.* sífilis, *f.*
syphon [SIPHON].
Syrian ['siriən], *a., n.* sirio.
syringe ['sirindʒ], *n.* jeringa.—*v.t.* jeringar.
syrup ['sirəp], *n.* jarabe; almíbar, *m.*
system ['sistim], *n.* sistema, *m.*; método.
systematic [sisti'mætik], *a.* sistemático, metódico.
systematize ['sistimətaiz], *v.t.* sistematizar; metodizar.

T

T, t [ti:], *n.* vigésima letra del alfabeto inglés; ***T-square,*** regla T.
tab [tæb], *n.* oreja; etiqueta; ***to keep tabs on,*** saber localizar.
tabernacle ['tæbənækl], *n.* tabernáculo.
table [teibl], *n.* mesa; tabla; lista; índice, *m.*; ***to lay the —,*** poner la mesa; ***to turn the tables,*** volverse la tortilla.—*v.t.* entablar (*una petición*); enumerar; (*U.S.*) aplazar.
table-cloth ['teiblklɔθ], *n.* mantel, *m.*
tableau ['tæblou], *n.* (*pl.* **tableaux**) cuadro.
table-lamp ['teibllæmp], *n.* quinqué, *m.*
table-land ['teibllænd], *n.* meseta.
table-linen ['teibllinin], *n.* mantelería.
tablespoon ['teiblspu:n], *n.* cuchara grande.
tablet ['tæblit], *n.* placa; losa; (*med.*) pastilla.
table-talk ['teiblto:k], *n.* conversación (*f.*) de sobremesa.
taboo [tə'bu:], *n.* tabú, *m.*
tabulate ['tæbjuleit], *v.t.* tabular, catalogar.
tacit ['tæsit], *a.* tácito.
taciturn ['tæsitə:n], *a.* taciturno.
tack [tæk], *n.* tachuela, puntilla; hilván, *m.* (*costura*); (*naut.*) bordada; (*fig.*) cambio de política.—*v.t.* clavar con tachuelas; hilvanar (*costura*); (*fig.*) añadir.—*v.i.* (*naut.*) virar; (*fig.*) cambiar de política.
tackle [tækl], *n.* aparejo; avíos *m.pl.*, (*sport*) carga entrada.—*v.t.* agarrar; (*sport*) entrar a, cargar; (*fig.*) abordar.
tact [tækt], *n.* discreción, *f.*
tactful ['tæktful], *a.* discreto.
tactical ['tæktikəl], *a.* táctico.
tactics ['tæktiks], *n.pl.* táctica.
tactile ['tæktail], *a.* tangible; táctil.
tactless ['tæktlis], *a.* indiscreto.
tadpole ['tædpoul], *n.* renacuajo.
taffeta ['tæfitə], *n.* tafetán, *m.*
tag (1) [tæg], *n.* herrete, *m.*; etiqueta; refrán, *m.*
tag (2) [tæg], *n.* ***to play —,*** jugar al marro.
tail [teil], *n.* cola, rabo; fin, *m.*—*pl.* cruz (*de una moneda*), *f.*, frac (*vestido*), *m.*; ***to turn —,*** volver la espalda.—*v.t.* seguir, pisar los talones a.—*v.i.* ***to — off,*** disminuir.
tail-coat ['teilkout], *n.* frac, *m.*
tail-end ['teil'end], *n.* extremo.
tail-light ['teil'lait], *n.* farol trasero.
tailor ['teilə], *n.* sastre, *m.*; ***tailor's shop,*** sastrería.—*v.t.* adaptar; entallar.
tailoress ['teiləres], *n.* sastra, modista.
tail-piece ['teil'pi:s], *n.* apéndice, *m.*
taint [teint], *n.* mancha; corrupción, contaminación, *f.*—*v.t.* corromper; contaminar.
take [teik], *v.t. irr.* tomar; coger; traer; llevar; aceptar; quitar; conducir; suponer; (*math.*) restar; sacar (*una fotografía*); dar (*un paseo*); ***to — aback,*** desconcertar; ***to — away,*** quitar; (*math.*) restar; ***to — back,*** (*fig.*) retractar; ***to — down,*** bajar; escribir al dictado; humillar; ***to — for granted,*** dar por sentado; ***to — in,*** comprender; admitir, dar asilo; encoger; (*fig.*) engañar; ***to — off,*** quitar; cortar; (*fam.*) imitar; arrancar; ***to — on,*** encargarse de; ***to — on trust,*** tomar a crédito; ***to — out,*** salir con; sacar; llevar afuera; extraer; ***to — over,*** encargarse de; ***to — to pieces,*** desarmar; ***to — up,*** subir;

empezar; ocupar (*un sitio*); adoptar; acortar (*un vestido*); ***to be taken with*** o ***to take a fancy to***, aficionarse a; ***to — care of***, cuidar; —*v.i.* lograr, tener éxito; prender; arraigarse. ***to — after***, parecerse a; ***to — off***, (*aer.*) despegar; ***to — to***, empezar a; aplicarse a; aficionarse a; ***to — up with***, trabar amistad con; ***to — care***, tener cuidado; ***to — the chair***, presidir; ***to — fright***, cobrar miedo; ***to — to one's heels***, huir; ***to — leave of***, despedirse de; ***to — no notice***, no hacer caso; ***to — pains***, darse molestia; esmerarse; ***to — pity on***, compadecerse de; ***to — place***, verificarse, suceder; ***to — shelter***, refugiarse.—*n.* toma; (*photo.*) tomada.

take-off [ˈteikɔf], *n.* caricatura; (*aer.*) despegue, *m.*

taken [ˈteikən] [TAKE].

taking [ˈteikiŋ], *a.* encantador, atractivo; contagioso.—*n.* toma; secuestro.—*pl.* ingresos, *m.pl.*

talcum powder [ˈtælkəmˈpaudə], *n.* polvo de talco.

tale [teil], *n.* cuento; ***old wives' —***, patraña, cuento de viejas; ***to tell tales***, contar historias; chismear.

tale-bearer [ˈteilbɛərə], *n.* chismoso.

talent [ˈtælənt], *n.* talento, ingenio.

talented [ˈtæləntid], *a.* talentoso.

talisman [ˈtælizmən], *n.* talismán, *m.*

talk [tɔ:k], *n.* conversación, *f.*; charla; rumor, *m.*—*v.t.*, *v.i.* hablar; ***to — into***, persuadir; ***to — out of***, disuadir; ***to — over***, discutir; persuadir.

talkative [ˈtɔ:kətiv], *a.* hablador, locuaz.

tall [tɔ:l], *a.* alto; (*fig.*) exagerado.

tallow [ˈtælou], *n.* sebo.

tally [ˈtæli], *n.* tarja; cuenta; ***to keep —***, llevar la cuenta.—*v.t.* llevar la cuenta.—*v.i.* concordar.

talon [ˈtælən], *n.* garra, uña.

tambourine [tæmbəˈri:n], *n.* pandereta.

tame [teim], *a.* manso; sumiso; soso.—*v.t.* domar; reprimir.

tameness [ˈteimnis], *n.* mansedumbre; sumisión, *f.*

tamer [ˈteimə], *n.* domador, *m.*

tamper [ˈtæmpə], *v.i.* meterse (en); estropear; falsificar (***with***).

tan [tæn], *a.* de color de canela.—*n.* bronceado.—*v.t.* curtir; poner moreno; tostar; (*fam.*) zurrar.—*v.i.* ponerse moreno, broncearse.

tandem [ˈtændəm], *n.* tándem, *m.*

tang [tæŋ], *n.* sabor, *m.*; dejo picante; retintín, *m.*

tangent [ˈtændʒənt], *a.*, *n.* tangente, *f.*

tangerine [tændʒəˈri:n], *n.* tangerina.

tangible [ˈtændʒibl], *a.* tangible.

tangle [tæŋgl], *n.* enredo, maraña.—*v.t.* enredar.—*v.i.* enredarse, enmarañarse.

tank [tæŋk], *n.* tanque, *m.*, cisterna; (*mil.*) tanque, *m.* carro (de combate).

tankard [ˈtæŋkəd], *n.* pichel, *m.*

tanker [ˈtæŋkə], *n.* petrolero.

tanned [tænd], *a.* bronceado moreno; curtido.

tanner [ˈtænə], *n.* curtidor, *m.*; (*fam.*) (moneda de) seis peniques.

tantalize [ˈtæntəlaiz], *v.t.* atormentar, provocar.

tantamount [ˈtæntəmaunt], *a.* ***to be — to***, equivaler a.

tantrum [ˈtæntrəm], *n.* perra, pataleta, berrinche, *m.*

tap (1) [tæp], *n.* palmadita.—*v.t.* dar una palmadita a.

tap (2) [tæp], *n.* grifo (*de agua*); ***on —***, en tonel; (*fig.*) a la mano.—*v.t.* decentar; horadar; sangrar; (*elec.*) derivar; escuchar (*conversaciones telefónicas*).

tape [teip], *n.* cinta.

tape-measure [ˈteipmeʒə], *n.* cinta métrica.

taper [ˈteipə], *n.* bujía; (*eccl.*) cirio.—*v.t.* afilar.—*v.i.* rematar en punta.

tape-recorder [ˈteiprikɔ:də], *n.* magnetófono.

tape-recording [ˈteiprikɔ:diŋ], *n.* grabación (*f.*) en cinta.

tapestry [ˈtæpəstri], *n.* tapiz, *m.*

tapeworm [ˈteipwə:m], *n.* tenia, lombriz solitaria.

tapioca [tæpiˈoukə], *n.* tapioca.

tar [tɑ:], *n.* alquitrán, *m.*—*v.t.* alquitranar, embrear; ***to — and feather***, embrear y emplumar.

tardiness [ˈtɑ:dinis], *n.* lentitud, *f.*, tardanza.

tardy [ˈtɑ:di], *a.* tardío; lento.

tare (1) [tɛə], *n.* (*bot.*) yero; (*Bibl.*) cizaña.

tare (2) [tɛə], *n.* (*com.*) tara.

target [ˈtɑ:git], *n.* blanco; ***— practice***, tiro al blanco.

tariff [ˈtærif], *n.* tarifa.

tarmac [ˈtɑ:mæk], *n.* (*aer.*) pista.

tarnish [ˈtɑ:niʃ], *n.* deslustre, *m.*—*v.t.* deslustrar.—*v.i.* deslustrarse.

tarpaulin [tɑ:ˈpɔ:lin], *n.* alquitranado, encerado.

tarry [ˈtæri], *v.i.* tardar; detenerse.

tart (1) [tɑ:t], *a.* ácido, agrio.

tart (2) [tɑ:t], *n.* tarta, pastelillo; (*low*) mujerzuela.

tartan [ˈtɑ:tən], *n.* tartán, *m.*

Tartar [ˈtɑ:tə], *a.*, *n.* tártaro.

tartar [ˈtɑ:tə], *n.* tártaro; ***cream of —***, crémor tártaro, *m.*

task [tɑ:sk], *n.* tarea; empresa; ***to take to —***, reprender, llamar a capítulo.

tassel [ˈtæsəl], *n.* borla.

taste [teist], *n.* gusto; sabor, *m.*; un poco; muestra; prueba; buen gusto; afición, *f.*; ***to have a — for***, tener afición a; ***in bad*** (***good***) ***—***, de mal (buen) gusto.—*v.t.* gustar; probar.—*v.i.* saber (***of***, a).

tasteful [ˈteistful], *a.* de buen gusto.

tasteless [ˈteistlis], *a.* insípido; de mal gusto.

tasty [ˈteisti], *a.* sabroso, apetitoso.

tatter [ˈtætə], *n.* andrajo.

tattered [ˈtætəd], *a.* andrajoso.

tatting [ˈtætiŋ], *n.* frivolité, *m.*

tattoo (1) [tæˈtu:], *n.* tatuaje, *m.*—*v.t.* tatuar.

tattoo (2) [tæˈtu:], *n.* (*mil.*) retreta.

tattooing (1) [tæˈtu:iŋ], *n.* tatuaje, *m.*

tattooing (2) [tæˈtu:iŋ], *n.* tamboreo.

taught [tɔ:t] [TEACH].

taunt [tɔ:nt], *n.* escarnio, mofa.—*v.t.* provocar; ***to — with***, echar en cara.

taut [tɔ:t], *a.* tieso.

tautness [ˈtɔ:tnis], *n.* tensión, *f.*

tautology [tɔ:ˈtɔlədʒi], *n.* tautología.

tavern [ˈtævən], *n.* taberna, mesón, *m.*

tawdry [ˈtɔ:dri], *a.* charro, chillón, cursi.

tawny [ˈtɔ:ni], *a.* leonado.

tax [tæks], *n.* impuesto; — ***collector,*** recaudador (*m.*) de contribuciones.—*v.t.* imponer contribuciones; (*jur.*) tasar; cargar; ***to — with,*** acusar de.
taxable ['tæksəbl], *a.* sujeto a impuestos.
taxation [tæk'seiʃən], *n.* imposición (*f.*) de contribuciones *o* impuestos.
tax-free ['tæks'fri:], *a.* libre de impuestos.
taxi ['tæksi], *n.* taxi, *m.*—*v.i.* ir en taxi; (*aer.*) correr por tierra.
taxidermist ['tæksidə:mist], *n.* taxidermista, *m.f.*
taxidermy ['tæksidə:mi], *n.* taxidermia.
taxi-driver ['tæksidraivə], *n.* taxista, *m.*
taximeter ['tæksimi:tə], *n.* taxímetro.
taxi-rank ['tæksi'ræŋk], *n.* parada de taxis.
tax-payer ['tækspeiə], *n.* contribuyente, *m.f.*
tea [ti:], *n.* té, *m.*; merienda; — ***-caddy,*** bote (*m.*) para té; — ***rose,*** rosa de té.
teach [ti:tʃ], *v.t. irr.* enseñar.—*v.i.* ser profesor.
teacher ['ti:tʃə], *n.* maestro, profesor, *m.*; maestra, profesora.
tea-chest ['ti:tʃest], *n.* caja para té.
teaching ['ti:tʃiŋ], *a.* docente.—*n.* enseñanza; doctrina.
tea-cosy ['ti:kouzi], *n.* cubretetera, *m.*
teacup ['ti:kʌp], *n.* taza para té.
teak [ti:k], *n.* teca.
team [ti:m], *n.* yunta, pareja (*bueyes*); equipo.—*v.t.* enganchar.—*v.i.* ***to — up*** (***with***), asociarse (con).
teamwork ['ti:mwə:k], *n.* cooperación, *f.*
teapot ['ti:pɔt], *n.* tetera.
tear (1) [tɛə], *n.* rasgón, *m.*—*v.t. irr.* romper; rasgar; despedazar; arañar; ***to — away,*** arrancar; ***to — down,*** derribar; ***to — up,*** desarraigar; hacer pedazos.—*v.i.* rasgarse; romper; correr precipitadamente; ***to — away,*** irse corriendo; ***to — down,*** bajar corriendo; ***to — oneself away,*** arrancarse; ***to — up,*** subir corriendo.
tear (2) [tiə], *n.* lágrima; gota; ***to shed tears,*** llorar.
tearful ['tiəful], *a.* lloroso.
tearfully ['tiəfuli], *adv.* entre lágrimas.
tear-gas ['tiəgæs], *n.* gas lacrimógeno.
tease [ti:z], *n.* fastidio; (*fam.*) guasa; (*fam.*) guasón, *m.*—*v.t.* fastidiar, embromar; tomar el pelo (a); cardar (*lana*).
tea-set ['ti:set], *n.* juego de té.
teaspoon ['ti:spu:n], *n.* cucharita.
teat [ti:t], *n.* pezón, *m.*; teta.
tea-time ['ti:taim], *n.* hora del té.
technical ['teknikəl], *a.* técnico.
technicality [tekni'kæliti], *n.* cosa técnica; tecnicismo; detalle técnico.
technician [tek'niʃən], *n.* técnico.
technique [tek'ni:k], *n.* técnica.
technological [teknə'lɔdʒikəl], *a.* tecnológico.
technologist [tek'nɔlədʒist], *n.* tecnólogo.
technology [tek'nɔlədʒi], *n.* tecnología.
tedious ['ti:djəs], *a.* tedioso, aburrido.
tedium ['ti:djəm], *n.* tedio.
teem [ti:m], *v.i.* rebosar; pulular; diluviar.
teeming ['ti:miŋ], *a.* prolífico, fecundo; torrencial.
teenager ['ti:neidʒə], *n.* adolescente, *m.f.*
teeter ['ti:tə], *v.i.* balancearse.
teeth [ti:θ] [TOOTH].
teethe [ti:ð], *v.i.* echar los dientes.
teething ['ti:ðiŋ], *n.* dentición, *f.*
teething-ring ['ti:ðiŋriŋ], *n.* chupador, *m.*
teetotal [ti:'toutl], *a.* abstemio.
teetotaller [ti:'toutlə], *n.* abstemio.
telegram ['teligræm], *n.* telegrama, *m.*
telegraph ['teligra:f, -græf], *n.* telégrafo; — ***pole,*** poste telegráfico.—*v.t., v.i.* telegrafiar.
telegraphy [ti'legrəfi], *n.* telegrafía.
telepathy [ti'lepəθi], *n.* telepatía.
telephone ['telifoun], *n.* teléfono; — ***directory,*** guía telefónica; — ***exchange,*** central telefónica, *f.*; — ***number,*** número de teléfono; — ***operator,*** telefonista, *m.f.*; ***to be on the —,*** estar comunicando; tener teléfono.—*v.t., v.i.* telefonear, llamar por teléfono.
telephone-box ['telifounbɔks], **telephone-kiosk** ['telifounki:ɔsk], *n.* cabina telefónica.
telephonic [teli'fɔnik], *a.* telefónico.
telephonist [ti'lefənist], *n.* telefonista, *m.f.*
telescope ['teliscoup], *n.* telescopio.—*v.t.* enchufar.—*v.i.* enchufarse.
telescopic [telis'kɔpik], *a.* telescópico.
televise ['telivaiz], *v.t.* transmitir por televisión.
television ['teliviʒən], *n.* televisión, *f.*
tell [tel], *v.t. irr.* contar; decir; expresar; manifestar; comunicar; revelar; marcar (*la hora*); ***to — off,*** regañar.—*v.i. irr.* decir; producir efecto.
teller ['telə], *n.* narrador; escrutador; pagador, *m.*
telling ['teliŋ], *a.* eficaz, notable.
tell-tale ['telteil], *a.* revelador.—*n.* soplón, *m.*
temerity [ti'meriti], *n.* temeridad, *f.*
temper ['tempə], *n.* temple; carácter, *m.*; mal genio; ***bad —,*** mal humor, *m.*; ***good —,*** buen humor; ***to lose one's —,*** enojarse.—*v.t.* templar; moderar.
temperament ['tempərəmənt], *n.* temperamento.
temperamental [tempərə'mentl], *a.* caprichoso; natural.
temperance ['tempərəns], *n.* templanza, moderación, *f.*; abstinencia.
temperate ['tempərit], *a.* moderado; templado.
temperature ['tempritʃə], *n.* temperatura; (*med.*) fiebre, *f.*
tempered ['tempəd], *a.* templado; ***hot —,*** irascible.
tempest ['tempist], *n.* tempestad, *f.*
tempestuous [tem'pestjuəs], *a.* tempestuoso.
temple (1) [templ], *n.* templo.
temple (2) [templ], *n.* (*anat.*) sien, *f.*
temporal ['tempərəl], *a.* temporal.
temporary ['tempərəri], *a.* provisional, interino.
temporize ['tempəraiz], *v.i.* contemporizar.
tempt [tempt], *v.t.* tentar; atraer.
temptation [temp'teiʃən], *n.* tentación, *f.*
tempter ['temptə], *n.* tentador, *m.*
tempting ['temptiŋ], *a.* tentador, atrayente.
temptress ['temptris], *n.* tentadora.
ten [ten], *a., n.* diez, *m.*
tenable ['tenəbl], *a.* defendible, sostenible.
tenacious [ti'neiʃəs], *a.* tenaz; adhesivo; porfiado.
tenacity [ti'næsiti], *n.* tenacidad, *f.*; porfía.
tenancy ['tenənsi], *n.* tenencia; inquilinato.
tenant ['tenənt], *n.* arrendatario, inquilino; morador, *m.*

tench [tentʃ], *n.* (*ichth.*) tenca.
tend [tend], *v.t.* guardar; cuidar; vigilar.—*v.i.* tender, propender.
tendency ['tendənsi], *n.* tendencia, propensión, *f.*
tendentious [ten'denʃəs], *a.* tendencioso.
tender (1) ['tendə], *a.* tierno; compasivo; blando; escrupuloso.
tender (2) ['tendə], *n.* (*com.*) oferta, propuesta; ***legal* —,** curso legal.—*v.t.* ofrecer; presentar.
tender (3) ['tendə], *n.* (*naut.*) falúa; (*rail.*) ténder, *m.*
tenderness ['tendənis], *n.* ternura; escrupulosidad, *f.*
tendon ['tendən], *n.* (*anat.*) tendón, *m.*
tendril ['tendril], *n.* zarcillo.
tenement ['tenimənt], *n.* vivienda; casa de vecindad.
tenet ['tenit], *n.* dogma, *m.*, principio.
tenfold ['tenfould], *a.* décuplo.—*adv.* diez veces.
tennis ['tenis], *n.* tenis, *m.*; **— *ball,*** pelota de tenis; **— *court,*** pista de tenis.
tenor ['tenə], *n.* curso; tenor, *m.*, contenido; (*mus.*) tenor, *m.*
tense (1) [tens], *a.* tieso; tirante; tenso.
tense (2) [tens], *n.* (*gram.*) tiempo.
tension ['tenʃən], *n.* tensión; (*pol.*) tirantez, *f.*
tent [tent], *n.* tienda; **— *pole,*** mástil (*m.*) de tienda.
tentacle ['tentəkl], *n.* tentáculo.
tentative ['tentətiv], *a.* tentativo.
tenterhooks ['tentəhuks], *n.pl.* ***on* —,** en ascuas.
tenth [tenθ], *a.* décimo.—*n.* décimo, décima parte; diez (*en las fechas*), *m.*
tenuous ['tenjuəs], *a.* tenue; delgado; sutil.
tenure ['tenjuə], *n.* tenencia; duración, *f.*
tepid ['tepid], *a.* tibio.
tercentenary [tə:sen'ti:nəri], *n.* tercer centenario.
term [tə:m], *n.* plazo, período; trimestre (*de escuela*); límite, *m.*; término.—*pl.* condiciones, *f.pl.*; tarifa; ***to be on good terms with,*** estar en buenas relaciones con; ***to come to terms,*** llegar a un arreglo.—*v.t.* llamar.
terminal ['tə:minl], *a.* terminal.—*n.* término; (*elec.*) borne, *m.*
terminate ['tə:mineit], *v.t.*, *v.i.* terminar.
termination [tə:mi'neiʃən], *n.* terminación, *f.*
terminology [tə:mi'nɔlədʒi], *n.* terminología.
terminus ['tə:minəs], *n.* estación terminal, *f.*
termite ['tə:mait], *n.* termita, *m.*
terrace ['teris], *n.* terraza.—*v.t.* terraplenar.
terra-cotta ['terə'kɔtə], *n.* terracota.
terrain [te'rein], *n.* terreno.
terrestrial [ti'restriəl], *a.* terrestre.
terrible ['teribl], *a.* terrible.
terrific [tə'rifik], *a.* espantoso; (*fam.*) estupendo.
terrify ['terifai], *v.t.* espantar, aterrar.
territorial [teri'tɔ:riəl], *a.* territorial.
territory ['teritəri], *n.* territorio; región, *f.*
terror ['terə], *n.* terror, *m.*, espanto; (*fam.*) fiera.
terrorism ['terərizm], *n.* terrorismo.
terrorist ['terərist], *n.* terrorista, *m.*
terrorize ['terəraiz], *v.t.* aterrorizar.
terse [tə:s], *a.* conciso, sucinto; brusco.
terseness ['tə:snis], *n.* concisión; brusquedad, *f.*
test [test], *n.* prueba; examen, *m.*; criterio; análisis, *m.*; ensayo; ***to put to the* —,** poner a prueba; ***to stand the* —,** soportar la prueba; **— *match,*** partido internacional de cricket *o* rugby; **— *pilot,*** piloto de pruebas; **— *tube,*** tubo de ensayo.—*v.t.* probar, poner a prueba; ensayar.
testament ['testəmənt], *n.* testamento; ***New Testament,*** Nuevo Testamento; ***Old Testament,*** Antiguo Testamento.
testicle ['testikl], *n.* testículo.
testify ['testifai], *v.t.*, *v.i.* declarar; (*jur.*) testificar.
testimonial [testi'mounjəl], *n.* recomendación, *f.*; certificado.
testimony ['testiməni], *n.* testimonio.
testiness ['testinis], *n.* mal humor, *m.*
testy ['testi], *a.* enojadizo, irascible.
tetanus ['tetənəs], *n.* tétano.
tether ['teðə], *n.* traba, maniota; ***to be at the end of one's* —,** quedar sin recursos; acabarse la paciencia.—*v.t.* trabar, atar.
Teuton ['tju:tən], *n.* teutón, *m.*
Teutonic [tju:'tɔnik], *a.* teutónico.
text [tekst], *n.* texto; tema, *m.*
text-book ['tekstbuk], *n.* libro de texto, manual, *m.*
textile ['tekstail], *a.* textil.—*n.* textil, *m.*; tejido.
textual ['tekstjuəl], *a.* textual.
texture ['tekstʃə], *n.* textura.
Thai [tai], *a.*, *n.* tailandés, *m.*
Thailand ['tailænd], *n.* Tailandia.
Thames [temz], *n.* Támesis, *m.*; ***to set the* — *on fire,*** inventar la pólvora.
than [ðæn], *conj.* que; de; del (de la, de los, de las) que; de lo que.
thank [θæŋk], *v.t.* dar las gracias a; **— *God,*** gracias a Dios; **— *you,*** gracias; ***to* — *for,*** agradecer.
thankful ['θæŋkful], *a.* agradecido.
thankless ['θæŋklis], *a.* ingrato.
thanks [θæŋks], *n.pl.* gracias; **— *to,*** gracias a.
thanksgiving ['θæŋksgiviŋ], *n.* acción (*f.*) de gracias.
that [ðæt], *a.* (*pl.* **those**) ese, *m.*; esa; aquel, *m.*; aquella.—*pron.* ése, *m.*; ésa; eso; aquél, *m.*; aquélla; aquello; (*replacing noun*) el; la; lo.—*rel. pron.* que; quien; el cual; la cual; lo cual; el que; la que; lo que.—*conj.* que; para que; para.
thatch [θætʃ], *n.* barda.—*v.t.* bardar.
thaw [θɔ:], *n.* deshielo.—*v.t.* deshelar; derretir; (*fig.*) ablandar.—*v.i.* deshelarse; derretirse; (*fig.*) ablandarse.
the [ðə *before vowel* ði:], *art.* el; la; lo; los; las.—*adv.* (*before a comparative*) cuanto . . . tanto (más).
theatre ['θiətə], *n.* teatro; quirófano (*hospital*); **— *attendant,*** acomodador, *m.*
theatrical [θi'ætrikəl], *a.* teatral.—*n.pl.* funciones teatrales, *f.pl.*; ***amateur theatricals,*** función (*f.*) de aficionados.
thee [ði:], *pron.* (*obs.*, *eccl.*) te; ti.
theft [θeft], *n.* robo, hurto.
their [ðɛə], *a.* su; sus; suyo; suya; suyos; suyas; de ellos, de ellas.
theirs [ðɛəz], *pron.* el suyo; la suya; los suyos; las suyas; de ellos, de ellas.
theism ['θi:izm], *n.* teísmo.
theist ['θi:ist], *n.* teísta, *m.f.*
them [ðem], *pron.* ellos; ellas; los; las; les.

theme [θi:m], *n.* tema, *m.*; tesis, *f.*
themselves [ðəm'selvz], *pron. pl.* ellos mismos; ellas mismas; sí mismos; se.
then [ðen], *adv.* entonces; luego, después; ***now and —,*** de vez en cuando; ***now —,*** ahora bien; ***and what — ?*** ¿y qué más? ***there and —,*** en el acto.—*conj.* pues; por consiguiente.
thence [ðens], *adv.* desde allí; por eso; por consiguiente.
thenceforth ['ðens'fɔ:θ], *adv.* de allí en adelante.
theocracy [θi'ɔkrəsi], *n.* teocracia.
theodolite [θi'ɔdəlait], *n.* teodolito.
theologian [θiə'loudʒən], *n.* teólogo.
theological [θiə'lɔdʒikəl], *a.* teológico.
theology [θi'ɔlədʒi], *n.* teología.
theorem ['θiərəm], *n.* teorema, *m.*
theoretical [θiə'retikəl], *a.* teórico.
theorist ['θiərist], *n.* teórico.
theorize ['θiəraiz], *v.i.* teorizar.
theory ['θiəri], *n.* teoría.
theosophy [θi'ɔsəfi], *n.* teosofía.
therapeutic [θerə'pju:tik], *a.* terapéutico.
therapy ['θerəpi], *n.* terapia.
there [ðɛə], *adv.* ahí, allí, allá; ***all —,*** (*fam.*) en sus cabales; ***down —,*** allí abajo; ***up —,*** allí arriba; ***who's — ?*** ¿quién llama? ***— is*** o ***are,*** hay; ***— they are,*** helos ahí.—*interj.* ¡vaya! ¡toma! ¡ya ves! ***—, — !*** ¡vamos!
thereabouts [ðɛərə'bauts], *adv.* por ahí; cerca de; aproximadamente.
thereafter [ðɛər'ɑ:ftə], *adv.* después de eso.
thereby [ðɛə'bai], *adv.* de ese modo; por allí cerca.
therefore ['ðɛəfɔ:], *adv.* por eso, por lo tanto.
therein [ðɛər'in], *adv.* allí dentro; en esto, en eso.
thereof [ðɛər'ɔv], *adv.* de esto, de eso.
thereupon [ðɛərə'pɔn], *adv.* encima; por consiguiente; luego, en eso.
therm [θə:m], *n.* unidad térmica.
thermal ['θə:məl], *a.* termal.
thermodynamics [θe:moudai'næmiks], *n.pl.* termodinámica.
thermometer [θə'mɔmitə], *n.* termómetro.
thermonuclear [θə:mou'nju:kljə], *a.* termonuclear.
thermos flask ['θə:məs'flɑ:sk], *n.* termos, *m.sg.*
thermostat ['θə:məstæt], *n.* termostato.
these [ði:z], *a.pl.* [THIS] estos; estas.—*pron. pl.* éstos; éstas.
thesis ['θi:sis], *n.* tesis, *f.*
Thespian ['θespjən], *a.* dramático.
they [ðei], *pron. pl.* ellos; ellas.
thick [θik], *a.* espeso; grueso; denso; turbio; apretado; numeroso; lleno; indistinto; estúpido; (*fam.*) íntimo; ***that's a bit — !*** ¡eso es un poco demasiado!—*n.* espesor, *m.*; lo más denso; ***the — of the fight,*** lo más reñido del combate; ***to go through — and thin,*** atropellar por todo; ***in the — of,*** en el centro de, en medio de.—*adv.* densamente; continuamente.
thicken ['θikən], *v.t.* espesar; aumentar.—*v.i.* espesarse; aumentar; complicarse.
thickening ['θikəniŋ], *n.* hinchamiento; (*cul.*) espesante, *m.*
thicket ['θikit], *n.* maleza, matorral, *m.*
thick-headed ['θik'hedid], *a.* torpe, estúpido.
thick-lipped ['θik'lipt], *a.* bezudo.
thickness ['θiknis], *n.* espesor, *m.*; densidad, *f.*; consistencia; pronunciación indistinta.
thickset ['θik'set], *a.* doblado; rechoncho.
thick-skinned ['θik'skind], *a.* paquidermo; (*fig.*) insensible.
thief [θi:f], *n.* ladrón, *m.*
thigh [θai], *n.* muslo.
thigh-bone ['θaiboun], *n.* fémur, *m.*
thimble [θimbl], *n.* dedal, *m.*
thin [θin], *a.* delgado; flaco; tenue; ligero; escaso; aguado; insubstancial; ***to grow —,*** enflaquecer.
thine [ðain], *pron.* (*obs.*, *eccl.*) el tuyo; la tuya; los tuyos; las tuyas.—*a.* tu; tus; tuyo; tuya; tuyos; tuyas.
thin-faced ['θin'feist], *a.* de cara delgada.
thing [θiŋ], *n.* cosa; ***poor — !*** ¡pobre! ***no such —,*** nada de eso; ***the —,*** lo que está de moda; ***to be just the —,*** venir al pelo.
think [θiŋk], *v.t.*, *v.i. irr.* pensar; creer; imaginar; considerar; ***to — of,*** pensar en; acordarse de; pensar de; ***as you — fit,*** como Vd. quiera; ***to — highly of,*** tener buen concepto de; ***to — proper,*** creer conveniente; ***what do you — of this?*** ¿qué le parece? ***to — out,*** resolver; proyectar; ***to — over,*** pensar.
thinker ['θiŋkə], *n.* pensador, *m.*
thinking ['θiŋkiŋ], *a.* pensador; inteligente.—*n.* pensamiento, reflexión, *f.*; juicio; ***to my way of —,*** a mi parecer.
thin-lipped ['θin'lipt], *a.* de labios apretados.
thinness ['θinnis], *n.* delgadez; flaqueza; tenuidad; escasez, *f.*; pequeño número; poca consistencia.
thin-skinned ['θin'skind], *a.* sensible.
third [θə:d], *a.* tercero; ***— party,*** tercera persona.—*n.* tercio, tercera parte; tres (*en las fechas*), *m.*; (*mus.*) tercera.
thirst [θə:st], *n.* sed, *f.*; (*fig.*) ansia.—*v.i.* tener sed (***for,*** de).
thirsty ['θə:sti], *a.* sediento; ***to be —,*** tener sed.
thirteen [θə:'ti:n], *a.*, *n.* trece, *m.*
thirteenth [θə:'ti:nθ], *a.* décimotercio.—*n.* décimotercio; trece (*en las fechas*), *m.*
thirtieth ['θə:tiəθ], *a.* trigésimo.—*n.* trigésimo; treinta (*en las fechas*).
thirty ['θə:ti], *a.*, *n.* treinta, *m.*
this [ðis], *a.* (*pl.* **these**) este; esta.—*pron.* éste; ésta; esto.
thistle [θisl], *n.* cardo.
thistle-down ['θisldaun], *n.* papo de cardo.
thither ['ðiðə], *adv.* allá, hacia allá; a ese fin.
Thomas ['tɔməs], *n.* Tomás, *m.*
thong [θɔŋ], *n.* correa.
thorax ['θɔ:ræks], *n.* (*pl.* **thoraces** [-æsi:z]) (*anat.*) tórax, *m.*
thorn [θɔ:n], *n.* espina; espino.
thorny ['θɔ:ni], *a.* espinoso.
thorough ['θʌrə], *a.* completo; perfecto; concienzudo.
thoroughbred ['θʌrəbred], *a.* de casta.
thoroughfare ['θʌrəfɛə], *n.* vía pública.
thoroughgoing ['θʌrəgouiŋ], *a.* completo; concienzudo.
thoroughness ['θʌrənis], *n.* esmero, minuciosidad, *f.*
those [ðouz], *a.pl.* [THAT] esos; esas; aquellos; aquellas.—*pron. pl.* ésos; ésas; aquéllos; aquéllas; los; ***— who,*** los que; las que; quienes; ***— which*** o ***— that,*** los que; las que.

thou [ðau], *pron.* (*obs.*, *eccl.*) tú.
though [ðou], *conj.* aunque; sin embargo; a pesar de que; ***as* —,** como si.
thought [θɔ:t], *n.* pensamiento; reflexión, *f.*; concepto; propósito; cuidado; (*fam.*) migaja; ***on second thoughts,*** después de pensarlo bien.
thoughtful ['θɔ:tful], *a.* pensativo; previsor; atento.
thoughtfulness ['θɔ:tfulnis], *n.* reflexión; previsión; atención, *f.*
thoughtless ['θɔ:tlis], *a.* descuidado; irreflexivo; inconsiderado; necio.
thoughtlessness ['θɔ:tlisnis], *n.* descuido; irreflexión; inconsideración; necedad, *f.*
thousand ['θauzənd], *a.* mil.—*n.* mil; millar, *m.*
thousandth ['θauzəndθ], *a.*, *n.* milésimo.
thrash [θræʃ], *v.t.* azotar; trillar; (*fam.*) derrotar; ***to* — *out,*** ventilar.
thrashing ['θræʃiŋ], *n.* paliza; trilla; **— *floor,*** era.
thrashing-machine ['θræʃiŋməʃi:n], *n.* trilladora.
thread [θred], *n.* hilo; hebra; filete, *m.*; (*fig.*) hilo.—*v.t.* enhebrar; ensartar; colarse a través de.
threadbare ['θredbɛə], *a.* raído; muy usado; (*fig.*) usado.
threat [θret], *n.* amenaza.
threaten [θretn], *v.t.*, *v.i.* amenazar (***to,*** con).
threatening ['θretniŋ], *a.* amenazador.
three [θri:], *a.*, *n.* tres, *m.*
three-cornered ['θri:'kɔ:nəd], *a.* triangular; **— *hat,*** sombrero de tres picos; tricornio.
threefold ['θri:fould], *a.* triple.
threepence ['θrepəns], *n.* tres peniques, *m.pl.*
three-ply ['θri:'plai], *a.* triple; de tres hilos *o* capas (*lana*).
threescore ['θri:'skɔ:], *a.*, *n.* sesenta, *m.*
thresh [θreʃ] [THRASH].
threshold ['θreʃould], *n.* umbral, *m.*; (*fig.*) principio.
threw [θru:] [THROW].
thrice [θrais], *adv.* tres veces.
thrift [θrift], *n.* ahorro; frugalidad, *f.*
thriftless ['θriftlis], *a.* manirroto.
thrifty ['θrifti], *a.* económico, frugal.
thrill [θril], *n.* estremecimiento; emoción, *f.*—*v.t.* emocionar.—*v.i.* estremecerse, emocionarse.
thriller ['θrilə], *n.* novela policíaca.
thrilling ['θriliŋ], *a.* emocionante; penetrante.
thrive [θraiv], *v.i. irr.* prosperar; crecer; desarrollarse con ímpetu.
thriving ['θraiviŋ], *a.* próspero; floreciente; vigoroso.
throat [θrout], *n.* garganta; ***to clear the* —,** aclarar la voz.
throaty ['θrouti], *a.* ronco.
throb [θrɔb], *n.* latido, pulsación, *f.*—*v.i.* latir, palpitar.
throbbing ['θrɔbiŋ], *a.* palpitante.—*n.* latido, pulsación, *f.*
throe [θrou], *n.* dolor, *m.*, agonía; ***throes of childbirth,*** dolores (*m.pl.*) de parto.
thrombosis [θrɔm'bousis], *n.* trombosis, *f.*
throne [θroun], *n.* trono; (*fig.*) corona.
throng [θrɔŋ], *n.* muchedumbre, multitud, *f.* —*v.t.* apretar; llenar de bote en bote.—*v.i.* apinarse.
throttle [θrɔtl], *n.* regulador, *m.*; estrangulador, *m.*—*v.t.* estrangular; (*fig.*) ahogar.
through [θru:], *prep.* por; a través de; por medio de; entre; por causa de; gracias a.—*adv.* a través; enteramente, completamente; desde el principio hasta el fin; de un lado a otro; ***to carry* —,** llevar a cabo; ***to fall* —,** (*fig.*) fracasar; ***to be wet* —,** mojarse hasta los huesos.—*a.* **— *train,*** tren directo.
throughout [θru:'aut], *adv.* en todas partes; de un extremo a otro.—*prep.* por todo.
throw [θrou], *n.* tiro; echada; lance, *m.* —*v.t. irr.* echar, lanzar, arrojar; derribar; desmontar; ***to* — *aside,*** desechar; ***to* — *away,*** tirar; desechar; ***to* — *back,*** devolver; ***to* — *down,*** echar al suelo; derribar; ***to* — *in,*** echar dentro; insertar; ***to* — *off,*** quitarse; despojarse de; ***to* — *open,*** abrir de par en par; ***to* — *out,*** echar fuera; emitir; rechazar; expeler; ***to* — *up,*** echar al aire; levantar; renunciar a; (*fam.*) vomitar arrojar.
throw-back ['θroubæk], *n.* atavismo.
thrown [θroun] [THROW].
thrush [θrʌʃ], *n.* (*orn.*) tordo.
thrust [θrʌst], *n.* golpe; ataque; empujón, *m.*; estocada; (*mech.*) empuje, *m.*, presión, *f.* —*v.t. irr.* introducir; meter; empujar; tirar; ***to* — *upon,*** imponer.—*v.i. irr.* acometer; meterse, introducirse; tirar una estocada; empujar.
thud [θʌd], *n.* ruido sordo.
thug [θʌg], *n.* rufián, criminal, *m.*
thumb [θʌm], *n.* pulgar, *m.*; ***under the* — *of,*** (*fig.*) en el poder de.—*v.t.* hojear (***through***); emporcar con los dedos.
thumb-stall ['θʌmstɔ:l], *n.* dedil, *m.*
thumb-tack ['θʌmtæk], *n.* (*U.S.*) [DRAWING PIN].
thump [θʌmp], *n.* golpe, *m.*, puñetazo.—*v.t.*, *v.i.* golpear; aporrear.
thunder ['θʌndə], *n.* trueno; estruendo.—*v.t.*, *v.i.* tronar; retumbar; (*fig.*) fulminar.
thunderbolt ['θʌndəboult], *n.* rayo.
thunderclap ['θʌndəklæp], *n.* trueno.
thundering ['θʌndəriŋ], *a.* de trueno; (*fam.*) terrible; muy grande.—*n.* trueno.
thunderstorm ['θʌndəstɔ:m], *n.* tormenta, tronada.
thunderstruck ['θʌndəstrʌk], *a.* estupefacto.
Thursday ['θə:zd(e)i], *n.* jueves, *m.*
thus [ðʌs], *adv.* así; de este modo; **— *far,*** hasta aquí; hasta ahora.
thwart [θwɔ:t], *v.t.* frustrar.
thy [ðai], *a.* (*obs.*, *eccl.*) tu; tus; tuyo; tuya; tuyos; tuyas.
thyme [taim], *n.* tomillo.
thyroid ['θairɔid], *a.* tiroideo; **— *gland,*** tiroides, *f.sg.*
thyself [ðai'self], *pron.* (*obs.*, *eccl.*) tú mismo; ti mismo.
tiara [ti'ɑ:rə], *n.* tiara.
tic [tik], *n.* tic nervioso.
tick (1) [tik], *n.* (*zool.*) ácaro.
tick (2) [tik], *n.* tictac, *m.*; contramarca.—*v.t.* marcar contra.—*v.i.* hacer tictac.
tick (3) [tik], *n.* funda de colchón.
tick (4) [tik], *n.* (*fam.*) crédito.

ticket ['tikit], *n.* billete, *m.*; entrada; papeleta; etiqueta; (*U.S. pol.*) candidatura; ***to buy a* —,** sacar un billete; **— *collector,*** revisor, *m.*; **—*office,*** taquilla.—*v.t.* marcar.
ticket-window ['tikit'windou], *n.* taquilla.
tickle [tikl], *n.* cosquillas, *f.pl.*—*v.t.* hacer cosquillas a; divertir; halagar.—*v.i.* hacer cosquillas.
tickling ['tikliŋ], *n* cosquillas, *f.pl.*
ticklish ['tikliʃ], *a.* cosquilloso; espinoso; ***to be* —,** tener cosquillas.
tidal [taidl], *a.* de marea; **— *wave,*** marejada.
tide [taid], *n.* marea; estación, *f.*, tiempo; corriente, *f.*; ***high* —,** marea alta, pleamar, *f.*; ***low* —,** marea baja, bajamar, *f.*; ***to go with the* —,** seguir la corriente.—*v.t.* ***to — over,*** ayudar; superar.
tidiness ['taidinis], *n.* aseo; buen orden, *m.*
tidy ['taidi], *a.* aseado; ordenado; (*fam.*) considerable.—*v.t.* asear, poner en orden; limpiar.
tie [tai], *n.* lazo, atadura; nudo; corbata; (*sport*) empate, *m.*; partido; (*fig.*) obligación, *f.*; **— *pin,*** alfiler (*m.*) de corbata.—*v.t.* atar; ligar; sujetar; limitar; anudar; ***to — up,*** atar; envolver; (*naut.*) amarrar.—*v.i.* atarse; (*sport*) empatar.
tier [tiə], *n.* fila.
tiger ['taigə], *n.* tigre, *m.*
tight [tait], *a.* apretado; tieso; estrecho; ajustado; bien cerrado; hermético; escaso; (*fam.*) borracho; (*fam.*) tacaño; **— *corner,*** (*fig.*) aprieto; ***to be tight-fisted,*** ser como un puño.—*adv.* fuertemente, estrechamente, bien; ***to hold* —,** tener bien.
tighten [taitn], *v.t.* apretar, estrechar.
tight-rope ['taitroup], *n.* cuerda de volatinero; **— *walker,*** volatinero, equilibrista, *m.f.*
tights [taits], *n.pl.* mallas, *f.pl.*, leotardos, *m.pl.*
tigress ['taigris], *n.* tigresa.
tile [tail], *n.* teja; baldosa; azulejo.—*v.t.* tejar, embaldosar.
till (1) [til], *n.* cajón (*m.*) de mostrador.
till (2) [til], *v.t.* cultivar.
till (3) [til], *prep.* hasta.—*conj.* hasta que.
tiller (1) ['tilə], *n.* labrador, *m.*
tiller (2) ['tilə], *n.* (*naut.*) caña del timón.
tilt [tilt], *n.* inclinación, *f.*; ladeo; justa.—*v.t.* inclinar; ladear.—*v.i.* inclinarse; ladearse; justar.
timber ['timbə], *n.* madera de construcción; viga; árboles, *m.pl.*
timbered ['timbəd], *a.* enmaderado; arbolado.
timbre [tɛ̃:mbr], *n.* timbre, *m.*
time [taim], *n.* tiempo; época, edad; estación, *f.*; hora; vez, *f.*; plazo; ocasión, *f.*; (*mus.*) compás, *m.*; (*mil.*) paso; ***at a* — o *at the same* —,** a la vez, al mismo tiempo; no obstante; ***at times,*** a veces; ***at any* —,** a cualquier hora; ***behind the times,*** pasado de moda; ***in* —,** a tiempo; con el tiempo; ***at no* —,** nunca; ***in the day-* —,** de día; ***in the night-* —,** de noche; ***every* —,** cada vez; ***in our times,*** en nuestros días; ***from — to* —,** de vez en cuando; ***from this — forward,*** desde hoy en adelante; ***out of* —,** (*mus.*) fuera de compás; ***for the — being,*** por ahora; ***to arrange a* —,** fijar un día; ***to mark* —,** (*mil., fig.*) marcar el paso; ***to have a good* —,** pasarlo bien; ***to take* —,** tardar; necesitar tiempo; ***to be on* —,** llegar en punto; ***what — is it?*** ¿qué hora es?—*v.t.* calcular el tiempo de; hacer con oportunidad; calcular.
time-exposure ['taimikspouʒə], *n.* exposición, *f.*
time-honoured ['taimonəd], *a.* venerable.
timeless ['taimlis], *a.* eterno.
timely ['taimli], *a.* oportuno.
time-piece ['taimpi:s], *n.* reloj, *m.*
time-table ['taimteibl], *n.* horario; itinerario.
timid ['timid], *a.* tímido.
timidity [ti'miditi], *n.* timidez, *f.*
timorous ['timərəs], *a.* timorato.
tin [tin], *n.* estaño; lata; hojalata; **— *can,*** lata.—*v.t.* estañar; envasar en lata; cubrir con hojalata.
tinder ['tində], *n.* yesca.
tinder-box ['tindəbɔks], *n.* yescas, *f.pl.*
tinfoil ['tinfɔil], *n.* papel (*m.*) de estaño.
tinge [tindʒ], *n.* matiz, tinte, *m.*; (*fig.*) dejo.—*v.t.* matizar.
tingle [tiŋgl], *n.* picazón, *f.*; hormigueo.—*v.i.* picar; estremecerse.
tinker ['tiŋkə], *n.* calderero.—*v.t., v.i.* remendar; ***to — with,*** chafallar.
tinkle [tiŋkl], *n.* retintín, *m.*; cencerreo.—*v.i.* tintinar.
tinned [tind], *a.* en lata, en conserva.
tin-opener ['tinoupnə], *n.* abrelatas, *m.sg.*
tin-plate ['tinpleit], *n.* hojalata.
tinsel ['tinsəl], *n.* oropel, *m.*
tint [tint], *n.* matiz; color; tinte, *m.*—*v.t.* matizar; colorar; teñir.
tiny ['taini], *a.* muy pequeño, minúsculo.
tip [tip], *n.* punta; cabo; extremidad, *f.*; depósito de basura; propina; aviso oportuno; golpecito.—*v.t.* inclinar; voltear; dar una propina a; poner regatón.—*v.i.* inclinarse; dar propina; ***to — over,*** volcarse.
tipple [tipl], *n.* bebida.—*v.i.* empinar el codo.
tipsy ['tipsi], *a.* achispado.
tiptoe ['tiptou], *n.* punta del pie; ***on* —,** de puntillas.
tiptop ['tip'tɔp], *a.* espléndido.
tirade [tai'reid], *n.* diatriba.
tire [taiə], *n.* (*U.S.*) [TYRE]—*v.t.* cansar; aburrir; ***to — out,*** agotar.—*v.i.* cansarse; aburrirse.
tired ['taiəd], *a.* cansado.
tiredness ['taiədnis], *n.* cansancio.
tireless ['taiəlis], *a.* incansable.
tiresome ['taiəsəm], *a.* molesto; aburrido.
tissue ['tisju:], *n.* tejido; tisú, *m.*; (*fig.*) sarta; **— *-paper,*** papel (*m.*) de seda.
tit (1) [tit], *n.* (*orn.*) paro.
tit (2) [tit], *n. only in* **— *for tat,*** tal para cual.
titbit ['titbit], *n.* golosina.
tithe [taið], *n.* diezmo.—*v.t.* diezmar.
titillate ['titileit], *v.t.* titilar.
titivate ['titiveit], *v.i.* emperifollarse; ataviarse.
title [taitl], *n.* título; derecho; documento.
titled [taitld], *a.* titulado.
title-page ['taitlpeidʒ], *n.* portada.
title-role ['taitlroul], *n.* papel principal, *m.*
titter ['titə], *n.* risita sofocada.—*v.i.* reír entre dientes.
titular ['titjulə], *a.* titular; nominal.

to [tu:], *prep.* a; hacia; por; para; de; en; hasta; con; que; (*hora*) menos; — ***his face,*** en cara; ***from town — town,*** de pueblo en pueblo.—*adv.* — ***and fro,*** de un lado a otro, de aquí para acullá; ***to come —,*** volver en sí.
toad [toud], *n.* sapo.
toadstool ['toudstu:l], *n.* hongo.
toady ['toudi], *n.* lameculos, *m.f.sg.*—*v.t.* adular (*to*).
toast [toust], *n.* pan tostado; brindis, *m.*—*v.t.* tostar; brindar.
tobacco [tə'bækou], *n.* tabaco; — ***pouch,*** tabaquera; — ***plantation,*** tabacal, *m.*
tobacconist [tə'bækənist], *n.* tabaquero, tabacalero; ***tobacconist's,*** estanco, tabaquería.
toboggan [tə'bɔgən], *n.* tobogán, *m.*
today [tə'dei], *n.* el día de hoy.—*adv.* hoy; hoy día; actualmente.
toddle [tɔdl], *v.i.* hacer pinitos.
toe [tou], *n.* dedo del pie; pie, *m.*; punta; ***big —,*** dedo gordo del pie; ***from top to —,*** de pies a cabeza.—*v.t.* ***to — the line,*** conformarse.
toffee ['tɔfi], *n.* caramelo.
together [tə'geðə], *a.* junto.—*adv.* juntamente; junto; al mismo tiempo; de seguida; — ***with,*** con; junto con; a la vez que.
toil (I) [tɔil], *n.* trabajo penoso.—*v.i.* afanarse; ***to — (up a hill),*** subir (*una cuesta*) con pena.
toil (2) [tɔil], *n.* (*usually pl.*) lazos, *m.pl.*; redes, *f.pl.*
toilet ['tɔilit], *n.* tocado; atavío; retrete, *m.*; — ***paper,*** papel higiénico, *m.*
token ['toukən], *n.* signo; muestra; recuerdo; ***as a — of,*** en señal de.
told [tould] [TELL].
tolerable ['tɔlərəbl], *a.* tolerable; regular.
tolerance ['tɔlərəns], *n.* tolerancia; indulgencia.
tolerant ['tɔlərənt], *a.* tolerante; indulgente.
tolerate ['tɔləreit], *v.t.* tolerar; permitir.
toleration [tɔlə'reiʃən], *n.* tolerancia.
toll (I) [toul], *n.* peaje, *m.*; derecho de molienda.
toll (2) [toul], *n.* tañido (*de campanas*).—*v.t., v.i.* tañer.
toll-gate ['toul'geit], *n.* barrera de peaje.
Tom [tɔm], *dimin.* Tomás.
tomato [tə'mɑ:tou], *n.* tomate, *m.*; — ***plant,*** tomatera.
tomb [tu:m], *n.* tumba.
tombstone ['tu:mstoun], *n.* piedra sepulcral.
tom-cat ['tɔmkæt], *n.* gato macho.
tome [toum], *n.* tomo.
tomfoolery [tɔm'fu:ləri], *n.* tontería.
tomorrow [tə'mɔrou], *adv., n.* mañana; ***the day after —,*** pasado mañana.
ton [tʌn], *n.* tonelada; ***tons of,*** (*fam.*) un montón de.
tone [toun], *n.* tono; acento; sonido; matiz, *m.*—*v.t.* entonar; ***to — down,*** amortiguar; suavizar; ***to — in with,*** armonizarse con; ***to — up,*** robustecer.
tongs [tɔŋz], *n.pl.* tenazas, *f.pl.*
tongue [tʌŋ], *n.* lengua; clavo (*de hebilla*); badajo (*de campana*); oreja (*de zapato*); ***to hold one's —,*** callarse.
tongue-tied ['tʌŋtaid], *a.* mudo; (*fig.*) turbado.
tongue-twister ['tʌŋtwistə], *n.* trabalenguas, *m.sg.*
tonic ['tɔnik], *a.* tónico.—*n.* (*med.*) tónico; (*mus.*) tónica.
tonight [tə'nait], *adv.* esta noche.
tonnage ['tʌnidʒ], *n.* tonelaje, *m.*
tonsil ['tɔnsil], *n.* amígdala.
tonsillitis [tɔnsi'laitis], *n.* tonsilitis, amigdalitis, *f.*
too [tu:], *adv.* demasiado; también, además.
took [tuk] [TAKE].
tool [tu:l], *n.* herramienta; instrumento; utensilio; (*fig.*) agente, *m.f.*—*v.t.* labrar con herramienta.
tooth [tu:θ], *n.* (*pl.* **teeth**) diente, *m.*; muela; púa (*de peine*); (*fig.*) paladar, *m.*; ***to cut one's teeth,*** echar los dientes; ***to gnash one's teeth,*** rechinarse los dientes; ***to have a sweet —,*** ser goloso; ***to pick one's teeth,*** limpiarse *o* curarse los dientes; ***in the teeth of,*** contra; ***false teeth,*** dentadura postiza; ***set of teeth,*** dentadura.
toothache ['tu:θeik], *n.* dolor (*m.*) de muelas.
toothbrush ['tu:θbrʌsh], *n.* cepillo para dientes.
toothless ['tu:θlis], *a.* desdentado; sin púas.
tooth-paste ['tu:θpeist], *n.* pasta de dientes.
toothpick ['tu:θpik], *n.* palillo, mondadientes, *m.sg.*
top (I) [tɔp], *a.* de encima; superior; principal; primero.—*n.* cima, cumbre, *f.*; copa (*de árbol*); ápice, *m.*; coronilla (*de cabeza*); superficie, *f.*; cabeza (*de página*); coronamiento; capota (*de vehículo*); ***from — to bottom,*** de arriba abajo; ***from — to toe,*** de pies a cabeza.
top (2) [tɔp], *n.* peonza; ***to sleep like a —,*** dormir como un tronco.
topaz ['toupæz], *n.* topacio.
top-coat ['tɔpkout], *n.* sobretodo.
top-dog ['tɔp'dɔg], *n.* (*fam.*) gallito.
toper ['toupə], *n.* borrachín, *m.*
top-hat ['tɔp'hæt], *n.* sombrero de copa.
topic ['tɔpik], *n.* tema, *m.*, asunto.
topical ['tɔpikəl], *a.* tópico; actual.
topmost ['tɔpmoust], *a.* más alto.
topography [tə'pɔgrəfi], *n.* topografía.
topple [tɔpl], *v.t.* derribar, hacer caer.—*v.i.* venirse abajo; tambalearse.
topsyturvy ['tɔpsi'tə:vi], *a.* trastornado.—*adv.* en desorden, patas arriba.
torch [tɔ:tʃ], *n.* antorcha, tea; ***electric —,*** linterna, lamparilla.
torch-bearer ['tɔ:ʃbεərə], *n.* hachero.
torchlight ['tɔ:tʃlait], *n.* luz (*f.*) de antorcha.
tore [tɔ:] [TEAR].
torment ['tɔ:ment], *n.* tormento, tortura; angustia.—[tɔ:'ment], *v.t.* atormentar, torturar.
torn [tɔ:n] [TEAR].
tornado [tɔ:'neidou], *n.* tornado.
torpedo [tɔ:'pi:dou], *n.* torpedo.—*v.t.* torpedear.
torpedo-boat [tɔ:'pi:doubout], *n.* torpedero.
torpedo-tube [tɔ:'pi:doutju:b], *n.* tubo lanzatorpedos.
torpid ['tɔ:pid], *a.* torpe; entorpecido.
torpor ['tɔ:pə], *n.* letargo; torpor, *m.*, entorpecimiento.
torrent ['tɔrənt], *n.* torrente, *m.*
torrential [tə'renʃəl], *a.* torrencial.
torrid ['tɔrid], *a.* tórrido.
tort [tɔ:t], *n.* (*jur.*) tuerto.

tortoise [ˈtɔːtəs], *n.* tortuga.
tortoise-shell [ˈtɔːtəʃel], *n.* carey, *m.*
tortuous [ˈtɔːtjuəs], *a.* tortuoso.
torture [ˈtɔːtʃə], *n.* tortura, tormento.—*v.t.* torturar; martirizar.
torturer [ˈtɔːtʃərə], *n.* atormentador, *m.*
toss [tɔs], *n.* sacudimiento; movimiento (*de cabeza*); cogida (*de toro*).—*v.t.* lanzar, echar; coger, acornear; mover (*la cabeza*); ***to — aside,*** echar a un lado; ***to — in a blanket,*** mantear; ***to — up,*** echar al aire; jugar a cara o cruz.—*v.i.* (*naut.*) cabecear.
tot (1) [tɔt], *n.* nene, *m.*; nena; copita.
tot (2) [tɔt], *v.t.* ***to — up,*** sumar.
total [toutl], *a.* total; entero, completo.—*n.* total, *m.*, suma.—*v.t.* sumar.—*v.i.* ascender a.
totality [touˈtæliti], *n.* totalidad, *f.*
totem [ˈtoutəm], *n.* totem, *m.*
totter [ˈtɔtə], *v.i.* bambolearse; estar para caerse.
tottering [ˈtɔtəriŋ], *a.* vacilante; tambaleante.
touch [tʌtʃ], *n.* tacto; contacto; toque, *m.*; ataque ligero; (*fam.*) sablazo; ***in — with,*** en contacto con.—*v.t.* tocar, tentar; alcanzar; conmover; importar; (*fam.*) dar un sablazo a; ***to — off,*** descargar; ***to — up,*** retocar; ***to — upon,*** tratar ligeramente de.—*v.i.* tocarse; ***to — down,*** aterrizar.
touching [ˈtʌtʃiŋ], *a.* conmovedor, patético. —*prep.* tocante a.
touch-line [ˈtʌtʃlain], *n.* (*sport*) línea de toque.
touchstone [ˈtʌtʃstoun], *n.* piedra de toque.
touchy [ˈtʌtʃi], *a.* susceptible.
tough [tʌf], *a.* duro; resistente; fuerte; (*fam.*) difícil.
toughen [tʌfn], *v.t.* endurecer.—*v.i.* -se.
toughness [ˈtʌfnis], *n.* dureza; fuerza; dificultad, *f.*
tour [tuə], *n.* viaje, *m.*, excursión, *f.*; ***on —,*** (*theat.*) de gira.—*v.t.*, *v.i.* viajar (por).
tourist [ˈtuərist], *n.* turista, *m.f.*
touristic [tuəˈristik], *a.* turístico.
tournament [ˈtuənəmənt], *n.* torneo.
tousle [tauzl], *v.t.* despeinar.
tout [taut], *n.* buhonero; revendedor (*de billetes*), *m.*—*v.i.* ***to — for,*** pescar, solicitar.
tow [tou], *n.* remolque, *m.*; ***on —,*** a remolque. —*v.t.* remolcar.
towards [təˈwɔːdz], *prep.* hacia; cerca de; para con; tocante a.
towel [ˈtauəl], *n.* toalla.
tower [tauə], *n.* torre, *f.*—*v.i.* elevarse; (*fig.*) destacarse.
towering [ˈtauəriŋ], *a.* elevado; dominante; (*fig.*) violento.
town [taun], *n.* ciudad, *f.*; pueblo, población, *f.*; ***— council,*** concejo municipal; ***— hall,*** ayuntamiento.
town-planning [ˈtaunˈplæniŋ], *n.* urbanismo.
townsman [ˈtaunzmən], *n.* ciudadano.
toxic [ˈtɔksik], *a.* tóxico.
toxin [ˈtɔksin], *n.* toxina.
toy [tɔi], *n.* juguete, *m.*—*v.i.* jugar.
toyshop [ˈtɔiʃɔp], *n.* juguetería.
trace [treis], *n.* huella; vestigio; tirante, *m.*; (*fig.*) dejo.—*v.t.* trazar; calcar; localizar; descubrir; ***to — back,*** hacer remontar.
tracing [ˈtreisiŋ], *n.* calco; ***— paper,*** papel (*m.*) para calcar.
track [træk], *n.* huella; pista; (*rail.*) vía; senda; ruta; ***beaten —,*** senda trillada; ***to keep — of,*** no perder de vista.—*v.t.* seguir la pista de; rastrear.
tract [trækt], *n.* tracto; región, *f.*; folleto; (*anat.*) vía.
tractable [ˈtræktəbl], *a.* dócil.
traction [ˈtrækʃən], *n.* tracción, *f.*
traction-engine [ˈtrækʃənˈendʒin], *n.* máquina de tracción.
tractor [ˈtræktə], *n.* tractor, *m.*
trade [treid], *n.* comercio; tráfico; profesión, *f.*; ***free —,*** libre cambio; cambio; ***— mark,*** marca de fábrica; ***— union,*** sindicato; ***— unionist,*** sindicalista, *m.f.*; ***— winds,*** vientos alisios.—*v.t.* cambiar.—*v.i.* comerciar, traficar; ***to — on,*** explotar.
trader [ˈtreidə], *n.* comerciante, traficante, *m.f.*; mercader, *m.*
tradesman [ˈtreidzmən], *n.* tendero; artesano; ***tradesman's entrance,*** puerta de servicio.
trading [ˈtreidiŋ], *a.* comerciante, mercantil. —*n.* comercio.
tradition [trəˈdiʃən], *n.* tradición, *f.*
traditional [trəˈdiʃənl], *a.* tradicional.
traduce [trəˈdjuːs], *v.t.* denigrar.
traffic [ˈtræfik], *n.* tráfico; circulación, *f.*; ***— island,*** salvavidas, *m.sg.*; ***— jam,*** atasco de la circulación; ***— lights,*** semáforo.—*v.i.* traficar.
tragedian [trəˈdʒiːdjən], *n.* trágico.
tragedy [ˈtrædʒidi], *n.* tragedia.
tragic [ˈtrædʒik], *a.* trágico.
tragi-comedy [ˈtrædʒiˈkɔmidi], *n.* tragicomedia.
trail [treil], *n.* pista, huella, rastro; sendero; cola.—*v.t.* arrastrar; rastrear.—*v.i.* arrastrar.
trailer [ˈtreilə], *n.* cazador; (*aut.*) remolque, *m.*; (*cine.*) anuncio de película; (*bot.*) tallo rastrero.
train [trein], *n.* tren, *m.*; séquito; cola (*de traje*); serie, *f.*—*v.t.* amaestrar; enseñar; (*sport*) preparar; entrenar; apuntar (*un cañón*).—*v.i.* educarse; entrenarse.
trainer [ˈtreinə], *n.* amaestrador; instructor; (*sport*) preparador, entrenador, *m.*
training [ˈtreiniŋ], *n.* instrucción, *f.*; (*sport*) entrenamiento; ***— college,*** escuela normal.
trait [trei(t)], *n.* rasgo, característica.
traitor [ˈtreitə], *n.* traidor, *m.*
trajectory [trəˈdʒektəri], *n.* trayectoria.
tram [træm], *n.* tranvía, *m.*
trammel [ˈtræməl], *n.* traba; estorbo.—*v.t.* trabar.
tramp [træmp], *n.* vagabundo; caminata; ruido de pisadas; ***— steamer,*** vapor volandero.—*v.t.* vagar por.—*v.i.* ir a pie; vagabundear; patear.
trample [træmpl], *n.* pisoteo.—*v.t.* pisotear; ***to — on,*** (*fig.*) atropellar, maltratar.
trance [trɑːns], *n.* rapto, arrobamiento; (*med.*) catalepsia.
tranquil [ˈtræŋkwil], *a.* tranquilo.
tranquillizer [ˈtræŋkwilaizə], *n.* (*med.*) tranquilizador, *m.*
tranquillity [træŋˈkwiliti], *n.* tranquilidad, *f.*
transact [trænˈzækt], *v.t.* despachar; llevar a cabo.
transaction [trænˈzækʃən], *n.* negocio; transacción, *f.*—*pl.* actas, *f.pl.*
transatlantic [ˈtrænzətˈlæntik], *a.* transatlántico.

transcend [træn'send], *v.t.* superar, trascender.
transcendence [træn'sendəns], *n.* trascendencia; superioridad, *f.*
transcendent [træn'sendənt], *a.* trascendental; superior.
transcribe [træns'kraib], *v.t.* transcribir.
transcript ['trænskript], *n.* traslado.
transcription [træns'kripʃən], *n.* transcripción, *f.*
transept ['trænsept], *n.* crucero.
transfer ['trænsfə:], *n.* transferencia; traslado; (*jur.*) cesión, *f.*; calcomanía.—[træns'fə:], *v.t.* trasladar, transferir; ceder.
transferable [træns'fə:rəbl], *a.* transferible.
transfiguration [trænsfigju'reiʃən], *n.* transfiguración, *f.*
transfigure [træns'figə], *v.t.* transfigurar.
transfix [træns'fiks], *v.t.* traspasar.
transform [træns'fɔ:m], *v.t.* transformar.
transformation [trænsfə'meiʃən], *n.* transformación, *f.*
transformer [træns'fɔ:mə], *n.* transformador, *m.*
transfusion [træns'fju:ʒən], *n.* transfusión, *f.*
transgress [træns'gres], *v.t.* traspasar; violar. —*v.i.* pecar.
transgression [træns'greʃən], *n.* transgresión, *f.*, pecado.
transgressor [træns'gresə], *n.* transgresor, pecador, *m.*
transient ['trænzjənt], *a.* transitorio.
transit ['trænsit], *n.* tránsito; ***in* —,** de tránsito.
transition [træn'siʃən], *n.* transición, *f.*
transitional [træn'siʃənl], *a.* de transición.
transitive ['trænsitiv], *a.* transitivo.
transitory ['trænsitəri], *a.* transitorio.
translatable [træns'leitəbl], *a.* traducible.
translate [træns'leit], *v.t.* traducir; (*eccl.*) trasladar.
translation [træns'leiʃən], *n.* traducción; versión, *f.*; (*eccl.*) traslado.
translator [træns'leitə], *n.* traductor, *m.*
translucent [trænz'lu:sənt], *a.* translúcido.
transmigration [trænzmai'greiʃən], *n.* transmigración, *f.*
transmission [trænz'miʃən], *n.* transmisión, *f.*
transmit [trænz'mit], *v.t.* transmitir; remitir.
transmitter [trænz'mitə], *n.* transmisor, emisor, *m.*
transmute [trænz'mju:t], *v.t.* transmutar.
transparency [træns'pærənsi], *n.* transparencia; transparente, *m.*
transparent [træns'pærənt], *a.* transparente.
transpire [træns'paiə], *v.i.* transpirar; (*fam.*) acontecer.
transplant [træns'plɑ:nt], *v.t.* trasplantar.
transport ['trænspɔ:t], *n.* transporte, *m.*; arrobamiento.—[træns'pɔ:t], *v.t.* transportar; deportar; arrebatar.
transportable [træns'pɔ:təbl], *a.* transportable.
transportation [trænspɔ:'teiʃən], *n.* transporte, *m.*; deportación, *f.*
transpose [træns'pouz], *v.t.* transponer; (*mus.*) trasportar.
transposition [trænspə'ziʃən], *n.* transposición, *f.*
transubstantiation [trænsʌbstænʃi'eiʃən], *n.* transubstanciación, *f.*
trap [træp], *n.* trampa; pequeño coche; (*mech.*) sifón, *m.*; (*low*) boca; ***to fall into a* —,** caer en la trampa.—*v.t.* coger con trampa; (*fig.*) tender un lazo a.—*v.i.* armar lazos. [TRAPS].
trapdoor ['træpdɔ:], *n.* escotillón, *m.*, trampa.
trapeze [trə'pi:z], *n.* trapecio.
trapper ['træpə], *n.* cazador (*con trampas*), *m.*
trappings ['træpiŋz], *n.pl.* jaeces, *m.pl.*; arreos, *m.pl.*
traps [træps], *n.pl.* (*fam.*) trastos, *m.pl.*
trash [træʃ], *n.* cachivaches, *m.pl.*; (*U.S.*, *fam.*) basura; gentuza; disparates, *m.pl.*
trashy ['træʃi], *a.* sin valor, despreciable.
traumatic [trɔ:'mætik], *a.* traumático.
travail ['træveil], *n.* dolores (*m.pl.*) de parto; afán, *m.*—*v.i.* estar de parto; afanarse.
travel [trævl], *n.* el viajar, viajes, *m.pl.*—*v.t.* recorrer.—*v.i.* viajar; andar.
traveller ['trævlə], *n.* viajero; (*com.*) viajante, *m.f.*; ***traveller's cheque,*** cheque (*m.*) de viajero.
travelling ['trævliŋ], *a.* de viaje; viajero.—*n.* viajes, *m.pl.*
traverse ['trævə:s], *a.* transversal.—*adv.* al través.—*n.* travesaño; (*jur.*) denegación, *f.*; (*mil.*) través, *m.*—*v.t.* atravesar, cruzar; (*jur.*) negar.
travesty ['trævisti], *n.* parodia.—*v.t.* parodiar.
trawl [trɔ:l], *n.* jábega.—*v.t.*, *v.i.* pescar a la rastra.
trawler ['trɔ:lə], *n.* barco pesquero de rastreo.
tray [trei], *n.* bandeja; cajón, *m.*
treacherous ['tretʃərəs], *a.* traidor, pérfido.
treachery ['tretʃəri], *n.* traición, *f.*, perfidia.
treacle [tri:kl], *n.* melado; melaza.
tread [tred], *n.* paso, pisada; huella (*de escalón*); llanta (*de neumático*).—*v.t. irr.* pisar; pisotear; hollar.—*v.i. irr.* pisar (*on*); ***to — under foot,*** pisotear.
treadle [tredl], *n.* pedal, *m.*
treadmill ['tredmil], *n.* molino de rueda de escalones; (*fig.*) tráfago.
treason [tri:zn], *n.* traición, *f.*
treasonable ['tri:znəbl], *a.* traidor.
treasure ['treʒə], *n.* tesoro; ***— trove,*** tesoro hallado.—*v.t.* atesorar.
treasurer ['treʒərə], *n.* tesorero.
Treasury ['treʒəri], **the,** *n.* Ministerio de Hacienda.
treasury ['treʒəri], *n.* tesorería.
treat [tri:t], *n.* regalo; placer, *m.*, gusto; festín, *m.*—*v.t.* tratar; convidar; obsequiar. —*v.i.* convidar; ***to — of,*** tratar de; ***to — with,*** negociar con.
treatise ['tri:tiz], *n.* tratado.
treatment ['tri:tmənt], *n.* tratamiento; conducta.
treaty ['tri:ti], *n.* tratado, pacto.
treble [trebl], *a.* triple; (*mus.*) atiplado.—*n.* (*mus.*) tiple, *m.*; ***— clef,*** clave (*f.*) de sol.—*v.t.* triplicar.—*v.i.* triplicarse.
tree [tri:], *n.* árbol, *m.*; horma (*de zapatos*); arzón (*de silla*), *m.*; ***fruit —,*** frutal, *m.*; ***to bark up the wrong —,*** (*fig.*) errar el tiro.
trek [trek], *n.* viaje, *m.*—*v.i.* viajar, caminar.
trellis ['trelis], *n.* enrejado; espaldera.
tremble [trembl], *n.* temblor, *m.*—*v.i.* temblar.
trembling ['trembliŋ], *a.* tembloroso; trémulo.
tremendous [tri'mendəs], *a.* tremendo.

tremor ['tremə], *n.* temblor, *m.*; estremecimiento.
tremulous ['tremjuləs], *a.* tembloroso, trémulo.
trench [trentʃ], *n.* foso, zanja; (*mil.*) trinchera. —*v.t.* atrincherar.—*v.i.* hacer fosos.
trenchant ['trentʃənt], *a.* penetrante.
trencher ['trentʃə], *n.* trinchero.
trend [trend], *n.* rumbo, curso; tendencia.
trepidation [trepi'deiʃən], *n.* trepidación, *f.*
trespass ['trespəs], *n.* pecado; violación, *f.*—*v.t.* pecar; entrar en propiedad sin derecho; infringir.
trespasser ['trespəsə], *n.* pecador, *m.*; intruso.
tress [tres], *n.* trenza, rizo.
trestle [tresl], *n.* caballete, *m.*
trial ['traiəl], *n.* prueba; tentativa; desgracia; (*jur.*) proceso, vista de una causa; ***on —***, a prueba; (*jur.*) en juicio; ***to stand —***, ser procesado; ***— run***, marcha de ensayo.
triangle ['traiæŋgl], *n.* triángulo.
triangular [trai'æŋgjulə], *a.* triangular.
tribal [traibl], *a.* de la tribu, tribal.
tribe [traib], *n.* tribu, *f.*
tribesman ['traibzmən], *n.* miembro de una tribu.
tribulation [tribju'leiʃən], *n.* tribulación, *f.*
tribunal [trai'bju:nl], *n.* tribunal, *m.*
tributary ['tribjutəri], *a.*, *n.* tributario.
tribute ['tribju:t], *n.* tributo; contribución, *f.*
trick [trik], *n.* engaño; maña; truco; ardid, *m.*; baza (*naipes*); ***dirty —***, perrada; ***to play a — on***, burlar.—*v.t.* engañar; adornar.—*v.i.* trampear.
trickery ['trikəri], *n.* engaño; adornos, *m.pl.*
trickle [trikl], *n.* chorrito.—*v.i.* gotear.
tricky ['triki], *a.* tramposo; (*fam.*) espinoso.
tricycle ['traisikl], *n.* triciclo.
trident ['traidənt], *n.* tridente, *m.*
tried [traid], *a.* probado, leal.
triennial [trai'enjəl], *a.* trienal.
trifle [traifl], *n.* bagatela, fruslería, poca cosa; (*cul.*) dulce (*m.*) de crema; (*fig.*) un poquito. —*v.i.* juguetear; ***to — with***, jugar con.
trifling ['traifliŋ], *a.* frívolo.
trigger ['trigə], *n.* gatillo.
trigonometry [trigə'nəmitri], *n.* trigonometría.
trilby ['trilbi], *n.* sombrero flexible.
trill [tril], *n.* trino; vibración, *f.*—*v.i.* trinar.
trillion ['triljən], *n.* trillón; (*U.S.*) billón, *m.*
trilogy ['trilədʒi], *n.* trilogía.
trim [trim], *a.* ajustado; en buen estado; elegante.—*n.* atavío; orden, *m.*, estado.—*v.t.* arreglar; ajustar; decorar; despabilar (*una lámpara*); recortar; (*carp.*) acepillar; (*naut.*) orientar.
trimming ['trimiŋ], *n.* guarnición, *f.*; ajuste, *m.*; (*naut.*) orientación, *f.*—*pl.* accesorios, *m.pl.*
trimness ['trimnis], *n.* aseo; esbeltez, *f.*
trinity ['triniti], *n.* trinidad, *f.*
trinket ['triŋkit], *n.* dije, *m.*
trio ['tri:ou], *n.* trío.
trip [trip], *n.* zancadilla; traspié, *m.*; excursión, *f.*, viaje, *m.*—*v.t.* hacer caer; dar una zancadilla a; (*fig.*) coger en falta (***up***).—*v.i.* tropezar; ir con paso ligero; (*fig.*) equivocarse.
tripartite [trai'pɑ:tait], *a.* tripartito.
tripe [traip], *n.* callos, *m.pl.*; (*fam.*) disparate, *m.*
triphthong ['trifθəŋ], *n.* triptongo.
triple [tripl], *a.* triple.—*v.t.* triplicar.—*v.i.* triplicarse.
triplet ['triplit], *n.* trillizo; (*mus.*) tresillo; (*poet.*) terceto.
triplicate ['triplikit], *a.* triplicado.—['triplikeit], *v.t.* triplicar.
tripod ['traipəd], *n.* trípode, *m.*
tripper ['tripə], *n.* excursionista, *m.f.*
trite [trait], *a.* trillado.
triumph ['traiəmf], *n.* triunfo.—*v.i.* triunfar.
triumphal [trai'ʌmfəl], *a.* triunfal.
triumphant [[trai'ʌmfənt], *a.* triunfante.
trivial ['triviəl], *a.* trivial; frívolo.
triviality [trivi'æliti], *n.* trivialidad; frivolidad, *f.*
trod [trəd], **trodden** [trədn] [TREAD].
troglodyte ['trəglədait], *n.* troglodita, *m.f.*
Trojan ['troudʒən], *a.*, *n.* troyano.
trolley ['trəli], *n.* trole, *m.*; carro.
trolley-bus ['trəlibʌs], *n.* trolebús, *m.*
trollop ['trələp], *n.* ramera; cochina.
trombone [trəm'boun], *n.* trombón, *m.*
troop [tru:p], *n.* tropa; tropel, *m.*; compañía; escuadrón, *m.*—*pl.* tropas, *f.pl.*—*v.i.* ir en tropel; apinarse; ***to — off***, retirarse en tropel.
trooper ['tru:pə], *n.* soldado de caballería.
trophy ['troufi], *n.* trofeo.
tropic ['trəpik], *a.*, *n.* trópico.
tropical ['trəpikəl], *a.* tropical.
trot [trət], *n.* trote, *m.*—*v.t.* hacer trotar; ***to — out***, (*fig.*) salir con.—*v.i.* trotar.
troth [trouθ], *n.* fe, *f.*; palabra de honor; ***to plight one's —***, desposarse.
trouble [trʌbl], *n.* pena; molestia; dificultad, *f.*; estorbo; inquietud, *f.*; ***to be in —***, hallarse en un apuro; (*fam.*) estar preñada; ***to cause —***, armar un lío; ***to be worth the —***, valer la pena.—*v.t.* molestar; turbar; incomodar; importunar; pedir, rogar.—*v.i.* darse molestia; incomodarse; apurarse.
troubled [trʌbld], *a.* turbado; preocupado.
troublesome ['trʌblsəm], *a.* molesto; fastidioso; importuno; difícil.
trough [trəf], *n.* artesa; gamella; tragadero (*del mar*).
trounce [trauns], *v.t.* zurrar.
troupe [tru:p], *n.* compañía.
trousers ['trauzəz], *n.pl.* pantalones, *m.pl.*
trousseau ['tru:sou], *n.* ajuar, *m.*
trout [traut], *n.* trucha.
trowel ['trauəl], *n.* paleta; desplantador, *m.*
Troy [trəi], *n.* Troya.
truancy ['tru:ənsi], *n.* tuna.
truant ['tru:ənt], *a.* tunante.—*n.* novillero; ***to play —***, hacer novillos.
truce [tru:s], *n.* tregua.
truck (1) [trʌk], *n.* carro; camión, *m.*; (*rail.*) vagón, *m.*
truck (2) [trʌk], *n.* cambio; relaciones, *f.pl.*; (*U.S.*) hortalizas, *f.pl.*
truculence ['trʌkjuləns], *n.* agresividad, *f.*; truculencia.
truculent ['trʌkjulənt], *a.* agresivo; truculento.
trudge [trʌdʒ], *v.i.* ir a pie; andar con pena.
true [tru:], *a.* verdadero; leal; sincero; a plomo.
truffle [trʌfl], *n.* trufa.

truism ['tru:izm], *n.* perogrullada.
trump (1) [trʌmp], *n.* triunfo (*naipes*); (*fam.*) joya.—*v.t.* cortar con el triunfo.—*v.i.* jugar triunfo.
trump (2) [trʌmp], *v.t.* ***to — up,*** inventar.
trump (3) [trʌmp], *n.* son de trompeta; ***the last —,*** el día del Juicio Final.
trumpet ['trʌmpit], *n.* trompeta; ***to blow one's own —,*** alzar el gallo.—*v.t.*, *v.i.* trompetear; (*fig.*) divulgar.
trumpeter ['trʌmpitə], *n.* trompetero, trompeta, *m.*
truncate [trʌŋ'keit], *v.t.* truncar.
truncation [trʌŋ'keiʃən], *n.* truncamiento.
truncheon ['trʌntʃən], *n.* porra.
trundle [trʌndl], *v.t.*, *v.i.* rodar.
trunk [trʌŋk], *n.* tronco; trompa (*de elefante*); baúl, *m.*—*pl.* taparrabo; bañador, *m.*; calzoncillos, *m.pl.*
trunk-call ['trʌŋk'kɔ:l], *n.* conferencia interurbana.
trunk-road ['trʌŋkroud], *n.* carretera principal.
truss [trʌs], *n.* haz, armazón, *m.*; (*med.*) braguero.
trust [trʌst], *n.* confianza; crédito; esperanza; (*jur.*) fideicomiso; (*com.*) trust, *m.*; ***to hold in —,*** guardar en depósito; ***on —,*** al fiado.—*v.t.* tener confianza en; creer en.—*v.i.* esperar; confiar (***in,*** en).
trustee [trʌs'ti:], *n.* guardián, *m.*; (*jur.*) depositario.
trustworthy ['trʌstwə:ði], *a.* fidedigno.
trusty ['trʌsti], *a.* leal; seguro; firme.
truth [tru:θ], *n.* verdad, *f.*; ***the plain —,*** la pura verdad.
truthful ['tru:θful], *a.* veraz; verdadero.
try [trai], *n.* prueba; tentativa; (*sport*) tiro.—*v.t.*, *v.i.* intentar, procurar, tratar de; probar; emprender; verificar; exasperar, fatigar; (*jur.*) ver, procesar; ***to — hard,*** esforzarse (***to,*** a, por); ***to — on,*** probar; ***to — out,*** poner a prueba; ensayar.
trying ['traiiŋ], *a.* difícil; molesto; fatigoso.
tryst [trist], *n.* cita; lugar (*m.*) de cita.
tsetse ['tsetsi], *n.* tsetsé, *f.*
tub [tʌb], *n.* cuba; artesón, *m.*
tuba ['tju:bə], *n.* tuba.
tube [tju:b], *n.* tubo; (*rail.*) metro; ***inner —,*** cámara de aire.
tuber ['tju:bə], *n.* (*bot.*) tubérculo.
tubercular [tju:'bə:kjulə], *a.* tuberculoso.
tuberculosis [tju:'bə:kju'lousis], *n.* tuberculosis, *f.*
tubing ['tju:biŋ], *n.* tubería.
tub-thumper ['tʌbθʌmpə], *n.* (*fam.*) gerundio.
tubular ['tju:bjulə], *a.* tubular.
tuck [tʌk], *n.* pliegue, *m.*; alforza; (*fam.*) dulces, *m.pl.*—*v.t.* alforzar; ***to — in,*** arropar.—*v.i.* ***to — into,*** (*fam.*) comerse.
Tuesday ['tju:zd(e)i], *n.* martes, *m.*
tuft [tʌft], *n.* manojo; moño; penacho; copete, *m.*
tug [tʌg], *n.* tirón; (*naut.*) remolcador, *m.*; ***— of war,*** lucha de la cuerda.—*v.t.*, *v.i.* tirar (de) (***at,*** de).
tuition [tju:'iʃən], *n.* instrucción, *f.*
tulip ['tju:lip], *n.* tulipán, *m.*
tulle [tju:l], *n.* tul, *m.*
tumble [tʌmbl], *n.* caída; voltereta.—*v.t.* derribar; desarreglar.—*v.i.* caer; voltear; ***to — down,*** venirse abajo; ***to — to it,*** (*fam.*) caer en la cuenta.
tumble-down ['tʌmbldaun], *a.* desvencijado, destartalado.
tumbler ['tʌmblə], *n.* volatinero; vaso.
tummy ['tʌmi], *n.* (*fam.*) barriguita, tripita.
tumour ['tju:mə], *n.* tumor, *m.*
tumult ['tju:mʌlt], *n.* alboroto; tumulto.
tumultuous [[tju:'mʌltjuəs], *a.* tumultuoso.
tun [tʌn], *n.* cuba, tonel, *m.*
tuna ['tju:nə], *n.* atún, *m.*
tune [tju:n], *n.* aire, *m.*, armonía; melodía; ***in —,*** afinado; (*fig.*) de acuerdo; ***out of —,*** desafinado; ***to the — of,*** (*fam.*) hasta la suma de.—*v.t.* afinar; sintonizar (*radio etc.*); ajustar (*motores*).—*v.i.* templar (***up***); sintonizar (***in***) (***to,*** con).
tuneless ['tju:nlis], *a.* discorde.
tuner ['tju:nə], *n.* afinador; (*rad.*) sintonizador, *m.*
tunic ['tju:nik], *n.* túnica.
tuning ['tju:niŋ], *n.* afinación; sintonización, *f.*
tuning-fork ['tju:niŋfɔ:k], *n.* diapasón, *m.*
Tunisia [tju:'niziə], *n.* Túnez, *f.*
Tunisian [tju:'niziən], *a.*, *n.* tunecino.
tunnel [tʌnl], *n.* túnel, *m.*—*v.t.*, *v.i.* construir un túnel; minar.
turban ['tə:bən], *n.* turbante, *m.*
turbine ['tə:bain], *n.* turbina.
turbojet ['tə:boudʒet], *n.* turborreactor, *m.*
turbot ['tə:bət], *n.* (*ichth.*) rodaballo.
turbulent ['tə:bjulənt], *a.* turbulento.
tureen [tju:'ri:n], *n.* sopera.
turf [tə:f], *n.* césped, *m.*; turba; carreras (*f.pl.*) de caballos.
turgid ['tə:dʒid], *a.* turgente; (*fig.*) hinchado.
Turk [tə:k], *n.* turco.
Turkey ['tə:ki], *n.* Turquía.
turkey ['tə:ki], *n.* pavo; pava.
Turkish ['tə:kiʃ], *a.*, *n.* turco.
turmoil ['tə:mɔil], *n.* tumulto, alboroto.
turn [tə:n], *n.* giro, vuelta; paseo; vez, *f.*; dirección, *f.*; inclinación, *f.*; oportunidad, *f.*, procedimiento; servicio; provecho; ***good —,*** favor, *m.*; ***bad —,*** mala pasada; ***at every —,*** a cada instante; ***to do a good —,*** prestar un servicio; ***to take a —,*** dar una vuelta; ***to take turns,*** turnar, alternar.—*v.t.* hacer girar, dar vueltas a; invertir; dar nueva dirección a; adaptar; convertir; volver; traducir; torcer; dar asco; infatuar; perturbar; tornear; redondear (*una frase*); ***to — against,*** hacerse enemigo de; ***to — aside,*** desviar; ***to — away,*** despedir, rechazar; ***to — back,*** volver atrás; ***to — one's back on,*** volver la espalda a; ***to — down,*** doblar, plegar; rechazar; ***to — from,*** desviar de; ***to — in,*** volver adentro; (*fig.*) entregar; ***to — into,*** cambiar en; ***to — off,*** cerrar; ***to — on,*** abrir; encender; ***to — out,*** arrojar; apagar; volver del revés; ***to — over,*** recorrer; invertir; volcar; entregar; ***to — round,*** volver; ***to — the stomach,*** dar asco; ***to — to good account,*** poner a provecho; ***to — up,*** volver arriba; revolver; ***to — upon,*** revolver sobre; ***to — upside down,*** trastornar.—*v.i.* volver; volverse; girar; ponerse; agriarse (*la leche*); infatuarse; perturbarse; resultar; tornearse; (*naut.*) virar; ***to — about,*** volverse; ***to — aside,*** desviarse; ***to — away,*** volverse; ***to — back,***

retroceder; ***to — in,*** volverse adentro; doblarse; (*fam.*) ir a la cama; ***to — into,*** entrar en; convertirse en; ***to — off,*** desviarse; torcer; ***to — out,*** resultar; suceder; salir; ***to — over,*** revolverse; ***to — round,*** volverse; ***to — to,*** ponerse a; dirigirse a; ***to — up,*** volver arriba; (*fam.*) llegar; acontecer; ***to — upon,*** volver sobre; depender de.
turncoat ['tə:nkout], *n.* renegado.
turning ['tə:niŋ], *n.* vuelta.
turning-point ['tə:niŋpɔint], *n.* punto decisivo.
turnip ['tə:nip], *n.* nabo.
turnout ['tə:naut], *n.* vestidos, *m.pl.*; entrada *o* salida de personas; (*com.*) producto neto.
turnover ['tə:nouvə], *n.* pastel, *m.*; (*com.*) ventas, *f.pl.*
turnstile ['tə:nstail], *n.* torniquete, *m.*
turntable ['tə:nteibl], *n.* plato.
turpentine ['tə:pəntain], *n.* trementina.
turpitude ['tə:pitju:d], *n.* infamia, torpeza.
turquoise ['tə:kwɔiz], *n.* turquesa.
turret ['tʌrət], *n.* torrecilla.
turtle [tə:tl], *n.* tortuga de mar; ***to turn —,*** voltear patas arriba; volcar(se).
turtle-dove ['tə:tldʌv], *n.* tórtola.
tusk [tʌsk], *n.* colmillo.
tussle [tʌsl], *n.* riña.—*v.i.* luchar.
tutelar ['tju:tilə], *a.* tutelar.
tutor ['tju:tə], *n.* preceptor, *m.*; ayo.—*v.t.* enseñar.—*v.i.* dar clases.
tutorial [tju:'tɔ:riəl], *n.* seminario.
tutoring ['tju:təriŋ], *n.* instrucción, *f.*
twain [twein], *n.* (*poet.*) dos, *m.f.pl.*
twaddle [twɔdl], *n.* disparates, *m.pl.*
twang [twæŋ], *n.* sonido vibrante; gangueo; punteado de una cuerda; acento.—*v.i.* ganguear.—*v.t.* rasguear.
'twas [twɔz] [IT WAS].
tweed [twi:d], *n.* cheviot, *m.*
tweezers ['twi:zəz], *n.pl.* tenacillas, pinzas, *f.pl.*
twelfth [twelfθ], *a.* duodécimo; ***Twelfth Night,*** día (*m.*) de los Reyes.—*n.* duodécimo, duodécima parte; doce (*en las fechas*), *m.*
twelve [twelv], *a.*, *n.* doce, *m.*
twentieth ['twentiiθ], *a.* vigésimo.—*n.* veintavo; vigésima parte; veinte (*en las fechas*), *m.*
twenty ['twenti], *a.*, *n.* veinte, *m.*
twice [twais], *adv.* dos veces.
twiddle [twidl], *v.t.* jugar con.
twig [twig], *n.* ramita.
twilight ['twailait], *a.* crepuscular.—*n.* crepúsculo.
twill [twil], *n.* tela asargada.
twin [twin], *a.*, *n.* mellizo, gemelo.
twine [twain], *n.* cordel, *m.*—*v.t.* enroscar; ceñir.—*v.i.* entrelazarse.
twin-engined ['twin'endʒind], *a.* bimotor.
twinge [twindʒ], *n.* punzada; (*fig.*) remordimiento.
twinkle [twiŋkl], *n.* centelleo; pestañeo.—*v.i.* centellear; brillar.
twinkling ['twiŋkliŋ], *n.* brillo; centelleo; (*fig.*) instante, *m.*; ***in the — of an eye,*** en un abrir y cerrar de ojos; en un santiamén.
twirl [twə:l], *n.* vuelta, rotación, *f.*; pirueta.—*v.t.* hacer girar; dar vueltas a.—*v.i.* girar; dar vueltas.
twist [twist], *n.* torzal, *m.*; mecha; sacudida; peculiaridad, *f.*; recodo; torsión, *f.*; trenza; rollo (*de tabaco*).—*v.t.* torcer; enroscar; trenzar; falsificar.—*v.i.* torcerse; serpentear; retorcerse.
twister ['twistə], *n.* torcedor; (*fam.*) estafador, *m.*
twisting ['twistiŋ], *a.* sinuoso.
twitch [twitʃ], *n.* tirón, *m.*; contracción nerviosa, *f.*—*v.t.* arrancar.—*v.i.* crisparse; moverse.
twitter ['twitə], *n.* piada, gorjeo.—*v.i.* piar, gorjear.
two [tu:], *a.*, *n.* dos, *m.*; ***to put — and — together,*** caer en la cuenta.
two-faced ['tu:'feist], *a.* de dos caras; (*fig.*) de dos haces.
twofold ['tu:fould], *a.* doble.—*adv.* doblemente.
two-headed ['tu:'hedid], *a.* de dos cabezas.
two-legged ['tu:'legid], *a.* bípedo.
twopence ['tʌpəns], *n.* dos peniques, *m.pl.*
twopenny ['tʌpni], *a.* de dos peniques; (*fig.*) de tres al cuarto.
two-ply ['tu:'plai], *a.* de dos hilos *o* capas.
two-seater ['tu:'si:tə], *a.* de dos asientos.
two-step ['tu:step], *n.* paso doble.
two-way ['tu:wei], *a.* de dos direcciones.
type [taip], *n.* tipo; letra de imprenta.—*v.t.*, *v.i.* escribir a máquina.
type-case ['taipkeis], *n.* caja de imprenta.
type-setter ['taipsetə], *n.* cajista, *m.f.*
typewriter ['taipraitə], *n.* máquina de escribir.
typewriting ['taipraitiŋ], *n.* mecanografía.
typewritten ['taipritn], *a.* escrito a máquina.
typhoid ['taifɔid], *n.* fiebre tifoidea.
typhoon [tai'fu:n], *n.* tifón, *m.*
typhus ['taifəs], *n.* tifus, *m.*
typical ['tipikəl], *a.* típico.
typify ['tipifai], *v.t.* simbolizar.
typist ['taipist], *n.* mecanógrafo.
typography [tai'pɔgrəfi], *n.* tipografía.
tyrannical [ti'rænikəl], *a.* tiránico.
tyrannize ['tirənaiz], *v.t.*, *v.i.* tiranizar.
tyrannous ['tirənəs], *a.* tiránico.
tyranny ['tirəni], *n.* tiranía.
tyrant ['taiərənt], *n.* tirano.
tyre [taiə], *n.* neumático; llanta (*de carro*).

U

U, u [ju:], *n.* vigésima primera letra del alfabeto inglés.
ubiquitous [ju:'bikwitəs], *a.* ubicuo.
udder ['ʌdə], *n.* ubre, *f.*
ugliness ['ʌglinis], *n.* fealdad, *f.*
ugly ['ʌgli], *a.* feo; repugnante.
Ukraine [ju:'krein], *n.* Ucrania.
Ukrainian [ju:'kreiniən], *a.*, *n.* ucranio.
ulcer ['ʌlsə], *n.* úlcera.
ulcerate ['ʌlsəreit], *v.t.* ulcerar.—*v.i.* ulcerarse.
ulterior [ʌl'tiəriə], *a.* ulterior; ***— motive,*** intención oculta.
ultimate ['ʌltimit], *a.* último; esencial, fundamental.

ultimatum [ʌlti'meitəm], *n.* ultimátum, *m.*
ultra ['ʌltrə], *a.* extremo, exagerado.—*prefix.* ultra-.
ultraviolet [ʌltrə'vaiəlit], *a.* ultravioleta.
umbrage ['ʌmbridʒ], *n.* (*poet.*) sombraje, *m.*; resentimiento; ***to take* —,** picarse (***at,*** de).
umbrella [ʌm'brelə], *n.* paraguas, *m.sg.*; **— *stand,*** paragüero.
umpire ['ʌmpaiə], *n.* (*sport*) árbitro; arbitrador, *m.*—*v.t.*, *v.i.* arbitrar.
un- [ʌn], *prefix, variously translated in Spanish by* in-, des-, no, sin, poco.
unabridged [ʌnə'bridʒd], *a.* no abreviado; íntegro.
unacceptable [ʌnək'septəbl], *a.* inaceptable.
unaccompanied [ʌnə'kʌmpənid], *a.* no acompañado, solo.
unaccomplished [ʌnə'kʌmpliʃt], *a.* inacabado, imperfecto, incompleto.
unaccountable [ʌnə'kauntəbl], *a.* inexplicable; irresponsable.
unaccustomed [ʌnə'kʌstəmd], *a.* desacostumbrado.
unacquainted [ʌnə'kweintid], *a.* desconocido; ***to be* — *with,*** no conocer; ignorar.
unadulterated [ʌnə'dʌltəreitid], *a.* sin mezcla, natural; puro.
unadventurous [ʌnəd'vəntʃərəs], *a.* nada aventurero; tímido.
unadvisable [ʌnəd'vaizəbl], *a.* poco conveniente; imprudente.
unaffected [ʌnə'fektid], *a.* sin afectación, natural, franco; no afectado.
unalterable [ʌn'ɔ:ltərəbl], *a.* inalterable; invariable.
unanimity [ju:nə'nimiti], *n.* unanimidad, *f.*
unanimous [ju:'næniməs], *a.* unánime.
unanswerable [ʌn'ɑ:nsərəbl], *a.* incontestable, incontrovertible.
unapproachable [ʌnə'proutʃəbl], *a.* inaccesible.
unarmed [ʌn'ɑ:md], *a.* desarmado; indefenso.
unashamed [ʌnə'ʃeimd], *a.* sin vergüenza.
unassuming [ʌnə'sju:miŋ], *a.* sin pretensiones, modesto.
unattainable [ʌnə'teinəbl], *a.* inasequible.
unattractive [ʌnə'træktiv], *a.* poco atractivo, antipático.
unavailing [ʌnə'veiliŋ], *a.* infructuoso, inútil, vano.
unavoidable [ʌnə'vɔidəbl], *a.* inevitable.
unaware [ʌnə'wɛə], *a.* ignorante; inconsciente.
unawares [ʌnə'wɛəz], *adv.* ***to take* —,** coger desprevenido.
unbearable [ʌn'bɛərəbl], *a.* intolerable, insoportable.
unbecoming [ʌnbi'kʌmiŋ], *a.* impropio, inconveniente; indecoroso; que sienta mal.
unbeliever [ʌnbi'li:və], *n.* incrédulo; descreído.
unbias(s)ed [ʌn'baiəst], *a.* imparcial.
unbidden [ʌn'bidn], *a.* no convidado; espontáneo.
unborn [ʌn'bɔ:n], *a.* no nacido todavía.
unbosom [ʌn'buzəm], *v.t.* confesar; ***to* — *oneself,*** abrir su pecho.
unbound [ʌn'baund], *a.* sin encuadernar.
unbounded [ʌn'baundid], *a.* ilimitado, infinito.
unbreakable [ʌn'breikəbl], *a.* inquebrantable.
unbridled [ʌn'braidld], *a.* desenfrenado.
unbroken [ʌn'broukən], *a.* intacto, entero; indomado; no interrumpido, ininterrumpido.
unbuckle [ʌn'bʌkl], *v.t.* deshebillar.
unburden [ʌn'bə:dn], *v.t.* descargar; aliviar; (*fig.*) ***to* — *oneself,*** desahogarse.
unbutton [ʌn'bʌtn], *v.t.* desabotonar, desabrochar.
uncanny [ʌn'kæni], *a.* misterioso; pavoroso.
unceasing [ʌn'si:siŋ], *a.* incesante, sin cesar.
uncertain [ʌn'sə:tn], *a.* incierto, dudoso; indeciso, irresoluto.
uncertainty [ʌn'sə:tnti], *n.* incertidumbre; irresolución, *f.*
unchain [ʌn'tʃein], *v.t.* desencadenar.
unchangeable [ʌn'tʃeindʒəbl], *a.* invariable, inmutable.
unchaste [ʌn'tʃeist], *a.* impúdico, incasto.
unchecked [ʌn'tʃekt], *a.* desenfrenado; no verificado.
unclaimed [ʌn'kleimd], *a.* no reclamado.
uncle [ʌŋkl], *n.* tío; (*fam.*) prestamista, *m.*
unclean [ʌn'kli:n], *a.* sucio, impuro; inmundo.
unclothe [ʌn'klouð], *v.t.* desnudar.
uncoil [ʌn'kɔil], *v.t.* desarrollar.—*v.i.* desovillarse.
uncomfortable [ʌn'kʌmfətəbl], *a.* incómodo; molesto, desagradable; preocupado.
uncommon [ʌn'kɔmən], *a.* poco común, raro, extraño; infrecuente; extraordinario.
uncompromising [ʌn'kɔmprəmaiziŋ], *a.* inflexible.
unconcerned [ʌnkən'sə:nd], *a.* indiferente, frío; despreocupado.
unconditional [ʌnkən'diʃənl], *a.* incondicional, absoluto.
unconquerable [ʌn'kɔŋkərəbl], *a.* invencible.
unconscious [ʌn'kɔnʃəs], *a.* inconsciente; sin sentido; espontáneo; ignorante.
unconstitutional [ʌnkɔnsti'tju:ʃənl], *a.* anticonstitucional.
uncontrollable [ʌnkən'trouləbl], *a.* irrefrenable, ingobernable.
unconventional [ʌnkən'venʃənl], *a.* poco convencional; excéntrico; original.
uncork [ʌn'kɔ:k], *v.t.* destapar.
uncouple [ʌn'kʌpl], *v.t.* desconectar; soltar.
uncouth [ʌn'ku:θ], *a.* tosco, grosero.
uncover [ʌn'kʌvə], *v.t.* descubrir; desabrigar; destapar.
unction ['ʌŋkʃən], *n.* unción, *f.*; ungüento; (*fig.*) hipocresía; fervor, *m.*
unctuous ['ʌŋktjuəs], *a.* untuoso, zalamero.
uncurl [ʌn'kə:l], *v.t.* desrizar.—*v.i.* desrizarse; destorcerse.
undamaged [ʌn'dæmidʒd], *a.* indemne.
undated [ʌn'deitid], *a.* sin fecha.
undaunted [ʌn'dɔ:ntid], *a.* intrépido; denodado.
undecided [ʌndi'saidid], *a.* indeciso; irresoluto.
undefended [ʌndi'fendid], *a.* indefenso.
undefined [ʌndi'faind], *a.* indefinido.
undeniable [ʌndi'naiəbl], *a.* incontestable, innegable.
under ['ʌndə], *a.* bajo; inferior; subordinado.—*adv.* abajo; debajo; menos; ***to keep* —,** subyugar.—*prep.* bajo, debajo de; inferior a; menos de; al mando de; **— *age,*** menor de edad; **— *arms,*** bajo las armas; **— *consideration,*** en consideración; **— *cover,*** al

abrigo; — ***pain of***, so pena de; — ***steam***, al vapor; — ***way***, en marcha.
underarm ['ʌndərɑ:m], *n.* sobaco, axila.
undercarriage ['ʌndəkæridʒ], *n.* (*aer.*) tren (*m.*) de aterrizaje.
underclothes ['ʌndəklouðz], *n.pl.* ropa interior.
undercurrent ['ʌndəkʌrənt], *n.* corriente (*f.*) submarina; (*fig.*) tendencia oculta.
undercut ['ʌndəkʌt], *n.* filete, *m.*—[ʌndə'kʌt], *v.t.* socavar; baratear.
under-developed ['ʌndədi'veləpt], *a.* subdesarrollado; (*phot.*) no revelado bastante.
underdog ['ʌndədɔg], *n.* víctima; débil, *m.*
underdone [ʌndə'dʌn], *a.* medio asado.
underestimate [ʌndər'estimeit], *v.t.* desestimar.
underfoot [ʌndə'fut], *adv.* debajo de los pies.
undergo [ʌndə'gou], *v.t. irr.* (*conjug. like* GO) padecer, sufrir; pasar por.
undergraduate [ʌndə'grædjuit], *n.* estudiante (*m.*) no licenciado.
underground ['ʌndəgraund], *a.* subterráneo. —*n.* metro.—[ʌndə'graund], *adv.* bajo tierra.
undergrowth ['ʌndəgrouθ], *n.* maleza.
underhand [ʌndə'hænd], *a.* clandestino, solapado.—*adv.* a escondidas bajo mano.
underlie [ʌndə'lai], *v.t. irr.* (*conjug. like* LIE) estar debajo de; ser la razón fundamental de.
underline [ʌndə'lain], *v.t.* subrayar.
underling ['ʌndəliŋ], *n.* subordinado, paniaguado.
underlying [ʌndə'laiiŋ], *a.* fundamental.
undermine [ʌndə'main], *v.t.* socavar; minar.
underneath [ʌndə'ni:θ], *adv.* debajo.—['ʌndəni:θ], *prep.* bajo, debajo de.
underpaid [ʌndə'peid], *a.* mal pagado.
underprivileged [ʌndə'privilidʒd], *a.* menesteroso.
underrate [ʌndə'reit], *v.t.* desestimar, menospreciar.
underside ['ʌndəsaid], *n.* revés, envés, *m.*
undersigned [ʌndə'saind], *a.*, *n.* infrascrito, abajo firmado.
understand [ʌndə'stænd], *v.t. irr.* (*conjug. like* STAND) comprender; saber; conocer; tener entendido; sobrentender.—*v.i.* comprender; tener entendido.
understandable [ʌndə'stændəbl], *a.* comprensible.
understanding [ʌndə'stændiŋ], *n.* entendimiento; comprensión, *f.*; acuerdo.
understatement ['ʌndəsteitmənt], *n.* moderación (*f.*) excesiva.
understudy ['ʌndəstʌdi], *n.* (*theat.*) sobresaliente, *m.f.*—*v.t.* sustituir.
undertake [ʌndə'teik], *v.t. irr.* (*conjug. like* TAKE) encargarse de, emprender.
undertaker ['ʌndəteikə], *n.* director (*m.*) de pompas fúnebres.
undertaking ['ʌndəteikiŋ], *n.* empresa funeraria; [ʌndə'teikiŋ], empresa; (*jur.*) garantía.
undertone ['ʌndətoun], *n.* voz baja, tonillo; (*art*) color apagado.
undervalue [ʌndə'vælju:], *v.t.* menospreciar.
underwear ['ʌndəwɛə], *n.* ropa interior.
underworld ['ʌndəwə:ld], *n.* infierno; heces (*f.pl.*) de la sociedad, hampa.
underwrite ['ʌndərait], *v.t. irr.* (*conjug. like* WRITE) (*com.*) asegurar, reasegurar.
underwriter ['ʌndəraitə], *n.* asegurador, reasegurador, *m.*
undeserved [ʌndi'zə:vd], *a.* inmerecido.
undesirable [ʌndi'zaiərəbl], *a.* no deseable; pernicioso, indeseable.
undigested [ʌndi'dʒestid], *a.* indigesto.
undignified [ʌn'dignifaid], *a.* sin dignidad.
undiminished [ʌndi'miniʃt], *a.* no disminuído; continuo; íntegro.
undisciplined [ʌn'disiplind], *a.* indisciplinado.
undisclosed [ʌndis'klouzd], *a.* no revelado.
undivided [ʌndi'vaidid], *a.* indiviso, íntegro, completo.
undo [ʌn'du:], *v.t.* (*conjug. like* DO) deshacer; desatar; anular; (*fig.*) arruinar.
undoing [ʌn'du:iŋ], *n.* anulación, *f.*; ruina.
undoubted [ʌn'dautid], *a.* indudable, evidente.
undress [ʌn'dres], *v.t.* desnudar, desvestir.—*v.i.* desnudarse.
undressed [ʌn'drest], *a.* desnudo; no preparado; (*com.*) en bruto.
undue [ʌn'dju:], *a.* excesivo, indebido; injusto.
undying [ʌn'daiiŋ], *a.* inmortal, imperecedero.
unearth [ʌn'ə:θ], *v.t.* desenterrar; (*fig.*) sacar a luz.
unearthly [ʌn'ə:θli], *a.* sobrenatural; misterioso; espantoso.
uneasiness [ʌn'i:zinis], *n.* inquietud, *f.*; malestar, *m.*; incomodidad, *f.*
uneasy [ʌn'i:zi], *a.* inquieto; incómodo; turbado.
uneatable [ʌn'i:təbl], *a.* incomible.
unemployed [ʌnim'plɔid], *a.* sin trabajo, desocupado.—*n.* desocupado, cesante, *m.*
unemployment [ʌnim'plɔiment], *n.* paro (forzoso), cesantía.
unending [ʌn'endiŋ], *a.* sin fin, perpetuo.
unequal [ʌn'i:kwəl], *a.* desigual; — ***to the task of***, incapaz de.
unequalled [ʌn'i:kwəld], *a.* sin igual, sin par.
unequivocal [ʌni'kwivəkəl], *a.* inequívoco.
unerring [ʌn'ə:riŋ], *a.* infalible.
uneven [ʌn'i:vən], *a.* desigual; impar; escabroso.
uneventful [ʌni'ventful], *a.* sin incidentes; tranquilo.
unexampled [ʌnig'zɑ:mpld], *a.* sin igual, único.
unexpected [ʌniks'pektid], *a.* imprevisto, inesperado; repentino.
unexpressed [ʌniks'prest], *a.* tácito, sobrentendido; no expresado.
unfading [ʌn'feidiŋ], *a.* inmarcesible; inmortal.
unfailing [ʌn'feiliŋ], *a.* inagotable; infalible, seguro.
unfair [ʌn'fɛə], *a.* injusto; desleal; parcial.
unfaithful [ʌn'feiθful], *a.* infiel; desleal; inexacto.
unfaithfulness [ʌn'feiθfulnis], *n.* infidelidad; deslealtad; inexactitud, *f.*
unfaltering [ʌn'fɔ:ltəriŋ], *a.* firme.
unfamiliar [ʌnfə'miljə], *a.* poco familiar; desconocido.
unfashionable [ʌn'fæʃnəbl], *a.* fuera de moda.
unfasten [ʌn'fɑ:sən], *v.t.* desatar; desabrochar; soltar.

unfathomable [ʌn'fæðəməbl], *a.* insondable, impenetrable.
unfavourable [ʌn'feivərəbl], *a.* desfavorable, adverso.
unfinished [ʌn'finiʃt], *a.* incompleto, inacabado.
unfit [ʌn'fit], *a.* inepto; impropio, inconveniente; indigno; enfermo.
unflagging [ʌn'flægiŋ], *a.* infatigable; persistente.
unflinching [ʌn'flintʃiŋ], *a.* determinado, resuelto.
unfold [ʌn'fould], *v.t.* desplegar; desenvolver.—*v.i.* descubrirse; desarrollarse; abrirse.
unforeseen [ʌnfɔ:'si:n], *a.* imprevisto.
unforgettable [ʌnfə'getəbl], *a.* inolvidable.
unforgivable [ʌnfə'givəbl], *a.* inexcusable.
unfortunate [ʌn'fɔ:tʃənit], *a., n.* desdichado, desgraciado, infeliz, *m.f.*
unfriendly [ʌn'frendli], *a.* hostil; perjudicial; insociable.
unfrock [ʌn'frɔk], *v.t.* exclaustrar.
unfurl [ʌn'fə:l], *v.t.* desplegar.
unfurnished [ʌn'fə:niʃt], *a.* desamueblado; desprovisto.
ungainly [ʌn'geinli], *a.* desgarbado.
ungentlemanly [ʌn'dʒentlmənli], *a.* de mal tono; indigno de un caballero.
ungodliness [ʌn'gɔdlinis], *n.* impiedad, *f.*
ungodly [ʌn'gɔdli], *a.* impío, irreligioso.
ungracious [ʌn'greiʃəs], *a.* desagradable, ofensivo.
ungrammatical [ʌngrə'mætikəl], *a.* antigramatical, incorrecto.
ungrateful [ʌn'greitful], *a.* ingrato; desagradable.
unguarded [ʌn'gɑ:did], *a.* indefenso; indiscreto; desprevenido.
unhappiness [ʌn'hæpinis], *n.* desgracia, infelicidad, *f.*
unhappy [ʌn'hæpi], *a.* desgraciado, infeliz; malhadado; inoportuno.
unharmed [ʌn'hɑ:md], *a.* ileso; indemne.
unhealthy [ʌn'helθi], *a.* enfermizo; malsano.
unheard [ʌn'hə:d], *a.* sin ser oído; desconocido.
unheard of [ʌn'hə:dəv], *a.* inaudito, sin ejemplo.
unhesitating [ʌn'heziteitiŋ], *a.* resuelto; pronto.
unhesitatingly [ʌn'heziteitiŋli], *adv.* sin vacilar, sin reservas.
unhinge [ʌn'hindʒ], *v.t.* desgoznar; (*fig.*) trastornar.
unholy [ʌn'houli], *a.* impío.
unhook [ʌn'huk], *v.t.* descolgar; desenganchar.
unhoped [ʌn'houpt], *a.* — ***for,*** inesperado.
unhurt [ʌn'hə:t], *a.* ileso, incólume, sano y salvo; indemne.
unicorn ['ju:nikɔ:n], *n.* unicornio.
unification [ju:nifi'keiʃən], *n.* unificación, *f.*
uniform ['ju:nifɔ:m], *a.* uniforme; invariable.—*n.* uniforme, *m.*
uniformity [ju:ni'fɔ:miti], *n.* uniformidad, *f.*
unify ['ju:nifai], *v.t.* unificar.
unimaginable [ʌni'mædʒinəbl], *a.* inimaginable.
unimpaired [ʌnim'pɛəd], *a.* no deteriorado; intacto.
unimpeachable [ʌnim'pi:tʃəbl], *a.* irreprensible, intachable.
unimportant [ʌnim'pɔ:tənt], *a.* insignificante, sin importancia.
uninformed [ʌnin'fɔ:md], *a.* ignorante.
uninhabited [ʌnin'hæbitid], *a.* inhabitado, desierto.
uninjured [ʌn'indʒəd], *a.* ileso.
uninspired [ʌnin'spaiəd], *a.* sin inspiración; pedestre.
unintelligible [ʌnin'telidʒibl], *a.* ininteligible.
unintentional [ʌnin'tenʃənl], *a.* involuntario.
uninterested [ʌn'intərestid], *a.* no interesado.
union ['ju:njən], *n.* unión, *f.*; ***Union of Soviet Socialist Republics,*** Unión (*f.*) de Repúblicas Socialistas Soviéticas.
unique [ju:'ni:k], *a.* único, sin igual.
unison ['ju:nizn], *n.* unisonancia; ***in —,*** al unísono.
unit ['ju:nit], *n.* unidad, *f.*
Unitarian [ju:ni'tɛəriən], *a., n.* unitario.
unite [ju:'nait], *v.t.* unir; incorporar; juntar.—*v.i.* unirse; incorporarse; juntarse.
united [ju:'naitid], *a.* unido; ***United Arab Republic,*** República Árabe Unida; ***United Kingdom,*** Reino Unido; ***United Nations,*** Naciones Unidas; ***United States,*** los Estados Unidos.
unity ['ju:niti], *n.* unidad, *f.*
universal [ju:ni'və:səl], *a.* universal; general; ***— joint,*** cardán, *m.*
universality [ju:nivə:'sæliti], *n.* universalidad; generalidad, *f.*
universe ['ju:nivə:s], *n.* universo.
university [ju:ni'və:siti], *n.* universidad, *f.*
unjust [ʌn'dʒʌst], *a.* injusto.
unjustifiable [ʌn'dʒʌstifaiəbl], *a.* injustificable.
unkempt [ʌn'kempt], *a.* despeinado; desaseado.
unkind [ʌn'kaind], *a.* poco amable; duro; desfavorable.
unknowingly [ʌn'nouiŋli], *adv.* sin saberlo; involuntariamente.
unknown [ʌn'noun], *a.* desconocido, ignoto.—*n.* (*math.*) incógnita.
unlace [ʌn'leis], *v.t.* desenlazar; desatar.
unladylike [ʌn'leidilaik], *a.* impropio de una señora; de mal tono.
unlawful [ʌn'lɔ:ful], *a.* ilegal.
unless [ʌn'les], *conj.* a menos que, a no ser que; excepto.
unlicensed [ʌn'laisənst], *a.* sin licencia; no autorizado.
unlike [ʌn'laik], *a.* disímil; diferente.—*prep.* a diferencia de, no como.
unlikely [ʌn'laikli], *a.* inverosímil, improbable.
unlimited [ʌn'limitid], *a.* ilimitado, inmenso.
unload [ʌn'loud], *v.t.* descargar; aligerar; deshacerse de.
unlock [ʌn'lɔk], *v.t.* abrir; (*fig.*) descubrir.
unlooked-for [ʌn'luktfɔ:], *a.* inopinado.
unloose [ʌn'lu:s], *v.t.* soltar; desatar.
unlucky [ʌn'lʌki], *a.* desgraciado, infeliz; funesto.
unmanageable [ʌn'mænidʒəbl], *a.* ingobernable, indomable.
unmanly [ʌn'mænli], *a.* afeminado.
unmannerly [ʌn'mænəli], *a.* mal educado.
unmarried [ʌn'mærid], *a.* soltero; célibe.

unmask [ʌn'mɑ:sk], *v.t.* desenmascarar; quitar el velo a, descubrir.
unmindful [ʌn'maindful], *a.* desatento; negligente.
unmistakable [ʌnmis'teikəbl], *a.* inequívoco, evidente.
unmoved [ʌn'mu:vd], *a.* fijo; firme; impasible.
unnatural [ʌn'nætʃərəl], *a.* innatural; desnaturalizado; artificial.
unnecessary [ʌn'nesisəri], *a.* innecesario, superfluo.
unnerve [ʌn'nə:v], *v.t.* acobardar.
unnoticed [ʌn'noutist], *a.* inadvertido, inobservado.
unobserved [ʌnəb'zə:vd], *a.* desapercibido.
unobtainable [ʌnəb'teinəbl], *a.* inasequible.
unobtrusive [ʌnəb'tru:siv], *a.* discreto.
unoccupied [ʌn'ɔkjupaid], *a.* desocupado; libre.
unofficial [ʌnə'fiʃəl], *a.* no oficial.
unorthodox [ʌn'ɔ:θədɔks], *a.* heterodoxo.
unpack [ʌn'pæk], *v.t.* desempaquetar; vaciar. —*v.i.* desempaquetar; deshacer las maletas.
unpalatable [ʌn'pælətəbl], *a.* desagradable.
unparalleled [ʌn'pærəleld], *a.* sin paralelo, sin igual.
unpardonable [ʌn'pɑ:dnəbl], *a.* imperdonable.
unpatriotic [ʌnpætri'ɔtik], *a.* antipatriótico.
unperturbed [ʌnpə'tə:bd], *a.* impasible.
unpleasant [ʌn'pleznt], *a.* desagradable.
unpopular [ʌn'pɔpjulə], *a.* impopular.
unpopularity [ʌnpɔpju'læriti], *n.* impopularidad, *f.*
unpractical [ʌn'præktikəl], *a.* impráctico.
unpractised [ʌn'præktist], *a.* inexperto.
unprecedented [ʌn'presidəntid], *a.* sin precedente.
unprejudiced [ʌn'predʒudist], *a.* imparcial.
unprepared [ʌnpri'pɛəd], *a.* sin preparación, desprevenido.
unpretentious [ʌnpri'tenʃəs], *a.* sin pretensiones, modesto.
unprincipled [ʌn'prinsipld], *a.* sin conciencia, inmoral.
unprofitable [ʌn'prɔfitəbl], *a.* improductivo; inútil.
unprotected [ʌnprə'tektid], *a.* sin protección.
unprovoked [ʌnprə'voukt], *a.* no provocado, sin motivo.
unpublished [ʌn'pʌbliʃt], *a.* inédito.
unpunished [ʌn'pʌniʃt], *a.* impune.
unqualified [ʌn'kwɔlifaid], *a.* incapaz; sin título; absoluto.
unquestionable [ʌn'kwestʃənəbl], *a.* indudable, indiscutible.
unravel [ʌn'rævəl], *v.t.* deshilar; (*fig.*) desembrollar.
unreadable [ʌn'ri:dəbl], *a.* ilegible.
unreal [ʌn'ri:əl], *a.* irreal; ilusorio; falso.
unreasonable [ʌn'ri:znəbl], *a.* irrazonable; extravagante; exorbitante.
unrelated [ʌnri'leitid], *a.* no relacionado; sin parentesco.
unreliable [ʌnri'laiəbl], *a.* indigno de confianza; informal; incierto.
unremitting [ʌnri'mitiŋ], *a.* incesante; incansable.
unrepentant [ʌnri'pentənt], *a.* impenitente.
unrequited [ʌnri'kwaitid], *a.* no correspondido.
unreserved [ʌnri'zə:vd], *a.* no reservado; franco.
unrest [ʌn'rest], *n.* inquietud, *f.*, desasosiego.
unrestrained [ʌnris'treind], *a.* desenfrenado.
unrestricted [ʌnris'triktid], *a.* sin restricción.
unrewarded [ʌnri'wɔ:did], *a.* no recompensado.
unrighteous [ʌn'raitʃəs], *a.* injusto, malo.
unrighteousness [ʌn'raitʃəsnis], *n.* injusticia, maldad, *f.*
unrivalled [ʌn'raivəld], *a.* sin igual.
unroll [ʌn'roul], *v.t.* desarrollar.—*v.i.* desarrollarse.
unruffled [ʌn'rʌfld], *a.* sereno; no arrugado, liso.
unruly [ʌn'ru:li], *a.* indomable, ingobernable.
unsaddle [ʌn'sædl], *v.t.* desensillar.
unsafe [ʌn'seif], *a.* inseguro; peligroso.
unsatisfactory [ʌnsætis'fæktəri], *a.* poco satisfactorio.
unsatisfied [ʌn'sætisfaid], *a.* descontento; no satisfecho; no convencido.
unsavoury [ʌn'seivəri], *a.* insípido; desagradable; (*fig.*) sucio, indeseable.
unscathed [ʌn'skeiðd], *a.* ileso.
unscrew [ʌn'skru:], *v.t.* destornillar.—*v.i.* destornillarse.
unscrupulous [ʌn'skru:pjuləs], *a.* poco escrupuloso.
unseasonable [ʌn'si:znəbl], *a.* fuera de sazón, intempestivo; inoportuno.
unseat [ʌn'si:t], *v.t.* derribar; (*pol.*) echar abajo.
unseemly [ʌn'si:mli], *a.* indecente; indecoroso; impropio.
unseen [ʌn'si:n], *a.* inapercibido; invisible; oculto.
unselfish [ʌn'selfiʃ], *a.* desinteresado; generoso.
unselfishness [ʌn'selfiʃnis], *n.* desinterés, *m.*; generosidad, *f.*
unserviceable [ʌn'sə:visəbl], *a.* inservible, inútil.
unsettle [ʌn'setl], *v.t.* desarreglar; agitar.
unsettled [ʌn'setld], *a.* inconstante; agitado; indeterminado; (*com.*) pendiente.
unshakable [ʌn'ʃeikəbl], *a.* firme; imperturbable.
unshaken [ʌn'ʃeikən], *a.* firme.
unsheathe [ʌn'ʃi:ð], *v.t.* desenvainar.
unshrinkable [ʌn'ʃriŋkəbl], *a.* que no se encoge.
unshrinking [ʌn'ʃriŋkiŋ], *a.* intrépido.
unsightly [ʌn'saitli], *a.* feo.
unskilled [ʌn'skild], *a.* inhábil, inexperto.
unsociable [ʌn'souʃəbl], *a.* insociable huraño.
unsophisticated [ʌnsə'fistikeitid], *a.* cándido inexperto.
unsound [ʌn'saund], *a.* podrido; defectuoso erróneo; enfermo; heterodoxo; ***of — mind***, insano.
unsparing [ʌn'spɛəriŋ], *a.* generoso; implacable.
unspeakable [ʌn'spi:kəbl], *a.* indecible execrable.
unspoilt [ʌn'spɔilt], *a.* intacto; no despojado ileso; no mimado.
unstable [ʌn'steibl], *a.* inestable; inconstante
unsteady [ʌn'stedi], *a.* inestable; inconstante inseguro.

unstudied [ʌn'stʌdid], *a.* no estudiado; natural.
unsuccessful [ʌnsək'sesful], *a.* sin éxito; infructuoso.
unsuitable [ʌn'sju:təbl], *a.* impropio, inconveniente; incongruo.
unsupported [ʌnsə'pɔ:tid], *a.* sin apoyo.
unsurmountable [ʌnsə'mauntəbl], *a.* insuperable.
unsurpassed [ʌnsə'pɑ:st], *a.* sin igual.
unsuspecting [ʌnsəs'pektiŋ], *a.* confiado.
unswerving [ʌn'swə:viŋ], *a.* constante; directo.
unsymmetrical [ʌnsi'metrikl], *a.* asimétrico.
unsympathetic [ʌnsimpə'θetik], *a.* incompasivo; antipático.
unsystematic [ʌnsistə'mætik], *a.* sin sistema.
untainted [ʌn'teintid], *a.* puro, no corrompido.
untamed [ʌn'teimd], *a.* indomado.
untenable [ʌn'tenəbl], *a.* insostenible.
unthinkable [ʌn'θiŋkəbl], *a.* inconcebible.
unthinking [ʌn'θiŋkiŋ], *a.* desatento, inconsiderado; indiscreto.
untidy [ʌn'taidi], *a.* desarreglado; desaseado.
untie [ʌn'tai], *v.t.* desatar, desligar.
until [ʌn'til], *prep.* hasta.—*conj.* hasta que.
untimely [ʌn'taimli], *a.* inoportuno, intempestivo; prematuro.
untiring [ʌn'taiəriŋ], *a.* infatigable.
unto ['ʌntu], *prep.* (*obs.*) hacia, a.
untold [ʌn'tould], *a.* no dicho; no narrado; incalculable; ***to leave* —,** no decir; dejar en el tintero.
untouched [ʌn'tʌtʃt], *a.* intacto.
untrained [ʌn'treind], *a.* inexperto; indisciplinado.
untranslatable [ʌntræns'leitəbl], *a.* intraducible.
untried [ʌn'traid], *a.* no experimentado.
untrodden [ʌn'trɔdn], *a.* no frecuentado; virgen.
untroubled [ʌn'trʌbld], *a.* tranquilo, calmo.
untrue [ʌn'tru:], *a.* falso; engañoso; infiel.
untrustworthy [ʌn'trʌstwə:ði], *a.* indigno de confianza.
untruth [ʌn'tru:θ], *n.* mentira.
untruthful [ʌn'tru:θful], *a.* mentiroso.
unusual [ʌn'ju:ʒuəl], *a.* poco común, inusitado, desacostumbrado.
unutterable [ʌn'ʌtərəbl], *a.* indecible.
unvarying [ʌn'vɛəriiŋ], *a.* invariable, uniforme.
unveil [ʌn'veil], *v.t.* quitar el velo; descubrir.
unversed [ʌn'və:st], *a.* inexperto.
unwarranted [ʌn'wɔrəntid], *a.* injustificable; (*com.*) no garantizado.
unwary [ʌn'wɛəri], *a.* incauto, imprudente.
unwavering [ʌn'weivəriŋ], *a.* resuelto, firme.
unwelcome [ʌn'welkəm], *a.* mal acogido; inoportuno; molesto.
unwell [ʌn'wel], *a.* indispuesto.
unwholesome [ʌn'houlsəm], *a.* insalubre, malsano.
unwilling [ʌn'wiliŋ], *a.* desinclinado, no dispuesto.
unwind [ʌn'waind], *v.t. irr.* (*conjug. like* WIND) desenvolver, desarrollar.—*v.i.* desenvolverse, desarrollarse.
unwise [ʌn'waiz], *a.* imprudente, indiscreto.
unwittingly [ʌn'witiŋli], *adv.* inconscientemente.
unwomanly [ʌn'wumənli], *a.* impropio de una mujer.
unwonted [ʌn'wountid], *a.* inusitado, insólito.
unworthiness [ʌn'wə:ðinis], *n.* indignidad, *f.*
unworthy [ʌn'wə:ði], *a.* indigno.
unwrap [ʌn'ræp], *v.t.* desenvolver.
unwritten [ʌn'ritn], *a.* no escrito.
unyielding [ʌn'ji:ldiŋ], *a.* firme, inflexible.
up [ʌp], *a.* ascendente; ***the* — *train*,** el tren ascendente.—*n.pl.* ***ups and downs*,** vicisitudes, *f.pl.*—*adv.* arriba; hacia arriba; levantado; de pie; (*fam.*) acabado; (*fam.*) enterado; **— *and down*,** arriba y abajo, por todas partes; **— *there*,** allá arriba; ***to go* —, *to take* —,** subir; ***to speak* —,** hablar alto; ***it's not* — *to much*,** (*fam.*) no vale gran cosa; ***it's* — *to you*,** a ti te toca; ***to be well* — *in*,** estar al corriente de; ***time's* —,** es la hora; ***what's* —?** ¿qué pasa? ***hard* —,** pobre; ***to be* — *in arms*,** sublevarse.—*prep.* en lo alto de; hacia arriba de; a lo largo de; en el interior de; ***to catch* —,** alcanzar; **— *to date*,** hasta la fecha; al corriente; de última moda; **— *to now*,** hasta ahora.
upbraid [ʌp'breid], *v.t.* reprender.
upbringing ['ʌpbriŋiŋ], *n.* crianza.
upheaval [ʌp'hi:vəl], *n.* trastorno.
uphill ['ʌphil], *a.* ascendente; penoso.—[ʌp'hil], *adv.* cuesta arriba.
uphold [ʌp'hould], *v.t. irr.* (*conjug. like* HOLD) apoyar, sostener; defender.
upholster [ʌp'houlstə], *v.t.* tapizar.
upholsterer [ʌp'houlstərə], *n.* tapicero.
upholstery [ʌp'houlstəri], *n.* tapicería.
upkeep ['ʌpki:p], *n.* manutención; conservación, *f.*
uplift ['ʌplift], *n.* elevación, *f.*; (*fam.*) fervor, *m.*—[ʌp'lift], *v.t.* elevar.
upon [ʌ'pɔn], *prep.* [ON].
upper ['ʌpə], *a. compar. of* UP; superior, más alto; **— *hand*,** (*fig.*) ventaja; **— *deck*,** (*naut.*) cubierta alta.
upper-cut ['ʌpəkʌt], *n.* golpe (*m.*) de abajo arriba.
uppermost ['ʌpəmoust], *a.* más alto; predominante.
upright ['ʌprait], *a.* derecho; vertical; recto.—*n.* soporte, montante, *m.*
uprightness ['ʌpraitnis], *n.* rectitud, *f.*
uprising [ʌp'raiziŋ], *n.* insurrección, *f.*
uproar ['ʌprɔ:], *n.* alboroto, conmoción, *f.*, estrépito.
uproarious [ʌp'rɔ:riəs], *a.* tumultuoso, estrepitoso.
uproot [ʌp'ru:t], *v.t.* desarraigar; (*fig.*) extirpar.
upset ['ʌpset], *n.* trastorno; vuelco.—[ʌp'set], *v.t. irr.* (*conjug. like* SET) trastornar; desarreglar; contrariar; derribar; volcar; perturbar.—*v.i.* volcarse.
upsetting [ʌp'setiŋ], *a.* perturbante; inquietante.
upshot ['ʌpʃɔt], *n.* resultado.
upside down ['ʌpsaid'daun], *adv.* de arriba abajo, al revés; en desorden, patas arriba.
upstairs [ʌp'stɛəz], *adv.* arriba.
upstanding [ʌp'stændiŋ], *a.* recto, honrado.
upstart ['ʌpstɑ:t], *a.*, *n.* advenedizo.
upstream ['ʌpstri:m], *adv.* agua arriba.
upward(s) ['ʌpwəd(z)], *adv.* hacia arriba.
uranium [juə'reinjəm], *n.* uranio.

urban ['ə:bən], *a.* urbano.
urbane [ə:'bein], *a.* urbano, fino.
urchin ['ə:tʃin], *n.* pilluelo.
urge [ə:dʒ], *n.* impulso; deseo.—*v.t.* empujar; estimular; pedir con ahinco, recomendar con urgencia.
urgency ['ə:dʒənsi], *n.* urgencia.
urgent ['ə:dʒənt], *a.* urgente.
urinate ['juərineit], *v.i.* orinar.
urine ['juərin], *n.* orina.
urn [ə:n], *n.* urna.
Uruguay [uru'gwai], *n.* el Uruguay.
Uruguayan [uru'gwaiən], *a.*, *n.* uruguayo.
us [ʌs], *pron.* nos; nosotros.
usable ['ju:zəbl], *a.* servible.
usage ['ju:zidʒ], *n.* uso, costumbre, *f.*; tratamiento.
use [ju:s], *n.* uso, empleo; costumbre; necesidad, *f.*; provecho; utilidad, *f.*; ***of no* —,** inútil; ***to make* — *of*,** aprovechar; utilizar; ***to have no* — *for*,** no necesitar; tener en poco; ***what is the* — *of it?*** ¿para qué sirve?—[ju:z], *v.t.* usar, emplear, utilizar; acostumbrar; manejar; gastar; tratar; ***to* — *up*,** agotar; ***to be used to*, *to* — *to*,** acostumbrar, soler.
useful ['ju:sful], *a.* útil; provechoso.
useless ['ju:slis], *a.* inútil; vano.
usher ['ʌʃə], *n.* ujier, (*theat.*) acomodador, *m.*—*v.t.* introducir; anunciar (***in***).
usherette [ʌʃə'ret], *n.* (*theat.*) acomodadora.
usual ['ju:ʒuəl], *a.* usual, acostumbrado; general; ***as* —,** como siempre, como de costumbre.
usurer ['ju:ʒurə], *n.* usurero.
usurious [ju:'zjuəriəs], *a.* usurario.
usurp [ju:'zə:p], *v.t.* usurpar; arrogarse.
usurper [ju:'zə:pə], *n.* usurpador, *m.*
usury ['ju:ʒuri], *n.* usura.
utensil [ju:'tensl], *n.* utensilio; herramienta.
utilitarian [ju:tili'tɛəriən], *a.*, *n.* utilitario.
utility [ju:'tiliti], *n.* utilidad, *f.*; ventaja.
utilize ['ju:tilaiz], *v.t.* utilizar, servirse de; explotar.
utmost ['ʌtmoust], *a.* extremo; más lejano; mayor.—*n.* todo lo posible.
Utopian [ju:'toupjən], *a.* utópico.
utter (1) ['ʌtə], *a.* completo; extremo.
utter (2) ['ʌtə], *v.t.* decir, pronunciar; dar.
utterance ['ʌtərəns], *n.* expresión; pronunciación, *f.*
uxorious [ʌk'sɔ:riəs], *a.* gurrumino.

V

V, v [vi:], *n.* vigésima segunda letra del alfabeto inglés.
vacancy ['veikənsi], *n.* vacío; vacancia; vacuidad, *f.*; laguna.
vacant ['veikənt], *a.* vacío; libre; vacante; distraído.
vacate [və'keit], *v.t.* dejar vacante; (*jur.*) rescindir.
vacation [və'keiʃən], *n.* vacación, *f.*, vacaciones, *f.pl.*
vaccinate ['væksineit], *v.t.* vacunar.
vaccination [væksi'neiʃən], *n.* vacunación, *f.*
vaccine ['væksi:n], *n.* vacuna.
vacillate ['væsileit], *v.i.* vacilar.
vacillating ['væsileitiŋ], *a.* vacilante.
vacillation [væsi'leiʃən], *n.* vacilación, *f.*
vacuity [væ'kju:iti], *n.* vacuidad, *f.*
vacuous ['vækjuəs], *a.* vacío; fatuo.
vacuum ['vækjuəm], *n.* vacío; ***— cleaner*,** aspiradora (*de polvo*); ***— flask*,** termos, *m.sg.*; ***— pump*,** bomba neumática.
vacuum-brake ['vækjuəmbreik], *n.* freno al vacío.
vagabond ['vægəbənd], *a.*, *n.* vagabundo.
vagary [və'gɛəri], *n.* capricho; divagación, *f.*
vagina [və'dʒainə], *n.* vagina.
vagrancy ['veigrənsi], *n.* vagancia.
vagrant ['veigrənt], *a.*, *n.* vagabundo.
vague [veig], *a.* vago.
vagueness ['veignis], *n.* vaguedad, *f.*
vain [vein], *a.* vano; vanidoso; ***in* —,** en vano, en balde.
vainglorious [vein'glɔ:riəs], *a.* vanaglorioso.
vainglory [vein'glɔ:ri], *n.* vanagloria.
vale [veil], *n.* valle, *m.*
valediction [væli'dikʃən], *n.* despedida; vale, *m.*
valedictory [væli'diktəri], *a.* de despedida.
Valencian [və'lensjən], *a.*, *n.* valenciano.
valet ['vælit, 'vælei], *n.* criado; sirviente, *m.*
valiant ['væljənt], *a.* valiente, animoso.
valid ['vælid], *a.* válido, valedero; vigente.
validate ['vælideit], *v.t.* validar.
validity [və'liditi], *n.* validez, *f.*
valise [və'li:z], *n.* maleta, saco de viaje.
valley ['væli], *n.* valle, *m.*
valorous ['vælərəs], *a.* valiente, valeroso.
valour ['vælə], *n.* valor, *m.*, valentía.
valuable ['væljuəbl], *a.* valioso; estimable.—*n.pl.* objetos (*m.pl.*) de valor.
valuation [vælju'eiʃən], *n.* valuación, tasación; estimación, *f.*
value ['vælju:], *n.* valor, *m.*—*v.t.* valorar, tasar; tener en mucho.
valueless ['væljulis], *a.* sin valor.
valuer ['væljuə], *n.* tasador, *m.*
valve [vælv], *n.* (*mech.*) válvula; (*biol.*) valva.
vamp (1) [væmp], *n.* pala (*de zapato*); remiendo; (*mus.*) acompañamiento improvisado.—*v.t.* poner palas; remendar; (*mus.*) improvisar un acompañamiento.
vamp (2) [væmp], *n.* (*fam.*) sirena, ninfa.—*v.t.* (*fam.*) engatusar.
vampire ['væmpaiə], *n.* vampiro.
van (1) [væn], *n.* vanguardia.
van (2) [væn], *n.* camioneta, furgoneta; ***delivery* —,** camión (*m.*) de reparto; ***removal* —,** carro de mudanzas; ***mail* —,** camión postal; ***guard's* —,** furgón, *m.*
vandal ['vændəl], *n.* vándalo.
vandalism ['vændəlizm], *n.* vandalismo.
vane [vein], *n.* veleta; aspa; paleta.
vanguard ['vængɑ:d], *n.* vanguardia.
vanilla [və'nilə], *n.* vainilla.
vanish ['væniʃ], *v.i.* desaparecer; desvanecerse.
vanishing ['væniʃiŋ], *a.*—***cream*,** crema (para el cutis).—*n.* desaparición, *f.*; ***— point*,** punto de fuga.
vanity ['væniti], *n.* vanidad, *f.*
vanquish ['væŋkwiʃ], *v.t.* vencer, derrotar.

vantage ['vɑ:ntidʒ], *n.* ventaja; — ***point,*** posición ventajosa.
vapid ['væpid], *a.* insípido, insulso.
vapidity [væ'piditi], *n.* insipidez, insulsez, *f.*
vaporization [veipərai'zeiʃən], *n.* vaporización, *f.*
vaporize ['veipəraiz], *v.t.* vaporizar.—*v.i.* vaporizarse.
vapour ['veipə], *n.* vapor, *m.*, humo, vaho.
variability [vɛəriə'biliti], *n.* variabilidad, *f.*
variable ['vɛəriəbl], *a.*, *n.* variable, *f.*
variance ['vɛəriəns], *n.* variación, *f.*; desacuerdo; ***at* —,** en desacuerdo.
variant ['vɛəriənt], *a.*, *n.* variante, *f.*
variation [vɛəri'eiʃən], *n.* variación, *f.*
varicose ['værikous], *a.* varicoso; — ***vein,*** várice, *f.*
varied ['vɛərid], *a.* variado.
variegate ['vɛərigeit], *v.t.* abigarrar, matizar.
variegated ['vɛərigeitid], *a.* abigarrado; jaspeado.
variegation [vɛəri'geiʃən], *n.* abigarramiento.
variety [və'raiəti], *n.* variedad, diversidad, *f.*
various ['vɛəriəs], *a.* vario.
varlet ['vɑ:lit], *n.* (*obs.*) lacayo; bribón, *m.*
varnish ['vɑ:niʃ], *n.* barniz, *m.*; ***nail* —,** esmalte (*m.*) de uñas.—*v.t.* barnizar; (*fig.*) disimular.
varnishing ['vɑ:niʃiŋ], *n.* barnizado; vidriado.
varsity ['vɑ:siti], *n.* (*fam.*) universidad, *f.*
vary ['vɛəri], *v.t.*, *v.i.* variar.
varying ['vɛəriiŋ], *a.* variante, diverso.
vase [vɑ:z], *n.* jarrón, *m.*; urna.
vassal ['væsəl], *a.*, *n.* vasallo.
vast [vɑ:st], *a.* vasto; inmenso.
vastness ['vɑ:stnis], *n.* inmensidad, *f.*
vat [væt], *n.* cuba, tina; ***wine* —,** lagar, *m.*
Vatican ['vætikən], *a.*, *n.* Vaticano.
vaudeville ['voudəvil], *n.* teatro de variedades.
vault (1) [vɔ:lt], *n.* bodega (*de vino*); (*arch.*) bóveda.—*v.t.* abovedar.
vault (2) [vɔ:lt], *n.* salto.—*v.t.* saltar.—*v.i.* (*sport*) saltar con pértiga.
vaunt [vɔ:nt], *n.* jactancia.—*v.t.* alardear, hacer gala de.—*v.i.* jactarse.
veal [vi:l], *n.* ternera.
veer [viə], *v.t.*, *v.i.* virar.
vegetable ['vedʒitəbl], *a.* vegetal.—*n.* legumbre, *f.*; ***green vegetables,*** hortalizas, *f.pl.*; — ***garden,*** huerto.
vegetarian [vedʒi'tɛərien], *a.*, *n.* vegetariano.
vegetate ['vedʒiteit], *v.i.* vegetar.
vegetation [vedʒi'teiʃən], *n.* vegetación, *f.*
vehemence ['vi:iməns], *n.* vehemencia; intensidad, *f.*
vehement ['vi:imənt], *a.* vehemente; apasionado.
vehicle ['vi:ikl], *n.* vehículo.
veil [veil], *n.* velo.—*v.t.* velar.
vein [vein], *n.* vena; (*geol.*) veta; (*carp.*) hebra; (*fig.*) rasgo; humor, *m.*
vellum ['veləm], *n.* vitela.
velocity [vi'lɔsiti], *n.* velocidad, rapidez, *f.*
velvet ['velvit], *a.* aterciopelado; de terciopelo; (*fig.*) dulce.—*n.* terciopelo.
venal ['vi:nəl], *a.* venal.
venality [vi:'næliti], *n.* venalidad, *f.*
vend [vend], *v.t.* vender.
vendor ['vendə], *n.* vendedor, *m.*
veneer [vi'niə], *n.* chapa; (*fig.*) apariencia.—*v.t.* chapear; (*fig.*) disimular.
veneering [vi'niəriŋ], *n.* chapeado.
venerable ['venərəbl], *a.* venerable.
venerate ['venəreit], *v.t.* venerar.
veneration [venə'reiʃən], *n.* veneración, *f.*
venereal [vi'niəriəl], *a.* venéreo; — ***disease,*** mal (*m.*) venéreo.
Venetian [vi'ni:ʃən], *a.*, *n.* veneciano; — ***blind,*** persiana.
Venezuelan [vene'zweilən], *a.*, *n.* venezolano.
vengeance ['vendʒəns], *n.* venganza.
vengeful ['vendʒful], *a.* vengativo.
venial ['vi:njəl], *a.* venial.
veniality [vi:ni'æliti], *n.* venialidad, *f.*
venison [venzn], *n.* venado.
venom ['venəm], *n.* veneno.
venomous ['venəməs], *a.* venenoso; malicioso.
vent [vent], *n.* abertura; respiradero; (*fig.*) desahogo; expresión, *f.*—*v.t.* ventilar; desahogar; dejar escapar; ***to* — *one's feelings,*** desahogarse.
ventilate ['ventileit], *v.t.* ventilar; (*fig.*) discutir.
ventilation [venti'leiʃən], *n.* ventilación, *f.*
ventilator ['ventileitə], *n.* ventilador, *m.*
ventriloquism [ven'triləkwizm], *n.* ventriloquia.
ventriloquist [ven'triləkwist], *n.* ventrílocuo.
venture ['ventʃə], *n.* ventura; riesgo; aventura; especulación, *f.*—*v.t.* aventurar, arriesgar; ***to* — *an opinion,*** expresar una opinión.—*v.i.* aventurarse, arriesgarse, correr riesgo; ***to* — *abroad,*** atreverse a salir; ***nothing ventured, nothing gained,*** quien no se aventura, no ha ventura.
venturesome ['ventʃəsəm], *a.* aventurero, atrevido; peligroso.
Venus ['vi:nəs], *n.* Venus, *f.*
veracious [ve'reiʃəs], *a.* veraz, verídico.
veracity [ve'ræsiti], *n.* veracidad, *f.*
verandah [və'rændə], *n.* veranda.
verb [və:b], *n.* verbo.
verbal ['və:bəl], *a.* verbal.
verbatim [və:'beitim], *a.*, *adv.* palabra por palabra.
verbose [və:'bous], *a.* verboso, prolijo.
verbosity [və:'bɔsiti], *n.* verbosidad, *f.*
verdant ['və:dənt], *a.* verde, floreciente.
verdict ['və:dikt], *n.* (*jur.*) veredicto, fallo.
verdure ['və:djə], *n.* verdura.
verge [və:dʒ], *n.* vara; borde, margen, *m.*; ***on the* — *of,*** al borde de; (*fig.*) a punto de.
verger ['və:dʒə], *n.* sacristán, *m.*; macero.
verification [verifi'keiʃən], *n.* verificación, *f.*
verily ['verili], *adv.* (*obs.*) en verdad.
verify ['verifai], *v.t.* verificar, averiguar.
verisimilitude [verisi'militju:d], *n.* verosimilitud, *f.*
veritable ['veritəbl], *a.* verdadero.
vermilion [və'miljən], *a.* bermejo.—*n.* bermellón, *m.*
vermin ['və:min], *n.* sabandijas, *f.pl.*
verminous ['və:minəs], *a.* verminoso.
vermouth ['və:məθ], *n.* vermut, *m.*
vernacular [və'nækjulə], *a.*, *n.* vernáculo.
vernal [və:nl], *a.* vernal, primaveral.
versatile ['və:sətail], *a.* versátil; de muchos talentos; adaptable.
versatility [və:sə'tiliti], *n.* adaptabilidad, *f.*; muchos talentos, *m.pl.*
verse [və:s], *n.* verso; estrofa; versículo.
versed [və:st], *a.* versado.
versification [və:sifi'keiʃən], *n.* versificación, *f.*

versifier ['vəːsifaiə], *n.* versificador, *m.*
versify ['vəːsifai], *v.t., v.i.* versificar.
version ['vəːʃən], *n.* versión; traducción, *f.*
versus ['vəːsəs], *prep.* contra.
vertebra ['vəːtibrə], *n.* (*pl.* **-brae** [-bri]) vértebra.
vertebrate ['vəːtibrit], *a., n.* vertebrado.
vertex ['vəːteks], *n.* (*pl.* **-tices** [-tisiːz]) (*geom., anat.*) vértice, *f.*; (*fig.*) cenit, *m.*
vertical ['vəːtikəl], *a.* vertical.
verve [vəːv], *n.* brío.
very ['veri], *a.* mismo; verdadero; perfecto.—*adv.* muy; mucho.
vespers ['vespəz], *n. pl.* (*eccl.*) vísperas, *f.pl.*
vessel [vesl], *n.* vasija, recipiente, *m.*; barco; (*anat.*) vaso.
vest [vest], *n.* camiseta; (*U.S.*) chaleco.—*v.t.* (*poet.*) vestir; revestir; ceder; ***vested interests,*** intereses (*m.pl.*) creados.
vestibule ['vestibjuːl], *n.* vestíbulo; zaguán, *m.*
vestige ['vestidʒ], *n.* vestigio.
vestment ['vestmənt], *n.* hábito.—*pl.* (*eccl.*) vestimentas, *f.pl.*
vestry ['vestri], *n.* sacristía; vestuario.
vet [vet], *n.* (*fam.*) veterinario.—*v.t.* (*fam.*) escudriñar.
veteran ['vetərən], *a., n.* veterano.
veterinary ['vetərinəri], *a.* veterinario; — ***science,*** veterinaria; — ***surgeon,*** veterinario.
veto ['viːtou], *n.* veto.—*v.t.* poner el veto; vedar.
vex [veks], *v.t.* irritar; enfadar.
vexation [vek'seiʃən], *n.* irritación, *f.*; enfado.
vexatious [vek'seiʃəs], *a.* irritante; enfadoso.
vexing ['veksiŋ], *a.* irritante; enfadoso.
V.H.F. [viːeitʃ'ef], (*abbrev.*) **very high frequency,** ondas (*f.pl.*) ultracortas.
via ['vaiə], *prep.* por, vía.
viability [vaiə'biliti], *n.* viabilidad, *f.*
viable ['vaiəbl], *a.* viable.
viaduct ['vaiədʌkt], *n.* viaducto.
vial ['vaiəl], *n.* frasco, ampolleta.
viaticum [vai'ætikəm], *n.* viático.
vibrant ['vaibrənt], *a.* vibrante.
vibrate [vai'breit], *v.t., v.i.* vibrar.
vibration [vai'breiʃən], *n.* vibración, *f.*
vicar ['vikə], *n.* cura anglicano; vicario.
vicarage ['vikəridʒ], *n.* vicaría.
vicarious [vai'kɛəriəs], *a.* vicario; experimentado *o* padecido por otro.
vice (1) [vais], *n.* vicio; defecto.
vice (2) [vais], *n.* tornillo de banco.
vice (3) [vais], *prefix.* vice.
vice-admiral ['vais'ædmərəl], *n.* vicealmirante, *m.*
vice-president ['vais'prezidənt], *n.* vicepresidente, *m.*
viceroy ['vaisrɔi], *n.* virrey, *m.*
viceroyalty [vais'rɔiəlti], *n.* virreinato.
vice versa ['vaisi'vəːsə], *adv.* viceversa.
vicinity [vi'siniti], *n.* vecindad; proximidad, *f.*
vicious ['viʃəs], *a.* vicioso.
viciousness ['viʃəsnis], *n.* viciosidad; depravación, *f.*
vicissitude [vi'sisitjuːd], *n.* vicisitud, *f.*
victim ['viktim], *n.* víctima.
victimization [viktimai'zeiʃən], *n.* tiranización, *f.*
victimize ['viktimaiz], *v.t.* hacer víctima; sacrificar; tiranizar.
victor ['viktə], *n.* víctor, vencedor, *m.*
Victorian [vik'tɔːriən], *a., n.* victoriano.
victorious [vik'tɔːriəs], *a.* victorioso, vencedor.
victory ['viktəri], *n.* victoria.
victuals ['vitəlz], *n.pl.* vituallas, *f.pl.*, víveres, *m.pl.*
videlicet [vɪz.].
vie [vai], *v.i.* competir, rivalizar.
Vienna [vi'enə], *n.* Viena.
Viennese [viə'niːz], *a., n.* vienés, *m.*
Vietnamese [vjetnæ'miːz], *a., n.* vietnamés, vietnamita, *m.*
view [vjuː], *n.* vista; panorama, *m.*; inspección, *f.*; parecer, *m.*, opinión, *f.*; apariencia; intención, *f.*; ***with a — to,*** con motivo de; ***in — of,*** en vista de; ***in the — of,*** en la opinión de—*v.t.* examinar; inspeccionar; mirar; considerar.
viewer ['vjuːə], *n.* espectador; inspector, *m.*; televidente, *m.f.*
view-finder ['vjuːfaində], *n.* enfocador, *m.*
vigil ['vidʒil], *n.* vigilia; vela; ***to keep — over,*** vigilar; velar.
vigilance ['vidʒiləns], *n.* vigilancia.
vigilant ['vidʒilənt], *a.* vigilante; despierto.
vignette [vi'njet], *n.* viñeta.
vigorous ['vigərəs], *a.* vigoroso, enérgico.
vigour ['vigə], *n.* vigor, *m.*
Viking ['vaikiŋ], *a., n.* vikingo.
vile [vail], *a.* vil; infame.
vileness ['vailnis], *n.* vileza; bajeza; infamia.
vilification [vilifi'keiʃən], *n.* difamación, *f.*, vilipendio.
vilify ['vilifai], *v.t.* difamar, vilipendiar.
villa ['vilə], *n.* villa, casa de campo.
village ['vilidʒ], *n.* aldea, pueblecito.
villager ['vilidʒə], *n.* aldeano, lugareño.
villain ['vilən], *n.* malvado.
villainous ['vilənəs], *a.* infame; malvado.
villainy ['viləni], *n.* infamia; maldad, *f.*
villein ['vilən], *n.* (*hist.*) villano.
vim [vim], *n.* (*fam.*) energía.
vindicate ['vindikeit], *v.t.* vindicar.
vindication [vindi'keiʃən], *n.* vindicación, *f.*
vindictive [vin'diktiv], *a.* vengativo; rencoroso.
vindictiveness [vin'diktivnis], *n.* deseo de venganza; rencor, *m.*
vine [vain], *n.* vid, *f.*, parra; enredadera.
vinegar ['vinigə], *n.* vinagre, *m.*
vinegary ['vinigəri], *a.* vinagroso.
vineyard ['vinjəd], *n.* viña, viñedo.
vinous ['vainəs], *a.* vinoso.
vintage ['vintidʒ], *a.* añejo; antiguo, veterano —*n.* vendimia.
vintner ['vintnə], *n.* vinatero.
viola (1) [vi'oulə], *n.* (*mus.*) viola.
viola (2) ['vaiələ], *n.* (*bot.*) viola.
violate ['vaiəleit], *v.t.* violar.
violation [vaiə'leiʃən], *n.* violación.
violence ['vaiələns], *n.* violencia.
violent ['vaiələnt], *a.* violento.
violet ['vaiəlit], *a.* violado.—*n.* (*bot.*) violeta.
violin [vaiə'lin], *n.* violín, *m.*
violinist [vaiə'linist], *n.* violinista, *m.f.*
violoncello [vaiələn'tʃelou], *n.* violoncelo.
viper ['vaipə], *n.* víbora.
viperish ['vaipəriʃ], *a.* viperino.
Virgil ['vəːdʒil], *n.* Virgilio.

Virgilian [və:'dʒiljən], *a.* virgiliano.
virgin ['və:dʒin], *a.*, *n.* virgen, *f.*
virginal ['və:dʒinl], *a.* virginal.—*n.pl.* (*mus.*) espineta.
virginity [və:'dʒiniti], *n.* virginidad, *f.*
virile ['virail], *a.* viril, varonil.
virility [vi'riliti], *n.* virilidad, *f.*
virtual ['və:tjuəl], *a.* virtual.
virtue ['və:tju:], *n.* virtud, *f.*; excelencia; ***by — of,*** en virtud de.
virtuosity [və:tju'ɔsiti], *n.* virtuosidad, *f.*
virtuoso [və:tju'ouzou], *n.* virtuoso.
virtuous ['və:tjuəs], *a.* virtuoso.
virulence ['virulǝns], *n.* virulencia.
virulent ['virulǝnt], *a.* virulento.
virus ['vairəs], *n.* virus, *m.*
visa ['vi:zə], *n.* visado.
visage ['vizidʒ], *n.* semblante, *m.*
viscount ['vaikaunt], *n.* vizconde, *m.*
viscountess ['vaikauntis], *n.* vizcondesa.
viscous ['viskəs], *a.* viscoso.
visibility [vizi'biliti], *n.* visibilidad, *f.*
visible ['vizibl], *a.* visible.
Visigoth ['vizigɔθ], *a.*, *n.* visigodo.
vision ['viʒən], *n.* visión, *f.*
visionary ['viʒənəri], *a.*, *n.* visionario.
visit ['vizit], *n.* visita.—*v.t.* visitar, hacer una visita a.—*v.i.* ***to go visiting,*** ir de visita.
visitation [vizi'teiʃən], *n.* visitación, *f.*
visiting ['vizitiŋ], *a.* de visita.—*n.* ***— card,*** tarjeta de visita.
visitor ['vizitə], *n.* visita; visitador, *m.*
visor ['vaizə], *n.* visera (*de casco*).
vista ['vistə], *n.* vista, perspectiva.
visual ['viʒjuəl], *a.* visual.
visualize ['viʒjuəlaiz], *v.t.* imaginar.
vital [vaitl], *a.* vital; escencial.—*n.pl.* partes vitales, *f.pl.*; (*fig.*) entrañas, *f.pl.*
vitality [vai'tæliti], *n.* vitalidad, *f.*
vitalize ['vaitəlaiz], *v.t.* vivificar, vitalizar.
vitamin ['vitəmin], *n.* vitamina.
vitiate ['viʃieit], *v.t.* viciar; infectar; invalidar.
vitreous ['vitriəs], *a.* vítreo, vidrioso.
vitriol ['vitriɔl], *n.* vitriolo.
vitriolic [vitri'ɔlik], *a.* vitriólico.
vituperate [vi'tju:pəreit], *v.t.* vituperar.
vituperation [vitju:pə'reiʃən], *n.* vituperio.
vivacious [vi'veiʃəs], *a.* animado, vivaracho.
vivacity [vi'væsiti], *n.* vivacidad, *f.*, viveza.
viva voce ['vaivə'vousi], *a.* oral.—*n.* examen (*m.*) oral.—*adv.* de viva voz.
vivid ['vivid], *a.* brillante; intenso; vivaz; gráfico.
vividness ['vividnis], *n.* brillantez; intensidad; vivacidad, *f.*
vivify ['vivifai], *v.t.* vivificar.
vivisection [vivi'sekʃən], *n.* vivisección, *f.*
vixen ['viksən], *n.* zorra; (*fig.*) arpía.
viz. [viz], *adv.* (*abbrev. of* **videlicet** [vi'deliset]) a saber.
vizier [vi'ziə], *n.* visir, *m.*
vocabulary [vou'kæbjuləri], *n.* vocabulario.
vocal ['voukəl], *a.*, *n.* vocal, *f.*
vocalist ['voukəlist], *n.* cantante, *m.f.*
vocalization [voukəlai'zeiʃən], *n.* vocalización, *f.*
vocalize ['voukəlaiz], *v.t.* vocalizar.
vocation [vou'keiʃən], *n.* vocación, *f.*
vocational [vou'keiʃənəl], *a.* profesional; práctico.
vocative ['vɔkətiv], *a.*, *n.* (*gram.*) vocativo.
vociferate [vo'sifəreit], *v.t.*, *v.i.* vociferar.
vociferation [vosifə'reiʃən], *n.* vociferación, *f.*
vociferous [vo'sifərəs], *a.* vocinglero, clamoroso.
vodka ['vɔdkə], *n.* vodca, *m.*
vogue [voug], *n.* boga, moda; ***in —,*** en boga, de moda.
voice [vɔis], *n.* voz, *f.*; ***in a loud —,*** en voz alta; ***in a low —,*** en voz baja.—*v.t.* proclamar; expresar; sonorizar.
void [vɔid], *a.* vacío; (*jur.*) nulo, inválido.—*n.* vacío.—*v.t.* invalidar, anular.
volatile ['vɔlətail], *a.* volátil; voluble.
volatilize [vɔ'lætilaiz], *v.t.* volatilizar.—*v.i.* volatilizarse.
volcanic [vɔl'kænik], *a.* volcánico.
volcano [vɔl'keinou], *n.* volcán, *m.*
vole [voul], *n.* ratón (*m.*) campestre; campañol, *m.*
volition [vo'liʃən], *n.* volición; voluntad, *f.*
volley ['vɔli], *n.* descarga, andanada; salva; (*sport*) voleo.
volt [voult], *n.* (*elec.*) voltio.
voltage ['voultidʒ], *n.* voltaje, *m.*
volubility [vɔlju'biliti], *n.* volubilidad, locuacidad, *f.*
voluble ['vɔljubl], *a.* gárrulo, locuaz.
volume ['vɔlju:m], *n.* tomo; volumen, *m.*
voluminous [və'lju:minəs], *a.* voluminoso.
voluntary ['vɔləntəri], *a.* voluntario.
volunteer [vɔlən'tiə], *a.*, *n.* (*mil.*) voluntario.—*v.t.* ofrecer; expresar.—*v.i.* ofrecerse; (*mil.*) alistarse.
voluptuary [və'lʌptjuəri], *a.*, *n.* voluptuoso.
voluptuous [və'lʌptjuəs], *a.* voluptuoso.
voluptuousness [və'lʌptjuəsnis], *n.* voluptuosidad, *f.*
vomit ['vɔmit], *n.* vómito.—*v.t.*, *v.i.* vomitar.
vomiting ['vɔmitiŋ], *n.* vómito.
voodoo ['vu:du:], *n.* vodú, *m.*
voracious [vɔ'reiʃəs], *a.* voraz.
voracity [vɔ'ræsiti], *n.* voracidad, *f.*
vortex ['vɔ:teks], *n.* vórtice, *m.*
votary ['voutəri], *n.* devoto; partidario.
vote [vout], *n.* voto; votación, *f.*; ***— of confidence,*** voto de confianza; ***— of thanks,*** voto de gracias; ***to put to the —,*** poner a votación.—*v.t.*, *v.i.* votar.
voter ['voutə], *n.* votante, *m.f.*; elector, *m.*
voting ['voutiŋ], *n.* votación, *f.*; ***— paper,*** papeleta de votación.
votive ['voutiv], *a.* votivo; ***— offering,*** exvoto.
vouch [vautʃ], *v.i.* afirmar; garantizar; responder (***for,*** de, por).
voucher ['vautʃə], *n.* fiador, comprobante, *m.*; abono; recibo.
vouchsafe [vautʃ'seif], *v.t.* otorgar, conceder.
vow [vau], *n.* voto; promesa solemne; ***to take a —,*** hacer un voto.—*v.t.* votar, jurar, hacer voto de.
vowel ['vauəl], *n.* vocal, *f.*
voyage ['vɔiidʒ], *n.* viaje, *m.*, travesía.—*v.i.* viajar por mar.
voyager ['vɔiədʒə], *n.* viajero (por mar).
Vulcan ['vʌlkən], *n.* Vulcano.
vulcanize ['vʌlkənaiz], *v.t.* vulcanizar.
vulgar ['vʌlgə], *a.* vulgar; grosero, de mal gusto; ***— fraction,*** fracción común, *f.*
vulgarism ['vʌlgərizm], *n.* vulgarismo; vulgaridad, *f.*

vulgarity [vʌl'gæriti], *n.* vulgaridad, *f.*; grosería.
vulgarize ['vʌlgəraiz], *v.t.* vulgarizar.
Vulgate ['vʌlgit], *n.* Vulgata.
vulnerability [vʌlnərə'biliti], *n.* vulnerabilidad, *f.*
vulnerable ['vʌlnərəbl], *a.* vulnerable.
vulture ['vʌltʃə], *n.* buitre, *m.*

W

W, w ['dʌblju:], *n.* vigésima tercera letra del alfabeto inglés.
wad [wɔd], *n.* taco; fajo; atado.
wadding ['wɔdiŋ], *n.* borra; relleno; algodón, *m.*
waddle [wɔdl], *n.* anadeo.—*v.i.* anadear.
wade [weid], *v.t., v.i.* vadear; andar en el agua; ***to — in,*** (*fig.*) meterse en; (*fig.*) ***to — through,*** leer con dificultad.
wader ['weidə], *n.* ave zancuda.—*pl.* botas (*f.pl.*) de vadear.
wafer ['weifə], *n.* (*eccl.*) hostia; oblea; barquillo.
waffle [wɔfl], *n.* fruta de sartén; (*fig.*) palabrería.
waft [wɔft], *n.* ráfaga.—*v.t.* llevar por el aire; hacer flotar.
wag (1) [wæg], *n.* coleada; meneo.—*v.t.* menear.—*v.i.* menearse.
wag (2) [wæg], *n.* bromista, *m.f.*
wage [weidʒ], *n.* jornal, *m.*, salario, sueldo. —*v.t.* hacer; emprender; ***to — war,*** hacer guerra.
wage-earner ['weidʒə:nə], *n.* jornalero, asalariado.
wager ['weidʒə], *n.* apuesta; ***to lay a —,*** hacer una apuesta.—*v.t., v.i.* apostar.
waggish ['wægiʃ], *a.* zumbón, guaso.
waggishness ['wægiʃnis], *n.* guasa.
waggle [wægl], *n.* meneo.—*v.t.* menear.—*v.i.* menearse.
waggon ['wægən], *n.* carro; (*rail.*) vagón, *m.*; ***on the —,*** (*fam.*) sin beber nada alcohólico.
waggoner ['wægənə], *n.* carretero.
wagtail ['wægteil], *n.* aguzanieves, *f.sg.*
waif [weif], *n.* expósito; animal abandonado.
wail [weil], *n.* gemido, lamento.—*v.t.* lamentar.—*v.i.* lamentarse, gemir.
wainscot ['weinskət], *n.* friso de madera.
waist [weist], *n.* cintura; corpiño; (*naut.*) combés, *m.*
waist-band ['weistbænd], *n.* pretina.
waistcoat ['weiskout], *n.* chaleco.
waist-deep ['weist'di:p], *a.* hasta la cintura.
waist-line ['weistlain], *n.* cintura.
wait [weit], *n.* espera; pausa; tardanza; ***to lie in —,*** acechar (*for*). —*v.t., v.i.* esperar, aguardar; servir; ***to — for,*** esperar a; ***to keep waiting,*** hacer esperar; ***to — at table,*** servir a la mesa.
waiter ['weitə], *n.* camarero, mozo.
waiting ['weitiŋ], *a.* que espera; de servicio. —*n.* espera; ***— room,*** sala de espera; antesala.
waitress ['weitris], *n.* camarera, criada.
waive [weiv], *v.t.* renunciar, abandonar.
wake (1) [weik], *n.* vigilia; velatorio.—*v.t. irr.* despertar.—*v.i. irr.* despertar(se).
wake (2) [weik], *n.* (*naut.*) estela; ***in the — of,*** en la estela de, después de.
wakeful ['weikful], *a.* despierto; vigilante.
waken ['weikən], *v.t., v.i.* despertar.
Wales [weilz], *n.* País de Gales, *m.*
walk [wɔ:k], *n.* paseo; modo de andar; avenida; paso; profesión, *f.*, carrera; ***to go for a —,*** dar un paseo.—*v.t.* hacer andar; sacar a paseo; recorrer; llevar al paso; ***to — the streets,*** callejear.—*v.i.* andar, ir a pie, caminar; pasear(se), dar un paseo; ***to — away,*** marcharse; ***to — back,*** volver a pie; ***to — down,*** bajar a pie; ***to — in,*** entrar; ***to — out,*** salir; salir en huelga; ***to — up,*** subir a pie; ***to — up and down,*** ir y venir.
walking ['wɔ:kiŋ], *n.* andar, pasear, *m.*; paseo; ***— pace,*** paso de andadura; ***— tour,*** excursión (*f.*) a pie.
walking-stick ['wɔ:kiŋstik], *n.* bastón, *m.*
walk-out ['wɔ:kaut], *n.* huelga.
walk-over ['wɔ:kouvə], *n.* triunfo fácil.
wall [wɔ:l], *n.* muro; pared, *f.*; muralla; ***garden —,*** tapia; ***partition —,*** tabique, *m.*; ***— socket,*** (*elec.*) enchufe, *m.*; ***walls have ears,*** las paredes oyen.—*v.t.* cercar con un muro; amurallar; ***to — in,*** murar; ***to — up,*** tapiar.
wallet ['wɔlit], *n.* cartera; bolsa de cuero.
wallflower ['wɔ:lflauə], *n.* alhelí, *m.*
wallop ['wɔləp], *n.* (*fam.*) golpe, *m.*, zurra; (*fam.*) cerveza.—*v.t.* (*fam.*) zurrar.
wallow ['wɔlou], *n.* revuelco.—*v.i.* revolcarse; (*fig.*) nadar.
wallpaper ['wɔ:lpeipə], *n.* papel pintado.
walnut ['wɔ:lnʌt], *n.* nogal (*árbol*), *m.*; nuez (*fruta*), *f.*
walrus ['wɔ:lrəs], *n.* morsa.
waltz [wɔ:l(t)s], *n.* vals, *m.*—*v.i.* valsar.
wan [wɔn], *a.* pálido, descolorido, macilento.
wand [wɔnd], *n.* vara; varita.
wander ['wɔndə], *v.i.* vagar, errar; extraviarse.
wanderer ['wɔndərə], *n.* vagabundo, vagamundo.
wandering ['wɔndəriŋ], *a.* errante; nómada; delirante.—*n.* vagar, errar, *m.*; divagación, *f.*; delirio.
wane [wein], *n.* diminución, decadencia; menguante, *f.*—*v.i.* disminuir; decaer; menguar.
want [wɔnt], *n.* necesidad, falta; escasez, *f.*; deseo; ***for — of,*** por falta de.—*v.t.* carecer de; necesitar; desear; pasarse sin; ***you are wanted,*** preguntan por Vd.—*v.i.* hacer falta; estar necesitado.
wanting ['wɔntiŋ], *a.* deficiente; ausente; escaso; ***to be —,*** faltar.—*prep.* sin.
wanton ['wɔntən], *a.* disoluto, lascivo; travieso.—*n.* libertino; prostituta.
war [wɔ:], *n.* guerra; ***cold —,*** guerra fría *o* tonta; ***— cry,*** alarido de guerra; ***— dance,*** danza guerrera; ***— memorial,*** monumento a los caídos; ***War Minister,*** Ministro de la Guerra; ***War Office,*** Ministerio de la Guerra; ***to declare —,*** declarar la guerra; ***to be at —,*** estar en guerra.—*v.i.* guerrear, hacer la guerra.
warble [wɔ:bl], *n.* gorjeo; trino.—*v.t., v.i.* gorjear; trinar.

ward [wɔ:d], *n.* pupilo; pupilaje, *m.*; distrito electoral; crujía, sala de hospital; guarda (*llave*).—*v.t.* proteger; parar; ***to — off,*** desviar, evitar.
warden [wɔ:dn], *n.* guardián, *m.*; alcaide, *m.*; director, *m.*
warder ['wɔ:də], *n.* guardián, *m.*; carcelero.
wardrobe ['wɔ:droub], *n.* guardarropa, *m.*; ropa; (*theat.*) vestuario.
ware [wɛə], *n.* mercadería; loza. —*pl.* mercancías, *f.pl.*
warehouse ['wɛəhaus], *n.* almacén, *m.*
warehouseman ['wɛəhausmən], *n.* almacenero.
warfare ['wɔ:fɛə], *n.* guerra.
wariness ['wɛərinis], *n.* prudencia, cautela.
warlike ['wɔ:laik], *a.* guerrero, belicoso.
warm [wɔ:m], *a.* caliente; caluroso; tibio; ardiente; furioso; (*fam.*) fresco; ***to be —,*** tener calor; hacer calor; estar caliente. —*v.t.* calentar; (*fig.*) entusiasmar.—*v.i.* calentarse; (*fig.*) entusiasmarse.
warm-blooded ['wɔ:m'blʌdid], *a.* de sangre caliente; apasionado.
warm-hearted ['wɔ:m'hɑ:tid], *a.* generoso, bondadoso.
warming-pan ['wɔ:miŋpæn], *n.* calentador, *m.*
warmth [wɔ:mθ], *n.* calor, *m.*; ardor, *m.*; cordialidad, *f.*
warn [wɔ:n], *v.t.* advertir; amonestar; avisar.
warning ['wɔ:niŋ], *n.* advertencia; amonestación, *f.*; aviso.
warp [wɔ:p], *n.* urdimbre, *f.*; torcimiento.—*v.t.* torcer; pervertir.—*v.i.* torcerse; desviarse.
warped [wɔ:pt], *a.* combo; desequilibrado.
warrant ['wɔrənt], *n.* autorización, *f.*; garantía; decreto; (*com.*) orden (*f.*) de pago; razón, *f.*—*v.t.* autorizar; garantir; asegurar; justificar.
warrantable ['wɔrəntəbl], *a.* justificable.
warrantor ['wɔrəntɔ:], *n.* garante, *m.f.*
warranty ['wɔrənti], *n.* garantía; autorización, *f.*
warren ['wɔrən], *n.* conejera; vivar, *m.*, madriguera.
warrior ['wɔriə], *n.* guerrero; soldado.
wart [wɔ:t], *n.* verruga.
wary ['wɛəri], *a.* cauto, cauteloso (***of,*** con).
was [wɔz] [BE].
wash [wɔʃ], *n.* lavado; ropa lavada; ropa sucia; ablución; loción, *f.*; (*naut.*) estela; (*art*) aguada.—*v.t.* lavar; bañar; (*art*) dar una capa de colora; ***to — away,*** quitar lavando; (*fam.*) anular.—*v.i.* lavarse; lavar ropa; ***to — up,*** fregar la vajilla.
wash-basin ['wɔʃbeisn], *n.* lavabo.
washer ['wɔʃə], *n.* lavador, *m.*; lavadora (*máquina*); (*mech.*) arandela.
washerwoman ['wɔʃəwumən], *n.* lavandera.
washing ['wɔʃiŋ], *n.* lavado; colada; ropa sucia.
washing-machine ['wɔʃiŋməʃi:n], *n.* lavadora.
washing-up ['wɔʃiŋ'ʌp], *n.* fregado de vajilla.
wash-leather ['wɔʃleðə], *n.* gamuza.
wash-out ['wɔʃaut], *n.* (*fam.*) fracaso.
wash-tub ['wɔʃtʌb], *n.* cuba de lavar.
wasp [wɔsp], *n.* avispa.
waspish ['wɔspiʃ], *a.* enojadizo, enconoso; mordaz.
wastage ['weistidʒ], *n.* pérdida, desgaste, *m.*
waste [weist], *a.* desierto; inútil; devastado; superfluo; ***— land,*** yermo; ***— paper,*** papel (*m.*) de desecho.—*n.* desperdicio; despilfarro; desierto; desechos, *m.pl.*; pérdida; inmensidad, devastación, *f.*—*v.t.* gastar; desperdiciar; malgastar; devastar; ***to — time,*** perder el tiempo.—*v.i.* gastarse, consumirse; ***to — away,*** demacrarse.
watch-chain ['wɔtʃtʃein], *n.* cadena de reloj.
watch-dog ['wɔtʃdɔg], *n.* perro guardián.
wasteful ['weistful], *a.* pródigo manirroto; ruinoso.
wastefulness ['weistfulnis], *n.* prodigalidad, *f.*, gasto inútil; pérdida.
waste-paper basket ['weist'peipəbɑ:skit], *n.* cesto para papeles.
watch [wɔtʃ], *n.* vigilancia; vela; guardia; centinela; sereno; ronda; reloj, *m.*; ***to be on the —,*** estar de acecho, estar de guardia. —*v.t.* mirar; acechar; ***to — over,*** vigilar.—*v.i.* velar; hacer guardia.
watchful ['wɔtʃful], *a.* vigilante; atento.
watchfulness ['wɔtʃfulnis], *n.* vigilancia; desvelo.
watch-glass ['wɔtʃglɑ:s], *n.* cristal (*m.*) de reloj.
watch-maker ['wɔtʃmeikə], *n.* relojero.
watchman ['wɔtʃmən], *n.* vigilante, *m.*, sereno; guardián, *m.*
water ['wɔ:tə], *n.* agua; ***fresh —,*** agua dulce; ***high —,*** marea alta; ***holy —,*** agua bendita; ***low —,*** marea baja; ***running —,*** agua corriente; ***salt —,*** agua salada; ***— level,*** nivel (*m.*) de agua; ***— main,*** cañería maestra; ***— man,*** barquero; ***— supply,*** traída de aguas; ***— tank,*** aljibe, *m.*; ***— tap,*** grifo; ***— wheel,*** rueda hidráulica; ***— wings,*** nadaderas, *f.pl.*; ***to make —,*** orinar.—*v.t.* regar; dar de beber; aguar.—*v.i.* tomar agua; hacerse agua; ***his mouth is watering,*** se le hace agua la boca; ***his eyes are watering,*** le lloran los ojos.
water-bottle ['wɔ:təbɔtl], *n.* cantimplora.
water-carrier ['wɔ:təkæriə], *n.* aguador, *m.*
water-cart ['wɔ:təkɑ:t], *n.* carro de regar.
water-closet ['wɔ:təklɔzit], *n.* (*abbrev.* **W.C.**) retrete, *m.*
water-colour ['wɔ:təkʌlə], *n.* acuarela.
watercress ['wɔ:təkres], *n.* berro, berros, *m.pl.*
watered ['wɔ:təd], *a.* regado; ***— silk,*** seda tornasolada.
waterfall ['wɔ:təfɔ:l], *n.* cascada.
watering ['wɔ:təriŋ], *n.* irrigación, *f.*, riego; lagrimeo (*de los ojos*); ***— can,*** regadera; ***— place,*** balneario.
water-lily ['wɔ:təlili], *n.* nenúfar, *m.*
waterlogged ['wɔ:təlɔgd], *a.* anegado en agua.
watermark ['wɔ:təmɑ:k], *n.* filigrana (*en el papel*); nivel (*m.*) de las aguas.
water-melon ['wɔ:təmelən], *n.* sandía.
water-mill ['wɔ:təmil], *n.* aceña.
water-polo ['wɔ:təpoulou], *n.* polo acuático.
water-power ['wɔ:təpauə], *n.* fuerza hidráulica.
waterproof ['wɔ:təpru:f], *a.*, *n.* impermeable, *m.*—*v.t.* hacer impermeable.
waterspout ['wɔ:təspaut], *n.* tromba marina, manga; canalón, *m.*

watertight ['wɔ:tətait], *a.* impermeable; (*fig.*) irrefutable.
waterworks ['wɔ:təwə:ks], *n.pl.* obras hidráulicas, *f.pl.*; establecimiento de abastecimiento de agua; (*fam.*) lloro.
watery ['wɔ:təri], *a.* acuoso; húmedo; lloroso; insípido.
watt [wɔt], *n.* (*elec.*) vatio.
wattage ['wɔtidʒ], *n.* vatiaje, *m.*
wattle [wɔtl], *n.* zarzo; barba.
wave [weiv], *n.* ola; onda; ondulación, *f.*; movimiento de la mano; ***sound* —,** onda sonora; ***short* —,** onda corta; ***long* —,** onda larga.—*v.t.* ondear; ondular; blandir, agitar. —*v.i.* ondear; ondular; hacer señales; flotar.
wave-band ['weivbænd], *n.* banda de frecuencias.
wave-length ['weivleŋθ], *n.* longitud (*f.*) de onda.
waver ['weivə], *v.i.* oscilar; vacilar.
wavering ['weivəriŋ], *a.* irresoluto, vacilante. —*n.* irresolución, vacilación, *f.*
wavy ['weivi], *a.* ondulado; sinuoso.
wax [wæks], *n.* cera; — ***paper*,** papel (*m.*) encerado; — ***taper*,** blandón *m.*—*v.t.* encerar.—*v.i.* crecer; ponerse.
waxen ['wæksən], *a.* de cera; color de cera.
waxwork ['wækswə:k], *n.* figura de cera.
way [wei], *n.* camino, senda; vía; dirección, *f.*, rumbo; viaje, *m.*; método, modo; manera; costumbre, *f.*; — ***in*,** entrada; — ***out*,** salida; ***by* — *of*,** pasando por; a manera de; ***that* —,** por ahí; ***this* —,** por aquí; ***which* —?** ¿por dónde? ***by the* —,** a propósito; ***right of* —,** derecho de paso; ***to be in the* —,** estorbar; ***on the* — *to*,** con rumbo a; ***out of the* —,** fuera del camino; (*fig.*) extraordinario; ***to get out of the* —,** quitarse de en medio; ***to get under* —,** (*naut.*) hacerse a la vela; ***to go out of one's* — *to*,** hacer todo lo posible para; ***to give* —,** ceder; romper; ***to get one's own* —,** salir con la suya; ***to lead the* —,** ir delante; ***to lose the* —,** extraviarse; ***a long* — *off*,** a lo lejos; ***a short* — *off*,** no muy lejos.
wayfarer ['weifɛərə], *n.* viandante, *m.f.*
waylay [wei'lei], *v.t.* asechar.
wayside ['weisaid], *n.* borde (*m.*) del camino.
wayward ['weiwəd], *a.* travieso; díscolo; caprichoso.
waywardness ['weiwədnis], *n.* travesura; desobediencia.
we [wi:], *pron.* nosotros, *m.pl.*; nosotras, *f.pl.*
weak [wi:k], *a.* débil; flojo; delicado; inseguro; poco convincente; — ***spot*,** lado débil; punto débil.
weaken ['wi:kən], *v.t.* debilitar; disminuir.—*v.i.* debilitarse.
weakling ['wi:kliŋ], *a.*, *n.* canijo; cobarde; alfeñique, *m.*
weakly ['wi:kli], *a.* débil; enfermizo.—*adv.* débilmente.
weakness ['wi:knis], *n.* debilidad; flojedad; imperfección, *f.*
wealth [welθ], *n.* riqueza; abundancia.
wealthy ['welθi], *a.* rico, adinerado.
wean [wi:n], *v.t.* destetar; separar.
weaning ['wi:niŋ], *n.* destete, *m.*
weapon ['wepən], *n.* arma.
wear [wɛə], *n.* uso; gasto; deterioro; moda; ***for summer* —,** para verano; — ***and tear*,** uso, depreciación, *f.*—*v.t. irr.* (*conjug. like* TEAR) llevar, llevar puesto; vestir; mostrar; gastar; deteriorar; usar; agotar; enfadar; ***to* — *away*,** usar; ***to* — *off*,** borrar.—*v.i. irr.* usarse; gastarse; perdurar; conservarse; pasar; ***to* — *away*,** usarse; ***to* — *off*,** borrarse, quitarse; ***to* — *on*,** pasar lentamente; ***to* — *out*,** usarse.
weariness ['wiərinis], *n.* cansancio.
wearing ['wɛəriŋ], *a.* cansado.—*n.* uso; desgaste, *m.*; deterioro.
wearisome ['wiərisəm], *a.* cansado; aburrido; pesado.
weary ['wiəri], *a.* cansado, fatigado; aburrido. —*v.t.* cansar; aburrir.—*v.i.* cansarse; aburrirse.
weasel [wi:zl], *n.* comadreja.
weather ['weðə], *n.* tiempo; ***what is the* — *like?*** ¿qué tiempo hace? ***the* — *is bad*,** hace mal tiempo; ***under the* —,** destemplado; — ***chart*,** carta metereológica; — ***forecast*,** pronóstico del tiempo.—*v.t.* curtir; aguantar; vencer; ***to* — *the storm*,** resistir a la tempestad.—*v.i.* curtirse a la intemperie.
weather-beaten ['weðəbi:tn], *a.* curtido por la intemperie.
weathercock ['weðəkɔk], *n.* veleta.
weave [wi:v], *n.* tejido; textura.—*v.t.*, *v.i. irr.* tejer.
weaver ['wi:və], *n.* tejedor, *m.*
weaving ['wi:viŋ], *n.* tejeduría; tejido.
web [web], *n.* tejido, tela; red, *f.*; lazo; (*zool.*) membrana interdigital.
web-footed ['web'futid], *a.* palmípedo.
wed [wed], *v.t.* casarse con; casar; (*fig.*) encadenar.—*v.i.* casarse.
wedding ['wediŋ], *n.* boda, casamiento; enlace, *m.*; — ***cake*,** pan (*m.*) de boda; — ***day*,** día (*m.*) de bodas; — ***dress*,** traje (*m.*) de boda; — ***ring*,** alianza, anillo de la boda.
wedge [wedʒ], *n.* cuña; calza.—*v.t.* acuñar; calzar; sujetar.
wedlock ['wedlɔk], *n.* matrimonio.
Wednesday ['wenzd(e)i], *n.* miércoles, *m.*
weed [wi:d], *n.* hierba mala; (*fam.*) tabaco; (*fam.*) madeja.—*pl.* ropa de luto.—*v.t.* escardar; (*fig.*) extirpar (***out***).
weeding ['wi:diŋ], *n.* escarda.
weedy ['wi:di], *a.* (*fig.*) raquítico.
week [wi:k], *n.* semana; ***once a* —,** una vez por semana.
weekday ['wi:kdei], *n.* día (*m.*) de entresemana.
weekend ['wi:kend], *n.* fin (*m.*) de semana.
weekly ['wi:kli], *a.* semanal.—*n.* revista semanal, semanario.
weep [wi:p], *v.t.*, *v.i. irr.* llorar.
weeping ['wi:piŋ], *a.* lloroso; — ***willow*,** sauce llorón, *m.*—*n.* lloro, lágrimas, *f.pl.*
weevil ['wi:vil], *n.* gorgojo.
weft [weft], *n.* trama.
weigh [wei], *v.t.* pesar; oprimir; comparar; ***to* — *anchor*,** levantar el ancla; ***to* — *down*,** sobrecargar; (*fig.*) oprimir (***on***).—*v.i.* pesar; ser de importancia.
weighing ['weiiŋ], *n.* peso; pesada; ponderación, *f.*
weighing-machine ['weiiŋməʃi:n], *n.* báscula, máquina de pesar.
weight [weit], *n.* peso; pesadez, *f.*; pesa; cargo; ***by* —,** al peso; ***gross* —,** peso bruto; ***net* —,** peso neto; ***to lose* —,** adelgazar; ***to put on* —,** engordar; ***to throw one's* —**

about, (*fam.*) darse importancia.—*v.t.* cargar; aumentar el peso de.
weightless ['weitlis], *a.* ingrávido.
weightlessness ['weitlisnis], *n.* ingravidez, *f.*
weighty ['weiti], *a.* de peso, pesado; (*fig.*) grave; importante.
weir [wiə], *n.* vertedero, presa de aforo.
weird [wiəd], *a.* extraño; fantástico.
welcome ['welkəm], *a.* bienvenido; grato, agradable; ***you are — to it,*** está a su disposición.—*n.* bienvenida; buena acogida.—*v.t.* dar la bienvenida a; saludar; acoger.—*interj.* ¡bien venido!
welcoming ['welkəmiŋ], *a.* acogedor.
weld [weld], *v.t.* soldar; (*fig.*) unir.
welder ['weldə], *n.* soldador, *m.*
welding ['weldiŋ], *n.* soldadura; unión, *f.*
welfare ['welfɛə], *n.* bienestar, *m.*; prosperidad; salud, *f.*; — ***work,*** servicio social.
well (1) [wel], *a.* bien; sano.—*adv.* bien; muy; ***as — as,*** tan bien como; ***as —,*** también.—*interj.* ¡bien! ¡bueno! ¡pues! — ***done!*** ¡bravo!
well (2) [wel], *n.* pozo; ***stair —,*** caja de escalera; (*naut.*) vivar, *m.*
well-aimed ['wel'eimd], *a.* certero.
well-behaved ['welbi'heivd], *a.* bien educado.
well-being ['wel'bi:iŋ], *n.* bienestar, *m.*
well-born ['wel'bɔ:n], *a.* de buena familia.
well-bred ['wel'bred], *a.* bien educado; de pura raza.
well-disposed ['weldis'pouzd], *a.* bien dispuesto.
well-educated ['wel'edjukeitid], *a.* instruído.
well-favoured ['wel'feivəd], *a.* de buen parecer.
well-founded ['wel'faundid], *a.* bien fundado.
wellingtons ['weliŋtənz], *n.pl.* botas (*f.pl.*) de goma.
well-known ['wel'noun], *a.* (bien) conocido.
well-meaning ['wel'mi:niŋ], *a.* bien intencionado.
well-read ['wel'red], *a.* erudito.
well-spent ['wel'spent], *a.* bien empleado.
well-spoken ['wel'spoukən], *a.* bien hablado; bien dicho.
well-stocked ['wel'stɔkt], *a.* bien provisto.
well-timed ['wel'taimd], *a.* oportuno.
well-to-do ['weltə'du:], *a.* acomodado.
well-wisher ['welwiʃə], *n.* bienqueriente, *m.f.*
well-worn ['wel'wɔ:n], *a.* usado; trillado.
Welsh [welʃ], *a.* galés, de Gales.—*n.* ***the —,*** los galeses.
Welshman ['welʃmən], *n.* galés, *m.*
welt [welt], *n.* ribete, *m.*; vira (*de zapato*).
welter ['weltə], *n.* tumulto; — ***weight,*** peso welter.
wench [wentʃ], *n.* (*obs.*) muchacha; (*fam.*) tía.
wend [wend], *v.t.* encaminar, dirigir; ***to — one's way,*** seguir su camino.
went [went] [GO].
wept [wept] [WEEP].
were [wə:] [BE].
west [west], *a.* occidental, del oeste; ***West Indies,*** las Antillas.—*n.* oeste, occidente, poniente, *m.*—*adv.* al oeste.
westerly ['westəli], *a.* occidental; del oeste; hacia el oeste.
western ['westən], *a.* occidental; del oeste.—*n.* novela *o* película del oeste.
westernized ['westənaizd], *a.* occidentalizado.
westward ['westwəd], *a.* occidental.—*adv.* hacia el oeste.
wet [wet], *a.* mojado; húmedo; lluvioso; (*fam.*) necio; — ***paint,*** recién pintado; ***to get —,*** mojarse; ***to be —,*** estar mojado; llover; — ***through,*** colado, mojado hasta los huesos.—*v.t.* mojar; ***to — one's whistle,*** (*fam.*) mojar el gaznate.
wetness ['wetnis], *n.* humedad, *f.*; lluvia.
whack [wæk], *n.* golpe, *m.*; tentativa; (*fam.*) porción, *f.*—*v.t.* golpear, pegar.
whale [weil], *n.* ballena; ***sperm —,*** cachalote, *m.*
whalebone ['weilboun], *n.* barba de ballena.
whaler ['weilə], *n.* ballenero; buque ballenero.
wharf [wɔ:f], *n.* muelle, *m.*, embarcadero, descargadero.
what [wɔt], *pron.* qué; que; cuál; cual; el cual, *etc.*, el que, *etc.*; cuanto; cuánto; — ***else?*** ¿y qué más? ***to know what's —,*** saber cuántas son cinco; ***what's-his-name,*** fulano de tal; ***what's up?*** ¿qué pasa? — ***with one thing and another,*** entre una cosa y otra.
whatever [wɔt'evə], *a.* todo . . . que; cualquier; cual.—*pron.* cuanto; todo lo que; cualquier cosa que; — ***happens,*** venga lo que venga; — ***you say,*** diga lo que diga.
wheat [wi:t], *n.* trigo.
wheaten [wi:tn], *a.* de trigo.
wheat-field ['wi:tfi:ld], *n.* trigal, *m.*
wheat-sheaf ['wi:tʃi:f], *n.* gavilla de trigo.
wheedle [wi:dl], *v.t.* halagar; engatusar.
wheedling ['wi:dliŋ], *a.* zalamero.—*n.* lagotería; halagos, *m.pl.*
wheel [wi:l], *n.* rueda; ***potter's —,*** rueda de alfarero; ***front —,*** rueda delantera; ***rear —,*** rueda trasera.—*v.t.* hacer rodar; poner ruedas en.—*v.i.* girar; dar vueltas.
wheelbarrow ['wi:lbærou], *n.* carretilla.
wheel-chair ['wi:ltʃɛə], *n.* silla de ruedas.
wheeze [wi:z], *n.* (*fam.*) truco.—*v.i.* jadear, respirar con dificultad.
wheezing ['wi:ziŋ], *a.* asmático.
whelk [welk], *n.* caracol (*m.*) de mar, buccino.
whelp [welp], *n.* cachorro.—*v.i.* parir.
when [wen], *adv.* cuando; cuándo; en cuanto; en que; que; y entonces.
whence [wens], *adv.* de dónde; de donde; de que; por lo que.
whenever [wen'evə], *adv.* cuandoquiera que; siempre que; cada vez que.
where [wɛə], *adv.* donde; dónde; adonde; adónde; en donde; en dónde; de donde; de dónde.
whereabouts ['wɛərəbauts], *n.* paradero.—[wɛərə'bauts], *adv.* dónde; donde.
whereas [wɛər'æz], *conj.* mientras (que); visto que, ya que.
whereby [wɛə'bai], *adv.* por (*o* con) el que; por qué; cómo.
wherefore ['wɛəfɔ:], *adv.* por lo cual; por qué.—*n.* porqué, *m.*
wherein [wɛər'in], *adv.* en donde; en dónde; en que; en qué.
whereof [wɛər'ɔv], *adv.* de que; cuyo.
whereon [wɛər'ɔn], *adv.* en que, sobre que.
whereupon [wɛərə'pɔn], *adv.* sobre lo cual, con lo cual.
wherever [wɛər'evə], *adv.* dondequiera (que); adondequiera (que); dónde.
wherewith [wɛə'wið], *adv.* con que; con qué.

wherewithal ['wɛəwiðɔ:l], *n.* dinero necesario, cumquibus, *m.*
whet [wet], *v.t.* afilar, aguzar; (*fig.*) estimular.
whether ['weðə], *conj.* si; que; — . . . **or** . . ., sea (que) . . . sea (que) . . .
whetstone ['wetstoun], *n.* (piedra) aguzadera, piedra de afilar.
whey [wei], *n.* suero de la leche.
which [witʃ], *pron.* que; qué; cuál; cuáles; el cual, *etc.*, el que, *etc.*; quien; — ***way?*** ¿por dónde?
whichever [witʃ'evə], *pron.* cualquiera; cualesquiera; el que, *etc.*; quienquiera; quienesquiera.
whiff [wif], *n.* soplo; fragancia.
while [wail], *n.* rato; momento; tiempo; ***a little — ago,*** hace poco tiempo; ***to be worth —,*** valer la pena.—*conj.* mientras (que), al mismo tiempo que; si bien.—*v.t.* ***to — away,*** matar, entretener (*el tiempo*).
whim [wim], *n.* capricho, antojo.
whimper ['wimpə], *n.* quejido, sollozo.—*v.i.* lloriquear, gemir.
whimsical ['wimzikəl], *a.* caprichoso, antojadizo; fantástico.
whine [wain], *n.* gimoteo.—*v.i.* gimotear.
whinny ['wini], *n.* relincho.—*v.i.* relinchar.
whip [wip], *n.* azote, *m.*; látigo; ***to have the — hand,*** (*fig.*) tener la sartén por el mango.—*v.t.* azotar; (*cul.*) batir; vencer; sacar; quitar; ***to — up,*** (*fig.*) excitar.
whippet ['wipit], *n.* perro lebrero.
whipping ['wipiŋ], *n.* azotamiento; — ***top,*** peonza.
whirl [wə:l], *n.* vuelta, rotación, *f.*, giro; (*fig.*) torbellino.—*v.t.* hacer girar.—*v.i.* girar; dar vueltas.
whirligig ['wə:ligig], *n.* perinola; tíovivo.
whirlpool ['wə:lpu:l], *n.* remolino.
whirlwind ['wə:lwind], *n.* torbellino.
whirr [wə:], *n.* zumbido.—*v.i.* zumbar; girar.
whisk [wisk], *n.* cepillo; batidor, *m.*; movimiento rápido.—*v.t.* cepillar, batir; mover rápidamente; ***to — away,*** arrebatar.—*v.i.* pasar rápidamente.
whisker ['wiskə], *n.* patilla.—*pl.* bigotes, *m.pl.*; barba.
whisky ['wiski], *n.* whisky, *m.*
whisper ['wispə], *n.* cuchicheo, susurro; ***in a —,*** en voz baja.—*v.t.*, *v.i.* susurrar, cuchichear; hablar al oído; murmurar.
whispering ['wispəriŋ], *n.* cuchicheo, susurro; murmullo.
whist [wist], *n.* whist, *m.*
whistle [wisl], *n.* silbo, silbido; pito; (*fam.*) gaznate, *m.*—*v.t.*, *v.i.* silbar; ***to — for,*** llamar silbando; (*fam.*) esperar en vano.
whistling ['wisliŋ], *n.* silbido.
whit [wit], *n.* pizca; ***not a —,*** ni pizca.
white [wait], *a.*, *n.* blanco; clara (*de huevo*); ***to go —,*** ponerse pálido; ***the — of the eye,*** lo blanco del ojo; — ***lie,*** mentirilla; — ***wine,*** vino blanco.
whiten [waitn], *v.t.* blanquear.—*v.i.* -se.
whiteness ['waitnis], *n.* blancura; palidez, *f.*
whitewash ['waitwɔʃ], *n.* jalbegue, *m.*; (*fig.*) disimulación, *f.*—*v.t.* enjalbegar; (*fig.*) encubrir.
whither ['wiðə], *adv.* adonde; adónde.
whitish ['waitiʃ], *a.* blanquecino.
Whit Sunday ['wit'sʌnd(e)i], *n.* domingo de Pentecostés.
Whitsuntide ['witsəntaid], *n.* Pentecostés, *m.*
whittle [witl], *v.t.* tallar; cercenar; afilar; (*fig.*) reducir.
whizz [wiz], *n.* silbido, zumbido.—*v.i.* silbar, zumbar.
who [hu:], *pron.* quién; quiénes; quien; quienes; que; el que, *etc.*
whoever [hu:'evə], *pron.* quienquiera (que), cualquiera (que).
whole [houl], *a.* todo; entero; sano.—*n.* todo; totalidad, *f.*; conjunto; ***on the —,*** en general.
wholeness ['houlnis], *n.* totalidad; integridad, *f.*
wholesale ['houlseil], *a.* al por mayor; (*fig.*) general.—*n.* venta al por mayor.
wholesome ['houlsəm], *a.* saludable; sano.
wholly ['houlli], *adv.* completamente, enteramente; del todo.
whom [hu:m], *pron.* que; el que, *etc.*, el cual, *etc.*; quien; quienes; quién; quiénes.
whoop [hu:p], *n.* alarido; (*med.*) estertor, *m.*—*v.i.* dar gritos; (*med.*) toser.
whooping ['hu:piŋ], *n.* alarido.
whooping-cough ['hu:piŋkɔf], *n.* tos ferina.
whore [hɔ:], *n.* puta, ramera.
whose [hu:z], *pron.* cuyo; del que, *etc.*, del cual, *etc.*; de quién; de quiénes.
why [wai], *n.* porqué, *m.*—*adv.* por qué; por el cual, *etc.*—*interj.* ¡cómo! ¡toma! ¡qué!
wick [wik], *n.* mecha.
wicked ['wikid], *a.* malo; perverso, malvado; malicioso.
wickedness ['wikidnis], *n.* maldad; perversidad, *f.*; pecado.
wicker ['wikə], *n.* mimbre, *m.*
wicket ['wikit], *n.* postigo; (*sport*) meta.
wide [waid], *a.* ancho; extenso; apartado; liberal; de ancho; ***six feet —,*** seis pies de ancho.—*adv.* lejos; completamente; ***far and —,*** por todas partes; — ***awake,*** bien despierto; — ***open,*** abierto de par en par.
wide-eyed ['waid'aid], *a.* con los ojos muy abiertos; asombrado; (*fig.*) inocente.
widen [waidn], *v.t.* ensanchar; extender.—*v.i.* ensancharse; extenderse.
widening ['waidniŋ], *n.* ensanche, *m.*; extensión, *f.*
widespread ['waidspred], *a.* difuso; esparcido; general.
widow ['widou], *n.* viuda.—*v.t.* enviudar, dejar viuda.
widowed ['widoud], *a.* viudo.
widower ['widouə], *n.* viudo.
widowhood ['widouhud], *n.* viudez, *f.*
width [widθ], *n.* anchura; ancho; amplitud, *f.*
wield [wi:ld], *v.t.* manejar, empuñar; ejercer.
wife [waif], *n.* (*pl.* **wives**) mujer, *f.*, esposa; señora; ***old wives' tale,*** cuento de viejas, patraña.
wig [wig], *n.* peluca; cabellera.
wild [waild], *a.* salvaje; silvestre; desierto; desordenado; violento; inconstante; borrascoso; loco; extravagante; ***to run —,*** volver al estado primitivo; desencadenarse; ***to sow one's — oats,*** correr sus mocedades; — ***beast,*** fiera; ***wild-cat strike,*** huelga irracional; — ***goose chase,*** caza de grillos.—*n.pl.* desierto, yermo; región remota.
wilderness ['wildənis], *n.* desierto, yermo.
wildfire ['waildfaiə], *n.* fuego fatuo; ***to spread like —,*** extenderse como el fuego.

wile ['wail], *n.* ardid, *m.*, engaño.
wilful ['wilful], *a.* obstinado; voluntarioso; premeditado.
wilfulness ['wilfulnis], *n.* obstinación; intención, *f.*
wiliness ['wailinis], *n.* astucia.
will [wil], *n.* albedrío; voluntad, *f.*; deseo; discreción, *f.*; testamento; ***at* —,** a voluntad; ***to do with a* —,** hacer con entusiasmo.—*v.t.* querer; mandar; legar; sugestionar.—*v. aux. irr.* querer; — ***you open the window?*** ¿quiere Vd. abrir la ventana? (*When it simply indicates the future, the future tense is used in Spanish*); — ***you come tomorrow?*** ¿Vd. vendrá mañana?
willing ['wiliŋ], *a.* dispuesto; servicial; deseoso; ***God* —,** si Dios quiere.
willingly ['wiliŋli], *adv.* de buena gana.
willingness ['wiliŋnis], *n.* buena voluntad, *f.*; consentimiento.
will-o'-the-wisp ['wiləðə'wisp], *n.* fuego fatuo.
willow ['wilou], *n.* sauce, *m.*
willowy ['wiloui], *a.* (*fig.*) cimbreño, esbelto.
will-power ['wilpauə], *n.* fuerza de voluntad.
willy-nilly ['wili'nili], *adv.* de buen o mal grado, que quiera o no.
wilt [wilt], *v.t.* marchitar; ajar.—*v.i.* marchitarse; (*fig.*) amansarse.
wily ['waili], *a.* astuto.
wimple [wimpl], *n.* toca, impla.
win [win], *n.* triunfo.—*v.t. irr.* ganar; vencer; persuadir.—*v.i. irr.* ganar; triunfar; prevalecer.
wince [wins], *n.* respingo.—*v.i.* recular; respingar.
winch [wintʃ], *n.* cabria; manubrio.
wind (1) [wind], *n.* viento; aliento; flatulencia; ***to get* — *of*,** husmear; ***following* —,** viento en popa.—*v.t.* dejar sin aliento.
wind (2) [waind], *v.t. irr.* dar cuerda a (*un reloj*); torcer; devanar, ovillar; ***to* — *off*,** devanar; ***to* — *round*,** envolver, ceñir; ***to* — *up*,** dar cuerda a; (*fig.*) atar cabos; (*com.*) liquidar.—*v.i. irr.* serpentear; arrollarse.
winded ['windid], *a.* jadeante.
windfall ['windfɔ:l], *n.* fruta caída del árbol; ganancia inesperada.
winding ['waindiŋ], *a.* sinuoso; tortuoso; serpentino; en espiral; — ***sheet*,** sudario; — ***staircase*,** escalera de caracol.—*n.* vuelta; tortuosidad, *f.*; (*elec.*) devanado.
winding-up ['waindiŋ'ʌp], *n.* conclusión; (*com.*) liquidación, *f.*
windmill ['windmil], *n.* molino (de viento).
window ['windou], *n.* ventana; ventanilla; vidriera; — ***frame*,** marco de ventana; — ***pane*,** cristal, *m.*; — ***sill*,** antepecho *o* repisa de ventana; ***to look out of the* —,** mirar por la ventana.
window-dresser ['windoudresə], *n.* decorador (*m.*) de escaparates.
windpipe ['windpaip], *n.* tráquea.
windscreen ['windskri:n], *n.* parabrisas, *m.sg.*; — ***wiper*,** limpiaparabrisas, *m.sg.*
windward ['windwəd], *a.* de barlovento.—*n.* barlovento.
windy ['windi], *a.* ventoso; (*fig.*) pomposo; cobarde; ***it is* —,** hace viento *o* aire.
wine [wain], *n.* vino.
wine-cellar ['wainselə], *n.* bodega.
wine-glass ['waingla:s], *n.* copa.
wine-grower ['waingrouə], *n.* viticultor *m.*
wine-press ['wainpres], *n.* lagar, *m.*
wineskin ['wainskin], *n.* odre, *m.*
wine-taster ['wainteistə], *n.* catavinos (*copa*), *m.sg.*; catador (*m.*) de vinos (*persona*).
wing [wiŋ], *n.* ala; (*theat.*) bastidor, *m.*; ***on the* —,** al vuelo; ***under one's* —,** (*fig.*) bajo su protección; ***in the wings*,** (*theat.*) entre bastidores.—*v.t.* proveer de alas; herir en el ala; herir en el brazo.—*v.i.* volar.
winged [wiŋd], *a.* alado; (*fig.*) rápido; elevado.
wing-span ['wiŋspæn], *n.* envergadura.
wing-tip ['wiŋtip], *n.* punta de ala.
wink [wiŋk], *n.* guiño; pestañeo; un abrir y cerrar de ojos; ***not to sleep a* —,** no pegar los ojos; ***to take forty winks*,** descabezar un *o* el sueño.—*v.i.* guiñar; pestañear; (*fig.*) centellear; ***to* — *at*,** guiñar el ojo a; (*fig.*) hacer la vista gorda a.
winner ['winə], *n.* ganador; vencedor, *m.*
winning ['winiŋ], *a.* vencedor; que gana.—*n.* ganancia; triunfo.—*pl.* ganancias, *f.pl.*
winnow ['winou], *v.t.* aventar.
winter ['wintə], *a.* de invierno; — ***sports*,** deportes (*m.pl.*) de nieve.—*n.* invierno.—*v.t.* hacer invernar.—*v.i.* invernar.
wintry ['wintri], *a.* de invierno; (*fig.*) glacial.
wipe [waip], *n.* limpión, *m.*—*v.t.* enjugar; limpiar; ***to* — *off*,** borrar; ***to* — *out*,** (*fig.*) extirpar; cancelar.
wire [waiə], *n.* alambre; (*fam.*) telegrama, *m.*; — ***netting*,** red (*f.*) de alambre.—*v.t.* atar con alambre; proveer de alambre; (*fam.*) telegrafiar; (*elec.*) alambrar.
wireless ['waiəlis], *a.* radiotelegráfico.—*n.* radio, *f.*; radiotelegrafía; ***portable* —,** radio portátil; — ***licence*,** permiso de radiorreceptor; — ***set*,** aparato de radio.
wire-pulling ['waiəpuliŋ], *n.* (*fam.*) intriga secreta.
wiring ['waiəriŋ], *n.* alambrado.
wiry ['waiəri], *a.* (*fig.*) nervudo.
wisdom ['wizdəm], *n.* sabiduría.
wise [waiz], *a.* sabio; sagaz; ***The Three Wise Men*,** los Reyes Magos; — ***guy*,** (*fam.*) sabelotodo.—*n.* guisa, modo.
wish [wiʃ], *n.* deseo, anhelo.—*v.t.* desear; querer; anhelar; ***to* — *good luck*,** desear mucha suerte (a); ***to* — *good morning*,** dar los buenos días; ***to* — *good-bye*,** despedirse (de); ***I* — *I knew!*** ¡ojalá (que) supiese!
wishful ['wiʃful], *a.* deseoso; — ***thinking*,** sueños dorados.
wishy-washy ['wiʃiwɔʃi], *a.* insípido, flojo.
wisp [wisp], *n.* mechón, *m.*; trocito.
wistful ['wistful], *a.* triste; pensativo; ansioso.
wit [wit], *n.* ingenio; sal, *f.*; gracia; hombre (*m.*) *o* mujer (*f.*) de ingenio; ***to* —,** a saber. —*pl.* juicio; ***to be at one's wits' end*,** no saber qué hacer; ***to be out of one's wits*,** perder el juicio; ***to live by one's wits*,** vivir de gorra.
witch [witʃ], *n.* bruja.
witchcraft ['witʃkra:ft], *n.* brujería.
witch-doctor ['witʃdɔktə], *n.* hechizador, *m.*, curandero.
with [wið], *prep.* con; entre; contra; de para con; — ***all speed*,** a toda prisa; — ***that*,** con esto; ***away* — *you!*** ¡anda!
withal [wið'ɔ:l], *adv.* con todo; además.

withdraw [wið'drɔ:], *v.t. irr* (*conjug. like* DRAW) retirar; quitar; retractar.—*v.i. irr.* retirarse; apartarse.
withdrawal [wið'drɔ:əl], *n.* retirada; retiro.
withdrawn [wið'drɔ:n], *a.* ensimismado.
wither ['wiðə], *v.t.* marchitar; (*fig.*) avergonzar.—*v.i.* marchitarse.
withered ['wiðəd], *a.* marchito; seco.
withering ['wiðəriŋ], *a.* que marchita; cáustico.
withers ['wiðəz], *n.pl.* cruz (*de caballo*), *f.*
withhold [wið'hould], *v.t. irr.* (*conjug. like* HOLD) retener; negar; ocultar.
within [wið'in], *adv.* dentro, adentro; en casa; (*fig.*) en el corazón.—*prep.* dentro de; — ***an ace of,*** por poco; — ***an inch of,*** (*fig.*) a dos dedos de; — ***hearing,*** al alcance de la voz; — ***reach of,*** al alcance de.
without [wið'aut], *adv.* fuera, afuera; por fuera; hacia fuera; exteriormente.—*prep.* sin; fuera de; a menos de.
withstand [wið'stænd], *v.t. irr.* (*conjug. like* STAND) oponerse a, resistir; soportar.
witless ['witlis], *a.* necio, tonto.
witness ['witnis], *n.* testigo; espectador, *m.*; testimonio; ***in — whereof,*** en testimonio de lo cual; ***to bear —,*** dar testimonio; — ***for the defence,*** testigo de descargo; — ***for the prosecution,*** testigo de cargo. —*v.t.* ser testigo de, presenciar; mostrar; (*jur.*) atestiguar.—*v.i.* dar testimonio.
witness-box ['witnisbɔks], *n.* puesto de los testigos.
witted ['witid], *a.* ***quick —,*** vivo de ingenio; ***slow —,*** lerdo.
witticism ['witisizm], *n.* agudeza, chiste, *m.*
witty ['witi], *a.* gracioso, salado.
wives [waivz] [WIFE].
wizard ['wizəd], *n.* brujo, hechicero, mago.
wizardry ['wizədri], *n.* brujería.
wizened ['wizənd], *a.* acartonado; marchito.
wobble [wɔbl], *v.i.* tambalearse.
woe [wou], *n.* dolor, *m.*; aflicción, *f.*; — ***is me!*** ¡ay de mí!
woeful ['wouful], *a.* desconsolado; funesto.
wolf [wulf], *n.* (*pl.* **wolves** [wulvz]) lobo; (*fam.*) tenorio; ***to keep the — from the door,*** cerrar la puerta al hambre.
woman ['wumən], *n.* (*pl.* **women**) mujer, *f.*; hembra.
woman-hater ['wumənheitə], *n.* misógino.
womanhood ['wumənhud], *n.* feminidad, *f.*; sexo femenino.
womanish ['wumənif], *a.* afeminado; mujeril.
womanizer ['wumənaizə], *n.* (*fam.*) mujeriego.
womankind ['wumənkaind], *n.* sexo femenino, la mujer.
womanly ['wumənli], *a.* mujeril.
womb [wu:m], *n.* matriz, *f.*, útero; (*fig.*) seno.
women ['wimin] [WOMAN].
won [wʌn] [WIN].
wonder ['wʌndə], *n.* admiración, *f.*; maravilla; prodigio.—*v.i.* admirarse, asombrarse (***at,*** de); preguntarse.
wonderful ['wʌndəful], *a.* maravilloso.
wondering ['wʌndəriŋ], *a.* admirado; perplejo.
wonderland ['wʌndəlænd], *n.* país (*m.*) de las maravillas.
wondrous ['wʌndrəs], *a.* maravilloso.

wont [wount], *n.* costumbre, *f.*; ***to be — to,*** soler.
won't [wount] [WILL NOT].
woo [wu:], *v.t.* cortejar; (*fig.*) solicitar.
wood [wud], *n.* bosque, *m.*; madera; leña.
wood-carving ['wudkɑ:viŋ], *n.* tallo *o* tallado de madera.
wooded ['wudid], *a.* arbolado, enselvado.
wooden [wudn], *a.* de madera; (*fig.*) torpe; — ***leg,*** pata de palo; — ***smile,*** sonrisa mecánica.
woodland ['wudlənd], *n.* bosques, *m.pl.*
woodpecker ['wudpekə], *n.* picamaderos *m.sg.*, pájaro carpintero.
woodshed ['wudʃed], *n.* leñera.
woodwind ['wudwind], *n.* (*mus.*) madera.
woodwork ['wudwə:k], *n.* maderaje, *m.*; carpintería.
woodworm ['wudwə:m], *n.* carcoma.
wooer ['wu:ə], *n.* galanteador, pretendiente, *m.*
wooing ['wu:iŋ], *n.* galanteo.
wool [wul], *n.* lana; ***to pull the — over someone's eyes,*** (*fig.*) embaucar (a uno).
wool-bearing ['wulbɛəriŋ], *a.* lanar.
wool-gathering ['wulgæðəriŋ], *a.* (*fig.*) distraído.
woollen ['wulən], *a.* de lana.—*n.* tela de lana.
woolly ['wuli], *a.* lanudo, lanoso; de lana; crespo; (*fig.*) flojo, impreciso.
woolsack ['wulsæk], *n.* fardo de lana; asiento del Presidente de la Cámara de los Lores.
word [wə:d], *n.* palabra; vocablo; orden, *f.*; recado; ***the Word,*** (*Bible*) el Verbo; ***by — of mouth,*** verbalmente; ***to bring —,*** traer la noticia; ***to keep one's —,*** cumplir su palabra; ***to give one's —,*** dar su palabra; ***to take someone's — for it,*** creer (a uno); ***to have a — with,*** hablar con; ***to have words with,*** tener palabras con; ***in other words,*** en otros términos.—*v.t.* expresar; redactar.
wordiness ['wə:dinis], *n.* verbosidad, *f.*
wording ['wə:diŋ], *n.* fraseología; estilo; términos, *m.pl.*; redacción, *f.*
wordy ['wə:di], *a.* verboso.
wore [wɔ:] [WEAR].
work [wə:k], *n.* trabajo; obra.—*pl.* obras; fábrica; mecanismo; — ***of art,*** obra de arte; ***to set to —,*** hacer trabajar; dar empleo a; ***out of —,*** desocupado.—*v.t.* trabajar; explotar; producir; tallar; manejar; hacer funcionar; cultivar; efectuar; (*naut.*) maniobrar; ***to — in,*** hacer penetrar; ***to — off,*** librarse de; ***to — on,*** influir en; obrar sobre; mover a compasión.—*v.i.* trabajar; funcionar; tener éxito; ser eficaz; moverse; ***to — at,*** ocuparse de; ***to — in,*** penetrar en, insinuarse en; ***to — out,*** resultar; ***not working,*** no funciona.
workable ['wə:kəbl], *a.* laborable; explotable; practicable.
workaday ['wə:kədei], *a.* ordinario, prosaico.
work-box ['wə:kbɔks], *n.* caja de labor.
workday ['wə:kdei], *n.* día (*m.*) laborable.
worker ['wə:kə], *n.* trabajador, *m.*; obrero.
workhouse ['wə:khaus], *n.* asilo (de pobres).
working ['wə:kiŋ], *a.* trabajador, que trabaja; de trabajo; obrero; — ***class,*** clase obrera; — ***clothes,*** ropa de trabajo.—*n.* trabajo; fermentación, *f.*; funcionamiento; explotación, *f.*; maniobra.
workman ['wə:kmən], *n.* obrero.

workmanlike ['wə:kmənlaik], *a.* hábil; esmerado.
workmanship ['wə:kmənʃip], *n.* habilidad, *f.*
workroom ['wə:kru:m], *n.* manufactura.
workshop ['wə:kʃɔp], *n.* taller, *m.*
world [wə:ld], *n.* mundo; — ***power,*** potencia mundial.
worldliness ['wə:ldlinis], *n.* mundanería.
worldly ['wə:ldli], *a.* mundano; humano; profano; ***to be worldly-wise,*** tener mucho mundo.
world-wide ['wə:ld'waid], *a.* mundial.
worm [wə:m], *n.* gusano; lombriz, *f.*; (*mech.*) tornillo sinfín.—*v.t.* ***to — out,*** sonsacar.—*v.i.* arrastrarse; insinuarse; ***to — one's way into,*** insinuarse en.
worm-eaten ['wə:mi:tən], *a.* carcomido.
wormwood ['wə:mwud], *n.* ajenjo.
worn [wɔ:n], **worn-out** ['wɔ:naut], *a.* usado; raído; fatigado; gastado. [WEAR].
worrier ['wʌriə], *n.* aprensivo; pesimista, *m.f.*
worry ['wʌri], *n.* preocupación, *f.*; cuidado.—*v.t.* preocupar; molestar; importunar; desgarrar.—*v.i.* preocuparse; estar preocupado.
worse [wə:s], *a.* (*compar. of* BAD) peor; inferior; ***so much the —,*** tanto peor; — ***than ever,*** peor que nunca; — ***and —,*** de mal en peor; ***to get —,*** empeorarse, ponerse peor.—*adv.* (*compar. of* BADLY) peor.—*n.* lo peor.
worsen ['wə:sən], *v.t.* hacer peor; exasperar; agravar.—*v.i.* hacerse peor; exasperarse; agravarse.
worship ['wə:ʃip], *n.* adoración; veneración, *f.*; culto.—*v.t.* adorar, venerar, reverenciar.—*v.i.* adorar; dar culto.
worshipful ['wə:ʃipful], *a.* venerable.
worshipper ['wə:ʃipə], *n.* adorador; fiel, *m.*
worst [wə:st], *a.* (*superl. of* BAD) el peor, *etc.*; pésimo.—*adv.* (*superl. of* BADLY) el peor, *etc.*—*n.* el peor, *etc.*; lo peor; ***the — of it is,*** lo peor es; ***if the — comes to the —,*** en el peor caso; ***to get the — of it,*** sacar el peor partido.—*v.t.* derrotar, vencer.
worsted ['wustid], *a.* de estambre.—*n.* estambre, *m.*
worth [wə:θ], *a.* digno; que vale; que merece; del precio de; ***to be —,*** valer; ser digno de; ***to be — while,*** valer la pena.—*n.* valor, *m.*; precio; mérito.
worthiness ['wə:ðinis], *n.* valor, *m.*, mérito.
worthless ['wə:θlis], *a.* sin valor; inútil; despreciable.
worthlessness ['wə:θlisnis], *n.* falta de valor; inutilidad, *f.*; vileza.
worthy ['wə:ði], *a.* digno; benemérito.—*n.* hombre ilustre, *m.*; benemérita.
would [wud], *pret., subj.* [WILL]; — ***that he were here!*** ¡ojalá (que) estuviese aquí! — ***to God!*** ¡plegue a Dios!
would-be ['wudbi:], *a.* supuesto; pretendiente; frustrado.
wouldn't [wudnt] [WOULD NOT].
wound (1) [wu:nd], *n.* herida, llaga.—*v.t.* herir; lastimar; ***to — to the quick,*** herir en lo vivo.
wound (2) [waund] [WIND].
wounding ['wu:ndiŋ], *a.* lastimador; ofensivo.
wove(n) [wouv(n)] [WEAVE].
wraith [reiθ], *n.* fantasma, *m.*
wrangle [ræŋgl], *n.* altercado; riña.—*v.i.* disputar, altercar; reñir; regatear.
wrap [ræp], *n.* bata; envoltorio.—*v.t.* envolver; embozar; ocultar; cubrir; ***to be wrapped up in,*** estar envuelto en; (*fig.*) estar absorto en.
wrapper ['ræpə], *n.* envoltura; embalaje, *m.*; cubierta; faja; bata.
wrapping ['ræpiŋ], *n.* envoltura; cubierta; — ***paper,*** papel (*m.*) de envolver.
wrath [rɔθ], *n.* furor, *m.*, ira.
wrathful ['rɔθful], *a.* enojado, furioso, airado.
wreak [ri:k], *v.t.* ejecutar; descargar; ***to — vengeance,*** tomar venganza.
wreath [ri:θ], *n.* guirnalda; corona; trenza.
wreathe [ri:ð], *v.t.* enguirnaldar; trenzar; entrelazar; ceñir.
wreck [rek], *n.* naufragio; barco naufragado; destrucción, *f.*; (*fig.*) ruina.—*v.t.* hacer naufragar; destruir; (*fig.*) arruinar.—*v.i.* naufragar.
wreckage ['rekidʒ], *n.* naufragio; restos, *m.pl.*
wren [ren], *n.* buscareta.
wrench [rentʃ], *n.* torcedura; tirón, arranque, *m.*; llave, *f.*—*v.t.* torcer, dislocar; arrancar.
wrest [rest], *v.t.* arrancar, arrebatar.
wrestle [resl], *v.i.* luchar.
wrestler ['reslə], *n.* luchador, *m.*
wrestling ['resliŋ], *n.* lucha.
wretch [retʃ], *n.* desgraciado, infeliz, *m.f.*
wretched ['retʃid], *a.* desgraciado; miserable; ruin; mezquino; despreciable.
wretchedness ['retʃidnis], *n.* miseria; ruindad *f.*; vileza.
wriggle [rigl], *v.i.* culebrear; retorcerse; ***to — out,*** escaparse; (*fig.*) extricarse.
wring [riŋ], *v.t. irr.* torcer; exprimir; ***to — one's hands,*** torcerse las manos; ***to — the neck of,*** torcer el pescuezo a.
wringer ['riŋə], *n.* torcedor; exprimidor, *m.*
wrinkle [riŋkl], *n.* arruga; pliegue, *m.*; (*fam.*) maña.—*v.t.* arrugar.—*v.i.* arrugarse.
wrinkly ['riŋkli], *a.* arrugado.
wrist [rist], *n.* muñeca.
wrist-watch ['ristwɔtʃ], *n.* reloj (*m.*) de pulsera.
writ [rit], *n.* escritura; (*jur.*) mandamiento; orden, *f.*; ***Holy Writ,*** la Sagrada Escritura.
write [rait], *v.t., v.i. irr.* escribir; ***to — back,*** contestar a una carta; ***to — down,*** apuntar; ***to — out,*** copiar; ***to — up,*** redactar.
writer ['raitə], *n.* escritor; autor, *m.*
writhe [raið], *v.i.* torcerse, retorcerse.
writing ['raitiŋ], *n.* escritura; escrito; letra; ***in —,*** por escrito; — ***paper,*** papel (*m.*) de escribir; — ***desk,*** escritorio; — ***pad,*** taco de papel.
written [ritn] [WRITE].
wrong [rɔŋ], *a.* malo; injusto; erróneo equivocado; falso; inoportuno; — ***side out,*** al revés; ***to be —,*** equivocarse; no tener razón; — ***number,*** número errado.—*n.* mal, *m.*; injusticia; agravio; culpa; error, *m.*; ***to be in the —,*** no tener razón; tener la culpa; ***to do —,*** hacer *o* obrar mal.—*adv.* mal; injustamente; equivocadamente; sin razón; al revés; ***to get it —,*** calcular mal; comprender mal.—*v.t.* ofender; hacer daño; agraviar; perjudicar.
wrong-doer ['rɔŋdu:ə], *n.* malhechor, *m.*
wrong-doing ['rɔŋdu:iŋ], *n.* maleficencia.

wrongful ['rɔŋful], *a.* injusto; falso.
wrong-headed ['rɔŋ'hedid], *a.* terco.
wrote [rout] [WRITE].
wrought [rɔ:t], *a.* forjado; trabajado; excitado.
wrung [rʌŋ] [WRING].
wry [rai], *a.* torcido; irónico; — ***face,*** mueca.

X

X, x [eks], *n.* vigésima cuarta letra del alfabeto inglés; ***X-rays,*** rayos X.—***v.t. to X-ray,*** radiografiar.
xenophobe ['zenəfoub], *n.* xenófobo.
xenophobia [zenə'foubjə], *n.* xenofobia.
Xmas ['krisməs], *n.* (*abbrev. of* **Christmas**) (*fam.*) Navidad, *f.*
xylophone ['zailəfoun], *n.* xilófono; marimba.

Y

Y, y [wai], *n.* vigésima quinta letra del alfabeto inglés.
yacht [jɔt], *n.* yate, *m.*; — ***club,*** club marítimo.
yachting ['jɔtiŋ], *n.* deporte (*m.*) de vela, yachting, *m.*
yachtsman ['jɔtsmən], *n.* yachtsman, *m.*
yak [jæk], *n.* yak, *m.*
Yank [jæŋk], **Yankee** ['jæŋki], *a., n.* (*fam.*) yanqui, *m.f.*
yank [jæŋk], *n.* tirón, *m.*—***v.t.*** dar un tirón a.
yap [jæp], *n.* ladrido.—***v.i.*** ladrar; (*fam.*) parlotear.
yard [jɑ:d], *n.* yarda; corral, *m.*, patio.
yard-arm ['jɑ:dɑ:m], *n.* penol (de la verga), *m.*
yard-stick ['jɑ:dstik], *n.* yarda de medir, criterio.
yarn [jɑ:n], *n.* hilo, hilaza; (*fam.*) historia, cuento; ***to spin a —,*** contar una historia.
yawl [jɔ:l], *n.* yola, bote, *m.*
yawn [jɔ:n], *n.* bostezo.—***v.i.*** bostezar; abrirse.
yawning ['jɔ:niŋ], *a.* abierto.—*n.* bostezo(s).
yea [jei] [YES].
year [jiə], *n.* año; ***last —,*** el año pasado; ***leap —,*** año bisiesto; ***next —,*** el año que viene, el año próximo; ***New Year,*** Año Nuevo; ***by the —,*** al año; ***— after —,*** año tras año; ***to be . . . years old,*** tener . . . años; ***to be getting on in years,*** envejecer, irse haciendo viejo.
year-book ['jiəbuk], *n.* anuario.
yearly ['jiəli], *a.* anual.—*adv.* anualmente, cada año, una vez al año.
yearn [jɔ:n], *v.i.* anhelar, suspirar.
yearning ['jə:niŋ], *a.* anhelante.—*n.* anhelo.
yeast [ji:st], *n.* levadura.
yell [jel], *n.* alarido, chillido; grito.—*v.i.* chillar; gritar.
yelling ['jeliŋ], *n.* chillido(s); gritería.
yellow ['jelou], *a.* amarillo; (*fam.*) cobarde.—*n.* amarillo.
yellowish ['jelouiʃ], *a.* amarillento.
yelp [jelp], *n.* gañido.—*v.i.* gañir.
yen [jen], *n.* (*fam.*) anhelo, gana.
yes [jes], *adv.* sí; ***—?*** ¿de verdad? ¿qué quiere? ¿qué hay?; ***to say —,*** decir que sí; dar el sí.
yes-man ['jesmæn], *n.* sacristán (*m.*) de amén.
yesterday ['jestəd(e)i], *n., adv.* ayer, *m.*; ***the day before —,*** anteayer.
yet [jet], *adv.* aún, todavía; ***as —,*** hasta ahora; ***not —,*** todavía no.—*conj.* pero, sin embargo, no obstante, con todo.
yew [ju:], *n.* tejo.
yield [ji:ld], *n.* producto; (*com.*) rédito; cosecha.—*v.t.* ceder; entregar; producir.—*v.i.* ceder; rendirse.
yielding ['ji:ldiŋ], *a.* flexible; dócil; complaciente.—*n.* rendición, *f.*, consentimiento.
yoke [jouk], *n.* yugo; canesú (*de un vestido*), *m.*; ***to throw off the —,*** sacudir el yugo.—***v.t.*** uncir, acoplar.
yokel ['joukəl], *n.* rústico, patán, *m.*
yolk [jouk], *n.* yema.
yonder ['jɔndə], *a.* aquel.—*adv.* allí, allá.
you [ju:], *pron.* tú, vosotros, usted, ustedes; te, os, le, la, les, las; ti; sí.
young [jʌŋ], *a.* joven; nuevo; — ***people,*** jóvenes, *m.pl.*; ***the night is —,*** la noche está poco avanzada.—*n.* cría, hijuelos, *m.pl.*: ***with —,*** preñada (*de animales*).
younger ['jʌŋgə], *a.* más joven; menor.
youngster ['jʌŋstə], *n.* jovencito, chiquillo.
your [jɔ:], *a.* tu, tus, vuestro, *etc.*; su, sus.
yours [jɔ:z], *pron.* el tuyo, la tuya, *etc.*; el vuestro, la vuestra, *etc.*; el suyo, la suya, *etc.*; ***yours faithfully,*** queda de Vd. su atentísimo seguro servidor (*usually abbrev. to* su att. s. s.); ***yours sincerely,*** queda de Vd. su afectuoso (*usually abbrev. to* aff.).
yourself [jɔ:'self], *pron.* tú mismo; vosotros mismos; Vd. mismo; Vds. mismos; te, os, se; ti, vosotros, usted, sí.
youth [ju:θ], *n.* juventud, *f.*; joven, *m.*, chico; jóvenes, *m.pl.*
youthful ['ju:θful], *a.* joven; vigoroso.
Yugoslav ['ju:gouslɑ:v], *a., n.* yugoeslavo.
Yugoslavia [ju:gou'slɑ:vjə], *n.* Yugoeslavia.
Yule [ju:l], *n.* (*obs.*) Navidad, *f.*
Yule-log ['ju:l'lɔg], *n.* noche bueno.
Yule-tide ['ju:ltaid], *n.* Navidades, *f.pl.*

Z

Z, z [zed, (*U.S.*) zi:], *n.* vigésima sexta letra del alfabeto inglés.
zany ['zeini], *a.* disparatado.—*n.* bufón, *m.*
zeal [zi:l], *n.* celo, entusiasmo.

zealot ['zelət], *n.* fanático.
zealous ['zeləs], *a.* entusiasta, apasionado.
zebra ['zi:brə, 'zebrə], *n.* cebra; — ***crossing,*** (tipo de) cruce (*m.*) de peatones.
zenith ['zeniθ], *n.* cenit, *m.*; apogeo.
zeppelin ['zepəlin], *n.* zepelín, *m.*
zero ['ziərou], *n.* cero; — ***hour,*** hora de ataque.
zest [zest], *n.* gusto, entusiasmo, deleite, *m.*
zigzag ['zigzæg], *v.t., v.i.* zigzaguear.
zinc [ziŋk], *n.* cinc, *m.*; — ***oxide,*** óxido de cinc.
Zion ['zaiən], *n.* Sión; Jerusalén, *m.*
Zionist ['zaiənist], *n.* sionista, *m.f.*
zip [zip], *n.* cremallera; (*fam.*) energía.—*v.i.* ***to — along,*** ir volando.
zircon ['zə:kən], *n.* circón, *m.*
zither ['ziðə], *n.* cítara.
zodiac ['zoudiæk], *n.* zodíaco.
zone [zoun], *n.* zona; ***temperate —,*** zona templada; ***frigid —,*** zona glacial.
zoo [zu:], *n.* zoo, *m.*, jardín zoológico.
zoological [zouə'lɔdʒikəl], *a.* zoológico.
zoologist [zou'ɔlədʒist], *n.* zoólogo.
zoology [zou'ɔlədʒi], *n.* zoología.
zoom [zu:m], *n.* zumbido.—*v.i.* zumbar; (*aer.*) empinarse.
Zulu ['zu:lu:], *a., n.* zulú, *m.*

ORTHOGRAPHIC CHANGING VERBS

Group **A.** abarcar: **c** changes to **qu** before **e.**

Present Indicative	*Participles*	*Imperative*	*Preterite*
abarco	abarcando		abar**qu**é
abarcas	abarcado	abarca	abarcaste
abarca			abarcó
abarcamos			abarcamos
abarcáis		abarcad	abarcasteis
abarcan			abarcaron

Group **B.** ahogar: **g** changes to **gu** before **e.**

Present Indicative	*Participles*	*Imperative*	*Preterite*
ahogo	ahogando		aho**gu**é
ahogas	ahogado	ahoga	ahogaste
ahoga			ahogó
ahogamos			ahogamos
ahogáis		ahogad	ahogasteis
ahogan			ahogaron

Group **C.** cazar: **z** changes to **c** before **e.**

Present Indicative	*Participles*	*Imperative*	*Preterite*
cazo	cazando		ca**c**é
cazas	cazado	caza	cazaste
caza			cazó
cazamos			cazamos
cazáis		cazad	cazasteis
cazan			cazaron

Group **D.** vencer and esparcir: **c** changes to **z** before **o** and **a.**

Present Indicative	*Participles*	*Imperative*	*Preterite*
ven**z**o	venciendo		vencí
vences	vencido	vence	venciste
vence			venció
vencemos			vencimos
vencéis		venced	vencisteis
vencen			vencieron
espar**z**o	esparciendo		esparcí
esparces	esparcido	esparce	esparciste
esparce			esparció
esparcimos			esparcimos
esparcís		esparcid	esparcisteis
esparcen			esparcieron

Group **E.** coger and afligir: **g** changes to **j** before **o** and **a.**

Present Indicative	*Participles*	*Imperative*	*Preterite*
co**j**o	cogiendo		cogí
coges	cogido	coge	cogiste
coge			cogió
cogemos			cogimos
cogéis		coged	cogisteis
cogen			cogieron
afli**j**o	afligiendo		afligí
afliges	afligido	aflige	afligiste
aflige			afligió
afligimos			afligimos
afligís		afligid	afligisteis
afligen			afligieron

Group **F.** delinquir: **qu** changes to **c** before **o** and **a.**

Present Indicative	*Participles*	*Imperative*	*Preterite*
delin**c**o	delinquiendo		delinquí
delinques	delinquido	delinque	delinquiste
delinque			delinquió
delinquimos			delinquimos
delinquís		delinquid	delinquisteis
delinquen			delinquieron

Present Subjunctive	*Imperfect Subjunctive*		*Future Subjunctive*
abarque	abarcara	abarcase	abarcare
abarques	abarcaras	abarcases	abarcares
abarque	abarcara	abarcase	abarcare
abarquemos	abarcáramos	abarcásemos	abarcáremos
abarquéis	abarcarais	abarcaseis	abarcareis
abarquen	abarcaran	abarcasen	abarcaren
ahogue	ahogara	ahogase	ahogare
ahogues	ahogaras	ahogases	ahogares
ahogue	ahogara	ahogase	ahogare
ahoguemos	ahogáramos	ahogásemos	ahogáremos
ahoguéis	ahogarais	ahogaseis	ahogareis
ahoguen	ahogaran	ahogasen	ahogaren
cace	cazara	cazase	cazare
caces	cazaras	cazases	cazares
cace	cazara	cazase	cazare
cacemos	cazáramos	cazásemos	cazáremos
cacéis	cazarais	cazaseis	cazareis
cacen	cazaran	cazasen	cazaren
venza	venciera	venciese	venciere
venzas	vencieras	vencieses	vencieres
venza	venciera	venciese	venciere
venzamos	venciéramos	venciésemos	venciéremos
venzáis	vencierais	vencieseis	venciereis
venzan	vencieran	venciesen	vencieren
esparza	esparciera	esparciese	esparciere
esparzas	esparcieras	esparcieses	esparcieres
esparza	esparciera	esparciese	esparciere
esparzamos	esparciéramos	esparciésemos	esparciéremos
esparzáis	esparcierais	esparcieseis	esparciereis
esparzan	esparcieran	esparciesen	esparcieren
coja	cogiera	cogiese	cogiere
cojas	cogieras	cogieses	cogieres
coja	cogiera	cogiese	cogiere
cojamos	cogiéramos	cogiésemos	cogiéremos
cojáis	cogierais	cogieseis	cogiereis
cojan	cogieran	cogiesen	cogieren
aflija	afligiera	afligiese	afligiere
aflijas	afligieras	afligieses	afligieres
aflija	afligiera	afligiese	afligiere
aflijamos	afligiéramos	afligiésemos	afligiéremos
aflijáis	afligierais	afligieseis	afligiereis
aflijan	afligieran	afligiesen	afligieren
delinca	delinquiera	delinquiese	delinquiere
delincas	delinquieras	delinquieses	delinquieres
delinca	delinquiera	delinquiese	delinquiere
delincamos	delinquiéramos	delinquiésemos	delinquiéremos
delincáis	delinquierais	delinquieseis	delinquiereis
delincan	delinquieran	delinquiesen	delinquieren

Spanish Verbs

Present Indicative	*Participles*	*Imperative*	*Preterite*
Group **G.** distinguir: **gu** changes to **g** before **o** and **a.**			
distingo	distinguiendo		distinguí
distingues	distinguido	distingue	distinguiste
distingue			distinguió
distinguimos			distinguimos
distinguís		distinguid	distinguisteis
distinguen			distinguieron
Group **H.** fraguar: **gu** changes to **gü** before **e.**			
fraguo	fraguando		fragüé
fraguas	fraguado	fragua	fraguaste
fragua			fraguó
fraguamos			fraguamos
fraguáis		fraguad	fraguasteis
fraguan			fraguaron
Group **I.** argüir: **üi** changes to **uy** before a vowel.			
arguyo	arguyendo		argüí
arguyes	argüido	arguye	argüiste
arguye			arguyó
argüimos			argüimos
argüís		argüid	argüisteis
arguyen			arguyeron
Group **J.** bullir: **i** is elided before a vowel.			
bullo	bullendo		bullí
bulles	bullido	bulle	bulliste
bulle			bulló
bullimos			bullimos
bullís		bullid	bullisteis
bullen			bulleron
Group **K.** tañer and ceñir: **i** is elided before a vowel; **e** in the stem sometimes changes to **i.**			
taño	tañendo		tañí
tañes	tañido	tañe	tañiste
tañe			tañó
tañemos			tañimos
tañéis		tañed	tañisteis
tañen			tañeron
ciño	ciñendo		ceñí
ciñes	ceñido	ciñe	ceñiste
ciñe			ciñó
ceñimos			ceñimos
ceñís		ceñid	ceñisteis
ciñen			ciñeron
Group **L.** variar: **i** takes an accent when the stress falls on it.			
varío	variando	varía	varié
varías	variado		variaste
varía			varió
variamos			variamos
variáis		variad	variasteis
varían			variaron
Group **M.** atenuar: **u** takes an accent when the stress falls on it.			
atenúo	atenuando	atenúa	atenué
atenúas	atenuado		atenuaste
atenúa			atenuó
atenuamos			atenuamos
atenuáis		atenuad	atenuasteis
atenúan			atenuaron

Present Subjunctive	*Imperfect Subjunctive*		*Future Subjunctive*
distinga	distinguiera	distinguiese	distinguiere
distingas	distinguieras	distinguieses	distinguieres
distinga	distinguiera	distinguiese	distinguiere
distingamos	distinguiéramos	distinguiésemos	distinguiéremos
distingáis	distinguierais	distinguieseis	distinguiereis
distingan	distinguieran	distinguiesen	distinguieren
fragüe	fraguara	fraguase	fraguare
fragües	fraguaras	fraguases	fraguares
fragüe	fraguara	fraguase	fraguare
fragüemos	fraguáramos	fraguásemos	fraguáremos
fragüéis	fraguarais	fraguaseis	fraguareis
fragüen	fraguaran	fraguasen	fraguaren
arguya	arguyera	arguyese	arguyere
arguyas	arguyeras	arguyeses	arguyeres
arguya	arguyera	arguyese	arguyere
arguyamos	arguyéramos	arguyésemos	arguyéremos
arguyáis	arguyerais	arguyeseis	arguyereis
arguyan	arguyeran	arguyesen	arguyeren
bulla	bullera	bullese	bullere
bullas	bulleras	bulleses	bulleres
bulla	bullera	bullese	bullere
bullamos	bulléramos	bullésemos	bulléremos
bulláis	bullerais	bulleseis	bullereis
bullan	bulleran	bullesen	bulleren
taña	tañera	tañese	tañere
tañas	tañeras	tañeses	tañeres
taña	tañera	tañese	tañere
tañamos	tañéramos	tañésemos	tañéremos
tañáis	tañerais	tañeseis	tañereis
tañan	tañeran	tañesen	tañeren
ciña	ciñera	ciñese	ciñere
ciñas	ciñeras	ciñeses	ciñeres
ciña	ciñera	ciñese	ciñere
ciñamos	ciñéramos	ciñésemos	ciñéremos
ciñáis	ciñerais	ciñeseis	ciñereis
ciñan	ciñeran	ciñesen	ciñeren
varíe	variara	variase	variare
varíes	variaras	variases	variares
varíe	variara	variase	variare
variemos	variáramos	variásemos	variáremos
variéis	variarais	variaseis	variareis
varíen	variaran	variasen	variaren
atenúe	atenuara	atenuase	atenuare
atenúes	atenuaras	atenuases	atenuares
atenúe	atenuara	atenuase	atenuare
atenuemos	atenuáramos	atenuásemos	atenuáremos
atenuéis	atenuarais	atenuaseis	atenuareis
atenúen	atenuaran	atenuasen	atenuaren

Present Indicative	*Participles*	*Imperative*	*Preterite*
Group **N.** creer: **i** changes to **y** before a vowel; before a consonant it takes an accent.			
creo	creyendo		creí
crees	creído	cree	creíste
cree			creyó
creemos			creímos
creéis		creed	creísteis
creen			creyeron
Group **O.** huir: **i** changes to **y** before a vowel.			
huyo	huyendo		huí[1]
huyes	huido	huye	huiste
huye			huyó
huimos			huimos
huís[1]		huid	huisteis
huyen			huyeron
Group **P.** aullar (all verbs, of any conjugation, having the diphthong **ai**, **au** or **eu** in the stem): **i** or **u** takes an accent when the stress falls on it.			
aúllo	aullando		aullé
aúllas	aullado	**aúlla**	aullaste
aúlla			aulló
aullamos			aullamos
aulláis		aullad	aullasteis
aúllan			aullaron
Group **Q.** garantir: defective, occurring only in those forms where the **i** is present in the verb ending, *viz.* the entire imperfect, preterite, future, conditional, both imperfect subjunctives, the future subjunctive and the forms of the present indicative and imperative given below.			
	garantiendo		garantí
	garantido		garantiste
			garantió
garantimos			garantimos
garantís		garantid	garantisteis
			garantieron

IRREGULAR VERBS

Present Indicative	*Participles*	*Imperative*	*Future Indicative*	*Preterite*
Group **1.** cerrar: **e** changes to **ie** when the stress falls on it.				
cierro	cerrando		cerraré	cerré
cierras	cerrado	**cierra**	cerrarás	cerraste
cierra			cerrará	cerró
cerramos			cerraremos	cerramos
cerráis		cerrad	cerraréis	cerrasteis
cierran			cerrarán	cerraron
Group **2.** perder: **e** changes to **ie** when the stress falls on it.				
pierdo	perdiendo		perderé	perdí
pierdes	perdido	**pierde**	perderás	perdiste
pierde			perderá	perdió
perdemos			perderemos	perdimos
perdéis		perded	perderéis	perdisteis
pierden			perderán	perdieron
Group **3.** cernir: **e** changes to **ie** when the stress falls on it.				
cierno	cerniendo		cerniré	cerní
ciernes	cernido	**cierne**	cernirás	cerniste
cierne			cernirá	cernió
cernimos			cerniremos	cernimos
cernís		cernid	cerniréis	cernisteis
ciernen			cernirán	cernieron

[1] The accents on these two forms may be omitted in **huir** but not in any other verb.

Present Subjunctive	*Imperfect Subjunctive*		*Future Subjunctive*
crea	creyera	creyese	creyere
creas	creyeras	creyeses	creyeres
crea	creyera	creyese	creyere
creamos	creyéramos	creyésemos	creyéremos
creáis	creyerais	creyeseis	creyereis
crean	creyeran	creyesen	creyeren
huya	huyera	huyese	huyere
huyas	huyeras	huyeses	huyeres
huya	huyera	huyese	huyere
huyamos	huyéramos	huyésemos	huyéremos
huyáis	huyerais	huyeseis	huyereis
huyan	huyeran	huyesen	huyeren
aúlle	aullara	aullase	aullare
aúlles	aullaras	aullases	aullares
aúlle	aullara	aullase	aullare
aullemos	aulláramos	aullásemos	aulláremos
aulléis	aullarais	aullaseis	aullareis
aúllen	aullaran	aullasen	aullaren
	garantiera	garantiese	garantiere
	garantieras	garantieses	garantieres
	garantiera	garantiese	garantiere
	garantiéramos	garantiésemos	garantiéremos
	garantierais	garantieseis	garantiereis
	garantieran	garantiesen	garantieren
cierre	cerrara	cerrase	cerrare
cierres	cerraras	cerrases	cerrares
cierre	cerrara	cerrase	cerrare
cerremos	cerráramos	cerrásemos	cerráremos
cerréis	cerrarais	cerraseis	cerrareis
cierren	cerraran	cerrasen	cerraren
pierda	perdiera	perdiese	perdiere
pierdas	perdieras	perdieses	perdieres
pierda	perdiera	perdiese	perdiere
perdamos	perdiéramos	perdiésemos	perdiéremos
perdáis	perdierais	perdieseis	perdiereis
pierdan	perdieran	perdiesen	perdieren
cierna	cerniera	cerniese	cerniere
ciernas	cernieras	cernieses	cernieres
cierna	cerniera	cerniese	cerniere
cernamos	cerniéramos	cerniésemos	cerniéremos
cernáis	cernierais	cernieseis	cerniereis
ciernan	cernieran	cerniesen	cernieren

Group 4. rodar: **o** changes to **ue** when the stress falls on it.

Present Indicative	Participles	Imperative	Future Indicative	Preterite
ruedo	rodando		rodaré	rodé
ruedas	rodado	rueda	rodarás	rodaste
rueda			rodará	rodó
rodamos			rodaremos	rodamos
rodáis		rodad	rodaréis	rodasteis
ruedan			rodarán	rodaron

Group 5. mover: **o** changes to **ue** when the stress falls on it.

Present Indicative	Participles	Imperative	Future Indicative	Preterite
muevo	moviendo		moveré	moví
mueves	movido	mueve	moverás	moviste
mueve			moverá	movió
movemos			moveremos	movimos
movéis		moved	moveréis	movisteis
mueven			moverán	movieron

Group 6. advertir: **e** (or in some cases **i**) changes to **ie** when the stress falls on it; **e** changes to **i** in some forms.

Present Indicative	Participles	Imperative	Future Indicative	Preterite
advierto	advirtiendo		advertiré	advertí
adviertes	advertido	advierte	advertirás	advertiste
advierte			advertirá	advirtió
advertimos			advertiremos	advertimos
advertís		advertid	advertiréis	advertisteis
advierten			advertirán	advirtieron

Group 7. dormir: **o** changes to **ue** when the stress falls on it; **o** changes to **u** in some forms.

Present Indicative	Participles	Imperative	Future Indicative	Preterite
duermo	durmiendo		dormiré	dormí
duermes	dormido	duerme	dormirás	dormiste
duerme			dormirá	durmió
dormimos			dormiremos	dormimos
dormís		dormid	dormiréis	dormisteis
duermen			dormirán	durmieron

Group 8. pedir: **e** changes to **i** when the stress falls on it and in some other cases.

Present Indicative	Participles	Imperative	Future Indicative	Preterite
pido	pidiendo		pediré	pedí
pides	pedido	pide	pedirás	pediste
pide			pedirá	pidió
pedimos			pediremos	pedimos
pedís		pedid	pediréis	pedisteis
piden			pedirán	pidieron

Group 9. padecer: **c** changes to **zc** before **o** and **a**.

Present Indicative	Participles	Imperative	Future Indicative	Preterite
padezco	padeciendo		padeceré	padecí
padeces	padecido	padece	padecerás	padeciste
padece			padecerá	padeció
padecemos			padeceremos	padecimos
padecéis		padeced	padeceréis	padecisteis
padecen			padecerán	padecieron

Group 10. agorar: **o** changes to **üe** when the stress falls on it.

Present Indicative	Participles	Imperative	Future Indicative	Preterite
agüero	agorando		agoraré	agoré
agüeras	agorado	agüera	agorarás	agoraste
agüera			agorará	agoró
agoramos			agoraremos	agoramos
agoráis		agorad	agoraréis	agorasteis
agüeran			agorarán	agoraron

Group 11. andar:

Present Indicative	Participles	Imperative	Future Indicative	Preterite
ando	andando		andaré	anduve
andas	andado	anda	andarás	anduviste
anda			andará	anduvo
andamos			andaremos	anduvimos
andáis		andad	andaréis	anduvisteis
andan			andarán	anduvieron

Present Subjunctive	*Imperfect Subjunctive*		*Future Subjunctive*
ruede	rodara	rodase	rodare
ruedes	rodaras	rodases	rodares
ruede	rodara	rodase	rodare
rodemos	rodáramos	rodásemos	rodáremos
rodéis	rodarais	rodaseis	rodareis
rueden	rodaran	rodasen	rodaren
mueva	moviera	moviese	moviere
muevas	movieras	movieses	movieres
mueva	moviera	moviese	moviere
movamos	moviéramos	moviésemos	moviéremos
mováis	movierais	movieseis	moviereis
muevan	movieran	moviesen	movieren
advierta	advirtiera	advirtiese	advirtiere
adviertas	advirtieras	advirtieses	advirtieres
advierta	advirtiera	advirtiese	advirtiere
advirtamos	advirtiéramos	advirtiésemos	advirtiéremos
advirtáis	advirtierais	advirtieseis	advirtiereis
adviertan	advirtieran	advirtiesen	advirtieren
duerma	durmiera	durmiese	durmiere
duermas	durmieras	durmieses	durmieres
duerma	durmiera	durmiese	durmiere
durmamos	durmiéramos	durmiésemos	durmiéremos
durmáis	durmierais	durmieseis	durmiereis
duerman	durmieran	durmiesen	durmieren
pida	pidiera	pidiese	pidiere
pidas	pidieras	pidieses	pidieres
pida	pidiera	pidiese	pidiere
pidamos	pidiéramos	pidiésemos	pidiéremos
pidáis	pidierais	pidieseis	pidiereis
pidan	pidieran	pidiesen	pidieren
padezca	padeciera	padeciese	padeciere
padezcas	padecieras	padecieses	padecieres
padezca	padeciera	padeciese	padeciere
padezcamos	padeciéramos	padeciésemos	padeciéremos
padezcáis	padecierais	padecieseis	padeciereis
padezcan	padecieran	padeciesen	padecieren
agüere	agorara	agorase	agorare
agüeres	agoraras	agorases	agorares
agüere	agorara	agorase	agorare
agoremos	agoráramos	agorásemos	agoráremos
agoréis	agorarais	agoraseis	agorareis
agüeren	agoraran	agorasen	agoraren
ande	anduviera	anduviese	anduviere
andes	anduvieras	anduvieses	anduvieres
ande	anduviera	anduviese	anduviere
andemos	anduviéramos	anduviésemos	anduviéremos
andéis	anduvierais	anduvieseis	anduviereis
anden	anduvieran	anduviesen	anduvieren

Present Indicative	*Participles*	*Imperative*	*Future Indicative*	*Preterite*
Group **12.** asir:				
asgo	asiendo		asiré	así
ases	asido	ase	asirás	asiste
ase			asirá	asió
asimos			asiremos	asimos
asís		asid	asiréis	asisteis
asen			asirán	asieron
Group **13.** caber:				
quepo	cabiendo		**cabré**	**cupe**
cabes	cabido	cabe	**cabrás**	**cupiste**
cabe			**cabrá**	**cupo**
cabemos			**cabremos**	**cupimos**
cabéis		cabed	**cabréis**	**cupisteis**
caben			**cabrán**	**cupieron**
Group **14.** caer:				
caigo	cayendo		caeré	caí
caes	caído	cae	caerás	caíste
cae			caerá	cayó
caemos			caeremos	caímos
caéis		caed	caeréis	caísteis
caen			caerán	cayeron
Group **15.** deducir:				
dedu**zco**	deduciendo		deduciré	**deduje**
deduces	deducido	deduce	deducirás	**dedujiste**
deduce			deducirá	**dedujo**
deducimos			deduciremos	**dedujimos**
deducís		deducid	deduciréis	**dedujisteis**
deducen			deducirán	**dedujeron**
Group **16.** dar:				
doy	dando		daré	**dí**[1]
das	dado	da	darás	**diste**
da			dará	**dio**[1]
damos			daremos	**dimos**
dais		dad	daréis	**disteis**
dan			darán	**dieron**
Group **17.** decir:				
digo	**diciendo**		**diré**	**dije**
dices	**dicho**	**di**	**dirás**	**dijiste**
dice			**dirá**	**dijo**
decimos			**diremos**	**dijimos**
decís		decid	**diréis**	**dijisteis**
dicen			**dirán**	**dijeron**
Group **18.** estar:				
estoy	estando		estaré	**estuve**
estás	estado	**está**	estarás	**estuviste**
está			estará	**estuvo**
estamos			estaremos	**estuvimos**
estáis		estad	estaréis	**estuvisteis**
están			estarán	**estuvieron**
Group **19.** haber:				
he	habiendo		**habré**	**hube**
has	habido	**hé**	**habrás**	**hubiste**
ha			**habrá**	**hubo**
hemos			**habremos**	**hubimos**
habéis		habed	**habréis**	**hubisteis**
han			**habrán**	**hubieron**

[1] In compounds **-dí, -dió.**

Present Subjunctive	*Imperfect Subjunctive*		*Future Subjunctive*
asga **asgas** **asga** **asgamos** **asgáis** **asgan**	asiera asieras asiera asiéramos asierais asieran	asiese asieses asiese asiésemos asieseis asiesen	asiere asieres asiere asiéremos asiereis asieren
quepa **quepas** **quepa** **quepamos** **quepáis** **quepan**	**cupiera** **cupieras** **cupiera** **cupiéramos** **cupierais** **cupieran**	**cupiese** **cupieses** **cupiese** **cupiésemos** **cupieseis** **cupiesen**	**cupiere** **cupieres** **cupiere** **cupiéremos** **cupiereis** **cupieren**
caiga **caigas** **caiga** **caigamos** **caigáis** **caigan**	cayera cayeras cayera cayéramos cayerais cayeran	cayese cayeses cayese cayésemos cayeseis cayesen	cayere cayeres cayere cayéremos cayereis cayeren
deduzca deduzcas deduzca deduzcamos deduzcáis deduzcan	dedujera dedujeras dedujera dedujéramos dedujerais dedujeran	dedujese dedujeses dedujese dedujésemos dedujeseis dedujesen	dedujere dedujeres dedujere dedujéremos dedujereis dedujeren
dé[2] des **dé**[2] demos deis[2] den	**diera** **dieras** **diera** **diéramos** **dierais** **dieran**	**diese** **dieses** **diese** **diésemos** **dieseis** **diesen**	**diere** **dieres** **diere** **diéremos** **diereis** **dieren**
diga **digas** **diga** **digamos** **digáis** **digan**	**dijera** **dijeras** **dijera** **dijéramos** **dijerais** **dijeran**	**dijese** **dijeses** **dijese** **dijésemos** **dijeseis** **dijesen**	**dijere** **dijeres** **dijere** **dijéremos** **dijereis** **dijeren**
esté **estés** **esté** estemos estéis **estén**	**estuviera** **estuvieras** **estuviera** **estuviéramos** **estuvierais** **estuvieran**	**estuviese** **estuvieses** **estuviese** **estuviésemos** **estuvieseis** **estuviesen**	**estuviere** **estuvieres** **estuviere** **estuviéremos** **estuviereis** **estuvieren**
haya **hayas** **haya** **hayamos** **hayáis** **hayan**	**hubiera** **hubieras** **hubiera** **hubiéramos** **hubierais** **hubieran**	**hubiese** **hubieses** **hubiese** **hubiésemos** **hubieseis** **hubiesen**	**hubiere** **hubieres** **hubiere** **hubiéremos** **hubiereis** **hubieren**

[2] In compounds **-de, -déis.**

Spanish Verbs

Present Indicative	*Participles*	*Imperative*	*Future Indicative*	*Preterite*
Group **20.** hacer:				
hago	haciendo		**haré**	**hice**
haces	**hecho**	**haz**	**harás**	**hiciste**
hace			**hará**	**hizo**
hacemos			**haremos**	**hicimos**
hacéis		haced	**haréis**	**hicisteis**
hacen			**harán**	**hicieron**
Group **21.** ir[1]:				
voy	**yendo**		iré	**fui**
vas	ido	**vé**	irás	**fuiste**
va			irá	**fue**
vamos			iremos	**fuimos**
vais		**id**	iréis	**fuisteis**
van			irán	**fueron**
Group **22.** oír:				
oigo	**oyendo**		oiré	oí
oyes	**oído**	**oye**	oirás	oiste
oye			oirá	oyó
oímos			oiremos	oímos
oís		**oíd**	oiréis	oísteis
oyen			oirán	oyeron
Group **23.** placer:				
plazco *or* **plazgo**	placiendo		placeré	plací
places	placido	place	placerás	placiste
place			placerá	plació *or* **plugo**
placemos			placeremos	placimos
placéis		placed	placeréis	placisteis
placen			placerán	placieron
Group **24.** poder:				
p**ue**do	**pudiendo**		**podré**	**pude**
p**ue**des	podido		**podrás**	**pudiste**
p**ue**de			**podrá**	**pudo**
podemos			**podremos**	**pudimos**
podéis			**podréis**	**pudisteis**
p**ue**den			**podrán**	**pudieron**
Group **25.** poner:				
pongo	poniendo		**pondré**	**puse**
pones	**puesto**	**pon**[3]	**pondrás**	**pusiste**
pone			**pondrá**	**puso**
ponemos			**pondremos**	**pusimos**
ponéis		poned	**pondréis**	**pusisteis**
ponen			**pondrán**	**pusieron**
Group **26.** querer:				
qu**ie**ro	queriendo		**querré**	**quise**
qu**ie**res	querido	**quiere**	**querrás**	**quisiste**
qu**ie**re			**querrá**	**quiso**
queremos			**querremos**	**quisimos**
queréis		quered	**querréis**	**quisisteis**
qu**ie**ren			**querrán**	**quisieron**

Group **27.** raer: Identical with caer (**14**) but has the following alternative forms: **raigo** *or* **rayo**

[1] Imperfect: **iba, -as, -a, íbamos, ibais, iban.**
[2] Jussive **vamos.**
[3] In compounds **-pón.**

Present Subjunctive	*Imperfect Subjunctive*		*Future Subjunctive*
haga	**hiciera**	**hiciese**	**hiciere**
hagas	**hicieras**	**hicieses**	**hicieres**
haga	**hiciera**	**hiciese**	**hiciere**
hagamos	**hiciéramos**	**hiciésemos**	**hiciéremos**
hagáis	**hicierais**	**hicieseis**	**hiciereis**
hagan	**hicieran**	**hiciesen**	**hicieren**
vaya	**fuera**	**fuese**	**fuere**
vayas	**fueras**	**fueses**	**fueres**
vaya	**fuera**	**fuese**	**fuere**
vayamos[2]	**fuéramos**	**fuésemos**	**fuéremos**
vayáis	**fuerais**	**fueseis**	**fuereis**
vayan	**fueran**	**fuesen**	**fueren**
oiga	**oyera**	**oyese**	**oyere**
oigas	**oyeras**	**oyeses**	**oyeres**
oiga	**oyera**	**oyese**	**oyere**
oigamos	**oyéramos**	**oyésemos**	**oyéremos**
oigáis	**oyerais**	**oyeseis**	**oyereis**
oigan	**oyeran**	**oyesen**	**oyeren**
plazca *or* **plazga**	placiera	placiese	placiere
plazcas	placieras	placieses	placieres
plazca	placiera *or* **pluguiera**	placiese *or* **pluguiese**	placiere *or* **pluguiere**
plazcamos	placiéramos	placiésemos	placiéremos
plazcáis	placierais	placieseis	placiereis
plazcan	placieran	placiesen	placieren
pueda	**pudiera**	**pudiese**	**pudiere**
puedas	**pudieras**	**pudieses**	**pudieres**
pueda	**pudiera**	**pudiese**	**pudiere**
podamos	**pudiéramos**	**pudiésemos**	**pudiéremos**
podáis	**pudierais**	**pudieseis**	**pudiereis**
puedan	**pudieran**	**pudiesen**	**pudieren**
ponga	**pusiera**	**pusiese**	**pusiere**
pongas	**pusieras**	**pusieses**	**pusieres**
ponga	**pusiera**	**pusiese**	**pusiere**
pongamos	**pusiéramos**	**pusiésemos**	**pusiéremos**
pongáis	**pusierais**	**pusieseis**	**pusiereis**
pongan	**pusieran**	**pusiesen**	**pusieren**
quiera	**quisiera**	**quisiese**	**quisiere**
quieras	**quisieras**	**quisieses**	**quisieres**
quiera	**quisiera**	**quisiese**	**quisiere**
queramos	**quisiéramos**	**quisiésemos**	**quisiéremos**
queráis	**quisierais**	**quisieseis**	**quisiereis**
quieran	**quisieran**	**quisiesen**	**quisieren**
raiga *or* **raya**			

Present Indicative	*Participles*	*Imperative*	*Future Indicative*	*Preterite*
Group **28.** reír:				
río	**riendo**		reiré	reí
ríes	reído	**ríe**	reirás	reíste
ríe			reirá	**rio**
reímos			reiremos	reímos
reís		**reíd**	reiréis	reísteis
ríen			reirán	**rieron**
Group **29.** roer:				
roo, **roigo** *or* **royo**	royendo		roeré	roí
roes	roído	roe	roerás	roíste
roe			roerá	royó
roemos			roeremos	roímos
roéis		roed	roeréis	roísteis
roen			roerán	royeron
Group **30.** saber:				
sé	sabiendo		**sabré**	**supe**
sabes	sabido	sabe	**sabrás**	**supiste**
sabe			**sabrá**	**supo**
sabemos			**sabremos**	**supimos**
sabéis		sabed	**sabréis**	**supisteis**
saben			**sabrán**	**supieron**
Group **31.** salir:				
salgo	saliendo		**saldré**	salí
sales	salido	**sal**	**saldrás**	saliste
sale			**saldrá**	salió
salimos			**saldremos**	salimos
salís		salid	**saldréis**	salisteis
salen			**saldrán**	salieron
Group **32.** ser[1]:				
soy	siendo		seré	**fui**
eres	sido	**sé**	serás	**fuiste**
es			será	**fue**
somos			seremos	**fuimos**
sois		**sed**	seréis	**fuisteis**
son			serán	**fueron**
Group **33.** tener:				
tengo	teniendo		**tendré**	**tuve**
tienes	tenido	**ten**[2]	**tendrás**	**tuviste**
tiene			**tendrá**	**tuvo**
tenemos			**tendremos**	**tuvimos**
tenéis		tened	**tendréis**	**tuvisteis**
tienen			**tendrán**	**tuvieron**
Group **34.** traer:				
traigo	trayendo		traeré	**traje**
traes	traído	trae	traerás	**trajiste**
trae			traerá	**trajo**
traemos			traeremos	**trajimos**
traéis		traed	traeréis	**trajisteis**
traen			traerán	**trajeron**
Group **35.** valer:				
valgo	valiendo		**valdré**	valí
vales	valido	**val** *or* vale	**valdrás**	valiste
vale			**valdrá**	valió
valemos			**valdremos**	valimos
valéis		valed	**valdréis**	valisteis
valen			**valdrán**	valieron

[1] Imperfect: **era, -as, -a, éramos, erais, eran.**
[2] In compounds **-tén.**

Present Subjunctive	*Imperfect Subjunctive*		*Future Subjunctive*
ría	**riera**	**riese**	**riere**
rías	**rieras**	**rieses**	**rieres**
ría	**riera**	**riese**	**riere**
riamos	**riéramos**	**riésemos**	**riéremos**
riáis	**rierais**	**rieseis**	**riereis**
rían	**rieran**	**riesen**	**rieren**
roa, **roiga** *or* **roya**	**royera**	**royese**	**royere**
roas	**royeras**	**royeses**	**royeres**
roa	**royera**	**royese**	**royere**
roamos	**royéramos**	**royésemos**	**royéremos**
roáis	**royerais**	**royeseis**	**royereis**
roan	**royeran**	**royesen**	**royeren**
sepa	**supiera**	**supiese**	**supiere**
sepas	**supieras**	**supieses**	**supieres**
sepa	**supiera**	**supiese**	**supiere**
sepamos	**supiéramos**	**supiésemos**	**supiéremos**
sepáis	**supierais**	**supieseis**	**supiereis**
sepan	**supieran**	**supiesen**	**supieren**
salga	saliera	saliese	saliere
salgas	salieras	salieses	salieres
salga	saliera	saliese	saliere
salgamos	saliéramos	saliésemos	saliéremos
salgáis	salierais	salieseis	saliereis
salgan	salieran	saliesen	salieren
sea	**fuera**	**fuese**	**fuere**
seas	**fueras**	**fueses**	**fueres**
sea	**fuera**	**fuese**	**fuere**
seamos	**fuéramos**	**fuésemos**	**fuéremos**
seáis	**fuerais**	**fueseis**	**fuereis**
sean	**fueran**	**fuesen**	**fueren**
tenga	**tuviera**	**tuviese**	**tuviere**
tengas	**tuvieras**	**tuvieses**	**tuvieres**
tenga	**tuviera**	**tuviese**	**tuviere**
tengamos	**tuviéramos**	**tuviésemos**	**tuviéremos**
tengáis	**tuvierais**	**tuvieseis**	**tuviereis**
tengan	**tuvieran**	**tuviesen**	**tuvieren**
traiga	**trajera**	**trajese**	**trajere**
traigas	**trajeras**	**trajeses**	**trajeres**
traiga	**trajera**	**trajese**	**trajere**
traigamos	**trajéramos**	**trajésemos**	**trajéremos**
traigáis	**trajerais**	**trajeseis**	**trajereis**
traigan	**trajeran**	**trajesen**	**trajeren**
valga	valiera	valiese	valiere
valgas	valieras	valieses	valieres
valga	valiera	valiese	valiere
valgamos	valiéramos	valiésemos	valiéremos
valgáis	valierais	valieseis	valiereis
valgan	valieran	valiesen	valieren

Present Indicative	*Participles*	*Imperative*	*Future Indicative*	*Preterite*
Group 36. venir:				
vengo	**viniendo**		**vendré**	**vine**
vienes	venido	**ven**[1]	**vendrás**	**viniste**
viene			**vendrá**	**vino**
venimos			**vendremos**	**vinimos**
venís		venid	**vendréis**	**vinisteis**
vienen			**vendrán**	**vinieron**
Group 37. ver[2]:				
veo	viendo		veré	vi
ves	**visto**	ve	verás	viste
ve			verá	vio
vemos			veremos	vimos
veis		ved	veréis	visteis
ven			verán	vieron

[1] In compounds **-vén.**
[2] Imperfect: **veía, -as, -a, -amos, -ais, -an.**

Present Subjunctive	*Imperfect Subjunctive*		*Future Subjunctive*
venga	**viniera**	**viniese**	**viniere**
vengas	**vinieras**	**vinieses**	**vinieres**
venga	**viniera**	**viniese**	**viniere**
vengamos	**viniéramos**	**viniésemos**	**viniéremos**
vengáis	**vinierais**	**vinieseis**	**viniereis**
vengan	**vinieran**	**viniesen**	**vinieren**
vea	viera	viese	viere
veas	vieras	vieses	vieres
vea	viera	viese	viere
veamos	viéramos	viésemos	viéremos
veáis	vierais	vieseis	viereis
vean	vieran	viesen	vieren

English Verbs

Presente	*Pronunciación*	*Pretérito*	*Participio Pasado*	*Español*

VERBOS IRREGULARES INGLESES

be				
I am (I'm)	[ai æm, aim]	was	been	ser, estar
you are (you're)	[ju: ɑ:; jɔ:, juə]	were		
he is (he's)	[hi: iz, hi:z]	was		
she is (she's)	[ʃi: iz, ʃi:z]	was		
it is (it's)	[it iz, its]	was		
we are (we're)	[wi: ɑ:, wiə]	were		
you are *véase arriba*		were		
they are (they're)	[ðei ɑ:, ðɛə]	were		

have				
I have (I've)	[ai hæv, aiv]	had	had	haber, tener
you have (you've)	[ju: hæv, ju:v]	had		
he has (he's)	[hi: hæz, hi:z]	had		
she has (she's)	[ʃi: hæz, ʃi:z]	had		
we have (we've)	[wi: hæv, wi:v]	had		
they have (they've)	[ðei hæv, ðeiv]	had		

Infinitivo	*Pretérito*	*Participio Pasado*	*Español*
abide	**abode**	**abode**	morar
awake	**awoke**	**awoken, awakened**	despertar
bear	**bore**	**borne**	llevar; parir
beat	**beat**	**beaten**	batir
begin	**began**	**begun**	empezar
bend	**bent**	**bent**	inclinar(se)
bereave	bereaved (**bereft**)	bereaved (**bereft**)	despojar
beseech	**besought**	**besought**	impetrar
bid	**bade, bid**	**bidden, bid**	mandar
bind	**bound**	**bound**	ligar
bite	**bit**	**bitten**	morder
bleed	**bled**	**bled**	sangrar
blow	**blew**	**blown**	soplar
break	**broke**	**broken**	quebrar
breed	**bred**	**bred**	criar
bring	**brought**	**brought**	traer
build	**built**	**built**	edificar
burn	**burned, burnt**	**burned, burnt**	quemar(se)
burst	**burst**	**burst**	reventar(se)

Infinitivo	*Pretérito*	*Participio Pasado*	*Español*
buy	**bought**	**bought**	comprar
cast	**cast**	**cast**	arrojar
catch	**caught**	**caught**	coger
chide	**chid**	**chid, chidden**	regañar
choose	**chose**	**chosen**	escoger
cleave	cleaved, **cleft, clove**	cleaved, **cleft, cloven**[1]	hender
cling	**clung**	**clung**	adherirse
clothe	clothed (*obs*. **clad**)	**clad,** clothed	vestir
come	**came**	**come**	venir
cost	**cost**	**cost**	costar
creep	**crept**	**crept**	arrastrarse
crow	crowed, **crew**	crowed	cacarear
cut	**cut**	**cut**	cortar
dare	dared (*obs*. **durst**)	dared	osar
deal	**dealt**	**dealt**	repartir
dig	**dug**	**dug**	cavar
do	**did**	**done**	hacer
draw	**drew**	**drawn**	tirar; dibujar
dream	dreamed, **dreamt**	dreamed, **dreamt**	soñar
drink	**drank**	**drunk**	beber
drive	**drove**	**driven**	conducir
dwell	**dwelt**	**dwelt**	morar
eat	**ate**	**eaten**	comer
fall	**fell**	**fallen**	caer
feed	**fed**	**fed**	(dar de) comer
feel	**felt**	**felt**	sentir
fight	**fought**	**fought**	combatir
find	**found**	**found**	encontrar
flee	**fled**	**fled**	huir
fling	**flung**	**flung**	arrojar

[1] *Cloven* hoof.

English Verbs

Infinitivo	*Pretérito*	*Participio Pasado*	*Español*
fly	**flew**	**flown**	volar
forbear	**forbore**	**forborne**	abstenerse
forbid	**forbad(e)**	**forbidden**	vedar
forget	**forgot**	**forgotten**	olvidar
forsake	**forsook**	**forsaken**	abandonar
freeze	**froze**	**frozen**	helar(se)
get	**got**	**got** (*U.S.* **gotten)**	obtener
gird	girded, **girt**	girded, **girt**	ceñir
give	**gave**	**given**	dar
go	**went**	**gone**	ir
grind	**ground**	**ground**	moler
grow	**grew**	**grown**	cultivar; crecer
hang[1]	**hung**	**hung**	colgar
hear	**heard**	**heard**	oír
heave	heaved, **hove**	heaved, **hove**	alzar
hew	hewed	hewed, **hewn**	debastar
hide	**hid**	**hidden**	esconder
hit	**hit**	**hit**	golpear
hold	**held**	**held**	tener
hurt	**hurt**	**hurt**	dañar
keep	**kept**	**kept**	guardar
kneel	**knelt**	**knelt**	arrodillarse
knit	**knit,** knitted	knitted	hacer punto
know	**knew**	**known**	saber
lay	**laid**	**laid**	poner
lead	**led**	**led**	conducir
[illegible]ean	**leant,** leaned	**leant,** leaned	apoyar(se)
[illegible]	leaped, **leapt**	leaped, **leapt**	saltar
[illegible]	learned, **learnt**	learned, **learnt**	aprender
[illegible]	**left**	**left**	dejar

[illegible]s regular en el sentido de *ahorcar*.

Infinitivo	*Pretérito*	*Participio Pasado*	*Español*
lend	**lent**	**lent**	prestar
let	**let**	**let**	dejar
lie[1]	**lay**	**lain**	yacer
light	**lit,** lighted	**lit,** lighted	iluminar
lose	**lost**	**lost**	perder
make	**made**	**made**	hacer
mean	**meant**	**meant**	querer decir
meet	**met**	**met**	encontrar(se)
melt	melted	melted	fundir
mow	mowed	**mown**	segar
pay	**paid**	**paid**	pagar
put	**put**	**put**	poner
quit	**quit,** quitted	**quit,** quitted	abandonar
read	**read**	**read**	leer
rend	**rent**	**rent**	desgarrar
rid	**rid**	**rid**	dezembarazar
ride	**rode**	**ridden**	montar
ring[2]	**rang**	**rung**	sonar
rise	**rose**	**risen**	levantarse
run	**ran**	**run**	correr
saw	sawed	**sawn**	aserrar
say	**said**	**said**	decir
see	**saw**	**seen**	ver
seek	**sought**	**sought**	buscar
sell	**sold**	**sold**	vender
send	**sent**	**sent**	enviar
set	**set**	**set**	fijar
sew	sewed	**sewn,** sewed	coser
shake	**shook**	**shaken**	sacudir
shear	sheared	**shorn,** sheared	tonsurar

[1] *Estar acostado.* En el sentido de *mentir* es regular.
[2] *Resonar.* En el sentido de *circundar* es regular.

English Verbs

Infinitivo	*Pretérito*	*Participio Pasado*	*Español*
shed	**shed**	**shed**	quitar(se de)
shine	**shone**	**shone**	relucir
shoe	**shod**	**shod**	herrar
shoot	**shot**	**shot**	disparar
show	showed	**shown**	indicar
shrink	**shrank**	**shrunk**	encoger(se)
shut	**shut**	**shut**	cerrar (se)
sing	**sang**	**sung**	cantar
sink	**sank**	**sunk, sunken**[1]	hundir(se)
sit	**sat**	**sat**	sentarse
slay	**slew**	**slain**	matar
sleep	**slept**	**slept**	dormir
slide	**slid**	**slid**	resbalar
sling	**slung**	**slung**	tirar
slink	**slunk**	**slunk**	escabullirse
slit	**slit**	**slit**	cortar
smell	**smelt,** smelled	**smelt**	oler
smite (*obs.*)	**smote**	**smitten**	herir
sow	sowed	**sown**	sembrar
speak	**spoke**	**spoken**	hablar
speed	**sped**	**sped**	correr
spell	**spelt,** spelled	**spelt,** spelled	deletrear
spend	**spent**	**spent**	gastar
spill	spilled, **spilt**	spilled, **spilt**	derramar
spin	**spun, span**	**spun**	hilar
spit	**spat**	**spat**	escupir
split	**split**	**split**	hender
spoil	**spoilt,** spoiled	**spoilt,** spoiled	estropear(se)
spread	**spread**	**spread**	tender
spring	**sprang**	**sprung**	brincar

[1] *Sunken* cheeks.

Infinitivo	*Pretérito*	*Participio Pasado*	*Español*
stand	**stood**	**stood**	estar (de pie)
steal	**stole**	**stolen**	robar
stick	**stuck**	**stuck**	fijar(se)
sting	**stung**	**stung**	picar
stink	**stank, stunk**	**stunk**	heder
strew	strewed	**strewn,** strewed	esparcir
stride	**strode**	**stridden**	andar a pasos largos
strike	**struck**	**struck**	golpear
string	**strung**	**strung**	ensartar
strive	**strove**	**striven**	esforzarse
swear	**swore**	**sworn**	jurar
sweep	**swept**	**swept**	barrer
swell	swelled	**swollen,** swelled	hinchar(se)
swim	**swam**	**swum**	nadar
swing	**swung**	**swung**	oscilar
take	**took**	**taken**	tomar
teach	**taught**	**taught**	enseñar
tear	**tore**	**torn**	romper
tell	**told**	**told**	contar
think	**thought**	**thought**	pensar
thrive	**throve,** thrived	thrived, **thriven**	prosperar
throw	**threw**	**thrown**	echar
thrust	**thrust**	**thrust**	empujar
tread	**trod**	**trodden**	pisar
wake	**woke**	**woken**	despertar(se)
wear	**wore**	**worn**	llevar
weave	**wove**	**woven**	tejer
weep	**wept**	**wept**	llorar
wet	wetted, **wet**	wetted, **wet**	mojar
win	**won**	**won**	ganar

English Verbs

Infinitivo	*Pretérito*	*Participio Pasado*	*Español*
wind	**wound**	**wound**	devanar
work	worked (*obs.* **wrought**)	worked (*obs.* **wrought**)	trabajar
wring	**wrung**	**wrung**	torcer
write	**wrote**	**written**	escribir

VERBOS DEFECTIVOS

Presente	*Pretérito*	*Participio Pasado*	*Español*
can	**could**	—	poder
may	**might**	—	tener permiso; poder
must	—	—	deber
shall	**should**	—	ir a (*futuro*)
will	**would**	—	querer; ir a (*futuro*)

THE STORY OF LANGUAGE 45p
C. L. Barber

'One of the best books of its kind to appear for years'
TIMES EDUCATIONAL SUPPLEMENT

Beginning with primitive man's first crude attempts at communication by sound, Dr Barber traces the development over thousands of years of organized language and its various families.

From the language groups emerging through the centuries he concentrates on the Indo-European as being of particular interest and describes the growth of the English language as we know it today. From each epoch – Old English, Middle English, the times of Chaucer, of Shakespeare, and later – he introduces pleasing examples of prose and verse to illustrate his arguments.

This new edition of an important book is made still more valuable by revisions and additions including the use of phonetic symbols from the international phonetic alphabet.

A PAN Original.

HOW TO STUDY 35p

Harry Maddox

'Probably one of the best texts of its kind now available'
NATIONAL FOUNDATION FOR EDUCATIONAL RESEARCH IN ENGLAND AND WALES

Successful study depends not only on ability and industry but on effective methods of working. This invaluable and comprehensive handbook tells you how to obtain the greatest benefit from your studies for the least expenditure of energy and effort.

Speed up your rate of reading
Do well in examinations
Think to some purpose
Benefit from Group Work/Discussions
Better your ability to memorize
Take accurate notes
Improve your written English
Understand elementary mathematics

Wherever you may be studying, the author will help you to work without supervision and realize your full potential.

A PAN Original.